$19.95

Twelfth Edition

Blue Book
of Gun Values™

By S.P. Fjestad

*S*houlder stocked pistols have traditionally been amongst the most coveted by pistol collectors. While the "broomhandle" Mauser enjoys the most widespread recognition, a later and more refined design of this classic arm was introduced by Unceta y Cia. (now Astra) in 1927. Referred to as the M900 series, several variations were to emerge during their relatively short production span. Although the design evolution makes for fascinating reading (see <u>Astra Automatic Pistols</u>, by L.M. Antaris), suffice to say that the craftsmanship of these pistols rivaled if not exceeded that of any competitor.

The cover gun for the 12th edition is a special order Astra M902, serial #22,486. Designed with an integral 20 shot magazine and issued with a "booted" shoulder stock, most M902 pistols were of selective fire design. Fewer than 100 (estimated) were manufactured as strict semi-automatics. Of these, only 2 are known to have been gold damascened.

Gold damascening is an elaborate decorative process whose form evolved in the Middle East and whose motifs are generally of Arabic inspiration. Its execution first involves marking the ornamental surface with fine cross hatched lines. The silhouetted designed is penned upon the scored surface followed by the hammered application of gold thread or foil. Punches and chisels are then used to preliminarily detail the inlaid area. The firearm is subsequently blued serving to darken the background. Finally, the embellished area is carefully burnished with the figurines finely detailed.

Extremely labor intensive and exacting, few artisans were capable of performing high quality work. One of the best, Adolfo Santos of Eibar, Spain, was frequently called upon to effect many of Astra's early orders. While unsigned, the details of his engraving and design pattern are signature enough. Deeply impressed by the Moorish inscriptions and motifs found in the walls of the Alhambra and Generalife palaces of Granada, Spain, Adolfo Santos elected to recreate those memorable views when designing the layout for this M902.

This extraordinary pistol, boxed together with shoulder stock, cleaning rod, and instruction booklet, was manufactured in 1932 and is thought to have been originally ordered by Egypt's King Farouk. Richly embellished with exquisite geometric patterns, the pistol also features elegant views from the terrace of the Alhambra palace accessing the reknowned Lion's Patio. The Arabic inscription, found in several locations about the pistol and in numerous locations about the palatial walls, directly translates as "There is no God but Allah".

Due to undisclosed delays, the pistol did not leave the Astra factory until January 7, 1949. Originally invoiced to a Spanish citizen, the pistol also found its way to Chile before its arrival into the United States. It presently rests in the collection of Leonardo M. Antaris, M.D.

It has often been said that a truly great arm is imbued with history, craftsmanship, and artistry. On these merits alone, this cased Astra M902 stands as the finest semiautomatic handgun to ever emerge from Spain. When further factoring in charisma, rarity, and condition, it transcends national considerations to becoming one of the world's finest pistols.

*B*ack cover photo courtesy of G. Allan Brown - Photographer. Colt engraved Buntline - Courtesy of Mr. Philip Lo Piccolo.

Twelth Edition

Blue Book
of Gun Values ™

Publisher's Note:

This book is the result of nonstop and continual firearms obtained by attending gun shows communicating with gun dealers and collectors throughout the country each year. This book represents an analysis of prices for which collectible firearms have actually been selling for during that period at an average retail level.

Although every reasonable effort has been made to compile an accurate and reliable guide, gun prices may vary significantly depending on such factors as the locality of the sale, the number of sales we were able to consider, and economic conditions.

Accordingly, no representation can be made that the guns listed may be bought or sold at prices indicated, nor shall the dealer or publisher be responsible for any error made in compiling and recording such prices.

All Rights Reserved
Copyright 1991, Blue Book Publications, Inc.
One Appletree Square, Minneapolis, MN. 55425
Phone no. (612)854-5229
FAX no. (612) 853-1486

Published and printed in the United States of America

ISBN No. 0-9625943-1-8

Library of Congress No. -pending as edition went to press.

No part of this publication may be reproduced in any form whatsoever, by photograph, mimeograph, FAX transmission, or any other mechanical or electronic means. Nor can it be broadcast or transmitted, by translation into any language, nor by recording electronically or otherwise, without the express written permission from the publisher - except by a reviewer, who may quote brief passages for critical articles and/or reviews.

The percentage breakdown by firearms condition factor with recpective values per condition and the Photo Percentage Grading System is copyrighted by Blue Book Publications, Inc. Any unauthorized usage of these systems for the evaluation of firearms values and color photo percentage breakdown is expressly forbidden by the publisher.

Blue Book of Gun Values Order Form
One Appletree Square
Minneapolis, MN 55425

-To Order-

Call : **TOLL FREE 1-800-877-GUNS (4867)** *or FAX (612) 854-1486 to use your* **VISA, MASTERCARD** *or* **DISCOVER** *charge cvards. (MN residents call (612) 854-5229) or send in this order card with payment.*

MN residents please include 6% sales tax - $1.44 per book)

☐ *12th edition sent 1st class U.S. Mail or UPS -* **$19.95** *each.($19.95/book plus $4.00 shipping and handling).*

Please allow 7 - 10 business days for delivery.

☐ *12th & 13th edition -* **$39.95** *per set (includes shipping and handling on both books). Advanced orders for the 13th edition get first priority next year. The 13th edition will be shipped in April of 1992.*

This offer expires March 1, 1992

Company Name _____

Name _____

Address _____

Phone _____

City _____ **State** _____ **Zip** _____

VISA/MASTERCARD # _____

Expiration Date of Card _____

Signature _____

Send with Payment to:
Blue Book of Gun Values
Department 522
One Appletree Square #1086
Minneapolis, MN 55425

Contents

How to Use This Book

The prices listed in this book are based on National average retail prices for both antique and modern firearms. This is not a wholesale pricing guide (I doubt if there could be such a thing). Percentages of original condition (with corresponding prices) are listed between 10%-100% for antiques (unless rarity and age preclude upper conditions) and 60%-100% on modern firearms since conditions below 60% is seldom encountered (or purchased). Please consult our expanded 32 page color grading insert (unnumbered color section appearing after page 32) to learn more about the condition of your firearm. This is the first time, to my knowledge, that color plates have been utilized to accurately illustrate the firearms percentage grading system. Since condition is the overriding factor in price evaluation, study these photos carefully to learn more about the condition of your specimen(s).

When looking up information in this text remember, it reads just like a good novel- turn the page to see if there is another good sentence waiting for you.

For your convenience the N.R.A. condition standards have been included making the conversion to percentage easier (page 30). This will especially be helpful when evaluating antiques.

For sake of simplicity the following organizational framework has been adopted throughout this publication.

1. Trademark, manufacturer, brand name, or importer is listed in bold face type alphabetically, i.e.,

ANSCHUTZ, BROWNING, WINCHESTER.

2. Manufacturer information is listed directly beneath the trademark heading, i.e., Manufacturer Located in New Haven, CT. Mfg began in 1866.

3. Next classification is type of gun, i.e.,

PISTOLS, REVOLVERS, RIFLES, SHOTGUNS.

4. Model names appear flush left, are bold faced, and capitalized in chronological (normally) order grouped under either pistol, rifle, or shotgun subheadings, i.e.,
SINGLE ACTION ARMY, MODEL 29, MODEL 12.

5 — Barrel lengths, guages, calibers and other descriptive data are further categorized adjacent to both models and submodels in this type face. This is where most of the information is listed for each specific model.

6. Variations within a model appear as sub-models and are indented, italicized, and are in upper and lower case to differentiate them from model headings, i.e.,
   PPK/S Durgarde, Mannlicher Type Full Stock, Engraved Carbine.

7. Manufacturer and model notes appear in smaller type and should be read since they contain important and other critical, up-to-date information, i.e.,
   This model was available with No. 3 factory engraving on a very limited special order basis. Add 40% to the above values.

8. Grading lines will appear at the top of each page an in the middle of the page if the pricing lines change. The most commonly encountered grading line in this text is from 100%-60%, i.e.,

Grading	100%	98%	95%	90%	80%	70%	60%

Antique grading lines have values listed for 100%-10%, or 80%-10%, i.e.,

100%	98%	95%	90%	80%	70%	60%	50%	40%	30%	20%	10%

or

Grading	80%	70%	60%	50%	40%	30%	20%	10%

Commemorative/limited edition grading lines will appear as follows:

Gradding	100%	issue	Price	qty	made

9. Price lines have been changed since the 10th Edition to allow the following - when the price line below is encountered,

Mfg.'s Sug. Retail	$170	$150	$130	$115	$105	$95	$85	$80

it automatically indicates that the gun is currently manufactured and the manufacturers' retail price is shown left of the 100% column. Following are the 100%-60% values. THe 100% price is what you can typically expect to pay for that model in new condition with normal discounting (if any). The 98%-60% remaining values represent actual retail selling prices - simply find to the correct column and refer to the price listed.

10. A currently manufactured gun without a retail price published by the manufacturer/importer (becoming more common every year) will appear as follows:

No. Mfg.'s Retail	$495	$450	$400	$350	$310	$280	$250

Obviously, the 100% price is the national average price a consumer will pay for a gun in new condition. The same situation for a stainless steel or limited mfg./special edition firearm withour retail pricing will appear as follows.

No Mfg.s Retail	$240	$185	$160	$145

11. A price line with 7 values listed (represented below) indicates a

	$715	$660	$605	$550	$440	$385	$330

discontinued, out or production model with values shown for 100%-60% conditions. Obviously, no "Mfg.'s Sug. Retail" will appear with the left margin but a model note may appear below the price line indicating what the last Mfg.'s Sug. Retail was before being discontinued.

12. A 4 value porice line indicates a current production gun, and

| Mfg.'s Sug. Retail | $822 | $665 | $545 | $465 |

prices are not shown in 90% or less condition since the specimen (notice model description) is either stainless steel, a commemorative, or limited production. Because these types of firearms are almost never encounterd 90% or less condition, values for lower conditions are not listed.

To find a particular gun in this book, first look under the name of the manufacturer, importer, or brand name. Next find the correct subdivision (either pistols, rifles, shotguns, etc.). When applicable, antiques will appear before modern guns and are subdivided like modern weapons. Once you find the correct model or sub-model under it's respective subheading, determine the weapon's percentage of original condition (see the Photo Percentage Grading System after page 32) and find the corresponding price. Commemoratives will appear last under a manufacturers heading.

Enlarged in the 12th edition are sections on Trademark Index, Modern Blackpowder Guns, Airguns, and Model Serialization breakdown by major trademarks. Three or four prices will be listed for both Black Powder and Airgun Models. When using the Model Serialization section make sure your model is listed and find the serial number within the yearly range listings.

Acknowledgments

Each edition, the **Blue Book of Gun Values** *gets a little bit bigger and takes on more responsibility as the firearms industry's foremost publication on values and related data. And every year, an increasing list of knowledgable people make the material on the pages more complete and informational. Remembering and listing everyone who has assisted me in the compilation of the 12th edition would be impossible, but go ahead and take a bow - you know who you are, and you have earned it. To the following a special thanks is in order:*

Dr. Leonardo Antaris
Donald M. Simmons
Leon Wier, Jr.
Dr. David & Pat Avery
R. L. Wilson
Dr. Richard Arnold
Marty Huber and
Kathleen Hoyt
  of Colt's Firearms
Thomas Koessl
Gerry Landskron
Evan Whildin
Jack Skeuse
  of Parker Reproductions
Jim Jasken
Mims Reed
Dr. Robert Beeman
  of Beeman Precision Arms
Keith Cochran
Bob Jones
Don Ware
the late Lt. Col. W. S. Brophy
  of Marlin Firearms
Harley Lindhus
Rick Kennerknecht
David Noll
Peter Hoffman
  of Walther Sportwaffen Fabrik
Christine Seidel
  of Mauser-Werke
Dr. Kam Nassar
Harry Akers
Patrick McKune
Keith Rolf
Dan Gibbons
Jim Austin
Remington Society of America

Patrick M. Lucking
A. O. Salvo
LeRoy Merz
Kevin Cherry
Robert Rayburn
Lowell Pauli
John Gyde
Richard Bauter
  of Browning
Damon Mills
David Buehn
Joyce Gentilo
  of Beretta U.S.A. Corp.
Don Criswell
the late David Adams
  of Sigarms, Inc.
Rudy Etchen
Jack Heath
  of Remington Arms Co.
Larry Baer
Bruno Pardee
  of U.S. Repeating Arms
Larry Del Greco
John C. Dugan
  Rugers Collectors Association
Richard Alexander
  of Interarms
Dan Sheil, Jr.
Jeff Brooks
Roy Jinks
  of Smith & Wesson
Robert White
Robert Saunders
  of American Derringer Corp.
Martin Vittitow
Colt Collectors Association
Browning Collcetors Association
Jim Supica, Jr.

and to

Bonnie Quick, whose quick scan, right-to-left proofreading style enabled this edition to be printed with the minimum of misplaced ink.

and to

"The Midnight Gourmet", a psuedonym for all of those food corporations whose mottos are 'We Deliver' and 'Open All Night', without them I would have never had been able feed the slaves.

and to

Ace Collier, Jr., now a part of the Blue Book Family, and the only registered Coon Ass at One Appletree Square to drive a convertible to work all winter with the windows part way down.

And to

Paul G. Wichtendahl, whose inability to say "No" to my coast-to-coast editing requests allowed this book to balloon to over 1,000 pages. Just one last thing Paul, and this will only take a minute......

and to

The staff of Blue Book Publications, Inc. whose rookie combat status performance during the past several weeks of intense hand-to-phone fighting has been exemplary. Next year, they'll be seasoned veterans, dug in well to avoid unplanned Scud attacks.

Dedication

The 12th edition of the Blue Book of Gun Values is dedicated to the late Lt. Col .William S. Brophy, an officer and gentleman. Those of us who were fortunate to know this walking firearms library are deeply saddened. We'll miss you Bill, and I hope all the elk up there have trophy racks.

The production of a publication brought to this level of quality and sophistication takes a good imagination, technical perfection, dedication to quality and deadlines, and a fat checkbook. The firms and individuals listed below are some of the best in the Minneapolis-St Paul area and are mentioned here because of their competance, commitment, concern and continual capacity to put up with my * * * *. Viking Press and Jack Dobihal- Printing, DPS's David & Debra - design, artwork & graphics, Northwest Color and Roger, Leslie, and Dick- for color separations, Prism Studios and Tom Farmer- Visuals and Trick Imagery. All of the people listed here deserve one round (two shots some days) of applause.

A Word About Pricing
in this Book

Undoubtedly, the most often asked question I get during the course of a year is "Steve, how do you come up with the prices in this book?" No simple question — and no simple answer. Coming up with over 40,000 accurate prices in this publication is no easy task. In addition to attending at least 15 gun/trade shows annually, I have a very knowledgeable dealer network and a "worried about higher prices" collector base to draw information from on a regular basis. Between the two, the axe gets sharpened pretty equally. Some prices are "mixed" for an "average national price" due to regional price fluctuations (i.e., Kentucky flintlocks sell for more money in PA than they would in Miami).

With prices settling down since the record highs of 1980-81, more and more guns are falling in their individual price "slots", making dealer retail pricing very competitive. Also, with much more firearms information and manufacturer data available for the collector today than even 10 years ago, production rarity premiums are also more predictable than previously.

Buying, selling, and trading for original top quality condition major trademarks such as Browning, Colt's, Winchester, and others is strong currently. I've talked to many collectors who feel now is the time to acquire some of those apparent "bargains" that are surfacing at this time. Whether these purchases today will keep up with the monetary appreciation afforded in the past remains to be seen - certainly a change in the inflation rate would go a long way in escalating firearms' prices.

It is important to note that prices listed for current production firearms include the manufacturer's suggested retail prices for 1990. They can be instantly recognized by the **"Mfg. Sug. Retail"** notation on the left margin of many price lines. With the erosion of profits on newly manufactured firearms due to agressive discount merchandising, almost all current production guns can be picked up at a sizeable discount. These discounts are reflected in the 100% column and indicate the discounted price you can typically expect to pay for a current production firearm in new condition.

Again - all values shown represent actual retail selling prices — dealer offers when you sell could be off by 15% - 50% of the values shown.

As much as I try to be more accurate every year, if you feel some price is out of line or I have omitted or misrepresented a particular model, by all means contact me and let's discuss it. Previous subscribers have been very kind in helping me with corrections of this nature in past editions. I hope your comments, observations, criticisms, and other ideas continue to come in. Most new suggestions get added to the next edition. Mistakes can happen, but they shouldn't happen twice. Direct technical and pricing correspondence to me at:

Blue Book of Gun Values
Research — Attn: S. P. Fjestad
One Appletree Square
Minneapolis, MN 55420
Phone No. 612-854-5229
FAX No. 612-853-1486

Once again, please allow 2-4 weeks normally for a reply.

Correspondence Inquiries

I have to apologize to many subscribers who have sent correspondence to me during the past. The good news is that after two years of being behind, I finally caught up with customer correspondence before Christmas! With the additional staff affording more research time, I'm glad to report that your letters regarding additional information should turn around within 30 days in the future. Remember, **the charge is $15.00 per gun** and payment must accompany your correspondence. Your letter(s)/FAXes will be answered in a FIFO system (first in—first out). Thank you for your patience.

Because of the flood of mail I get yearly, I can no longer perform free evaluations. To take advantage of this new service, send in information, including: trademark, model description, pertinent data (including caliber, type and condition of finish, barrel length, and any other special features) along with your name, address, phone number, and payment. Also, if possible, a couple of clear pictures would help tremendously. Please, do not send your firearm(s) unless you have talked to me directly. If you are desperate, you can FAX me this information along with a Visa/Mastercard number, expiration date, and your signature authorizing payment. **FAXed questions with payment will be answered within 48 hours, unless the *gun doctors* are out on a trade show or holiday.**

As always, we will try to answer your question(s) in as short a time as possible using this new system.

All Correpsondence should be directed to:

Blue Book Publications
Attn: Research Department
One Appletree Square
Minneapolis, MN 55425

FAXed reasearch questions (accompanied by credit card number
***AND** expiration date) will be the fastest.*

SORRY- NO ORDER OR REQUEST FOR RESEARCH PAID BY CREDIT CARD WILL BE PROCESSED WITHOUT A CREDIT CARD EXPIRATION DATE.

FOREWORD

*F*ive months, 10 reams of paper, 20 domestic and international flights totalling 30,000+ miles, 1 Operation Desert Storm, and more last minute "fine tuning" than the staff could have ever imagined, the 12th Edition is in your hands. I remember struggling for 341 pages in the 3rd Edition which cost $12.95 in 1982. This edition has 1,024 pages, contains over 1/2 million words and prices, includes 30 pages of full-color, and sells for $19.95. Those improvements and additions make this 12th Edition the best **Blue Book of Gun Values** published to date.

*T*he past 12 months have not been kind to the firearms industry - especially those involved in the manufacture of new guns. It seems the new gun business in America has been to the summit, and is now descending to a lower base camp each year. The problem is there seems to be no higher peaks in sight. As our domestic and a few international gun companies get re-acclimated to the lower altitude, some are readjusting but others are having to call 911.

*T*imes have changed, the Bull Market of the 60's and 70's is over, and those companies who are awaiting its return without making internal adjustments may not get another chance. The nineties will demand sharper marketing, leaner operations, continual technological improvements, and a positive acceptance in realizing that the development of a variety of shooting sports will eventually overtake the demand factor that hunting has enjoyed for centuries.

*I*nterestingly enough, the collectible gun business has been insulated from the recession that the rest of our economy has been experiencing. Many dealers are reporting sales equal or better than previous years. Quality merchandise is selling, sometimes at record prices. I can't think of one good collector gun that hasn't increased in value during the past five years. The reasons for this are simple- investment dollars are not in control of most collectible firearms and rampant speculation has not affected the firearms marketplace.

*T*arget and sport shooting are attracting more new American shooters annually than anything else, just as they have done in Europe for decades. The development and growth of these new shooting sports will be instrumental for the firearms industry to maintain a strong pulse. Those companies who continue to rely on hunters only for the sale of their products will be dissapointed sooner or later.

I mproved in the 12th Edition is the 32 page "Photo Percentage Grading System", now with 60 color plates to assist you in the grade of almost any type of firearm (un-numbered section after pg. 32). Also, the Trademark Index has been updated and enlarged plus new serialization tables have also been added. Thousands of prices were changed/added to reflect the most up-to-date information taken from the most recent IWA Trade Show held in Nuremberg (European Shot Show equivalent) and the Robert Howard Auction held recently in San Francisco (almost 700 fine quality Winchesters and Colts were sold). I feel fortunate that this new data could be published so quickly.

I n closing, I would encourage you to get involved in the continual battles involving local, state, and federal gun laws. Being indifferent at this point in our firearms evolution is actually helping the other side pass more restrictive gun laws. Let your politicians and other officials know how you feel regarding the issues.

A s in the past, I appreciate your support in this project and keep those cards and letters coming in. Our Delta flight to the NRA Annual Convention in San Antonio is making its final approach and once again I must return my tray to its locked position for landing.

Sincerely,

Steven P. Fjestad
Author and Publisher
Blue Book of Gun Values

A Unique Concept

The Blue Book of Gun Values is the only book that:

- Utilizes the professionals' grading system of percentage of original finish remaining. (Eliminates confusing descriptions such as "Good", "Excellent", "Fair".)

- Is updated annually for up-to-date prices.

- Is based on actual selling prices. (These are the prices you can expect to pay — not artificial list prices or some "expert's" opinion.)

- Offers you personal consultation by mail on special questions you may have! (No book can cover everything.)

In the past I have offered one free consultation per book order. With the growth of this project (not to mention the hundreds of letters and phone calls I am already behind on), this is no longer possible. Individual appraisals and/or additional research can be performed for $15.00 per gun. Please include a detailed description with all pertinent information about the gun(s) in question in your letter/fax. Good quality photos of the receiver, special markings, etc. would also be appreciated.

Interested in buying or selling a particular firearm(s)? Depending on what you are interested in, a referral will be made that will enable you to be sure that you are getting what you paid for (or getting paid a fair price). This service is designed to help all those people who are worried or scared about purchasing a potentially "bad gun" or getting "ripped off" when selling. Please phone or write the Blue Book of Gun Values for both availability and dealer referrals that can be relied upon for both buying and selling. All replies are treated strictly confidential. Replies should be directed to:

Blue Book
of Gun Values TM
Attn: Steven Fjestad or Ace Collier, Jr.
One Appletree Square
Minneapolis, MN 55425
Phone No. 612-854-5229
FAX NO. 612-853-1486

If we're not available, please leave a message.

A Word about
Blue Book Publications

This may seem a lot like last years introduction, so in order to avoid repetition, let me put it this way- "It has been another year of transition here at Blue Book Publications, Inc.". We are still in the same office space as we were last year, the carpet is still blue and Steve's desk is still probably one of the largest in the Twin Cities (for that matter the upper midwest) but that is about all that has stayed constant. Mayhem is the order of the day - but we like it that way. We have a new computer system (AGAIN?) for all of the same reasons that we bought the last one. This time we can actually see progress in speed of processing, records tracking, customer service and all those other buzz words of business. We are justifiably proud of what we have accomplished. The Powers that Be were not thrilled with the idea at the beginning but they like the results. In- house typesetting has made this 12th edition bulge to 1,024 pages including the Color Photo Precentage Grading insert which DOUBLED in size for this edition. As always, the Human Resources aspect is what has made this year better than ever and the pictures that follow will give you an image to go with the voice at the other end of the line. Our office hours are slightly longer than last year. We are ready for your phone call/FAX between 8:30 AM to 5:00 PM CST, Monday through Friday. We are hoping to add a 24 hour order line for your convenience, but like so many things its on the "drawing board" right now. At worst, you'll get the answering machine. Below are the non-machines ready to help you.

Capt A. (Ace) H. Jerry Collier Jr.

One of the New Additions to the staff. In name he is the Associate Editor and also part of the Research team. Actually, he is that and if you ask him he is also the house GPN. You'll have to ask him what that means. Ace has been contributing to the book for years and we are very happy to have him as a part of the permanent team now.

Paul G. Wichtendahl

Another of the new additions. He replaced Carolyn Laughlin, Doris Johnson, and Vicki Schmeling. Paul is responsible for the accounting, computer systems, customer database, and general operations. Every page of the book you are holding was typeset by him. Paul also contributes to advertising layout and planning.

Lisa Winkels

"**T**his will just take a minute, Lisa " is one of her favorite quotes. Lisa handles daily order processing and also did a great deal of the input for this edition. Lisa is also new this year, but has adapted to this ordered madness exceptionally well. If you got your book on time or got your questions answered promptly you probably have Lisa to thank. She keeps the office clean and orderly as well as keeping the rest of us in line.

Beth Marthaler

Beth has been involved with the Blue Book before and we were glad to have her back again as part-time. She came in in 1991 to help cover the phones and lend a hand where it was needed. Having her here kept it all from getting out of control as we pushed towards the deadline. By the time the next edition rolls around she will be a Mom (again). Congratulations.

Steven Fjestad

So many of you know and love him that he really needs no introduction. Mr. Guns is no longer the only male in the office but still spends his time talking about Cosmo articles. He still is responsible for writing each edition and facilitating the advertising and marketing plan. This year was new for him, instead of escaping to the Sunshine Belt to write the book he did it all in the luxury of the "Ranch" here in the Twin Cities. *Hope it was **painful** Steve.*

Introduction

How to Start Gun Collecting

In every part of this country, there are firearms-collecting associations. You can benefit from membership/affiliation in such an association, since you can use it to meet other collectors and firearms experts who are an excellent source of information, help, guidance and invaluable education. In most major cities, there are regularly scheduled firearms shows where you can buy, sell or swap your weapons and gain insight into general prices and values. Also, at the larger national shows, you'll find many prominent and reputable dealers who usually have high-quality merchandise for sale.

I personally recommend that you attend at least one major weapons show each year. When you do, you'll be able to see everything from ultra-rare antiques to modern commemoratives. This will help you to determine where your interest lies. You can also make price comparisons. Shows are a place to meet collectors, investors and dealers from all over the nation. Once you have decided what you want to collect, we recommend you talk to everyone who could have any knowledge and provide you with information in this area. You must do the homework.

Recently, I wrote a dealer friend of mine on what a beginning collector should do to start this fascinating hobby. His comments were: collect what you really like, buy books and read, get out and look with a magnifying glass, be involved in a collecting fraternity, know your dealer(s)— pick them carefully, listen to them and knowledgeable others, avoid speculation, and get a receipt. These are good measures to follow.

For your benefit, we've included a mini-directory of recommended reading material and reference works as well as trade publications that will further assist you in gathering the knowledge needed for your choosen area(s) of interest.

Starting Tips

My advice would be to pick out an area where knowledge or interest already exist. Once you have found an area that you find interesting and want to collect, formulate a plan on what you would like to purchase as an overall collection. Expand this established base with additional knowledge. Buy the necessary books, magazines, and trade periodicals to make yourself informed as possible in the niche you've chosen. Most advanced collectors and dealers have expansive reference libraries for fast, fingertip accessibility. Don't worry about the price for reference material — one book can easily pay for itself in one gun trade. And the books themselves become investments as they go out of print and command increased prices. No one individual can know everything about every gun — reference works are a must.

Once you're "book trained" the next step is to start looking — not buying — at guns in the field you've chosen. Attend a few gun shows or visit dealers that have inventories of items you're looking for. *Don't* get side-tracked by other fascinating merchandise. Pay close attention to the coloration of blueing, crispness of metal markings (proof marks, barrel address, etc.), wood to metal fit, bore condition, and possible non- factory alterations. In this business, the experience gained in running through your hands has no substitute. I have known people who would quote from memory every gauge, choke, barrel, stock variation available for the Model 12 Winchester, yet these sample people can't spot a reblued gun. Knowing the correct factory bluing color, style of wood, and finish, production variation etc., does not come overnight. It takes experience and a well-trained eye. If in doubt about "original finish someone claims, consult a dealer or collector who does know the difference. Only after you've taken these steps are you ready to become a buyer. Anything less could result in a "long-term" investment.

Where and How to Buy and Sell Guns

This "Art" has changed drastically over the last 30 years. Dealer showrooms, gun shows, and local advertising were the only means of buying or selling guns for many years. Trading was more localized and regional price differences were more evident. Many fine weapons stayed in one locality for long periods of time. With the advent of the 5 second long distance telephone call and overnight express mail, the firearms marketplace now reaches coast to coast. International marketing is even possible where regulations permit. All this means increased merchandise exposure, more universal grading standards, and higher levels of competition in pricing firearms fairly.

Buying

It's been said that good guns are wherever you find them. Nothing could be truer. The following listing will give an idea of where to purchase collector guns:

A) Gun shows — these shows exist throughout the United States and are usually well- attended. With hundreds of showings being held yearly (check your gun shop or trade publications for dates), it is possible to take in two shows on a single weekend — locations permitting.

Advantages include:

1. Physically inspecting potential purchases.

2. Comparing prices, against other similar items at the same show.

3. Having a large selection from which to choose.

4. Providing unequaled opportunity to meet fellow collectors and other experts in the field to exchange information.

5. Displaying the broadest base of firearms, accessories, and memorabilia from which to develop new interests.

6. Haggle for better prices, especially for items still unsold late in the show.

7. Offer "trade-in" potential with prices established at the show — rather hard and lenghty to do by mail.

Disadvantages include:

1. A good chance of running into fakes, reblued items, and non-factory alterations or conversions. Higher prices over the last 5 years have resulted in many common models being "upgraded" to a model much rarer. Be careful on purchases where this type of activity might exist.

2. Most sales are final. Once the cash has been transformed, your inspection is over. A collector pays for his "mistakes" in this business. If a sale is contingent on a yet-to-come factory letter, part(s), or additional accessories make sure the seller includes them in his bill-of- sale. It's simply good business for both parties. When contemplating a purchase, ask the seller what he/she knows about the specimen(s) you are considering, including finish condition (and if original), possible alterations, and how it was obtained. If those answers pass your screening test, then you are ready to ask what the seller would take in payment for the gun OR if they would be interested in trading. Asking a seller what their lowest cash price would be and then offering a "pretty good old 12 ga. double barrel" in trade will not put you on the Christmas card list of your average firearms dealer.

3. "Show Pressure" forces you into decisions that have to be made in a few minutes — oftentimes with 2 other people simultaneously bargaining for the same gun.

4. Being side-tracked into other areas. Know what you want, what you want to pay for it, and don't impulse buy. Keep a level head, and stick to the areas you're familiar with. This is important with merchandise ranging from stuffed animal heads to Browning .50 calibers.

Remember — most good gun show "buys" occur during the gun show's opening hours, or the night previous to opening before the public is admitted. An apparent bargain found on Sunday afternoon sounds skeptical at best, although many dealers will "negotiate" a price very late in the show, depending on their cash flow and desire to haul a potential sale to yet another gun show. Get to the show at the opening, walk the aisles with orderly precision, avoid back tracking, and when you find a specimen that meets *all* of your criteria *and* is on your shopping list: Buy it. Too many times I've walked back to a table ready to buy and an empty spot is all that remains. Truly good guns that are fairly priced sell fast because dealers are competing with collectors. One last item — don't interrupt an exhibitor engaged in selling (even if it's one you want). It's not in the gun circuit code of ethics. Be patient.

B) Gun Shops — Many modern gun shops have good selections of collector guns in stock. Take one gun at a time here — and make sure that gun is within your field of expertise. Sometimes dealers selling mostly new guns get items in on trade that they know very little about — including trade-ins that "aren't right". Be able to know the difference before you buy. Again, don't get sidetracked. While you are likely to get a fair deal at a gun shop, you may find an item in your field once every five years.

C) Auctions — While not as major as gun shows or gun shops in the marketplace, auctions can be used to your advantage in buying. Large auction houses such as Christie's and Sotheby's deal in only extremely fine and rare specimens that carry big price tags. Know what you want and your monetary limit before conducting business at this level. Some auction guns are "dogs" with hidden defects that preclude their sale through reputable dealers. Estate, household, and farm auctions can be used with some success if you know previously which guns will be sold. Frequently, no "gun" will be in attendance and prices could be quite low. Make sure that condition is at par with your standards. With all auctions, attend the preliminary exhibition and be sure you make a careful inspection of all guns you might bid on. Mail order bids are sometimes an option to being at the auction. Before bids are submitted, know everything about what you're potentially purchasing.

D) Other Collectors — Buying from other collectors is dependent on how comfortable you are with his knowledge, expertise, honesty, and previous dealings. Serious collectors usually sell their finest guns last. Make sure the gun you're considering isn't a poor duplicate in the collection or one of his "mistakes". Obviously, it is to a collectors advantage to sell to another collector and thereby avoid the "middleman" dealer markup. find out if the guns were carefully chosen originally, part of an estate settlement, or other important past history. Also, big collections don't necessarily guarantee good collections. More than a few "collections" are gathered around poor quality, high quantity odds and ends.

E) Mail Order Dealer — This area has really grown in the past 10 years. These dealers send out regular inventory listings to previous customers and much business is out- of-state. It is to the dealer's advantage to accurately grade his guns very carefully to avoid misrepresentation and eliminate customer fears in not being able to see the gun. Good mail-order dealers *always* give an inspection period. Returned guns don't make anyone happy so the dealer is always faced with selling as good a gun as possible for a competitive price. Anything less results in stagnating inventory levels. Many of these dealers specialize in specific areas. Their specialization usually insures the buyer of good condition original guns made possible by the dealers thorough "screening" used before buying. Getting as many dealer inventory listings as possible will give you a chance to "shop" around and check prices. A dealers reputation is a big factor in this area. Deal with those you're comfortable with and will listen when you want to trade in something previously purchased.

F) Classified Ads — Rarely anymore do good quality, collector guns show up under the "Guns for Sale" Ad in the local newspaper. The "steals" of the 60's and 70's are mostly gone. Still keep your eyes open and follow every lead. These wild goose chases can sometimes be very rewarding. An "advertised"

WWII Luger for $485.00 is certainly worth buying if it turns out to be a Kreighoff. Be fast — don't hesitate when real "buys" do pop up.

G) Trade Periodicals — Magazines, such as *Shotgun News, Gun Report, Gun List, American Rifleman, Guns and Ammo, Man at Arms,* and others, contain valuable firearms information. Some listed fireamrs are good buys — others are out and out rip-offs. Know who you are buying from, insist on an inspection period covering all purchases, and get a receipt. See References/Periodicals Section for addresses and subscription costs.

Selling

Certainly as many considerations confront the potential seller as the potential buyer. Different approaches must be used when selling a single gun, a few guns, or an extensive collection. Locality, modern or antique status, and proper grading all have to be studied. No standard format is applicable to every situation here.

Knowing the market and prices should be an advantage in selling. The collector is familiar with gun values, knows dealers that handle his type of guns, and has established contact with fellow collectors of similar merchandise. These potential buyers increase the liquidity base.

When selling more than one gun and similar items are involved, either the piecemeal or "sold only as a group" method should be determined first. Selling a collection intact is certainly cleaner than taking one-at-a-time. More money can be extracted selling individually — if you have the patience.

In 1981 when gold and silver were fluctuating large amounts daily, a woman called in and asked me "What's the spot price of Winchesters today?" After my initial laugh, I told her collector gun values have always been dictated by marketplace supply and demand. Just as a spot price for a Winchester will never appear in the *Wall Street Journal,* a fair market price tag on your 98% P.38 will not necessarily guarantee you instant liquidity. Lack of inflation has caused a drop in asking prices for many collector guns that are available in good supply.

When selling use the same general headings listed under buying as possibilities. Certainly an obvious place to sell a valuable gun is to the dealer who might have originally sold you the item. Since he considered it worthy of ownership previously, restocking the gun should be in his scope of interest. How much will you get? This will depend on length of ownership, any change of condition, that gun's increased market appeal (if any), and the dealers current inventory levels. Unless the funds generated in selling a gun are needed immediately, never be in a rush to sell a nice gun. Patience will reward you over panic. When that right person shows genuine interest, offer the gun professionally and stick close to your asking price — you'll probably get it.

Many major trade publications offer national exposure — and larger exposure generally means higher prices. It makes sense that 75,000 people reading *Shotgun News* will generate more interest than 300 tire-kickers at a hometown gun show. While results may take more time (3-6 weeks), the added dollars on the sale price usually justify the wait.

Trends to be Aware Of

Collecting firearms as a hobby originally started because of nostalgia over antique firearms and their place in history. Modern collectible firearms are today the fastest-growing area. If you spend time studying these modern guns, you will see there are many excellent choices to be made from Colts, Lugers, Mausers, Smith & Wessons and Winchesters. Much interst is also developing in .22-caliber pistols from antiques through modern variations.

Another area showing increasing collector interest is high- grade quality Damascus-barrelled shotguns.

Firearms Laws

There are four legal classifications of firearms used by the Bureau of Alcohol, Tobacco, and Firearms of the Treasury Department.

1) Antique — Any firearm manufactured in or before 1898, and replicas that do not fire rim-fire or center-fire cartridges readily available in commercial trade. Anyone can legally own an antique and no paperwork has to be completed during their purchase.

2) Modern — Firearms manufactured after 1898, excluding replica antiques, and with special regulations for class III fully automatic arms. Any modern gun sold in the United States today must be registered if bought from a dealer. Private sales preclude this (check local and state laws). A modern gun — Can be shipped state to state by dealers to other dealers May be shipped to an out-of-state dealer by a private individual Must be registered upon sale by dealer Is governed not only by the regulations of The Gun Control Act of 1968, but also by the appropriate local and state laws pertaining to the same Cannot be shipped interstate to a private individual, only other licensed dealers

3) Curios and Relics — Certain specified modern firearms that can be sent interstate to licensed collectors. These include guns manufactured at least 50 years prior to the current date (not replicas thereof). Check current curio and relic listings the the BATF.

4) Class III Arms — Includes machine guns, silencers, short barreled shotguns (under 18"), short barreled rifles (under 16"), modern smoothbore handguns, and modern arms with a rifled bore diameter greater than .5 inches. The first three items may be legally owned, not withstanding federal regulations and local restrictions in a few areas. Class III items are illegal in some states. For further information, contact your local office of the BATF.

What to Collect — The Answers Depend on You

Firearms offer something for everyone. There are different-purpose fire-arms with many designs. Some have historical value and are quite fascinating. History has often been changed because some faction or culture had superior firearms to influence or force its culture and politics on another.

To a certain extent, there is no right or wrong area in which to collect. Pick the category you prefer and then do some studying before you make a choice and begin buying. Be sure you're comfortable with the area you ultimately decide to go with.

I would suggest that you keep your collection orderly and coherent. Collect one marker or one model in all its variations (if possible). You could also base a collection on type, such as Kentucky dueling pistols or military automatic handguns. Collections have been based on firearms of one caliber, such as the 9mm Parabellum or .22-caliber Rim Fire. The variations are numerous, but the collection will have greater appeal if there is a visible purpose to it. This should not stop you from purchasing something outside your collection if you like it — and it is a genuine bargain.

When buying for your collection, you will be much better off if you pur-chase quality items. Owning only one extremely high-quality collector fire-arm is preferable to owning two or three lesser ones. The greatest demand and appreciation will always be with the highest-quality pieces. Guns in poor ndition may show smaller increases in value. Current production firearms and those just out of production have collector value only if in close to new condition or in the original box. The corresponding ratings shown herein would be 95%, 98% or 100%. *See section "How to Use and Apply Grading System." Commemoratives, for example, must be new (100%) or they have lost much of their collector value. If a commemorative is no more than the standard-issue firearm but with minor trim added, its chance of appreciating is about nil. At the other extreme, an antique or possibly a military firearm may be found with no remaining finish, and if there is demand because of rarity, it could be an excellent addition to a collection. The main consideration is how they are normally found and collector demand. Study my price value guidelines for a better indication of rarity and values.

A shrewd collector may look for a firearm not actively collected but with growing interest.

Antique Arms — A Very Exciting Area to Look At

Antiques span hand cannons and matchlocks to the earlier modern designs. They can be found in all states of condition and show strong appreciation even though they are expensive. High-quality Flintlock and Percussions arms, civil and military, are an excellent example of collectible antique weaponry. In later antiques, Colts and Winchesters are the perennial favorites. Civil War period arms are very popular, as are Volcanics, Henrys, Remingtons, Smith & Wessons, Sharps, etc. Again I recommend that you spend the time thoroughly to study this book.

Modern Arms — Offering Something for Nearly Everyone

Modern arms are those manufactured after 1898. Due to this arbitrary cutoff date, there are a few later antiques which carry over to the modern category. Where this happens, I will list known accepted cutoff models or serial number information in the text. The modern arms era brought the development of some of the most popular arms ever developed. Many are still with us today in commercial versions, often because they were adopted at one time as a military arm. In some of the more collectible later designs, we find important cutoff dates where quality designs were modified to take advantage of less expensive production. These facts will be detailed in the text while explaining their significance. Currently, the fastest-growing collector area centers around either production arms, arms recently out of production or arms recently discontinued. The following text will list in detail models of these, including Auto Mag, Browning, Colt, Ruger, Smith & Wesson, Winchester, etc.

Military Arms

At the end of World War II, unique firearms became available. Many were brought home as souvenirs. Since they were armed forces firearms, few survived in original condition. Military firearms provide a vast field of study, especially since many of them are directly tied to our nation's history. Late in 1984, Federal legislation once again allowed importation of non-domestic WWI and WWII military handguns. As a result, many military Lugers (including DWM and Mauser variations), Mauser Broomhandles, Browning Hi-Powers and P.38's, have been recently imported in some quantities. Condition on most of these recent imports is 80% or lower (with pitting on some) and prices typically start in the $200 range. While many of these newer imports would make workable shooters, they have in no way lowered prices on 90%+ condition specimens due to normal collector activity in top quality only military pistols. Recently imported pistols should have the importers name visibly stamped on an exterior surface. Most of these imports are surplus WWII or European police guns that have been liquidated through domestic distribution. Machine guns offer a rather elite form of military arms for the collector. Their high prices and the strict federal laws make them less appealing, however, and a Class III license has to be obtained from the BATF. In some states, they are banned by law.

What Dictates Value — A Combination of Factors

Condition, rarity, demand, special features and historical significance determine current value. All values are based on the premise that the firearm is authentic and original. The value of a collector arm is always in relation to the condition of other examples of the same make, model and variation. Condition is the amount of over-all original finish remaining on all parts of the firearm and condition of wood, if stocked, which can run from 0 to 100%. The collector is encouraged to acquire the better examples of what is available. If you find one better than the norm and it can be purchased at a fair price, you have had a stroke of luck. Most modern arms should be in the premium class, 95% to 100%, for collector purposes and definitely for maximum appreciation.

Rarity — A Word About Its Importance to the Collector/Investor

Rarity is very much like condition in the sense that the rarer pieces are highly prized and, just as guns in the best condition, are in great demand.

Demand — Who Wants What and Why

Demand for a collector arm exists because of nostalgia, rarity, history or unusual features. Demand dictates higher prices.

Special Features

Special features can increase value. Non-standard or experimental parts, special-order options or finish can make a price difference. The most desirable of all special features is engraving and precious metal inlays.

Historical Signifance

Arms are important for the roles they played in wars. Demand also exists for arms owned by famous persons. Guns owned by Western heroes and outlaws have sold for $30,000 to $50,000. The key here is authenticity and documentation. This can be in the form of factory shipping ledger entries or original signed bills of sale, etc.

Identification and Authentication

Reference books are available on almost any firearm. They offer a wealth of information and can be used to help identify through component parts, manufacturing variations, serial numbers, etc. Authentication should be done by someone knowledgeable. See guide to reference books and recommended reading.

Restoration

Restoration occurs mainly in antiques but can be found with any popular arms. In most cases, a restored or refinished firearm does not deserve the status of a collectible firearm. Once a firearm has been restored, it can never be returned to its original condition. Restoration of antiques is accepted by many people because of the scarcity of good original arms. Such guns should be so marked and explicitly sold as restored pieces. Unfortunately, as they pass through several owners, this information tends to be lost. Replacement or repair done with current original parts should not affect the value.

Modification and Conversion

Many collector arms have been modified for personal taste and not with the intent to defraud or produce a fake. Often, it was done before a collector demand developed. Usually, it was done to copy a much scarcer variation of the same firearm. At a recent gun show, I found offered for sale as the genuine item six of the same rare variations of a modern handgun. All were priced in the correct range, were they authentic. Each was a fake made from a more common model. Their true value was about 20% of the asking price. Upgrading can take place in most firearms but can cost the most with engraved guns. Most often a low-grade shotgun is engraved to simulate a much-scarcer, higher-grade gun. Conversions are most common with antiques. Disagreement exists on whether it is permissible to reconvert guns such as Percussions back to their original Flintlock condition. Guns so converted should be noted as such and sold on that basis.

Dealers and Gun Prices

Although you may be concerned with wholesale/retail price breaks, such a price structure can only be applied to modern firearms — shooters you buy in the gun shop. It certainly does not apply to collectible firearms. In the first place, practically all collectibles are out of production. That means you'll have to wait until someone decides to part with, say, a Luger he "liberated" during the war. Now the problem is: how do you find the man who want to sell his no-longer-made Luger? Your chances of meeting him are pretty slim — so you go to a legitimate dealer with your request. Now it's the dealer's job to find the gun you want, at a fair price — and to assure you that the Luger is original and authentic. In fact, your broker or dealer is really responsible for the Luger's meeting all criteria of collectible value. Since the dealer has performed a valuable service for you, he naturally adds a fee to the price you eventually pay for your Luger. Without the fee- paid service, you might be spending your time running around the country looking for the gun — and still end up with a "fake!" So, although I've tried my hardest to formulate realistic prices in this guide, please remember that you may have to pay more merely because you are utilizing someone else's valuable services.

The NRA

If you own guns — or are thinking about owning guns — you face more challenges every year. One is your *"right* to keep and bear arms". If you're like most people, you've probably let others do the fighting for you: the National Rifle Association, your state rifle and pistol association, and the several new organizations formed to meet the threat from the gun-grabbers.

If you have not joined the NRA in the past year, this is the year to do so. Recent legislation against "assault" rifles has crippled yet another classification of firearms for the law-abiding U.S. citizen. We cannot afford to lose our rights as gun owners one classification at a time. If it was not for the NRA, many battles would have already been lost to preserve this greatest of American freedoms. Giving the NRA $25 is the *first* $25 firearms enthusiasts should spend annually. Without a well funded, professionally run organization to combat this threat, our individual efforts will not be enough.

Well, the time is past when *any* gun owner — hunter to collector of expensive antiques — can sit back and ignore this threat. The anti-gun movement is professionally run, heavily financed, and supported by a majority of the news media. I strongly recommend that you become a member of the National Rifle Association. Besides being the strongest lobbying organization in America today, the NRA also offers its members firearms insurance policies, magazines and information keeping you abreast of proposed legislation changes, plus many other benefits. The United States is the only country in the world that constitutionally guarantees her citizens the right to keep and bear arms. Preserving that right is the fundamental principle behind the NRA. If you want to enjoy and continue to collect firearms, join the NRA and let them help. After all, can you imagine this fascinating and rewarding hobby legislated out of existence?

To join, write:

National Rifle Association
1600 Rhode Island Ave. N.W.
Washington, D.C. 20036

Yearly membership is $25.00 (includes annual subscription to monthly American Rifleman magazine.

Or send in this coupon

National Rifle Association Membership Application
Please send in with payment (choose one below) to:

1 yr. - $25
3 yr. - $68
5 yr. - $100

NRA of America
1600 Rhode Island
Avenue, N.W.
Washington, DC
20036
Attn: Membership

Date _____

Company Name _____

Name_____

Street_____

City _____

State_____ Zip _____

Phone_____

The Second Amendment Foundation is a tax-exempt publicly supported foundation organized under 501(c)(3) of the Internal Revenue Code.

The Foundation is dedicated to promoting a better understanding about our constitutional heritage to privately own and possess firearms. To that end, we carry on many educational and legal action programs designed to better inform the public about the gun control debate.

This critique was made possible by the generosity of many citizens who want to preserve the Second Amendment of the U.S. Contistution.

All contributions to the Foundation are tax-deductible.

For more information about the foundation write to:

Second Amendment Foundation
James Madison Building
12500 N.E. Tenth Place
Bellevue, Eashington 98005
Phone No.: (206) 454- 7012

To make a contribution, use the coupon below:

Second Amendment Foundation
12500 N.E. 10th Place, Bellevue, WA 98005

Contributing Membership Application

IN DEFENSE OF
THE RIGHT TO KEEP
AND BEAR ARMS

Please accept my personal commitment to help preserve and protect our Right to Keep and Bear Arms.

I have enclosed my contribution of:
☐ $15   ☐ $25   ☐ $50   ☐ $100   ☐ $ other _____

I have enclosed my membership fee:
☐ $15 Annual   ☐ $100 Defenders Club   ☐ $1000 Committee of One Thousand

Name _____

Street Address _____ Apt. _____

City _____ State _____ Zip _____

Phone _____

Grading Criteria for Firearms

The old, NRA method of firearms grading — by relying upon adjectives such as "Excellent" or "Fair" — served the firearms fraternity for a long time. Today's collectors, however, are turning away from such a subjective system. One man's "Fair" is another man's "Good!"

The leading professionals in the grading of firearms now utilize what is essentially an objective method for deciding the price range of a gun: THE PERCENTAGE OF ORIGINAL FACTORY BLUING REMAINING ON THE GUN. After looking critically at a few firearms, and carefully studying the Photo Percentage Grading System (starts after page 32), even the novice can soon tell whether a piece has 100%, 98%, 95%, or less bluing remaining.

Of course, factors such as "depth" and quality of the bluing, engraving and embellishment, historical significance, and even the condition of the stock can and do affect the price. But the basic "condition" — and therefore the price — is best determined by the percentage of original bluing remaining. The key word here is "original," for if anyone other than the factory has reblued the gun, its value as a collector's item is greatly diminished, with the exception of rare and historical pieces that have been properly restored.

Study the drawings on these pages. Note how the bluing in certain areas of the firearm wears off first. These are usually places where the gun rubs against the holster, hand or body. We have chosen a Luger and a Winchester as examples, but the principles apply to almost any firearm.

It should be noted that the older a collectible firearm is, the smaller the percentage of original bluing one can expect to find. Some very old and/or very rare firearms are acceptable to collectors in almost any condition! The average collector, however, will probably never have the opportunity to purchase such a specimen.

For your convenience, NRA Condition Standards are shown below. Converting from this grading system to percentages can now be done accurately.

CONVERTING TO NRA MODERN STANDARDS

When converting from NRA Modern Standards, the following rules generally apply:

Perfect — 100% with or without box. Not mint - new.
Excellent — 95%+ - 99% (typically).
Very Good — 80 - 95% - all original.
Good — 60 - 80% - all original.
Fair — 20 - 60% - May not be original (shootable, not very collectible).
Poor — Under 20%.

NRA Condition Standards

MODERN CONDITIONS —

New — not previously sold at retail, in same condition as current factory production.

Perfect — in new condition in every respect

Excellent — new condition, used but little, no noticeable marring of wood or metal, bluing perfect (except at muzzle or sharp edges).

Very Good — in perfect working condition, no appreciable wear on working surfaces, no corrosion or pitting, only minor surface dents or scratches.

Good — in safe working condition, minor wear on working surfaces, no broken parts, no corrosion or pitting that will interfere with proper functioning.

Fair — in safe working condition, but well worn, perhaps requiring replacement of minor parts or adjustments which should be indicated in advertisement, no rust, but may have corrosion pits which do not render article unsafe or inoperable.

ANTIQUE CONDITIONS —

Factory New — all original parts; 100% original finish; in perfect condition in every respect, inside and out.

Excellent — all original parts; over 80% original finish; sharp lettering, numerals and design on metal and wood; unmarred wood; fine bore.

Fine — all original parts; over 30% original finish; sharp lettering, numerals and design on metal and wood; minor marks in wood; good bore.

Very Good — all original parts; none to 30% original finish; original metal surfaces smooth with all edges sharp; clear lettering, numerals and design on metal; wood slightly scratched or bruised; bore disregarded for collectors firearms.

Good — some minor replacement parts; metal smoothly rusted or lightly pitted in places, cleaned or reblued; principal lettering, numerals and design on metal legible; wood refinished, scratched, bruised or minor cracks repaired; in good working order.

Fair — some major parts replaced; minor replacement parts may be required; metal rusted, may be lightly pitted all over, vigorously cleaned or reblued; rounded edges of metal and wood; principal lettering, numerals and design on metal partly obliterated; wood scratched, bruised, cracked or repaired where broken; in fair working order or can be easily repaired and placed in working order.

Poor — major and minor parts replaced; major replacement parts required and extensive restoration needed; metal deeply pitted; principal lettering, numerals and design obliterated, wood badly scratched, bruised, cracked or broken; mechanically inoperative, generally undesirable as a collectors firearm.

These NRA conditions have been used by the author as the guidelines for the value ranges in this work. In order to use this book correctly, the reader is urged to constantly consult these condition standards when assessing a gun before applying a value to it. They stand as the crux of the valuation matter.

Common Abbreviations

ACP	Automatic Colt Pistol		PPD	Post Paid
ADJ	Adjustable		P.O.R.	Price on Request
AE	Automatic Ejectors		QD	Quick Detachable
BR	Bench Rest		RB	Round Barrel
BPE	Black Power Express		REM	Remington
B	Blue		RF	Rimfire
BAC	Browning Arms Company		RFM	Rim Fire Magnum
BP	Butt Plate		RN	Round Knob
BT	Beavertail		RNLT	Round Knob Long Tang
CAL	Caliber		RR	Red Ramp
CCA	Colt Collectors Association		SAE	Selective Automatic Ejectors
CC	Case Colors			
CF	Centerfire		S.R.C.	Saddle Ring Carbine
CH	Cross Hair		SR	Solid Rib
CYL	Cylinder		S/N	Serial Number
DSL	Detachable Side Locks		SMLE	Short Magazine Lee Enfield Rifle
DISC	Discontinued			
DA	Double Action		SA	Single Action
DB	Double Barrel		SAA	Single Action Army
DST	Double Set Triggers		SNT	Single Non-Selective Trigger
DT	Double Trigger			
DW	DeutscheWaffen and Munitions Fabrik		SST	Single Selective Trigger
			SS	Single Shot or Stainless Steel
EXC	Excellent			
EXT	Extractors		ST	Single Trigger
FBT	Full Beavertail Forearm		SK	Skeet
F&M	Full & Modified		SPEC	Special
FE	Fore End		SPL	Special
FFL	Federal Firearms License		S.G.	Straight Grip
FN	Fabrique Nationale		SMG	Sub Machine Gun
HB	Heavy Barrel		S&W	Smith & Wesson
H&H	Holland & Holland		SXS	Side by Side
HP	Hollow Point		TD	Take Down
IC	Improved Cylinder		TGT	Target
LC	Long Colt		TH	Target Hammer
LT	Long Tang or Light		TT	Target Trigger
LTRK	Long Tang Round Knob		UMC	Union Metallic Cartridge Co.
MAG	Magnum			
mag.	Magazine		VG	Very Good
MC	Monte Carlo		VR	Ventilated Rib
MK	Mark		WC	Wad Cutter
MR	Matted Rib		WFF	Watch For Fakes
M&P	Military & Police		WBY	Weatherby
NM	National Match		WIN	Winchester
N	Nickel		WCF	Winchester Center Fire
NIB	New in Box		WFF	Watch For Fakes
O&U	Over and Under		WRA	Winchester Repeating Arms Co.
OA	Overall			
OBF	Octagon Barrel w/full mag.		WRF	Winchester Rim Fire
OBO	Or Best Offer		WO	White Outline
OCT	Octagon		WW	World War
PG	Pistol Grip			

THE **BLUE BOOK OF GUN VALUES**™

PHOTO PERCENTAGE GRADING SYSTEM©

Hopefully, this might be the end of an era. I'm glad I can't remember the months I've spent (wasted?) through various telecommunication devices trying to figure out the condition of a wide array of firearms (i.e., could you hold it closer to the microphone so I can see it better?) Other related fields have the same problem - try calling up a coin, car, stamp, baseball card, or antique furniture dealer and ask him what he will pay you in C-notes for your favorite collectible artifact. The answer is always the same: "Sir, I will have to see it before I can make that determination. Your described excellent condition may only be good to me." In other words, a collectible object's value is always determined by its unique condition factor. And most of the time, it's original condition that counts.

In real estate they say there are three things to look for when purchasing property: Location, Location, and Location. In firearms the three criteria are: Original condition, Original condition, and Original condition. With most firearms models in good supply, if there is little original condition remaining, there is no desirability - and if there is no desirability, there is no price. In the past 3-5 years, prices of many specimens in superb original condition that are rare and are of major trademarks have banked enough profits to rate them as the magna-cum-laude graduates of the collectible fraternity (battleground is probably more accurate).

The photos on the following pages are in high-resolution 4-color and have individual descriptions listing percentages of condition and other notations, comments, and grading tips that are critical when describing a firearms condition accurately. To date, I do not think anyone has tried to show the percentage firearms grading system using color plates. Although expensive, I hope it will be responsible for collectors, investors, and dealers to do business faster and more accurately, while lowering your long distance phone bill concurrently.

Three categories of guns are represented in these photo grading illustrations: Rifles, Shotguns, and Handguns. Chosen category representative models are as follows: Rifles - various Winchester lever actions, Shotguns - Model 12's, L.C. Smith's, Parker, Browning, and Winchester, Handguns - German P.38's, Model 1911's and 1911A1's (Colt and other manufacturers), Colt revolvers, and older Colt percussion models. Each photo has its own caption. Simply compare your guns against these photos to find out the corresponding condition in percentages. If your particular configuration is not pictured, try to interpolate areas of wear to the closest category shown (i.e., a double barrel shotgun should be compared to the Model 12's pictured).

It is extremely important when examining wear in any firearm to think about how that wear occurred after a period of normal (and possibly abnormal) use. You will notice in the following Winchester grading photographs that regardless of the amount of receiver bluing, the barrel (magazine tube, if rifle) usually retains over 90% finish. This is because when the owner(s) carried this gun his/her hand(s) came in contact with the receiver metal just in front of the lever or trigger guard - in other words, where the rifle/shotgun naturally balances when holding it. You don't carry a gun in the field by its barrel or stock, and that explains why they typically show wear last. For these reasons, the receiver on a rifle or shotgun is the kingpin when ascertaining condition. A long gun with only 30% barrel blue and 95% receiver finish with crisp checkering simply doesn't add up, unless the barrel has been replaced. I have always said that firearms collecting became harder after Eli Whitney introduced interchangeable parts.

On a handgun, wear also starts where it is held when shooting or carrying - on the front and rear grip straps and grips themselves. Worn finish on the sides accumulates after holster use, rubbing or movement against hard, abrasive surfaces, corrosion from gun powder residue, cleaning, etc. On any firearm, the first area to show wear is the sharp corners and places of mechanical movement or contact (i.e., breech block "primer rings" and striations, lockup notches on cylinders, gun powder corrosion in the breech area, etc.). I have examined many guns that have been fired very little but are in 98% condition because the proud owner(s) has worn off 2% over-zealously cleaning his/her pride and joy every month for the last ten years! Thinking about how a gun's finish naturally wears or ages is critical when examining any specimen for condition and originality - I cannot emphasize this point enough. On every gun you examine, ask yourself "Is the cumulative condition overall the sum of its individual parts?"

We are lucky that the consistency and uniformity of firearms grading standards have not changed. In the coin business, just when you thought those easy, short-term profits were in your sights, the coin industry changed the grading system making your numismatics fall (not to mention profits) a grade or two. A 98% gun from 1960 is still a 98% gun today. Nothing has changed except for the values going up considerably and the really good stuff has never been harder to find because gun collectors usually dispose of their firearms as their last financial alternative. The first thing an investor sells after 4 or 5 years is his worst investment. The last thing a gun collector will sell is his/her best specimen(s) - unless a cash offer gets tendered that can't be refused. Because collectors and shooters in general rule the roost in the firearms industry, the frequency between turnovers is much longer than if investors were in control.

Always try to buy as much original condition as you can afford. Remember however, that you can overpay for those last couple of percentage points of a firearm's condition. Don't forget about those crazed investment (non-collector) diamond buyers who purchased 1 Carat, D-Flawless certified stones (the best quality) for over $80,000 in the early 1980's and flushed them down their portfolio toilets several years later for $12,000. As in any other area of collecting, it is typically wise to stay away from a model, area, or category that has gone up faster than an F-15 in an alarmingly short time. While it's true that these short-term boomers may continue to rise and take you with them, chances are you may be dropped off at the summit of Mt. Everest with no oxygen for the way down.

If you have any questions regarding either the photos or accompanying captions, please contact me or the dealer who sent you this **Blue Book of Gun Values** photo percentage grading system. While no grading system is perfect, hopefully this will enable you to ascertain the approximate grade of your individual firearms. Only after learning the correct condition of a firearm can you accurately determine its true value.

Sincerely,

Steven P. Fjestad

Author - **Blue Book of Gun Values**

P.S. - I would like to thank LeRoy Merz and Richard Ellis for their firearms, contributions, and expertise in helping with this improved Photo Percentage Grading System. Also, Martin Mandall (Mandall's Shooting Supplies), Patrick McKune, and Robert White also get "hats off" treatment for supplying some of the firearms pictured in this section.

All photos in this section were taken by S.P. Fjestad and Paul Goodwin/Richard Ellis

The "Photo Percentage Grading System" is copyrighted by Blue Book Publications, Inc. All rights reserved.

RIFLE PHOTO PERCENTAGE GRADING SYSTEM

Photo No. 1 - Model 71 Deluxe Rifle with 99½%+ bright shiny original blue overall. Most dealers would consider this a mint specimen. Note how sharp the points of the checkering are. While this gun is not 100%, it is extremely close. Observe the slight wear on rear hammer curvature.

Photo No. 2 - Model 1894 Carbine with 98% + bright shiny original receiver finish and 100% barrel/mag. bluing. Winchester collectors will recognize this as a very fine early gun by the bright vivid case colors still intact on the lever and hammer. This is an extremely desirable specimen – many dealers would call this mint, but corners of frame/loading gate and wood show a litle wear.

RIFLE PHOTO PERCENTAGE GRADING SYSTEM

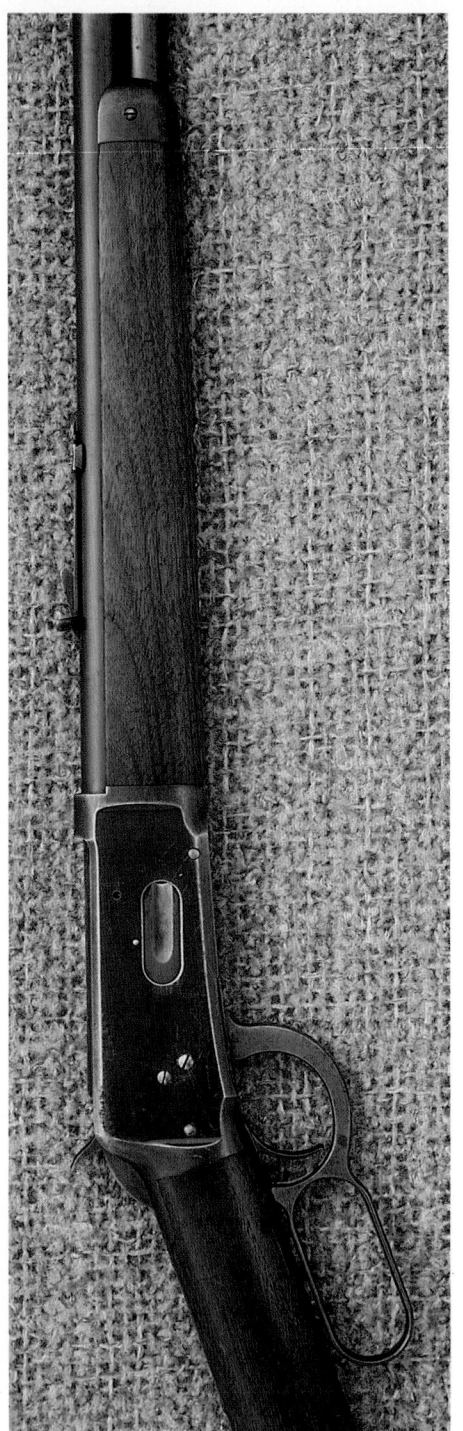

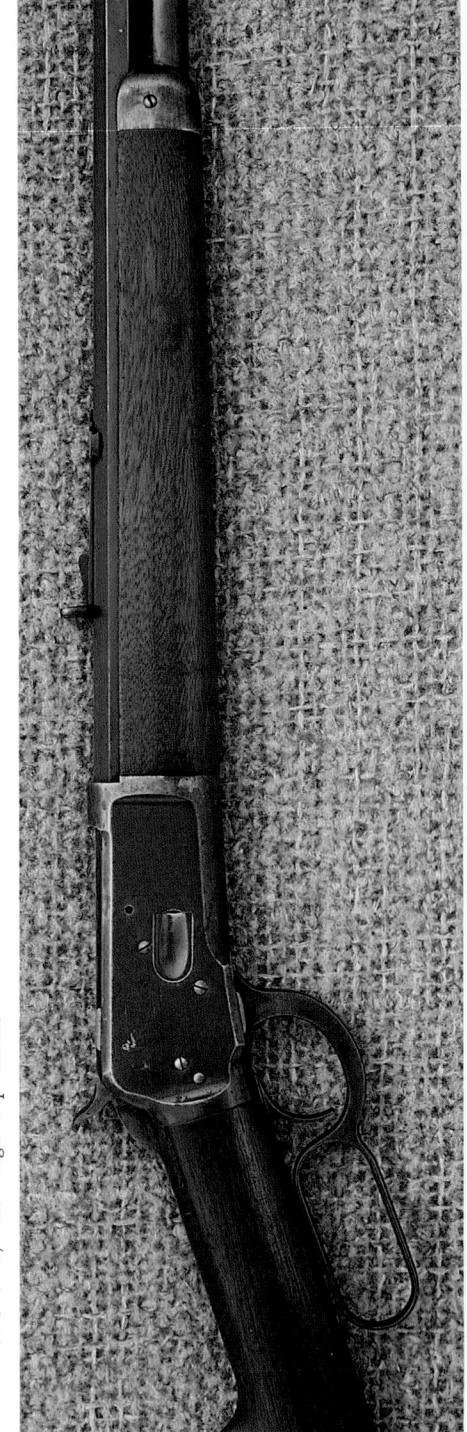

Photo No. 3 - Model 1894 Rifle with 95% bright shiny original blue on receiver and 98% barrel/mag. blue. Compare almost faded case colors on lever and hammer to Photo No. 2 - again indicating an early gun. Wood is also excellent with perfect fit to metal.

Photo No. 4 - Model 1892 Rifle with 90%+ original bluing with some light handling and storage marks. Note the darkness of the wood and the mostly shiny forearm cap. Also, observe the color of the bluing is turning a light patina (oxidized bluing which turns a plum-brown color after aging) compared to Photo No. 5. Overall, a nice original specimen.

RIFLE PHOTO PERCENTAGE GRADING SYSTEM

Photo No. 5 - Model 1892 Pistol Grip Takedown Rifle with 80%+ original receiver bluing. This is a clean sharp gun showing no abuse - only normal wear. Notice that the checkering shows wear on the stock and forearm, and the lever has turned shiny due to use.

Photo No. 6 - Model 1873 Deluxe Rifle with 70% vivid receiver case colors and 95% barrel blue. Observe the natural color mottling on sideplate and receiver rear - also some small brown rust spots from improper storage can be seen on receiver front. Original bright case colors are extremely desirable on any older firearm.

RIFLE PHOTO PERCENTAGE GRADING SYSTEM

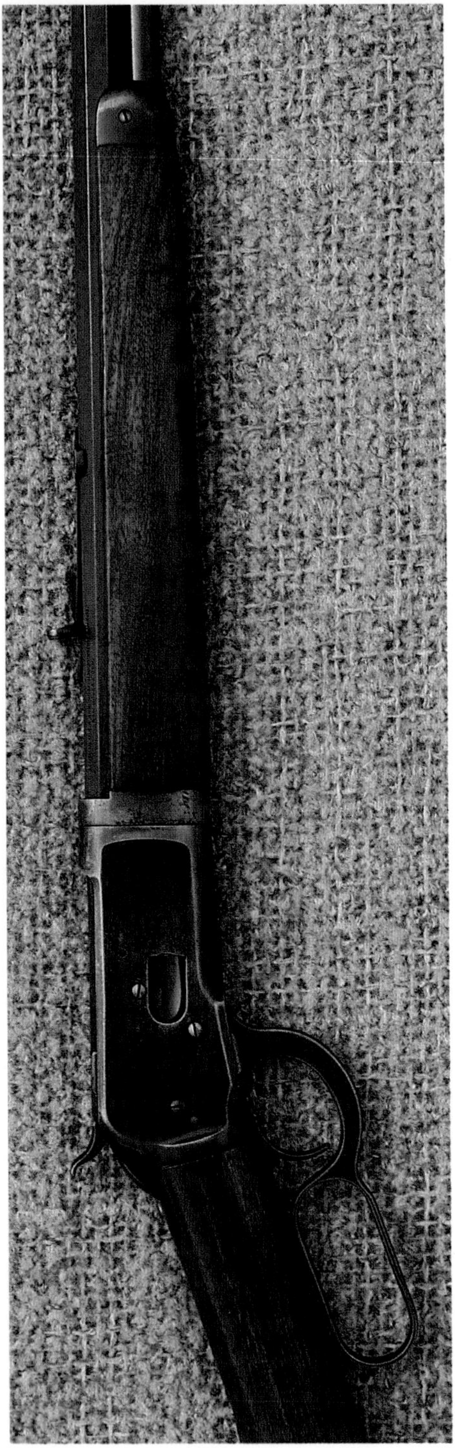

Photo No. 7 - Model 1892 Takedown Rifle showing 60% receiver finish and 95% barrel blue. Notice that the balance of the receiver has flaked and turned brown. Also, close observation indicates that the frame screws have never been damaged by a screwdriver.

Photo No. 8 - Model 55 Takedown Rifle retaining 50% of what appears to be an older reblued finish. The dark wood is generally in good condition. Notice that the top frame screw shows damage and that the lever has been bent (is not flush against lower tang) due to older abuse.

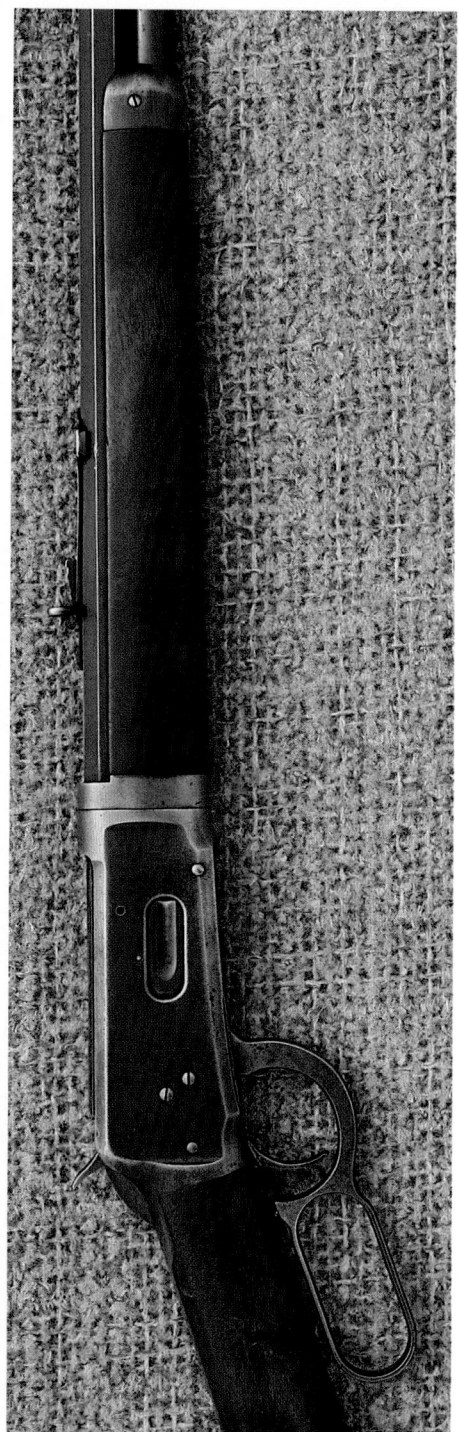

Photo No. 9 - Model 1894 Takedown Rifle with 40% original blue turning brown on frame and 90% barrel blue. The bottom and top of receiver and takedown ring have turned silvery from handling. This is normal wear and consistent with the rest of the gun's condition.

Photo No. 10 - Model 1894 Carbine depicting 20% receiver blue and 90% barrel/mag. blue. Notice the pattern of wear and how the balance of finish is turning a gun metal grey, including the barrel band. This carbine's condition is typical of many older Winchesters. A well used specimen showing no abuse.

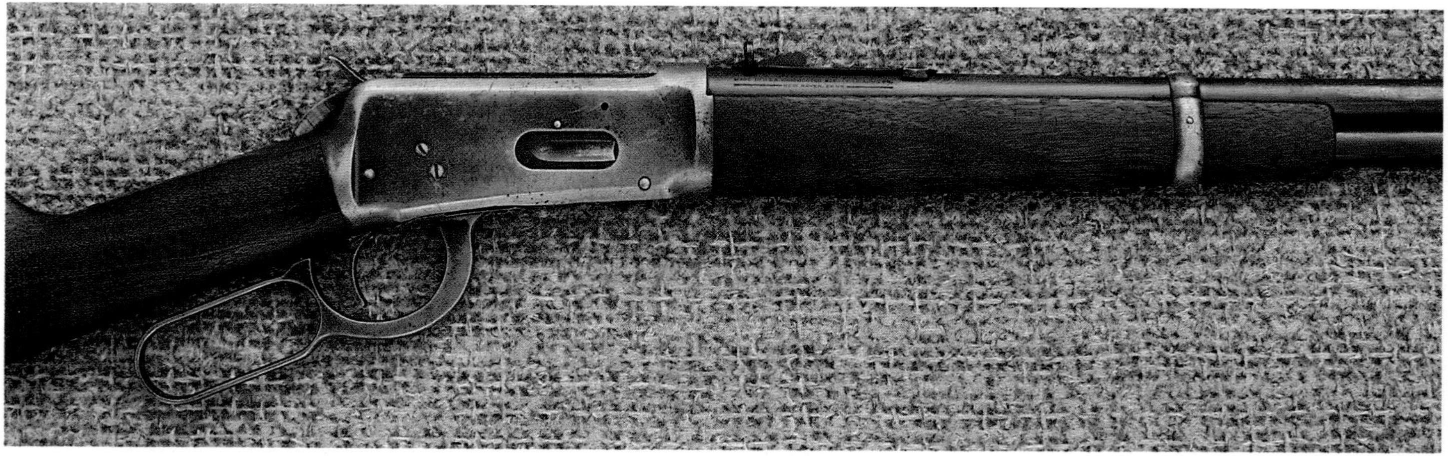

RIFLE PHOTO PERCENTAGE GRADING SYSTEM

Photo No. 11 - Model 55 Takedown Rifle with no receiver blue remaining (it has flaked off) and 50% barrel/mag. blue. The wood is in very good condition. This is commonly referred to as a "shiny gun". While this gun appears in poor condition due to flaking, it is still a lot more desirable than the Model 1892 pictured in Photo No. 12.

Photo No. 12 - Model 1892 Rifle showing a lot of wear with all metal surfaces having turned a dark brown heavy patina due to much use, some abuse (note nails in front of forearm), and neglect. In the business this is called a "brown gun" or "roach" and is the least desirable from a condition standpoint.

SHOTGUN PHOTO PERCENTAGE GRADING SYSTEM

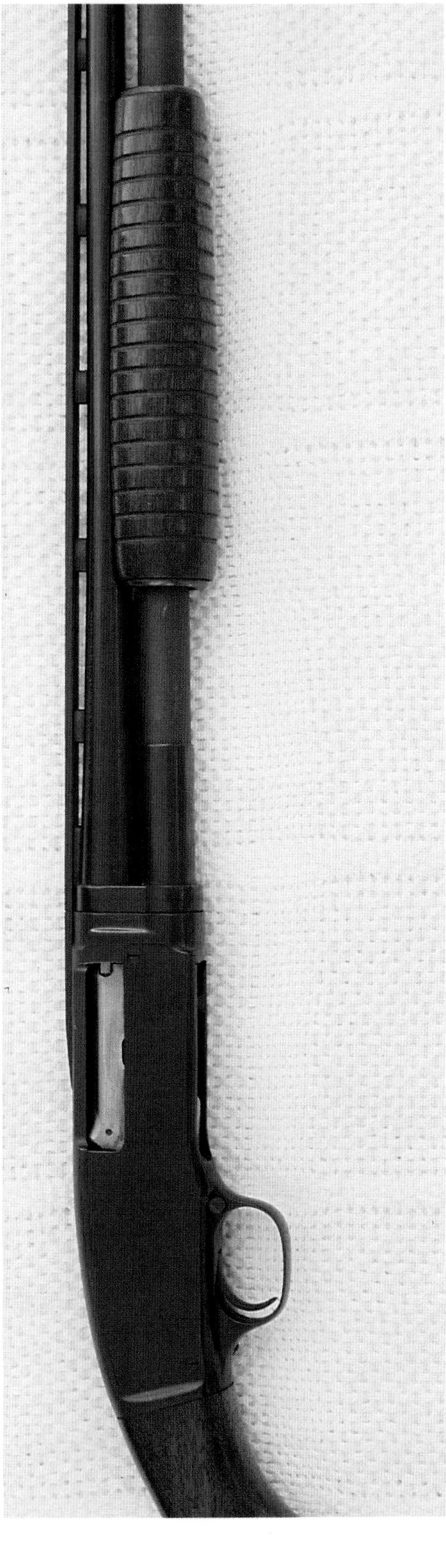

Photo No. 13 - Winchester Model 42 in mint condition. Collectors will note the addition of a Simmons ventilated rib which means that the receiver and barrel have been refinished. This subtracts from the value compared to an original, but the excellent original condition of the wood and other sharp features make this specimen desirable.

Photo No. 14 - Winchester Model 12 in 98% original condition. Observe wear on receiver corners and horizontal striation on magazine tube where slide action contacts metal. Nice original older dark wood (notice that stock is slightly oversized where it meets frame metal indicating not sanded) with "corncob" forearm.

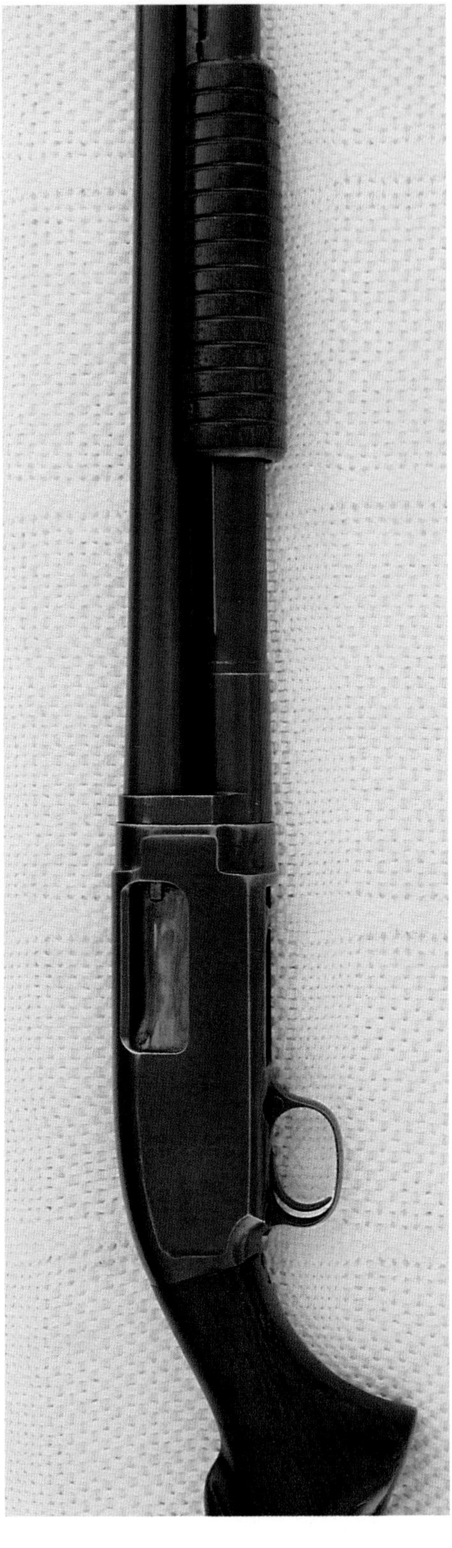

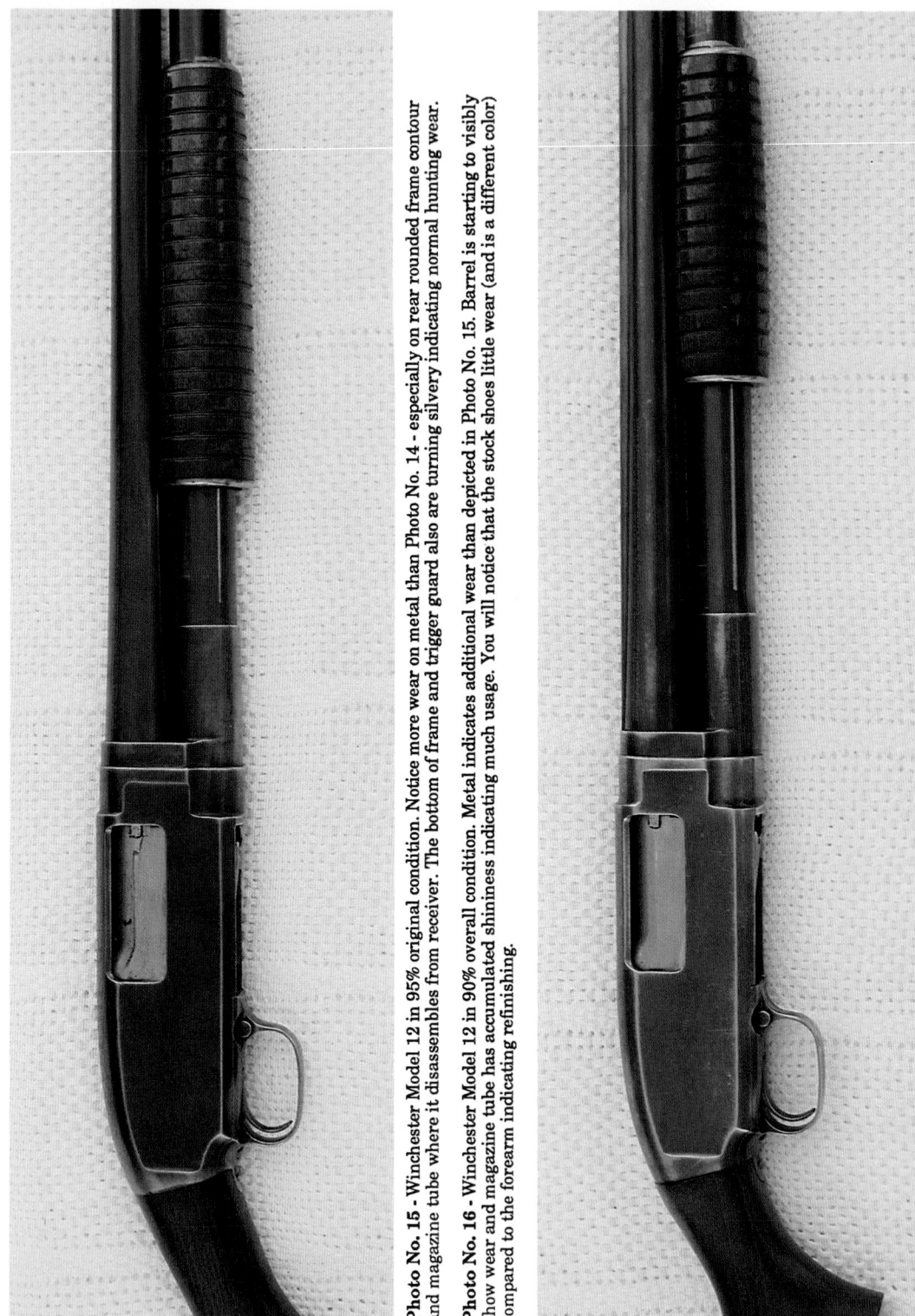

Photo No. 15 - Winchester Model 12 in 95% original condition. Notice more wear on metal than Photo No. 14 - especially on rear rounded frame contour and magazine tube where it disassembles from receiver. The bottom of frame and trigger guard also are turning silvery indicating normal hunting wear.

Photo No. 16 - Winchester Model 12 in 90% overall condition. Metal indicates additional wear than depicted in Photo No. 15. Barrel is starting to visibly show wear and magazine tube has accumulated shininess indicating much usage. You will notice that the stock shoes little wear (and is a different color) compared to the forearm indicating refinishing.

SHOTGUN PHOTO PERCENTAGE GRADING SYSTEM

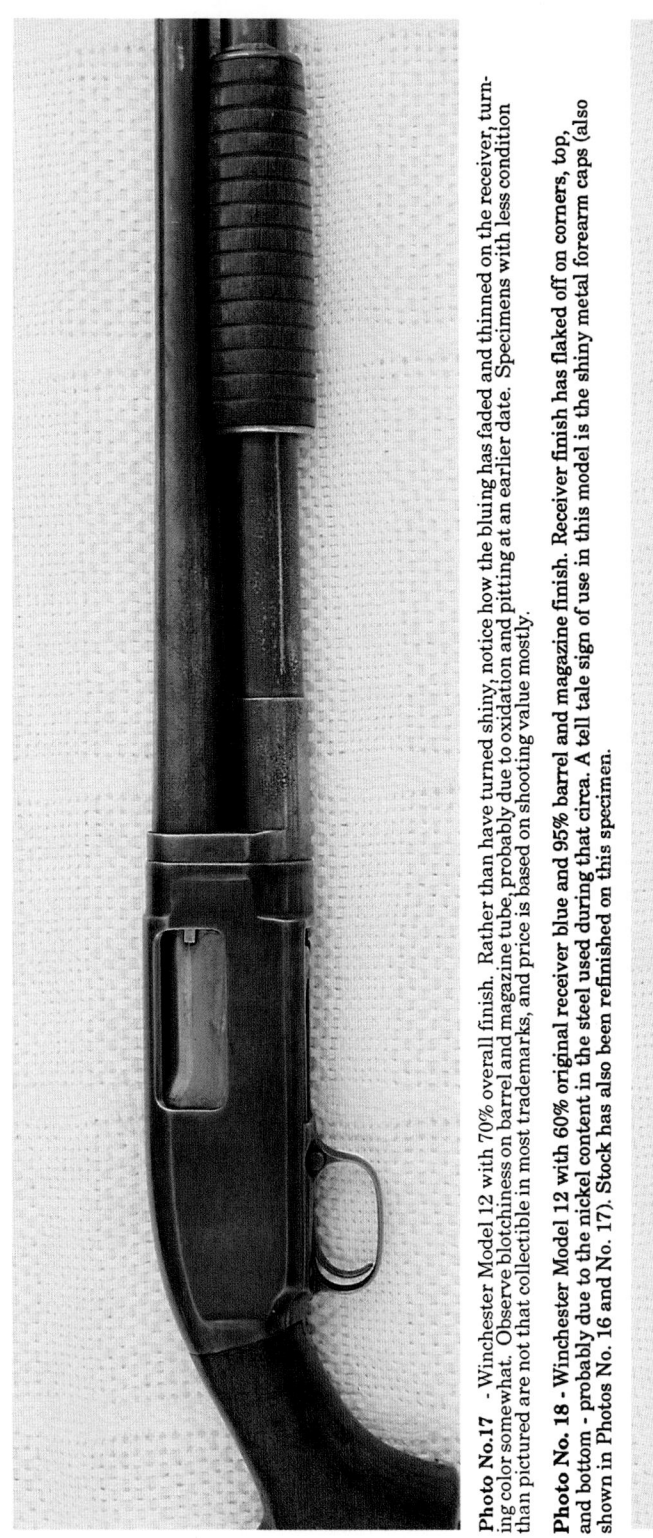

Photo No.17 - Winchester Model 12 with 70% overall finish. Rather than have turned shiny, notice how the bluing has faded and thinned on the receiver, turning color somewhat. Observe blotchiness on barrel and magazine tube, probably due to oxidation and pitting at an earlier date. Specimens with less condition than pictured are not that collectible in most trademarks, and price is based on shooting value mostly.

Photo No. 18 - Winchester Model 12 with 60% original receiver blue and 95% barrel and magazine finish. Receiver finish has flaked off on corners, top, and bottom - probably due to the nickel content in the steel used during that circa. A tell tale sign of use in this model is the shiny metal forearm caps (also shown in Photos No. 16 and No. 17). Stock has also been refinished on this specimen.

SHOTGUN PHOTO PERCENTAGE GRADING SYSTEM

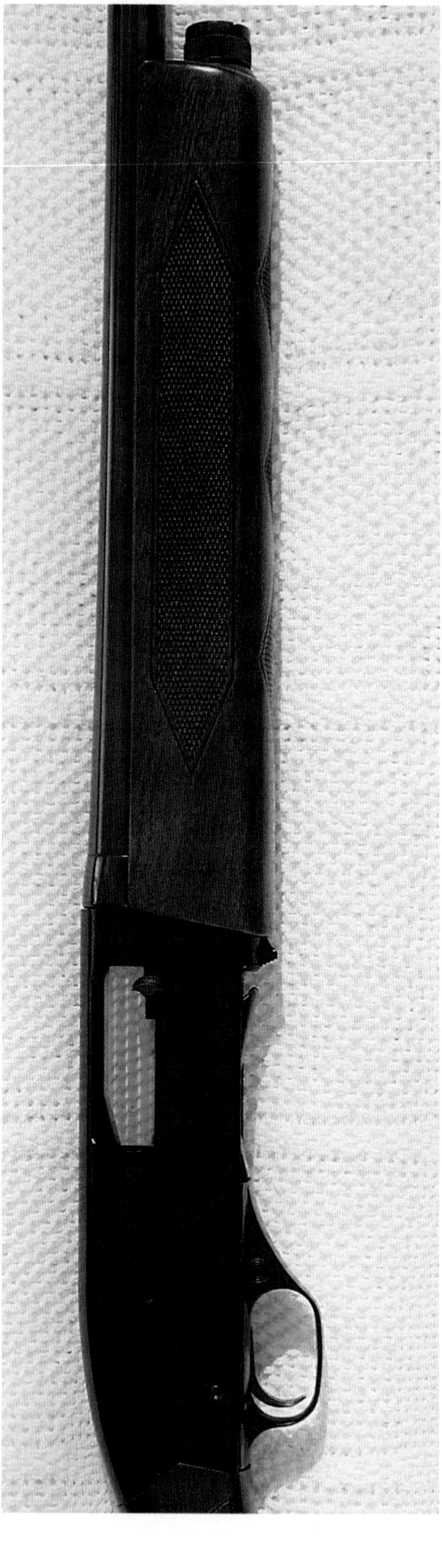

Photo No.19 - Winchester Model 1400 in new condition or 100%. Notice no wear on any visible part. Close examination will show checkering is pressed in rather than hand-cut. Swirl marks on breech block indicates engine-turning. Receiver appears black because it is an alloy and takes bluing differently than the steel barrel.

Photo No.20 - Browning A-5 in mint condition (over 99%+ original condition). Note round knob pistol grip and safety location (indicative of an early gun). Checkering is sharp on pistol grip but slightly worn on forearm. Close inspection will reveal a dark hairline crack on bottom of forearm next to frame (common in this model).

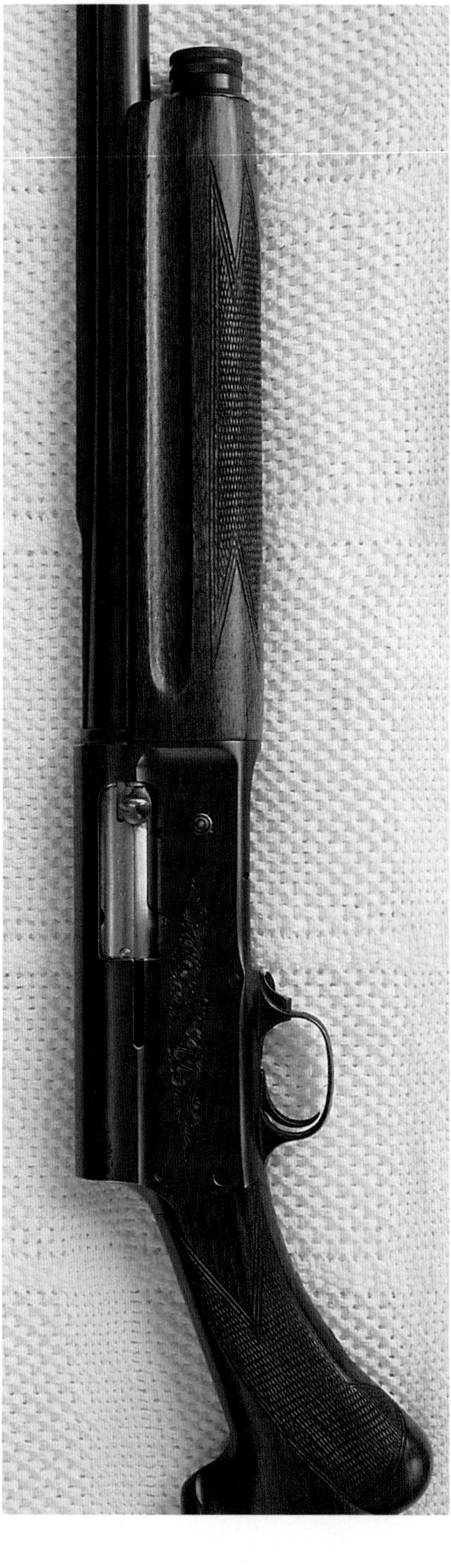

SHOTGUN PHOTO PERCENTAGE GRADING SYSTEM

Photo No. 21 - Bottom view of L.C. Smith Field Grade with hammers. No argument about this gun's condition – it's mint! A Field Model hammer gun with all the original case colors and bluing remaining is ultra rare.

Photo No. 22 - L.C. Smith Field Grade (hammerless). Again, another mint specimen of an L.C. Smith. Notice the way the case colors on frame top are mottled, wood to metal fit, and the checkering without points (common on field grades).

SHOTGUN PHOTO PERCENTAGE GRADING SYSTEM

Photo No. 23 - L.C. Smith Ideal Grade with approximately 30% original case colors remaining. Notice the stock cracks around the sideplate (somewhat common with older well-used L.C. Smiths) and case colors next to frame shoulder.

Photo No. 24 - This is the bottom view of Photo 21. Notice the shininess on the front and bottom of frame indicating much usage. Also note the "LONGRANGE" and "HUNTER ONE TRIGGER" markings on receiver bottom with stock cracking also visible.

SHOTGUN PHOTO PERCENTAGE GRADING SYSTEM

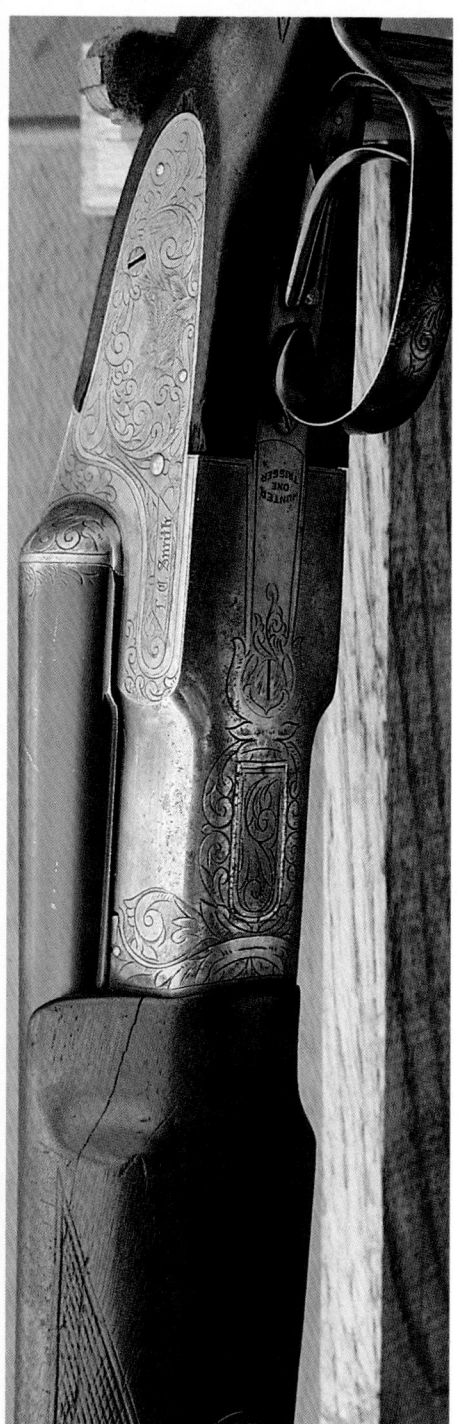

Photo No. 25 - Another L.C. Smith in Specialty Grade with traces of original case colors barely remaining. Notice light pitting around bottom front of receiver and hairline crack in forearm.

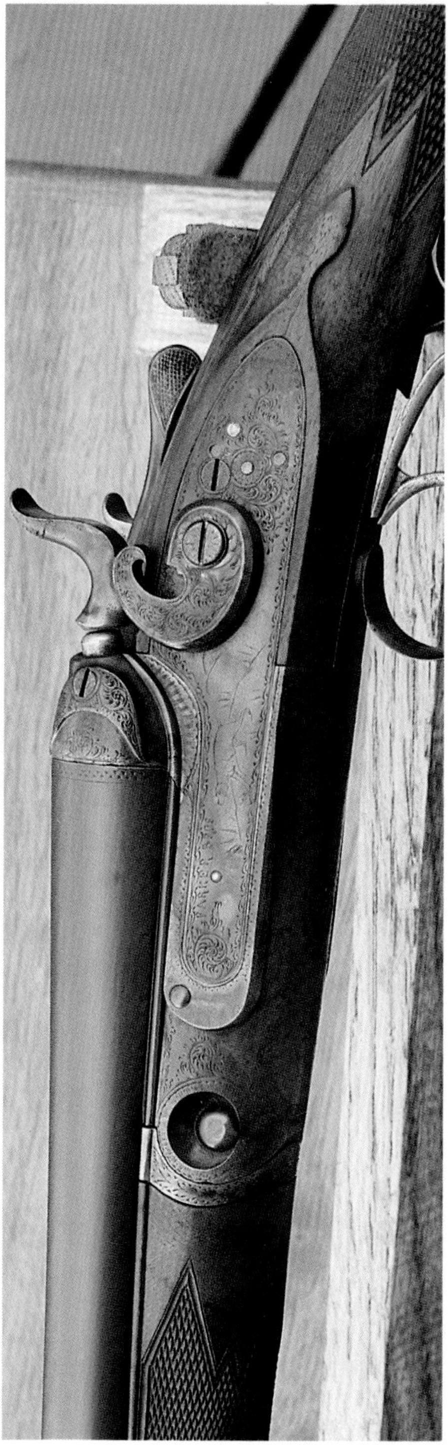

Photo No. 26 - Older Parker Brothers D-Grade hammer gun with fluid steel barrels. While appearing original, this shotgun has been professionally refurbished. Note the light scroll engraving and scalloped shoulders of frame.

HANDGUN PHOTO PERCENTAGE GRADING SYSTEM

Photo No. 27 - Colt Series 80 National Match Model in new condition (100%). No observable wear on any visible part. Note how roll-die stamp put the slide logo at different depths along the length of the legend. Compare color difference in bluing to Photo No. 35 and No. 36, indicating the differences in metallurgy, machining, polishing, and bluing solvents.

Photo No.28 - Walther Post-War P1 (commercial variation of the P.38) in 98% original condition. Observe wear on slide edges, top of trigger, and hold-open lever. The color difference between frame and slide bluing is normal since the frame is an alloy and the upper slide is steel, and each metal reacts to the bluing differently.

HANDGUN PHOTO PERCENTAGE GRADING SYSTEM

Photo No. 29 - Walther Post-War P1 in 95% original condition. Note more wear than Photo No. 28 on slide edges. Barrel, trigger guard, safety, takedown lever and bottom of grips also show additional usage. Silvery scratching above serial number remains where some "craftsman" tried to "erase" an Operation ID number - this decreases value 30%+.

Photo No.30 - Walther WWII ac-44 Model in 90% condition. While it appears to be original, close inspection reveals a refinished gun (note how tops of slide serial numbers and P.38 logo have disappeared when the gun was polished during refinishing). Because P.38's are in good supply in original 90%+ condition, this lowers the value to shooting status.

HANDGUN PHOTO PERCENTAGE GRADING SYSTEM

Photo No.31 - Mauser WWII byf-43 Model in 70% original condition. This specimen shows dark areas of blotchiness from older oxidation on slide and frame. While this pistol offers little collector value (most commonly available handguns in this condition are the same), it still maintains a minimum "spot price" as a shooter.

Photo No.32 - Korth Revolver (W. German mfg.) in new condition (100%). This revolver has been cropped to show the exceptional metal machining, polishing, and translucent-like bluing. Metal parts almost resemble polished black marble. This is perhaps the finest (and most expensive) new revolver available in today's marketplace.

HANDGUN PHOTO PERCENTAGE GRADING SYSTEM

Photo No. 33 - Model 1911 Springfield Armory in 96-97% original condition. Notice markings and trigger wear. Also note scratch from top of trigger guard to slide stop lever indicating careless reassembly.

Photo No. 34 - Model 1911 Springfield Armory in 60% original condition. As wear has accumulated, the metal has become a duller grayish color. Notice martial markings next to trigger and rear of slide on both guns.

HANDGUN PHOTO PERCENTAGE GRADING SYSTEM

Photo No. 35 - Model 1911A1 manufactured by Singer for WW II contract. This pistol is ultra-rare in this condition factor – 98%. A very "crisp" specimen, considering only 500 were manufactured in 1942 only.

Photo No. 36 - Model 1911 manufactured by North American Arms Co. Limited. In this condition (99% overall), it can be considered one of the "Holy Grails" of Colt semi-auto collecting.

HANDGUN PHOTO PERCENTAGE GRADING SYSTEM

Photo No. 37 - Another Model 1911 North American Arms in approximately 85-90% original condition. Observe pitting on slide top and great condition of frame.

Photo No. 38 - Model 1911 manufactured by North American Arms in approximately 75% original condition. Compare this pistol against Photo 37 and notice additional wear on front grip strap and grip safety.

HANDGUN PHOTO PERCENTAGE GRADING SYSTEM

Photo No. 39 - North American Arms Model 1911 in approximately 60% original condition. Again, notice the additional bluing wear compared to Photo 38.

Photo No. 40 - Another Model 1911 manufactured by North American Arms in approximately 20-30% original condition. This pistol's rarity factor, despite its condition, still makes it very desirable.

HANDGUN PHOTO PERCENTAGE GRADING SYSTEM

Photo No. 41 - Model 1911 manufactured under military contract by Remington U.M.C. in 98% original condition. Notice ordnance proofing and condition of walnut grips.

Photo No. 42 - Colt Model 1911 Military manufactured in 1913. This gun is in mint (99% +) condition overall.

HANDGUN PHOTO PERCENTAGE GRADING SYSTEM

Photo No. 43 - Pre-War Colt commercial in .38 Super caliber (very desirable). This "creampuff" is in mint condition.

Photo No. 44 - Colt Pre-War Government Model .45 that has been reblued. Note thinning of "patent legend" on slide side with slight corner rounding.

HANDGUN PHOTO PERCENTAGE GRADING SYSTEM

Photo No. 45 - Colt Model 1911A1 with correct darker parkerized finish in mint condition. Observe dark plastic grips.

Photo No. 46 - A.J. Savage slide Model 1911 with almost all the original finish worn off. This pistol would grade 5-10%.

HANDGUN PHOTO PERCENTAGE GRADING SYSTEM

Photo No. 47 - Colt Pre-War New Service revolver in mint overall original condition. Notice the grip condition on the specimen.

Photo No. 48 - Colt Model 1917 Army in 98% original condition. Note direction of polishing by front sight blade.

HANDGUN PHOTO PERCENTAGE GRADING SYSTEM

Photo No. 49 - Colt New Service in 99% overall original condition. Notice how fine the metal has been polished and high lustre bluing.

Photo No. 50 - Colt Model 1909 U.S.M.C. in 93-95% original condition. Observe polishing and coloration of bluing.

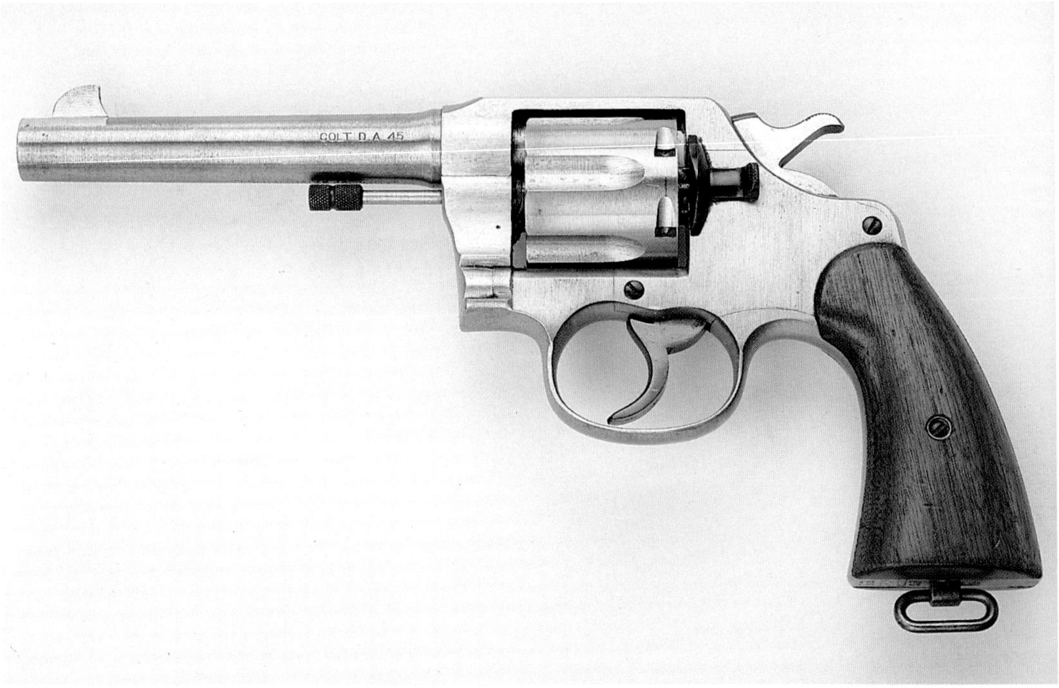

HANDGUN PHOTO PERCENTAGE GRADING SYSTEM

Photo No. 51 - Model 1917 Army "in the white" from the factory. This gun was never blued, notice vertical striations in polishing.

Photo No. 52 - Colt Model 1909 U.S.M.C. in 90% overall original condition. Note holster wear on barrel tip and striations between cylinder cutouts.

HANDGUN PHOTO PERCENTAGE GRADING SYSTEM

Photo No. 53 - Colt Early Officer's Model with factory engraving and Mother-of-Pearl grips. This specimen is in approximately 80% original condition.

Photo No. 54 - Colt Model 1889 Double Action in approximately 60% original condition. Notice amount and location of wear.

HANDGUN PHOTO PERCENTAGE GRADING SYSTEM

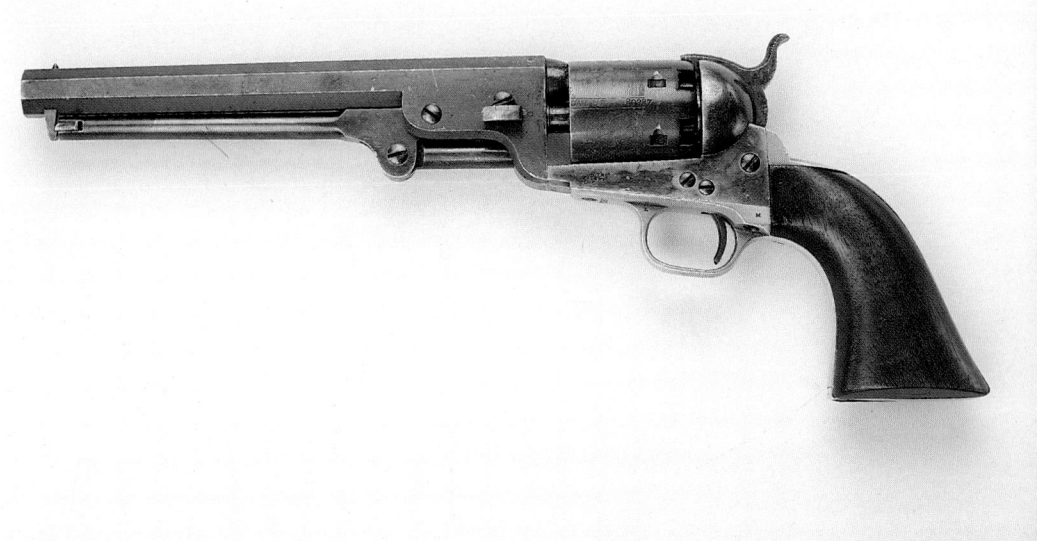

Photo No. 55 - Colt Model 1851 U.S. Army contract in 90% + overall condition, note case colors remaining and brass grip straps.

Photo No. 56 - Colt Model 1851 U.S. Navy contract in approximately 70-80% original condition.

HANDGUN PHOTO PERCENTAGE GRADING SYSTEM

Photo No. 57 - Colt Model 1851 U.S. Navy contract in 30-40% original condition. Note thinning and greyish patina color of bluing.

Photo No. 58 - Colt Antique (pre-1899 manufacture) Single Action Army (SAA) manufactured in 1875. Note high lustre finish and case colors on this 95% gun-also observe barrel and cylinder "freckling".

HANDGUN PHOTO PERCENTAGE GRADING SYSTEM

Photo No. 59 - Colt 3rd Model Dragoon in approximately 80% overall condition. A beautiful specimen considering 1851 manufacture.

Photo No. 60 - Colt 2nd Model Dragoon with no finish remaining. While appearing original, this pistol has been artificially aged giving it an older appearance. Fakes in rarer Colt models have become more elaborate.

Glossary

ACTION — The heart of the gun, receiver, bolt or breech block feeding and fire-arm mechanism.

ADJUSTABLE CHOKE — A device built into the muzzle of a shotgun to change from one choke to another.

AIR GUN—A gun which utilizes compressed air or gas to launch the projectile.

AUTO LOADING— See semi-automatic.

AUTOMATIC EJECTOR — A single-shot or double-barrel action that is equipped to hurl fired casses clear of the breech.

BEAVERTAIL FOREND — A wider than normal forend.

BLUING — The blue or black finish of the metal parts of a gun. The process is actually one of controlled rusting and brushing and is usually created with an acid bath. Blueing minimizes light reflection, gives a "finish" to the bare metal, and protects somewhat against rust.

BUCKHORN SIGHT — An open, metallic rear sight with sides that curl upward and inward.

BULL BARREL — A heavier, thicker than normal barrel with little or no taper.

BUTT PLATE — A protective plate attached to the butt.

CALIBER — The diameter of the bore.

CHECKERING — A functional decoration applied to pistol grips and forends consisting of pointed pyramids cut into the wood.

CHOKE — The muzzle constriction on a shotgun to control spread of the shot.

COCKING INDICATOR — A device which can be seen and/or felt when a gun is cocked.

COLOR OR CASE HARDEN — A hardening process which imparts colorful swirls to metal surfaces.

COMB — The portion of the stock on which the shooter's cheek rests.

COMBINATION GUN — One shotgun and one rifle barrel.

COMPENSATOR — A recoil-reducing device which mounts on the muzzle of a gun to deflect part of the powder gasses up and rearward. Also called a "muzzle brake".

DAMASCUS BARREL — A barrel made by twisting, forming and welding thin strips of steel around a mandrel.

DERRINGER — A small, usually large-caliber pistol.

DOUBLE ACTION — The principle in a revolver or auto-loading pistol wherein the hammer can be cocked and dropped by a single pull of the trigger. Most of these actions also provide capability for single action fire. In auto-loading pistols, double action normally applies only to the first shot of any series, the hammer being cocked by the slide for subsequent shots.

DOUBLE-BARRELLED — A gun consisting of two barrels joined either side by side or one over the other.

DOUBLE-SET TRIGGER — A device which consists of two triggers — one to cock the mechanism that spring-assists the other trigger, substantially lightening trigger pull.

DRILLING — German for "triple", which is their designation for a three-barrel gun.

EJECTOR — Mechanical device used to eject empty cartridges from chamber(s).

ENGINE TURNING — Overlapped spots of circular polishing.

ENGLISH STOCK — A very straight, slender-gripped stock.

ETCHING — A method of decorating metal gun parts.

EXTRACTOR — A device that withdraws the fired case from the chamber.

FALLING BLOCK — A single-shot action where the breech block drops straight down when the lever is actuated.

FIT AND FINISH — Terms used to describe over-all firearm workmanship.

FLOATING BARREL — A barrel bedded to avoid contact with any point on the stock.

FLOOR PLATE — The piece which closes the bottom of the magazine body.

FOREND — The forward portion of a rifle or shotgun stock.

FREE RIFLE — A rifle designed for international-type target shooting. The only restriction on design is weight — maximum 8 kilograms (17.6 lbs.).

GAUGE — The bore diameter of a shotgun.

LAMINATED STOCK — A gunstock made of many layers of wood glued together under pressure. They are very resistant to warpage.

MAGAZINE — The container which holds cartridges under spring pressure to be fed into the gun's chamber.

MAGNUM — A modern cartridge with a higher-velocity load or heavier projectile than standard.

MANNLICHER STOCK — A full-length slender forend extending to the muzzle.

MICROMETER SIGHT — A finely adjustable target sight.

MONTE CARLO STOCK — A stock with an elevated comb used primarily for scoped rifles.

MUZZLE BRAKE — A recoil-reducing device attached to the muzzle.

OVER-UNDER — A two-barrel gun in which the barrels are stacked one on top of the other.

PARKERIZING — A matted rust-resistant oxide finish, usually gray or gray-green in color, found on military guns.

PEEP SIGHT — A rear sight consisting of a hole or aperture through which the front sight and target are aligned.

RELEASE TRIGGER — A trap shooting trigger that fires the gun when the trigger is released.

RIB — A raised sighting plane affixed to the top of a barrel.

SCHNABEL — A decorative sculptured knob at the end of a forend — usually European style.

SHORT ACTION — A rifle designed for shorter cartridges.

SIDE LOCK — A type of action, usually shotgun, when the moving parts are located on the lock plates inletted in the stock. Usually found only on high-quality guns.

SIDE PLATES — Ornamental additions to simulate a side lock gun on a boxlock.

SINGLE ACTION — A revolver design which requires the hammer to be manually cocked for each shot. Also an auto-loading pistol design which requires manual cocking of the hammer for the first shot only.

SINGLE TRIGGER — One trigger on a double-barrel gun. It fires both barrels singly by successive pulls.

SLING SWIVELS — Metal loops affixed to the gun on which a carrying strap is attached.

TAKE DOWN — A gun which can be easily taken apart for carrying or shipping.

TANG — An extension of the receiver into the stock.

TRAP STOCK — A shotgun stock with greater length and less drop for trap shooting.

VENTILATED RIB — A sighting plane affixed along the length of a shotgun barrel with gaps or slots milled for cooling purposes.

Firearms in the Nineties

Editorial by S. P. Fjestad

Things have changed. Since the last time I departed from this airport, typing has taken the place of writing, the dollar is worth 12% less, domestic gas has risen sharply from 79.9 cents per gallon, 43 days after it started, Operation Desert Storm has come and gone, and I can no longer talk about West and East Germany. Certainly the 90's have already delivered changes that have impacted our lives greatly.

During Operation Desert Storm, firearms and other related weaponry regained some positive exposure in our society. After all, the hero of the war in the Middle East was not a battalion or skilled diplomacy- rather the Patriot Missile represented the Red, White and Blue in Purple Heart form. It's been awhile since a weapon has been considered an invaluable tool in this country. This fact alone was worth watching all those hours of CNN.

Despite the fact that our superior weaponry was responsible for such a short war, the positive status has not carried over on domestic firearms and their "aura". America continues to struggle with the many issues involving citizens and their rights (and fights) regarding firearms ownership. If the "Anti's" continue to politically leverage the legalities of owning firearms, we could be down to slingshots (steel shot only of course) by the time the party favors are dusted off at the end of 1999.

For so many years shooting and hunting have been best first cousins, but as Americans continue to change their thinking about the morality of harvesting game, the media and anti-gun elements are starting to portray hunting as a sort of twisted internship for a professional career in serial killing. Read my Dad's article on the following pages for a more representative view on this subject.

This winter a friend of mine (I think) gave me a clipped out ad out of one of the local newspapers. I have re-created an image of it below:

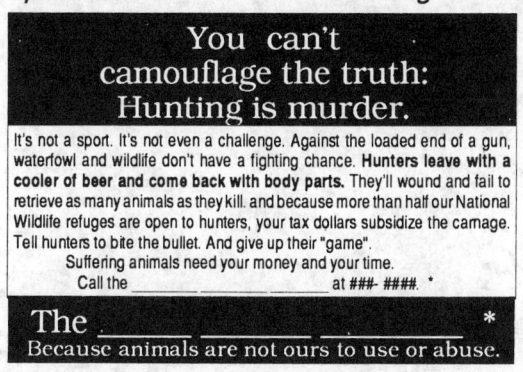

Little shocks me any more, but I thought this type of advertising sensation-alism, coupled with a "Don't confuse us with the facts" attitude was in poor taste. As this form of cancer grows in the nineties, more and more hunters will put their guns in the cabinet for the last time. I'm a hunter, and I don't know who these guys are talking about.

To offset this decline in hunting (and hunters), the development and growth of alternative shooting sports (Sporting Clays, Biathlon events, air rifle, black powder, etc.) will have to be pumped up. Hopefully, major sponsors will support major shooting events. After all, shooting does not mean hunt-ing.

The director of the Walther company told me in Germany during IWA last month that West Germany has over 300,000 registered airgun shooters. At the same time the U.S. has less than 3,000. It's important that all of us gun enthusiasts (including antique collectors) get out and shoot in different events and sports this decade. If not, I'm afraid the museums next century will be filled with 20th century "illegal art forms with barrels" that no one ever used.

Steven P. Fjestad

NOTE: The name of the organization has been withheld. We at Blue Book Publications have no desire to slander, mislabel, categorize or prejudice your attitudes towards ANY group of individuals because of their opinions, affiliations or politics.

HARVESTING
by Norman Fjestad

*M*y brother and I were lucky to have parents that encouraged outdoor activities, which included hunting. This probably came about naturally as we were raised on the family farm that was was settled by my Grandfather in 1869. This farm had 3 duck sloughs with over 2 miles of lakeshore, their names are Johnson Lake, Fjestad Lake, & the Muskrat slough. I will try to relate some of the true stories going back to the early '30's and before.

*T*he Johnson Lake was so named after a person who drowned during a duck-hunting mishap right before World War 1. No one could recover the body so an "Indian John" was hired to try find the unlucky Mr. Johnson. The Indian arrived at the lake in the morning carrying only a box with some type of trained animal inside. He demanded to be paid first and requested that all spectators had to clear out as he had a secret. Two hours after he and the "box" waded into the cold September waters, Johnson's body was laying on the lake shore. To this day, they're still speculating what kind of animal the wooden box contained.

Norman, Frank & Trixie, circa 1938

*W*e started hunting at age 10. My first gun was a Damascus double with one hammer missing. During my lifetime I have shot two old double barrels (names I've forgotten), a 20 ga. Marlin repeater and a 16 ga. Model 12 Winchester. The Winchester was the first gun I owned, cost of $25 with three boxes of shells. I also shot an old Remington automatic with bottom ejector, a Fox Sterlingworth double, a Winchester Model 1200 repeater and a Browning 12 ga. Superposed.

*T*he cost of shells limited our hunting, even though they were 75 cents a box for the better shells. Dad was a true disciplinarian when it came to gun safety. If we ever pointed a gun at any one, including any dog, there was no more hunting that year.

*A*t one time, Dad, Frank, and I each had a dog - Trixie, Tony, and Duke. Mother would allow all three in the house (two American spaniels and a black lab). Sometimes I have a hard time recalling my own name, but remember all the dogs back to 1930.

*F*or some uknown reason, very few of our neighbors hunted. Dad used the Winchester Model's 97 and 12 for many decades, then switched to a Browning A-5 after World War 2. He was an excellent shot and went hunting almost every day during the season. He always shot Winchester shells also, even though Montgomery Ward shells were selling for 35 cents a box.

O n opening day of Duck Hunting Dad's friends, Judge Roger Dell, Dr. Bell would come out eight miles from Fergus Falls. They would always have a case of Winchester shells in a wood box. During World War 2 shells were very hard to get. We also had several hunters come up from Minneapolis. They would stay for several days and enjoy the hunting and hospitality at our house. Mother did the duck cleaning and cooking (usually 40-50 during opening day). She also did all her cooking from scratch, so there were some real duck dinners with all the trimmings. It takes a patient wife to be married to a hunter.

M y hunting memories should include a J.H. Haddock, a hunter from Minneapolis. Dad saw Haddock hunting on a neighbors property and invited him to hunt and stay for duck supper. This was in 1917, and for the next 50 years he came to our farm two times during each hunting season. Each time he would stay for 3 days. His good English manner fascinated Frank and myself. Mother would serve a whole duck or more to each of us and Haddock would compliment my mother how tasty the food was between every other mouthful. He would always bring a basket of grapes and a box of Fanny Farmer candy. No money was ever exchanged for these privileges of hunting. That is the way it was back then.

Theodore, with Model 97, watching an upcoming hunter, Norman.

M any area hunters have also enjoyed the hunting at our farm over the years - Cliff Maxwell from the YMCA in Fergus, Bill Berghuis from Gamble Robinson, the Anderson brothers, and many others have truly enjoyed their hunting trips with us and the fellowship it provides.

G oing back to 1920 there was always an opening day duck supper. This tradition hs been carried on ever since. Our two sons, Steven and Greg, have helped carry on the tradition.

M y wife Harriet, took over the duck hunting cooking in 1953 and carried on the tradition up until last year. Our annual duck supper grew to 24 people. Last season Minneapolis hunters have rented our property and Harriet and I, Greg and his wife Becky were treated to a local restaurant for an excellent steak dinner. Times do change, but I still miss the annual duck supper.

G reg is engaged in farming on the home farm, and Steve is the author and publisher of this book. Harriet and I are retired and living in Fergus Falls, MN. There are many pleasant memories of hunting over the years and I consider myself lucky to have been part of it. Steve and Greg remind me yearly of the time they chased up 4 green-wing teal that flew by me and I never got a feather. Now that I'm retired and only helping part-time with farming, I spend considerable time on local and state conservation issues and other ways to help our environment so future generations can also enjoy.

Norman Fjestad

The Holding Pattern

In Texas they have an expression for having a lot of guns and no money - it is called being "gun poor". This page is for those individuals who find themselves in this predicament. Since it is rather hard for a collector/investor to walk into a bank and use $20,000 of high grade Browning shotguns and rifles as collateral for even a $4,000 short-term loan, gun owners in the past have had limited choices.

The Holding Pattern, Inc., located in Nashville, TN has an alternative to this situation. They can make loans available on investment quality firearms exclusively. To my knowledge this has never been attempted before, and this author feels that such a unique loan arrangement is long overdue. At last you can retain the value of your important firearm(s) while using them as collateral (and be reassured that they are being stored very securely in a bank vault).

Rather than explain the details, I would recommend that you contact The Holding Pattern, Inc. to learn more about this industry first service.. The Holding Pattern's address is:

The Holding Pattern, Inc., 401 Church St.,

1020 L&C Tower,Nashville, TN 37219
Phone: 615-255-0691   FAX: 615-255-0693

In addition to contacting them directly using the above listed channels, Holding Pattern representatives will be at the following gun shows:

June 14-16, Las Vegas Sahara

July 11-14 CADA Las Vegas Riviera

September 28- 29, CADA Denver

October 25- 27, Las Vegas Sahara

December 12 - 15, CADA Chicago

January 1991, Las Vegas Sahara

The Holding Pattern is owned by Dr. Paul and Cindy McCombs, longtime residents of Nashville, TN. They are reputable people and I would recommend your talking to them personally for this unique and needed service. For other firearms industry trade endorsements, please contact them directly for a listing.

FIREARMS PUBLICATIONS

When people ask me how I have learned so much about firearms, much of the credit goes to the extensive library I have accumulated (see photo). Recently, I took an inventory of these gun related publications with current replacement values. The total came to over $30,000.00! Once I got over that shock, I wanted to know what I had approximately paid for them originally and how they had performed as an investment. The results are impressive - many of my books have outperformed my guns in terms of price appreciation. How is this possible? Most of these books are rarer than the guns inside and each time they are reprinted (some are not) the price usually goes up substantially.

If you are a firearms collector or investor, quality reference works in the area(s) you are interested in are a must. Not only will they probably pay for themselves by saving you money (not to mention mistakes), but as stated above, they also perform as a solid investment. It's like getting paid to get educated. I always chuckle when I hear someone complain about the "high price" of a particular book when it could have saved him hundreds of dollars on the non-original gun he bought several weeks before. Unless you like to learn by making expensive mistakes, good quality firearms publications will give you the knowledge needed to make intelligent choices when buying or selling.

I would encourage you to look at the following book listing describing many of the best reference works available today on many important trademarks. To order, simply call us **TOLL-FREE 1-800-877-4867**, to use your **VISA/MASTERCARD/DISCOVER** or use the enclosed order form. Remember, books also make great gifts for any shooter or firearms enthusiast.

If I had to make one book recommendation this year, it would be R.L. Wilson's new <u>Winchester Engraving</u> book. This is the second edition of this publication, and while the retail price is $115.00, it is worth every penny (both as a reference and an investment). I paid $45.00 fifteen years ago for a firwt edition - today it is very liquid at $300.00+. I'm sure the second edition will perform the same way.

Having these reference works at fingertip accessibility will make you a better firearms buyer/seller, and sooner or later, they will pay for themselves. When people ask me how to start collecting firearms, my reply is to go out and buy a 2'x 4' bookcase and do not stop buying firearms related publications until it is full. One last thing, if you are interested in publications not listed on the following pages, please call/FAX/write us with your request(s).

Steven P. Fjestad

Before you make your next move...

The publications available on the following pages
are available from

Blue Book Publications, Inc.

and will help to make your gun collection or firearms
related business more up-to-date and accurate.
The following books have been hand picked
to insure your satisfaction.

Why *guess* when you can be *sure*?

Firearms Publications

012 - THE BLUE BOOK OF GUN VALUES, by Steven P. Fjestad

The 12th edition Blue Book of Gun Values is now the definitive firearms pricing guide with related data. It lists both current and discontinued domestic, foreign and military guns, major trademark antiques, commemoratives, and new models. Also includes extensive model information, serialization, cartridge interchangeability tables, collectors' overview, firearms inventory record keeping system, and more. New for 1991 is a 32 page, 4 color Photo Percentage Grading System insert that enables gun owners to ascertain the condition of their firearms accurately. Purchased separately, this information/data would cost over $100! Soft cover. Over 1,000 pages.

* **Price $19.95**

099 - BLUE BOOK OF GUN VALUES / COMBINATION PACKAGE

Also available is a combination package enabling you to purchase the current 12th Edition and next year's 13th Edition (to be published in April, 1992) for $39.95. This includes both books and shipping charges.

* **Price $39.95**

101 - THE BLUE BOOK OF GUITAR VALUES, by Dwight G. Bode; edited by Steven P. Fjestad

This is the PRIEMERE EDITION of a comprehensive book that focuses on the collectable value of guitars and gives the serious collector of guitars an alternative guide to the price for their instruments. It covers presently produced, antique and out of production guitars. This book is edited by Steven P. Fjestad and carries the Blue Book tradition in dedication to quality, realism and completeness. To be published in the summer of 1991.

500 - THE AK 47 STORY, by Edward Clinton Ezell

The story of the evolution of the Kalashnikov family of weapons. Because of the recent interest in this configuration of firearms, this book has become more popular than ever. "Clear, coherent, highly readable." — *Soldier of Fortune*. Paperback. 256 pages, 150 photos, 25 drawings.

* **Price $12.95**

505 - AFRICAN RIFLES & CARTRIDGES, by Taylor

A study of the various rifles and cartridges used on African safaris during the past century. Taylor explains the development and application of firearms/cartridges and how effective they are in a dangerous situation. Fascinating history of "Magnum" hunting in Africa since the turn of the century. Hardcover. Many photo's and illustrations.

- **Price** **$29.95**

510 - ASTRA AUTOMATIC PISTOLS, by L.M. Antaris

The first complete, top-quality reference text devoted exclusively to Astra's Automatic Pistols and their accessories. Pistol production is detailed from 1911 and reviewed through the 1980's. Individual models are discussed from both a historical and technical perspective, followed by extensively tabulated production data. Destination tables itemize specific pistols shipped to the Spanish military, German Condor Legion, Nazi Germany, Chilean Air Force, Portuguese Navy, and other foreign militaries. Also covered are prototypes, shipping boxes, holsters, shoulder stocks, etc. Hardbound. 250 pages including 400 B&W photos.

- **Price** **$40.00**

520 - BERETTA AUTOMATIC PISTOLS, by J.B. Wood

The definitive book on semi-auto Beretta pistols. This book includes important models from 1915 through Models 70, 80, 90, up to and including Model 92F (with commercial variations) chosen by the military. Hardbound. 192 pages including photos and charts.

- **Price** **$19.95**

525 - BROWNING DATES OF MANUFACTURE, by George Madis

Covers most models from 1824 to present. This book gives the date codes and product codes for all Browning models from the forerunners to the present. Differentiates the Belgian from the Japanese models and eliminates the confusion that exists even among Browning specialists. Paperback. 48 pages.

- **Price** **$5.00**

526 - THE BROWNING HIGH-POWER AUTOMATIC PISTOLS, by Blake

This hardcover is the definitive study of the Browning High-Power pistol, the most popular military contract pistol of all time. Blake goes on a explain the variations and give you good quality photos as well. A must book for any High-Power collector! Hardcover.

- **Price** **$47.50**

529 - CARTRIDGES OF THE WORLD, by Frank Barnes

The definative text on both foreign and domestic cartridges, including dimensions, ballistics data, development and history, and other pertinent data. Hundreds of cartridges are listed in an easily read format. This is the only book you will need for gaining more knowledge on cartridges.

- **Price**   **$18.95**

530 - COLT DATES OF MANUFACTURE, by R.L. Wilson

Compilation of all Colt dates from 1847 to 1978. Includes complete serial ranges for each year enabling you obtain the exact year of manufacture for any Colt pistolrevolver, rifle, or shotgun. Pocket size, softcover. 61 pages.

- **Price**   **$5.00**

532 - COLT PEACEMAKER BRITISH MODEL, by Keith Cochran

A complete history of the Colt Single Action and its distribution and sales in England from 1874 through the turn of the century. This text follows the evolution of this revolver in England and has much history regarding the variations (of which there were many). Caliber rarities are also broken down and known serial number listings are provided. A chronological rundown of changes completes this unique publication. Hardcover, multiple B&W photos and assorted graphics, 159 pages.

- **Price**   **$35.00**

533 - COLT CAVALRY ARTILLERY, by Keith Cochran

This hardcover publication on Colt's Cavalry, Artillery, and Militia SAA's is laid out simular to the Colt Peacemaker Encyclopedia. Alphabetized sections include features and other items of interest that are described in detail. Much new information is covered within these pages. This is the only book devoted strictly to Government procured Colt Single Action Army's and will be a welcome addition to Colt handgun enthusiasts. Hardcover, many B&W photos and related graphics, 288 pages.

- **Price**   **$45.00**

534 - COLT PEACEMAKER YEARLY VARIATIONS, by Keith Cochran

A pocket chronology of the Colt Peacemaker includes annual production totals, caliber introductions, cavalry and or militia markings, chamber dimensions, commemorative issues with totals, factory inspector markings, frame types, Government contracts, and overall quantities of pistols. Also included is a serialization breakdown and caliber production chart. A very handy reference work. Softcover.

- **Price** **$12.95**

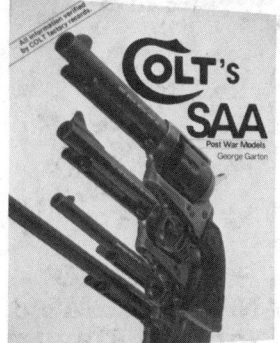

535 - COLT'S SAA POST WAR MODELS, by George Garton

Provides the collector/investor with complete facts on the Post War Single Action Army Revolver. Also has information on caliber, production totals, and variations taken from factory records. Hardbound. 176 pages with many B&W photos.

- **Price** **$29.95**

536 - COLT PEACEMAKER YEARLY VARIATIONS, by Keith Cochran

A pocket chronology of the Colt Peacemaker includes annual production totals, caliber introductions, cavalry and or militia markings, chamber dimensions, commemorative issues with totals, factory inspector markings, frame types, Government contracts, and overall quantities of pistols. Also included is a serialization breakdown and caliber production chart. A very handy reference work. Hardcover, limited B&W photos, 76 pages.

- **Price** **$17.95**

537 - COLT - AN AMERICAN LEGEND, by R.L.Wilson

A true American classic - R.L. Wilson takes you literally and photographically through Col. Sam Colt's amazing life's story with the guns that earned him legendary status in 3 decades! A beautiful hardcover that will be off your coffee table more than on. Hardcover. Over 400 pages.

- **Price** **$65.00**

538 - COLT PEACEMAKER ENCYCLOPEDIA, VOL. 2, by Keith Cochran

An entire reference work devoted strictly to the Colt Single Action Army revolver. This publication has a unique alphabetical format that lists all pertinent SAA headings in order. In addition, many B&W photos depict important features/options of this most collectible revolver. A must for Colt SAA fanciers. This 2nd Edition has been expanded to include much new information and photo's.

* **Price $65.00**

540 - KNOW YOUR COLT .45 AUTO PISTOLS/ MODELS 1911 & A1, by E.J. Hoffschmidt

Over 79 photographs of military and commercial models plus foreign copies provide the reader with detailed illustrations to accompany the fact- filled text. Takedown, repair and national match guns are shown in detail. A must for the .45 enthusiast! Softcover. 60 pages with photos and illustrations.

* **Price $6.95**

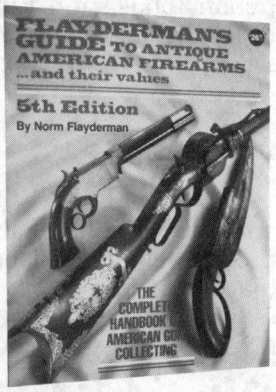

545 - FLAYDERMAN'S GUIDE TO ANTIQUE AMERICAN FIREARMS & THEIR VALUES by Norman Flayderman

How to identify, value, & collect domestic antique firearms. Greatly expanded coverage, updated prices & detailed specifications. Paperback. 624 pages with extensive photos/illustrations.

* **Price $23.95**

550 - GERMAN PISTOLS AND HOLSTERS 1934/1945 MILITARY-POLICE-NSDAP, by Lt. Col. Robert D. Whittington III

Lists most Nazi pistols used during WWII. Includes many photographs of these pistols with respective descriptions. Also graphically depicts acceptance stamps and proof marks which enable the reader to readily identify the broad categories of organizations for which these pistols were procured. Includes illustrations of holsters and identification list of holster manufacturer's codes. Hardbound. 224 pages.

* **Price $19.95**

551 - GERMAN PISTOLS AND HOLSTERS, VOL. II by Lt. Col. Robert D.Whittington III

A continuation of Vol. I of German Pistols and Holsters. Much new information. A must for German miltary pistol collectors. Hardcover. B & W photos with illustrations.

- **Price** **$45.00**

552 - GERMAN PISTOLS AND HOLSTERS, VOL. III by Lt. Col. Robert D. Whittington III

A continuation of Vol. II of German Pistols and Holsters. Much new information. This edition contains some of the information from Vol.'s I and II in addition to new research. B & W photos with illustrations.

- **Price** **$50.00**

555 - THE GOVERNMENT MODELS, by William H.D. Goddard

Perhaps the definitive work on the development of the early Colt Models including 1900, 1902, 1903 Pocket Hammer, 1905 Military, 1909, 1911, 1911-A1, with variations of each. An interesting story of the development of the greatest pistol design of the 20th Century. Hardbound. 293 pages with over 60 B&W photos/illustrations, and 7 color plates.

- **Price** **$58.50**

560 - AMERICAN GUNSMITHS, by Frank Sellers

This is one of the more useful books that the research staff at Blue Book Publications uses during the course of the year. After having this copy for only 3 years, ours is almost worn out! Mr. Sellers gives us the ultimate "grocery listing" of thousands of American firearms manufacturers and gunsmiths - over 10,000 separate listings with dates also. Hardcover. CHECK pages.

- **Price** **$39.95**

565 - HANDGUNS OF THE WORLD, by Edward Clinton Ezell

Practical information and solid facts, from production figures, to the photographs of each model. Includes a handy reference guide listing all cartridges in use which make this publication an invaluable tool for any handgun enthusiast. Hardbound. 704 pages with photos/illustrations.

- **Price** **$39.95**

566 - HATCHER'S NOTEBOOK, by Hatcher

This classic has been out of print for the past year or more - we are happy to be able to offer this definitive publication to our customers again. Hatcher studies the many technical aspects of firearms and ammunition throughout the past 150 years. Many little humerous anecdotes are also included involving historically significant events. Simply a must for every firearms bookshelf! Hardcover with many B&W photos and illustrations. Over 600 pages

- **Price** **$24.95**

567 - HIGH STANDARD AUTOMATIC PISTOLS (1932-1950), by Charles Petty

This is the only reference work currently available on one of the most popular collector handguns - the High Standard Semi-Auto Pistol. Only today are shooters and collectors realizing how well manufactured this limited series of .22 LR rimfires was during its day. This book lists most variations that were manufactured between 1932 and 1950. Good quality B&W photos also let both the collector and shooter disseminate between models. Although incomplete in post-1950 production, this book is still the only watering hole for High Standard Semi-Auto collectors. Hardcover, B&W photos, 124 pages.

- **Price** **$19.95**

575 - THE SHOOTING FIELD - 150 YEARS WITH HOLLAND & HOLLAND, by Peter King

This elegant deluxe Blacksmith book tells the fascinating story of Holland & Holland's first century and a half. Founded in 1935, Holland & Holland quickly became the chosen arms maker to the rich and the powerful. In keeping with the Holland & Holland tradition of perfection, no expense has been spared in the creation of this definitive, authorized history of the firm and its guns. For the arms enthusiast and collector, the tables and charts provide a unique and invaluable reference. Serial number information, production data, gun descriptions, and a wealth of other details so essential to the collector or fine arms dealer, is now available for the very first time. Hardbound. 176 pages, with over 100 color and B&W photos/illustrations.

- **Price** **$49.95**

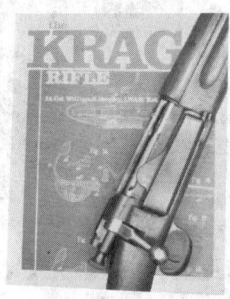

580 - THE KRAG RIFLE, by Lt. Col. William S. Brophy, USAR, Ret.

This definitive text provides information necessary to understand the Krag rifle and variations (Models 1892 Rifle and Carbine, 1896 Rifle and Carbine, 1898 Rifle and variations, 1899, etc.) Also includes prototypes, foreign contracts, accessories (including bayonets and scabbards), and accoutrements. Hardbound. 258 pages with extensive B&W model photos, charts and related illustrations.

- **Price**   **$35.00**

585 - L.C. SMITH SHOTGUNS, by Lt. Col. William S. Brophy, USAR, Ret.

The definitive work on L.C. Smith shotguns (including Hunter Arms Co. and Baker Shotguns.) Traces the history of the company and thoroughly covers each grade and variation of L.C. Smiths from beginning to end with production figures and dates. Hardcover. 254 pages, including many B&W photos/illustrations, and 8 color plates.

- **Price**   **$35.00**

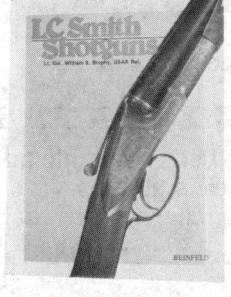

587 - LUGERS AT RANDOM, by Charles Kenyon, Jr.

The most difinitive book written on Lugers. Contains over 400 photos and illustrations covering the Luger in all of its variations. Hardcover. Over 400 pages.

- **Price**   **$39.95**

590 - KNOW YOUR M1 GARAND RIFLES, by E.J. Hoffschmidt

This classic Hoffschmidt book is illustrated with original line drawings and photographs. All M1 models are covered from experimental T and E models to M14 match guns, plus troubleshooting and takedown. Softcover. 80 pages with photos, charts and illustrations.

- **Price**   **$6.95**

591 - COLLECTOR'S GUIDE TO THE M1 GARAND AND THE M1 CARBINE, by Bruce N. Canfield

This comprehensive guide is essential to the novice and expert alike. It includes all markings, features, accessories and variations. Included is production figures and serial number combinations. Hardcover. Over 150 pages with many B & W photos and illustrations.

- **Price** **$35.00**

595 - MARLIN FIREARMS, by Lt. Col. William S. Brophy, USAR, Ret.

New! Finally, a complete and definitive reference work on Marlin Firearms. Covers the model history from 1863 to present. Also elaborates on the men and events which made the company world-famous. Written by the foremost authority on Marlin Arms, its curator, Lt. Col. William S. Brophy. Hardbound. 704 pages with over 1,900 B&W photos and line drawings.

- **Price** **$59.95**

596 - THE MARLIN 336, by Murray

The only book available on Marlin's most popular lever-action rifle. Included are production statistics, rare production variations, many B&W photo's, and other data. Softcover. With many B&W photo's and illustrations.

- **Price** **$17.00**

600 - KNOW YOUR BROOMHANDLE MAUSERS, by Robert J. Berger

Never before published photographs, drawings, and reproductions, from the original Mauser factory manuals and other sources, are skillfully used by Berger to present the fascinating story of the big Mauser pistols and their many variations. A valuable addition to Mauser literature. Softcover. 96 pages with photos/illustrations.

- **Price** **$6.95**

605 - SYSTEM MAUSER, by John W. Breathed, Jr. and Joseph J. Schroeder, Jr.

Extensively covers the Model 1896 self-loading Broomhandle pistol. Nearly 100 variations are pictured and described, detailing the mechanics and markings. Also covers many accouterments for the pistol. Hardbound. 273 pages with many photos/illustrations depicting most variations.

- **Price** **$29.95**

606 - MAUSER RIFLES & PISTOLS, by William Smith

Smith explains most of the Mauser-Werke production rifles and pistols (both commercial and military). Out of print for many years, this revised edition is a good "first text" for the beginning Mauser collector studying this famous trademark. Hardcover. With photo's and illustrations.

- **Price** $30.00

607 - MAUSER BOLT RIFLES, by Olson

This new 3rd edition is the definitive study of the most popular bolt action ever manufactured - Mauser Model 98. The preceeding models are listed first, followed by a very thorough recap of the many commercial and military Model 98's built before 1950. This book is a must if you are a Model 98 collector. Hardcover. Over 300 pages with many B&W photo's, illustrations, and production tables.

- **Price** $47.25

610 - THE NAVY LUGER, by Joachim Gortz and John Walter

Concise illustrated history of the German Naval Luger with variations (including Models 1904, 1906, and 1914–1918 dated). Hardbound. 128 pages with extensive B&W photos, charts and illustrations.

- **Price** $24.95

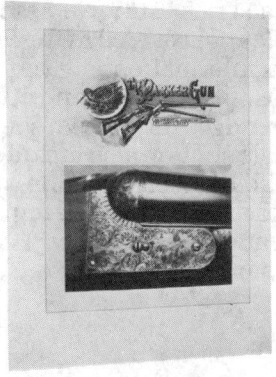

615 - THE PARKER GUN, by Larry L. Baer

This is the most important work published on America's most famous shotgun trademark. Includes detailed photographs of all grades and gauges of shotguns. While primarily a study of the hammerless Parker with fluid steel barrels, it also covers some hammer guns and damascus guns with related background and history of Parker Bros. Hardbound. 196 pages with extensive B&W photos, charts and illustrations.

- **Price** $35.00

620 - THE STANDARD DIRECTORY OF PROOF MARKS, by G. Wirnsberger

This concise directory contains most of the important proof marks from various European countries. Each country's (listed in alphabetical order) proof marks are listed in chronological sequence. This is a very valuable publication since it establishes the approximate age of most European proofed guns. Hundreds of line drawings, charts, and indices make this book the world's most valuable proof mark reference work. Softcover. 192 pages.

- **Price $9.95**

625 - SINGLE SHOT RIFLES, by James J. Grant

A concise study of the single shot rifle including Ballards, Remingtons, Sharps, Stevens, F. Wessons, and Winchesters. Also lists foreign actions/trademarks including Martinis, German Schuetzens, and others. Hardbound. 385 pages with 175 illustrations.

- **Price $25.00**

626 - MORE SINGLE SHOT RIFLES, by James J. Grant

This is the second in a series listing an assortment of single shot rifles not covered in the first publication. Detailed information is given on calibers, barrel lengths, descriptions and other pertinent data. Cartridges for these sometimes limited mfg. single shots is also included. Good quality B&W photos depict actions, advertising brochures, cartridges, etc. An important follow-up publication. Hardcover, B&W photos, approx. 400 pages.

- **Price $25.00**

631 - SAVAGE MODEL 99, by Murray

A very complete softcover on Savage's most collectible rifle - the Model 99. Murray lays this book out much like the Marlin Model 336 text. If you are a Savage Model 99 collector, you can wear this book out in a hurry! Soft cover. With many photo's and illustrations.

- **Price $23.00**

52

635 - SHARPS FIREARMS, by Frank Sellers

The best and most complete book about Christian Sharps and the guns he made. Includes the early percussion models, slant breech variations, Civil War contracts, Philadelphia rifles and pistols, conversions, and Models 1874, 1875, 1877, and 1878. Mention is also made of the Sharps Magazine Rifle and SxS shotgun. Hardbound. 358 pages with many B&W identifying photos, historical pictures and illustrations.

- **Price $45.00**

637 - HISTORY OF SMITH AND WESSON, by Roy Jinks

The definitive reference text on Smith and Wesson firearms. This publication starts out by detailing the early history and formulation of Horace Smith and Daniel Wesson. It evolves through their partnership and initial production of revolvers. Chronological model histories are provided along with explanations of their development. Many good illustrations and B&W photos are included to make sure both the S&W novice and advanced collector can visually see model differences. This is the only book available in print on the entire S&W firearms history. Hardcover, B&W photos, 290 pages.

- **Price $21.95**

640 - THE SPRINGFIELD 1903 RIFLES, by Lt. Col. William S. Brophy, USAR, Ret.

This book is the massive lifetime work of the rifle's premier authority, William Brophy. This high quality publication includes descriptions of some of the rarest collections in existence. A MUST for any Springfield collector/investor. Hardbound. 624 pages with 1,500 B&W photos and diagrams.

- **Price $49.95**

645 - TRAPDOOR SPRINGFIELD, by M.D. Waite & B.D. Ernst

The first comprehensive work on the testing, development, and evolution of this famous military longarm of the 1870's and 1880's. These rifles and carbines served as the standard U.S. Army shoulder weapon for nearly 20 years and helped shape the American West. Describes variations of the Springfield. Hardbound. 257 pages with extensive illustrations.

- **Price** **$35.00**

646 - U.S. MILITARY ARMS DATES OF MANUFACTURE, by George Madis

A pocket chronology of U.S. Military Arms manufacture including Springfield Armory manufacture. Also included is World War I and II military production as well as subcontractor listings. An invaluable pocket book listing of major U.S. Military manufacturers with serialization breakdowns.

- **Price** **$5.00**

650 - KNOW YOUR WALTHER P.38 PISTOLS, by E.J. Hoffschmidt

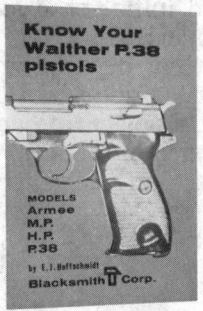

From experimental models and pre-war production to post-World War II .22 caliber and silenced pistols, over 80 illustrations provide the necessary visual aides to assist in the understanding of these firearms. Takedown information and factory data on proof marks. Softcover. 77 pages.

- **Price** **$6.95**

655 - KNOW YOUR WALTHER PP & PPK PISTOLS, by E.J. Hoffschmidt

This work includes pre-war catalogue sheets, correspondence, and advertisements. Hoffschmidt explored drawings, field stripping information, ammunition, and proof marking details, to produce this complete reference guide to all common and unusual models of the famous Walther PP & PPK Pistols. Softcover. 87 pages with B&W photos/illustrations.

- **Price** **$6.95**

660 - WEBLEY REVOLVERS, revised from W.C. Dowell's The Webley Story by Gordon Bruce and Christian Reinhart

Since the first publication of Dowell's The Webley Story in 1962, there has been a growing interest in the subject of Webley firearms. New line illustrations have been added with more detailed information. Hardbound. 256 pages with B&W photos/illustrations.

- **Price $59.95**

670 - WINCHESTER ENGRAVING, by R. L. Wilson

This publication is the definitive work for the study and appreciation of engraved Winchester firearms. More than a record of the great firearms engravers, this work is a chronology of Winchester factory-engraved rifles and shotguns, some of which are the most elaborately decorated firearms ever manufactured in this country. The first edition was published in 1974 and had a retail price of $45.00 – currently it is selling for $350.00. Even though $115.00 is expensive, once this edition sells out (and it won't take long), premiums will be paid immediately. Don't wait until they're $200.00. Deluxe hardcover. 512 pages with many color plates and B&W photos/illustrations.

- **Price $115.00**

675 - THE HISTORY OF WINCHESTER FIREARMS 1866-1980, by Duncan Barnes

Simply a must book for any Winchester collector/investor. Chronologically lists every Winchester model manufactured, with production data, through 1980. Many rare production variances are listed in addition to special order features. This book is highly recommended. Hardcover. 239 pages with most models pictured in B&W.

- **Price $19.95**

680 - THE WINCHESTER BOOK, by George Madis

The most complete and authoritative book on Winchester firearms. Contains individual chapters on most rifle models, with many special order features and production variances both pictured and described. Also lists many shotguns and accoutrements (including sights, catalogs, and factory literature.) Deluxe hardbound, 1 of 1,000 edition, each copy personally autographed.654 pages with many photos/illustrations.

*   **Price $45.00**

685 - WINCHESTER DATES OF MANUFACTURE, by George Madis

The source for all dates for all collectors of Winchesters. Over 80 models listed by date with all production year by year. Softcover pocketsized. 51 pages.

*   **Price $5.00**

690 - THE WINCHESTER ERA, by George Madis

An overview of Winchester history including a discussion of Mr. Winchester's involvement with firearms manufacture and the empire developed. Deluxe limited first edition, 1 of 1,000, hardbound, autographed. 167 pages with many historical photos, drawings, and illustrations.

*   **Price $14.95**

693 - WINCHESTER - THE GOLDEN AGE by R.L. Wilson

A very well written text outlining the golden years of Winchester gun manufacturing in America. Generous photo's enhance this publication written by an author who is an expert in the field. Hardcover. Hardcover with color and B&W photo's.

*   **Price $20.00**

694 - WINCHESTER MODEL 21, by Ned Schwing

Finally - a comlete analysis of Winchester's famous Model 21. Much new information and factory production data is given in this 1991 new release. If you collect this American classic, this book will pay for itself after a trade/purchase or two. Long awaited - now finally available. Hardcover. Over 350 pages including many B&W and color photos.

- **Price** **$49.95**

695 - THE WINCHESTER MODEL 42, by Ned Schwing

Traces the development and manufacture of the Winchester Model 42 .410 ga. slide action shotgun. Many variations are both described and pictured in this most recent Winchester book. Included are serialization charts from 1933-1963. A perfect compliment to the Model 12 book. Hardcover, B&W photos, tables, illustrations, and related graphics, 169 pages.

- **Price** **$34.95**

700 - THE WINCHESTER HANDBOOK, by George Madis

A condensed version of The Winchester Book. Contains extensive coverage of all models. While not as complete as The Winchester Book, this publication is an invaluable quick-reference guide for most Winchesters. 1 of 1,000 deluxe hardbound edition, autographed. 288 pages including 600 photographs.

- **Price** **$19.95**

705 - THE WINCHESTER MODEL TWELVE, by George Madis

Complete coverage of the most collectible slide action shotgun ever manufactured, the Winchester Model 12. Hardbound, deluxe autographed edition, 1 of 1,000. 176 pages including photos/illustrations.

- **Price** **$19.95**

715 - WINCHESTER - AN AMERICAN LEGEND by R.L. Wilson

This is simply one of the best laid out and most beautiful gun books ever published! Random House has produced a Winchester book that both collectors, investors, and coffee table purveyors alike can use and display with a great deal of pride. Perhaps the best new release in 1991. A perfect gift also! Hardcover. Over 500 pages with hundreds of color and B&W photo's depicting some of the most elaborate and historically significant longarms ever produced in New Haven, CT.

* **Price $85.00**

750 - OLD FISHING LURES & TACKLE IDENTIFICATION & VALUES, by Luckey.

A very comprehensive guide to American fishing lures, tackle, and accessories. Many photo's and illustrations to help identify and price most of the popular lures and other fishing equipment. Softcover. Over 200 pages with hundeds of B&W photos and illustrations.

* **Price $14.95**

775 - GUIDE TO POCKET KNIVES AND RAZORS by Sargent

This softcover gives you much information on most of the collectible knives and razors in America today. Contains many photo's, illustrations, and accurate data on many of the most popular trademarks in this new field of collecting. Softcover. Over 200 pages including B&W photos.

* **Price $19.95**

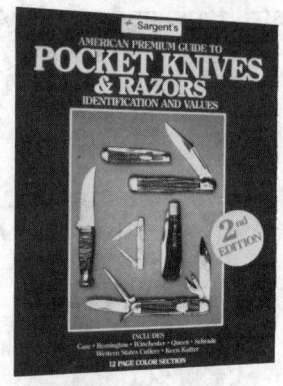

800 - MILITARY SWORDS OF JAPAN 1868-1945, by R. Fuller & R. Gregory

A fascinating study of early Japanese swords through World War II manufacture. As swords are gaining popularity with both collectors and investors, this reference will be invaluable in ascertaining knowledge regarding features that are rare and desirable, provenance on earlier makers, and illustrations which provide the reader with visual identification. Learn what the Japanese have known for years. Hardcover, 128 pages.

* **Price $24.95**

BLUE BOOK PUBLICATIONS, INC.

One Appletree Square, Minneapolis, MN 55425

To use your **VISA, MASTERCARD, or DISCOVER**
Call TOLL FREE 1- 800- 877- 4867
or FAX you order to 1- 612- 853- 1486

DATE: _____

NAME: _____

COMPANY NAME: _____

STREET: _____

CITY_____

STATE: _____ ZIP _____

PHONE NUMBER (required): _____

CREDIT CARD NO.: _____

EXPIRATION DATE _____ SIGNATURE:_____

-or- CHECK NUMBER: _____

Catalog #	Quan-tity	Description	Author	Price
		TOTAL FROM ABOVE		
		Shipping & Handling Charges		
		MN Residents add 6% Sales Tax		
		TOTAL AMOUNT DUE		

SHIPPING CHARGES IN THE CONTINENTAL US ARE:
up to $10.00 in Total value of books = **$3.25**
for each additional $10.00 of books add **$1.25**

SPECIAL OFFERING UNTIL DECEMBER 1, 1991!!
Purchase the "Winchester Book of Engraving" by R. L. Wilson and you will get a complimentary copy of "The History of Winchester Firearms 1866- 1980" by Duncan Barnes. It's the perfect Christmas package.

Firearms Associations

Alaska Gun Collectors Association
> c/o Wayne Anthony Ross, President
> P.O. Box 101522
> Anchorage, Alaska 99510

Arkansas Gun and Cartridge Collectors Club
> No Current Address

Ark - La - Tex - Gun Collectors
> Thomas L. Baird, President
> 9601 Blom Blvd.
> Shreveport, LA 71118

Bay Colony Weapons Collectors, Inc.
> Ronald B. Santurjian
> 47 Homer Road
> Belmont, MA 02178

Bayou Gun Club, The
> No Current Address

Boardman Valley Collectors Guild
> Secretary Jack Johnson
> County Road 600
> Manton, MI 49663

Browning Collectors Assn.
> Mrs. Judy A. Rogers, Secretary
> 4928 Merrick Avenue
> Grand Island, NE 68801

C.A.D.A.(Collector Arms Dealer Association)
> P.O. Box 427
> Thomson, IL 61285

California Rifle & Pistol Association, Inc.
> Executive Director
> 12062 Valley View St.
> Garden Grove, CA 92645

Central Illinois Gun Collectors Assn. Inc.
> Russ Gardner Sec.- Treas.
> Box 875
> Jacksonville, IL 62651-0875

Central Penn Antique Arms Association
> John E. Holman Jr.
> 978 Thistle Road
> Elizabethtown, PA 17022

Chisholm Trail Antique Gun Association
> E.D. Stone
> 1906 Richmond
> Wichita, KS 67203

Civil War Round Table of North New Jersey
> James F. Elliott
> 124 Conover Lane
> Red Bank, NJ 07701

Colt Collectors Association
> Sydna Guest, Secretary
> 3200 Westminster
> Dallas, TX 75205
> Annual Membership $20
> Lifetime Membership $250

The Corpus Christi Antique Gun Collectors Association
> Corpus Christi Antique Gun Collectors
> P.O. Box 9392
> Corpus Christi, TX 78410

Dallas Arms Collectors Assoc., Inc.
> Richard Shea
> RT 1 Box 282-B
> DeSoto, TX 75115

Delaware Antique Arms Collectors Assoc.
> No Current Address

Denver Muzzle Loading Gun Club, Inc.
> Bill Rutherford
> P.O. Box 888
> Englewood, CO 80151

Derringer Collectors Association
> Mr. J. Michael Hall
> 500 E. Old 66
> Shamrock, TX 79079

Ducks Unlimited
> One Waterfowl Way
> Long Grove, Il 60047

Forks of the Delaware W.A.
> No Current Address

Fort LFort Lee Arms Collectors
> P.O. Box 1716
> South Hackensack, NJ 07606

Georgia Arms Collectors Association
> No Current Address

Golden Eagle Collectors Association
> P.O. Box 62213
> Sunnyvale, CA 94086-2213

Gun Owners Civil Rights Alliance
> Mr. Joseph E. Olson, President
> P.O. Box 131254
> St. Paul, MN 55113

Gun Owners of America
> 8001 Forbes Pl., Suite 102
> Springfield, VA 22151

Hawaii Historic Arms Association
> Box 1733
> Honolulu, HI 96806

Houston Gun Collectors Association

P.O. Box 53435
Houston, TX 77052

Hunter Education Association

Box 525
Draper, UT 84020
Phone No.: 801-571-9461

Indianhead Firearms Assn.

R#9 Box 186
Chippewa Falls, WI 54729

Indian Territory Gun Collectors Association

Box 4491
Tulsa, OK 74159

Iroquois Arms Collectors Association

Kenneth Keller-sec.
Susann Keller-show sec.
214 70th St.
Niagara Falls, NY 14304

Jefferson State Arms Collectors

Al Perry
521 South Grape
Medford, OR 97501

Jersey Shore Antique Arms Collectors

Joe Sisia
P.O. Box 100
Bayville, NJ 08721

Kansas Cartridge Collectors Association

Vic Suetter
Route 1
Lincoln, KS 67455

Kentuckiana Arms Collectors Assoc.

Wanda Jones, Secretary
P.O. Box 1776
Louisville, KY 40201

Kentucky Gun Collectors Association

Ruth Johnson, Exec. Sec.
P.O. Box 64
Owensboro, KY 42302

Kentucky State Rifle and Pistol Association, Inc.

P.O. Box 773
Elizabethtown, KY 42701

Lancaster Muzzle Loading Rifle Association

James H. Frederick, Jr.
R.D. #2 Box 402
Columbia, PA 17512

Lehigh Valley Military Collectors Association

No Current Address

Long Island Antique Gun Collectors Assoc.

Frederick R. Wilkens
35 Beach Street
Farmingdale, L.I., NY 11735

Louisiana Gun Collectors Association, Inc.

No Current Address

The Mannlicher Collectors Association

P.O. Box 7144
Salem, OR 97303

Marlin Firearms Collectors Association, Ltd.

Mr. Dick Paterson, Secretary/Treasurer
407 Lincoln Bldg.
44 Main Street
Champaign, IL 61820

Maryland Arms Collectors Assoc. (MACA)

Mr. D. Kuzemchak, Secretary
33 S. Main Street
P.O. Box 206
Loganville, PA 17342-0206
$25 annual membership fee

Memphis Antique Weapons Association

Lonnie Griffin
108 Clark Place
Memphis, TN 38104

Minnesota Rifle and Revolver Association

Karin A. Ostrand, President
10 Pheasant Ln.
North Oaks, MN 55127

Minnesota Weapons Collectors Association

Gail Foster, Executive Secretary
P.O. Box 662
Hopkins, MN 55343

Missouri Valley Arms Collectors Association, Inc.

L.P. Brammer, Secretary
P.O. Box 33033
Kansas City, MO 64114
(816) 333-6509
Annual membership $12.50— ages 21-65;
$7.50— under 21 or over 65 "fully retired"

Montana Arms Collectors Association

Lewis E. Yearout
308 Riverview Drive
East Great Falls, MT 59404
$20 annual membership fee

Mossberg Collectors Association

P.O. Box 22156
St. Louis, MO 63116

N.A.P.C.A.

c/o Automag
Box 15738 TGS
St. Louis, MO 63163

National Alliance of Stocking Gun Dealers

P.O. Box 187
Havelock, NC 28532

National Rifle Association (NRA)

1600 Rhode Island Avenue N.W.
Washington, D.C. 20036
Membership dues $25 a year
$68 for 3 years
$100 for 5 years

New Hampshire Arms Collectors, Inc.

Warren Thayer
P.O. Box 6
Harrisville, N.H. 03450

North Eastern Arms Collectors Assoc., Inc.

Thomas J. Mulligan, President
P.O. Box 185
Amityville, NY 11701

Northwest Montana Arms Collectors Association (NWMACA)

Paul C. Beckstrom
P.O. Box 653
Kalispell, MT 59901

Ohio Gun Collectors Association

P.O. Box 24F
Cincinnati, OH 45224

Old Fort Gun Collectors Association

No Current Address

Oregon Arms Collectors

Ted Dowd
P.O. Box 25103
Portland, OR 97225

Pelican Arms Collectors Association

Bob Thompson
P.O. Box 747
Clinton, LA 70722

Pennsylvania Antique Gun Collectors Assoc.

Mrs. Kathleen Beyer Secy./Treas.
28 Fulmer Avenue
Havertown, PA 19083
$10 annual membership fee

Pikes Peak Gun Collectors Guild

Charles Cell
406 E. Uintah
Colorado Springs, CO 80903

Potomac Arms Collectors Association

Bruce D. Feinberg
P.O. Box 2676
Laurel, MD 20811

Quail Unlimited

Rt. #3 - Box 29B
Edgefield, SC 29824

Remington Society of America

Marv Adams, Secretary-Treasurer
967 Maple Street
Perrysburg, OH 43551
Annual Membership $15

Ruger Collectors Association, Inc.

P.O. Box 1778
Chino Valley, AZ 86323
$25 annual membership fee

Safari Club International

4800 W. Gates Pass Rd.
Tucson, AZ 85745

Sako Collectors Association, Inc.

Mims C. Reed
1725 Woodhill Lane
Bedford, TX 76021
$20 annual membership fee
$200 life membership

Santa Barbara Historical Arms Coll. Assoc.

P.O. Box 6291
Santa Barbara, CA 93160-6291
$10 annual membership fee
$10 initiation fee

San Bernardino Valley Arms Collectors

Harold R.F. Thrasher
1970 Mesa Street
San Bernardino, CA 92405

Santa Fe Gun Collectors Association

Ernie Lang
1085 Nugget
Los Alamos, NM 87544

San Fernando Valley Arms Coll. Assoc.

Harold Ball
P.O. Box 65
North Hollywood, CA 91603

San Gabriel Valley Arms Collectors

No Current Address

Second Amendment Foundation/Gun Week

12500 Northeast 10 Pl.
Bellevue, WA 98005

Shasta Arms Collectors Association

No Current Address

Smith & Wesson Collectors Association

R. & M. Kolesar, Secretaries
P.O. Box 321
Bellevue, WA 98009

The Stark Gun Collectors, Inc.

Pat F. McDonald
602 Summerdale N.W.
Massillon, OH 44646

Tampa Bay Arms Collectors Association

John J. Tuvell, Secretary
2461-67th Avenue South
St. Petersburg, FL 33712

Texas Gun Collectors Association

85 Wells Fargo Trail
Austin, TX 78737
(512) 288-5039

The Thompson Center Association

Hilary Wright, Secretary
P.O. Box 792
Northboro, MA 01532
$25 annual membership fee

Washington Arms Collectors, Inc.

J. Dennis Cook
P.O. Box 7335
Tacoma, WA 98407

Weapons Collectors Society of Montana

3100 Bancroft
Missoula, MT 59801

Weatherby Collectors Association, Inc.

P.O. Box 128
Moira, NY 12957

Williamette Valley Arms Collectors Association, Inc.

Murry Brooks, Executive Secretary
P.O. Box 5191
Eugene, OR 97405

Winchester Arms Collectors Association, Inc.

Richard A. Berg, Exec. Sec.
P.O. Box 6754
Great Falls, MT 59406

Winchester Club of America

Larry Jones
2190 So. Kalamath
Denver, CO 80223

Ye Connecticut Gun Guild

Robert L. Harris
U.S. Route 7-Kent Road
Cornwall Bridge, CT 06754

Zumbro Valley Arms Collectors, Inc.

Box 6621
Rochester, MN 55901

PERIODICALS LISTINGS

American Airgunner P.O. Box 1459 , Abilene, TX 79604-1459, Phone No.: 915-673-6538, Annual Subscription - $15.00. Published quarterly

American Firearms Industry 2801 E. Oakland Park Blvd., Ft. Lauderdale, FL 33306. Phone No.: 305-561-3505. Trade publications and related material.

American Rifleman Published by the NRA, 1600 Rhode Island Ave., Washington, DC 20036. Phone No.: 202-828-5138. Subscription included in price of NRA Membership ($25). Published monthly

Field & Stream Magazine 2 Park Ave., New York, NY 10016. Phone No.: 212-779-5000. Subscription rate $15.94 annually. Published monthly.

Gun Report P.O. Box 111, Aledo, IL 61231 Phone No.: 309-582-5311. Published monthly

Guns and Ammo 8490 Sunset Blvd., Los Angeles, CA 90069. Phone No. 213-854-2222 Published monthly

Gun Week P.O.Box 488, Station C, Buffalo, NY 14209. Annual Subscription - $27. Published weekly. Phone No.: 716- 885- 6408

Man at Arms 222 W. Exchange St., Providence, RI 02903 . Published bi-monthly ($20 yearly). Phone No. 401-726-8011

National Alliance of Stocking Gun Dealers P.O. Box 187, Havelock, NC 28532. Phone No.: 919-447-1313

North American Hunter 12301 Whitewater Dr., Minnetonka, MN 55343. Phone No.: 612-936-9333. Published monthly (included in membership).

Outdoor Life Magazine Two Park Ave., New York, NY 10016. Phone No.: 212-779-5000

Publishers Development Corportation 591 Camino De La Reina #200, San Diego, CA 92108. Publisher of: Shooting Industry, American Handgunner and Guns magazines. Phone No.: 800-537-3006, call for subscription rates

Shotgun News P.O. Box 669, Hastings, NE 68901. Subscription - $18 yearly (36 issues). 402-463-4589

Safari Club International 4800 W. Gates Pass Rd., Tucson, AZ 85745. Phone No.: 602-620-1220. Publications: Safari magazine, Safari Africa, Deer of the World, Sheep of the World, International Record Book of Trophy Animals, Record Book Field Edition.

Shooting Sportsman 1037 W. 8th Ave., W. Williamsport, PA 17701. Phone No.: 717-326-4869

Sporting Clays Magazine Suite 21-J, Airport Office Park, Airport Road, Hilton Head, SC 29928. Phone No.: 803-681-2219. Published bi-monthly

The Sporting Goods Dealer 1212 N. Lindbergh Blvd., St. Louis, MO 63132. Phone No.: 314-997-7111

Sporting Goods Business 1515 Broadway, New York, NY 10036. Phone No.: 212-869-1300

Sports Afield Magazine 250 W. 55th St., New York, NY 10019. Phone No.: 212-649-4300

Women & Guns Published by Second Amendment Foundation, James Madison Bldg., 12500 NE 10th Pl., Bellevue, WA 98005. Phone No.: 206-454-7012

A

A.A.
Previously manufactured by Azanza & Arrizablaga located in Eibar, Spain.

Grading	100%	98%	95%	90%	80%	70%	60%
A.A. — semi-auto pistol, 7.65mm, slide marked Azanza & Arrizablaga Model 1916, A.A. in oval on frame.	$130	$105	$85	$65	$55	$50	$45
REIMS — semi-auto pistol, 6.35mm or 7.65mm, copies of M1906 Browning, marked 1914 Model.	$120	$100	$75	$65	$55	$50	$45

A.A.A.
Previously manufactured by Aldazabal located in Spain.

M1919 — semi-auto pistol, 7.65mm.

	100%	98%	95%	90%	80%	70%	60%
	$110	$100	$85	$70	$65	$60	$55

A & R SALES
Previous manufacturer located in South El Monte, CA.

HANDGUN — .45 ACP cal., semi-auto patterned after Colt Model 1911 Gov.'t, less weight than normal Colt .45.

	100%	98%	95%	90%	80%	70%	60%
	$225	$205	$175	$155	$145	$135	$125

RIFLE: MARK IV SPORTER — semi-auto, .308 Winchester, M-14 action-clip fed, adj. sights.

	100%	98%	95%	90%	80%	70%	60%
	$295	$260	$225	$200	$175	$155	$140

A F C
Previously manufactured by Auguste Francotte located in Liege, Belgium, 1912-1914.

SEMI-AUTO PISTOL — 6.35mm, 6 shot mag., frame marked "Francotte Liege".

	100%	98%	95%	90%	80%	70%	60%
	$275	$250	$220	$165	$140	$110	$85

A. J. ORDNANCE
THOMAS — .45 double action, .45 ACP, 6 shot, 3½ in. barrel, fixed sights, checkered plastic grips, delayed blowback action, each shot double action, stainless steel barrel. Disc.

	100%	98%	95%	90%	80%	70%	60%
	$470	$415	$385	$360	$330	$275	$220
Chrome	$525	$470	$440	$415	$385	$330	$275

A K S (AK-47's)
Semi-auto paramilitary design rifle originally designed in Russia (1947). Currently manufactured by several arsenals in China including Norinco and Poly Technologies, Inc. Also manufactured in other countries including Yugoslavia, Czechoslovakia, and Hungary. U.S. importation was discontinued for commercial sales in 1989 due to federal legislation.

Since the Federal ban on this type of paramilitary designed rifle, demand initially surged (summer and fall of 1989) and currently is at more predictable levels. AK-47's are not rare - over 700 million have been manufactured in China alone since WW II. Limited U.S. importation coupled with fluctuating political activity has been responsible for unpredictable pricing on this and other para-military configured models.

Grading	100%	98%	95%	90%	80%	70%	60%

AK-47 MODELS

Also refer to separate listings under Poly Technologies, Inc., Norinco, Federal Ordnance, American Arms, Inc., and others who imported this configuration until March, 1989. Values below are for generic imports with average quality in mfg.

AK-47 STANDARD MILITARY RIFLE — 7.62mm x 39mm (standard Russian military cal.) or .223 cal., semi-auto Kalashnikov action, 16½ in. barrel, 5 or 30 shot mag., wood stock and forearm except on folding stock model, is supplied with bayonet, sling, cleaning kit, standard military production rifle of China and Russia.

$550	$495	$450	$395	$350	$300	$265

Folding stock models are now commanding a 10-15% premium.

Yugoslavian, Czechoslavakian, or Hungarian manufactured AK-47's will command a $100-$200 premium over Norinco mfg. rifles. Poly Technologies mfg. (see separate heading) also command a premium. Presently, the .223 cal. is more desireable than 7.62 x 39mm.

Values may change significantly due to regional demand for this rifle configuration (i.e. values will be less in Montana than in California).

A M A C

See Iver Johnson section in this text. AMAC stands for American Military Arms Corporation manufactured in Jacksonville, AR.

A M T

Manufactured by Arcadia Machine & Tool located in Irwindale, CA. Also see Auto-Mag for discontinued models.

PISTOLS: SEMI-AUTO

LIGHTNING — .22 LR, semi-auto, stainless steel only, 5 (bull only), 6½, 8½, 10½, or 12½ (disc. 1987) in. bull or tapered barrels, adj. sights and trigger, pistol based on semi-auto Ruger action, tapered barrels. Mfg. 1984-87.

$240	$200	$150

Last Mfg.'s Sug. Retail was $289.

This model features a frame grooved for scope mounts, Clarke trigger, Millett sights, and either Pachmayr rubber or Wayland wood grips as standard equipment.

Bull's Eye Regulation Target — similar to 6½ in. Lightning with bull barrel, except has vent rib, wooden grips, extended rear sight. Mfg. 1986 only.

$350	$285	$220

Last Mfg.'s Sug. Retail was $436.

AUTOMAG II — .22 Mag., stainless steel only, 3⅜, 4½, or 6 in. barrel, gas assisted action, Millett adj. sights with white outline, grooved Lexan grips, 9 shot mag. New 1987.

Mfg.'s Sug. Retail	$350	$280	$225	$195

BABY AUTOMAG — .22 LR, semi-auto, stainless steel only, 8½ in. vent rib barrel, Millett adj. sights, smooth walnut grips, 1,000 mfg.

$450	$400	$350

BACKUP PISTOL — .22 LR (disc. 1987) or .380 ACP cal., semi-auto action, 2½ in. barrel, stainless steel, Lexan grips, formerly TDE, 5 shot mag. in .380, 8 shot mag. in .22 LR, 18 oz. Older disc. walnut grip models are worth a slight premium.

Mfg.'s Sug. Retail	$256	$200	$165	$135

This model is now manufactured by Irwindale Arms, Inc. and can also be found under their own heading.

Grading	100%	98%	95%	90%	80%	70%	60%

.45 ACP GOVERNMENT MODEL — .45 ACP, similar to Colt semi-auto Gov't model, stainless steel, 5 in. barrel, fixed rear sight, loaded chamber indicator, adj. trigger, wrap-around neoprene grips.

HARDBALLER — .45 ACP, similar to Colt Gold Cup Model, stainless steel, 5 in. barrel, adj. Millett rear sight, serrated rib, loaded chamber indicator, adj. trigger, wrap-around neoprene grips.

Mfg.'s Sug. Retail	$506	$390	$340	$295			

Hardballer Long Slide — same as Hardballer, except 7 in. barrel and longer slide assembly.

Mfg.'s Sug. Retail	$540	$410	$350	$300			

Note: Long slide kit is also available to convert regular Hardballer — $347 retail.

SKIPPER — similar to Hardballer, except approx. 1 in. shorter slide on pre-'84 mfg, re-released in 1991 with choice of .40 S&W or .45 ACP cal., 4¼ in. barrel, checkered walnut grips, matte finish stainless steel, Millett adj. rear sight, 7 shot mag., 33 oz.

Mfg.'s Sug. Retail	$450	$350	$285	$250			

COMBAT SKIPPER — same as Skipper, only with fixed sights. Disc. 1984.

		$375	$330	$295			

BULL'S EYE TARGET MODEL — .40 S&W, similar to Hardballer with 5 in. barrel, 8 shot mag., adj. Millett sights, wrap around Neoprene grips, 38 oz. New 1991.

Mfg.'s Sug. Retail	$500	$400	$340	$295			

"ON DUTY" DOUBLE ACTION — 9mm Para. or .40 S&W cal., stainless steel slide and barrel, 4½ in. barrel, 13 shot mag., 3-dot sighting system, anodized aluminum frame, trigger disconnect safety with inertia firing pin, carbon fiber grips, 32 oz. New 1991.

Mfg.'s Sug. Retail	$506	$400	$340	$295			

RIFLES

LIGHTNING (25/22) — .22 LR, semi-auto based on Ruger 10-22 action, stainless steel, 30 shot mag., 17½ in. bull or tapered barrel, nylon pistol grip handle and forearm, folding stock with recoil pad or youth stock, fixed sights, 6 lbs. New 1986.

Mfg.'s Sug. Retail	$280	$210	$175	$150			

Small Game Hunter (SGH) — .22 LR, same mechanical action as Lightning, except has matte black nylon stock with checkered forearm and grip, 22 in. barrel, 10 shot mag., no sights, removable recoil pad allows storage in stock, 6 lbs. New 1986.

Mfg.'s Sug. Retail	$270	$210	$185	$160			

While advertised in .22 Mag., this caliber was never manufactured.

A-SQUARE

Manufacturer located in Madison, IN.

A-Square also offers at extra cost different grades of walnut, different metal finishes, and various sights/scope rings. Custom calibers are also available upon special order. Values of these special order options can be obtained by contacting A-Square directly.

RIFLES: BOLT ACTION

In 1990, the below listed Groupings have been priced equally. Previously, value differences occurred between the smaller and larger calibers. The 1989 retail values for Groups 1-4 were $1,500, $1,550, $1,580, and $1,600 respectively.

HANNIBAL MODEL — bolt action built on a P-17 Enfield receiver, various cal.'s, 22-26 in. barrel, 9 - 11¼ lbs., select walnut wood with pistol grip and recoil pad. New 1986.

Group 1 — .270 Win. (disc. 1990), .30-06, or 9.3 X 62 (new 1988) cal.

Mfg.'s Sug. Retail	$1,860	$1,860	$1,500	$1,225	$1,100	$995	$900	$850

Group 2 — .300 Win. Mag., .308 Norma Mag. (disc. 1987), .338 Win. Mag., .416 Taylor (new 1988), .425 Express (new 1989), .458 Win. Mag., or 7mm Rem. Mag. cal.

Mfg.'s Sug. Retail	$1,860	$1,860	$1,500	$1,225	$1,100	$995	$900	$850

Grading	100%	98%	95%	90%	80%	70%	60%

Group 3 — .300 Wby. Mag., .300 H&H (new 1988), .340 Wby. Mag., .375 Wby. Mag., .375 H&H, .375 JRS (1990 mfg. only), .404 Jeffrey (new 1991), .416 Hoffman, .416 Rem Mag. (new 1989), .450 Ackley Mag., .458 Lott (new 1989), .470 Ruark (1990 mfg. only), 7mm STW (1990 mfg. only), 8mm Rem. Mag. (new 1988), or 9.3 X 64 (new in 1988) cal.

Mfg.'s Sug. Retail	$1,860	$1,860	$1,500	$1,225	$1,100	$995	$900	$850

Group 4 — .338 A-Square, .375 A-Square, .378 Wby. Mag., .404 Jeffrey (1988-90 mfg.), .416 Rigby, .416 Wby. (new 1989), .460 Short A-Square, .460 Long A-Square (disc. 1987), .460 Wby. Mag., .495 A-Square, or .500 A-Square cal.

Mfg.'s Sug. Retail	$1,860	$1,860	$1,500	$1,225	$1,100	$995	$900	$850

Above listed A-Square proprietary calibers are available in Group 4 Models only.

CAESAR MODEL — bolt action built on a Remington M-700 receiver, various cal.'s, 22-26 in. barrel, 9 - 10¾ lbs., select walnut with pistol grip and recoil pad. Also available in left-hand action at no extra charge. New 1986.

Group 1 — .270 Win. (disc. 1990) or .30-06, 9.3 X 62 (new 1988) cal.

Mfg.'s Sug. Retail	$1,900	$1,900	$1,525	$1,250	$1,125	$1,000	$900	$840

Group 2 — .300 Win. Mag., .308 Norma Mag. (disc. 1987), .338 Win. Mag., .416 Taylor (new 1988), .425 Express (new 1989), .458 Win. Mag., or 7mm Rem. Mag. cal.

Mfg.'s Sug. Retail	$1,900	$1,900	$1,525	$1,250	$1,125	$1,000	$900	$840

Group 3 — .300 Wby. Mag., .300 H&H (new 1988), .340 Wby. Mag., .375 Wby. Mag., .375 H&H, .375 JRS (1990 mfg. only), .404 Jeffrey (new 1991), .416 Hoffman, .416 Rem Mag. (new 1989), .450 Ackley Mag., .458 Lott (new 1989), .470 Ruark (1990 mfg. only), 7mm STW (1990 mfg. only), 8mm Rem. Mag. (new 1988), or 9.3 X 64 (new in 1988) cal.

Mfg.'s Sug. Retail	$1,900	$1,900	$1,525	$1,250	$1,125	$1,000	$900	$840

ATCSA

Maker: Armas De Tiro Y Casa.

COLT POCKET PISTOL COPY — revolver, .38 cal., 6 shot.

	$155	$140	$110	$100	$90	$75	$65

SINGLE SHOT REVOLVER — target pistol.

	$195	$165	$145	$110	$100	$90	$75

AYA (AGUIRRE Y ARANZABAL)

Current manufacture (limited exportation) by AYA and previous manufacture by Diarm located in Eibar, Spain. Last imported and distributed by American Arms, Inc. located in North Kansas City, MO.

Exportation of all AYA shotguns ceased in 1988. Limited manufacture of AYA shotguns is still occurring in Eibar, Spain at the original plant (non-Diarm and without U.S. exportation currently).

SHOTGUNS: O/U

AUGUSTA — 12 ga. only, deluxe O/U sidelock, arabesque engraving in deep relief, select walnut. Disc. 1985.

	$7,500	$6,500	$5,500	$5,000	$4,000	$3,350	$2,950

Last Mfg.'s Sug. Retail was $10,000.

CORAL "A" — 12 or 16 ga., boxlock action with Kersten cross bolt, vent rib, ejectors, double triggers. Disc. 1985.

	$1,275	$1,050	$875	$775	$695	$625	$560

Last Mfg.'s Sug. Retail was $2,195.

CORAL "B" — same as A, except for coin-wash engraved receiver. Disc. 1985.

	$1,395	$1,100	$925	$820	$720	$650	$595

Last Mfg.'s Sug. Retail was $2,450.

MODEL 37 SUPER — 12, 16, or 20 ga., various barrel lengths and chokes, vent rib, sidelock, auto ejector, elaborate engraving, high grade wood. Merkel style action. Prices below reflect older models.

12 ga.	$2,600	$2,350	$2,100	$1,900	$1,700	$1,500	$1,250

Grading	100%	98%	95%	90%	80%	70%	60%
16 ga.	$2,550	$2,200	$2,000	$1,700	$1,500	$1,350	$1,150
20 ga.	$3,000	$2,500	$2,000	$1,900	$1,700	$1,600	$1,475

New Model 37 Super A — game scene engraved, detachable sidelock action, nickel steel receiver. Disc. 1985.

	$5,000	$4,750	$4,300	$3,750	$3,250	$2,650	$2,175

Last Mfg.'s Sug. Retail was $7,300.

New Model 37 Super B — fine scroll engraved, detachable sidelock action, nickel steel receiver. Disc. 1985.

	$5,250	$4,750	$4,300	$3,720	$3,350	$2,650	$2,175

Last Mfg.'s Sug. Retail was $7,795.

79 "A" — 12 ga. only, boxlock with double locking lugs, sel. trigger, ejectors. Disc. 1985.

	$1,275	$1,075	$965	$880	$790	$705	$640

Last Mfg.'s Sug. Retail was $1,595.

79 "B" — same as 79 "A", only more elaborate engraving. Disc. 1985.

	$1,395	$1,200	$1,085	$990	$890	$790	$695

Last Mfg.'s Sug. Retail was $1,795.

79 "C" — same as 79 "B", only more elaborate engraving, double triggers on request. Disc. 1985.

	$2,050	$1,825	$1,605	$1,460	$1,315	$1,165	$1,000

Last Mfg.'s Sug. Retail was $2,650.

77 — 12 ga. only, Merkel style O/U sidelock with Greener crossbolt, deluxe engraving-checkering. Disc. 1985.

	$3,100	$2,750	$2,500	$2,255	$2,030	$1,805	$1,600

Last Mfg.'s Sug. Retail was $4,100.

SHOTGUNS: SxS

U.S. importation ceased in 1988 on all AYA shotguns.

BOLERO— same as Matador, with non-selective single trigger and extractors. Disc. 1984.

	$440	$360	$330	$305	$275	$250	$220

IBERIA — 12 or 20 ga., 3 in., boxlock, double triggers, plain walnut. Disc. 1984.

	$566	$440	$370	$315	$285	$255	$230

IBERIA II — 12 or 16 ga., 28 in. barrels, 2¾ in. chamber only, double triggers, plain walnut. Mfg. 1984-1985 only.

	$515	$430	$370	$315	$285	$255	$230

Last Mfg.'s Sug. Retail was $570.

MATADOR — 12, 16, 20, 28, or .410 ga., 26, 28, or 30 in. barrel, various chokes, Anson & Deeley boxlock, auto ejectors, beavertail forearm, SST, checkered pistol grip stock. Mfg. 1955-1963.

	$500	$450	$400	$350	$300	$275	$250

Add 20% for .410 or 28 ga.

MATADOR II —similar to Matador, with vent rib, 12 or 20 ga. only. Disc.

	$550	$500	$450	$400	$350	$325	$300

MATADOR III — 12 or 20 ga., 3 in. chamber in 20 ga. only, boxlock, vent rib, ejectors, SST. Disc. 1985.

	$930	$805	$725	$650	$560	$495	$430

Last Mfg.'s Sug. Retail was $1,235.

SENIOR — 12 ga. only, self-opener, engraved sidelock action, select walnut. Top-of-the-line quality, made to special order only. Lighter up-land version also available. Disc. 1987.

	$15,500	$12,000	$10,000	$8,000	$6,500	$5,500	$4,500

Last Mfg.'s Sug. Retail was $21,000.

Grading	100%	98%	95%	90%	80%	70%	60%

NO. 1 — 12 or 20 ga., full sidelock action with third lever fastener, straight grip, ejectors, DT's, elaborate fine scroll engraving. Disc. 1987.

	$2,600	$2,225	$1,950	$1,600	$1,300	$1,000	$875

Add $145 for SST.
Last Mfg.'s Sug. Retail was $3,750.

28 and .410 ga.'s — disc. 1987.

	$2,800	$2,400	$1,995	$1,650	$1,350	$1,050	$900

Last Mfg.'s Sug. Retail was $3,895.

NO. 2 — 12, 16 (disc. 1985), 20, 28 or .410 ga., 3 in. chambers, English-style sidelock, ejector, cocking indicators, DT's, third lever fastener. Disc. 1987.

	$1,250	$1,050	$850	$700	$575	$500	$425

Add 25%-35% for 28 or .410 ga.
Last Mfg.'s Sug. Retail was $1,650.

No. 2 - 2 Barrel Set — available in either 20/28 ga., or 28/.410 ga. Imported 1986-87 only.

	$1,995	$1,775	$1,600	$1,400	$1,200	$995	$850

Last Mfg.'s Sug. Retail was $2,440.

NO. 3-A — 12, 16, 20, 28, or .410 ga., boxlock, extractors, double triggers. Disc. 1985.

	$640	$540	$495	$450	$400	$375	$350

Add 25%-35% for 28 or .410 ga.
Last Mfg.'s Sug. Retail was $850.

NO. 4-A — 12, 16 (disc. 1985), 20, 28, or .410 ga., 3 in. chambers, English-style straight stock, boxlock action, ejectors, double trigger, straight grip. Disc. 1987.

	$600	$530	$475	$440	$410	$365	$325

Add 25%-35% for 28 or .410 ga.
Last Mfg.'s Sug. Retail was $835.

4-A DELUXE — English-style, boxlock ejector. Stock, forearm, trigger to order. Disc. 1985.

	$1,700	$1,400	$1,225	$1,000	$800	$650	$525

Add 25%-35% for 28 or .410 ga.
Last Mfg.'s Sug. Retail was $2,195.

XXV BOXLOCK (BL) — 12 or 20 ga. only, similar to 4-A Deluxe, except 25 in. barrels, Churchill rib. Disc. 1986.

	$995	$900	$840	$785	$740	$680	$615

Add $85 for SST.
Last Mfg.'s Sug. Retail was $1,350.

XXV SIDELOCK (SL) — 12, 16, 20, 28 or .410 ga., sidelock ejector, 25 in. barrels, Churchill rib. Stock, forearm, trigger to order. Disc. 1986.

12, 16, or 20 ga.

	$1,600	$1,350	$1,175	$950	$750	$600	$500

Add $85 for SST.
Add 25%-35% for 28 or .410 ga.
Last Mfg.'s Sug. Retail was $2,195.

53-E — 12, 16, or 20 ga., engraved sidelock ejector, sideclips, third lock. Stock, forearm, trigger to order. Disc. 1986.

	$1,440	$1,195	$1,025	$925	$820	$700	$620

Add $85 for SST.
Last Mfg.'s Sug. Retail was $1,795.

56 — 12, 16, or 20 ga., sidelock action-engraved, ejectors, sel. trigger. Disc. 1985.

	$4,895	$4,100	$3,700	$3,450	$3,100	$2,750	$2,500

Last Mfg.'s Sug. Retail was $5,750.

Grading	100%	98%	95%	90%	80%	70%	60%

106 — 12, 16, or 20 ga., English-style boxlock, double trigger, pistol grip, 28 in. barrels. Disc. 1985.

| | $530 | $440 | $400 | $360 | $320 | $300 | $275 |

Last Mfg.'s Sug. Retail was $585.

107-LI — 12 or 16 ga., English-style boxlock, double trigger, straight grip, light English scroll engraving. Disc. 1985.

| | $675 | $560 | $520 | $480 | $425 | $400 | $360 |

Last Mfg.'s Sug. Retail was $745.

MODEL 116 — 12, 16, or 20 ga., 27-30 in. barrels, any choke, hand detachable H&H sidelocks, double triggers, engraved, select checkered walnut pistol grip stock. Disc. 1985.

| | $1,000 | $845 | $795 | $750 | $675 | $600 | $500 |

Last Mfg.'s Sug. Retail was $1,125.

MODEL 117 — 12, 16 or 20 ga., 3 in. chambers, 26-30 in. barrels, any choke, hand detachable H&H sidelocks, ejectors, SST, engraved, select checkered walnut pistol grip stock. Disc. 1986.

| | $835 | $715 | $660 | $620 | $585 | $545 | $500 |

Last Mfg.'s Sug. Retail was $1,075.

QUAIL UNLIMITED MODEL 117 — 12 ga. only, 26 in. barrels choked IC/M with 3 in. chambers, upgraded wood and checkering, high gloss bluing, gold colored ST, engraved by Baron Technologies in PA, only 42 mfg. for Quail Unlimited of North America.

| | $1,650 | $1,400 | $1,150 | $975 | $875 | $800 | $725 |

This model had a retail price of $1,700 but was made available to Quail Unlimited members for approx. $1,200.

MODEL 210 — 12 or 16 ga., boxlock, exposed hammers, double triggers, plain walnut, light engraving. Disc. 1985.

| | $795 | $675 | $550 | $475 | $435 | $395 | $350 |

Last Mfg.'s Sug. Retail was $900.

711 BOXLOCK — 12 ga. only, boxlock, selective trigger, ejectors, vent rib. Disc. 1984.

| | $880 | $680 | $575 | $490 | $445 | $395 | $350 |

711 Sidelock — sidelock action. Mfg. 1985 only.

| | $995 | $850 | $775 | $695 | $625 | $550 | $475 |

Last Mfg.'s Sug. Retail was $1,250.

ABADIE

Maker: Several Belgian makers for Portuguese Military.

MODEL 1878 (OFFICER'S MODEL) — 9.1mm, solid frame revolver, 6 shot, ejector rod, officer's issue A.

| | $220 | $195 | $165 | $130 | $120 | $110 | $100 |

MODEL 1886 (TROOPER'S MODEL) — similar to 1878, but larger, trooper issue A.

| | $195 | $175 | $160 | $120 | $110 | $100 | $90 |

ABBEY, GEORGE T.

Utica, NY from 1845-1852. Chicago, Il from 1852-1874. Percussion and breechloading firearms.

100%	98%	95%	90%	80%	70%	60%	50%	40%	30%	20%	10%

PERCUSSION RIFLE

.44 cal. — 32 in. octagon barrel.

| $605 | $550 | $470 | $415 | $370 | $340 | $305 | $275 | $250 | $220 | $195 | $165 |

.44 cal. — octagon barrel, brass trimmed.

| $770 | $735 | $695 | $605 | $550 | $485 | $450 | $405 | $365 | $330 | $275 | $220 |

100%	98%	95%	90%	80%	70%	60%	50%	40%	30%	20%	10%

.44 cal. — 31 in. double barrel.

100%	98%	95%	90%	80%	70%	60%	50%	40%	30%	20%	10%
$1,210	$1,100	$880	$770	$715	$650	$595	$550	$515	$475	$430	$360

.44 cal. — double barrel O/U, brass trimmed.

100%	98%	95%	90%	80%	70%	60%	50%	40%	30%	20%	10%
$1,485	$1,295	$1,130	$990	$910	$855	$770	$715	$660	$605	$495	$330

ABBEY, F.J. & COMPANY

Chicago, IL, 1858-1878. Muzzle and breechloading shotguns and pistols.

PERCUSSION RIFLE — several variations.

100%	98%	95%	90%	80%	70%	60%	50%	40%	30%	20%	10%
$605	$550	$470	$415	$360	$305	$275	$250	$210	$175	$145	$110

PERCUSSION SHOTGUN — several variations.

100%	98%	95%	90%	80%	70%	60%	50%	40%	30%	20%	10%
$800	$715	$635	$550	$470	$415	$360	$320	$285	$250	$210	$155

ACCU-TEK

Manufacturer located in Chino, CA.

Grading	100%	98%	95%	90%	80%	70%	60%

PISTOLS: SEMI-AUTO

MODEL AT-32 — .32 ACP cal., single action design, 2½ in. barrel, 5 shot mag. with finger extension, manual hand safety with firing pin block and trigger disconnect, side mag. release, exposed hammer, 16 oz. Mfg. in U.S. New 1990.

Mfg.'s Sug. Retail	100%	98%	95%	90%	80%	70%	60%
	$250	$220	$195	$175	$150	$135	$120	$110

MODEL AT-380 — .380 ACP cal., same specifications as the model AT-32. New 1990.

Mfg.'s Sug. Retail	$250	$220	$195	$175	$150	$135	$120	$110

MODEL ATL-380 — similar to Model AT-380, except has different metal finish and various colored synthetic grips popular with ladies. New 1990.

Mfg.'s Sug. Retail	$250	$220	$195	$175	$150	$135	$120	$110

ACHA

Maker: Domingo Acha, Spain.

MODEL 1916 — semi-auto pistol, 7.76mm, 7 shot mag., 1903 Browning copy.

$220	$165	$100	$85	$65	$55	$45

ATLAS — semi-auto pistol, 6.35mm, 6 shot mag., slide marked ATLAS, 1906 Browning copy.

$165	$140	$125	$95	$75	$65	$50

LOOKING GLASS — semi-auto pistol, 6.35mm, 6 shot mag., blued or nickel, 1906 Browning copy, side marked "Looking Glass", many variations.

$220	$165	$130	$100	$85	$70	$55

LOOKING GLASS — semi-auto pistol, 7.65mm, exposed hammer.

$220	$165	$140	$105	$90	$75	$65

ACME

Trade name of Davenport Arms Company Shotguns, Maltby Henley & Co. Revolvers, and Merwin and Hulburt & Co. Owl Head Revolvers.

100%	98%	95%	90%	80%	70%	60%	50%	40%	30%	20%	10%

SEVEN SHOT REVOLVER — single action, .22 Short rimfire.

100%	98%	95%	90%	80%	70%	60%	50%	40%	30%	20%	10%
$360	$310	$240	$185	$165	$150	$120	$110	$100	$90	$65	$55

FIVE SHOT REVOLVER — single action, .32 Short rimfire.

$360	$320	$255	$200	$175	$160	$120	$110	$100	$90	$65	$55

100%	98%	95%	90%	80%	70%	60%	50%	40%	30%	20%	10%

ACME ARMS
Trade name for Cornwall Hardware Co., NY.
REVOLVERS
SEVEN SHOT — single action, .22 Short rimfire.

| $275 | $250 | $210 | $185 | $165 | $155 | $140 | $125 | $110 | $90 | $85 | $75 |

FIVE SHOT — single action, .32 Short rimfire.

| $285 | $255 | $215 | $195 | $175 | $165 | $145 | $120 | $100 | $90 | $85 | $75 |

SHOTGUN
SIDE-BY-SIDE — 12 ga., damascus barrel.

| $275 | $240 | $195 | $165 | $145 | $125 | $110 | $95 | $65 | $60 | $50 | $45 |

ACME HAMMERLESS
Maker: Hopkins & Allen, for Hulbert Brothers, 1893.
REVOLVERS
FIVE SHOT — double action, top break, .32 centerfire, non-ejecting.

| $145 | $125 | $100 | $90 | $80 | $70 | $60 | $50 | $40 | $30 | $20 | $15 |

Also known as Forehand Model 1891, can be hammer or hammerless.

FIVE SHOT — double action, top break, .38 centerfire, non-ejecting.

| $145 | $125 | $100 | $90 | $80 | $70 | $60 | $50 | $40 | $30 | $20 | $15 |

Also known as Forehand Model 1891, can be hammer or hammerless.

ACTION (M.S.)
Maker: Modesto Santos, Eibar, Spain.

Grading	100%	98%	95%	90%	80%	70%	60%
MODEL 1915 — semi-auto pistol (French Military), 7.65mm.	$175	$145	$120	$85	$70	$60	$45
MODEL 1920 — semi-auto pistol (action), 6.35mm.	$195	$150	$110	$85	$65	$45	$40

ACTION ARMS LTD.
Importer and distributor located in Philadelphia, PA.
Only Action Arms Models AT84S, AT88S, and Timberwolf will be listed under this heading. Uzi and Galil trademarks can be located in their respective sections.
PISTOLS
AT-84S — 9mm Para., selective double action design, patterned after the CZ-75, 4.8 in. barrel, 15 shot mag., originally introduced in 1985.

| $470 | $415 | $385 | $360 | $330 | $275 | $220 |

The AT-84S Series was mfg. in Switzerland by Industrial Technology & Machines A.G. and was sold by Action Arms between June of 1987 and 1989. Serial number range is 01201-06000. No P or H models were ever mfg. in this series (2 or 3 prototypes only).

Grading	100%	98%	95%	90%	80%	70%	60%

AT-88S — 9mm or .41 Action Express (available early 1990) cal., selective double action design patterned after CZ-75, 4.8 in. barrel, 15 shot (9mm) or 10 shot (.41 AE) mag., can be "cocked and locked", fixed sights, blued metal, walnut grips, 35.3 oz. Introduced in 1987 with original shipments not occuring until 1989.

	$495	$435	$385	$360	$330	$275	$220

The .41 AE cal. is more desireable in this model currently.

A very small quantity of AT-88S's was made by I.T.M. of Switzerland and finishes included all blue, all chrome, or 2-tone. These pistols may exhibit both I.T.M. and A.A.L. markings. More recent manufacture was performed by Muller of England.

AT-88P — compact variation of the Model AT-88S, 3.7 in. barrel, 13 shot (9mm) or 8 shot (.41 AE) mag., 32.1 oz. Importation began 1989.

	$495	$435	$385	$360	$330	$275	$220

AT-88H — 9mm or .41 Action Express cal., ultra compact variation of the Model AT-88S, 3.5 in. barrel, 10 shot (9mm) or 7 shot (.41 AE) mag., 30.5 oz. Importation began 1989.

	$495	$435	$385	$360	$330	$275	$220

RIFLES

TIMBERWOLF — .357 Mag. or .44 Mag. (new 1991) cal., slide action, straight grip shotgun style stock with adj. drop, takedown, 18.5 in. barrel, 10 shot tube mag., pushbutton trigger guard, sear locking and firing pin safeties, integral scope base, approx. 5½ lbs. New 1989.

Mfg.'s Sug. Retail	$425	$365	$330	$295	$260	$230	$200	$175

Add $70 for chrome finish.

Add $20 for .44 Mag. cal. (blue finish only).

ADAMS

Maker: Deane, Adams, & Deane, located in London, Eng.

PERCUSSION REVOLVERS

100%	98%	95%	90%	80%	70%	60%	50%	40%	30%	20%	10%

MODEL 1851 — double action, .38 cal., 4½ in. barrel.

$1,375	$1,265	$1,100	$990	$855	$745	$690	$605	$550	$440	$385	$330

MODEL 1851 — double action, .44 cal., 6 in. barrel.

$935	$880	$800	$690	$550	$495	$440	$395	$340	$305	$275	$255

MODEL 1851 — Dragoon, double action, .50 cal., 8 in. barrel.

$1,375	$1,265	$1,100	$990	$855	$715	$690	$605	$550	$385	$360	$340

MODEL 1851 — .38 cal., cased with accessories.

$1,760	$1,595	$1,375	$1,100	$990	$910	$825	$745	$660	$605	$550	$525

MODEL 1851 — .44 cal., cased with accessories.

$1,295	$1,155	$990	$880	$770	$690	$635	$550	$440	$385	$360	$330

MODEL 1851 — Dragoon, .50 cal., cased with accessories.

$1,680	$1,485	$1,210	$1,185	$990	$880	$800	$715	$635	$550	$495	$470

ADAMS, JOSEPH

Birmingham, England.

OFFICER MODEL — flintlock pistol, musket caliber .65, Brown Bess.

$2,850	$2,500	$2,250	$2,000	$1,800	$1,600	$1,400	$1,100	$900	$825	$725	$600

ADAMY, GEBRUDER
Suhl, Germany, 1920's and 1930's.

Grading	100%	98%	95%	90%	80%	70%	60%

SHOTGUN — O/U, double trigger, engraved, cased.

		100%	98%	95%	90%	80%	70%	60%
		$1,815	$1,650	$1,375	$1,155	$990	$880	$770

ADIRONDACK ARMS COMPANY
Plattsburgh, NY, 1870-1874.

Magazine loaded repeating rifle, .44 cal., brass or iron frame, later model, may also be marked A.S. Babbitt, Plattsburgh, N.Y., absorbed by Winchester in 1874, then disc.

> This rifle was designed in 1870 and patented by Orvill M. Robinson in Upper Jay, NY. It was available in .38 and .44 cal. rimfire rifles without a wooden forend and had a high cyclic rate of fire. Original models were made in Plattsburgh, NY at which time A.S. Babbitt became one of several additional partners. In 1872, Robinson was granted a patent for a second model rifle. It was similar to the 1870, except a wooden forend was added and the operating mechanism was changed considerably. Following these improvements, Mr. Oliver Winchester contacted Mr. Robinson and purchased the entire Robinson company, discontinuing manufacture.

100%	98%	95%	90%	80%	70%	60%	50%	40%	30%	20%	10%

EARLY MODEL — finger holds on hammer.

100%	98%	95%	90%	80%	70%	60%	50%	40%	30%	20%	10%
$2,400	$2,100	$1,750	$1,450	$1,325	$1,200	$1,075	$975	$875	$775	$675	$600

LATE MODEL — action worked by buttons top of receiver mid-section.

100%	98%	95%	90%	80%	70%	60%	50%	40%	30%	20%	10%
$2,200	$1,950	$1,675	$1,300	$1,200	$1,100	$975	$875	$775	$675	$550	$495

ADLER
Maker: Engelbrecht & Wolff located in Blasii, Germany, 1905-1907.

Grading	100%	98%	95%	90%	80%	70%	60%

SEMI-AUTO PISTOL — 7mm Adler, 8 shot mag., cocking lever on top of frame, not competitive in its price range.

	100%	98%	95%	90%	80%	70%	60%
	$2,200	$1,925	$1,540	$1,045	$770	$495	$330

ADVANTAGE ARMS USA, INC.
Previous manufacturer located in St. Paul, MN. Advantage Arms USA, Inc. was distributed by Wildfire Sports, Inc. also located in St. Paul.

MODEL 422 — .22 LR and Mag., 4 barrel double action derringer, rotating firing pin, 2½ in. barrel, high grade alloy frame and barrel, 4 shot, available in blue, nickel, or QPQ (heat treated but appears blued) finish, 15 oz. Mfg. 1986-87 only.

	$150	$135	$115	$105	$95	$85	$75

Add $10 for .22 Mag. cal.

Add $6 for nickel finish.

Add $11 for QPQ finish.

Last Mfg.'s Sug. Retail was $166.

AETNA
Previously manufactured by Harrington & Richardson located in Worchester, MA.

Type: single action revolvers, all of the same general size and configuration, solid frame, spur trigger, so called "Suicide Specials" during their day.

100%	98%	95%	90%	80%	70%	60%	50%	40%	30%	20%	10%

AETNA NO. 2 — .32 rimfire, 5 shot.

100%	98%	95%	90%	80%	70%	60%	50%	40%	30%	20%	10%
$330	$275	$215	$185	$170	$155	$145	$120	$100	$85	$75	$55

AETNA NO. 2½ — .32 rimfire, 5 shot.

100%	98%	95%	90%	80%	70%	60%	50%	40%	30%	20%	10%
$330	$275	$215	$185	$170	$155	$145	$120	$100	$85	$75	$55

100%	98%	95%	90%	80%	70%	60%	50%	40%	30%	20%	10%

MODEL 1876 — .22 rimfire, 7 shot.

100%	98%	95%	90%	80%	70%	60%	50%	40%	30%	20%	10%
$330	$275	$210	$195	$175	$165	$155	$130	$110	$95	$90	$65

MODEL 1876 — .32 rimfire, 5 shot.

100%	98%	95%	90%	80%	70%	60%	50%	40%	30%	20%	10%
$330	$275	$210	$175	$165	$155	$145	$120	$105	$90	$75	$55

MODEL 1876 — .38 rimfire, 5 shot.

100%	98%	95%	90%	80%	70%	60%	50%	40%	30%	20%	10%
$330	$275	$220	$205	$195	$175	$165	$145	$120	$105	$95	$85

AETNA ARMS COMPANY

Manufacturer located in New York, 1869-1883.

Single action pocket revolver, blued or nickel, birdshead grip, copy of S&W models 1-3, models marked ALLING are worth a slight premium.

SEVEN SHOT — .22 rimfire.

100%	98%	95%	90%	80%	70%	60%	50%	40%	30%	20%	10%
$250	$235	$210	$195	$175	$165	$155	$130	$110	$95	$90	$65

FIVE SHOT — .32 rimfire.

100%	98%	95%	90%	80%	70%	60%	50%	40%	30%	20%	10%
$230	$220	$205	$175	$165	$155	$145	$120	$105	$90	$75	$55

AGNER

Manufactured by Saxhoj Products Inc. in Denmark. Imported until 1986 by Beeman Arms, Inc. located in Santa Rosa, CA.

PISTOL: SEMI-AUTO

Grading	100%	98%	95%	90%	80%	70%	60%

M 80 — .22 LR only, stainless steel, semi-auto target pistol, new design features unique security key safety feature, adj. French walnut grips, dry fire mechanism, 5.9 in. barrel, 5 shot mag., limited production, 2.4 lbs. Imported 1981-1986.

100%	98%	95%
$1,125	$1,040	$950

Add $100 for left-hand action.
Last Mfg.'s Sug. Retail was $1,295.

AIR MATCH

Previously imported by Kendall International, located in Paris, KY.

AIR MATCH 500 — .22 cal. match single shot pistol, target grips, adj. front counterweight, 10½ in. barrel. Imported 1984-86.

100%	98%	95%	90%	80%	70%	60%
$695	$575	$540	$510	$475	$440	$410

Last Mfg.'s Sug. Retail was $788.

AJAX ARMY

Distributed by E.C. Meacham Co., maker unknown, 1880's Circa.

100%	98%	95%	90%	80%	70%	60%	50%	40%	30%	20%	10%

SINGLE ACTION — .44 rimfire, spur trigger, solid frame.

100%	98%	95%	90%	80%	70%	60%	50%	40%	30%	20%	10%
$550	$440	$360	$315	$275	$255	$230	$210	$185	$170	$155	$140

AKRILL, E.

French, 1800's.

FLINTLOCK RIFLE — breech loaded, .69 cal., damascus octagon barrel.

100%	98%	95%	90%	80%	70%	60%	50%	40%	30%	20%	10%
$3,300	$2,750	$2,200	$1,980	$1,460	$1,320	$1,240	$1,075	$935	$800	$745	$660

ALAMO RANGER

Grading	100%	98%	95%	90%	80%	70%	60%

REVOLVER — .38 cal., Spanish copy of Colt Model 1929.

	100%	98%	95%	90%	80%	70%	60%
	$140	$120	$110	$100	$90	$85	$75

ALASKA

Maker: Hood Firearms Company, Norwich, CT, 1873-1884.

Dubbed "Suicide Specials" in their day.

REVOLVERS

100%	98%	95%	90%	80%	70%	60%	50%	40%	30%	20%	10%

SINGLE ACTION — .22 rimfire, 7 shot, spur trigger, solid frame.

100%	98%	95%	90%	80%	70%	60%	50%	40%	30%	20%	10%
$275	$220	$195	$145	$140	$125	$110	$100	$90	$75	$70	$65

FIVE SHOT — .32 Short rimfire.

100%	98%	95%	90%	80%	70%	60%	50%	40%	30%	20%	10%
$220	$195	$160	$155	$150	$140	$125	$105	$95	$85	$75	$70

ALDAZABAL

Maker: Aldazabal, Leturiondo & Cia.

Grading	100%	98%	95%	90%	80%	70%	60%

SEMI-AUTOMATIC PISTOL — 7.65mm, 7 shot, Eibar style.

	100%	98%	95%	90%	80%	70%	60%
	$195	$165	$110	$100	$90	$75	$65

ALERT

Maker: Hood Firearms Company, Norwich, CT, 1873-1881.

These revolvers were dubbed "Suicide Specials" in their day.

REVOLVERS

100%	98%	95%	90%	80%	70%	60%	50%	40%	30%	20%	10%

SINGLE ACTION — .22 rimfire, 7 shot, spur trigger, solid frame.

100%	98%	95%	90%	80%	70%	60%	50%	40%	30%	20%	10%
$220	$195	$165	$145	$130	$125	$110	$100	$90	$75	$70	$65

FIVE SHOT — .32 Short rimfire.

100%	98%	95%	90%	80%	70%	60%	50%	40%	30%	20%	10%
$170	$165	$160	$155	$150	$140	$125	$105	$95	$85	$75	$70

ALEXIA

Maker: Hopkins & Allen, Norwich, CT, 1867-1915.

Also known as: Blue Jacket, Captain Jack, Chichester, Defender, Dictator, Monarch, Mountain Eagle, Hopkins & Allen, Towers Police Safety, and Universal.

Description: single action revolver, solid frame, spur trigger, inexpensive vest pocket pistol issued under numerous names for private companies, octagon barrel.

REVOLVERS

.22 RIMFIRE — 7 shot.

100%	98%	95%	90%	80%	70%	60%	50%	40%	30%	20%	10%
$165	$160	$155	$145	$130	$125	$110	$100	$90	$75	$70	$65

.32 SHORT RIMFIRE — 5 shot.

100%	98%	95%	90%	80%	70%	60%	50%	40%	30%	20%	10%
$170	$165	$160	$155	$150	$140	$125	$105	$95	$85	$75	$70

SINGLE ACTION38 SHORT RIMFIRE — 5 shot.

100%	98%	95%	90%	80%	70%	60%	50%	40%	30%	20%	10%
$195	$180	$170	$165	$160	$145	$140	$120	$110	$100	$90	$85

.41 SHORT RIMFIRE — 5 shot.

100%	98%	95%	90%	80%	70%	60%	50%	40%	30%	20%	10%
$220	$210	$205	$195	$180	$170	$160	$145	$125	$110	$100	$90

ALFA

Maker: Armero Especialistas Reunidas, located in Eibar, Spain, 1920's.

All revolvers are marked Alfa on grips.

Grading	100%	98%	95%	90%	80%	70%	60%
EARLY MODEL — .32, .38, or .44 cal., copies of S&W No. 2 by O. Hermanos.							
	$145	$130	$120	$110	$105	$95	$75
LATE MODEL — .22 LR, .32 S&W, or .38 S&W cal., copies of Colt Police Positive and S&W Military and Police.							
	$160	$150	$130	$120	$110	$100	$90

ALKARTASUNA FABRICA DE ARMAS, S.A.

Manufacturer located in Guernica, Spain.

ALKARTASUNA RUBY AUTOMATIC — 7.65mm, 9 shot, 3⅝ in. barrel, blue, fixed sights, checkered wood or hard rubber grips, used by French Army in WWI and WWII. Mfg. 1917-1922.

$220	$195	$165	$110	$65	$55	$45

ALLEN & THURBER

Note: Ethan Allen started many plants to keep up with expanding business after 1832. Listed below is a chronological order of the firms constituting the family dynasty founded by Ethan Allen.

E. Allen — Grafton, Mass. 1832-1837

Allen & Thurber — Grafton, Mass. 1837-1842

Allen & Thurber — Norwich, Conn. 1842-1847

Allen & Thurber — Worcester, Mass. 1847-1854

Allen, Thurber, & Co. — Worcester, Mass. 1854-1856

Allen & Wheelock — Worcester, Mass. 1856-1865

E. Allen & Co. — Worcester, Mass. 1865-1871

Forehand & Wadsworth — Worcester, Mass. 1871-1890

Forehand Arms Co. — Worcester, Mass. 1890-1902

No other 19th century American firm produced a wider variety of firearms than did Ethan Allen & subsidiaries.

ALLEN FIREARMS

Previous importer located in Santa Fe, NM importing A. Uberti Firearms until early in 1987. After Allen Firearms closed, Cimarron F.A. Mfg. Co. located in Houston, TX purchased the remaining inventory (in addition to ordering new products under their name).

Allen Firearms was formerly called Western Arms and manufactured both modern and black powder reproduction firearms and accessories patterned after famous older models. Only modern cartridge guns will be shown in this section. Black powder guns will appear under Modern Black Powder Guns.

REVOLVERS: SINGLE ACTION

Available in either black powder or modern configured frames.

CATTLEMAN — available in .45 LC, .44-40, .38 Spl., .357 Mag., .22 LR, or .22 Mag cal., 4¾, 5½, or 7½ in. barrel lengths, brass or steel backstraps and trigger guard.

$325	$265	$225	$190	$175	$150	$140

Last Mfg.'s Sug. Retail was $289.

Also could be ordered with A, B, or C grade engraving and nickel finish.

Sheriff's Model — .44-40 or .45 LC cal., 3 in. barrel.

$325	$265	$225	$190	$175	$160	$150

Last Mfg.'s Sug. Retail was $289.

Grading	100%	98%	95%	90%	80%	70%	60%

Target Model — same as Cattleman Model, only fully adj. rear blade sight.

	$335	$285	$230	$200	$185	$170	$150

Last Mfg.'s Sug. Retail was $299.

CATTLEMAN BUNTLINE — .45 LC, .44-40, or .357 Mag. cal., 18 in. barrel, backstrap cut for shoulder stock.

	$335	$285	$230	$200	$185	$175	$165

Last Mfg.'s Sug. Retail was $299.

BUCKHORN — .44 Mag., .44 Spl., or .44-40 cal., various barrel lengths, Buntline and revolving carbine models, also available in the Buckhorn series — add approx. $60, add $30 for convertible cylinders.

	$325	$265	$225	$205	$190	$180	$170

Last Mfg.'s Sug. Retail was $299.

"OUTLAW" 1875 REMINGTON — .45 LC, .44-40, or .357 Mag. cal., 7½ barrel. Add $40 for nickel plating.

	$285	$240	$195	$180	$170	$155	$140

Last Mfg.'s Sug. Retail was $279.

1890 REMINGTON — available in .45 LC, .44-40, or .357 Mag. cal., 5½ barrel. New 1986.

	$290	$245	$200	$180	$170	$155	$140

Last Mfg.'s Sug. Retail was $289.

PHANTOM MODEL — .357 or .44 Mag. only, 10 in. barrel for silhouette use. New 1985.

	$365	$315	$260	$230	$215	$190	$170

Last Mfg.'s Sug. Retail was $369.

REVOLVERS: DOUBLE ACTION

INSPECTOR MODEL — .32 S&W or .38 Sp. cal., 3, 4, or 6 in. barrels, double action, blued or chrome finish. New 1985. Add $20 for target sights.

	$255	$215	$170	$145	$125	$110	$95

Last Mfg.'s Sug. Retail was $279.

TARGET PISTOLS

1871 ROLLING BLOCK TARGET PISTOL — available in .357 Mag., .22 LR, or 22 Mag. cal., 9½ in. barrel. Also available in carbine model (22 in. barrel) - add $35.

	$240	$205	$170	$150	$135	$120	$100

Last Mfg.'s Sug. Retail was $229.

RIFLES AND CARBINES

CATTLEMAN REVOLVING CARBINE S.A. — available in .45 LC, .44-40, .357 Mag., or .22 LR/Mag. (convertible) cal., 18 in. barrel.

	$350	$275	$235	$210	$190	$175	$160

Last Mfg.'s Sug. Retail was $339.

1875 REMINGTON CARBINE S.A. — 18 in. barrel - same cal.'s as above, except .22 LR/Mag.

	$375	$295	$250	$230	$200	$180	$165

Last Mfg.'s Sug. Retail was $389.

HENRY RIFLE OR CARBINE — .44-40 cal., brass frame, 24½ in. barrel on rifle, 22½ in. barrel on carbine.

	$550	$495	$450	$415	$360	$320	$260

Could also be special ordered with grade A engraving ($250 extra), grade B engraving ($400 extra), and grade 3 engraving ($500 extra).

Last Mfg.'s Sug. Retail was $569.

Grading	100%	98%	95%	90%	80%	70%	60%

Henry 1 of 1,000 — premiums are slightly higher than a C engraved gun.

1866 CARBINE — .44-40, .38 Spl., .22 Mag. or .22 LR cal., brass receiver, 19 in. round barrel. "Indian" model - add $40.

	100%	98%	95%	90%	80%	70%	60%
	$425	$380	$335	$285	$260	$235	$210

Last Mfg.'s Sug. Retail was $429.

1866 Trapper Carbine — .44-40 cal. only, 16 in. barrel.

	$425	$380	$335	$285	$260	$235	$210

Last Mfg.'s Sug. Retail was $429.

Red Cloud Commemorative carbine — same cal.'s, special engraving and brass tacks in forearm and stock.

	$475	$425	$370	$310	$275	$240	$220

Last Mfg.'s Sug. Retail was $469.

1866 RIFLE — brass receiver, same cal.'s as the carbine, 24¼ in. oct. barrel.

	$450	$400	$350	$300	$265	$235	$210

Last Mfg.'s Sug. Retail was $449.

1873 CARBINE — .44-40, .357 Mag., .22 Mag., or .22 LR cal., steel receiver, 19 in. round barrel. Add $70 for nickel.

	$495	$450	$400	$360	$320	$280	$240

Last Mfg.'s Sug. Retail was $499.

1873 Trapper Carbine — .44-40 cal. only, 16 in. barrel.

	$495	$450	$400	$360	$320	$280	$240

Last Mfg.'s Sug. Retail was $499.

1873 RIFLE — casehardened receiver, same cal.'s as the carbine, 24¼ in. oct. barrel.

	$540	$475	$415	$365	$325	$285	$245

Last Mfg.'s Sug. Retail was $569.

SHARPS/GEMMER SPORTING RIFLE — .45-70 cal. only, copy of the famous Sharp's rifle. New 1985.

	$575	$515	$430	$375	$320	$295	$270

Last Mfg.'s Sug. Retail was $599.

1979 JUSTIN CENTENNIAL COMMEMORATIVE — includes specially engraved 1866 sporting rifle and 1873 single action revolver (7½ in. barrel) with gold plated parts and inlay. Both guns are chambered for .44-40 cal. Also includes special hand signed pair of Justin boots, serial numbered belt buckle and presentation oak case. All serial numbers are matching.

Grading	100%	Issue	Price	Qty.	Made

MODEL 1873 1 of 1,000 — .44-40 cal, special wood, only 1,000 manufactured. Disc. 1985.

	100%	Issue	Price	Qty.	Made
	$1,350		$1,500		1,000

ALPHA ARMS INC.

Previous manufacturer located in Flower Mound, TX from 1983-87.

Retail price included custom hard case.

Grading	100%	98%	95%	90%	80%	70%	60%

RIFLES: BOLT ACTION

Many special order options including an octagonal barrel, various finishes, and special sights were available at extra cost on the models listed below. These options, while not listed separately by price, will add value to the prices shown below.

ALPHA JAGUAR — available in most calibers from .222 Rem. through .338 Win., Mauser-type barreled action, Alphawood laminate stock, 20 to 24 in. barrel lengths, approx. 6 lbs. New 1987.

Grade I Jaguar — slide safety, supplied with luggage case.

	$900	$800	$700	$625	$560	$500	$425

Last Mfg.'s Sug. Retail was $995.

Grading	100%	98%	95%	90%	80%	70%	60%

Grade II Jaguar — similar to Grade I Jaguar, except has Douglas premium barrel.

	100%	98%	95%	90%	80%	70%	60%
	$995	$900	$800	$700	$625	$560	$500

Last Mfg.'s Sug. Retail was $1,095.

Grade III Jaguar — similar to Grade II Jaguar, except has Model 70-type 3-position safety, honed trigger and action.

	$1,125	$995	$900	$800	$700	$625	$560

Last Mfg.'s Sug. Retail was $1,395.

Grade IV Jaguar — similar to Grade III Jaguar, except has fully lightened action and installed swivel studs.

	$1,250	$1,050	$930	$825	$725	$640	$560

Last Mfg.'s Sug. Retail was $1,595.

ALPHA CUSTOM — available in most calibers from .222 Rem. through .338-284, many other calibers available on special order, 20 to 24 in. barrel lengths, limited production, right or left-hand, approx. 6 lbs. New 1984.

	$1,525	$1,200	$975	$850	$725	$640	$560

Last Mfg.'s Sug. Retail was $1,735.

ALPHA GRAND SLAM — same general specifications as the Alpha Custom, except comes standard with laminated wood stock, fluted bolt and non-glare matte finished metal parts, right or left-hand, approx., 6½ lbs. New 1985.

	$1,200	$950	$875	$750	$650	$600	$525

Last Mfg.'s Sug. Retail was $1,465.

ALPHA ALASKAN — .308 Win., .350 Rem. Mag., .358 Win., or .458 Win. cal.. Action is similar to Alpha Grand Slam, except barrel, receiver, bolt and safety are stainless steel, right or left-hand, approx. 6¾ - 7½ lbs. New 1985.

	$1,525	$1,200	$975	$850	$725	$640	$560

Last Mfg.'s Sug. Retail was $1,735.

ALPHA BIG-FIVE — .300 H&H thru .375 H&H or .458 Win. cal., action is similar to Alpha Jaguar Grade IV, except has reinforced stock and decelerator 0recoil pad. Mfg. 1987 only.

	$1,575	$1,250	$1,050	$895	$750	$640	$560

Last Mfg.'s Sug. Retail was $1,795.

AMERICAN ARMS

Previous manufacturer located in Garden Grove, CA.

EAGLE 380 — .380 ACP only, stainless steel semi-auto, copy of Walther PPK/S, 6 shot mag., 3¼ in. barrel, 20 oz.

	$295	$250	$215

Add $25 for black teflon finish (disc. 1985).
Last Mfg.'s Sug. Retail was $289.

AMERICAN ARMS CO.

Manufacturer located in Boston, MA from 1870-1901. 1893 to 1904 at Milwaukee, WI. Acquired by Marlin In 1901.

100%	98%	95%	90%	80%	70%	60%	50%	40%	30%	20%	10%

HANDGUNS

O/U DESIGN — Wheeler Pat. Action, brass frame, spur trigger, .22 Short R.F., .32 Short R.F., .41 Short R.F.

100%	98%	95%	90%	80%	70%	60%	50%	40%	30%	20%	10%
$800	$750	$700	$650	$575	$500	$420	$360	$300	$225	$160	$110

SHOTGUNS

HAMMERLESS MODEL — 12 ga., semi-hammerless.

$600	$550	$500	$450	$350	$275	$225	$175	$150	$125	$100	$75

100%	98%	95%	90%	80%	70%	60%	50%	40%	30%	20%	10%

WHITMORE PATENT — 10 or 12 ga., hammerless, checkering, SxS. Add 10% for 10 ga. ($2\frac{7}{8}$ in. chambers).

| $685 | $625 | $575 | $520 | $460 | $400 | $340 | $270 | $200 | $150 | $125 | $100 |

SINGLESHOT — 12 ga., semi-hammerless, damascus barrel.

| $260 | $225 | $200 | $175 | $150 | $125 | $90 | $70 | $50 | $40 | $30 | $20 |

AMERICAN ARMS, INC.

Importer/manufacturer/distributor of Quality Firearms including various Spanish shotguns (Grulla, Indesal, Norica, and Zabala Hermanos), several European pistols and rifles, and exclusive importation of Sites Handguns (new 1990) mfg. in Torino, Italy. American Arms also manufactures several pistols in North Kansas City, MO. American Arms previously imported (1988-89 only) Norica Airguns that may be found under the Norica heading in the Modern Airguns section in the back of this publication. headquartered in North Kansas City, MO.

AMERICAN ARMS ALSO IMPORTS FRANCHI O/U AND SEMI-AUTO SHOTGUNS WHICH CAN BE FOUND UNDER THE FRANCHI LISTING IN THIS TEXT.

Grading	100%	98%	95%	90%	80%	70%	60%

PISTOLS

MODEL TT-9MM TOKAREV — 9mm Para., semi-auto single action, $4\frac{1}{2}$ in. barrel, 9 shot mag., hammer block external safety, 31 oz. Imported 1988-89 only.

| | $250 | $230 | $210 | $195 | $180 | $170 | $160 |

Last Mfg.'s Sug. Retail was $289.

This model is patterned after the Tokarev action and is made from machined steel parts in Yugoslavia.

MODEL EP-380 — .380 ACP, semi-auto double action, stainless steel, $3\frac{1}{2}$ in. barrel, 7 shot mag., wood checkered grips, adj. rear sight, 25 oz. Imported 1988-90 only.

| | $375 | $325 | $250 |

This model was made in West Germany.

Last Mfg.'s Sug. Retail was $449.

MODEL PK-22 CLASSIC — .22 LR, semi-auto double action, styled after Gov't .45 ACP, $3\frac{1}{3}$ in. barrel, 8 shot finger extension mag., black polymer grips, 22 oz. New 1988.

| Mfg.'s Sug. Retail | $199 | $175 | $150 | $125 | $110 | $100 | $90 | $80 |

This model is made in North Kansas City, MO. It has patented safety features such as external hammer block and internal blocking of the firing pin until the trigger is pulled.

MODEL CX-22 CLASSIC — .22 LR, style patterned after Walther PPK, $3\frac{1}{3}$ in. barrel, 8 shot finger extension mag., 22 oz. New 1990.

| Mfg.'s Sug. Retail | $187 | $165 | $140 | $115 | $100 | $90 | $85 | $75 |

This model is made in North Kansas City, MO. It has patented safety features such as external hammer block and internal blocking of the firing pin until the trigger is pulled.

CXC-22 — similar to CX-22 Classic, except has chrome slide. Mfg. in 1990 only.

| | $170 | $150 | $125 | $110 | $100 | $90 | $80 |

Last Mfg.'s Sug. Retail was $189.

MODEL PX-22/25 CLASSIC — .22 LR or .25 ACP (new in 1991) cal., compact variation of the Model PK-22, $2\frac{3}{4}$ in. barrel, 7 shot finger extension mag., 15 oz. New 1989, PX-25 was introduced in 1991.

| Mfg.'s Sug. Retail | $189 | $170 | $150 | $125 | $110 | $100 | $90 | $80 |

Add $10 for .25 ACP cal.

This model is made in North Kansas City, MO. It has patented safety features such as external hammer block and internal blocking of the firing pin until the trigger is pulled.

Grading	100%	98%	95%	90%	80%	70%	60%

MODEL P-98 CLASSIC — .22 LR, semi-auto double action patterned after Walther P.38, 5 in. barrel, 8 shot mag., blue/black finish, grooved wrap around grips, 26 oz. New 1990.

Mfg.'s Sug. Retail	$219	$190	$170	$140	$120	$110	$100	$90

SABRE — 9mm Para. or .40 S&W cal. semi-auto double action only featuring slim line design and blow back short recoil operation, 3¾ in. barrel with polygonal rifling, soft polymer grips, thumb activated mag release, available in matte finish stainless steel or blue ordnance steel, manual safety, 8 shot (.40 S&W) or 9 shot (9mm) mag., 26 oz. Mfg. in Italy by Sites - importation began in 1991.

Mfg.'s Sug. Retail	$309	$275	$250	$225	$200	$185	$170	$160

Add $30 for stainless steel finish.

SPECTRE — 9mm Para. or .40 S&W cal., semi-auto double action, 6 in. barrel with polygonal rifling, 30 shot mag., ambidextrous safety, decocking lever, 4½ lbs., mfg. in Italy by Sites. New in 1990.

Mfg.'s Sug. Retail	$375	$335	$290	$265	$235	$200	$185	$170

This model was previously imported by F.I.E. located in Hialeah, FL.

RIFLES

MODEL ZCY 308 — .308 cal., gas operated semi-auto AK-47 type action, Yugoslavian mfg. Imported 1988 only.

	$775	$650	$550	$450	$400	$375	$350

Last Mfg.'s Sug. Retail was $825.

MODEL AKY 39 — 7.62 x 39mm cal., gas operated semi-auto AK-47 type action, Teakwood fixed stock and grip, flip up Tritium night front sight and rear, Yugoslavian mfg. Imported 1988-89 only.

	$550	$495	$440	$395	$350	$300	$270

Last Mfg.'s Sug. Retail was $559.

This model was supplied with sling and cleaning kit.

Model AKF 39 Folding Stock — 7.62 x 39mm cal., folding stock variation of the Model AKY-39. Imported 1988-89 only.

	$575	$500	$450	$400	$350	$300	$270

Last Mfg.'s Sug. Retail was $589.

EXP-64 SURVIVAL RIFLE — .22 LR, semi-auto, takedown rifle stores in oversize synthetic stock compartment, 21 in. barrel, 10 shot clip mag., open sights, receiver grooved for scope mounting, cross bolt safety, 40 in. overall length, 7 lbs. Imported 1989-90 only.

	$150	$135	$125	$115	$105	$95	$85

Last Mfg.'s Sug. Retail was $169.

MINI-MAX — .22 LR, semi-auto, 18¾ in. barrel, wood or black synthetic stock, 10 shot mag., adj. rear sight, 4⅓ lbs. Imported in 1990 only.

	$85	$75	$65	$55	$45	$40	$35

Add $6 for wood stock.
Last Mfg.'s Sug. Retail was $99.

SM 64 TD SPORTER — .22 LR, semi-auto, takedown barrel, 21 in. barrel, checkered walnut finished hardwood stock and forend, hooded front sight and adj. rear sight, 7 lbs. Imported 1989-90 only.

	$130	$115	$105	$95	$85	$75	$65

Last Mfg.'s Sug. Retail was $149.

SHOTGUNS: OVER AND UNDER

American Arms is currently importing Spanish shotguns manufactured by Zabala Hermanos, Lanber, and Indesal. Italian shotguns are also imported mfg. by Stefano Fausti (Models Silver, Waterfowl, and Turkey Special). American Arms imported Franchi Black Magic semi-auto and O/U shotguns will appear under the Franchi section in this text. Older Diarm models have been listed below.

Grading	100%	98%	95%	90%	80%	70%	60%

LINCE — 12 or 20 ga., 3 in. chambers, boxlock with Greener crossbolt, various barrel lengths and chokings, available in either blue or shiny chrome finish, SST, VR, ejectors. Imported 1986 only.

	$510	$400	$380	$360	$340	$320	$300

Add $70 for choke tubes.
Last Mfg.'s Sug. Retail was $610.

SILVER MODEL — 12 or 20 ga. only, similar to Lince Model, except has brushed aluminum finished receiver, no engraving. Imported 1986-87 only.

	$495	$450	$390	$360	$330	$300	$285

Add $50 for multi-chokes.
Last Mfg.'s Sug. Retail was $545.

SILVER I — similar to Silver Model, except also available in 28 or .410 ga. (both new 1988), single selective trigger became standard in 1988, extractors, fixed chokes, recoil pad. New 1986.

Mfg.'s Sug. Retail	$489	$415	$380	$340	$300	$285	$270	$255

Add $60 for 28 or .410 ga.
Engraved frame became standard in 1987.

SILVER II — similar to Silver Model, except is supplied with choke tubes, deluxe walnut, and ejectors. New 1987.

Mfg.'s Sug. Retail	$629	$560	$510	$455	$395	$360	$330	$300

28 and .410 ga. (fixed chokes only) are available at no extra charge.

Small Gauge Combo — includes 28 and .410 ga. barrels bored IC/M. New 1989.

Mfg.'s Sug. Retail	$998	$890	$815	$675	$595	$550	$495	$450

SILVER LITE — 12 or 20 ga., 2¾ in. chambers, boxlock action, 26 in. vent. barrels with VR andchoke tubes, blued alloy receiver, SST, ejectors, gold trigger, checkered walnut stock and forearm, 5 lbs. 14 oz. or 6 (12 ga.) lbs. Importation began 1990.

Mfg.'s Sug. Retail	$699	$595	$525	$460	$400	$360	$330	$300

SILVER SPORTING — 12 ga. only, Sporting Clay model, boxlock action, 28 in. vent. barrels with channelled broadway VR and choke tubes, nickel finished engraved receiver, SST, ejectors, figured walnut stock and forearm with handcut checkering, 7 lbs. 6 oz. Importation began 1990.

Mfg.'s Sug. Retail	$819	$740	$660	$560	$495	$450	$400	$360

STERLING/BRISTOL — 12 or 20 ga., 3 in. chambers, boxlock with Greener crossbolt and false side plates, various barrel lengths and choke tubes, chrome finished receiver with moderate game scene engraving, SST, VR, ejectors. Imported 1986-89.

	$695	$550	$495	$450	$400	$375	$350

Last Mfg.'s Sug. Retail was $825.

Until 1989, this model was designated the Bristol. In 1988, the engraving pattern was changed from game scene to elaborate scroll type.

SIR — 12 or 20 ga., 3 in. chambers, sidelock with Greener crossbolt, various barrel lengths and chokings, chrome finished receiver with game scene engraving, ST, VR, ejectors, deluxe checkered pistol grip stock and forearm. Imported 1986 only.

	$900	$725	$660	$610	$565	$520	$485

Add $75 for choke tubes.
Last Mfg.'s Sug. Retail was $1,090.

ROYAL — 12 or 20 ga., 3 in. chambers, sidelock with Greener crossbolt, chrome finished receiver with elaborate scroll engraving, ST, VR, ejectors, oil finished deluxe checkered pistol grip and forearm. Imported 1986-87 only.

	$1,595	$1,310	$1,080	$960	$850	$750	$675

Add $65 for choke tubes.
Last Mfg.'s Sug. Retail was $1,730

Grading	100%	98%	95%	90%	80%	70%	60%

EXCELSIOR — 12 or 20 ga., 3 in. chambers, sidelock with Greener crossbolt, various barrel lengths and chokings, chrome finished receiver with elaborate deep relief engraving and multiple gold inlays, ST, VR, ejectors, oil finished deluxe checkered pistol grip and forearm. Imported 1986-87 only.

	$1,775	$1,510	$1,250	$1,100	$975	$885	$780

Add $70 for choke tubes.
Last Mfg.'s Sug. Retail was $1,925.

WATERFOWL SPECIAL — 12 ga. only, Mag. chambers (3½ in. was added in 1989), 28 in. barrels with choke tubes, SST, ejectors, parkerized metal finish, matte finished stock and forearm, sling swivels, recoil pad. New 1987.

Mfg.'s Sug. Retail	$639	$585	$515	$460	$425	$395	$375	$350

10 ga. Waterfowl — 10 ga. Mag., double triggers, extractors, matte finishes similar to 12 ga. Waterfowl, beavertail forearm. Imported 1988-89 only.

	$750	$625	$550	$495	$450	$390	$360

Last Mfg.'s Sug. Retail was $829.

TURKEY SPECIAL — 10 ga., 3½ in. Mag., 26 in. barrels with choke tubes, double triggers, extractors, recoil pad, non-glare metal finish. New 1988.

Mfg.'s Sug. Retail	$859	$750	$625	$525	$500	$450	$390	$360

F.S. 200 — 12 ga., trap or skeet model, 26 or 32 in. separated barrels only, SST, ejectors, boxlock with Greener crossbolt, black or chromed receiver, checkered walnut stock and forearm. Imported 1986-87 only.

	$690	$560	$500	$450	$410	$375	$350

Last Mfg.'s Sug. Retail was $835.

F.S. 300 — 12 ga., trap or skeet model, 26, 30, or 32 in. separated barrels only, SST, ejectors, boxlock with Greener crossbolt and false side plates lightly engraved, chromed receiver, checkered walnut stock and forearm. Imported 1986 only.

	$825	$675	$610	$555	$510	$470	$440

Last Mfg.'s Sug. Retail was $995.

F.S. 400 — 12 ga., trap or skeet model, 26, 30, or 32 in. separated barrels only, ST, ejectors, sidelock with Greener crossbolt, lightly engraved chromed receiver, checkered walnut stock and forearm. Imported 1986 only.

	$1,145	$945	$860	$800	$740	$680	$620

Last Mfg.'s Sug. Retail was $1,360.

F.S. 500 — same specifications as FS 400. Importation disc. 1985.

	$1,175	$950	$860	$795	$730	$660	$595

Last Mfg.'s Sug. Retail was $1,360.

SHOTGUNS: SIDE-BY-SIDE

American Arms is currently importing Spanish shotguns manufactured by Zabala Hermanos and Grulla. Older discontinued Diarm models will also be shown in this section.

GENTRY/YORK — 12, 16 (disc. 1990), 20, 28, or .410 ga., 3 in. chambers, boxlock, ejectors (extractors after 1986), double triggers, chromed receiver features fine scroll engraving, pistol grip stock with recoil pad and beavertail forearm. New 1986.

Mfg.'s Sug. Retail	$549	$465	$385	$335	$300	$280	$260	$240

Add $30 for 28 or .410 ga.
Before 1988 this model was designated York (case coloring began 1988).

BRITTANY — 12 or 20 ga., boxlock action, 25 (20 ga.) or 27 (12 ga.) in. barrels, SST, ejectors, matted solid rib, choke tubes, engraved case colored frame, checkered walnut straight grip stock with recoil pad and semi-beavertail forearm, 6½ or 7 lbs. New 1989.

Mfg.'s Sug. Retail	$669	$590	$520	$475	$435	$400	$375	$350

The wood finish was changed in this model from oil to semi-gloss in 1991.

Grading	100%	98%	95%	90%	80%	70%	60%

SHOGUN — 10 ga., 3½ in. chambers, boxlock, ejectors, double triggers, chromed receiver features fine scroll engraving. Imported 1986 only.

	$440	$350	$325	$300	$280	$260	$240

Last Mfg.'s Sug. Retail was $525.

DERBY — 12, 20, 28, or .410 ga., 3 in. chambers, sidelock, ejectors, double (disc. 1989) or single trigger, chromed receiver features fine scroll engraving, straight grip walnut stock and forearm. New 1986.

Mfg.'s Sug. Retail	$929	$825	$715	$600	$500	$425	$385	$350

Add $20 for 28 or .410 ga.

Subtract $50 for DT.

Add approx. $200 for 2-barrel set (20 and 28 ga.) - disc. 1990.

This model featured a case-colored receiver between 1988-90 and was changed to coin finish in late 1991. At the same time, the wood finish was changed from oil to semi-gloss.

GRULLA -2 — 12, 20, 28, or .410 ga., hand fitted sidelock action, 26 or 28 in. barrels, DT's, ejectors, fixed chokes, concave rib, case colored receiver with elaborate engraving, deluxe English style straight stock and splinter forearm (checkered and hand rubbed), between 5¾ - 6¼ lbs. New 1989.

Mfg.'s Sug. Retail	$2,798	$2,400	$2,100	$1,675	$1,350	$1,050	$900	$800

This model is individually handcrafted with less than 1,000 mfg. each year.

Small Gauge Set — includes choice of 20/28 ga. or 28/.410 ga. barrel combination (26 in. fixed choke barrels). New 1989.

Mfg.'s Sug. Retail	$3,679	$3,275	$2,850	$2,300	$1,975	$1,650	$1,325	$1,150

WATERFOWL SPECIAL — 10 ga. only, 3½ in. chambers, 32 in. barrels, DT's, parkerized finish, sling swivels and camouflaged sling, extractors, fixed chokes, recoil pad. New 1987.

Mfg.'s Sug. Retail	$589	$550	$500	$460	$425	$395	$375	$350

TURKEY SPECIAL — 10 or 12 ga., Mag. chambers (3½ in. 12 ga. introduced in 1989), 26 in. barrels only, double triggers, parkerized finish, dull finish stock and forearm, sling swivels, recoil pad, choke tubes. New 1987.

Mfg.'s Sug. Retail	$589	$500	$450	$400	$360	$330	$300	$285

Add $30 for 10 ga.

COMBINATION GUNS

RS COMBO — choice of .222 Rem. or .308 rifle barrel under 12 ga. barrel, engraved boxlock frame with antique silver finish, DT's, 24 in. VR barrels with shotgun choke tubes, rifle sights, grooved for scope mounting, Monte Carlo stock, 7 lbs. 14 oz. Imported 1989 only.

	$675	$595	$550	$495	$450	$420	$385

Last Mfg.'s Sug. Retail was $749.

SHOTGUNS: SINGLE SHOT

SINGLE SHOT MODEL — 12, 20, or .410 ga., 3 in. Mag., non-exposed hammer, pistol grip stock, non-reflective finish. Imported 1988-89 only.

	$90	$80	$70	$60	$55	$50	$45

Last Mfg.'s Sug. Retail was $99.

Camper Special — 12, 20, or .410 ga., 3 in. Mag., folding design, 21 in. barrel, pistol grip. Imported 1988-89 only.

	$95	$80	$70	$60	$55	$50	$45

Last Mfg.'s Sug. Retail was $107.

Slugger — 12 or 20 ga., 24 in. Slug shotgun barrel with adj. rear sight and blade front, recoil pad. Imported 1989 only.

	$100	$85	$75	$65	$55	$50	$45

Last Mfg.'s Sug. Retail was $115.

Youth — 20 or .410 ga., 26 in. barrel, 12½ in. stock dimensions, recoil pad. Imported 1989 only.

	$100	$85	$75	$65	$55	$50	$45

Last Mfg.'s Sug. Retail was $115.

Grading	100%	98%	95%	90%	80%	70%	60%
Combo — interchangeable rifle and shotgun barrels, choice of .22 Hornet/12 ga. with 28 in. barrel or .22 LR/20 ga. with 26 in. barrel, includes fitted hard case. Imported 1989 only.	$195	$165	$130	$115	$100	$90	$80

Last Mfg.'s Sug. Retail was $235.

	100%	98%	95%	90%	80%	70%	60%
10 Ga. Model — 10 ga. only, 3½ in. chambers, 26 in. multi-choke or 32 in. full fixed choke barrel, non-exposed hammer, non-reflective finish. Imported 1988-89 only.	$135	$115	$95	$80	$70	$60	$55

Add $30 for multi-chokes (26 in. barrel).
Last Mfg.'s Sug. Retail was $149.

AMERICAN BARLOCK WONDER
Manufactured by Crescent Arms for Sears Roebuck & Co.

SHOTGUNS

SIDE-BY-SIDE — various gauges, hammerless or outside hammer, damascus or steel barrels. Add 15% for steel barrels, smaller gauges.

	100%	98%	95%	90%	80%	70%	60%
	$240	$225	$200	$175	$140	$100	$75

SINGLE SHOT — various gauges, hammer, steel barrel. Add 35% for smaller gauges.

	100%	98%	95%	90%	80%	70%	60%
	$125	$115	$100	$90	$75	$60	$50

AMERICAN DERRINGER CORPORATION
Manufacturer located in Waco, TX 1980-present.

DERRINGERS: STAINLESS STEEL

MODEL 1 — available in over 55 cal.'s including .22 LR through .45-70, also 2½ in. .410 shot shell, O/U stainless steel derringer, 3 in. barrels, automatic barrel selection, "hammer block" type safety, 15 oz., spur trigger, rosewood grips. New 1980.

Regular Cal.'s — most cal.'s between .22 LR and .38 Spl.

Mfg.'s Sug. Retail	$200	$180	$160	$130

Add approx. $175 for .22 Hornet (disc. 1989), .223 Rem., or .30-30 cal.

Larger Cal.'s — typically .41 cal. and larger.

Mfg.'s Sug. Retail	$320	$270	$220	$180

Subtract approx. $75 for .357 Mag. or .45 ACP cal.

Add approx. $65 for .41 - .45 Mag. cal.'s.

This model can be ordered with special ser. no.'s and other custom features at additional cost(s).

LADY DERRINGER — .32 Mag. or .38 Spl. standard cal.'s, also available in .22 LR, .22 Mag., .357 Mag., .380 ACP, 9mm Para., .45 ACP, or .45 LC/.410 shotshell cal. at a small premium, high polished finish with synthetic ivory grips, handfitted action allowing easy cocking, cased in French styled jewelry box. New 1990.

Standard Grade — standard model as described above, 1990 mfg. only.

	$215	$185	$160

Last Mfg.'s Sug. Retail was $250.

Deluxe Grade — similar to Standard Grade, except take grips are scrimshawed in a cameo or rose design, choice of walnut case or French jewelry box.

Mfg.'s Sug. Retail	$250	$215	$185	$160

Deluxe Engraved — similar to Deluxe Grade, except hand engraved with circa 1880 patterns.

Mfg.'s Sug. Retail	$695	$625	$500	$400

Mother of pearl grips and personalized engraving are available as extra cost options on this model.

14 KT. Gold Engraved — entire Derringer manufactured out of a 14 KT. gold bar (contains approx. 20 oz. of 14 KT. gold and 3 oz. of stainless steel), custom engraved with diamond sights, special order only.

Mfg.'s Sug. Retail	$110,000	$110,000	$70,000	$49,500

MODEL 1 TEXAS COMMEMORATIVE — .38 Spl., .44-40, or .45 LC cal., similar to Model 1 except has brass frame, stainless steel barrel, and stag grips. 500 mfg. in each cal. starting in 1986.

Grading	100%	Issue Price	Qty. Made
44-40 cal.	$280	$320	500
.45 cal.	$285	$320	500
.32 Mag. (disc.)	$185	$200	500
.38 Spl.	$185	$213	500
.22 LR (new 1991)	$200	$238	500
.41 Rimfire (not shootable)	$235	$295	500
Fully engraved model	$995	$1,100	limited

Add $79 for 125th Anniversary "Book" pistol case.

MODEL 3 — .32 Mag. (new 1990 - limited availability) or .38 Spl. cal., single shot, 2½ in. barrel, 8½ oz., spur trigger, rosewood grips.

Grading	100%	98%	95%	90%	80%	70%	60%
Mfg.'s Sug. Retail	$120	$95	$70	$55			

MODEL 4 — .357 Mag. through .45 Colt cal.'s on upper barrel, 3 in. .410 shot shell lower barrel, O/U derringer combination pistol, 4¹⁄₁₀ in. barrel, rosewood grips, 16½ oz. New 1985.

Mfg.'s Sug. Retail	$350	$310	$250	$210

This model is also available on special order in either .50-70 or .50 Saunders cal. (new 1989 - single shot only). Retail is $395.

Alaskan Survival Model — same as Model 4, except choice of .45-70 or .44 Mag. cal. upper or lower barrel.

Mfg.'s Sug. Retail	$388	$340	$295	$260

This model is also available in a .45-70 O/U configuration. Retail is $450.

MODEL 6 — .45 Colt/.410 ga. O/U, 6 in. barrel, 21 oz. Available in high polish, satin, or gray matte finish (standard). New 1986.

Mfg.'s Sug. Retail	$350	$295	$260	$220

Add $13 for satin finish.

Add $38 for high polish finish.

Add $35 for oversized grips.

MODEL 7 — .22 LR, .32 Mag., .38 Spl., .38 S&W (disc. 1989), .380 ACP, or .44 Spl. cal., O/U, same basic specifications as Model 1, except ultra lightweight (7½ oz.).

Mfg.'s Sug. Retail	$200	$165	$140	$115

Add $13 for .22 LR cal.

.44 Special Cal. — .44 Spl. cal. only.

Mfg.'s Sug. Retail	$500	$445	$410	$350

MODEL 10 — .45 ACP or .45 LC, O/U, 3 in. barrels, aluminum frame, matte finish, 10 oz. New 1988.

Mfg.'s Sug. Retail	$250	$215	$175	$145

Add $70 for .45 LC cal.

MODEL 11 — .38 Spl. only, same basic specifications as Model 1, matte gray finish, only 11 oz.

Mfg.'s Sug. Retail	$195	$165	$145	$125

HIGH STANDARD DOUBLE ACTION — .22 LR or .22 Mag. cal., 3½ in. O/U barrels, double action trigger, dual extraction, hammerless, blue finish with black synthetic grips, 11 oz. New 1990.

Mfg.'s Sug. Retail	$150	$135	$110	$95

This O/U Derringer duplicates the original High Standard design.

DA 38 DOUBLE ACTION — .357 Mag. (new 1991), .38 Spl. or 9mm Para. cal., 3 in. O/U barrels, satin stainless steel with aluminum grip frame, double action trigger design, hammer-block thumb safety, choice of checkered rosewood, walnut, or other hardwood grips, 14.5 oz. New 1990.

Mfg.'s Sug. Retail	$245	$205	$170	$145

Grading	100%	98%	95%	90%	80%	70%	60%

Add $12 for 9mm Para. cal.
Add $124 for .357 Mag. cal.

MINI-COP — .22 Mag. cal., 4 shot double action design, stainless steel construction, patterned after the original Mini-Cop mfg. in Torrance, CA. New 1990.

Mfg.'s Sug. Retail	$250	$220	$185	$155			

COP STAINLESS — .357 Mag. cal., double action, similar design to Mini-Cop. New 1991.

Mfg.'s Sug. Retail	$313	$265	$240	$220			

CUSTOM TARGET MODELS — .38 Spl. Wadcutter or 9mm Federal cal., mfg. for End of Trail Derringer Match, limited production. New 1990.

Mfg.'s Sug. Retail	$1,000	$895	$750	$600			

PISTOLS: SEMI-AUTO

STANDARD MODEL

.25 Mag. Cal. — .25 Mag., semi-auto single action, less than 100 manufactured in stainless steel only.

	$500	$400	$300				

.25 ACP Cal. — .25 ACP, semi-auto single action, less than 400 manufactured in stainless steel, less than 50 in blued steel.

Stainless	$400	$300	$250				
Blue	$550	$400	$325				

LM-4 — see separate listing under Semmerling.

AMERICAN FIREARMS MANUFACTURING COMPANY, INC.

Previous manufacturer located in San Antonio, TX between 1972-1974.

AMERICAN .25 AUTOMATIC — .25 auto, 8 shot, $2\frac{1}{10}$ in. barrel, smooth walnut grips, mfg. 1966-74.

Stainless	$195	$180	$165				
Blue	$165	$150	$140	$120	$100	$90	$85

AMERICAN .38 SPL. — .38 Spl., O/U configuration, approx. 3,000-4,000 mfg. between 1972-74.

	$200	$165	$135				

AMERICAN .380 AUTOMATIC — .380 auto, 8 shot, $3\frac{1}{2}$ in. barrel, stainless steel, smooth walnut grips. Mfg. 1972-1974.

	$700	$500	$300				

This model is extremely rare — only 10 were manufactured. Prices hard to evaluate.

AMERICAN GUN CO.

Manufactured by Crescent Firearms Co. distributed by H. & D. Folsom Co.

HANDGUNS

REVOLVER — .32 S&W, 5 shot, double action, top break-open action.

	$175	$160	$140	$120	$95	$65	$50

SHOTGUNS

SxS — various gauges, hammer or hammerless, damascus or steel barrels.

	$240	$225	$200	$175	$140	$100	$75

Add 15% for small gauges or steel barrels.

Grading	100%	98%	95%	90%	80%	70%	60%

AMERICAN HISTORICAL FOUNDATION, THE

A private organization which markets military commemoratives and subcontracts manufacturers. AHF is located in Richmond, VA.

AHF limited edition models are not necessarily all manufactured at one time. Rather, guns are fabricated as demand dictates.

COMMEMORATIVE ISSUES

Due to insufficient and inconsistent collector/investor demand, The American Historical Foundation should be contacted directly to ascertain values for older and current models in the secondary marketplace. Please refer to the Trademark Index in the back of this text for their address and telephone number. Values listed below reflect either AHF's original issue price or last retail price before discontinuance.

PISTOLS

ARMED FORCES MODEL 1911A1 SERIES — .45 ACP cal., consists of four Model 1911A1's (one for each U.S. armed service branch), custom designed artwork with selective etchings, grips are finished in different woods and medallions, 1,911 mfg. for each branch by Auto Ordnance Corp.

Mfg.'s Sug. Retail $995

Add $119 for display case.

AIRBORNE JUBILEE MODEL 1911A1 — .45 ACP cal., high polished bluing with etched commemorative inscriptions, 24 Kt. gold plated selected parts, 500 mfg. by Auto Ordnance Corp.

Mfg.'s Sug. Retail $995

Add $145 for display case.

D-DAY COMMEM. M1911A1 — .45 ACP cal., mfg. by Auto-Ordnance Corp. and patterned after the Colt Gov't. Model, various 24 Kt. plated small parts, polymer grips with medallions, serial numbered DDAY 0001 - DDAY 1,000. Introduced 1989.

Mfg.'s Sug. Retail $995

Add $149 for walnut display case.

VIETNAM WAR LIMITED EDITION M1911A1 — .45 ACP, patterned after the Colt Gov.'t Model 1911A1, mfg. by Auto Ordnance Corp., engraved frame with mirror polished slide featuring 24 KT. selective etchings and gold plated small parts. Issued in 1983.

Mfg.'s Sug. Retail $1,095

40TH ANNIVERSARY COMMEM. RUGER MARK II — .22 LR, features 24 Kt. gold etched receiver and barrel with plating on various small parts, polymer ivory grips with both red and black Ruger medallions, ser. numbered 40th 1-40th 950. Issued 1990.

Mfg.'s Sug. Retail $995

Add $149 for walnut display case.

REVOLVERS

Texas Patterson — .36 cal., 5 shot, hand engraved and 24 Kt. gold plating, first issue of the "Samuel Colt Golden Tribute Collection", limited edition of 950, mfg. by D. Pedersoli of Italy.

Mfg.'s Sug. Retail $1,895

Add $259 for display case.

WALKER — .44 cal., 6 shot, second issue of the "Samuel Colt Golden Tribute Collection", limited edition of 950, mfg. by A. Uberti, located in Italy.

Mfg.'s Sug. Retail $1,895

Add $229 for display case.

CIVIL WAR COLT DRAGOONS — .44 cal., available as either Union (hand engraved and 24 Kt. gold plating) or Confederate Model (hand engraved and silver plated). 125 mfg. of each, entire edition is sold out.

Last Mfg.'s Sug. Retail was $2,495.

Grading	100%	98%	95%	90%	80%	70%	60%

JEFFERSON DAVIS MODEL 1851 NAVY — .36 cal., patterned after the Colt 1851 Navy presented to J. Davis in 1858, hand engraved with sterling silver plated selected parts, complete with detatchable shoulder stock, limited edition of 250, mfg. by A. Uberti.

Mfg.'s Sug. Retail $2,995

Add $395 for display case.

WILD BILL HICKOK MODEL 1851 NAVY — .36 cal., high quality reproduction of the 1851 Navy revolvers carried by Wild Bill Hickok, hand engraved and sterling silver plated, limited edition of 500, mfg. by A. Uberti.

Mfg.'s Sug. Retail $1,995

Add $119 for display case.

COL. J. S. MOSBY MODEL 1860 ARMY — .44 cal., stainless steel construction, hand engraved with selected 24 Kt. gold plated parts, limited edition of 150, mfg. by Colt Firearms. Last Mfg.'s Sug. Retail was $2,495. The entire edition is sold out.

J.E.B. STUART LEMAT — .44 cal., 9 shot, includes single shot .65 cal. shotgun barrel, blued surfaces with selective etching and 24 Kt. gold plating, limited edition of 500, mfg. by Navy Arms beginning 1987.

Mfg.'s Sug. Retail $2,695

Add $179 for display case.

200TH COMMEMORATIVE REVOLVER — .44 Mag., Dan Wesson manufactured revolver with extensive 24Kt. gold inlays and etchings, 10 in. barrel, ivory polymer grips, serial numbered CC001-CC950 (950 mfg.), 4 lbs. Released 1987.

Collector's Edition

Last Mfg.'s Sug. Retail was $995. This variation is now sold out.

Deluxe Museum Edition — this model is now sold out, only 500 were mfg., issue price is unknown on this variation.

2ND AMENDMENT COMMEM. REVOLVER — .44 Mag., 10 in. barrel, mfg. by Dan Wesson to AHF specifications, 2 different models, walnut stocks with medallions. Released 1989.

Collector's Edition — fully etched coverage, blued frame and barrel with 24 Kt. gold plated small parts, 1,500 mfg. serial numbered 2AC 0001 - 2AC 1500.

Mfg.'s Sug. Retail $1,495

Add $149 for walnut display case.

Deluxe Museum Edition — fully etched coverage, all metal parts 24 Kt. gold plated, 750 mfg. serial numbered 2AD 001 - 2AD 750.

Mfg.'s Sug. Retail $1,895

Add $149 for walnut display case.

AMERICAN DEER HUNTER COMMEMORATIVE — .44 Mag., mfg. by Dan Wesson, 10 in. barrel, 4 lbs. Issued 1990.

Deluxe Trophy Grade Edition — deeply blued finish with 24 Kt. gold plated hammer, trigger, front sight, cylinder release, and grip screws, Herrett finger groove grips, 250 mfg. serial numbered 001T-250T with "DEER" prefix.

Mfg.'s Sug. Retail $1,995

Add $149 for walnut display case.

This variation is also available in a bear, moose, elk, or sheep edition.

Sportsman's Edition — field grade version with high polished bluing and gold gilt etching on barrel, 750 mfg. serial numbered 001S-750S with "DEER" prefix.

Mfg.'s Sug. Retail $995

Add $149 for walnut display case.

This variation is also available in a bear, moose, elk, or sheep edition.

GENERAL PATTON SAA — .45 LC, 5½ in. barrel, silver plated finish with extensive scroll hand engraving, 2500 mfg. in limited edition beginning 1988, serial numbered P0001-P2500, polymer grips combined with ivory, lanyard ring. Mfg. by A. Uberti in Italy.

Mfg.'s Sug. Retail $1,895

Add $169 for walnut/glass display case.

Grading	100%	98%	95%	90%	80%	70%	60%

TEDDY ROOSEVELT SAA — .44-40 cal., reproduction of Teddy Roosevelt's famous Colt engraved SAA, hand engraved on both sides with a 24 Kt. inlay of Roosevelt's initials on left recoil shield, entire gun is 24 Kt. gold and sterling silver plated, 750 mfg. by A. Uberti.

Mfg.'s Sug. Retail $1,995

Add $149 for display case.

RIFLES AND CARBINES

MODEL 1861 SPRINGFIELD MUSKET — .58 cal., issued to commemorate 125th anniversary of the Civil War, selected parts are hand engraved and 24 Kt. gold plated, furniture grade walnut stock, 125 mfg. by Ezechiele and Rino Chiappa.

Mfg.'s Sug. Retail $3,495

Add $295 for display case.

CONSTITUTION COMMEMORATIVE HENRY — .44-40 cal., patterned after the famous Henry rifle, brass frame, hand engraved with 24 Kt. gold plating, 200 mfg. by A. Uberti. Entire edition is sold out.

Last Mfg.'s Sug. Retail was $2,395.

Add $249 for display case.

CIVIL WAR COMMEMORATIVE HENRYS — similar to Constitution Commemorative Henry, choice of either Abraham Lincoln (hand engraved brass frame with gold plating and blued barrel) or Jefferson Davis (hand engraved brass frame with silver plating and brown barrel), 250 of each model mfg. by A. Uberti.

Mfg.'s Sug. Retail $3,495

Add $249 for display case.

MODEL 94 CARBINE — .30-30 cal., issued to commemorate the closing of the West.

Collector's Edition — hand engraved receiver with 24 Kt. antiqued gold plating, special stock medallion, 750 mfg. by Winchester.

Mfg.'s Sug. Retail $1,795

Add $249 for a display case.

Deluxe Museum Edition — mirror polished, hand engraved receiver with 24 Kt. gold plating, deluxe walnut stocks, 250 mfg. by Winchester.

Mfg.'s Sug. Retail $2,595

Add $249 for display case.

WWII M1 GARAND RIFLE — .30-06 cal., mfg. from original pre-WWII Garands, various 24Kt. plated parts, high polish blue, walnut cased, released in 1984, serial numbered WW0001-WW2500, 9½ lbs.

Last Mfg.'s Sug. Retail was $1,895.

AIRBORNE GOLDEN JUBILEE M1A1 CARBINE — .30 carbine, mfg. from original WWII circa carbines with folding stock, special commemorative etchings, 24 Kt. gold plated selected parts, 500 unit limited edition.

Mfg.'s Sug. Retail $1,295

Add $249 for display case.

AIRBORNE GOLDEN JUBILEE THOMPSON — .45 ACP, issued to commemorate 50th anniversary of the Airborne, special commemorative etchings and medallions, 500 mfg. by Auto Ordnance Corp.

Mfg.'s Sug. Retail $1,995

Add $249 for display case.

KOREAN WAR THOMPSON RIFLE — .45 ACP, semi-auto (also in fully auto with class III license) reproduction of the famous military Thompson sub-machine gun, mfg. by Auto-Ordnance Corp., four models commemorating the four U.S. service branches (Air Force, Army, Marine Corps. and Navy), special finished high grade walnut stock, pistol grip, and forearm, multiple 24Kt. plated parts, walnut cased, 2,000 manufactured 1984, serial numbered KW0001-KW3000.

Add $249 for display case.

Last Mfg.'s Sug. Retail was $1,995.

Total production on this model was 3,000 units - 750 total for each U.S. service branch.

Grading	100%	98%	95%	90%	80%	70%	60%

Thompson Engraved Model — similar to above, except has full engraving coverage. 50 available within the edition limit (2,000).
Last Mfg.'s Sug. Retail was $2,000.

VIETNAM M14 RIFLE — .308 cal., manufactured by Federal Ordnance, 24Kt. gold etched and gilted metal parts, mfg. limited to 500 of each edition. Released 1987.

Collectors Edition
Mfg.'s Sug. Retail $2,195

Deluxe Museum Edition
Mfg.'s Sug. Retail $2,495

Add $249 for display case on either edition.

M16 VIETNAM WAR COMMEMORATIVE — .223 cal., semi-auto version of the M16, mfg. by B.F.I., four models commemorating the four U.S. service branches (Air Force, Army, Marine Corps., and Navy), hand engraved, 24 Kt. gold plated small parts, medallions in stock, bipod included, 1,500 mfg. 1988 serial numbered V 0001 - V 1000. This set is now sold out.

Mfg.'s Sug. Retail $2,995

Add $249 for glass display case.
Each service branch model had 250 mfg.

M16 AIRBORNE — .223 cal., carbine variation with hand engraving and 24 Kt. gold plated selected parts, specially finished stocks with heavily textured black finish, 950 mfg. by B.F.I.

Mfg.'s Sug. Retail $2,795

Add $249 for display case.

AMERICAN ARMED FORCES UZI — 9mm, semi-auto, carbine variation, gold plated small parts and numerous 24 Kt. inlays, 1,500 mfg. in 1988, serial numbered UZI 001 - UZI 1,500, mfg. by I.M.I., includes detachable wooden stock.
Last Mfg.'s Sug. Retail was $2,195. This model sold out late 1990.

SPECIAL FORCES MAC-10 — .45 ACP, issued to commemorate 25th anniversary of the MAC-10, semi-auto, special etching and engraving, 1,500 mfg. by Military Armament Corporation.

Mfg.'s Sug. Retail $1,595

Add $169 for display case.

LAW ENFORCEMENT THOMPSON — .45 ACP, each set contains a policeman and sheriff model, appropriatly 24 Kt. gold etching and gilting, deluxe walnut stocks with custom medallions, 1,500 of each mfg. by Auto Ordnance Corp.

Mfg.'s Sug. Retail $1,595

Add $249 for display case.

SHOTGUNS

VIETNAM WAR COMBAT SHOTGUN — 12 ga., hand engraved receiver with 24 Kt. gold plated small parts, 750 mfg. 1988, serial numbered VN 001 - VN 750, mfg. by Savage Industries.

Mfg.'s Sug. Retail $1,595

Add $225 for walnut/glass display case.

AMERICAN INDUSTRIES

Please refer to the Calico section in this text.

AMERICAN INTERNATIONAL

Austria.

Grading	100%	98%	95%	90%	80%	70%	60%

AMERICAN 180 AUTO CARBINE — a specialized .22 LR, designed for para military use, 177 round drum mag., 16½ in. barrel, aperture sight, high impact plastic stock.

	100%	98%	95%	90%	80%	70%	60%
	$660	$550	$440	$360	$330	$305	$275

Add $550 for Laser Lok System.

Add $125 for Extra Drum Mag. and Winder.

Note: This gun was available in a selective fire version for law enforcement only. The gun also was available with a laser assisted sighting system which, when affixed to the weapon, projects a beam to point of impact.

ANCIENS ETABLISSEMENTS PIEPER

Please refer to the Bayard section in this text for Bayard Models 1908, 1923, And 1930. In addition, Bergmann-Bayard Models 1908 and 1910 mfg. in Gaggenau, Germany will appear under the Bergman heading.

ANSCHUTZ

Manufacturer located in Ulm, Germany. Imported and distributed exclusively in the U.S. by Precision Sales International Inc., located in Westfield, MA.

PISTOLS

EXEMPLAR — .22 LR, bolt action, Match 64 left-hand action (for right-hand shooters), 10 in. barrel, 5 shot mag., two stage trigger, adj. rear sight, receiver grooved for scope, contoured grip and forestock are stippled, 3⅓ lbs., also available for left-hand shooters. New 1987.

Mfg.'s Sug. Retail	$460	$395	$340	$285	$250	$225	$200	$180

Add $12 for left-hand model.

Exemplar Magnum — while advertised in 1987, the .22 Mag. was never manufactured.

Exemplar XIV — .22 LR, similar to Exemplar, except has 14 in. barrel, 4.15 lbs. New 1988.

Mfg.'s Sug. Retail	$489	$420	$360	$300	$250	$225	$200	$180

Exemplar Hornet — .22 Hornet cal., 5 shot mag., Match 54 left hand-action, 10 in. barrel, no sights - tapped and grooved, 4.35 lbs. New 1988.

Mfg.'s Sug. Retail	$822	$745	$650	$575	$525	$475	$415	$365

RIFLES: DISCONTINUED BOLT ACTION

Savage imported Anschutz rifles were available from 1963-1981. While some of those models might not be listed below, refer to models of similar caliber and quality that are listed to ascertain values.

During the period when Savage was importing Anschutz rifles, certain models in the Anschutz line were designated "Savage-Anschutz" for sales by Savage in the U.S. Conversely, certain models manufactured by Savage were designated "Anschutz-Savage" for sale by Anschutz in Europe. Some of these models did not have any modifications but others were restocked, supplied with different sights, and had other different features from their original counterparts. In most cases, the original model numbers were used.

Some "Anschutz-Savage" rifles have made their way into the U.S. While somewhat rare, these rifles are typically based on the Savage Model 110 action. They are not as desirable as those "Savage-Anschutz" marked rifles utilizing the superior Anschutz action. Anschutz also manufactured between 1,000-2,000 rifles utilizing SAKO actions in .222 Rem. cal. in the late 50's-early 60's. These guns will approximate values shown on the discontinued centerfire models listed below.

MARK 10 TARGET RIFLE — .22 LR cal., single shot, 26 in. heavy barrel, adj. sights, globe front, target stock with full pistol grip, adj. palm stop, mfg. 1963-1981.

		$350	$320	$290	$260	$230	$210	$195

MODEL 1407 — .22 LR cal. "I.S.U." model, heavy barrel, no sights, disc.

		$375	$340	$300	$260	$230	$210	$195

Grading	100%	98%	95%	90%	80%	70%	60%

MODEL 1408 — .22 LR cal., heavy barrel, no sights. Disc.

	$375	$340	$300	$260	$230	$210	$195

Add $150 for 1408 ED Model.

MODEL 1411 — .22 LR cal., prone position target model, heavy barrel, no sights. Disc.

	$360	$320	$290	$260	$230	$210	$195

MODEL 1413 MATCH — .22 LR cal., adj. cheek piece, heavy target barrel with no sights, competition model. Disc.

	$550	$475	$420	$375	$325	$285	$240

MODEL 1418 MANNLICHER — .22 LR cal., hunting model, fine checkering, clip mag.

	$650	$575	$500	$450	$365	$315	$275

MODEL 1418/19 — .22 LR cal., sporter variation, previous importation by Savage Arms.

	$300	$260	$225	$200	$175	$150	$125

MODEL 1518 MANNLICHER — deluxe model of Model 1418.

	$700	$595	$540	$485	$430	$375	$325

MODEL 1574 SPORTER — .22 Mag., .222 Rem., .22-250 Rem., .223 Rem., .243 Win., or .308 Win. cal., mfg. by Krico (Kreigeskorte) located at Stuttgart and distributed by Anschutz, approx. 1,000 imported during 1970-73.

	$795	$695	$595	$540	$485	$430	$375

MODEL 153 — .222 Rem., 24 in. barrel, folding leaf rear sight, French walnut stock, rosewood forend tip and pistol grip cap. Mfg. 1963-1981.

	$550	$475	$400	$375	$350	$300	$280

MODEL 153-S — .222 Rem., 24 in. barrel, double set triggers, otherwise, same as 153.

	$600	$525	$450	$425	$385	$330	$305

MODEL 184 — .22 LR, 21½ in. barrel, Monte Carlo combination, checkered pistol grip, Schnabel forend, folding leaf sight. Mfg. 1963-1981.

	$350	$320	$290	$260	$230	$210	$195

MODEL 54 SPORTER — .22 LR, 5 shot clip, 24 in. round tapered barrel, Monte Carlo roll over combination, folding leaf sight, checkered pistol grip. Mfg. 1963-1981.

	$625	$550	$475	$425	$395	$360	$320

MODEL 54M — .22 Win. Mag., otherwise same as Sporter.

	$695	$575	$525	$475	$425	$395	$350

MODEL 141 — .22 LR, 5 shot clip, 23 in. round tapered barrel, Monte Carlo stock, folding leaf sight. Disc.

	$345	$280	$240	$200	$180	$160	$140
Model 141M (Mag.)	$365	$300	$265	$225	$200	$180	$160

MODEL 164 — .22 LR, 5 shot clip, 23 in. round tapered barrel, Monte Carlo stock, folding leaf sight. Mfg. 1963-1981.

	$345	$280	$240	$200	$180	$160	$140

MODEL 164M — same as 164, only .22 Win. Mag.

	$365	$300	$265	$225	$200	$180	$160

SPORTER RIFLES: RECENT MANUFACTURE

Prices below reflect the recent devaluation of the U.S. dollar against some foreign currencies. While the manufacturer's suggested retails have gone up considerably, prices for used specimens (98% or less original condition) have not increased proportionately, and in some cases, have changed very little.

Grading	100%	98%	95%	90%	80%	70%	60%

THE KADETT — .22 LR, bolt action, 22 in. barrel, 5 shot clip mag., folding leaf rear sight, single stage trigger, grooved receiver, checkered hard-wood stock, 5½ lbs. Mfg. 1987 only.

	$235	$200	$180	$165	$150	$135	$120

Last Mfg.'s Sug. Retail was $265.

THE ACHIEVER — .22 LR, bolt action, 19½ in. barrel, single shot, folding leaf rear sight, two stage trigger, grooved receiver, stippled hard-wood stock with vented forearm and adj. length of pull, 5¼ lbs. New 1987.

Mfg.'s Sug. Retail	$395	$340	$280	$230	$205	$185	$165	$150

MODEL 1449D YOUTH — .22 LR, bolt action design, 16¼ in tappered barrel with adj. rear sight, receiver is grooved for scope mounting, 5 shot clip mag. with single shot clip adapter available, European hardwood stock, 12¼ in. trigger pull, 3½ lbs. New 1990.

Mfg.'s Sug. Retail	$249	$210	$185	$165	$150	$135	$120	$110

MODEL 1416D CUSTOM — .22 LR, bolt action, 22½ in. barrel, 5 or 10 shot mag., Monte Carlo walnut stock, folding leaf sight.

Mfg.'s Sug. Retail	$675	$575	$475	$400	$350	$295	$240	$225

This model utilizes the Match 64 action, similar to the Anschutz Model 1403 Target.

Model 1416D Fiberglass — similar to Model 1416D Custom, except has McMillan fiberglass stock in hunter brown color and includes roll-over cheekpiece and checkered Wundhammer swell pistol grip, 5¼ lbs. New 1991.

Mfg.'s Sug. Retail	$842	$755	$650	$575	$525	$475	$415	$365

1416DCL Classic — same specifications as 1416D Custom, except regular stock.

Mfg.'s Sug. Retail	$624	$560	$475	$400	$350	$295	$240	$225

Add $102 for left-hand action.

MODEL 1418D — .22 LR, Mannlicher full stock, skipline checkering, 19¾ in. barrel, same action as Model 1416D.

Mfg.'s Sug. Retail	$979	$850	$750	$650	$550	$495	$425	$360

Add $40 for set trigger (mfg. 1985-89).

MODEL 1700D/1422D CUSTOM — .22 LR, bolt action, 5 shot mag., 24 in. barrel, iron sights, heavy barrel, Monte Carlo stock with skipline checkering, 7¼ lbs.

Mfg.'s Sug. Retail	$1,229	$1,095	$895	$750	$650	$550	$450	$375

Add $195 for Meistergrade (select walnut and gold etched trigger guard).

This model was designated 1422D until 1989 when it was changed to the Model 1700D. The Model 1400D Meistergrade was disc. 1987 - the last advertised retail price was $930.

This rifle employs the Anschutz Match 54 action.

1700D Graphite — similar to Model 1700D Custom, except has McMillan black graphite reinforced stock with Monte Carlo roll-over cheekpiece, includes sling and swivels, 22 in. barrel, 7¼ lbs. New 1991.

Mfg.'s Sug. Retail	$1,205	$1,075	$850	$750	$650	$550	$450	$375

1700D/1422DCL Classic — same general specifications as 1422D Custom, except smaller diameter barrel and regular stock.

Mfg.'s Sug. Retail	$1,199	$1,075	$850	$750	$650	$550	$450	$375

Add $195 for Meistergrade (select walnut and gold etched trigger guard).

This model was designated 1422DCL Classic until 1989 when it was changed to the Model 1700D Classic. The Model 1422DCL Classic Meistergrade was disc. 1987 - the last advertised retail price was $875.

1700D FEATHERWEIGHT — similar to Model 1700D Custom, except has matte black McMillan fiberglass stock configured like the Custom Model, 22 in. barrel, no sights, 6¼ lbs. New 1989.

Mfg.'s Sug. Retail	$1,174	$1,050	$850	$750	$650	$550	$450	$375

1700D Featherweight Deluxe — similar specification to the 1700D Featherweight, except has skip-line checkered Fibergrain synthetic stock with realistic wood grain. New 1990.

Mfg.'s Sug. Retail	$1,384	$1,195	$1,050	$875	$775	$650	$550	$450

Grading	100%	98%	95%	90%	80%	70%	60%

DIE MEISTERMACHER — .22 LR, similar action and specifications as Model 1422D Custom, limited edition of 25 guns, select wood, extra polish on metal parts, hand-lapped barrel, with numerous gold inlays including Olympic wreath. Mfg. 1985.

			$2,500	**$2,000**	**$1,600**		

Last Mfg.'s Sug. Retail was $2,475. This variation sold out in late 1988.

MODEL 1700D/1432D CUSTOM — .22 Hornet, 24 in. barrel, folding leaf sight, Monte Carlo stock with skipline checkering and rosewood grip cap, 4 shot mag., 7¾ lbs. Model 1432D was disc. 1987, and the Model 1700D was introduced 1989.

Mfg.'s Sug. Retail	$1,379	$1,195	$1,050	$875	$775	$650	$550	$450

Add $195 for Meistergrade variation (select walnut).

This model was designated 1432D until 1987 and then reintroduced 1989 as the Model 1700D. The Model 1432D Custom Meistergrade was disc. 1986 - the last advertised retail price was $770.

This model comes standard with the Anschutz Match 54 action.

1700D/1432DCL Classic — same general specifications as 1432D Custom, except regular stock and 23½ (1432DCL) or 24 (1700D) in. barrel.

Mfg.'s Sug. Retail	$1,350	$1,175	$995	$835	$735	$615	$500	$400

Add $195 for Meistergrade variation (select walnut).

This model was designated 1432D until 1987 and then reintroduced 1989 as the Model 1700D. This model comes standard with the Anschutz Match 54 action.

Last Mfg.'s Sug. Retail was $849 on the Model 1432DCL.

MODEL 1433D — .22 Hornet, special order only, Match 54 target action, Mannlicher full stock, 4 shot mag. Set trigger new 1985 — add $15. Disc. 1986.

	$995	$840	$740	$640	$525	$425	$350

Last Mfg.'s Sug. Retail was $826.

MODEL 1516D CUSTOM — .22 Mag., otherwise the same as Model 1416D, 4 shot mag.

Mfg.'s Sug. Retail	$698	$595	$495	$400	$350	$295	$240	$225

This model utilizes the Match 64 action, similar to the Anschutz Model 1403 Target.

1516DCL Classic — same specifications as 1516D Custom, except regular stock.

Mfg.'s Sug. Retail	$685	$585	$490	$400	$350	$295	$240	$225

MODEL 1518D — .22 Mag. otherwise same as Model 1418D (Mannlicher stock), 4 shot mag.

Mfg.'s Sug. Retail	$998	$875	$750	$625	$525	$440	$375	$325

Add $40 for set trigger (disc.).

MODEL 1700D/1522D CUSTOM — .22 Mag., bolt action, 5 shot mag., 24 in. barrel, iron sights, heavy barrel, Monte Carlo stock with skipline checkering, 7¼ lbs.

Mfg.'s Sug. Retail	$1,229	$1,095	$895	$750	$650	$550	$450	$375

Add $195 for Meistergrade variation (select walnut).

This model was designated 1522D until 1989 and then reintroduced as the Model 1700D. The Model 1522D Custom Meistergrade was disc. 1985 - last advertised retail price was $678.

1700D/1522DCL Classic — same general specifications as 1522D Custom, except smaller diameter barrel and regular stock.

Mfg.'s Sug. Retail	$1,199	$1,075	$875	$725	$625	$525	$425	$350

Add $195 for Meistergrade variation (select walnut).

This model was designated 1522DCL until 1989 and then reintroduced as the Model 1700D. The Model 1522DCL Classic Meistergrade was disc. 1985 - the last advertised retail price was $660.

BAVARIAN 1700 — .22 LR, .22 Mag., .22 Hornet, or .222 Rem. cal., 24 in. barrel, clip mag., checkered European style stock with European Monte Carlo cheek piece and schnabel forend, 7½ lbs. New 1988.

Mfg.'s Sug. Retail	$1,229	$1,095	$895	$750	$650	$550	$450	$375

Add $150 for .22 Hornet or .222 Rem. cal.

Add $195 for Meistergrade variation (select walnut).

Grading	100%	98%	95%	90%	80%	70%	60%

MODEL 1700D/1532D CUSTOM — .222 Rem., otherwise same as Model 1700D/1432D Custom.

Mfg.'s Sug. Retail	$1,379	$1,195	$1,050	$875	$775	$650	$550	$450

Add $195 for Meistergrade variation (select walnut).
Last Mfg.'s Sug. Retail was $909 on the Model 1532D.

This model was designated 1532D until 1987 and then reintroduced 1989 as the Model 1700D. The Model 1532D MG Custom Meistergrade was disc. 1986 - the last advertised retail price was $770.

1700D/1532DCL Classic — same as Model 1700D/1532D Custom, except regular stock.

Mfg.'s Sug. Retail	$1,350	$1,175	$995	$835	$735	$615	$500	$400

Add $195 for Meistergrade variation (select walnut).
This model was designated 1532DCL until 1987 and then reintroduced 1989 as the Model 1700D.

Last Mfg.'s Sug. Retail was $849 on Model 1532DCL.

RIFLES: SINGLE SHOT SILHOUETTE

MODEL 64S RIFLE — single shot, .22 LR, 26 in. round barrel, beavertail forearm, adj. single stage receiver, aperture sights, target stock with Wundhammer grip and adj. butt plate, checkered pistol grip, mfg. 1963-1981.

		$475	$425	$375	$325	$285	$240	$220

Subtract 15% if without sights (Model 64).
This was model was available in left or right hand action.

MODEL 64MS — .22 LR, single shot silhouette target model, 21¼ in. barrel, no sights, Wundhammer swell stippled pistol grip stock, adj. trigger, 8 lbs.

Mfg.'s Sug. Retail	$885	$775	$640	$525	$450	$375	$350	$285

Add $63 for left-hand action.
This variation employs the Model 1403 action.

Model 64MS - FWT — similar to Model 64MS, except single stage trigger, 6¼ lbs. Disc. 1988.

		$550	$475	$425	$350	$325	$260	$230

Last Mfg.'s Sug. Retail was $596.

MODEL 54.18MS — .22 LR, silhouette target model, 22 in. barrel, match 54 single shot action, walnut Wundhammer stock is stippled on pistol grip and entire forearm, no sights, 8 lbs. 6 oz.

Mfg.'s Sug. Retail	$1,449	$1,200	$1,050	$875	$750	$650	$550	$475

Add $72 for left-hand action.
This model employs the Super Match 54 action.

Model 54.18MS ED — same action as Model 54.18MS, except has 19¼ in. barrel (⅞ in. diameter) with 14¼ in. extension tube, 3 removable muzzle weights. Disc. 1988.

		$1,075	$900	$775	$675	$575	$485	$410

Add $100 for left-hand action.
Last Mfg.'s Sug. Retail was $1,215.

MODEL 54.18MS REP — similar to Model 54.18MS, except has repeating action, 5 shot mag., thumbhole wood stock with vented forestock, 7¾ lbs. This model was introduced in 1989 with a wood stock and a retail price of $1,650. In 1990, the stock was changed to a synthetic McMillan fiberglass finished in grey.

Mfg.'s Sug. Retail	$1,789	$1,525	$1,250	$1,000	$895	$785	$695	$595

Add 10% for wood stock (1989 mfg. only).
This model features a 54 Super Match action with clip mag.

Model 54.18MS REP Deluxe — deluxe version of the Model 54.18MS REP featuring Fibergrain McMillan stock with advanced thumbhole design and stippled checkering. New 1990.

Mfg.'s Sug. Retail	$2,079	$1,775	$1,495	$1,200	$1,000	$895	$785	$695

Grading	100%	98%	95%	90%	80%	70%	60%

MATCH RIFLES: BOLT ACTION - RECENT PRODUCTION

MODEL 2000 MK — .22 LR, single shot match, 26 in. barrel, aperture sights, 7½ lbs. Disc. 1988.

	$340	$290	$250	$210	$180	$160	$145

Last Mfg.'s Sug. Retail was $400.

MODEL 1403D — .22 LR, improved Model 645 match rifle, single shot, no sights, adj. trigger, 8 lbs. 6 oz. Importation disc. in 1990.

	$600	$525	$450	$360	$300	$260	$225

Add $50 for left-hand action (disc. 1988).
Last Mfg.'s Sug. Retail was $700.

MODEL 1803D — .22 LR, Match 64 action, 25½ in. target barrel, single stage adj. trigger, blond finished wood with dark stippling on pistol grip and forearm, adj. cheek piece and butt plate, 8.6 lbs. New 1987.

Mfg.'s Sug. Retail	$1,012	$850	$725	$625	$525	$430	$365	$310

Add $70 for left-hand action (disc. 1989).

MODEL 1808D RT (RUNNING TARGET) — .22 LR, single shot running target model, 32½ in. barrel, adj. stock, cheek piece, trigger, heavy beavertail forend, no sights, muzzle barrel weights, 9¼ lbs.

Mfg.'s Sug. Retail	$1,631	$1,395	$1,195	$950	$800	$695	$580	$500

Add $50 for left-hand action.
This model was previously designated the Model 1808 ED Super during 1990 and earlier mfg.

MODEL 1903D — .22 LR, similar specifications to the Model 1803D, except has new improved target stock and adj. checkpiece made from walnut finished European hardwood, full length stippled checkering on forend and contoured pistol grip, fully adj. new style butt plate, 8.6 lbs. New 1990.

Mfg.'s Sug. Retail	$1,039	$865	$725	$625	$525	$430	$365	$310

Add $66 for left-hand action.

MODEL 1907 ISU — .22 LR, single shot match "I.S.U." model, 26 in. barrel, prone and position shooting, removable cheek piece, adj. butt plate, hand stippled stock with ventilated forearm and blond wood finish, 11 lbs.

Mfg.'s Sug. Retail	$1,729	$1,500	$1,250	$995	$825	$695	$580	$500

Add $105 for left-hand action.
This variation was designated Model 1807 before 1989.

MODEL 1910 SUPER MATCH II — .22 LR, single shot, 27¼ in. barrel, diopter sights, thumbhole stock is fully adj., 12 lbs., model down from 1813 (or 1913), special order only.

Mfg.'s Sug. Retail	$2,585	$2,150	$1,800	$1,400	$1,050	$875	$725	$625

Add $148 for left-hand action.
This variation was designated as Model 1810 before 1988.

MODEL 1911 PRONE MATCH — .22 LR, single shot match prone rifle, 27¼ in. barrel, adj. cheek piece, butt plate, no sights.

Mfg.'s Sug. Retail	$2,026	$1,750	$1,475	$1,175	$1,000	$895	$785	$695

Add $120 for left-hand action.
This variation was designated Model 1811 before 1988.

MODEL 1913 SUPER MATCH — .22 LR single shot, top-of-the-line match rifle, every possible refinement, international diopter sights, 27¼ in. barrel, hand and palm rest, 13.9 lbs.

Mfg.'s Sug. Retail	$2,895	$2,500	$1,800	$1,400	$1,050	$875	$725	$625

Add $164 for left-hand action.
This variation was designated Model 1813 before 1988.

Grading	100%	98%	95%	90%	80%	70%	60%

BIATHLON RIFLES

MODEL 1403B — .22 LR bolt action, Match 64 action, 21½ in. barrel, blonde finished European hardwood with stippled pistol grip, Biathlon design allows 4 mag.'s to be stored in a housing attached to the forend on right side, entry level Biathlon gun, 8½ lbs. New 1990.

Mfg.'s Sug. Retail	$998	$850	$730	$660	$525	$450	$375	$335

MODEL 1827B — .22 LR bolt action, biathlon rifle, carries four 5 shot mag.'s in stock, special biathlon features, 21½ in. barrel, limited production.

Mfg.'s Sug. Retail	$2,256	$1,900	$1,475	$1,175	$1,025	$895	$785	$695

Add $120 for left-hand action (disc. 1989).

In 1990, the stock design was changed permitting 8 mag.'s to be stored in two housings attached to both the stock and forend on right side.

Model 1827BT Fortner — same general specifications as Model 1827B, except has Fortner straight pull-through bolt action, 9 lbs. New 1986.

Mfg.'s Sug. Retail	$3,860	$3,375	$2,875	$2,475	$2,150	$1,895	$1,650	$1,400

Add $320 for left-hand action.

In 1990, the stock design was changed permitting 8 mag.'s to be stored in two housings attached to both the stock and forend on right side.

RIFLES: SEMI-AUTO

MODEL 520/61 — .22 LR, semi-auto, 24 in. barrel, 10 shot mag., Monte Carlo stock, 6½ lbs. Disc. 1983.

	$260	$205	$185	$155	$145	$130	$120

MARK 525 SPORTER RIFLE — .22 LR, semi-auto, 24 in. barrel, 10 shot mag., adj. rear sight, Monte Carlo stock, 6½ lbs. New 1984.

Mfg.'s Sug. Retail	$514	$450	$385	$350	$295	$250	$215	$175

Mark 525 Carbine — similar to Mark 525 Rifle, except has 20 in. barrel. Disc. 1986.

	$385	$310	$260	$220	$195	$160	$145

ANSCHUTZ SHOTGUNS

Anschutz marked O/U shotguns that were manufactured by Miroku of Japan were distributed previously in Europe. Several grades of these shotguns were manufactured and while rarely seen in the U.S., values approximate other Miroku O/U's of similar quality and features ($650 - $1,000 assuming 95% or better condition).

APACHE

Previous importer, mfg. by Ojanguren Y Vidosa, Eibar, Spain.

HANDGUN

SEMI-AUTO — 6.35mm., clip fed.

	$190	$175	$160	$140	$120	$95	$75

ARMALITE INCORPORATED

Costa Mesa, CA.

RIFLES

AR-7 EXPLORER — semi-auto, .22 LR, 16 in. aluminum barrel with steel liner, aperture sight, gun takes down and can be stored in hollow plastic stock, gun will float, mfg. 1959-1973, now made by Charter Arms.

	$101	$90	$80	$75	$70	$65	$60

AR-7 CUSTOM — same as above, only with custom walnut stock including cheek piece, pistol grip. Mfg. 1964-1970.

	$165	$140	$120	$100	$90	$80	$70

Grading	100%	98%	95%	90%	80%	70%	60%

AR-180 — .223 Rem. cal., semi-auto, gas operated, 18¼ in. barrel, folding stock. Manufactured by Armalite in Costa Mesa, CA, 1969-1972, Howa Machinery Ltd., Nagoya, Japan 1972 and 1973. Since 1976 the AR-180 has been made by Sterling Armament Co. Ltd., Dagenham, Essex, England.

Sterling Mfg.

	$850	$775	$695	$625	$550	$495	$450

Costa Mesa Mfg.

	$995	$875	$750	$675	$600	$550	$500

Howa Mfg.

	$1,350	$1,110	$995	$875	$795	$725	$650

SHOTGUN

AR-17 — 12 ga., semi-auto, 24 in. barrel, interchangeable choke tubes, gas operated, high strength aluminum barrel and receiver, plastic stock and forearm, either gold anodized or black finish. Only 2000 mfg. between 1964-1965.

	$575	$460	$420	$360	$310	$260	$220

ARMES DE CHASSE

Importer/distributor/retailer located in Chadds Ford, PA., 19137.

Armes de Chasse also exclusively imports Chapuis (French) rifles and shotguns, A. Francotte and G. Merkel long guns. These trademarks will appear under their own headings in this text.

Because of international currency exchange rates being rather volatile recently, the values listed below could change rapidly if the importer was to experience price increases from the manufacturer.

DOUBLE RIFLES

ARMES DE CHASSE SAFARI EXPRESS — available in cal.'s up to 470 Nitro Express, boxlock action, English scroll or border engraving, coin finished or case colored receiver, oil finished walnut stock with checkering. These guns are manufactured to Armes de Chasse specifications by several different European manufacturers, custom order only. Importation disc. 1989.

	$3,300	$2,800	$2,500	$2,200	$2,000	$1,850	$1,700

Add $600 for English scroll engraving.
Last Mfg.'s Sug. Retail was $3,300.

ARMES DE CHASSE NORTH AMERICAN SAFARI EXPRESS — available in most standard U.S. cal.'s, otherwise similar to Safari Express model. Importation disc. 1989.

	$3,300	$2,800	$2,500	$2,200	$2,000	$1,850	$1,700

This rifle was available on a custom order basis only. Options included a set of 20 ga. shotgun barrels with factory scope mounts.

Last Mfg.'s Sug. Retail was $3,300.

SHOTGUNS: SIDE-BY-SIDE

BALMORAL — 12, 16, or 20 ga., boxlock with color case hardened side plates, can be chambered for 3½ in. (12 ga.), checkered English stock and splinter forearm, ST, auto safety. Imported 1989 only.

	$735	$625	$560	$495	$450	$420	$395

Last Mfg.'s Sug. Retail was $780.
This model was mfg. in Italy in association with Dr. F. Beretta.

CHESAPEAKE — 12 ga., 3½ in. chambers, designed for steel shot, boxlock action, auto ejectors, DT's, manual safety, mfg. in Italy in association with Dr. F. Beretta. Mfg. 1989 only.

	$715	$600	$540	$495	$450	$420	$395

Last Mfg.'s Sug. Retail was $765.

Grading	100%	98%	95%	90%	80%	70%	60%

HIGHLANDER — 20 ga., boxlock action, upland game gun, extractors, DT's, manual safety, checkered English stock and splinter forearm, mfg. in Italy in association with Dr. F. Beretta. Mfg. 1989 only.

	$600	$525	$465	$430	$400	$360	$315

Last Mfg.'s Sug. Retail was $675.

SHOTGUNS: SXS & O/U - SIMSON/SUHL MFG.

While advertised, Models 70E, 74E, 76E, EJ, and EU were never imported into this country.

ARMINEX LTD.
Previous manufacturer located in Scottsdale, AZ.

TRI-FIRE — .45 ACP, 9mm Para., and .38 Super cal.'s, single action auto, interchangeable barrels allow caliber conversion. Available in 5, 6, or 7 (disc. 1984) in. stainless barrel lengths, no grip safety, steel frame construction, ambidextrous thumb safety (on Target and Presentation only), smooth walnut grips, 38 oz. Approx. 250 mfg. between 1981-85.

	$525	$475	$425	$400	$375	$350	$325

Add $50 if presentation cased.

Add approx. $130/conversion unit.

Last Mfg.'s Sug. Retail was $396.

Target Model — same specifications as Tri-Fire, except has 6 or 7 (disc. 1984) in. barrel, very limited mfg.

	$595	$550	$495	$450	$400	$360	$320

Last Mfg.'s Sug. Retail was $448.

ARMINIUS
Zella-Mehlis, Germany 1922-present. Currently imported by Fie Corp. in Hialeah, FL. — see the Fie section for current production models.

HANDGUNS: SINGLE SHOT

MODEL 1 — .22 LR Target, adj. sights.

	$275	$210	$195	$165	$155	$140	$110

MODEL 2 — Same as Model 1, except has set trigger.

	$340	$255	$225	$190	$170	$155	$140

HANDGUNS: REVOLVER

MODEL 3 — .25 ACP, folding trigger, hammerless.

	$175	$135	$125	$105	$100	$90	$80

MODEL 8 — .320 Revolver, folding trigger, hammerless.

	$175	$135	$125	$105	$100	$90	$80

MODEL 9 — .32 ACP.

	$185	$140	$130	$115	$105	$95	$85

MODEL 10 — .32 ACP, hammerless.

	$165	$125	$120	$100	$95	$85	$75

TARGET — .22 LR.

	$90	$70	$65	$55	$50	$45	$45

ARMITAGE INTERNATIONAL, LTD.
Manufacturer located in Seneca, SC.

Grading	100%	98%	95%	90%	80%	70%	60%

SCARAB SKORPION — 9mm Para., paramilitary design patterned after the Czech Model 61, direct blow back action, 4.63 in. barrel, matte black finish, 12 shot (standard) or 32 shot (optional) mag., 3.5 lbs. Mfg. in U.S. 1989-90 only.

	$375	$330	$295	$260	$240	$220	$200

Add $45 for threaded flash hider or imitation suppressor.
Only 602 Scarab Skorpions were manufactured during 1989-90.

Last Mfg.'s Sug. Retail was $400.

ARMS CORPORATION OF THE PHILIPPINES

Manufacturer located in Manila, Philippines since 1980. Currently imported and distributed by Armscor Precision, Inc. located in Foster City, CA.

REVOLVERS

Many of the current models listed below will have limited availability initially because of an existing military contract which is consuming most of the hand gun production.

MODEL M100 — .22 LR, .22 Mag., or .38 Spl., double action revolver, 6 shot, 4 in. vent rib barrel, blued finish only, adj. sights, checkered hardwood grips, 33 oz. Imported 1985-1989.

	$185	$150	$125	$115	$105	$95	$85

Formerly designated as M100TC or Special Edition. .22 LR and .22 Mag. cal.'s were disc. 1988.

MODEL 200 P (POLICE) — .38 Spl., 6 shot, double action, 4 in. half shroud barrel, fixed sights, rubber or wood grips, 26 oz. New 1990.

Mfg.'s Sug. Retail	$200	$185	$160	$145	$130	$120	$110	$100

MODEL 200 TC (THUNDER CHIEF) — .38 Spl., 6 shot, double action, 4 in. full shroud barrel, adj. rear sight, checkered wood grips, 28 oz. New 1990.

Mfg.'s Sug. Retail	$234	$210	$185	$160	$145	$130	$120	$110

RIFLES

MODEL M14P — .22 LR, bolt action, 5 shot mag., 23 in. barrel, open sights, 6 lbs. New 1986.

Mfg.'s Sug. Retail	$96	$85	$70	$60	$50	$45	$40	$35

MODEL M14D — .22 LR, bolt action, similar to Model 14P, except has adj. rear sight and rear checkered mahogany stock. Mfg. 1987 initially and reintroduced 1990.

Mfg.'s Sug. Retail	$109	$95	$85	$70	$60	$50	$45	$40

MODEL M1400LW — .22 LR, similar action to Model 14P, except has checkered stock and Schnabel forend, 10 shot mag., hard rubber pad, 6 lbs. New 1990.

Mfg.'s Sug. Retail	$200	$170	$150	$130	$115	$100	$90	$80

MODEL M1400SC (SUPER CLASSIC) — .22 LR, otherwise similar to Model M1500SC, except has 10 shot mag. and 23 in. barrel, 6 lbs. Introduced late 1990.

Mfg.'s Sug. Retail	$240	$210	$180	$155	$135	$115	$100	$90

MODEL M1500 — .22 Mag., bolt action, 5 shot mag., 21½ in. barrel, checkered mahogany stock, open sights, 6½ lbs. New 1986.

Mfg.'s Sug. Retail	$234	$205	$175	$155	$135	$115	$100	$90

Model 1500LW (Lightweight) — similar to Model M1500, except has lightweight classic European styled stock made of checkered American Walnut, with butt pad. New 1990.

Mfg.'s Sug. Retail	$220	$195	$160	$145	$130	$110	$100	$90

Model 1500SC (Super Classic) — checkered American Walnut stock with hard rubber pad and Monte Carlo cheek piece, hardwood forend tip, engine turned bolt, 6½ lbs. New 1990.

Mfg.'s Sug. Retail	$262	$230	$195	$175	$155	$135	$115	$100

MODEL M1600 — .22 LR, semi-auto, 15 shot mag., 18 in. barrel, copy of the Armalite M16, ebony stock, 5¼ lbs. New 1986.

Mfg.'s Sug. Retail	$111	$95	$85	$70	$60	$50	$45	$40

Grading	100%	98%	95%	90%	80%	70%	60%

M1600R — same as M1600, except has stainless steel retractable butt stock and vent. barrel hood, 7¼ lbs. New 1986.

Mfg.'s Sug. Retail	$130	$115	$95	$75	$65	$50	$45	$40

M1600C — same as M1600, except has 20 in. barrel, fiberglass stock, barrel enclosing forearm, 7½ lbs. Mfg. 1986 only.

	$135	$115	$95	$85	$75	$65	$55

Last Mfg.'s Sug. Retail was $150.

M1600W — same as 1600C, except has wood stock. Mfg. 1986 only.

	$135	$115	$95	$85	$75	$65	$55

Last Mfg.'s Sug. Retail was $150.

M1800 — .22 Hornet, bolt action, 5 shot clip mag., 23 in. barrel, checkered mahogany stock with Monte Carlo cheek piece, 6½ lbs. A few samples mfg. 1986 only.

	$165	$145	$125	$110	$100	$90	$85

Last Mfg.'s Sug. Retail was $176.

MODEL M20P — .22 LR, semi-auto, 15 shot mag., 20¾ in. barrel, open sights, 5½ lbs. New 1986.

Mfg.'s Sug. Retail	$91	$80	$70	$60	$50	$45	$40	$35

Add $3 for Model M20PC.

Model M20C — similar to Model M20P, except has carbine style stock with barrel band and curved steel butt plate, 16½ in. barrel, 5¼ lbs. New 1990.

Mfg.'s Sug. Retail	$119	$100	$90	$75	$60	$50	$45	$40

MODEL M2000 — same specifications as Model M20P, except has checkered mahogany stock and adj. rear sight. Mfg. 1986 only.

	$85	$70	$60	$50	$45	$40	$35

Last Mfg.'s Sug. Retail was $99.

Model M2000SC (Super Classic) — similar to Model M2000, except has checkered American Walnut stock with cheek piece and hardwood forend tip, engine turned bolt, 6 lbs. New 1990.

Mfg.'s Sug. Retail	$244	$210	$180	$160	$140	$120	$100	$90

MODEL M-50 S — .22 LR, semi-auto design, 16½ in. shrouded barrel, 25 or 30 shot mag., uncheckered mahogany stock, 6½ lbs.

Mfg.'s Sug. Retail	$146	$125	$105	$90	$75	$65	$50	$45

This model was designated PPS-50 until 1991.

MODEL AK22 S — .22 LR, semi-auto, copy of the famous Russian Kalashnikov AK-47 rifle, 18½ in. barrel, 15 shot mag., mahogany stock and forearm, 7 lbs. New 1986.

Mfg.'s Sug. Retail	$162	$140	$120	$95	$85	$75	$65	$55

Model AK22 F — similar to Model AK22 S, except has metal folding stock. New 1989.

Mfg.'s Sug. Retail	$206	$175	$155	$135	$115	$100	$90	$80

SHOTGUNS

MODEL M30 D — 12 ga. only, slide action, 28 or 30 in. plain barrel, 6 shot mag., all steel receiver, checkered mahogany stock and forearm, 7.3 lbs. Imported 1986-89.

	$185	$155	$135	$115	$95	$85	$80

MODEL M30 IC (INTERCHANGEABLE CHOKES) — 12 ga. only, 28 in. plain barrel with choke tubes, 5 shot mag., uncheckered stock and forearm. New 1990.

Mfg.'s Sug. Retail	$208	$175	$155	$135	$115	$100	$90	$80

Model M30 D/IC (Deluxe) — similar to Model M30 IC, except has checkered mahogany stock.

Mfg.'s Sug. Retail	$206	$175	$155	$135	$115	$100	$90	$80

MODEL M30 DG (DEER GUN) — 12 ga. only, law enforcement version of Model M30, 20 in. plain barrel, iron sights, 7 shot mag., about 7 lbs. Introduced 1986.

Mfg.'s Sug. Retail	$174	$150	$130	$105	$95	$80	$70	$60

Grading	100%	98%	95%	90%	80%	70%	60%

MODEL M30 R (RIOT) — 12 ga. only, similar to Model M30DG, except has front bead sight only, 5 shot mag. New 1986.

Mfg.'s Sug. Retail	$174	$150	$130	$105	$95	$80	$70	$60

MODEL M30 K (COMBAT) — 12 ga., 21 in. barrel, 7 shot mag., combat olive green butt stock and forearm, 7.4 lbs. New 1990.

Mfg.'s Sug. Retail	$174	$150	$130	$105	$95	$80	$70	$60

MODEL M30 C (COMBO) — 12 ga., 20 in. barrel, 5 shot mag., unique detachable black synthetic butt stock that separates allowing pistol grip only operation. New 1990.

Mfg.'s Sug. Retail	$200	$175	$155	$135	$115	$100	$90	$80

MODEL M30 FS (FOLDING STOCK) — 12 ga., 20 in. barrel, 5 shot mag., features 3 piece matte black folding stock and grooved forearm, grooved pistol grip, 7 lbs. New 1990.

Mfg.'s Sug. Retail	$208	$175	$155	$135	$115	$100	$90	$80

MODEL M30 RP (COMBO) — 12 ga. only, same action as M30 DG, interchangeable black pistol grip, 18¼ in. plain barrel w/front bead sight, 6¼ lbs. Imported 1987-90.

	$175	$155	$135	$110	$95	$85	$80

Last Mfg.'s Sug. Retail was $210.

ARMS RESEARCH ASSOCIATES
Manufacturer located in Stone Park, IL.

KF SYSTEM — 9mm, paramilitary design carbine, 18½ in. barrel, vent barrel shroud, 20 or 36 shot mag., matte black finish, 7½ lbs., select fire-class III transferable only.

Mfg.'s Sug. Retail	$379	$340	$295	$275	$250	$230	$210	$195

ARMI TECNICHE OF EMILIO RIZZINI
Manufacturer located in Brescia, Italy.

This trademark has had limited importation to date and currently, there is no exclusive U.S. importer/distributor. Most Armi Techniche of E. Rizzini O/U shotguns that have been imported recently have sold in the $475-$695 range.

ARMSCORP OF AMERICA, INC.
Manufacturer/importer located in Baltimore, MD.

PISTOLS: SEMI-AUTO

HI POWER — 9mm, patterned after Browning design, 4⅔ in. barrel, military finish, 13 shot mag., synthetic checkered grips, spur hammer, 2 lbs. Imported 1989-90 only, mfg. in Argentina.

	$350	$295	$275	$250	$230	$215	$200

Add $15 for round hammer.

Add $50 for hard chrome finish w/combat grips (disc. 1989).

Last Mfg.'s Sug. Retail was $435.

Compact Detective HP — similar to Hi Power, except has 3½ in. barrel, 1.9 lbs. Mfg. 1989 only.

	$375	$325	$295	$275	$250	$225	$210

Last Mfg.'s Sug. Retail was $475.

SD-9 — 9mm Para., double action only, blowback mechanism, 3.07 in. barrel, 6 shot mag., frame is fabricated mostly of heavy gauge sheet metal stampings, chamber indicator, Israeli mfg., 1½ lbs. Imported 1989-90 only.

	$295	$250	$230	$210	$195	$180	$170

This pistol has also been manufactured by Sirkus Industries - refer to their section in this text.

Last Mfg.'s Sug. Retail was $350.

Grading	100%	98%	95%	90%	80%	70%	60%

P22 — .22 LR, patterned after the Colt Woodsman, 4 or 6 in. barrel, 10 shot mag., checkered wooden grips, mfg. in Argentina. Imported 1989-90 only.

	$190	$150	$130	$115	$100	$95	$85

Last Mfg.'s Sug. Retail was $225.

RIFLES: SEMI-AUTO

M-14RP — .308 cal., 20 shot mag., newly manufactured M-14 using original excellent condition forged G.I. parts including used fiberglass stock. New 1986.

Mfg.'s Sug. Retail	$938	$825	$700	$600	$525	$465	$420	$375

Add $125 for new walnut stock (Model M-14RNS).

Subtract approx. 25% for rifle mfg. from Norinco parts.

M-14 NATIONAL MATCH — .308 cal., built in accordance with A.M.T.U. MIL spec.'s, 3 different barrel weights to choose from, national match rear sight system, calibrated mag., leather sling. New 1987.

AMTU Model

Mfg.'s Sug. Retail	$1,875	$1,475	$1,275	$1,050	$950	$875	$795	$700

M21 Match Rifle

Mfg.'s Sug. Retail	$2,188	$1,875	$1,500	$1,150	$975	$875	$795	$725

T-48 FAL STANDARD RIFLE — .308 (7.62 NATO) cal., mfg. in the U.S. to precise original metric dimensions (parts are interchangeable with original Belgium FAL), forged receiver, hammer forged chrome lined Mil-spec. 21 in. barrel with flash surpressor, adj. front sight, aperture rear sight, 10 lbs. New 1990.

Mfg.'s Sug. Retail	$1,244	$1,075	$900	$775	$625	$525	$465	$425

This model is guaranteed to shoot within 2.5 MOA with match ammunition.

T-48 BUSH MODEL — similar to T-48 FAL, except has 18 in. barrel, 9¾ lbs. Mfg. 1990 only.

	$1,100	$925	$800	$650	$525	$465	$425

Last Mfg.'s Sug. Retail was $1,250.

FRHB — .308 (7.62 NATO) cal., Israeli mfg. with heavy barrel and bipod. Imported 1990 only.

	$1,725	$1,450	$1,150	$975	$875	$795	$725

Last Mfg.'s Sug. Retail was $1,895.

FAL — .308 cal., Armscorp forged receiver, 21 in. Argentinian rebuilt barrel, manufactured to military spec.'s, supplied with one military 20 shot mag., aperture rear sight, 10 lbs. Mfg. 1987-89.

	$850	$750	$600	$540	$465	$420	$375

Subtract $55 if without flash hider.

Add $75 for heavy barrel with bipod (14 lbs.).

Add $400 (last retail) for .22 LR conversion kit.

This model is guaranteed to shoot within 2.5 MOA with match ammunition.

Last Mfg.'s Sug. Retail was $875.

FAL Bush Model — similar to FAL, except has 18 in. barrel with flash suppressor, 9¾ lbs. Mfg. 1989 only.

	$875	$760	$625	$550	$465	$420	$375

Last Mfg.'s Sug. Retail was $900.

FAL Para Model — similar to FAL Bush Model, except has metal folding stock, leaf rear sight. Mfg. 1989 only.

	$900	$775	$635	$550	$465	$420	$375

Last Mfg.'s Sug. Retail was $930.

FAL Factory Rebuilt — factory (Argentine) rebuilt FAL without flash suppressor in excellent condition with Armscorp forged receiver, 9 lbs. 10 oz. Disc. 1989.

	$695	$625	$560	$520	$450	$400	$360

Last Mfg.'s Sug. Retail was $675.

M-21 — .308 (7.62 NATO) cal., semi-auto. New 1990.

Mfg.'s Sug. Retail	$2,188	$1,950	$1,675	$1,400	$1,150	$975	$875	$795

Grading	100%	98%	95%	90%	80%	70%	60%

M36 ISRAELI SNIPER RIFLE — .308 cal., gas operated semi-auto, Bullpup configuration, 22 in. free floating barrel, Armscorp M14 receiver, 20 shot mag., includes flash suppressor and bipod, 10 lbs. Civilian offering 1989 only.

	$2,900	$2,500	$2,275	$2,050	$1,900	$1,775	$1,600

Last Mfg.'s Sug. Retail was $3,000.

EXPERT MODEL — .22 LR, semi-auto, 20.9 in. barrel, 10 shot mag., wood stock with one - screw takedown, iron sights with grooved receiver, 5.1 lbs. New 1989.

Mfg.'s Sug. Retail	$225	$195	$150	$125	$115	$105	$95	$85

ARMSPORT

Current importer and distributor located in Miami, FL. Specializing in European manufacturers.

Armsport also imports black powder firearms. They are listed in the Black Powder section of this book.

COMBINATION GUNS

2781 AND 2782 — 12 ga./.222 cal., O/U turkey gun, blued receiver. Model 2782 has chrome receiver. Model 2782 was imported 1985 only. Model 2782 new 1985. Disc. 1989.

	$650	$550	$495	$440	$395	$350	$300

Last Mfg.'s Sug. Retail on Model 2781 was $650.

Last Mfg.'s Sug. Retail on Model 2782 was $750 (disc. 1989).

2783 — similar to Model 2782, except is deluxe model with lateral rib. Imported 1986-1988.

	$1,350	$1,075	$925	$820	$750	$680	$600

Last Mfg.'s Sug. Retail was $1,600.

2784 — same action as Model 2783, except is chambered for .243 Win. Imported 1986-1988.

	$1,350	$1,075	$925	$820	$750	$680	$600

Last Mfg.'s Sug. Retail was $1,600.

2785 — same action as Model 2783, except is chambered for .270 Win. Imported 1986-1988.

	$1,350	$1,075	$925	$820	$750	$680	$600

Last Mfg.'s Sug. Retail was $1,600.

2786 — 20 ga./.222 cal., O/U turkey gun, otherwise same specifications as Model 2783. Mfg. 1986 only.

	$1,350	$1,075	$925	$820	$750	$680	$600

Last Mfg.'s Sug. Retail was $1,350.

2787 — same as Model 2786, except is chambered for .243 Win. Mfg. 1986 only.

	$1,350	$1,075	$925	$820	$750	$680	$600

Last Mfg.'s Sug. Retail was $1,350.

2788 — same as Model 2786, except is chambered for .270 Win. Mfg. 1986 only.

	$1,350	$1,075	$925	$820	$750	$680	$600

Last Mfg.'s Sug. Retail was $1,350.

4043 — 12, 16, or 20 ga./rifle O/U combination gun, choice of caliber, select walnut, 23½ in. barrels, relief engraved. Disc. 1983.

	$1,675	$1,260	$1,090	$925	$840	$755	$670

4651 — Tikka deluxe O/U shotgun/rifle, exposed hammers, combo. 12 ga./.222. 12 ga. is chambered for 3 in. shells. Disc. 1984.

	$750	$565	$490	$415	$375	$340	$300

4690 — Tikka deluxe O/U shotgun/rifle, hammerless, combo 12 ga./.222. 12 ga. is chambered for 3 in. shells. Disc. 1984.

	$1,095	$820	$750	$700	$650	$575	$500

Grading	100%	98%	95%	90%	80%	70%	60%

RIFLES: BOLT-ACTION

2801 — .30-06 cal., 24 in. barrel, iron sights, checkered walnut stock and forearm. Imported 1986 only.

	$725	$600	$495	$430	$380	$335	$285

Last Mfg.'s Sug. Retail was $895.

2802 — same as Model 2801, except chambered for .308 cal.

	$725	$600	$495	$430	$380	$335	$285

Last Mfg.'s Sug. Retail was $895.

2803 — same as Model 2801, except chambered for .270 Win. cal.

	$725	$600	$495	$430	$380	$335	$285

Last Mfg.'s Sug. Retail was $895.

2804 — same as Model 2801, except chambered for .243 Win. cal.

	$725	$600	$495	$430	$380	$335	$285

Last Mfg.'s Sug. Retail was $895.

2805 — same as Model 2801, except chambered for 7mm Rem. Mag.

	$725	$600	$495	$430	$380	$335	$285

Last Mfg.'s Sug. Retail was $895.

2806 — same as Model 2801, except chambered for .300 Win. Mag.

	$725	$600	$495	$430	$380	$335	$285

4601, 4603, 4605, & 4606 — Tikka deluxe, .30-06 cal., bolt action. Model 4603 is .270 Win. Model 4605 is 7mm Rem. Model 4606 is 300 Win. Mag. Disc. 1984.

	$725	$545	$450	$380	$340	$295	$260

4602, 4604, & 4607 — Tikka deluxe .308 Win. bolt action. Model 4604 is .243 Win. Model 4607 .222 Rem. Disc. 1983.

	$675	$510	$450	$420	$390	$350	$310

RIFLES: DOUBLE & COMBINATION

4020 — Express set O/U double rifle with ejectors plus an extra set of O/U shotgun barrels. Disc. 1986.

	$3,850	$3,300	$2,860	$2,420	$2,200	$1,980	$1,760

Last Mfg.'s Sug. Retail was $4,400.

4021 — same combination as Model 4020, except rifle has extractors. Disc. 1986.

	$3,400	$2,910	$2,520	$2,135	$1,940	$1,745	$1,550

Last Mfg.'s Sug. Retail was $3,875.

4022 — Express O/U rifle only with ejectors, choice of calibers. Disc. 1986.

	$3,450	$2,945	$2,555	$2,160	$1,965	$1,770	$1,570

Last Mfg.'s Sug. Retail was $3,925.

4023 — same as Model 4022, except has extractors. Disc. 1986.

	$2,925	$2,515	$2,180	$1,845	$1,675	$1,510	$1,340

Last Mfg.'s Sug. Retail was $3,350.

4010 — Emperor SxS, double rifle with extra set of 20 ga. barrels and forearm. Completely hand made and finished using the best materials and craftsmen, choice of caliber, leather fitted case. Disc. 1983.

	$16,300	$12,225	$10,595	$8,965	$8,150	$7,335	$6,520

4011 — same as Model 4010, except rifle only, 9.3 x 74R cal. Disc. 1984.

	$12,750	$9,565	$8,290	$7,015	$6,375	$5,740	$5,100

4012 — Emperor "One-of-a-Kind" SxS rifle/shotgun set. Special engraving finishing per individual customer order, choice of gauges, calibers. Leather fitted case. Rare. Disc. 1983.

	$26,000	$19,500	$16,900	$14,300	$13,000	$11,700	$10,400

Grading	100%	98%	95%	90%	80%	70%	60%

4013 — same as Model 4012, but SxS double rifle only. Disc. 1983.

| | $22,850 | $17,140 | $14,855 | $12,570 | $11,425 | $10,285 | $9,140 |

RIFLES: LEVER-ACTION

4500 & 4501 — .44-40 cal., deluxe copy of Winchester Model 1873 Rifle, engraved. Model 4501 is .357 Mag. Model 4500 (.44-40) disc. in 1984. Model 4501 (.357 Mag.) disc. 1986.

| | $1,135 | $975 | $845 | $715 | $650 | $585 | $520 |

Last Mfg.'s Sug. Retail was $1,296.

4502 & 4503 — .44-40 cal., deluxe copy of Winchester Model 1873 Carbine, engraved. Model 4503 is .357 Mag. Model 4502 (.44-40) disc. in 1984. Model 4503 (.357 Mag.) disc. 1986.

| | $960 | $825 | $715 | $605 | $550 | $495 | $440 |

Last Mfg.'s Sug. Retail was $1,095.

4504 — .357 Mag., standard copy of Winchester Model 1873 carbine. Disc. 1986.

| | $555 | $470 | $410 | $345 | $315 | $285 | $250 |

Last Mfg.'s Sug. Retail was $625.

RIFLES: SEMI-AUTO

2785 & 2786 — .22 LR cal., semi-auto, 10 shot mag. Model 2786 is military type with 15 shot mag. Imported 1985 only.

| | $150 | $125 | $100 | $90 | $80 | $70 | $60 |

Last Mfg.'s Sug. Retail was $170.

SHOTGUNS: O/U

Armsport choking codes (on rear left of barrels) designate the following: * indicates full choke, ** identifies improved choking, *** refers to modified, **** is improved cylinder, ***** indicates cylinder bore.

The models listed below that have -3 suffixes indicate 1988 importation.

2528 — 12 ga., 3 in. Mag., 28 in. barrels, single trigger with auto ejectors. Disc. 1983.

| | $595 | $450 | $390 | $330 | $300 | $270 | $240 |

2626 — 20 ga., 3 in. Mag., 26 in. barrels, single trigger with auto ejectors. Disc. 1983.

| | $595 | $450 | $390 | $330 | $300 | $270 | $240 |

2697 & 2698 — 10 ga., 3½ in. Mag., similar to Models 2699 & 2700 except have 3 screw in choke tubes, Model 2698 has 32 in barrels. New 1989.

| Mfg.'s Sug. Retail | $1,295 | $1,100 | $850 | $675 | $575 | $520 | $495 | $475 |

2699/2700C & 2700 — 10 ga., 3½ in. Mag., 27 (2699 - new 1989), 28 (2700C), or 32 (2700) in. barrels with 12mm vent rib, extractors, DT's. New 1986.

| Mfg.'s Sug. Retail | $1,175 | $995 | $775 | $625 | $550 | $475 | $430 | $395 |

2700B — similar to Model 2700, except has deluxe walnut (32 in. barrels only). Mfg. 1987 only.

| | $660 | $575 | $480 | $430 | $395 | $370 | $350 |

Last Mfg.'s Sug. Retail was $795.

2701/2702 & 2703/2704 — 12 and 20 ga., 3 in. Mag., 26 and 28 in. barrels, double triggers, extractors. Disc. 1985, and reintroduced 1989.

| Mfg.'s Sug. Retail | $650 | $550 | $450 | $375 | $295 | $265 | $230 | $200 |

2705 — .410 ga., double triggers, 26 in. barrels, bored F & F, extractors. Importation began 1986.

| Mfg.'s Sug. Retail | $750 | $650 | $525 | $425 | $350 | $300 | $275 | $235 |

2706 — 12 ga. only, law enforcement model, 20 in. barrels, double triggers, extractors. Imported 1986 only.

| | $330 | $280 | $260 | $240 | $220 | $200 | $185 |

Last Mfg.'s Sug. Retail was $375.

Grading	100%	98%	95%	90%	80%	70%	60%

2707 — 28 ga., otherwise similar to Model 2705. New 1990.

Mfg.'s Sug. Retail	$750	$650	$525	$425	$350	$300	$275	$235

2708 — 12 ga. only, slug gun, 23 in. barrels, single trigger, ejectors. Importation began 1986.

Mfg.'s Sug. Retail	$800	$665	$550	$450	$385	$325	$300	$280

A Model 2708-3 was mfg. 1986-1989. This variation had 20 in. barrels, double triggers, and extractors. Values of this earlier variation will be approx. 30-40% less than listed above.

2711, 2713-3, 2721, & 2723 — 12 or 20 ga., 3 in. Mag., 26 or 28 in. barrels, extractors. Models 2721 and 2723 have ejectors and were disc. 1985. Models 2711 and 2713-3 were disc. 1989.

	$445	$385	$340	$310	$275	$250	$230

Add 25% with ejectors.

Last Mfg.'s Sug. Retail was $375 on Models 2721/2723.

Last Mfg.'s Sug. Retail was $535 on Models 2711/2713-3.

2717, 2719, 2720, & 2725 — 12 (Model 2717), 20 (Model 2719), 28 (Model 2725 - new 1990), or .410 (Model 2720) ga., 3 in. Mag. (except Model 2725), 26 or 28 in. barrels, SST.

Mfg.'s Sug. Retail	$735	$625	$525	$450	$385	$325	$300	$280

Add $65 for 28 or .410 ga.

2712, 2714-3, 2722, & 2724 — 12 or 20 ga., 3 in. Mag., 26 or 28 in. barrels. Models 2712 and 2722 are 12 ga., engraved with 12mm vent rib. Models 2722 and 2724 have ejectors. Importation of Models 2712, 2722, and 2724 were disc. 1986. Model 2714-3 was disc. 1988.

	$500	$395	$350	$300	$275	$235	$200

Last Mfg.'s Sug. Retail was $615 on Model 2714-3.

Last Mfg.'s Sug. Retail was $395 on Models 2712/2722/2724.

2715-3 & 2716-3 — 12 ga. only, 28 in. barrels with 3 choke tubes, auto ejectors, single trigger. Imported 1988 only.

	$575	$465	$400	$350	$295	$265	$245

Last Mfg.'s Sug. Retail was $680.

2718, 2733, & 2735 — 12 and 20 ga., 3 in. Mag., 26 and 28 in. barrels, SST, extractors. Models 2733/2735 have deluxe Boss actions. Model 2718 was disc. 1985.

Mfg.'s Sug. Retail	$750	$630	$530	$450	$385	$325	$300	$280

Last Mfg.'s Sug. Retail was $390 on Model 2718.

2734 & 2736 Sporting Clays — 12 (2734) or 20 (2736) ga., similar to Models 2733 and 2735, except has 3 choke tubes.

Mfg.'s Sug. Retail	$850	$695	$560	$450	$385	$325	$300	$280

2745, 2746 & 2747 — 12 ga., 3½ in. chambers, 24 (2745), 27/28 (2746) or 31/32 (2747) in. barrels with wide rib and 3 choke tubes, auto extractors, Boss type action. New 1989.

Mfg.'s Sug. Retail	$850	$695	$560	$450	$385	$325	$300	$280

Add $15 for 31/32 in. barrels.

These models are mfg. by Armi Techniche of Emilio Rizzini located in Italy.

2726, 2728, 2742, & 2744 — 12 and 20 ga., 3 in. Mag., 26 and 28 in. barrels, SST, ejectors. Models 2726 & 2728 were disc. 1985.

Mfg.'s Sug. Retail	$900	$725	$585	$475	$400	$350	$315	$290

Last Mfg.'s Sug. Retail on Models 2726 & 2728 was $440.

2727-3 & 2729-3 — 1986 designations for Models 2726 & 2728 respectively. -3 suffixes indicate 1988 designations. Importation disc. 1988.

	$550	$450	$385	$330	$295	$265	$245

Last Mfg.'s Sug. Retail was $615.

2727 & 2729 — 12 (Model 2727) or 20 (Model 2729) ga., field model, boxlock action, 26 or 28 in. barrels with wide rib and fixed chokes. New 1990.

Mfg.'s Sug. Retail	$830	$680	$560	$450	$385	$325	$300	$280

These models have evolved from Models 2726/2728 and Models 2727-3 and 2729-3.

Grading	100%	98%	95%	90%	80%	70%	60%

2730 — 12 ga., skeet gun, 27 in. barrel, has six interchangeable chokes, Boss-type action.

Mfg.'s Sug. Retail	$1,010	$795	$650	$550	$495	$450	$425	$395

These models are mfg. by Armi Techniche of Emilio Rizzini located in Italy.

2731 — same as Model 2730, except is 20 ga. and has 26 in. barrels.

Mfg.'s Sug. Retail	$1,010	$800	$675	$565	$525	$465	$435	$400

2732 & 2732/3 — 12 ga. only, competition trap model, 30 in. barrel. New 1990.

Mfg.'s Sug. Retail	$1,150	$925	$700	$600	$525	$470	$440	$415

Add $100 for Model 2732/3.

These two models are mfg. by Emilio Rizzini located in Italy.

2741 & 2743 — 12 (Model 2741) or 20 (Model 2743) ga., field model, 26 or 28 in. barrels with wide rib and fixed chokes, Boss type action. New 1990.

Mfg.'s Sug. Retail	$810	$660	$550	$450	$385	$325	$300	$280

These models are mfg. by Armi Techniche of Emilio Rizzini located in Italy.

2750 & 2751 — 12 (Model 2750) or 20 (Model 2751) ga., Sporting Clays configuration, 26 or 28 in. barrels with 5 choke tubes, includes engraved sideplates. New 1990.

Mfg.'s Sug. Retail	$1,035	$825	$675	$575	$525	$475	$445	$400

2760 — 12 ga., tournament trap model with choke tubes. Mfg. by Ferlib beginning 1991.

Mfg.'s Sug. Retail	$1,795	$1,550	$1,250	$1,000	$800	$675	$600	$540

2763 — 12 ga., sporting clays configuration, includes 5 choke tubes, mfg. by Ferlib in Italy - importation began in 1991.

Mfg.'s Sug. Retail	$1,825	$1,565	$1,250	$1,000	$800	$675	$600	$540

2765 — similar to Model 2763, except is 20 ga. with 26 in. barrels. Importation began in 1991.

Mfg.'s Sug. Retail	$2,000	$1,700	$1,350	$1,100	$850	$700	$625	$550

4014 — Emperor Grade SxS. Individually fitted per customer H&H type action, engraved, fitted leather case, choice of gauge, barrel lengths, etc. Completely hand finished.

	$9,175	$6,885	$5,965	$5,050	$4,590	$4,130	$3,670

Emperor Grade models are disc. Limited availability.

4015 — Emperor "One-of-a-Kind" SxS. Similar to Model 4014, except that every part of the gun is made per customer order. Specifications including style of engraving, dimensions, wood configuration, special requests, etc. No expense spared. Disc. 1984.

	$18,000	$13,500	$11,700	$9,900	$9,000	$8,100	$7,200

4016 — Emperor SxS with outside hammers, fitted leather case, extensively engraved, any gauge. Disc. 1983.

	$4,550	$3,415	$2,960	$2,505	$2,275	$2,050	$1,820

4017 — Emperor "One-of-a-Kind" SxS with outside hammers. Flexibility of options is similar to Model 4015. Disc. 1984.

	$12,750	$9,565	$8,290	$7,015	$6,375	$5,740	$5,100

4030 & 4031 — 12 ga. SxS, Holland-style detachable locks, English walnut, ejectors, engraved. Model 4031 is 20 ga. Disc. 1983.

	$3,950	$2,965	$2,570	$2,175	$1,975	$1,780	$1,580

4032 & 4033 — 12 ga. Premier Mono Trap Gun, 32 in. barrel, ejector. Model 4033 is same, except for 34 in. barrel. Disc. 1986.

	$1,810	$1,560	$1,350	$1,145	$1,040	$935	$830

Last Mfg.'s Sug. Retail was $2,075.

4034 & 4035 — 12 ga. Premier Mono Trap Set, 32 in. single, 30 in. O/U. Model 4035 is same, except has 34 in. single, 32 in. O/U. Disc. 1986.

	$2,565	$2,215	$1,920	$1,625	$1,475	$1,330	$1,180

Last Mfg.'s Sug. Retail was $2,950.

Grading	100%	98%	95%	90%	80%	70%	60%

4040 — 12 ga. Slug Special SxS, 23 in. barrels. Disc. 1984.

	100%	98%	95%	90%	80%	70%	60%
	$1,325	$995	$865	$730	$665	$600	$530

4046 & 4047 — 12 ga. trap gun, 34 in. barrel, extra trigger mechanism. Model 4047 is 32 in. Disc. 1986.

	100%	98%	95%	90%	80%	70%	60%
	$2,860	$2,460	$2,100	$1,850	$1,700	$1,500	$1,300

Last Mfg.'s Sug. Retail was $3,275.

4050 — Pigeon Grade O/U, 12 ga., engraved. Disc. 1986.

	100%	98%	95%	90%	80%	70%	60%
	$2,375	$2,025	$1,755	$1,485	$1,350	$1,215	$1,080

Last Mfg.'s Sug. Retail was $2,700.

4055 & 4056 — Premier Skeet 12 ga., selective trigger, ejectors, engraved, select wood. Model 4056 is 20 ga. Disc. 1983.

	100%	98%	95%	90%	80%	70%	60%
	$2,000	$1,500	$1,300	$1,100	$1,000	$900	$800

4061 & 4062 — .410 ga. SxS, single trigger, selective ejectors. Model 4062 is 28 ga. Disc. 1983.

	100%	98%	95%	90%	80%	70%	60%
	$995	$750	$650	$550	$500	$450	$400

4063 & 4064 — .410 ga. O/U, single trigger, selective ejectors. Model 4064 is 28 ga. Disc. 1983.

	100%	98%	95%	90%	80%	70%	60%
	$995	$750	$650	$550	$500	$450	$400

SHOTGUNS: REPEATING

2755 — 12 ga., 7 shot, Atis mfg., black anodized receiver, 24 or 28 in. barrel with VR. Mfg. 1985-87 only.

	100%	98%	95%	90%	80%	70%	60%
	$335	$260	$225	$195	$180	$160	$145

Last Mfg.'s Sug. Retail was $395.

2755A — same as Model 2755, except has 30 in. barrel. Mfg. 1986-87 only.

	100%	98%	95%	90%	80%	70%	60%
	$335	$260	$225	$195	$180	$160	$145

2756 — 12 ga., 28 in. VR barrel, 3 interchangeable chokes. Mfg. 1986-87 only.

	100%	98%	95%	90%	80%	70%	60%
	$390	$335	$280	$230	$205	$190	$175

Last Mfg.'s Sug. Retail was $465.

2756A — same as Model 2756, except has 30 in. vent rib barrel. Mfg. 1986-87 only.

	100%	98%	95%	90%	80%	70%	60%
	$390	$335	$280	$230	$205	$190	$175

Last Mfg.'s Sug. Retail was $465.

2757 — 12 ga. only, law enforcement model, 20 in. barrel, black receiver. Mfg. 1986-87 only.

	100%	98%	95%	90%	80%	70%	60%
	$310	$250	$205	$190	$175	$155	$140

Last Mfg.'s Sug. Retail was $375.

2766, 2767, & 2768 — 12 ga., Fabarms mfg., 25 in. barrel. Model 2768 has 20 in. barrel. Imported 1985 only.

	100%	98%	95%	90%	80%	70%	60%
	$260	$220	$200	$180	$160	$140	$120

Last Mfg.'s Sug. Retail was $300.

SHOTGUNS: SEMI-AUTO

2751 — 12 ga., 3 in. Mag., semi-auto, Atis mfg., black anodized receiver, 28 in. barrel. Mfg. 1985-87 only.

	100%	98%	95%	90%	80%	70%	60%
	$430	$340	$310	$285	$255	$230	$200

Last Mfg.'s Sug. Retail was $575.

2751A — same as Model 2751, except has 30 in. full choke barrel. Mfg. 1986-87 only.

	100%	98%	95%	90%	80%	70%	60%
	$430	$340	$310	$285	$255	$230	$200

Last Mfg.'s Sug. Retail was $575.

2752 — same action as Model 2751, except chrome receiver and engraving. Mfg. 1986-87 only.

	100%	98%	95%	90%	80%	70%	60%
	$440	$345	$310	$285	$255	$230	$200

Last Mfg.'s Sug. Retail was $600.

Grading	100%	98%	95%	90%	80%	70%	60%

2752A — same as Model 2752, except has 30 in. barrel. Mfg. 1986-87 only.

	$440	$345	$310	$285	$255	$230	$200

Last Mfg.'s Sug. Retail was $600.

2753 — same action as Model 2751, except has 28 in. barrel with 3 interchangeable chokes. Mfg. 1986-87 only.

	$460	$355	$315	$285	$255	$230	$200

Last Mfg.'s Sug. Retail was $650.

2753A — same as Model 2753, except has chrome receiver and engraving. Mfg. 1986-87 only.

	$470	$365	$320	$285	$255	$230	$200

Last Mfg.'s Sug. Retail was $675.

2761 & 2762 — 12 ga., black or chrome receiver, Fabarms made, engraved action, 27 in. barrel. Add $75 for interchangeable choke tubes. Imported during 1985 only.

	$410	$360	$315	$295	$270	$245	$215

Last Mfg.'s Sug. Retail was $475.

SHOTGUNS: SINGLE AND SIDE-BY-SIDE

1033 — 10 ga. SxS, 3½ in. Mag., 32 in. full and full chokes. Disc. 1985.

	$395	$340	$315	$275	$250	$225	$200

Last Mfg.'s Sug. Retail was $450.

1050-1 — 1986 designation for the Model 1051. -1 suffix designates 1988 and later importation.

Mfg.'s Sug. Retail	$760	$635	$530	$450	$385	$325	$300	$280

1051 & 1052 — 12 ga. SxS, 3 in. Mag., 28 in. mod. & full chokes. Model 1052 is 20 ga., 3 in. Mag., 26 in. Imp. & Mod. Disc. 1985.

	$330	$280	$260	$240	$225	$205	$180

Last Mfg.'s Sug. Retail was $375.

1053-1 — 1986 designation for the Model 1052. -1 suffix designates 1988 and later importation.

Mfg.'s Sug. Retail	$760	$635	$530	$450	$385	$325	$300	$280

1054-1 & 1055-1 — .410 (1054) or .28 (1055) ga. -1 suffix designates 1988 and later importation.

Mfg.'s Sug. Retail	$860	$700	$600	$500	$450	$400	$365	$330

1055 & 1057 — 28 and .410 ga. SxS, 3 in. Mag., 26 in. barrel, Imp. and Mod. chokes. Model 1057 is 28 ga., 3 in. Mag., 26 in. Imp. & Mod. Disc. 1985.

	$330	$280	$260	$240	$225	$205	$180

Last Mfg.'s Sug. Retail was $375.

Model 1057 was redesignated 1055 in 1985 and Model 1055 was changed to 1054.

1101, 1102, 1103, & 1104 — 12 ga., folding single barrel w/vent rib. Model 1102 is 20 ga. Model 1103 is .410 ga. Model 1104 is 28 ga. Disc. 1985.

	$125	$105	$90	$75	$70	$65	$60

Last Mfg.'s Sug. Retail was $140.

1107 & 1108 — 12 ga., folding single barrel 19 in., pistol grip. Model 1108 is 20 ga. Disc. 1983.

	$135	$105	$95	$85	$75	$70	$65

1125, 1126, & 1127 — 12 or 20 ga., single barrel, 3 in. chamber, bottom lever opening, Model 1127 is 20 ga. New 1987.

Mfg.'s Sug. Retail	$90	$75	$55	$50	$45	$40	$35	$30

The Model 1125 was disc. 1989.

1128 — .410 ga., otherwise similar to Models 1125/1126/1127. Importation disc. 1990.

	$75	$55	$50	$45	$40	$35	$30

Last Mfg.'s Sug. Retail was $90.

Grading	100%	98%	95%	90%	80%	70%	60%

1212 & 1213 — 12 ga., SxS, outside hammers, engraved action, 20 in. barrels. Model 1213 is 20 ga. Disc. 1983.

	$450	$340	$295	$250	$225	$205	$180

1225 — 12 ga. only, O/U configuration, folding action, top lever break. Mfg. 1986-87 only.

	$275	$235	$200	$185	$170	$165	$150

Last Mfg.'s Sug. Retail was $345.

1226 — 20 ga. only, O/U configuration, folding action, top lever break. Mfg. 1986-87 only.

	$275	$235	$200	$185	$170	$165	$150

Last Mfg.'s Sug. Retail was $345.

SHOTGUNS: TRI-BARREL

MODEL 2900 TRILLING — 12 ga., 3 barrel shotgun with 28 in. barrels bored F & M or choke tubes over IC/choke tubes. Importation began 1986-87 and was resumed in 1990.

Mfg.'s Sug. Retail	$3,400	$2,900	$2,375	$2,000	$1,650	$1,400	$1,200	$995

Subtract 25% for fixed chokes (1986-87 mfg.).

This model was re-introduced in 1990 and includes choke tubes on all 3 barrels.

ARRIETA, S.L.

Manufacturer located in Elgoibar, Spain. Currently imported by several importers including Morton's Limited, Quality Arms, New England Arms, Griffin & Howe, Orvis (catalog sales), and Jack Jansma.

Prices could differ from values shown below because of the fluctuating U.S. dollar.

More information can be obtained on Arietta by either contacting the factory or the above listed importers.

SHOTGUNS: DISCONTINUED SxS

Values listed below are for 12 or 16 ga. Add 10% for either 20, 28 or .410 ga. Also add 10% for matched pair.

490 EDER — 12, 16, or 20 ga., boxlock, double triggers, extractors, light engraving. Disc. 1986.

	$475	$405	$350	$300	$270	$245	$220

Last Mfg.'s Sug. Retail was $540.

500 TITAN — 12, 16, or 20 ga., Purdey type action with H&H pattern double safety sidelocks, satin receiver engraved, double triggers, extractors. Disc. 1986.

	$575	$495	$430	$365	$330	$300	$265

Last Mfg.'s Sug. Retail was $660.

501 PALOMERA — 12, 16, or 20 ga., same action as 500, fine border engraving, blued or casehardened action. Disc. 1986.

	$680	$570	$495	$420	$380	$345	$305

Last Mfg.'s Sug. Retail was $760.

505 ALASKA — 12, 16, or 20 ga., same action as 501, blued action extensively engraved. Disc. 1986.

	$750	$645	$560	$475	$430	$390	$345

Last Mfg.'s Sug. Retail was $860.

SHOTGUNS: CURRENT SxS

The models listed below are essentially custom ordered per individual specifications - delivery time is approx. 9 months (12 months for small gauges).

All Arrieta shotguns have frames scaled to individual guages. Various special options are available by custom order, and a few are listed below. On the models listed below, there are 4 qualities of action. Fourth quality is used on the Model 550. Third quality is used on Models 557-588. Second quality is used on Models 590 and 595 (designed for heavy use). First quality is used on Models 600-903, except for Model 900 (557 action).

Grading	100%	98%	95%	90%	80%	70%	60%

ADD THE FOLLOWING AMOUNTS FOR CURRENTLY MANUFACTURED SHOTGUNS.
Add 10% for small gauges (20, 28, or .410).
Add approx. $750 for single trigger depending on action.
Add 10% for matched pair.
Add 10% for rounded action on standard models.
Extra barrels are priced from $975-$1,600/set depending on model.

510 MONTANA — 12, 16, or 20 ga., H&H-type sidelocks, all inner parts gold-plated.

Mfg.'s Sug. Retail	$2,350	$2,350	$1,725	$1,350	$1,000	$800	$675	$615

550 FIELD — 12, 16, or 20 ga., best hand fitted double safety Holland-type sidelocks, hand detachable, blue finish, moderate engraving.

Mfg.'s Sug. Retail	$2,350	$2,350	$1,725	$1,350	$1,000	$800	$675	$615

557 STANDARD — 12, 16, or 20 ga., Demi-Bloc steel barrels, detachable engraved sidelocks, double triggers, ejectors.

Mfg.'s Sug. Retail	$2,650	$2,650	$1,850	$1,425	$1,100	$900	$750	$640

558 PATRIA — 12, 16, or 20 ga., same as 557, except frame, tangs, and sidelocks 100% engraved.

Mfg.'s Sug. Retail	$2,850	$2,850	$1,950	$1,475	$1,125	$900	$750	$640

560 CUMBRE — 12, 16, or 20 ga., same as 558, except is more elaborately engraved.

Mfg.'s Sug. Retail	$3,050	$3,050	$2,100	$1,575	$1,200	$950	$800	$700

570 LIEJA — 12, 16, or 20 ga., same as 560, except has non-detachable sidelocks.

Mfg.'s Sug. Retail	$3,275	$3,275	$2,250	$1,725	$1,325	$1,075	$850	$750

575 SPORT — 12, 16, or 20 ga., same as 560, except is more elaborately engraved.

Mfg.'s Sug. Retail	$3,300	$3,300	$2,275	$1,725	$1,325	$1,075	$850	$750

578 VICTORIA — 12, 16, or 20 ga., same as 570 except is fine English scrollwork engraved.

Mfg.'s Sug. Retail	$3,600	$3,600	$2,425	$1,775	$1,375	$1,100	$925	$850

585 LIRIA — 12, 16, or 20 ga., same as 575, except has profuse engraving.

Mfg.'s Sug. Retail	$4,100	$4,100	$2,775	$2,200	$1,875	$1,550	$1,250	$1,025

588 CIMA — similar to M585 Liria, except has more engraving.

Mfg.'s Sug. Retail	$4,200	$4,200	$2,825	$2,250	$1,900	$1,575	$1,250	$1,025

590 REGINA — 12, 16, or 20 ga., same as 570, except has more profuse engraving.

Mfg.'s Sug. Retail	$4,350	$4,350	$2,900	$2,275	$1,925	$1,600	$1,275	$1,050

595 PRINCIPE — all gauges, sidelock action, relief engraved hunting scenes, ejectors, DT's.

Mfg.'s Sug. Retail	$6,600	$6,600	$4,700	$3,950	$3,400	$2,925	$2,500	$2,000

600 IMPERIAL — 12, 16, or 20 ga., top-of-the-line self-opening action, very ornate engraving throughout.

Mfg.'s Sug. Retail	$5,800	$5,800	$4,100	$3,700	$3,150	$2,750	$2,400	$1,950

600-1 IMPERIAL — 12, 16, or 20 ga., similar to 600 Imperial, except has light border engraving around sidelocks, tangs, trigger guard. Importation disc. 1988.

	$4,600	$3,825	$3,500	$3,175	$2,835	$2,460	$2,000

Last Mfg.'s Sug. Retail was $5,380.

601 TIRO — all gauges, sidelock action with nickle plating, ejectors, SST, self-opening action, border engraving.

Mfg.'s Sug. Retail	$6,850	$6,850	$4,825	$4,000	$3,400	$2,950	$2,500	$2,000

801 — all gauges, Holland-style detachable sidelocks, self-opening action, ejectors, coin-wash finish, finest Churchill style engraving.

Mfg.'s Sug. Retail	$9,800	$9,800	$7,100	$6,000	$5,100	$4,600	$4,000	$3,450

Model's 801 through 875 are also available with self-opening actions as an option — add $800.

Grading	100%	98%	95%	90%	80%	70%	60%

802 — 12, 16, or 20 ga., similar to 801 only non-detachable sidelocks, finest Holland-style engraving.

Mfg.'s Sug. Retail $9,800 $9,800 $7,100 $6,000 $5,100 $4,600 $4,000 $3,450

803 — all gauges, similar to 801, finest Purdey-style engraving.

Mfg.'s Sug. Retail $6,600 $6,600 $4,700 $3,950 $3,400 $2,925 $2,500 $2,000

863 DUNN'S FINE GRADE — all gauges, sidelock, special model for American upland hunter, level rib, scroll engraved, this model sold exclusively through Dunn's.

Add 10% for 20, 28, or .410 ga.

This model has been redesignated the Model 900.

Mfg.'s suggested retail price is $1,995.

871 — all gauges, rounded frame sidelock action with Demi-Block barrels, scroll engraved, ejectors, DT's.

Mfg.'s Sug. Retail $4,650 $4,650 $3,200 $2,650 $2,150 $1,750 $1,450 $1,275

872 — all gauges, rounded frame sidelock action with Demi-Block barrels, elaborate scroll engraving with third lever fastener.

Mfg.'s Sug. Retail $11,400 $11,400 $8,500 $7,250 $5,950 $5,200 $4,400 $3,600

873 — all gauges, sidelock action with Demi-Block barrels, game scene engraving, ejectors, SST.

Mfg.'s Sug. Retail $6,875 $6,875 $4,825 $4,000 $3,400 $2,950 $2,500 $2,000

874 — all gauges, sidelock action with Demi-Block barrels, action is gold line engraved.

Mfg.'s Sug. Retail $8,500 $8,500 $6,100 $4,750 $3,850 $3,425 $3,000 $2,600

875 — all gauges, top-of-the-line quality, built to individual customer spec.'s only, elaborate engraving with gold inlays.

Mfg.'s Sug. Retail $15,000 $15,000 $10,750 $8,950 $7,850 $6,850 $5,900 $4,950

SHOTGUNS: 900 SERIES

The 900 series is made exculsively for Morton's Limited and replaces the 600 and 800 series guns in 1988.

Add $1,950 retail for self-opening action on the 900 series.

900 — all gauges, sidelock, Purdey style scroll engraving, sold exclusively through Dunn's/Jaeger Inc.

Mfg.'s Sug. Retail $2,400 $2,400 $1,800 $1,400 $1,050 $800 $675 $615

This model is sold by Dunn's and is designated the Fine Grade.

901 — all gauges, sidelock, Churchill style engraving, best quality.

Mfg.'s Sug. Retail $8,575 $8,575 $6,125 $4,800 $3,850 $3,425 $3,000 $2,600

902 — all gauges, sidelock, Holland & Holland style engraving, best quality.

Mfg.'s Sug. Retail $8,575 $8,575 $6,125 $4,800 $3,850 $3,425 $3,000 $2,600

903 — all gauges, sidelock, Purdey style engraving, best quality.

Mfg.'s Sug. Retail $4,500 $4,500 $3,675 $3,050 $2,550 $2,155 $1,825 $1,655

This model is sold through Dunn's located in Grand Junction, TN and is designated the Best Grade.

904 — all gauges, sidelock, rounded frame, scroll engraving, best quality. Disc. 1989.

                 $6,900 $5,700 $4,400 $3,750 $3,350 $3,000 $2,600

Last Mfg.'s Sug. Retail was $7,850.

905 — all gauges, sidelock, scroll engraving with game scenes cameos. Disc. 1989.

                 $7,400 $5,900 $4,500 $3,800 $3,400 $3,000 $2,600

Last Mfg.'s Sug. Retail was $8,325.

Grading	100%	98%	95%	90%	80%	70%	60%

906 — all gauges, sidelock, border engraving, special field gun available for either lead or steel shot. Disc. 1989.

$2,100	$1,700	$1,375	$1,050	$850	$675	$615

Last Mfg.'s Sug. Retail was $2,450.

907 — all gauges, sidelock, Purdey style engraving, special field gun available for either lead or steel shot. Disc. 1989.

$3,450	$2,700	$2,225	$1,900	$1,600	$1,275	$1,050

Last Mfg.'s Sug. Retail was $4,000.

908 — all gauges, sidelock, Purdey style engraving. Disc. 1989.

$3,475	$2,700	$2,225	$1,900	$1,600	$1,275	$1,050

Last Mfg.'s Sug. Retail was $4,020.

909 — all gauges, sidelock, round frame, large scroll engraving. Disc. 1989.

$3,900	$3,000	$2,500	$2,100	$1,775	$1,550	$1,300

Last Mfg.'s Sug. Retail was $4,500.

ARRIZABLAGA

Manufacturer located in Eibar, Spain since 1940. Morton's Limited located in Lexington, KY has imported this trademark on a limited basis in the past.

More information can be obtained on Arrizablaga by contacting the factory directly (refer to Trademark Index).

The models listed below are essentially custom ordered per individual specifications - delivery time is approx. 9 months (12 months for small gauges).

ADD THE FOLLOWING AMOUNTS ON ARRIZABLAGA SHOTGUNS:

All Arrizablaga shotguns have self-opening (assisted) actions.

Add 10% for matched pair.

Add $2,630 (retail) for extra barrels.

Add $448 for 28 ga.

Add $1,146 for .410 ga.

Add $1,095 for single trigger.

Add $235 for pistol grip stock.

HEAVY SCROLL MODEL — 12, 16, or 20 ga., sidelock action, elaborate engraving, deluxe oil finished stock and forearm.

Mfg.'s Sug. Retail	$8,674	$8,674	$6,150	$5,400	$4,750	$4,300	$3,850	$3,325

ENGLISH SCROLL MODEL — 12, 16, or 20 ga., sidelock action, English scroll engraving, deluxe oil finished walnut stock and forearm.

Mfg.'s Sug. Retail	$9,140	$9,140	$6,500	$5,650	$4,950	$4,500	$4,000	$3,450

SPECIAL MODEL — 12, 16, or 20 ga., sidelock top of the line model, best quality wood and engraving.

Mfg.'s Sug. Retail	$13,694	$13,694	$8,975	$8,200	$7,400	$6,600	$5,900	$4,950

ASTRA

Manufactured by Unceta Y Cia., Guernica, Spain. Currently imported by Interarms located in Alexandria, VA.

PISTOLS: CURRENT MANUFACTURE

CONSTABLE — double action, .22 LR (10 shot, disc. in 1990.), .32 auto (8 shot, disc. 1984), .380 ACP (7 shot), exposed hammer, 3½ in. barrel, fixed sight, 28 or 40 (.380 ACP) oz., blue or chrome (disc.) finish, plastic grips. Mfg. 1965-present.

Mfg.'s Sug. Retail	$380	$310	$250	$210	$180	$165	$150	$135

Add $10 for chrome finish or wood grips (disc. in 1990).

Grading	100%	98%	95%	90%	80%	70%	60%

Constable Stainless — .380 ACP only, stainless version of the Constable. Mfg. 1986 only.

	$350	$300	$240	$220	$200	$175	$150

Last Mfg.'s Sug. Retail was $345.

Constable Sport — same as Constable, except has 6 in. barrel, blue finish only, 35 oz. Mfg. 1986-87 only.

	$325	$245	$210	$180	$165	$150	$135

Last Mfg.'s Sug. Retail was $330.

Blue Engraved Constable — blue engraved. Importation disc. 1987.

	$375	$295	$250

Add $20 for .22 LR or checkered wood grips.
Last Mfg.'s Sug. Retail was $375.

Chrome Engraved Constable — chrome engraved. Importation disc. 1987.

	$350	$295	$250

Add $20 for .22 LR or checkered wood grips.
Last Mfg.'s Sug. Retail was $390.

CONSTABLE A-60 — .380 ACP, double action, 3½ in. barrel, 13 shot mag., ambidextrous safety, adj. rear sight, blue finish only. New 1986.

Mfg.'s Sug. Retail	$475	$395	$325	$280	$245	$220	$185	$160

MODEL A-80 — 9mm Para, .38 Super (disc.) or .45 ACP cal., double action, semi-auto, 15 shot mag. (9 for .45 ACP), 3¾ in. barrel. Imported 1982-89.

	$370	$320	$285	$265	$240	$210	$185

Add $35 for chrome finish (disc.).
.38 Super cal. in chrome finish will command a premium (10%-20%).
Last Mfg.'s Sug. Retail was $425.

MODEL A-90 — 9mm Para. or .45 ACP cal., 1986 designation for Model A-80 with updated slide mounted safety and pushbutton mag. release, 3¾ in. barrel, 15 shot mag. (9mm) or 9 shot (.45 ACP), blue only, 48 oz. Imported 1986-90, replaced by Model A-100.

	$400	$340	$300	$275	$245	$225	$200

Last Mfg.'s Sug. Retail was $500.

Model A-100 — replaced the Model A-90 in 1990, with similar specifications.

Mfg.'s Sug. Retail	$540	$430	$350	$300	$265	$245	$225	$200

MODEL 4000 FALCON — .22 LR, .32 ACP, or .380 ACP cal., 4 in. barrel, fixed sights, blue, plastic grips, exposed hammer. Mfg. 1956-1986.

	$450	$400	$330	$260	$235	$200	$150

Add 50% for .22 cal.
Add 100% for engraved M-4000.
Last Mfg.'s Sug. Retail was $340.

Model 4000 Tri-cal. Kit — includes .22 LR, .32 ACP, and .380 ACP cal.'s, either rust blued or salt blued finish, less than 200 mfg. Boxed.

	$1,100	$875	$750

PISTOLS: DISCONTINUED

MODEL 1911 — .25 ACP or .32 ACP cal., semi-auto, may have external or internal hammer.

	$300	$200	$155	$135	$125	$110	$100

Add 20% if with external hammer.

MODEL 1915/1916 — .32 ACP cal., semi-auto.

	$250	$180	$170	$145	$135	$120	$110

Note: Models 1915/1916 were later referred to as Model 100 Special.

CAMPO GIRO 1913 — mfg. 1913.

	$2,250	$1,600	$1,200	$1,000	$800	$600	$400

Grading	100%	98%	95%	90%	80%	70%	60%

CAMPO GIRO 1913-16 — mfg. 1913-16.

	$1,350	$1,100	$800	$675	$550	$450	$300

MODEL 200 FIRECAT AUTOMATIC PISTOL — .25 ACP cal., 2¼ in. barrel, 6 shot, blue, plastic grips, mfg. 1920-present, U.S. importation stopped by GCA 68.

	$240	$190	$165	$145	$125	$110	$100

Add 50% for engraved M-200.

MODEL 300 — .32 ACP or .380 ACP cal., semi-auto.

	$450	$350	$270	$240	$210	$180	$150

Add 20% if Nazi-proofed.

Add 100% for engraved M-300.

MODEL 400 AUTOMATIC PISTOL — 9mm Bayard long, 9 shot, 6 in. barrel, blue, fixed sights, plastic grips, mfg. 1921-1945.

	$400	$325	$230	$200	$170	$135	$100

Add 200% for Navy variation.

Add 100% for Nazi accepted specimens.

Approx. serial range of Nazi accepted specimens (no markings) is S/N 92,851 - 98,850.

MODEL 600 MOD. AUTOMATIC — 9mm Luger, 8 shot, 5¼ in. barrel, blue, fixed sights, wood or plastic grips, mfg. 1944-1945.

	$300	$250	$200	$175	$155	$140	$130

Add a 100%+ premium for Nazi Waffenamt proofing (approx. serial range 1 - 10,500).

MODEL 700 SPECIAL — .32 ACP cal., semi-auto.

	$500	$465	$425	$350	$275	$215	$170

MODEL 800 CONDOR AUTOMATIC — same as 600, except has exposed hammer, 9mm, mfg. 1958-1965.

	$1,350	$1,000	$800	$650	$550	$450	$350

MODEL 900 — 7.63 Mauser cal., Broomhandle copy, parts non-interchangeable with Mauser. Mfg. from 1928-1936.

	$2,500	$1,850	$1,350	$850	$700	$525	$425

Add $500 for matching detachable stock.

Add 50% for early Bolo grip variation.

Add 20% for specimens with Japanese characters.

MODEL 902 — 7.63 Mauser cal., semi-auto, similar to 900 except 20 shot mag.

	$8,000	$6,125	$4,250	$3,000	$2,500	$2,100	$1,700

Add $1,250 for original "booted" stock.

Deduct 50% for selective fire version.

MACHINE PISTOLS — class III, transferrable only, 10 or 20 shot detachable mag., several variations.

	$3,000	$2,500	$1,900	$1,600	$1,250	$900	$600

MODEL 3000 POCKET AUTOMATIC — .32 auto or .380 auto, 4 in. barrel, fixed sights, blue, plastic grips, mfg. 1947-1956.

	$450	$325	$240	$210	$180	$150	$120

Add 100% for engraved M3000.

MODEL 1000 OR 1000 SPECIAL —semi-auto, .32 ACP.

	$475	$420	$365	$310	$280	$255	$225

Grading	100%	98%	95%	90%	80%	70%	60%

MODEL 2000 CUB — .22 Short or .25 auto cal., 2¼ in. barrel, fixed sights, blue, plastic grips, also chrome finish, mfg. 1954-present, U.S. importation stopped by GCA 68. Astra also made 2000 Cubs for Colt called Jr. Model {see Colt section}.

	$200	$170	$140	$115	$95	$85	$75

Add 25% for chrome finish.
Add 50% for engraved M-2000.

MODEL 2000 CAMPER — same as Cub, .22 Short only, with 4 in. barrel, mfg. 1955-1960.

	$325	$265	$200	$160	$125	$90	$70

ASTRA CADIX DOUBLE ACTION REVOLVER — .22 LR, 9 shot, .38 Spl., 5 shot, 4 or 6 in. barrel, adj. sights, blue, plastic grips, mfg. 1960-1968.

	$165	$155	$140	$120	$110	$85	$55

REVOLVERS

.357 D/A REVOLVER — .357 Mag., 6 shot, 3, 4, 6 or 8½ in. barrel (add $10), adj. sights, blue, checkered wood grips, mfg. 1972-1988.

	$250	$215	$185	$170	$155	$140	$125

Last Mfg.'s Sug. Retail was $295.
Stainless Steel. — 4 in. barrel only. Disc. 1987.

	$285	$245	$205

Last Mfg.'s Sug. Retail was $330.

.44/.45 CAL D/A REVOLVER — .41 Mag. (disc. 1985), .44 Mag. or .45 ACP (disc. 1987), 6 shot, 6 or 8½ in. (.44 Mag. only) barrels. Mfg. 1980-87.

	$280	$235	$210	$190	$180	$170	$160

Last Mfg.'s Sug. Retail was $315.
Stainless Steel — .44 Mag. only, 6 in. barrel only, 2½ lbs.

Mfg.'s Sug. Retail	$450	$370	$300	$265

CONVERTIBLE REVOLVER — 9mm with extra .357 Mag. cylinder, 6 shot, 3 in. barrel, blue only, checkered walnut grips, 2¼ lbs. Mfg. 1986 - present.

Mfg.'s Sug. Retail	$395	$335	$275	$250	$225	$200	$180	$160

TERMINATOR — .44 Mag. or .44 Spl. (disc.) cal., 6 shot, adj. rear sight, Roberts rubber grips, 2¾ in. shrouded barrel only. Inventories were depleted in 1989.
Blue finish

	$250	$225	$190	$175	$160	$150	$140

Last Mfg.'s Sug. Retail was $250.
Stainless steel

	$275	$235	$190

These models were distributed by Sile Distributors, Inc. located in New York, NY.
Last Mfg.'s Sug. Retail was $275.

AUSTRALIAN AUTOMATIC ARMS PTY. LTD.

Manufacturer located in Tasmania, Australia. Currently imported and distributed by California Armory, Inc. located in San Bruno, CA.

SAR — .223 cal., semi-auto paramilitary design rifle, 16¼ or 20 in. (new 1989) barrel, 5 or 20 shot M-16 style mag., fiberglass stock and forearm, 7½ lbs. Imported 1986-89.

	$725	$625	$550	$510	$465	$410	$370

Add $25 for 20 in. barrel.
Also available in fully auto version (AR) — same values as shown above.
Last Mfg.'s Sug. Retail was $663.

Grading	100%	98%	95%	90%	80%	70%	60%

SAC — .223 cal., semi-auto paramilitary design carbine, 10½ in. barrel, 20 shot mag., fiberglass stock and forearm, 6.9 lbs. New 1986.
This model is available to class III dealers and law enforcement agencies only.

SAP — .223 cal., semi-auto paramilitary design pistol, 10½ in. barrel, 20 shot mag., fiberglass stock and forearm, 5.9 lbs. New 1986.

Mfg.'s Sug. Retail	$995	$900	$775	$675	$615	$550	$500	$465

SP — .223 cal., semi-auto, sporting configuration, 16¼ or 20 in. barrel, wood stock and forearm, 5 or 20 shot M-16 style mag., 7.5 lbs. Importation began late 1991.
Although retail values had not been established as this edition went to press, prices will be very similar to the SAP Model listed above.

AUTO MAG

Short recoil rotary bolt system made entirely of stainless steel. Most pistols were sold in .44 AMP cal. although .357 AMP was also a popular factory option. Several other calibers and variations were marketed through Lee Jurras including exotics like the .44 Condor (16 in. barrel and scoped - one of a kind). Also, a .30 cal. Cougar with 12 in. barrel and highly polished metal was a one of a kind item. Other limited Jurras variations include The Custom 100 Series, The Grizzly, The Backpacker, and Metallic Silhouette. Other manufacturers logo's include Auto Mag Corp., TDE, High Standard, and AMT.

A unique handgun, the Auto Mag has never been a commercial success due to high manufacturing costs and functioning problems. Initial reaction to Dirty Harry's use of this weapon in the movie "Sudden Impact" made prices escalate considerably, but most values appear to have stablized since 1986. Be aware of fakes - especially of the XP variety (re-serialized, re-stamped, location of markings,etc.). Also, the ease of barrel swapping should be considered when deciding a potential purchase.

Serial number ranges for the various models are as follows: Pasadena mfg. - A0000 through A03300. TDE North Hollywood - mostly A03400 through A05015 although some were marked with very low ser. no.'s. TDE El Monte mfg. - A05016 through A08300. High Standard guns were originally marked with "H" prefix serial numbers (only 132 made), after which they carried standard "A0" prefix serial numbers. The "H" prefix guns remain a collectors item and command a 25% premium over values listed below. TDE/OMC marked pistols - B00001 through B00370 are known as the "B" series or solid bolt models (only 370 manufactured). This "B" series also commands collector premiums.

AMT manufactured the last two lots of Auto Mags; the first was the "C" series and was basically the same as the "B" except that only 50 guns were fabricated. The last Auto Mags made by AMT were appropriately serial numbered LAST 1 through LAST 50. These guns had the reputation of being the poorest quality but do carry collector premiums. One interesting variation is the North Hollywood "two-line" model. Also, the first .357 cal. pistols manufactured did not have the words AUTO MAG appearing on the gun. These are also collectors items.

LESS THAN 10,000 AUTO MAGS WERE PRODUCED BY ALL MANUFACTURERS.

In addition to the above calibers, a very few non-factory .22 and .25 cal. prototypes were fabricated by Kent Lomont in addition to several engraved models. These specimens will usually demand a premium over the values listed below. Also, some barrels and pistols were made in Covina, CA.

Values below represent the "top-of-the-market". In many regions where there is less demand for this specialized pistol, values will be less than shown below.

ORIGINAL PASADENA — .44 AMP only, 6½ in. VR barrel.

	$1,700	$1,500	$1,250

TDE NORTH HOLLYWOOD
.44 AMP — 6½ in. VR barrel.

	$1,700	$1,500	$1,250

.357 AMP — two line address.

	$1,750	$1,525	$1,275

Grading	100%	98%	95%	90%	80%	70%	60%

TDE EL MONTE

.44 AMP — 6½ VR, 8, or 10 in. tapered barrel.

	$1,600	$1,450	$1,200

.357 AMP — 6½ VR, 8, or 10 in. tapered barrel.

	$1,450	$1,300	$1,050

HIGH STANDARD — "H" prefixed serial numbers.

	$1,900	$1,675	$1,350

TDE/OMC "B" SERIES — 6½ VR or 10 in. barrel.

	$1,700	$1,500	$1,250

AMT "C" SERIES — 6½ VR or 10 in. barrel.

	$1,775	$1,550	$1,275

Add 50%+ for L.E. Jurras custom models.

Add 10% for Jurras Lion marked models.

Lee Jurras added his Lion's head logo (from 1977 on) on TDE manufactured guns.
Add $500 for shoulder stock.

Note: guns were cased (plastic attache style) with accessories. Original Auto-Mag ammo (mfg. by CDM in Mexico) is currently selling for approx. $75 a box.

AUTO-ORDNANCE CORP.
Manufacturer located in West Hurley, NY.

Auto-Ordnance Corp. manufactures an exact reproduction of the original 1927 Thompson machine gun. They are currently available in semi-auto only since production ceased on fully automatic variations in 1986 (mfg. 1975-1986).

CARBINES: SEMI-AUTO

1927 A1 STANDARD — .45 ACP, 16 in. plain barrel, solid steel construction, standard military sight, walnut stock and horizontal forearm. Disc. 1986.

	$570	$490	$430	$360	$315	$290	$270

Last Mfg.'s Sug. Retail was $575.

1927 A1 DELUXE — 10mm (new 1991) or .45 ACP cal., 16 in. finned barrel, solid steel construction, adj. rear sight, walnut stock and hand grips.

Mfg.'s Sug. Retail	$735	$610	$515	$440	$370	$320	$295	$275

Add $10 for 10mm cal.

Add $140 (retail) for 50 shot drum mag. or $345 for 100 shot drum mag. (new in 1990) on this model and other 1927 variations. Also add $124 (retail) for Thompson hard case (violin type).

THOMPSON M1 — .45 ACP, combat model, 16½ in. smooth barrel, side-cocking lever, flat black finish, walnut stock, pistol grip, and grooved forearm, 11½ lbs. New 1986.

Mfg.'s Sug. Retail	$713	$600	$505	$435	$360	$310	$285	$265

1927 A1C LIGHTWEIGHT — .45 ACP, same as 1927 A-1 Deluxe, except receiver made of a lightweight alloy. 20% weight reduction. New 1984.

Mfg.'s Sug. Retail	$707	$595	$500	$430	$350	$310	$285	$265

1927 A5 PISTOL/CARBINE — .45 ACP, 13 in. finned barrel, alloy construction, overall length 26 in., 30 shot mag., 7 lbs.

Mfg.'s Sug. Retail	$704	$595	$495	$425	$350	$300	$275	$260

1927 A3 22 CAL — .22 LR, 16 in. finned barrel, alloy frame and receiver, walnut stock, pistol grip, and forearm pistol grip, 7 lbs.

Mfg.'s Sug. Retail	$488	$425	$365	$320	$285	$260	$230	$200

Grading	100%	98%	95%	90%	80%	70%	60%

PISTOLS: SEMI-AUTO

1911 A1 — .38 Super, 9mm Para., .40 S&W (new in 1991), or .45 ACP cal., 4½ (.40 S&W cal. only) or 5 in. barrel, parts interchange with the original Colt Gov't Model, blue only, checkered plastic grips, 39 oz.

Mfg.'s Sug. Retail	$369	$315	$275	$250	$235	$225	$215	$200

Add $47 for .40 S&W cal.

Add $35 for .38 Super or 9mm Para. cal.

Add $22 for satin nickel finish (.45 ACP only, new 1990).

1911 A1 "Pit Bull" — .45 ACP only, compact variation of the 1911 A1, 3½ in. barrel, 7 shot mag., 36 oz. New 1988.

Mfg.'s Sug. Retail	$404	$335	$285	$250	$235	$225	$215	$200

AUTO — POINTER

Manufactured by Yamamoto Co. formerly imported by Sloans.

SEMI-AUTO SHOTGUN — 12 or 20 ga., gas operated. Disc.

$275	$240	$220	$195	$180	$160	$145

NOTES

B

BSA GUNS LIMITED

Birmingham Small Arms, located in Birmingham, England. Manufactured 1861-current in England. Imported until 1985 by Precision Sports, from Ithaca, NY And 1986 by BSA Guns Ltd., located in Grand Prairie, TX. Imported and distributed until 1989 by Samco Global Arms, Inc., located in Miami, FL (small quantities of certain models still remain). Currently, BSA Firearms and Airguns are not being imported.

Samco also imports various military surplus bolt action rifles including Hakim, Lee Enfield, Loewe, Mauser, Steyr, and others. In addition to these imports, Samco also sells sporterized variations of the above trademarks and these can be found under the Samco section in this text.

RIFLES: RECENT IMPORTATION

Importation of all BSA rimfire and centerfire rifles were disc. 1987.

Grading	100%	98%	95%	90%	80%	70%	60%

CF-2 ACTION — .222 R., .22-250, .243 Win., 6.5 x 55mm, 7 x 57, 7 x 64mm, 7mm Rem. Mag., .270 Win., .308 Win., .30-06, or .300 Win. Mag. cal., bolt action, barrel length 23-26 in., 7½ -8 lbs. CF-2 nomenclature designates an action rather than a model. CF-2 actioned models are listed below. Add $70 for double set trigger option on the below listed models. Limited quantities of English mfg. models remain.

Sporter/Classic — same cal.'s as above, checkered oil finished walnut stock. Imported 1986-87.

	100%	98%	95%	90%	80%	70%	60%
	$325	$275	$250	$225	$210	$195	$180

Sporter Model features Monte Carlo stock, rosewood capped forearm and pistol grip stock, and swivels.

Last Mfg.'s Sug. Retail was $360.

Classic Varminter — available in .222R-.243 W. cal.'s only, heavy barrel, matte finish, with swivels. Imported 1986 only.

	100%	98%	95%	90%	80%	70%	60%
	$325	$275	$250	$225	$210	$190	$175

Last Mfg.'s Sug. Retail was $345.

Heavy Barrel Model — .222R, .22-250, or .243W cal., approx. 9 lbs., no sights.

	100%	98%	95%	90%	80%	70%	60%
	$375	$300	$260	$240	$225	$210	$180

Last Mfg.'s Sug. Retail was $410.

Carbine Model — 20 in. barrel. Disc. 1985.

	100%	98%	95%	90%	80%	70%	60%
	$350	$325	$295	$270	$250	$225	$200

Last Mfg.'s Sug. Retail was $480.

Stutzen Rifle — Mannlicher style full length stock, same general specifications as Sporter/Classic, 20½ in. barrel. Not available in 7mm Rem. Mag. or .300 Win. Mag cal.

	100%	98%	95%	90%	80%	70%	60%
	$375	$325	$275	$250	$225	$210	$180

Last Mfg.'s Sug. Retail was $385.

Regal Custom — similar to Sporter Model, except has slim classic European style stock with Schnabel forend, deluxe walnut with extra checkering, ebony forend cap, engraved action and floorplate. Limited importation (1986 only).

	100%	98%	95%	90%	80%	70%	60%
	$875	$795	$685	$590	$550	$500	$450

Last Mfg.'s Sug. Retail was $950.

This model was custom made by special order only.

CFT TARGET RIFLE — 7.62mm, single shot, bolt action, globe front and aperture rear sights, 26½ in. barrel, 11 lbs. Disc. 1987.

	100%	98%	95%	90%	80%	70%	60%
	$675	$590	$550	$500	$450	$400	$360

Last Mfg.'s Sug. Retail was $780.

Grading	100%	98%	95%	90%	80%	70%	60%

RIFLES: DISCONTINUED, SINGLE SHOT

NO. 12 MARTINI — .22 LR, 29 in. barrel, target sights, straight stock, pre-WWII.

	100%	98%	95%	90%	80%	70%	60%
	$360	$275	$250	$210	$175	$155	$130

MODEL 15 — same as 12, except pistol grip stock, better grade target sights, pre-WWII.

	$385	$305	$275	$240	$200	$175	$155

CENTURION MATCH RIFLE — same as 15, except Centurion guarantee — 1½ in. grouping at 100 yards, 24 in. barrel, pre-WWII.

	$440	$385	$330	$275	$240	$220	$175

MATCH 12/15 — similar to 15, except made after WWII.

	$385	$305	$275	$240	$200	$175	$155

MODEL 12/15 — heavy barrel.

	$415	$330	$305	$270	$230	$195	$165

MODEL 13 — lighter version of 12.

	$340	$265	$235	$200	$165	$150	$125

MODEL 13 SPORTER — same as 13, except has sport sights.

	$330	$240	$220	$175	$155	$140	$120
.22 Hornet.	$385	$305	$275	$240	$200	$175	$155

MARTINI INTERNATIONAL MATCH — .22 LR, 29 in. heavy barrel, international sights, mfg. 1950-1953.

	$415	$360	$320	$275	$255	$230	$200

INTERNATIONAL LIGHT — 26 in. lightweight barrel.

	$415	$360	$320	$275	$255	$230	$200

INTERNATIONAL MKII — improved trigger, ejectors and stock design, mfg. 1953-1959.

	$425	$375	$340	$315	$285	$255	$220

INTERNATIONAL MKIII — longer action, floating barrel, mfg. 1959-1967.

	$495	$430	$385	$360	$330	$305	$265

INTERNATIONAL ISU — modeled to meet ISU standards, 28 in. barrel, mfg. 1968-disc.

	$495	$430	$385	$360	$330	$305	$265

INTERNATIONAL MARK V — same as ISU, but heavier barrel, mfg. 1976-disc.

	$525	$460	$430	$375	$350	$330	$305

RIFLES: DISCONTINUED, BOLT ACTION

MAJESTIC FEATHERWEIGHT DELUXE — .243, .270, .308, or .30-06 cal., bolt action, 22 in. barrel, folding sight, checkered European style stock, mfg. 1959-1965.

	$330	$250	$220	$195	$180	$165	$145
.458 Mag.	$445	$375	$305	$275	$220	$210	$200

MAJESTIC DELUXE — .222, .22 Hornet, .243, 7 x 57, .308, or .30-06 cal., heavier barrel.

	$330	$250	$220	$195	$180	$165	$145

MONARCH DELUXE — same as Majestic Deluxe, but American design stock, mfg. 1965-1974.

	$350	$275	$250	$220	$195	$180	$165

MONARCH DELUXE VARMINT — same as Monarch Deluxe, except .222 or .243 cal., 24 in. heavy barrel. Disc.

	$370	$305	$275	$250	$210	$195	$180

Grading	100%	98%	95%	90%	80%	70%	60%

MARTINI ISU MATCH .22 — single shot, bolt action, .22 cal. only, similar to CFT Model. Add $100 for Mk. V.H.B. Model. Disc. 1985.

	$825	$700	$600	$530	$475	$435	$400

Last Mfg.'s Sug. Retail was $1,000.

BAFORD ARMS, INC.
Manufactured by Baford Arms, Inc. located in Bristol, TN. Distributed by C.L. Reedy & Associates, Inc. located in Melbourne, FL.

MODEL 35 FIRE POWER — 9mm Para., semi-auto single action, patterned after the Browning Hi-Power, total stainless steel construction, 4¾ in. barrel, combat hammer and safety, Pachmayr grips, removable barrel bushing, Millett Mk. II sights, 14 shot mag., 32 oz. New late 1988.

Mfg.'s Sug. Retail	$495	$575	$475	$395

This model has had limited manufacture to date (only 55 total mfg.).

THUNDER DERRINGER — .44 Spl./.410 shotshell, single shot, tip out action, 3 in. barrel, blued steel finish, spur trigger, wood grips. New 1988.

Mfg.'s Sug. Retail	$130	$130	$110	$95	$90	$85	$80	$75

Add $90 for interchangable barrel kit.

Interchangeable pistol barrels are chambered in various calibers between .22 Short and 9mm Para. There are two types: one fits flush while the other facilitates a scope mounting.

BAIKAL
Manufactured in the U.S.S.R. Current importer is KBI Inc. located in Harrisburg, PA. As this edition goes to press, KBI Inc. is still waiting for Russia to be granted Most Favored Nation Status before regular importation resumes (importation taxes would be reduced 66%).

Baikal shotguns have limited importation into the U.S. In recent years, however, a few O/U's have been seen for sale and have no doubt been "imported" into this country one at a time. Quality is in the intermediate level and collector interest is not particularly great. Most O/U shotguns fall into the $400 - $1,000 range if quality is at par with other more famous trademarks. The most commonly encountered Baikal models are the 650, 650E, and the 750 series. The MC series represent their top-of-the-line models (No.'s 5, 6, 7, 8, 109, 110, 111) and retailed from $1,500 (MC-5) to $5,850 (MC-111) when offered in 1983. Currently, collector interest is not sufficient to support the older retail prices and demand is very limited.

SHOTGUNS: RECENT IMPORTATION

SINGLE BARREL — 12, 20, or .410 ga.

No Mfg.'s Retail	$75	$65	$55	$45	$40	$35	$30

SIDE X SIDE FIELD MODEL — 12 ga. only, double triggers, extractors.

No Mfg.'s Retail	$295	$260	$220	$190	$160	$130	$95

Add $70 for automatic ejectors.

OVER & UNDER FIELD MODEL — 12 ga. only, double triggers, extractors.

No Mfg.'s Retail	$350	$295	$260	$220	$180	$150	$125

Add $115 for single trigger and automatic ejectors.

BAILONS GUNMAKERS LIMITED
Manufacturer and refurbisher located in Birmingham, England. Limited exportation into the U.S. (see Trademark Index in back for more information)

Bailons also makes to special order, both boxlock and sidelock shotguns in most popular gauges. Prices are subject to negotiation and dependent upon the amount and type of engraving specified as well as quality of the wood. Also, Bailons repairs and refurbishes English shotguns using original materials and old world finishing techniques.

Grading	100%	98%	95%	90%	80%	70%	60%

HUNTING RIFLE — various cal.'s, modified Mauser bolt action, 24 in. barrel, set triggers, sights, engraving, and types of finishes are at optional cost, prices below reflect standard rifle with no options. New 1986.

Mfg.'s Sug. Retail	$1,850	$1,675	$1,475	$1,350	$1,200	$1,075	$900	$795

BAKER GUN & FORGING CO.

Previous manufacturer located in Batavia, NY. 1889-1933.

SHOTGUNS: SIDE BY SIDE

Note: Original damascus guns in 80% or better condition with bright case colors will approach the values of steel barrel counterparts.

BATAVIA SPECIAL — 12, 16, or 20 ga., 26, 28, 30, or 32 in. barrels, any standard choke, checkered pistol grip stock, sidelock, extractors.

	$385	$305	$275	$260	$250	$220	$200

BATAVIA LEADER — same as Special, except has deluxe finish.

	$440	$360	$335	$305	$285	$265	$220
Auto ejectors	$525	$440	$415	$385	$370	$330	$305

BLACK BEAUTY SPECIAL — same as Leader, except has engraved, select wood.

	$745	$650	$615	$590	$550	$525	$495
Auto ejectors	$855	$760	$725	$700	$660	$635	$605

BATAVIA EJECTOR — same as Leader, but finer finish.

	$880	$770	$745	$715	$690	$660	$635
Damascus barrels	$440	$330	$305	$275	$250	$220	$165

BAKER S GRADE — same as Leader, but finer finish, better grade wood.

	$880	$775	$745	$715	$690	$650	$635
Auto ejectors	$1,100	$990	$965	$935	$910	$880	$745

BAKER R GRADE — same as Leader, except scroll and game scene engraved, Krupp barrels, fancy wood.

	$1,100	$990	$965	$935	$910	$880	$745
Auto ejectors	$1,320	$1,210	$1,155	$1,100	$1,075	$1,045	$965
Damascus barrel	$550	$415	$385	$360	$330	$275	$230

PARAGON GRADE — custom order only to customer specifications.

	$1,650	$1,430	$1,320	$1,210	$1,155	$1,045	$770
Auto ejectors	$1,815	$1,595	$1,485	$1,375	$1,210	$1,100	$990

EXPERT GRADE — auto ejectors standard, overall finer grade wood and engraving.

	$2,500	$2,100	$1,850	$1,500	$1,250	$1,000	$750

DELUXE GRADE — best quality.

	$3,750	$3,250	$2,950	$2,650	$2,300	$2,000	$1,600

Add $200 for single trigger.

Damascus barrels — also known as Early Paragon Grade. If condition is 50% or less subtract 50% or more. If 90% original condition or better, prices will be the same as for damascus L.C. Smith guns.

SHOTGUNS: SINGLE BARREL TRAP

Baker single barrel trap guns, although more rare than their side by side counterparts, are not as desirable as those models listed above. Typically, values will be 50%-75% of a side by side model of equal grade.

BARRETT FIREARMS MANUFACTURING, INC.

Manufacturer located in Murfreesboro, TN.

Grading	100%	98%	95%	90%	80%	70%	60%

MODEL 82 RIFLE — .50 Browning machine gun cartridge, semi-auto recoil operation, 33-37 in. barrel, 11 shot mag., 2,850 FPS muzzle velocity, scope sight only, parkerized finish, 35 lbs. Mfg. 1985-87.

	100%	98%	95%	90%	80%	70%	60%
	$4,350	$3,950	$3,450	$2,700	$2,150	$1,800	$1,500

Last Mfg.'s Sug. Retail for consumers was $3,180 in 1985.

This model underwent design changes since initial production.

MODEL 82A1 — .50 BMG, current military configuration, variant of the original Model 82, available to civilians, back-up iron sights provided, 2 mags., and fitted hard case, 29 (new late 1989) or 33 (disc. 1989) in. barrel, 10 shot mag., 32½ lbs. for 1989 and older mfg., 28½ lbs. for 1990 mfg.

Mfg.'s Sug. Retail	$6,195	$5,950	$4,950	$4,250	$3,650	$3,150	$2,650	$2,200

Add $225 for camo backpack carrying case.

Add $975 for new 12X scope and mounts.

Add $800 for older disc. Leupold M3 Ultra 10X scope.

MODEL 90 — .50 BMG, bolt action design, 29 in. match grade barrel with muzzle brake, 5 shot detachable box mag., includes extendible bi-pod legs, Sorbothane recoil pad, scope optional, 22 lbs. New 1990.

Mfg.'s Sug. Retail	$3,350	$3,200	$2,850	$2,400	$2,150	$1,875	$1,600	$1,500

Add $975 for new 12X scope and mounts.

BAR-STO

Previous manufacturer of semi-auto pistols.

BAR-STO .25 ACP — .25 ACP, patterned after the Baby Browning, brushed stainless steel finish, walnut grips, approx. 250 manufactured in the 1974 circa.

	$195	$165	$125

BAUER FIREARMS CORPORATION

Previous manufacturer located in Fraser, MI.

BAUER .25 AUTOMATIC — .25 auto, 2½ in. barrel, 6 shot, fixed sights, checkered walnut or pearlite grips, mfg. 1972-1984.

	$150	$130	$110

Note: These guns are identical to the Baby Browning, except stainless steel.

THE RABBIT — combination gun, all metal construction, .22 cal. and .410 ga., O/U configuration. Mfg. 1982-1984.

	$125	$100	$90	$80	$70	$60	$50

BAVARIAN RIFLES

Manufactured in Germany. Imported by Caliber, Inc. located in Middlefield, CT. Distributed by H & S, Inc. located in Durham, CT.

Until 1989, these rifles were named "Prinz" and may be found under that heading in this text.

BAVARIAN CLASSIC RIFLE — .243 Win., .30-06, .308 Win., .300 Win. Mag., or 7mm Rem. Mag. cal., Mauser 98 action with Heym match barrel, Monte Carlo walnut stock with custom checkering and Pachmayr pad, single trigger, includes 1 in. rings and bases. Importation began 1990.

No Mfg.'s Retail	$561	$450	$415	$385	$360	$340	$320

Bavarian Classic Carbine — similar to Bavarian Classic Rifle, except has shorter barrel. Importation began 1990.

No Mfg.'s Retail	$686	$550	$485	$440	$400	$375	$350

BAVARIAN CUSTOM GRADE — same cal.'s as Bavarian Classic Rifle, includes gold inlays, custom checkering, and presentation case with custom I.D. Importation has been delayed to 1992 due to recent political changes in Germany.

No Mfg.'s Retail	$1,250	$995	$850	$725	$600	$525	$475

Grading	100%	98%	95%	90%	80%	70%	60%

BAYARD

Previously manufactured by Anciens Etablissements Pieper located in Herstal, Belgium.

Even though Bayard Models 1908, both 1923's, and 1930 were manufactured only by Anciens Etablissements Pieper of Herstal, Belgium these pistols are listed under this heading as they are most commonly referred to by this trademark designation.

.25 and .380 cal.'s are more rare than the .32's and will command a 20%+ premium above values listed below unless indicated differently.

MODEL 1908 POCKET AUTOMATIC — .25 auto, .32 auto, .380 auto, 6 shot, 2¼ in. barrel, fixed sights, blue, hard rubber grips.

	$220	$195	$165	$100	$85	$70	$55

MODEL 1923 POCKET AUTOMATIC — .25 auto, 2½ in. barrel, blue, fixed sights, checkered hard rubber grips.

	$220	$195	$140	$100	$85	$70	$55

BAYARD 1923 POCKET AUTOMATIC — .32 auto, .380 auto, 6 shot, 3⁵⁄₁₆ in. barrel, fixed sights, blue, checkered hard rubber grips.

	$220	$165	$140	$130	$120	$110	$100

Add 50% for .380 cal.

BAYARD 1930 POCKET AUTOMATIC — slight modification of 1923.

	$220	$165	$140	$130	$120	$110	$100

BEEMAN PRECISION ARMS, INC.

Importer and distributor located in Santa Rosa, CA.

Beeman is a large importer, specializing in high quality European rifles and pistols mostly. Trademarks currently being distributed in the U.S. are manufacturers: Agner (disc. 1986), Erma (disc. 1985), FAS, Fabarm, Feinwerkbau, Korth, Krico, Unique, and Weihrauch. These trademarks will appear under their respective alphabetical headings. Air rifles, pistols, and/or black powder firearms will appear under those headings in the back of the book.

Below listed firearms are manufactured to Beeman specifications, and are therefore listed under the Beeman Heading.

PISTOLS: SEMI-AUTO

BEEMAN MP-08 — .380 ACP, Luger type toggle action, 3½ in. barrel, 6 shot mag., blue, 1.4 lbs. Mfg. 1968-present.

Mfg.'s Sug. Retail	$390	$335	$275	$240	$185	$145	$115	$95

In 1988, Beeman took over importation of these two models (MP-08 and P-08). These revised models have new Luger style checkered walnut grips and 3½ in. barrel. Previous variations had plastic grips. While importation was disc. in 1990, limited quantities of this model still remain.

BEEMAN P-08 — .22 LR, Luger type toggle action, 8 shot mag., 3.8 in. barrel, blue, checkered walnut grips, 1.9 lbs. Mfg. 1969-present.

Mfg.'s Sug. Retail	$390	$335	$275	$240	$185	$145	$115	$95

While importation was disc. in 1990, limited quantities of this model still remain.

PISTOLS: SINGLE SHOT

SP STANDARD — .22 LR cal., sidelever action, 8, 10, 12, or 15 in. barrel, adj. sights and walnut grips, single shot. Made in W. Germany. Imported 1985-86 only.

	$230	$200	$180	$170	$160	$150	$140

Add $10 or $30 for 12 or 15 in. barrel respectively.
Last Mfg.'s Sug. Retail was $250.

Grading	100%	98%	95%	90%	80%	70%	60%

SP DELUXE — similar to SP Standard, except has forearm, about 3½ lbs. Made in W. Germany. Imported 1985-86 only.

	100%	98%	95%	90%	80%	70%	60%
	$260	$220	$200	$185	$170	$155	$145

Add $10 or $30 for 12 or 15 in. barrel respectively.
Last Mfg.'s Sug. Retail was $300.

BEHOLLA PISTOL
Previously manufactured by Becker & Hollander located in Suhl, Germany.

BEHOLLA POCKET AUTOMATIC — .32 auto, 7 shot, 2.9 in. barrel, blue, serrated wood or rubber grips, mfg. 1915-1920, from 1920-1925 the same gun was mfg. by Stenda-Werke.

	100%	98%	95%	90%	80%	70%	60%
	$225	$170	$150	$135	$120	$100	$90

BENELLI
Manufacturer located in Urbino, Italy. Shotguns currently imported by Heckler And Koch, Inc. located in Chantilly, Va. handguns currently imported by Sile Distributors, Inc., located in New York, NY. Previously imported by Saco located in Arlington, VA.

PISTOLS

MODEL B-76 — 9mm Luger, selective double action, all steel, 4¼ in. barrel, 8 shot mag., 34 oz. Importation disc. in 1990.

	100%	98%	95%	90%	80%	70%	60%
	$390	$340	$295	$245	$225	$210	$190

Last Mfg.'s Sug. Retail was $428.

MODEL B-76S TARGET — 9mm, similar to B-76 except has 5½ barrel, target grips, and adj. rear sights. Importation disc. 1990.

	100%	98%	95%	90%	80%	70%	60%
	$475	$425	$395	$350	$325	$300	$280

Last Mfg.'s Sug. Retail was $595.

MODEL B-77 — .32 ACP, selective double action, all steel, 4¼ in. barrel, 8 shot mag.

Mfg.'s Sug. Retail	$399	$275	$245	$225	$200	$180	$170	$160

MODEL B-80 — .30 Luger, selective double action, all steel, 4¼ in. barrel, 8 shot mag., 34 oz.

Mfg.'s Sug. Retail	$385	$275	$245	$225	$200	$180	$170	$160

MODEL B-80S TARGET — similar to B-80, except has 5½ barrel, target grips, and adj. rear sights.

Mfg.'s Sug. Retail	$785	$475	$395	$350	$325	$295	$275	$250

MODEL MP3S — .32 Smith & Wesson Long Wad Cutter, target variation with 5½ in. barrel, high gloss bluing, target grips, and adj. rear sights.

Mfg.'s Sug. Retail	$785	$475	$395	$350	$325	$295	$275	$250

SHOTGUNS: SEMI-AUTO

Older models (disc. before 1986) may have a parts availability problem if repairs are needed. Approx. 50,000 SL-80 series shotguns were mfg. before discontinuance.

SL80 SERIES MODEL SL-121V — 12 ga., mechanically like SL-123V, various barrel lengths, black receiver finish, 3 in. Mag.— no extra charge. Disc. 1985.

	100%	98%	95%	90%	80%	70%	60%
		$360	$295	$260	$245	$215	$190	$175

Last Mfg.'s Sug. Retail was $397.

SL80 SERIES MODEL SL-121 SLUG — 12 ga., mechanically like SL-123V, only 21¹/₁₆ in. cylinder bore barrel, approx. 7 lbs. 3 oz. Disc. 1985.

	100%	98%	95%	90%	80%	70%	60%
		$395	$315	$275	$250	$220	$195	$175

Last Mfg.'s Sug. Retail was $434.

Grading	100%	98%	95%	90%	80%	70%	60%

SL80 SERIES MODEL SL123V AND DELUXE — 12 ga. fast "3rd generation" action, lower receiver Ergal special aluminum alloy, various chokes, approx. 6 lbs. 13 oz. Disc. 1985.

	$400	$325	$285	$255	$225	$200	$180

Last Mfg.'s Sug. Retail was $464.

SL80 SERIES MODEL 123V SPECIAL TRAP AND SKEET — 12 ga., choice of photo-engraving and frame finish, 32 in. barrel, approx. 7 lbs. 10 oz. Disc. 1985.

	$500	$425	$365	$330	$300	$275	$245

Add $115 for Skeet Model.
Last Mfg.'s Sug. Retail was $584.

Very limited quantities of the EXL Trap were mfg. (similar to 123 Trap Model, except has hand engraved receiver).

MODEL 80 SPECIAL SKEET — 12 ga. only, skeet variation, nickel plated receiver, limited importation, disc. 1989.

	$450	$350	$315	$275	$250	$225	$195

Last Mfg.'s Sug. Retail was $531.

MODEL 80 SPECIAL TRAP — 12 ga only, supplied with nickel plated receiver, disc. 1989.

	$425	$335	$300	$265	$240	$215	$185

SL80 SERIES MODEL SL201 — 20 ga., 26 in. barrel bored imp. mod., approx. 5 lbs. 10 oz. Disc. 1985.

	$375	$300	$260	$240	$215	$190	$165

Last Mfg.'s Sug. Retail was $399.

M1 SUPER 90 SLUG — 12 ga. only, 3 in. Mag., semi-auto, incorporates improvements on the Benelli action, including rotating Montefeltro bolt system, 19¾ in. cyl. bore barrel with iron sights, 7 shot mag., fiberglass stock and forearm, 7¼ lbs. New 1986. Imported exclusively by H&K.

Mfg.'s Sug. Retail	$659	$565	$400	$350	$310	$295	$270	$240

Add $55 for pistol grip stock (Defense Model).

Add $45 for ghost-ring sighting system on either model.

M1 SUPER 90 FIELD — similar to M1 Super 90, except has 21 (new 1990), 24 (new 1990), 26, or 28 in. vent rib barrel and 3-shot plug, includes 3 screw in choke tubes.

Mfg.'s Sug. Retail	$729	$595	$450	$375	$330	$295	$275	$260

This model is available with either a short or extended magazine tube. The short tube is available in all barrel lengths - an extended mag. tube is available in 26 or 28 in. barrel only.

MONTEFELTRO SUPER 90 STANDARD HUNTER — 12 ga. only, 3 in. chamber, 26 or 28 in. VR barrel with 3 choke tubes, matte black metal finish, checkered walnut stock and forearm with choice of high gloss or satin finish, 5 shot mag., 7¼ lbs. New 1988.

Mfg.'s Sug. Retail	$729	$595	$450	$375	$330	$295	$275	$260

Add $70 for left-hand action.

Montefeltro Turkey Gun — similar to Montefeltro Standard Hunter except has 24 in. VR barrel with 3 choke tubes, satin finish wood only, 7 lbs. Imported 1989 only.

	$575	$440	$370	$330	$295	$275	$260

Last Mfg.'s Sug. Retail was $675.

Montefeltro Uplander — similar to Montefeltro Turkey Gun except has 21 or 24 in. VR barrel with 3 choke tubes, satin finish wood only, 7 lbs. New 1989.

Mfg.'s Sug. Retail	$729	$595	$450	$375	$330	$295	$275	$260

BLACK EAGLE — 12 ga., Montefeltro action, similar to Montefeltro Super 90 Standard Hunter except has black synthetic stock and forearm, 21, 24, 26, or 28 (new 1990) in. VR barrel with 3 choke tubes, right hand only. Imported 1989-90, configuration changed to competition in 1991 (see Black Eagle Competion Model).

	$675	$575	$475	$395	$340	$300	$275

Last Mfg.'s Sug. Retail was $807.

Grading	100%	98%	95%	90%	80%	70%	60%

Black Eagle Competition Model — 12 ga. only, designed for competition shooting with action adj. for lighter loads, 26 or 28 in. VR barrel with 5 choke tubes and wrench provided, includes buttstock drop adjustment kit, new 1991.

Mfg.'s Sug. Retail	$995	$850	$735	$625	$500	$395	$340	$300

Black Eagle Slug Gun — 12 ga., 24 in. rifled barrel with receiver scope mount. New 1990.

Mfg.'s Sug. Retail		$859	$735	$625	$475	$395	$340	$300	$275

SUPER BLACK EAGLE — 12 ga. only, 3½ in. chamber, updated Montefeltro action accepts all 12 ga. loads, 26 or 28 in. VR barrel with 5 choke tubes and wrench provided, choice of dull finish and satin stock (28 in. barrel only) or blued finish and high gloss wood finish (26 in. barrel only), with recoil pad, includes buttstock drop adjustment kit, approx. 7 lbs. 5 oz. New 1991.

Mfg.'s Sug. Retail		$989	$850	$735	$625	$500	$395	$340	$300

M3 SUPER 90 — 12 ga. only, defense configuration incorporating convertible (fingertip activated) pump or semi-auto action, 19¾ in. cyl. bore barrel with rifle sights, choice of standard polymer stock or integral pistol grip, 7½ lbs. New 1989.

Mfg.'s Sug. Retail		$859	$735	$625	$475	$395	$340	$300	$275

Add $55 for ghost-ring sighting system.

Add $100 for folding stock (new 1990).

Add $320 for Model 200 Laser Sight System with bracket.

BENSON FIREARMS LTD.

Manufactured by Aldo Uberti in Italy. Previously imported and distributed from 1987-1989 by Benson Firearms Ltd. located in Seattle, WA. Benson Firearms Ltd. combined with A. Uberti USA Inc. In early 1989 and discontinued importation.

Benson Firearms can be differentiated from other A. Uberti imports by the "Benson Firearms Seattle, WA" barrel marking. Many of the models listed below are similar to those models imported by Allen Firearms (disc. 1987) and A. Uberti USA, Inc., (current importer).

REVOLVERS: SINGLE ACTION

Can be ordered with either black powder or modern configured frames.

CATTLEMAN — available in .45 LC, .44-40, .38 Spl., .357 Mag., .22 LR, or .22 Mag cal., 4¾, 5½, or 7½ in. barrel lengths, brass or steel backstraps and trigger guard. Disc. 1989.

			$325	$235	$190	$175	$160	$150	$135

Add $30 for steel backstrap.

Add $64 for stainless steel construction (Disc. 1987).

Last Mfg.'s Sug. Retail was $359.

Sheriff's Model — .44-40 or .45 LC cal., 3 in. barrel, brass backstrap. Disc. 1989.

			$250	$210	$190	$175	$160	$150	$135

Add $24 for steel backstrap.

Last Mfg.'s Sug. Retail was $295.

Target Model — same as Cattleman Model, only fully adj. rear blade sight, brass backstrap. Disc. 1989.

			$345	$240	$200	$185	$170	$150	$135

Add $26 for steel backstrap.

Add $60 for stainless steel construction (Disc. 1987).

Last Mfg.'s Sug. Retail was $389.

CATTLEMAN BUNTLINE — .45 LC or .357 Mag. cal., 18 in. barrel, brass backstrap cut for shoulder stock. Disc. 1989.

			$350	$250	$210	$185	$175	$165	$150

Add $30 for target sights.

Add $30 for steel backstrap.

Last Mfg.'s Sug. Retail was $395.

Grading	100%	98%	95%	90%	80%	70%	60%

BUCKHORN — .44 Mag., .44 Spl., or .44-40 cal., various barrel lengths, brass backstrap, Buntline and revolving carbine models, also available in the Buckhorn series - add approx. $65, add $30 for convertible cylinders. Disc. 1989.

	$310	$210	$205	$190	$180	$170	$160

Add $30 for steel backstrap.

Add $36 for target sights.

Last Mfg.'s Sug. Retail was $369.

1873 STALLION — .22 LR/ .22 Mag. convertible, 4¾, 5½, or 6½ in. barrel, case hardened frame. Disc. 1989.

	$315	$210	$195	$170	$155	$140	$120

Add $27 for steel backstrap and trigger guard.

Add $26 for target sights.

Add $50 for stainless steel.

Last Mfg.'s Sug. Retail was $389.

"OUTLAW" 1875 REMINGTON — available in .45 LC, .44-40, or .357 Mag. cal., 7½ in. barrel. Disc. 1989.

	$325	$225	$195	$170	$155	$140	$120

Add $43 for nickel plating.

Last Mfg.'s Sug. Retail was $369.

The quality (tolerances and finish) should be inspected on this model before purchasing.

1890 REMINGTON — available in .45 LC, .44-40, or .357 Mag. cal., 5½ in. barrel. New 1986. Disc. 1989.

	$340	$220	$190	$175	$155	$140	$120

Add $43 for nickel plating.

Last Mfg.'s Sug. Retail was $385.

The quality (tolerances and finish) should be inspected on this model before purchasing.

PHANTOM MODEL — .357 or .44 Mag. cal., 10 in. barrel for silhouette use. New 1985. Disc. 1989.

	$490	$395	$325	$290	$260	$230	$215

Last Mfg.'s Sug. Retail was $559.

REVOLVERS: DOUBLE ACTION

INSPECTOR MODEL — .32 S&W or .38 Sp. cal., 3, 4, or 6 in. barrels, double action, blued or chrome finish. Mfg. 1985-1989.

	$400	$295	$245	$210	$170	$145	$125

Add $40 for target sights.

Add $30 for chrome plating.

Last Mfg.'s Sug. Retail was $445.

TARGET PISTOLS

1871 ROLLING BLOCK TARGET PISTOL — available in .357 Mag., .22 LR, .22 Mag., or .22 Hornet cal., 9½ in. barrel. Also available in carbine model (22 in. barrel) - add $54. Disc. 1989.

	$275	$205	$175	$150	$135	$120	$100

Last Mfg.'s Sug. Retail was $315.

CARBINES AND RIFLES

CATTLEMAN REVOLVING CARBINE S.A. — available in .45 LC, .44-40, .357 Mag., or .22 LR/Mag. (convertible) cal., 18 in. barrel, fixed sights. Disc. 1989.

	$425	$285	$230	$200	$185	$180	$175

Add $40 for target sights.

Last Mfg.'s Sug. Retail was $475.

Grading	100%	98%	95%	90%	80%	70%	60%

1875 REMINGTON CARBINE S.A. — 18 in. barrel — same cal.'s as above, except .22 LR/Mag. Disc. 1989.

	$440	$285	$230	$200	$230	$185	$175

Add $80 for nickel plating.
Last Mfg.'s Sug. Retail was $540.

HENRY RIFLE OR CARBINE — .44-40 cal., brass frame, 24½ in. barrel on rifle, 22½ in. barrel on carbine. Disc. 1989.

	$750	$580	$490	$415	$360	$320	$260

Can also be special ordered with grade A engraving ($234 extra), grade B engraving ($412 extra), and grade 3 engraving ($635 extra).

Last Mfg.'s Sug. Retail was $875.

Henry 1 of 1,000 — discontinued several years ago, premiums are slightly higher than a C engraved gun.

1866 CARBINE — .44-40, .38 Spl., .22 Mag. or .22 LR cal., brass receiver, 19 in. round barrel. "Indian" model - add $80. Disc. 1989.

	$565	$420	$340	$285	$260	$235	$210

Last Mfg.'s Sug. Retail was $649.

1866 Trapper Carbine — .22 LR, .38 Spl., or .44-40 cal., 16 in. barrel. Disc. 1989.

	$565	$420	$340	$285	$260	$235	$210

Last Mfg.'s Sug. Retail was $649.

Red Cloud Commemorative Carbine — same cal.'s, special engraving and brass tacks in forearm and stock. Disc. 1989.

	$650	$475	$385	$310	$275	$240	$220

Last Mfg.'s Sug. Retail was $729.

1866 RIFLE — brass receiver, same cal.'s as the carbine, 24¼ in. oct. barrel. Disc. 1989.

	$610	$445	$370	$300	$260	$235	$210

Add $61 for "Indian" model (19 in. barrel).
Last Mfg.'s Sug. Retail was $689.

1873 CARBINE — .44-40, .357 Mag., .22 Mag., or .22 LR cal., steel receiver, 19 in. round barrel. Disc. 1989.

	$675	$525	$450	$395	$360	$320	$280

Add $120 for nickel finish.
Last Mfg.'s Sug. Retail was $795.

1873 Trapper Carbine — .44-40 cal. only, 16 in. barrel. Disc. 1989.

	$675	$525	$450	$395	$360	$320	$280

Last Mfg.'s Sug. Retail was $795.

1873 RIFLE — case hardened receiver, same cal.'s as the carbine, 24¼ in. oct. barrel. Disc. 1989.

	$725	$535	$460	$400	$360	$320	$280

Last Mfg.'s Sug. Retail was $855.

BERETTA, DR. FRANCO

Current manufacturer located in Brescia, Italy. Previously distributed exclusively through Double M Shooting Sports located in Guilford, CT until 1988.

BLACK DIAMOND SHOTGUNS: O/U

Black Diamond target guns were imported exclusively by Double M Shooting Sports. Double M Shooting Sports stopped importation in 1988 of all Dr. Franco Beretta shotguns. Prices have been discontinued as current importation is limited. For further information (including 1991 prices and model availability) regarding Dr. Franco Beretta shotguns, please write the manufacturer directly at the address listed in the Trademark Index in the back of this text.

Grading	100%	98%	95%	90%	80%	70%	60%

FIELD MODEL — 12, 16, 20, 28, or .410 ga., variety of chokes, coin finish receiver.

	$720	$630	$570	$510	$455	$430	$410

Last Mfg.'s Sug. Retail was $960.

GRADE ONE — 12, 16, 20, 28, or .410 ga., variety of chokes, coin finish receiver with acid etched engraving, French walnut. Trap or skeet model also available, except in 16 ga.

	$1,020	$900	$810	$720	$630	$570	$525

Last Mfg.'s Sug. Retail was $1,440.

GRADE TWO — 12, 16, 20, 28, or .410 ga., variety of chokes, coin finish receiver with moderate engraving, French walnut. Trap or skeet model also available, except in 16 ga.

	$1,475	$1,320	$1,200	$1,080	$930	$815	$750

Last Mfg.'s Sug. Retail was $2,040.

GRADE THREE — 12, 16, 20, 28, or .410 ga., variety of chokes, coin finish receiver with scrollwork engraving, French walnut. Trap or skeet model also available, except in 16 ga.

	$2,100	$1,920	$1,775	$1,560	$1,410	$1,200	$1,035

Last Mfg.'s Sug. Retail was $3,000.

GRADE FOUR — 12, 16, 20, 28, or .410 ga., variety of chokes, coin finish receiver with elaborate engraving, French walnut. Trap or skeet model also available, except in 16 ga.

	$2,760	$2,520	$2,280	$2,100	$1,920	$1,740	$1,560

Last Mfg.'s Sug. Retail was $3,960.

SKEET SET — includes 12, 20, 28, and .410 barrels, available in Grades One through Four.
Multiply values on Grades One - Four by 275% for 4 ga. Skeet sets.

SHOTGUNS: CURRENT MANUFACTURE

The models listed below were imported and distributed by Excam located in Hialeah, FL until 1988.

GAMMA STANDARD O & U — 12, 16, or 20 ga., 26 or 28 in. barrels, coin finish receiver with extensive engraving, Italian walnut. Add $83 with single trigger and ejectors. Imported 1984-1988.

	$400	$360	$330	$300	$275	$260	$240

Last Mfg.'s Sug. Retail was $445.

Gamma Standard — with interchangeable choke tubes. Importation disc. 1988.

	$580	$515	$475	$430	$395	$360	$335

Last Mfg.'s Sug. Retail was $630.

GAMMA DELUXE O & U — 12, 16, or 20 ga., 26 or 28 in. barrels, coin finish receiver with extensive engraving, Italian walnut. Add $84 with single trigger and ejectors. Imported 1984-1988.

	$445	$405	$370	$350	$325	$300	$275

Last Mfg.'s Sug. Retail was $480.

Gamma Deluxe — with interchangeable choke tubes. Importation disc. 1988.

	$635	$570	$530	$490	$450	$420	$390

Last Mfg.'s Sug. Retail was $685.

GAMMA TARGET O & U — 12 ga. only, SST, ejectors, Wundhammer swell pistol grip, English walnut stock and beavertail forearm. Imported 1986-1988.

	$550	$505	$455	$410	$370	$350	$325

Last Mfg.'s Sug. Retail was $595.

ALPHA TWO STANDARD O & U — 12, 16, or 20 ga., 26 or 28 in. barrels, coin finish receiver with extensive engraving, Italian walnut. Add $76 with single trigger and ejectors. Imported 1984-1988.

	$360	$330	$300	$275	$250	$230	$210

Last Mfg.'s Sug. Retail was $395.

Grading	100%	98%	95%	90%	80%	70%	60%

ALPHA TWO DELUXE O & U — 12, 16, or 20 ga., 26 or 28 in. barrels, coin finish receiver with extensive engraving, sling swivels, Italian walnut. Add $75 with single trigger and ejectors, $80 for interchangeable choke tubes (disc. 1985). Imported 1984-1988.

	$395	$355	$330	$300	$275	$250	$230

Last Mfg.'s Sug. Retail was $435.

AMERICA STANDARD O & U — .410 ga. only, 26 or 28 in. barrels, coin finish receiver with extensive engraving, Italian walnut. Add $85 for Deluxe model. Imported 1984-1988.

	$305	$280	$265	$240	$215	$205	$190

Last Mfg.'s Sug. Retail was $335.

EUROPA O & U — .410 ga. only, 26 in. barrels, coin finish receiver with some engraving, Italian walnut. Add $95 for Deluxe model (disc. 1985). Imported 1984-1988.

	$275	$250	$235	$220	$210	$200	$185

Last Mfg.'s Sug. Retail was $295.

FRANCIA STANDARD SXS — .410 ga. only, double triggers, extractors, checkered walnut. Imported 1986-1988. Add $19 for Deluxe Model.

	$235	$220	$210	$200	$185	$175	$160

Last Mfg.'s Sug. Retail was $255.

ALPHA THREE STANDARD SXS — 12, 16, or 20 ga., 26 or 28 in. barrels, coin finish receiver with extensive engraving, Italian walnut. Add $25 for Single trigger (disc. 1985), add $100 for ejectors. Imported 1984-1988.

	$390	$355	$325	$300	$275	$250	$235

Last Mfg.'s Sug. Retail was $425.

BETA THREE SINGLE BARREL — single barrel field gun, available in 12, 16, 20, 24, 28, 32, or .410 ga., vent rib, chrome finish receiver. Imported 1985-1988.

	$155	$145	$140	$130	$125	$120	$115

Last Mfg.'s Sug. Retail was $190.

BERETTA, PIETRO

Manufactured in Brescia, Italy 1526-present and Accokeek, MD 1978 to date. Beretta U.S.A. Corp. was formed in 1977 and is located in Accokeek, MD. Beretta U.S.A. Corp. has been importing Beretta Firearms exclusively since 1980. 1970-1977 manufacture was imported exclusively by Garcia.

SEMI-AUTO PISTOLS: DISC.

MODEL 1910 — .25 ACP cal., single action, 7 shot, fixed sights, wood grips, mfg. 1910-1934.

	$300	$275	$250	$195	$165	$145	$110

MODEL 1915 — .32 ACP, 8 shot, 3.3 in. barrel, fixed sights, blue, wood grips, mfg. 1915-1919.

	$300	$305	$275	$250	$195	$165	$110

MODEL 1915 — 9mm Glisenti, second variation - larger version, mfg. 1915.

	$400	$385	$330	$275	$220	$195	$140

9mm Para. is not interchangeable and potentially dangerous if interchanged with 9mm Glisenti.

MODEL 1923 — 9mm, 8 shot, 4 in. barrel, fixed sights, steel grips, mfg. 1923-1935.

	$650	$500	$400	$300	$250	$200	$150

Add 25% for slotted rear grip strap.

MODEL 1934 — .380 ACP (9mm Kurz), 3⅜ in. barrel, fixed sights, blue, plastic grips, Italy's service weapon in WWII, military models have poorer finish, mfg. 1934-1959.

	$290	$275	$250	$195	$165	$140	$110
Commercial model	$290	$330	$275	$220	$195	$165	$140

Grading	100%	98%	95%	90%	80%	70%	60%

MODEL 1935 — .32 ACP, 3½ in. barrel, fixed sights, blue, plastic grips, the wartime model had poor finish, mfg. 1935-1959.

	100%	98%	95%	90%	80%	70%	60%
	$250	$225	$200	$180	$160	$140	$120
Commercial model	$275	$250	$215	$185	$165	$145	$125

MODEL 318 — .25 ACP, 2½ in. barrel, fixed sights, blue, plastic grips, mfg. 1934-1939.

	100%	98%	95%	90%	80%	70%	60%
	$275	$250	$220	$195	$165	$140	$110

MODEL 418 — .25 ACP, fixed sights.

	100%	98%	95%	90%	80%	70%	60%
	$220	$190	$170	$145	$125	$110	$100

MODEL 420 — .25 ACP, chrome finish, small coverage engraving.

	100%	98%	95%	90%	80%	70%	60%
	$350	$300	$260	$230	$200	$175	$160

MODEL 421 — .25 ACP, gold plated, elaborate engraving.

	100%	98%	95%	90%	80%	70%	60%
	$475	$430	$400	$360	$320	$280	$230

PISTOLS: POST WWII

100% values on below listed models assume NIB condition.

MODEL 948 — .22 LR, 3½ or 6 in. barrel, fixed sights, hammer.

	100%	98%	95%	90%	80%	70%	60%
	$175	$150	$125	$100	$75	$60	$50

MODEL 949 OLYMPIC TARGET — .22 S or LR, 8¾ in. barrel, target sights, adj. barrel weights, blue, muzzle brake, checkered wood grips with thumbrest, limited mfg. 1959-1964.

	100%	98%	95%	90%	80%	70%	60%
	$660	$550	$495	$385	$305	$250	$195

MODEL 950CC MINX M2 — .22 Short, hinged 2⅜ in. barrel, fixed sights, blue, plastic grips. Mfg. 1955-disc.

	100%	98%	95%	90%	80%	70%	60%
	$135	$115	$105	$95	$85	$75	$70

MODEL 950CC SPECIAL MINX M4 — same as M2, with 4 in. barrel.

	100%	98%	95%	90%	80%	70%	60%
	$135	$115	$105	$95	$85	$75	$70

MODEL 950B JETFIRE — same as M2, in .25 ACP.

	100%	98%	95%	90%	80%	70%	60%
	$135	$115	$105	$95	$85	$75	$70

MODEL 951 BRIGADIER — 9mm, 4½ in. barrel, fixed sights, blue, plastic grips, current Italian service pistol. Mfg. 1952-present.

	100%	98%	95%	90%	80%	70%	60%
	$250	$215	$195	$175	$150	$130	$115

Add $350 for "Brigadier" or "Israeli" Model.

MODEL 20 — .25 ACP, double action, alloy frame, 9 shot, 2½ in. barrel, plastic or walnut grips, 10.9 oz. Disc. 1985.

	100%	98%	95%	90%	80%	70%	60%
	$160	$140	$125	$115	$95	$85	$75

Last Mfg.'s Sug. Retail was $214.

MODEL 70 PUMA OR COUGAR — .32 ACP or .380 ACP cal., 3½ in. barrel, fixed sights, blue, plastic grips, .32 Puma alloy frame, .380 Cougar steel frame. Disc.

	100%	98%	95%	90%	80%	70%	60%
	$200	$180	$165	$150	$130	$110	$90

This model is more desirable in .380 ACP cal.

MODEL 70T — same as 70, .32 ACP, target sights. Disc.

	100%	98%	95%	90%	80%	70%	60%
	$275	$250	$220	$195	$165	$150	$140

MODEL 70S — .22 LR or .380 ACP cal., single action, 3½ in. barrel, 9 shot, blued finish, plastic grips, weight .22 cal. — 18 oz., .380 ACP — 23 oz., steel frame, .22 LR has adj. rear sight. Disc. 1985.

	100%	98%	95%	90%	80%	70%	60%
	$240	$210	$185	$170	$155	$140	$125

Last Mfg.'s Sug. Retail was $295.

Grading	100%	98%	95%	90%	80%	70%	60%

MODEL 71 JAGUAR — alloy frame, .22 LR version of 70. Disc.

	$220	$195	$180	$160	$150	$140	$110

MODEL 72 JAGUAR — same as 71, with 6 in. barrel. Disc.

	$220	$195	$180	$160	$150	$140	$110

MODEL 76P-76W TARGET PISTOL — .22 LR, single action, 11 shot, steel frame, 6 in. barrel, adj. sights, blued finish, thumbrest plastic grips (76-P). Disc. 1985.

	$345	$300	$275	$245	$220	$195	$170

Add $40 for thumbrest wood grips (Model 76-W).
Last Mfg.'s Sug. Retail was $395.

MODEL 80 — .22 Short cal., target pistol with limited importation into the U.S.

	$750	$675	$595	$550	$495	$450	$395

MODEL 81P-81W — .32 ACP, double action, 13 shot, 3.8 in. barrel, fixed sights, blue. Imported 1976-1984.

	$300	$250	$225	$195	$175	$155	$135

Add $90 for nickel finish.
Add $20 for wood grips (W Suffix).

MODEL 82W — .32 ACP, double action, more compact than Model 81, 10 shot, walnut grips, 17 oz. Importation disc. 1984.

	$300	$250	$225	$195	$175	$155	$135

Add $75 for nickel finish.

MODEL 84W-EL — same as Model 84 only specially engraved, select walnut grips. Presentation case. Disc. 1984.

	$1,025	$770	$720	$615	$565	$520	$460

MODEL 86P-86W — .380 ACP only, double action, tip-up 4⅓ in. barrel, 8 shot mag., plastic or walnut grips, 23 oz. Add $80 for walnut grips (86-W). This model was advertised, but never released.
Mfg.'s Sug. Retail was $480 in 1986.

MODEL 90 DOUBLE ACTION AUTOMATIC — .32 ACP, 3⅝ in. barrel, fixed sights, blue, plastic grips. Mfg. 1969-1983.

	$275	$195	$175	$155	$130	$110	$95

MODEL 92 — same general specifications as current Model 92SB, originally mfg. 1976 until disc.

	$400	$350	$315	$280	$255	$240	$220

Early production Model 92's had a frame mounted safety and mag. release button at base of pistol grip in addition to a serial number suffix. The Model 92's design evolved from the Beretta Model 951. Military contracts have normally specified steel frame fabrication.

Model 92S — same as Model 92, second model. Disc.

	$375	$325	$260	$230	$200	$180	$165

MODEL 92SB-P — 9mm Luger, double action, 16 shot, 4.92 in. barrel, fixed sights, alloy frame, high-polish blued finish, plastic grips (Model 92SB-P), 34½ oz. Mfg. 1980-1985.

	$475	$425	$385	$345	$310	$285	$260

Last Mfg.'s Sug. Retail was $600.

Model 92SB-W — same as above, only with wooden grips. Disc. 1985.

	$495	$430	$390	$355	$330	$290	$260

Last Mfg.'s Sug. Retail was $620.

Grading	100%	98%	95%	90%	80%	70%	60%

MODEL 92SB-P COMPACT — same as Model 92SB, except has 4.3 in. barrel, 14 shot, plastic grips (Model 92SB-P), 31 oz. Disc. 1985.

| | $500 | $440 | $385 | $345 | $310 | $285 | $260 |

Add $60 for nickel finish.
Last Mfg.'s Sug. Retail was $620.

Model 92SB-W Compact — same as above only with wooden grips. Disc. 1985.

| | $525 | $465 | $395 | $355 | $335 | $300 | $280 |

Last Mfg.'s Sug. Retail was $635.

MODEL 100 — .32 ACP, fixed sights. Disc.

| | $250 | $220 | $195 | $165 | $150 | $140 | $130 |

MODEL 101 — same as 70T, in .22 LR. Disc.

| | $250 | $220 | $195 | $165 | $150 | $140 | $130 |

SEMI-AUTO PISTOLS: RECENT MFG.

MODEL 21-W — .22 LR or .25 ACP, double action, alloy frame, 7 shot mag. (.22 LR) or 8 shot mag. (.25 ACP), 2½ in. barrel, walnut grips, 12.3 oz.

| Mfg.'s Sug. Retail | $225 | $190 | $155 | $140 | $130 | $115 | $95 | $85 |

Add $25 for nickel finish.

Add $50 for engraving.

This model is manufactured by Beretta U.S.A. Corp. in Accokeek, MD.

Lady Beretta — .22 LR only, similar to Model 21-W, except is specially serial numbered and has gold etching on top of frame and slide sides. Supplied with a blue velvet drawstring bag. 1990 issue.

| | $245 | $185 | $160 | $140 | $130 | $115 | $100 |

This model was sold exclusively by Lew Horton Distributing Co.

Last Mfg.'s Sug. Retail was $285.

MODEL 71 — .22 LR, single action, 8 shot, 6 in. barrel, plastic grips with thumbrest, finger extension mag. Imported 1987 only.

| | $190 | $160 | $140 | $130 | $115 | $95 | $85 |

Last Mfg.'s Sug. Retail was $215.

MODEL 84P-84W — .380 ACP cal., double action semi-auto, 3.82 in. barrel, alloy frame, steel slide, 13 shot mag., firing pin block, ambidextrous manual safety (also used as a decocking lever), low dot profile sights, curved trigger guard, plastic or wood grips, blue or nickel finish, 23 oz.

| Mfg.'s Sug. Retail | $495 | $395 | $335 | $300 | $270 | $240 | $210 | $190 |

Add $25 for wooden grips (Model 84W).

Add $65 for nickel finish (includes checkered wooden grips).

Model 84F — similar specifications to the Model 84P-84W, except patterned after the Model 92F Gov.'t Model, matte black Bruniton finish, squared off trigger guard, plastic or wood grips, 23 oz. Mfg. 1990 only.

| | $395 | $330 | $300 | $270 | $240 | $210 | $190 |

Last Mfg.'s Sug. Retail was $479.

MODEL 85P-85W — same general specifications as the Model 84, except 8 shot mag., Model 85P has plastic grips, 22 oz.

| Mfg.'s Sug. Retail | $455 | $365 | $300 | $270 | $240 | $210 | $190 | $175 |

Add $60 for nickel finish.

Add $25 for wooden grips (Model 85W).

Model 85F — similar specifications to the Model 85P-85W, except patterned after the Model 92F Gov.'t Model, matte black Bruniton finish, squared off trigger guard, plastic or wood grips, 21.8 oz. Mfg. in 1990 only.

| | $375 | $300 | $270 | $240 | $210 | $190 | $175 |

Add $25 for wooden grips.
Last Mfg.'s Sug. Retail was $440.

Grading	100%	98%	95%	90%	80%	70%	60%

MODEL 87 — .22 LR, double action semi-auto, 7 shot mag., 3.82 or 6 in. target barrel with counterweight, wood grips, 20 oz. (3.82 in. barrel). Importation began 1986.

Mfg.'s Sug. Retail	$460	$375	$325	$280	$245	$210	$190	$175

Model 87 Target — single action only target variation of the Model 87 with 6 in. barrel, 23 oz.

Mfg.'s Sug. Retail	$480	$385	$335	$285	$245	$210	$190	$175

MODEL 89 — .22 LR, single action target semi-auto, matte black finish on metal parts, 10 shot mag., anatomical wood grips, adj. sights, 41 oz. Importation began 1988.

Mfg.'s Sug. Retail	$685	$550	$475	$400	$350	$300	$275	$250

MODEL 92F — 9mm Para., official U.S. military variation of 92 Series, 4.9 in. barrel, alloy frame, steel slide, 15 shot mag., chamber loaded indicator, matte black Bruniton finish, squared off trigger guard to facilitate two-hand shooting, extended mag. base, 3 dot sights became an option in 1991. Model 92F-P has plastic grips. Model 92F-W has wood grips. New 1984.

Mfg.'s Sug. Retail	$630	$545	$445	$410	$375	$335	$300	$275

Add $25 for checkered wood grips.

Add $100 for Trijicon Sight System.

Add $70 for gold engraving/accenting.

Plastic grips are currently as desirable as wood, even though wood adds $25 to the retail price.

Older Italian mfg. Model 92's are commanding slight premiums in some areas.

The U.S. military on January 15, 1985 announced that the Model 92F would replace the Colt Gov't. Model .45 ACP as the standard government issue sidearm. Because of domestic political pressures, Congress requested that a new sidearm competition be conducted again in 1988. The result of this second trial was that the Department of the Army announced on May 22, 1989 that Beretta had won again. This military contract with Beretta U.S.A. Corp. involves over 315,000 Model 92SB-F's being manufactured for U.S. military consumption by the early 1990's. Because of the emphasis on military production, commercial models have been somewhat limited to date and may command premiums over the values listed above. The Model 92F and Model 92F Compact (reintroduced 1989) are the only variations available for commercial sale currently. Actual delivery of commercial Model 92's began in January of 1986.

Model 92F Stainless — similar to Model 92F, except is mfg. from stainless steel, satin finish with plastic grips, initially released to law enforcement agencies only, a limited amount have found their way into the commercial market (usually with premiums being asked).

Mfg.'s Sug. Retail	$706	$695	$595	$495				

MODEL 92F COMPACT — similar to Model 92F, except has 4.3 in. barrel and 13 shot mag., plastic or wood grips, 31½ oz. While temporarily suspended in 1986, production was resumed 1989.

Mfg.'s Sug. Retail	$625	$570	$450	$415	$375	$335	$300	$275

Add $30 for checkered walnut grips (Model 92F Wood).

Model 92SB Compact 8 Shot — similar to Model 92F Compact, except has 8 shot straight line mag., plastic grips only. New 1990.

Mfg.'s Sug. Retail	$640	$575	$455	$415	$375	$335	$300	$275

MODEL 92G — 9mm Para., identical to the Model 92F, except features a spring loaded decocking lever that safely lowers the hammer allowing fire-ready when unholstering the pistol. New 1990.

The Model 92G is sold to law enforcement agencies only and no commercial prices are available. This pistol has been used by French Gendarmes since 1987.

MODEL 950 BS — .22 Short or .25 ACP cal., single action, alloy frame, 8 shot (.25 cal. only) or 6 shot mag., tip-up 2½ and 4 in. (.22 only) barrel, plastic grips, thumb safety, 8-10 oz.

Mfg.'s Sug. Retail	$175	$145	$125	$110	$100	$90	$80	$70

Add $30 for nickel finish.

Add $75 for engraved variation.

This model is manufactured by Beretta U.S.A. Corp. in Accokeek, MD.

Grading	100%	98%	95%	90%	80%	70%	60%

Model 950 EL — same general specifications as Model 950 BS, only with wooden grips and gold plated parts. Importation disc. 1988.

	$190	$175	$150	$140	$130	$115	$105

Last Mfg.'s Sug. Retail was $210.

BOLT-ACTION RIFLES: RECENT MFG.

MODEL 500 CUSTOM — .222 Rem., .223 Rem., .243 Win., .270 Win., .30-06, or .308 Win. cal., 3 action length, 24 in. barrel, iron sights, checkered walnut stock with recoil pad. Importation was resumed 1988 only.

	$595	$530	$450	$395	$350	$315	$275

Last Mfg.'s Sug. Retail was $725.

Model 500S — same as Model 500, except is equipped with iron sights. Imported 1986 only.

	$615	$560	$460	$400	$350	$315	$275

Last Mfg.'s Sug. Retail was $700.

Model 500 DL — same specifications as Model 500, only better walnut and light engraving. Disc. 1986.

	$1,395	$1,260	$1,000	$875	$795	$725	$650

Last Mfg.'s Sug. Retail was $1,595.

Model 500 DLS — same as Model 500 DL, except is equipped with iron sights. Imported 1986 only.

	$1,420	$1,285	$1,020	$875	$795	$725	$650

Last Mfg.'s Sug. Retail was $1,625.

Model 500 EELL — same specifications as Model 500 DL, only select walnut and more engraving. Disc. 1986.

	$1,550	$1,260	$1,150	$1,000	$875	$800	$725

Last Mfg.'s Sug. Retail was $1,745.

Model 500 EELLS — same as Model 500 EELL, except is equipped with iron sights. Imported 1986 only.

	$1,575	$1,425	$1,200	$1,120	$875	$800	$725

Last Mfg.'s Sug. Retail was $1,785.

MODEL 501 — available in either .243 or .308 Win. cal., medium bolt action, 6 shot, 23 in. barrel, no sights, checkered walnut stock. Disc. 1986.

	$595	$530	$465	$395	$350	$315	$275

Last Mfg.'s Sug. Retail was $665.

Model 501 S — same as Model 501, except is equipped with iron sights. Imported 1986 only.

	$615	$560	$460	$400	$350	$315	$275

Last Mfg.'s Sug. Retail was $700.

Model 501 DL — same specifications as Model 501, only better walnut and light engraving. Disc. 1986.

	$1,395	$1,260	$1,000	$875	$795	$725	$650

Last Mfg.'s Sug. Retail was $1,575.

Model 501 DLS — same as Model 501 DL, except is equipped with iron sights. Imported 1986 only.

	$1,420	$1,285	$1,020	$875	$795	$725	$650

Last Mfg.'s Sug. Retail was $1,625.

Model 501 EELL — same specifications as Model 501 DL, only select walnut and more engraving. Disc. 1986.

	$1,550	$1,260	$1,150	$1,000	$875	$800	$725

Last Mfg.'s Sug. Retail was $1,745.

Model 501 EELLS — same as Model 501 EELL, except is equipped with iron sights. Imported 1986 only.

	$1,575	$1,425	$1,200	$1,120	$875	$800	$725

Last Mfg.'s Sug. Retail was $1,785.

Grading	100%	98%	95%	90%	80%	70%	60%

MODEL 502 — available in either .30-06, .270 or 7mm Rem. Mag. cal., long bolt action, 5 or 6 shot, 24 in. barrel, no sights, checkered walnut stock. Disc. 1986.

	$625	$565	$490	$440	$395	$360	$330

Last Mfg.'s Sug. Retail was $710.

Model 502 S — same as Model 502, except is equipped with iron sights. Imported 1986 only.

	$650	$595	$525	$460	$395	$360	$330

Last Mfg.'s Sug. Retail was $745.

Model 502 DL — same specifications as Model 502, only better walnut and light engraving. Also available in .375 H&H Mag. Disc. 1986.

	$1,495	$1,310	$1,175	$1,025	$900	$775	$695

Last Mfg.'s Sug. Retail was $1,640.

Model 502 DLS — same as Model 502, except is equipped with iron sights. Imported 1986 only.

	$1,410	$1,325	$1,175	$1,025	$900	$775	$695

Last Mfg.'s Sug. Retail was $1,660.

Model 502 EELL — same specifications as Model 502 DL, only select walnut and more engraving. Also available in .375 H&H Mag. Disc. 1986.

	$1,575	$1,425	$1,200	$1,120	$875	$800	$725

Last Mfg.'s Sug. Retail was $1,785.

Model 502 EELLS — same as Model 502 EELL, except is equipped with iron sights. Imported 1986 only.

	$1,575	$1,425	$1,200	$1,120	$875	$800	$725

Last Mfg.'s Sug. Retail was $1,785.

SEMI-AUTO RIFLES: RECENT MFG.

AR 70 — .222 or .223 cal., semi-auto paramilitary design rifle, 5, 8 or 30 shot mag.'s, Diopter sights, epoxy finish, 17.72 in. barrel, 8.3 lbs.

	$1,050	$875	$725	$600	$500	$450	$400

Last Mfg.'s Sug. Retail was $1,065. 1989 Federal legislation banned the importation of this model into U.S.

CUSTOM RIFLES: RECENT MFG.

Older specimens in this SO/689 series (not custom ordered within the last several years) could have values considerably lower than those listed below since values went up substantially before they were discontinued.

MODEL S689 O/U — 9.3 x 74R or 30-06 cal., boxlock action, nickel (disc. 1985) or case hardened (new 1986) receiver, double triggers, 23 in. barrels, auto ejectors, sling swivels, 7.7 lbs. Importation disc. in 1990.

	$3,700	$2,600	$2,200	$1,850	$1,550	$1,275	$1,050

Add $1,000 for scope and claw mounts.
Last Mfg.'s Sug. Retail was $4,907.

SSO EXPRESS O/U — .375 H&H or .458 Win. Mag. cal., sidelock action, case hardened receiver, double triggers, 23 in. barrels, auto ejectors, 11 lbs., cased. Importation disc. 1989.

	$12,500	$9,500	$8,250	$6,950	$6,100	$5,600	$4,875

Add $425 for claw mounts.
Last Mfg.'s Sug. Retail was $17,533.

SSO5 EXPRESS O/U — similar to SSO Express except has more elaborate engraving and better walnut.

	$14,250	$11,750	$8,750	$7,500	$6,750	$6,100	$5,600

Last Mfg.'s Sug. Retail was $19,600.

SSO6 EXPRESS O/U — .375 H&H or .458 Win. Mag. cal., top of the line sidelock double rifle, individually built to the customers specifications. New 1990.

Since each gun is a special order, prices are available by quotation by contacting Beretta U.S.A. Corp. directly.

Grading	100%	98%	95%	90%	80%	70%	60%

MODEL 455 SIDE-BY-SIDE — .375 H&H or .458 Win. Mag. cal., top of the line sidelock double rifle, individually built to the customers specifications. New 1990.
Since each gun is a special order, prices are available by quotation by contacting Beretta U.S.A. Corp. directly.

O/U SHOTGUNS: DISC.

BL-1 — 12 ga., 26, 28, or 30 in. barrels, various chokes, boxlock, extractors, double triggers, checkered pistol grip stock. Mfg. 1968-1973.

	$385	$330	$275	$220	$190	$175	$160

BL-2 — same as BL-1, with single selective trigger, more engraving.

	$420	$385	$360	$305	$265	$225	$185

BL-2 Stake-Out — riot configuration with 18 in. barrels, DT.

	$385	$330	$275	$220	$190	$175	$160

BL-2/S — same as BL-2, with vent rib and speed trigger. Mfg. 1974-1976.

	$440	$385	$330	$305	$265	$225	$185

BL-3 — O/U, same as BL-2, with more engraving, vent rib and ejectors, also available in 20 ga. Mfg. 1968-1976.

	$595	$550	$525	$470	$440	$385	$350

BL-3 SKEET

	$660	$605	$580	$525	$470	$415	$370

BL-3 TRAP

	$580	$520	$495	$450	$415	$375	$335

BL-4 — deluxe version of BL-3, more engraving, better wood.

	$695	$650	$595	$550	$495	$450	$395

BL-4 SKEET

	$745	$690	$635	$550	$495	$450	$395

BL-4 TRAP

	$675	$625	$580	$525	$475	$425	$360

BL-5 — higher grade version of BL-4.

	$910	$855	$800	$715	$650	$575	$475

BL-5 SKEET

	$960	$910	$855	$760	$675	$600	$500

BL-5 TRAP

	$850	$820	$775	$695	$595	$525	$430

BL-6 — auto ejectors, sidelock, elaborate engraving.

	$1,250	$1,100	$990	$935	$850	$765	$680

BL-6 SKEET

	$1,295	$1,100	$990	$935	$850	$765	$680

BL-6 TRAP

	$1,100	$950	$885	$810	$755	$670	$580

MODEL S55B — 12 or 20 ga., O/U, 26, 28, or 30 in. barrels, various chokes, boxlock, extractors, selective trigger, checkered pistol grip stock. Disc.

	$550	$495	$440	$385	$330	$300	$280

MODEL S56 E — same as S55B, with engraved receiver and auto ejectors. Disc.

	$605	$555	$515	$460	$415	$365	$330

Grading	100%	98%	95%	90%	80%	70%	60%

MODEL S58 SKEET — same as S56E, with 26 in. Bohler steel barrels, skeet bore, wide vent rib, skeet.

| | $770 | $695 | $630 | $550 | $495 | $445 | $395 |

MODEL S58 TRAP — same as S58 Skeet, with 30 in. barrels, imp. mod. and full choke, Monte Carlo stock with pad.

| | $700 | $625 | $550 | $495 | $450 | $410 | $365 |

SILVER SNIPE — 12 or 20 ga., 26, 28, or 30 in. barrels, boxlock, extractors, trigger optional, checkered pistol grip stock. Mfg. 1955-1967.

| | $415 | $370 | $330 | $295 | $265 | $230 | $210 |

   Silver Snipe SST — with vent. rib and SST.

| | $550 | $495 | $440 | $415 | $360 | $330 | $295 |

     Add 25% for ejectors.

GOLDEN SNIPE — same as Silver Snipe, with auto ejectors and vent. rib standard.

| | $660 | $605 | $550 | $525 | $470 | $430 | $385 |

   Golden Snipe SST — with SST.

| | $715 | $660 | $605 | $580 | $525 | $465 | $410 |

MODEL 57 E — higher quality version of Golden Snipe. Mfg. 1955-1967.

| | $825 | $770 | $660 | $635 | $550 | $495 | $450 |

   Model 57 E SST — with single selective trigger.

| | $880 | $825 | $715 | $690 | $605 | $540 | $495 |

ASEL MODEL — 12 or 20 ga., 26, 28, or 30 in. barrels, various chokes, single trigger, checkered pistol grip stock, auto ejectors. Mfg. 1947-1964.

| | $1,340 | $1,100 | $990 | $880 | $800 | $720 | $650 |

GRADE 100 — 12 ga., 26, 28, or 30 in. barrels, any choke, sidelock, double trigger, auto ejectors, checkered pistol grip or straight stock.

| | $1,820 | $1,550 | $1,300 | $1,100 | $900 | $775 | $695 |

MODEL 200 — same as 100, with chrome lined bores and action parts, higher quality engraving.

| | $2,310 | $2,000 | $1,870 | $1,650 | $1,375 | $1,100 | $875 |

MODEL 680 — competition trap and skeet model, .12 ga. only, boxlock, various chokes. Mono-trap model available. Silver finish receiver, hand engraved, premium walnut. Disc.

| | $1,215 | $1,030 | $870 | $790 | $715 | $635 | $550 |

     Add $60 for 2 barrel combo. package.

FIELD SHOTGUNS: O/U RECENT MFG.

MODEL 685 — 12 or 20 ga. 2¾ or 3 in. chambers, matte chromed receiver, extractors, single trigger. Disc. 1986.

| | $650 | $575 | $495 | $450 | $400 | $360 | $320 |

   Last Mfg.'s Sug. Retail was $875.

MODEL 686 — 12 (disc. 1990), 20 (disc. 1990), or 28 ga., field model, boxlock action, various barrels/chokes, ejectors, single trigger, engraved silver finished receiver, special walnut, pistol or straight grip stock. Fixed-chokes disc. 1987.

| Mfg.'s Sug. Retail | $1,225 | $995 | $800 | $650 | $575 | $525 | $460 | $415 |

   Subtract $100 if fixed chokes.

MODEL 686 ONYX — 12 or 20 ga., 3 in. chambers, boxlock action, 26 or 28 in. barrels with multi-chokes, matte finish on metal parts, single trigger, ejectors. New 1988.

| Mfg.'s Sug. Retail | $1,225 | $995 | $825 | $675 | $595 | $550 | $480 | $425 |

This model is also available with a straight grip English stock at no extra charge.

Grading	100%	98%	95%	90%	80%	70%	60%

Model 686 Onyx Combo — same as Model 686 Field, except is supplied with 1 set each of 20 ga. (28 in.) and 28 ga. (26 in.) barrels. Introduced 1986.

Mfg.'s Sug. Retail	$1,840	$1,500	$1,275	$1,125	$950	$875	$820	$775

Model 686 Onyx Magnum — 12 ga. only, similar to Model 686 Onyx, except has 3½ in. chambers. New 1990.

Mfg.'s Sug. Retail	$1,260	$1,100	$925	$800	$700	$650	$575	$525

MODEL 687 L — 12 or 20 ga., boxlock, various barrels/chokes, ejectors, floral engraved nickel finished receiver, select walnut, fitted case.

Mfg.'s Sug. Retail	$1,655	$1,295	$1,015	$825	$700	$635	$575	$525

Subtract $100 without multi-chokes.

MODEL 687 L ONYX — 12 or 20 ga., 3 in. chambers, same game scene engraving as standard Model 687 L, except has Onyx blackened receiver, multi-chokes standard. Mfg. 1990 only.

	$1,250	$995	$825	$700	$635	$575	$525

Last Mfg.'s Sug. Retail was $1,590.

MODEL 687 GOLDEN ONYX — 12 or 20 ga., 3 in. chambers, similar to Model 686 Onyx, except has more engraving, better walnut, and several gold inlays. Imported 1988-89 only.

	$1,375	$1,075	$875	$775	$685	$635	$575

Last Mfg.'s Sug. Retail was $1,800.

MODEL 687 EL — same general specifications as Model 687L Field, except available in 20, 28 (new 1990), or .410 (new 1990) ga. also, 2¾ or 3 in. chambers, boxlock with sideplates, better walnut, and more engraving.

Mfg.'s Sug. Retail	$2,740	$2,335	$2,000	$1,725	$1,500	$1,350	$1,150	$1,000

Add $760 for small frame 28 or .410 ga.

MODEL 687 EL ONYX — 12 or 20 ga., 3 in. chambers, simulated sidelock plates with classic scroll engraving. Mfg. 1990 only.

	$2,295	$2,000	$1,725	$1,500	$1,350	$1,150	$1,000

Last Mfg.'s Sug. Retail was $2,660.

MODEL 687 EELL — 12, 20, or 28 ga., same general specifications as Model 687EL, except has extra select walnut, game scene engraving, 3 in. chambers and gold plated trigger, multi-chokes introduced 1988.

Mfg.'s Sug. Retail	$4,015	$3,325	$2,695	$2,300	$1,950	$1,725	$1,500	$1,250

Subtract $100 if without multi-chokes (except 28 ga.).

This model is also available with a straight grip English stock at no extra charge (20 ga. only).

Model 687 EELL Combo — includes one set of 28 ga. (26 in. barrels with multi-chokes) and one set of 20 ga. (choice of 26 or 28 multi-choke) barrels.

Mfg.'s Sug. Retail	$4,455	$3,725	$2,900	$2,425	$1,925	$1,725	$1,500	$1,250

Subtract $250 for fixed chokes.

Multi-chokes became standard in 1991.

SKEET SHOTGUNS: O/U RECENT MFG.

MODEL 682 SKEET — competition skeet model, 12, 20, 28 (disc. 1988), or .410 ga. (disc. 1988), 26 (12 ga. only) or 28 in. barrels, boxlock, skeet chokes, silver finish receiver, hand engraved, premium walnut, cased. New 1984.

Mfg.'s Sug. Retail	$2,180	$1,775	$1,525	$1,250	$1,050	$950	$895	$800

Model 682 Super Skeet — 12 ga. only, 28 in. VR barrels bored SK/SK featuring factory porting, stock has separate adj. comb cheekpiece. New 1991.

Mfg.'s Sug. Retail	$2,535	$2,200	$1,900	$1,650	$1,475	$1,275	$1,050	$950

Model 682 Skeet Deluxe — same as Model 682, except deluxe walnut and elaborate engraving. Disc. 1986.

	$2,650	$2,300	$2,100	$1,850	$1,600	$1,400	$1,200

Last Mfg.'s Sug. Retail was $3,000.

Grading	100%	98%	95%	90%	80%	70%	60%

Model 682 2-Barrel Skeet Set — 12 ga. only, two barrel set bored for skeet and sporting play competition. Imported 1988 only.

	$4,950	$4,200	$3,675	$3,175	$2,850	$2,500	$2,175

Last Mfg.'s Sug. Retail was $6,650.

Model 682 4-Ga. Skeet Set — four barrel skeet set comes with interchangeable barrels (28 in.) in 12, 20, 28, and 410 ga.'s. New 1985.

Mfg.'s Sug. Retail	$5,160	$4,325	$3,725	$3,200	$2,850	$2,500	$2,175	$1,900

MODEL 687 EELL SKEET — 12 ga. only, fixed chokes, 28 in. barrels.

Mfg.'s Sug. Retail	$3,715	$3,125	$2,550	$2,250	$1,900	$1,725	$1,500	$1,250

Model 687 EELL 4-Ga. Skeet Set — four ga. skeet set, cased. New 1988.

Mfg.'s Sug. Retail	$7,105	$5,650	$4,750	$3,950	$3,400	$3,000	$2,700	$2,450

SPORTING CLAYS: O/U RECENT MFG.

These variations have been specifically designed for sporting clay target shooting.

MODEL 682 SPORTING — 12 ga. only, similar specifications to Model 682, 28 or 30 (new 1989) in. VR barrels, except over-field stock dimensions and hand engraved silver finished receiver. Multichokes are standard.

Mfg.'s Sug. Retail	$2,260	$1,815	$1,575	$1,275	$1,050	$950	$895	$800

Add $765 for extra set of barrels (combo. package - new 1990).

MODEL SUPER SPORT — 12 ga. only, 28 or 30 in. VR barrels with multi-chokes, similar to Model 682 Sporting. New 1989.

Mfg.'s Sug. Retail	$2,400	$2,075	$1,775	$1,525	$1,250	$1,050	$950	$875

MODEL 686 SPORTING — 12 ga. only, deluxe checkered walnut stock and forearm with over-field dimensions, 28 or 30 (new 1991) in. barrels only, multi-chokes standard. New 1987.

Mfg.'s Sug. Retail	$1,735	$1,425	$1,250	$1,050	$925	$875	$775	$695

Add $585 for extra set of barrels (combo. package - new 1991).

Model 686 English Course — 12 ga. only, features 28 in. VR barrels and special tapered VR with special sighting plane designed for English courses. New 1991.

Mfg.'s Sug. Retail	$1,800	$1,500	$1,300	$1,100	$925	$875	$775	$695

MODEL 687 SPORTING — 12 or 20 ga. only, deluxe checkered walnut stock and forearm with over-field dimensions, 28 in. barrels only, multi-chokes standard. New 1987.

Mfg.'s Sug. Retail	$2,285	$2,000	$1,725	$1,500	$1,250	$1,050	$950	$875

Add $775 for extra set of barrels (combo. package - new 1991).

Model 687 English Course — 12 ga. only, features 28 in. VR barrels and special tapered VR with special sighting plane designed for English courses. New 1991.

Mfg.'s Sug. Retail	$2,355	$2,050	$1,750	$1,500	$1,250	$1,050	$950	$875

MODEL 687 EELL SPORTING — 12 or 20 (disc. 1989) ga. only, deluxe checkered walnut stock and forearm with over-field dimensions, 28 in. barrels only, multi-chokes standard. New 1987.

Mfg.'s Sug. Retail	$4,200	$3,550	$2,795	$2,375	$1,925	$1,725	$1,500	$1,250

Add $875 for extra set of barrels (combo. package - 1990 mfg. only).

TRAP SHOTGUNS: O/U RECENT MFG.

MODEL 682 TRAP O/U — 12 ga. only, competition trap model, silver or Bruniton finish (matte black), 30 or 32 in. barrels, adj. trigger, supplied with case. New 1985.

Mfg.'s Sug. Retail	$2,160	$1,765	$1,500	$1,250	$1,050	$950	$895	$800

Add $65 for multi-chokes.

This model is designated the Model 682 X if with Bruniton matte black finish.

Model 682 Mono — single under-barrel trap model, high post vent rib, 32 or 34 in. barrel. No extra charge for multi-chokes. Imported 1985-1988.

	$1,530	$1,400	$1,200	$1,025	$925	$875	$775

Last Mfg.'s Sug. Retail was $1,890.

Grading	100%	98%	95%	90%	80%	70%	60%

Model 682 Pigeon Trap — 12 ga. only, includes features for international style pigeon and competition shooters including international style stock, flat VR, and mid-rib sights, silver (new 1991) or matte black (disc.) metal finish, semi-gloss American walnut stock, light scroll engraving, sliding trigger, includes multi-chokes. New 1990.

Mfg.'s Sug. Retail	$2,400	$1,925	$1,625	$1,300	$1,075	$950	$895	$800

Model 682 Top Single — 12 ga. only, single over-barrel trap model, 32 or 34 in. barrel. New 1986.

Mfg.'s Sug. Retail	$2,300	$1,750	$1,500	$1,275	$1,025	$925	$875	$775

Subtract $75 if without multi-chokes.
Multi-chokes became standard in 1989.

Model 682 Mono/Top Combo — 12 ga. only, supplied with mono under or upper single barrel and O/U barrel sets. Otherwise same specifications as Model 682 Trap. Cased.

Mfg.'s Sug. Retail	$2,965	$2,325	$2,050	$1,725	$1,525	$1,375	$1,200	$1,000

Subtract $50 if without multi-chokes.

MODEL 682 SUPER TRAP O/U — 12 ga. only, competition trap model, 30 in. barrels, step tapered rib, factory porting, length of pull and separate stock cheekpiece are adjustable. New 1991.

Mfg.'s Sug. Retail	$2,505	$2,000	$1,675	$1,350	$1,075	$950	$895	$800

This model gives you a choice of fixed or multi-chokes at no extra charge.

Model 682 Top Single Super — 12 ga. only, single over-barrel trap model, 32 or 34 in. barrel with choice of fixed or multi-chokes. New 1991.

Mfg.'s Sug. Retail	$2,665	$2,125	$1,775	$1,400	$1,095	$975	$900	$800

Model 682 Top Combo Super — 12 ga. only, supplied with upper single barrel and O/U barrel sets. Otherwise same specifications as Model 682 Super Trap. Cased.

Mfg.'s Sug. Retail	$3,315	$2,650	$2,175	$1,800	$1,600	$1,375	$1,200	$1,000

Add $65 for multi-chokes on both barrels.

MODEL 687 EELL O/U — 12 ga. only, boxlock action with engraved silver finished side plates, Monte Carlo stock with recoil pad, 30 in. barrels with choke tubes.

Mfg.'s Sug. Retail	$4,045	$3,440	$2,750	$2,350	$1,925	$1,725	$1,500	$1,250

MODEL 687 EELL TOP SINGLE TRAP — 12 ga. only, single over-barrel trap model, 32 or 34 in. barrel. New 1988.

Mfg.'s Sug. Retail	$4,245	$3,500	$2,850	$2,400	$1,975	$1,725	$1,500	$1,250

Add $50 for multi-chokes.

Model 687 EELL Top Trap Combo — 12 ga. only, supplied with 30 or 32 in. O/U barrels and a mono trap upper barrel, multi-chokes standard. New 1988.

Mfg.'s Sug. Retail	$5,080	$4,350	$3,850	$3,425	$3,000	$2,775	$2,550	$2,250

Add $40 for multi-chokes.

Model 687 EELL Mono Trap Combo — 12 ga. only, supplied with 30 or 32 in. O/U barrels and a mono trap bottom barrel. Imported 1986-1988.

	$4,175	$3,725	$3,395	$3,000	$2,775	$2,550	$2,250

Add $140 for multi-chokes.
Last Mfg.'s Sug. Retail was $4,900.

CUSTOM GRADE SHOTGUNS: O/U RECENT MFG.

Older specimens in this SO series (not custom ordered within the last several years) could have values considerably lower than those listed below since values went up substantially before they were discontinued.

SO-2 — 12 ga., 26-30 in. barrels, sidelock, any chokes, vent rib, auto ejectors, SST, checkered stock in various configurations (field, skeet, or trap), grades differ in wood, engraving, and finish, cased. Mfg. 1948-present.

	$4,900	$4,200	$3,500	$2,850	$2,200	$1,900	$1,750

SO-3 — 2nd grade of the SO series. Disc. 1987.

	$7,850	$6,800	$5,980	$5,475	$4,450	$3,875	$3,400

Last Mfg.'s Sug. Retail was $8,250.

Grading	100%	98%	95%	90%	80%	70%	60%

SO-3 EL — grade-up from SO-3 with better wood and engraving. Disc. 1985.

| | $8,250 | $6,900 | $6,000 | $5,500 | $4,450 | $3,900 | $3,500 |

Last Mfg.'s Sug. Retail was $8,100.

SO-3 EELL — best quality model, custom specifications, choice of engraving motifs. Disc. 1987.

| | $8,995 | $7,975 | $6,700 | $5,750 | $5,000 | $4,500 | $3,950 |

Add $1,375/set of O/U barrels.
Last Mfg.'s Sug. Retail was $11,625.

SO-4 — 12 ga., sidelock, available in field, skeet, or trap configurations, custon spec.'s, fluorescent sights, wide rib, cased. Disc. 1987.

| | $8,350 | $7,000 | $6,100 | $5,500 | $4,500 | $4,000 | $3,500 |

Add $2,300 for extra set of O/U barrels.
Last Mfg.'s Sug. Retail was $8,700.

SO-5 COMPETITION — best quality O/U, extensively engraved, top quality checkered walnut stock (semi-pistol grip) and forearm, available in either Trap, Skeet, or Sporting configurations, limited importation, last published retail price was in 1989.

| | $10,000 | $8,500 | $7,800 | $6,750 | $5,950 | $5,200 | $4,500 |

Add $3,500 for extra set of barrels.
Add $3,250 for Trap Combo set.
Add $700 for SST.
Last Mfg.'s Sug. Retail was $13,693.

SO-5 EELL — next to top-of-the-line model, available in either Trap, Skeet, or Sporting configurations, custom built to customer dimensions. Importation disc. 1988.

| | $15,950 | $12,250 | $10,500 | $8,500 | $7,800 | $6,750 | $5,950 |

Last Mfg.'s Sug. Retail was $21,750.

SO-6 FIELD — best quality O/U, extensively engraved, top quality checkered walnut stock (semi-pistol grip) and forearm, field dimensions, built to customer specifications, limited importation, last published retail price was in 1989.

| | $11,250 | $8,750 | $7,850 | $6,750 | $5,950 | $5,200 | $4,500 |

Add $4,000 for extra set of barrels.
Add $733 for SST.
Last Mfg.'s Sug. Retail was $15,480.

SO-6 EELL — current top-of-the-line model, field dimensions, custom built to customer specifications. Importation disc. 1989.

| | $17,300 | $12,750 | $11,000 | $8,500 | $7,800 | $6,750 | $5,950 |

Last Mfg.'s Sug. Retail was $23,973.

SO-9 — 12, 20, 28, or .410 ga., first time the SO series has been offered in smaller gauges, 28 or .410 ga. models have smaller proportionate frames. New 1990.
Since each gun is a special order, prices are available by quotation by contacting Beretta U.S.A. Corp. directly.

SIDE-BY-SIDE SHOTGUNS: DISC.

MODEL 409 PB — 12, 16, 20, or 28 ga., 27, 28, and 30 in. barrels, various chokes, double triggers, plain extractors, checkered pistol grip stock. Mfg. 1934-1964.

| | $770 | $660 | $605 | $550 | $495 | $440 | $385 |

MODEL 410 E — higher quality, auto ejector version of 409PB.

| | $880 | $770 | $715 | $660 | $605 | $550 | $495 |

MODEL 410 — same as 410 E, except 10 ga. Mag., 32 in. barrel, full choke, heavier construction, mfg. 1934. Disc.

| | $990 | $880 | $825 | $770 | $715 | $660 | $550 |

Grading	100%	98%	95%	90%	80%	70%	60%

MODEL 411 E — same as 409 PB, with false sideplates and finer finishing. Mfg. 1934-1964.

	100%	98%	95%	90%	80%	70%	60%
	$1,210	$1,100	$1,045	$990	$880	$825	$770

MODEL 424-426 — 12 and 20 ga. (Model 426 only), 26 and 28 in. barrels, various chokes, boxlock, extractors, double triggers, light engraving, checkered straight stock. Add $115 for Model 426.

	$900	$715	$660	$635	$550	$495	$415

MODEL 426 E — same as 424, with auto ejectors, SST, select wood and more intricate engraving, silver pigeon inlay. Disc. 1983.

	$1,115	$935	$880	$855	$770	$715	$635

MODEL 625 — 12 or 20 ga., 26-30 in. barrels, various chokes, boxlock, extractors, double triggers, light engraving, checkered straight stock. Imported 1984-1986.

	$795	$745	$660	$580	$530	$485	$440

Last Mfg.'s Sug. Retail was $835.

MODEL GR-2 — 12 and 20 ga.'s, 26 and 28 in. barrels, various chokes, boxlock, extractors, double triggers, checkered pistol grip stock. Mfg. 1968-1976.

	$660	$605	$550	$495	$385	$330	$275

MODEL GR-3 — same as GR-2, with select wood and more engraving. Mfg. 1968-1976.

	$770	$715	$660	$605	$495	$440	$385

MODEL GR-4 — same as GR-3, with auto ejectors. Mfg. 1968-1976.

	$880	$825	$770	$715	$605	$550	$495

SILVER HAWK — 12 ga. Mag. & 10 ga. Mag. with double triggers and extractors. Disc. 1967.

	$495	$380	$325	$275	$250	$225	$200

Add $100 for 10 ga.

SILVER HAWK FEATHERWEIGHT — 12, 16, 20, or 28 ga., 26-32 in. barrels, high solid rib, various chokes, double triggers, checkered pistol grip stock, beavertail forearm. Disc. 1967.

	$495	$440	$415	$385	$360	$330	$275
Single trigger	$550	$495	$440	$415	$385	$360	$330

SO-6 DOUBLE BARREL — same general specifications and embellishments as the SO series O/U guns, but S x S. Mfg. 1948-1982.

	$5,900	$5,500	$5,280	$5,060	$4,840	$4,400	$3,850

SO-7 DOUBLE BARREL — top of the line S x S, finest quality wood, more elaborate engraving. Disc.

	$8,250	$7,700	$7,150	$6,600	$6,050	$5,500	$4,620

SIDE-BY-SIDE SHOTGUNS: RECENT MFG.

MODEL 626 FIELD — 12 or 20 (disc. 1987) ga., 2¾ in. chambers, 26 and 28 in. barrels, various chokes, boxlock, ejectors, single trigger, moderate engraving, pistol grip or straight checkered stock. Imported 1984-1988.

	$895	$800	$740	$685	$595	$540	$490

Last Mfg.'s Sug. Retail was $995.

MODEL 626 ONYX — 12 or 20 ga., 3 in. chambers, 26 or 28 (new 1990) in. VR barrels with multi-chokes, matte finished metal parts, select checkered walnut stock and forearm. New 1988.

Mfg.'s Sug. Retail	$1,640	$1,260	$1,025	$850	$750	$685	$595	$540

Model 626 Onyx Magnum — 12 ga. only, 3½ in. chambers. New 1990.

Mfg.'s Sug. Retail	$1,675	$1,275	$1,050	$900	$800	$700	$600	$550

MODEL 627 EL FIELD — 12 and 20 (disc. 1987) ga., 2¾ (disc. 1990) or 3 in. (became standard in 1991) chambers, 26 and 28 in. barrels, various chokes, boxlock, ejectors, single trigger, extensive engraving, pistol grip or straight checkered stock, cased. New 1985.

Mfg.'s Sug. Retail	$2,785	$2,275	$1,850	$1,625	$1,300	$1,100	$925	$795

Grading	100%	98%	95%	90%	80%	70%	60%

Subtract $200 for fixed chokes and 2¾ in. chambers.

Model 627 EL Sport — same as Model 627 EL Field, except 12 ga. only, knurled rib, sporting clays dimensions. Importation disc. 1988.

	100%	98%	95%	90%	80%	70%	60%
	$1,800	$1,625	$1,500	$1,300	$1,100	$925	$795

Last Mfg.'s Sug. Retail was $1,995.

MODEL 627 EELL — 12 or 20 (disc. 1987) ga., 2¾ or 3 (12 ga. only) in. chambers, 26 or 28 in. barrels, various chokes, boxlock, ejectors, single trigger, elaborate engraving, pistol grip or straight checkered stock, cased. New 1985.

Mfg.'s Sug. Retail	$4,735	$3,900	$3,225	$2,600	$2,125	$1,750	$1,600	$1,450

Subtract $200 if fixed chokes only.
Multi-chokes became standard in 1991.

CUSTOM GRADE SHOTGUNS: SIDE-BY-SIDE

Older specimens in this SO series (not custom ordered within the last several years) could have values considerably lower than those listed below since values went up substantially before they were discontinued.

MODEL 451 SERIES — 12 ga., totally hand-made, sidelock action, ejectors, scroll engraving. Custom made to order with fitted luggage case, various grades have increasing embellishments in EL Models.

Model 451 — disc. 1987.

	$6,000	$5,200	$4,875	$4,600	$4,300	$3,995	$3,600

Last Mfg.'s Sug. Retail was $12,375.

Model 451 E — 12 ga. only, double triggers, specifications furnished by individual customer. Imported 1989 only.

	$14,650	$10,950	$9,750	$8,500	$7,800	$6,750	$5,800

Add $4,000 for extra set of barrels.
Add $750 for SST.
Last Mfg.'s Sug. Retail was $20,467.

Model 451 EL — disc. 1984.

	$6,450	$5,400	$4,875	$4,600	$4,300	$4,000	$3,600

Model 451 EELL — previous top-of-the-line model, choice of engraving motifs per customer specifications. Disc. 1987, reintroduced 1989 only.

	$17,500	$12,950	$11,000	$8,500	$7,800	$6,750	$5,950

Last Mfg.'s Sug. Retail in 1989 was $24,367.

Last Mfg.'s Sug. Retail in 1987 was $14,925.

MODEL 452 — 12 ga. only, top of the line side-by side shotgun featuring H&H style detachable locks. New 1990.

Since each gun is a special order, prices are available by quotation by contacting Beretta U.S.A. Corp. directly.

SINGLE BARREL SHOTGUNS: DISC.

MARK II TRAP — 12 ga., 32 or 34 in. wide vent rib, full choke, boxlock with auto ejector, Monte Carlo stock, recoil pad. Mfg. 1972-1976.

	$660	$605	$580	$550	$495	$440	$385

MODEL FS-1 SINGLE BARREL — 12, 16, 20, 28, or .410 ga., 26 or 28 in. barrels, full choke, checkered semi-pistol grip, under lever break open, folds to length of barrel (also known as Companion).

	$225	$200	$175	$125	$100	$85	$65

TR-1 TRAP — 12 ga., 32 in. full choke barrel, under lever break open, Monte Carlo pistol grip stock with pad, engraved. Mfg. 1968-1971.

	$275	$250	$220	$195	$140	$110	$100

TR-2 TRAP — same as TR-1, with high rib, mfg. 1969-1973.

	$290	$260	$230	$205	$150	$120	$110

Grading	100%	98%	95%	90%	80%	70%	60%

MODEL 412 — 12, 20, 28, or .410 ga., monobloc construction, folding action, sling swivels, checkered walnut stock and forearm, 5 lbs. Importation disc. 1988.

	$190	$170	$125	$100	$85	$70	$60

Last Mfg.'s Sug. Retail was $215.

SLIDE ACTION SHOTGUNS: DISC.

MODEL SL-2 — 12 ga., 26, 28, or 30 in. barrels, various chokes, vent rib, checkered pistol, grip stock. Mfg. 1968-1971.

	$300	$275	$250	$220	$195	$165	$140

SILVER PIGEON — 12 ga., various chokes, light engraving.

	$250	$200	$175	$160	$150	$140	$130

GOLD PIGEON — 12 ga., various chokes, vent rib, engraved. Add $200 for deluxe models.

	$475	$375	$310	$275	$240	$215	$195

RUBY PIGEON — 12 ga., various chokes, vent rib, elaborately engraved, special deluxe walnut.

	$600	$475	$395	$350	$295	$260	$230

SEMI-AUTO SHOTGUNS: DISC.

SILVER LARK — 12 ga., various chokes.

	$295	$260	$240	$220	$200	$185	$170

GOLD LARK — 12 ga., vent rib, light scroll engraving, select walnut.

	$480	$400	$325	$260	$230	$210	$195

RUBY LARK — 12 ga., vent rib, heavy engraving, deluxe walnut.

	$675	$550	$475	$395	$350	$295	$260

MODEL AL-1 — 12 and 20 ga., semi-auto gas operated, 26, 28, and 30 in. plain barrel, various chokes, checkered pistol grip stock. Mfg. 1971-1973.

	$385	$360	$330	$305	$250	$195	$165

MODEL AL-2 — 12 or 20 ga., 26, 28, or 30 in. barrels, vent rib, various chokes, gas operated, checkered pistol grip stock. Mfg. 1968-1975.

	$330	$305	$275	$250	$220	$195	$165

MODEL AL-2 SKEET — same as AL-2, with 26 in. wide rib skeet bored barrel, mfg. 1969-1975.

	$395	$360	$320	$275	$220	$200	$185

MODEL AL-2 TRAP — same as AL-2, with 30 in. full choke barrel, wide rib, Monte Carlo stock, with recoil pad. Mfg. 1969-1975.

	$375	$345	$315	$285	$250	$195	$165

MODEL AL-2 MAGNUM — 12 ga., 28 and 30 in. mod. or full choke, 3 in. chambers. Mfg. 1973-1975.

	$415	$385	$330	$275	$250	$230	$210

MODEL AL-3 — continuation of the AL-2 series. Mfg. 1975-1976.

	100%	98%	95%	90%	80%	70%	60%
Field grade	$395	$360	$330	$260	$240	$220	$190
Magnum grade	$425	$385	$330	$275	$250	$230	$210
Skeet grade	$400	$360	$330	$260	$240	$220	$190
Trap grade	$385	$350	$295	$250	$225	$210	$185

MODEL AL-3 DELUXE TRAP — same as AL-3, with fully engraved receiver, premium grade wood. Mfg. 1975-1976.

	$770	$715	$660	$605	$550	$495	$440

MODEL 301 — continuation of the AL-3 series, scroll engraved receiver. Mfg. 1977-1982.

	100%	98%	95%	90%	80%	70%	60%
Field grade	$395	$360	$330	$260	$240	$220	$190

Grading	100%	98%	95%	90%	80%	70%	60%
Magnum grade	$425	$385	$330	$275	$250	$230	$210
Skeet grade	$400	$360	$330	$260	$240	$220	$190
Trap grade	$385	$350	$295	$250	$225	$210	$185

MODEL 301 SLUG GUN — 22 in. barrel, with sights. Disc.

	100%	98%	95%	90%	80%	70%	60%
	$395	$360	$330	$305	$265	$230	$190

SEMI-AUTO SHOTGUNS: RECENT MFG.

MODEL 1200 FIELD — 12 ga., inertia recoil system, 28 in. VR barrels with multi-chokes, checkered European walnut stock and forearm (pre-1989), matte black polymer stock and forearm (starting 1989), recoil pad, 4 shot mag., approx. 8 lbs. Imported 1984-1989.

	100%	98%	95%	90%	80%	70%	60%
	$475	$415	$350	$295	$250	$225	$200

Last Mfg.'s Sug. Retail was $580.

Model 1200 Magnum — 12 ga., 3 in. chamber, 28 in. VR barrel with multi-chokes (2), matte black polymer stock and forearm. New 1989.

Mfg.'s Sug. Retail	$540	$430	$365	$310	$260	$230	$200	$185

Model 1200 Riot — 12 ga. only, 2¾ or 3 in. chamber, 20 in. cyl. bore barrel with iron sights, extended mag. New 1989.

Mfg.'s Sug. Retail	$575	$475	$415	$350	$295	$250	$225	$200

MODEL 302 — 12 or 20 ga., self-compensating gas operation semi-auto, designed for both 2¾ and 3 in. shells, available with interchangeable chokes, slug barrel, trap and skeet models (disc.), VR, mag. cut-off. Mfg. 1982-1987. This model was superseded by the Model 303.

		100%	98%	95%	90%	80%	70%	60%
		$395	$365	$340	$310	$280	$255	$225

Add $30 for multi-choke set.
Last Mfg.'s Sug. Retail was $480.

Model 302 Super Lusso — same specifications as Model A302, but includes hand engraved receiver, many gold plated parts, and stock and forearm made from presentation grade walnut. Disc. 1986.

	$2,150	$1,950	$1,750	$1,550	$1,300	$1,050	$895

Last Mfg.'s Sug. Retail was $2,500.

MODEL A-303 — 12 or 20 ga., 2¾ or 3 in. chambers, same gas operation as the Model 302, 26, 28, 30, or 32 in. VR barrel, high-strength alloy receiver, select wood with choice pistol grip or straight English stock, beavertail forearm, multi-chokes became standard 1987.

Mfg.'s Sug. Retail	$665	$530	$425	$375	$335	$300	$270	$240

Subtract $70 without multi-chokes.

A-303 Upland — 24 in. VR barrel with multi-chokes, English style straight stock. New 1989.

Mfg.'s Sug. Retail	$665	$540	$450	$395	$350	$300	$270	$240

A-303 Waterfowl/Turkey — 12 ga. only, 3 in. chamber, choice of 24, 26, 28, or 30 in. VR barrel, matte finished wood and metal, multi-chokes are standard. New 1991.

Mfg.'s Sug. Retail	$665	$540	$450	$395	$350	$300	$270	$240

A-303 Sporting — 12 or 20 (new 1991) ga. only, 2¾ in. chambers, sporting clay dimensions, 28 in. VR barrel with multi-chokes. New 1988.

Mfg.'s Sug. Retail	$745	$580	$475	$425	$365	$310	$280	$250

A-303 Skeet — 12 or 20 ga., 26 in. VR barrel with fixed skeet choking.

Mfg.'s Sug. Retail	$685	$545	$440	$375	$335	$300	$270	$240

A-303 Super Skeet — 12 ga. only, 28 in. VR fixed choke barrel, features factory porting, adj. length of pull, and adj. separate cheekpiece on stock. New 1991.

Mfg.'s Sug. Retail	$1,000	$875	$700	$600	$500	$425	$365	$300

A-303 Trap — 12 ga. only, 30 or 32 in. VR barrel with fixed choking or multi-chokes.

Mfg.'s Sug. Retail	$685	$545	$400	$360	$325	$280	$250	$220

Add $40 for multi-chokes (with Monte Carlo stock).

A-303 Super Trap — 12 ga. only, 30 or 32 in. VR multi-choke barrel with step tapered rib, features factory porting, adj. length of pull, and adj. separate cheekpiece on stock. New 1991.

Mfg.'s Sug. Retail	$1,045	$900	$725	$615	$500	$425	$365	$300

Grading	100%	98%	95%	90%	80%	70%	60%
A-303 Slug — 12 or 20 ga., 3 in. chamber (12 ga. only), 22 in. cylinder bore barrel, iron sights.							
Mfg.'s Sug. Retail	$665	$540	$425	$360	$325	$295	$265	$240
A-303 Youth — 20 ga. only, 3 in. chamber, 24 in. VR barrel with multi-chokes. New 1988.							
Mfg.'s Sug. Retail	$680	$550	$435	$370	$330	$300	$270	$240

COMMEMORATIVES

MODEL A-303 DUCKS UNLIMITED — 12 or 20 ga., D.U. serialization, 5,500 mfg. in 12 ga. 1986-87, 3,500 mfg. in 20 ga. 1987-88.

	100%	98%	95%
12 ga.	$575	$450	$350
20 ga.	$675	$475	$375

These D.U. Models had no retail pricing from Beretta. Rather, they were auctioned off at D.U. dinners, and as a result, prices could vary substantially from region to region.

MODEL 687 O/U SHOTGUN TERCENTENNIAL — 12 ga., comes with S.S.T. and ejectors. Limited production, only 300 manufactured.

	100%	98%	95%
	$2,500	$1,950	$1,400

MODEL 84 PISTOL TERCENTENNIAL — commemorative, only 300 manufactured. Fully engraved with gold inlays. Presentation case. Only 100 imported to U.S.

	100%	98%	95%
	$1,450	$1,100	$850

BERGMANN

Manufacturer located in Gaggenau, Germany 1892-1944. Re-established in 1931 under Bergmann Erben.

100%	98%	95%	90%	80%	70%	60%	50%	40%	30%	20%	10%

SEMI-AUTO

Prices established are for original guns with matching parts.

MODEL 1894 (ANTIQUE) — 5mm or 8mm. Extremely rare. Add 50% for 5mm.

100%	98%	95%	90%	80%	70%	60%	50%	40%	30%	20%	10%
$4,500	$3,750	$3,350	$2,860	$2,550	$2,200	$1,900	$1,600	$1,250	$995	$925	$850

MODEL 1896-NO. 2 — 5mm, smaller type frame.

100%	98%	95%	90%	80%	70%	60%	50%	40%	30%	20%	10%
$2,100	$1,900	$1,600	$1,300	$1,100	$895	$715	$660	$610	$565	$515	$450

MODEL 1896-NO. 3 — 6.5mm - 80mm barrel.

100%	98%	95%	90%	80%	70%	60%	50%	40%	30%	20%	10%
$2,200	$1,950	$1,650	$1,350	$1,125	$925	$750	$700	$665	$630	$600	$565

MODEL 1896-NO. 4 — 8mm, military contract.

100%	98%	95%	90%	80%	70%	60%	50%	40%	30%	20%	10%
$2,275	$2,000	$1,650	$1,350	$1,125	$925	$750	$700	$665	$630	$600	$565

MODEL 1897-NO. 5 — 7.8mm, commercial manufacture.

100%	98%	95%	90%	80%	70%	60%	50%	40%	30%	20%	10%
$2,600	$2,275	$2,000	$1,650	$1,350	$1,125	$925	$750	$700	$665	$630	$600

MODEL 2 — .25 cal., small frame. Add $100 for Model 2A.

100%	98%	95%	90%	80%	70%	60%	50%	40%	30%	20%	10%
$300	$285	$260	$240	$215	$180	$160	$135	$115	$95	$80	$65

MODEL 3 — .25 cal., small frame. Add $100 for Model 3A.

100%	98%	95%	90%	80%	70%	60%	50%	40%	30%	20%	10%
$300	$285	$260	$240	$215	$180	$160	$135	$115	$95	$80	$65

ERBEN — Models I, II, and Special, .25 Cal. except Special .32 Cal.

100%	98%	95%	90%	80%	70%	60%	50%	40%	30%	20%	10%
$335	$300	$285	$260	$240	$215	$180	$160	$135	$115	$95	$80

BERGMANN-BAYARD PISTOLS

Even though the below listed Bergmann-Bayard models were manufactured only by Anciens Etablissements Pieper of Herstal, Belgium these pistols are listed under this heading as they are most commonly referred to by this trademark designation.

100%	98%	95%	90%	80%	70%	60%	50%	40%	30%	20%	10%

MODEL 1908 STANDARD COMMERCIAL — 9mm Bergmann, identified by a mounted knight on the left magazine housing and is without finger cuts at base of magazine housing.

| $1,500 | $1,250 | $1,000 | $750 | $600 | $500 | $400 | $360 | $335 | $310 | $285 | $260 |

Add 25% if backstrap is slotted for shoulder stock.

Add $2,500 for excellent original leather/wood shoulder stock.

MODEL 1908 SPANISH CONTRACT — 9mm Bergmann, total contract was for 3,000 pistols, can be identified from standard commercial pistols by the Spanish military acceptance stamp struck on the receiver.

| $1,350 | $1,100 | $900 | $750 | $600 | $450 | $350 | $315 | $280 | $265 | $245 | $225 |

MODEL 1910 STANDARD COMMERCIAL — 9mm Bergmann, mechanically similar to Model 1908 Standard Commercial except has finger cuts in bottom of magazine housing, circular grooves are present on each side of magazine base.

| $1,100 | $900 | $700 | $600 | $500 | $400 | $350 | $315 | $280 | $265 | $245 | $225 |

MODEL 1910 DANISH GOVERNMENT CONTRACT — 9mm Bergmann, Trolit grips were used for the original conversion, followed later by wood replacements, total contract was for 4,840 pistols with delivery mfg. 1911-1914. This variation can be identified from the usual commercial pistols by the Danish proof mark on the left receiver side and Danish inventory number on right side of receiver.

| $1,250 | $1,000 | $850 | $700 | $575 | $450 | $350 | $315 | $280 | $265 | $245 | $225 |

Deduct 20% if converted and overstamped M.1910/21.

MODEL 1910/21 TOJHUS — 9mm Bergmann, these pistols are marked "Haerens Tojhus" and are numbered from 1-900, original grips were black Trolit, replacement grips are either all smooth or with checkered circles above and below grip screw.

| $1,250 | $1,000 | $850 | $700 | $575 | $450 | $350 | $315 | $280 | $265 | $245 | $225 |

This contract was manufactured by the Danish Royal Arsenal located in Copenhagen.

MODEL 1910/21 RUSTKAMMER — 9mm Bergmann, pistols are marked "Haerens Rustkammer", and numbered 901-2204, grip replacements are the same as noted for Haerens Tojhus.

| $1,100 | $900 | $700 | $600 | $500 | $400 | $350 | $315 | $280 | $265 | $245 | $225 |

This contract was manufactured by the Danish Royal Arsenal located in Copenhagen.

BERNARDELLI, VINCENZO

Manufactured since 1721 in Brescia, Italy. Imported and distributed exclusively by Magnum Research, Inc. located in Minneapolis, MN beginning in 1989. Long Arms were previously imported and distributed in the U.S. by Quality Arms Inc. located in Houston, TX, Armes De Chasse located in Chadds Ford, PA., and by Stoeger located in New York, NY.

Grading	100%	98%	95%	90%	80%	70%	60%

COMBINATION GUNS

MODEL 190 — combination rifle/shotgun chambered for 12, 16, or 20 ga. under .243, .30-06, or .308 cal., boxlock action, DT's, extractors. Imported 1989 only.

| | | | $1,295 | $1,025 | $895 | $800 | $700 | $600 | $525 |

Add $700 for extra set of 12 ga. O/U barrels.

Mfg.'s Sug. Retail was $1,393.

MODEL COMB 2000 — 12, 16, or 20 ga. under choice of rifle cal.'s, ejectors, set trigger. Importation began 1990.

| Mfg.'s Sug. Retail | $2,441 | $2,075 | $1,775 | $1,550 | $1,350 | $1,100 | $925 | $800 |

Add $621 for extra set of O/U shotgun barrels (Model COMB 2000S).

Grading	100%	98%	95%	90%	80%	70%	60%

MODEL 120 — 12 ga. over choice of 12 cal.'s, deluxe checkered walnut stock and forearm, iron sights, double triggers, vent recoil pad, coin washed receiver with light engraving.

	$1,950	$1,585	$1,300	$1,050	$850	$760	$650

Add $130 for extra set of shotgun barrels.
Last Mfg.'s Sug. Retail was $2,411.

PISTOLS: SEMI-AUTO, DISCONTINUED

VEST POCKET MODEL — .25 auto, 2⅛ in. barrel, fixed sights, blue, bakelite grips. Mfg. 1945-1948.

	$250	$195	$165	$140	$110	$90	$65

BABY SEMI-AUTO — .22 S or L, 2⅛ in. barrel, fixed sights, blue, bakelite grips. Mfg. 1949-1968.

	$250	$175	$150	$130	$100	$90	$80

SPORTER MODEL — .22 LR, 6, 8, or 10 in. barrels, target sights, blue, wood grips. Mfg. 1949-1968.

	$305	$275	$220	$165	$140	$110	$85

MODEL 60 — .22 LR, .32 auto, or .380 auto cal., 3½ in. barrel, fixed sights, blue, bakelite grips. Mfg. 1959-present.

	$220	$195	$180	$165	$155	$135	$120

This model is not imported domestically.

MODEL 68 — .22 Short or .22 LR cal., vest pocket model, 6 shot, bakelite grips, 8½ oz. Current mfg.

	$140	$120	$110	$100	$90	$80	$70

This model is not imported domestically.

PISTOLS: SEMI-AUTO, RECENT MFG.

Prices could differ from values shown below because of the fluctuating U.S. dollar.

MODEL 80 — .22 LR or .380 auto cal., 3½ in. barrel, adj. sights, blue, thumbrest plastic grips. Imported 1968-1988.

	$185	$160	$150	$140	$130	$115	$100

Add $5 for .380 ACP.
Note: This model was produced to conform to import regulations of GCA 1968. Importation of this model was disc. 1988.

MODEL USA — .22 LR, .32 (disc.), or .380 ACP. cal., semi-auto, single action, steel frame, chamber indicator, adj. sights, target bakelite grips, 7 shot (.380 ACP) or 10 shot (.22 LR) mag.

Mfg.'s Sug. Retail	$289	$265	$240	$220	$195	$175	$150	$130

This model has the same technical specifications as the Model 60.

MODEL AMR — .22 LR, .32 (disc.), or .380 ACP cal., similar action to USA Model except has 6 in. barrel and adj. rear sight.

Mfg.'s Sug. Retail	$309	$290	$245	$225	$195	$175	$150	$130

MODEL 90 SPORT TARGET — same as 80, only .32 ACP or .22 LR, with 6 in. barrel. Imported 1968-1988.

	$210	$185	$170	$155	$140	$120	$110

Last Mfg.'s Sug. Retail was $245.

MODEL 69 TARGET — .22 LR, target semi-auto, single action, 5.9 in. heavy barrel, 10 shot mag., wrap-around checkered wooden grips, 38 oz.

Mfg.'s Sug. Retail	$459	$420	$360	$320	$285	$240	$200	$185

This model was previously designated Model 100.

MODEL 100 TARGET — .22 LR, 5.9 in. barrel, adj. sight, blue, checkered wood, thumbrest grips, cased. Imported 1968-1988.

	$395	$325	$295	$260	$225	$190	$175

Last Mfg.'s Sug. Retail was $360.

Grading	100%	98%	95%	90%	80%	70%	60%

MODEL P010 TARGET — .22 LR, single action, 5.9 in. barrel, adj. sights and trigger, matte black finish, large anatomic walnut stippled grips with thumbrest, 10 shot mag., 40.5 oz. New 1989.

Mfg.'s Sug. Retail	$519	$475	$395	$350	$320	$285	$260	$240

Add $60 for wooden case.

MODEL P018 — 7.65mm (disc. 1988) or 9mm Luger, double action, semi-auto, steel construction, 4⅞ in. barrel, 16 shot mag., plastic (standard) or walnut checkered grips, 36 oz. Imported 1985-present.

Mfg.'s Sug. Retail	$499	$450	$385	$340	$300	$275	$250	$230

Add $40 for walnut grips.

Add $30 for carrying case w/combination lock (disc. 1989).

This model was extensively redesigned in 1989 and includes a " cocked and locked" feature, thumb mag. release, loaded chamber indicator, as well as other improvements.

P018 Compact — similar to Model P018 except has 4 in. barrel and 14 shot mag., approx. 2 lbs. New 1989.

Mfg.'s Sug. Retail	$519	$465	$395	$345	$300	$275	$250	$230

This model was also redesigned in 1989 to incorporate the same features as the Model P018.

DOUBLE RIFLES

EXPRESS VB — various cal.'s, side-by-side sidelock action, ejectors, double triggers. Importation began 1990.

Mfg.'s Sug. Retail	$7,033	$6,150	$5,100	$4,675	$4,100	$3,600	$3,100	$2,650

Add $207 for single trigger (Model Express VB M).

RIFLES: SEMI-AUTO

SEMI-AUTO .22 — .22 LR, blow back action. Importation began 1990.

Mfg.'s Sug. Retail	$438	$385	$295	$250	$210	$170	$150	$135

SHOTGUNS: SIDE-BY-SIDE, DISCONTINUED

MODEL 110 — 12 ga., trap or skeet model, separated barrels, high post rib.

$2,000	$1,500	$1,300	$1,100	$1,000	$900	$800

MODEL 110 EXTRA — same as Model 110, except engraved.

$3,021	$2,265	$1,970	$1,665	$1,510	$1,360	$1,210

S. UBERTO 1 GAMECOCK — 12, 16, 20, or 28 ga., 25¾ in. imp. cyl. and mod., 27½ in. full and mod., hammerless, boxlock, extractors, two triggers, English style stock, checkered.

$853	$635	$605	$550	$495	$440	$415

Add 20% for ejectors.

SHOTGUNS: SIDE-BY-SIDE, CURRENT MFG.

Bernardelli side-by-side shotguns are manufactured with straight grip, English-style stocks with pistol grip available as a special order. Importation of Bernardelli shotguns has been inconsistent in the past and current dealer inventories of older merchandise might be priced less than similar models currently imported.

A wide variety of special order options is available on these shotguns. Individual price quotations are available by contacting Magnum Research, Inc. in Minneapolis, MN directly.

Barrel choke markings for V. Bernardelli shotguns are as follows; Full: *, Impr. Mod: **, Mod: ***, Impr. Cyl: ****, Cylinder: CL.

BRESCIA HAMMER DOUBLE BARREL — 12, 16, or 20 ga., 25¾, 27½ and 29½ in. mod. and full, 12 ga., 25½ in. imp. cyl. and mod., sidelock, extractors, two triggers, straight English stock, splinter forearm, checkered.

Mfg.'s Sug. Retail	$2,482	$2,050	$795	$600	$450	$425	$395	$375

Sudden drop in values reflects desirability factor in today's marketplace.

Grading	100%	98%	95%	90%	80%	70%	60%

ITALIA HAMMER DOUBLE BARREL — same as Brescia, except higher grade engraving and wood.

Mfg.'s Sug. Retail	$2,844	$2,275	$1,200	$900	$735	$650	$600	$550

Sudden drop in values reflects desirability factor in today's marketplace.

ITALIA EXTRA HAMMER — hammer double, 12, 16, or 20 ga. Top-of-the-line hammer model.

Mfg.'s Sug. Retail	$7,861	$6,400	$3,150	$2,200	$1,650	$1,375	$1,050	$800

Sudden drop in values reflects desirability factor in today's marketplace.

MODEL 112 — 12 ga., entry-level model with extractors and DT's. Imported 1989 only.

	$850	$750	$675	$625	$550	$495	$450

Add $64 for single trigger (Model 112 M - disc.).
Last Mfg.'s Sug. Retail was $998.

MODEL 112E — 12 ga., Anson & Deeley action, light engraving. Importation disc. 1989.

	$995	$850	$775	$695	$625	$550	$495

Last Mfg.'s Sug. Retail was $1,108.

MODEL 112 EM — similar to Model 112E, except has single trigger.

Mfg.'s Sug. Retail	$1,798	$1,475	$950	$825	$725	$650	$540	$495

Model 112 EM - MC — similar to Model 112 EM, except has 3 in. chambers and 5 choke tubes. Importation began 1990.

Mfg.'s Sug. Retail	$1,971	$1,600	$1,000	$850	$775	$675	$575	$495

Model 112 EM-MC-WF — includes 3½ in. chambers, waterfowl model with matte finish, single trigger and 3 choke tubes. Importation disc. 1990.

	$1,275	$975	$850	$775	$675	$575	$495

Last Mfg.'s Sug. Retail was $1,444.

S. UBERTO 1 — 12, 16, 20, or 28 ga., Anson & Deeley action, Purdey locks, light engraving, case hardened receiver, double triggers, extractors.

	$1,050	$900	$800	$700	$625	$550	$495

Add $65 for single trigger (Model S. Uberto 1M).
Last Mfg.'s Sug. Retail was $1,164.

S. Uberto 1E — same as S. Uberto 1, except with ejectors. Importation disc. 1990.

	$1,175	$950	$850	$740	$650	$565	$495

Add $65 for single trigger (Model S. Uberto 1EM).
Last Mfg.'s Sug. Retail was $1,357.

S. UBERTO 2 — 12, 16, 20, and 28 ga.'s, Anson & Deeley action, Purdey locks, light scroll engraving, silver finished receiver, double triggers, extractors. Importation disc. 1989.

	$1,075	$925	$820	$720	$650	$540	$495

Add $35 for single trigger (Model S. Uberto 2M).
Last Mfg.'s Sug. Retail was $1,260.

S. Uberto 2E — same as S. Uberto 2, except with ejectors.

Mfg.'s Sug. Retail	$1,924	$1,575	$975	$850	$750	$665	$550	$500

Add $81 for single trigger (Model S. Uberto 2EM).

S. UBERTO FS — 12, 16, 20, or 28 ga., Purdey locks, relief engraved with hunting scenes on silver finished receiver, double triggers, extractors. Importation disc. 1989.

	$1,275	$1,025	$900	$775	$670	$560	$500

Add $65 for single trigger (Model S. Uberto FSM - disc. 1989).
Last Mfg.'s Sug. Retail was $1,421.

S. Uberto FSE — same as S. Uberto F.S., except with ejectors. Importation disc. 1989.

	$1,375	$1,100	$975	$850	$750	$625	$550

Add $65 for single trigger (Model S. Uberto FSEM).
Last Mfg.'s Sug. Retail was $1,537.

Grading	100%	98%	95%	90%	80%	70%	60%

ROMA 3 — same as S. Uberto, double triggers, extractors, false sideplates, casehardened receiver. Importation disc. 1989.

| | $1,150 | $950 | $850 | $740 | $650 | $565 | $475 |

Add $65 for single trigger (Model Roma 3M).
Last Mfg.'s Sug. Retail was $1,274.

Roma 3E — same as Roma 3, except with ejectors.

| Mfg.'s Sug. Retail | $1,986 | $1,625 | $1,000 | $850 | $775 | $675 | $575 | $495 |

Add $81 for single trigger (Model Roma 3EM).

ROMA 4 — more deluxe model than Roma 3, false sideplates, scroll engraved, silver finished receiver. Importation disc. 1989.

| | $1,250 | $1,025 | $900 | $800 | $700 | $625 | $550 |

Add $65 for single trigger (Model Roma 4M).
Last Mfg.'s Sug. Retail was $1,439.

Roma 4E — same as Roma 4, except with ejectors.

| Mfg.'s Sug. Retail | $2,276 | $1,825 | $1,225 | $950 | $850 | $750 | $650 | $595 |

Add $78 for single trigger (Model Roma 4EM).

ROMA 6 — 12, 16, 20, or 28 ga., fully engraved sideplates, Purdey locks, silver finish receiver, single trigger, finely figured English walnut. Importation disc. 1989.

| | $1,395 | $1,150 | $975 | $875 | $775 | $675 | $600 |

Add $175 for single trigger (Model Roma 6M).
Last Mfg.'s Sug. Retail was $1,619.

Roma 6E — same as Roma 6, except with ejectors, 16 ga. was disc. 1989.

| Mfg.'s Sug. Retail | $2,482 | $1,975 | $1,325 | $1,050 | $950 | $810 | $720 | $630 |

Add $81 for single trigger (Model Roma 6EM).

ELIO — 12 ga. only, lightweight, extractors, fine English style scroll engraving on silver finish receiver. Importation disc. 1989.

| | $1,125 | $925 | $850 | $740 | $650 | $565 | $475 |

Add $65 for single trigger (Model Elio M).
Last Mfg.'s Sug. Retail was $1,238.

Elio E — same as Elio, except with ejectors. Importation disc. 1989.

| | $1,200 | $1,000 | $895 | $795 | $695 | $595 | $500 |

Add $65 for single trigger (Model Elio EM).
Last Mfg.'s Sug. Retail was $1,353.

SLUG GUN — 12 ga. only, 23¾ in. slug bored barrels, extractors, Anson & Deeley action, Purdey locks, lightly engraved, silver finish receiver. Importation disc. 1990.

| | $1,325 | $1,000 | $895 | $795 | $695 | $595 | $500 |

Add $65 for single trigger (Model Slug M).
Last Mfg.'s Sug. Retail was $1,575.

SLUG LUSSO — 12 ga. only, 23¾ in. slug bored barrels, sideplates, with extensive engraving featuring hunting scenes, cheek piece, ejectors, silver finished receiver.

| Mfg.'s Sug. Retail | $2,793 | $2,325 | $1,550 | $1,200 | $995 | $875 | $750 | $650 |

Add $80 for single trigger (Model Slug Lusso M).
This model was previously designated Slug Deluxe (1988 or earlier).

HEMINGWAY — 12 or 20 ga., boxlock action, coin finished receiver with game scene engraving, 23½ in. barrels, DT's, deluxe checkered walnut stock and forearm, 6¼ lbs.

| Mfg.'s Sug. Retail | $2,172 | $1,750 | $1,250 | $950 | $850 | $750 | $650 | $600 |

Add $81 for single trigger (Model Hemingway M).

HEMINGWAY DE LUXE — similar to Hemingway, except is also available in 16 ga. and has sideplates, better wood, and more engraving.

| Mfg.'s Sug. Retail | $2,482 | $2,025 | $1,400 | $1,000 | $925 | $810 | $720 | $630 |

Add $81 for single trigger (Model Hemingway De Luxe M).

Grading	100%	98%	95%	90%	80%	70%	60%

LAS PALOMAS PIGEON — 12 ga. live pigeon gun, single trigger, special dimensions for live pigeon shooting.

Mfg.'s Sug. Retail	$3,930	$3,375	$2,400	$1,850	$1,625	$1,500	$1,375	$1,195

Add $81 for single trigger (Model Las Palomas M).

HOLLAND V.B. LISCIO — 12 ga. only, Holland type sidelocks, light engraving, silver finish receiver, single trigger, ejectors, select walnut.

Mfg.'s Sug. Retail	$10,757	$8,700	$6,000	$4,750	$4,450	$3,900	$3,350	$2,850

HOLLAND V.B. INCISO — 12 ga. only, H&H sidelock action, Purdey locks, various barrel lengths, single trigger, ejectors, straight or pistol grip stock, 100% engraved on coin finished receiver.

Mfg.'s Sug. Retail	$12,929	$10,700	$7,000	$5,500	$4,700	$4,200	$3,500	$3,000

HOLLAND V.B. LUSSO — 12 ga. only, H&H sidelock action, Purdey locks, various barrel lengths, single trigger, ejectors, straight or pistol grip stock, same features as Holland V.B. Inciso, only extra select wood and game scene engraving.

Mfg.'s Sug. Retail	$14,377	$11,500	$8,100	$6,300	$5,200	$4,750	$4,000	$3,450

HOLLAND V.B. EXTRA — 12 ga. only, H&H style action, any barrel length and choke, double triggers, auto ejectors, straight or pistol grip stock, 100% engraved on coin finished receiver. Prices are completely dependent upon individual customer specifications. Values listed below are for engraving pattern No. 3.

Mfg.'s Sug. Retail	$16,549	$13,250	$9,700	$7,450	$6,150	$5,200	$4,600	$3,950

Add $1,034 for engraving pattern No. 4.

Add $4,551 for engraving pattern No. 12.

Add $8,895 for engraving pattern No. 20.

Add $621 for single trigger.

Older specimens (not custom ordered within the last 2 years) could have values considerably lower than those listed above.

HOLLAND V.B. GOLD — top-of-the-line model, made to individual order. Very limited production and ultra-rare.

Mfg.'s Sug. Retail	$57,922	$47,500	$32,500	$24,000	$18,500	$13,000	$11,500	$9,950

Older specimens (not custom ordered within the last 2 years) could have values considerably lower than those listed above.

SHOTGUNS: OVER & UNDER, RECENT MFG.

A wide variety of special order options is available on these shotguns. Individual price quotations are available by contacting Magnum Research, Inc. in Minneapolis, MN directly.

MODEL 115 HUNTING — 12 ga. only, boxlock action, monoblock frame, inclined plane lockings, blued receiver, single trigger, ejectors. Importation disc. 1989.

	$1,770	$1,425	$1,225	$1,000	$895	$750	$650

Last Mfg.'s Sug. Retail was $1,915.

Model 115S — same as 115, except moderate engraving.

	$2,150	$1,925	$1,745	$1,500	$1,250	$1,025	$950

Last Mfg.'s Sug. Retail was $2,500.

Model 115L — same as 115S, except extensive scroll engraving on silver finish receiver.

	$2,600	$2,375	$2,050	$1,750	$1,450	$1,100	$850

Last Mfg.'s Sug. Retail was $3,170.

Model 115E — sideplate, boxlock action, ejector, bulino game scene engraving.

	$4,650	$4,125	$3,600	$3,100	$2,650	$2,200	$1,800

Last Mfg.'s Sug. Retail was $5,200.

MODEL 115 TARGET — 12 ga. only, same specifications as Model 115, except trap dimensions. Importation disc. 1989.

	$1,800	$1,595	$1,375	$1,175	$1,000	$895	$750

Last Mfg.'s Sug. Retail was $2,160.

Grading	100%	98%	95%	90%	80%	70%	60%

Model 115S — same specifications as 115 Target, except light engraving.

Mfg.'s Sug. Retail	$3,920	$3,275	$2,425	$1,825	$1,500	$1,250	$1,025	$895

This model is available in either Pigeon, Skeet, Sporting Clays, or Trap configuration.

Model 115L — same as 115S, except extensive scroll engraving on silver finish receiver. Importation disc.1990.

	$3,700	$2,995	$2,600	$2,375	$2,050	$1,750	$1,450

Last Mfg.'s Sug. Retail was $4,201.

Model 115E — same specifications as 115S, except with extensively engraved sideplates. Importation disc. 1990.

	$5,950	$4,800	$4,125	$3,600	$3,100	$2,650	$2,200

Last Mfg.'s Sug. Retail was $6,827.

Model 115S Monotrap — 12 ga. only, single barrel. Imported 1989 only.

	$2,600	$2,150	$1,900	$1,700	$1,500	$1,250	$1,025

Add $1,000 for extra trap barrel.
Last Mfg.'s Sug. Retail was $2,976.

MODEL 190 TARGET
— 12 ga, SST, ejectors, engraved silver receiver, select checkered walnut stock and forearm. Imported 1986-1989.

	$1,425	$1,095	$925	$800	$700	$600	$525

Last Mfg.'s Sug. Retail was $1,572.

Model 190 MC — similar to Model 190 Target except has Monte Carlo stock. Imported 1989 only.

	$1,000	$825	$700	$600	$525	$475	$450

Last Mfg.'s Sug. Retail was $1,155.

Model 190 Special — 12 ga. only, similar to Model 190 Target, except has better walnut and engraving. Imported 1988-1989.

	$1,335	$1,000	$895	$800	$700	$600	$525

Add $75 for single trigger (Model 190 Special MS).
These variations are hunting models.

Last Mfg.'s Sug. Retail was $1,456.

MODEL 192 MS COMPETITION
— 12 ga. only, ejectors, selective or non-selective triggers, multi-chokes standard on Sporting Clays Model. New 1990.

Mfg.'s Sug. Retail	$2,307	$1,925	$1,400	$1,075	$900	$825	$725	$625

This model is available in either Pigeon, Skeet, Sporting Clays, or Trap configuration.

MODEL 192 MS-MC HUNTING
— 12 ga. only, boxlock action with engraved coin finished receiver, 3 in. chambers, ejectors, SST, 26¾ or 28 in. VR barrels with choke tubes, steel shot compatible. Importation began 1990.

Mfg.'s Sug. Retail	$1,833	$1,400	$995	$825	$700	$600	$525	$475

Model 192 MS-MC-WF — waterfowler variation which includes 3½ in. chambers, 3 choke tubes, and SST. Imported 1990 only.

	$1,275	$950	$875	$775	$675	$575	$500

Last Mfg.'s Sug. Retail was $1,444.

MODEL 200 LIGHTWEIGHT MS
— 12 ga. only, silver gray finished receiver with game scene engraving. Imported 1988-1989.

	$1,075	$895	$800	$700	$600	$525	$475

Last Mfg.'s Sug. Retail was $1,211.

MODEL 220 MS HUNTING
— 12 (disc. 1989) or 20 ga., silver gray finished receiver with engraving. New 1988.

Mfg.'s Sug. Retail	$1,812	$1,395	$975	$825	$700	$600	$525	$475

Add $700 for extra set of 12 ga. barrels (disc. 1990).
This model is available with either a pistol grip or English grip (straight) stock.

Grading	100%	98%	95%	90%	80%	70%	60%

SATURNO MS-MC COMPETITION — 12 ga. only, sporter configuration, boxlock action with lightly engraved side plates. Importation began 1991.

Mfg.'s Sug. Retail	$2,927	$2,475	$1,650	$1,150	$975	$810	$720	$630

This model is available in either Pigeon, Skeet, Sporting Clays, or Trap configuration.

SATURNO MS-MC HUNTING — 12 ga. only, boxlock action with lightly engraved side plates, ejectors, SST, includes multi-chokes. Importation began 1991.

Mfg.'s Sug. Retail	$2,609	$2,275	$1,525	$1,050	$875	$750	$695	$600

ORIONE — 12 ga., double Purdey lock, vent rib, case hardened receiver, double triggers, extractors. Importation disc. 1989.

	$1,150	$995	$850	$750	$640	$555	$495

Last Mfg.'s Sug. Retail was $1,380.

ORIONE S — same as Orione, except ejectors, engraved nickel finish receiver. Importation disc. 1989.

	$1,175	$1,025	$860	$760	$650	$560	$510

Last Mfg.'s Sug. Retail was $1,425.

ORIONE L — same as Orione S, single trigger, finer engraving, English or pistol type select walnut stock. Importation disc. 1989.

	$1,285	$1,125	$950	$840	$750	$650	$550

Last Mfg.'s Sug. Retail was $1,550.

ORIONE E — top-of-the-line, deep relief engraving. Importation disc. 1989.

	$1,375	$1,200	$1,020	$900	$820	$710	$650

Last Mfg.'s Sug. Retail was $1,660.

SHOTGUNS: SEMI-AUTO

MODEL 9MM FLOBERT — 9mm rimfire shot cartridge, 24.4 in. smooth bore barrel, 3 shot mag., steel receiver, walnut stock and forearm with sling and swivels, 5 lbs. 3 oz.

Mfg.'s Sug. Retail	$393	$325	$225	$175	$150	$125	$105	$95

SHOTGUNS: FOLDING MODELS

SINGLE BARREL — 12, 16, 20, 24, 28, 32 or .410 ga., gun folds in half. Importation disc. 1990.

	$230	$185	$150	$135	$125	$115	$100

Last Mfg.'s Sug. Retail was $265.

DOUBLE BARREL — 12 and 16 ga., gun folds in half, double triggers. Current manufacture, but available in Europe only.

	$570	$430	$370	$315	$285	$260	$230

BERSA

Currently imported and distributed exclusively by Eagle Imports, Inc., located in Ocean, NJ. Previously imported and distributed before 1988 by Rock Island Armory located in Geneseo, IL and Outdoor Sports Headquarters, Inc. located in Dayton, OH.

MODEL 223 — .22 LR, single action semi-auto, 10 shot mag., 3½ in. barrel, squared-off trigger guard, nylon grips, blued action. Importation disc. 1987.

	$200	$170	$150	$125	$115	$105	$95

Last Mfg.'s Sug. Retail was $239.

MODEL 23 — .22 LR, double action semi-auto, 9 shot mag., 3½ in. barrel, walnut grips, 24½ oz. New 1988.

Mfg.'s Sug. Retail	$267	$225	$180	$150	$125	$115	$105	$95

Add $30 for satin nickel finish.

Grading	100%	98%	95%	90%	80%	70%	60%

MODEL 224 — similar to Model 223, except has 4 in. barrel. Imported 1987 only.

	100%	98%	95%	90%	80%	70%	60%
	$200	$170	$150	$125	$115	$105	$95

Last Mfg.'s Sug. Retail was $239.

MODEL 225 — similar to Model 223, except has 5 in. barrel and 10 shot mag. Disc. 1987.

	100%	98%	95%	90%	80%	70%	60%
	$155	$135	$125	$115	$105	$95	$85

Last Mfg.'s Sug. Retail was $170.

MODEL 226 — similar to Model 225, except has 6 in. barrel. Importation disc. 1987.

	100%	98%	95%	90%	80%	70%	60%
	$200	$170	$150	$125	$115	$105	$95

Last Mfg.'s Sug. Retail was $239.

MODEL 323 — .32 ACP, single action semi-auto, 8 shot mag., thumbrest plastic grips, 25 oz. Disc. 1987.

	100%	98%	95%	90%	80%	70%	60%
	$105	$95	$85	$75	$65	$55	$45

Last Mfg.'s Sug. Retail was $125.

MODEL 383 — .380 ACP, single action semi-auto, 3½ in. barrel, blued finish, nylon grips, 7 shot mag. Importation disc. 1988.

	100%	98%	95%	90%	80%	70%	60%
	$120	$95	$90	$80	$70	$60	$50

Last Mfg.'s Sug. Retail was $188.

MODEL 383 — .380 ACP, double action semi-auto, 3½ in. barrel, blued finish, custom wood grips, 7 shot mag. Importation disc. 1988.

	100%	98%	95%	90%	80%	70%	60%
	$135	$105	$95	$85	$75	$65	$55

Last Mfg.'s Sug. Retail was $239.

MODEL 83 — .380 ACP, double action semi-auto, 3½ in. barrel, blued finish, custom walnut grips, 6 shot mag., 24½ oz. New 1988.

		100%	98%	95%	90%	80%	70%	60%
Mfg.'s Sug. Retail	$267	$225	$180	$150	$125	$115	$105	$95

Add $30 for satin nickel finish.

MODEL 85 — .380 ACP, similar specifications to Model 83 except has 12 shot mag., 30½ oz. New 1988.

		100%	98%	95%	90%	80%	70%	60%
Mfg.'s Sug. Retail	$315	$275	$245	$220	$195	$170	$150	$130

Add $60 for satin nickel finish.

MODEL 86 — .380 ACP cal., matte finish, undercover model, wrap around rubber grips, 12 shot mag. Importation began 1991.

		100%	98%	95%	90%	80%	70%	60%
Mfg.'s Sug. Retail	$359	$310	$265	$225	$200	$170	$150	$130

Add $33 for nickel finish.

MODEL 90 — 9mm Para., single action, semi-auto, steel frame, checkered walnut grips, 13 shot mag., deep blue finish. New 1990.

		100%	98%	95%	90%	80%	70%	60%
Mfg.'s Sug. Retail	$384	$325	$280	$250	$220	$195	$170	$150

BERTUZZI

Manufacturer located in Brescia, Italy since 1886. Imported and distributed by New England Arms Co. located in Kittery Point, ME.

SHOTGUNS: S X S

Grading	100%	98%	95%	90%	80%	70%	60%

MODEL ORIONE — 12 ga., scalloped Anson & Deeley boxlock action, beavertail forearm, single trigger, auto ejector. This model is available on special order only — contact the distributor listed above for availability, prices, and options. Prices start at $3,500.

BEST QUALITY SIDELOCK — various gauges, best quality sidelock model with extensive engraving. Prices start at $7,500.

HAMMER GUN — all gauges, upper tang safety, double triggers, fine quality engraving. Prices start at $3,500 and approach $6,000 with ejectors and single trigger. The self-cocking mechanism is popular in this model and prices can vary between $6,500-$15,000.

SHOTGUNS: O/U

ZEUS — 12 ga., sidelock, auto ejector, deluxe engraving, deluxe wood checkering, SST. This model is available on special order only — contact the distributor listed above for availability, prices, and options. Prices generally range from $8,500-$10,000.

ZEUS EXTRA LUSSO — 12 ga., sidelock, auto ejector, deluxe wood, deluxe checkering and engraving, SST. This model is available on special order only — contact the distributor listed above for availability, prices, and options. Prices generally range from $10,000-$15,000.

BIG HORN ARMS CORP.

Previous manufacturer located in Watertown, SD.

TARGET PISTOL — .22 Short only, unique action permitting auto. ejection, ambidextrous stock made of molded Tufflex with carvings, 26 oz. Approx. 1,200 mfg. Disc. in the late 60's.

	$225	$200	$180	$160	$140	$120	$100

LIL' MAGNUM SHOTGUN — .410 diameter reloadable shot cartridge, single shot open bolt operation, included reloading equipment, approx. 2,000 mfg. in the late 60's.

	$100	$85	$75	$65	$55	$50	$45

BIGHORN RIFLE CO.

Previous manufacturer located in Orem, UT.

BIGHORN RIFLE — Mauser action, choice of calibers, custom made bolt action of high quality, interchangeable barrels (gun is supplied with 2 barrels), adj. trigger, deluxe walnut stock, many custom options. Mfg. 1984 only.

	$2,100	$1,800	$1,600	$1,400	$1,200	$1,000	$850

BIGHORN PISTOL — .22 LR, bolt action design, research is underway to gather more information concerning this model.

BINGHAM, LTD.

Manufacturer located in Norcross, GA 1976-1985.

RIFLES

PPS 50 — .22 LR only, blowback action, 50 round drum mag., standard model has Beechwood stock. Add $20 for deluxe model with walnut stock. Duramil model has chrome finish and walnut stock — add $30. Disc. 1985.

	$195	$160	$145	$135	$125	$110	$100

This model was styled after the Soviet WWII Model PPSH Sub Machine Gun.

Last Mfg.'s Sug. Retail was $230.

AK-22 — .22 LR only, blowback action, styled after AK-47, 15 shot mag. standard, 29 shot mag. available. Standard model has Beechwood stock. Deluxe model has walnut stock — add $20. Disc. 1985.

	$225	$195	$160	$145	$135	$125	$110

Last Mfg.'s Sug. Retail was $230.

BANTAM — .22 LR or 22 Mag., bolt action single shot, 18½ in. barrel. Disc. 1985.

	$110	$90	$75	$65	$55	$45	$40

Last Mfg.'s Sug. Retail was $120.

Grading	100%	98%	95%	90%	80%	70%	60%

FG-9 — 9mm only, blowback action, semi-auto paramilitary design carbine, 20½ in. barrel. New design for 1984. While advertised this model was never manufactured.

BITTNER

Manufactured by Gustav Bittner located in Vieprty, Bohemia, (Austria, Hungary).

BITTNER MODEL 1893 — 7.7mm Bittner cal., pistol with hand activated repeater mechanism, box magazine, checkered grips, limited manufacture in 1893 circa.

	$4,500	$3,800	$3,100	$2,700	$2,300	$1,900	$1,500

BLAND, THOMAS & SONS GUNMAKERS LTD.

English manufacturer located in England since 1840. This firm was purchased in 1990 by Woodcock Hill located in Benton, PA.

Woodcock Hill should be contacted directly (address listed in Trademark Index) for more information (including current models and prices) regarding Thomas Bland & Sons firearms. Prices will vary depending on the exchange rate between the pound/dollar.

SHOTGUNS

Both boxlock and sidelock best quality shotguns are available in all gauges with prices ranging between $5,000 - $40,000 depending upon type, finish, and accessories.

RIFLES

Double rifles are available in almost all calibers and specifications. Prices vary between $12,000 - $45,000 depending upon type, finish, and accessories. Bolt action rifles are available in any type of action, most calibers, and other special options. The bolt action models are not manufactured in England. Prices range between $1,100 - $11,000.

BLASER

Manufactured by Blaser Jagdwaffen Gmbh in Isny/Allgau, Germany. Currently imported and distributed in the U.S. by Autumn Sales Inc. located in Fort Worth, TX.

Prices could differ from values shown below because of the fluctuating U.S. dollar.

Blaser Jagdwaffen manufactures a large variety of rifles, drillings, and combination guns for the European market. The models below have been selected for domestic sales. More information is available on the European models by contacting Autumn Sales (see Trademark Index).

MODEL R-84 — .22-250, .243 Win., 6mm Rem., .25-06 Rem., .270 Win., .280 Rem., or .30-06 standard cal.'s, .257 Wby. Mag., .264 Win. Mag., 7mm Rem. Mag., .300 Win. Mag., .300 Wby. Mag., .338 Win. Mag., or .375 H&H Magnum cal., 23 or 24 (Mag. cal.'s only) in. barrel. short bolt action with 60 degree rotation, checkered walnut stock and forearm, approx. 7 lbs. Introduced 1988.

Mfg.'s Sug. Retail	$1,850	$1,725	$1,450	$1,200	$1,050	$975	$895	$825

Add $50 for left-hand action.

Add $545 per interchangeable barrel.

ULTIMATE BOLT ACTION — .22-250, .243, .25-06, .270, .308, .30-06, 7 x 57, 7 x 64, .264 Win. Mag., 7mm Rem. Mag., 300 Win. Mag., .338 Win. Mag., or .375 H&H cal., unique bolt action design with 60 degree bolt throw, interchangeable barrel capability, 3 locking lugs, safety lever cocks and uncocks the firing pin spring, exposed hammer, aluminum receiver, 22 or 24 in. barrel, single set trigger, silver finished receiver has light engraving, select checkered walnut stock and forearm, 6¾ lbs. Extra interchangeable barrels are $545 each, extra bolt heads are $175 each. Mfg. 1985-1989.

	$1,350	$1,100	$975	$925	$825	$750	$675

All models were available in left-hand version at no extra charge.

Last Mfg.'s Sug. Retail was $1,495.

Grading	100%	98%	95%	90%	80%	70%	60%

MODEL K77 A SINGLE SHOT — .22-250, .243 Win., 6.5 x 55mm, .270 Win., 7 x 57R, 7 x 65R, or .30-06 standard cal.'s, 7mm Rem. Mag., .300 Win. Mag. or .300 Wby. Magnum cal., break open action, 23 or 24 in. barrel, 3 piece take down, upper tang safety, checkered walnut stock and forearm, engraved silver finished receiver, sling swivels, 5½ lbs. Imported 1988-90.

	$2,000	$1,675	$1,475	$1,300	$1,100	$925	$800

Add $50 for Mag. calibers.
Add $730-$778 per interchangeable barrel.
Last Mfg.'s Sug. Retail was $2,280.

ULTIMATE: SPECIAL ORDER

All of the below listed models may have been ordered with a butt stock cartridge trap — add $250-$500 depending on model. Special order guns required 3 to 9 months to hand fabricate. Mfg. was disc. 1989 on all models.

Ultimate Deluxe — same as Ultimate, except better wood and game scene engraving.

	$1,425	$1,175	$1,000	$950	$850	$775	$700

Last Mfg.'s Sug. Retail was $1,595.

Ultimate Deluxe Carbine — .243 Win. or .308 Win. cal. only, 19½ in. barrel with full length forearm. New 1986.

	$1,600	$1,375	$1,150	$1,000	$900	$825	$750

Last Mfg.'s Sug. Retail was $1,800.

Ultimate Super Deluxe — similar to Ultimate Deluxe, except features better wood and game scene engraving. New 1986.

	$3,750	$3,250	$2,900	$2,600	$2,300	$2,100	$1,850

Last Mfg.'s Sug. Retail was $4,030.

Ultimate Exclusive — similar to Ultimate Super Deluxe, except features better wood and game scene engraving. New 1986.

	$4,850	$4,300	$3,500	$2,975	$2,600	$2,275	$1,975

Add $700 per interchangeable barrel.
Last Mfg.'s Sug. Retail was $5,655.

Ultimate Super Exclusive — similar to Ultimate Exclusive, except features better wood and game scene engraving. New 1986.

	$7,700	$6,800	$5,750	$4,700	$3,950	$3,450	$2,950

Add $950 per interchangeable barrel.
Last Mfg.'s Sug. Retail was $8,905.

Ultimate Royal — best quality Ultimate, featuring Bavarian cheek piece and checkering/carving on stock and forearm, elaborate game scene engraving, gold plated hammer. New 1986.

	$9,000	$7,500	$6,750	$6,000	$5,375	$4,600	$4,000

Add $1,200 per interchangeable barrel.
Last Mfg.'s Sug. Retail was $11,500.

BOITO

Manufacturer located in Brazil. Previously imported by F.I.E. Corp. located in Hialeah, FL.

Boito shotguns were inexpensive, utilitarian shotguns that are shootable, but not collectible. Because of this, prices typically range between $100 - $225, depending on the gauge and condition.

BORCHARDT

Manufacturer located in Germany From 1894 - 1897

PISTOL: SEMI-AUTO

These prices are established with matching parts and original finish guns.

MODEL 1893 — 7.65mm, with accessories, cased. Subtract 40% if uncased and without accessories.

Ludwig Loewe mfg. — serial numbered 1-1104.

	$13,500	$10,500	$8,500	$6,000	$5,000	$4,500	$4,000

Grading	100%	98%	95%	90%	80%	70%	60%

DWM mfg. — starting approx. 1895, serial numbered 1105-3000.

	100%	98%	95%	90%	80%	70%	60%
	$12,500	$10,000	$8,500	$6,000	$5,000	$4,500	$4,000

BOSS & COMPANY

Manufacturer located in London, England. 1832 to date.

Boss is one of the world's finest shotguns. It has always been custom built to customer specifications. Less than 10,000 have been manufactured to date. We will list the basic models with approximate values, but should the opportunity for purchase or sale arise, competent appraisals should be secured.

SHOTGUNS

BOSS SIDE-BY-SIDE — all gauges, barrel lengths and chokes to specifications, bar-action sidelock, checkered stock, pistol or straight grip stock, standard with either double or non-selective single trigger.

	$22,500	$18,750	$15,000	$13,000	$12,000	$10,000	$9,000

20 gauge — add 20%.

28 gauge — add 40%.

.410 gauge — add 60%+.

SST — add $1,000. Patented "3 pull" system.

Add 10% for opening assist.

Add appropriate price ($500 on up) if properly cased.

BOSS O/U — all ga.'s, barrel lengths and chokes to specifications, shell-framed sidelock, auto ejectors, SST, stock to specifications.

	$29,500	$25,000	$21,500	$18,500	$15,870	$13,800	$12,000

20 gauge — add 30%.

28 gauge — add 65%.

.410 gauge — add 75%+.

SST — add $1,000. Patented "3 pull" system.

Add 10% for opening assist.

Add appropriate price ($500 on up) if properly cased.

Note: above values represent base gun only. Any additional engraving and/or special orders will add considerably to the above prices.

BOSWELL, CHARLES

Previously manufactured in London, England. In 1988 Charles Boswell was purchased by U.S. interests and Cape Horn International located in Charlotte, NC has been retained to sell and manufacture the Boswell Guns in the U.S. In addition to aquiring their entire inventory of English manufactured firearms, Cape Horn International is currently fabricating new shotguns and double rifles in the U.S. using the best materials including English lock mechanisms snd will retain the Charles Boswell Co. Trademark. Every gun will be Ccstom ordered to an individual client's requirements/specifications. Previously imported by Saxon Arms, Ltd., located in Clearwater, FL.

SHOTGUNS: SIDE-BY-SIDE

BOXLOCK SXS — made to individual order, choice of engraving - including game scenes with gold, Anson & Deeley boxlock actions, select European hybrid walnut, double triggers, leather cased, currently mfg. While each shotgun is priced per individual special order, the below listed prices represent standard features and embellishments.

Best Quality

Mfg.'s Sug. Retail	$8,500	$8,500	$6,500	$5,650	$4,800	$4,200	$3,750	$3,250

Grading	100%	98%	95%	90%	80%	70%	60%

Deluxe Grade — game scene engraved.
Mfg.'s Sug. Retail $9,500 $9,500 $7,250 $6,000 $5,000 $4,400 $3,750 $3,250
Add $900 for single trigger.
Add $1,800 for extra set of barrels.
Add $1,500 for smaller gauges.

FEATHERWEIGHT MONARCH GRADE — lavishly engraved with gold game scenes, light-weight model, specifications per individual customer special order. Mfg. began 1989.
Boxlock Model
Mfg.'s Sug. Retail $12,000 $12,000 $9,500 $7,250 $6,000 $5,000 $4,400 $3,750
Sidelock Model
Mfg.'s Sug. Retail $22,000 $22,000 $17,500 $15,000 $12,750 $10,000 $7,950 $6,250

SIDELOCK SXS — made to individual order, choice of game scene engraving, H&H sidelock action, select European hybrid walnut, double triggers, leather cased, currently mfg. While each shotgun is priced per individual special order, the below listed values represent standard features and embellishments.
Mfg.'s Sug. Retail $17,500 $17,500 $15,000 $12,750 $10,000 $9,000 $8,500 $7,750
Add $4,000 for smaller gauges except .410 — add $5,000.
Add $900 for extra set of barrels.
Add $1,800 for extra set of .410 ga. barrels.

DOUBLE RIFLES

BOXLOCK SXS RIFLE — made to individual order, .300 Express, .375 H&H, or .458 Win. Mag. cal., choice of game scene engraving, Anson & Deeley boxlock actions, select European hybrid walnut, double triggers, leather cased.
Mfg.'s Sug. Retail $40,000 $40,000 $31,500 $25,000 $21,000 $17,500 $16,500 $15,000
.600 Nitro Express
This model is priced by quotation only.

SIDELOCK SXS RIFLE — made to individual order, .300 Express, .375 H&H, or .458 Win. Mag. cal., choice of game scene engraving, H&H sidelock action, select European hybrid walnut, double triggers, leather cased.
Mfg.'s Sug. Retail $55,000 $55,000 $42,000 $35,000 $31,000 $25,000 $21,500 $18,750
.600 Nitro Express
Mfg.'s Sug. Retail $85,000 $85,000 $65,000 $49,500 $40,000 $37,500 $31,000 $27,000
Premiums are often times paid for these models due to extreme rarity and slow fabrication time.

BREDA, ERNESTO

Manufacturer located in Milan, Italy. Previous importation by Diana Imports Co., located in San Francisco, CA.

SHOTGUNS: SEMI-AUTO

GOLD SERIES SEMI-AUTO — 12 ga. semi-auto, 2¾ in., 25 or 27 in. barrels, gas operated. Current model has interchangeable choke tubes, vent rib is standard. Add $26 for choke tubes (each).
Antares Standard — all steel construction. Importation disc. 1988.
$440 $375 $340 $310 $285 $260 $240
Last Mfg.'s Sug. Retail was $495.
Argus — lightweight standard, weighs only 6.6 lbs. Importation disc. 1988.
$450 $380 $340 $310 $285 $260 $240
Last Mfg.'s Sug. Retail was $510.
Aries — Magnum, 3 in. chambers, 7.9 lbs. Importation disc. 1988.
$460 $395 $350 $320 $295 $270 $250
Last Mfg.'s Sug. Retail was $525.

Grading	100%	98%	95%	90%	80%	70%	60%

STANDARD — 12 ga., semi-auto, 2¾ in., 25 or 27 in. barrels, recoil operated, lightly engraved. Current model has interchangeable choke tubes. Add $35 for vent rib, $20 for choke tubes (each). Disc.

	$300	$275	$255	$230	$215	$200	$180

GRADE 1 — 12 ga., same as standard, except with fancier wood and engraving.

	$575	$530	$485	$440	$410	$380	$350

GRADE 2 — 12 ga., exceeds Grade 1 on embellishments.

	$685	$620	$560	$500	$460	$420	$375

GRADE 3 — 12 ga., top-of-the-line semi-auto.

	$850	$790	$700	$640	$590	$540	$480

MAGNUM MODEL — 12 ga. only, chambered for 3 in. shells. Add $20 for vent rib.

	$470	$415	$380	$350	$315	$290	$265

ALTAIR SPECIAL — 12 ga. semi-auto, 2¾ in., 25 or 27 in. barrels, gas operated, alloy construction. Current model has interchangeable choke tubes, vent rib is standard. Add $25 for choke tubes (each). Choice of blued or chromed receiver.

	$440	$375	$340	$310	$285	$260	$240

Last Mfg.'s Sug. Retail was $495.

SHOTGUNS: OVER AND UNDER

VEGA SPECIAL — 12 ga. only, boxlock action, 26 or 28 in. barrels, single trigger, ejectors, blue only.

	$575	$495	$460	$440	$400	$375	$350

Last Mfg.'s Sug. Retail was $650.

VEGA SPECIAL TRAP — 12 ga. only, boxlock action, triggers and locks designed for competition shooting, 30 or 32 in. barrels, single trigger, ejectors, blue only.

	$885	$820	$760	$720	$675	$635	$575

Last Mfg.'s Sug. Retail was $1,114.

SIRIO STANDARD — 12 ga. only, boxlock action, 26 or 28 in. barrels, single trigger, ejectors, blue only, action extensively engraved. Also available in skeet model (28 in. barrels).

	$2,000	$1,850	$1,630	$1,480	$1,320	$1,200	$1,050

Last Mfg.'s Sug. Retail was $2,225.

SHOTGUNS: SIDE-BY-SIDE

ANDROMEDA SPECIAL — 12 ga. only, single trigger, ejectors, select checkered walnut, satin finish receiver with elaborate engraving.

	$640	$550	$480	$420	$365	$300	$250

Last Mfg.'s Sug. Retail was $685.

BREN

Manufactured 1983-86 by Dornaus & Dixon Ent., Inc., located in Huntington Beach, CA.

Note: the Bren 10 shoots a Norma factory loaded 10mm auto. cartridge. Ballistically, it is very close to a .41 Mag. Bren pistols also have unique power seal rifling, with five lands and grooves.

Since the discontinuance of the Bren pistol in 1986, collector interest has accelerated, driving prices up substantially. Some of this interest has been created by its appearance in both movies and television, much like the S & W Model 29 and Auto Mag exposure in the past. Values below reflect the current, short term interest in these models.

ORIGINAL BREN 10 MAGAZINES ARE CURRENTLY SELLING FOR $150-$175 IF NEW.

100% VALUES IN THIS SECTION ASSUME NIB CONDITION. SUBTRACT 10% WITHOUT BOX/MANUAL.

Grading	100%	98%	95%	90%	80%	70%	60%

BREN 10 STANDARD MODEL — 10mm only, semi-auto selective double action design, brushed satin finish, 5 in. barrel, 11 shot, stainless steel frame. Mfg. 1984-86.

	$1,250	$995	$725				

Last Mfg.'s Sug. Retail was $500.

BREN 10 POCKET MODEL — 10mm only, semi-auto selective double action design, stainless frame, compact version of the full-size Bren 10, 4 in. barrel, 28 oz., 9 shot. Mfg. 1984-86.

	$1,325	$1,000	$750				

Last Mfg.'s Sug. Retail was $600.

BREN 10 MILITARY/POLICE MODEL — 10mm only, identical to standard model, except has matte black finish. Mfg. 1984-86.

	$1,300	$995	$725				

Last Mfg.'s Sug. Retail was $550.

BREN 10 SPECIAL FORCES MODEL — 10mm only, commercial version of the military pistol submitted to the U.S. gov't. Model D has dark finish. Model L has light finish. Disc. 1986.

	$1,450	$1,100	$800				

Last Mfg.'s Sug. Retail was $600.

BREN 10 DUAL-MASTER PRESENTATION MODEL — 10mm and .45 ACP, supplied with extra slide and barrel to accommodate the .45 ACP, same Mag. for both cal.'s, extra fine finish, with wood presentation case. Disc. 1986.

	$1,775	$1,300	$850				

Last Mfg.'s Sug. Retail was $800.

BREN 10 INITIAL COMMEMORATIVE — 10mm only, 2,000 annnounced mfg.(exact amount unknown), 22Kt. gold plated detailing, laser engraved stocks, special presentation chest. Disc. 1986.

	$2,850	$2,000	$1,600				

Last Mfg.'s Sug. Retail was $2,000.

MARKSMAN MODEL — .45 ACP, 250 mfg. for a retail shop in Chicago called "The Marksman", action similar to Bren 10 Standard Model.

	$1,125	$850	$600				

BRETTON

Manufactured in Saint-Etienne, France. Imported and distributed by Mandall Shooting Supplies, Inc. located in Scottsdale, AZ and Quality Arms, Inc., located in Houston, TX.

SHOTGUNS: OVER AND UNDER

All Bretton shotguns are extremely lightweight and well balanced because of their unique design (permitting total disassembly including barrels) and use of various composition alloys.

BABY STANDARD (SPRINT MODEL) — 12 or 20 ga. only, sliding breech action allows barrels to move straight forward, 27½ separated barrels, double triggers, side opening lever, blued action and barrels, recoil pad, checkered walnut stock and forearm, 4.8 lbs.

Mfg.'s Sug. Retail	$865	$815	$700	$625	$575	$475	$430	$395

Available from Mandall Shooting Supply, Inc. only.

SPRINT DELUXE — 12, 16 (disc.), or 20 ga., action same as Baby Standard, engraved coin finished receiver, 271/2 separated barrels, deluxe checkered walnut stock and forearm, extremely lightweight, 4.8 lbs.

Mfg.'s Sug. Retail	$975	$895	$750	$675	$600	$550	$500	$460

Available from Quality Arms, Inc. and Mandall Shooting Supply, Inc.

FAIR PLAY MODEL — 12 or 20 ga., differs from Sprint Models in that action pivots like normal O/U, 27½ separated barrels, lightweight construction, 4.8 lbs.

Mfg.'s Sug. Retail	$1,025	$925	$775	$695	$600	$550	$500	$460

Grading	100%	98%	95%	90%	80%	70%	60%

BRITARMS

Manufacturer located in England. Previously imported and distributed by Mandall Shooting Supplies, Inc. located in Scottsdale, AZ.

Britarms Target Pistols have had very limited importation to date in the U.S. While Britarms has manufactured other models, only the Model 2000 is listed since it has been formally imported through a U.S. firm.

Model 2000 (MK II) — .LR, standard fire target semi-auto pistol, adj. trigger and rear sight, anatomical adj. grips, limited importation.

Mfg.'s Sug. Retail	$1,295	$1,175	$925	$775	$695	$600	$550	$500

Above values represent 1990 pricing information from Mandall's.

BRNO ARMS

Manufactured in Brno & Uherski Brod, Czechoslovakia. Currently imported and distributed by T.D. Arms located in New Baltimore, MI. Pragotrade located in Ontario, Canada also imports this trademark in greater quantities since Canadian - Czechoslovakian politics do not tax Brno firearms of Canadian import. Recently, inexpensive Pragotrade pricing has lowered the "base price" on some of the CZ-70 and CZ-85 variations. Previously imported by Saki International located in Rocky River, OH.

Since Czechoslovakia is still on non-favored nation status in the U.S., current domestic importation of CZ pistols and rifles is very limited. Even though there is a reduced supply of CZ-75 pistols, the many copies of this design being imported currently have absorbed some of the demand.

PISTOLS

CZ-70 — 7.65mm, double action, similar to Walther PP, 8 shot mag., 1 lb. 9 oz. Disc.

	$400	$350	$300	$275	$250	$225	$200

A very limited quantity of this model was imported.

CZ-75 — 9mm Para., Poldi steel, selective double action, thumb safety, 4¾ in. barrel, 15 shot mag., available in baked enamel, matte blue, high polished blue, nickel, or parkerized finish, 35 oz.

Mfg.'s Sug. Retail	$699	$550	$440	$375	$335	$310	$285	$260

Add $50 for walnut grips.

Add 15% for earlier non-import marked specimens.

This model will have limited availability in 1990 since importer is currently out of stock.

"First Model" variations, mostly imported by Pragotrade of Canada, are identifiable by short slide rails, no half-cock feature, and were mostly available in high polish blue only. These early pistols sell for $1,000 if N.I.B. condition.

CZ-85 — variation of the CZ-75 with ambidextrous controls, new plastic grip design, sight rib. Available in matte blue, black enamel, or a combination finish.

	$800	$700	$625	$550	$475	$400	$325

While this gun has not officially been imported into the U.S., limited samples have been brought in by U.S. servicemen stationed in Europe and other sources.

CZ-83 — 7.65mm (.32 ACP) or .380 ACP (new 1986) cal., modern design, 15 shot mag. Mfg. began 1985.

	$595	$540	$475	$415	$350	$295	$250

This model has had very limited importation. 1986 retail was $415.

CZ-82 — 9 x 18mm Makarov, current Czech military sidearm, recent exportation to W. Germany in Makarov chambering.

This model is the same as the CZ-83 except for cal. Prices are similar to the model CZ-83.

PAV — .22 LR, single shot, 9¾ in. barrel, all steel construction. Imported 1986 only.

	$95	$85	$75	$65	$60	$55	$50

Last Mfg.'s Sug. Retail was $105.

Grading	100%	98%	95%	90%	80%	70%	60%

DRULOV 70 — .22 cal., single shot. Add $30 for set trigger. Disc. 1986.

	$105	$95	$85	$75	$70	$65	$60

Last Mfg.'s Sug. Retail was $115.

DRULOV 75 — .22 cal., single shot with set trigger & micrometer sights. Also available in left-hand.

Mfg.'s Sug. Retail	$349	$300	$250	$215	$185	$155	$140	$120

DRULOV 78 — .22 cal., similar to Drulov 75. Imported 1986 only.

	$275	$240	$200	$175	$150	$130	$110

Last Mfg.'s Sug. Retail was $180.

RIFLES: BOLT ACTION

The Brno Lightweight Sporter was introduced in the late 1930's. A small quantity was manufactured during pre-war and WWII. Most production occured between 1946-1955. Total production of this model was approx. 40,000+ units. A design change was implemented at approximate serial number 23,000, at which time the receiver was changed to a double square bridge dovetailed to accept scope mounts. Earlier mfg. had a rounded receiver and some had claw type scope mounts installed. These guns were referenced as Models 21 and 22 domestically, but no model designation appears on the gun. Available cal.'s were 6.5 x 57, 7 x 57, 7 x 64, 8 x 57, or 8 x 60mm. Configuration was small ring Mauser 98 receiver with double set triggers, butterknife bolt, checkered walnut pistol grip stock (half or full length), with cheekpiece and sling swivels, late production incorporated four variations and two barrel lengths (20.5 or 23.6 in.).

HORNET SPORTER (MODEL ZKW 465) — miniature Mauser action, .22 Hornet, 22¾ in. barrel, 5 shot mag., 3-leaf express sight, double set trigger, double set triggers, checkered pistol grip stock, also called Z-B Mauser, approx. 40,000 mfg. between 1949-1973.

	$875	$700	$600	$470	$385	$305	$220

There are few examples in .218 Bee and .222 Rem. cal. - premiums can be added.

MODEL ZG-47 — cal.'s included .270 Win., .30-06, 7 x 57, 7 x 64, 8 x 64S, 9.3 x 62, and other metric cal.'s, large ring Mauser 98 action with double square bridge dovetailed for scope mounts, rollover type safety, checkered pistol grip walnut stock with sling swivels and Schnabel forend, approx. 20,000 mfg. world wide between 1955-1965.

MODEL 21H — 6.5 x 57, 7 x 57, or 8 x 57 cal., 20½ in. barrel, double set trigger, 2-leaf sight, checkered pistol grip stock. Disc.

	$850	$675	$575	$470	$385	$305	$220

MODEL 22F — same as 21H, with full length stock. Disc.

	$1,050	$900	$700	$525	$440	$360	$275

MODEL 1 — .22 LR, 22¾ in. barrel, 3-leaf sight, 5 shot clip mag., checkered pistol, 6 lbs. Mfg. 1946-1957.

	$595	$540	$485	$405	$375	$320	$265

MODEL 2 — same as Model 1, with checkered deluxe walnut stock.

	$635	$570	$515	$430	$405	$350	$295

MODEL 3 — .22 LR, target rifle model with 27½ in. heavy barrel, adj. click target sights, 5 shot clip mag., plain target style stock with large swivels, 9½ lbs. Mfg. 1949-1956.

	$635	$570	$515	$430	$405	$350	$295

MODEL 4 — similar to Model 3, except has improved trigger design and safety. Mfg. 1957-1962.

	$700	$635	$570	$515	$430	$405	$350

MODEL 5 — similar to Model 1, except has improved trigger design and safety. Mfg. 1957-1973.

	$650	$570	$515	$430	$405	$350	$295

Grading	100%	98%	95%	90%	80%	70%	60%

MODEL ZKM-452 — .22 LR, bolt action, 5 or 10 shot mag., 25 in. barrel, w/beechwood stock, 6 lbs. 10 oz. Importation disc. 1986.

	100%	98%	95%	90%	80%	70%	60%
	$210	$175	$160	$140	$120	$105	$90

Last Mfg.'s Sug. Retail was $239.

MODEL ZKM-452D (DELUXE) — same as ZKM-452 only with walnut Monte Carlo stock. Limited availability as importer is currently out of stock.

Mfg.'s Sug. Retail	$399	$350	$295	$260	$230	$195	$170	$150

ZKB 680 (FOX II) — .22 Hornet or .222 Rem. (disc.) cal., 23½ in. barrel, 5 shot mag., set triggers, 5 lbs. 12 oz.

Mfg.'s Sug. Retail	$499	$445	$380	$340	$295	$255	$230	$200

ZKK 600 — .30-06, .270 Win., 7 x 57mm (disc.), or 7 x 64mm (disc.) cal., improved Mauser type action, 23½ in. barrel, both adj. set trigger and standard trigger included, 7 lbs. 2 oz.

Mfg.'s Sug. Retail	$599	$530	$430	$395	$360	$330	$300	$275

Add $50 for Monte Carlo stock.

ZKK 601 — .223 Rem., .243 Win. or .308 Win. (disc.) cal., otherwise same as ZKK 600.

Mfg.'s Sug. Retail	$599	$530	$430	$395	$360	$330	$300	$275

Add $60 for Monte Carlo stock (disc.).

ZKK 602 — .300 Win. Mag., .375 H&H, 8 x 68mm (disc.), .416 Rigby (disc.), or .458 Win. Mag. (disc.) cal., otherwise same as ZKK 600. Limited availability.

Mfg.'s Sug. Retail	$689	$625	$500	$450	$395	$350	$310	$280

Add $60 for Monte Carlo stock.

This model with standard stock will have limited availability in 1991 as importer is currently out of stock.

RIFLES: SEMI-AUTO

CZ-511 — .22 LR, semi-auto, select walnut stock, adj. sights. Disc. 1986.

	100%	98%	95%	90%	80%	70%	60%
	$280	$250	$230	$215	$200	$190	$180

Last Mfg.'s Sug. Retail was $310.

MODEL 581 — .22 LR, semi-auto, select walnut stock, adj. sights, 5 shot mag. Disc.

	100%	98%	95%	90%	80%	70%	60%
	$600	$540	$495	$440	$395	$350	$295

RIFLES: O/U

SUPER EXPRESS — 7 x 65R, 9.3 x 74R (disc.), .375 H&H (disc.), or .458 Win. Mag. (disc.) cal., sidelock action with Kersten breech crossbolt, hand engraved, approx. 9 lbs.

Mfg.'s Sug. Retail	$3,900	$3,450	$2,875	$2,300	$1,875	$1,600	$1,375	$1,200

Add $190 for disc. cal.'s.

This model previously could be ordered with 6 different types of engraving options. They were: Grade I — add $2,060, Grade II — add $1,030, Grade III — add $1,545, Grade IV — add $1,030, Grade V — add $620, Grade VI — add $660.

SHOTGUNS/COMBINATIONS GUNS: O/U

ZH-SERIES

ZH series over and unders are unique in that they permit 8 different interchangeable barrels including rifle and shotgun sets, interrupter on double trigger, blued action, engraved, diamond checkered walnut.

Add $25 for Monte Carlo stock (disc.).

Add for $45 for set triggers (disc.).

ZH-300 — 12 ga. only, double triggers with rear trigger doubling as single trigger, 27½ in. barrels, 7 lbs. New 1986.

Mfg.'s Sug. Retail	$599	$530	$430	$395	$360	$330	$300	$275

This model is available in skeet, trap, or field configuration.

Grading	100%	98%	95%	90%	80%	70%	60%

ZH-301 — 12 ga. field, 27½ in. barrels. Disc. 1986.

| | $570 | $505 | $460 | $435 | $410 | $390 | $370 |

Last Mfg.'s Sug. Retail was $605.

ZH-302 — 12 ga., skeet model, 26 in. barrels. Disc. 1986.

| | $575 | $510 | $465 | $440 | $415 | $395 | $375 |

Last Mfg.'s Sug. Retail was $615.

ZH-303 — 12 ga., trap model, 30 in. barrels. Disc. 1986.

| | $575 | $510 | $465 | $440 | $415 | $395 | $375 |

Last Mfg.'s Sug. Retail was $615.

ZH-304 — 7 x 57R mm x 12 ga., combination rifle/shotgun. Disc. 1986.

| | $640 | $570 | $500 | $450 | $410 | $380 | $350 |

Last Mfg.'s Sug. Retail was $685.

ZH-305 — 5.6 x 52R mm x 12 ga., combination rifle/shotgun. Disc.

| | $685 | $640 | $585 | $520 | $460 | $415 | $360 |

ZH-306 — 5.6 x 50mm Mag. x 12 ga., combination rifle/shotgun. Disc.

| | $685 | $640 | $585 | $520 | $460 | $415 | $360 |

ZH-321 — 16 ga. field, 27 in. barrels. Disc. 1986.

| | $570 | $505 | $460 | $435 | $410 | $390 | $370 |

Last Mfg.'s Sug. Retail was $605.

ZH-324 — 7 x 57R mm x 16 ga., combination rifle/shotgun. Disc. 1986.

| | $640 | $570 | $530 | $495 | $475 | $450 | $420 |

Last Mfg.'s Sug. Retail was $685.

MODEL ZH-300 COMBO SET — Model ZH-300 style engraving and features, equipped with 8 interchangeable barrels that include various O/U configurations including shotgun/shotgun and shotgun/rifle configurations in various ga.'s and cal.'s. New 1986.

| Mfg.'s Sug. Retail | $3,500 | $3,150 | $2,675 | $2,300 | $2,000 | $1,800 | $1,600 | $1,450 |

MODEL 500 — 12 ga. only, ejectors, field tubes, acid etched engraving. New 1986.

| Mfg.'s Sug. Retail | $629 | $545 | $450 | $400 | $365 | $330 | $300 | $275 |

Model 500 Combo Set — shotgun/rifle set comprised of 4 barrels including 12 ga. over barrels with choice of 5.6 x 52R (disc.), 7 x 57R, 7 x 65R mm's, or 12 ga. under barrels (in either field, skeet, or trap chokings), sling swivels, set trigger on rifle/shotgun combo, chemically engraved, about 7½ lbs. New 1987.

| Mfg.'s Sug. Retail | $2,169 | $1,925 | $1,625 | $1,400 | $1,200 | $1,075 | $950 | $825 |

This model is available in limited quanitity.

CZ-581 — 12 ga., boxlock with Greener crossbolt, Poldi steel action, 28 in. barrels, vent rib, sel. ejectors, sling swivels.

| Mfg.'s Sug. Retail | $649 | $525 | $440 | $400 | $370 | $355 | $340 | $320 |

Add $30 for single trigger (disc.)

CZ-584 — 12 ga. and 7 x 57R mm rifle/shotgun combination , .222 Rem. and .308 Win. cal.'s also available, 24½ in. barrels, ejectors. Disc. 1986.

| | $920 | $820 | $750 | $700 | $650 | $600 | $550 |

Last Mfg.'s Sug. Retail was $999.

SUPER SERIES — available in 12 ga. field, skeet, and trap configuration as well as combination shotgun/rifle in 12 ga. x 7 x 57R or 7 x 65R cal.

| Mfg.'s Sug. Retail | $899 | $800 | $700 | $640 | $590 | $550 | $515 | $475 |

Add $70 for single trigger or trap/skeet configuration (disc.).

Add $700 for extra set of 12 ga. field barrels.

Add $1,101 for hand engraving.

Grading	100%	98%	95%	90%	80%	70%	60%

Super Combo — 3 barrel set including 12 ga., 7 x 57R mm, and 7 x 65R mm barrels. New 1987.

Mfg.'s Sug. Retail	$2,169	$1,925	$1,640	$1,425	$1,250	$1,100	$1,000	$925

This model is currently out of stock from the importer.

SHOTGUNS: SIDE-BY-SIDE

ZP-49 — 12 ga. only, ejectors, double triggers, true sidelock, Purdey-type top bolt, cocking indicators, walnut stock, swivels. Imported since 1986.

Mfg.'s Sug. Retail	$589	$535	$460	$420	$385	$350	$320	$290

Add $20 for engraving.

ZP-149 — similar to ZP-49, except plain receiver. Imported 1986-1989.

	$525	$460	$420	$385	$350	$320	$290

Add $20 for engraving.
Last Mfg.'s Sug. Retail was $589.

ZP-349 — 12 ga. only, extractors, double triggers, true sidelock, Purdey-type top bolt, cocking indicators, walnut stock with cheek piece, beavertail forearm, swivels, 7.3 lbs. Imported 1986 only.

	$450	$390	$360	$325	$300	$270	$250

Add $20 for engraving.
Last Mfg.'s Sug. Retail was $520.

BRONCO
Echave Y Arizmendi, Eibar, Spain.

MODEL 1918 POCKET AUTOMATIC — 7.65mm, 6 shot, 2½ in. barrel, fixed sights, blue, hard rubber grips. Mfg. 1918-1925.

	$175	$150	$100	$80	$70	$60	$50

VEST POCKET AUTOMATIC — 6.35mm, small frame. Disc.

	$160	$125	$110	$95	$80	$60	$40

BROWN PRECISION INC.
Manufacturer located in Los Molinos, CA Since 1967.

Brown Precision Inc. manufactures primarily rifles using Remington or Winchester actions and restocks them using a combination of Kevlar and Graphite (wrinkle finish) to save weight. Stock colors are green, brown, gray, black, camo brown, camo green, or camo gray.

STANDARD HIGH COUNTRY BOLT ACTION RIFLE — Rem. Model 700 BDL action, .243, .25-06, .270, 7mm Mag., .308, or .30-06 cal., 22 in. standard barrel, no sights, Kevlar stock, swivels and pad. Mfg. 1975-present.

Mfg.'s Sug. Retail	$986	$940	$850	$700	$600	$525	$440	$400

Add $120 for factory barrel recontouring.

Add $40 for camouflage or $80 for full camouflage treatment.

Add $100 for left hand BDL action.

Custom High Country — similar to High Country, except has ADL action and 20 or 22 in. stainless steel barrel and electroless nickel black wrinkle finish, 5 lbs. 11 oz.

Mfg.'s Sug. Retail	$1,059	$995	$900	$750	$650	$575	$500	$450

Add $100 for left hand BDL action.

Add $350 for stainless steel barrel.

Add $160 for nickel or Teflon metal finish.

Add $27 for left-hand action (700 BDL only).

MODEL 7 SUPER LIGHT — .243 cal., Model 7 action, 18 in. factory barrel, no sights, 5 lbs. 4 oz.

Mfg.'s Sug. Retail	$1,059	$995	$900	$750	$650	$575	$500	$450

Grading	100%	98%	95%	90%	80%	70%	60%

LAW ENFORCEMENT SELECTIVE TARGET — .308 cal., Model 700 Varmint action with 20, 22, or 24 in. factory barrel, O.D. green camouflage treatment.

Mfg.'s Sug. Retail	$1,059	$995	$900	$750	$650	$575	$500	$450

OPEN COUNTRY VARMINT RIFLE — uses Rem. VS hardware that is tuned and precision bedded. New 1989.

Mfg.'s Sug. Retail	$1,086	$1,000	$900	$750	$650	$575	$500	$450

PRO-HUNTER — .375 H & H or .458 Win. Mag. cal., Model 7 ADL action, 20 or 22 in. stainless steel barrel, with or without claw extractor conversion, dull electroless nickel, blue, or teflon finish, express sights, synthetic stock (four different colors), 6 lbs. 7 oz. New 1988.

Mfg.'s Sug. Retail	$1,823	$1,823	$1,575	$1,425	$1,250	$1,100	$1,000	$925

Add $100 for left-hand action.

BROWN PRECISION WINCHESTER 70 — .270 or .30-06 cal., 22 in. featherweight barrel, camo stock in four colors with black recoil pad, 6¼ lbs. New 1989.

Mfg.'s Sug. Retail	$599	$599	$525	$465	$420	$385	$325	$300

Add $20 for 7mm Rem. Mag. (24 in. sporter barrel).

BLASER BOLT ACTION RIFLE — standard Camex Blaser cal.'s and action, fiberglass stock and nickel plated barrel. Disc. 1989.

	$1,395	$1,150	$995	$875	$750	$675	$600

Last Mfg.'s Sug. Retail was $1,395.

BROWNING ARMS

Established Circa 1880 in Ogden, UT. BAC Headquarters (not manufacturing) are currently located in Morgan, UT. manufactured by Fabrique Nationale in Herstal and Liege, Belgium: Also since 1976 by Miroku in Japan and A.T.I. in Salt Lake City, UT.

The Browning section in this text has been arranged in the following order—PISTOLS, RIFLES, SHOTGUNS: SEMI-AUTO, SHOTGUNS: O/U, OTHER SHOTGUNS, LIMITED EDITIONS-COMMEMORATIVES.

The Browning firm, first known as J.M. Browning & Bro., was established in Ogden, Utah about 1880. Later known as Browning Brothers and Browning Arms Company (BAC), the firm actually manufactured only one gun — the Model 1878 Single Shot which was John M.'s first patent. Winchester bought the production and distribution rights to this gun in 1883, bringing it out as the Winchester M1885. From that time until 1900 Mr. Browning sold Winchester the exclusive rights to 31 rifles and 13 shotguns, of which Winchester produced only 7 rifles (M1885SS: the lever actions M1886, 1892, 1894 and 1895: and the slide action .22's M1890 and 1906) and 3 shotguns (M1887, M1893 and M1897). The other models were bought from Browning simply to keep them out of the hands of other arms makers.

John M. Browning, perhaps the greatest firearms inventor the world has ever known, was directly responsible for an estimated 80 separate firearms that evolved from his 128 patents. During his most prolific period from 1894 to 1910, Browning sold the rights to his rifles, semi-auto pistols, shotguns and machine guns to Winchester, Remington, Colt's and Stevens in this country and to Fabrique Nationale for sale outside the U.S. Every Colt and FN semi-auto pistol is based on a Browning patent. In 1902 Browning broke off relations with Winchester when the company refused to negotiate a royalty arrangement for his new semi-auto shotgun(A-5). Browning took the prototype to FN where it became the most commercially successful of all his inventions. FN has produced 6 automatic pistols, 3 rifles and 2 shotguns designed by John M. Browning and is still a major producer of arms sold by Browning in the U.S. and by FN distributors world wide.

Our American military was armed for many years with Browning designed weaponry, not the least of which is the venerable "Old Slabside" 1911 Gov't Model .45 ACP. Today, the firm that bears the Browning name still stands at the forefront with the other makers of fine sporting weapons.

Note: Between 1966-1974 Browning used a salt-curing process to speed the drying time needed for their walnut stock blanks. Unfortunately, the salt would be released from the wood and oxidize the metal surface(s) after a period of time. These guns, especially bolt action rifles in all grades, some BAR's, Superposed shotguns, and T-bolt models should be examined carefully around the edges of the wood for signs of freckling and rust. Discount guns that show evidence

Grading	100%	98%	95%	90%	80%	70%	60%

of salt corrosion 15-50%, depending on how bad rusting has occurred. Check screws and wood under butt plate as well.

Editor's Note: It is important to note the differences in values of Browning weapons manufactured in Belgium by F.N. and those made recently in Japan by Miroku. We feel that these values are somewhat higher because of collector interest in Browning guns made in Belgium and not as the result of any inferiority of the quality of Browning guns made anywhere else.

BROWNING SERIALIZATION

In addition to the Browning serialization listed in the back of this text, the following codes will determine the year and origin of those guns made from 1975 to date. The 2 letters in the middle of the serial number are the code designations for year of manufacture. They represent the following: RV - 1975, RT - 1976, RR - 1977, RP - 1978, RN - 1979, PM - 1980, PZ - 1981, PY - 1982, PX - 1983, PW - 1984, PV - 1985, PT -1986, PR - 1987, PP - 1988, PN - 1989, NM - 1990, NZ - 1991. Since most Brownings use a 3-digit model identification code (appearing first on European or U.S. mfg. guns and last on Japanese mfg.), both where and when the specimen was made can easily be determined (i.e. Ser. No. 611RP2785 would be a Model B-2000 made in either Belgium or Portugal in 1978 with 2785 being the Ser. No.— Ser. No. 1479PX368 indicates a BSS 20 ga. mfg. in Japan in 1983 with Ser. No. 1479).

AS A FINAL NOTE: most post-war Brownings are collectible only if in 95% or better condition as most models have relatively high mfg. and are not that old. Condition under 95% is normally very shootable, but not as collectible and values for 95% or less condition could be lower than shown in some areas.

Most 100% values in this section assume N.I.B. condition. Subtract 10% without box/manual. Also, all add-ons or deductions in this section reflect retail pricing without any discounting.

PISTOLS: SEMI-AUTO, F.N. PRODUCTION UNLESS OTHERWISE NOTED

MODEL 1900-FN — 7.65mm cal., first Belgium Browning, 4 in. barrel. Mfg. 1899-1910. 724,500 mfg.

	100%	98%	95%	90%	80%	70%	60%
	$325	$300	$275	$250	$225	$195	$150

Add 30% for early pistols with "pistol logo" grips.

MODEL 1903-FN — 9mm Browning Long cartridge, 5 in. barrel. Mfg. 58,400, 1903-1939.

	100%	98%	95%	90%	80%	70%	60%
	$450	$400	$350	$300	$260	$220	$180

Add 50% if slotted to accept shoulder stock.

This variation was also manufactured with a detachable shoulder stock — this accessory is rare and can add as much as $2,000 to values listed above.

MODEL 1903-SWEDISH CONTRACT — 9mm cal., manufactured by Husqvarna and Swedish Arsenal (so marked), many were imported into U.S. and converted to .380 ACP from original Browning 9mm Long. Deduct 25% for .380 ACP conversion.

	100%	98%	95%	90%	80%	70%	60%
	$300	$260	$230	$200	$180	$150	$125

MODEL 1905-FN (VEST POCKET) — 6.35mm (.25 ACP), dubbed "Vest Pocket" model, manufactured by Fabrique Nationale, Herstal, Belgium. Mfg. 1,086,133, 1906-1959.

First Variation — no slide lock/safety lever.

	100%	98%	95%	90%	80%	70%	60%
	$375	$325	$300	$280	$225	$195	$150

Add 10% for nickel finish.

Second Variation — post 1908, with slide lock/safety lever.

	100%	98%	95%	90%	80%	70%	60%
	$325	$300	$275	$250	$225	$195	$150

Add 10% for nickel finish.

MODEL 1910-FN — 7.65mm (.32 ACP) and Browning 9mm short (.380 ACP) 4 in. barrel. FN manufacture. Made 1912-1980. 701,266 mfg. Add 25% for Browning import .32 ACP.

	100%	98%	95%	90%	80%	70%	60%
	$325	$300	$275	$250	$225	$195	$150

Grading	100%	98%	95%	90%	80%	70%	60%

Add 20% if BAC marked and .380 ACP.

Add 30% for BAC marked and 7.65 mm.

BAC marked pistols were imported 1954-1968.

This model is also referred to as the Model 1955.

MODEL 1922 OR 10/22 FN — 7.65mm or .380 ACP cal., modified Model 1910 with 4½ in. barrel, longer grip frame and mag., made for commercial sale as well as military contracts. Several hundred thousand made by Nazis during the occupation of Liege, Belgium 1940-1944. Mfg. between 1912-1959.

	$240	$215	$195	$175	$150	$125	$110

Add 10% for .380 ACP or Waffenampt proofing.

Add 20% for foreign contracts.

The Model 10/22 and M1922 are the same pistol. The Model 1910 was modified by FN technicians for sale to Serbian arm forces in 1923. Also sold to France, Holland, Yugoslavia, and other countries. Also made by the German military 1940-1944.

FN "BABY" MODEL — 6.35mm (.25 ACP) cal., lighter, smaller modification of Browning Model 1905 Vest Pocket .25, has no grip safety or slide lock, imported under BAC trademark from 1954-1970 in standard blue finish, lightweight nickel and engraved Renaissance models. Mfg. 1931-1983. Total production is over 510,000.

FN Marked — slide marked Fabrique Nationale, blued finish standard.

	$395	$350	$310	$280	$245	$225	$200

BAC Marked — slide marked Browning Arms Co., blued finish standard.

	$300	$265	$225	$195	$180	$165	$150

Lightweight model — nickel frame, with pearl grips.

	$395	$350	$310	$280	$245	$225	$200

Renaissance model — engraved, satin grey finish.

	$875	$760	$600				

FN/BROWNING MODEL 10/71 — 4½ in. barrel, modified version of Model 1922 (10/22) in .380 ACP cal., grip safety, includes target sights and grips in addition to incorporating a magazine finger tip extension designed to comply with GCA of 1968. Sold in U.S. by BAC 1970-1974 as the "Standard .380", still mfg. by FN as Model 125.

	$375	$295	$250	$220	$205	$190	$160

Renaissance or Gold Line model

	$995	$850	$775				

MODEL 1935 HI-POWER — 9mm, 13 shot mag. 4⅝ in. barrel, Browning's last pistol design, millions made 1927 to date in variations for commercial, military, and police use in over 68 countries, first imported under BAC trademark in 1954.

Please refer to the Fabrique Nationale section of this book for pre-1954 variations (including WWII and earlier commercial models).

HI-POWER: POST-1954 MFG. — 9mm, same as FN model 1935, has BAC slide marking, 13 shot mag., 4⅝ in. barrel, polished blue finish, checkered walnut stocks, fixed sights, molded grips were introduced in 1986, ambidextrous saftey was added to all models in 1989. Mfg. 1954-present.

Polished Blue Finish — includes fixed sights.

Mfg.'s Sug. Retail	$498	$440	$365	$325	$300	$280	$260	$240

Subtract $31 for molded grips (disc. 1990).

This model has been produced with both a spur (disc.) or round (current mfg.) hammer configuration. The round cone hammer variation is more desirable but does not necessarily command a higher value. Older specimens in original black pouches (especially with gold metal zipper) will command slight premiums over boxed guns.

Adj. sights

Mfg.'s Sug. Retail	$544	$480	$395	$350	$325	$300	$280	$255

Matte Blue Finish — non-glare matte finish, ambidextrous safety, fixed sights only. New 1985.

Mfg.'s Sug. Retail	$459	$405	$340	$300	$280	$260	$240	$225

Grading	100%	98%	95%	90%	80%	70%	60%

Recently, Hi-Power's that appear to have a "black" finish have been noticed. These guns are painted rather than blued and some parties have been selling them as original military FN's. Do not confuse these painted specimens for original pistols and remember, original guns will be worth more than refinished pistols.

Silver Chrome Finish — entire gun finished in silver chrome, includes adj. sights and Pachmayr rubber grips. New 1991.

Mfg.'s Sug. Retail	$550	$480	$395	$350	$325	$300	$280	$255

HP - Practical — features blued slide, silver - chromed frame finish, wrap around Pachmayr rubber grips, round style serrated hammer, and removable front sight, 36 oz. New 1991.

Mfg.'s Sug. Retail	$550	$480	$395	$350	$325	$300	$280	$255

Nickel/Silver Chrome finish — not to be confused with stainless steel (never offered in the Hi-Power). Also, this finish is different from the silver chrome finish released in 1991. Disc. 1985.

	$550	$475	$415	$375	$360	$340	$315

Last Mfg.'s Sug. Retail was $525.

.30 Luger Hi-Power — .30 Luger cal., mfg. for European sales 1986-87 (most are marked F.N. on slide), approx. 1,500 imported late 1986-89, similar specifications as 9mm model.

	$475	$420	$365	$315	$275	$240	$215

This model was never cataloged for sale by BAC in the U.S. A few specimens have been noted with B.A.C. slide markings and are more desirable than F.N. marked pistols.

GP Competition — 9mm, competition model with 6 in. barrel, detent adj. rear sight, rubber wrap-around grips, front counterweight, improved barrel bushing, decreased trigger pull, approx. 36½ oz.

	$625	$550	$475	$425	$395	$350	$325

The original GP Competition came in a black plastic case w/accesories and are more desirable than later imported specimens which were computer serial numbered and came in a styrafoam box. Above prices are for older models — deduct 10% if newer model (computer serial numbered).

This model was never cataloged for sale by BAC in the U.S.

Tangent rear sight model — manufactured from 1965-1978. Adj. rear sight to 500 meters. A total of approx. 7,000 were imported by Browning Arms Co. A variation with grip strap slotted to accommodate a shoulder stock was also available from Browning on special order; approx. 250 were imported. This variation will command a premium; beware of fakes, however (carefully examine slot milling).

	$700	$600	$525	$440	$400	$370	$340

Add $150 for original slotted rear grip strap.

This variation is worth a slight premium if with "T" ser. no. prefix (mfg. 1964-1969).

BCA EDITION HI-POWER — limited edition made specifically for the Browning Collectors Association.

	$600	$495	$400

RENAISSANCE HI-POWER — extensive scroll engraving on gray silver receiver, synthetic pearl grips, gold plated trigger. Disc. 1980.

Round Hammer	$1,250	$900	$725
Spur Hammer/adj. sights	$1,050	$860	$700
Spur Hammer/fixed sights	$975	$825	$650

Add 5% for adj. sights.

CASED RENAISSANCE SET — one each .25 auto, .380 auto, and Hi-Power Renaissance models in walnut case. Mfg. 1955-1969.

	$3,400	$2,750	$2,100

CENTENNIAL MODEL HI-POWER — same as fixed sight Hi-Power, chrome plated with inscription "Browning Centennial/1878-1978", engraved on side, cased, 3,500 mfg. in 1978. Original issue price was $500.

	$600	$500	$425

Grading	100%	98%	95%	90%	80%	70%	60%

LOUIS XVI MODEL — 9mm, chemically etched throughout in leaf scroll patterns, satin finish, checkered grips, walnut case. Disc. 1984.

	$850	$675	$525

Add 5% for adj. sights.

9 MM CLASSIC SERIES - PISTOL — 9mm, Hi-Power action, less than 2,500 manufactured in Classic model and under 350 manufactured in Gold Classic. Both editions feature multiple engraved scenes, and a special silver grey finish, presentation grips, cased. Mfg. 1984-86.

	$850	$675	$495

Last Mfg.'s Sug. Retail was $1,000.

Gold Classic — 5 gold inlays, select walnut grips are both checkered and carved. Mfg. 1984-86.

	$1,800	$1,450	$1,150

Last Mfg.'s Sug. Retail was $2,000.

HI-POWER DOUBLE ACTION — this model was first listed in the Browning catalog in 1985 but was never manufactured. The proposed 1985 retail price was $494.

BDM DOUBLE ACTION — 9mm Para., new double mode design featuring slide selector allowing choice between pistol (true double action operation) or revolver mode (full hammer decocking after each shot), dual purpose decocking lever/safety, 4.73 in. barrel, 15 shot mag., matte blue finish, black molded wrap around grips, unique breech block allows visible cartridge inspection, adj. rear sight, 31 oz. New 1991-mfg. in U.S.A.

Mfg.'s Sug. Retail	$505	$445	$385	$350	$325	$300	$280	$260

This model features hammer block and firing pin block safeties.

BDA-380 — .380 ACP, double action, 14 shot, 3¹³⁄₁₆ in. barrel, fixed sights, smooth walnut grips, 23 oz., introduced 1982-current production, mfg. by Beretta.

Mfg.'s Sug. Retail	$523	$395	$325	$265	$240	$220	$200	$180

Nickel finish

Mfg.'s Sug. Retail	$550	$425	$340	$275	$250	$225	$205	$185

BDA MODEL — 9mm (9 shot) — 2,740 mfg., .38 Super — 752 mfg., .45 ACP (7 shot), mfg. from 1977-1979 by Sig-Sauer of W. Germany (same as Sig-Sauer 220).

9mm	$500	$450	$400	$340	$300	$260	$220
.38 Super	$650	$575	$495	$450	$390	$350	$320
.45 ACP	$500	$440	$380	$320	$280	$260	$220

NOMAD MODEL — .22 LR, 10 shot, 4½ and 6¾ in. barrels, steel frame, adj. sights, blued finish, black plastic grips. Mfg. 1962-1974 by FN.

	$295	$250	$200	$180	$165	$150	$135

CHALLENGER MODEL — .22 LR, 10 shot, 4½ and 6¾ in. barrels, steel frame, adj. sights, checkered wrap-around walnut grips, gold plated trigger. Mfg. 1962-1975 by FN.

	$350	$295	$250	$215	$190	$170	$155

Renaissance — engraved satin nickel finish.

	$1,150	$895	$700

Gold Line — blued finish, gold lining on perimeter of frame surfaces.

	$1,150	$895	$700

CHALLENGER II — .22 cal., Salt Lake City mfg., 6¾ in. barrel, alloy frame, plastic impregnated hardwood grips, 38 oz. Mfg. 1975-1982.

	$260	$180	$170	$145	$135	$120	$110

CHALLENGER III — .22 cal., Salt Lake City mfg., 5½ in. bull barrel, 11 shot, alloy frame, adj. sights, 35 oz. Mfg. 1982-1985.

	$220	$190	$170	$145	$135	$120	$110

Last Mfg.'s Retail was $240.

Grading	100%	98%	95%	90%	80%	70%	60%

CHALLENGER III SPORTER — same as Challenger III, except 6¾ in. round barrel, wide trigger, 29 oz. Mfg. 1982-85.

| | $220 | $190 | $170 | $145 | $135 | $120 | $110 |

Last Mfg.'s Sug. Retail was $240.

BUCK MARK .22 — .22 LR, 11 shot, 5½ in. bull barrel, composite grips with skipline checkering (disc. 1990) or molded rubber grips (new 1991), adj. sights, gold trigger, matte blued finish. New 1985.

| Mfg.'s Sug. Retail | $220 | $175 | $155 | $130 | $120 | $110 | $100 | $90 |

Add $30 for nickel finish (new 1991).

Buck Mark models are manufactured in Salt Lake City, UT.

Buck Mark Plus — similar to Buck Mark, except has uncheckered wooden grips and high polish blue. New 1987.

| Mfg.'s Sug. Retail | $266 | $220 | $175 | $145 | $135 | $120 | $110 | $100 |

Buck Mark 5.5 Target — same action as Buck Mark, 5½ in. barrel with serrated top rib allowing adj. sight positioning, target sights, matte blue finish, 35½ oz. New 1990.

| Mfg.'s Sug. Retail | $360 | $285 | $240 | $210 | $180 | $160 | $140 | $125 |

Add $20 for Gold Target Model.

The Gold Target Model includes gold anodized frame and top rib. Introduced in 1991.

Buck Mark 5.5 Field — same action and barrel as the Target 5.5, except sights are designed for field use, anodized blue finish, contoured walnut grips, 35½ oz. New 1991.

| Mfg.'s Sug. Retail | $360 | $285 | $240 | $210 | $180 | $160 | $140 | $125 |

Buck Mark Varmint — same action as Buck Mark, 9⅞ in. barrel with serrated top rib allowing adj. sight positioning, laminated wood grips, optional detachable forearm, matte blue, 48 oz. New 1987.

| Mfg.'s Sug. Retail | $335 | $270 | $230 | $200 | $175 | $155 | $135 | $120 |

Buck Mark Silhouette — silhouette variation of the Buck Mark, 9⅞ in. bull barrel with serrated top rib allowing adj. sight positioning, hooded target sights, laminated wood stocks and forearm, matte blue, 53 oz. New 1987.

| Mfg.'s Sug. Retail | $380 | $315 | $265 | $225 | $195 | $170 | $150 | $135 |

Buck Mark Unlimited Silhouette (Match) — similar to Silhouette Model featuring 14 in. barrel with set back front sight, 64 oz. New 1991.

| Mfg.'s Sug. Retail | $450 | $380 | $315 | $265 | $225 | $195 | $170 | $150 |

MEDALIST TARGET MODEL — .22 LR, 6¾ in. barrel, vent rib, adj. target sights and barrel weights (3 supplied), blued finish, target walnut grips with thumbrest, dry-fire mechanism, 46 oz., cased. Mfg. 1962-1975 by FN.

	$625	$525	$450	$400	$375	$325	$300
Gold Line (407 mfg. 1963)	$1,650	$1,200	$875				
Renaissance Model	$2,150	$1,850	$1,400				
BCA Edition Engraved (60 mfg.)	$2,350	$1,900	$1,400				

Deduct 15% if without case and accessories.

INTERNATIONAL MEDALIST — early model manufactured 1971 and 1974, 5.9 in. barrel, only 681 made with BAC markings and blued finish. Currently manufactured by FN in the parkerized international configuration.

| | $615 | $535 | $475 | $410 | $350 | $300 | $275 |
| Early Model | $650 | $615 | $550 | $425 | $360 | $330 | $280 |

RIFLES: SINGLE SHOT

Grading	100%	98%	95%	90%	80%	70%	60%

MODEL 1878 — .38 Long (rare), .40-72, or .45-70 cal., J.M. Browning's first patent, fewer than 600 made by Browning Brothers in Ogden, Utah between 1878-1883, various stocks with and without pistol grips, full and half length, with or without ramrod, several receiver configurations, a very few were made in the deluxe model, seldom found in unused condition.

	$5,000	$4,250	$3,650	$3,075	$2,700	$2,300	$1,850

Add 10% for ramrod model with pistol grip and checkered stock.

MODEL 78 — .22-250, 6mm, .243, .25-06, 7mm Mag., .30-06, or .45-70 cal., 24 or 26 in. round or octagon barrel, lever activated falling block, no sights except .45-70, checkered walnut stock, approx. 24,000 mfg. 1973-1982.

	$425	$350	$320	$295	$275	$265	$250
.45-70 cal.	$470	$375	$325	$300	$275	$265	$250

The Model 78 was reintroduced as the Model 1885 in 1985.

MODEL 1885 — .22-250, .223R., .270 Win., .30-06, 7mm Rem. Mag., or .45-70 cal., falling block action, sear safety, 28 in. octagonal barrel, adj. trigger, no sights, checkered walnut stock and Schnabel forearm, exposed hammer, gold trigger, 8¾ lbs. Introduced 1985.

Mfg.'s Sug. Retail	$772	$600	$500	$400	$360	$330	$295	$275

This model in .45-70 cal. is equipped with open sights.

RIFLES: SEMI-AUTO .22 LR

GRADES I - III — .22 LR or .22 Short, takedown design, 11 shot (16 for .22 Short) tube mag. in butt stock, 19¼ in. barrel in LR, 22¼ in. barrel in short (rare), checkered pistol grip stock, semi-beavertail forearm, stock has hole machined halfway to allow partial filling of tube mag., adj. folding rear sight, grades differ in finish, amount of engraving, and grade of wood, 4¾ lbs. Mfg. 1914-1976 by FN, 1976-present by Miroku in Japan.

Grade I — FN

	$425	$350	$275	$225	$195	$165	$150

Add 10-15% for "Shorts only" or thumb wheel rear sight older models if in 95% or better condition.

FN Grade I's have a lightly engraved blued steel receiver, checkered walnut, blued trigger, and a variety of rear sights.

Grade I — Miroku

Mfg.'s Sug. Retail	$345	$280	$230	$200	$175	$160	$150	$140

Miroku manufactured .22's can be determined by year of manufacture in the following manner: RV suffix - 1975, RT - 1976, RR - 1977, RP - 1978, RN - 1979, PM - 1980, PZ - 1981, PY - 1982, PX - 1983, PW - 1984, PV - 1985, PT - 1986, PR - 1987, PP - 1988, PN - 1989, NM - 1990, NZ-1991.

Grade II — FN

	$795	$575	$450	$360	$325	$295	$260

FN Grade II's have gray chromed receiver, deluxe wood with finer checkering, gold plated trigger, and engraving depicting two squirrels and two prairie dogs. Signed or unsigned by engraver.

Grade II — Miroku — disc. 1984.

	$425	$350	$295	$225	$200	$180	$160

Grade III — FN

	$1,395	$1,100	$875	$825	$770	$715	$605

FN Grade III's have coin finish or gray chromed receiver, extra deluxe walnut with skipline checkering, gold plated trigger, and more elaborate game scene engraving usually featuring a dog flushing ducks or upland game. Signed or unsigned by engraver. A few were also special ordered with blued finish and special engraving — these command an extra premium.

Grade III — Miroku — disc. 1983.

	$750	$650	$540	$495	$450	$400	$360

Grade VI — Miroku — game scene engraved with gold plating, choice of blued or grayed receiver, deluxe walnut. New 1987.

Mfg.'s Sug. Retail	$709	$600	$500	$400	$360	$325	$295	$260

Grading	100%	98%	95%	90%	80%	70%	60%

BAR-22 — .22 LR, 20¼ in. barrel, 15 shot tube mag., folding leaf sight, high polish alloy receiver, checkered pistol grip stock, 5 lbs. 13 oz. Mfg. 1977-1985 by Miroku.

| | $215 | $185 | $165 | $150 | $135 | $120 | $105 |

Last Mfg.'s Sug. Retail was $245.

BAR-22 GRADE II — engraved model of BAR-22 featuring game scenes on silver greyed alloy receiver, select French walnut. Disc. 1985.

| | $305 | $265 | $245 | $210 | $195 | $175 | $160 |

Last Mfg.'s Sug. Retail was $350.

RIFLES: BAR HIGH POWER

BROWNING PATENT 1900 HIGH POWER — .35 Rem. only, manufactured by FN from 1910-1931, only 4,913 made in standard and deluxe grades, similar to Remington Model 8 auto-loading rifle.

| | $650 | $575 | $495 | $440 | $385 | $340 | $300 |

Deluxe model — with checkered walnut stock and adj. sights on solid rib barrel.

| | $750 | $650 | $550 | $525 | $470 | $440 | $415 |

BAR SEMI-AUTO — .243, .270, .280 Rem. (new 1990), .308, or .30-06 cal. available in standard model, Mag. cal.'s include 7mm Rem., 300 Win., and .338 Win. (reintroduced 1990), gas operated, blued receiver, 22 or 24 (Mag. only) in. barrel, rotary bolt with seven lugs, folding leaf sight, walnut stock. Grades differ in engraving, finish, and grade of wood, approx. 7 lbs. 6 oz. Mfg. 1967-present.

Note: Original .338's were limited production, mostly seen in the deluxe Grade II only. During the last year of FN .338 production, several were delivered in a Grade I by FN. Although being rarer than the Grade II, it is not as desirable. The following prices are for Portugese assembled guns, manufactured by FN, and are so stamped on the barrel.

Add 10% for FN mfg. and assembled BAR's (marked "FN manufactured and assembled").

Add 25% for .338 Win. Mag. cal. (FN mfg. only).

Grade I — current manufacture, no engraving, blued finish, ordering this model without sights became an option in 1988.

| Mfg.'s Sug. Retail | $633 | $540 | $450 | $395 | $350 | $325 | $300 | $280 |

Subtract $16 without sights.

FN mfg. and assembled Grade I's can be denoted by light scroll engraving on the receiver.

Grade I Magnum — current manufacture, no engraving, with recoil pad, 8 lbs. 6 oz.

| Mfg.'s Sug. Retail | $680 | $575 | $495 | $425 | $375 | $350 | $330 | $310 |

Subtract $16 without sights.

Ordering this gun without sights became an option in 1988.

Grade II — blued receiver, engraved with big game heads. Mfg. 1967-1974.

| | $725 | $625 | $550 | $525 | $470 | $440 | $415 |

This model was previously designated Deluxe.

Grade II Magnum — magnum version of Grade II. Mfg. 1967-1974.

| | $795 | $675 | $595 | $550 | $510 | $460 | $430 |

Grade III — features elk and sheep game scenes etched on greyed steel receiver, select checkered stock and forearm. Disc. 1984.

| | $925 | $800 | $660 | $620 | $580 | $560 | $540 |

Grade III Magnum — magnum version of Grade III. Disc. 1984.

| | $1,025 | $850 | $700 | $660 | $620 | $595 | $580 |

Grade IV — engraved satin finish greyed receiver depicts big game animal scenes and trigger guard, carved boarders on checkering. Disc. 1989.

| | $1,475 | $1,300 | $1,150 | $1,000 | $900 | $825 | $750 |

Last Mfg.'s Sug. Retail on this model was $1,670.

Grade IV Magnum — magnum version of Grade IV. Disc. 1984.

| | $1,675 | $1,495 | $1,225 | $1,050 | $950 | $850 | $775 |

Last Mfg.'s Sug. Retail on this model was $1,720.

Grading	100%	98%	95%	90%	80%	70%	60%

Grade V — more elaborate engraving than Grade IV, with gold inlays. Mfg. 1971-1974.

	$3,000	$2,600	$2,250	$1,850	$1,600	$1,450	$1,250

Grade V Magnum — magnum version of Grade V.

	$3,650	$2,900	$2,400	$1,950	$1,700	$1,595	$1,400

BAR NORTH AMERICAN DEER RIFLE ISSUE — .30-06 cal. only, BAR style action with silver grey finish and engraved action, 600 total production, walnut cased with accessories. Disc. 1983 but were sold through 1989.

	$2,495	$2,100	$1,700

Last Mfg.'s Sug. Retail was $3,550.

RIFLES: FAL

The following semi-auto FAL's were imported by BAC in limited numbers. Current production FAL's can be found under the Fabrique Nationale heading.

FAL G SERIES STANDARD — 7.62mm, paramilitary design rifle, wood butt stock, wood or nylon forearm, milled receiver.

	$3,200	$2,850	$2,300	$1,950	$1,650	$1,350	$1,040

G Series Heavy Barrel — wood furniture, milled receiver with special bipod.

	$6,000	$5,250	$4,700	$4,160	$3,600	$3,100	$2,650

G Series Lightweight — lightweight variation of the FAL.

	$4,000	$3,500	$3,000	$2,500	$2,100	$1,875	$1,600

The Lightweight Model had the trigger frame, magazine, and return spring tube made out of aluminum.

Browning Arms Co. Import — milled receiver, wood or nylon furniture.

	$2,400	$2,000	$1,700	$1,550	$1,400	$1,275	$1,150

CAL Prototype — originally imported in 1980, prototype to the current FN FNC, at first declared illegal but later given amnesty, only 20 imported.

	$6,000	$5,250	$4,700	$4,160	$3,600	$3,100	$2,650

G series FAL's were imported between 1959-1962 by Browning Arms Co. This rifle was declared illegal by the GCA of 1968 and was exempted 5 years later. Total numbers exempted are: Standard model-1822, Heavy Barrel model-21, Paratrooper model-5.

RIFLES: LEVER ACTION

BL-22 GRADE I — .22 S, L, and LR, 20 in. barrel, short throw lever, folding leaf sight, 15 shot (LR) mag., exposed hammer, Western style stock and forearm, 5 lbs. Mfg. 1970-present by Miroku.

Mfg.'s Sug. Retail	$302	$240	$205	$175	$150	$125	$110	$100

BL-22 Grade II — same general specifications as BL-22, except scroll engraved blue receiver and checkered select walnut.

Mfg.'s Sug. Retail	$344	$280	$235	$195	$165	$140	$125	$115

MODEL 52 LIMITED EDITION — .22 LR cal., virtually identical to the original Winchester Model 52C Sporter, except for minor safety enhancements, bolt action, 24 in. drilled and tapped barrel, 5 shot detachable mag., high grade pistol grip walnut stock with oil style finish, deep blue finish, adj. trigger, two position safety, 7 lbs. 5,000 mfg. in 1991 only.

Mfg.'s Sug. Retail	$500	$500	$425	$375

MODEL 53 DELUXE LIMITED EDITION — .32-20 cal. (round nose or hollow point bullets only), patterned after the original Winchester Model 53 (redesigned Model 1892), 7 shot tube mag., high polished blued metal, open sights, 22 in. tapered barrel, high grade checkered walnut stock featuring full pistol grip cap and shotgun style metal butt plate, 6½ lbs. Only 5,000 mfg. in 1990, the inventory still remains however.

Mfg.'s Sug. Retail	$675	$675	$550	$475

MODEL 65 GRADE I LIMITED EDITION — .218 Bee, patterned after the Winchester Model 65, round tapered 24 in. barrel, open sights (hooded front), blued metal finish, 7 shot tube mag., uncheckered pistol grip stock and semi-beavertail forearm, metal butt plate, 6¾ lbs. 3,500 total mfg. for Grade I in 1989 only, inventory depleted in 1990.

	$550	$465	$425

Grading	100%	98%	95%	90%	80%	70%	60%

Last Mfg.'s Sug. Retail was $550.

Model 65 High Grade — grayed receiver (and lever) with scroll engraving and gold plated animals, gold plated trigger, deluxe checkered walnut stock and semi-beavertail forearm. 1,500 total mfg. in 1989, inventory depleted in 1990.

| | | | $850 | $775 | $700 | | |

Last Mfg.'s Sug. Retail was $850.

MODEL 71 LIMITED EDITION CARBINE — .348 Win., reproduction of the Winchester Model 71 carbine, 20 in. barrel, open sights, 4 shot mag., 8 lbs. New 1987 with inventory depleted in 1990.

Grade I — uncheckered satin finished walnut stock and forearm. 4,000 mfg. 1986-87 only.

| | $595 | $475 | $410 | $365 | $340 | $320 | $300 |

Last Mfg.'s Sug. Retail was $600.

High Grade — deluxe checkered walnut stock and forearm with high gloss finish, scroll engraved-gray receiver with gold inlays and trigger. 3,000 mfg. 1986-87 only.

| | | | $895 | $735 | $660 | | |

Last Mfg.'s Sug. Retail was $980.

MODEL 71 LIMITED EDITION RIFLE — .348 Win. reproduction of the Winchester Model 71 rifle, 24 in. barrel, open sights, 4 shot mag., 8 lbs. 2 oz. Mfg. 1986-87 only with inventory depleted in 1990.

Grade I — uncheckered satin finished walnut stock and forearm. 3,000 mfg. 1986-87 only.

| | $595 | $475 | $410 | $365 | $340 | $320 | $300 |

Last Mfg.'s Sug. Retail was $600.

High Grade — deluxe checkered walnut stock and forearm with high gloss finish, scroll engraved-gray receiver with gold inlays and trigger. 3,000 mfg. 1986-87 only.

| | | | $895 | $735 | $660 | | |

Last Mfg.'s Sug. Retail was $980.

MODEL 81 BLR — .22-250, .222R. (disc. 1989), .223R., .243 Win., .257 Roberts, 7mm-08 Rem., .284 Win., .308 Win., or .358 Win. cal., rotary bolt locking lugs, 20 in. barrel, 4 shot detachable mag., adj. sight, checkered stock, recoil pad, 1971 mfg. in Belgium, 1972-present by Miroku. No sights optional 1988-89.

| Mfg.'s Sug. Retail | $487 | $390 | $330 | $285 | $250 | $220 | $195 | $165 |

Add 15%+ for Belgium mfg. (1971 only).

Subtract $15 without sights.

.243 Win., .308 Win. and 7mm-08 Rem. cal.'s are the most popular in this model.

This model was also manufactured by TRW in Cleveland, OH for a very limited production in .243 and .308 cal.'s. While they are rare, they are not widely collected and premiums currently do not exist.

Model 81 BLR Long Action — .270 Win., 30-06, or 7mm Rem Mag. cal., 22 or 24 in. barrel, approx. 8½ lbs. New 1991.

| Mfg.'s Sug. Retail | $530 | $425 | $350 | $300 | $270 | $240 | $220 | $200 |

MODEL 1886 LIMITED EDITION GRADE I — .45-70 Gov't. only, patterned after the Winchester Model 1886, blued receiver, 26 in. octagon barrel, full mag., crescent butt plate, open sights. 7,000 mfg. 1986 only.

| | | | $775 | $600 | $475 | | |

Last Mfg.'s Sug. Retail was $578.

Model 1886 Limited Edition High Grade — same general specifications as Model 1886, except has checkered high grade walnut stock and forearm, greyed steel receiver, with game scene engraving including elk and American Bison, gold accenting with "1 of 3,000" engraved on top of barrel. 3,000 mfg. 1986 only.

| | | $1,100 | $875 | $675 | | | |

Last Mfg.'s Sug. Retail was $935.

Model 1886 Montana Centennial — similar to Model 1886 High Grade. 2,000 mfg. 1986 only to commemorate Montana Centennial.

| | | $1,050 | $850 | $650 | | | |

Grading	100%	98%	95%	90%	80%	70%	60%

Last Mfg.'s Sug. Retail was $935.

B-92 CARBINE — .357 Mag. or .44 Rem. Mag. cal., 20 in. barrel, patterned after the Winchester Model 92, 11 shot mag. (tubular), blued finish. Disc. 1986.

	$325	$275	$225	$200	$175	$160	$150

Last Mfg.'s Sug. Retail was $342.

B-92 Centennial — .44 Mag., limited quantities.

	$395	$325	$275				

Last Mfg.'s Sug. Retail was $295.

MODEL 1895 LIMITED EDITION GRADE I — .30/40 Krag or .30-06 cal. only, patterned after the Winchester Model 1895, blued receiver, 24 in. barrel, 4 shot mag.(box type), select walnut, rear buckhorn sight, 8 lbs. Mfg. 1984 only.

.30/40 Krag	$550	$475	$375	$325	$300	$280	$260
.30-06	$650	$525	$400	$350	$325	$300	$280

Production totaled 6,000 in the .30-06 cal. and 2,000 in .30/40 Krag for this model.

Model 1895 Limited Edition High Grade — same general specifications as Model 1895, except gold plated game scenes on satin finish receiver, gold trigger, and finely checkered select French walnut.

	$995	$895	$795				

Production totaled 1,000 in the .30-06 cal. and 1,000 in .30/40 Krag for this model.

RIFLES: BOLT ACTION

A-BOLT HUNTER MODEL — available in .25-06, .270 Win., .280 Rem. (new 1988), .30-06, 7mm Rem Mag., .300 Win. Mag., or .338 Win. Mag. cal. in long action, short action available in .223 Rem. (new 1988), .22-250, .243 Win., .257 Roberts, .284 Win. (new 1989), 7mm-08 Rem., or .308 Win. cal., matte blue finish, 3 lug rotary bolt locking, 22 (short action only), 24 in. (disc. 1987), or 26 in. barrel (new 1988 - long action Mag. cal.'s only), 60 degree bolt throw, adj. trigger, hidden detachable mag., no sights, top tang thumb safety, checkered pistol grip stock. Mfg. since 1985 by Miroku.

Mfg.'s Sug. Retail	$493	$405	$340	$295	$265	$240	$225	$210

Add $63 for open sights.

Medallion Model — same A-Bolt specifications, except also available in .375 H&H cal., features better grade walnut stock with rosewood pistol grip and forend caps, synthetic floor plate, high lustre bluing, no sights.

Mfg.'s Sug. Retail	$572	$455	$380	$330	$290	$265	$250	$235

Add $25 for left-hand action.

Add $97 for .375 H&H cal. (open sights only).

Left hand action available in .270 Win., .30-06, 7mm Rem. Mag., or .300 Win. Mag. only.

Micro Medallion Model — .22 Hornet (new late 1991), .223 Rem. (new 1988), .22-250 Rem., .243 Win., .257 Roberts, .284 Win., .308 Win., or 7mm-08 Rem. cal., scaled down variation of the A-Bolt Hunter Model, 20 in. barrel, short action only, 13⁵⁄₁₆ in. length of pull, 3 shot mag., no sights. Introduced 1988.

Mfg.'s Sug. Retail	$572	$455	$380	$330	$290	$265	$250	$235

Gold Medallion Model — .270 Win., .30-06, or 7mm Rem. Mag. cal., similar to Medallion Model, except has extra select walnut stock with continental style cheek piece, gold lettering and light engraving, no sights. New 1988.

Mfg.'s Sug. Retail	$775	$640	$525	$430	$360	$330	$300	$265

Stainless Stalker — .25-06 Rem., .270 Win., .280 Rem., .30-06, 7mm Rem. Mag., .300 Win. Mag., .338 Win. Mag. or .375 H&H (new 1990) cal., action and barrel are stainless steel, matte black graphite fiberglass composite stock, dull stainless finish, no sights. New 1987.

Mfg.'s Sug. Retail	$640	$560	$425	$350				

Add $95 for .375 H&H cal.

Add $20 for left hand action.

Originally, this model was offered in .270 Win., .30-06, or 7mm Rem. Mag. cal. only.

Camo Stalker — .270 Win., .30-06, or 7mm Rem. Mag. cal., laminated black and green wood stock, matte finish on metal parts, no sights. Mfg. 1987-1989.

	$400	$340	$310	$285	$250	$230	$215

Grading	100%	98%	95%	90%	80%	70%	60%

Last Mfg.'s Sug. Retail was $483.

Composite Stalker — .25-06 Rem., .270 Win., .280 Rem.,.30-06, 7mm Rem. Mag., .300 Win. Mag., or .338 Win. Mag. cal., black graphite fiberglass composite stock, matte non-glare metal finish. New 1988.

Mfg.'s Sug. Retail	$493	$390	$330	$290	$265	$240	$225	$210

A-BOLT BIGHORN SHEEP ISSUE — .270 Win. only, 22 in. barrel, high grade walnut stock with gloss finish and skipline checkering, deep relief engraving on receiver barrel, floorplate, and trigger guard, two 24Kt. inlays depicting bighorn sheep. 600 mfg. 1986-87 only.

	$1,000	$800	$625

Last Mfg.'s Sug. Retail was $1,365.

A-BOLT PRONGHORN ISSUE — .243 Win., presentation grade walnut with skipline checkering and pearl borders, receiver and barrel engraving, multiple gold inlays on receiver top and floor plate. 500 mfg. 1987 only.

	$995	$800	$625

Last Mfg.'s Sug. Retail was $1,302.

A-BOLT GRADE I RIMFIRE — .22 LR or .22 Mag. (new 1989), 60 degree bolt throw, 22 in. barrel, checkered walnut stock and forearm, 5 shot mag., adj. trigger, available with or without open sights, 5 lbs. 9 oz. New 1986.

.22 LR cal.

Mfg.'s Sug. Retail	$375	$290	$235	$190	$175	$160	$145	$130

Add $10 for open sights.

A 15 shot mag. is also available for this model at $15 retail.

.22 Win. Mag. cal.

Mfg.'s Sug. Retail	$430	$335	$270	$215	$190	$175	$160	$150

Add $10 for open sights.

GOLD MEDALLION .22 A-BOLT — similar to A-Bolt, except has high grade select walnut stock checkered 22 lines per inch, rosewood pistol and forend cap, high gloss finish, gold filled lettering and moderate engraving, solid recoil pad. New 1988.

Mfg.'s Sug. Retail	$497	$415	$340	$300	$265	$240	$225	$210

MODEL BBR — .25-06, .270, .30-06, 7mm Mag., .300 or .338 Win. Mag. cal., short action available in .22-250, 243 W., 257 Roberts, 7mm-08 Rem., or 308 Win. cal., 24 in. barrel, 60 degree throw, fluted bolt, adj. trigger, hidden detachable mag., no sights, checkered pistol grip, Monte Carlo stock. Mfg. 1978-1984 by Miroku.

	$470	$360	$330	$305	$250	$220	$200

Some rare production calibers will add premiums to the values listed above (i.e., add 50% for .243 Win. cal.).

BBR LIGHTNING GOLD RIFLE ISSUE (ELK) — 7mm Rem. Mag., bolt action rifle, 1,000 manufactured, deeply blued receiver which has multiple animals gold inlaid, high grade walnut stock and forearm feature skipline checkering. Disc. 1986.

	$1,195	$950	$795

Last Mfg.'s Sug. Retail was $1,395.

T-BOLT T-1 — .22 LR, straight pull bolt action, 5 shot mag., 22 in. barrel, adj. rear sight, 5½ lbs., plain pistol grip stock. Mfg. 1965-1974 by FN.

	$350	$300	$255	$210	$180	$160	$140

An aperture rear sight was standard for the first nine years of production.

T-BOLT T-2 — same as T-1, only with select checkered walnut stock (lacquer finished), 24 in. barrel, 6 lbs.

	$400	$350	$295	$240	$200	$180	$160

Add $100 for aperture rear sight.

Late production T-2 — features oil finished stock, plastic front sight, and Browning computerized serialization.

	$300	$255	$210	$180	$160	$140	$120

Grading	100%	98%	95%	90%	80%	70%	60%

HIGH-POWER BOLT ACTION MODEL — .222 R. (Sako action), .22-250 (Sako action), .243 Win., .257 Roberts, .264 Win. Mag., .270, .284 Win. (Sako action), .30-06, .308 Win., 7mm Mag., .300 Win. Mag., .308 Norma Mag., .300 H&H, .338 Mag., .375 H&H, or .458 Win. Mag. cal., standard Mauser type action with either short or long (more desirable) extractor, 22 or 24 in. (heavy available) barrel, folding leaf sight (except on .222 R. and .22-250), checkered pistol grip stock. Mfg. 1959-1974 by FN.

The .243 and .308 Win. cal.'s were built on the small ring Mauser action prior to using the Sako medium action. The .222 Rem. Mag. was also furnished less the rear sight.

Note: Grades differ in engraving, finish, checkering, and grade of wood. It should be noted that the salt wood problem is more common in these high powered models. Guns should be checked carefully for rust below wood surfaces.

Safari Grade — basic model with blued finish.

	100%	98%	95%	90%	80%	70%	60%
Standard cal.'s	$795	$675	$550	$450	$400	$350	$325
Mag. cal.'s	$900	$750	$650	$595	$525	$450	$400
.257 Roberts	$1,295	$1,050	$825	$700	$600	$525	$450
.284 Win.	$1,550	$1,200	$950	$800	$700	$600	$500
.308 Norma Mag.	$1,050	$850	$700	$600	$525	$450	$400
.338 Win. Mag.	$1,050	$850	$735	$650	$595	$525	$450
.375 H&H	$1,300	$1,000	$800	$700	$600	$525	$450
.458 Win. Mag.	$1,095	$995	$895	$750	$625	$525	$450

Deduct 10%-15% for short extractor.

Between 1963 and 1974, Browning also offered short and medium barrelled actions in the Safari, Medallion and Olympian Grades. These models have Sako barrelled actions and were stocked by FN. Medium weight barrels could also be ordered.

Safari Grade - Short Sako Action — short action, .222 Rem. or .222 Rem. Mag. cal.

	100%	98%	95%	90%	80%	70%	60%
	$800	$675	$550	$450	$400	$350	$325

Safari Grade - Medium Sako Action — medium action, .22-250, .243, .284 or .308 cal.

	100%	98%	95%	90%	80%	70%	60%
	$800	$675	$550	$450	$400	$350	$325

Only 192 rifles (in Safari, Medallion, and Olympian grades) were mfg. in .284 cal. between 1965-1976.

Medallion Grade — features select figured walnut with skipline checkering, rosewood grip and forearm caps, blue/black lustre bluing, receiver and barrel portion scroll engraved, ram's head engraved on floor plate.

	100%	98%	95%	90%	80%	70%	60%
	$1,450	$1,195	$1,000	$925	$830	$700	$575

Add 10%-50% for rare calibers.

Add 20% for pencil barrel in Sako actions.

Add 15% for long extractor.

This model was also available with a Sako short or long action - cal.'s are the same as listed for the Sako Safari.

Olympian Grade — top-of-the-line model featuring highly figured walnut stock that is both checkered and carved. Receiver, floor plate, and trigger guard are chrome plated in a satin finish that have deep relief animal scenes engraved, as well as deep scroll work on other metal parts.

	100%	98%	95%	90%	80%	70%	60%
	$2,250	$2,000	$1,875	$1,700	$1,550	$1,350	$1,175

Add 10%-50% for rare calibers (.284 is among the rarest).

Add 20% for pencil barrel in Sako actions.

Add 15% for long extractor.

This model was also available with a Sako short or long action - cal.'s are the same as listed for the Sako Safari.

RIFLES: SLIDE ACTION

BPR-22-MAGNUM — .22 Mag., short-stroke action, 20¼ in. barrel, 11 shot tube mag., mfg. 1977-1982.

	100%	98%	95%	90%	80%	70%	60%
	$270	$195	$170	$160	$140	$130	$100

Grading	100%	98%	95%	90%	80%	70%	60%

BPR-22 Grade II — same as BPR-22, only engraved action, select walnut.

	$380	$295	$265	$250	$230	$200	$150

TROMBONE MODEL — .22 LR only, slide action with tube mag., fixed sights, takedown, 24 in. barrel, hammerless, similar to Win. Model 61, with either F.N. or U.S. (rare) barrel address.

FN Barrel Address

	$550	$475	$395	$350	$295	$260	$225

BAC Barrel Markings

	$650	$540	$460	$410	$345	$295	$250

Over 150,000 "Trombones" were mfg. by FN from 1922-1974. About 3,200 were imported by BAC in late 1960's. Very rare with factory engraving.

BCA GRADE III FN TROMBONE — only 60 manufactured for the Browning Collectors Association 1985-86, silver engraved frame with deluxe walnut.

	$2,295	$1,995	$1,600

RIFLES: O/U

EXPRESS RIFLE — .270 Win. or .30-06 cal., superposed style action. 24 in. barrels, auto ejectors, Fleur-de-lis engraving, single trigger, folding leaf rear sight, 6 lbs. 14 oz., cased. Disc. 1986.

	$1,995	$1,750	$1,600	$1,475	$1,300	$1,100	$900

Last Mfg.'s Sug. Retail was $3,125.

SHOTGUNS: DISC. SEMI-AUTO

BROWNING CHOKES AND THEIR CODES (ON REAR LEFT-SIDE OF BARREL)

* designates full choke (F).

*- designates improved modified choke (IM).

** designates modified choke (M).

**- designates improved cylinder choke (IC).

**$ designates skeet (SK).

*** designates cylinder bore (CYL).

INV. designates barrel is threaded for Browning Invector choke tube system.

AUTO-5 STANDARD - 1903-1939 MFG. — 12 or 16 ga.(introduced in U.S. in 1923), 26-32 in. barrel, recoil operated, various chokes, checkered pistol grip stock, mfg. 1903-1939 by FN, grades differ in engraving, inlays, and grade of wood. Approx. ser. range 1-229,000 (12ga.), 1-128,000 (16 ga.).

	100%	98%	95%	90%	80%	70%	60%
Grade 1	$475	$425	$375	$325	$285	$250	$200
Solid matte rib	$575	$495	$425	$375	$325	$275	$250
With vent rib	$695	$500	$450	$400	$350	$300	$250
Grade 2.(disc.1940)	$1,250	$1,000	$875	$750	$625	$550	$495
Solid matte rib	$1,450	$1,150	$1,000	$875	$750	$625	$575
With vent rib	$1,625	$1,300	$1,200	$1,000	$850	$750	$650
Grade 3.(disc. 1940)	$2,500	$2,200	$1,975	$1,775	$1,500	$1,250	$995
Solid matte rib	$2,700	$2,400	$2,100	$1,850	$1,650	$1,375	$1,100
With vent rib	$2,950	$2,550	$2,250	$2,000	$1,775	$1,500	$1,225
Grade 4.(disc. 1940)	$3,995	$3,655	$3,300	$2,995	$2,550	$2,050	$1,600
Solid matte rib	$4,150	$3,885	$3,450	$3,175	$2,700	$2,200	$1,800

Pre-WWII 16 ga. A-5's are chambered for $2\frac{9}{16}$ in. shells. These shotguns are considerably less desirable than 16 ga. A-5's chambered for $2\frac{3}{4}$ in. modern shotshells. Since some guns have been modified to $2\frac{3}{4}$ in., careful inspection is advised before purchasing or shooting.

Grading	100%	98%	95%	90%	80%	70%	60%

"AMERICAN BROWNING" AUTO-5 — 12, 16, or 20 ga., Remington-produced model of the Auto 5, very similar to the Remington Model 11, except with Browning logo, mag. cut-off, and different engraving, over 45,000 mfg. in 12 ga., over 25,000 in 16 ga., and 20,000 in 20 ga., stocks have Remington style round knob pistol grips with black plastic caps. Mfg. 1940-1942 and ser. numbered approx. 229,000-346,000 (12 ga.) with "B" prefix.

	$395	$345	$295	$225	$200	$185	$170

Add 10% for vent rib and/or 20 ga.

AUTO-5 STANDARDWEIGHT — 12, 20, or 16 ga., recoil operation, 26-32 in. barrels, standard production gun between 1952-1969, various chokes, checkered walnut stock and forearm, synthetic Browning marked butt plate, lacquer (until approx. 1966) or polyurethane finish, butt stock has either round knob pistol grip (1952-1976) or flat knob (introduced 1967), watch for cracked forearms on all A-5's (due to barrel recoil), between 7⅓-8 lbs.

	100%	98%	95%	90%	80%	70%	60%
Plain barrel	$435	$395	$360	$325	$295	$270	$240
Matted Rib	$475	$410	$370	$330	$300	$275	$245
Vent Rib	$525	$440	$395	$350	$315	$295	$260

Add 10% for N.I.B. condition.

Barrel addresses appeared as follows: 1952-1958 "St. Louis, Missouri", 1959-1968 "St. Louis, Missouri and Montreal P.Q.", 1969-1975 "Morgan, Utah and Montreal, P.Q.". Make sure barrel address circa matches year of mfg (see listings in the back of this text). Standardweight models had H or M prefixes.

SHOTGUNS: SEMI-AUTO RECENT MFG.

Miroku manufactured A-5's can be determined by year of manufacture in the following manner: RV suffix - 1975, RT - 1976, RR - 1977, RP - 1978, RN - 1979, PM - 1980, PZ - 1981, PY - 1982, PX - 1983, PW - 1984, PV - 1985, PT - 1986, PR - 1987, PP - 1988, PN - 1989, NM - 1990, NZ - 1991.

NOTE: Barrels are interchangeable between older Belgium A-5 models and recent Japanese A-5's mfg. by Miroku. A different barrel ring design might necessitate some minor sanding of the inner forearm on the older model, but otherwise, these barrels are fully interchangeable.

NOTE: The use of steel shot is recommended ONLY in those recent models manufactured in Japan incorporating the Invector choke system - NOT in the older Belgium variations.

AUTO-5 LIGHTWEIGHT — 12 or 20 ga., recoil operated, 26, 28, and 30 in. barrels, various chokes, scroll engraved receiver, checkered pistol grip stock, approx. 10 oz. lighter than Standardweight, mfg. 1952-1976 by FN, mfg. 1976-present by Miroku in Japan. Over 2,750,000 A-5's were mfg. by FN in all configurations between 1902-1976.

	100%	98%	95%	90%	80%	70%	60%
FN model	$450	$400	$375	$325	$295	$270	$240
FN-vent rib	$550	$460	$410	$370	$330	$295	$260

Add 10% for N.I.B. condition.

Add 10% for 20 ga. with VR.

Light 12 Miroku — 12 ga. only, now standard with vent rib (1986) and Invector choke system.

	100%	98%	95%	90%	80%	70%	60%
Mfg.'s Sug. Retail	$720	$580	$450	$400	$350	$300	$280	$260

Subtract $40 without Invector chokes.

Light 20 Miroku — 20 ga. only, 2¾ in. chamber, similar to original Belgium Light 20, VR, Invector choke standard. New 1987.

	100%	98%	95%	90%	80%	70%	60%
Mfg.'s Sug. Retail	$720	$580	$475	$420	$380	$340	$300	$270

AUTO-5 MAGNUM — 12 or 20 ga., 3 in. chamber, 26, 28, 30, or 32 in. barrels, various chokes, vent rib, similar to Standard. Mfg. 1958-1976 by FN, mfg. 1976-present by Miroku.

	100%	98%	95%	90%	80%	70%	60%
FN model.	$550	$450	$400	$350	$320	$260	$240
FN, vent rib.	$675	$575	$525	$480	$430	$340	$315

Add 10% for N.I.B. condition.   Add 15% for 20 ga. with VR if NIB.

Between 1976-1985 approx. 2,000 Belgian 12 ga. A-5 Mag.'s were imported into the U.S. These late models can be differentiated by serialization — also, slight premiums may be asked. The 20 ga. Mag. was not introduced until 1967.

Grading	100%	98%	95%	90%	80%	70%	60%

A-5 Mag. Miroku — 12 or 20 ga., VR barrel with Invector choke system.

Mfg.'s Sug. Retail	$743	$620	$510	$430	$385	$350	$325	$290

Subtract $40 without Invector chokes.

AUTO-5 LIGHT 12 BUCK SPECIAL — same as Standard only with 24 in. barrel, slug bore, adj. sight, mfg. 1958-1976 by FN, mfg. 1976-1984 and 1989 again by Miroku. Between 1985-1988, Buck Special barrels were available at extra cost.

FN Mfg.

	$550	$460	$410	$370	$330	$295	$240

Miroku model

Mfg.'s Sug. Retail	$725	$585	$465	$400	$360	$320	$290	$260

Add $23 for Buck Special on 3 in. Mag. receiver.

AUTO-5 SKEET — same as Standard Light only with 26 or 28 in. skeet bored, vent rib barrel. Pre-1976 mfg. by FN, 1976-1983 mfg. by Miroku.

FN Mfg.

	$450	$400	$375	$325	$295	$270	$240

Add 20% for vent rib.

Standard Miroku

	$460	$420	$380	$340	$300	$270	$250

AUTO-5 TRAP MODEL — same as Standard, 12 ga. only, 30 in. full vent rib barrel, 8½ lbs., mfg. by FN until 1971.

	$535	$460	$410	$335	$320	$295	$270

AUTO-5 SWEET 16 — similar to Standardweight Model, except 16 ga.(2¾ in. chamber) only and approx. 10 oz. lighter, gold plated trigger. Mfg. 1950-1976 by Fabrique Nationale.

Plain Barrel

	$500	$395	$350	$295	$250	$220	$195

Solid Matte Rib

	$660	$525	$450	$350	$275	$250	$225

Vent Rib

	$795	$695	$600	$525	$450	$375	$325

Sweet 16 Miroku — 16 ga. only, similar to original Belgium Sweet 16, VR, invector choke standard. New 1987.

Mfg.'s Sug. Retail	$720	$580	$475	$420	$380	$340	$300	$270

AUTO-5 2-MILLIONTH COMMEMORATIVE — 12 ga., 2,500 mfg., 1971-74 mfg., special walnut, engraving, high-luster bluing, cased with Browning book. Issue price — $550-$700.

	$1,195	$900	$750

A-5 CLASSIC SERIES SHOTGUN — 12 ga., 5,000 mfg. in Classic model, 500 mfg. in Gold Classic. Both editions feature game scenes, John M. Browning's profile, and other inscriptions, special silver grey finished receiver. Introduced 1984.

Classic Model — no inlays. Factory inventories were depleted in 1987.

	$895	$750	$600

Last Mfg.'s Sug. Retail was $1,260.

Gold Classic Model — features 5 inlays depicting duck hunting scenes. Mfg. 1986 with inventory depleted 1989.

	$4,000	$3,500	$2,950

Last Mfg.'s Sug. Retail was $6,500.

Grading	100%	98%	95%	90%	80%	70%	60%

A-5 DU 50TH ANNIVERSARY

A-5 DU Light 12 — 12 ga. only, 5,500 mfg. in 1987 only for Ducks Unlimited chapters throughout North America. Prices will fluctuate greatly from chapter to chapter as these guns were auctioned to the highest bidder. Receiver is specially engraved and has "Fiftieth year" depicted on right side of receiver, deluxe checkered stock and forearm, high gloss blue. Reports on guns having been resold recently indicate price ranges from $850 - $1,100.

A-5 DU Sweet Sixteen — 16 ga. only, companion 1988-89 DU auction gun, 4500 mfg. 1988 only. Early indications show a limited amount of resales occuring in the $850 - $900 range.

A-5 DU Light 20 — 20 ga. only, companion 1990 DU auction gun, 4500 mfg. 1990 only. Prices will vary depending on auction price of individual DU Chapters. A secondary price range should be slightly higher than the Sweet Sixteen DU A-5 gun since it is newer.

DOUBLE AUTOMATIC SHOTGUN — short recoil action, 12 ga. only, 2 shot, 26, 28, or 30 in. barrel, various chokes, checkered pistol grip stock, blued steel receiver. Mfg. 1952-1971.

	100%	98%	95%	90%	80%	70%	60%
	$435	$400	$350	$300	$260	$220	$195
w/vent rib	$550	$495	$420	$375	$325	$295	$245

TWELVETTE DOUBLE AUTO — similar to Double Auto, except hiduminum (aircraft alloy) frame and color anodized in blue, silver, brown, green, and black, approx. 7 lbs. without rib. Approx. 67,000 (all variations) mfg. 1952-1971.

	100%	98%	95%	90%	80%	70%	60%
	$450	$400	$350	$295	$250	$220	$200
w/vent rib	$575	$495	$425	$395	$340	$280	$250

For dark red, royal blue, brown, or gold colored receivers — add 10% (rare).

TWENTYWEIGHT DOUBLE AUTO — similar to Twelvette, but ¾ pound lighter, 26½ in. barrel only. Mfg. 1952-1971.

	100%	98%	95%	90%	80%	70%	60%
	$475	$400	$350	$285	$235	$220	$200
w/vent rib	$625	$525	$450	$400	$350	$295	$260

B/2000 STANDARD — 12 or 20 ga., 26, 28, or 30 in. barrel, various chokes, vent rib, gas operated, checkered pistol grip stock, Belgium manufactured but assembled in Portugal, approx. 115,000 imported into the U.S. between 1974-1983.

100%	98%	95%	90%	80%	70%	60%
$395	$360	$340	$320	$295	$275	$220

B/2000 MAGNUM — same as B/2000 Auto Shotgun, with 3 in. chambers, recoil pad, vent rib.

100%	98%	95%	90%	80%	70%	60%
$420	$380	$360	$330	$305	$285	$230

B/2000 SKEET — same as Standard, with 26 in. skeet bored barrel, floating vent rib, skeet stock, pad.

100%	98%	95%	90%	80%	70%	60%
$400	$350	$330	$310	$285	$260	$210

B/2000 TRAP — same as Standard, with 30 or 32 in. barrel bored F or IM, floating rib, Monte Carlo trap stock.

100%	98%	95%	90%	80%	70%	60%
$400	$350	$330	$310	$285	$260	$210

B/2000 BUCK SPECIAL — 12 or 20 ga., barrel sights on 24 in. barrel.

100%	98%	95%	90%	80%	70%	60%
$410	$360	$340	$320	$295	$270	$220

1976 CANADIAN OLYMPICS B2000 — 12 ga., 100 manufactured in 1976 for Canadian sales only, high polish blue with multiple gold inlays including Olympic crest, 30 in. barrel, cased. Issue price was $1,295.

100%	98%	95%
$1,395	$995	$695

MODEL B-80 — 12 or 20 ga., 3 in. capability by changing barrel, gas operation, 4 shot, hunting models use choice of steel or aluminum receiver, anodized aluminum was used in the Superlight (12 ga. mfg. 1984 only), 6 to 8 lbs. 1 oz. Buck special disc. 1984. Components manufactured by Beretta of Italy and finished and assembled FN's plant in Portugal. Mfg. 1981-late 1988, final inventory was sold in 1991. Invector chokes became standard in 1985.

100%	98%	95%	90%	80%	70%	60%
$450	$375	$325	$295	$275	$250	$230

Steel frames were reintroduced into production again in 1988.

Grading	100%	98%	95%	90%	80%	70%	60%

Last Mfg.'s Sug. Retail was $562.

Model B-80 Upland Special — 12 or 20 ga., 2¾ in. chamber, 22 in. vent. rib barrel, straight grip stock, invector chokes. Mfg. 1986-1988.

	$475	$390	$340	$305	$280	$260	$240

Last Mfg.'s Sug. Retail was $562.

MODEL B 80 DU COMMEMORATIVE — mfg. for American DU Chapters (The Plains and others), price fluctuates greatly as collector support is sometimes limited. Unless new, this models' values approximate those of the regular Model B-80. If NIB, values recently have been in the $700-$995 range.

A-500 — 12 ga. only, recoil operation self adjusting for any load, 3 in. chamber, 26, 28, or 30 in. invector choked barrel with vent rib, checkered walnut stock and forearm with recoil pad, rotary bolt lock-up, magazine cut-off, high polished blue, light engraving, approx. 7 lbs. 5 oz. Mfg. 1987-1989.

	$465	$390	$345	$305	$280	$260	$240

This model was renamed the A-500R (see listing below) with the introduction of the A-500G.

Last Mfg.'s Sug. Retail was $560.

A-500G — similar to A-500, except has improvements incorporated, distinguishable by "A-500G" in gold accents on receiver, capable of shooting all 2¾ or 3 in. shells interchangeably, approx. 8 lbs. New 1990.

Mfg.'s Sug. Retail	$640	$550	$425	$375	$325	$295	$275	$250

A-500R — 12 ga. only, 3 in. chamber, new design utilizing short recoil system with a four-lug rotary bolt design, capable of shooting all 12 gauge loads interchangeably, magazine cut-off, 26, 28, or 30 in. VR barrel with Invector chokes standard, 24 in. barrel on Buck Special (fixed choke), high polished blued finish with red accents on receiver sides, gold trigger, checkered semi-pistol grip walnut stock with vent. recoil pad, approx. 8 lbs. New 1990.

Mfg.'s Sug. Retail	$560	$475	$425	$375	$325	$295	$275	$250

This model features fewer moving parts than many other semi-auto shotguns due to the short recoil operating system.

SHOTGUNS: O/U

SUPERPOSED SHOTGUN: 1931-1976 MANUFACTURE — 12, 20, 28, or .410 ga., 26½, 28, 30, or 32 in. barrels, various chokes, boxlock, auto ejectors, SST, DT, or twin single triggers (early mfg.), checkered pistol grip stock, mfg. 1931-1940 and 1949-1976 by FN, grades differ in amount of engraving, inlay, general quality of workmanship and wood. Currently, shorter barrel (26½ in.) superposed models are bringing a small premium over a 30 in. F & M model. Prices below assume vent rib models, earlier matted rib guns will be 5-10% less, depending on condition.

NOTE: The use of steel shot is NOT recommended in the older Superposed Series manufactured in Belgium.

BROWNING CHOKES AND THEIR CODES (ON BARREL)

* designates full choke (F).

*- designates improved modified choke (IM).

** designates modified choke (M).

**- designates improved cylinder choke (IC).

**$ designates skeet (SK).

*** designates cylinder bore (CYL).

SKEET MODELS were available in every ga. and grade - values are the same as listed below.

TRAP MODELS were available in every grade in 12 ga. only - DEDUCT 5-10% from values shown below. BROADWAY TRAP MODELS with ⅝ in. wide vent rib were also available in every grade - DEDUCT 10-15%.

Add 15%-20% for 20 ga. on all grades.

Add 100% for 28 ga. on Grade I, 30% on higher grades.

Grading	100%	98%	95%	90%	80%	70%	60%

Add 50% for .410 ga. on Grade I, 20% on higher grades.

Deduct 25% for early DT models.

Grade I Standard — the Grade I has a blued steel frame with hand engraved scroll and rosette patterns, checkered walnut stock and forearm. Grade I Standard was disc. 1973.

	$1,395	$1,075	$925	$840	$775	$650	$550

Grade I Lightning — similar to Grade I Standard. Disc. 1976.

	$1,450	$1,150	$975	$870	$810	$690	$600

Grade I Magnum — 3 in. chambers with standard Browning recoil pad. Disc. 1976.

	$1,395	$1,075	$900	$825	$760	$635	$525

Because of the wide spread use of steel shot in recent years, values for Magnum and Lightning models have gone down (these models are not compatible with steel shot).

Pigeon Grade — also designated Grade II temporarily after WWII and renamed Pigeon in 1960. This grade featured a silver grey receiver with 2 flying pigeons surrounded by fine scroll engraving on each side of the frame. The receiver bottom and tangs also exhibit fine scroll work. The Pigeon Grade was disc. 1974.

	$2,650	$2,250	$1,950	$1,825	$1,650	$1,570	$1,485

Grade III — 12 or 20 ga., satin finished receiver with game scene engraving featuring pheasants and fighting cocks on receiver, receiver bottom has a retriever and pheasant. Disc. 1960.

	$2,400	$2,150	$2,000	$1,815	$1,650	$1,570	$1,485

Pointer Grade — also designated Grade III, manufactured post-war only until renamed Pointer in early 1960. Features engraved silver grey receiver with a Pointer depicted on each frame side, select walnut. Disc. 1966.

	$3,300	$2,850	$2,450	$2,050	$1,850	$1,700	$1,625

Grade IV — limited manufacture between 1950-1955, engraving usually featured a dog and bird scene in deep relief.

	$3,150	$2,700	$2,450	$2,125	$1,875	$1,750	$1,650

Diana Grade — also designated Grade V in post-war manufacture until renamed Diana in 1960. Pre-WWII Grade V's featured more delicate scroll engraving with deer adorning the right side and wild bore shown on the left. Post-WWII guns exhibit deep relief engraving with duck and pheasant game scenes on each frame side, select checkered walnut stock and forearm. Disc. 1976.

	$3,550	$3,100	$2,650	$2,150	$1,900	$1,800	$1,700

Midas Grade — also designated Grade VI during post-war manufacture until renamed Midas in 1960. Pre-WWII Midas Grades featured an inlaid pigeon with outstretched wings on blued frame sides and bottom plus trigger guard. This earlier Midas also exhibited multiple gold escutcheons and gold lining. Post-war models feature deep relief scroll engraving with gold inlaid ducks and pheasants on frame sides and a grouse on the bottom. Ejector trip rods, ejector hammers and firing pins are also 18Kt. gold plated. Finest checkered walnut. Disc. 1976.

	$4,650	$4,100	$3,500	$3,000	$2,700	$2,500	$2,300

Grade VI — offered from 1955-1960 only. Elaborate deep relief scroll engraved with multiple gold inlays.

	$5,500	$4,500	$4,000	$3,500	$3,200	$3,000	$2,600

SUPERPOSED WITH EXTRA BARREL(S) OR SUPER-TUBES

Could be ordered from the factory in the following combinations: 12 or 20 ga. with one extra set of barrels in same ga. 12 ga. with one extra set in 20 ga. 12 or 20 ga. with two extra barrel sets of same ga. 20 ga. with one extra set in either 28 or .410 ga. 20 ga. with both 28 and .410 ga. barrel sets. 28 ga. with extra set of .410 barrels. Super-Tubes were adaptable on 12 ga. guns only; came from the factory cased with accessories, 16½ in. long, factory installation.

Extra barrel set(s) — add 40-50% of the guns' value for each extra set.

Super-Tubes — available for 12 ga. only, single ga. — add $250.

Super-Tube Set — 3 ga. set (20, 28 and .410 ga.'s) — add $400.

Exposition/Exhibition Model

This specially manufactured Superposed saw limited production from the late 60's through 1976. This model had its own serial range (usually 3 digit) with a "C" prefix. Grades A through G ranged from fairly simple scroll designs without gold inlays up to extremely ornate designs featuring multi-colored gold inlaid game figures. Most of these guns were produced by FN for

Grading	100%	98%	95%	90%	80%	70%	60%

display purposes, potential production models, or potential engraving standardization. Many of these Exhibition/Exposition superposed models were consigned to Browning Arms Co. during the 1970's because of the depressed market conditions of that time. Prices are determined by the embellishments and engraving per individual gun (A Grade being the lowest, G Grade with gold being the highest). Prices usually start at around $5,000, while a G Grade with extensive gold inlays could reach 5 digits.

BICENTENNIAL SUPERPOSED SUPERLIGHT SHOTGUN — specially engraved limited edition Model, 51 mfg. — one for each state and Washington, D.C. Left side has U.S. Flag, bald eagle and state emblem inlaid in gold. Right side has gold inlaid hunter and turkey. Blued receiver, fancy checkered English stock, Schnabel forend, velvet lined wood case. Made 1976 by FN.

	$14,000	$10,000	$8,750

WATERFOWL SUPERPOSED SHOTGUN SERIES — 12 ga., 500 made of each issue. Gold inlays with extensive engraving, lightning action, 28 in. barrels, walnut cased, factory depleted Pintail and Black Duck Issues in 1989.

1981 Mallard Issue

	$4,650	$3,995	$3,250

Last Mfg.'s Sug. Retail was $7,000. This issue was sold out in 1988.

1982 Pintail Issue

	$4,500	$3,850	$3,100

Last Mfg.'s Sug. Retail was $8,800.

1983 Black Duck Issue

	$4,500	$3,850	$3,100

Last Mfg.'s Sug. Retail was $8,800.

OVER/UNDER CLASSIC SERIES SHOTGUN — 20 ga. only, 26 in. barrels, less than 2,500 manufactured in Classic model and under 350 manufactured in Gold Classic. Both editions feature multiple engraved scenes and a special silver grey finish. Select American walnut featuring oil finish. Available 1986 only.

	$1,750	$1,500	$1,200

Last Mfg.'s Sug. Retail was $2,000.

Gold Classic — 8 gold inlays, select walnut forearm and stock are both checkered and carved. Available 1986 only.

	$4,750	$3,950	$3,150

Last Mfg.'s Sug. Retail was $6,000.

SUPERPOSED SUPERLIGHT — 12 or 20 ga., 26½ in. solid or VR barrels, lightened slimmer firearm and straight grip stock. Mfg. 1967-1976 by FN.

	100%	98%	95%	90%	80%	70%	60%
12 gauge	$1,600	$1,395	$1,225	$1,110	$1,025	$925	$800
20 gauge	$1,995	$1,750	$1,575	$1,350	$1,250	$1,000	$850

For Pigeon, Diana, and Midas grade Superlight 12 ga. models use previous values on standard model high-grades and add approx. 25% (plus gauge premiums).

There is also a Quail Unlimited limited edition in the Superlight series. Values are somewhat higher but difficult to ascertain because so few are bought and sold each year.

SUPERPOSED SHOTGUN: 1983-86 MANUFACTURE — 12 or 20 ga. In 1983, Browning announced renewed production of the famous Belgium "Superposed" O/U in Grade I only. Available in Lightning or Superlight models, 3 in. chambers in Lightning 20 ga., 26½ or 28 in. barrels. Belgium manufactured from 1983-86.

Grade I — limited availability.

	$1,795	$1,375	$1,100	$975	$850	$725	$595

Last Mfg.'s Sug. Retail was $1,995.

SUPERPOSED CONTINENTAL — 20 ga. O/U shotgun w/extra set of .30-06 O/U rifle barrels. Shotgun barrels are 26½ in., rifle barrels are 24 in., SST, ejectors, elaborate scroll engraved receiver, special oil finish walnut, cased. 500 mfg. Disc. 1986.

	$2,995	$2,700	$2,350	$1,950	$1,600	$1,250	$1,000

Last Mfg.'s Sug. Retail was $4,375.

Grading	100%	98%	95%	90%	80%	70%	60%

SUPERPOSED PRESENTATION MODELS (P1-P4) — custom made versions of the Lightning Field, Super Light, Trap, and Skeet guns, specifications the same as Standard models, with differences in finish, engraving and inlay(s), and grade of wood and checkering. These guns were introduced by FN in 1977 and were disc. after 1984. Add $1,775 for extra set of barrels, add $3,600 for 2 sets of extra barrels.

P Series Trap — deduct 10% from values listed below.

P Series Broadway Trap — deduct 15-20% from values listed below.

P Series Skeet 12 and 20 ga. — add 5-10% to values listed below.

Since P Series Superposed were disc. 1985, collector interest will undoubtedly increase and prices might be increased somewhat. BAC has no remaining inventory of this model. Interestingly, the P series models are rarer than most of the pre-1976 high grade Superposed models. Add 20% for 20 ga.

Add 30% for 28 ga.

Add 40% for .410 ga.

Presentation 1 — silver grey or blued receiver, oak leaf and fine scroll engraved, choice of 6 different animal scenes.

	$2,650	$2,250	$1,995	$1,750	$1,500	$1,250	$1,000

Presentation 1 w/gold inlays — same as Presentation 1, only with gold inlays.

	$3,150	$2,700	$2,300	$2,000	$1,825	$1,700	$1,500

Presentation 2 — silver grey or blued receiver, high relief engraving, choice of 3 different sets of game scenes.

	$2,995	$2,450	$2,100	$1,850	$1,725	$1,600	$1,400

Presentation 2 w/gold inlays — same as Presentation 2, only with gold inlays.

	$3,475	$3,150	$2,700	$2,300	$2,000	$1,825	$1,700

Presentation 3 — silver grey or blued receiver, more elaborate high relief engraving with choice of partridges, mallards or geese depicted on frame sides in 18Kt. gold.

	$4,950	$4,100	$3,600	$3,200	$2,875	$2,300	$2,000

Presentation 4 — features engraved side plates in either silver grey or blued finish, engraved game scenes include waterfowl on right frame side, 5 pheasants on left frame side, 2 quail on receiver bottom, and a retriever's head on trigger guard. Extra figure walnut stock and forearm.

	$5,480	$4,385	$3,900	$3,600	$3,300	$3,000	$2,750

Presentation 4 w/gold inlays — same as Presentation 4, only with game scenes inlaid in 18Kt. gold.

	$6,580	$5,265	$4,750	$4,250	$3,800	$3,500	$3,200

Only 8 blue/gold guns were mfg. in this configuration - 2 each in 12, 20, 28, or .410 ga. As a result, healthy premiums exist since most of the guns sold were the grey/gold finish.

P SERIES SUPERLIGHT — available in various configurations including multi-barrel sets. Typically, add 20-25% onto the values listed for the regular P series as shown above. Also add 20-40% for the 28 ga. and .410 ga. respectively.

LIEGE O/U — 12 ga., 26½, 28 or 30 in. barrels, various chokes, boxlock, auto ejectors, non-selective single trigger, vent rib, checkered pistol grip stock. Approx. 10,000 mfg. 1973-1975 by FN.

	$700	$600	$550	$500	$425	$400	$375

This model is also known as the B 26.

B 27 — F.N. manufactured modified B 26, recently imported into the U.S., same action as Liege (B 26), blued or satin finished receiver with light engraving, no BAC markings.

Standard Game — 28 in. barrels, 9/32 in. vent rib, pistol grip stock, Schnabel forearm, SST, blued receiver, choking M/F only.

	$775	$675	$600	$550	$475	$425	$400

Also available in Skeet model with gold "Browning" logo on blued receiver. Prices are the same.

Deluxe Game (Grade II) — same as Standard Grade, except has 30 in. barrels, better wood and English scroll engraved satin finished receiver, choking M/F only.

	$875	$725	$625	$575	$510	$475	$445

Grading	100%	98%	95%	90%	80%	70%	60%

Grand Deluxe Game — 28 in. IC/IM & M/F choked barrels, game scene engraved, signed by the engraver, 90% receiver coverage.

	$1,100	$850	$775	$700	$640	$580	$520

This model was also available in a Trap configuration — values are about the same as above.

Deluxe Skeet — same as Deluxe, except is designed for skeet shooting.

	$850	$725	$625	$575	$510	$475	$445

International Skeet is also available at same price; hand fit pistol grip with stippling and International Type recoil pad.

Deluxe Trap — same as Deluxe, except is configured for trap shooting.

	$750	$650	$560	$530	$500	$475	$445

City of Liege Commemorative —limited edition of 250 units manufactured to commemorate the 1,000th anniversary of the city of Liege, cased. Only 29 imported into the U.S.

	$1,125	$975	$910	$850	$775	$700	$600

ST-100 — 12 ga., Belgian mfg., O/U trap configuration with separated barrels and adj. point of impact, manufactured 1979-1983 for European sale mostly, floating VR, ST, deluxe checkered walnut stock and forearm, non-B.A.C. model.

	$2,250	$1,950	$1,700	$1,400	$1,200	$975	$825

SUPERPOSED HIGH GRADES: 1985-PRESENT

Browning, in 1985, resumed production of the Superposed in Pigeon, Pointer, Diana, and Midas grades. They are available in 12 and 20 ga. only, in either a Lightning or Superlight configuration. These higher grades are custom ordered from the factory with delivery ranging from 8 to more than 12 months. Custom options can be special ordered on each grade with corresponding prices being higher than shown below. B-25 engraving patterns on these various grades will nearly duplicate those styles manufactured before 1976. Skeet models are not available.

B-25 — 12 or 20 ga. only, original Superposed Model manufactured entirely from parts fabricated in Herstal, Belgium. Also available in Superlight configuration.

Pigeon Grade

Mfg.'s Sug. Retail	$5,450	$4,750	$2,450	$1,950	$1,800	$1,650	$1,525	$1,450

Add $2,725 for an extra set of barrels.

Pointer Grade

Mfg.'s Sug. Retail	$6,580	$5,775	$2,650	$2,150	$1,900	$1,750	$1,625	$1,550

Add $2,920 for an extra set of barrels.

Diana Grade

Mfg.'s Sug. Retail	$7,000	$6,150	$3,150	$2,450	$2,150	$1,900	$1,800	$1,625

Add $3,450 for an extra set of barrels.

Midas Grade

Mfg.'s Sug. Retail	$9,340	$7,950	$4,450	$3,500	$3,100	$2,700	$2,500	$2,200

Add $4,260 for an extra set of barrels.

B-125 — 12 or 20 ga. only, retains all the features of the original Superposed, except parts are subcontracted worldwide to decrease production costs and are assembled "in the white" at Herstal's Custom Gun Shop in Belgium, choice of three different engraving styles and two receiver finishes. Introduced 1988.

Hunting Model — available in either Lightweight or Superlight configuration.

A STYLE ENGRAVING - blued receiver with border engraving featuring Browning logo engraved on each side.

Mfg.'s Sug. Retail	$3,190	$2,800	$1,950	$1,700	$1,450	$1,275	$1,050	$950

B STYLE ENGRAVING - coined finished receiver with smaller game scene engravings.

Mfg.'s Sug. Retail	$3,450	$2,995	$2,150	$1,825	$1,500	$1,275	$1,050	$950

C STYLE ENGRAVING - coined finished receiver with elaborate scroll work and game scene engraving.

Mfg.'s Sug. Retail	$3,735	$3,195	$2,275	$1,900	$1,550	$1,300	$1,100	$1,000

Grading	100%	98%	95%	90%	80%	70%	60%

Sporting Clays Model — 12 ga. only, designed for sporting clays competition and includes Invector plus choke tube system.

A STYLE ENGRAVING - blued receiver with border engraving featuring Browning logo engraved on each side.

Mfg.'s Sug. Retail	$3,300	$2,875	$2,000	$1,700	$1,450	$1,275	$1,050	$950

B STYLE ENGRAVING - coined finished receiver with smaller game scene engravings.

Mfg.'s Sug. Retail	$3,550	$3,050	$2,175	$1,825	$1,500	$1,275	$1,050	$950

C STYLE ENGRAVING - coined finished receiver with elaborate scroll work and game scene engraving.

Mfg.'s Sug. Retail	$3,800	$3,200	$2,300	$1,900	$1,575	$1,325	$1,100	$1,000

Trap Model — standard F-1 style engraving.

Mfg.'s Sug. Retail	$3,350	$2,900	$2,000	$1,700	$1,450	$1,275	$1,050	$950

SHOTGUNS: CITORI SERIES O/U

All Citori shotguns which incorporate the Invector choke tube system may be used with steel shot.

On some Citori models, the retail value for a currently manufactured 28 or .410 ga. is less than for a 12 ga. When evaluating these smaller gauges in used condition, values will generally be higher than those listed below.

CITORI HUNTING MODELS — 12, 20, 28 or .410 ga., 26, 28, or 30 in. barrels, various chokes, boxlock, auto ejectors, SST, vent rib, features checkered semi-pistol grip stock with grooved semi-beavertail forearm, grades differ in amount of engraving, finish, and wood. Mfg. 1973-present by Miroku.

Grade I

Mfg.'s Sug. Retail	$1,065	$825	$675	$575	$495	$450	$395	$350

Subtract $40 without Invector chokes.

Invector chokes became standard on this model in 1988.

3½ in. Magnum Model — 12 ga., 3½ in. chambers, 28 or 30 in. VR barrels with back-bored Invector plus choke tubes, with recoil pad, 8 lbs. 9 oz. New 1989.

Mfg.'s Sug. Retail	$1,135	$950	$850	$775	$700	$625	$575	$525

Upland Special — 12, 16 (mfg. 1989 only), or 20 ga., checkered straight grip stock, 24 in. barrels, Invector chokes standard. New 1984.

Mfg.'s Sug. Retail	$1,110	$800	$675	$575	$495	$450	$425	$395

Grade II — 12, 20, 28, or .410 ga. Disc. 1983.

	$995	$810	$740	$685	$610	$570	$540

Grade III — 12, 20, 28, or .410 ga., greyed steel with engraved game scenes, Invector chokes standard. New 1985.

Mfg.'s Sug. Retail	$1,565	$1,200	$975	$825	$725	$625	$585	$550

Add 15-25% for .410 or 28 ga. (disc. 1989).

Grade V — 12, 20, 28, or .410 ga., extensive deep relief engraving with game scenes on satin grey receiver. Disc. 1984.

	$1,425	$1,265	$1,100	$990	$880	$795	$695

Grade VI — 12, 20, 28, or .410 ga., blued or grayed receiver with extensive engraving including 8 gold inlays.

Mfg.'s Sug. Retail	$2,250	$1,695	$1,325	$1,150	$1,000	$895	$795	$695

Add 15-25% for 28 or .410 ga. (disc. 1989).

CITORI SUPERLIGHT MODELS — 12, 20, 28, or .410 ga., 2¾ in. chambers except for .410, English stock, 6 lbs. 9 oz., oil finish, Invector chokes became standard in 1988. Mfg. 1983-present.

Grade I

Mfg.'s Sug. Retail	$1,110	$835	$700	$575	$495	$450	$425	$395

Subtract $80 without Invector chokes.

Add $5 for 28 or .410 ga.

Grade III — same gauges as Grade I, Invector chokes standard on 12, 16, or 20 ga. New 1986.

Mfg.'s Sug. Retail	$1,600	$1,250	$1,025	$850	$725	$625	$585	$550

Add $150 for 28 or .410 ga.

Grading	100%	98%	95%	90%	80%	70%	60%

Grade V — sideplate available. Disc. 1984.

	$1,425	$1,265	$1,100	$990	$880	$795	$695

Grade VI — Invector chokes standard, except not available on 28 or .410 ga.

Mfg.'s Sug. Retail $2,300 $1,775 $1,400 $1,175 $1,000 $895 $795 $695

Add $150 for 28 or .410 ga.

CITORI SPORTER MODELS — same as Citori Field, only with 26 in. barrels, various chokes, straight grip stock, Schnabel forearm. Disc. 1983.

	$875	$740	$600	$550	$495	$440	$385

Add $50 for 28 or .410 ga.

Sporter Grade II — 12, 20, 28, or .410 ga.

	$1,130	$1,075	$1,020	$965	$880	$770	$715

Sporter Grade V — 12, 20, 28, or .410 ga.

	$1,500	$1,395	$1,225	$1,100	$990	$880	$825

CITORI LIGHTNING MODELS — 12, 16, 20, 28, or .410 ga., (3½ in. 12 ga. was introduced 1989), 26, 28, or 30 in. barrels, Invector chokes standard in 12, 16, or 20 ga., boxlock, auto ejectors, SST, vent rib, features checkered round knob pistol grip stock and slimmer forearm, grades differ in amount of engraving, finish, and quality of wood. Introduced 1988.

Grade I

Mfg.'s Sug. Retail $1,095 $800 $675 $575 $495 $450 $425 $395

Add $5 for 28 or .410 ga.

Grade III — 12, 16, 20, 28, or .410 ga., greyed steel receiver with engraved game scenes, Invector chokes standard. New 1988.

Mfg.'s Sug. Retail $1,595 $1,250 $1,000 $825 $725 $625 $585 $550

Add $145 for 28 or .410 ga.

Grade VI — 12, 16, 20, 28, or .410 ga., blued or greyed receiver with extensive engraving including 8 gold inlays.

Mfg.'s Sug. Retail $2,285 $1,775 $1,425 $1,175 $1,000 $895 $795 $695

Add $150 for 28 or .410 ga.

GRAN LIGHTNING MODEL — 12 or 20 ga. only, 3 in. chambers, similar to Lightning Model, except has higher grade walnut stock and forearm with satin/oil finish, includes recoil pad, 26 or 28 in. barrels, 6¾ - 8 lbs. New 1990.

Mfg.'s Sug. Retail $1,485 $1,225 $1,000 $850 $725 $625 $585 $550

MICRO LIGHTNING — 20 ga. only, 2¾ in. chambers, 24 in. Invector choked barrels, Grade I only, 6 lbs. 3 oz. New 1991.

Mfg.'s Sug. Retail $1,120 $850 $700 $600 $525 $450 $425 $395

SPORTING CLAYS MODELS

GTI — 12 ga. only, 28 or 30 in. barrel with 13 mm vent. rib and barrels, red lettering on receiver during 1989 only - changed to gold lettering and borders with Browning logo in 1990, checkered stock and semi-beavertail forearm, Invector chokes standard, back-bored Invector plus chokes became standard in 1990, approx. 8 lbs. New 1989.

Mfg.'s Sug. Retail $1,240 $1,075 $850 $700 $600 $525 $495 $450

Add $55 for ported barrels (new 1990).

Grade I Special Sporting — target dimensions, high post tapered rib, 28, 30, or 32 in. barrels, full pistol grip with palm swell, approx. 8 lbs. 3 oz. New 1989.

Mfg.'s Sug. Retail $1,225 $1,060 $835 $700 $600 $525 $495 $450

Add $55 for ported barrels (new 1990).

Add $800 for 2 barrel set (28 and 30 in. barrels), disc. 1990.

In 1990, the Grade I designation was added to this model. Changes include back-bored barrels with Invector plus choke tubes.

Grade I Lightning Sporting — features rounded pistol grip, Lightning style forearm, high or low post vent. rib, "Lightning Sporting Clays Edition" inscribed and gold-filled on receiver, 30 in. barrels. New 1989.

Mfg.'s Sug. Retail $1,170 $1,015 $800 $700 $600 $525 $495 $450

Add $55 for high-post rib or ported barrels (new 1990).

Grading	100%	98%	95%	90%	80%	70%	60%

In 1990, the Grade I designation was added to this model. Changes include back-bored barrels with Invector plus choke tubes.

CITORI SKEET MODELS — 12, 20, 28, or .410 ga., same action as Citori Field, only with high post target rib (standard 1985), 26 and 28 in. skeet barrels, recoil pad, Invector chokes became standard in 1990.

Mfg.'s Sug. Retail	$1,200	$975	$795	$675	$600	$525	$495	$450

Subtract $50 if without Invector chokes.

Add $10 for 28 or .410 ga. on new retail values only.

Earlier mfg. skeet guns had a low profile, wide VR.

Grade II — 12, 20, 28, or .410 ga., high rib. Disc. 1983.

	$1,000	$850	$800	$740	$690	$650	$600

Grade III — 12, 20, 28, or .410 ga., Invector chokes only. New 1986.

Mfg.'s Sug. Retail	$1,700	$1,325	$1,050	$850	$725	$625	$550	$495

Grade V — 12, 20, 28, or .410 ga., high rib. Disc. 1984.

	$1,495	$1,265	$1,100	$990	$880	$795	$650

Grade VI — Skeet gauges, choice of blue or grey finished receiver with multi gold inlays, deluxe walnut.

Mfg.'s Sug. Retail	$2,400	$1,925	$1,575	$1,325	$1,100	$960	$875	$825

CITORI 3 GAUGE SKEET SETS — 12 ga. only, comes with 1 removable forearm and 3 sets of barrels consisting of 20, 28 and .410 ga.'s, cased. New 1987.

Grade I — with high post target rib.

Mfg.'s Sug. Retail	$2,780	$2,325	$1,975	$1,650	$1,450	$1,275	$1,050	$975

Grade III — with high post target rib.

Mfg.'s Sug. Retail	$3,200	$2,525	$2,125	$1,800	$1,550	$1,395	$1,250	$1,125

Grade VI — with high post target rib.

Mfg.'s Sug. Retail	$3,925	$3,375	$2,625	$2,200	$1,875	$1,700	$1,675	$1,495

CITORI 4 GAUGE SKEET SETS — 12 ga. only, comes with 1 removable forearm and 4 sets of barrels consisting of 12, 20, 28 and .410 ga.'s, cased. New 1985.

Grade I — with high post target rib.

Mfg.'s Sug. Retail	$4,000	$3,250	$2,525	$1,950	$1,695	$1,500	$1,400	$1,295

Grade III — with high post target rib.

Mfg.'s Sug. Retail	$4,550	$3,600	$2,800	$2,250	$1,950	$1,800	$1,675	$1,500

Grade VI — with high post target rib.

Mfg.'s Sug. Retail	$5,100	$4,000	$3,250	$2,750	$2,400	$2,000	$1,850	$1,700

CITORI TRAP MODELS — same as Standard Citori, with 12 ga., 30 and 32 in. barrels, trap chokes, Monte Carlo stock, recoil pad. Invector chokes became standard in 1988.

Mfg.'s Sug. Retail	$1,195	$985	$800	$600	$525	$440	$415	$360

Subtract $45 without Invector chokes or high rib.

Grade I Plus Trap — features adj. rib and stock, back-bored barrels, Invector Plus choke system. New 1990.

Mfg.'s Sug. Retail	$2,010	$1,550	$1,125	$925	$800	$700	$600	$500

Add $25 for ported barrels.

In 1991 this model included a travel vault gun case at no extra charge. Subtract $50 for older mfg. without travel case.

Grade II — high post rib. Disc. 1983.

	$1,000	$850	$800	$740	$690	$650	$600

Grade III — 12 ga. only, high post rib. New 1986.

Mfg.'s Sug. Retail	$1,700	$1,325	$1,025	$850	$715	$625	$550	$495

Grade V — high post rib. Disc. 1984.

	$1,395	$1,125	$990	$880	$795	$710	$620

Grade VI — 12 ga. only, Invector chokes became standard in 1985.

Mfg.'s Sug. Retail	$2,400	$1,825	$1,495	$1,225	$1,100	$960	$875	$825

Trap Combination Set — Grade I only, 32 in. O/U and 34 in. single barrel, cased. Disc.

	$1,185	$1,100	$1,045	$990	$910	$855	$800

Grading	100%	98%	95%	90%	80%	70%	60%

SHOTGUNS: SINGLE BARREL

BT-99 COMPETITION TRAP GUN — 12 ga., 32 or 34 in. vent. rib barrel, mod., imp. mod., or full choke, boxlock, auto ejector, checkered pistol grip stock, beavertail forearm, mfg. 1968-present by Miroku. Invector chokes became standard in 1986, and values below assume Invector choking.

Mfg.'s Sug. Retail	$1,070	$860	$675	$540	$460	$400	$360	$330

Subtract $25 without Invector chokes.

Grade I BT-99 Plus — same action as BT-99 except has adj. rib to control point of impact and new recoil reduction system that reduces felt recoil by 50%, stock has adj. comb and butt plate (recoil pad), back-bored barrel, Invector chokes, 8¾ lbs. New 1989.

Mfg.'s Sug. Retail	$1,875	$1,495	$1,100	$925	$775	$675	$595	$550

Add $25 for ported barrel.

In 1990, the Grade I designation was added to this model. Changes include back-bored barrels with Invector plus choke tubes. In 1991 this model was supplied with a travel vault gun case as standard equipment. Older mfg. will not have these cases as an original accessory.

BT-99 Micro Plus — similar to Grade I BT-99 Plus, except has youth dimensions and choice of 28 or 30 in. barrel, 8 lbs. 6 oz. New 1991.

Mfg.'s Sug. Retail	$1,875	$1,495	$1,100	$925	$775	$675	$595	$550

Add $25 for ported barrel.

BT-99 2 Barrel Set — disc. 1983.

	$1,030	$880	$825	$750	$700	$650	$600

BT-99 Pigeon Grade — satin grey receiver with deep relief, engraved pigeons in fleur-de-lis background. Disc. 1984.

	$1,200	$900	$800	$700	$600	$525	$440

RECOILLESS SINGLE BARREL TRAP — 12 ga., special bolt action design that eliminates 70% of felt recoil, 27 or 30 in. vent. rib Invector barrel, rib adjusts for 3 points of impact, stock has adj. pull (2 sizes) and comb height, about 8½ lbs.

While advertised in 1989, this model has yet to be produced.

SHOTGUNS: DISCONTINUED, SIDE-BY-SIDE

BSS MODEL — 12 or 20 ga., 26, 28, or 30 in. barrels, various chokes, boxlock, auto ejectors, checkered pistol grip stock, beavertail forearm, selective single trigger. Mfg. 1971-1988 by Miroku.

	$550	$495	$450	$400	$365	$330	$300

Add 10%-15% for 20 ga.
Last Mfg.'s Sug. Retail was $775.

Early guns had a single non-selective trigger (silver plated) — subtract 10%.

Grade II — satin greyed steel receiver featuring an engraved pheasant, duck, quail and dogs. Disc. 1983.

	$1,025	$925	$800	$700	$600	$525	$450

Sporter Model — has straight grip stock and slim forearm, oil finish, 26 or 28 in. barrels. Disc. 1988.

	$595	$550	$495	$450	$395	$360	$320

Add 10%-15% for 20 ga.
Last Mfg.'s Sug. Retail was $775.

BSS SIDELOCK — 12 or 20 ga., engraved sidelock action in satin grey finish, ST, 26 or 28 in. barrels, English select walnut stock, splinter forend. Mfg. 1983-1988 in Korea.

12 ga.	$1,795	$1,295	$1,125	$975	$825	$750	$675
20 ga.	$1,995	$1,500	$1,350	$1,100	$900	$800	$700

Last Mfg.'s Sug. Retail was $2,000.

SHOTGUNS: SLIDE ACTION

Grading	100%	98%	95%	90%	80%	70%	60%

BPS MODELS — 12 or 20 ga., gauges are chambered for Mag. ammunition. Invector option (standard for 1985) allows 6 screw-in choke tubes to be interchanged, bottom ejection, double action bars, top tang safety, 5 shot capacity, vent rib, all steel receiver. Mfg. by Miroku 1977-to-date.

Hunting Model — 12 or 20 ga., 3 in. chambers

Mfg.'s Sug. Retail	$443	$355	$295	$250	$225	$200	$185	$175

3½ in. Magnum Model (Hunting & Stalker) — 10 or 12 ga., 3½ in. chamber, 12 ga. 3½ in. chamber was new 1989, 26 (10 ga. only), 28 or 30 in. barrel with Invector chokes and vent. rib, 4 shot mag., 8¾ (12 ga.) or 9½ (10 ga.) lbs.

Mfg.'s Sug. Retail	$573	$495	$440	$410	$375	$340	$310	$290

In 1990, the back-bored Invector plus choke tube system became standard in 12 ga. 3½ in. chamber only.

Stalker Model — 10 or 12 ga., 3½ in. chamber, all metal parts have a dull matte finish, non-glare black synthetic composite stock and forearm. New 1987.

Mfg.'s Sug. Retail	$443	$355	$295	$250	$225	$200	$185	$175

Upland Special — 12 or 20 ga., 22 in. barrel, straight grip stock with Schnabel forearm, 6½ - 7½ lbs. New 1985.

Mfg.'s Sug. Retail	$443	$355	$295	$250	$225	$200	$185	$175

Youth and Ladies Model — 20 ga. only, 22 in. vent rib barrel, straight grip shortened stock, 6¾ lbs. New 1986.

Mfg.'s Sug. Retail	$443	$355	$295	$250	$225	$200	$185	$175

Buck Special — 12 or 20 (disc. 1984) ga., 3 in. chamber, 24 in. barrel with Invector chokes, iron sights. Reintroduced 1988.

Mfg.'s Sug. Retail	$449	$365	$300	$250	$225	$200	$185	$175

3½ in. Buck Special — 10 or 12 ga., 3½ in. chambers, 24 in. barrel. New 1990.

Mfg.'s Sug. Retail	$578	$500	$430	$400	$360	$330	$310	$290

Trap Model — 12 ga., 30 in. barrel. Disc. 1984 but trap barrels were available separately for several years.

	$360	$300	$270	$230	$210	$190	$170

Wild Turkey Federation Commemorative — only 500 manufactured. Disc. 1991.

	$495	$395	$325

Pacific Edition DU — limited mfg., DU serialization, cased.

	$595	$475	$350

The Coastal DU — limited mfg., DU serialization, cased.

	$595	$475	$350

Waterfowl Deluxe — 12 ga. Mag., gold trigger and etching, invector chokes, limited mfg.

	$625	$525	$450

MODEL 12 LIMITED EDITION SERIES

Grade I 20 Ga. — 20 ga. only, 2¾ in. chamber only, reproduction of the famous Winchester Model 12 with slight design improvements, 26 in. VR barrel bored modified, 5 shot mag., high post floating rib, walnut stock and forearm with semi-gloss finish, take down, 7 lbs. 1 oz. 8,000 mfg. in 1988 with inventory depleted 1990.

	$735	$665	$575

Last Mfg.'s Sug. Retail was $735.

Browning Arms Company is limiting manufacture to 8,000 Grade I 20 Ga.'s.

Grade I 28 Ga. — 28 ga. only, similar to Grade I 20 Ga., except in 28 ga., 26 in. VR modified choke barrel.

Mfg.'s Sug. Retail	$772	$772	$700	$595

Browning Arms Company is limiting manufacture to 7,000 Grade I 28 Ga.'s.

Grade V 20 Ga. — similar specifications to Grade I, except has select walnut checkered 22 lines per inch with high gloss finish, extensive game scene engraving including multiple gold inlays. mfg. 1988 only.

	$1,175	$975	$825

Last Mfg.'s Sug. Retail was $1,187.

Grading	100%	98%	95%	90%	80%	70%	60%

Browning Arms Company is limiting manufacture to 4,000 Grade V 20 Ga.'s.

Grade V 28 Ga. — 28 ga. only, similar to Grade V 20 Ga., except in 28 ga., 26 in. VR modified choke barrel.

Mfg.'s Sug. Retail	$1,246	$1,246	$1,050	$895

Browning Arms Company is limiting manufacture to 5,000 Grade V 28 Ga.'s.

MODEL 42 LIMITED EDITION — .410 ga., 3 in. chamber, reproduction of the Winchester Model 42 with slight design improvements, 26 in. VR full choke barrel, select walnut stock, 6 lbs. 12 oz. New in late 1991.

Mfg.'s Sug. Retail	$800	$800	$700	$595

Browning Arms Company is limiting manufacture to 6,000 Grade I Model 42's.

Model 42 Grade 5 — engraving and embellishments similar to the Model 12 Grade 5 in 20 ga. New in late 1991.

Mfg.'s Sug. Retail	$1,360	$1,360	$1,075	$895

Browning Arms Company is limiting manufacture to 6,000 Grade V Model 42's.

LIMITED EDITION SETS INCLUDING BLACK POWDER

BICENTENNIAL 1876-1976 SET — .45-70 Model 78 rifle with specially engraved receiver, silver finish, fancy wood, cased, with engraved knife and medallion, 1,000 sets mfg. in 1976. Issue price — $1,500.

	$1,350	$875	$600

CASED RENAISSANCE SET — one each .25 auto, .380 auto, and Hi-Power Renaissance models in walnut case. Mfg. 1955-1969.

	$3,400	$2,750	$2,100

JONATHAN BROWNING MOUNTAIN RIFLE — 50 cal., percussion, 30 in. octagon barrel, single set trigger, engraved lock plate, select walnut stock, cased with medallion, 1,000 mfg. in 1978. Issue price — $650.

	$650	$500	$440

MOUNTAIN RIFLE — same as Jonathan Browning Mountain Rifle, without Centennial embellishments, not cased. Also in .45 or .54 cal.

	$300	$250	$200	$170	$150	$135	$125

CENTENNIAL O/U RIFLE/SHOTGUN — superposed 20 ga. action fitted with .30-06, 24 in. barrels, folding leaf sight, 26½ in. mod. and full, 20 ga. barrels, auto ejectors, SST, elaborately engraved, gold inlaid, high grade checkered walnut stock, deluxe walnut case, 500 mfg. to commemorate Browning Centennial — 1878-1978.

	$3,500	$2,850	$2,250	$1,950	$1,600	$1,250	$1,000

CENTENNIAL SET — complete Browning set mfg. in 1978, included various models and other accessories.

	$4,995	$2,800	$1,995

1 OF 50 BICENTENNIAL RIFLE — .30-06 cal., Model 78 single shot with 26 in. octagon barrel, includes special engraving by Neil Hartliep (non-factory), extra fine walnut, 4X wide angle scope, special luggage case. 50 mfg. (one for each state) during 1976 only and sold by silent mail order bidding (minimum bid was $3,100 in 1976).

As very few specimens are bought or sold each year, pricing is rather unpredictable. A few specimens have been sold in the $3,250 - $5,000 range recently. Remember, the work on this gun was subcontracted by Centennial Guns (division of Frigon Guns located in Clay Center, KS).

BRUCHET

Manufacturer located in Saint Etienne. Distributed exclusively from 1982-1989 by Wes Gilpin located in Dallas, TX. In 1989, Bruchet was able to get permission to use the

Grading	100%	98%	95%	90%	80%	70%	60%

older Darne trademark and all new manufacture will be entered under the Darne listing.

Paul Bruchet has been manufacturing his shotguns patterned after the Darne action since 1981, following his tenure at Darne as line foreman until 1979 (at which time the Darne plant closed). These new Bruchet Models were designated "A" or "B". All shotguns were totally hand made with approx. 50 guns being mfg. each year.

Since Paul Bruchet was able to retain the Darne trademark in 1989, please refer to the Darne section in this text for all manufacture after 1989 (current prices will also be listed).

MODEL A — 12, 16, 20, 28, or .410 ga., small key opening, ejectors, double triggers only, basically 4 variations (1, 1A, 2, and 2A), wide assortment of customer specified special orders.

Retail values are as follows: Model 1A starts at under $2,000, the Model 2 starts at $3,000, and the Model 2A starts at $3,500. Each additional grade represents more embellishments and better grade of walnut. Magnum chambers can be ordered at a small surcharge. Importation began 1982, values above represent the last published retail prices from 1989.

MODEL B — 12, 16, 20, 28, or .410 ga., large key opening, self-opening (assisted) action, ejectors, double triggers only, basically special ordered to individual customer specifications.

Retail values are as follows: Model B starts at $5,800 and includes deluxe carrying case. Each additional upgrade represents more embellishments and a better grade of walnut. Magnum chambers can be ordered at a small surcharge. Importation began 1982, values above represent the last published retail prices from 1989.

BRYCO ARMS

Manufacturer located in Irvine, CA. Distributed by Jennings Firearms, Inc. located in Carson City, NV.

Pistols listed below are single action design.

BRYCO 38 — .22 LR (disc. 1990), .32 ACP, or .380 ACP cal., semi-auto, 2.8 in. barrel, choice of nickel, chrome, or black teflon finish, alloy receiver, 16 oz. New 1988.

Mfg.'s Sug. Retail	$110	$90	$75	$60	$55	$50	$45	$40

Add $20 for .380 ACP cal.

BRYCO 48 — .22 LR, .32 ACP (disc. 1990), or .380 ACP, semi-auto, black or chrome finish, black grips, 4 in. barrel, 24 oz. New 1989.

Mfg.'s Sug. Retail	$139	$120	$95	$75	$60	$55	$50	$45

BUDISCHOWSKY

Previous manufacturer located in Mt. Clemens, MI.

PISTOLS: SEMI-AUTO

TP-70 — .22 LR, double action, 2½ in. barrel, stainless steel, fixed sights, plastic grips. Mfg. 1973-1977.

	$440	$385	$330

TP-70 — .25 ACP, same as .22 LR, except for caliber. Mfg. 1973-1977.

	$330	$275	$220

Note: In 1977, Norton Arms marketed this pistol. Quality of workmanship is not on a par with the early Budischowsky and values are approx. 35% less.

SEMI-AUTO PISTOL — .223 cal., 11⅝ in. barrel, 20 or 30 shot mag., fixed sights, a novel paramilitary designed type pistol.

	$470	$415	$385	$360	$305	$250	$220

PARAMILITARY DESIGN RIFLE — .223 cal., semi-auto, 18 in. barrel, wooden paramilitary stock.

	$505	$440	$415	$385	$330	$275	$250

Grading	100%	98%	95%	90%	80%	70%	60%

PARAMILITARY DESIGN RIFLE FOLDING STOCK

	$525	$470	$440	$415	$360	$305	$275

BUSHMASTER FIREARMS INC.

Originally manufactured by Gwinn Arms Co., Winston-Salem, N.C. 1972-1974. Previously manufactured by Bushmaster Firearms Inc. located in North Windham, ME. 1974-1990. The Quality Parts Co. gained control in 1990 and the Bushmaster Pistol and Rifle are now discontinued.

Bushmaster pistols and rifles had limited mfg. during the past several years because they are also manufacturing an AR-15 type rifle (see the Quality Parts Co. heading in the "Q" section of this text).

BUSHMASTER PISTOL — .223 Rem., semi-auto., top bolt (older models with aluminum receivers) or side bolt (current mfg.) operation, steel frame (current mfg.), 11½ in. barrel, parkerized finish, adj. sights, wood stock, 5¼ lbs.

	$350	$280	$250	$225	$180	$140	$120

Add $40 for electroless nickel finish (disc. 1988).

This model uses a 30 shot M-16 mag. and the AK-47 gas system.

Last Mfg.'s Sug. Retail was $375.

BUSHMASTER RIFLE — .223 Rem., semi-auto., top bolt (older models with aluminum receivers) or side bolt (current mfg.) operation, steel frame (current mfg.), 18½ in. barrel, parkerized finish, adj. sights, wood stock, 6¼ lbs., base values are for folding stock model.

	$295	$260	$230	$200	$180	$140	$120

Add $40 for electroless nickel finish (disc. 1988).

Add $65 for fixed rock maple wood stock.

This model uses a 30 shot M-16 mag. and the AK-47 gas system.

Last Mfg.'s Sug. Retail was $350.

Rifle Combination System — includes rifle with both metal folding stock and wood stock with pistol grip.

	$400	$370	$330	$310	$275	$235	$200

Last Mfg.'s Sug. Retail was $450.

NOTES

CETME

Grading	100%	98%	95%	90%	80%	70%	60%

AUTOLOADING RIFLE — .308 cal., 17¾ in. barrel, gas operated, roller cam action, similar to HK-91 in appearance, wood military style stock, aperture rear sight.

	$715	$660	$605	$550	$440	$385	$330

C Z

Previously manufactured in Strakonice, Czechoslovakia, 1921 to approx. 1958.

PISTOLS: SEMI-AUTO

"DUO" POCKET AUTOMATIC — .25 auto, 6 shot, 2⅛ in. barrel, fixed sights, blue or nickel, plastic grips. Mfg. 1926-present (current Z pistol by Brno).

	$200	$185	$170	$150	$125	$100	$75

Add 40% for WWII years.

This model was manufactured by Dushek and is the same as the Z pistol equivalent by Brno.

CZ 22 — .380 cal., derived from Mauser Nickle Pistol and manufactured under license from Mauser. Mfg. 1923 only.

	$400	$350	$320	$300	$275	$235	$200

CZ 24 — .380 cal.

Standard Frame — 8 shot mag. Over 175,000 mfg. 1924-38. Over half issued to Czech Army. Same general design as CZ 22 except no gap between trigger and frame. Add $50 if Nazi proofed. Production continued to 1941.

	$350	$320	$290	$260	$230	$195	$150

A small number were Kriegsmarine proofed. Add 200%. Beware of counterfeit markings.

Long Frame — 9 shot mag.

	$600	$550	$500	$450	$375	$300	$225

Add $750 if fit with stock slot (either standard frame or long frame).

CZ 27 — .32 cal.

"CESKA" Slide Legend Variation — slanted slide grooves, high polish. Ser. range 16,000-21,500

	100%	98%	95%	90%	80%	70%	60%
Prewar Commercial	$450	$400	$350	$300	$250	$200	$150
DR Proofed	$450	$400	$350	$300	$250	$200	$150
Nazi Proofed	$450	$400	$350	$300	$250	$200	$150

"BOHMISCHE" Slide Legend Variation — vertical slide grooves, high or medium polish. Ser. range 21,500-261,000. Nazi proofed.

	$225	$200	$175	$150	$135	$120	$110

Nazi Police pistols dated 1941, 1942, or 1943 marked with Eagle/K on left trigger guard web, add 125% for 1941 date, add 100% for 1942 and 1943 date.

A small number were Kriegsmarine proofed. Add 200%. Beware of counterfeit markings.

"fnh" Slide Legend Variation — Medium polish or phosphate. Ser. range 261,000-476,000.

	$200	$175	$150	$125	$100	$85	$70

"Phosphate" finish — a small number of phosphate pistols were fit with an extended barrel for silencer attachment. Usually in 450,000-460,000 Ser. range.

	$550	$500	$450	$400	$375	$350	$325

Post WWII mfg. — dated 1945, 1946, 1947, 1948, 1949, 1950, 1951. These models will have the "NARODNI PODNIK" inscription on slide.

Currently, these variations average $250 in 95%+ condition while reworks (very common) average under $200.

Grading	100%	98%	95%	90%	80%	70%	60%

VZ 38 DOUBLE ACTION AUTOMATIC — .380 auto, 9 shot, double action only, 4⅝ in. barrel, fixed sights, blue, plastic grips. Mfg. 1938-1939.

	$350	$300	$250	$200	$170	$140	$125

For Waffenampt proofed (E/WaA76 on barrel and left frame), usually phosphate finished and either unnumbered or in B291,000-B293,000 Ser. range — add $1,000.

Changed to Model 39T after 1939.

VZ 38 "BULGARIAN CONTRACT" — .380 auto, 9 shot, single or double action, prominent safety on left frame. Usually in 420,000-423,000 range.

	$1,350	$1,100	$900	$750	$600	$500	$400

MODEL 1945 DOUBLE ACTION AUTOMATIC — .25 auto, 8 shot, 2½ in. barrel, fixed sights, blue, plastic grips. Double action only. Mfg. between 1945-1952.

	$200	$175	$165	$150	$140	$130	$120

NEW MODEL .006 DOUBLE ACTION AUTOMATIC — .32 auto, 8 shot, 3⅜ in. barrel, fixed sight, blue, plastic grips, called VZ-50 in Czechoslovakia, used by National Police.

	$500	$425	$350	$300	$265	$230	$190

CZ HANDGUNS: CURRENT MFG.

Note: modern commercial CZ handguns are located in the Brno section of this book.

RIFLES: MILITARY

G 33-40 — 8mm, mfg. between 1940-42, most have been sporterized.

	$350	$295	$260	$230	$200	$175	$150

This model is Brno mfg., not CZ.

CZ RIFLES: CURRENT MFG.

Note: modern commercial Czeskoslovenska rifles are located in the Brno section of this book.

CABANAS

Manufactured by Industrias Cabanas, S.A. in Aguilas, Mexico. Distributed and retailed by Mandall Shooting Supplies Inc. located in Scottsdale, AZ.

.22 BLANK POWERED RIFLE — shoots oversize .177 pellets/BB's powered by .22 blanks, 1,150 fps, single shot bolt action operation, iron sights, models vary in barrel lengths, stock configurations, etc. Transfer requires FFL.

Mini-82 Youth Pony

Mfg.'s Sug. Retail	$70	$70	$65	$55	$50	$45	$40	$35

R-83 Larger Youth

Mfg.'s Sug. Retail	$80	$80	$75	$65	$55	$45	$40	$35

Safari

	$100	$90	$80	$70	$60	$50	$40

Last Mfg.'s Sug. Retail was $100 (disc. 1990).

Varmint

	$100	$90	$80	$70	$60	$50	$40

Espronceda IV

Mfg.'s Sug. Retail	$135	$120	$110	$100	$90	$80	$70	$60

Leyre

Mfg.'s Sug. Retail	$150	$150	$120	$110	$100	$90	$80	$70

Master — top-of-the-line model, 19⅔ in. barrel, adj. iron sights. Disc. 1990.

	$135	$120	$110	$100	$90	$80	$70

Blanks (6mm) and BB's (4.5mm) are available at $3.50 for 50 of each.

Last Mfg.'s Sug. Retail was $150.

Phaser — features thumb hole stock with Monte Carlo cheek piece and finger contoured pistol grip, automatic latch, barrel weight compensator. Importation began 1991.

Mfg.'s Sug. Retail	$160	$160	$125	$110	$100	$90	$80	$70

Grading	100%	98%	95%	90%	80%	70%	60%

CABELA'S INC.
Sporting Goods Dealer located in Sidney, NB.

SHOTGUNS: SIDE BY SIDE

HEMINGWAY MODEL — mfg. for Cabela's by V. Bernardelli located in Italy, ST, ejectors.

Mfg.'s Sug. Retail	$975	$925	$775	$700	$640	$575	$525	$465

AYA GRADE II CUSTOM — mfg. for Cabela's by AYA located in Eibar, Spain, ST, ejectors, similar to AYA Model II with Model 53 engraving and trim. Disc. and sold out.

	$1,295	$1,150	$895	$775	$700	$640	$575

CALICO
Manufacturer located in Bakersfield, CA.

Calico also makes select-fire machine gun pistols and carbines that are mfg. for military or law enforcement use only. These models do not appear in this publication.

A complete line of accessories is available for all Calico carbines and pistols.

CARBINES

M-100 — .22 LR, semi-auto carbine, paramilitary design with folding butt stock, 100 shot helical feed mag., alloy frame, ambidextrous safety, 16.1 shrouded barrel with flash suppressor/muzzle brake, 4.2 lbs. empty. New 1986.

Mfg.'s Sug. Retail	$345	$285	$240	$210	$190	$175	$160	$150

M-101 — similar to M-100, except has synthetic buttstock. New 1991.

Mfg.'s Sug. Retail	$350	$290	$245	$215	$190	$175	$160	$150

M-105 SPORTER — similar to M-100, except has walnut distinctively styled butt stock and forend, 4¾ lbs. empty. New 1989.

Mfg.'s Sug. Retail	$374	$310	$250	$225	$200	$175	$160	$150

M-106 — same as M-105 Sporter, except includes folding stock kit. Mfg. 1990 only.

	$325	$275	$235	$210	$180	$160	$150

Last Mfg.'s Sug. Retail was $376.

MODEL M-900 — 9mm Para., retarded blowback action, paramilitary design with folding butt stock, cast aluminum receiver with stainless steel bolt, static cocking handle, 16 in. barrel, fixed rear sight with adj. post front, 50 (standard) or 100 shot helical feed mag., ambidextrous safety, black polymer pistol grip and forend, 3.7 lbs. empty. Mfg. 1989- 1990.

	$495	$395	$340	$320	$300	$285	$260

Last Mfg.'s Sug. Retail was $582.

M-951 TACTICAL CARBINE — 9mm Para., 16.1 in. barrel, similar appearance to M-900 Carbine, except has muzzle brake and extra pistol grip on front of forearm, 4¾ lbs. New 1990.

Mfg.'s Sug. Retail	$676	$580	$460	$375	$325	$300	$285	$270

M-951S — similar to M-951, except has synthetic buttstock. New 1991.

Mfg.'s Sug. Retail	$681	$585	$460	$375	$325	$300	$285	$270

PISTOLS: SEMI-AUTO

M-110 — .22 LR, same action as M-100 Carbine, 6 in. barrel with muzzle brake, 100 round helical feed mag., includes notched rear sight and adj. windage front sight, 10½ in. sight radius, ambidextrous safety, pistol grip storage compartment, 2.21 lbs. empty. New 1989.

Mfg.'s Sug. Retail	$244	$220	$195	$175	$160	$150	$140	$130

M-950 — 9mm Para., same operating mechanism as the M-900 Carbine, 6 in. barrel, 50 (standard) or 100 shot helical feed mag., 2¼ lbs. empty. New 1989.

Mfg.'s Sug. Retail	$597	$500	$375	$320	$300	$285	$270	$255

Many accessories are also available for this model.

Grading	100%	98%	95%	90%	80%	70%	60%

CAMEX-BLASER USA, INC.
Previous importer/distributor of Blaser Jagwaffen Gmbh rifles.

Previously imported Camex-Blaser rifles can be located in the Blaser section in this text.

CARTRIDGE FIREARMS
Unknown maker.

Many models of pistols, rifles, and shotguns — antique and modern. Many poor quality copies in addition to a few high quality, nicely engraved guns. Most of these firearms that are average quality, trade in the $100-$300 area. Engraved models can add as much as 150%. High mfg.

CASARTELLI, CARLO
Manufactured in Brescia, Italy. Imported and distributed by New England Arms Co. located in Kittery Point, ME.

> Casartelli rifles and shotguns are available through special order only. Details can be obtained by writing the above importer/distributor.

RIFLES

AFRICA MODEL — BOLT ACTION — various heavy and Mag. cal.'s, action is square B ridge type Mauser, full coverage game scene engraving appropriate to caliber, takedown, limited production.

Mfg.'s Sug. Retail	$10,650	$10,650	$9,100	$6,700	$5,900	$5,300	$4,700	$4,100

SAFARI MODEL — BOLT ACTION — standard cal.'s, regular Mauser action, full coverage game scene engraving, limited production.

Mfg.'s Sug. Retail	$8,250	$8,250	$6,250	$5,900	$5,250	$4,950	$4,150	$3,650

KENYA — DOUBLE RIFLE — most standard and Mag. cal.'s, sidelock action, elaborate game scene and/or scroll engraving, limited production.

Mfg.'s Sug. Retail	$34,500	$34,500	$23,750	$20,500	$18,000	$14,750	$12,000	$9,950

SHOTGUNS

SIDELOCK MODEL — various ga.'s, elaborate game scene and/or scroll engraving, limited production.

Mfg.'s Sug. Retail	$17,000	$17,000	$11,500	$9,200	$7,900	$6,500	$5,200	$4,250

CASPIAN ARMS LTD.
Current manufacturer located in Hardwick, VT.

> Besides manufacturing limited quantities of pistols (listed below), Caspian Arms also fabricates both steel and stainless steel high quality frames and related small parts for the Colt Government Model 1911-A1. Caspian Arms frames are also used by Glades Gun Works for their finished pistols. Custom guns may also be ordered on a limited basis by contacting Caspian Arms Ltd. directly.

GOVERNMENT MODEL — .45 ACP, similar to Colt Model 1911, available in either stainless steel or regular steel, specifications similar to Colt Model 1911, extra slides also available in .38 Super or 9mm Para., checkered walnut grips, high profile sights, adj. trigger. Mfg. 1986-1989.

	$550	$485	$425	$390	$365	$345	$325

Last Mfg.'s Sug. Retail was $550.

Vietnam Commemorative — .45 ACP, total production is 1,000, hand engraved by J.J. Adams, nickel plated, branch service medallion installed in grips. Mfg. began 1986, limited quantities remain.

Mfg.'s Sug. Retail	$1,200	$1,200	$995	$795

Add $350 for gold plating.

Add $200 for serial numbers below RVN100.

This Vietnam Commemorative is also available in 24Kt. gold hand inlay edition for $14,000 — very limited production.

Grading	100%	98%	95%	90%	80%	70%	60%

MODEL 110 — .38 Super (limited) or .45 ACP, similar to Colt Model 1911, stainless steel barrel, extended safety, adj. National Match trigger, Combat Commander hammer, Bo-Mar low mount sights, beavertail grip safety, throated and polished feed ramp, hand fitted slide, tuned extractor, checkered front strap and trigger guard, hand checkered stocks, chrome receiver with matte blue slide. Introduced in mid-1988, limited mfg.

	100%	98%	95%	90%	80%	70%	60%
Mfg.'s Sug. Retail	$899	$899	$800	$740	$675	$600	$550	$495

This model is also available in .38 Super with limited availability.

CENTURY GUN DISTRIBUTING, INC.
Manufactured by Century Manufacturing, Inc. located in Greenfield, IN. Distributed By Century Gun Distributing Inc., Also Located In Greenfield, IN.

REVOLVERS
Less than 1,200 Model 100's have been manufactured since 1976. Values below are for .45-70 cal. Other calibers are priced from $1,500 on up.

MODEL 100 — .30-30 (new 1987), .375 Win. (new 1986) and .444 Marlin (new 1986), .45-70, or .50-70 Gov't (new 1987) cal., single action 6 shot, manganese bronze frame, steel cylinder, 6½, 8, 10, or 12 in. round barrel, crossbolt safety with unique hammer safety, adj. sights, walnut grips.

	100%	98%	95%	90%	80%	70%	60%
Mfg.'s Sug. Retail	$850	$785	$685	$595	$550	$495	$450	$395

Limited quantities of this revolver manufactured from stainless steel will be available in late 1991. Price is POR.

This model was originally made in Evansville, IN and production was halted at ser. no. 524. The second series is being made in Greenfield, IN with limited production resuming in 1986. Earlier handmade "Evansville" Model 100's (disc.) are currently selling for between $2,500-$3,500, depending on the region.

CENTURY INTERNATIONAL ARMS, INC.
Importers and distributors located in St. Albans, VT.

Century Arms imports a variety of used military rifles and pistols, including various Mauser rifle contract models, French Lebels and MAS models, Mannlichers, F.N. Model 49's, Lee Enfields, Hakims, Mosin-Nagants, Egyptian Rashid's, Chinese SKS-56's, arsenal refinished M-1 carbines/Garands and various WWI and WWII used military pistols (including Mauser Broomhandles, Argentine mfg. M1911's, and French PA 35's). Because most of these items range in the $95-$200 price range, individual listings are not listed in this text. Most of these models are in good to like new condition overall. In addition, surplus and currently manufactured ammunitions are available at very competitive prices. Generally these models offer good values to the shooter and a few are collectible.

PISTOLS

HI-POWER — 9mm Para., copy of the FN Browning Hi-Power, mfg. in Argentina by Fabrica Militar under license from FN, matte finish, 13 shot mag., 4.6 in barrel, 32 oz. Importation began 1991.

	100%	98%	95%	90%	80%	70%	60%
No Mfg.'s Retail		$330	$275	$240	$210	$185	$160	$145

PARKER PISTOL — 10mm or .45 ACP cal., design similar to Colt M1911, mfg. by Wyoming Arms Inc., stainless steel fabrication, ribbed synthetic grips, 7 shot mag., 5 in. barrel. New 1991.

	100%	98%	95%	90%	80%	70%	60%
No Mfg.'s Retail		$330	$275	$240	$210	$185	$160	$145

RIFLES

CBC MODEL N66 — .22 LR, semi-auto design patterned after the Remington Nylon 66, 14 shot tube mag., 19½ in. barrel. Importation began 1989.

	100%	98%	95%	90%	80%	70%	60%
No Mfg.'s Retail		$110	$85	$75	$65	$60	$55	$50

Grading	100%	98%	95%	90%	80%	70%	60%

NORINCO JW-8 — .22 LR, bolt action, 5 shot mag., 23 in. barrel, sling swivels. Importation began 1989.

No Mfg.'s Retail	$100	$75	$65	$60	$55	$50	$45

CENTURION P14 SPORTER — .300 Win. Mag., .303 British, or 7mm Rem. Mag. (disc.) cal., P-14 action with sporterized stock and 24 in. barrel, checkered beechwood stock, tapped and drilled for scope mounts. New 1987.

No Mfg.'s Retail	$210	$165	$140	$130	$120	$110	$100

Add $30 for .300 Win. Mag. cal.

MAS 36 SPORTER — 7.5mm, Mas 36 action with shorter barrel, military stock has been sporterized, reblued metal, positive safety. Importation disc.

	$135	$115	$95	$85	$80	$75	$70

SWEDISH CONTRACT M38 — 6.5 X 55mm, Swedish Mauser M38 with new Monte Carlo stock, 24 in. barrel, 5 shot fixed mag.

No Mfg.'s Retail	$195	$150	$135	$125	$115	$105	$95

ENFIELD SPORTER NO. 4 — .303 British, new checkered stock with Monte Carlo cheek piece, 25.2 in. barrel, 10 shot detach. mag.

No. Mfg.'s Retail	$165	$135	$125	$115	$105	$95	$90

JUNGLE SPORTER NO. 5 — .303 British, 20.5 in.barrel with flash eliminator, new checkered Monte Carlo stock and forearm, detach. mag. Importation disc.

	$190	$150	$135	$125	$115	$105	$95

MAS .223 — .223 cal., civilian version of the FAMAS 5.56mm paramilitary design rifle, made by Giat in France, switchable ejection port, rubber covered cheek piece, bullpup configuration, protected sights, with bipod, 20 shot mag. Imported 1986-89.

	$2,250	$1,850	$1,600	$1,400	$1,200	$1,000	$850

This model has been banned from domestic importation due to 1989 Federal legislation.

M-1 GARAND — .30-06, 24 in. barrel, arsenal repaired stocks, good to very good condition. Importation disc.

	$350	$275	$250	$235	$215	$200	$190

CHAMPLIN FIREARMS, INC.

Custom manufacturer/gunsmith located in Enid, OK. Champlin Firearms was established In 1966.

Champlin Firearms, Inc. manufactures handcrafted rifles built around a patented bolt action of their own design and manufacture. Most guns are built per individual customer order and specifications. Values will vary greatly depending on the configuration, desirability, and special order specifications. All Champlin rifles are built along classic lines with best quality wood and exemplary workmanship. They have been used successfully on safaris and have shot dangerous game throughout the world.

Champlin Firearms, Inc. also inventories a wide selection of high grade, top quality shotguns and rifles (especially top trademark doubles and bolt actions). Contact George Caswell (owner) directly for a current listing. Additional services include a complete gunsmithing service for all grades of English double rifles and shotguns. Custom stocks are also built to individual customer specifications. All double rifles are test fired and checked thoroughly upon completion of manufacture or repair. Again, Champlin Firearms should be contacted for consultation and quotation regarding this additional work.

BOLT ACTION RIFLE — standard, all calibers, round or octagon barrel, adj. trigger, each rifle is built to customer specifications. Values below represent base gun with standard wood, no options, and no engraving.

Mfg.'s Sug. Retail	$8,500	$8,500	$8,000	$7,000	$6,750	$6,000	$5,250	$4,500

Many additional special order options are available on this model and Champlin Firearms should be contacted directly for price quotations.

Grading	100%	98%	95%	90%	80%	70%	60%

CHAPUIS ARMES

Manufacturer located in St. Bonnet Le Chateau, France. Currently imported by Armes De Chasse located in Chadds Ford, PA 19317.

Chapuis rifles and shotguns are manufactured on a limited basis. Most of their emphasis is on high quality double rifles and shotguns. For further information regarding this respected French trademark, please contact the importer listed above. The below listed models are imported exclusively by Armes de Chasse.

RIFLES/COMBINATION GUNS

EXPRESS PROGRESS AGEX JUNGLE SxS DOUBLE RIFLE — .375 H&H cal., boxlock action, special reinforced receiver with double underbites, 25½ in. barrels, fine English scroll engraving, ejectors, select French walnut with compartment in pistol grip cap.

Mfg.'s Sug. Retail	$10,000	$10,000	$8,450	$6,750	$5,600	$4,775	$4,100	$3,575

EXPRESS PROGRESS AGEX SAVANNA SxS DOUBLE RIFLE — deluxe version of the Agex Jungle, except has hand engraved leaves on action sides and Cape Buffalo head on floorplate of action.

Mfg.'s Sug. Retail	$11,000	$11,000	$9,700	$8,250	$6,850	$5,500	$4,600	$3,850

RG EXPRESS MODEL SXS DOUBLE RIFLE — 7 X 65R, 8 X 57JRS, 9.3 X 74R, or .375 H&H, double rifle, ejectors, boxlock action, 23.6 in. barrels, deluxe checkered walnut stock with cheek piece, full line of options are available, 7 lbs. 6 oz. Importation began 1989.

Mfg.'s Sug. Retail	$7,000	$7,000	$6,500	$5,500	$4,775	$4,100	$3,575	$3,100

Add $1,069 for REXPress option.

RGP CAPE GUN COMBINATION — 12 or 20 ga., choice of 7 x 65R, 8 x 57JRS, or 9.3 x 74R cal.

Mfg.'s Sug. Retail	$4,511	$4,511	$3,375	$2,800	$2,300	$1,950	$1,600	$1,400

RG PROGRESS SHOTGUN/COMBINATION — 12, 16, 20 ga. or rifled slug, rifled barrel option available as well as combination guns. Importation began 1989.

Mfg.'s Sug. Retail	$3,000	$3,000	$2,500	$2,100	$1,800	$1,600	$1,400	$1,200

SHOTGUNS: SxS

On both Chapuis SxS and O/U shotguns, the following options are available: hand-rubbed oil finish - add $193, engraved long trigger guard tang - add $332, hand-checkered Brazilian rosewood buttplate - add $112, recoil pad - add $235. Also, a variety of other special order options is available by contacting the importer directly.

RG PROGRESS — 12 or 20 ga., boxlock action with notched action zone, coin finished receiver, 22, 23.6, 26.8, 27.6, or 31.5 in. barrels, ejectors, raised solid rib, VR or ultra-light rib, deluxe checkered walnut stock and forearm, 5-10 lbs. depending on gauge.

Mfg.'s Sug. Retail	$3,149	$3,149	$2,600	$2,100	$1,800	$1,600	$1,400	$1,200

Add $331 for 20 ga. Mag.

R PROGRESS — 12 or 20 ga., features flat tapered English hunting rib, boxlock action.

Mfg.'s Sug. Retail	$4,065	$4,065	$3,250	$2,600	$2,100	$1,850	$1,550	$1,350

Add $258 for 20 ga. Mag.

SIDE-BY-SIDE MODEL — 12, 16, or 20 ga., boxlock action with notched action zone, coin finished receiver, 22, 23.6, 26.8, 27.6, or 31.5 in. barrels, ejectors, raised solid rib, VR, or ultra-light rib, deluxe checkered walnut stock and forearm, 5-8 lbs. depending on gauge.

Mfg.'s Sug. Retail	$3,500	$3,500	$2,850	$2,300	$1,950	$1,700	$1,400	$1,200

Various options can add $1,000 to the retail price listed above.

SHOTGUNS: O/U

UG ALFA GRADE I — 12 ga., boxlock action, extractors, approx. 6½ lbs.

Mfg.'s Sug. Retail	$2,564	$2,564	$2,150	$1,850	$1,575	$1,275	$1,000	$750

Grading	100%	98%	95%	90%	80%	70%	60%

RG ALFA GRADE II — 12 or 16 ga., ejectors, English style engraving.

Mfg.'s Sug. Retail	$3,149	$3,149	$2,600	$2,100	$1,800	$1,600	$1,400	$1,200

Add $331 for 20 ga. Mag.

R ALFA GRADE III — 12 or 20 ga., similar to RG Alfa Grade II, except has deluxe French walnut stock and forearm.

Mfg.'s Sug. Retail	$4,063	$4,063	$3,250	$2,600	$2,100	$1,850	$1,550	$1,350

Add $260 for 20 ga. Mag.

OVER & UNDER MODEL —12, 16, or 20 ga., boxlock action with notched action zone, coin finished receiver, 22, 23.6, 26.8, 27.6, or 31.5 in. barrels, ejectors, raised solid rib, VR, or ultra-light rib, deluxe checkered walnut stock and forearm, 5-8 lbs. depending on gauge.

Mfg.'s Sug. Retail	$3,500	$3,500	$2,850	$2,300	$1,950	$1,700	$1,400	$1,200

Various options can add $1,000 to the retail price listed above.

CHAPUIS, P. ARMES ET FILS
Manufacturer located in Saint-Bonnet le Chateau, France.

Paul Chapuis specializes in custom order rifles and shotguns. Currently, this manufacturer has no U.S. importer and should be contacted directly (see Trademark Index) for more model information and current pricing. This is a different company than Chapuis Armes.

CHARLIN ARMS
Previously manufactured in France.

Charlin Arms previously made shotguns which were patterned after Darne firearms. Typically, they are very high quality and values seem to approximate the Darne guns. Once you have determined the comparable model in Darne, please refer to the Darne section in this book.

CHARLES DALY
See Daly, Charles.

CHARTER ARMS
Manufacturer located in Stratford, CT.

As this edition goes to press, Charter Arms is in the process of refinancing. Even though the models below are listed as current mfg., the production of all models is discontinued at this time.

REVOLVERS: DOUBLE ACTION
All Charter Arms revolvers have a hammer block safety system, 8 groove rifling, unbreakable beryllium copper firing pin, triple safety features, no sideplate, steel frames, and lifetime warranty to the original owner.

BONNIE & CLYDE SET — .32 H&R Mag. (Bonnie) and .38 Spl. (Clyde), matched pair, 6 shot, 2½ in. fully shrouded barrel, wood laminate grips (color coordinated), blued finish, pistols individually marked Bonnie or Clyde on barrels, supplied with gun rugs. New 1989.

No Mfg.'s Retail	$535	$395	$360	$330	$295	$260	$240

PATHFINDER — .22 LR or .22 Mag. (disc. 1989), 6 shot, 2, 3, or 6 (disc. 1985) in. barrels, round butt, adj. sights, walnut grips, wide trigger and spur hammer.

No Mfg.'s Retail	$225	$165	$150	$140	$130	$120	$110

Pathfinder — Square Butt — .22 LR or 22 Mag. (disc. 1989), 6 in. barrel, square butt, otherwise same as Pathfinder.

No Mfg.'s Retail	$230	$175	$145	$130	$120	$105	$90

Pathfinder Stainless — stainless variation, .22 LR or .22 Mag. (disc. 1989), 3½ in. shrouded barrel.

No Mfg.'s Retail	$290	$225	$190	$175

Grading	100%	98%	95%	90%	80%	70%	60%

UNDERCOVER — .32 S&W (disc. 1989) or .38 Spl. cal., 5 shot in .38 Spl., 6 shot in .32 S&W, 2 (.38 Spl.) or 3 in. barrel, wide trigger and spur hammer, fixed sights, .38 Spl. can also be ordered with pocket hammer.

No Mfg.'s Retail	$216	$155	$145	$135	$125	$115	$100

Undercover Stainless — 2 in. shrouded barrel only.

No Mfg.'s Retail	$273	$195	$180	$165			

UNDERCOVERETTE — same as Undercover, in .32 S&W long, 6 shot, 2 in. barrel, blue. Disc.

	$155	$140	$110	$100	$90	$70	$55

BULLDOG — .44 Spl., 5 shot, 2½ or 3 (disc. 1988) in. barrels, wide trigger and spur or pocket hammer, checkered bulldog grips (walnut or neoprene).

No Mfg.'s Retail	$232	$160	$145	$130	$120	$110	$105

Bulldog Stainless — 2½ in. bull or 3 (disc. 1989) in. regular barrel.

No Mfg.'s Retail	$286	$205	$180	$160			

Target Bulldog — .357 Mag. or .44 Spl. cal., 5 shot, 4 in. shrouded barrel, adj. sights, square butt only, blued finish. Mfg. 1986-1988.

	$225	$180	$165	$150	$130	$115	$100

Subtract $10 for .357 Mag. cal.
Last Mfg.'s Sug. Retail was $255.

Target Bulldog Stainless — 9mm Federal, .357 Mag. or .44 Spl. cal., 5 shot, 5½ in. shrouded VR barrel, adj. sights, square butt target grips only, matte finished, 28 oz. New 1989.

No Mfg.'s Retail	$375	$265	$235	$200			

BULLDOG PUG — .44 Spl., 5 shot, 2½ in. shrouded barrel, fixed sights, walnut or neoprene grips. New 1986.

No Mfg.'s Retail	$250	$185	$160	$145	$130	$115	$100

Bulldog Pug Stainless — 2½ in. shrouded barrel. New 1987.

No Mfg.'s Retail	$300	$210	$175	$160			

BULLDOG TRACKER — .357 Mag. (.38 Spl.), 5 shot, 2½, 4 (disc. 1989), and 6 (disc. 1989) in. bull barrels, adj. sights, blue only, checkered bulldog grips, square butt on 4 or 6 in. barrel only. Disc. 1986 - reintroduced 1989.

No Mfg.'s Retail	$250	$185	$160	$145	$130	$115	$100

POLICE BULLDOG — .32 H&R Mag., .38 Spl. or .44 Spl. cal., 5 (.44 Spl. only) or 6 shot, fixed sights, blue only, 3½ or 4 in. barrel, Neoprene grips or square butt (.44 Spl. only).

No Mfg.'s Retail	$234	$175	$145	$130	$120	$110	$105

Add $20 for either .44 Spl. cal or 3½ in. shrouded barrel.

Stainless Police Bulldog — .32 Mag., .357 Mag. (new 1989), .38 Spl. (disc. 1988 - reintroduced 1990) or .44 Spl. (new 1989), 5 (.357 Mag. or .44 Spl.) or 6 (.32 Mag. or .38 Spl.) shot, square butt, 3½ or 4 in. shrouded barrel. New 1987.

No Mfg.'s Retail	$287	$205	$180	$160			

Add $20 for .357 Mag. or .44 Special cal.
Neoprene grips are standard on these models except for the .357 Mag. (square butt).

POLICE UNDERCOVER — .32 H&R Mag. or .38 Spl. cal., 6 shot, spur or pocket hammer, 2 in. shrouded barrel, checkered walnut grips, fixed sights, blue only.

No Mfg.'s Retail	$250	$185	$160	$145	$130	$115	$100

Stainless Police Undercover — similar to Police Undercover.

No Mfg.'s Retail	$280	$205	$180	$160			

OFF DUTY — .22 LR (new 1990) or .38 Spl. cal., 5 (.38 Spl.) or 6 (.22 LR) shot, 2 in. barrel, fixed sights, blue only, matte black finish.

No Mfg.'s Retail	$184	$125	$115	$105	$100	$95	$90

Stainless Off Duty — similar to Off Duty.

No Mfg.'s Retail	$240	$185	$160	$145			

Grading	100%	98%	95%	90%	80%	70%	60%

PIT BULL — 9mm Federal, .357 Mag. (disc. 1989), or .38 Spl. (disc. 1989) cal., 5 shot, 2½, 3½, or 4 (disc. 1989) in. full shrouded barrel, Neoprene grips, approx. 26 oz. New 1989.

No Mfg.'s Retail	$286	$205	$180	$160	$140	$125	$115

Stainless Pit Bull — 2½ or 3½ in. shrouded barrel.

No Mfg.'s Retail	$312	$225	$190	$165			

PISTOLS: SEMI-AUTO

MODEL 40 — .22 LR only, double action semi-auto., 3.3 in. barrel, 8 shot mag., 21½ oz., fixed sights, stainless steel. Mfg. 1984-86.

	$265	$240	$220				

Last Mfg.'s Sug. Retail was $319.

MODEL 79K — .32 or .380 ACP cal., double action semi-auto., 3.6 in. barrel, 7 shot mag., 24½ oz., fixed sights, stainless steel. Mfg. 1984-86.

	$325	$300	$280				

Last Mfg.'s Sug. Retail was $390.

EXPLORER II & S II PISTOL — .22 LR, semi-auto survival pistol, barrel unscrews, 8 shot mag., black, gold (disc.), silvertone, or camouflage finish, 6, 8, or 10 in. barrels, simulated walnut grips. Disc. 1986.

	$90	$80	$70	$60	$55	$50	$45

Last Mfg.'s Sug. Retail was $109.

This model uses a modified AR-7 action.

Manufacture of this model is by Survival Arms located in Cocoa, FL.

TARGET PISTOLS

MODEL 42T (COMPETITION II TARGET) — .22 LR only, single action, 5.9 in. barrel, target model with checkered walnut grips, adj. sights, blue finish only. Mfg. 1984-1985 only.

	$490	$450	$395	$350	$300	$260	$220

Last Mfg.'s Sug. Retail was $599.

RIFLES

AR-7 EXPLORER RIFLE — .22 LR cal., takedown, barreled action stores in Cycolac sythetic stock, 8 shot mag., adj. sights, 16 in. barrel, black finish on AR-7, silvertone on AR-7S. Camouflage finish new 1986 (AR-7C).

No Mfg.'s Retail	$146	$115	$100	$85	$75	$65	$550

Manufacture of this model is by Survival Arms located in Cocoa, FL.

CHINESE FIREARMS

Most Chinese firearms for U.S. export are currently being manufactured by two companies: Poly Technologies, Inc. and Norinco. Poly Technologies, Inc. is currently being imported by Keng's Firearms Specialty located in Riverdale, GA and is distributed by Ptk International, Inc. in Atlanta, GA. Norinco is imported and distributed by China Sports, Inc. located in Dallas, TX. Please refer to the Poly Technologies, Inc. and Norinco sections in this text to find out more about these firearms. In addition to these two trademarks, other Chinese models have been manufactured under various subcontracts with the Chinese Arsenals. These guns (typically aks copies) are generally unmarked and quality can vary greatly.

CHIPMUNK MANUFACTURING INC.

Previous manufacturer located in Medford, OR until 1990.

CHIPMUNK SINGLE SHOT RIFLE — .22 LR or .22 Mag. (disc. 1987) cal., manually cocked single shot, 16⅛ in. barrel, iron sights (adj. aperture rear), 30 in. overall length, 2½ lbs.

	$125	$110	$90	$80	$70	$60	$50

Last Mfg.'s Sug. Retail was $130.

Grading	100%	98%	95%	90%	80%	70%	60%

Deluxe Rifle — similar to standard rifle, except has deluxe hand checkered walnut. New 1987.

| | $165 | $145 | $125 | $110 | $85 | $70 | $60 |

Last Mfg.'s Sug. Retail was $180.

SILHOUETTE PISTOL — .22 LR, bolt action design with 14⅞ in. barrel, iron sights, rear grip walnut stock. New 1987.

| | $135 | $115 | $95 | $80 | $70 | $60 | $50 |

Last Mfg.'s Sug. Retail was $150.

CHURCHILL, E.J., (GUNMAKERS) LTD.

Previously manufactured in London, England. The company underwent various trading forms until Churchill, Atkin, Grant & Lang Ltd. closed in 1981. Currently, E.J. Churchill side by side shotguns are manufactured in Surrey, England and while they are not imported into the U.S., these models are shown with U.S. prices if purchased in England. Prices are subject to fluctuating U.S. dollar.

Churchill Guns are among the world's finest with many custom features. We will list both discontinued and current models and approximate values, but strongly urge competent appraisal if purchase or sale is contemplated.

Prices could differ from values shown below because of the fluctuating U.S. dollar.

SHOTGUNS AND RIFLES

All below models were built or finished to customer specifications pertaining to choking, chambers, barrel lengths, stock measurements, weight, engraving patterns. Standardized patterns did exist, however, for each model. The "XXV" designation referred to the 25 in. barrel length which was a Churchill specialty and was also a registered trademark.

PREMIER QUALITY SXS — all ga.'s, best quality, easy opening or standard opening, 25, 28, 30, or 32 in. barrels, any choke, sidelock, auto ejectors, standard with double triggers, engraved, checkered, straight or pistol grip stock. Also mfg. in some double rifles. Disc.

| | $17,000 | $15,000 | $12,000 | $10,000 | $9,000 | $7,500 | $6,500 |

20 ga. — add 20%.
28 ga. — add 40%.
SST — add $1,000.
16 ga. — deduct 10%.
Double rifle — add 35%.

Premier Grade — 12 ga. only, sidelock, assisted opening, limited current mfg.

| Mfg.'s Sug. Retail | $18,750 | $16,000 | $14,000 | $12,000 | $10,000 | $9,000 | $7,500 | $6,500 |

IMPERIAL SXS — all ga.'s, most barrel lengths, second quality sidelock model, ejectors, mostly standard opening, a few made as easy opening. Also mfg. in some double rifles. Disc.

| | $13,500 | $11,500 | $9,500 | $7,500 | $6,500 | $5,250 | $4,000 |

20 ga. — add 20%.
28 ga. — add 40%.
SST — add $1,000.
16 ga. — deduct 10%.
Double rifle — add 35%.

Imperial Grade — 12 or 20 ga., second quality sidelock model, ejectors, standard opening, limited current mfg.

| Mfg.'s Sug. Retail | $14,250 | $12,000 | $9,950 | $7,700 | $6,600 | $5,600 | $4,500 | $3,500 |

FIELD MODEL — 12 ga. only, most barrel lengths, third quality sidelock model. Disc.

| | $9,000 | $8,000 | $7,000 | $6,000 | $5,000 | $4,500 | $3,500 |

20 ga. — add 20%.
28 ga. — add 40%.
SST — add $1,000.
16 ga. — deduct 10%.

Grading	100%	98%	95%	90%	80%	70%	60%

HERCULES MODEL — all ga.'s, 25-30 in. barrels, best quality boxlock model, ejectors, easy opening or standard opening. Also made in some double rifles in .22 Hornet and similar cal.'s.

	100%	98%	95%	90%	80%	70%	60%
	$9,000	$8,000	$7,000	$6,000	$5,000	$4,500	$3,500

20 ga. — add 20%.

28 ga. — add 40%.

SST — add $1,000.

16 ga. — deduct 10%.

Double rifle — add 35%.

UTILITY MODEL — mostly 12 ga., 25-30 in. barrels, second quality boxlock model, ejectors, checkered straight or pistol grip stock. Disc.

	100%	98%	95%	90%	80%	70%	60%
	$6,250	$4,500	$3,500	$3,000	$2,500	$2,000	$1,800

20 ga. — add 20%.

28 ga. — add 40%.

.410. — add 60%.

SST — add $500.

16 ga. — deduct 10%.

CROWN MODEL — 12, 16, 20, or .410 (rare) ga., third quality boxlock model, various barrel lengths. Disc.

	100%	98%	95%	90%	80%	70%	60%
	$4,500	$3,500	$3,000	$2,500	$2,000	$1,600	$1,200

20 ga. — add 20%.

28 ga. — add 40%.

.410 — add 60%.

SST — add $500.

16 ga. — deduct 10%.

REGAL — 12, 16, 20, 28, or .410 ga., second quality boxlock model introduced after WWII, released after Utility Model was disc. Premium for 28 or .410 ga.

	100%	98%	95%	90%	80%	70%	60%
	$6,000	$4,300	$3,750	$3,100	$2,500	$2,000	$1,800

20 ga. — add 20%.

28 ga. — add 40%.

.410 ga. — add 60%.

SST — add $500.

16 ga. — deduct 10%.

Regal Grade — 12, 20, 28, or .410 ga., best quality boxlock model, ejectors, standard opening, limited current production.

	100%	98%	95%	90%	80%	70%	60%
Mfg.'s Sug. Retail	$5,625	$4,800	$4,000	$3,500	$3,000	$2,500	$2,000	$1,800

PREMIER QUALITY O/U — 12, 16, or 20 ga., same barrel and bore as Premier Double, engraved, sidelock, auto ejectors, checkered pistol grip or straight stock. Disc.

	100%	98%	95%	90%	80%	70%	60%
	$17,000	$15,000	$12,000	$10,000	$9,000	$7,500	$6,500

20 ga. — add 20%.

28 ga. — add 40%.

SST — add $1,000.

Vent rib — add $500.

16 ga. — deduct 10%.

RIFLES

"ONE OF ONE THOUSAND RIFLE" — Mauser type bolt action, .270, 7mm Rem. Mag., .308, .30-06, .300 Win. Mag., .375 H&H Mag., or .458 Win. Mag. cal., 5 shot standard, 3 shot mag. Magnum, 24 in. barrel, classic French walnut stock, swivel recoil pad with trap, trap pistol grip cap. Mfg. 1973 for Interarms 20th Anniversary, limited, 100 mfg.

	100%	98%	95%	90%	80%	70%	60%
	$1,400	$1,250	$1,000	$900	$750	$700	$600

CHURCHILL

Currently imported and distributed by Ellett Brothers located in Chapin, SC. Previously imported (until 1988) by Kassnar Imports, Inc. located in Harrisburg, PA. Not affiliated with E.J. Churchill Gunmakers, Ltd.

In late 1988 the Churchill trademark was sold to Ellett Brothers located in Chapin, SC.

RIFLES

HIGHLANDER — .25-06 Rem., .243 Win., .270 Win., .308 Win., .30-06, 7mm Rem. Mag., or .300 Win. Mag. cal., bolt action, 22 in. barrel, thumb safety, no sights, 3 or 4 shot mag., checkered walnut stock, 7½ lbs.

Mfg.'s Sug. Retail	$460	$395	$350	$330	$300	$270	$240	$215

Add $30 for iron sights (disc).

REGENT — same cal.'s as Highlander, deluxe checkered walnut with Monte Carlo comb and cheek piece. Last imported by Kassner in 1988.

	$555	$455	$385	$340	$300	$280	$260

Add $30 for iron sights.
Last Mfg.'s Sug. Retail was $610.

ROTARY 22 — .22 LR, beginners rifle, bolt hold-open device, adj. rear sight, 10 shot rotary mag. Imported 1989 only.

	$120	$105	$95	$85	$75	$65	$55

Last Mfg.'s Sug. Retail was $130.

SHOTGUNS: SIDE BY SIDE

WINDSOR I — 10 (disc. 1988), 12, 16, 20, 28, or .410 ga., double barrel, 23-32 in. barrels, Anson and Deeley boxlock, antique silver finish receiver with fine scroll engraving, extractors, double triggers, checkered pistol grip and forend.

Mfg.'s Sug. Retail	$653	$550	$465	$450	$385	$300	$250	$230

Add $150 for 10 ga.

Add $55 for 28 or .410 ga.

Add $30 for Flyweight Models (25 in. barrels - disc. 1988).

WINDSOR II — 12 or 20 ga., double barrel, 26-30 in. barrels, Anson and Deeley boxlock, antique silver finish receiver with fine scroll engraving, ejectors, double triggers, checkered pistol grip and forend. Add $100 for 10 ga. (disc.). Importation disc. 1987.

	$595	$485	$415	$350	$315	$270	$240

Last Mfg.'s Sug. Retail was $638.

WINDSOR VI — 12 or 20 (disc.) ga., double barrel, 25 or 28 in. barrels, sidelock, antique silver finish receiver with fine scroll engraving, ejectors, double triggers, checkered pistol grip and forend. Disc. 1987.

	$840	$700	$600	$550	$510	$460	$420

Last Mfg.'s Sug. Retail was $900.

ROYAL — available in 10, 12, 20, 28, or .410 ga., DT's, extractors, checkered walnut stock and forearm, case hardened receiver. New late 1988.

Mfg.'s Sug. Retail	$540	$485	$405	$370	$310	$275	$250	$230

Add $20 for 28 ga.

Add $74 for .410 ga.

SHOTGUNS: OVER/UNDER

MONARCH — 12, 20, 28, or .410 ga., 25, 26 or 28 in. vent rib barrels, SST, extractors, boxlock action, DT, silver finish receiver with fine scroll engraving, checkered European walnut stock and forearm, 6½-7½ lbs.

Mfg.'s Sug. Retail	$529	$460	$370	$340	$300	$250	$230	$210

Add $67 for .410 ga. with 26 in. barrels.

Deduct $40 without SST.

Deduct $33 for 28 ga.

Grading	100%	98%	95%	90%	80%	70%	60%

Monarch Turkey Gun — 12 ga. only, 24 in. barrels with matte finish. New 1990.

Mfg.'s Sug. Retail	$529	$460	$370	$340	$300	$250	$230	$210

WINDSOR III — 12, 20, or .410 ga. (disc.), double barrel, 27 or 30 in. barrels, double bottom lock, antique silver finish receiver with fine scroll engraving, extractors, SST, vent rib, checkered pistol grip and forend.

Mfg.'s Sug. Retail	$625	$550	$495	$450	$380	$340	$300	$280

Add $140 for Flyweight Model or choke tubes (disc.).

Add $75 for .410 ga.

WINDSOR IV — 12, 20, 28, or .410 ga., double barrel, 26-30 in. barrels, double bottom lock, antique silver finish receiver with fine scroll engraving, ejectors, SST, vent rib, checkered pistol grip and forend. Interchangeable chokes became standard in 1989.

Mfg.'s Sug. Retail	$852	$725	$640	$530	$470	$430	$395	$360

Deduct $52 for 28 or .410 ga.

Deduct $100 if without choke tubes.

REGENT V — 12 or 20 ga., double barrel, 27 in. barrels, double bottom lock, antique silver finish receiver with extra fine scroll engraving, ejectors, single trigger, vent rib, checkered pistol grip and forend. Interchangeable choke tubes standard. Disc. 1986, reintroduced 1990.

Mfg.'s Sug. Retail	$1,100	$895	$795	$700	$620	$560	$510	$470

This model was previously designated Regent VII until 1989 when it changed to the Regent V.

REGENT TRAP AND SKEET — 12 or 20 ga., double barrel, 26 or 30 in. barrels, double bottom lock, antique silver finish receiver with sideplates engraved in fine scroll, ejectors, SST, vent rib, checkered pistol grip and forend.

Mfg.'s Sug. Retail	$963	$795	$650	$575	$540	$485	$440	$390

Add $40 for trap variation.

REGENT GRADE SHOTGUN/RIFLE COMBINATION — 12 ga. over either .222 Rem., .223, .243 Win. (disc.), .270 Win., .30-06, or .308 Win. cal., double barrel, 25 in. barrels, double bottom lock, antique silver finish receiver with extra fine scroll engraving, ejectors, single trigger, vent rib, checkered pistol grip and forend.

Mfg.'s Sug. Retail	$927	$800	$700	$635	$560	$510	$475	$440

SHOTGUNS: SEMI-AUTO

STANDARD MODEL — 12 ga. only, gas operated and shoots different loads interchangeably without alterations, 24, 26, 28 in. VR barrel, magazine cut-off, hand checkered walnut with satin finish, matte metal finish, includes ICT choke tubes. New 1990.

Mfg.'s Sug. Retail	$550	$495	$415	$375	$310	$275	$250	$230

Turkey Model — similar to Standard Model, except has 24 in. barrel only. New 1990.

Mfg.'s Sug. Retail	$570	$510	$425	$380	$315	$275	$250	$230

WINDSOR GRADE — 12 ga. only, 26, 28, or 30 in. barrels, gas operation, anodized alloy receiver, vent rib, checkered pistol grip and forend, 7½ lbs. Deluxe model includes polished receiver with etching.

	$380	$320	$300	$275	$250	$225	$200

Add $35 for choke tubes.

Add $55 for Deluxe model.

Last Mfg.'s Sug. Retail was $420.

REGENT GRADE — 12 ga. only, 26, 28, or 30 in. barrels, gas operation, anodized alloy receiver, vent. rib, checkered pistol grip and forend, 7½ lbs. Deluxe model includes polished receiver with etching. Disc. 1986.

	$440	$365	$340	$320	$300	$285	$270

Add $35 for choke tubes.

Add $55 for Deluxe model.

Last Mfg.'s Sug. Retail was $495.

Grading	100%	98%	95%	90%	80%	70%	60%

SHOTGUNS: SLIDE ACTION

WINDSOR GRADE — 12 ga. only, 26, 27, 28, or 30 in. barrels, double slides, anodized alloy receiver, vent rib, checkered pistol grip and forend, 7½ lbs. Disc. 1986.

	$385	$330	$310	$275	$250	$225	$200

Last Mfg.'s Sug. Retail was $430.

CIMARRON F.A. MFG. CO.

Importer/distributor/retailer located in Houston, TX. Currently importing Aldo Uberti Modern and Black Powder Firearms. Black Powder Reproductions can be located in the Black Powder section under Cimarron Arms in the back of this text. Previously named Old-West Guns Co.

REVOLVERS & CARBINES: SINGLE ACTION REPRODUCTIONS

The Cimarron Arms reproduction of the 1873 Colt Peacemaker is available in two configurations listed below. These pistols are extremely accurate reproductions of the original Colt pre-war Peacemaker and are marked (and machined) the same as the originals including serial numbers on frames, backstrap, trigger guard, and cylinder. Barrels are radiused and cylinders are beveled. Frames are color case hardened, stocks are walnut - choice of 4¾, 5½, or 7½ in. barrel. All Cimarron SAA's are barrel marked "- CIMARRON F.A. MFG. Co. HOUSTON, TX. U.S.A. -".

The "Old Model" configuration has the older style black powder frame, screw in cylinder pin retainer, and circular "bullseye" ejector head.

The Standard Model includes the post-1890 style frame with spring loaded cross-pin cylinder retainer and "half-moon" ejector head.

Both the Old Model and Standard Model are available in the authentic old style "charcoal blue" finish (sometimes referred to as fire-bluing).

Add $325 for "A" style engraving (30% coverage) on SAA's listed below.

Add $425 for "B" style engraving (50% coverage) on SAA's listed below.

Add $750 for "C" style engraving (100% coverage) on SAA's listed below.

Add $800 for "Texas Cattlebrands" engraving pattern.

CIMARRON SAA & VARIATIONS — available in .45 LC, .44-40, .38 Spl., .357 Mag., .22 LR, or .22 Mag cal., 4¾, 5½, and 7½ in. barrel lengths, steel backstraps and trigger guard.

Standard or Old Model

Mfg.'s Sug. Retail	$429	$370	$285	$250	$220	$195	$175	$160

Sheriff's Model — .44-40 or .45 LC cal., 3 or 4 in. barrel, steel backstraps and trigger guard.

Mfg.'s Sug. Retail	$390	$345	$275	$250	$220	$195	$175	$160

Target Model — similar to Standard Model, except has fully adj. target rear sight, brass or steel backstrap.

Mfg.'s Sug. Retail	$400	$355	$280	$255	$220	$195	$175	$160

Add $40 for .357 Mag. cal.

This variation is available in the Standard Model configuration only and with standard finish.

BUNTLINE MODEL — .45 LC, .44-40, or .357 Mag. cal., 18 in. barrel, brass or steel backstrap cut for shoulder stock. Disc. 1989.

	$355	$280	$255	$220	$195	$175	$160

Add $10 for target sights.

Last Mfg.'s Sug. Retail was $400.

BUNTLINE CARBINE — similar cal.'s to Buntline Model, except also includes .22 LR/.22 Mag. (convertible cylinders), 18 in. barrel, includes non-detachable shoulder stock with brass hardware and finger extension trigger guard.

Mfg.'s Sug. Retail	$440	$380	$295	$260	$225	$195	$175	$160

Add $20 for target sights.

Add $20 for .22 LR/.22 Mag. combo.

Grading	100%	98%	95%	90%	80%	70%	60%

BUCKHORN — .44 Mag. or .44 Spl., reinforced variation of the Cimarron SAA designed for more powerful cartridges, 4¾, 6 or 7½ in. barrel, brass or steel backstap.

Mfg.'s Sug. Retail	$400	$355	$285	$260	$220	$195	$175	$160

Buckhorn Convertible Model — includes .44 Mag./.44-40 cylinders, 4¾, 6 or 7½ in. barrel. Disc. 1989.

		$375	$295	$265	$220	$195	$175	$160

Add $12 for target sights.
Last Mfg.'s Sug. Retail was $427.

Buckhorn Target Model — .44 Mag. or .44 Spl. cal., 4¾, 6 or 7½ in. barrel, adj. rear sight.

Mfg.'s Sug. Retail	$420	$370	$290	$265	$225	$195	$175	$160

Buckhorn Buntline — .44 Mag., .44 Spl., or .44-40 cal., 18 in. barrel, fixed or target sights. Disc. 1989.

		$370	$285	$265	$220	$195	$175	$160

Add $30 for target sights.
Last Mfg.'s Sug. Retail was $419.

Buckhorn Carbine — .44 Mag., .44 Spl., or .44-40 cal., 18 in. barrel, includes non-detachable shoulder stock with brass hardware and lanyard ring. Disc. 1990.

		$375	$290	$265	$220	$195	$175	$160

Add $30 for target sights.
Last Mfg.'s Sug. Retail was $429.

SPECIAL EDITION SAA'S

U.S. CAVALRY MODEL — authentic reproduction of original Colt military cavalry contract, 7½ in. barrel, marked U.S. on lower left frame, one piece walnut grips with military cartouche.

Mfg.'s Sug. Retail	$459	$400	$330	$300	$280	$260	$240	$220

U.S. ARTILLERY MODEL — Renaldo A. Carr 1895 U.S. Artillery Model Commemorative, limited mfg.

Mfg.'s Sug. Retail	$459	$400	$330	$300	$280	$260	$240	$220

7TH CAVALRY CASED SET — U.S. Cavalry Model in case with accessories. Disc. 1990.

		$695	$625	$550	$500	$460	$420	$385

Last Mfg.'s Sug. Retail was $780.

JUDGE ROY BEAN COMMEMORATIVE — mfg. to commemorate Judge Roy Bean's Texas cattlebrand.

Mfg.'s Sug. Retail	$1,695	$1,500	$1,175	$995	$875	$750	$625	$550

REMINGTON REPRODUCTIONS

These guns are reproductions of the Models 1875 and 1890.

MODEL 1875 — available in .45 LC, .44-40, or .357 Mag. cal., 7½ barrel.

Mfg.'s Sug. Retail	$390	$340	$250	$200	$170	$155	$140	$120

Add $90 for nickel plating.

Model 1875 Carbine — same cal.'s as Model 1875, 18 in. barrel, includes non-detachable shoulder stock with brass hardware and lanyard ring. Importation disc. 1990.

		$410	$340	$300	$265	$230	$200	$180

Last Mfg.'s Sug. Retail was $460.

MODEL 1890 — .45 LC, .44-40, or .357 Mag. cal., 5½ barrel.

Mfg.'s Sug. Retail	$390	$340	$250	$210	$175	$160	$145	$125

1871 ROLLING BLOCK TARGET PISTOL — .357 Mag., .22 LR, .22 Hornet (new 1990), or .22 Mag. cal., 9½ in. barrel. Importation disc. 1990.

		$250	$200	$180	$160	$140	$125	$110

Last Mfg.'s Sug. Retail was $280.

Grading	100%	98%	95%	90%	80%	70%	60%

1871 Rolling Block Baby Carbine — same cal.'s as Target Pistol, has 22 in. barrel and walnut stock and forearm, brass trigger guard and butt plate. Importation disc. 1990.

	$310	$245	$205	$170	$155	$140	$120

Last Mfg.'s Sug. Retail was $340.

ROLLING BLOCK SPORTING RIFLE — .45-70 cal., 30 in. barrel, walnut stock and forearm. Imported 1989-1990 only.

	$565	$430	$395	$350	$320	$300	$275

Last Mfg.'s Sug. Retail was $620.

Deluxe Rolling Block Sporting Rifle — similar to standard model, except has select wood. Importation disc. 1990.

	$640	$485	$450	$375	$340	$320	$295

Last Mfg.'s Sug. Retail was $720.

RIFLES: WINCHESTER REPRODUCTIONS

Add $20 for Charcoal Blue finish for below listed models.

HENRY RIFLE/CARBINE — .44-40 cal., brass frame, 24½ in. barrel on rifle, 22½ in. barrel on carbine.

Mfg.'s Sug. Retail	$800	$695	$550	$465	$415	$360	$325	$295

Can also be special ordered with Grade A engraving ($350 extra), Grade B engraving ($550 extra), and Grade C engraving ($725 extra).

1866 SPORTING RIFLE — .22 LR, .22 Mag., or .44-40 cal., brass receiver, 24 in. octagon barrel.

Mfg.'s Sug. Retail	$690	$575	$450	$375	$325	$275	$240	$200

Add $375 (retail) for A engraving, $595 for B engraving, $940 for C engraving.

1866 YELLOWBOY CARBINE — includes .38 Spl. cal., otherwise similar to Model 1866 Sporting Rifle, features 19 in. round barrel with 2 bands, saddle ring, uncheckered walnut stock and forearm.

Mfg.'s Sug. Retail	$650	$540	$425	$350	$300	$250	$235	$200

1866 Trapper Carbine — .44-40 cal., 16 in. round barrel. Importation disc. 1990.

	$465	$385	$340	$320	$275	$240	$200

Last Mfg.'s Sug. Retail was $538.

1866 Yellowboy Indian Carbine — .22 LR, .22 Mag., .38 Spl., or .44-40 cal., 19 in. round barrel. Disc. 1989.

	$575	$475	$400	$350	$300	$260	$220

This model has a photo engraved brass frame and has brass tacks in stock and forearm.

Last Mfg.'s Sug. Retail was $649.

Red Cloud Commemorative Carbine — same cal.'s as Yellowboy Indian Carbine, includes special engraving representing Oglalla Indian tribe symbols, brass tacks in forearm and stock. Disc. 1989.

	$575	$475	$400	$350	$300	$260	$220

Last Mfg.'s Sug. Retail was $649.

1873 SPORTING RIFLE — .22 LR, .22 Mag., .357 Mag., .44-40, or .45 LC cal., 24½ in. octagon barrel, case hardened reciever, full mag., iron sights.

Mfg.'s Sug. Retail	$800	$695	$550	$465	$415	$360	$325	$295

Add $375 (retail) for A engraving, $595 for B engraving, $940 for C engraving, or $1,095 for "1 of 1000" engraving.

1873 Long Range Rifle — .44-40 or .45 LC cal., includes 30 in. octagon barrel with full mag., case hardened receiver, iron sights. New 1990.

Mfg.'s Sug. Retail	$820	$695	$550	$475	$425	$395	$370	$345

1873 Short Rifle — .44-40 or .45 LC cal., features 20 in. octagon barrel, case hardened receiver, iron sights. New 1990.

Mfg.'s Sug. Retail	$800	$695	$550	$465	$415	$360	$325	$295

Grading	100%	98%	95%	90%	80%	70%	60%

1873 Saddle Ring Carbine — .22 LR, .22 Mag., .357 Mag., .44-40, or .45 LC cal., blued steel receiver, saddle ring, 19 in. round barrel.

Mfg.'s Sug. Retail	$730	$625	$500	$400	$350	$300	$260	$220

Add $90 for nickel plating (disc.).

1873 Trapper Carbine — .357 Mag. (new 1990), .44-40, or .45 LC (new 1990) cal., 16 in. barrel, blue finish only. Importation disc, 1990.

	$575	$475	$400	$350	$300	$260	$220

Last Mfg.'s Sug. Retail was $650.

CLARIDGE HI-TEC INC.

Manufacturer located in Northridge, CA Since 1990.

In 1990, Claridge Hi-Tec, Inc. was created - this new company took over Goncz Armament, Inc. Warranties from Goncz Armament, Inc. are not transferrable to Claridge Hi-Tec, Inc.

All Claridge Hi-Tec firearms utilize match barrels mfg. in house that are button-rifled. The Claridge action is an original design and does not copy other actions.

PISTOLS & CARBINES

The models listed below are also available using stainless steel construction.

L MODEL PISTOL — 9mm Para. or .45 ACP cal., semi-auto paramilitary design, 9½ in. shrouded barrel, aluminum receiver, choice of black matte, satin aluminum, or two-tone combination finish, one piece grip, safety locks firing pin in place, 10 or 18 shot double row mag., adj. sights, 3 lbs. 1 oz. New 1991.

Mfg.'s Sug. Retail	$775	$675	$495	$375	$300	$260	$220	$200

A trigger activated laser sighting scope is available in Models M, L, and C.

S MODEL PISTOL — similar to L Model, except has 5 in. non-shrouded barrel, 2 lbs. 9 oz.

Mfg.'s Sug. Retail	$720	$625	$465	$350	$300	$260	$220	$200

M MODEL PISTOL — similar to L Model, except has 7½ in. barrel, 3 lbs.

Mfg.'s Sug. Retail	$720	$625	$465	$350	$300	$260	$220	$200

C MODEL CARBINE — same cal.'s as L and S Model pistols, 16¼ in. shrouded barrel, choice of composite or uncheckered walnut stock and forearm, 4 lbs. 14 oz. New in 1991.

Mfg.'s Sug. Retail	$895	$750	$625	$525	$450	$395	$350	$300

CLASSIC DOUBLES

Previously manufactured in Tochigi City, Japan. Previously imported and distributed by Classic Doubles International, Inc. located in St. Louis, MO. The factory closed in 1987, and all Classic Doubles remaining in inventory were sold to GU Wholesalers located in Omaha, NE in 1990. while a few models are still available through GU Wholesalers (call for availability), all values listed below reflect discontinuance of mfg. to date, there has been little collectibility in the Classic Doubles trademark. As a result, values are determined by the shooting value each model has to offer. Also, in some regions of the country, 98% and lower values are lower than prices listed below.

In late 1987, Winchester/Olin discontinued importation of their Japanese shotgun models (Models 101 and 23). At that point, Classic Doubles International, Inc. became the sole importer of these shotguns. There have been very few changes made during this changeover of importation. However, the new Classic Double shotguns (Models 101 and 201) do not have the Winchester trademark or definitive Winchester proofmark stamped on the barrels. The Model 201 is a new model designation.

SHOTGUNS: O/U - MODEL 101

All newly imported Classic Doubles have an interchangeable choke tube system compatible with the older Winchester manufatctured models. Prices listed include a luggage style carrying case.

Grading	100%	98%	95%	90%	80%	70%	60%

CLASSIC FIELD GRADE I — 12 or 20 ga., 3 in. chambers, vent rib, 25½ or 28 in. vent. barrels with choke tubes, blued receiver with moderate scroll engraving, ejectors, checkered pistol grip or English stock and forearm, 6¼ - 7 lbs.

	$1,400	$1,250	$1,100	$1,000	$900	$825	$750

Last Mfg.'s Sug. Retail was $1,905.

WATERFOWL MODEL — 12 ga. only, 3 in. chambers, 30 in. barrels with vent rib and choke tubes, matte blued receiver with moderate engraving, low gloss walnut stock with vent recoil pad, 7 ¾ lbs.

	$1,150	$995	$895	$800	$700	$600	$500

Last Mfg.'s Sug. Retail was $1,520.

CLASSIC SPORTER — 12 ga. only, made for Sporting Clays competition, 28 or 30 in. vent barrels and rib with choke tubes, quick detachable stock system, border engraved coin finished receiver with non-reflective matte surface on top frame and lever, checkered walnut stock and forearm, 7¾ lbs.

	$1,500	$1,295	$1,150	$1,000	$900	$825	$750

Add $965 for extra barrel.
Last Mfg.'s Sug. Retail was $1,980.

CLASSIC FIELD GRADE II — 12, 20, 28 or .410 ga., 28 in. choke tube vent. barrels and rib, deluxe walnut with round knob pistol grip stock and forearm with fine fleur-de-lis checkering, coin finished receiver (different sizes) with game scene engraving featuring hunting motifs on receiver sides and bottom, .410 ga. bored M/F only, 6¼ - 7lbs.

	$1,675	$1,425	$1,245	$1,100	$1,000	$900	$795

The .410 and 28 ga.'s are more desirable in this model.

Last Mfg.'s Sug. Retail was $2,190.

CLASSIC FIELD GRADE II TWO BARREL SET — 12 and 20 ga. barrels, both with Winchokes, 26 in. barrels - 20 ga., 28 in. barrels - 12 ga., coin finished receiver with game scene engraving and borders, 6½ (20 ga.) or 7 (12 ga.) lbs.

	$2,500	$2,100	$1,825	$1,550	$1,375	$1,200	$1,075

Last Mfg.'s Sug. Retail was $3,420.

TARGET GUNS

CLASSIC TRAP SINGLE — 12 ga. only, over single 32 or 34 in. barrel with vent. rib and choke tubes, blued receiver with light engraving, choice of Monte Carlo or regular stock, recoil pad, 8½ lbs.

	$1,425	$1,250	$1,100	$1,000	$900	$825	$750

Last Mfg.'s Sug. Retail was $2,070.

CLASSIC TRAP O/U — 12 ga. only, 30 or 32 in. vent. barrels and rib with choke tubes, finish and engraving similar to Classic Trap Single, choice of Monte Carlo or standard stock with recoil pad, 8¾ or 9 lbs.

	$1,300	$1,125	$1,000	$900	$825	$750	$675

Last Mfg.'s Sug. Retail was $1,905.

CLASSIC TRAP COMBO — includes one set of O/U barrels (30 or 32 in.) and one over single barrel (32 or 34 in.), choke tubes, choice of Monte Carlo or standard stock, 8¾ or 9 lbs.

	$2,125	$1,875	$1,600	$1,475	$1,300	$1,175	$995

Last Mfg.'s Sug. Retail was $2,825.

CLASSIC SKEET — 12 or 20 ga., 27½ in. vent. barrels and rib, choke tubes on 12 ga. only, smaller ga.'s are bored SK/Sk, similar metal finish to Classic Trap models, 7¼ or 7¾ lbs.

	$1,450	$1,275	$1,125	$1,000	$900	$825	$750

Last Mfg.'s Sug. Retail was $1,905.

Grading	100%	98%	95%	90%	80%	70%	60%

Classic Skeet 4 ga. Set — similar to Classic Skeet except has 4 barrels (12, 20, 28, or .410 ga.), 12 ga. has choke tubes, smaller ga.'s are bored SK/SK.

	$3,900	$3,500	$3,100	$2,875	$2,600	$2,300	$1,995

Last Mfg.'s Sug. Retail was $4,765.

SHOTGUNS: SIDE BY SIDE

MODEL 201 CLASSIC — 12 or 20 ga., 3 in. chambers, forged steel monoblock with improved lug design, 26 in. choke tube barrels with vent. rib, high lustre bluing, no engraving, SST, ejectors, premium walnut stock and beavertail forearm with fancy checkering pattern, solid red rubber recoil pad, 6¾ - 7 lbs.

	$1,650	$1,450	$1,275	$995	$875	$775	$625

Add $120 for 20 ga.

The 12 ga. can be ordered with choke tubes at no extra charge.

Last Mfg.'s Sug. Retail was $2,190.

Model 201 Classic Small Bore Set — 28 and .410 ga. two barrel set, similar to Model 201 Classic except has smaller frame and overall dimensions, 28 in. VR barrels only bored IC/M on 28 ga. and M/F on .410 ga., 6 or 6½ lbs

	$2,650	$2,250	$1,900	$1,700	$1,550	$1,350	$1,150

Last Mfg.'s Sug. Retail was $3,675.

CLERKE PRODUCTS

Santa Monica, CA.

HI-WALL — single shot rifle, falling block replica of Winchester 1885 High Wall, lever operated, case hardened receiver, 26 in. barrel, available in most modern calibers, no sights, checkered walnut pistol grip stock, Schnabel forearm. Mfg. 1972-1974.

	$250	$225	$185	$175	$150	$140	$125

DELUXE HI-WALL — same as Hi-Wall, except half octagon barrel, select wood and recoil pad.

	$300	$275	$235	$210	$180	$160	$145

CLIFTON ARMS

Manufacturer and retailer of Custom Rifles located in Grand Prairie, TX. Clifton Arms mostly specializes in composite atocks (with or without integral, retractable bipod).

Clifton Arms mostly manufactures composite, hand laminated stocks that are patterned after the Dakota 76 stock configuration. However, custom rifles can be ordered by contacting the company and specifying the type of action, caliber, barrel and stock configuration and/or color. Price quotations vary per individual, special ordered rifle.

COBRAY INDUSTRIES

See listing under S.W.D. in the S section of this text.

COGSWELL & HARRISON, LIMITED

London, England. 1770 to date.

SHOTGUNS

REGENCY — 12, 16, or 20 ga., double barrel, 26, 28, or 30 in. barrels, any choke combination, hammerless Anson & Deeley system, boxlock, double triggers, auto ejectors, straight English stock. Mfg. 1970-present.

Mfg.'s Sug. Retail	$3,200	$2,750	$2,500	$2,250	$2,000	$1,800	$1,600	$1,375

Grading	100%	98%	95%	90%	80%	70%	60%

AMBASSADOR MODEL — double barrel, same gauges and barrels as Regency, boxlock with false sideplates, auto ejectors, double triggers, engraved game scene or scroll rose motif, English stock.

Mfg.'s Sug. Retail	$4,000	$3,650	$3,100	$2,850	$2,700	$2,500	$2,250	$1,995

MARKOR — 12, 16, or 20 ga., double barrel, 27½ or 30 in. barrel and choke, boxlock, double trigger, English stock. Disc.

	$1,500	$1,350	$1,200	$1,000	$950	$825	$700
Auto ejectors	$1,750	$1,500	$1,350	$1,200	$1,100	$900	$700

HUNTIC MODEL — 12, 16, or 20 ga., double barrel, 25, 27, or 30 in. barrels, any choke, sidelock, auto ejectors, English style stock. Disc.

	$3,500	$3,200	$3,000	$2,800	$2,500	$2,175	$1,850

SST — add $400.

AVANT TOUT SERIES — 12, 16, or 20 ga., double barrel, 25, 27½, or 30 in. barrels, boxlock, false sideplates, straight English stock, auto ejectors, series disc.

	$2,250	$1,925	$1,700	$1,495	$1,350	$1,200	$1,075

REX OR AVANT TOUT III — no sideplates.

	$1,800	$1,650	$1,500	$1,350	$1,200	$1,075	$895

SANDHURST OR AVANT TOUT II

	$2,500	$2,300	$2,150	$2,000	$1,750	$1,500	$1,225

KONOR OR AVANT TOUT I

	$2,850	$2,700	$2,500	$2,250	$2,000	$1,775	$1,500

SST — add $400.
20 ga. — add 20%.
16 ga. — deduct 10%.

BEST QUALITY — 12, 16, or 20 ga.'s, double barrel, 25, 26, 28, or 30 in. barrels, any choke, hand detachable sidelock, auto ejectors, double triggers standard, English stock.
Primic Model — disc.

	$5,750	$4,650	$4,150	$3,650	$3,050	$2,500	$1,950

Victor Model

Mfg.'s Sug. Retail	$10,000	$8,600	$6,250	$5,000	$4,350	$3,740	$3,000	$2,375

SST — add $400.
20 ga. — add 20%.
16 ga. — deduct 10%.
Note: Degree of engraving and grade of wood are the basic differences among models.

COLT'S MANUFACTURING COMPANY, INC.

Manufacturer located in Hartford, CT.

Manufactured from 1836-1841 in Paterson, NJ; 1847 to 1848 in Whitneyville, CT; 1854 to 1864 in London, England; and from 1848 to date in Hartford, CT. Colt Firearms became a division of Colt Industries in 1964. In March, 1990, the Colt Firearms Division was sold to C.F Holding Corp. located in Hartford, CT. The new company is called Colt's Manufacturing Company, Inc.

PERCUSSION REVOLVERS

Prices shown for percussion Colt's are for guns only. Original cased guns with accessories will bring a healthy premium over non-cased models (200-350% over a gun only is common). Be very careful when buying an "original" cased gun, as many fake cases have shown up in recent years.

100%	98%	95%	90%	80%	70%	60%	50%	40%	30%	20%	10%

Prices shown on the following pages for extremely rare Colt's firearms might not include values in the 90% or greater condition column. Prices are very hard to establish since these excellent to mint specimens are seldomly seen or sold.

BABY PATERSON — nicknamed "Baby Paterson", .28 and .31 cal., 5 shot, 2½ in. to 4¾ in. barrels, blued metal with walnut varnished grips, serial range 1-500, marked Patent Arms M'g Co., Paterson, N.J., Colt's Pt. Mfg. 1837-1838.
Without loading lever

100%	98%	95%	90%	80%	70%	60%	50%	40%	30%	20%	10%
$30,000	$26,000	$22,000	$18,500	$16,000	$14,000	$12,000	$10,750	$9,800	$8,950	$8,100	$7,500

Add 10-15% if cased with accessories.
Factory modified — with loading lever.

$34,000	$30,000	$26,000	$22,000	$18,500	$16,000	$14,000	$12,000	$10,750	$9,800	$8,950	$8,100

Add 10-15% if cased with accessories.

POCKET MODEL PATERSON — .31 or .34 cal., 2½ in. to 4¾ in. octagon barrels, larger gauge than the "Baby" model, serial range 1-800, blued metal with walnut varnished grips. Mfg. 1837-1840.
Without loading lever

$34,000	$30,000	$26,000	$22,000	$18,500	$16,000	$14,000	$12,000	$10,750	$9,800	$8,950	$8,100

Add 10-15% if cased with accessories.
With loading lever

$37,000	$34,000	$30,000	$26,000	$22,000	$18,500	$16,000	$14,000	$12,000	$10,750	$9,800	$8,950

Add 10-15% if cased with accessories.

BELT MODEL PATERSON — .31 or .34 cal., 5 shot, 4-6 in. barrels, can be found with Pocket Model straight grip or flared grip, blued metal with walnut varnished stocks, some may have case hardened hammer, marked with the Paterson, N.J. address.
Straight grip — without loading levers.

$31,500	$28,500	$24,550	$21,000	$17,500	$15,000	$13,000	$11,000	$10,000	$9,500	$8,850	$8,250

Flared grip — without loading lever.

$28,500	$26,000	$23,000	$19,250	$16,500	$14,250	$12,000	$10,750	$9,800	$9,200	$8,600	$8,100

Add 10% for loading lever.

TEXAS PATERSON — .36 cal., 4-12 in. octagon barrels, 7½ and 9 in. barrels are most common, serial range 1-1000, blued metal with case hardened hammer and frame and walnut varnished grips, this model has the greatest collector appeal of the Patersons, stagecoach holdup scene rolled on cylinder and flared grip style.

Grading		80%	70%	60%	50%	40%	30%	20%	10%

Without loading lever

	80%	70%	60%	50%	40%	30%	20%	10%
	$75,000	$65,000	$55,000	$47,500	$40,000	$35,000	$30,000	$25,000

With loading lever

	$85,000	$75,000	$62,500	$51,000	$44,000	$39,500	$35,000	$30,000

Note: Authentic martially marked models have considerable added value and should be appraised individually.

WALKER COLT — .44 cal., 6 shot, 9 in. round and octagon barrel, designed for military use, blued metal, case hardened frame, lever, hammer, brass trigger guard, cylinder unfinished with Texas Ranger and Indian battle scene, all numbered in companies A, B, C, D, and E, one piece walnut grips, with inspectors marks, all inspector's marks well worn, as are revolvers, top of barrel marked, "ADDRESS SAM COLT NEW YORK CITY". Mfg. 1847.
Military model

	$115,000	$99,500	$87,500	$73,500	$61,500	$52,000	$42,000	$31,500

Civilian model — serial numbered from 1001-1100.

	$105,000	$92,500	$82,500	$71,500	$58,500	$49,500	$40,000	$29,500

Grading	80%	70%	60%	50%	40%	30%	20%	10%

WHITNEYVILLE HARTFORD DRAGOON — .44 cal., 6 shot, 7½ in. octagon and round barrel, some of the left-over Walker parts were used in Dragoons, blued metal with casehardened frame, lever, hammer, brass trigger guard and steel cylinder bears Texas Ranger and Indian battle scene.
Rear frame cut out for grips

	80%	70%	60%	50%	40%	30%	20%	10%
	$75,000	$69,500	$65,000	$60,000	$55,000	$50,000	$45,000	$40,000

Straight rear frame

	$42,500	$38,250	$34,500	$31,000	$27,800	$26,000	$23,400	$21,000

FIRST MODEL DRAGOON — .44 cal., 6 shot, 7½ in. round and octagon barrel, blued metal with case hardened frame, lever, hammer, brass grip straps, silvered straps for civilian market, serial range numbered after Hartford Dragoon, 1341 to around 8000. Mfg. 1848-1850.
Military model

	$13,500	$11,500	$9,950	$9,000	$8,150	$7,500	$6,900	$6,000

Civilian model

	$11,500	$9,500	$7,500	$6,500	$5,500	$4,500	$3,750	$2,950

FLUCK MODEL DRAGOON — basically a First Model Dragoon, with 7½ in. altered Walker barrels and fully martially marked, should be extensively checked over, used to replace defective Walkers. Mfg. 1848.

	$22,000	$18,500	$16,000	$14,000	$12,000	$10,750	$9,800	$8,950

SECOND MODEL DRAGOON — .44 cal., 6 shot, 7½ in. round and octagon barrel, serial range following the First Model Dragoon 8000-10,700. Mfg. 1850-1851.
Military model

	$25,000	$21,000	$17,500	$14,250	$11,750	$9,850	$8,350	$7,000

Civilian model

	$18,500	$15,000	$12,000	$10,000	$8,500	$7,000	$5,750	$4,750

New Hampshire or Massachusetts — notice state markings on front portion of trigger guard.

	$25,000	$21,000	$17,500	$14,250	$11,750	$9,850	$8,350	$7,000

THIRD MODEL DRAGOON — .44 cal., 6 shot, 7½ in. round or octagon barrel, same basic features as earlier models, but with round trigger guard and rectangular cylinder slots, serial range approx. 10,200-19,600, some overlapping of numbers, with approx. 10,500 mfg. from 1851-1861.
Third model Dragoon

	$14,250	$12,000	$10,250	$9,400	$8,600	$7,550	$6,500	$5,350

Martially marked U.S.

	$15,000	$13,250	$11,500	$9,950	$8,650	$7,650	$6,600	$5,600

Third model — 8 in. barrel.

	$15,500	$12,850	$11,250	$10,000	$9,150	$8,250	$7,350	$6,750

First and second variation — shoulder stock model.

	$12,500	$10,250	$8,750	$7,700	$6,500	$5,500	$4,400	$3,300

C.L. Dragoon

	$13,000	$11,350	$9,150	$8,000	$6,850	$5,700	$4,600	$3,500

ENGLISH HARTFORD DRAGOON — basically a Third Model Dragoon, assembled at Colt's London factory, with unique serial range 1-700, some were assembled from earlier parts inventories, easy to spot with British proofs of crown over V and crown over GP, the blue was of the English type, many were engraved.

	$11,000	$9,750	$8,500	$7,500	$6,500	$5,500	$4,500	$3,500

Recently, several 10-20% condition factory engraved English Dragoons have auctioned off at between $6,000-$8,500, depending on the amount of engraving.

1848 BABY DRAGOONS — .31 cal., 5 shot, 3, 4, 5, or 6 in. octagon barrels, most without loading lever, serial range 1-15,500, a scaled down version of the .44 caliber Dragoons, early ones with Texas Ranger scene and later ones with the holdup scene.

100%	98%	95%	90%	80%	70%	60%	50%	40%	30%	20%	10%

Type I — left hand barrel stamping, Texas Ranger and Indian scene, approx. serial range 1-150.

| $10,750 | $9,200 | $8,750 | $7,900 | $7,000 | $6,500 | $5,750 | $4,950 | $4,150 | $3,350 | $2,750 | $2,250 |

Type II — with Texas Ranger and Indian scene, 11,600 serial range, without loading lever.

| $9,500 | $8,750 | $7,900 | $7,000 | $6,500 | $5,750 | $4,950 | $4,150 | $3,350 | $2,750 | $2,250 | $1,750 |

Type III — with Stagecoach scene and oval cylinder slots, serial range 10,400-12,000.

| $7,400 | $6,750 | $6,150 | $5,500 | $4,950 | $4,350 | $3,750 | $3,000 | $2,500 | $2,150 | $1,800 | $1,500 |

Type IV — with Stagecoach holdup scene, rectangle cylinder slots, serial range 11,000-12,500.

| $7,750 | $7,150 | $6,650 | $6,150 | $5,500 | $4,950 | $4,350 | $3,750 | $3,000 | $2,500 | $2,150 | $1,800 |

Type V — with Stagecoach holdup scene, rectangle cylinder slots and loading lever, serial range 11,600-15,500.

| $7,550 | $6,850 | $6,250 | $5,600 | $4,950 | $4,350 | $3,750 | $3,000 | $2,500 | $2,150 | $1,800 | $1,500 |

1849 POCKET MODEL — .31 cal., 5 or 6 shot, 3, 4, 5, and 6 in. octagon barrels, most with loading levers, blued metal with case hardened frame, lever and hammer, grip straps of brass (silver plated), or steel (silver plated or blued), serial range 12,000 to 340,000. Mfg. 1850-1873.

First Type — 4, 5, or 6 in. barrel, loading lever and small or large brass trigger guard.

| $3,950 | $3,500 | $3,150 | $2,700 | $2,400 | $2,050 | $1,775 | $1,400 | $1,150 | $850 | $600 | $400 |

Second Type — 4, 5, or 6 in. barrel, loading lever and steel grip straps.

| $4,250 | $3,800 | $3,500 | $3,150 | $2,700 | $2,400 | $2,050 | $1,600 | $1,300 | $900 | $600 | $400 |

Wells Fargo Model — 3 in. barrel, without loading lever and with small round trigger guard.

| $10,750 | $9,500 | $8,750 | $7,900 | $7,000 | $6,200 | $5,300 | $4,250 | $3,350 | $2,400 | $1,600 | $995 |

1849 LONDON POCKET MODEL — London pistols were of the same general configuration, but of better finish, serial range 1-11,000. Mfg. 1853-1857.

Early Type — serial numbered under 1500, with small trigger guard and brass grip straps.

| $3,950 | $3,600 | $3,200 | $2,850 | $2,600 | $2,300 | $2,050 | $1,800 | $1,575 | $1,350 | $1,175 | $1,000 |

Late Type — oval trigger guard and steel grip straps.

| $2,850 | $2,600 | $2,300 | $2,050 | $1,800 | $1,575 | $1,350 | $1,175 | $1,000 | $800 | $725 | $575 |

1851 NAVY — .36 cal., 6 shot, 7½ in. octagon barrel and loading lever, blued metal with casehardened frame, lever and hammer, one piece walnut finished grips, cylinder scene of Texas Navy battle with Mexico, serial range 1-highest recorded number was 215,348, three barrel addresses 1-74,000 (ADDRESS SAM COLT, HARTFORD, CT.), 74,000-101,000 (ADDRESS SAM COLT, HARTFORD, CT.) 101,000-215,348 (ADDRESS COL. SAM COLT, NEW YORK, U.S. AMERICA). Mfg. 1850-1873.

Grading	80%	70%	60%	50%	40%	30%	20%	10%

First Model — square back trigger guard, bottom wedge screw, serial range 1-1,250.

| | $15,000 | $12,000 | $10,000 | $8,250 | $7,000 | $5,750 | $4,500 | $3,500 |

Second Model — square back trigger guard, top wedge screw, serial range 1,250-4,000.

| | $8,750 | $7,500 | $6,850 | $5,500 | $4,600 | $3,900 | $3,100 | $2,500 |

Third Model — small round brass trigger guard, serial range 4,200-85,000.

| | $4,950 | $3,950 | $3,250 | $2,750 | $2,350 | $2,000 | $1,750 | $1,350 |

Fourth Model — large round brass trigger guard, serial range 85,000-215,348.

| | $4,950 | $3,950 | $3,250 | $2,750 | $2,350 | $2,000 | $1,750 | $1,350 |

Iron Gripstrap Model — most often seen in fourth model.

| | $5,450 | $4,600 | $3,850 | $3,350 | $2,650 | $2,200 | $1,800 | $1,550 |

Martially Marked U.S. Navies — brass or iron gripstrap.

| | $4,950 | $3,950 | $3,250 | $2,750 | $2,350 | $2,000 | $1,750 | $1,350 |

Cut for shoulder stock — first and second type (like third model Dragoon).

| | $8,750 | $7,450 | $6,500 | $5,150 | $4,600 | $4,100 | $3,350 | $2,650 |

Third Type — four screw frame.

| | $5,950 | $4,950 | $3,900 | $3,000 | $2,450 | $1,900 | $1,650 | $1,320 |

Grading	80%	70%	60%	50%	40%	30%	20%	10%

51 NAVY LONDON MODEL — basically the same gun as the Hartford piece with London barrel address, with British proof marks in serial range 1-42,000. Mfg. 1853-1857.
Early First Model — serial range below 2000, brass grip straps and small trigger guard.

	$5,750	$4,600	$3,850	$3,150	$2,700	$2,350	$1,950	$1,650

Late Second Model — balance of production, large round trigger guard, steel grip straps, all London parts.

	$4,600	$3,800	$3,000	$2,600	$2,200	$1,850	$1,500	$1,175

1860 MODEL ARMY — .44 cal., 6 shot, 7½ and 8 in. round barrels with loading lever, blued metal with case hardened frame, lever and hammer, one piece walnut grips, normally blued steel back strap and brass trigger guard, barrel markings were (ADDRESS SAM COLT, HARTFORD, CT.) on early productions and (ADDRESS COL. SAM COLT, NEW YORK, U.S. AMERICA) on balance, serial range 1-about 200,500, Texas Navy scene on round cylinder model. Mfg. 1860-1873.
Fluted Cylinder Model — Fluted Cylinder Model, full length cylinder flutes and no cylinder scene, 7½ or 8 in. barrel, grips of Navy (very rare) or Army size, usually 4 screw frames.

	$8,750	$7,700	$6,900	$5,750	$4,800	$3,900	$3,100	$2,500

Round Cylinder Model — roll engraved Texas Navy scene, some with early Hartford address, Army grips, four screw frame to about 50,000 range, most were sold to the U.S. Government and will be martially marked.

	$6,000	$5,400	$4,400	$3,850	$3,000	$2,450	$1,950	$1,350

Civilian Model — same general configurations as Round Cylinder Model, but with 3 screw frame, no shoulder stock cuts and better blue finish than military pieces, late New York barrel address.

	$6,000	$5,400	$4,400	$3,850	$3,000	$2,450	$1,950	$1,350

1861 MODEL NAVY — .36 cal., 6 shot, 7½ in. round barrel with loading lever, blued metal with case hardened frame, lever and hammer, silver plated brass grip straps, the barrel address was (ADDRESS COL. SAM COLT, NEW YORK, U.S. AMERICA), serial range 1 - 38,843, cylinder scene of Texas Navy and MEXICO BATTLE, MADE 1861-1873.
Regular production model

	$5,800	$4,750	$4,150	$3,500	$2,950	$2,450	$2,000	$1,500

Martially Marked Navies — will bear the U.S. stamp and inspector's marks, those marked U.S.N. on butt were of a 650 piece order for the Navy.

	$7,500	$6,250	$5,400	$4,500	$3,750	$2,950	$2,500	$2,000

London Mark Navy — with (ADDRESS COL. COLT, LONDON), for barrel address.

	$4,800	$4,250	$3,500	$2,900	$2,450	$2,150	$1,800	$1,400

Shoulder Stock Cut Navy — 4 screw frames in serial range 11,000-14,000, made for third style stock (see Dragoon stocks).

	$8,750	$7,500	$6,850	$5,850	$5,100	$4,300	$3,700	$3,200

Fluted Cylinder Navy — in serial range 1-100, with fluted cylinder and without rolled cylinder scene.

	$25,000	$20,000	$17,500	$15,000	$12,000	$10,750	$9,800	$8,500

1862 POLICE MODEL — .36 cal., 4½, 5½, and 6½ in. barrels, 5 shot, semi-fluted cylinder, last design of the Colt Percussion Pistols, mostly seen with brass trigger guards and grip straps, streamlined design, mfg. 1861-1873.

	$3,500	$3,000	$2,525	$2,035	$1,650	$1,320	$1,100	$935

DERRINGERS

100%	98%	95%	90%	80%	70%	60%	50%	40%	30%	20%	10%

FIRST MODEL DERRINGER — .41 rimfire, single shot, 2½ in. barrel, scroll engraving standard, blued, nickel, or silver plated barrel, downward pivoting barrel, no grips, serial numbered 1-6,500. Mfg. approx. 1870-1890.

$850	$820	$750	$675	$600	$540	$495	$440	$395	$340	$295	$250

100%	98%	95%	90%	80%	70%	60%	50%	40%	30%	20%	10%

SECOND MODEL DERRINGER — .41 rimfire or centerfire, single shot, 2½ in. barrel, scroll engraving standard, blued, nickel, or silver plated barrel, downward pivoting barrel, checkered and varnished walnut grips, "No 2" marked on top of barrel, serial numbered 1-9,000. Mfg. approx. 1870-1890.

100%	98%	95%	90%	80%	70%	60%	50%	40%	30%	20%	10%
$1,450	$1,200	$975	$825	$750	$675	$600	$540	$495	$440	$395	$340

.41 Centerfire — add 100%.

THIRD MODEL DERRINGER (THUER MODEL) — .41 rimfire or centerfire (rare), single shot, side pivoting 2½ in. barrel, varnished walnut grips, blued barrels, bronze frames were either nickel or silver plated, engraving optional, Colt-barrel address, spur trigger, serial numbered approx. 1-45,000. Mfg. approx. 1875-1910.

100%	98%	95%	90%	80%	70%	60%	50%	40%	30%	20%	10%
$1,450	$1,200	$975	$750	$650	$550	$450	$350	$250	$175	$125	$100

.41 centerfire is worth an additional 30-50% and early models are worth considerably more.

Grading			100%	98%	95%

FOURTH MODEL DERRINGER — .22 Short, single shot similar in appearance to the 3rd Model, 2½ in. barrel, approx. 112,000 mfg. between 1959-1963 with either D or N suffix. A few were put in books, picture frames, penholders, bookends, etc. (these will command premiums).

			$100	$85	$65

LORD DERRINGER — .22 Short only, side pivoting Thuer action, gold plated with black chrome barrel and walnut grips. Mfg. approx. 1959-1963 by Colt, cased.

			$125	$85	$65

LADY DERRINGER — .22 Short only, side pivoting Thuer action, full gold plated finish with pearlite grips. Mfg. approx. 1959-1963 by Colt, cased.

			$125	$85	$65

LORD & LADY CASED SET — one each of the Lord & Lady derringers or combinations, consecutive serial numbers.

			$275	$175	$125

LADY CASED SET — cased pair of Lady Derringers.

			$250	$175	$125

LORD CASED SET — cased pair of Lord Derringers.

			$250	$175	$125

BOOKCASE DERRINGER PAIR — includes consecutively numbered .22 Short derringers with synthetic ivory grips and nickel finish, cased inside unique hard cover "Colt Derringers" labeled book with red velvet lining, limited mfg. in early 60's.

			$285	$225	$150

POCKET PISTOLS

100%	98%	95%	90%	80%	70%	60%	50%	40%	30%	20%	10%

CLOVERLEAF HOUSE PISTOL — .41 Short or long rimfire, cloverleaf configured 4 shot cylinder, spur trigger, 1½ or 3 in. barrel, approx. 7,500 mfg. in ser. no. range 1-8,300 during 1871-1876.

100%	98%	95%	90%	80%	70%	60%	50%	40%	30%	20%	10%
$1,250	$995	$875	$750	$675	$575	$495	$440	$395	$340	$295	$250

This model is sometimes referred to as the Jim Fisk model as he was murdered by Edward Stokes with a Cloverleaf.

5-shot Cloverleaf — similar to 4-shot model, except has round 5-shot cylinder and 2⅜ in. barrel only, approx. 2,500 mfg. in ser. no. range 6,160-9,950 during 1871-1876.

100%	98%	95%	90%	80%	70%	60%	50%	40%	30%	20%	10%
$1,500	$1,200	$995	$825	$700	$600	$550	$495	$440	$395	$340	$295

100%	98%	95%	90%	80%	70%	60%	50%	40%	30%	20%	10%

OPEN TOP REVOLVER (OLD LINE) — .22 Short or long rimfire, 2⅜ or 2⅞ in. barrel, without topstrap on frame, with or without integral ejector, blued or nickel plated, varnished walnut grips, approx. 114,200 mfg. 1871-1877.

$575	$450	$395	$350	$300	$280	$255	$230	$200	$175	$150	$125

NEW LINE REVOLVER AND VARIATIONS

1ST MODEL — .22, .30, .32, .38, or .41 cal. rim and centerfire, mfg. 1873-1876, 7 (.22 cal. only) or 5 shot, short cylinder flutes, cylinder stop slots cut on exterior of cylinder, 1¾, 2¼, or 4 in. barrel, full nickel or blue/case hardened finish, spur trigger, many thousands mfg. 1873-1876.

$475	$395	$325	$275	$250	$225	$200	$185	$170	$160	$145	$120

2ND MODEL — similar to 1st Model, except has longer cylinder flutes and cylinder stop slots are on the back of cylinder, may or may not have loading gate. Mfg. 1876-1884.

$475	$395	$325	$275	$250	$225	$200	$185	$170	$160	$145	$120

Caliber rarity on both models from highest mfg. to lowest is: .22, .32, .30, .41, and .38.

NEW HOUSE MODEL — .38 or .41 cal. centerfire, 5 shot, 2¼ in. barrel, spur trigger, checkered hard rubber grips. Approx. 4,000 mfg. 1880-1886 starting at ser. no. 10,300.

$1,350	$1,050	$925	$850	$725	$650	$575	$495	$440	$395	$325	$260

NEW POLICE MODEL — .32, .38, or .41 cal. centerfire, 5 shot, 2¼, 4½, 5, or 6 in. barrel, spur trigger, with or without ejector, stamped or etched "NEW POLICE" on barrel. Approx. 4,000 mfg. 1882-1886.

$950	$875	$775	$675	$600	$540	$495	$440	$395	$340	$295	$250

PERCUSSION CONVERSIONS

Research is currently underway to categorize the many variations (including Thuer) that exist on Percussion revolvers which were converted for centerfire capability. Over 46,000 conversions were made on the following models listed in order of highest mfg. to lowest: 1862 Police and Pocket Navy, Model 1860 Army Richards, Thuer's patent conversions, Model 1851 Navy, Model 1861 Navy, Model 1860 Army Richards-Mason. Out of these, the Models 1862 Police and Pocket Navy accounted for slightly over 50%. Be wary of "2nd" generation alterations. Prices generally are in the $650-$2,500+ range with rarer variations selling for considerably more. Cased models will command 175-300%+ premiums.

"OPEN TOP" REVOLVERS

Grading	80%	70%	60%	50%	40%	30%	20%	10%

1871-72 OPEN TOP MODEL RIMFIRE — .44 cal. rimfire, 6 shot, 7½ in. barrel, without frame topstrap, blued metal with casehardened hammer, serial range 1-approx. 7000, barrel address (ADDRESS COL. SAM COLT, NEW YORK, U.S. AMERICA), forerunner of the single action Army, quite desirable. Mfg. 1871-1872.

Regular Production Model — 7½ in. barrel, New York address, Army grips.

		$9,750	$8,000	$6,500	$5,500	$4,250	$3,000	$1,950	$1,250

Regular Production — with Navy grips.

		$10,250	$8,250	$6,750	$5,750	$4,500	$3,250	$2,000	$1,400

Late Production — with address (COLT PT. F. A. MANUFACTURING CO., HARTFORD, CT., U.S.A.).

		$7,750	$6,300	$5,350	$4,300	$3,000	$2,000	$1,500	$1,250

Note: Models with 8 in. barrel of COLTS/PATENT frame markings have added value.

REVOLVERS: SINGLE ACTION ARMY — 1873-1940 MFG. (SER. NO.'S 1 - 357,000)

Note: The Colt SAA was produced in over 30 Calibers with just about any special order feature or combination of special orders available directly from the factory. All of these special orders act independently and interdependently to determine a correct value for a particular Colt SAA. Single action Colt's rank at the top for revolver collectors. When contemplating a purchase in the 4 digit plus price range, several professional opinions should be secured. Caliber rarities make a major difference in pricing single actions.

Grading	80%	70%	60%	50%	40%	30%	20%	10%

It is advisable to procure a factory letter when buying or selling older or recently manufactured Colt Single Action's (hence guaranteeing authenticity and value credibility). These watermarked letters are available by writing Colt Firearms in Hartford, CT, with a charge of $35 per serial number - if Colt cannot provide you with proper documentation after conducting research, they will refund you $10. Include your name and address, Colt model name, serial number, and check to: COLT HISTORIAN, P.O. BOX 1868, HARTFORD, CT 06101. Please allow adequate time for proper response.

Values shown below are for guns without special order features. Factory engraving, ivory grips, very rare special order barrel lengths, and special finishes would add considerably to the values shown below. One final word on single action Colts: Black Powder Colts (pre 182,000 serial range) should be scrutinized carefully for restamped serial numbers on various parts. This makes a major difference in pricing the SAA, as a true, original collector's gun differs greatly in value from a restamped "parts gun". .44-40 and .45 cal.'s in the pre 182,000 serial range will bring premiums over other calibers, especially in shorter barrel lengths. The .44-40 caliber is very collectible since this ammunition at inception was interchangeable with the most popular rifle/carbine of its circa - the Winchester Model 1873.

EARLY MODEL SAA (PINCH FRAME) — serial range 1-100, with frame pinched to make rear sight, .45 cal., 7½ in. barrel. Mfg. 1813.

$17,500	$15,000	$13,000	$11,000	$9,250	$8,000	$6,750	$5,400

EARLY MARTIAL MARKED SAA — serial range to 24,000, .45 cal., 7½ in. barrel, U.S. marked.

$9,750	$8,250	$7,000	$6,300	$5,700	$4,950	$3,950	$2,950

.44 RIMFIRE SAA — mostly in .44 Henry rimfire, 7½ in. barrel, serial numbered in own range 1-1863, mfg. 1875-1880, most specimens were shipped to Mexico and saw hard use, rare in any original condition.

$14,000	$12,000	$10,500	$9,000	$7,600	$6,300	$5,000	$3,500

This variation is one of the most frequently faked Colt revolvers — be careful (and get a receipt).

SINGLE ACTION ARMY (SAA) — single action, 6 shot revolver, over 30 calibers, 3 in. (Sheriff's model), 4¾, 5½, 7½, and 12 in. (Buntline model) barrels. Blue, nickel, or case hardened frame, walnut or hard rubber grips, total production 357,000. Mfg. 1873-1940.

SAA'S with serial numbers before 182,000 are antiques and are generally more collectible than post-1898 SAA'S. Values for both periods of manufacture in the 10%-80% condition range are similar. Antique SAA revolvers in 80%-100% condition will average 15%-30% higher than modern mfg. (post-1898).

100%	98%	95%	90%	80%	70%	60%	50%	40%	30%	20%	10%

.45 cal.

$5,500	$4,500	$3,850	$3,000	$2,400	$1,950	$1,600	$1,225	$995	$785	$715	$660

.44-40 cal. — roll-die "Colt Frontier Six Shooter" marking on left side of barrel.

$6,750	$5,750	$4,600	$3,800	$3,100	$2,450	$2,000	$1,650	$1,375	$1,000	$875	$725

Colt changed from the etched barrel marking to a roll die in approx. 1881.

.41 cal.

$5,250	$4,300	$3,750	$2,800	$2,200	$1,750	$1,450	$1,050	$900	$700	$640	$550

.38-40 cal.

$5,000	$4,200	$3,650	$2,650	$2,050	$1,600	$1,300	$950	$825	$675	$600	$550

.32-20 cal.

$5,000	$4,200	$3,650	$2,650	$2,050	$1,600	$1,300	$950	$825	$675	$600	$550

.22 cal.

$13,500	$11,250	$8,750	$7,175	$6,600	$5,500	$4,400	$3,300	$2,750	$2,425	$2,050	$1,775

SAA IN .38 SPECIAL CAL. — only 82 made, plus 7 in. target version, pre-war.

$3,700	$3,450	$2,875	$2,300	$1,725	$1,265	$920	$850	$780	$720	$680	$630

CAVALRY MODEL SAA — .45 Colt, 7½ in. barrel, marked U.S. on left lower frame. With one piece walnut grips, military cartouche.

$13,500	$11,250	$8,750	$7,175	$6,600	$5,500	$4,400	$3,300	$2,750	$2,425	$2,050	$1,775

100%	98%	95%	90%	80%	70%	60%	50%	40%	30%	20%	10%

ARTILLERY MODEL SAA — .45 Colt, 5½ in. barrel, marked U.S. on left lower frame. With one piece walnut grips, military cartouche. These guns are the original artillery model Colts returned to the factory or Springfield Armory. Barrels were shortened to 5½ in. and the guns were refinished and reissued to the military. Very seldom do the serial numbered parts on these guns match. A factory letter on this model will designate factory refurbishing.

$6,750	$5,750	$4,600	$3,800	$3,100	$2,450	$2,150	$1,850	$1,575	$1,325	$1,175	$995

ETCHED BARREL .44-40 SAA — Colt Frontier, "Colt Frontier Six Shooter" acid etched into barrel instead of stamped, 21,000-65,000 ser. no. range.

$10,750	$9,600	$8,400	$7,200	$5,760	$4,500	$3,600	$3,000	$2,400	$2,000	$1,600	$1,200

This variation was only mfg. from 1876-1881. Watch for fake, replaced, or re-etched barrels.

SHERIFF'S MODEL SAA — 3, 4, or 4¾ (ultra rare) in. barrel, without ejector rod. Mfg. stopped 1927. Watch For Fakes.

$13,500	$11,000	$9,500	$8,400	$7,250	$6,100	$5,000	$4,000	$3,100	$2,500	$2,000	$1,800

Fakes can be detected on this model by re-welded frames.

A mint 4¾ in. Sheriff's Model recently brought an auction price of $21,000.

FLAT-TOP TARGET SAA — various calibers from .22 to .476 Eley, approx. 925 mfg., 1888-1896.

$14,500	$12,200	$11,000	$9,900	$8,800	$8,250	$7,700	$6,600	$6,050	$5,500	$4,750	$3,950

Note: Different calibers make a substantial difference in pricing for this model.

BISLEY MODEL SAA — differs from single action Army by hump backed grip frame and raked hammer, approx. 44,350 mfg., 1894-1915.

.32-20 cal.

$4,100	$3,600	$3,000	$2,600	$2,275	$1,900	$1,300	$1,100	$895	$715	$650	$550

.38-40 cal.

$4,500	$3,850	$3,250	$2,850	$2,450	$2,100	$1,400	$1,200	$925	$715	$650	$550

.41 cal.

$4,750	$4,000	$3,450	$2,950	$2,500	$2,250	$1,550	$1,250	$995	$800	$700	$625

.44-40 cal.

$5,000	$4,400	$3,750	$3,350	$2,900	$2,500	$2,100	$1,850	$1,600	$1,300	$995	$875

.45 cal.

$4,850	$4,100	$3,500	$2,950	$2,500	$2,250	$1,550	$1,250	$1,025	$850	$750	$650

.455 Eley — mfg. for the international revolver contests held in Bisley, England.

$6,000	$5,250	$4,650	$4,100	$3,650	$2,950	$2,650	$2,350	$1,950	$1,700	$1,400	$1,175

BISLEY TARGET FLAT-TOP — flat top frame, removable target sights, 976 mfg., 1894-1913. Values are 150% greater than respective Standard Bisley Models.

POST-WAR 1ST GENERATION SAA — approx. 860 manufactured in various configurations after 1945. These specimens in 98%+ condition will approximate values on the pre-war models. Ser. no. range 357,000-357,860.

2ND GENERATION SINGLE ACTION ARMY: 1956-1975 MFG.

Popular demand brought back the Single Action Army in 1956 with minor modifications, most not noticeable except to experts. Serial numbers began at 0001SA and continue to 73,000SA before the "New Model" was introduced in 1976 (ser. no. 80000 SA). Premiums are paid for rare production variances if NIB condition. Prices stated assume 7½ barrel length. It should be noted that many "premium niches" exist in this model as collectors are establishing premiums paid for rarer production variances (the inter- relation of barrel length, caliber, frame type, finish quality, year of manufacture, and other special features).

The order of desirability on standard 2nd generation SAA'S is as follows: 4¾ barrels are the most desirable, followed by 5½ in., and then 7½ in. Caliber desirability is as follows: .45 LC has the most demand followed by .44 Spl., .38 Spl., and then .357 Mag. It follows that desirable calibers found with desirable barrel lengths will command healthy premiums — especially if production was unusually low in a particular combination. Reference books specifically on the post-war SAA are a must when determining the rarity factors (or if they exist) on these multiple production combinations. Buntlines, Sheriff's models, and special orders through the Custom Gun Shop are in a class by themselves and have to be evaluated one at a time.

It is advisable to procure a factory letter when buying or selling older or recently manufactured Colt Single Action's (hence guaranteeing authenticity and value credibility). These water-marked letters are available by writing Colt Firearms in Hartford, CT, with a charge of $35 per serial number - if Colt cannot provide you with proper documentation after conducting research, they will refund you $10. Include your name and address, Colt model name, serial number, and check to: COLT HISTORIAN, P.O. BOX 1868, HARTFORD, CT 06101. Please allow adequate time for proper response.

Grading	100%	98%	95%	90%	80%	70%	60%

SINGLE ACTION ARMY

— SA suffix, .357 Mag., .38 Special, .44 Special., or .45 LC cal., 3 (Sheriff's Model), 4¾, 5½, 7½, or 12 in. (Buntline) barrel lengths, all blue, blue/case hardened, or nickel finishes, hard rubber stocks (standard until 1970).

	100%	98%	95%	90%	80%	70%	60%
.357 Mag.	$825	$725	$600	$550	$500	$475	$450
.38 Spl.	$975	$850	$750	$650	$615	$575	$550
.44 Spl.	$900	$800	$700	$625	$600	$575	$550
.45 LC	$1,100	$925	$775	$675	$625	$595	$550

Add 20-25% for 4¾ in. barrel.

Add 10-15% for nickel finish.

Add $200+ for original ivory grips.

Add $50-$75 for those pistols with original "black box".

100% assumes NIB condition for this model.

Earlier 2nd generations with the Rampant Colt grips (serial numbered under 50,000 approx.) are a little more desirable than those SAA's with Eagle grips (serial numbered over 50,000 approx.).

Early 2nd generation SAA's in 98%+ original condition with the black box (pre-1965) will command a premium over values listed above. "Stagecoach" boxes were used approx. 1965-1973 and are not quite as desirable as the one piece black box. Original "Stagecoach" boxes in excellent condition are currently selling for approx. $50.

Factory Engraved 2nd Generation SAA's — since approx. only 350 SAA's were factory engraved (with almost 90% being in .45 LC cal.), accurate pricing with this degree of rarity factor is difficult to ascertain with any degree of accuracy. Prices overall will be at least 50% higher than their 3rd generation engraved counterparts.

Factory engraved 2nd generation SAA's are at least 10 times rarer than 3rd generation engraved pistols.

Sheriff's Model — SM suffix, .45 cal., 3 in. barrel without ejector rod housing, casehardened finish, many custom options were ordered in this variation. Approx. 500 mfg. 1960-1975.

	100%	98%	95%	90%	80%	70%	60%
	$1,275	$975	$800	$750	$695	$625	$550

Add 20% for nickel finish.

Add $200 for ivory grips.

Buntline Special — .45 Colt only, 12 in. barrel, case hardened frame, hard rubber (rarer) or walnut grips. Over 3,900 mfg. between 1957-1975.

	100%	98%	95%	90%	80%	70%	60%
	$850	$700	$635	$600	$575	$550	$525

Add 50% for nickel finish (rare).

NEW FRONTIER

— "NF" suffix, flat-top frame, adj. rear sight, .357 Mag., .38 Spl. (rare), .44 Spl., or .45 cal., 4¾ (rare), 5½ (rare) or 7½ (common) in. barrel, uncheckered walnut grips, case-hardened frame, over 4,200 mfg. 1961-1975.

	100%	98%	95%	90%	80%	70%	60%
	$675	$600	$575	$550	$525	$500	$475

Nickel or full-blue finish is very rare in this model.

New Frontier Buntline Special — .45 Colt only, 12 in. barrel, flat-top frame, adj. rear sight. Approx. 70 mfg. 1962-1967.

	100%	98%	95%	90%	80%	70%	60%
	$1,550	$1,300	$995	$850	$725	$600	$500

3RD GENERATION SINGLE ACTION ARMY: 1976-1985 MFG.

Values below assume 7½ in. barrel (most frequently encountered barrel length).

The order of desirability on standard 3rd generation SAA'S is as follows: 4¾ barrels are the most desirable, followed by 5½ in., and then 7½ in. Caliber desirability is as follows: .44-40

Grading	100%	98%	95%	90%	80%	70%	60%

and .45 LC have the most demand followed by .44 Spl., .38 Spl., and then .357 Mag. It follows that desirable calibers found with desirable barrel lengths will command healthy premiums — especially if production was unusually low in a particular combination. Reference books specifically on the post-war SAA are a must when determining the rarity factors(or if they exist) on these multiple production combinations. Buntlines, Sheriff's models, and special orders through the Custom Gun Shop are in a class by themselves and have to be evaluated one at a time.

SINGLE ACTION ARMY — .357 Mag., .44 Spl., .44-40, or .45 LC cal., 3 (Sheriff's Model), $4\frac{3}{4}$, $5\frac{1}{2}$, $7\frac{1}{2}$, or 12 in. (Buntline) barrel lengths, all blue, blue/case hardened, or nickel finishes, walnut or rubber stocks.

3rd model production began in 1976 with ser. no. 80000SA and reached no. 99999SA in 1978. At this point the SA suffix changed to a prefix (beginning with SA01001).

It is advisable to procure a factory letter when buying or selling older or recently manufactured Colt Single Action's (hence guaranteeing authenticity and value credibility). These water-marked letters are available by writing Colt Firearms in Hartford, CT, with a charge of $35 per serial number - if Colt cannot provide you with proper documentation after conducting research, they will refund you $10. Include your name and address, Colt model name, serial number, and check to: COLT HISTORIAN, P.O. BOX 1868, HARTFORD, CT 06101. Please allow adequate time for proper response.

Standard Model

	100%	98%	95%	90%	80%	70%	60%
.357 Mag.	$675	$575	$515	$480	$460	$440	$420
.44 Spl.	$775	$675	$625	$550	$515	$485	$450
.44-40	$895	$750	$675	$600	$550	$500	$460
.44-40 Black Powder Frame	$975	$850	$700	$625	$575	$525	$475
.45 LC	$825	$700	$650	$575	$535	$495	$460

100% assumes NIB condition for this model.

Add 10% for $5\frac{1}{2}$ in. barrel.

Add 25%-30% for $4\frac{3}{4}$ in. barrel.

Add $200 for ivory grips.

Add $100 for nickel finish.

Buntline Special — .45 Colt only, 12 in. barrel, case hardened frame.

	$750	$650	$625	$600	$575	$535	$500

Add 10% for nickel finish.

New Frontier — "NF" suffix, flat-top frame, adj. rear sight, .44 Spl., .44-40 (rare), or .45 cal., $4\frac{3}{4}$ (rare), $5\frac{1}{2}$ (rare) or $7\frac{1}{2}$ (common) in. barrel, uncheckered walnut grips, case hardened frame. Mfg. 1978-1981.

	$525	$450	$425	$410	$395	$380	$365

3rd generation NF serialization can be differentiated from 2nd by 5 digits (starting with 0) followed by the NF suffix. 2nd generation guns had 4 digit numbers.

For factory engraved New Frontier Models, refer to above SAA engraved listing and subtract 25%.

New Frontier Buntline Special — .45 Colt only, 12 in. barrel, flat-top frame, adj. rear sight. Rare.

	$675	$575	$550	$525	$500	$485	$460

Sheriff's Model — .44-40 or .45 LC cal., 3 in. barrel without ejector rod housing, casehardened, nickel, or royal blue finish, approx. 4,560 guns mfg. 1980-85.

	$795	$695	$650	$575	$535	$495	$460

Add 10% for extra convertible cylinder.

Add 10% for nickel finish.

Add $200 for ivory grips.

This model was also available with two cylinders (.45 LC & .45 ACP or .44 Spl. & .44-40) — add $200. The .45 LC/.45 ACP is perhaps more desirable.

Storekeepers Model — .45 LC cal. only, black powder frame, 4 in. barrel, without ejector rod, casehardened, royal blue, or nickel finish, approx. 280 mfg. 1984-85.

	$1,195	$900	$795	$700	$650	$575	$535

Premiums will exist for nickel finish.

Grading	100%	98%	95%	90%	80%	70%	60%

FACTORY ENGRAVED 3RD GENERATION SAA'S

3rd generation factory engraved SAA's were produced in much greater numbers than their 2nd generation counterparts. As a result, pricing is also more predictable - especially on .45 LC cal. Since over 80% of all engraved 3rd generation SAA's are in .45 LC, values listed below represent this caliber. Engraved specimens encountered in other calibers (especially .44-40, approx. 2% of engraved production) will be considerably more expensive. Most specimens encountered are in 7½ in. barrel length. Pistols with 4¾ (most desirable) or 5½ in. barrels will add additional premiums (15%-30%).

SAA Class A Engraved — with class A engraving (25% coverage on gun).

	$1,275	$975	$875	$800	$725	$650	$575

Add 10% for nickel finish.

SAA Class B Engraved — with class B engraving (50% coverage on gun).

	$1,475	$1,130	$1,050	$975	$880	$760	$650

Add 10% for nickel finish.

SAA Class C Engraved — with class C engraving (75% coverage on gun).

	$1,650	$1,295	$1,125	$1,025	$925	$825	$725

Add 10% for nickel finish.

SAA Class D Engraved — with class D engraving (100% coverage on gun).

	$2,100	$1,625	$1,300	$1,125	$995	$875	$795

Add 15% for nickel finish.

SINGLE ACTION ARMY: CURRENT MFG. (1985-PRESENT)

Most collector interest in recently manufactured SAA's is for either mint or NIB specimens.

STANDARD SINGLE ACTION ARMY — .44-40 or .45 cal., 3 (special order only), 4 (disc. 1988), 4¾, 5 (disc. 1987), 5½, 7½ or 10 (special order only) in. barrel, blue, royal blue, color case hardened (reintroduced 1989), or nickel finish, blackpowder frame, 3 line patent date, custom order only.

Values below are for base gun with $271 of additional custom work already included in the price. While the price of the base gun is $879, a SAA custom order MUST EXCEED $1,120 RETAIL for Colt to accept the order.

Mfg.'s Sug. Retail	$1,120	$1,000	$775	$650	$575	$500	$450	$425

Popular SAA Special Order Options:

Add $127 for nickel finish.

Add $209 for royal blue finish.

Add $238 for mirror brite finish.

Add $386 for gold or silver plating.

Add $73-$110 for optional walnut/rosewood grips.

Add $405-$514 for ivory grips.

Add $75 for consecutive serial numbers (pair).

Add $225 for individual unique serial number.

Add $250 for custom barrel shortening.

Quotations upon request for color case hardening/metal finish mixing.

CUSTOM SHOP ENGRAVING — previous to 1990, Colt furnished retail values for their standard A, B, C, and D Custom Shop engraving patterns. In 1990, Colt engraving prices are available by quotation only. Values are determined by model and the other work to be performed on the gun.

Values below represent the last Colt factory advertised retail (1989).

Add $999 for Class "A" engraving (¼ metal coverage).

Add $1,996 for Class "B" engraving (½ metal coverage).

Add $2,995 for Class "C" engraving (¾ metal coverage).

Add $3,992 for Class "D" engraving (full metal coverage).

Add an additional 13% (approx.) for buntline engraving.

Grading	100%	98%	95%	90%	80%	70%	60%

Additional SAA Custom Order Options — the Colt Custom Shop will perform additional work (special orders including engraving, custom stocks, non-standard barrel lengths, gold or silver plating, and other custom features) if the individual work order totals over $1,120 retail. Quotations are supplied at $25/each for these special order guns. Please contact the Colt Custom Gun Shop for this written estimate regarding these custom built SAA's. Their address is: Colt Customer Service Dept., Attn: SAA Quotation, P.O. Box 1868, Hartford, CT 06101.

SCOUT MODEL SAA

FRONTIER SCOUT (Q or F SUFFIX) — .22 LR or .22 Mag. (introduced after 1960) cal., "Q" or "F" suffix, blue with bright alloy frame, all blue, or duotone ("Q" models only) finish (rare), 4¾ or 9½ (Buntline) barrel, available with interchangeable cylinders after 1964, black composition or walnut grips, approx. 246,000 mfg. 1957-1970.

	$325	$275	$225	$190	$170	$150	$140

Add 10% for extra cylinder.

Add 20% for Buntline model.

Add 25% for "Q" suffix - mfg. 1957-58 only.

FRONTIER SCOUT (K SUFFIX) — Zamac alloy frame version of "Q" Model with "K" suffix, blue or nickel finish with walnut stocks, approx. 44,000 mfg. 1960-1970.

	$350	$280	$250	$220	$195	$170	$150

Add 25% for nickel finish.

This model used the alloy Zamac for manufacture (as opposed to aluminum in the "Q" and "F" suffix models), and specimens are 6 oz. heavier as a result.

FRONTIER SCOUT '62 (P SUFFIX) — blue finish version of "K" Model, except has "P" suffix, staglite grips, approx. 68,000 mfg. 1962-1970.

	$350	$280	$250	$220	$195	$170	$150

PEACEMAKER — .22 LR/.22 Mag., color casehardened steel frame, 4⅜, 6, or 7½ (nicknamed Buntline Model but may be marked Peacemaker or Buntline) in. barrel, black composition grips, furnished with interchangeable .22 LR/.22 Mag. cylinders, approx. 190,000 mfg. 1970-1977.

	$300	$260	$225	$185	$160	$140	$130

Add 20% for Buntline model or 4¾ in. barrel.

Subtract $35 if without extra cylinder.

This model can be denoted by a "G" or "L" prefix.

NEW FRONTIER — similar features as Peacemaker Model, except with flat top frame, ramp front and adj. rear sight, mfg. 1970-1977. Reintroduced in 1982 without convertible .22 Mag. cylinder and added cross bolt safety, available in Coltguard finish, all blue finish became standard in 1985, mfg. disc. 1986.

	$280	$240	$200	$175	$155	$140	$130

Add 15% for Buntline model or 4¾ in. barrel.

This model can be denoted by a "G" or "L" prefix.

Last Mfg.'s Sug. Retail was $181.

PISTOLS: SEMI-AUTO

Until several years ago, the Single Action Army revolver commanded the most attention among Colt handgun collectors. Since 1987, Colt Semi-Auto's have been in tremendous demand and have out-accelerated every other area of Colt collecting. Because condition and originality play such a key role in determining Colt Semi-Auto prices, many variations have had their values pushed upward to the point where it is difficult to accurately determine a realistic price - especially on those models in 98% original condition or better. As a result, 95% through 100% values in this section are meant to be used only as a guideline. It is important to notice the spread in values in this section, since pistols in 95%+ original condition get very expensive. Four years ago I doubt whether the same specimen would have brought $1,500. As always, the hardest prices to ascertain when firearms market conditions are bullish are the 98-100% values.

Grading	100%	98%	95%	90%	80%	70%	60%

MODEL 1900 — .38 ACP, 6 in. barrel, blue, fixed sights, plain walnut grips - checkered hard rubber grips after S/N 2,450, high spur hammer, sight safety. Mfg. 1900-1903.

	100%	98%	95%	90%	80%	70%	60%
	$6,750	$5,350	$3,850	$2,500	$1,400	$925	$750

Add 60%+ for USN marked.

Add 50% for US marked with inspector initials.

Deduct 30%-50% for sight safety altered (factory refinished).

This model is serial numbered approx. between 1-4,274.

MODEL 1902 SPORTING — .38 ACP, 6 in. barrel, blue, fixed sights, checkered hard rubber grips, no safety, high spur hammer and round hammer. Mfg. 1902-1908.

			95%	90%	80%	70%	60%
	$3,800	$2,600	$1,300	$975	$750	$625	$450

This model is serial numbered approx. 4,275-11,000 and 30,000-30,190.

MODEL 1902 MILITARY — .38 ACP, 6 in. barrel, blue, similar to 1902 Sporting, hammer changed to spur type in 1908, checkered black hard rubber grips, Lanyard swivel on bottom rear ofleft grip. Mfg. 1902-1929.

			95%	90%	80%	70%	60%
	$2,250	$1,600	$900	$700	$625	$550	$425

Add 10% for front slide checkering.

This model is serial numbered approx. 11,000-16,000 and 30,200-43,266.

MODEL 1902 MILITARY-U.S. ARMY MARKED — similar specifications to 1902 Military, only serial number range 15,001-15,200.

			95%	90%	80%	70%	60%
	$8,500	$6,500	$5,000	$4,000	$3,500	$2,750	$1,950

MODEL 1903 POCKET (MODEL M 38 ACP) — .38 ACP, 4½ in. barrel, blue finish, checkered black hard rubber grips, similar to 1902 Sporting, but 4½ in. barrel, 7½ in. overall. Mfg. 1903-1929.

			95%	90%	80%	70%	60%
	$1,200	$850	$700	$600	$475	$400	$350

Add 10% for early round hammer.

This model is serial numbered approx. 16,000-47,226.

MODEL 1903 POCKET (MODEL M 32 ACP) — .32 ACP, 4 in. barrel, wood blue, checkered hard rubber grips, hammerless, slide lock and grip safety, barrel lock bushing. Mfg. 1903-1940.

			95%	90%	80%	70%	60%
	$475	$375	$325	$275	$230	$200	$175

Add $50 for nickel finish (mostly w/pearl grips).

Add 20% for first model (Type I) mfg. 1903-1911.

Type I - 32 ACP's have a 4 in. barrel, barrel bushing, no magazine safety, and are serial numbered 1-71,999.

Type II - 32 ACP's still retain their barrel bushing but have a 3¾ in. barrel and were mfg. from 1908-1910. They are serial numbered 72,000-105,050.

Type III - 32 ACP's do not have a barrel bushing and were mfg. from 1910-1926. They are serial numbered 105,051-468,096.

Type IV - 32 ACP's have the added magazine safety (of which there are both the commercial and "U.S. Property" variations). They are serial numbered 468,097-554,446.

Model 1903 Parkerized — U.S. property, 3¼ in. barrel, no barrel bushing, magazine safety, serial numbered 554,447-572,214.

			95%	90%	80%	70%	60%
	$925	$750	$625	$475	$375	$320	$275

MODEL 1905 — .45 ACP, 5 in. barrel, blue fixed sights, checkered walnut stocks, similar to 1902 .38 ACP. Mfg. 1905-1911.

			95%	90%	80%	70%	60%
	$3,150	$2,400	$1,750	$1,250	$800	$650	$500

Add 100% for 1907 U.S. Military Contract variation.

The shoulder stock option for this pistol is exceedingly rare. Depending on the condition, this accessory can add $5,000-$10,000 to the price of the gun.

Grading	100%	98%	95%	90%	80%	70%	60%

MODEL 1908 POCKET (MODEL M 380 ACP) — .380 ACP, first issue, 3¾ in.barrel only, same as Pocket Model .32 ACP (32 ACP), except chambered for .380 ACP. Mfg. 1908-1940.

	$750	$600	$425	$350	$300	$250	$225

Add 15% for Type II (see explanation below).

Add $50 for nickel finish (mostly w/pearl grips).

Type II - 380 ACP's with barrel bushing and were mfg. 1908-1910 (6,251 mfg.). They are serial numbered 1-6,251.

Type III - 380 ACP's do not have a barrel bushing and were mfg. 1910-1926. They are serial numbered 6,252-92,893.

Type IV - 380 ACP's have the added magazine safety (of which there are both the commercial and "U.S. Property" variations). They are serial numbered 92,894-134,499.

Model 1908 "U.S. Property" — blue finish only, U.S. property. Serial numbered 134,500-138,000.

	$1,250	$950	$775	$600	$500	$400	$300

VEST POCKET MODEL 1908-HAMMERLESS — .25 ACP, 2 in. barrel, fixed sights, checkered hard rubber grips on early models, walnut on later, magazine disconnect added on guns made after 1916. Mfg. 1908-1941.

	100%	98%	95%	90%	80%	70%	60%
Blue finish	$450	$375	$315	$270	$240	$200	$155
Nickel finish	$475	$375	$295	$260	$220	$165	$130

100% values assume NIB condition. Deduct 15% if without cardboard box.

MODEL 1909 — .45 ACP, straight handle design, 5 in. barrel, checkered walnut grips, approx. 22 mfg., ultra rare.

Extreme rarity factor precludes accurate price evaluation by individual condition factors. Specimens that are original and over 90% have sold for over $35,000 recently.

GOV.'T MODEL 1911 COMMERCIAL VARIATIONS

MODEL 1911 — .45 ACP, 5 in. barrel, fixed sights, 7 shot mag., flat main spring housing, polished blue finish only (commercial and original military), checkered walnut grips. Colt licensed other companies to manufacture under government contracts, 39 oz. Mfg. 1912-1925.

Most M1911 variations listed below are not as collectible if under 60% original condition. However, they are still very desirable as shooters and values (if in original condition) will approximate the 60% prices if in good mechanical condition.

Add 20% for 4-digit ser. no., 40% for 3-digit, 60%+ for 2-digit.

Colt Model 1911's are enjoying high demand as of this writing and prices have increased the most in the 95%-100% condition factors. Be careful on the 98%+ condition specimens, especially the rarer variations. Some collectors are now requiring a potential high-dollar Model 1911 to pass an X-ray or fluroscope test (detects welding and other metalurgical alterations) before purchasing.

Model 1911 Commercial — denoted by "C" preceding serial number, approx. ser. number range C1-C138,532. Watch for fakes.

	100%	98%	95%	90%	80%	70%	60%
1912-1914 mfg.	$2,150	$1,600	$1,200	$875	$595	$450	$395
1914-1925 mfg.	$1,850	$1,400	$995	$775	$550	$425	$375

Approx. 138,532 were mfg. between 1912-1925.

GOV.'T MODEL 1911 .45 ACP MILITARY VARIATIONS

COLT MFG. MODEL 1911 MILITARY — right side of slide marked "MODEL OF 1911 U.S. ARMY", blue finish only (NOT parkerized unless reworked).

	100%	98%	95%	90%	80%	70%	60%
1912-1913 mfg.	$1,850	$1,300	$795	$675	$475	$450	$400
1914-1925 mfg.	$1,350	$995	$750	$595	$540	$425	$375

Over 2,550,000 M1911 pistols were ordered during WWI by U.S. Government but approx. 650,000 were mfg. between 1911-1925. Those pistols with a parkerized finish will indicate post-WWI reworking, usually marked with an arsenal code (ie. AA-AUGUSTA ARSENAL, SA-SPRINGFIELD ARSENAL, etc.). These reworks do not have the same values as original, unaltered specimens and prices generally are in the $295-$475 range.

Grading	100%	98%	95%	90%	80%	70%	60%

NORTH AMERICAN ARMS COMPANY — less than 100 mfg. in Quebec, Ontario during 1918 only, blued finish. Be very wary of fakes as this variation is perhaps the most desirable Colt WWI Gov't semi-auto.

	$10,750	$8,750	$7,950	$7,100	$6,000	$5,250	$4,500

REMINGTON - UMC — over 21,500 mfg. (ser. numbered 1-21,676) in 1918-1919 only, blued finish.

	$1,375	$1,075	$800	$625	$550	$495	$450

SPRINGFIELD ARMORY — approx. 30,000 mfg. between 1914-1915, blued finish.

	$1,275	$995	$775	$575	$500	$465	$425

Serialization is 72,751-83,855, 102,597-107,596, 113,497-120,566, and 125,567-133,186.

U.S. NAVY — over 31,000 mfg. for U.S. Navy contract between 1911-1914 in defined serial ranges, blued finish. Marked "MODEL OF 1911 U.S. NAVY" on right slide side.

	$2,750	$2,200	$1,800	$1,500	$1,200	$995	$750

U.S. Navy specimens are seldomly found in over 80% original condition because of the corrosive factor encountered while at sea.

U.S. MARINE CORPS. — approx. 13,500 mfg. between 1911-1913 and 1916-1918 in defined serial ranges, blued finish, right side of slide marked "MODEL OF 1911 U.S. ARMY".

	$2,750	$2,200	$1,800	$1,500	$1,200	$995	$750

WWI BRITISH SERIES — .455 cal., serialized W10001-W21000, marked "CALIBRE 455", blued finish, proofed with broad arrow British Ordnance punch Mfg. 1915-1916.

	$1,350	$1,000	$850	$750	$625	$525	$475

Add 25% for variations with either Navy or Marine markings. Many WWI British-series M1911's were exported back to the U.S. following WWI and were converted to .45 ACP. Usually, a "5" has been crossed-out of the original cal. designation. These reworks are not as collectible and prices range from $350-$500.

BRITISH RAF REWORK — this variation is the WWI British series re-issued to RAF officers in the early 1920's, blued finish, differentiated by hand-stamped "RAF" or "R.A.F." on left side of frame.

	$975	$875	$825	$675	$575	$495	$460

A.J. SAVAGE MUNITIONS CO. — mfg. slides only, blued finish, marked in middle on left side of slide with flaming ordnance bomb with "S" in center.

	$1,275	$1,000	$850	$750	$675	$600	$525

NORWEGIAN TRIAL MODEL 1911 COLT — 11.25mm cal., approx. 300 mfg. with "C" prefix in 1913-14 only, usually encounterd in 90% or less condition.

	$1,500	$1,250	$950	$850	$775	$685	$595

These guns were ordered for Norwegian service evaluation and were mfg. by Colt's in Hartford, CT.

NORWEGIAN MODEL 1912 11.25MM — 11.25mm cal., mfg. under license from Colt's between 1917-1919, "M1912" slide designation, approx. 500 mfg.

	$1,250	$950	$850	$775	$685	$595	$495

NORWEGIAN 1914 11.25MM — This model has a distinctive extended slide release, approx. 20,000 mfg. between 1919-1932.

	$850	$700	$600	$525	$475	$425	$375

Add 100% for Waffenamt Nazi mfg. (mfg. 1945 only).
Nazi production of the M1914 began in 1941, with serialization beginning where 1932 mfg. left off (approx. 21,000 range). Between 1941-42, approx. 7,000 pistols were mfg. without Waffenamt stampings. Nazi stamped guns (all 1945 dated) began in the mid-29,000 serial range and existing specimens indicate that approx. 1,000 were mfg. with the Nazi Eagle.

ARGENTINE CONTRACT — mfg. 1917-1925, ser. no.'s are in C20,001-21,000 and C110,000-130,000 range, slide marked "Pistola Automatica Sistema Colt, Calilbre 11,25 mm, Modelo 1916", usually marked with Argentine seal.

	$825	$625	$540	$495	$450	$410	$350

Grading	100%	98%	95%	90%	80%	70%	60%

This variation is not to be confused with the Ballestar Molina Model with integral grip strap (.45 ACP or .22 LR) that resembles a Colt 1911, but was not licensed or mfg. by Colt. 100% value for the .45 ACP is $400 - add 100% for .22 LR Target Model.

RUSSIAN CONTRACT — approx. 50,000 mfg. with frame marked "ANGLO ZAKAZIVAT", blued finish. Mfg. 1915-1917, seldomly encountered - watch for fakes.

	$2,450	$1,825	$1,575	$1,350	$1,200	$1,100	$1,000

GOV.'T MODEL 1911A1 & VARIATIONS

MODEL 1911 A1 — .45 ACP, blue or parkerized, checkered walnut grips, plastic on later military guns, checkered arched mainspring housing and longer grip safety spur. As in the Model 1911, Colt licensed other companies to produce under gov't contract during WWII. Mfg. 1925-1970.
Inspect carefully for arsenal reworks (so marked by proofing, normally on left side of frame above or behind trigger), and reparkerizing.

Most M1911 A1 variations listed below are not as collectible if under 60% original condition. However, they are still very desirable as shooters and values (if in original condition) will approximate the 60% prices if in good mechanical condition.

PRE-WWII COLT COMMERCIAL — "C" preceding serial number, mfg. 1925-1942. Approx. ser. no. range C138,533-C215,000.

	$1,150	$950	$750	$620	$575	$495	$400

1946-1969 COLT COMMERCIAL — "C" prefix until 1950 when changed to "C" suffix, approx. 196,000 mfg. 1946-1970.

	$575	$495	$425	$395	$360	$330	$295

Add 20% for "C" prefix models after ser. no. 221,000.

SUPER .38 AUTOMATIC PISTOL — identical to Gov't Model .45, except chambered for .38 Super automatic. Mfg. 1928-1970.

	100%	98%	95%	90%	80%	70%	60%
Pre-War	$2,000	$1,600	$1,250	$1,000	$875	$775	$675
Post-War	$600	$500	$425	$365	$325	$300	$280

Pre-war variations are serialized below 34,450.

SUPER MATCH .38 — same as Super .38, but hand honed action, match grade barrel. Mfg. 1935-1941. Examine carefully for fakes.

	100%	98%	95%	90%	80%	70%	60%
Fixed sights	$3,500	$2,750	$2,000	$1,600	$1,200	$1,000	$850
Add 10% for adj. sights.							

SUPER MATCH .38 MS — .38 Super cal., 1961 mfg., serial numbered 101MS - 855MS, 754 total manufactured, same configuration as the .38 Midrange.

	$2,400	$1,950	$1,675	$1,495	$1,375	$1,175	$1,000

1968-1969 BB TRANSITIONAL

	$775	$695	$600	$550	$495	$425	$375

.45 ACP TO .22 LR CONVERSION UNIT — consists of slide assembly, barrel, bushing, floating chamber ejector, recoil spring and guide, magazine and slide stop. Mfg. 1938-present. Add 100% for pre-war manufacture ("U"-prefix serial on slide). Over 5,000 mfg. in all variations.

	100%	98%	95%	90%	80%	70%	60%
Adj. sight	$295	$250	$175	$150	$140	$120	$100
Fixed sight	$235	$190	$160	$140	$120	$110	$100

.22 LR TO .45 ACP CONVERSION UNIT — converted service Ace .22 to .45 ACP. Mfg. 1938-1942. Very rare — 112 mfg.

	$2,500	$2,000	$1,500	$1,000	$800	$700	$600

These units are serial numbered on top of slide.

GOV.'T MODEL 1911A1 MILITARY VARIATIONS

Grading	100%	98%	95%	90%	80%	70%	60%

COLT MFG. MODEL 1911A1 MILITARY — approx. 1,643,068 mfg. between 1924-1945, ser. no.'s 700,000 - on up, right side of frame marked "M1911A1 U.S. ARMY".

	$600	$525	$465	$400	$350	$325	$295

Add 30% for SA marked post-WWII National Match.
On early 1911 A1 military models with bright blue finish — add 100% if condition is 98% or better.

ITHACA — approx. 369,129 mfg. 1943-1945 in Ithaca, NY, ser. no. ranges 856,101 - 916,404, 1,208,674 - 1,279,673, 1,441,431 - 1,471,430, 1,816,642 - 1,890,503, and 2,619,014 - 2,693,613. Parkerized finish.

	$550	$495	$450	$395	$355	$330	$300

UNION SWITCH AND SIGNAL — approx. 55,000 mfg. 1943 only in Swissvale, PA, ser. no. range 1,041,405 - 1,096,404. Parkerized finish.

	$975	$825	$650	$525	$475	$425	$395

REMINGTON RAND — approx. 1,086,624 mfg. 1943-1945 in Syracuse, NY, ser. no. ranges 916,405 - 1,041,404, 1,279,649 - 1,441,430, 1,471,431 - 1,609,528, 1,743,847 - 1,816,641, 1,890,504 - 2,075,103, 2,134,404 - 2,244,803, and 2,380,014 - 2,619,013. Parkerized finish.

	$550	$475	$435	$375	$340	$320	$295

SINGER MFG. CO. — 500 mfg. 1942 in Elizabeth, NJ, ser. no. range S800,001 - S800,500. Parkerized finish.

	$12,750	$10,750	$9,150	$8,375	$7,500	$6,750	$5,875

The Singer 1911A1 variation is one of the most sought after Colt models. In recent years, values have increased significantly and as a result, many fakes have emerged. Most specimens are now recognized by ser. no. and be very cautious when contemplating a purchase. Some collectors unsure of authenticity are now requiring X-ray testing to determine originality (slide restampings, ser. no. changes, etc.).

MEXICAN CONTRACT — mfg. approx. 1921-1927 with "C" prefix ser. no.'s, frames marked "EJERCITO MEXICANO", most surviving examples show much use.

	$1,200	$1,000	$825	$700	$625	$550	$495

BRAZILIAN

	$995	$895	$795	$695	$595	$550	$495

ARGENTINE CONTRACT — mfg. 1927-early 30's, ser. no.'s are in low C140,000 range, slide marked "EJERCITO ARGENTINO COLT.CAL.45 MOD.1927" checkered walnut grips. This variation has recently been imported again.

	$550	$495	$425	$385	$350	$325	$295

In 1927, the Argentina Arsenal began manufacturing the Model 1911A1. The slide marking is two lines and reads "EJERCITO ARGENTINO SYST.COLT.CAL. 11.25 mm MOD.1927". Values will approximate those shown above.

ACE MODELS: PRE-WWII

COMMERCIAL ACE — .22 LR, similar to Government .45 ACP, but in .22LR cal., 4¾ in. barrel, blue, adj. sights, checkered walnut grips, almost 11,000 mfg. (ser. no. range 1-10,935) 1931-1941 and 1947.

	$1,650	$1,400	$995	$800	$625	$475	$425

SERVICE MODEL ACE — .22 LR, 5 in. barrel, blue or parkerized finish, same as .45 ACP National Match except for caliber, has floating chamber to simulate .45 ACP recoil, limited mfg. 1935-1945.

	$1,800	$1,425	$1,150	$875	$675	$525	$460

This variation is marked "SERVICE MODEL" on left frame, serial numbers have "SM" prefix and have ranges to approx. 13,800. Parkerized finish seems to be less desirable.

Grading	100%	98%	95%	90%	80%	70%	60%

PRE-WWII NATIONAL MATCH MODELS

NATIONAL MATCH — .45 ACP, same as Government Model, except has hand honed action, match grade barrel, blue. Mfg. 1933-1941 within ser. no. range C164,800 - C215,000.
Fixed sights

	$1,800	$1,375	$1,050	$750	$625	$550	$500

Adj. sights

	$2,500	$2,000	$1,750	$1,475	$1,200	$995	$750

DRAKE CUSTOM NATIONAL MATCH — while Drake made slides, they did not produce any complete pistols.
An original Drake conversion sells in the $850-$1,150 range, depending on condition.

GOVERNMENT NATIONAL MATCH REWORKS — assembled by government armorers, all parts marked "NM", parkerized finish.

		$1,100	$950	$800	$675	$585	$510	$450

These pistols were made specifically for the U.S. shooting team at Camp Perry.

POST-WWII NATIONAL MATCH MODELS

GOLD CUP NATIONAL MATCH — .45 ACP, match grade barrel, new design bushing, flat mainspring housing, long adj. stop trigger, hand fitted slide with enlarged ejection port, adj. target sights, gold medallions in grips, "NM" suffix. Mfg. 1957-1970.

		$725	$625	$550	$450	$405	$380	$350

Note: This model was the first National Match Model manufactured following WW II.

GOLD CUP MKIII NATIONAL MATCH — .38 Spl., same as Gold Cup National Match, except chambered for .38 Spl., mid-range wadcutter. Mfg. 1961-1974.

	$825	$750	$695	$625	$575	$475	$435

MKIV/SERIES 70 GOLD CUP NATIONAL MATCH — .45 ACP, flat mainspring housing, accurizer barrel and bushing, adj. trigger, target hammer, solid rib, Colt Elliason sight. Mfg. 1970-1983.

		$595	$550	$495	$465	$435	$395	$360

MKIV/SERIES 70 GOLD CUP 75TH ANNIVERSARY NATIONAL MATCH — same as Gold Cup except for commemorative aspect for Camp Perry, 1978, 200 made; add 100% to standard Mark IV/Series 70 Gold Cup prices.

GOLD CUP MKIV SERIES 80 NATIONAL MATCH — .45 ACP, 5 in. barrel, 7 shot mag., 39 oz., Colt-Elliason adj. rear sight, wide grooved adj. target trigger, under cut front sight, flat mainspring housing, critical internal parts are hand honed. Mfg. 1983-present.

Mfg.'s Sug. Retail	$820	$660	$530	$450	$400	$380	$350	$325

Stainless Gold Cup National Match — similar to Gold Cup, only manufactured from stainless steel, matte finish, released late in 1986.

Mfg.'s Sug. Retail	$875	$700	$550	$450

Add $65 for "Ultimate" bright stainless steel finish.

BULLSEYE NATIONAL MATCH — .45 ACP cal., hand built, tuned, and adjusted by Colt's custom gunsmiths for precise match accuracy, includes factory installed Bomar sights, equipped with carrying case and 2 extra mag.'s. 1991 release.

Mfg.'s Sug. Retail	$1,500	$1,325	$1,075	$895	$800	$725	$650	$600

PRESENTATION GOLD CUP — .45 ACP cal., similar to regular Gold Cup Series 80 National Match, except has a deep blue-mirror bright finish accented by custom jeweled hammer, trigger, and barrel hood. Supplied with oak and velvet custom case. 1991 release.

Mfg.'s Sug. Retail	$1,195	$1,075	$895	$800	$725	$650	$600	$550

PISTOLS: SEMI-AUTO, RECENT MFG.

The values listed below are the last published factory engraving prices - factory specified "Class A - Class D" pricing was discontinued late 1990. Beginning in 1991, factory engraving on the models listed below is done per individual price quotation. Quotations from Colt are available at $25 each (deductible from work order). These prices (disc. 1990) should

Grading	100%	98%	95%	90%	80%	70%	60%

be added to the cost of each engraved production gun (NIB condition only) to determine an approximate value.

MODEL'S MUSTANG, .380 ACP GOVERNMENT, DETECTIVE SPECIAL, AND DIAMONDBACK

CLASS "A" ENGRAVING (¼ METAL COVERAGE) — ADD $587.

CLASS "B" ENGRAVING (½ METAL COVERAGE) — ADD $793.

CLASS "C" ENGRAVING (¾ METAL COVERAGE) — ADD $1,026.

CLASS "D" ENGRAVING (FULL METAL COVERAGE) — ADD $1,203.

MODEL'S .45 ACP GOLD CUP, GOVERNMENT MODEL, OFFICER'S ACP, PYTHON, COMBAT COMMANDER, KING COBRA, TROOPER MKV, LAWMAN MKV, AND DELTA ELITE.

CLASS "A" ENGRAVING (¼ METAL COVERAGE) — ADD $734.

CLASS "B" ENGRAVING (½ METAL COVERAGE) — ADD $997.

CLASS "C" ENGRAVING (¾ METAL COVERAGE) — ADD $1,231.

CLASS "D" ENGRAVING (FULL METAL COVERAGE) — ADD $1,495.

Beginning in 1991, Colt began shipping all models in a distinctive blue plastic carrying case/shipping container.

SPECIAL ENGRAVING/OPTIONS — Also available: inlays, seals, custom grips, lettering, prices quoted on request. Smooth ivory grips are $215 extra (1990 retail).

JUNIOR POCKET MODEL — 2¼ in. barrel, blue, checkered walnut grips, made by Astra in Spain from 1958-1968.

	100%	98%	95%	90%	80%	70%	60%
.22 Short	$295	$265	$240	$210	$180	$160	$140
.25 ACP	$250	$225	$200	$180	$150	$140	$130

Add 10% for nickel finish.

A very few conversion kits were offered for this model. They are rare and asking prices are $225-$300 if in mint condition.

COLT AUTOMATIC CALIBER .25 — .25 ACP cal., mfg. by Firearms International for Colt between 1970-1973.

	100%	98%	95%	90%	80%	70%	60%
	$275	$240	$215	$185	$150	$140	$130

MKIV/SERIES 70 GOVERNMENT MODEL — .45 ACP, .38 Super, 9mm, or 9mm Steyr, 5 in. barrel, checkered walnut grips/medallion. A slight premium might be asked for the Series 70 models if NIB. Series 70 models were mfg. 1970-1983 and were serial numbered with with "70G" prefixes 1970-1976, "G70" suffixes 1976-1980, "B70" suffixes 1979-1981, and "70B" prefixes 1981-1983.

	100%	98%	95%	90%	80%	70%	60%
Blue finish	$495	$425	$375	$330	$300	$275	$250
Nickel finish	$525	$450	$400	$345	$315	$285	$260

9mm Steyr was made for European exportation only. However, a few specimens have found their way into the United States. Prices for NIB specimens usually start in the $595+ range.

Series 70 Combat Gov.'t —.45 ACP cal., bluish-black metal finish, features modifications for combat shooting, forerunner to the Combat Elite.

	100%	98%	95%	90%	80%	70%	60%
	$495	$450	$415	$380	$360	$340	$320

Conversion Unit — converts .45 ACP to .22 LR

	100%	98%	95%	90%	80%	70%	60%
	$250	$230	$210	$190	$170	$155	$140

POST-WAR ACE SERVICE MODEL — .22 LR, similar specifications to previous Pre-WWII manufacture, "SM" prefix, approx. 30,000 mfg. between 1978-1982.

	100%	98%	95%	90%	80%	70%	60%
	$575	$495	$450	$415	$380	$360	$340

This model is serial numbered SM14,001-SM43,830.

MKIV/SERIES 80 GOVERNMENT MODEL — .45 ACP, .38 Super or 9mm Para. cal., single action, 5 in. barrel, 7 shot mag. in .45, approx. 38 oz., action has new firing pin safety, checkered walnut grips with medallion. Production started in 1983 with ser. no. FG01000.

Blue Finish

	100%	98%	95%	90%	80%	70%	60%
Mfg.'s Sug. Retail	$640	$520	$450	$375	$340	$315	$295	$275

Add $10 for 9mm Para. or .38 Super cal.

Grading	100%	98%	95%	90%	80%	70%	60%

Nickel Finish — available in .45 ACP (disc. 1986) or .38 Super (disc. in 1987) cal.

	100%	98%	95%	90%	80%	70%	60%
	$525	$465	$380	$350	$315	$285	$260

Last Mfg.'s Sug. Retail was $600.

Satin Nickel/Blue — is supplied with Colt-Pachmayr grips. Disc. 1986.

	$510	$445	$370	$345	$310	$280	$255

Last Mfg.'s Sug. Retail was $557.

Stainless Steel — 9mm Para. (new 1991), .38 Super (new 1990), or .45 ACP cal.

Mfg.'s Sug. Retail	$685	$560	$480	$425			

Add $5 for 9mm Para. or 38 Super cal.

"Ultimate" Bright Stainless Steel — . 38 Super (new 1991) or .45 ACP cal., high polish stainless finish. New 1986.

Mfg.'s Sug. Retail	$750	$610	$500	$450			

Conversion Unit — converts .45 ACP to .22 LR (Series 70 and 80) or 9mm (Series 80 only). Disc. 1987.

	$270	$240	$210	$190	$170	$155	$140

Last Mfg.'s Sug. Retail was $305.

MKIV/SERIES 80 GOLD CUP NATIONAL MATCH — .45 ACP, flat mainspring housing, accurizer barrel and bushing, adj. trigger, target hammer, solid rib, Colt-Elliason sight, made 1983-present.

Mfg.'s Sug. Retail	$820	$660	$530	$450	$400	$380	$350	$325

Stainless Gold Cup National Match — similar to Gold Cup, only manufactured from stainless steel, matte finish, released late in 1986.

Mfg.'s Sug. Retail	$875	$700	$550	$450			

Add $65 for "Ultimate" bright stainless steel finish.

Bullseye National Match — .45 ACP cal., hand built, tuned, and adjusted by Colt's custom gunsmiths for precise match accuracy, includes factory installed Bomar sights, equipped with carrying case and 2 extra mag.'s. 1991 release.

Mfg.'s Sug. Retail	$1,500	$1,325	$1,075	$895	$800	$725	$650	$600

Presentation Gold Cup — .45 ACP cal., similar to regular Gold Cup Series 80 National Match, except has a deep blue-mirror bright finish accented by custom jeweled hammer, trigger, and barrel hood. Supplied with oak and velvet custom case. 1991 release.

Mfg.'s Sug. Retail	$1,195	$1,075	$895	$800	$725	$650	$600	$550

Combat Elite — similar to Gold Cup, only with Colt-Pachmayr wrap around rubber grips, beveled magazine well, stainless steel receiver with carbon steel slide, and 3 dot fixed sighting system.

Mfg.'s Sug. Retail	$775	$650	$580	$450	$400	$360	$330	$300

.380 SERIES 80 GOVERNMENT MODEL — .380 ACP only, single action, 3¼ in. barrel, 7 shot mag., fixed sights, composition stocks, 21¾ oz. New 1985.

Blue Finish

Mfg.'s Sug. Retail	$420	$335	$290	$235	$215	$200	$190	$180

Nickel Finish — bright polish nickel finish with white composite grips.

Mfg.'s Sug. Retail	$470	$385	$320	$270	$240	$220	$210	$200

Coltguard Finish — employs a high strength electroless matte nickel finish. Mfg. 1986-1989.

	$325	$300	$260	$235	$210	$200	$185

Last Mfg.'s Sug. Retail was $406.

Stainless Steel — new 1989.

Mfg.'s Sug. Retail	$450	$360	$320	$270			

GOVT. POCKETLITE — similar to .380 Series 80 Govt. Model, except frame is mfg. with alloy, blue finish only, black composition grips, 14 ¾ oz. New 1991.

Mfg.'s Sug. Retail	$420	$350	$300	$250	$215	$200	$190	$180

Grading	100%	98%	95%	90%	80%	70%	60%

DOUBLE EAGLE SERIES 90 — 9mm Para. (new 1991), .38 Super (new 1991), .45 ACP, or 10mm cal., double action semi-auto that operates on the Browning/Colt short recoil, link pivot locking system used by the Gov.'t Model, 5 in. barrel, matte stainless steel only, 3 dot sighting system, checkered synthetic Xenoy grips, 8 shot mag. (9 shot in 9mm Para. or .38 Super cal.), decocking lever, squared off combat trigger guard, 39 oz. New 1990.

Mfg.'s Sug. Retail	$696	$585	$495	$425

Add $4 for 9mm Para. or .38 Super cal.

Add $20 for 10mm cal.

Add $30 for Accro adj. rear sight (new 1991).

Double Eagle Combat Commander — .45 ACP, 4¼ in. barrel, 8 shot mag., white dot sights, 36 oz. New 1991.

Mfg.'s Sug. Retail	$696	$585	$495	$425

Officers Model — .40 S&W or .45 ACP cal., 3½ in. barrel, 8 shot mag. 35 oz. New 1991.
As this edition goes to press, prices have yet to be established on this model.

Officers Lightweight Model — .45 ACP cal. only, 3½ in. barrel, alloy frame with blue finish only, white dot sights, 25 oz. New 1991.

Mfg.'s Sug. Retail	$640	$575	$500	$450	$400	$360	$330	$295

ALL AMERICAN MODEL 2000 — 9mm Para. only, double action semi-auto, new design features roller-bearing mounted trigger allowing double action only trigger pull every shot, hammerless, 4½ in. barrel, matte finished steel slide and polymer receiver, 15 shot mag., 3-dot sighting system, ambidextrous mag. release, black synthetic checkered grips, internal striker block safety, checkered trigger guard and front grip strap, 29 oz. New 1991.

Mfg.'s Sug. Retail	$600	$575	$500	$460	$425	$385	$350	$325

This model utilizes a recoil operated rotary action featuring integral locking lugs similar to the military M16 rifle.

MUSTANG — similar to .380 Series Gov't., except has 2¾ in. barrel, 5 shot mag., blue finish only, 18½ oz. New 1986.

Mfg.'s Sug. Retail	$420	$330	$290	$235	$215	$200	$190	$180

Nickel finish — bright polish nickel finish with white composite grips. New 1987.

Mfg.'s Sug. Retail	$470	$385	$320	$270	$240	$220	$210	$200

Stainless Steel — stainless steel variation of the Mustang. New 1990.

Mfg.'s Sug. Retail	$450	$365	$320	$270

Coltguard finish — employs a high strength electroless matte nickel finish. Mfg. 1987.

	$330	$300	$260	$235	$210	$200	$185

Last Mfg.'s Sug. Retail was $406.

MUSTANG PLUS II — .380 ACP only, 2¾ in. barrel, blued finish, black composition grips, 7 shot mag., 20 oz. New 1988.

Mfg.'s Sug. Retail	$420	$330	$290	$235	$215	$200	$190	$180

This model has the full grip length of the .380 Government Model.

Stainless Steel — stainless steel variation of the Mustang Plus II. New 1990.

Mfg.'s Sug. Retail	$450	$365	$320	$270

MUSTANG POCKETLITE — similar to Mustang, except has aluminum alloy receiver, blue only, black composite grips, 12½ oz. Introduced 1987.

Mfg.'s Sug. Retail	$420	$330	$290	$235	$215	$200	$190	$180

Nickel/Stainless Steel Finish — similar to Mustang Pocketlite, except has nickel finish frame and stainless steel slide. New 1991.

Mfg.'s Sug. Retail	$420	$350	$310	$250	$225	$200	$190	$180

LIGHTWEIGHT COMMANDER — .45 ACP, 4¼ in. barrel, same as Government Model, except shorter and lighter alloy frame, 27½ oz., round spur hammer. Mfg. 1951-present, fixed sights.

Mfg.'s Sug. Retail	$640	$520	$450	$385	$350	$300	$265	$240

Add 10% for .38 Super or 9mm Para. (disc. cal.'s).

Grading	100%	98%	95%	90%	80%	70%	60%

COMBAT COMMANDER — same as Lightweight, except steel frame, .45 ACP, .38 Super, or 9mm.

Blued Finish

| Mfg.'s Sug. Retail | $640 | $520 | $450 | $385 | $350 | $300 | $265 | $240 |

Add $10 for 9mm Para. or .38 Super cal.

Stainless Steel — .45 ACP cal. only. New 1990.

| Mfg.'s Sug. Retail | $690 | $565 | $475 | $425 |

Satin Nickel — disc. 1986.

| | $500 | $450 | $410 | $365 | $310 | $275 | $250 |

Last Mfg.'s Sug. Retail was $550.

Gold Cup Commander — .45 ACP cal., features custom shop alterations including heavy duty adj. target sights, beveled mag. well, serrated front strap, checkerd mainspring housing, wide grip safety, and Palo Alto wood grips. 1991 release.

| Mfg.'s Sug. Retail | $960 | $875 | $725 | $600 |

OFFICER'S ACP — .45 ACP only, 3½ in. barrel, 34 oz., 6 shot mag., short version of the Government Model. New 1985.

Blued Finish

| Mfg.'s Sug. Retail | $640 | $520 | $450 | $385 | $350 | $300 | $265 | $240 |

Matte Blued Finish

| Mfg.'s Sug. Retail | $625 | $510 | $440 | $370 | $330 | $280 | $250 | $225 |

Officers Stainless Steel — matte stainless steel finish. New 1986.

| Mfg.'s Sug. Retail | $680 | $555 | $480 | $415 |

Add $70 for "Ultimate" bright stainless steel finish (new 1987).

Officers Lightweight — similar to Officers ACP, except has alloy frame and weighs 24 oz. New 1986.

| Mfg.'s Sug. Retail | $640 | $520 | $450 | $390 | $350 | $300 | $265 | $240 |

Officers Satin Nickel — disc. 1985.

| | $470 | $410 | $370 | $320 | $280 | $260 | $235 |

Last Mfg.'s Sug. Retail was $513.

DELTA ELITE — 10mm Norma, 5 in. barrel, black neoprene grips, high profile 3 dot sights, blue finish, 7 shot mag., 38 oz. Introduced 1987.

| Mfg.'s Sug. Retail | $705 | $600 | $500 | $450 | $385 | $350 | $330 | $310 |

Stainless Steel — matte stainless steel finish, new 1989.

| Mfg.'s Sug. Retail | $715 | $610 | $500 | $450 |

Add $70 for "Ultimate" brite stainless steel finish.

DELTA GOLD CUP STAINLESS — 10mm Norma, target variation, includes Accro adj. rear sight and trigger (serrated also), wrap around combat grips. New 1989.

| Mfg.'s Sug. Retail | $900 | $760 | $625 | $525 |

Delta Gold Cup Blue — similar to Delta Gold Cup Stainless, except has blue finish. New 1991.

| Mfg.'s Sug. Retail | $870 | $730 | $600 | $500 | $450 | $400 | $360 | $330 |

PISTOLS: SEMI-AUTO .22 CAL. (WOODSMAN SERIES)

The Colt Woodsman was made for 62 years, and included a multitude of variations/options in models, sights, barrels, grips, markings, etc. Many of the variations are quite scarce and desirable, but generally known only to specialized collectors. The following price guidelines are for standard production models, and only for those specimens in unmodified, factory original condition.

Note: All 100% condition Woodsmans with the original serial numbered box, test target, instruction folder, hang tag, and screw driver command a 10-25% premium, depending on the model's rarity.

Over 690,000 Woodsmans with variations were mfg. between 1915-1977.

PRE-WOODSMAN — .22 LR, 6½ in. barrel. Mfg. 1915-1927, production totaled about 54,000.

| | $750 | $600 | $500 | $400 | $325 | $275 | $250 |

Grading	100%	98%	95%	90%	80%	70%	60%

This model was manufactured to use standard velocity ammunition only (not high speed). Colt did offer a conversion kit for high velocity ammo after the transition.

Woodsmans mfg. between 1915-1922 had a lightweight pencil barrel (approx. serial range 1-31,000). The medium barrel was introduced approx. 1922 and was retained until the 90,000 serial range (approx. mfg. 1922-1934).

WOODSMAN 1ST SERIES — .22 LR, 10 shot Mag., blue only, bottom mag. release, checkered wood grips, marked "The Woodsman" on receiver, adj. sights, mfg. from 1927-1947, total production was approx. 112,000.
Note: guns made prior to 1922 were designed for standard velocity .22 LR ammunition only. The new style main spring housing, designed for high velocity ammunition, began appearing at approx. ser. no. 80,000 and was completely phased in by approx. ser. no. 85,000. Later guns, INCLUDING ALL PISTOLS MADE AFTER WWII, were designed for high velocity ammunition.

Between 1934 and 1947 a tapered barrel was standard production (approx. ser. range 90,000-187,423).

Sport Model — 4½ in. barrel, this model was introduced in 1933.

	$700	$595	$450	$400	$325	$275	$250

Approx. serial range on this variation is 86,105 - 187,423. Sport Model was disc. 1947.

Target Model — 6½ in. barrel.

	$600	$535	$475	$400	$325	$275	$250

Note: Colt discontinued the 1st Model series in 1947. These guns are quite different from the 2nd Model series started in 1948.

WOODSMAN 1ST SERIES MATCH TARGET — .22 LR only, 6½ in. heavy barrel, commonly called "Bullseye" Match Target, mfg. 1938-1944, production totaled around 16,000. Difficult to find in mint condition.

	$1,400	$1,150	$925	$750	$575	$475	$400

"U.S. Property" Marked — gray parkerized finish with U.S. Ordnance stamp, rare.

	$2,000	$1,700	$1,400	$1,150	$925	$750	$575

WOODSMAN 2ND SERIES — .22 LR only, slide stop and hold open, push button mag. release on this model is located on the top side of frame, Coltwood plastic grips (mfg. 1948-1950) or brown plastic grips (mfg. 1950-1955), mfg. between 1948-1955, total production on all 2nd Series was approx. 146,000.

Sport Model — 4½ in. barrel.

	$450	$375	$325	$300	$250	$225	$200

Target Model — 6 in. barrel.

	$350	$300	$275	$250	$225	$200	$175

Match Target Model — 4½ in. heavy barrel. This variation will command a premium over the 6 in. barrel.

	$650	$550	$495	$425	$395	$370	$335

Match Target Model — 6 in. heavy barrel.

	$500	$450	$410	$370	$335	$295	$275

WOODSMAN 3RD SERIES — .22 LR only, slide stop and hold open, mfg. between 1955-1977, black plastic grips (mfg. 1955-1960) or walnut grips (1960-1977), 3rd Models an be differentiated from 2nd Models because of their bottom mag. release.

Sport Model — 4½ in. barrel.

	$395	$365	$335	$300	$275	$225	$200

Target Model — 6 in. barrel.

	$350	$300	$275	$250	$225	$200	$175

Match Target Model — 4½ in. heavy barrel.

	$595	$495	$450	$400	$350	$325	$295

Match Target Model — 6 in. heavy barrel.

	$500	$460	$400	$375	$350	$325	$295

Grading	100%	98%	95%	90%	80%	70%	60%

CHALLENGER MODEL — similar to Woodsman 2rd Series, only with fixed sights, without hold open, and bottom mag. release, 4½ and 6 in. barrels, mfg. between 1950-1955 with total production reaching approx. 77,000.

	$350	$300	$275	$250	$225	$210	$180

HUNTSMAN MODEL — .22 LR only, fixed sights and no hold open, 4½ and 6 in. barrels, black plastic grips to serial number 1411940C - walnut grips after that cutoff, mfg. between 1955-1977 with total production reaching over 100,000.

	$325	$285	$260	$240	$220	$200	$180

The Huntsman is very similar to the Challenger Model, except is built on a 3rd series frame.

Huntsman Model S Master Series — mfg. in limited production runs during 1983 and 1985, 1983 mfg. pistols were equipped with automatic slide stock and Elliason rear sight, either straight non-tapered Huntsman barrel (285 mfg.) or tapered Woodsman barrel with pinned front sight (115 mfg.). 1985 parts clean-up mfg. totaled less than 50 units, mostly in high-grade special orders through the Custom Shop.

1983 mfg.	$550	$475	$425	$375	$350	$325	$295

1985 mfg. must be price evaluated per individual gun.

TARGETSMAN MODEL — similar to the Huntsman, except has adj. rear sight and thumbrest on left grip, 6 in. barrel only, approx. 65,000 mfg. 1959-1977.

	$350	$300	$280	$260	$240	$220	$200

REVOLVERS: DOUBLE ACTION

100%	98%	95%	90%	80%	70%	60%	50%	40%	30%	20%	10%

MODEL 1877 LIGHTNING — .38 Colt or .32 Colt (very rare), 2, 2½, 3½, 4½, or 6 in. barrels without ejector. 4½, 5, 6, 7, or 7½ in. barrels with ejector, 6 shot double action, long cylinder fluting, blued finish with case hardened frame and hammer, full nickel plating also available. Mfg. from 1877-1910. Over 166,000 mfg.

$1,100	$895	$800	$740	$660	$575	$495	$425	$340	$265	$185	$130

MODEL 1877 THUNDERER — .41 Colt cal. only, otherwise same general specifications as Model 1877 Lightning.

$1,250	$975	$860	$795	$695	$600	$510	$430	$350	$275	$195	$140

MODEL 1878 FRONTIER — .32-20 WCF, .38-40 WCF, .44-40 WCF, .45 Colt, or .450-.455-.476 Eley cal., 3½ or 4 in. barrels without ejector, 4¾, 5½, or 7½ in. with ejector. 6 in. is 1902 U.S. Revolver. 6 shot cylinder with long flutes, pinched frame, removable trigger guard, early guns have checked walnut stocks, later guns have hard black rubber. Mfg. 1878-1905. Over 51,000 made.

$1,350	$1,000	$875	$800	$700	$600	$510	$430	$350	$275	$200	$150

MODEL 1889 "NAVY" — .38 Short and Long Colt, and .41 Short and Long Colt, 3, 4½, and 6 in. barrel, wood or rubber grips, blue or nickel finish, the first solid frame, swing out cylinder (counter-clockwise rotation) Colt produced, approx. 28,000 made 1889-1894, 1st 5,000 were ordered by U.S. Navy - hence name.

Blue finish

$1,150	$950	$850	$795	$675	$500	$425	$330	$295	$265	$245	$225

Nickel finish

$1,350	$1,100	$995	$850	$700	$525	$450	$330	$295	$265	$245	$225

MODEL 1892 "NEW ARMY & NAVY" (2ND ISSUE) — similar to 1889 Navy, but double cylinder notches, double locking bolt, and shorter flutes, square cyl. release thumb catch, .38 Special added in 1904, .32-20 added in 1905, mfg. 1892-1907. Add $100 for U.S.N. markings.

$975	$850	$725	$650	$550	$475	$395	$330	$295	$265	$245	$225

This model also had sub-variations that included Models 1894, 1895, 1896, 1901, & 1903. Values will approximate those shown above.

	95%	90%	80%	70%	60%	50%	40%	30%	20%	10%

...ODEL TARGET FIRST ISSUE — .38 Spl., 6 in. barrel, adj. sights, blue. Mfg. 1904-

	$995	$875	$750	$650	$550	$450	$400	$365	$335	$305	$275

'FICER'S MODEL TARGET SECOND ISSUE — .22 LR, .32 Police Positive, and .38 Spl., 4, 4½, 5, 6, and 7½ in. barrels, 7½ in. barrel in .38 Spl. only, adj. sights, checkered walnut grips. Mfg. 1908-1940.

$750	$625	$525	$425	$365	$335	$305	$275	$245	$215	$180	$160

Add $75 for .22 LR cal.

This model was also produced in "single action only" in limited numbers with wide hammer - add a 25%-40% premium, depending on condition.

MODEL 1905 MARINE CORPS — same as New Navy Second Issue, except has a round butt, in .38 short, long, and special, only 6 in. barrel. Mfg. 1905-1909 in approx. ser. no. range 10,000-10,925, about 925 mfg.

$2,250	$1,950	$1,600	$1,400	$1,200	$995	$875	$775	$675	$600	$525	$480

This model was available in both civilian and military configurations.

ARMY SPECIAL MODEL — .32-20, .38 (various), and .41 Colt, 4, 4½, 5, and 6 in. barrels, hard rubber grips, fixed sights, rounded cylinder release thumb catch, has heavier frame than New Navy, approx. ser. no. range 291,000-540,000, mfg. 1908-1927.

Blue finish

$495	$425	$350	$295	$265	$245	$225	$205	$190	$175	$160	$150

Nickel finish

$575	$495	$425	$330	$295	$265	$245	$225	$205	$190	$175	$160

NEW SERVICE MODEL — .38 Spl., .357 Mag., .38-40, .44-40, .44 Russian, .44 Spl., .45 ACP, .45 Colt, .450 Eley, .455 Eley, or .476 Eley, 4, 5, or 6 in. barrels in .38 Spl., 4½, 5½, and 7½ in. barrel in all others, blue or nickel finish, walnut stock. Mfg. 1898-1942. Rare cal.'s (Eley cal.'s and .44 Russian) will command premiums over values listed below.

Commercial

$875	$725	$625	$575	$495	$445	$400	$365	$335	$310	$285	$265

Magnum

$675	$575	$495	$425	$375	$345	$325	$305	$290	$275	$260	$250

1917 Army

$875	$700	$600	$525	$475	$425	$375	$335	$310	$285	$260	$245

New Service Target — similar to New Service Model, except hand honed action and adj. sights, 7½ in. barrel only, square butt, blue only. Mfg. 1900-1940.

$1,150	$900	$775	$675	$600	$525	$475	$440	$395	$360	$330	$275

Shooting Master — various cal.'s from 38 Spl. through .45 LC, 6 in. barrel, checkered walnut grips with Colt Medallion, machined grip straps, trigger, hammer, and ejector rod head, round butt, approx. ser. no. range 333,000 - 350,000.

$950	$825	$725	$625	$525	$475	$440	$395	$360	$330	$295	$260

The Shooting Master could be ordered with a square butt after 1933.

OFFICIAL POLICE — .32-20 (disc. 1942), .41 long (disc. 1930), .38 Spl., or .22 LR (introduced 1930), 6 shot, square butt, 4, 5, or 6 in. barrels, 2 in. barrel in .38 Spl., checkered walnut grips, fixed sights. Mfg. 1927-1969.

Blue finish

$375	$300	$265	$245	$225	$205	$190	$175	$160	$150	$140	$120

Nickel finish

$425	$350	$300	$265	$245	$225	$205	$190	$175	$160	$150	$140

Add 15% for .22 LR cal.

Marshall Model — .38 Special, 2 or 4 in. barrel, round butt, differentiated by "M" suffix and "COLT MARSHALL" on barrel, about 2,500 mfg. 1954-1956 in approx. ser. no. range 833350-M through 845320-M.

$575	$500	$425	$375	$335	$305	$275	$245	$215	$180	$160	$140

100%	98%	95%	90%	80%	70%	60%	50%	40%	30%	20%	10%

Commando Model— .38 Special, 2 in. (rare), 4 in. (common), or 6 in. (rare) barrel, parkerized finish, about 50,000 mfg. between 1942-1945, 32 oz., marked "COLT COMMANDO" on barrel.

| $400 | $350 | $295 | $260 | $225 | $205 | $190 | $175 | $160 | $150 | $140 | $120 |

OFFICIAL POLICE MKIII — .38 Spl., 4, 5, or 6 in. barrels. Mfg. 1969-1975.
Blue finish

| $250 | $190 | $175 | $150 | $135 | $125 | $115 | $105 | $100 | $95 | $90 | $85 |

Nickel finish

| $275 | $215 | $195 | $175 | $165 | $155 | $145 | $135 | $125 | $115 | $105 | $100 |

METROPOLITAN MKIII — .38 Spl., similar to Official Police, except heavier and 4 in. heavy barrel only, blue finish. Mfg. 1969-1972.

| $250 | $190 | $175 | $150 | $135 | $125 | $115 | $105 | $100 | $95 | $90 | $85 |

OFFICER'S MODEL SPECIAL — .22 LR or .38 Spl., 6 in. barrel, blue, similar to Second Issue, only heavier non-tapered barrel, new style hammer and "Coltmaster Sight", checkered plastic grips. Mfg. 1949-1953.

| $575 | $500 | $450 | $375 | $325 | $295 | $265 | $245 | $225 | $205 | $190 | $175 |

Add $75 for .22 LR cal.

OFFICER'S MODEL MATCH — .22 LR, .22 Mag, or .38 Spl., 6 in. barrel, tapered heavy barrel, wide spur hammer, Accro sight, large target grips (walnut). Mfg. 1953-1970.

| $475 | $425 | $375 | $325 | $300 | $275 | $250 | $225 | $200 | $185 | $170 | $155 |

Add $75 for .22 LR cal.

Add 100% for .22 Mag. cal. (approx. 850 mfg.).

This model was also produced in "single action only" in limited numbers - add a 25%-40% premium, depending on condition.

NEW POCKET — .32 Short and long Colt, 2½, 3½, or 6 in. barrel, rubber grips. Mfg. 1895-1905.
Blue finish

| $350 | $300 | $265 | $245 | $225 | $205 | $190 | $175 | $160 | $150 | $140 | $120 |

Nickel finish

| $395 | $350 | $295 | $265 | $245 | $225 | $205 | $190 | $175 | $160 | $150 | $140 |

POCKET POSITIVE — same as New Pocket, except has positive lock feature, also chambered for .32 Colt, .32 S&W, and .32 Colt New Police. Mfg. 1905-1940.
Blue finish

| $395 | $350 | $295 | $265 | $245 | $225 | $205 | $190 | $175 | $160 | $150 | $140 |

Nickel finish

| $425 | $375 | $325 | $295 | $265 | $245 | $225 | $205 | $190 | $175 | $160 | $150 |

NEW POLICE — .32 Colt and .32 Colt New Police, 2½, 4, and 6 in. barrels, fixed sights, same frame as New Pocket, except larger grips, rubber grips. Mfg. 1896-1905.
Blue finish

| $325 | $275 | $240 | $220 | $200 | $185 | $175 | $160 | $150 | $140 | $120 | $110 |

Nickel finish

| $350 | $295 | $250 | $225 | $205 | $190 | $175 | $160 | $150 | $140 | $120 | $110 |

NEW POLICE TARGET — 6 in. barrel, blue.

| $475 | $395 | $350 | $295 | $265 | $245 | $225 | $205 | $190 | $175 | $160 | $150 |

POLICE POSITIVE — .32 Colt, .32 New Police, .38 New Police, or .38 S&W, 2½ in. (.32 only), 4, 5, or 6 in. barrels, improved "positive lock" version of the New Police, walnut or rubber grips. Mfg. 1905-1947.
Blue finish

| $400 | $350 | $300 | $265 | $245 | $225 | $205 | $190 | $175 | $160 | $150 | $140 |

Nickel finish

| $475 | $415 | $350 | $295 | $265 | $245 | $225 | $205 | $190 | $175 | $160 | $150 |

	95%	90%	80%	70%	60%	50%	40%	30%	20%	10%

POSITIVE TARGET MODEL — .22 LR, .22 WRF, .32 Colt, or .32 New Police, 6 in. barrel, ~, adj. sight, checkered walnut grips. Mfg. 1905-1940.

~5	$595	$550	$500	$450	$395	$360	$330	$295	$260	$220	$180

Add 10% for .22 WRF cal.

POLICE POSITIVE SPECIAL — .32-20, .32 New Police, .38 New Police, or .38 Spl., 4, 5, or 6 in. barrels, fixed sights, frame longer to permit longer cylinder, wood, rubber, or plastic grips. Mfg. 1907-1973.

$375	$325	$275	$250	$225	$205	$190	$175	$160	$150	$140	$120

CAMP PERRY MODEL — .22 LR, 8 in. (rare) or 10 in., Officer's Model frame modified to accept a flat single shot chamber. The model name was stamped on the left side of the chamber, the only single shot Colt on a revolver frame. 2,488 mfg. between 1926-1941.

$1,195	$995	$915	$860	$810	$750	$685	$620	$540	$460	$395	$340

Add 25% for 8 in. barrel.

BANKER'S SPECIAL — 2 in. barrel, blue, rounded butt. Mfg. 1926-1940.

.38 cal.

$625	$525	$450	$375	$335	$305	$275	$245	$215	$180	$160	$140

.22 cal.

$1,100	$950	$850	$750	$600	$500	$440	$395	$360	$330	$295	$260

COURIER — .22 S, L, & LR, .32 New Police, double action, 6 shot, 3 in. barrel. Disc. after a limited production in 1956.

$895	$825	$775	$675	$550	$450	$395	$350	$325	$295	$260	$230

Add 10% for .22 cal.

Even though fewer .22 cal. Couriers were mfg. than Banker's Specials, the Banker's Specials are still more desireable as they are less frequently encountered in 95-100% condition.

AIRCREWMAN SPECIAL — .38 Spl., double action, aluminum frame, 2 in. barrel, 11 oz., fixed sights, checkered walnut grips, mfg. 1951 mostly.

$850	$750	$675	$595	$525	$475	$440	$400	$370	$345	$325	$295

Approx. 1,200 mfg. within ser. no. range 2,900LW - 7,775LW. Original U.S. or A.F. will command large premiums.

BORDER PATROL — .38 Spl., double action, 6 shot, 4 in. heavy barrel, 400 mfg. during 1952 only in 610,000 ser. no. range.

$875	$725	$600	$550	$475	$400	$365	$335	$305	$275	$245	$215

DETECTIVE SPECIAL — .38 Spl., .32 New Police, and .38 New Police, 2 in. barrel, blue, wood or plastic grips. Mfg. 1926-1972.

$450	$375	$300	$275	$250	$225	$205	$190	$175	$160	$140	$125

COBRA (ROUND BUTT) — first issue, 2 or 3 in. barrel, blue, same as Detective Special, only alloy frame and available in .22 LR.

$395	$350	$295	$250	$225	$200	$185	$170	$160	$150	$140	$120

Add 20% for .22 LR cal.

COBRA (SQUARE BUTT) — blue, same as Cobra Round Butt, only 4 in. barrel, square butt. Mfg. 1951-1973.

$450	$375	$325	$250	$225	$200	$185	$170	$160	$150	$140	$120

AGENT FIRST ISSUE — .38 Spl., same as Cobra first issue, except shorter grip frame. Mfg. 1955-1973.

$350	$300	$250	$225	$205	$190	$175	$160	$150	$140	$120	$110

AGENT L.W. — .38 Spl., same as First Issue, except shrouded ejector rod, alloy frame, matte finish since 1982. Mfg. 1973-86.

$295	$250	$200	$175	$160	$150	$140	$130	$120	$115	$110	$100

Last Mfg.'s Sug. Retail was $260.

100%	98%	95%	90%	80%	70%	60%	50%	40%	30%	20%	10%

COBRA SECOND ISSUE — .38 Spl., same as Cobra first issue, except shrouded ejector rod. Mfg. 1973-1981.

| $375 | $325 | $275 | $250 | $225 | $200 | $190 | $175 | $160 | $150 | $140 | $120 |

DETECTIVE SPECIAL SECOND ISSUE — .38 Spl., same as first issue, shrouded ejector rod, 2 and 3 in. barrels, fixed sights, wrap-around wood grips. Mfg. 1973-86.

| $375 | $325 | $275 | $250 | $225 | $200 | $190 | $175 | $160 | $150 | $140 | $120 |

Add $50 for nickel.
Last Mfg.'s Sug. Retail was $429.

Also available with class A engraving - add $590 if in 98% condition or better.

COMMANDO SPECIAL — .38 Spl., steel frame, shrouded ejector rod, 2 in. barrel, matte parkerized finish, rubber grips. Mfg. 1984-86.

| $275 | $225 | $185 | $160 | $150 | $140 | $130 | $120 | $110 | $100 | $95 | $90 |

Last Mfg.'s Sug. Retail was $260.

POLICE POSITIVE SECOND ISSUE — same as Detective Special Second Issue, except 4 in. barrel, .38 Spl.

| $275 | $225 | $195 | $175 | $160 | $150 | $140 | $130 | $120 | $115 | $110 | $105 |

DIAMONDBACK — .22 LR or .38 Spl., 2½ (very rare in .22 LR), 4, or 6 in. VR barrel, adj. sights, steel frame, checkered walnut grips, made 1966-86.

| $375 | $325 | $295 | $265 | $245 | $225 | $205 | $190 | $175 | $160 | $150 | $140 |

Add $55 for nickel finish.
Add 20% for .22 LR cal.
Last Mfg.'s Sug. Retail was $461.

Note: Approx. 2,200 Diamondbacks were made with 6 in. barrels and nickel finish in .22 cal. - made 1979. Add additional $150 for 100% specimens.

VIPER MODEL — .38 Spl., alloy frame, 4 in. barrel. Mfg. 1977-1984.

| $275 | $225 | $190 | $175 | $160 | $150 | $140 | $130 | $120 | $110 | $105 | $100 |

COLT .357 MAG — 4 in. or 6 in. barrel, heavy frame, Accro sight, blue, checkered walnut grips. Later guns marked Trooper. Mfg. 1953-1961.

Standard hammer

| $425 | $350 | $300 | $285 | $270 | $260 | $250 | $240 | $230 | $220 | $210 | $200 |

Wide hammer w/target grips

| $475 | $400 | $350 | $300 | $285 | $265 | $255 | $245 | $235 | $225 | $215 | $205 |

TROOPER — .22 LR (rare) or .38 Spl., 4 in. barrel, blue, quick draw ramp front sight, adj. rear sight, checkered walnut grips. Mfg. 1953-1969.

Standard hammer

| $325 | $275 | $225 | $210 | $200 | $190 | $180 | $170 | $165 | $160 | $155 | $150 |

Wide hammer and target grips

| $375 | $325 | $275 | $225 | $210 | $200 | $190 | $180 | $170 | $165 | $160 | $155 |

Add $75-$125 for .22 LR cal., depending on condition.

Grading				100%	98%	95%	90%	80%	70%	60%

TROOPER MK III — .22 LR, .22 Mag., or .357 Mag. cal., 4, 6, or 8 in. barrel, adj. sights, walnut target grips, redesigned lock work to reduce amount of hand fitting needed on earlier predecessors. Mfg. 1969-1983.

				100%	98%	95%	90%	80%	70%	60%
Blue finish				$325	$275	$190	$180	$170	$160	$150
Nickel finish				$345	$275	$200	$190	$180	$170	$160

TROOPER MK V — .357 Mag., 4 or 6 in. barrel, adj. sights, walnut target grips, improved version of Mark III action, vent rib barrel, redesigned 1980. Disc. 1986.

Blue finish

				100%	98%	95%	90%	80%	70%	60%
				$330	$290	$250	$215	$185	$170	$160

Last Mfg.'s Sug. Retail was $362.

Grading	100%	98%	95%	90%	80%	70%	60%
Nickel finish							
	$365	$315	$285	$235	$200	$185	$170

Last Mfg.'s Sug. Retail was $396.

LAWMAN MK III — .357 Mag., 2 in. and 4 in. barrel, shrouded ejector rod for 2 in. barrel, fixed sights, checkered walnut grips. Mfg. 1969-1983.

	100%	98%	95%	90%	80%	70%	60%
Blue finish	$295	$240	$190	$180	$170	$160	$150
Nickel finish	$315	$250	$200	$190	$180	$170	$160

LAWMAN MK V — .357 Mag., 2 or 4 in. barrel, shrouded ejector rod for 2 in. barrel, fixed sights, checkered walnut grips, improved version of MK III action. Mfg. 1984 and 1985 only.

Blue finish

	100%	98%	95%	90%	80%	70%	60%
	$295	$250	$200	$175	$160	$150	$140

Last Mfg.'s Sug. Retail was $309.

Nickel finish

	100%	98%	95%	90%	80%	70%	60%
	$325	$280	$225	$200	$180	$170	$160

Last Mfg.'s Sug. Retail was $328.

BORDER PATROL 2ND ISSUE — .357 Mag., 4 in. heavy barrel, Mark III Trooper frame, limited mfg. in 1970-71.

Blue Finish — 5,356 mfg.

	100%	98%	95%	90%	80%	70%	60%
	$375	$325	$275	$235	$200	$180	$170

Nickel Finish — 1,152 mfg.

	100%	98%	95%	90%	80%	70%	60%
	$450	$375	$325	$275	$235	$200	$180

PEACEKEEPER — .357 Mag. only, 4 or 6 in. barrel, matte blue finish, rubber combat grips, adj. rear sight, about 42 oz. Mfg. 1985-1987.

	100%	98%	95%	90%	80%	70%	60%
	$320	$275	$245	$205	$195	$180	$165

Last Mfg.'s Sug. Retail was $330.

BOA — .357 Mag., deep blue polish, full length ejector shroud with Mark V action, 600 each mfg. in 4 and 6 in. barrel lengths. Entire production run was purchased by Lew Horton Distributing Co., Inc. located in Southboro, MA. 1985 retail was $525.

	100%	98%	95%	90%	80%	70%	60%
	$595	$525	$450	$415	$375	$350	$325

Boa Set — 100 sets mfg. including 4 and 6 in. barrels with fully shrouded ejector rod housing, consecutive serial numbers, and cherry wood presentation case. 1985 retail was $1,200.

	100%	98%	95%	90%	80%	70%	60%
	$1,450	$1,100	$875				

COMBAT COBRA — .357 Mag., 2½ in. barrel, special edition for Lew Horton with CC prefix and stainless steel construction.

	100%	98%	95%	90%	80%	70%	60%
	$475	$440	$395	$350	$315	$280	$250

KING COBRA — .357 Mag., blued metal, black neoprene round butt grips, 2 ½ (new 1990), 4 or 6 in. solid rib barrel only, outline sights, approx. 42 oz. (4 in. barrel). New 1988.

	100%	98%	95%	90%	80%	70%	60%
Mfg.'s Sug. Retail	$410	$335	$295	$260	$235	$210	$200	$185

KING COBRA STAINLESS — .357 Mag., stainless steel construction, black neoprene round butt grips, 2 (disc. 1987), 2½ (new 1988), 4, 6, or 8 (new 1990) in. solid rib barrel, outline sights, approx. 36 oz. (2½ in. barrel). New late 1987.

	100%	98%	95%	90%	80%	70%	60%
Mfg.'s Sug. Retail	$435	$370	$325	$265			

King Cobra "Ultimate" Bright Stainless — similar to King Cobra, except for bright stainless steel, 2 ½ (new 1990), 4 or 6 in. barrel. New 1988.

	100%	98%	95%	90%	80%	70%	60%
Mfg.'s Sug. Retail	$470	$400	$340	$280			

PYTHON — .357 Mag., 2½, 3 (disc.), 4, 6, or 8 in. barrel with vent rib, royal blue finish, full shrouded ejector rod, checkered walnut grips. Mfg. 1955-present.

Blue finish

	100%	98%	95%	90%	80%	70%	60%
Mfg.'s Sug. Retail	$776	$550	$415	$350	$325	$300	$275	$250

Early 2½, 4 or 6 in. Pythons without letter prefix before ser. no. will bring a small premium if in 100% condition or N.I.B., as well as the disc. 3 in. barrel.

Grading	100%	98%	95%	90%	80%	70%	60%

Also available with Class A, B, C, or D engraving — prices are the same as the .45 ACP Government Models listed previously under the Pistols: Semi-Auto, Recent Manufacture.

Nickel finish — available in polished or satin nickel, disc. 1985.

	$550	$460	$415	$365	$325	$300	$275

Last Mfg.'s Sug. Retail was $693.

Stainless Steel Python — stainless steel construction, matte finish, neoprene combat stocks, 2½, 4, 6 or 8 (new 1989) in. barrel. Introduced 1983.

Mfg.'s Sug. Retail	$865	$660	$565	$450

The 6 in. barrel includes neoprene target stocks.

"Ultimate" Stainless Steel — deluxe, highly polished stainless model. New 1985.

Mfg.'s Sug. Retail	$895	$675	$575	$450

ULTIMATE PYTHON — .357 Mag., specially tuned by the custom gun shop, supplied with both Elliason target and Accro white outline sighting systems, walnut and rubber grips also included, choice of Colt Royal Blue or Ultimate Stainless finish, 6 in. barrel only. 1991 release.

Mfg.'s Sug. Retail	$1,040	$1,025	$850	$775	$695	$625	$550	$475

Add $120 for Ultimate Stainless Model.

PYTHON HUNTER — .357 Mag., 8 in. barrel, includes EER Leupold 2X scope, Halliburton aluminum case and accessories. Mfg. 1981 only.

	$900	$775	$700	$650	$595	$540	$495

Last Mfg.'s Sug. Retail was $995.

PYTHON .38 SPECIAL — 8 in. barrel, blued. Disc.

	$595	$500	$425	$375	$350	$325	$300

ANACONDA .44 MAG. — .44 Mag., double action, 4 (new 1991), 6, or 8 (new 1991) in. VR barrel, transfer bar safety system, 6 shot, matte stainless steel only, black neoprene combat grips with Colt medallion, red ramp front sight, full length ejector rod housing, white outline rear adj. sight, 53 oz. New 1990.

Mfg.'s Sug. Retail	$540	$460	$400	$350

Anaconda Hunter — .44 Mag., supplied with Leupold 2X scope, carrying case, cleaning accessories, and both walnut and rubber grips, 8 in. barrel only. 1991 release.

Mfg.'s Sug. Retail	$1,200	$1,095	$895	$725

RIFLES: DISCONTINUED

Grading	80%	70%	60%	50%	40%	30%	20%	10%

FIRST MODEL RING LEVER — .34, .36, .38, .40, or .44, 8 or 10 shot revolving cylinder, 32 in. octagon barrel, walnut stock, no forend, 200 mfg., Percussion. Mfg. 1837-1838.

Standard Model

	$10,450	$9,350	$8,250	$7,150	$6,050	$5,500	$4,950	$3,850

Altered Model — attached loading lever.

	$11,000	$9,900	$8,800	$7,700	$6,600	$6,050	$5,500	$4,400

SECOND MODEL RING LEVER — same as First Model, without top strap over cylinder, .44 caliber only, Percussion, 5000 mfg., 1838-1841.

Standard Model

	$10,450	$9,350	$8,250	$7,150	$6,050	$5,500	$4,950	$3,850

Altered Model

	$11,000	$9,900	$8,800	$7,700	$6,600	$6,050	$5,500	$4,400

MODEL 1839 CARBINE — .525 smooth bore, 6 shot cylinder, 24 in. barrel, exposed hammer for cocking, blued, walnut stock, Percussion, approx. 950 mfg., 1838-1841.

Standard Model

	$7,700	$6,600	$5,500	$4,950	$4,400	$4,235	$3,960	$3,520

Early Model — no loading lever.

	$13,200	$12,100	$10,450	$9,350	$8,250	$7,260	$6,600	$5,500

Grading				80%	70%	60%	50%	40%	30%	20%	10%

MODEL 1855 REVOLVING — .36, .44, or .56 cal., various barrel lengths and stock styles, 5 or 6 shot cylinder, blued with walnut butt stock, no forend, percussion. Mfg. 1856-1864.

½ Stock Sporter — 24, 27, or 30 in. barrel, approx. 1500 mfg.

				$3,080	$2,860	$2,640	$2,200	$1,925	$1,650	$1,430	$1,210

Full Stock Sporter — 21, 24, 27, 30, or 31 in. barrel, approx. 2000 mfg.

				$3,740	$3,520	$3,300	$2,970	$2,420	$1,925	$1,760	$1,540

Military Model, U.S. — marked, 21-37 in. barrel, 9310 mfg.

				$5,280	$4,950	$4,400	$3,850	$3,300	$2,750	$2,420	$1,980

.36 Caliber Carbine Model — 15, 18, or 21 in. barrel, 4400 mfg.

				$6,050	$5,500	$4,400	$3,300	$2,475	$1,925	$1,650	$1,430

.56 Caliber Artillery Carbine — 24 in. barrel.

				$7,150	$6,050	$4,950	$3,850	$3,300	$2,860	$2,475	$2,200

Shotgun Model — .60 or .75 cal., smooth bore, 27, 30, 33, or 36 in. barrels, 1100 mfg.

				$3,850	$3,300	$3,025	$2,750	$2,200	$1,870	$1,650	$1,375

100%	98%	95%	90%	80%	70%	60%	50%	40%	30%	20%	10%

MODEL 1861 MUSKET — .58 cal., Percussion, muzzle loader, 40 in. barrel, with 3 bands, metal parts, white walnut stock, 75,000 mfg., 1861-1865.

$1,320	$1,100	$990	$880	$825	$770	$715	$605	$495	$330	$295	$275

COLT-BURGESS LEVER ACTION — .44-40 cal., 25½ in. barrel, 15 shot tube mag., blue with case hardened lever and hammer, walnut stock, 6400 mfg., 1883-1885.

$1,650	$1,540	$1,320	$1,100	$935	$770	$660	$605	$550	$470	$415	$385

COLT-BURGESS CARBINE — same as Rifle, with 20 in. barrel.

$2,200	$1,980	$1,760	$1,375	$1,265	$1,100	$990	$880	$825	$715	$605	$550

COLT-BURGESS BABY CARBINE — same as Carbine, with lightened frame.

$2,750	$2,420	$2,200	$1,650	$1,430	$1,320	$1,155	$1,045	$935	$880	$825	$715

LIGHTNING SLIDE ACTION — small frame, .22 cal., 24 in. barrel, open sights, walnut straight stock, round or octagon barrel, 90,000 mfg. Mfg. 1887-1904.

$1,875	$1,650	$1,540	$1,320	$1,100	$935	$770	$660	$605	$550	$470	$415

LIGHTNING SLIDE ACTION — medium frame, same as small frame, in .32-20, .38-40, or .44-40, with larger frame.

$1,600	$1,350	$1,175	$1,025	$875	$675	$575	$450	$375	$325	$300	$275

LIGHTNING CARBINE MEDIUM FRAME — same as Rifle, with 20 in. barrel.

$1,870	$1,760	$1,540	$1,320	$935	$825	$715	$605	$525	$440	$415	$330

LIGHTNING BABY CARBINE MEDIUM FRAME — lightened version of Carbine.

$4,400	$3,850	$3,300	$2,750	$1,650	$990	$880	$770	$660	$550	$525	$440

LIGHTNING SLIDE ACTION — large frame, .38-56 - .50-95, express, large version of previously described Lightnings, 6500 mfg. Mfg. 1887-1894.

$2,200	$1,980	$1,760	$1,430	$1,265	$1,100	$880	$660	$550	$495	$440	$330

LIGHTNING CARBINE LARGE FRAME — 22 in. barrel.

$3,300	$3,025	$2,750	$2,200	$1,925	$1,650	$1,485	$1,100	$990	$880	$715	$550

BABY CARBINE LARGE FRAME — lightened version.

$8,250	$7,700	$6,600	$4,950	$4,125	$3,575	$3,080	$2,750	$2,420	$2,200	$1,925	$1,650

Note: .50-95 express will bring premium of 20%.

DOUBLE RIFLE SXS — Various cal.'s in the .45 range, hammers, very limited production between 1878-1880. Most guns were owned by friends of Caldwell Colt — Sam Colt's son, the original designer. Colt Double Rifles are extremely rare and desirable, and should be examined carefully. Prices typically range between $15,000-$25,000, if all original.

.22 CAL RIFLES

Grading	100%	98%	95%	90%	80%	70%	60%

COLTEER 1-22 — .22 LR and Mag., single shot bolt action, 20 or 20 in. round barrel, adj. rear sight, plain walnut stock. Approx. 50,000 mfg. 1957-1966.

	100%	98%	95%	90%	80%	70%	60%
	$275	$215	$175	$140	$110	$95	$80

STAGECOACH — .22LR, semi-auto, 16½ in. barrel, 13 shot mag. deluxe walnut, saddle ring w/leather thong, roll-engraved hold-up scene. Over 25,000 mfg. 1965-mid 70's.

	100%	98%	95%	90%	80%	70%	60%
	$325	$275	$215	$175	$140	$110	$90

COURIER — similar to Colteer semi-auto, except pistol-grip stock and enlarged forearm. Mfg. 1970-mid 70's.

	100%	98%	95%	90%	80%	70%	60%
	$275	$215	$175	$140	$110	$95	$80

COLTEER — .22 LR, similar to Stagecoach, except 19 3/8 in. barrel, 15 shot mag., no engraving and plain walnut. Over 25,000 mfg. 1965-mid 70's.

	100%	98%	95%	90%	80%	70%	60%
	$275	$215	$175	$140	$110	$95	$80

BOLT ACTION CENTERFIRE RIFLES

COLT "57" — .243 or .30-06 cal., FN Mauser action, mfg. by Jefferson Mfg. Co. in N. Haven, CT during 1957, approx. 5,000 mfg starting at ser. no. 1, checkered American Monte Carlo walnut stock, wrap-around front sight.

	100%	98%	95%	90%	80%	70%	60%
	$550	$450	$400	$350	$300	$265	$230

This model was also available in a deluxe version with deluxe hand checkered walnut stock — add 15%.

COLTSMAN STANDARD RIFLE — .243 Win., .30-06, .300 Mag., or .308 cal., mfg. by Kodiak, Mauser or Sako-action, 22 in. or 24 in.(.300 Mag.), 5 or 6 shot mag. Approx. 10,000 (both models) mfg. 1958-1966.

	100%	98%	95%	90%	80%	70%	60%
	$475	$400	$350	$300	$265	$230	$210

COLTSMAN CUSTOM RIFLE — deluxe variation including deluxe walnut with skipline checkering and rosewood forearm cap.

	100%	98%	95%	90%	80%	70%	60%
	$700	$600	$500	$450	$390	$340	$300

COLT SAUER RIFLE (STANDARD ACTION) — non-rotating bolt action, manufactured in Germany by J. P. Sauer & Son, .25-06, .270 Win. or .30-06, 24 in. barrel, 4 round mag., no sights, checkered walnut stock with rosewood forend tip and pistol grip cap, recoil pad. Disc. 1985.

	100%	98%	95%	90%	80%	70%	60%
	$1,150	$975	$800	$700	$660	$620	$575

Last Mfg.'s Sug. Retail was $1,257.

COLT SAUER SHORT ACTION — same as the standard except in .22-250, .243 Win. or .308 Win. Disc. 1985.

	100%	98%	95%	90%	80%	70%	60%
	$1,200	$975	$800	$700	$660	$620	$575

Last Mfg.'s Sug. Retail was $1,257.

COLT SAUER MAGNUM — same as the standard except in 7mm Rem. Mag., 300 Win. Mag., or 300 Weatherby Mag. Disc. 1985.

	100%	98%	95%	90%	80%	70%	60%
	$1,250	$1,000	$800	$700	$660	$620	$575

Last Mfg.'s Sug. Retail was $1,300.

COLT SAUER GRAND ALASKAN — heavier version in .375 H&H Mag., adj. sights.

	100%	98%	95%	90%	80%	70%	60%
	$1,375	$1,125	$995	$900	$820	$740	$690

COLT SAUER GRAND AFRICAN — .458 Win. Mag., 4 round capacity, 9 lb. 12 oz. Disc. 1985.

	100%	98%	95%	90%	80%	70%	60%
	$1,450	$1,150	$995	$900	$820	$740	$690

Last Mfg.'s Sug. Retail was $1,400.

Grading	100%	98%	95%	90%	80%	70%	60%

DRILLINGS

COLT SAUER DRILLING — 12 ga./.30-06 or .243 Combo gun, 25 in. barrels, engraved, 8 lbs. Disc. 1985.

	$2,950	$2,500	$2,100	$1,800	$1,500	$1,250	$1,000

Last Mfg.'s Sug. Retail was $4,228.

RIFLES: SINGLE SHOT CENTERFIRE

COLT-SHARPS RIFLE — .17 Bee, .22-250, .243, .25-06, 7mm Rem. Mag., .30-06, or .375 H&H cal., Sharps falling block action, high-gloss bluing, deluxe checkered walnut stock and forearm. Approx. 500 mfg. 1970-1977.

	$2,295	$1,950	$1,650	$1,200	$1,000	$800	$650

RIFLES: RECENT MFG.

AR - 15A2 SPORTER LIGHTWEIGHT (R6530) — .223 Rem., features 16 in. barrel and shorter stock and handguard, adj. rear sight for windage and elevation, includes 2 detachable 5 shot mag's., 6.7 lbs. New 1991.

Mfg.'s Sug. Retail	$860	$815	$750	$675	$595	$525	$475	$425

Add $160 for .22 LR conversion kit.

AR - 15A2 TARGET GOV'T MODEL RIFLE (R6550/6551) — .223 Rem. (5.56mm), semi-auto version of the M-16 rifle with forward bolt assist, gas operated, 20 in. barrel, straight line black nylon stock, aperture rear, post front sight, 5, 20, or 30 shot detachable box mag. (supplied with two 5 shot mag.'s starting in 1989), 7 ½ lbs.

Mfg.'s Sug. Retail	$880	$825	$750	$675	$595	$525	$475	$425

Add $160 for .22 LR conversion kit (new 1990).

Subtract $70 for older field-style rear sight assembly (pre-1987).

In 1987, Colt replaced the AR-15A2 Sporter II Rifle with the AR-15A2 Gov't Model. This new model has the 800 meter rear sighting system housed in the receivers carrying handle (similar to the M-16 A2).

The AR-15A1 did not have a forward bolt assist and was mfg. until 1963-84. Finishes included parkerizing and electroless nickel. Some dealers are asking premiums for this earlier variation.

AR - 15A2 MATCH H-BAR (R6600/6601) — similar to AR-15A2 Gov't Model Rifle, except has heavy 20 in. barrel, 8 lbs. New 1986.

Mfg.'s Sug. Retail	$920	$875	$795	$725	$625	$550	$495	$450

Add $168 for .22 LR conversion kit (new 1990).

AR - 15A2 Match Delta H-Bar (M6600DH/6601DH) — similar to AR-15A2 H-Bar, except has 3-9X rubber armored variable scope, removable cheek piece, adj. scope mount, and leather sling. Aluminum cased. New 1987.

Mfg.'s Sug. Retail	$1,460	$1,300	$1,100	$995	$825	$750	$695	$650

Add $160 for .22 LR conversion kit (new 1990).

AR - 15A2 Sporter II — standard 20 in. barrel, rear sight adj. for windage only, 7½ lbs. Disc. 1989.

	$995	$900	$800	$700	$600	$525	$470

Last Mfg.'s Sug. Retail was $740.

AR - 15A2 CARBINE — similar to older AR-15A2 Sporter II Rifle, except has collapsible butt stock, field sights, 16 in. barrel, shortened forearm, 5 lbs. 13 oz. Disc. 1988.

	$995	$900	$800	$700	$600	$525	$470

Last Mfg.'s Sug. Retail was $770.

AR - 15A2 GOV'T MODEL CARBINE (R6520) — similar to AR-15A2 Gov't Model Rifle, except has collapsible butt stock, 800 meter adj. rear sight, 16 in. barrel, 5 lbs. 13 oz., shortened forearm. Mfg. 1988-1990 (civilian sales disc. because of Federal/State regulations).

	$995	$895	$800	$700	$600	$525	$470

Last Mfg.'s Sug. Retail was $880.

Grading		100%	98%	95%	90%	80%	70%	60%

AR-15 9mm Carbine — same as 5.56mm Carbine, except 9mm with 20 shot Mag., 6 lbs. 5 oz. Mfg. 1985-86 only.

		$1,100	$975	$850	$775	$675	$595	$550

Last Mfg.'s Sug. Retail was $696.

AR - 15 SCOPE (4X) AND MOUNTS

Mfg.'s Sug. Retail	$290	$220	$175	$160

SHOTGUNS: DISCONTINUED

Strong, original case colors and vivid damascus barrel patterning will make the difference when determining values on the Models 1878 and 1883. Remember, these are black powder shotguns.

100%	98%	95%	90%	80%	70%	60%	50%	40%	30%	20%	10%

MODEL 1878 HAMMER SHOTGUN SXS — 10 or 12 ga., 28-32 in. blued or browned damascus barrels, double triggers, sideplates, case hardened breech, non-automatic ejectors, semi-pistol grip stock, 22,683 mfg. between 1878-1889. Many of these guns were ordered with special features - these original guns command premiums above the prices listed below.

$3,350	$2,995	$2,675	$2,200	$1,925	$1,650	$1,485	$1,100	$990	$880	$715	$550

MODEL 1883 HAMMERLESS SXS — 8, 10 or 12 ga., 28-32 in. barrels, many deluxe custom orders occur in this model. Mfg. from 1883-1895. Approx. serial range is No. 1-3,050 and 4,055-8,365. Seldom encountered in mint condition.

$3,750	$3,350	$2,995	$2,675	$2,200	$1,925	$1,650	$1,485	$1,100	$990	$880	$715

This model was generally a custom order gun with no standard grades being designated. Quality was extremely high, and the high cost of manufacture is a large reason why the gun never sold in large numbers commercially. The Model 1883 was discontinued after only 12 years of manufacture (it was one of the most expensive shotguns during its day). Values above assume moderate engraving and above average walnut.

Grading		100%	98%	95%	90%	80%	70%	60%

STANDARD AUTO SHOTGUN — 12 or 20 ga. (also available in Mag.'s), mfg. by Franchi of Italy, aluminum frame, 26, 28, 30, or 32 in. plain or VR barrel, almost 5,300 mfg. (both models) 1962-1966.

	$375	$350	$325	$295	$260	$230	$200

Add $50 for VR barrel.

CUSTOM AUTO SHOTGUN — similar to Standard Model, except deluxe walnut, hand engraved receiver. Mfg. 1962-1966.

	$475	$425	$375	$350	$325	$295	$260

COLTSMAN PUMP SHOTGUN — 12, 16, or 20 ga., Franchi frame assembled by both Kodiak and Montgomery Wards, 26 or 28 in. plain barrel, aluminum frame. Approx. 2,000 mfg. 1961-1965.

	$325	$295	$260	$230	$200	$180	$165

COMMEMORATIVES, SPECIAL EDITIONS, & LIMITED MFG.

During the course of a year, I receive many phone calls and letters on special editions and limited editions that do not appear in this section. It should be noted that a commemorative issue is a gun that has been manufactured, marketed, and sold through the auspices of the specific trademark (in this case Colt). There have literally been hundreds of special and limited editions which, although mostly made by Colt (some were subcontracted), were not marketed or retailed by Colt. These guns are not Colt commemoratives and for the most part, do not have the desirability factor that the factory commemoratives have. Typically, special and limited editions are made for an organization, state, special event, personality, etc. and are sold and marketed through a company/individual to those people who want to purchase them. These special editions may or may not have a retail price and oftentimes, since demand is regional, values decrease rapidly in other areas of the country. Desirability is the key to determining values on these editions. More information on these special and limited editions not listed in the following pages can be obtained by contacting the factory. The fee

Grading	100%	Issue Price	Qty. Made

for this research is $35 per serial number ($10 refunded if no information is found). Please send name and address, Colt model name, serial number, and check to: COLT HISTORIAN, P.O. BOX 1868, HARTFORD, CT 06101. Allow adequate time for proper response.

As a reminder on commemoratives, I would like to repeat a few facts, especially for the beginning collector, applicable to all manufacturers of commemoratives. Commemoratives are current production guns designed as a reproduction of an historically famous gun model, or as a tie-in with historically famous persons or events. They are generally of very excellent quality and often embellished with select woods and finishes such as silver, nickel, or gold plating. Obviously, they are manufactured to be instant collectibles and to be pleasing to the eye. As with firearms in general, not all commemorative models have achieved collector status, although most enjoy an active market. Consecutive-numbered pairs as well as collections based on the same serial number will bring a premium. Remember that handguns usually are in some type of wood presentation case, and that rifles may be cased or in packaging with graphics styled to the particular theme of the collectible. The original factory packaging and papers should always accompany the firearm as they are necessary to realize full value at the time of sale. All commemorative firearms should be absolutely new, unfired, and as issued since any obvious use or wear removes it from collector status and lowers its value significantly. Many owners have allowed their commemoratives to sit in their boxes for years without inspecting them for corrosion or oxidation damage. Periodic inspection should be implemented to insure no damage occurs - this is important, since even light "freckling" created from touching the metal surfaces can reduce values significantly. A fired gun with obvious wear or without its original packaging can lose as much as 50% of its normal value.

Until recently, commemoratives in general have experienced poor liquidity and an overall reduction of prices. Commemorative production in some trademarks has totalled well over 250,000 units, and some collectors are weighing the "limited production" factor on each model before paying a premium over the standard production model of that particular commemorative. The following values reflect average purchase prices made in various areas of the U.S. In some regions it is possible to purchase an SAA commemorative made in substantial quantity for almost no premium over a standard production SAA. Because of this, prices could fluctuate over 25% depending on the geographic location of purchase or sale.

A final note on commemoratives: As a rule, what determines the bottom of the market in commemoratives is the top of the market for their standard model production relatives. A problem with limited editions is that over the years of ownership, most of the original amount manufactured stays in the same N.I.B. condition. Thus, if supply always is constant and in one condition, demand has to increase before price appreciation can occur. Taking into consideration the inflation factor during the past 2 decades, many older, high manufacture commemoratives/limited editions have not performed very well as investments. Yet, others have. Many commemorative dealers have told me that recent changes in overseas currency rates have made domestic guns less expensive to own for Europeans especially. For this reason, many commemoratives are being sold overseas resulting in less supply for the domestic market. This secondary demand factor has strengthened commemorative prices. After 29 years of special edition production, many models' performance record can be accurately analyzed and any appreciation (or depreciation) can be compared against other purchases of equal vintage. You be the judge.

LEW HORTON SPECIAL EDITIONS — some Lew Horton Special Editions appear within the Colt section by individual model name. In addition, the following special editions have been issued by Lew Horton.

Editions include: Ultimate Officers .45 ACP - 500 mfg. 1989 - $777 retail; Lt. Commander .45 ACP - 800 mfg. 1985 - $590 retail; Combat Cobra 2½ in. - 1,000 mfg. - $500 retail; The Lady Colt (MKIV .380 ACP) - 1,000 mfg. 1989 - $547 retail; Night Commander .45 ACP - 250 mfg. 1989 - $725 retail; El Presidente .38 Super Stainless Gov.'t - 350 mfg. 1990 - $800 retail.

Grading	100%	Issue Price	Qty. Made

1961 GENESEO, ILLINOIS 125TH ANNIVERSARY DERRINGER

	$550	$28	104

1961 SHERIFF'S MODEL — blue and case hardened.

	$1,995	$130	478

Grading	100%	Issue Price	Qty. Made
1961 SHERIFF'S MODEL — nickel.			
	$5,000	$140	25
1961 125TH ANNIVERSARY MODEL SAA			
	$850	$150	7,390
1961 KANSAS STATEHOOD SCOUT			
	$325	$75	6,201
1961 PONY EXPRESS CENTENNIAL SCOUT			
	$450	$80	1,007
1961 CIVIL WAR CENTENNIAL PISTOL .22 SHORT			
	$175	$33	24,114
1962 ROCK ISLAND ARSENAL CENTENNIAL SCOUT			
	$250	$39	550
1962 COLUMBUS, OHIO SESQUICENTENNIAL SCOUT			
	$550	$100	200
1962 FORT FINDLAY, OHIO SESQUICENTENNIAL SCOUT			
	$650	$90	110
1962 FORT FINDLAY CASE PAIR — .22 LR - .22 Mag.			
	$2,500	$185	20
1962 NEW MEXICO GOLDEN ANNIVERSARY SCOUT			
	$350	$80	1,000
1962 FORT MCPHERSON, NEBRASKA CENTENNIAL DERRINGER			
	$395	$29	300
1962 WEST VIRGINIA STATEHOOD CENTENNIAL SCOUT			
	$325	$75	3,452
1963 WEST VIRGINIA STATEHOOD CENTENNIAL SAA .45			
	$850	$150	600
1963 ARIZONA TERRITORIAL CENTENNIAL SCOUT			
	$325	$75	5,355
1963 ARIZONA TERRITORIAL CENTENNIAL SAA .45			
	$850	$150	1,280
1963 CAROLINA CHARTER TERCENTENARY SCOUT			
	$395	$75	300
1963 CAROLINA CHARTER TERCENTENARY 22/45 COMBO			
	$1,195	$240	251
1963 H. COOK "1 TO 100" 22/45 COMBO			
	$1,495	$275	100
1963 FORT STEPHENSON, OHIO SESQUICENTENNIAL SCOUT			
	$550	$75	200
1963 BATTLE OF GETTYSBURG CENTENNIAL SCOUT			
	$325	$90	1,019
1963 IDAHO TERRITORIAL CENTENNIAL SCOUT			
	$350	$75	902

Grading	100%	Issue Price	Qty. Made
1963 GEN. JOHN HUNT MORGAN INDIANA RAID SCOUT			
	$650	$75	100
1964 CHERRY'S SPORTING GOODS 35TH ANNIVERSARY 22/45 COMBO			
	$1,495	$275	100
1964 NEVADA STATEHOOD CENTENNIAL SCOUT			
	$325	$75	3,984
1964 NEVADA STATEHOOD CENTENNIAL SAA .45			
	$850	$150	1,688
1964 NEVADA STATEHOOD CENTENNIAL 22/45 COMBO			
	$1,195	$240	189
1964 NEVADA ST. CENT. 22/45 COMBO W/EXTRA ENGR. CYL.'S			
	$1,295	$350	577
1964 NEVADA "BATTLE BORN" SCOUT			
	$325	$85	981
1964 NEVADA "BATTLE BORN" SAA .45			
	$1,195	$175	80
1964 NEVADA "BATTLE BORN" 22/45 COMBO			
	$2,595	$265	20
1964 MONTANA TERRITORIAL CENTENNIAL SCOUT			
	$325	$75	2,300
1964 MONTANA TERRITORIAL CENTENNIAL SAA .45			
	$950	$150	851
1964 WYOMING DIAMOND JUBILEE SCOUT			
	$325	$75	2,357
1964 GENERAL HOOD CENTENNIAL SCOUT			
	$325	$75	1,503
1964 NEW JERSEY TERCENTENARY SCOUT			
	$325	$75	1,001
1964 NEW JERSEY TERCENTENARY SAA .45			
	$950	$150	250
1964 ST. LOUIS BICENTENNIAL SCOUT			
	$325	$75	802
1964 ST. LOUIS BICENTENNIAL SAA .45			
	$850	$150	200
1964 ST. LOUIS BICENTENNIAL 22/45 COMBO			
	$1,295	$240	250
1964 CALIFORNIA GOLD RUSH SCOUT			
	$350	$80	500
1964 PONY EXPRESS PRESENTATION SAA .45			
	$1,095	$250	1,004
1964 CHAMIZAL TREATY SCOUT			
	$395	$85	450

Grading	100%	Issue Price	Qty. Made
1964 CHAMIZAL TREATY SAA .45	$1,295	$170	50
1964 CHAMIZAL TREATY 22/45 COMBO	$1,995	$280	50
1964 COL. SAM COLT SESQUICENTENNIAL PRESENTATION SAA .45	$850	$225	4,750
1964 COL. SAM COLT SESQUICENTENNIAL DELUXE PRES. SAA .45	$1,950	$500	200
1964 COL. SAM COLT SESQUICENTENNIAL SPEC. DELUXE PRES. SAA .45	$2,950	$1,000	50
1964 WYATT EARP BUNTLINE SAA .45	$1,795	$250	150
1965 OREGON TRAIL SCOUT	$325	$75	1,995
1965 JOAQUIN MURIETTA 22/45 COMBO	$1,595	$350	100
1965 FORTY-NINER MINER SCOUT	$325	$85	500
1965 OLD FT. DES MOINES RECONSTRUCTION SCOUT	$350	$90	700
1965 OLD FT. DES MOINES RECONSTRUCTION SAA .45	$995	$170	100
1965 OLD FT. DES MOINES RECONSTRUCTION 22/45 COMBO	$1,595	$290	100
1965 APPOMATTOX CENTENNIAL SCOUT	$325	$75	1,001
1965 APPOMATTOX CENTENNIAL SAA .45	$850	$150	250
1965 APPOMATTOX CENTENNIAL 22/45 COMBO	$1,195	$240	250
1965 GENERAL MEADE CAMPAIGN SCOUT	$325	$75	1,197
1965 ST. AUGUSTINE QUADRACENTENNIAL SCOUT	$325	$85	500
1965 KANSAS COWTOWN SERIES — Wichita Scout.	$325	$85	500
1966 KANSAS COWTOWN SERIES — Dodge City Scout.	$325	$85	500
1966 COLORADO GOLD RUSH SCOUT	$325	$85	1,350
1966 OKLAHOMA TERRITORY SCOUT	$325	$85	1,343

Grading	100%	Issue Price	Qty. Made
1966 DAKOTA TERRITORY SCOUT			
	$325	$85	1,000
1966 GENERAL MEADE SAA .45			
	$895	$165	200
1966 ABERCROMBIE & FITCH "TRAILBLAZER" — New York.			
	$1,000	$275	200
1966 KANSAS COWTOWN SERIES — Abilene Scout.			
	$325	$95	500
1966 INDIANA SESQUICENTENNIAL SCOUT			
	$325	$85	1,500
1966 PONY EXPRESS .45 SAA 4-SQUARE SET (4 GUNS)			
	$3,850	$1,400	unknown
1966 CALIFORNIA GOLD RUSH SAA .45			
	$1,195	$175	130
1966 ABERCROMBIE & FITCH "TRAILBLAZER" — Chicago.			
	$1,000	$275	100
1966 ABERCROMBIE & FITCH "TRAILBLAZER" — San Francisco.			
	$1,000	$275	100
1967 LAWMAN SERIES — Bat Masterson Scout.			
	$350	$90	3,000
1967 LAWMAN SERIES — Bat Masterson SAA .45.			
	$1,200	$180	500
1967 ALAMO SCOUT			
	$325	$85	4,250
1967 ALAMO SAA .45			
	$850	$165	750
1967 ALAMO 22/45 COMBO			
	$1,195	$265	250
1967 KANSAS COWTOWN SERIES — Coffeyville Scout.			
	$325	$95	500
1967 KANSAS TRAIL SERIES — Chisolm Trail Scout.			
	$325	$100	500
1967 WWI SERIES — Chateau Thierry .45 Auto.			
	$650	$200	7,400
1967 WWI SERIES — Chateau Thierry Deluxe.			
	$1,350	$500	75
1967 WWI SERIES — Chateau Thierry Spec. Deluxe.			
	$2,750	$1,000	25
1968 NEBRASKA CENTENNIAL SCOUT			
	$325	$100	7,001
1968 KANSAS TRAIL SERIES — Pawnee Trail Scout.			
	$325	$110	501

Grading	100%	Issue Price	Qty. Made
1968 WWI SERIES — Belleau Wood.	$650	$200	7,400
1968 WWI SERIES — Belleau Wood Deluxe.	$1,350	$500	75
1968 WWI SERIES — Belleau Wood Special Deluxe.	$2,750	$1,000	25
1968 LAWMAN SERIES — Pat Garrett Scout.	$350	$110	3,000
1968 LAWMAN SERIES — Pat Garrett .45 SAA.	$995	$220	500
1969 GEN. NATHAN BEDFORM FORREST SCOUT	$325	$110	3,000
1969 KANSAS TRAIL SERIES — Santa Fe Trail Scout.	$325	$120	501
1969 WWI SERIES — Battle of 2nd Marne .45 Auto.	$650	$220	7,400
1969 WWI SERIES — Battle of 2nd Marne Deluxe.	$1,350	$500	75
1969 WWI SERIES — Battle of 2nd Marne Spec. Deluxe.	$2,750	$1,000	25
1969 ALABAMA SESQUICENTENNIAL SCOUT	$325	$110	3,001
1969 ALABAMA SESQUICENTENNIAL .45 SAA	$15,000	unknown	1
1969 GOLDEN SPIKE SCOUT	$325	$135	11,000
1969 KANSAS TRAIL SERIES — Shawnee Trail Scout.	$325	$120	501
1969 WWI SERIES — Meuse-Argonne .45 Auto.	$650	$220	7,400
1969 WWI SERIES — Meuse-Argonne .45 Deluxe.	$1,350	$500	75
1969 WWI SERIES — Meuse-Argonne Spec. Deluxe.	$2,750	$1,000	25
1969 ARKANSAS TERRITORIAL SESQUICENTENNIAL SCOUT	$325	$110	3,500
1969 LAWMAN SERIES — .45 SAA Wild Bill Hickock.	$995	$220	500
1969 LAWMAN SERIES — Wild Bill Hickock Scout.	$350	$117	3,000
1969 CALIFORNIA BICENTENNIAL SCOUT	$325	$135	5,000

Grading	100%	Issue Price	Qty. Made
1970 KANSAS FORT SERIES — Ft. Learned Scout.			
	$325	$120	500
1970 WWII SERIES — European Theatre.			
	$650	$250	11,500
1970 WWII SERIES — Pacific Theatre.			
	$650	$250	11,500

Note: A complete set of the WWI and WWII Series standard grade models (6 guns) with matching serial numbers in NIB condition is currently selling in the $4,000 range.

Grading	100%	Issue Price	Qty. Made
1970 TEXAS RANGER SAA .45			
	$1,795	$650	1,000
1970 TEXAS RANGER GRADE II			
	$3,995	$2,250	unknown
1970 TEXAS RANGER GRADE II			
	$4,500	$2,950	unknown
1970 KANSAS FORTS — Ft. Hays Scout.			
	$325	$130	500
1970 MAINE SESQUICENTENNIAL SCOUT			
	$325	$120	3,000
1970 MISSOURI SESQUICENTENNIAL SCOUT			
	$325	$125	3,000
1970 MISSOURI SESQUICENTENNIAL .45 SAA			
	$795	$220	900
1970 KANSAS FORTS — Ft. Riley Scout.			
	$325	$130	500
1970 LAWMAN SERIES — Wyatt Earp Scout.			
	$395	$125	3,000
1970 LAWMAN SERIES — Wyatt Earp .45 SAA.			
	$1,650	$395	500
1971 NRA CENTENNIAL .45 SAA			
	$895	$250	5,000
1971 NRA CENTENNIAL .357 SAA			
	$695	$250	5,000
1971 NRA CENTENNIAL GOLD CUP .45 ACP			
	$750	$250	2,500
1971 1851 NAVY — U.S. Grant.			
	$595	$250	4,750
1971 1851 NAVY — Robert E. Lee.			
	$595	$250	4,750
1971 1851 NAVY — Lee-Grant Set.			
	$1,495	$500	250
1971 KANSAS SERIES — Ft. Scott Scout.			
	$325	$130	500

Grading	100%	Issue Price	Qty. Made

1972 FLORIDA TERRITORY SESQUICENTENNIAL SCOUT

| | $325 | $125 | 2,001 |

1972 ARIZONA RANGER SCOUT

| | $325 | $135 | 3,001 |

1975 PEACEMAKER CENTENNIAL .45

| | $950 | $300 | 1,500 |

1975 PEACEMAKER CENTENNIAL 44.40

| | $950 | $300 | 1,500 |

1975 PEACEMAKER CENT. CASED PAIR

| | $1,995 | $625 | 500 |

USS TEXAS BATTLESHIP SPECIAL EDITION (1975) — .45 ACP, Model 1911A1 with special embillishments, nickel finish, this model is not a factory commemorative.

| | $895 | unknown | 500 |

USS ARIZONA BATTLESHIP SPECIAL EDITION (1975) — .45 ACP, Model 1911A1 with special embillishments, nickel finish, this model is not a factory commemorative.

| | $895 | unknown | 500 |

1976 U.S. BICENTENNIAL SET — includes SAA .45, Python .357 Mag., and black powder Dragoon in walnut display case with drawers.

| | $1,725 | $1,695 | 1,776 |

1976 BICENTENNIAL SAA FREEDOM COLTS — consisted of A, B, and C sets, set A's were engraved, B's had gold work and accessories, C's were similar to B's, but had shoulder stock. Set A prices averaged $1,500-$3,000 in 1976, set B prices varied between $3,500-$20,000, and set C prices started at $5,000. Total mfg. was 4 set A's, 6 set B's, and 1 set C. These sets in today's marketplace are too rare to accurately evaluate and pricing is literally "what the market will bare".
These guns were all manufactured by Dwain Wright located in Sisters, OR.

1977 2ND AMENDMENT .22

| | $325 | $195 | 3,020 |

1977 U.S. CAVALRY 200TH ANNIVERSARY SET

| | $1,250 | $995 | 3,000 |

1978 STATEHOOD 3RD MODEL DRAGOON

| | $8,000 | $12,500 | 52 |

1979 NED BUNTLINE .45 SAA

| | $795 | $895 | 3,000 |

OHIO PRESIDENT'S SPECIAL EDITION (1979) — .45 ACP, Model 1911A1 with special Ohio embellishments, this is not a factory commemorative.

| | $850 | unknown | 250 |

1979 TOMBSTONE CENTENNIAL .45 SAA — .45 LC cal., 7½ in. barrel, nickel finish, two-piece walnut stocks, P-1876 Model, etched with scroll engraving and Western scenes. 300 mfg. (200 singles and 50 pairs).

| | $675 | $550 | 300 |

A pair of the above would sell in the $1,400-$1,550 price range.
This model was not sold retail through the auspices of Colt.

1980 DRUG ENFORCEMENT AGENCY (DEA) .45 AUTO

| | $1,100 | $550 | 910 |

This model was not sold retail through the auspices of Colt.

Grading	100%	Issue Price	Qty. Made

1980 OLYMPICS ACE MODEL SPECIAL EDITION

	$1,150	$1,000	200

This model was not sold retail through the auspices of Colt.

1980 HERITAGE-WALKER .44 PERCUSSION

	$950	$1,475	1,847

1981 "JOHN M. BROWNING" .45 AUTO

	$795	$1,100	3,000

1980-81 .45 ACP GOV.'T SIGNATURE SERIES — .45 ACP cal., blue finished Gov.'t slide with gold auroplated slide or nickel finish. 250 mfg. in both finishes.

	$750	$833	250

Add $50 for blue finish.

1980-81 ACE SIGNATURE SERIES — .22 LR cal., featured Cocobolo grips with medallions, blued finish with photo engraving, cased. 1,000 mfg.

	$900	$955	1,000

1982 JOHN WAYNE SAA STANDARD

	$1,995	$2,995	3,100

While advertising literature indicated 3,100 were mfg., 3,041 were sold.

1982 JOHN WAYNE SAA DELUXE

	$5,500	$10,000	500

While advertising literature indicated 500 were mfg., only 90 were sold.

1982 JOHN WAYNE SAA PRESENTATION

	$12,000	$20,000	100

While advertising literature indicated 100 were mfg., only 47 were sold.

Note: Each grade of the above John Wayne commemoratives has its own serial number range.

1983 BUFFALO BILL WILD WEST SHOW CENTENNIAL SAA .45

	$1,100	$1,350	500

1983 CCA LIMITED EDITION SAA — .44-40 cal., 4¾ in. barrel, nickel finish, fleur-de-lis checkered wood grips, 250 mfg. in 1983 to commemorate Colt Collector's Assn.

	$1,100	$825	250

This model was not sold retail through the auspices of Colt.

1983 "ARMORY MODEL" SAA .45 ACP — this model had limited production, and should not be confused as being a commemorative. So called because was shipped with extra .45 long Colt cylinder and the "Colt Armory Edition" book by E. Grant, presentation cased.

	$1,395	$1,125	500

Armory model commemoratives available with class A engraving — $2,062, B engraving — $2,395, C engraving — $2,995, D engraving — $3,500. 20 total available.

1983 PYTHON SILVER SNAKE SPECIAL EDITION — .357 Mag., 6 in. barrel, black chrome stainless steel, Pachmayr grips with custom shop pewter medallions, etched engraving, includes custom gun pouch.

	$1,225	$1,150	250

1984 1ST EDITION GOV'T MODEL .380 ACP

	$425	$425	1,000

Serial range RC00000-01000.

1984 JOHN WAYNE "DUKE" FRONTIER .22

	$450	$475	5,000

1984 COLT/WINCHESTER SET — 1 ea. of the Model 1894 Winchester carbine and Colt Peacemaker, serial numbered 1WC-4440WC, .44-40 cal., elaborate gold etching, cased. Pistol became available for sale individually in 1986 - see individual listing below for values. Please refer to 1984 Winchester/Colt Set in the Winchester Commemorative section in this text.

Grading	100%	Issue Price	Qty. Made

WINCHESTER/COLT SAA — .44-40 cal., 7½ in. barrel, gold etching, this commemorative was originally made as part of the 1984 Winchester/Colt rifle-pistol set but now can be purchased individually. Originally mfg. 1984.

	$795	N/A	4,000

1984 USA EDITION SAA — .44-40 cal., 7½ in. barrel, old style black powder frame, bullseye ejector rod head, 3 line patent date, high polished blue with gold line engraving. 100 guns total mfg. — 1 for each state and its capitol.

	$2,750	$4,995	100

1984 KIT CARSON .22 NEW FRONTIER — 6 in. barrel, color case hardened frame, gold artwork, serial numbered KCC0001-KCC1000, cased.

	$350	$550	1,000

1984 SECOND EDITION GOV'T MODEL .380 ACP — serial numbered 00000-01000RC.

	$495	$525	1,000

1984 OFFICER'S COMMENCEMENT ISSUE — Officer's ACP with Marine Corps emblem, rosewood grips, silver plated oak leaf scroll, cased.

	$650	$700	1,000

This model was not sold retail through the auspices of Colt.

1984 THEODORE ROOSEVELT COMMEMORATIVE SAA — .44-40 cal., 7½ in. barrel, black powder frame, case colored receiver, factory "B" hand engraving, ivory stocks, cased.

	$1,495	$1,695	500

1984 NORTH AMERICAN OILMEN SAA BUNTLINE — .45 Long Colt, 12 in. barrel, non-fluted cylinder, elaborate gold etching, ebony grips with ivory inlays, stand-up glass case, ser. no.'s 1-100 mfg. for Canada, 101-200 for the U.S.

	$3,250	$3,900	200

This model was not sold retail through the auspices of Colt.

1985 TEXAS 150th SESQUICENTENNIAL SAA — .45 cal., Sheriff's model, 4 in. barrel, gold etching, smooth ivory grips, French fit oak presentation case. Mfg. 1985 only.
Premier Model — elaborate engraving, 150 mfg.

	$3,500	$7,995	150

Standard Model — 1,000 mfg.

	$895	$1,836	1,000

1986 150th ANNIVERSARY SAA — .45 Long Colt, 10 in. barrel, 50% engraved, royal blue finish, Goncalo Alves smooth grips, 150th anniversary logo in stocks, cherrywood case. 1,000 mfg. 1986 only.

	$1,300	$1,595	1,000

1986 150th ANNIVERSARY ENGRAVING SAMPLER SAA — various cal.'s, 4 different engraving styles on metal surfaces, 75% coverage, ivory grips, signed by the engraver, available with either blue or nickel finish. Add $120 for nickel. New 1986.

	$1,650	$1,613	unknown

1986 150th ANNIVERSARY ENGRAVING SAMPLER .45 M1911 A1 — .45 ACP, 4 different engraving styles on metal surfaces, 75% coverage, ivory grips, signed by the engraver, available with either blue or nickel finish. Add $60 for nickel. New 1986.

	$1,095	$1,155	unknown

1986 MUSTANG FIRST EDITION — .380 ACP, 1,000 manufactured serialized MU00001-MU01000 (the first thousand of production), rosewood stocks, walnut presentation case. Mfg. 1986 only.

	$450	$475	1,000

Grading	100%	Issue Price	Qty. Made

OFFICER'S ACP HEIRLOOM EDITION — .45 ACP, personalized with individual's choice for serial number (ie. John Smith 1), mirror brite bluing, jeweled barrel, hammer, and trigger, ivory grips, with historical letter and mahogany case. New 1986.

	$1,550	$1,643	open

1986 DOUBLE DIAMOND SET — set is comprised of a Python Ultimate .357 Mag. revolver and Officer's Model .45 ACP, both guns in stainless steel, smooth rosewood grips, presentation cased. 1,000 sets mfg. 1986 only, serial numbered 1-1,000 (matched).

	$1,595	$1,575	1,000

DELTA MATCH H-BAR RIFLE — AR-15 A2 H-Bar rifle selectively chosen and equipped with 3 x 9 variable power rubber armored scope, leather sling, shoulder stock cheek piece, cased. Mfg. 1987.

	$1,500	$1,425	open

12TH MAN-'SPIRIT OF AGGIELAND' — .45 ACP, mfg. to commemorate Texas A & M University, serial numbered TAM001-TAM999, 24Kt gold plating including wreaths on left frame and inscription on right, cherrywood glass top presentation case, includes personalized class graduation inscription. Available 1987 only.

	$950	$950	999

This model was not sold retail through the auspices of Colt.

KLAY-COLT 1851 NAVY — .36 cal., cased reproduction of the 3rd Model 1851 Navy, special fabrication insuring old world quality, charcoal bluing, heat treated screws and accessories, cased. Introduced 1986.

Standard Edition — no engraving.

	$1,850	$1,850	150

Engraved Edition — choice of engraving.

	$3,150	$3,150	50

Optional engraving patterns with or without gold inlays available at extra cost.

COMBAT ELITE CUSTOM EDITION — .45 ACP, with ambidextrous thumb safety, wide grip safety, hand honed action, and carrying case, ser. numbered CG00001 - CG00500. Mfg. 1987.

	$900	$900	500

1987 SHERIFF'S EDITION — set of 5 SAA Sheriff's configuration pistols in .45 LC cal., barrel lengths include 2, 2½, 3, 4, and 5½ in., royal blue finish, smooth rosewood grips with medallions, supplied with glass top display case which displays the revolvers in a circle around a brass sheriff's badge. Serialization has 3 numeral prefix (which is the same in each set), followed by the letters "SE", followed by 1 or 2 numerals (indicating barrel length) - i.e. serial number 002SE25 indicates the second set built, Sheriff's Edition (SE), and a barrel length of 2½ inches).

	$4,200	$7,500	100 sets

1989 SNAKE EYES LIMITED EDITION — includes two Python revolvers (2½ in. barrels), one finished in brite stainless steel and the other in royal blue finish, grips are ivory like with scrimshaw "snake eyes" dice on left side and royal flush poker hand on right, includes chips and playing cards, 500 sets only of consecutive serial numbers. New 1989.

	$1,950	$2,950	500

1990 SAA HEIRLOOM II EDITION.—.45 LC cal., 7 ½ in. barrel, color case hardened frame and hammer, balance of metal finished in Colt Royal Blue, one piece American Walnut grips with cartouche on lower left side, personalized inscription on backstrap, walnut cased. Available 1990 only.

	$1,395	$1,600	open

Grading	100%	Issue Price	Qty. Made

1990 JOE FOSS LIMITED EDITION .45 ACP GOV'T MODEL—.45 ACP cal., first limited edition in Colt's All American Hero Series, commemorates Joe Foss, famous American WWII Marine Fighter Pilot, gun features gold etched scenes on slide sides, smooth walnut grips, 2,500 mfg. serial numbered JF 0001 - JF 2,500, French fitted walnut presentation case, 38 oz. Mfg. 1990 only.

	100%	Issue Price	Qty. Made
	$1,200	$1,375	2,500

COMMANDO ARMS

Manufactured previously in Knoxville, TN.

Commando Arms became the new name for Volunteer Enterprises in the late 1970's.

Grading	100%	98%	95%	90%	80%	70%	60%

MARK 45 — .45 ACP, carbine styled after the Thompson sub-machine gun, 16½ in. barrel.

	100%	98%	95%	90%	80%	70%	60%
	$350	$315	$280	$225	$195	$175	$160

CONNECTICUT VALLEY ARMS, INC.

Manufacturer located in Norcross, GA.

CVA manufactures mostly percussion/flintlock/finished and kit guns in either rifle or shotgun configurations. Black powder firearms can be found in the back of this text.

CONTENTO/VENTURA

Previously imported by Ventura Imports in Seal Beach, CA. Ventura also imported Bertuzzi and Piotti.

SHOTGUNS

CONTENTO O/U — 12 ga., 32 in. barrels, boxlock, optional screw in choke tubes, high vent rib, SST, auto ejectors, hand checkered Monte Carlo trap stock.

	100%	98%	95%	90%	80%	70%	60%
	$1,045	$990	$935	$880	$770	$690	$635

MK 2 — 2 barrel, O/U, with extra single barrel.

	$1,375	$1,320	$1,265	$1,210	$1,100	$1,020	$965

MK 2 — leather cased, combination set.

	$1,705	$1,650	$1,595	$1,540	$1,430	$1,350	$1,295

MK 3 — engraved, O/U.

	$1,650	$1,570	$1,485	$1,375	$1,295	$1,185	$1,100

MK 3 — 2 barrel, O/U, with extra single barrel.

	$2,200	$2,035	$1,925	$1,815	$1,650	$1,595	$1,515

MK 3 — leather cased, combination set.

	$2,750	$2,420	$2,200	$2,090	$1,955	$1,815	$1,760

MODEL 51 SXS — 12, 16, 20, 28, or .410 ga., 26-32 in. barrels, various chokes, extractors, boxlock, double triggers, checkered straight stock.

	$385	$360	$330	$305	$250	$220	$165
Auto ejectors	$495	$440	$385	$360	$305	$275	$220

MODEL 52 SXS — 10 ga., double triggers only, otherwise similar to 51.

	$525	$495	$470	$415	$360	$305	$250

MODEL 53 SXS — deluxe version of 51, scalloped frame, auto ejectors.

	$470	$440	$415	$385	$330	$275	$220
SST	$605	$550	$525	$495	$440	$385	$330

Grading	100%	98%	95%	90%	80%	70%	60%

MODEL 61 SXS — 12 or 20 ga., 26, 27, 28, or 30 in. barrels, H&H sidelocks, various chokes, floral engraved, hand detachable locks, cocking indicators, select walnut pistol grip stock, auto ejectors.

	100%	98%	95%	90%	80%	70%	60%
	$880	$825	$770	$745	$690	$605	$550
SST							
	$1,020	$965	$910	$855	$800	$715	$660

MODEL 65 SXS — same as 61, with elaborate engraving and quality hand finishing.

	$1,100	$1,045	$990	$965	$880	$825	$770

CONTINENTAL ARMS CORPORATION
Previous importer located in New York. mfg. in Belgium.

DOUBLE RIFLE — .270, .303, .30-40, .348, .30-06, .375 H&H, .400 Jeffreys, .465, .475, .500, or .600, Nitro Express cal., 24 or 26 in. barrels, Anson & Deeley boxlock system, double triggers, checkered stock.

	$5,500	$4,620	$3,850	$3,300	$2,970	$2,750	$2,420

COOEY MACHINE & ARMS CO. LTD.
Previous manufacturer located in Cobourg, Ontario - Canada. Winchester acquired Cooey sometime in the 70's, at which time, production ceased.

There is limited information available on the variety of shotguns and rifles manufactured by this company (most distribution occurred in Canada). To date, there is limited collector demand for this trademark and values should be based on the shooting utility rather than collector premiums due to rarity. Most values will range between $75-$150.

COONAN ARMS, INC.
Manufacturer located in St. Paul, MN.

COONAN .357 MAG. MODEL B — .357 Mag. only, stainless steel and alloy construction, single action, semi-auto, design based on the Colt Model 1911, 7 shot mag., 5 in. barrel, smooth walnut grips, 42 oz. New 1983.

Mfg.'s Sug. Retail	$700	$675	$530	$425

Add $50 for 6 in. barrel (new 1989).

Add $118 for adj. rear sight.

Add $130 for BoMar sight.

Add $41 for .38 Spl. conversion kit (new 1986).

This model can be differentiated from the Model A in that it has an extended grip safety lever, linkless barrel system, trigger bar slot is enclosed, and recontoured rear grip strap. This model became standard in 1985.

Model B Compensated — 6 in. barrel with compensator, new 1990.

Mfg.'s Sug. Retail	$1,050	$925	$795	$650

COONAN .357 MAG. MODEL A — original model without above listed improvements, special order only, inventory depleted in 1991. Serialization is under 2,000 for this model (less than 1,200 were mfg.). No further production is being planned.

	$995	$775	$550

This variation will also shoot .38 + P loads.

Last Mfg.'s Sug. Retail was $625.

COP
Previous manufacturer located in Torrance, CA.

COP DERRINGER — .357 Mag., 4 shot, 3 in. barrel, stainless steel mfg., wood grips, COP stands for Compact Off-Duty Police. Disc.

	$350	$325	$285	$260	$240	$220	$200

Grading	100%	98%	95%	90%	80%	70%	60%

COSMI, AMERICO & FIGLIO

Manufactured in Torretti, Italy since 1930. Imported and distributed by New England Arms Co. located in Kittery Point, ME.

Approximately 6,800 Cosmi shotguns have been manufactured since 1930.

SEMI-AUTO MODEL — 12 or 20 ga., 2¾ or 3 in. chamber, semi-auto, unique pivoting break open action loads cartridges into stock chamber from inside of receiver, 8 shot mag. with 3 shot option, VR Boehler steel barrel available with or without choke tubes, all internal parts are mfg. from special chrome-nickel steel, custom order gun only with dimensions specified by individual customer (approx. 4-6 month delivery time).

Standard Grade — barrel and attatched receiver assembly are blued, frame is chromed-nickel steel. In 1991, Cosmi introduced a new variation with solid titanium frame - more information can be obtained by contacting Cosmi directly in Italy.

Mfg.'s Sug. Retail	$5,200	$5,200	$4,650	$3,950	$3,350	$2,850	$2,400	$2,000

Add $700 for De Luxe Model with #3 engraving.

Add $1,800 for Extra De Luxe Model with #2 engraving.

Add $2,100 for Extra De Luxe Model with #4 engraving.

Add $2,300 for Extra De Luxe Model with #1 engraving.

Add $2,600 for Extra De Luxe Model with #5 engraving.

Cosmi also manufactures an Extra Series with more elaborate engraving. Series C specimens start at $12,000, Series B start at $10,000, and Series A (top of the line) start at $18,000.

Extra Luso Models — available with various styles and amounts of engraving. Prices are quoted individually and can be obtained by contacting New England Arms Co.

CRESCENT FIRE ARMS COMPANY

Manufactured 1888-1893 in Norwich, CT. Sold to H&D Folsom in 1893 and became a division of Stevens Arms & Tool in 1926.

Values below assume standard models with double triggers, extractors, original finish, and 100% working order. Sidelock actions were also available and will command premiums from prices listed below. Shotguns with exposed hammers can equal their hammerless counterparts if condition is 80% or better.

SXS SHOTGUN

12 ga.

	100%	98%	95%	90%	80%	70%	60%
	$195	$175	$150	$125	$100	$85	$65

16 ga.

	$195	$175	$150	$125	$100	$85	$65

20 ga.

	$295	$265	$230	$200	$170	$150	$125

28 ga.

	$375	$325	$280	$250	$200	$150	$100

.410 ga.

	$400	$350	$300	$250	$200	$150	$100

Inexpensive, but hard to duplicate at today's prices. Later bought out by Folsom and became maker of "house" guns for various companies.

CUSTOM GUN GUILD

Manufactured in Doraville, GA.

WOOD'S MODEL IV SINGLE SHOT — Various cal.'s, custom manufactured, falling block type single shot, lightweight, only 5½ lbs. Mfg. 1984 only.

	$2,975	$2,500	$2,250	$2,000	$1,850	$1,700	$1,050

NOTES

D

D W M
Deutsche Waffen And Munitions Fabriken. Berlin, Germany 1900-1930.

Grading	100%	98%	95%	90%	80%	70%	60%

POCKET AUTOMATIC — 7.65mm, 3½ in. barrel, blue, hard rubber grips. Mfg. 1921-1931.

	$700	$630	$580	$500	$420	$380	$330

DAEWOO
Manufacturer located in Korea. Previously imported by Stoeger Industries of Hackensack, NJ. Daewoo makes a variety of firearms, most of which are not imported into the U.S. To date, this limited importation has resulted in minimum collector interest for this trademark. Prices on most models must be determined by the shooting value rather than any collectible value.

MAX II (K2) — 5.56 cal. (.223), paramilitary design rifle, 18 in. barrel, gas operated rotating bolt, folding fiberglass stock, interchangeable mag.'s with the Colt M16, 7 lbs. Importation disc. 1986.

	$495	$425	$375	$350	$325	$295	$270

Last Mfg.'s Sug. Retail was $609.

  MAX I (K1A1) — similar to above, except has retractable stock. Importation disc. 1986.

	$475	$395	$375	$350	$325	$295	$270

Last Mfg.'s Sug. Retail was $592.

DAISY
Manufacturer located in Rogers, AR. Also see Daisy section under Modern Air Rifles & Pistols.

RIFLES: DISCONTINUED

V/L STANDARD RIFLE — single shot, .22 V/L, a caseless air ignited cartridge, 18 in. barrel, plastic stock, 19,000 mfg., 1968-1969.

	$110	$90	$75	$65	$55	$45	$30

V/L PRESENTATION — same as Standard, but walnut stock, 4,000 mfg.

	$165	$130	$110	$90	$70	$55	$45

V/L PRESENTATION KIT — comes with case, gun cradles, 300 rounds of ammo, and a gold plate on the butt with owner's name and serial number of gun.

	$275	$165	$130	$110	$90	$70	$55

Note: The Daisy .22 V/L is the only commercial caseless ammo system. It was discontinued because the BATF ruled that the gun constituted a firearm, and since Daisy is federally licensed to manufacture air weapons only, the factory decided to discontinue manufacture.

LEGACY RIFLES: CURRENT MFG.

All Legacy models have a removable trigger, slings and swivels, takedown barrel, dovetail receiver for scope mounting, rifled inner steel barrel with 12 lands and grooves, and an adj. rear sight. Weight is between 6½ - 7 lbs.

MODELS 2201/2211/2221 — .22 LR cal., single shot, bolt action, models vary in features, prices range from $80-$130. New 1988.
Model 2201 has copolymer stock with adj. butt plate. Model 2211 has walnut finished hardwood stock. Model 2221 was disc. 1988.

Grading	100%	98%	95%	90%	80%	70%	60%

MODELS 2202/2212/2222 — .22 LR cal., bolt action repeater, 10 shot rotary mag., models vary in features, prices range from $90-$135. New 1988.
Model 2202 has copolymer stock with adj. butt plate, 10 shot rotary mag. Model 2212 has a walnut finished hardwood stock. Model 2222 was disc. 1988.

MODELS 2203/2213 — .22 LR cal., semi-auto, 7 shot clip mag., models vary in features, prices range from $95-$140. New 1988.
Model 2203 has copolymer stock with adj. butt plate. Model 2213 has American hardwood stock.

DAKIN GUN CO.
San Francisco, CA. 1960's.
SHOTGUNS

MODEL 100 SXS — 12 or 20 ga., boxlock, engraved, double trigger.

	$340	$255	$240	$205	$190	$170	$155

MODEL 147 SXS — 12 or 20 ga., boxlock, engraved, vent rib, double trigger.

	$385	$290	$270	$235	$215	$195	$175

MODEL 160 SXS — 12 or 20 ga., boxlock, single trigger, ejectors, vent rib.

	$460	$345	$300	$255	$230	$210	$185

MODEL 215 SXS — 12 or 20 ga., sidelock, heavy engraving, special walnut, single trigger, ejectors, vent rib.

	$960	$720	$625	$530	$480	$435	$385

MODEL 170 O&U — 12, 16, or 20 ga., boxlock, light engraving, double triggers, vent rib.

	$485	$365	$325	$270	$245	$220	$195

DAKOTA ARMS INC.
Manufacturer and distributor located in Sturgis, SD.
RIFLES

Dakota Arms models listed below are also available with many custom options. Actions (barreled or unbarreled) may also be purchased separately. Please contact the manufacturer directly for individual quotations.

DAKOTA 76 CLASSIC GRADE — .257 Roberts, .270 Win., .280 Rem., .30-06, 7mm Rem. Mag., .300 Win. Mag., .338 Win. Mag., .375 H&H, or .458 Win. Mag. cal., custom frame incorporating many Win. Model 70 features, 21 or 23 in. barrel, Mauser type extractor, checkered deluxe walnut stock, 7½ lbs. Left-hand action available at no extra charge. New 1987.

Mfg.'s Sug. Retail	$2,150	$2,000	$1,600	$1,375	$1,150	$990	$880	$770

This Model is also available with a composite stock at no extra charge.

Short Action Classic Grade — same cal.'s as Alpine Grade, 21 in. barrel, short action receiver similar to Alpine Grade, right or left hand action. New 1989.

Mfg.'s Sug. Retail	$1,850	$1,775	$1,450	$1,300	$1,075	$925	$800	$700

Other calibers are available on a special order basis.

SAFARI GRADE — .300 Win. Mag., .338, 7mm Rem. Mag., .375 H&H, .416 Hoffman, or . 458 Win. Mag. cal., 23 in. barrel, one piece drop trigger guard assembly with hinged floor plate, checkered walnut stock with ebony forearm tip. Left-hand action available at no extra charge. New 1987.

Mfg.'s Sug. Retail	$2,950	$2,725	$2,375	$2,150	$1,850	$1,600	$1,350	$1,050

Subtract $400 (retail) if ordered with composite stock.

.416 RIGBY AFRICAN GRADE — .416 Rigby, 4 shot mag., select wood with cross bolts in the stock, other features similar to Safari Grade Model, 24 in. barrel, "R" prefix on serial number. New 1989.

Mfg.'s Sug. Retail	$3,500	$3,300	$2,925	$2,600	$2,300	$1,950	$1,675	$1,400

Grading	100%	98%	95%	90%	80%	70%	60%

ALPINE GRADE — .22-250, .243 Win., 6mm Rem., 250-3000, 7mm/08, .308, or .358 cal., short action variation of the Classic Grade, lighter weight model featuring a blind 4 shot mag., slimmer stock and barrel, serial numbered with a "K" prefix, 6½ lbs. New 1989.

Mfg.'s Sug. Retail	$1,995	$1,875	$1,495	$1,300	$1,075	$925	$800	$700

Other calibers are available on a special order basis.

SINGLE SHOT MODEL — available in most rimmed and rimless commercially loaded cal.'s., Farquharson action, 23 in. round barrel, removeable trigger plate, top tang safety, deluxe checkered walnut stock and forearm, 6 lbs. New 1990.

Mfg.'s Sug. Retail	$1,950	$1,875	$1,550	$1,375	$1,150	$990	$880	$770

DAKOTA SINGLE ACTION REVOLVERS

Manufactured in Italy, imported and distributed by E.M.F. Co., Inc. located in Santa Ana, CA.

Note: Other firearms imported by E.M.F. Co., Inc. will be found in the E section of this book.

SAA VARIATIONS

Old Model — .22 LR-.45 LC cal.'s, copy of the Colt S.A.A., 4⅝, 5½, and 7½ in. barrels, blue finish, case hardened frame, 1-piece walnut grips, solid brass backstrap and trigger guard.

Mfg.'s Sug. Retail	$450	$325	$250	$200	$175	$150	$135	$120

Add $100 for nickel finish (disc.).

Add $110 for convertible cylinders.

New Model — .357 Mag., .44-40, or .45 LC cal., features forged steel frame, black nickel backstrap and trigger guard, 4¾, 5½, or 7½ in. barrel, choice of case hardened or nickel frame, one piece walnut grips, original Colt type hammer (without transfer bar safety). Importation began 1991.

Mfg.'s Sug. Retail	$490	$340	$270	$225	$175	$150	$135	$120

Dakota Premier — .45 LC, black powder frame, initial mfg. was with 4⅝ or 5½ in. barrel, set screw cylinder pin release, steel backstrap and trigger guard, one piece grips. This model was the predecessor to the New Hartford Model.

	$375	$295	$250	$190	$170	$160	$150

Last Mfg.'s Sug. Retail was $520.

New Hartford Model — .22 LR, .32-20, .357 Mag., .38-40, .44-40, .44 Spl., or .45 LC cal., features forged steel frame, backstrap, and trigger guard, exact reproduction of Colt's 1st or 2nd generation SAA, choice of black powder (with base pin frame set screw) or 2nd generation (push button cylinder pin release) frame, case hardened frame, original Colt markings, 4¾, 5½ or 7½ in. barrel. Importation began 1991.

Mfg.'s Sug. Retail	$600	$425	$350	$275	$225	$175	$150	$130

Add $60 for nickel finish.

Add $400 for Cattlebrand engraving.

Add $240 for Hartford scroll engraving.

Cavalry Model — .45 LC cal., 7½ in. barrel, faithful reproduction of the original Colt Cavalry Model, one piece walnut grips with inspector cartouche, case hardened frame and hammer. Importation began 1991.

Mfg.'s Sug. Retail	$655	$425	$325	$275	$220	$185	$160	$150

Artillery Model — .45 LC cal., similar to Cavalry Model, except has 5½ in. barrel. Importation began 1991.

Mfg.'s Sug. Retail	$655	$425	$325	$275	$220	$185	$160	$150

Texas Sesquicentennial — .45 LC cal., 4¾ in. barrel, 50 mfg. for Texas Sesquicentennial with special engraving, includes numbered belt buckle and presentation case.

No Mfg.'s Retail	$1,200	$925	$725	$550				

Original list price was $4,550.

Target Model — .357 Mag., .44-40, or .45 LC cal., 5½ or 7½ in. barrel, case hardened frame, brass backstrap. Imported 1987-90.

	$325	$240	$185	$150	$140	$130	$120

Last Mfg.'s Sug. Retail was $500.

Grading	100%	98%	95%	90%	80%	70%	60%

Buntline Model — 12 in. barrel, .357, .44-40, or .45 LC cal., blue only. Importation disc. 1990.

| | | $300 | $250 | $175 | $160 | $150 | $140 | $130 |

Last Mfg.'s Sug. Retail was $520.

Buckhorn Model — 16¼ in. barrel, otherwise same as Buntline. Importation disc. 1987.

| | | $295 | $250 | $180 | $170 | $160 | $150 | $140 |

Last Mfg.'s Sug. Retail was $495.

Engraved Old Model — .32-20, .357, .38-40, .44-40, or .45 cal., 4¾, 5½ or 7½ in. barrel.

Mfg.'s Sug. Retail $530 $335 $275 $225 $175 $150 $135 $120

Add $90 for nickel finish.

Sheriff's Old Model — .357 Mag., .44-40, or .45 cal., 3½ in. barrel only.

Mfg.'s Sug. Retail $450 $295 $225 $165 $150 $135 $125 $110

U.S. Army — variety of cal.'s, premium quality construction. Disc. 1985.

| | | $300 | $205 | $180 | $165 | $155 | $145 | $135 |

Last Mfg.'s Sug. Retail was $395.

Convertible Model — available with .22 LR/.22 Mag., .32-20/.32 H & R Mag., .357 Mag./9mm, or .44-40/.44 Spl. cal., .45 LC/.45 ACP double cylinders. Imported 1986-90.

| | | $380 | $310 | $260 | $220 | $195 | $170 | $150 |

Last Mfg.'s Sug. Retail was $580.

Fast Draw Model — .22 LR, .22 Mag., .32-20, .32 H & R Mag., .357 Mag., .38-40, 9mm, .44 Spl., .44-40, .45 ACP, or .45 LC cal., case hardened frame, 4⅝ in. barrel. Importation disc. 1990.

| | | $300 | $225 | $165 | $150 | $135 | $125 | $110 |

Last Mfg.'s Sug. Retail was $480.

Bisley Model — .22 LR, .22 Mag., .32-20, .32 H & R Mag., .38-40, .357 Mag., 9mm, .44 Spl., .44-40, .45 ACP, or .45 LC cal., 4⅝, 5½, or 7½ in. barrel lengths. New 1986.

Mfg.'s Sug. Retail $495 $325 $250 $225 $200 $185 $160 $145

Add $30 for nickel finish.

Engraved Bisley — .32-20, .38-40, .357 Mag., .44-40, or .45 LC cal. (disc. 1990), 4¾, 5½ or 7½ in. barrel, action engraved throughout. New 1987.

Mfg.'s Sug. Retail $570 $350 $275 $250 $225 $200 $180 $160

Add $100 for nickel finish.

U.S. Army Commemorative — .45 cal., 7½ in. barrel, serial numbered 1-500, blue finish, case hardened frame, steel backstrap and trigger guard, 1-piece walnut grips. Importation disc. 1987.

| | | $350 | $265 | $185 | $170 | $160 | $150 | $135 |

Last Mfg.'s Sug. Retail was $495.

CARBINES

TEXAS CARBINE — .22 LR, action patterned after Remington revolving carbine, 21 in. octagon barrel, wood stock and forearm, brass frame. Also available with extra .22 Mag. cylinder.

Mfg.'s Sug. Retail $420 $250 $210 $165 $150 $135 $125 $110

DALY, CHARLES

Manufactured by B.C. Miroku, Japan.

SHOTGUNS

In the early sixties, C. Daly guns were manufactured by the firm of B.C. Miroku in Tokyo, Japan. This Japanese gun manufacturing company has produced guns for many companies, Browning being the current biggest customer. Miroku guns are high quality with excellent fit and finish. Many of them are highly engraved and are fine examples of the gunmaker's art. Charles Daly Miroku Guns are becoming quite collectible in some areas (smaller gauges with open chokes). Their production ceased in 1976.

Grading	100%	98%	95%	90%	80%	70%	60%

O/U SHOTGUN — 12, 20, 28, or .410 ga., 26, 28, or 30 in. vent rib barrels, various chokes, boxlock, auto ejectors, SST, select walnut checkered pistol grip stock, superior and diamond grade trap have Monte Carlo stocks, the grades differ in amount of engraving and wood. Mfg. 1963-1976 by Miroku.
Add 10% for 20 ga. on models listed below.
Add 30% for 28 ga. on models listed below.
Add 40% for .410 ga. on models listed below.

VENTURE GRADE

	$550	$495	$470	$440	$415	$360	$305

VENTURE SKEET — 26 in. skeet and skeet.

	$575	$525	$495	$470	$440	$385	$330

VENTURE TRAP — 30 in. imp. mode. and full.

	$530	$495	$470	$415	$360	$330	$300

FIELD GRADE — 12 or 20 ga., field gun.

	$625	$550	$525	$500	$450	$400	$375

SUPERIOR GRADE

	$725	$660	$635	$605	$550	$495	$440

SUPERIOR TRAP

	$640	$590	$550	$500	$460	$425	$390

This model had an optional selective ejection system enabling the shooter to deactivate the ejectors.

DIAMOND GRADE FIELD

	$1,070	$990	$935	$880	$770	$715	$660

DIAMOND GRADE SKEET

	$1,095	$990	$910	$800	$745	$690	$635

DIAMOND GRADE TRAP

	$925	$885	$800	$740	$685	$620	$560

WIDE RIB DIAMOND GRADE FLAT-TOP TRAP

	$960	$920	$840	$815	$760	$700	$640

DIAMOND REGENT GRADE — mostly 12 ga., extensive frame engraving with gold inlays, rare.

	$2,000	$1,700	$1,425	$1,275	$1,100	$990	$880

EMPIRE DOUBLE BARREL SHOTGUN — 12, 16, or 20 ga., 26, 28, or 30 in. barrels, various chokes, boxlock, extractors, single trigger, checkered pistol grip stock. Mfg. 1968-1971.

	$545	$495	$470	$415	$360	$305	$250
Vent rib	$595	$535	$500	$450	$400	$350	$300

SUPERIOR GRADE SINGLE BARREL TRAP — 12 ga., 32 or 34 in. vent rib, full choke barrel, auto ejector, Monte Carlo stock with recoil pad. Mfg. 1968-1976.

	$550	$525	$495	$440	$385	$330	$305

1974 WILDLIFE COMMEMORATIVE — duck scene engraved, Diamond grade, Trap, or Skeet, limited to 500 guns. Mfg. 1974.

	$1,650	$1,430	$1,320	$1,100	$990	$880	$770

DALY, CHARLES: 1976 TO PRESENT

Currently imported by Outdoor Sports Headquarters, Inc. located in Dayton, OH. Italian manufacturer.

Note: The Charles Daly "Noramatic" shotguns were produced in 1968 by Breda in Italy. Current production shotguns have been manufactured in Italy since 1976 by Breda in Milan.

Grading	100%	98%	95%	90%	80%	70%	60%

SHOTGUNS: SEMI-AUTO

The Noramatic series was not imported by Outdoor Sport Headquarters, Inc.

NORAMATIC LIGHTWEIGHT MODEL — 12 ga., 26 or 28 in. barrel, various chokes, available with quick choke interchangeable tubes, checkered pistol grip stock, same as the Breda shotgun. Mfg. 1968 only.

| | $305 | $275 | $250 | $220 | $195 | $165 | $140 |

Add $25 for vent rib.
Add $15 for quick choke.

NORAMATIC SUPER LIGHTWEIGHT — 12 or 20 ga., same as Lightweight, except approx. ½ lb. lighter.

| | $330 | $305 | $275 | $250 | $220 | $195 | $165 |

Add $25 for vent rib.
Add $15 for quick choke.

NORAMATIC MAGNUM — same as Lightweight, with 3 in. 12 or 20 ga. chambers, 28 or 30 in. vent rib barrel, full choke.

| | $330 | $305 | $275 | $250 | $220 | $195 | $165 |

NORAMATIC TRAP — same as Lightweight, with 30 in. full vent rib barrel, Monte Carlo stock.

| | $360 | $330 | $305 | $275 | $250 | $220 | $195 |

CHARLES DALY AUTOMATIC — 12 ga., 2¾ or 3 in. chambers, gas operation, alloy frame, pistol grip (high gloss) or English stock, vent rib, 5 shot mag. Also available as slug gun with iron sights. Invector chokes became standard in 1986. Disc. 1988.

| | $320 | $275 | $235 | $205 | $190 | $170 | $150 |

Add $15 for oil finished English stock.
Last Mfg.'s Sug. Retail was $365.

MULTI-XII — 12 ga. only, 3 in. chamber, 27 in. vent rib multichoke barrel, self adjusting gas operation, deluxe checkered walnut stock with recoil pad and forearm. Imported 1987-88 only.

| | $425 | $360 | $320 | $285 | $250 | $225 | $195 |

Last Mfg.'s Sug. Retail was $498.

SHOTGUNS: O/U

Indesol from Spain currently manufactures the new models listed below.

PRESENTATION MODEL — 12 or 20 ga., with choke tubes, Purdey double underlug locking action with decorative engraved sideplates, French walnut, single trigger, ejectors. Disc. 1986.

| | $995 | $840 | $750 | $670 | $615 | $560 | $520 |

Last Mfg.'s Sug. Retail was $1,165.

LUXE MODEL — 12, 20, 28, or .410 ga., boxlock with self adj. crossbolt, 26 or 28 chrome lined VR barrels with internal choke tubes, SST, ejectors, antique silver finish on receiver, deluxe hand checkered walnut stock and forearm. New 1989.

| Mfg.'s Sug. Retail | $650 | $575 | $500 | $460 | $425 | $400 | $375 | $350 |

This model is mfg. by Indesul of Spain.

FIELD MODEL — similar to Luxe Grade except has fixed chokes, extractors, machine stock checkering, and blued receiver, not available in 28 or .410 ga. New 1989.

| Mfg.'s Sug. Retail | $450 | $395 | $370 | $340 | $315 | $285 | $260 | $230 |

DIAMOND FIELD — 12 or 20 ga. (disc. 1986) Mag.'s, with choke tubes. Same action as Presentation model without sideplates, engraved, select walnut, single trigger, ejectors. Disc. 1986.

| | $695 | $600 | $550 | $510 | $460 | $420 | $380 |

Last Mfg.'s Sug. Retail was $895.

Grading	100%	98%	95%	90%	80%	70%	60%

Diamond Trap or Skeet — 12 ga. only, 26 or 30 in. barrels only. Disc. 1986.

	$850	$700	$550	$500	$475	$450	$425

Deduct $50 for Skeet Model.
Last Mfg.'s Sug. Retail was $1,050.

SUPERIOR II — 12 or 20 ga., various chokes, boxlock action, single trigger, ejectors, engraved. Disc. 1988.

	$675	$575	$475	$425	$395	$375	$350

Add $35 for 12 ga. Mag. (disc. 1987).
Last Mfg.'s Sug. Retail was $875.

FIELD III — 12 or 20 ga., various chokes, boxlock action, single trigger. Disc. 1989.

	$395	$370	$340	$315	$285	$260	$230

Last Mfg.'s Sug. Retail was $450.

SHOTGUNS: SIDE-BY-SIDE

SUPERIOR — 12 or 20 ga., boxlock action, various chokes, single trigger. Disc. 1985.

	$550	$470	$405	$345	$315	$280	$250

Last Mfg.'s Sug. Retail was $624.

LUXE MODEL — 12 or 20 ga., boxlock action, SST, ejectors, 26 in. barrels with choke tubes, checkered pistol grip walnut stock with semi-beavertail forearm, recoil pad. New 1990.

Mfg.'s Sug. Retail	$650	$550	$450	$395	$350	$315	$285	$260

This model is manufactured by Hermanos located in Spain.

DALY, CHARLES: PRUSSIAN MANUFACTURE

Charles Daly was an importer whose goal was to give the U.S. shotgun consumer a European manufactured gun of similar quality to the premier American shotguns of the circa. In that behalf, he had various European firms fabricate shotguns with American shooting features and preferences. Many "Prussian" Daly's were built by various firms in Suhl, Germany. Importation ceased prior to WWII. These Prussian Charles Daly's utilized the finest materials and best workmanship of their time.

SHOTGUNS

EMPIRE O&U — 12, 16, or 20 ga., various barrel lengths, Anson & Deeley boxlock, ejectors and double triggers, fine engraving, deluxe walnut. Disc. 1933.

	$4,000	$3,400	$2,740	$2,380	$2,010	$1,825	$1,645

DIAMOND O&U — same as Empire model, only finer workmanship and materials.

	$5,000	$4,300	$3,475	$3,000	$2,600	$2,300	$2,000

SUPERIOR SXS — 10, 12, 20, 28, or .410 ga., Anson & Deeley boxlock, various barrel lengths, ejectors (except superior model). Disc. 1933.

	$1,050	$790	$690	$580	$525	$475	$420

EMPIRE SXS — same as Superior, only more engraving and better wood.

	$2,300	$1,725	$1,495	$1,265	$1,150	$1,035	$920

DIAMOND SXS — like Empire model, only more elaborate.

	$4,000	$3,300	$2,700	$2,300	$1,900	$1,645	$1,460

REGENT DIAMOND SXS — top-of-the-line Prussian side by side.

	$5,250	$4,650	$3,800	$3,200	$2,700	$2,250	$2,025

EMPIRE SINGLE BARREL TRAP — 12 ga., 30-34 in. barrel, Anson & Deeley boxlock, ejector, vent rib, finely engraved with select walnut, chopper lump extension, top quality. Disc. 1933.

	$2,150	$1,675	$1,375	$1,100	$960	$850	$750

Grading	100%	98%	95%	90%	80%	70%	60%

SEXTUPLE SINGLE BARREL TRAP — 12 ga., 30-34 in. barrel, six locking bolts, ejector, vent rib, elaborately engraved and checkered. Regent Diamond Model has better engraving and wood.
Empire Quality

	$2,600	$2,100	$1,700	$1,400	$1,100	$900	$750

Regent Diamond Quality

	$3,300	$2,850	$2,400	$1,950	$1,650	$1,350	$995

DRILLING MODEL — 3 barrel combination gun, available in 12, 16, 20 ga.'s and .25-20, .25-35, and .30-30 cal.'s, extractors, double triggers, engraved action, select walnut. Disc. 1933.
Superior Quality

	$2,600	$1,950	$1,690	$1,430	$1,300	$1,170	$1,040

Diamond Quality — deluxe engraving and walnut.

	$4,200	$3,150	$2,730	$2,310	$2,100	$1,750	$1,425

Regent Diamond Quality — top-of-the-line model.

	$5,500	$4,125	$3,575	$3,025	$2,750	$2,475	$2,200

COMMANIDER O&U — 12, 16, 20, 28, or .410 ga., Anson & Deeley boxlock action, single or double triggers, ejectors. Mfg. in Belgium circa 1939.
Model 100

	$500	$375	$325	$275	$250	$225	$200

Add $100 for single trigger.
Model 200 — similar to Model 100, except has deluxe walnut.

	$650	$490	$425	$360	$325	$300	$260

For 28 and .410 ga.'s — add 10% - 30%.

RIFLES

BOLT ACTION GRADE I — .22 Hornet, mfg. by F. Jaeger & Co. of Suhl, Germany, 5 shot mag., 24 in. barrel, miniature Mauser bolt action, deluxe walnut. Disc.

	$820	$615	$535	$455	$410	$370	$330

DAN ARMS OF AMERICA

Manufactured in Italy By Silma. Imported by Dan Arms of America, located in Allentown, PA. Previously imported by Dan Arms of North America (previously called Sportsman's Emporium Ltd.)

Firearms previously imported by the former Dan Arms of North America (Sportsman's Emporium Ltd.) do not carry their warranty periods into current Dan Arms of America importation.
All shotguns listed below were discontinued in early 1988. Dan Arms of America has limited quantities remaining of these models, and values below reflect discontinuance.

SHOTGUNS: OVER AND UNDER

LUX GRADE I — 12 or 20 ga., 3 in. Mag. chambers, 26, 28, or 30 in. barrels, vent rib, extractors, pistol grip, double trigger, European walnut.

	$280	$220	$210	$200	$190	$180	$170

Last Mfg.'s Sug. Retail was $350.

LUX GRADE II — 12 ga. only, 3 in. Mag. chambers, 26, 28, or 30 in. barrels, vent rib, extractors, pistol grip, single trigger, European walnut.

	$320	$250	$240	$230	$215	$200	$190

Last Mfg.'s Sug. Retail was $395.

LUX GRADE III — 20 or 12 ga., 3 in. Mag. chambers, 26, 28, or 30 in. barrels, vent rib, ejectors, pistol grip, single trigger, checkered European walnut.

	$375	$300	$285	$270	$255	$240	$220

Last Mfg.'s Sug. Retail was $450.

Grading	100%	98%	95%	90%	80%	70%	60%

LUX GRADE IV — 12 ga. only, 3 in. Mag. chambers, 28 in. barrels, vent rib, ejectors, pistol grip, single trigger, checkered European walnut, multi-choked with 5 tubes.

	$460	$390	$350	$310	$285	$265	$245

Last Mfg.'s Sug. Retail was $550.

SKEET MODEL — 12 ga. only, 26½ in. barrels, 10mm vent rib, anatomical pistol grip.

	$550	$450	$400	$355	$320	$300	$285

Last Mfg.'s Sug. Retail was $650.

TRAP MODEL — 12 ga. only, 30 in. barrels, 10mm vent rib, anatomical pistol grip.

	$550	$450	$400	$355	$320	$300	$285

Last Mfg.'s Sug. Retail was $650.

SILVERSNIPE — 12 or 20 ga., made to customer specifications, sideplates, select high grade walnut, name engraving upon request.

	$1,300	$1,200	$1,050	$900	$800	$700	$600

Last Mfg.'s Sug. Retail was $1,475.

SHOTGUNS: SIDE-BY-SIDE

FIELD MODEL — 12, 16, 20, 28, or .410 ga., double triggers, extractors, 26 or 28 in. barrels.

	$285	$220	$210	$200	$190	$180	$170

Last Mfg.'s Sug. Retail was $350.

DELUXE FIELD MODEL — 12 or 20 ga., single triggers, ejectors, 26 or 28 in. barrels.

	$440	$375	$340	$310	$290	$260	$230

Last Mfg.'s Sug. Retail was $500.

DARDICK

Previously manufactured in Hamden, CT.

PISTOLS

SERIES 1100 — .38 Dardick Tround, double action, 10 shot mag.

	$560	$420	$365	$310	$255	$225	$200

Dardick ammunition in itself is collectible - currently, individual rounds are selling in the $5-$10 range.

SERIES 1500 — .22, .30, or .38 Dardick Tround, double action.

	$875	$660	$570	$490	$440	$395	$350

Subtract $400 for .30 cal.
Note: carbine conversion units (.22 or .38 cal) add $175 — $400.

DARNE S.A.

Manufactured between 1881-1979 and 1989 to date in Saint Etienne, France.

Please refer to the Bruchet section for 1982-1989 mfg. utilizing the Darne action.

SHOTGUNS: PRE-1980 MFG.

DARNE SLIDING BREECH SHOTGUN — 12, 16, 20, or 28 ga., double barrel, S x S, unique action utilizes sliding breech lock-up, high quality mfg., 27½ in. barrel standard with other lengths available, any choke combination, either straight grip or pistol grip stock, checkered, models differ in amount of engraving and grade of wood.

Bird Hunter Model R11

	$1,000	$715	$635	$550	$495	$440	$360

Pheasant Hunter Model R15

	$2,300	$1,950	$1,750	$1,625	$1,500	$1,425	$1,300

Magnum Model R16

	$1,650	$1,450	$1,350	$1,250	$1,125	$1,000	$900

Grading	100%	98%	95%	90%	80%	70%	60%
Quail Hunter Model V19							
	$3,350	$2,750	$2,500	$2,250	$2,000	$1,800	$1,650
Model V22							
	$3,750	$3,300	$3,000	$2,600	$2,300	$2,050	$1,850
Hors Series No. 1 Model V							
	$4,400	$3,850	$3,575	$3,300	$3,080	$2,750	$2,200

SHOTGUNS: 1989 TO DATE MFG.

In 1989, Peter Bruchet (the old Darne plant superintendant) retained permission to once again use the Darne trademark. Hence, all 1989 and later mfg. has been produced by Peter Bruchet.

All new mfg. Darnes can be choked to the customers choice. All models listed below have automatic ejectors, are oil finished by hand, and may be barreled to any length (except for Models R 11, 12, and 13). All prices are subject to change without notice.

R 11 — 12 or 16 ga., half pistol grip stock, light engraving.

Mfg.'s Sug. Retail	$2,750	$2,500	$2,100	$1,870	$1,760	$1,650	$1,375	$1,225

R 12 — same as above, except with better engraving.

Mfg.'s Sug. Retail	$3,300	$3,150	$2,500	$2,100	$1,870	$1,760	$1,650	$1,375

R 13 — 12, 16, or 20 ga., straight or pistol grip stock, traditional action with bouquet engraving.

Mfg.'s Sug. Retail	$3,750	$3,500	$2,875	$2,450	$2,100	$1,870	$1,760	$1,500

R 14 — 12, 16, or 20 ga., slug gun, choice of forends, light engraving, and optional cheek rest pistol grip stock is also available.

Mfg.'s Sug. Retail	$3,450	$3,250	$2,550	$2,100	$1,870	$1,760	$1,650	$1,375

R 15 — 12, 16, 20, 24, or 28 ga., select walnut stock and forearm with fine checkering, large scroll engraving, obturator disks.

Mfg.'s Sug. Retail	$4,150	$3,800	$3,000	$2,575	$2,300	$2,000	$1,775	$1,475

R 17 — 12 or 20 ga., Magnum model (3 in. chambers), customer's choice of full coverage engraving, superior quality walnut and checkering.

Mfg.'s Sug. Retail	$5,150	$4,700	$3,500	$2,950	$2,575	$2,250	$1,925	$1,600

V 19 — all gauges, easy opening large key action, top quality walnut and checkering, full coverage rose and scroll engraving with chiseled fences.

Mfg.'s Sug. Retail	$7,650	$7,250	$6,400	$5,150	$4,700	$3,500	$2,950	$2,575

V 21 — similar to V 19, except has large scroll rosace engraving and chiseled fences.

Mfg.'s Sug. Retail	$8,100	$7,600	$6,875	$5,475	$4,950	$3,675	$3,100	$2,675

V 22 — similar to V 21, except has bulino style engraving featuring hunting scenes, ornamental borders, and gold inlays (if specified).

Mfg.'s Sug. Retail	$10,250	$9,500	$8,000	$6,300	$5,400	$4,000	$3,475	$3,000

VHS — all gauges, top of the line model incorporating customers choice of engraving style, type of inlays, and checkering pattern, best quality wood. The values below represent base prices without options.

Mfg.'s Sug. Retail	$11,550	$10,750	$8,800	$7,000	$6,100	$4,800	$3,950	$3,375

DAVIDSON FIREARMS

Maker: Fabrica De Armas, Eibar, Spain.

MODEL 63B — 12, 16, 20, 28, or .410 ga., double barrel, 25, 26, 28, or 30 in. barrels, Anson & Deeley boxlock, engraved and nickel plated frame, various chokes, walnut checkered stock. Mfg. 1963-disc.

	$275	$260	$220	$200	$175	$165	$155

Model 63B Magnum — similar to 63B, except 10 ga. Mag., 12, or 20 ga. Mag., 32 in. barrel.

12 or 20 ga.	$360	$340	$310	$275	$230	$195	$165

Grading	100%	98%	95%	90%	80%	70%	60%
10 ga.	$385	$370	$340	$305	$250	$220	$195

MODEL 69SL — 12 or 20 ga., true detachable sidelock action, engraved nickel plated action, 26 in. and 28 in. barrels, imp. cyl. and mod., mod. and full, checkered walnut stock. Mfg. 1963-1976.

	$415	$395	$375	$340	$320	$290	$260

MODEL 73 STAGECOACH — 12 or 20 ga., detachable sidelock exposed hammers, 3 in. chambers, 20 in. mod. and full barrels, checkered walnut stock. Mfg. 1976-disc.

	$275	$260	$220	$200	$175	$165	$155

DAVIS INDUSTRIES
Manufacturer located in Chino, CA.

Davis Industries provides a lifetime warranty to the original purchaser of all models listed below.

D-22/D-25/D-32 SERIES DERRINGER — .22 LR, .22 Mag., .25 ACP, or .32 ACP cal., O/U steel construction, 2.4 in. vent rib barrel, 9½ oz., black teflon or chrome finish.

Mfg.'s Sug. Retail	$65	$55	$50	$45	$40	$35	$30	$30

In this series, the .25 ACP cal. is the Model D-25 and the .32 ACP cal. is the Model D-32.

P-32 — .32 ACP, single action semi-auto, 6 shot mag., 2.8 in. barrel, black teflon or chrome finish, 22 oz. New 1987.

Mfg.'s Sug. Retail	$87	$75	$65	$55	$45	$40	$35	$30

P-380 — .380 ACP, single action semi-auto, similar to P-32, 5 shot mag., 2.8 in. barrel, 22 oz., bright chrome or black Teflon finish, internal shock resister for recoil, wood grips. New 1989.

Mfg.'s Sug. Retail	$98	$85	$75	$65	$55	$45	$40	$35

DEMRO
Manufacturer located in Manchester, CT.

T.A.C. MODEL 1 RIFLE — .45 ACP or 9mm Luger, blow back operation, 16⅞ in. barrel, also available in carbine model and fully auto.

	$360	$310	$260	$220	$200	$180	$165

XF-7 WASP CARBINE — .45 ACP or 9mm Luger, blow back operation, 16⅞ in. barrel, also available in fully auto.

	$360	$310	$260	$220	$200	$180	$165

Add $45 for case.

DETONICS FIREARMS INDUSTRIES
Detonics Firearms Industries was a previous manufacturer located in Bellevue, WA 1976-1988. Detonics was sold in early 1988 to the New Detonics Manufacturing Corporation, a wholly owned subsidiary of "1045 Investers Group Limited".

Please refer to the New Detonics Manufacturing Corporation in the "N" section of this text for complete model listings of both companies.

DIARM S.A.
Manufacturing conglomerate (25 companies) located in Deba, Spain. Previously imported and distributed by American Arms, Inc. located in North Kansas City, MO. Older Diarm models can be found under the American Arms, Inc. heading in this publication. Diarm importation began in 1986. At Publication release, Diarm is on strike and all production has stopped.

DIXIE GUN WORKS
See "Modern Black Powder Guns" Section.

Grading	100%	98%	95%	90%	80%	70%	60%

DOMINGO ACHA
Manufactured in Spain.

LOOKING GLASS — .25 and .32 cal. auto pistol.

	$150	$125	$105	$85	$75	$60	$50

DOMINO, IGI
Previously imported from Italy by Mandall Shooting Supplies located in Scottsdale, AZ. This firm was absorbed by FAS (see separate listing in F section) in 1990.

MODEL OP 601 MATCH PISTOL — .22 Short, 5 shot, 5.6 in. barrel, match sights, full target grips, vent barrel and slide to reduce recoil, adj. and removable trigger.

	$1,225	$1,000	$715	$635	$550	$495	$440

Last Mfg.'s Sug. Retail was $1,295.

MODEL SP 602 MATCH PISTOL — .22 LR, 5½ in. barrel, same as 601, but .22 LR and slightly different trigger.

	$1,225	$1,000	$715	$635	$550	$495	$440

Last Mfg.'s Sug. Retail was $1,295.

DREYSE PISTOL
Manufactured by Rheinische Metallwaren and Machinenfabrik, located in Sommerda, Germany.

MODEL 1907 AUTOMATIC — 7.65mm, 8 shot, 3½ in. barrel, blue, fixed sights, hard rubber grips. Mfg. 1907-1914.

	$200	$170	$150	$120	$95	$75	$50

MODEL 1910 — 9mm Luger, 3½ in. barrel. Mfg. 1912-1915.

	$760	$570	$495	$420	$380	$345	$305

VEST POCKET AUTOMATIC — .25 ACP, 6 shot, 2 in. barrel, blue, fixed sights, hard rubber grips. Mfg. 1912-1915.

	$225	$190	$165	$130	$100	$75	$50

DRILLINGS
A Drilling is a three-barrel combination gun (two shotgun barrels and a rifle barrel, vice versa, or three shotgun barrels). Normally, two triggers fire the shotgun barrels and one of them activates the rifle barrel when the barrel selector is moved forward (usually located on the upper tang). Most well made Drillings in above average condition are surprisingly accurate when using the rifle barrel(s).

Please refer to illustrations below depicting the most commonly encountered Drilling configurations.

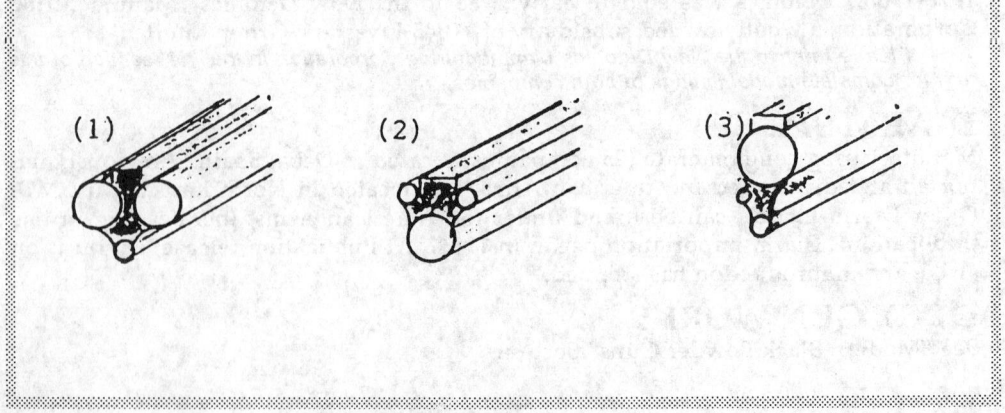

Grading	100%	98%	95%	90%	80%	70%	60%

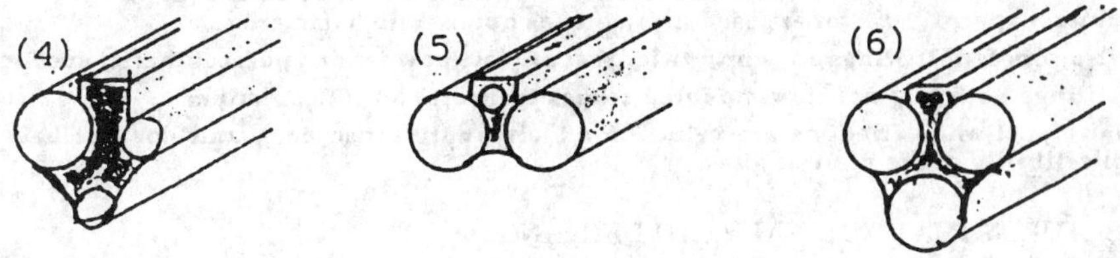

Illustration No. 1 - Normal Drilling configuration with 2 shotgun barrels over a rimmed, centerfire rifle (most are 16 ga. x 16 ga. by either 9.3 x 72R or 8 x 57JR cal.).

Illustration No. 2 - Two rifle barrels over a shotgun. This configuration will normally command twice the price as No. 1.

Illustration No. 3 - Three barrels with no two being the same gauge or caliber. This configuration is very collectible, especially if the smallest caliber is .22LR. Again, price will be double of No. 1.

Illustration No. 4 - Sometimes called a "cross-eyed" Drilling with one shotgun and two rifle barrels. This variation brings a good premium over No. 1.

Illustration No. 5 - Rib Drilling with rifle caliber generally small (.22LR or .22 Hornet).

Illustration No. 6 - Three shotgun barrels with the same gauge. This configuration is quite rare and healthy premiums are charged over No. 1.

For over 125 years Drillings have been the classic hunting gun of many European countries, especially Germany and Austria. Because a single hunting trip may require shooting both wildfowl and animals (oftentimes within several hours), Europeans have long favored a single long-arm that could afford both rifle and shotgun shooting, be reliable, and not wear the hunter out while transporting it in the field. Americans, on the other hand, have not placed as much emphasis on this combination gun principle, and more often than not, have chosen to buy both a rifle and shotgun for each specific hunting application. Since Drillings generally have not been as popular in the U.S., collectibility has been somewhat limited in this country, except for those who see the utility and functionability of these mostly hand assembled weapons. Very few Drillings manufactured before WWII are alike today in configuration and condition.

DRILLING VALUES

Rather than list the various manufacturers of Drillings (there are hundreds), it should be noted that guns with major trademarks and established provenences (i.e. Charles Daly, Colt Sauer, Ferlach addressed, Heym, Krieghoff, J.P. Sauer, Suhl addressed, etc.) will be more collectible than other lesser known brands - even if the quality of worksmanship is similar. Pre-war specimens are generally more desireable (and expensive) than post-war variations and to date, have outperformed post-war specimens in price appreciation. Many older pre-war specimens were designed for rimmed cartridges with lower breech pressures and should not be re-bored or reloaded for the "hotter" cartridges/loads available today. It should be noted that since Drillings are more complex than a typical shotgun, most of the manufacture

Grading	100%	98%	95%	90%	80%	70%	60%

has been done by hand - some guns have taken individual craftsmen over a year to fabricate! Ordering a new Drilling today would be a very expensive proposition, and buying a good used specimen will save you thousands of dollars (and maybe a year wait). For these reasons, many collectors feel Drillings today are under-priced since they can be purchased at a fraction of the cost for a new one (and may well be better quality also).

GENERAL OBSERVATIONS CONCERNING DRILLING COLLECTIBILITY

Subtract approx. 50% for exposed hammers (as opposed to hammerless).

Nitro-proofed Drillings are worth twice that of blackpowder or damascus barrel specimens.

Drillings with original claw-mounted scopes are worth 30-40% premiums.

Many post-war variations are valued for their hunting use only, and do not have the collectibility of the pre-war guns.

FEATURES THAT ADD VALUE TO DRILLINGS

Drillings with American calibers and smaller gauges will be more desirable (and expensive) than the European metric calibers (i.e. a gun configured 20 ga. x 20 ga. by .243 Win. will outperform a similar gun in 16 ga. x 16 ga. by 9.3 x 72R cal.). The most commonly encountered gauges and calibers are 16 ga. (most pre-war guns are chambered for $2\frac{9}{16}$ in. and would have to be re-chambered for $2\frac{3}{4}$ in. to be shootable today). In addition, a sidelock action will be more desirable than a boxlock, and a lot more expensive if the locks are also detachable.

Features and embellishments become very critical in ascertaining Drilling values also - a gun with deep relief engraving, carved stock, claw mounts w/scope, buffalo horn trigger guard and butt plate, cocking indicators, two position front sight (i.e. night sight), middle set of express sights, adj. trigger, concealed upper tang peep sight, a non-Greener safety system, lightweight (under 6½ lbs.), separate rifle cocking, shotgun barrel inserts in .22LR or .22 Mag. cal. (approx. 8 or 11 in. long), cartridge trap, etc. is going to be A LOT more collectible than a plain-Jane hammer model with a loose action.

FEATURES THAT DETRACT VALUE FROM DRILLINGS

These include exposed hammers, damascus or blackpowder only guns, bottom lever break, calibers for which ammo is not readily available or cannot be easily made from other more common brass, loose action, mechanical problems which hinder shooting, etc.

CONDITION FACTORS

Condition is another major consideration - a gun that shows much use and is not operationally intact/correct may bring several thousand dollars less than another similar specimen showing little wear and excellent original finish (including the case colors). Most good boxlock Drillings in the above mentioned trademarks start in the $1,750 range and can go to $4,000 and higher if the configuration, features, and condition are all desirable. Average Drillings usually sell in the $650 - $1,500 range assuming worn condition, metric calibers and few features. For these reasons, Drillings have to be evaluated one at a time and a COMPETENT appraisal/evaluation should be procurred before buying or selling a specimen.

DUBIEL ARMS COMPANY

Manufacturer located in Sherman, TX. Dubiel Arms has been making custom bolt action rifles for many years (since 1973 in Sherman, TX).

BOLT ACTION RIFLE — custom made bolt action, .22-250-.458 Win. Mag. cal's available, barrel length and weight to order, no sights, Canjar trigger, all steel parts, custom made rifle stocks available in five styles.

	100%	98%	95%	90%	80%	70%	60%
Mfg.'s Sug. Retail	$2,500	$2,500	$2,100	$1,870	$1,760	$1,650	$1,375	$1,225

Grading	100%	98%	95%	90%	80%	70%	60%

DUMOULIN, ERNEST

Manufacturer located in Herstal, Belgium. Previously imported (until 1990) and retailed on a very limited basis by Midwest Gun Sport located in Zebulon, NC. (formerly from Ellisville, MO.). Older importation was by Abercrombie & Fitch located in New York, NY.

Note: Most Ernest Dumoulin rifles and shotguns are essentially custom ordered firearms with a long list of options available which, in some cases, can easily double the values of models shown below. Because of this, these options are not listed individually. To determine the exact price on a specific model with certain options, Ernest Dumoulin (see Trademark Index) should be contacted to obtain a firm price (dependent on the fluctuation of the U.S. dollar and other domestic and foreign regulations). Written correspondence should include a SASE (a FAX will be faster).

Current retail prices listed reflect 1989 information since almost no importation has occured since that time.

RIFLES: BOLT ACTION

BAVARIA DELUXE — .243 Win. through .458 Win. cal.'s, 21½, 24, or 25½ in. octagonal barrel, French walnut stock with rosewood forend tip and pistol grip cap, no sights, custom made essentially with Sako (disc.) or Mauser action. Many engraving options available from $510-$1,900. Disc. 1985.

Series I	$995	$890	$775	$650	$575	$530	$460

Add 15% for .375 H&H or .458 Win. Mag. cal. Last Mfg.'s Sug. Retail was $1,080.

RIFLE MOUSQUETON — .240 Win. through .338 Win. cal.'s, 20 in. barrel, Mannlicher style, French walnut stock and pistol grip cap, no sights, custom made essentially with Sako or Mauser action. Many engraving options available from $510 - $1,900. Disc.

	$720	$620	$560	$510	$470	$420	$360

CENTURION MODEL — .270 Win. through .458 Win. cal.'s, 21½, 24, or 25½ in. barrels, French walnut stock with rosewood forearm tip and pistol grip cap, no sights, custom made essentially with Sako or Mauser action. Many engraving options available from $510 - $1,900. Importation disc. 1986.

	$660	$590	$535	$480	$425	$390	$360

Last Mfg.'s Sug. Retail was $740.

CENTURION CLASSIC — similar to Centurion, standard cal.'s only, Mauser 98 action only and has better wood.

Mfg.'s Sug. Retail	$1,525	$1,525	$1,375	$1,175	$975	$800	$700	$600

These models are also available in Mag. cal.'s that are divided into 4 groups — 1, 2, 3, and 4 Mag. Series. These options retail in the $50 - $300 price range.

Diane — grade up from Centurion Classic, 22 in. barrel, Mauser 98 action, M-70 safety, adj. steel trigger.

Mfg.'s Sug. Retail	$1,450	$1,450	$1,250	$1,000	$825	$700	$600	$500

Above values represent base price with no options.

Amazone — grade up from Diane, 20 in. barrel, full stock.

Mfg.'s Sug. Retail	$1,750	$1,750	$1,525	$1,325	$1,075	$865	$750	$600

Above values represent base price with no options.

Bavaria Deluxe — .243 Win. through .458 Win. cal.'s, 21½, 24, or 25½ in. octagonal barrel, French walnut stock with rosewood forend tip and pistol grip cap, no sights, custom made essentially with Sako (disc.) or Mauser action. Many engraving options available from $510 - $1,900.

Mfg.'s Sug. Retail	$1,900	$1,900	$1,675	$1,450	$1,200	$995	$775	$650

Above values represent base price with no options.

Safari — Mag. cal.'s only.

Mfg.'s Sug. Retail	$2,350	$2,350	$1,775	$1,475	$1,200	$995	$775	$650

Above values represent base price with no options.

Grading	100%	98%	95%	90%	80%	70%	60%

MANNLICHER MODEL — Mauser type bolt action, various cal.'s, full stocked. Disc. 1985.

	$730	$660	$580	$520	$470	$430	$395

Last Mfg.'s Sug. Retail was $825.

Mannlicher Classic — same as basic Mannlicher, except has better walnut. Disc. 1985.

	$995	$890	$775	$650	$575	$530	$460

Last Mfg.'s Sug. Retail was $1,065.

MATCH MODEL — match target rifle, adj. sights and stock. Disc. 1985.

	$1,640	$1,490	$1,300	$1,050	$900	$800	$700

Last Mfg.'s Sug. Retail was $1,860.

Match NATO — 7.62 cal. match rifle. Disc. 1985.

	$2,640	$2,400	$2,175	$1,850	$1,595	$1,400	$1,195

Last Mfg.'s Sug. Retail was $3,000.

ST. HUBERT MODEL — Sako action, various cal.'s and barrel lengths. Disc. 1985.

	$1,900	$1,700	$1,495	$1,300	$1,150	$995	$850

Last Mfg.'s Sug. Retail was $2,125.

SAFARI SPORTSMAN — Mauser 98 action, .416 Rigby, .375 H&H, .505 Gibbs, or .404 Jeffreys cal., 4 shot mag., limited availability in 1986.

Mfg.'s Sug. Retail	$4,000	$4,000	$3,550	$3,250	$2,800	$2,400	$2,000	$1,750

Add $300 for .505 Gibbs cal.
Above values represent base price with no options.

AFRICAN PRO — similar to Safari Sportsman except has ebony or buffalo horn forearm tip, tilting hood for the front sight, multiple folding rear sight.

Mfg.'s Sug. Retail	$4,800	$4,800	$4,000	$3,550	$3,250	$2,800	$2,400	$2,000

Above values represent base price with no options.

DOUBLE RIFLES

EUROPA I — .22 Hornet, .222 Rem., .222 Rem. Mag., 6mm Rem., .243 Win., .25-06, .30-06, 6.5 X 57R, 7 X 57R, 8 X 57JRS, or 9.3 X 74R cal., Anson & Deeley boxlock action, moderate engraving. New 1989.

Mfg.'s Sug. Retail	$4,800	$4,800	$4,200	$3,800	$3,500	$3,250	$2,995	$2,700

Above values represent base price with no options.

CONTINENTAL I — same calibers as Europa I, sidelock action, 12 engraving options to choose from, many options available on special order. New 1989.

Mfg.'s Sug. Retail	$8,600	$8,600	$7,700	$6,995	$6,400	$5,600	$4,750	$4,150

Above values represent base price with no options.

"PIONNIER" JUXTAPOSED EXPRESS RIFLES – assorted cal.'s from .22 Hornet through .600 Nitro Express, S x S configuration, heavily engraved, select walnut. Limited production, Anson & Deeley triple lock action, sideplates available at extra charge.

P-I and P-II — English style scroll or bouquet (P-II) engraving.

Mfg.'s Sug. Retail	$7,850	$7,850	$6,500	$5,825	$5,200	$4,650	$4,160	$3,700

Add $400 for P-II engraving.

P III — English style lace engraving (tapestry style).

Mfg.'s Sug. Retail	$8,640	$8,640	$7,750	$7,000	$6,400	$5,600	$4,750	$4,150

P-IV through P-VIII — various styles of royal engraving with or without hunting scenes.

Mfg.'s Sug. Retail	$9,100	$9,100	$7,995	$7,450	$6,800	$6,000	$5,000	$4,350

Add $400 for gold inlays.

P-IX through P-XII — Louis XVI style engraving.

Mfg.'s Sug. Retail	$9,540	$9,540	$8,600	$7,800	$7,250	$6,400	$5,250	$4,500

Pionnier Magnum — .338 Win. Mag., .375 H&H, .416 Rigby, .416 Hoffman, .458 Win. Mag., .577 Nitro Express, or .600 Nitro Express. Boxlock action with Greener crossbolt.

Mfg.'s Sug. Retail	$10,900	$10,900	$9,400	$8,650	$7,800	$7,000	$6,450	$5,825

Above values represent base price with no options.

Grading	100%	98%	95%	90%	80%	70%	60%

ARISTOCRATE MODEL — available in all cal.'s up to .375 H&H (also in 20 ga.), single shot action with low profile, exhibition oil finished walnut stock and forearm. Values below assume standard model (12 engraving options available). Imported 1987-1988 only.

	100%	98%	95%	90%	80%	70%	60%
	$9,100	$8,450	$7,775	$7,000	$6,450	$5,825	$5,275

Last Mfg.'s Sug. Retail was $10,400.

Above values represent base price with no options.

PRESTIGE RIFLE (SIDELOCK) — best quality sidelock, various cal.'s, triple locking, 10 different presentation options available, values below reflect standard model without options. Custom order only, 1 year waiting period. New 1986.

	100%	98%	95%	90%	80%	70%	60%
Mfg.'s Sug. Retail	$17,900	$17,900	$15,000	$12,500	$9,995	$8,000	$7,000	$6,000

Add $600 for Mag. cal.'s over .416 Rigby.

SHOTGUNS

EUROPA MODEL — 12, 20, 28, or .410 ga., Anson & Deeley boxlock action, single or double trigger, moderately engraved, oil finished stock and forearm, choice of 6 engraving options. New 1989.

	100%	98%	95%	90%	80%	70%	60%
Mfg.'s Sug. Retail	$3,300	$3,300	$2,750	$2,350	$2,000	$1,800	$1,575	$1,400

LEIGE JUXTAPOSED SHOTGUN (SxS) — 12, 16 (disc. 1986), 20, or 28 ga., Anson & Deeley locking action, elaborate engraving, deluxe walnut. New 1986.

Luxe Model

	100%	98%	95%	90%	80%	70%	60%
	$5,300	$4,600	$3,900	$3,300	$2,900	$2,600	$2,300

Last Mfg.'s Sug. Retail was $5,900 (disc. 1988).

Grand Luxe

	100%	98%	95%	90%	80%	70%	60%
Mfg.'s Sug. Retail	$6,900	$6,900	$6,000	$5,000	$4,300	$3,600	$3,200	$2,875

Add 15% for 28 ga.

Add 15% for sideplates.

Many engraving options and other special order features can be added to the above models.

CONTINENTAL MODEL — 12, 20, 28, or .410 ga., sidelock action, double or single trigger, deluxe oil finished walnut stock, choice of 6 engraving options. New 1989.

	100%	98%	95%	90%	80%	70%	60%
Mfg.'s Sug. Retail	$7,400	$7,400	$6,250	$5,200	$4,400	$3,700	$3,200	$2,875

Above values represent base price with no options.

ETENDART JUXTAPOSED SHOTGUN (SxS) — 12, 20 and 28 ga., full sidelock, exhibition grade walnut, double triggers, top-of-the-line quality, built to special order. Values listed assume standard gun (12 engraving options available). New 1987.

	100%	98%	95%	90%	80%	70%	60%
Mfg.'s Sug. Retail	$14,400	$14,400	$12,250	$9,995	$9,100	$8,450	$7,775	$7,000

Add 6% for 28 ga.

BOSS ROYAL SUPERPOSED (O/U) — 12, 20 or 28 ga., full sidelock, exhibition grade walnut, double triggers, top-of-the-line quality, built to special order. Values listed assume standard gun (12 engraving options available). New 1987.

	100%	98%	95%	90%	80%	70%	60%
Mfg.'s Sug. Retail	$18,500	$18,500	$16,000	$13,750	$11,000	$9,775	$8,000	$6,950

Add 6½% for 28 ga.

SUPERPOSED EXPRESS "INTERNATIONAL" — O/U shotgun, includes extra set of rifle barrels, 20 ga., 7 choices of rifle cal.'s, deluxe walnut. Elaborate engraving patterns available at extra charge, limited production. Disc. 1985.

	100%	98%	95%	90%	80%	70%	60%
	$2,400	$2,000	$1,800	$1,575	$1,400	$1,200	$1,050

Last Mfg.'s Sug. Retail was $2,490.

COMBINATION GUNS

EAGLE MODEL — O/U configuration (shotgun barrel on bottom), 12 or 20 ga., .22 Hornet, .222 Rem., .222 Rem. Mag., 6mm Rem., .243 Win., .25-06, .30-06, 6.5 X 57R, 7 X 57R, 8 X 57JRS, or 9.3 X 74R cal., boxlock action. New 1989.

	100%	98%	95%	90%	80%	70%	60%
Mfg.'s Sug. Retail	$2,700	$2,700	$2,400	$2,175	$1,850	$1,595	$1,400	$1,195

Above values represent base price with no options.

Grading	100%	98%	95%	90%	80%	70%	60%

DUMOULIN, HENRI & FILS

Manufacturer located in Herstal, Belgium. Imported and distributed by New England Arms, Co. located in Kittery Point, ME.

H. Dumoulin has manufactured firearms in Liege/Herstal, Belgium since 1947. They have specialized in bolt action rifles, generally built on Mauser 98 or commercial Mauser actions. The Imperial Magnum action was developed and introduced in 1987.

RIFLES

GRAND LUXE BOLT ACTION — .300 Wby., .338 Win. Mag., .375 H&H, .378 Wby., .404 Jeffrey, .416 Rigby, .460 Wby., or .505 Gibbs cal., 24, 25.6, or 26 in. barrel, European walnut stock with ebony forend tip and pistol grip cap, folding leaf sights with hooded front, custom made on the Dumoulin Imperial Magnum double square bridge action. Many engraving options available.

Mfg.'s Sug. Retail	$6,750	$6,500	$6,200	$5,500	$4,950	$4,300	$3,600	$3,200

Add $500 for left hand action.

Add $850 for extended top and bottom tang.

Add $800 for claw mounts.

Add $700 for .505 Gibbs cal.

SOVERIGN — available in same cal.'s as Grand Luxe Bolt Action, except with a higher quality finish, knurled bolt handles, gold inlayed lettering. Many engraving options available. Pricing on this model depends on engraving, wood and other options. Imperial Magnum is also available in various stages of completion, barreled actions, actions in the white, etc. Please contact New England Arms, Co. directly for quotation.

SXS BOXLOCK RIFLE — boxlock action, best quality double rifle, highly figured European walnut, finely hand checkered with standard scroll engraving. Custom ordered to customer's dimensions. Prices start at $9,500.

SXS SIDELOCK RIFLE — sidelock action, best quality hand detachable locks, top quality European walnut, finely hand checkered with standard scroll engraving. Additional engraving or deluxe wood quoted on request. Prices start at $15,000.

SHOTGUNS

BOXLOCK MODEL — available in most ga.'s, individually built per customer special order. The importer should be contacted directly for more information and a price quotation.

SIDELOCK MODEL — available in most ga.'s, individually built per customer special order. The importer should be contacted directly for more information and a price quotation.

E

E.M.F. CO., INC.

Current importer and distributor located in Santa Ana, CA.

Grading	100%	98%	95%	90%	80%	70%	60%

REVOLVERS: REPRODUCTIONS

1875 REMINGTON OUTLAW — .357 Mag., .44-40, or .45 LC cal., copy of the Rem. Model 1875 SA, 7½ in. barrel only, casehardened frame, walnut grips, blue only.

Mfg.'s Sug. Retail	$465	$325	$250	$185	$165	$155	$145	$135

Add $60 for nickel plating.

Add $135 for engraving.

1890 REMINGTON SINGLE ACTION — .357 Mag., .44-40, or .45 LC cal., 5½ in. barrel, lanyard ring in butt stock, blue frame, walnut grips. New 1986.

Mfg.'s Sug. Retail	$470	$330	$255	$185	$165	$155	$145	$135

Add $60 for nickel plating.

Add $150 for engraving.

DERRINGERS: REPRODUCTIONS

STANDARD MODEL — .38 Spl., Rem. Model 41 copy, top hinged, vent rib, spur trigger, teflon blue finish. Disc. 1986.

	$60	$50	$40	$35	$30	$25	$20

Add $7 for nickel finish.
Last Mfg.'s Sug. Retail was $75.

RIFLES: MODERN REPRODUCTIONS

The models listed below, being of a paramilitary design, were disc. 1989 due to Federal legislation as a result of the controversy with this type of firearms configuration.

These models are authentic shooting reproductions mfg. in Italy.

AP 74 — .22 LR or .32 ACP cal., copy of the Colt AR-15, semi-auto, 15 shot mag., 20 in. barrel, 6¾ lbs. Importation disc. 1989.

	$295	$250	$200	$175	$155	$145	$135

Add $25 for .32 cal.
Last Mfg.'s Sug. Retail was $295.

Sporter Carbine — wood sporter stock, .22 LR only. Importation disc. 1989.

	$320	$275	$225	$195	$175	$160	$140

Last Mfg.'s Sug. Retail was $320.

Paramilitary Paratrooper Carbine — .22 LR only, folding wire stock, black nylon on paramilitary design model. Importation disc. 1987.

	$260	$190	$175	$165	$155	$145	$135

Add $10 for wood folding stock.
Last Mfg.'s Sug. Retail was $325.

"Dressed" Military Model — with Cyclops scope, Colt bayonet, sling, and bipod. Disc. 1986.

	$330	$265	$240	$220	$200	$185	$170

Last Mfg.'s Sug. Retail was $450.

ISRAELI GALIL — .22 LR only, reproduction of the Israeli Galil, semi-auto. Importation disc. 1989.

	$295	$250	$200	$175	$155	$145	$135

Last Mfg.'s Sug. Retail was $295.

Grading	100%	98%	95%	90%	80%	70%	60%

KALASHNIKOV AK-47 — .22 LR only, reproduction of the Russian AK-47, semi-auto. Importation disc. 1989.

	100%	98%	95%	90%	80%	70%	60%
	$295	$250	$200	$175	$155	$145	$135

Last Mfg.'s Sug. Retail was $295.

FRENCH M.A.S. — .22 LR only, reproduction of the French Bull-Pup Combat Rifle, semi-auto with carrying handle, 29 shot mag. Importation disc. 1989.

	100%	98%	95%	90%	80%	70%	60%
	$320	$265	$240	$220	$200	$185	$170

Last Mfg.'s Sug. Retail was $320.

M1 CARBINE — .30 cal. only, copy of the U.S. Military M1 Carbine. Disc. 1985.

	100%	98%	95%	90%	80%	70%	60%
	$175	$150	$140	$130	$120	$110	$100

Add $43 for Paratrooper variation.
Last Mfg.'s Sug. Retail was $205.

RIFLES: REMINGTON REPRODUCTIONS

ROLLING BLOCK CARBINE — .45-70 cal., authentic reproduction of the Remington Rolling Block Carbine. Importation began 1991.

	100%	98%	95%	90%	80%	70%	60%
Mfg.'s Sug. Retail	$820	$585	$400	$325	$250	$235	$220	$200

RIFLES: SHARPS REPRODUCTIONS

SHARPS OLD RELIABLE RIFLE — .45-70 cal., copy of the Sharp's Single Shot, 28 in. octagonal barrel, case hardened frame, double set triggers.

	100%	98%	95%	90%	80%	70%	60%
Mfg.'s Sug. Retail	$950	$725	$575	$440	$330	$295	$260	$230

Carbine Model — saddle-ring carbine with 22 in. round barrel, single trigger.

	100%	98%	95%	90%	80%	70%	60%
Mfg.'s Sug. Retail	$950	$725	$575	$440	$330	$295	$260	$230

RIFLES: WINCHESTER REPRODUCTIONS

DELUXE HENRY RIFLE — .44-40 cal. only, deluxe walnut, reproduction of New Haven Arms Co.'s Henry Rifle. New 1987.

	100%	98%	95%	90%	80%	70%	60%
Mfg.'s Sug. Retail	$1,111	$850	$600	$450	$330	$295	$260	$230

Engraved Henry Rifle — similar to deluxe Henry Rifle except has hand engraved receiver. Imported 1987-90.

	100%	98%	95%	90%	80%	70%	60%
	$1,200	$975	$700	$525	$400	$340	$295

Last Mfg.'s Sug. Retail was $1,598.

1866 YELLOWBOY CARBINE — .22 LR (disc.), .38 Spl., or .44-40 cal., 19 in. barrel, saddle-ring carbine, brass frame.

	100%	98%	95%	90%	80%	70%	60%
Mfg.'s Sug. Retail	$805	$575	$400	$325	$250	$235	$220	$200

1866 Rifle — same cal.'s as 1866 Yellowboy Carbine, 24¼ in. barrel.

	100%	98%	95%	90%	80%	70%	60%
Mfg.'s Sug. Retail	$835	$585	$400	$325	$250	$235	$220	$200

Engraved Yellowboy Carbine — .38 Spl., or .44-40 cal. only. Importation disc. 1990.

	100%	98%	95%	90%	80%	70%	60%
	$800	$575	$440	$330	$295	$260	$230

Last Mfg.'s Sug. Retail was $1,080.

1873 CARBINE — .22 Mag. (disc.), .357 Mag., .44-40, or .45 LC cal., 19 in. barrel, copy of the Winchester Model 1873, case hardened receiver.

	100%	98%	95%	90%	80%	70%	60%
Mfg.'s Sug. Retail	$980	$750	$575	$440	$330	$295	$260	$230

1873 Rifle — 24¼ in. barrel, available only in .357 Mag. or .44-40 cal.

	100%	98%	95%	90%	80%	70%	60%
Mfg.'s Sug. Retail	$1,110	$800	$575	$440	$330	$295	$260	$230

Engraved Rifle — available in .357 Mag. or .44-40 cal. only. Importation disc. 1987.

	100%	98%	95%	90%	80%	70%	60%
	$895	$635	$500	$450	$400	$360	$325

Last Mfg.'s Sug. Retail was $850.

Grading	100%	98%	95%	90%	80%	70%	60%

PREMIER 1873 CARBINE & RIFLE — .45 LC, case hardened frame, uncheckered walnut stock and forearm, full mag., rifle has 24¼ in. barrel, carbine has 19 in. barrel. Imported 1988-1989 only.

	$850	$595	$450	$330	$295	$260	$230

Add $38 for rifle variation.
Last Mfg.'s Sug. Retail was $1,160.

84 GUN CO.
Eighty Four, PA. Early 1970's.

RIFLES

CLASSIC RIFLE — Bolt action, various calibers. Grades 1-4.

	100%	98%	95%	90%	80%	70%	60%
Grade 1	$420	$315	$275	$235	$210	$190	$170
Grade 2	$780	$585	$512	$430	$390	$355	$315
Grade 3	$860	$645	$560	$475	$430	$390	$345
Grade 4	$1,580	$1,185	$1,030	$870	$790	$715	$640

LOBO RIFLE — bolt action, various calibers. Grades standard, 1-4.

	100%	98%	95%	90%	80%	70%	60%
Standard	$415	$315	$270	$230	$210	$190	$170
Grade 1	$540	$405	$355	$300	$270	$245	$220
Grade 2	$795	$600	$520	$440	$400	$360	$320
Grade 3	$1,600	$1,200	$1,040	$880	$800	$720	$640
Grade 4	$2,350	$1,765	$1,530	$1,295	$1,175	$1,060	$940

PENNSYLVANIA RIFLE — bolt action, various calibers. Grades standard, 1-4.

	100%	98%	95%	90%	80%	70%	60%
Standard	$420	$315	$275	$235	$210	$190	$170
Grade 1	$540	$405	$355	$300	$270	$245	$220
Grade 2	$795	$600	$520	$440	$400	$360	$320
Grade 3	$1,600	$1,200	$1,040	$880	$800	$720	$640
Grade 4	$2,350	$1,765	$1,530	$1,295	$1,175	$1,060	$940

EAGLE ARMS INC.
Manufacturer located in Coal Valley, IL.

The desirability of the models listed below may change regionally. As a result, values could fluctuate from one area to another due to the buyer demand on this paramilitary configuration.

MODEL EA-15 E-1 RIFLE — .223 cal., patterned after the Colt AR-15A2, 20 in. barrel, forward bolt assist, 7 lbs. New 1990.

Mfg.'s Sug. Retail	$825	$775	$675	$575	$475	$400	$365	$325

EA-15 E-1 Carbine — similar to EA-15 E-1 Rifle, except has sliding butt stock and 16 in. barrel, 5 lbs. 14 oz. New 1990.

Mfg.'s Sug. Retail	$845	$795	$695	$575	$475	$400	$365	$325

Add $50 for E-2 accessory kit.

EA-15 E-2 H-BAR Rifle — similar to Model EA-15 E-1, except has heavy barrel, 8 lbs. 9 oz., includes E-2 accessories. New 1990.

Mfg.'s Sug. Retail	$895	$825	$725	$600	$525	$450	$400	$375

EA-15 E-2 H-BAR Golden Eagle — similar to EA-15 H-BAR, except has 20 in. Douglas premium extra heavy barrel, 12 lbs. 12 oz. New 1991.

Mfg.'s Sug. Retail	$1,075	$975	$850	$725	$600	$525	$450	$400

EGO ARMAS, S.A.
Manufacturer located in Eibar, Spain. No current U.S. importation.

Grading	100%	98%	95%	90%	80%	70%	60%

Ego Armas manufactures high quality sidelock double rifles and both boxlock and sidelock shotguns. More information, including current models and approximate U.S. pricing, can be obtained by writing this manufacturer directly (see Trademark Index).

ENFIELD
Royal Small Arms Factory, Middlesex, England.

NO. 2 MK. I REVOLVER — .380 British Service (based on .38 S&W with a 200 grain bullet), double action, 6 shot, 5 in. barrel, fixed sights, blue, composition grips, top break, issued to British army 1932.

$235	$195	$175	$140	$130	$120	$110

RIFLES
SMLE stands for Rifle, Short, Magazine, Lee-Enfield. The SMLE rifles served the British Military from 1902-1954.

NO. 1 MK. III SMLE — .303 British, bolt action, 10 shot mag., 25.2 in. barrel, open sights, long range volley sights, magazine cut-off, adopted by British Army in 1907.

$225	$190	$150	$125	$100	$90	$75

NO. 1 MK. III SMLE — a simplified rifle adopted by the British during WWI, volley sights and magazine cut-off deleted, the most common variation of SMLE.

$225	$190	$150	$125	$100	$90	$75

NO. 3 MK. I PATTERN 14 RIFLE — modified Mauser type bolt action, .303 British, issued as substitute standard by British Army during WWI, manufactured in U.S. (the later U.S. 1917 Enfield is identical except for caliber and sights).

$225	$190	$150	$125	$100	$90	$75

NO. 3 MK. I — .22 cal., single shot military training model.

$350	$300	$275	$250	$225	$200	$175

NO. 4 MK. I — an improved SMLE with aperture rear sight, stronger receiver and more easily manufactured parts, adopted in 1939 by the British Army.

$215	$185	$145	$120	$95	$75	$55

This model was manufactured during WWII in Canada, England, and the U.S. To determine which armory manufactured this model, the following information should be studied. Savage-Stevens mfg. is denoted by "US Property S" with a C in ser. no., Canadian mfg. (Long Branch, Ontario) is indicated by "Long Branch" - no code, British mfg. was by B.S.A., Shirley and marked "M.47C"., Royal Ordnance Factory (near Liverpool) marked "ROF(F)", or Royal Ordnance Factory (near Sheffield) marked"ROFM" or "RM" or "M".

Sniper Model — cased, with or without scope.

Cased	$900	$750	$675	$595	$540	$480	$420
Uncased	$750	$600	$535	$480	$420	$350	$295

NO. 5 MK. I JUNGLE CARBINE — a shorter, lighter version of the No. 4 MK. I with a 20.5 in. barrel, flash hider, recoil pad and shortened forend and hand guard, 7.2 lbs., developed during WWII.

$295	$250	$200	$150	$125	$100	$85

ENFIELD AMERICA, INC.
Manufacturer located in Atlanta, GA.

MP-45 — .45 ACP, semi-auto paramilitary design pistol, 4½, 6, 8, 10, or 18½ in. shrouded barrel, Parkerized finish, 10, 30, 40, or 50 shot mag., 6 lbs. Mfg. 1985 only.

$295	$260	$240	$220	$200	$185	$170

Last Mfg.'s Sug. Retail was $350.

ERA
Manufacturer located in Brazil.

Grading	100%	98%	95%	90%	80%	70%	60%

ERA O/U SHOTGUN — 12 or 20 ga., 28 in. vent rib barrel, full and mod., double triggers, extractors, checkered hardwood stock.

	100%	98%	95%	90%	80%	70%	60%
	$275	$250	$225	$200	$170	$150	$125
Trap version	$300	$275	$250	$225	$200	$175	$150
Skeet version	$300	$275	$250	$225	$200	$175	$150

ERA DOUBLE BARREL — 12, 20, or .410 ga., 26, 28, or 30 in. barrels, various chokes, double triggers, extractors, checkered pistol grip stock.

100%	98%	95%	90%	80%	70%	60%
$165	$150	$135	$125	$110	$100	$85

ERA DOUBLE RIOT MODEL — same as Double Barrel, except 12 or 20 ga., 18 in. barrel.

100%	98%	95%	90%	80%	70%	60%
$185	$175	$150	$140	$125	$110	$95

ERA QUAIL MODEL — same as Standard, except 12 or 20 ga., 20 in. barrel.

100%	98%	95%	90%	80%	70%	60%
$185	$175	$150	$140	$125	$110	$95

ERMA-WERKE

Manufacturer located in Dachau, Germany. Currently, pistols and revolvers are imported and distributed by Mandall's Shooting Supplies, Inc. located in Scottsdale, AZ and Precision Sales International, Inc. located in Westfield, MA. Previously distributed by Excam located in Hialeah, FL.

Erma-Werke rifles are not currently imported into the U.S. Erma-Werke also private labels handguns for American Arms (refer to their section for listings).

PISTOLS: SEMI-AUTO

MODEL LA 22 — .22 LR, semi-auto, action patterned after the Luger, mfg. 1964-1967.

100%	98%	95%	90%	80%	70%	60%
$395	$335	$275	$240	$200	$175	$140

ERMA KGP68A/BEEMAN MP-08 — Luger type toggle action, .32 ACP (disc. 1987) or .380 ACP, 3½ (Beeman) or 4 in. barrel, 6 shot mag., blue, 1.4 lbs. Mfg. 1968-present.

100%	98%	95%	90%	80%	70%	60%
$335	$275	$240	$185	$145	$115	$95

Last Mfg.'s Sug. Retail was $390.

From 1988-90, Beeman took over importation of this model in .380 ACP cal. only with new Luger style checkered walnut grips and 3½ in. barrel. Previous models had plastic grips.

ERMA KGP69/BEEMAN P-08 — Luger type toggle action, .22 LR, 8 shot mag., 3¾ in. barrel, blue, plastic (disc.) or checkered walnut grips. Mfg. 1969-present.

100%	98%	95%	90%	80%	70%	60%
$335	$275	$240	$185	$145	$115	$95

Last Mfg.'s Sug. Retail was $390.

Beeman was the sole importer of this model between 1988-90.

MODEL ESP 85A SPORTING PISTOL — .22 LR and .32 S&W Long Wadcutter, blow back semi-auto, 6 in. barrel, 5 or 8 (.32 S&W only) shot mag., adj. stippled match grips with thumbrest, fully adj. and interchangeable sights, gun is supplied with 2 barrels (.22 LR and .32 S&W), several extra mag.'s, sights, disassembly tools, and attache style case with foam rubber cut-outs, 2½ lbs. Importation began 1989.

	100%	98%	95%	90%	80%	70%	60%
Mfg.'s Sug. Retail	$1,250	$1,050	$900	$800	$700	$625	$550	$495

Add $56 for .32 S&W cal.

Add $117 for Match Model.

Add $775 for conversion unit.

Add approx. $220 for chrome finish.

Add $30 for left-hand action (Match Model only).

This model is distributed by Precision Sales International, Inc. and Mandall Shooting Supplies, Inc.

Model ESP 85A Complete Set — includes both .22 LR and .32 S&W Long Wadcutter barrels and mag.'s, cased with accessories.

	100%	98%	95%	90%	80%	70%	60%
Mfg.'s Sug. Retail	$1,995	$1,775	$1,525	$1,350	$1,125	$950	$825	$750

Grading	100%	98%	95%	90%	80%	70%	60%

ET-22 LUGER CARBINE — .22 LR, 11¾ in. barrel, blue rear ramp sight, checkered walnut grips and uncheckered forearm, adj. artillery type rear sight, rarely seen.

	$395	$335	$275	$240	$200	$175	$140

Add 20% for leatherette case.

REVOLVERS: DOUBLE ACTION

These models are distributed by Precision Sales International, Inc. only.

ER 777 — .357 Mag., 6 shot, 4 or 5½ in. barrel, solid rib and full barrel shroud, adj. target rear sight, blued steel, checkered sport grips, 2¾ lbs. Importation began 1990.

Mfg.'s Sug. Retail	$1,093	$975	$825	$700	$625	$550	$495	$450

ER 772 MATCH — .22 LR, match gun with special adj. contoured grips with stippling, 6 in. barrel, action similar to ER 777, fully adj. and extended rear sight, interchangeable front sight, 3 lbs. Importation began 1990.

Mfg.'s Sug. Retail	$1,225	$995	$830	$700	$625	$550	$495	$450

ER 773 MATCH — .32 S & W Long, otherwise same as ER 772 Match, 2.9 lbs. Importation began 1990.

Mfg.'s Sug. Retail	$1,225	$995	$830	$700	$625	$550	$495	$450

RIFLES

EM1 .22 CARBINE — M1 copy .22 LR cal., 10 or 15 shot mag., 18 in. barrel, rear adj. aperature sight, 5.6 lbs. Mfg. 1966-current.

Mfg.'s Sug. Retail	$389	$340	$275	$240	$215	$190	$175	$160

This model is distributed by Mandall Shooting Supplies, Inc. on a limited basis only.

EGM-1 — same as EM1 except for unslotted butt stock, 5 shot mag.

	$195	$155	$145	$130	$120	$110	$100

EG72 PUMP — outside hammer, .22 LR cal., 15 shot mag., 18½ in. barrel. Mfg. 1970-1976.

	$125	$95	$90	$75	$70	$65	$60

EG712 LEVER-ACTION — Win. Model 94 copy, .22 LR cal., tube mag., 18½ in. barrel. Mfg. 1976 to date.

	$204	$160	$145	$130	$120	$110	$100

EG-73 — same as EG712 except .22 Mag. cal., 12 shot mag. Mfg. 1973 to date.

	$229	$180	$160	$155	$130	$115	$100

EUROPEAN AMERICAN ARMORY CORP.

Importer/distributor located in Hialeah, FL beginning late 1990.

European American Armory Corp. will repair the following older Excam and FIE models: late Model TZ-75 series 88, TA-90, E380 (steel frame), GT380 (steel frame), E15, and TA-76 handguns. This IS NOT warranty work, and repair prices start at $30 per gun (not including major parts).

REVOLVERS: BOUNTY HUNTER SERIES

MODEL EASAB SAA — .22 LR, single action revolver, 6 shot, 4¾ in. barrel, blued or chrome finish, wood grips.

Mfg.'s Sug. Retail	$65	$60	$45	$40	$35	$35	$35	$35

Add $10 for chrome finish.

MODEL EASAMB SAA COMBO — includes .22 LR and .22 Mag. cylinders, 4¾ (standard), 6, or 9 in. barrel, blue finish, wood grips.

Mfg.'s Sug. Retail	$75	$65	$55	$50	$45	$45	$45	$45

Add $10 for 9 in. barrel.

Add $15 for gold finish (4¾ in. barrel only).

Add $10 for chrome plated finish (4¾ in. barrel only).

Add $10 for brass backstrap and trigger guard (6 in. barrel only).

Grading	100%	98%	95%	90%	80%	70%	60%

PISTOLS: SEMI-AUTO - WITNESS SERIES

EA 9 SERIES — 9mm Para. cal., action patterned after the CZ-75, standard double action, 4¾ in. barrel, steel frame, 16 shot mag., blue, blue/chrome, or matte chrome finish, combat sights, black neoprene grips, 38 oz. Importation began late 1990.

| Mfg.'s Sug. Retail | $336 | $305 | $255 | $230 | $215 | $185 | $170 | $155 |

Add $24 for blue/chrome or matte chrome finish.

Model EA 9 Compact — similar to EA 9, except has 3½ in. barrel and 13 shot mag.

| Mfg.'s Sug. Retail | $336 | $305 | $255 | $230 | $215 | $185 | $170 | $155 |

Add $24 for blue/chrome or matte chrome finish.

Model EA 9 Ported — ported variation of the Model EA 9, except has 5 in. ported barrel and slide, blue finish, competition sights, 40 oz.

| Mfg.'s Sug. Retail | $490 | $450 | $375 | $345 | $320 | $300 | $275 | $260 |

EA 40 SERIES — .40 S&W cal., action patterned after the CZ-75, standard double action, 4¾ in. barrel, steel frame, 12 shot mag., blue, blue/chrome, or matte chrome finish, combat sights, black neoprene grips, 38 oz. Importation began late 1990.

| Mfg.'s Sug. Retail | $424 | $375 | $310 | $275 | $250 | $225 | $205 | $185 |

Add $20 for blue/chrome or matte chrome finish.

Model EA 40 Compact — similar to EA 40, except has 3½ in. barrel and 9 shot mag.

| Mfg.'s Sug. Retail | $424 | $375 | $310 | $275 | $250 | $225 | $205 | $185 |

Add $20 for blue/chrome or matte chrome finish.

Model EA 40 Ported — ported variation of the Model EA 41, except has 5 in. ported barrel and slide, blue finish, competition sights, 40 oz.

| Mfg.'s Sug. Retail | $515 | $470 | $385 | $350 | $325 | $300 | $275 | $255 |

EA 41 SERIES — .41 Action Express cal., action patterned after the CZ-75, standard double action, 4¾ in. barrel, steel frame, 11 shot mag., blue, blue/chrome, or matte chrome finish, combat sights, black neoprene grips, 38 oz. Importation began late 1990.

| Mfg.'s Sug. Retail | $424 | $375 | $310 | $275 | $250 | $225 | $205 | $185 |

Add $20 for blue/chrome or matte chrome finish.

Model EA 41 Compact — similar to EA 41, except has 3½ in. barrel and 8 shot mag.

| Mfg.'s Sug. Retail | $424 | $375 | $310 | $275 | $250 | $225 | $205 | $185 |

Add $20 for blue/chrome or matte chrome finish.

Model EA 41 Ported — compensated variation of the Model EA 41, except has 5 in. ported barrel and slide, blue finish, competition sights, 40 oz.

| Mfg.'s Sug. Retail | $515 | $470 | $385 | $350 | $325 | $295 | $275 | $260 |

EA 45 SERIES — .45 ACP cal., action patterned after the CZ-75, standard double action, 4¾ in. barrel, steel frame, 11 shot mag., blue, blue/chrome, or matte chrome finish, combat sights, black neoprene grips, 38 oz. Importation began late 1990.

| Mfg.'s Sug. Retail | $472 | $425 | $360 | $320 | $285 | $255 | $220 | $205 |

Add $15 for blue/chrome or matte chrome finish.

Model EA 45 Compact — similar to EA 45, except has 3½ in. barrel and 8 shot mag.

| Mfg.'s Sug. Retail | $472 | $425 | $360 | $320 | $285 | $255 | $220 | $205 |

Add $15 for blue/chrome or matte chrome finish.

Model EA 45 Ported — ported variation of the Model EA 45, except has 5 in. ported barrel and slide, blue finish, competition sights, 40 oz.

| Mfg.'s Sug. Retail | $515 | $455 | $385 | $350 | $325 | $300 | $275 | $255 |

PISTOLS: SINGLE ACTION - EUROPEAN SERIES

MODEL EA22-T — .22 LR cal., 6 in. barrel, 12 shot mag., single action, steel frame, target model, 26 oz. Importation began 1991.

| Mfg.'s Sug. Retail | $290 | $250 | $215 | $195 | $175 | $160 | $145 | $130 |

Grading	100%	98%	95%	90%	80%	70%	60%

MODEL EA32 — .32 ACP cal., 3.88 in. barrel, 7 shot mag., single action, steel frame, 26 oz., either satin chrome or standard blue, wooden grips. Importation began 1991.

Mfg.'s Sug. Retail	$150	$130	$110	$100	$90	$80	$65	$55

Add $14 for chrome finish (Model EA32C).

MODEL EA380 — .380 ACP cal., 3.88 in. barrel, 7 shot mag., single action, steel frame, either satin chrome or standard blue, wooden grips, 26 oz. Importation began 1991.

Mfg.'s Sug. Retail	$150	$130	$110	$100	$90	$80	$65	$55

Add $14 for chrome finish (Model EA380).

EXCAM

Previous importer and distributor located in Hialeah, FL that went out of business late 1990. Excam distributed Dart, Erma, Tanarmi, Targa, & Warrior exclusively for the U.S. These trademarks will appear under Excam only in this book. All importation of Excam firearms ceased in 1990.

All Targa and Tanarmi pistols were manufactured in Gardone V.T., Italy. All Erma and Warrior pistols and rifles were manufactured in W. Germany. Senator O/U shotguns were manufactured by A. Zoli located in Brescia, Italy.

ERMA PISTOLS

RX 22 — .22 LR only, double action-Walther copy, 3¼ in. barrel, 8 shot mag., blue only, plastic grips, 17 oz. Assembled in the U.S. Disc. 1986.

	$140	$125	$105	$95	$90	$85	$80

Last Mfg.'s Sug. Retail was $139.

KGP 22 — .22 LR only, Luger type toggle action, 3.78 in. barrel, 8 shot mag., blue only, plastic grips, 29 oz. Importation disc. 1986.

	$220	$195	$175	$155	$135	$120	$105

Last Mfg.'s Sug. Retail was $220.

KGP 380 — .380 ACP only, Luger type toggle action, 3½ in. barrel, 5 shot mag., blue only, plastic grips, 23 oz. Disc. 1986.

	$250	$215	$185	$160	$145	$135	$125

Last Mfg.'s Sug. Retail was $230.

ERMA RIFLES

EG 712 — .22 LR only, lever action copied after the Win. Model 92, 18½ barrel, 15 shot, iron sights. Disc. 1985.

	$180	$160	$140	$125	$115	$100	$90

Last Mfg.'s Sug. Retail was $204.

EG 712L — .22 LR only, lever action copied after the Win. Model 92, 18½ octagonal barrel, deluxe walnut silver plated receiver and barrel bands, 15 shot, iron sights. Disc.

	$300	$241	$220	$180	$150	$130	$115

EG 73 — .22 Mag. only, lever action copied after the Win. Model 92, 19¼ barrel, 12 shot, iron sights, blue only. Disc. 1985.

	$205	$185	$160	$140	$130	$120	$105

Last Mfg.'s Sug. Retail was $229.

EG 722 — .22 LR only, slide action, 18½ barrel, 15 shot, iron sights, blue only. Disc. 1985.

	$180	$160	$140	$125	$115	$100	$90

Last Mfg.'s Sug. Retail was $204.

EM 1 CARBINE — .22 LR or .22 Mag., gas semi-auto, copy of the original M1 carbine, 19½ in. barrel, 15 shot, iron sights, blue only. ESG 22 is 22 Mag. (12 shot) — add $100. Disc. 1985.

	$175	$155	$140	$125	$115	$100	$90

Last Mfg.'s Sug. Retail was $195.

Grading	100%	98%	95%	90%	80%	70%	60%

SENATOR OVER/UNDER SHOTGUNS

SENATOR MODEL — 12, 20, or .410 ga., 3 in. chambers, 26 or 28 in. F/M barrels, folding action, double triggers, extractors, vent barrels and rib, checkered walnut stock and forearm, engraved silver finished receiver. Imported 1986-1987.

	$235	$200	$180	$165	$150	$140	$130

Last Mfg.'s Sug. Retail was $275.

TANARMI HANDGUNS

MODEL TA 22 — .22 LR, 6 shot, 4¾ in. barrel, brass trigger guard and grip straps, blued finish, wood grips, 34 oz.

	$85	$70	$60	$55	$50	$45	$40

Last Mfg.'s Sug. Retail was $99.

MODEL TA 76 S.A.A. — .22 LR, single action revolver, 4¾ in. barrel, 6 shot, blue finish only, wood grips, 32 oz.

	$85	$65	$55	$50	$45	$40	$35

Add $4 for chrome finish or brass backstrap and trigger guard.
Last Mfg.'s Sug. Retail was $95.

Model TA 76M Combo — includes .22 LR and .22 Mag. cylinders, 4¾ (standard), 6, or 9 in. barrel, blue finish, wood grips.

	$95	$75	$65	$60	$55	$50	$45

Add $6 for chrome plated finish (4¾ in. barrel only).

Add $10 for 6 (Model TA 766) or 9 (Model TA 769) in. barrel.

Add $16 for brass backstrap and trigger guard (N/A in 9 in. barrel).
Last Mfg.'s Sug. Retail was $105.

TA 38SB O/U DERRINGER — 38 Spl. only, O/U Derringer-copy of Rem. Model 41, 3 in. barrels, 14 oz., with safety, blue finish only, checkered nylon grips. Importation disc. 1985.

	$90	$75	$65	$55	$50	$45	$40

Last Mfg.'s Sug. Retail was $80.

TA 41 SERIES SEMI-AUTO — .41 Action Express cal., action similar to TA 90 Series, 11 shot mag., matte blue (Model TA 41B) or matte chrome (Model TA 41C) finish, combat sights, black neoprene grips, 38 oz. Importation began 1989.

	$450	$390	$360	$330	$295	$265	$240

Add $70 for adj. target sights (Model TA 41BT).
Last Mfg.'s Sug. Retail was $490.

Model TA 41C — matte chrome finish.

	$485	$430	$395	$360	$330	$295	$270

Add $50 (retail) for adj. target sights (Model TA 41CT).
Last Mfg.'s Sug. Retail was $550.

Model TA 41 SS — .41 AE, compensated variation of the Model TA 41 except has 5 in. ported barrel and slide, blue/chrome finish, competition sights, 40 oz. Importation began 1989.

	$575	$450	$420	$385	$350	$325	$300

Last Mfg.'s Sug. Retail was $650.

TA 90 SERIES SEMI-AUTO — 9mm, double action, copy of the CZ-75, 4¾ in. barrel, steel frame, 15 shot mag., matte blue (Model TA 90B) or matte chrome finish (Model TA 90C), combat sights, wood (disc. 1985) or neoprene grips, 38 oz. New 1985.

	$365	$300	$260	$225	$205	$190	$180

Add $85 for adj. target sights (TA 90BT).
Earlier models featured a polished blue finish and nickel steel alloy frame (35 oz.).

Last Mfg.'s Sug. Retail was $415.

Model TA 90C — matte chrome finish.

	$380	$315	$270	$235	$210	$190	$180

Add $95 for adj. target sights (TA 90CT).
Last Mfg.'s Sug. Retail was $430.

Grading	100%	98%	95%	90%	80%	70%	60%

Model BTA 90B and C — 9mm, smaller version of TA 90, 3½ in. barrel, 12 shot mag., neoprene grips. New 1986.

	$380	$315	$270	$235	$210	$190	$180

Add $20 for chrome finish (BTA 90C).

Last Mfg.'s Sug. Retail was $430.

Model TA 90 SS — 9mm, compensated variation of the Model TA 90 except has 5 in. ported barrel and slide, blue/chrome finish, competition sights, 40 oz. Importation began 1989.

	$575	$450	$420	$385	$350	$325	$300

Last Mfg.'s Sug. Retail was $650.

TA 90BK — convertible kit including 2 barrels (9mm and .41 AE) and 2 mag.'s. While advertised, this combination never saw production.

TARGA PISTOLS

GT 22 SERIES — .22 LR, 3.88 in. barrel, 10 shot mag., single action 26 oz., steel frame, either satin chrome (GT 22C) or standard blue (GT 22B) finish, wooden grips became standard in 1986. GT 22T is 6 in. barrel target version (12 shot mag.).

	$170	$140	$125	$110	$95	$80	$70

Add $15 for chrome finish (Model GT 22C).

Last Mfg.'s Sug. Retail was $200.

GT 26 and GT 27B OR C — .25 ACP, 2½ in. barrel, 6 shot mag., single action, 13 oz., available in standard blue alloy, satin chrome alloy (GT 27B or C), or steel frame (GT 26S), wooden grips became standard in 1986.

	$50	$45	$35	$30	$30	$25	$25

Add $59 for steel frame (Model GT 26S).

Add $13 for chrome alloy (Model GT 27C).

Last Mfg.'s Sug. Retail was $56.

GT 28 SERIES — .25 ACP, 2½ in. barrel, 5 shot mag., single action, blue alloy, wood grips. New 1990.

	$45	$35	$30	$30	$25	$25	$20

Add $18 for chrome finish (Model GT 28C).

Last Mfg.'s Sug. Retail was $51.

GT 32 SERIES — 32 ACP, 3.88 in. barrel, 7 shot mag., single action, steel frame, 26 oz., either satin chrome (GT 32C) or standard blue (GT 32B), wooden grips became standard in 1986.

	$170	$140	$125	$110	$95	$80	$70

Add $15 for chrome finish (Model GT 32C).

Last Mfg.'s Sug. Retail was $200.

GT 380 ACP SERIES — .380 ACP, 3.88 in. barrel, 6 shot mag., single action, steel frame, 26 oz., either satin chrome (GT 380C) or standard blue (GT 380B), wooden grips became standard in 1986.

	$175	$145	$135	$125	$115	$105	$95

Add $8 for chrome finish (Model GT 380C).

Last Mfg.'s Sug. Retail was $212.

GT 380 LW — similar to GT 380 Series except has light alloy receiver and 3¼ in. barrel.

	$100	$85	$70	$60	$55	$50	$45

Last Mfg.'s Sug. Retail was $119.

GT 380 BE or CE — engraved models, either blue (BE) or chrome (CE) finish, wood grips. Importation disc. 1989.

	$180	$155	$145	$135	$125	$115	$105

Add $25 for chrome finish (Model GT 380 CE).

Last Mfg.'s Sug. Retail was $220.

GT 380 XE — .380 ACP, 3.88 in. barrel, 11 shot mag., blue only, wood grips, 28 oz.

	$190	$165	$155	$145	$135	$125	$115

Last Mfg.'s Sug. Retail was $235.

Grading	100%	98%	95%	90%	80%	70%	60%

GT 32 XEB — same as GT 380 XE, only 32 ACP, 12 shot mag. Disc. 1985.

	100%	98%	95%	90%	80%	70%	60%
	$165	$145	$135	$125	$115	$100	$95

Last Mfg.'s Sug. Retail was $189.

REVOLVERS: CURRENT MFG.

RX 38 B — .38 Spl., double action, 6 shot, 2 in. barrel, blue finish only. Importation began 1990.

	100%	98%	95%	90%	80%	70%	60%
	$85	$65	$55	$50	$45	$40	$35

Last Mfg.'s Sug. Retail was $95.

UBERTI REVOLVERS

Importation of these revolvers by Excam was stopped in 1986.

ALDO UBERTI CATTLEMAN SA REVOLVER — .375 Mag., .44 Mag., or 45 long Colt cal., 6 shot, single action, 5½, 6, or 7½ in. barrels, target sights, wood grips, blued finish. New 1985. Disc. 1986.

	100%	98%	95%	90%	80%	70%	60%
	$295	$250	$195	$165	$150	$140	$130

Add $10 for .44 Mag. cal.
Last Mfg.'s Sug. Retail was $222.

ALDO UBERTI DA INSPECTOR — .38 Spl., double action, 3 or 4 in. barrel, blue finish, wood grips, 6 shot. Disc. 1986.

	100%	98%	95%	90%	80%	70%	60%
	$325	$250	$200	$180	$165	$150	$140

Add $17 for adj. sights.
Last Mfg.'s Sug. Retail was $240.

WARRIOR REVOLVERS

Importation of these revolvers by Excam was stopped in 1986.

WARRIOR DOUBLE ACTION MODEL W 722 (B) — .22 LR or 22 Mag. only, double action, 6 in. barrel, 8 shot, blue only, plastic grips, 35 oz. Disc. 1986.

	100%	98%	95%	90%	80%	70%	60%
	$100	$80	$70	$65	$60	$55	$50

Add $50 for 22 Mag. extra cyl.
Last Mfg.'s Sug. Retail was $98.

WARRIOR DOUBLE ACTION MODEL W 384 (B) — 38 Spl. only, double action, 4 or 6 in. barrels, 6 shot, blue only, plastic grips, 30 oz. Vent rib standard. Disc. 1986.

	100%	98%	95%	90%	80%	70%	60%
	$135	$110	$100	$90	$80	$70	$65

Add $5 for 6 in. barrel (W 386 B).
Last Mfg.'s Sug. Retail was $125.

WARRIOR DOUBLE ACTION MODEL W 357 — 357 Mag. only, double action, 4 or 6 in. barrels, 6 shot, blue only, plastic grips, 36 oz. Vent rib standard. 6 in. barrel (W 3576). Disc. 1986.

	100%	98%	95%	90%	80%	70%	60%
	$190	$165	$145	$135	$130	$125	$120

Last Mfg.'s Sug. Retail was $185.

EXEL ARMS OF AMERICA, INC.

Previous importer located in Gardener, MA. Exel Arms previously imported Lanber (Series 100), Ugartechea (Series 200), and Laurona (Series 300) shotguns. Lanber, Ugartechea, and Laurona, are listed alphabetically below.

LANBER SHOTGUNS: OVER AND UNDER

Lanber shotguns are not being imported currently. The last Mfg.'s Sug. Retail on all models listed below reflects 1987 pricing, the last year they were imported. Any future importation could reflect pricing changes.

EXEL SERIES 100: MODELS 101 THROUGH 104 — 12 ga., boxlock action, vent rib, extractors, single trigger. Add $16 for 103 Mag., $92 for ejectors (Model 104 only).

	100%	98%	95%	90%	80%	70%	60%
	$400	$350	$310	$270	$240	$225	$200

Last Mfg.'s Sug. Retail was $451.

These models were previously designated the 844ST Series.

Grading	100%	98%	95%	90%	80%	70%	60%

EXEL MODEL 105 — 12 ga., boxlock action, single trigger, ejectors, Lanber screw-in chokes, deluxe wood, engraved satin finish action.

	$575	$495	$440	$405	$370	$345	$310

Last Mfg.'s Sug. Retail was $644.

This model was previously designated the Model 2004LCH.

EXEL MODELS 106 AND 107 — 12 ga., similar to 105, only more deluxe version with vent barrels and rib, blued receiver only, interchangeable Lanber screw-in chokes. Trap model is Model 107.

	$725	$625	$550	$500	$475	$450	$425

Last Mfg.'s Sug. Retail was $845.

These models were previosly designated 2008LCH and 2009LCH respectively.

UGARTECHEA SHOTGUNS: SIDE-BY-SIDE

Ugartechea shotguns are not being imported currently. The last Mfg.'s Sug. Retail on all models listed below reflects 1986-87 pricing, the last years they were imported. Any future importation could reflect pricing changes.

EXEL 200 SERIES — these side by sides are available in 12 or 20 ga. (3 in.) only. Model 201 is basic gun with 213 being the highest grade.

Model 201, 202, and 203 — double triggers, extractors, straight grip, matted rib, various chokes and barrel lengths.

	$375	$325	$260	$240	$215	$180	$165

Last Mfg.'s Sug. Retail was $429.

Previously designated Model 30.

Model 281 — same as 201 series, except 28 ga.

	$420	$325	$275	$250	$235	$210	$195

Last Mfg.'s Sug. Retail was $472.

Previously designated Model 30.

Model 240 — same as 201 series, except .410 ga.

	$450	$355	$295	$270	$250	$235	$210

Last Mfg.'s Sug. Retail was $472.

Previously designated Model 30.

Models 204, 205, and 206 — single trigger optional, ejectors, straight grip, silver finish, various chokes and barrel lengths. Importation disc. 1986.

	$550	$470	$415	$370	$340	$315	$280

Last Mfg.'s Sug. Retail was $627.

Models 207 and 207A — 12 ga. only, sidelock, case hardened action. 207A is deluxe model with ejectors. Model 201 disc. 1986.

	$725	$650	$580	$515	$465	$400	$345

Last Mfg.'s Sug. Retail was $836.
Deduct 33% without ejectors (Model 207).
Previously designated Milano EX.

Models 208 and 208A — same as 207/207A, only engraved coin finished receiver. 208A is deluxe model with ejectors. Model 208 disc. 1986.

	$775	$695	$625	$550	$485	$420	$360

Last Mfg.'s Sug. Retail was $925.
Deduct 33% without ejectors (Model 208).
Previously designated Model 75 EX.

Models 209 and 210 — better engraving and walnut than 207/207A. Model 210 is 20 ga. Importation disc. 1986.

	$580	$505	$450	$415	$375	$340	$310

Last Mfg.'s Sug. Retail was $672.

Grading	100%	98%	95%	90%	80%	70%	60%

Models 211, 212, and 213 — top-of-the-line model, best quality engraving and walnut. Special order only.

	100%	98%	95%	90%	80%	70%	60%
	$2,350	$2,000	$1,780	$1,475	$1,200	$1,000	$850

Last Mfg.'s Sug. Retail was $3,100.

Previously designated Model 110.

MODEL 251 — .410-3 in. ga., folding design, 26 in. barrels only, DT's, extractors, walnut stock and forearm. New 1987.

	100%	98%	95%	90%	80%	70%	60%
	$185	$165	$140	$120	$105	$95	$85

Last Mfg.'s Sug. Retail was $215.

LAURONA SHOTGUNS: OVER AND UNDER

Laurona shotguns are no longer being imported by Exel Arms of America, Inc. Currently, Laurona shotguns are being imported by Galaxy Imports located in Victoria, TX and these new models can be located in the Laurona section of this text. Model nomenclature has changed from the discounted Exel 300 Series below.

EXEL 300 SERIES — These over and unders are available in 12 or 20 ga. only. Model 301 is basic gun with 310 being the highest grade.

Models 301 and 302 — 12 ga., double selective trigger system, ejectors, pistol grip, vent rib, lightly engraved chrome finish receiver, various chokes and barrel lengths. Importation disc. 1986.

	100%	98%	95%	90%	80%	70%	60%
	$485	$415	$380	$340	$300	$275	$250

Models 303 and 304 — 12 ga., similar to 301/302, except has better engraving on coin finish receiver, vent barrels. Importation disc. 1987.

	100%	98%	95%	90%	80%	70%	60%
	$545	$470	$430	$385	$340	$315	$270

Previously designated Model 82G Super.

Models 305(A) and 306(A) — 12 or 20 ga., similar to 303/304, except has better engraving on coin finish receiver, screw-in choke tubes. Importation disc. 1987.

	100%	98%	95%	90%	80%	70%	60%
	$625	$535	$470	$430	$390	$350	$315

Previously designated Models 83MG and 85MS.

Models 307 and 308 — 12 ga., trap model, 29 in. barrels, extensive engraving, Monte Carlo stock. Importation disc. 1987.

	100%	98%	95%	90%	80%	70%	60%
	$580	$500	$460	$420	$380	$340	$300

Last Mfg.'s Sug. Retail was $668.

Previously designated Model 82U Trap.

Models 309 and 310 — super trap model, 29 in. vent barrels, more extensive engraving than Models 307/308. Importation disc. 1987.

	100%	98%	95%	90%	80%	70%	60%
	$630	$545	$495	$460	$415	$385	$340

Last Mfg.'s Sug. Retail was $726.

Previously designated Model 82 S. Trap.

Model 82 — double selective trigger system, ejectors, pistol grip, vent rib, various chokes and barrel lengths. Disc.

	100%	98%	95%	90%	80%	70%	60%
	$549	$410	$380	$340	$300	$275	$250

F

FAS

Manufacturer located in Italy. Currently imported and distributed by Mandall's Shooting Supplies Inc. located in Scottsdale, AZ. Previously imported by Beeman Precision Arms, Inc. located in Santa Rosa, CA and Osborne's located in Cheboygan, MI.

Grading	100%	98%	95%	90%	80%	70%	60%

PISTOLS: SEMI-AUTO

MODEL 601 — .22 Short only, semi-auto competition pistol, 5½ in. barrel, 5 shot mag., wrap-around matchwood grips, 41½ oz.

Mfg.'s Sug. Retail	$1,595	$1,425	$1,200	$995	$875	$695	$640	$565

MODEL 602 — .22 LR only, semi-auto competition pistol, 5.6 in. barrel, 5 shot mag., wrap-around match wood grips, 40 oz.

Mfg.'s Sug. Retail	$1,525	$1,400	$1,200	$995	$875	$695	$640	$565

MODEL 603 — .32 S&W wadcutter only, semi-auto competition pistol, 5.6 in. barrel, 5 shot mag., wrap-around adj. or non-adj. match wood grips, 40 oz. Importation disc. 1987.

	$975	$850	$725	$640	$565	$480	$420

Last Mfg.'s Sug. Retail was $942.

FEG

These models can be found under the Interarms section in this text.

F.I.E.

Firearms import & export previously located in Hialeah, FL.

F.I.E. filed bankrupcy in November of 1990 and all models are discontinued. Parts and service for these older firearms may be obtained through Quality Firearms, Inc. (see Trademark Index), even though all warranties on F.I.E. guns are void.

ARMINIUS REVOLVERS: DOUBLE ACTION

All pistols under this heading are manufactured in W. Germany under the trademark Arminius. .22 cal. is 8 shot, 32 S&W is 7 shot, all others 6 shot.

MODEL 522TB — .22 LR, blue finish, 4 in. barrel, 8 shot.

	$130	$100	$85	$75	$70	$65	$60

Add $23 for walnut grips.
Last Mfg.'s Sug. Retail was $174.

722 SERIES — .22 LR, blue (standard) or chrome finish (disc. 1985), 6 in. barrel, 8 shot.

	$125	$100	$90	$80	$70	$65	$60

Add $23 for walnut grips.
Add $49 for .22 LR/.22 Mag. combo.
Add $15 for chrome finish.
Last Mfg.'s Sug. Retail was $161.

Grading	100%	98%	95%	90%	80%	70%	60%

STANDARD REVOLVER — .22 LR, .22 Mag., .32 Mag. or .38 Spl., 2 or 4 in. barrel, blued finish, fixed sights, without ejector assembly. Mfg. in U.S. starting 1989.

	$80	$70	$65	$60	$55	$50	$45

Add $19 for chrome finish (2 in. barrel only).

Add $38 for gold plated finish (2 in. barrel only).

Add $23 for .22 Combo package (2 cylinders - 4 in. barrel only).

Models with 4 in. barrels are available in blued finish only.

Last Mfg.'s Sug. Retail was $101.

MODEL 532TB — .32 S&W, blue (standard) or chrome finish (disc. 1985), adj. sights, 4 in. barrel, 7 shot.

	$145	$120	$100	$80	$75	$70	$65

Add $23 for walnut grips.

Add $15 for chrome finish.

Last Mfg.'s Sug. Retail was $183.

MODEL 732B — similar to Model 532TB, except has 6 in. barrel and fixed sights. Imported 1988 only.

	$120	$100	$90	$80	$70	$65	$60

Last Mfg.'s Sug. Retail was $140.

MODEL N-38 (TITAN TIGER) — .38 Spl., blue (standard) or chrome finish (disc. 1985), 2 or 4 in. barrel, fixed sights. Mfg. in U.S.

	$130	$110	$95	$80	$75	$65	$60

Add $23 for walnut grips.

Add $15 for chrome finish.

Last Mfg.'s Sug. Retail was $176.

ZEPHYR — .38 Spl., 5 shot, aluminum construction, 2 in. barrel, blue finish, checkered grips, 14 oz. New 1990.

	$145	$120	$100	$80	$75	$70	$65

Last Mfg.'s Sug. Retail was $189.

Lady Zephyr — similar to Zephyr except has gold trimmed parts, scrimshawed red rose on ivory polymer grips, and gold case. New 1990.

	$250	$210	$180	$155	$135	$115	$95

Last Mfg.'s Sug. Retail was $295.

MODEL 384TB — .38 Spl., blue (standard) or chrome finish (disc. 1985), 6 shot, 4 in. barrel.

	$150	$125	$105	$85	$80	$70	$65

Add $23 for walnut grips.

Add $13 for chrome finish.

Last Mfg.'s Sug. Retail was $195.

MODEL 386TB — .38 Spl., blue (standard) or chrome finish (disc. 1985), 6 shot, 6 in. barrel.

	$150	$125	$105	$85	$80	$70	$65

Add $23 for walnut grips.

Add $13 for chrome finish.

Last Mfg.'s Sug. Retail was $195.

.357 MAG. SERIES — .357 Mag., blue (standard) or chrome finish (disc. 1985), 6 shot, 3 (Model 3573TB), 4 (Model 3574TB), or 6 (Model 3576TB) in. barrels.

	$200	$170	$135	$120	$110	$100	$90

Add $23 for walnut grips.

Add $15 for chrome finish.

Last Mfg.'s Sug. Retail was $255.

REVOLVERS: DISCONTINUED SNUB-NOSE

Currently manufactured 2 in. snub-nosed revolvers are listed in the previous category under Standard Revolver, Titan Tiger, and Zephyr.

Grading	100%	98%	95%	90%	80%	70%	60%

222 SERIES — .22 LR & .22 Mag. cal., blue (standard) or chrome finish, 2 in. snub-nose barrel. Disc. 1985.

	$135	$115	$90	$85	$75	$65	$60

Add $15 for walnut grips.

Add $45 for .22 LR/.22 Mag. combo.

Last Mfg.'s Sug. Retail was $120.

222B SERIES — .22 LR only starting 1989, similar to 222 Series, reintroduced 1987-1989.

	$150	$120	$105	$85	$80	$70	$65

Add $45 for .22 LR/.22 Mag. combo (disc. 1988).

Last Mfg.'s Sug. Retail was $185.

232 SERIES — .32 S&W, blue (standard) or chrome finish, 2 in. barrel. Disc.

	$120	$90	$85	$75	$65	$60	$55

Add $15 for walnut grips.

Add $14 for adj. sights.

Add $28 for chrome finish.

232B SERIES — similar to 232 Series, 2 in. barrel. Reintroduced 1987-1989.

	$150	$125	$110	$95	$85	$75	$70

Add $5 for adj. sights.

Last Mfg.'s Sug. Retail was $185.

MODEL 382TB — .38 Spl., blue (standard) or chrome finish, 2 in. barrel. Disc. 1985.

	$125	$110	$100	$90	$80	$75	$65

Add $15 for walnut grips.

Add $16 for chrome finish.

Last Mfg.'s Sug. Retail was $145.

MODEL 3572 — .357 Mag., blue (standard) or chrome finish, 2 in. barrel. Disc. 1984.

	$223	$170	$160	$135	$125	$115	$100

Add $15 for walnut grips.

Add $17 for chrome finish.

REVOLVERS: SINGLE ACTION

Combo designations on below listed models indicate 2 cylinders (.22 LR/.22 Mag.).

COWBOY — .22 LR or .22 LR/Mag. combo, 3¼ or 6 in. barrel, blued finish, square butt grip, without ejector tube, fixed sights. Mfg. in the U.S. starting 1989.

	$75	$65	$50	$45	$40	$35	$30

Add $23 for combo.

Last Mfg.'s Sug. Retail was $95.

GOLD RUSH — .22 LR or .22 LR/Mag. combo, 3¼, 4¾, or 6½ in. barrel, round (3¼ in. barrel only) or square butt grip, gold band on barrel and cylinder, ivory-tex grips. Mfg. in U.S. starting 1989.

	$155	$125	$110	$95	$85	$75	$70

Add $47 for combo.

Last Mfg.'s Sug. Retail was $189.

TEXAS RANGER (TEX 22 SERIES) — .22 LR or .22 Mag. (combo only), 3¼ (new 1986), 4¾, 6½ (new 1989), 7, or 9 in. barrel, 6 shot, blue only. Mfg. U.S.

	$80	$70	$60	$50	$45	$40	$35

Add $23 for combo.

Add $6 for 9 in. barrel.

This model with a 3¼ in. barrel is called the Little Ranger.

Last Mfg.'s Sug. Retail was $108.

Grading	100%	98%	95%	90%	80%	70%	60%

BUFFALO SCOUT (E15 SERIES) — .22 LR or .22 Mag., blue (standard) or chrome finish, 4¾ in. barrel. Mfg. Brescia, Italy.

	$75	$55	$45	$35	$35	$30	$30

Add $23 for walnut grips.

Add $23 for combo.

Add $9 for chrome or blue/gold finish.

Last Mfg.'s Sug. Retail was $98.

The Yellow Rose Combo — all metal parts 24 Kt. gold plated, smooth walnut grips. New 1986.

	$130	$110	$95				

Add $151 for scrimshawed ivory polymer grips - walnut cased (new 1989).

Last Mfg.'s Sug. Retail was $161.

LEGEND S.A.A. (PL-22 SERIES) — .22 LR or .22 Mag., blue only. Mfg. Brescia, Italy. Disc. 1984.

	$120	$90	$85	$75	$65	$60	$55

Add $3 for walnut grips.

Add $17 for combo.

HOMBRE MODEL — .357 Mag., .44 Mag., or .45 cal., color case hardened receiver, 5½ (disc. 1985), 6, or 7½ in. barrel, 45 oz., smooth walnut grips. Mfg. W. Germany.

	$220	$180	$145	$130	$120	$110	$100

Add $25 for brass back strap and trigger guard (disc.).

Last Mfg.'s Sug. Retail was $265.

Golden Hombre — same general specifications as Hombre, except all metal surfaces are plated in 24Kt. gold.

	$300	$210	$145				

Add $65 for ivory polymer grips (new 1989).

Last Mfg.'s Sug. Retail was $350.

TITAN PISTOLS: SEMI-AUTO

TITAN II (E32 SERIES) — .32 ACP (disc. 1988), or .380 ACP, single action, blue (standard) or chrome finish. Mfg. USA.

	$195	$160	$135	$120	$105	$95	$85

Add $25 for walnut grips.

Add $10 for chrome finish.

This series was redesigned in 1988 to be shorter and more compact. Older series Titans are worth approx. $50 less than values shown above.

Last Mfg.'s Sug. Retail was $220.

SUPER TITAN II — .32 ACP (disc. 1988), or .380 ACP, single action, 12 shot mag. in .32 ACP, 11 for .380 cal., walnut grips, standard blue only. Mfg. U.S.

	$215	$185	$155	$135	$120	$105	$95

Last Mfg.'s Sug. Retail was $260.

.22 TITAN II (E22) — .22 LR, single action, 10 shot mag., blue finish only. Walnut grips standard.

	$130	$105	$90	$80	$70	$65	$60

Last Mfg.'s Sug. Retail was $161.

Lady .22 — similar to .22 TITAN II except has combination blue/gold finish with scrimshawed red rose on ivory polymer grips. New 1990.

	$185	$155	$130	$120	$105	$95	$85

Last Mfg.'s Sug. Retail was $208.

THE BEST (A27) — .25 ACP, single action, blue only, deluxe finish, walnut grips, steel frame, 6 shot mag. Mfg. in Spain by Astra. Importation disc. 1988.

	$125	$105	$90	$80	$70	$65	$60

Last Mfg.'s Sug. Retail was $155.

Grading	100%	98%	95%	90%	80%	70%	60%

.25 TITAN (E27 SERIES) — .25 ACP, single action, blue (disc. 1989) or Dyna-chrome finish (standard 1990).

	$60	$50	$45	$40	$35	$30	$30

Subtract $5 for blued finish.
Add $26 for gold trim (new 1986).
Add $62 for Misty Gold finish (1988 only).
Last Mfg.'s Sug. Retail was $77.

Titan Tigress — similar to .25 Titan except is entirely gold plated and cased, ladies pistol. Importation began 1989.

	$130	$110	$95

Last Mfg.'s Sug. Retail was $153.

.25 TITAN (E38 SERIES) — .25 ACP, similar to E27 series except has standard blue finish. New 1990.

	$50	$45	$40	$35	$30	$30	$25

Add $9 for Dyna-chrome finish.
Last Mfg.'s Sug. Retail was $59.

SSP SERIES — .32 ACP or .380 ACP cal., single action semi-auto, $3\frac{1}{8}$ in. barrel, 5 shot mag., blue or chrome finish, composition grips, 25 oz. Mfg. U.S. New 1990.

	$120	$95	$85	$75	$65	$60	$55

Add $19 for chrome finish.
Last Mfg.'s Sug. Retail was $146.

Lady SSP — similar to SSP except has gold trimmed parts, scrimshawed red rose on ivory polymer grips, and gold case. New 1990.

	$210	$180	$155	$135	$120	$105	$95

Last Mfg.'s Sug. Retail was $250.

TZ-75 — 9mm Para., double action, 4.72 in. barrel, steel frame and slide, 15 shot mag., patterned after the CZ-75 action, 35 oz. Imported 1982-1989. This model was updated in 1988 (Series 88).

	$375	$325	$290	$270	$250	$235	$220

Add $20 for satin chrome finish (new 1986).
Add $20 for black rubber grips.
Last Mfg.'s Sug. Retail was $440.

TZ-75 SERIES 88 — 9mm Para. or .41 Action Express cal., improved TZ-75 action, 4.72 in. barrel, steel frame and slide, 11 (.41 AE) or 17 (9mm) shot mag., fixed removable rear sight, choice of matte blue, satin chrome, or blue slide/chrome frame finish, updated CZ-75 action, 35 oz. New 1988.

	$435	$360	$330	$295	$280	$260	$240

Add $97 for .41 Action Express cal.
Add $20 for satin chrome on 9mm, $29 on .41 AE.
Add $14 for black rubber grips.
This model is also available with a blue slide/chrome frame (I.P.S.C. configuration) at no extra charge.

The TZ-75 Series 88 was re-engineered in 1988 to include: frame mounted sear locking safety (cocked and locked), Colt style firing pin safety block, improved recessed slide serrations, muzzle barrel swell, bobbed hammer design, elongated combat style slide stop, new mag. release, and removable rear sight. Last Mfg.'s Sug. Retail was $519.

TZ-75 Combo — includes both .41 Action Express cal. and 9mm Para. barrels. New 1990.

	$615	$535	$475	$430	$395	$370	$350

Add $29 for satin chrome or blue slide/chrome frame finish.
Last Mfg.'s Sug. Retail was $709.

Grading	100%	98%	95%	90%	80%	70%	60%

TZ-75 Series 88 Gov.'t Model — 9mm Para. only, compact variation of the TZ-75 Series 88, 3⅗ in. barrel, 12 shot mag., checkered walnut grips, 33½ oz. New 1990.

	$435	$360	$330	$295	$280	$260	$240

Add $20 for satin chrome or blue slide/chrome frame finish.
Last Mfg.'s Sug. Retail was $519.

TZ-75 Series 88 with ported barrel — similar to the TZ-75 Series 88 except has 5 in. ported barrel and slide. New 1990.

	$615	$535	$475	$430	$395	$370	$350

Last Mfg.'s Sug. Retail was $709.

Compensated TZ-75 Series 88 — similar to the TZ-75 Series 88 except has 5¾ in. compensated barrel, 42 oz. New 1990.

	$700	$615	$535	$475	$430	$395	$370

Last Mfg.'s Sug. Retail was $804.

MODEL 722 TP SILHOUETTE PISTOL — .22 LR, bolt action target pistol, 10 in. free-floating barrel, 4-way adj. trigger, micro adj. rear sight, 6 or 10 shot mag., stippled pistol grip and forearm, supplied with 2-piece scope mount, 3.4 lbs. New 1990.

	$220	$190	$160	$140	$125	$115	$100

Last Mfg.'s Sug. Retail was $263.

SPECTRE PISTOL — 9mm Para., double action, unique triple action blowback system with two piece bolt, 6 in. barrel, military style configuration, adj. sights, 30 or 50 (opt.) shot mag. (unique 4 column configuration), 4.8 lbs. New 1989.

	$600	$475	$395	$340	$295	$260	$230

Add $14 for mag. loading tool.
Last Mfg.'s Sug. Retail was $718.

KG-99 — 9mm, paramilitary design pistol, 36 shot mag. Mini-99 also available with 20 shot mag. and 3 in. barrel. Disc. 1984.

	$450	$340	$300	$250	$225	$210	$180

This model was not manufactured by F.I.E. - only sold.

DERRINGERS

MODEL D38 — .38 Spl., O/U, chrome finish only, no transfer bar. Disc. 1985.

	$70	$60	$55	$45	$40	$35	$30

Add $17 for walnut grips.
Last Mfg.'s Sug. Retail was $82.

MODEL D86 — .38 Spl., single shot, 3 in. barrel, internal transfer bar safety, ammo storage compartment, blue or Dyna-chrome finish, 11 oz. New 1986.

	$80	$65	$55	$50	$45	$40	$35

Add $9 for Dyna-chrome finish.
Add $25 for deluxe model (walnut stocks).
Add $60 for Misty Gold finish (disc.).
Last Mfg.'s Sug. Retail was $95.

RIFLES: SEMI-AUTO

GR-8 BLACK BEAUTY — .22 cal. only, 14 shot, 19½ in. barrel, 64 oz., tubular feed, black nylon stock, patterned after Rem. Nylon 66. Mfg. by C.B.C. of Brazil. F.I.E. Importation disc. 1988, now imported by K.B.I.

	$90	$75	$70	$65	$60	$55	$50

Last Mfg.'s Sug. Retail was $100.

Grading	100%	98%	95%	90%	80%	70%	60%

PARA RIFLE — .22 LR, paramilitary designed rifle with case, takedown, 11 shot, matte black receiver finish. Mfg. by L. Franchi between 1979-1984. Imported into the U.S. from 1985-88.

	$275	$225	$195	$155	$140	$130	$120

8,000 of this model were manufactured by L. Franchi. 5,000 went to the Italian Government and were used as training rifles (with German scopes). The remainder has been imported by F.I.E. (without scopes).

Last Mfg.'s Sug. Retail was $225.

SPECTRE CARBINE — 9mm Para., same action as Spectre pistol, paramilitary design carbine, collapsible metal butt stock, 30 or 50 (opt.) shot mag., adj. rear sight, with pistol and forearm grip. New 1989.

	$595	$450	$395	$340	$295	$260	$230

Last Mfg.'s Sug. Retail was $700.

RIFLES: BOLT-ACTION

MODEL 122 — .22 LR, 6 or 10 shot clip mag., 21 in. tapered barrel, Monte Carlo walnut stock, adj. sights. Mfg. by Hamilton & Hunter. New 1986.

	$100	$80	$70	$60	$55	$50	$45

Last Mfg.'s Sug. Retail was $115.

MODEL 322 — .22 LR, competition model, 26.2 in. floating barrel, adj. trigger, 6 or 10 shot mag., stippled pistol grip, 7 lbs. New 1990.

	$580	$425	$380	$340	$295	$260	$230

Last Mfg.'s Sug. Retail was $665.

MODEL 422 — similar to Model 322 except has heavy barrel, 9 lbs. New 1990.

	$580	$425	$380	$340	$295	$260	$230

Last Mfg.'s Sug. Retail was $665.

SHOTGUNS

All Franchi shotguns can be located in the Franchi section of this text.

S.O.B. — 12, 20, or .410 ga., 18½ in. single barrel, pistol grip only. Disc. 1984.

	$100	$90	$80	$70	$60	$55	$50

COMPETITOR SEMI-AUTO — 12 or 20 ga., gas operated semi-auto, various barrel lengths with screw-in chokes standard. Mfg. in the U.S. New 1990.
Pricing on this model was not available before publication release.

THE STURDY O/U — 12 or 20 ga., 3 in. chambers, 28 in. barrels, vent rib and barrels, engraved silver finish receiver, double triggers, extractors, manufactured by Maroccini of Italy. Imported 1985-1988.

	$300	$275	$250	$235	$220	$205	$190

Last Mfg.'s Sug. Retail was $350.

Sturdy Deluxe Priti — similar to The Sturdy model except has deluxe walnut. Importation disc. 1988.

	$325	$290	$260	$240	$225	$205	$195

Add $70 for ejectors, SST, and choke tubes.
Last Mfg.'s Sug. Retail was $380.

Model 12 Deluxe — 12 ga. only, SST, auto ejectors, multi-choked barrels, select walnut. Imported 1988 only.

	$320	$290	$260	$240	$225	$205	$195

Last Mfg.'s Sug. Retail was $380.

THE BRUTE — 12, 20, or .410 ga., 19 in. barrels, 30 in. overall length. Side x side action, disc. 1984.

	$195	$150	$140	$120	$110	$100	$90

Grading	100%	98%	95%	90%	80%	70%	60%

SPAS-12 — this model appears under the Franchi heading in the F section.

SAS-12 — this model appears under the Franchi heading in the F section.

LAW-12 — this model appears under the Franchi heading in the F section.

FABARM

Manufacturer located in Brescia, Italy. Currently imported and distributed by St. Lawrence Sales Inc. (starting in 1988) located in Lake Orion, MI. Previously imported until 1986 by Beeman Precision Arms, Inc. located in Santa Rosa, CA.

Values and information listed below reflect 1990 data as this publication was not afforded 1991 prices/changes by press time.

SHOTGUNS: DISCONTINUED O/U

The Field Model and Skeet/Trap Combination Set listed below were previously imported by Beeman Precision Arms, Inc.

FIELD MODEL — 12 ga. only, 29⅛ in. barrels, VR, single trigger ejectors, silver finished receiver, also available in Skeet and Trap models. Disc. 1985.

		100%	98%	95%	90%	80%	70%	60%
		$695	$595	$550	$500	$460	$420	$390

Last Mfg.'s Sug. Retail was $795.

SKEET/TRAP COMBINATION SET — 12 ga. only, is supplied with both skeet and trap barrel assemblies, cased. Disc. 1986.

	100%	98%	95%	90%	80%	70%	60%
	$1,050	$900	$840	$780	$720	$670	$600

Last Mfg.'s Sug. Retail was $1,195.

Models below have boxlock actions with coin finished receivers and light engraving. A high gloss wood finish is also available at $39 extra, and auto safety is an additional $30.

GAMMA SPORTING COMPETITON — 12 ga. only, designed for sporting clays competition, SST, 29 in. VR, (10mm) and barrels supplied with 5 innerchokes, special recoil pad, ejectors, checkered walnut stock and forearm. Importation began 1989.

Mfg.'s Sug. Retail	$961	$850	$775	$725	$650	$575	$495	$400

Add $17 for stock and forend trap (includes 28 in. barrels with 5 choke tubes).

GAMMA SKEET — 12 ga. only, 27½ in. VR, and barrels, SST, ejectors, supplied with 5 inner-chokes, special recoil pad, checkered walnut stock and forearm. Importation began 1989.

Mfg.'s Sug. Retail	$921	$825	$750	$700	$635	$550	$450	$375

GAMMA TRAP — 12 ga. only, 29 in. VR, and barrels with special trap chokes, SST, ejectors, checkered Monte Carlo stock and forearm, 7½ lbs. Importation began 1989.

Mfg.'s Sug. Retail	$921	$825	$700	$650	$600	$525	$425	$350

EURALFA TRAP — 12 ga. only, 3 in. chambers, 30 in. barrels bored IM/F. New 1990.

Mfg.'s Sug. Retail	$636	$550	$495	$460	$430	$400	$360	$320

SHOTGUNS: SPORTING O/U

Models below have boxlock actions with coin finished receivers and light engraving.

GAMMA FIELD — 12 or 20 ga., SST, ejectors, 26, 28, or 29 in. VR, and barrels (fixed chokes), checkered walnut stock and forearm, 6½ lbs. Importation began 1989.

Mfg.'s Sug. Retail	$913	$840	$695	$625	$550	$475	$400	$325

Add $40 for 5 innerchokes with wrench (3 in. chambers in 12 ga.).

Add $48 for 20 ga. (3 in. chambers).

Gamma AL Superlight — 12 ga. only, similar to Gamma Field except receiver is made from Ergal light alloy, 6 lbs. Importation began 1989.

Mfg.'s Sug. Retail	$970	$875	$760	$695	$625	$550	$450	$375

Add $41 for 5 innerchokes with wrench.

Add $66 for 20 ga. with 3 in. chambers. New 1990.

This model is chambered for 2¾ in. shells only.

Grading	100%	98%	95%	90%	80%	70%	60%

GAMMA PARADOX — 12 ga. only, 25 in. VR and barrels with top barrel rifled and lower barrel supplied with 3 innerchokes, SST, ejectors, checkered walnut stock and forearm, 6 lbs. 6 oz. Importation began 1989.

Mfg.'s Sug. Retail	$945	$850	$750	$695	$625	$550	$450	$375

Gamma Paradox AL Superlight — similar to Gamma Paradox except receiver is made from Ergal light alloy, 5 lbs. 7 oz. Importation began 1989.

Mfg.'s Sug. Retail	$960	$875	$760	$695	$625	$550	$450	$375

EURALFA — 12 ga., 2¾ in. chambers, 26 or 28 in. VR barrels with fixed chokes, DT or SNT, extractors, blued receiver with photo engraving, 6½ lbs. Importation began 1989.

Mfg.'s Sug. Retail	$571	$495	$460	$420	$390	$350	$310	$275

Euralfa AL Superlight — 12 ga., similar to Euralfa except receiver is made from Ergal light alloy, 6 lbs. Importation began 1989.

Mfg.'s Sug. Retail	$603	$515	$475	$430	$400	$360	$320	$285

Euralfa Magnum — 12 ga., 3 in. chambers, 26, 28, or 29 in. VR (10mm wide) barrels with fixed chokes, rubber recoil pad. Importation began 1989.

Mfg.'s Sug. Retail	$587	$515	$475	$430	$400	$360	$320	$285

Euralfa Innerchoke — 12 ga. only, 3 in. chambers, 28 in. barrels. New 1990.

Mfg.'s Sug. Retail	$652	$560	$500	$460	$430	$400	$360	$320

Euralfa Slug — 12 ga. only, 24 in. barrels bored cyl./cyl. New 1990.

Mfg.'s Sug. Retail	$571	$500	$475	$430	$400	$360	$320	$285

EURALFA PARADOX — 12 ga. only, similar to Euralfa except 25 in. VR barrels with top barrel rifled and lower barrel supplied with 3 innerchokes, 6 lbs. 6 oz. Importation began 1989.

Mfg.'s Sug. Retail	$636	$550	$495	$460	$430	$400	$360	$320

Euralfa Paradox AL Superlight — similar to Euralfa Paradox except receiver is made from Ergal light alloy, 5 lbs. 7 oz. Importation began 1989.

Mfg.'s Sug. Retail	$636	$550	$495	$460	$430	$400	$360	$320

SHOTGUNS: SEMI-AUTO

The models listed below are gas operated self compensating, have 4 shot mag.'s, aluminum receivers, twin action bars, blued receiver with photo etched game scene engraving, and checkered walnut stock and forearm. Add $25 for De Luxe engraving or camouflage wood finish.

ELLEGI STANDARD — 12 ga. only, 28 in. VR barrel with fixed choke, blued receiver, gold trigger, 6 lbs. 9 oz. Importation began 1989.

Mfg.'s Sug. Retail	$619	$525	$450	$375	$325	$300	$275	$250

Ellegi Multichoke — similar to Ellegi Standard except 5 different choke tubes extend length of barrel up to 6 in., average weight is 6 lbs. 9 oz. Importation began 1989.

Mfg.'s Sug. Retail	$644	$540	$475	$395	$350	$325	$300	$265

The standard barrel length on this model is 24½ in. (30½ in. with full extra-long choke tube).

Ellegi Innerchoke — 12 ga. only, 3 in. chamber, 28 in. VR barrel with 5 innerchokes supplied, 7 lbs. Importation began 1989.

Mfg.'s Sug. Retail	$644	$540	$475	$395	$350	$325	$300	$265

Ellegi Magnum — 12 ga. only, 3 in. chamber, 30 in. VR barrel with fixed choke, recoil pad, 7¼ lbs. Importation began 1989.

Mfg.'s Sug. Retail	$619	$525	$450	$375	$325	$300	$275	$250

Ellegi Super Goose — 12 ga. only, 3 in. chamber, 35½ in. VR (12mm wide) barrel with fixed choke, adj. rifle rear sight, supplied with rail for mounting scope rings, rubber recoil pad, designed especially for long range shooting, 7½ lbs. Importation began 1989.

Mfg.'s Sug. Retail	$734	$625	$495	$425	$375	$340	$315	$280

Ellegi Slug — 12 ga. only, 24½ in. barrel, adj. rear sight and bead front, 6 lbs. 9 oz. Importation began 1989.

Mfg.'s Sug. Retail	$652	$545	$475	$395	$350	$325	$300	$265

Add $200 for combo set (includes innerchoked 28 in. barrel).

Grading	100%	98%	95%	90%	80%	70%	60%

Ellegi Police — 12 ga. only, 20 in. cylinder bored barrel, matte black receiver, non-glare stock and forearm. Importation began 1989.

Mfg.'s Sug. Retail	$587	$495	$425	$360	$300	$275	$250	$225

SHOTGUNS: SIDE X SIDE

The models listed below have boxlock actions with added sideplates.

BETA MODEL — 12 ga. only, 2¾ in. chambers, standard model with checkered walnut stock and forearm, ST, ejectors. Imported 1989 only.

	$695	$625	$550	$450	$375	$300	$250

Last Mfg.'s Sug. Retail was $920.

This model was replaced by the Beta Lux in 1990.

BETA LUX — 12 ga. only, 3 in. chambers, 28 in. barrels bored F/M, 6.6 lbs. New 1990.

Mfg.'s Sug. Retail	$913	$840	$695	$625	$550	$475	$400	$325

Add $114 for competition trap/pigeon model.

BETA EUROPE — 12 ga. only, deluxe model with coin finished game scene engraved sideplates, 26½ or 27½ in. barrels with fixed chokes, ejectors, DT or SST, checkered English stock and splinter forearm, 6 lbs. 6 oz. Importation began 1989.

Mfg.'s Sug. Retail	$1,711	$1,400	$1,100	$850	$700	$575	$495	$450

Add $33 for semi-beavertail forend.

Add $130 for competition trap/pigeon model.

SHOTGUNS: SLIDE ACTION

The models listed below are variations of the same action based on a twin bar slide system, alloy receiver with anti-glare finish (including barrel), rear trigger guard safety, and 2¾ or 3 in. shell interchangeability.

Add $25 for camouflage wood finish on the models listed below.

MODEL S.D.A.S.S. — 12 ga. only, 3 in. chamber, originally designed for police and self defense use, 8 shot tube mag., 20 or 24½ in. barrel threaded for external choke tubes, approx. 6 lbs. 6 oz. Importation began 1989.

Mfg.'s Sug. Retail	$415	$325	$285	$260	$230	$195	$160	$140

This model with 24½ in. barrel is threaded for external multi-chokes which can add up to 6 in. to the barrel length - available for a $17 extra charge.

Special Police — similar to Model S.D.A.S.S. except has special heavy 20 in. cylinder bored barrel VR, cooling jacket, 6 shot mag., rubber recoil pad. Importation began 1989.

Mfg.'s Sug. Retail	$440	$340	$295	$265	$230	$195	$160	$140

Martial — 12 ga. only, 18, 20, 28, 30, or 35½ (disc. 1989) in. barrel, fixed sights and choke, approx. 6¼ lbs. Importation began 1989.

Mfg.'s Sug. Retail	$424	$330	$290	$260	$225	$190	$160	$140

Add $41 for VR.

Add $20 for 35½ (disc. 1989) in. barrel.

Add $33 for multi-choke (plain rib with 1 choke and wrench).

Add $65 for innerchoke (includes 1 choke and wrench - VR barrel only).

SHOTGUNS: SINGLE BARREL

The models listed below have receivers made out of aluminum alloy, rear trigger guard safety, and matte black finish metal surfaces.

OMEGA STANDARD — 12, 20, or .410 ga., 3 in. chamber, 26 or 28 (12 ga. only) in. barrel, checkered beech stock and forearm, approx. 5 lbs. 5 oz. Importation began 1989.

Mfg.'s Sug. Retail	$139	$120	$95	$80	$70	$60	$55	$50

Goose Gun — similar to Omega Standard except is 12 ga. only with a 35½ in. barrel, 6 lbs. Importation began 1989.

Mfg.'s Sug. Retail	$156	$135	$115	$90	$80	$70	$60	$55

Grading	100%	98%	95%	90%	80%	70%	60%

FABBRI, ARMI

Manufacturer located in Gordone V.T., Italy. Can be ordered from New England Arms Co. located in Kittery Point, ME.

SIDE BY SIDE SHOTGUN — 12 or 20 ga., one of the world's best current production guns, highest-quality sidelock, ejectors, full engraving.

Mfg.'s Sug. Retail	$27,500	$22,000	$17,500	$15,000	$13,500	$10,000	$7,200	$6,100

O/U SHOTGUN — 12 or 20 ga., top-of-the-line quality with any combinationof engraving, wood, and other options.

Mfg.'s Sug. Retail	$44,000	$40,000	$34,500	$29,500	$25,000	$20,000	$16,000	$13,500

FABRIQUE NATIONALE

Manufacturer located in Herstal and Liege, Belgium. Established a contract with John M. Browning in 1902 for exclusive manufacture of various Browning Patent Firearms.

Also See: Browning Arms under Rifles, Shotguns, and several Pistols.

There will be some overlapping of models found in this section and under Browning Arms.

PISTOLS: SEMI-AUTO

MODEL 1900 — 7.65mm cal., first Belgium Browning, 4 in. barrel. Mfg. 724,500, 1899-1910.

	$325	$300	$275	$250	$225	$195	$150

Add 30% for early pistols with "pistol logo" grips.

MODEL 1903 — 9mm Browning Long cartridge, 5 in. barrel. Mfg. by Fabrique Nationale, Herstal-Belgium. Mfg. 58,400, 1903-1939.

	$450	$400	$350	$300	$260	$220	$180

Add 50% if slotted to accept shoulder stock.

This variation was also manufactured with a detachable shoulder stock — this accessory is rare and can add as much as $2,000 to values listed above.

MODEL 1903-SWEDISH CONTRACT — 9mm cal., mfg. by Husqvarna and Swedish Arsenal (so marked), many were imported into U.S. and converted to .380 ACP from original Browning 9mm Long.

	$300	$260	$230	$200	$180	$150	$125

Subtract 25% for .380 ACP conversion.

MODEL 1905 (VEST POCKET) — 6.35 mm (.25 ACP), dubbed "Vest Pocket" model, manufactured by Fabrique Nationale, Herstal-Belgium. Mfg. 1,086,133 between 1906-1959.

First Variation — no slide lock/safety lever.

	$375	$325	$300	$280	$225	$195	$150

Add 10% for nickel finish.

Second Variation — post-1908, with slide lock/safety lever.

	$325	$300	$275	$250	$225	$195	$150

Add 10% for nickel finish.

MODEL 1910 — 7.65mm (.32 ACP) and Browning 9mm Short (.380 ACP) 4 in. barrel. FN manufacture. Mfg. 701,266, 1912-19806. This model was sold 1954-68 with BAC trademark — commonly designated the Model 1955.

	$325	$300	$275	$250	$225	$195	$150

Add 20% if BAC marked and .380 ACP.

Add 30% if BAC marked and 7.65mm.

BAC marked pistols were imported 1954-1968.

Grading	100%	98%	95%	90%	80%	70%	60%

MODEL 1922 OR 10/22 — 7.65mm or .380 ACP cal., modified Model 1910 with 4½ in. barrel, longer grip frame and mag., made for commercial sale as well as military contracts. Several hundred thousand made by Nazis during the occupation of Liege, Belgium 1940-1944. Mfg. 1912-1959.

	$240	$215	$195	$175	$150	$125	$110

Add 10% for .380 ACP.

Add 10% for Waffenamt proofing.

Add 20% for foreign contracts.

The Model 10/22 and M1922 are the same pistol, Model 1910 modified by FN technicians for sale to Serbian Armed Forces in 1923. Also sold to France, Holland, Yugoslavia, and other countries. Also mfg. by the German military 1940-1944.

"BABY" MODEL — 6.35mm (.25 ACP) cal., lighter, smaller modification of Browning Model 1905 Vest Pocket .25, has no grip safety or slide lock, imported under BAC trademark from 1954-1970 in standard blue finish, lightweight nickel and engraved Renaissance models. Mfg. 1931-1983. Total production is over 510,000.

FN Marked — slide marked Fabrique Nationale, blued finish standard.

	$395	$350	$310	$280	$245	$225	$200

BAC Slide Marked — slide marked Fabrique Nationale, blued finish standard.

	$300	$265	$225	$195	$180	$165	$150

Lightweight Model — nickel frame, with pearl grips.

	$395	$350	$310	$280	$245	$225	$200

Renaissance Model — engraved, satin grey finish.

	$875	$760	$600

FN/BROWNING MODEL 10/71 — 4½ in. barrel, modified version of Model 1922 (10/22) in .380 ACP cal. with target sights and grips in addition to incorporating a magazine finger tip extension designed to comply with GCA of 1968. Sold in U.S. by BAC 1970-1974 as the "Standard .380", still mfg. by FN as Model 125.

	$375	$295	$250	$220	$205	$190	$160

Renaissance or Gold Line Model

	$995	$850	$775

PISTOLS: HI-POWERS

The F.N. Hi-Power (also known as P-35) was Browning's last pistol design. A single action semi-auto 9mm pistol, it was the first to incorporate a staggered high capacity magazine. It has a 4⅝ in. barrel, 13 shot mag., hammer and mag. safeties, a wide variety of finishes and sight options. It's probably the most widely used military pistol in the world.

PRE-WAR COMMERCIAL HP — semi-auto pistol, 9mm, blue, wood grips, fixed or tangent rear sight, 13 shot mag., slotted for stock.

	100%	98%	95%	90%	80%	70%	60%
Fixed sight	$650	$575	$500	$450	$400	$350	$300
Tangent sight	$1,000	$850	$750	$600	$500	$400	$375

Add $300 for wooden holster stock.

PRE-WAR MILITARY CONTRACT — mfg. under military contract for various European countries.

	100%	98%	95%	90%	80%	70%	60%
Lithuanian Crest	$1,300	$1,175	$950	$750	$600	$450	$375
Latvian Contract	$1,550	$1,325	$1,150	$950	$800	$550	$400
Estonian Contract	$1,200	$1,000	$850	$700	$600	$500	$400

Since so many variations have been manufactured for military contract, the listing above represents a few of the more interesting (and collectable) models.

WWII Production: Waffenamt Proofed

There is a range of finishes during Nazi production that varies from the excellent pre-war commercial finish on early guns assembled from captured parts to the roughly milled, poorly

Grading	100%	98%	95%	90%	80%	70%	60%

finished specimens mfg. late in the war. Values below assume all major parts (slide, barrel, and frame) are matching.

In recent years, many Nazi production Hi-Powers have had the rear grip strap milled out and slotted to accept a shoulder stock. Careful observation is advised before purchasing a "rare" (and expensive) slotted and tangent sight specimen.

Type I: Tangent sights — slotted — assembled from existing pre-war Belgian army parts, quality is excellent, correct ser. range is quite limited, approx. 48,000-52,000. All are proofed WaA 613.

	100%	98%	95%	90%	80%	70%	60%
	$1,750	$1,450	$1,200	$1,000	$800	$600	$500

Type II — tangent rear sight only, approx. 50,000 mfg. with generally good quality finish.

	100%	98%	95%	90%	80%	70%	60%
	$1,000	$800	$620	$475	$450	$400	$325

Type III Standard Fixed Sights

	100%	98%	95%	90%	80%	70%	60%
	$490	$445	$410	$350	$310	$275	$240

POST-WAR COMMERCIAL CONTRACT — not manufactured until 1950, first imported with BAC markings in 1954 (see Browning HP section).
Add $50 if round hammer.

Tangent sight only

	100%	98%	95%	90%	80%	70%	60%
	$725	$670	$645	$590	$535	$425	$350

Tangent sight — slotted for stock.

	100%	98%	95%	90%	80%	70%	60%
	$1,200	$950	$835	$780	$725	$500	$450

Fixed sight — ring hammer.

	100%	98%	95%	90%	80%	70%	60%
	$450	$400	$375	$350	$325	$300	$275

Add $50 for pre-1970 models with round hammer.

POST-WAR MILITARY CONTRACT — mfg. from 1946-present, early models are identifiable by an "A" serial number prefix and are not fitted with a magazine safety. In 1947 the rear slide bushing became hardened by a new heat treatment process. Other design modifications were added in 1950 making post 1950 barrels not interchangeable with earlier frames. Many thousands manufactured under various government contracts.

Tangent sight and slotted

	100%	98%	95%	90%	80%	70%	60%
	$1,200	$950	$890	$725	$650	$600	$525

Tangent sight only

	100%	98%	95%	90%	80%	70%	60%
	$780	$725	$670	$550	$525	$500	$475

Fixed sight

	100%	98%	95%	90%	80%	70%	60%
	$550	$450	$425	$325	$300	$275	$250

MUSCAT AND OMAN CONTRACT
First Model — 9 guns.

	100%	98%	95%
	$4,500	$2,750	$1,495

Second Model — 27 guns.

	100%	98%	95%
	$3,000	$1,700	$995

INGLIS MANUFACTURED HI-POWERS — SEE INGLIS SECTION.

RIFLES

MODEL 1949 — semi-auto, 7mm, 7.65mm, 7.92mm, or .30-06 cal., gas operated 10 shot mag., 23 in. barrel, military rifle, tangent rear sight, military stock. Mfg. 160,000.

	100%	98%	95%	90%	80%	70%	60%
	$425	$350	$275	$250	$225	$185	$155

Add 10% for .30-06 cal.
Add 100% for sniper variation.

FN SNIPER RIFLE (BOLT ACTION) — .308 cal., this model was a Mauser actioned Sniper Rifle equipped with 20 in. extra heavy barrel, flash hider, diopter sights, Hensoldt 4X scope, hard case, bipod, and sling. Approx. 50 were imported into the U.S. with the last retail price (1988) being $2,950. When encountered today, values will range from $3,500 and higher (depending on condition).

Grading	100%	98%	95%	90%	80%	70%	60%

RIFLES: FAL/LAR/FNC SERIES

After tremendous price increases between 1985-1988, Fabrique Nationale decided in 1988 to discontinue this series completely. Not only are these rifles not exported to the U.S. any longer, but all production has ceased in Belgium as well. The only way FN will produce these models again is if they are given a large military contract - in which case a "side-order" of commercial guns may be built. 1989 Federal legislation regarding this type of paramilitary design also helped push up prices to their current level.

F.N. FAL — semi-auto, French designation for the FN L.A.R. (light automatic rifle), otherwise same as LAR. See values for LAR model listed below.

F.N. L.A.R. COMPETITION (LIGHT AUTOMATIC RIFLE) — .308 Win. (7.62 x 51), semi-auto, competition rifle with match flash hider, 21 in. barrel, adj. 4 position fire selector on automatic models, wood stock, aperture rear sight adj. from 100-600 meters, 9.4 lbs. Mfg. 1950-1988.

	$2,000	$1,750	$1,600	$1,450	$1,300	$1,175	$1,000

This model was designated by the factory as the 50.00 Model.

Mid-1987 retail on this model was $1,258. The last Mfg.'s Sug. Retail was $3,179 (this price reflected the last exchange rate and special order status of this model).

Heavy barrel rifle — barrel is twice as heavy as standard LAR, includes wood or synthetic stock, short wood forearm, and bi-pod, 12.2 lbs. Importation disc. 1988.

	$2,500	$2,150	$1,850	$1,500	$1,350	$1,200	$1,050

Add $400 for walnut stock.

There were 2 variations of this model. The Model 50.41 had a synthetic butt stock while the Model 50.42 had a wood butt stock with steel butt plate incorporating a top extension used for either shoulder resting or inverted grenade launching.

Mid-1987 retail on this model was $1,497 (Model 50.41) or $1,654 (Model 50.42). The last Mfg.'s Sug. Retail was $3,776 (this price reflected the last exchange rate and special order status of this model).

Paratrooper rifle — similar to LAR model, except has folding stock, 8.3 lbs. Mfg. 1950-1988.

	$1,200	$1,000	$850	$750	$650	$575	$500

There were 2 variations of the Paratrooper LAR Model. The Model 50.63 had a stationary aperture rear sight and 18 in. barrel. The Model 50.64 was supplied with a 21 in. barrel and had a rear sight calibrated for either 150 or 200 meters. Both models retailed for the same price.

Mid-1987 retail on this model was $1,310 (both the Model 50.63 and 50.64). The last Mfg.'s Sug. Retail was $3,239 (this price reflected the last exchange rate and special order status of this model).

FNC MODEL — .223 Rem. (5.56mm), lightweight combat carbine, 18½ in. barrel, NATO approved, 30 shot mag., 8.4 lbs. Disc. 1987.

	$1,100	$975	$825	$725	$625	$550	$500

Add $50 for Paratrooper model (16 or 18½ in. barrel).

While rarer, the 16 in. barrel model incorporated a flash hider that did not perform as well as the flash hider used on the standard 18½ in. barrel.

Mid-1987 retail on this model was $749 (Standard Model) and $782 (Paratrooper Model). The last Mfg.'s Sug. Retail was $2,204 (Standard Model) and $2,322 (Paratrooper Model) - these prices reflected the last exchange rate and special order status of these models.

F.N. MAUSER SPORTER DELUXE — available in popular American and European calibers, 24 in. barrel, adj. sight, checkered pistol grip stock. Mfg. 1947-1963.

		$650	$550	$495	$460	$300	$275	$250

F.N. PRESENTATION GRADE — same as Deluxe, except engraved and select wood.

		$1,150	$935	$855	$770	$500	$475	$450

F.N. SUPREME BOLT ACTION — .243, .270, 7mm, .308, or .30-06, 24 in. barrel, peep sight, checkered pistol grip stock. Mfg. 1957-1975.

		$650	$550	$495	$460	$300	$275	$250

Grading	100%	98%	95%	90%	80%	70%	60%

F.N. SUPREME MAGNUM — same as Bolt Action, .264 Mag., 7mm Mag., or .300 Win. Mag.

	$675	$575	$540	$495	$325	$275	$250

FALCON FIREARMS

Manufacturer located in Northridge, CA. Distributed by Falcon Firearms located in Northridge, CA. New 1986.

Values and information listed below reflect 1990 data as this publication was not afforded 1991 prices/changes by press time.

PORTSIDER — .45 ACP, patterned after Colt M 1911 A-1, stainless steel, fixed sights, 5 in. barrel, 7 shot mag., available in left only. New 1986.

Mfg.'s Sug. Retail $580 $500 $425 $375

Portsider Set — features right and left hand models with matching serial numbers. Only 100 sets mfg. 1986-1987.

Mfg.'s Sug. Retail $1,400 $1,400 $1,150 $925

GOLD FALCON — .45 ACP, machined receiver made from solid 17 Kt gold alloy, stainless steel slide, diamond sighting system, choice of grips, standard or personalized engraving options. Only 50 mfg.

Mfg.'s Sug. Retail $30,500 $30,500 $22,500 $16,400

FAMARS, ABBIATICO & SALVINELLI

Manufacturer located in Gardone, Italy. Imported exclusively in the U.S. by Mr. Joe Bojalad located in Pittsburgh, PA.

A & S Famars manufactures some of the world's finest shotguns - only 50-60 are fabricated yearly. Values listed below are for base models with no extra embellishments or special orders. Because every A & S Famars longarm is an individual custom order, each Famars firearm must have its value ascertained on an individual appraisal basis.

Due to the recent devaluation of the U.S. dollar, prices may fluctuate rapidly on this trademark.

RIFLES: CUSTOM MANUFACTURE

Sidelock rifles are all best quality and range in calibers between .22 LR and .600 Nitro Express. Each gun is manufactured per individual customer special order, and further information and price quotations are available by contacting the above listed U.S. agent directly.

SHOTGUNS: CUSTOM MANUFACTURE

HAMMER SHOTGUN — double barrel, SxS only, hammers, double triggers, various gauges. Prices usually start at $6,500 for a custom ordered gun.

BOXLOCK SHOTGUN — SxS only, available with Anson-Deeley boxlock action, scalloped or rounded frame, various engraving patterns available.

SIDELOCK SHOTGUN — SXS or O/U, hammerless, DT or ST, various gauges. Prices usually start at approx. $9,000 for a custom ordered gun.

FAUSTI, STEFANO

Manufacturer located in Marcheno, Italy.

S. Fausti manufactures shotguns in O/U, SxS, and single shot configurations. To date there has been little importation, but American Arms is private labeling a .410 and 10 gauge O/U (please refer to American Arms section in this text).

FEATHER INDUSTRIES, INC.

Manufacturer located in Boulder, CO.

DERRINGERS

GUARDIAN ANGEL 9mm/.38 Spl. — 9mm Para., O/U design, stainless steel, double action backup derringer. Mfg. 1988-1989 only.

	$130	$95	$75

Grading	100%	98%	95%	90%	80%	70%	60%

Last Mfg.'s Sug. Retail was $140.

This model has interchangeable loading blocks that allow shooting 9mm Para. or .38 Spl. There is no exposed hammer and trigger is totally enclosed.

GUARDIAN ANGEL .22 LR/.22 Mag..22 LR or .22 Mag., design is similar to 9mm/.38 Spl. model, 2 in. barrel, fixed sites, 12 oz. New in 1990.

Mfg.'s Sug. Retail	$120	$90	$75	$60			

Add $30 for individual extra loading blocks.

This model has interchangeable loading blocks that allow shooting .22LR or .22 Mag. There is no exposed hammer and the trigger is totally enclosed.

PISTOLS

MINI-AT — .22 LR, pistol variation of the AT-22, 5½ in. shrouded barrel, 20 shot mag., approx. 2 lbs. Mfg. 1986-1989.

	$195	$165	$145	$135	$130	$125	$115

Last Mfg.'s Sug. Retail was $220.

RIFLES

AT-22 — .22 LR, semi-auto blowback action, 17 in. detachable shrouded barrel, collapsible metal stock, adj. rear sight, with sling and swivels, 20 shot mag., 3¼ lbs. New 1986.

Mfg.'s Sug. Retail	$250	$225	$175	$155	$145	$135	$125	$115

AT-9 — 9mm Para., semi-auto blowback action, 16 in. barrel, paramilitary design, available with either 32 or 100 (optional) mag., 5 lbs. New 1988.

Mfg.'s Sug. Retail	$500	$440	$375	$310	$280	$260	$240	$200

Add $80 for 100 round drum mag (disc. 1989).

SATURN 30 — 7.62 x 39mm Kalashnikov cal., semi-auto, gas operated, 19½ in. barrel, composite stock with large thumbhole pistol grip, 5 shot detachable mag., drilled and tapped for scope mounts, adj. rear sight, 8½ lbs. Mfg. in 1990 only.

	$625	$525	$450	$375	$325	$280	$260

Last Mfg.'s Sug. Retail was $695.

KG-9 — 9mm Para., semi-auto blowback action, 25 or 50 shot mag., assualt configuration. Mfg. 1989 only.

	$495	$425	$375	$325	$275	$240	$200

Last Mfg.'s Sug. Retail was $560.

SAR-180 — .22 LR, semi-auto blowback action, 17½ in. barrel, 165 shot drum mag., fully adj. rear sight, walnut stock with combat style pistol grip and forend, 6¼ lbs. Mfg. 1989 only.

	$450	$395	$350	$295	$260	$240	$200

Add $105 for retractable stock.
Add $395 for laser sight.
Last Mfg.'s Sug. Retail was $500.

KG-22 — .22 LR, similar to KG-9 except is .22 LR and has 20 shot mag. Mfg. 1989 only.

	$295	$250	$200	$175	$155	$145	$135

Last Mfg.'s Sug. Retail was $300.

FEDERAL ENGINEERING CORPORATION

Previous manufacturer located in Chicago, IL.

Values below represent changes due to 1989 Federal legislation regarding this paramilitary configuration of firearm. Mfg. of these models has been disc.

XC-220 — .22 LR semi-auto paramilitary design rifle, 16⁵⁄₁₆ in. barrel length, 28 shot mag., machined steel action, 7½ lbs. New 1984.

	$395	$350	$300	$275	$250	$230	$210

Grading	100%	98%	95%	90%	80%	70%	60%

XC-450 — .45 ACP only, semi-auto paramilitary design carbine, 16½ in. barrel length, 30 shot mag., fires from closed bolt, machined steel action, 8½ lbs. New 1984.

	$950	$825	$750	$675	$600	$550	$500

XC-900 — 9mm only, semi-auto paramilitary design carbine, 16½ in. barrel length, 32 shot mag., fires from closed bolt, machine steel action, 8 lbs. New 1984.

	$950	$825	$750	$675	$600	$550	$500

FEDERAL ORDNANCE INC.
Manufacturer/importer/distributor located in South El Monte, CA.

Federal Ordnance has been importing or distributing both foreign and domestic military handguns and rifles since 1966. In addition, they also fabricate firearms using mostly original older parts. Listed below are those models which have been recently manufactured or remanufactured.

In addition to the models listed below, Fed. Ord. also distributes used M-1 Carbines, AK-47's, SKS's, Finnish 39's, Lee Enfields, Baby Carbines, P-14's, M-1 Garands, Hakims, Mauser 98's, and other rifles. Most of these are in good to excellent overall condition and prices typically are in the $165-$400 range (except the M-1 Garand), depending on the model and quality.

CARBINES

MODEL 713 DELUXE MAUSER CARBINE — 7.63 Mauser or 9mm Para. cal., 16 in. barrel, detachable stock, one 10 shot and one 20 shot detachable mag., deluxe walnut, leather case with accessories, adj. sights to 1,000 meters, 5 lbs. 1,500 mfg. 1986.

Mfg.'s Sug. Retail	$1,986	$1,775	$1,450	$1,050			

Field Grade Mauser Carbine — 7.63 Mauser or 9mm Para. (new 1989) cal., 16 in. barrel, 10 shot fixed mag., nondetachable walnut stock. New 1987.

Mfg.'s Sug. Retail	$1,200	$995	$795	$695	$595	$500	$450	$400

PISTOLS

In addition to the Broomhandle models listed below, Federal Ordnance also manufactures other special editions. These models include the British Model, Cut-Away, Cartridge Counter, Para La Guerra, and others. Prices are in the $800-$950 price range (retail).

MODEL 714 BROOMHANDLE — 7.63 Mauser or 9mm Para. cal., 5½ in. barrel, new frame, exterior completely refinished, 10 shot detachable mag., "fair" bore, adj. rear sight. New 1986.

Mfg.'s Sug. Retail	$820	$750	$595	$500	$440	$400	$375	$350

Add $100 for new barrel.

Model 714 Para La Guerra — 7.63 Mauser or 9mm Para., remanufactured to duplicate Spanish Civil War configuration Broomhandle, includes 10 in. barrel with "Para La Guerra" engraved on side. New 1990.

Mfg.'s Sug. Retail	$890	$775	$625	$525	$450	$400	$375	$350

Model 714 Bolo — similar to Model 714 Broomhandle, except has smaller grips, 3.9 in. barrel, 10 shot mag. standard. Mfg. 1988 only.

	$775	$600	$500	$440	$400	$375	$350

Last Mfg.'s Sug. Retail was $890.

STANDARD BROOMHANDLE — 7.63 Mauser or 9mm Para. cal., refurbished (new barrels, completely refinished, etc.) C-96 pistols, replaced springs, includes original Chinese shoulder/holster stock.

Mfg.'s Sug. Retail	$735	$625	$500	$460	$430	$400	$375	$350

Subtract $195 without shoulder/holster stock.

Standard Bolo — similar to Standard Broomhandle, except Bolo configuration (3.9 in. barrel and smaller grips). New 1990.

Mfg.'s Sug. Retail	$530	$480	$385	$350	$310	$280	$260	$240

Grading	100%	98%	95%	90%	80%	70%	60%

RANGER 1911A1 GI — .45 ACP, 5 in. barrel, 7 shot mag., steel construction throughout, checkered walnut grips, 40 oz. New 1988.

Mfg.'s Sug. Retail	$440	$385	$350	$310	$280	$260	$240	$200

Add $20 for Ranger Extended Model (40 oz. - new 1990).

Add $40 for Ranger Ambo (ambidextrous safety, 40 oz. - new 1990).

Add $25 for lightweight Ranger Lite Model (32 oz. - new 1990).

These pistols are new manufacture and patterned after the Colt 1911A1 Gov.'t Model.

Ranger Ten — 10mm cal., otherwise same as regular Ranger 1911A1. New 1990.

Mfg.'s Sug. Retail	$780	$675	$525	$475	$450	$420	$395	$370

RANGER SUPERCOMP — .45 ACP or 10mm cal., compensated variation of the Ranger 1911A1 with 6 in. compensated barrel, slide, tuned trigger, and other competition features, 42 oz. New 1990.

Mfg.'s Sug. Retail	$1,390	$1,250	$875	$775	$675	$600	$550	$495

Add $10 for 10mm cal.

THE RANGER ALPHA — .38 Super, 10mm, or .45 ACP cal., 5 or 6 in. barrel, patterned after the Colt Gov.'t Model. New 1990.

Mfg.'s Sug. Retail	$1,000	$900	$775	$675	$575	$475	$425	$380

Add $16 for 10mm cal.

Add $16 for 6 in. barrel.

Add $9-$25 for ported 5 or 6 in. barrel depending on cal.

PETERS STAHL PS-07 — 10mm or .45 ACP cal., mfg. by Peters Stahl of W. Germany to exacting standards, 6 in. barrel with polygonal rifling, top-of-the-line competition model with compensated barrel and other advanced competition features, 45 oz. New 1990.

Mfg.'s Sug. Retail	$2,600	$2,350	$1,800	$1,500	$1,200	$995	$825	$700

Add $51 for 10mm cal.

RIFLES

M-14 S.A. — .308 cal., legal for private ownership (no selector), 20 shot mag., refinished original M-14 parts, available in either filled fiberglass, G.I. fiberglass, refinished wood, or new walnut stock. New 1986.

Mfg.'s Sug. Retail	$700	$625	$550	$495	$450	$395	$335	$285

Add $50 for filled fiberglass stock.

Add $110 for refinished wood stock.

Add $190 for new walnut stock with handguard.

CHINESE RPK 86S-7 — 7.62 X 39mm cal., semi-auto version of the P.R.C.-RPK light machine gun, 75 shot drum mag., 23¾ in. barrel, with bipod. Imported 1989 only.

	$1,000	$875	$725	$650	$575	$525	$475

Last Mfg.'s Sug. Retail was $500.

FEINWERKBAU

Manufacturer located in Oberndorf, West Germany. Currently imported exclusively by Beeman Precision Arms located in Santa Rosa, CA.

Feinwerkbau manufactures some of the world's finest quality target rifles and pistols (.22 LR rimfire and airgun).

Prices below reflect the recent devaluation of the U.S. dollar against some foreign currencies. While the manufacturer's suggested retails have gone up considerably, prices for used specimens (98% or less original condition) have not increased proportionately, and in some cases, have changed very little.

Grading	100%	98%	95%	90%	80%	70%	60%

MODEL 2000 — .22 LR only, single shot, match target bolt action rifle, fully adj. trigger, walnut stocks, four variations featuring different specifications. Importation disc. 1988.

Universal Model — 26⅜ in. barrel, aperture sights, stippled pistol grip and forearm, 9¾ lbs.

	$1,150	$925	$850	$735	$650	$595	$550

Add $350 for electronic trigger.

Add $160 for left-hand variation.

Last Mfg.'s Sug. Retail was $1,395.

Mini 2000 (Junior) — 22 in. barrel, aperture sights, stippled pistol grip, 9⅛ lbs.

	$1,025	$875	$825	$700	$625	$575	$525

Add $350 for electronic trigger.

Add $150 for left-hand variation.

Last Mfg.'s Sug. Retail was $1,225.

Match Model — 26¼ in. barrel, adj. cheek piece on stock, stippled pistol grip and forearm, aperture sights.

	$1,075	$895	$825	$700	$625	$575	$525

Add $390 for electronic trigger.

Add $113 for left-hand variation.

Last Mfg.'s Sug. Retail was $1,285.

Running Target — adj. cheek piece on stock, thumbhole stippled pistol grip, no sights, for running bore competition.

	$1,150	$925	$850	$735	$650	$595	$550

Add $142 for left-hand variation.

Last Mfg.'s Sug. Retail was $1,398.

MODEL 2600 UNIVERSAL — .22 LR only, similar design to Model 600 air rifle, single shot, 26.3 in. barrel, aperture sights, 10.6 lbs. New 1986.

Mfg.'s Sug. Retail	$1,398	$1,125	$925	$850	$735	$650	$595	$550

Add $175 for left-hand variation.

MODEL 2600 ULTRA MATCH FREE RIFLE — .22 LR, single shot match gun based on Model 2600 action, 26.1 in. barrel, laminate stock with thumbhole, fully adj. aperture sights, 14 lbs. 1 oz. New 1986.

Mfg.'s Sug. Retail	$1,998	$1,795	$1,400	$1,150	$925	$850	$735	$650

Add $250 for electronic trigger (disc. 1988).

Add $150 for left-hand variation.

FERLACH GUNS

Includes those firearms manufactured in Ferlach, Austria from the mid-1600's to present.

Many people are confused that Ferlach is a trademark - it is not. Rather, it is a small village in Austria where a gun guild was started as early as 1558. At that time, it was absolutely neccesary that all the people involved in fabricating a firearm were located together in close proximity. This enabled the barrel maker, the stock maker, and the lock mechanism maker to work together closely to ensure that everyone was performing their task(s) correctly, effectively and efficiently. As the individual skills became better and more refined, more and more firearms were manufactured. Eventually, individual gunsmiths began to put their name on the barrel or frame of those guns which they had either manufactured solely or with the help of their fellow Ferlach craftsman. Since all Ferlach firearms are essentially hand made per individual special order, very few are exactly alike. In the past the gunsmiths of Ferlach have produced almost every type of shoulder arm imaginable including such modern weapons as superposed and juxtaposed rifles and shotguns, hammerless drillings, repeating rifles, 3 barrel rifles, combination guns, 4 barrel rifles/shotguns/combination guns (called Vierlings), hammer guns of every type, etc. Some of these specimens represent the highest refinement in the gunmakers trade. Because of the almost unlimited variety of Ferlach variations, it is recommended that a COMPETENT appraisal is procurred before buying or selling a specimen.

Grading	100%	98%	95%	90%	80%	70%	60%

As is the case with many other European weapons, those models with desirable American features will outperform those with European specifications (i.e. a Ferlach sidelock combination gun that is 20 ga. x .243 Win. will be more valuable than a similar specimen chambered for 16 ga. x 5.6 by 50R mm with sling swivels). Things to consider when contemplating buying or selling a Ferlach long arm are: type of action, difficulty of fabrication (Vierlings are very complicated to construct), caliber/gauge desirability, notoriety of gunsmith on barrel legand, elaborateness of embellishments, condition, rarity, accessories, and any provenance a specimen might have.

Today's master gunsmiths of Ferlach carry on the old world tradition of quality in every respect. Most guns manufactured today are by individual special order with a wide range of calibers/gauges and other special features and options. As of this writing, these gunsmiths in alphabetical order are: LUDWIG BOROVNIK, JOHANN FANZOJ, WILFRIED GLANZNIG, JOSEF HAMBRUSCH, KARL HAUPTMANN, GOTTFRIED JUCH, JOSEF JUST, JAKOB KOSCHAT, JOHANN MICHELITSCH, WALTER OUTSCHAR, HERBERT SCHEIRING, BENEDIKT WINKLER, AND JOSEF WINKLER. Anyone wishing to contact these master gunmakers should either write to the guild or address them individually at: Ferlach, Waagplatz,6, A-9170 Ferlach, AUSTRIA. Please allow at least 4-6 weeks for a response.

FEMARU

Previously manufactured by Femaru-Febyver-Es Gepgyar R.T. located in Budapest, Hungary.

MODEL 1910 — 7.65mm Roth/Steyr cal., rare and only infrequently encountered.

	100%	98%	95%	90%	80%	70%	60%
	$1,750	$1,550	$1,350	$1,150	$975	$850	$725

MODEL 1937 — 7.65mm, 3.93 in. barrel, 8 shot mag., commercial blue finish, 2-piece walnut grips, Nazi marked jhv 41-jhv 44.

	100%	98%	95%	90%	80%	70%	60%
	$275	$240	$215	$190	$175	$160	$145

Add 35% for Waffenamt proofing.

FROMMER STOP POCKET AUTO — .32 ACP, .380 ACP, 6 or 7 shot, $3\frac{7}{8}$ in. barrel, fixed sights, blue, rubber grips, locked breech, outside hammer. Mfg. 1912-1920.

	100%	98%	95%	90%	80%	70%	60%
	$150	$135	$125	$110	$90	$75	$50

FROMMER BABY POCKET AUTO — similar to Stop Pocket Auto, except 2 in. barrel, 5 or 6 shot.

	100%	98%	95%	90%	80%	70%	60%
	$175	$165	$150	$135	$100	$85	$65

FROMMER LILIPUT AUTO — blowback action, .25 auto, 6 shot, 2.14 in. barrel, blue, hard rubber grips. Mfg. in early twenties.

	100%	98%	95%	90%	80%	70%	60%
	$225	$200	$175	$145	$115	$90	$75

FERLIB

Manufacturer located in Gordone V.T., Italy. Distributed by Quality Arms located in Houston, Tx, and New England Arms Co. located in Kittery Point, ME. Previously imported by W.L. Moore & Company located in Westlake Village, CA.

SHOTGUNS: SIDE-BY-SIDE

HAMMER GUN — boxlock action, exposed hammers, deluxe checkered walnut stock and forearm, blued action.

	100%	98%	95%	90%	80%	70%	60%
Mfg.'s Sug. Retail	$3,750	$3,500	$3,175	$2,850	$2,350	$2,100	$1,800	$1,500

MODEL F.VI — 12, 16, 20, 28, or .410 ga., Anson & Deeley scalloped boxlock action, ejectors, double triggers, case hardened frame, select checkered stock and forearm.

	100%	98%	95%	90%	80%	70%	60%
Mfg.'s Sug. Retail	$2,950	$2,750	$2,200	$1,975	$1,600	$1,250	$1,000	$750

Add $375 for single trigger.
Add 12% for .28 or .410 ga.

Grading	100%	98%	95%	90%	80%	70%	60%

MODEL F.VII — 12, 16, 20, 28, or .410 ga., Anson & Deeley scalloped boxlock action, ejectors, double triggers, coin finish, full coverage English scroll or game scene engraving, select checkered stock and forearm.

Mfg.'s Sug. Retail	$3,950	$3,700	$3,000	$2,600	$2,200	$1,800	$1,625	$1,475

Add 12% for 28 or .410 ga.

Add $375 for single trigger.

MODEL F.VII/SC — 12, 16, 20, 28, or .410 ga., Anson & Deeley scalloped boxlock action, ejectors, double triggers, coin finish, game scene with scroll accent engraving with gold inlays, select checkered stock and forearm.

Mfg.'s Sug. Retail	$5,250	$5,000	$3,950	$3,400	$2,800	$2,300	$2,000	$1,600

Add $375 for single trigger.

MODEL F.VII SIDEPLATE — 12, 16, 20, 28, or .410 ga., Anson & Deeley boxlock action with sideplates, ejectors, single trigger, coin finish, extensive game scene and scroll accent engraving, select checkered stock and forearm.

Mfg.'s Sug. Retail	$5,650	$5,300	$4,300	$3,800	$3,200	$2,750	$2,500	$2,100

F.VII/SC Gold — same as F.VII Sideplate, except with gold inlays.

Mfg.'s Sug. Retail	$6,750	$6,450	$5,100	$4,200	$3,850	$3,200	$2,950	$2,650

Add 12% for .28 or .410 ga. on both models.

F.V. SIDELOCK — various ga.'s, full sidelock action, special order to customer specifications. Values start in the $10,000 range and go up.

FIALA OUTFITTERS INCORPORATED
New York City, NY.

FIALA REPEATING PISTOL — .22 LR, 10 shot, 3, 7½, or 20 in. barrels, blue, plain wood grips, resembles an auto loader, but is actually hand operated by moving the slide to eject load and cock. Mfg. 1920-1923.

	$475	$400	$340	$280	$230	$200	$175

Add 50% for 3-barrel set.

Add $150 for original case.

Add $250 for stock.

Add $300 for canvas holster stock.

FINNISH LION
Manufactured by Valmet (now Tikka) located in Sweden. Limited importation into the U.S by Mandall's Shooting Supplies, Inc. Scottsdale, AZ.

RIFLES

MATCH RIFLE — .22 LR, bolt action, single shot, 29 in. barrel, extended aperture sight, globe front sight, thumbhole stock, adj. hook butt. Mfg. 1937-1972.

	$495	$415	$360	$305	$250	$210	$195

CHAMPION FREE RIFLE — .22 LR, bolt action, single shot, 29 in. barrel, double set trigger, full target and accessories. Mfg. 1965-1972.

	$580	$495	$440	$385	$330	$290	$265

STANDARD ISU TARGET RIFLE — .22 LR, bolt action, single shot, 27 in. barrel, full target stock and accessories. Mfg. 1966-1977.

	$330	$275	$250	$205	$180	$165	$150

TARGET RIFLE — .22 LR, target rifle with adj. stock and trigger, bolt action, single shot, aperture sights.

Mfg.'s Sug. Retail	$695	$650	$575	$495	$440	$385	$340	$295

FIOCCHI OF AMERICA, INC.
Importer and distributor located In Ozark, MO.

Fiochi of America imports Pardini target pistols and manufactures a wide variety of ammunition domestically. Unitl 1988, Fiochi imported Antonio Zoli shotguns. These trademarks can be found in their respective sections of this text.

FIREARMS INTERNATIONAL (F I)

Previous importer/assembler located in Washington, D.C.

F.I. imported various shotguns and pistols including the Star D and Iver Johnson Pony handguns. F.I. sold less than 100 .380 ACP's that were marked Colt before the Mustang was introduced - these are rare. While some models are relatively rare, collectability to date has been minimal and most models sell in the $125-$250 range.

FOX, A. H.

Previously manufactured in Philadelphia, PA 1903-1930. Manufactured by Savage since 1930.

Mr. Ansley H. Fox first started manufacturing shotguns in the 1896 circa. This first company was called the Fox Gun Co. located in Baltimore, MD. Relatively few guns were made and surviving specimens today are very rare. After this venture he was employed by the Baltimore Gun Co. for several years (approx. circa 1900-1903). Following this period, he formed the Philadelphia Gun Co. where the predecessors to the A.H. Fox Gun Co. were manufactured. These Philadelphia Gun Co. models (circa 1904) were the same as the newer Fox shotguns except that the hinge pin was removed. Sources indicate that the lowest grade was an "A" with the highest being an "E" (fully engraved and ultra rare). Following this tenure, Mr. Fox went on to form the A.H. Fox Gun Co. that was started approx. 1905. In addition to being an entrepreneur and trend setter, Mr. Fox also had the reputation of being an expert shot in his own right, winning more than a few events on the East Coast around the turn of the century.

The A.H. Fox Gun Company of Philadelphia, Pennsylvania, began production in 1905 and produced high quality double barrel shotguns until 1930. The Savage Arms Company, then of Utica, New York, acquired the Fox Company and produced these guns until 1942, when all but the utilitarian model B series guns were discontinued.

A.H. Fox guns are rapidly being considered an American classic as is the L.C. Smith and Parker. Collector interest is high and will undoubtedly grow. The guns do not command quite as high a price as the Smith and Parker guns, but represent a fine investment collectible value.

The Savage made guns from 1930-1942 usually are valued at about 25% less than the early A.H. Fox guns. The current production B series are just not in the same class and are obviously not intended to be. They are lower priced by today's standards and are designed as a utility grade hunting gun.

SHOTGUNS

A.H. Fox serialization indicates the following: 12 ga. guns are encountered in the 100,000 up to 200,000 serial range, 20 ga. shotguns are in the 200,000 up to 300,000 serial range, and 16 ga. specimens are encountered in the 300,000 serial range.

100%	98%	95%	90%	80%	70%	60%	50%	40%	30%	20%	10%

STERLINGWORTH SXS — 12, 16, or 20 ga., 26, 28, or 30 in. barrels, various chokes, boxlock, extractors, double trigger, checkered pistol grip stock. Mfg. 1905-1930.

100%	98%	95%	90%	80%	70%	60%	50%	40%	30%	20%	10%
$1,200	$900	$825	$750	$625	$525	$400	$365	$335	$300	$275	$250

Add 33% for auto ejectors.

Add 50% for 20 ga.

A single trigger is a very desireable option on this model.

STERLINGWORTH DELUXE — same as Sterlingworth, with recoil pad and ivory bead, 32 in. barrel available.

100%	98%	95%	90%	80%	70%	60%	50%	40%	30%	20%	10%
$1,500	$1,200	$950	$850	$775	$675	$600	$540	$460	$400	$365	$330

Add $200 for auto ejectors.

Add 50% for 20 ga.

A single trigger was not an option on this model.

100%	98%	95%	90%	80%	70%	60%	50%	40%	30%	20%	10%

STERLINGWORTH SKEET — same as Sterlingworth, with 26 or 28 in. skeet boring, straight grip stock.

This model is very scarce (only several are known) and the extreme rarity factor precludes accurate price evaluation.

SUPER HE GRADE — 12 ga., 2¾ (very rare) or 3 in. chambered long range gun, 30 and 32 in. full choke, auto ejectors, otherwise same as Sterlingworth.

100%	98%	95%	90%	80%	70%	60%	50%	40%	30%	20%	10%
$2,500	$2,000	$1,700	$1,400	$1,100	$995	$900	$825	$750	$675	$600	$550

Add $300 for SST.

Original 3 in. chambered HE grades are marked "not warranteed, see instruction tag" on barrel flats. The HE grade was also manufactured in 20 ga. but is extremely rare. 2¾ in. chambers are rarer than 3 in. guns in this model.

HIGHER GRADE MODELS (A-F) — the following higher grade Fox shotguns are similar to the Sterlingworth in configuration. The grades differ in engraving and inlays, grade of wood and general workmanship. The E designation means auto ejectors.

Early A and B grades have very little engraving and are much less desirable than later models. Values below are for later guns.

Values below are for 12 ga. Notice ga. add-ons listed below FE grade.

A Grade

100%	98%	95%	90%	80%	70%	60%	50%	40%	30%	20%	10%
$1,500	$1,200	$950	$850	$775	$675	$600	$540	$460	$400	$365	$330

AE Grade (ejectors)

$1,800	$1,500	$1,200	$1,000	$900	$800	$725	$650	$575	$500	$450	$400

BE Grade (ejectors)

$3,000	$2,500	$2,200	$1,800	$1,500	$1,150	$995	$900	$825	$750	$675	$600

This model is rarely encountered.

CE Grade (ejectors)

$3,000	$2,500	$2,200	$1,800	$1,500	$1,150	$995	$900	$825	$750	$675	$600

XE Grade (ejectors)

$6,000	$5,000	$4,000	$3,000	$2,500	$2,200	$1,800	$1,500	$1,150	$995	$900	$825

DE Grade (ejectors)

$9,000	$8,000	$6,500	$5,500	$4,500	$3,500	$2,500	$2,200	$1,800	$1,500	$1,250	$1,000

FE Grade (ejectors) — top-of-the-line model, only infrequently encountered.

$25,000	$20,000	$15,000	$12,000	$10,000	$9,000	$8,000	$7,250	$6,500	$5,800	$5,250	$4,500

Add $200-$1,000 for vent. rib, depending on grade.

Add $200-$1,000 for SST, depending on grade.

Add $200-$1,000 for beavertail forearm, depending on grade.

16 ga. guns were made on same frame as 20 ga. - add 30%.

Add 60% for 20 ga.

Subtract 25% for Savage mfg.

Note: These guns were disc. in 1942 by Savage Arms after they mfg. them for 12 years. Pre-1930 guns were made by A.H. Fox Company.

Grading	100%	98%	95%	90%	80%	70%	60%

SINGLE BARREL TRAP — 12 ga., 30 or 32 in. vent. rib barrel, full choke, boxlock, auto ejector, checkered trap style stock and recoil pad. The grades differ in wood, engraving, and overall quality. ME grade is custom built and extremely high quality with gold inlays. These models were disc. 1942. Guns mfg. between 1932-1942 have Monte Carlo stock. Even though trap guns may be rarer than their side X side counterparts, to date their desirability is less since there are simply fewer collectors.

	100%	98%	95%	90%	80%	70%	60%
Grade JE	$1,760	$1,540	$1,430	$1,320	$1,100	$990	$880
Grade KE	$2,420	$2,200	$2,090	$1,980	$1,760	$1,650	$1,540
Grade LE	$3,300	$3,080	$2,970	$2,860	$2,640	$2,420	$2,200
Grade ME	$8,250	$7,700	$7,150	$6,600	$6,050	$5,500	$4,950

Grading	100%	98%	95%	90%	80%	70%	60%

MODEL B DOUBLE BARREL — 12, 16, 20, or .410 ga., 24-30 in. barrels, various chokes, vent rib on newer models, boxlock, extractors, double triggers, checkered pistol grip stock. Mfg. 1940-1986.

	$230	$210	$205	$185	$165	$145	$120

Last Mfg.'s Sug. Retail was $250.

MODEL B-ST — same as model B, with single trigger. Mfg. 1955-1966.

	$275	$250	$220	$195	$165	$140	$120

MODEL B-DL — same as model B-ST, with satin chrome receiver, select wood. Mfg. 1962-1965.

	$315	$275	$240	$220	$195	$165	$140

MODEL B-DE — same as B-DL, with less checkering. Mfg. 1965-1966.

	$295	$255	$230	$210	$180	$155	$125

MODEL B-SE — 12, 20, or .410 ga., single trigger, selective ejectors, vent. rib, beavertail forend, select walnut. Mfg. 1966-88.

	$415	$370	$325	$280	$240	$210	$180

Add 20% for .410 ga.
Last Mfg.'s Sug. Retail was $525.

Even though there were multiple series designations assigned to this model, there seems to be little difference in desirability. For that reason, other designations will be priced similarly to values shown above.

FRANCHI, LUIGI

Manufacturer located in Brescia, Italy. Currently imported exclusively by American Arms, Inc. located in North Kansas City, MO. Some models were previously imported by FIE firearms located in Hialeah, FL.

Also see Sauer/Franchi heading in the S section.

RIFLES

CENTENNIAL SEMI-AUTO — .22 LR, 21 in. barrel, open sight to commemorate Franchi's 100th anniversary. Mfg. 1968 only.

	$330	$250	$220	$195	$165	$150	$140

Engraved deluxe model

	$415	$330	$305	$275	$240	$200	$165

Gallery model

	$220	$195	$160	$120	$100	$80	$60

SHOTGUNS: SEMI-AUTO

BLACK MAGIC GAME — 12 ga. only, 3 in. chamber with gas metering system, interchangeable shell handling without adjustments, two-tone black alloy receiver with gold accents and trigger, 24, 26, or 28 in. VR barrel with Franchokes, checkered walnut stock and forearm, 7 lbs. Importation began 1989.

Mfg.'s Sug. Retail	$659	$550	$450	$395	$330	$300	$270	$240

Black Magic Skeet — skeet variation of the Black Magic Game, 2¾ in. chamber, 26 in. ported VR barrel with fixed Tula skeet choke, skeet dimensioned stock, 7¼ lbs. Importation began 1989.

Mfg.'s Sug. Retail	$699	$580	$475	$425	$350	$325	$295	$265

Black Magic Trap — trap variation of the Black Magic Game, 2¾ in. chamber, 30 in. VR barrel with Franchoke system, trap dimensioned stock, 7½ lbs. Importation began 1989.

Mfg.'s Sug. Retail	$739	$615	$495	$430	$350	$325	$295	$265

Grading	100%	98%	95%	90%	80%	70%	60%

STANDARD MODEL (48/AL) — 12 or 20 ga., 24, 26, 28, or 30 (disc. in 1990) in. VR barrel, recoil operated, alloy frame, checkered pistol grip stock, VR standard, Franchokes became available in 1989, 12 ga., 6 lbs. 4 oz. and 20 ga., 5 lbs. 2 oz. Mfg. 1950-present.

	100%	98%	95%	90%	80%	70%	60%
Mfg.'s Sug. Retail	$529	$445	$375	$300	$270	$250	$230	$210

Subtract $40 if without Franchokes.

Starting in 1990, this model comes standard with black receiver and gold accents. Franchokes became standard in 1990.

STANDARD MAGNUM (48/AL) — same as Standard, except 28 in. (disc. 1988) or 32 in. VR barrel, Mag. chamber, recoil pad, Mfg. 1954-1990.

			95%	90%	80%	70%	60%
	$415	$360	$300	$270	$250	$230	$210

Last Mfg.'s Sug. Retail was $482.

This model was replaced by the Combo S/T currently imported by American Arms, Inc. located in North Kansas City, MO.

COMBO S/T 12 ga. only, 3 in. chamber, Model 48/AL recoil action, 23 in. barrel with external interchangeable Franchoke system (X-full and rifled slug), fully adj. open type rifle sights, non-reflective barrel and receiver finish, checkered walnut pistol grip stock and forend. Importation began in 1990.

	100%	98%	95%	90%	80%	70%	60%
Mfg.'s Sug. Retail	$559	$465	$385	$310	$270	$250	$230	$210

HUNTER MODEL (48/AL) — same as Standard, except etched receiver, better wood, VR standard, Franchokes became available in 1989. Mfg. 1950-1990.

			95%	90%	80%	70%	60%
	$415	$360	$300	$270	$250	$230	$210

Add $35 for internal Franchokes (3).
Last Mfg.'s Sug. Retail was $482.

This model was imported exclusively by FIE Firearms located in Hialeah, FL.

HUNTER MAGNUM — mfg. 1954-1973.

			95%	90%	80%	70%	60%
	$430	$380	$370	$340	$315	$290	$275

PRESTIGE MODEL — 12 ga. only, gas operated, vent. rib, various barrel lengths, alloy receiver, Franchokes became available in 1989. Imported 1985-1989.

			95%	90%	80%	70%	60%
	$575	$475	$395	$325	$310	$295	$275

Add $40 for internal Franchokes (3).
Last Mfg.'s Sug. Retail was $720.

This model was imported exclusively by FIE Firearms located in Hialeah, FL.

Turkey Model — similar to Prestige Model except has dull matte black finish, Franchokes standard. Imported 1989 only.

			95%	90%	80%	70%	60%
	$615	$515	$425	$350	$320	$300	$280

Last Mfg.'s Sug. Retail was $760.

This model was imported exclusively by FIE Firearms located in Hialeah, FL.

ELITE MODEL — same general specifications as the Prestige Model, only etched receiver, Franchokes became available in 1989. Imported 1985-1989.

			95%	90%	80%	70%	60%
	$595	$500	$425	$350	$320	$300	$280

Add $45 for internal Franchokes (3).
Last Mfg.'s Sug. Retail was $740.

This model was imported exclusively by FIE Firearms located in Hialeah, FL.

SPAS-12 — 12 ga., 2¾ in. chamber, combat shotgun that offers pump or semi-auto operation, 8 shot tube mag., alloy receiver, synthetic stock with built-in pistol grip, one-button switch to change from semi-auto to slide action operation, 21½ in. barrel, 8.12 lbs.

	100%	98%	95%	90%	80%	70%	
Mfg.'s Sug. Retail	$589	$495	$450	$400	$360	$320	$300

This model was imported exclusively by FIE Firearms located in Hialeah, FL until 1990.

Grading	100%	98%	95%	90%	80%	70%	60%

SPAS-15 — 12 ga. only, 2¾ in. chamber, operates as either semi-auto or slide action that is convertible with a one-button switch, 6 shot detachable box mag., 21½ in. barrel, lateral folding skeleton stock, carrying handle, 10 lbs. Limited importation 1989 only.
This model had very limited importation (less than 200) as the BATF disallowed further importation almost immediately. Even though the retail was in the $700 range, demand and rarity has pushed prices past the $2,000 level already.

SAS-12 — 12 ga. only, 3 in. chamber, slide action only, synthetic stock with built-in pistol grip, 8 shot tube mag., 21½ in. barrel, 6.8 lbs. Imported 1988-90 only.

| | $415 | $360 | $300 | $270 | $250 | $230 | $210 |

Last Mfg.'s Sug. Retail was $473.

This model was imported exclusively by FIE Firearms located in Hialeah, FL.

LAW-12 — 12 ga. only, 2¾ in. chamber, gas operated semi-auto, synthetic stock with built-in pistol grip, 8 shot tube mag., 21½ in. barrel, 6.12 lbs. Imported 1988-90 only.

| | $500 | $450 | $400 | $360 | $320 | $300 | $280 |

Last Mfg.'s Sug. Retail was $643.

This model was imported exclusively by FIE Firearms located in Hialeah, FL.

TURKEY GUN — same as Standard Mag., 12 ga., 3 in. barrel only, turkey scene engraved. Mfg. 1963-1965.

| | $415 | $385 | $370 | $340 | $315 | $290 | $275 |

SLUG GUN — 22 in. plain barrel, and rifle sights.

| | $360 | $330 | $315 | $295 | $275 | $255 | $240 |

SKEET GUN — 26 in. skeet choke, vent rib, select wood. Mfg. 1972-1974.

| | $385 | $370 | $350 | $330 | $310 | $285 | $265 |

ELDORADO — fancy wood and gold filled engraved receiver. Mfg. 1954-1975.

| | $450 | $420 | $395 | $380 | $360 | $340 | $320 |

CROWN GRADE — engraved hunting scene. Mfg. 1954-1975.

| | $1,540 | $1,320 | $1,210 | $1,045 | $965 | $910 | $855 |

DIAMOND GRADE SILVER INLAID SCROLL — mfg. 1954-1975.

| | $1,980 | $1,735 | $1,540 | $1,430 | $1,210 | $1,045 | $965 |

IMPERIAL GRADE — gold inlaid hunting scene.

| | $2,420 | $2,090 | $1,925 | $1,760 | $1,595 | $1,485 | $1,320 |

Note: Standard, Skeet and Slug with steel frame mfg. 1965-1972, designated "Dynamic" 12 in., values are the same.

MODEL 500 STANDARD — 12 ga,, 26 or 28 in. barrel, various chokes, vent rib, gas operated, checkered pistol grip stock. Mfg. 1976-present.

| | $330 | $310 | $305 | $265 | $230 | $195 | $165 |

MODEL 520 DELUXE — engraved receiver.

| | $385 | $365 | $330 | $290 | $260 | $220 | $195 |

MODEL 520 ELDORADO GOLD — fine wood, engraved gold, inlaid receiver. Mfg. 1977-present.

| | $990 | $770 | $715 | $660 | $580 | $525 | $470 |

MODEL 530 AUTO TRAP — similar to 500, except 30 in. and 32 in. full, very high rib, special trap stock, pad.

| | $660 | $550 | $525 | $440 | $415 | $385 | $330 |

SHOTGUNS - O/U

Grading	100%	98%	95%	90%	80%	70%	60%

DE LUXE MODEL PRITI — 12 or 20 ga., boxlock action, ST, ejectors, 26 or 28 in. VR barrels with fixed chokes. Imported 1988-1989 only.

| | $395 | $350 | $315 | $285 | $240 | $215 | $185 |

Last Mfg.'s Sug. Retail was $460.

This model was imported exclusively by FIE Firearms located in Hialeah, FL.

ALCIONE MODEL — 12 ga., 28 in. barrels, less engraving than Alcione SL, separated barrels. Importation disc. 1989.

| | $675 | $550 | $495 | $460 | $430 | $380 | $335 |

Last Mfg.'s Sug. Retail was $800.

Previously designated Diamond Model.

This model was imported exclusively by FIE Firearms located in Hialeah, FL.

ALCIONE SL — 12 ga., 27 or 28 in. barrels, 6 lbs. 13 oz., separated barrels, ejectors, single trigger, silver finished receiver engraved with luggage case. Importation disc. 1986.

| | $1,150 | $995 | $875 | $800 | $725 | $640 | $550 |

Last Mfg.'s Sug. Retail was $1,595.

BLACK MAGIC SPORTING HUNTER — 12 ga. only, 3 in. chambers, 28 in. separated barrels with VR and Franchokes, black receiver with gold accents and trigger, SST, ejectors, checkered walnut stock and forearm, 7 lbs. Importation began 1989.

| Mfg.'s Sug. Retail | $1,249 | $1,060 | $875 | $800 | $725 | $650 | $575 | $495 |

The Black Magic Model Series is imported exclusively by American Arms, Inc. located in North Kansas City, MO.

Black Magic Lightweight Hunter — similar to Black Magic Sporting Hunter except 2¾ in. chambers only, 26 in. separated barrels with VR and Franchokes, alloy receiver, 6 lbs. Importation began 1989.

| Mfg.'s Sug. Retail | $1,209 | $1,035 | $850 | $775 | $700 | $625 | $550 | $475 |

ARISTOCRAT FIELD — 12 ga., 26, 28, or 30 in. barrels, various chokes, vent rib, auto ejectors, boxlock, selective single trigger, checkered pistol grip stock. Mfg. 1960-1969.

| | $660 | $470 | $440 | $395 | $375 | $340 | $310 |

ARISTOCRAT MAGNUM — same as Field, except 32 in. barrel, 3 in. chamber, full choke, pad. Mfg. 1962-1965.

| | $660 | $470 | $440 | $395 | $375 | $340 | $310 |

ARISTOCRAT SKEET — same as Field, but 26 in. vent rib, bored skeet no. 1 and no. 2. Mfg. 1960-1969.

| | $715 | $525 | $495 | $450 | $430 | $395 | $365 |

ARISTOCRAT TRAP — 30 in. vent rib barrel, bored mod. and full, trap stock Mfg. 1960-1969.

| | $745 | $550 | $525 | $480 | $455 | $415 | $380 |

ARISTOCRAT SILVER KING — select wood, engraved coin finished receiver. Mfg. 1962-1969.

| | $750 | $560 | $535 | $485 | $470 | $430 | $400 |

ARISTOCRAT DELUXE — finer wood, more engraving. Mfg. 1960-1966.

| | $990 | $870 | $835 | $810 | $770 | $715 | $660 |

ARISTOCRAT SUPREME — gold inlaid game birds. Mfg. 1960-1966.

| | $1,430 | $1,265 | $1,155 | $1,075 | $990 | $935 | $880 |

ARISTOCRAT IMPERIAL — high grade wood, more engraving. Mfg. 1967-1969.

| | $2,640 | $2,200 | $2,090 | $1,925 | $1,815 | $1,650 | $1,430 |

ARISTOCRAT MONTE CARLO — highest grade wood, elaborate engraving and inlay, mfg. 1967-1969.

| | $3,520 | $3,080 | $2,915 | $2,640 | $2,420 | $2,090 | $1,870 |

Grading	100%	98%	95%	90%	80%	70%	60%

FALCONET S — 12 ga., lightweight model of the Alcione SL, 27 or 28 in. barrels, 6 lbs. 1 oz., separated barrels, moderate engraving on silver finish receiver. Disc. 1985.

	$895	$765	$660	$560	$510	$460	$410

Last Mfg.'s Sug. Retail was $1,015.

FALCONET FIELD — 12, 16, 20, 28, or .410 ga., 24-30 in. barrels, various chokes, auto ejectors, select single trigger, engraved alloy receiver, checkered walnut stock. Mfg. 1968-1975.

	100%	98%	95%	90%	80%	70%	60%
Buckskin (light)	$550	$495	$470	$440	$415	$385	$360
Ebony (black)	$550	$495	$470	$440	$415	$385	$360
Silver	$605	$550	$525	$495	$470	$415	$385

28 ga. and .410 — add 25%.

FALCONET SKEET — 26 in. barrels, bored skeet no. 1 and no. 2, wide vent rib, case hardened steel receiver. Mfg. 1970-1974.

	$935	$855	$825	$770	$715	$690	$650

FALCONET INTERNATIONAL SKEET — higher grade wood, more engraving. Mfg. 1970-1974.

	$1,045	$935	$865	$825	$770	$745	$700

FALCONET STANDARD TRAP — 12 ga., 30 in. mod. and full, wide vent rib, trap stock, pad. Mfg. 1970-1974.

	$935	$855	$825	$770	$715	$690	$650

FALCONET INTERNATIONAL TRAP — higher grade wood, more engraving. Mfg. 1970-1974.

	$1,045	$935	$865	$825	$770	$745	$700

PEREGRINE MODEL 451 — 12 ga., 26-28 in. barrels, various chokes, vent rib, auto ejectors, alloy receiver, selective single trigger, checkered pistol grip stock. Mfg. 1975.

	$605	$550	$525	$495	$440	$415	$360

PEREGRINE MODEL 400 — same as 451, except steel receiver. Mfg. 1975.

	$660	$605	$570	$540	$495	$460	$385

MODEL 2003 TRAP — 12 ga., 30 or 32 in. barrels, imp. mod. and full, or full and full, boxlock, auto ejectors, single selective trigger, high vent rib, trap style stock, pad, cased. Mfg. 1976. Disc.

	$1,205	$1,090	$1,045	$910	$855	$770	$660

MODEL 2004 TRAP — same as 2003, except single barrel, cased. Mfg. 1976. Disc.

	$1,205	$1,090	$1,045	$910	$855	$770	$660

MODEL 2005 COMBINATION TRAP — two sets of barrels, one single, one O/U, cased. Mfg. 1976. Disc.

	$1,815	$1,595	$1,515	$1,320	$1,210	$1,075	$935

MODEL 2005/3 COMBINATION TRAP — three sets of barrels, cased. Mfg. 1976. Disc.

	$2,420	$2,090	$1,980	$1,705	$1,515	$1,485	$1,320

UNDERGUN MODEL 3000 — radical competition trap, very high rib separated barrels, single and O/U, set cased. Disc.

	$2,750	$2,530	$2,310	$2,090	$1,980	$1,870	$1,760

SHOTGUNS: SIDE-BY-SIDE

AIRONE — .12 ga., double barrel, choice of barrel length and chokes, box lock, Anson & Deeley, auto ejectors, double triggers, checkered English style stock, engraved. Mfg. 1940-1950.

	$1,320	$1,100	$935	$825	$745	$715	$660

ASTORE — double barrel, similar to Airone, except less engraving, extractors. Mfg. 1937-1960.

	$990	$910	$770	$715	$635	$580	$550

Grading	100%	98%	95%	90%	80%	70%	60%

ASTORE 5 — same as Astore, except higher grade wood, more engraving, auto ejectors. Disc.

	$2,200	$1,925	$1,650	$1,540	$1,460	$1,375	$1,320

ASTORE II — similar to Astore 5, except less elaborate, currently mfg. in Spain for Franchi.

	$1,210	$1,045	$935	$880	$800	$715	$660

SIDELOCK DOUBLE BARREL — 12, 16, or 20 ga., barrels and choke custom order, stock to order, hand detachable side lock, self-opening action, auto ejectors, six grades offered, they differ only in overall quality and ornamentation, and grade of wood used.

	100%	98%	95%	90%	80%	70%	60%
Condor	$7,700	$6,600	$6,050	$5,720	$5,500	$4,620	$3,960
Imperial	$10,450	$9,350	$8,800	$8,250	$7,480	$6,600	$5,720
Imperiales	$10,670	$9,570	$9,020	$8,470	$7,700	$6,820	$5,940

SIDE-LOCK DOUBLE BARREL

No. 5 Imperial Monte Carlo

	$15,400	$13,200	$11,000	$9,900	$9,350	$8,250	$7,150

No. 11 Imperial Monte Carlo

	$16,500	$14,300	$12,100	$11,000	$10,450	$9,350	$8,250

Imperial Monte Carlo Extra

	$19,800	$17,050	$14,300	$13,200	$12,650	$11,000	$9,900

Note: Imperial Monte Carlo Extra is currently being mfg. on special order only; the other models are disc.

FRANCOTTE, AUGUSTE & CIE. S.A.

Manufacturer located in Liege, Belgium since 1805. Currently imported exclusively by Armes De Chasse located in Chadds Ford, PA. Previously imported by VL&O between 1900-1930's, Abercrombie & Fitch until approx. 1982.

Prices below reflect the recent devaluation of the U.S. dollar against some foreign currencies. While the manufacturer's suggested retails have gone up considerably, prices for used specimens (98% or less original condition) have not increased proportionately, and in some cases, have changed very little.

SHOTGUNS

The models listed below are also available in 24 or 32 ga. upon special order.

BOXLOCK SXS — premium grade Belgium side-by-side, double triggers standard, auto ejectors, sideplates (except Knockabout). Available in 12, 16, 20, 28, or .410 ga., with gold inlaid bird scenes, Anson & Deeley boxlock action.

Mfg.'s Sug. Retail	$15,642	$14,850	$11,000	$8,000	$6,250	$5,000	$4,000	$3,250

Add $1,531 for 28 or .410 ga.

Add $1,449 for sideplates with engraving.

Deluxe Anson & Deeley — gold inlaid game scenes.
Prices and options are quoted per individual request.

SIDELOCK SXS — true sidelock action, available in 12, 16, 20, 28, or .410 ($1,200 extra) ga., Arabesque scroll engraving, various chokes and barrel lengths, custom order only.

Mfg.'s Sug. Retail	$27,310	$26,000	$21,500	$18,500	$15,000	$12,000	$9,000	$7,750

Add $2,724 for 28 or .410 ga.

Deluxe sidelock — same as above, except with gold inlaid game scenes.
Prices and options are quoted per individual request.

JUBILEE

	100%	98%	95%	90%	80%	70%	60%
	$1,595	$1,430	$1,265	$1,100	$990	$825	$715
No. 14	$2,000	$1,900	$1,800	$1,650	$1,500	$1,450	$1,200
No. 18	$2,500	$2,400	$2,250	$2,000	$1,800	$1,600	$1,300
No. 20	$3,000	$2,600	$2,350	$2,100	$1,900	$1,700	$1,500
No. 25	$3,500	$3,000	$2,500	$2,200	$2,100	$1,900	$1,700
No. 30	$5,000	$4,500	$4,000	$3,500	$2,500	$2,200	$2,000

Grading	100%	98%	95%	90%	80%	70%	60%

KNOCKABOUT

	$1,265	$1,100	$935	$825	$715	$635	$550

Add 20% for 20 ga.
Add 30% for 28 ga.
Add 40% for .410 ga.

NO. 45 EAGLE GRADE

	$5,850	$4,950	$4,250	$3,800	$3,000	$2,650	$2,250

RIFLES

All newly mfg. rifles in this section are custom made to the purchaser's individual specifications.

BOLT ACTION MODEL — many calibers available between .222 Rem. and .505 Gibbs Mag., select checkered walnut stock, engraved mag. floor plate, available by special order only.

Short Bolt Action — .222 Rem., .243 Win., .308 Win., short action.

Mfg.'s Sug. Retail	$10,173	$9,100	$7,250	$6,000	$4,950	$4,100	$3,300	$2,700

Standard Model — .30-06, .270 Win., or 7 x 64mm cal., medium action.

Mfg.'s Sug. Retail	$8,173	$7,575	$6,000	$4,950	$4,100	$3,300	$2,700	$2,000

Magnum Action — .416 Rigby, .460 Wby., .505 Gibbs, long action.

Mfg.'s Sug. Retail	$14,068	$13,150	$10,650	$9,250	$7,750	$6,400	$4,950	$3,950

SINGLE SHOT MOUNTAIN RIFLE — available in a variety of cal.'s, boxlock or sidelock action, custom order only, rimless cal.'s are also available upon request.

Boxlock Mountain Rifle — 5.6 x 60, 5 x 57R, or 7 x 65R cal.

Mfg.'s Sug. Retail	$14,482	$13,400	$10,850	$9,350	$7,850	$6,500	$5,000	$4,000

Add $1,449 for optional sideplates.

Sidelock Mountain Rifle — 7 x 65R or 7mm Rem. Mag. cal.

Mfg.'s Sug. Retail	$26,275	$24,000	$20,000	$16,500	$13,000	$10,500	$9,000	$8,000

STANDARD SXS BOXLOCK RIFLE — available in a variety of cal.'s, custom order only.

Mfg.'s Sug. Retail	$19,103	$18,000	$15,250	$11,250	$8,750	$6,950	$5,750	$5,000

Add $1,449 for optional sideplates.
Add $1,788 for .375 H&H or .458 Win. Mag. cal.

STANDARD SXS SIDELOCK RIFLE — available in a variety of cal.'s, custom order only.

Mfg.'s Sug. Retail	$30,034	$28,250	$24,500	$20,000	$16,500	$13,000	$10,500	$9,000

Add $6,586 for larger cal.'s.
A special Safari Sidelock is also available upon special request.

FRASER, DANL. & CO.

Manufacturer located in Europe. Limited importation into the United States.

Danl. Fraser & Co. has been building rifles since 1873 (originally in Edinburgh, Scotland).

HIGHLANDER SINGLE SHOT — .22 LR or .22 Hornet cal., underlever falling block action (color case hardened), 24 in. (½ round, ½ octagon) barrel, folding express-style sights, pistol grip walnut stock with fine checkering. Disc.

	$415	$335	$300	$280	$260	$240	$220

Last Mfg.'s Sug. Retail was $475.

Royal Highlander — .22 LR or .22 Hornet cal., mfg. in Scotland, rose and scroll engraving with 18Kt. inlays. Special order only — prices available upon request.

FRASER FIREARMS CORP.

Previously manufactured by R.B. Industries, Ltd. until 1990. Previously distributed by Fraser Firearms Corp. located in Fraser, MI.

Grading	100%	98%	95%	90%	80%	70%	60%

FRASER 25 CAL. — .25 cal. only, copy of the Bauer semi-auto pocket model, 6 shot mag., 2¼ in. barrel, stainless steel construction.

	$120	$100	$90				

Add $17 for Model 2 (black nylon grips).

Add $115 for Model 3 (24 Kt. gold plated).

Last Mfg.'s Sug. Retail was $133.

FREEDOM ARMS
Manufacturer located in Freedom, WY.

Percussion mini-revolvers can be found in the Blackpowder Section of this text.

MINI-REVOLVERS: STAINLESS STEEL

Because Freedom Arms' manufacturing capacity has been maximized due to the success of the .454 Casull revolver, the mini-revolver series has been temporarily discontinued starting in 1989. As a result, prices have escalated on these models due to no production and normal demand.

FA-S-22LR (PATRIOT) — .22 LR cal., 5 shot, 1, 1¾ (disc. 1988), or 3 (disc. 1988) in. barrel, Hi-Gloss finish.

	$175	$125	$95				

Add $15 for 3 in. barrel model (FA-BG-22LR, Minute-Man, disc. 1988).

Last Mfg.'s Sug. Retail was $153.

FA-S-22M (IRONSIDES) — .22 Mag. cal., 4 shot, 1, 1¾ (disc. 1988), or 3 in. barrel, Hi Gloss finish.

	$190	$150	$110				

Add $43 for 3 in. barrel model (Bostonian).

Last Mfg.'s Sug. Retail was $177.

FA-S-22-LR BUCKLE/REVOLVER COMBINATION — .22 LR, 1 in. barrel, pistol is housed in belt buckle.

	$210	$165	$135				

Last Mfg.'s Sug. Retail was $193.

.22 Mag. cal.

	$240	$185	$150				

Last Mfg.'s Sug. Retail was $216.

CASULL SA REVOLVERS: STAINLESS STEEL

MODEL 252 — .22 LR cal., 5 shot, unique two point firing pin, choice of 7½ (Varmint Class Model with express sights, black/green laminated hardwood grips) or 10 in. (Silhouette Class Model with competition sights and black micarta grips), approx. 3¾ lbs. New 1991.

Mfg.'s Sug. Retail	$1,248	$1,080	$850	$725			

Add $189 for extra .22 Mag. cylinder.

Add $47 for 10 in. barrel (Silhouette Class).

.454 CASULL FIELD GRADE — .44 Mag. (new 1991) or .454 Casull cal., 4¾ (fixed sight only), 6, 7½, or 10 in. barrel, stainless steel matte finish with Pachmayr presentation grips. New 1988.

Mfg.'s Sug. Retail	$882	$775	$640	$525			

Add $84 for adj. sights.

Add $189 for extra .45 LC or .45 ACP (new 1990) cylinder.

Add $84 for .44 Mag. cal. (7½ or 10 in. barrel only).

Silhouette Pak — .44 Mag., includes 10 in. barrel revolver, silhouette competition sight, honed action with 3 lb. trigger pull, plastic grips, locking aluminum carrying case with cleaning kit and tool. Mfg. 1990 only.

	$1,000	$850	$750				

Last Mfg.'s Sug. Retail was $1,180.

Grading	100%	98%	95%	90%	80%	70%	60%

Hunter Pak — .454 Casull, 7½ in. barrel, plastic grips, field grade low profile adj. sight, sling and studs, locking aluminum carrying case with cleaning kit and tool. New 1990.

Mfg.'s Sug. Retail	$1,194	$1,060	$875	$750

Add $224 for Leupold 2X scope with rings and base.

.454 CASULL PREMIER GRADE — .44 Rem. Mag., .44 Win. Mag. (disc. 1989), .45 LC (disc. 1990), or .454 Casull cal., 5 shot, stainless steel with brushed finish, single action revolver, the .454 Casull shoots 225 grain bullet at over 2000 fps., 4¾, 6, 7½, 10, and 12 (disc. 1988) in. barrels, walnut (older mfg.) or impregnated hardwood grips. Mfg. 1983-present.

Mfg.'s Sug. Retail	$1,133	$995	$800	$650

Add $66 for no sights.

Add $109 for .44 Mag. cal.

The no sights model is available in 7½ in. barrel only -receiver is drilled and tapped for scope base - new 1990.

Adj. sights

Mfg.'s Sug. Retail	$1,242	$1,075	$850	$725

Add $88-$114 for Mag-na-porting.

Add $112 for SSK Industries T'SOB 3-ring scope mount.

.44 Rem. Mag. or .45 LC cal. is available through the custom shop and are priced on quotation.

Silhouette Pak — .44 Mag., includes 10 in. barrel revolver, silhouette competition sight, honed action with 3 lb. trigger pull, hardwood grips, locking aluminum carrying case with cleaning kit and tool. Mfg. 1990 only.

	$1,275	$995	$850	

Last Mfg.'s Sug. Retail was $1,395.

Hunter Pak — .454 Casull, 7½ in. barrel, ebony micarta grips, premier grade adj. sight, sling and studs, locking aluminum carrying case with cleaning kit and tool. New 1990.

Mfg.'s Sug. Retail	$1,504	$1,340	$995	$850

Add $224 for Leupold 2X scope with rings and base.

U.S. DEPUTY MARSHALL — 3 in. barrel only with no ejector, fixed sights, U.S. Marshall medallion in left hardwood grip. New 1990.

Mfg.'s Sug. Retail	$1,257	$1,075	$825	$725

Add $120 for adj. sights.

SIGNATURE EDITION — .454 Casull, high polish stainless steel, 7½ in. barrel only, rosewood grips, cased with accessories ser. no.'s DC1-2000. Limited mfg.

Mfg.'s Sug. Retail	$2,650	$2,300	$1,750	$1,300

PRIMUS INTER PARES — 1 of every 100 guns is made in this variation, includes octagonal barrel, ivory grips, 7½ in. barrel, and cased. Contact the factory directly for prices on this model.

FRENCH MILITARY

Manufactured in various locations In France.

MODEL 1886 LEBEL — bolt action, 8mm Lebel, 32 in. barrel, adj. sight, military stock. Mfg. 1886 - WWII.

	$125	$100	$75	$65	$50	$40	$25

1936 MAS MILITARY RIFLE — bolt action, 7.5mm MAS, 22 in. barrel, adj. sight, military stock, bayonet in forearm. Mfg. 1936-1940.

	$125	$100	$75	$65	$50	$40	$25

MODEL 1935A AUTO PISTOL — 7.65mm long, 8 shot, 4.3 in. barrel, fixed sights, blue, checkered wood grips, French service sidearm. Mfg. 1935-1945.

	$195	$175	$150	$125	$110	$100	$90

M.A.B. MODEL C — 7.65mm, design based on FN Browning Model 1910, 6.1 in. barrel. Introduced 1933.

	$250	$220	$190	$170	$150	$125	$110

Grading	100%	98%	95%	90%	80%	70%	60%

M.A.B. MODEL D — 7.65mm, 7 in barrel, single action, similar to Model C, mfg. commercially 1933-1940, many thousands mfg. for the German military during WWII (marked "Pistole MAB Kaliber 7.65mm")

	100%	98%	95%	90%	80%	70%	60%
	$275	$225	$200	$175	$150	$125	$110

MODEL M.A.B. PA - 15 — 9mm, single action semi-auto, 16 shot, currently used by French military.

	100%	98%	95%
	$700	$595	$450

MODEL M.A.B. PA - 15 TARGET — rare target variation of PA-15, adj. sight, 6 in. barrel, cased.

100%	98%	95%
$1,600	$1,200	$750

FRIGON

Manufactured by Marocchi in Italy. Imported and distributed by Frigon Guns located in Clay Center, KS.

FT I — 12 ga. only, single barrel trap gun, blued finish, 32 or 34 in. VR barrel, quick-change stock. New 1986.

Mfg.'s Sug. Retail	$975	$825	$600	$495	$435	$375	$350	$295

FTC — 12 ga. only, quick-change stock, trap combination gun includes 1 single barrel and 1 set of O/U barrels, cased. New 1986.

Mfg.'s Sug. Retail	$1,775	$1,500	$1,225	$1,025	$875	$775	$685	$620

FS-4 — 4-barrel skeet set including 12, 20, 28, or .410 ga., individual forearms, quick-change stock, vent barrels (except for .410 ga.), cased. New 1986.

Mfg.'s Sug. Retail	$2,600	$2,250	$1,850	$1,650	$1,475	$1,350	$1,250	$1,150

FROMMER PISTOLS

Femaru-Febyver-Es Gepgyar R.T., Budapest, Hungary.

Please refer to the Femaru listing in this section.

FURR ARMS

Manufacturer located in Orem, UT.

Please refer to the Gatling Gun Company listing in this text.

G

GALEF SHOTGUNS

Previous importer of Zabal Hermanos (Spanish) and Antonio Zoli (Italian) shotguns.

Grading	100%	98%	95%	90%	80%	70%	60%

COMPANION FOLDING SINGLE BARREL — 12, 16, 20, 28, or .410 ga., 28 in. barrel, full choke, 30 in. full, 12 ga. only, hammerless, underlever, checkered pistol grip stock.

	$110	$95	$85	$75	$65	$55	$45

MONTE CARLO TRAP — 12 ga., single barrel, 32 in. full vent rib, hammerless, underlever, recoil pad, checkered pistol grip Monte Carlo stock, disc.

	$225	$185	$175	$150	$135	$125	$100

SILVER SNIPE — 12 or 20 ga., O/U, 3 in. chambers, 26, 28, or 30 in. barrels, imp. cyl. and mod. or full and mod. vent rib, checkered pistol grip stock, boxlock, extractors, single trigger, mfg. by Angelo Zoli, disc.

	$450	$400	$350	$295	$275	$250	$220

GOLDEN SNIPE — O/U, same as Silver Snipe, except auto ejectors.

	$525	$475	$425	$375	$325	$300	$275

SILVER HAWK — 12 or 20 ga., SxS, 3 in. chambers, 26, 28, or 30 in. barrels, imp. cyl. and mod. or mod. and full, boxlock, extractors, checkered pistol grip and beavertail forearm. Mfg. by Angelo Zoli, 1968-1972.

	$395	$365	$325	$285	$255	$225	$200

GALEF ZABALA DOUBLE — 10, 12, 16, or 20 ga., S x S, 22, 26, 28, or 30 in. barrels, boxlock, extractors.

	100%	98%	95%	90%	80%	70%	60%
10 gauge	$250	$230	$200	$175	$150	$140	$125
Other gauges	$200	$175	$150	$130	$120	$110	$100

GALIL

Manufactured by Israel Military Industries (IMI). Currently imported by Springfield Armory located in Geneseo, IL starting in 1991. Previous importers were Action Arms, Ltd. located in Philadelphia, PA. and Magnum Research, Inc., located In Minneapolis, MN.

MODEL AR — .223 cal. or .308 cal., semi-auto paramilitary design rifle, gas operated - rotating bolt, 16.1 in. (.223 only) or 19 in. (.308 only) barrel, parkerized, folding stock. Flip-up Tritium night sights. 8.6 lbs.

	$1,050	$900	$775	$650	$575	$500	$425

Last Mfg.'s Sug. Retail was $950.

GALIL SPORTER — similar to above, except has one-piece thumbhole stock and 5 shot mag. Importation began 1991.

Mfg.'s Sug. Retail	$1,423	$1,320	$1,125	$995	$825	$700	$600	$500

MODEL ARM — similar to Model AR, except includes folding bipod, vented hardwood handguard, and carrying handle.

	$1,150	$950	$825	$700	$600	$525	$450

Last Mfg.'s Sug. Retail was $1,050.

HADAR II — .308 cal., gas operated, hunting rifle configuration, 1 piece walnut thumbhole stock with pistol grip and forearm, 18½ in. barrel, adj. rear sight, recoil pad, 4 shot (standard) or 25 shot mag., 10.3 lbs. Imported 1989 only.

	$950	$850	$750	$650	$600	$540	$475

Last Mfg.'s Sug. Retail was $998.

Grading	100%	98%	95%	90%	80%	70%	60%

SNIPER OUTFIT — .308 cal., semi-auto, limited production, sniper model built to exact specifications for improved accuracy, 20 in. heavy barrel, hardwood folding stock (adj. cheek piece) and forearm, includes Tritium night sights, bipod, detachable 6 X 40mm Nimrod scope, two 25 shot mag.'s, carrying/storage case, 14.1 lbs. Imported 1989 only.

	$4,000	$3,500	$3,000	$2,650	$2,150	$1,750	$1,300

Last Mfg.'s Sug. Retail was $3,995.

GAMBA, RENATO

Manufacturer located in Gardone V.T., Italy. Pistols were previously imported and distributed (until 1990) by Armscorp Of America, Inc. located in Baltimore, MD. Gamba shotguns are currently imported and distributed by Heckler & Koch, Inc. located in Sterling, VA.

Renato Gamba firearms have had limited importation since 1986. In 1989, several smaller European firearms companies were purchased by R. Gamba and are now part of the Renato Gamba Group. The importation of R. Gamba guns changed in 1990 to reflect their long term interest in exporting firearms to America. Earlier imported models may be rare but have not enjoyed much collectability to date.

PISTOLS

R. Gamba pistols are currently not being imported into the U.S. Importation was discontinued in 1990.

SAB G90 STANDARD — 7.65 P (disc.), 9 x 18mm Ultra (disc.), or 9mm Para. cal., double action, 4.72 in. barrel, 15 shot side release mag., blue or chrome (disc.) finish, hammer drop safety on frame, smooth walnut grips, 2.2 lbs.

	$415	$325	$300	$280	$260	$240	$225

Add $65 for chrome finish (disc.).
Last Mfg.'s Sug. Retail was $475.

SAB G90 Competition — 9mm Para., similar to SAB G90 Standard, except has adj. rear sight, "cocked and locked" operation, and checkered walnut grips. Imported 1990 only.

	$465	$375	$325	$300	$275	$250	$230

Last Mfg.'s Sug. Retail was $550.

SAB G91 COMPACT — similar to SAB G90, except has 3.54 in. barrel, 12 shot mag., 1.87 lbs.

	$430	$340	$315	$295	$270	$250	$230

Add $65 for chrome finish (disc.).
Last Mfg.'s Sug. Retail was $500.

SAB G91 Competition — 9mm Para., similar to SAB G91 Compact, except has adj. rear sight, "cocked and locked" operation, and checkered walnut grips. Imported 1990 only.

	$475	$380	$330	$300	$275	$250	$230

Last Mfg.'s Sug. Retail was $575.

REVOLVERS

R. Gamba revolvers have not been imported since 1986.

TRIDENT FAST ACTION — .32 S&W or .38 Spl. cal., 2½ or 3 in. barrel, double action, blued receiver with checkered walnut grips, 6 shot, 23 oz.

	$495	$395	$360	$330	$295	$270	$245

Last Mfg.'s Sug. Retail was $595.

TRIDENT SUPER — .32 S&W or .38 Spl. cal., 4 in. vent rib barrel, 6 shot, double action, checkered walnut grips, 25 oz.

	$530	$425	$380	$345	$300	$270	$245

Last Mfg.'s Sug. Retail was $645.

TRIDENT MATCH 900 — .32 W.C. or .38 Spl. cal., match gun featuring 6 in. heavy barrel and anatomically compatible checkered walnut grips, target sights, 2.2 lbs.

	$750	$660	$590	$525	$475	$430	$390

Last Mfg.'s Sug. Retail was $995.

Grading	100%	98%	95%	90%	80%	70%	60%

Trident Match 901 — similar to Trident Match 900.

	100%	98%	95%	90%	80%	70%	60%
	$750	$660	$590	$525	$475	$430	$390

Last Mfg.'s Sug. Retail was $995.

RIFLES

R. Gamba rifles have not been imported since 1986.

SAFARI EXPRESS — 7 x 65R, 9.3 x 74R, or .375 H&H cal., 25 in. barrels with open sights, underlug locking with Greener crossbolt, ejectors except on .375 H&H, coin finished receiver with scroll work and game scene engraving, DT's, deluxe checkered walnut stock with cheek piece and recoil pad, 9.9 lbs.

	100%	98%	95%	90%	80%	70%	60%
	$5,685	$4,575	$3,950	$3,575	$3,175	$2,850	$2,500

Last Mfg.'s Sug. Retail was $6,630.

MUSTANG — 5.6 x 50, 6.5 x 57R, 7 x 65R, .222 Rem., .270 Win., or .30-06 cal., single 25½ in. barrel configuration with highly engraved sidelock action, double-set triggers, best quality checkered walnut stock and forearm, 6.17 lbs.

	100%	98%	95%	90%	80%	70%	60%
	$11,000	$8,750	$7,950	$7,275	$6,600	$6,000	$5,450

Last Mfg.'s Sug. Retail was $12,930.

RGZ 1000 — 7 x 64, .270 Win., 7mm Rem. Mag., .300 Win. Mag., modified Mauser K-98 action, 20½ in. barrel, pistol grip stock with cheek piece, 7 lbs.

	100%	98%	95%	90%	80%	70%	60%
	$1,100	$885	$825	$760	$700	$640	$575

Last Mfg.'s Sug. Retail was $1,310.

RGX 1000 Express — similar to RGZ 1000, except has 23¾ in. barrel and double set triggers, 7.7 lbs.

	100%	98%	95%	90%	80%	70%	60%
	$1,255	$960	$875	$795	$725	$650	$575

Last Mfg.'s Sug. Retail was $1,475.

SHOTGUNS: OVER AND UNDER

Heckler & Koch, Inc. located in Sterling, VA is the exclusive importer for R. Gamba shotguns. Most O/U models (except for the Daytona Trap Model) listed below were discontinued in 1990 when H&K became the exclusive importer for R. Gamba shotguns.

COUNTRY MODEL — 12 or 20 ga., DT's, extractors, checkered walnut stock and forearm.

	100%	98%	95%	90%	80%	70%	60%
	$650	$520	$485	$455	$430	$395	$365

Last Mfg.'s Sug. Retail was $765.

GRIFONE MODEL — 12 or 20 ga., engraved, silver finished boxlock action, vent barrels and rib, deluxe checkered walnut, SST, ejectors, 7.05 lbs.

	100%	98%	95%	90%	80%	70%	60%
	$795	$630	$575	$525	$475	$430	$390

Add $50 for single trigger.
Add $98 for multi-choke option.
Last Mfg.'s Sug. Retail was $935.

EUROPA 2000 — 12 ga. only, engraved, silver finished boxlock action with sideplates, vent rib, single trigger, ejectors, deluxe checkered stock and forearm, 6.84 lbs.

	100%	98%	95%	90%	80%	70%	60%
	$1,250	$995	$895	$835	$775	$715	$650

Last Mfg.'s Sug. Retail was $1,475.

EDINBURGH SUPER SLUG — 12 ga. only, trap model, SST, ejectors, engraved action, deluxe checkered stock and forearm.

	100%	98%	95%	90%	80%	70%	60%
	$1,225	$980	$895	$835	$775	$715	$650

Last Mfg.'s Sug. Retail was $1,425.

GRIFONE SPORTING TRAP — 12 ga. only, trap model, SST, ejectors, moderately engraved action, deluxe checkered stock and forearm.

	100%	98%	95%	90%	80%	70%	60%
	$1,225	$980	$895	$835	$775	$715	$650

Last Mfg.'s Sug. Retail was $1,425.

Grading	100%	98%	95%	90%	80%	70%	60%

GRINTA TRAP/SKEET — 12 ga. only, trap/skeet model, SST, ejectors, medium engraving coverage.

	$1,460	$1,250	$995	$895	$835	$775	$715

Last Mfg.'s Sug. Retail was $1,710.

VICTORY TRAP/SKEET — similar to Grinta Model, except has better walnut and more engraving.

	$1,620	$1,295	$1,100	$995	$895	$835	$775

Last Mfg.'s Sug. Retail was $1,905.

EDINBURG MATCH — similar to Victory Model, except has different style of engraving.

	$1,630	$1,300	$1,100	$995	$895	$835	$775

Last Mfg.'s Sug. Retail was $1,930.

MONTREAL MODEL 81 — 12 ga. only, boxlock, interchangeable trigger assembly, select walnut, vent rib. Available in International Trap, American Skeet, Sporting, and Field models. Add $50 for adj. single barrel.

	$1,995	$1,500	$1,300	$1,100	$1,000	$900	$800

MONTREAL 81 AMERICAN TRAP COMBO — 12 ga. only, 32 in. barrels and adj. impact, single 34 in. barrel, interchangeable trigger assembly.

	$2,800	$2,100	$1,820	$1,540	$1,400	$1,260	$1,120

SINGLE BARREL TRAP-MODEL 496 — 12 ga. only, boxlock, vent rib.

	$1,150	$865	$750	$635	$575	$520	$460

S. VINCENT 580 EXTRA DELUXE SXS — 12 ga. only, custom made to individual preferences, very high quality, sidelock action, engraving coverage 100%.

	$3,250	$2,440	$2,115	$1,790	$1,625	$1,465	$1,300

DAYTONA MODEL — 12 ga. only, boxlock action, SST, ejectors, available in either Trap, Skeet, or Sporting Clays configuration, deluxe walnut with fine English scroll engraving with game scenes. Importation began 1990.

Mfg.'s Sug. Retail	$5,400	$4,800	$3,950	$3,300	$2,800	$2,350	$1,900	$1,500

Add approx. $1,750-$2,000 for extra set of competition barrels.

Daytona SL — deluxe variation of the Daytona Model, except has sidelocks and sideplates with extensive engraving, includes case. Importation began 1990.

Mfg.'s Sug. Retail	$16,380	$14,900	$11,750	$9,750	$8,000	$6,500	$5,000	$4,250

Daytona SL HH — H&H style sidelocks, top of the line model, includes case. Importation began in 1990.

Mfg.'s Sug. Retail	$28,000	$24,250	$19,995	$15,750	$12,450	$10,000	$8,750	$7,950

BAYERN 88 COMBINATION GUN — 12 ga. over same cal.'s listed for Mustang Model, coin finished boxlock action with game scene engraving, double DT's, extractors, deluxe checkered walnut stock with recoil pad, 7½ lbs.

	$1,365	$1,050	$950	$860	$775	$715	$665

Last Mfg.'s Sug. Retail was $1,595.

SHOTGUNS: SIDE X SIDE

Previous to 1989, most of the models listed below were available in 28 ga. on a 28 ga. frame by option. These 28 ga. guns will command 15%+ premiums over values listed below.

HUNTER SUPER — 12 ga. only, Anson & Deeley engraved boxlock action with silver finish, DT's, extractors, 6.84 lbs.

	$1,395	$1,100	$865	$760	$630	$575	$525

Last Mfg.'s Sug. Retail was $1,506.

PRINCIPESSA — 12 or 20 ga., similar to Hunter Super except has English straight grip stock and better engraving, 6.62 lbs. Previously imported (until 1989) by Armes de Chasse located in Chadds Ford, PA.

Mfg.'s Sug. Retail	$2,120	$1,900	$1,650	$1,400	$1,200	$995	$800	$625

Add $340 for single trigger.

Grading	100%	98%	95%	90%	80%	70%	60%

OXFORD 90 — 12 or 20 ga., boxlock action with Purdey locking system, DT's, ejectors, scroll engraving, deluxe checkered straight grip walnut stock with recoil pad or checkered butt, 6.84 lbs. Previously imported (until 1989) by Armes de Chasse located in Chadds Ford, PA.

Mfg.'s Sug. Retail	$2,540	$2,300	$1,900	$1,650	$1,400	$1,200	$995	$800

Add $335 for single trigger.

LONDON — 12 or 20 ga., H&H side-lock system, ejectors, DT or SST, deluxe checkered straight grip stock and forearm, 6.84 lbs. Previously imported (until 1989) by Armes de Chasse located in Chadds Ford, PA.

Mfg.'s Sug. Retail	$8,665	$7,900	$6,250	$5,000	$4,000	$3,600	$3,200	$2,950

LONDON ROYAL — similar to London Model except has less extensive game scene engraving.

	$5,250	$4,350	$3,750	$3,300	$3,050	$2,800	$2,500

Last Mfg.'s Sug. Retail was $6,730.

AMBASSADOR GOLDEN BLACK — 12 or 20 ga., H&H side-lock system, gold-line engraving on barrels and receiver, single trigger, ejectors, deluxe checkered walnut stock and forearm, 6.4 lbs.

Mfg.'s Sug. Retail	$16,460	$13,750	$11,000	$8,950	$7,950	$7,275	$6,600	$6,000

Add $255 for English style engraving.

AMBASSADOR EXECUTIVE — 12 or 20 ga. only, top-of-the-line model, made to individual order only, every possible refinement.

Mfg.'s Sug. Retail	$27,150	$23,410	$19,995	$15,750	$12,450	$10,000	$8,750	$7,950

Add $5,695 for extra barrel set when ordered with gun.

SHOTGUNS: FOLDING ACTION

These models had limited importation. All models were disc. 1990.

MILANO 1 — all gauges, single barrel with vent rib, checkered stock and forearm with sling swivels, 5¾ lbs.

	$315	$250	$220	$185	$150	$125	$105

Last Mfg.'s Sug. Retail was $365.

Milano 2 — similar to Milano 1.

	$320	$255	$220	$185	$150	$125	$105

Last Mfg.'s Sug. Retail was $380.

Milano 3 — similar to Milano 2.

	$320	$255	$220	$185	$150	$125	$105

Last Mfg.'s Sug. Retail was $390.

LS 2000 — 12, 20, 28, or .410 ga., O/U configuration, single trigger, extractors, vent rib, engraved action, 6.3 lbs.

	$545	$390	$330	$295	$260	$235	$205

Last Mfg.'s Sug. Retail was $630.

SHOTGUNS: SLIDE ACTION

MODEL 2100 — 12 ga. Mag., 19½ in. barrel, 7 shot mag., law enforcement configuration with matte black metal and wood, 6.62 lbs. Limited importation.

	$610	$480	$390	$330	$275	$220	$195

Last Mfg.'s Sug. Retail was $715.

GARBI

Manufacturer located in Eibar, Spain. Distributed by W.L. Moore & Co. located in Westlake Village, CA.

SHOTGUNS: DISCONTINUED SIDE-BY-SIDE

Currently, Garbi is mfg. 400-500 shotguns per year.

Grading	100%	98%	95%	90%	80%	70%	60%

MODEL 51 A — 12 ga. only, extractors, case hardened finish, straight grip.

	100%	98%	95%	90%	80%	70%	60%
	$450	$350	$325	$300	$280	$260	$240

MODEL 51 B — 12, 16, or 20 ga., ejectors, case hardened or coin finish receiver, straight grip.

	$850	$650	$590	$540	$500	$460	$420

MODEL 60 A — 12 ga. only, extractors, case hardened finish, true sidelock, large scroll engraving, cocking indicators, hand checkered butt, choice of grip.

	$725	$575	$530	$475	$440	$400	$360

MODEL 60 B — 12, 16, or 20 ga., ejectors, case hardened or coin finish receiver, extensive engraving, straight grip.

	$1,200	$850	$790	$735	$680	$630	$575

MODEL 62 A — 12 ga. only, extractors, case hardened finish, true sidelock, light engraving, cocking indicators, hand checkered butt, choice of grip.

	$725	$575	$530	$475	$440	$400	$360

MODEL 62 B — 12, 16, or 20 ga. only, ejectors, case hardened or coin finish receiver, extensive engraving, straight grip.

	$1,200	$850	$790	$735	$680	$630	$575

SHOTGUNS: SXS RECENT MFG.

Garbi currently manufactures between 400 - 500 shotguns yearly.

For the following models — add $250 for 28 ga., $300 for single trigger, $75-$150 for beavertail forearm, $600-$1,300 per extra set of barrels (depending on grade), and $150 for Churchill style level file-cut rib.

MODEL 71 — 12, 16, or 20 ga., Holland-pattern detachable sidelock ejector double, fine English scroll engraving, oil finish, select walnut, articulated trigger. Importation disc. 1988.

	$2,250	$1,825	$1,500	$1,300	$1,075	$980	$900

Last Mfg.'s Sug. Retail was $2,600.

MODEL 100 — 12, 16, or 20 ga., Holland-pattern detachable sidelock ejector double, Purdy style scroll engraving, chopper lump barrels, oil finish, select walnut, articulated trigger.

Mfg.'s Sug. Retail	$3,850	$3,400	$2,700	$2,100	$1,650	$1,450	$1,200	$1,025

MODEL 101 — 12, 16, or 20 ga., Holland-pattern sidelock ejector double with chopper lump barrels, Continental style floral and scroll engraving, selected walnut stock.

Mfg.'s Sug. Retail	$4,500	$4,050	$3,300	$2,700	$2,250	$1,900	$1,650	$1,400

MODEL 102 — 12, 16, 20, or 28 ga., Holland-pattern sidelock ejector double with chopper lump barrels, Holland-type large scroll engraving, selected walnut stock. Importation disc. 1988.

	$4,100	$3,250	$2,500	$2,200	$1,900	$1,650	$1,400

Last Mfg.'s Sug. Retail was $4,500.

MODEL 103A — 12, 16, 20, or 28 ga., Holland-pattern sidelock ejector double with chopper lump barrels, Purdey-type fine scroll and rosette engraving, selected walnut stock.

Mfg.'s Sug. Retail	$6,100	$5,500	$4,400	$3,450	$2,700	$2,350	$2,000	$1,750

MODEL 103B — 12, 16, 20, or 28 ga., Holland-pattern sidelock ejector double with chopper lump barrels of nickel-chrome steel, H&H type easy opening mechanism, Purdey-type fine scroll and rosette engraving, well figured walnut stock.

Mfg.'s Sug. Retail	$8,300	$7,500	$6,000	$5,150	$4,250	$3,500	$2,750	$2,250

MODEL 120 — 12, 16, 20, or 28 ga., Holland-pattern sidelock ejector double with chopper lump barrels of nickel-chrome steel, H&H type easy opening mechanism, game scene engraving-3 patterns available. Well figured walnut stock.

Mfg.'s Sug. Retail	$7,700	$6,925	$5,700	$4,750	$4,000	$3,250	$2,500	$2,100

Grading	100%	98%	95%	90%	80%	70%	60%

MODEL 200 — 12, 16, 20, or 28 ga., Holland-pattern sidelock ejector double with chopper lump barrels of nickel-chrome steel, heavy-duty locks, magnum proofed, very fine Continental style floral and scroll engraving, well figured walnut stock.

	100%	98%	95%	90%	80%	70%	60%
Mfg.'s Sug. Retail	$8,200	$7,500	$5,950	$4,875	$4,125	$3,375	$2,600	$2,200

SPECIAL WLM — 12, 16, 20, or 28 ga., top-of-the-line Holland-pattern sidelock ejector double with chopper lump barrels, full coverage large scroll engraving, fancy-figured walnut stock. Importation disc. 1988.

	$5,400	$4,325	$3,500	$3,150	$2,700	$2,300	$2,000

Last Mfg.'s Sug. Retail was $6,250.

SPECIAL AG — 12, 16, 20, or 28 ga., top-of-the-line Holland-pattern sidelock ejector double with chopper lump barrels, large scroll engraving patterned after Labeau-Courally, fancy figured walnut stock.

Mfg.'s Sug. Retail	$8,400	$7,625	$6,100	$5,200	$4,300	$3,550	$2,750	$2,300

GASTINE RENETTE

Manufacturer and retailer located in Paris, France.

Currently being manufactured with limited importation and distribution. No Manufacturer's list price is shown in this section. Gastine Renette should be contacted directly (see Trademark Index) for an up-to-date quotation or information on their current model line-up.

RIFLES: BOLT ACTION

MAUSER ACTION — disc. 1989.

	$2,700	$2,000	$1,850	$1,580	$1,430	$1,260	$1,000

DELUXE MAUSER ACTION

No Mfg.'s Retail	$7,500	$5,750	$4,800	$3,750	$2,600	$2,200	$1,750

SHOTGUNS SXS

MODEL 105 — 12 or 20 ga., Anson and Deeley type triple bolt action, ejectors, double triggers, case hardened frame, 6 lbs. 8 oz.

	$1,800	$1,400	$1,250	$1,125	$1,000	$900	$800

MODEL 98 — 12 and 20 ga., Purdey type triple bolt action, ejectors, double triggers, case hardened frame, 6 lbs. 8 oz.

	$2,500	$2,000	$1,850	$1,580	$1,430	$1,260	$1,000

MODEL 202 — 12 or 20 ga., Purdey type triple bolt action, sidelocks, fine English engraving, first grade French walnut, ejectors, double triggers, coin finished receiver, 6 lbs. 10 oz.

	$4,500	$3,950	$3,250	$2,500	$2,175	$1,875	$1,580

MODEL 353 — 12 or 20 ga., Purdey type triple bolt action, hand detachable sidelocks, Chopper lump barrels, fine English engraving, first grade French walnut, ejectors, double triggers, case hardened receiver, best quality, 6 lbs. 10 oz.

	$17,500	$13,650	$11,000	$8,900	$6,700	$6,250	$5,780

DOUBLE RIFLES

The models listed below are older, disc. models.

STANDARD TYPE G — 9.3 x 74R, 7.65R, .30-06, or .375 H&H cal., double bolt action, ejectors, reinforced stock, 23¾ in. barrels, bouquet style engraving with deluxe walnut stock and forearm, 7lbs. 6 oz.

	$2,270	$1,700	$1,560	$1,480	$1,340	$1,250	$1,125

DELUXE TYPE R — 9.3 x 74R, 7.65R, .30-06, or .375 H&H cal., double bolt action, true sideplates, ejectors, reinforced stock, 23¾ in. barrels, animal engraving with deluxe walnut stock and forearm, 7 lbs. 6 oz.

	$2,700	$2,050	$1,850	$1,700	$1,520	$1,390	$1,260

Grading	100%	98%	95%	90%	80%	70%	60%

PRESIDENT TYPE PT — 9.3 x 74R, 7.65R, .30-06, or .375 H&H cal., double bolt action, true sideplates, ejectors, reinforced stock, 23¾ in. barrels, light engraving with gold line inlays, best quality walnut, 7 lbs. 6 oz.

	100%	98%	95%	90%	80%	70%	60%
	$3,160	$2,370	$2,060	$1,850	$1,690	$1,570	$1,400

GATLING GUN COMPANY

Manufactured since 1961 by Furr Arms located in Orem, UT. Distributed by J & G Sales, Inc. located in Prescott, AZ.

The Gatling Gun Company manufactures high quality ⅙, ⅓, ½, ¾ and full scale brass reproductions of famous, antique machine guns and cannons. Models include the 1874 Gatling Gun on carriage (includes 225 round Broadwell feed drum and 10 exposed barrels), 1876 Camel Gun (includes 225 round Broadwell feed drum), 1883 Gatling Gun on carriage (Accles feed drum, 10 enclosed barrels), 1893 Police, British Naval Cannon, and the James Six Pounder. Prices vary according to the complexity of each model, and are available by contacting the distributor.

⅙ *Scale 1874 Carriage Gatling*

Mfg.'s Sug. Retail	$5,000	$5,000	$4,000	$3,500

⅓ *Scale 1874 Carriage Gatling*

Mfg.'s Sug. Retail	$6,500	$6,500	$5,250	$4,250

½ *Scale 1876 Carriage Gatling*

Mfg.'s Sug. Retail	$12,000	$12,000	$9,000	$7,500

¾ *Scale 1876 Carriage Gatling*

Mfg.'s Sug. Retail	$19,000	$19,000	$15,000	$12,000

⅙ *Scale 1874 Camel Tripod*

Mfg.'s Sug. Retail	$4,000	$4,000	$3,000	$2,500

⅓ *Scale 1874 Camel Tripod*

Mfg.'s Sug. Retail	$4,500	$4,500	$3,500	$2,800

½ *Scale 1876 Camel Tripod*

Mfg.'s Sug. Retail	$8,000	$8,000	$6,500	$5,250

¾ *Scale 1876 Camel Tripod*

Mfg.'s Sug. Retail	$12,000	$12,000	$9,000	$7,500

Full *Scale 1876 Camel Tripod*

Mfg.'s Sug. Retail	$18,000	$18,000	$14,500	$11,500

⅙ *Scale 1893 Police Gatling*

Mfg.'s Sug. Retail	$2,500	$2,500	$2,100	$1,650

⅓ *Scale 1893 Police Gatling*

Mfg.'s Sug. Retail	$3,200	$3,200	$2,550	$2,000

⅙ *Scale 1883 Carriage Gatling*

Mfg.'s Sug. Retail	$5,000	$5,000	$4,000	$3,500

⅓ *Scale 1883 Carriage Gatling*

Mfg.'s Sug. Retail	$6,500	$6,500	$5,250	$4,250

⅙ *Scale James Six Pounder Cannon*

Mfg.'s Sug. Retail	$900	$900	$750	$575

⅕ *Scale James Six Pounder Cannon*

Mfg.'s Sug. Retail	$2,200	$2,200	$1,850	$1,400

⅓ *Scale James Six Pounder Cannon*

Mfg.'s Sug. Retail	$3,200	$3,200	$2,550	$2,000

⅒ *Scale H.M.S. Victory Naval Cannon*

Mfg.'s Sug. Retail	$500	$500	$375	$325

⅒ *Scale H.M.S. Victory Naval Cannon* — this cannon is mounted on an oak ship deck section complete with planking, port lid, and working block and tackle.

Mfg.'s Sug. Retail	$900	$900	$750	$575

Grading	100%	98%	95%	90%	80%	70%	60%
⅓ Scale H.M.S. Victory Naval Cannon							
Mfg.'s Sug. Retail	$3,200	$3,200	$2,550	$2,000			

GAUCHER

Manufacturer located in St. Etienne, France. Currently imported and distributed by Mandall's Shooting Supplies located in Scottsdale, AZ.

PISTOLS: TARGET

MODEL GN1 — .22 LR cal., single shot silhouette pistol featuring 10 in. barrel, adj. sights, anatomically shaped grips, monoblock lever cocking, 2.42 lbs. Importation began 1991.

Mfg.'s Sug. Retail	$380	$360	$325	$290	$260	$230	$200	$185

MODEL GP — similar to Model GN1, except has forearm integrated into grip. Importation began 1991.

Mfg.'s Sug. Retail	$323	$300	$275	$250	$225	$200	$185	$160

GAVAGE

Previous manufacturer located in Liege, Belgium between 1936-1943 approximately.

GAVAGE PISTOL — 7.65mm, patterned after the "Clement", fixed barrel, limited mfg.

	$375	$325	$250	$200	$175	$150	$125

This pistol is very rare if encountered with Waffenamt proofmarks - healthy premiums are being asked.

GENTRY, DAVID

Custom rifle gunmaker located in Bellgrade, MT.

David Gentry is a current custom rifle builder who usually fabricates rifles to individual custom order requests. In addition to special orders, he also builds the Rough Rider Model ($995 retail) and Outfitter's Rifle ($2,400 retail). Mr Gentry should be contacted directly (see Trademark Index) for more information on options/prices.

GERMAN WWII MILITARY PISTOLS

Also See: Fabrique Nationale, Luger, Mauser, and Walther for other military pistols.

P.38 — double action, 9mm, 5 in. barrel, 8 shot mag., fixed sights, brown or black composite grips, blued finish. Many variations exhibiting a variety of metal finishes and codings, 34 oz. Over 1,000,000 manufactured during WW II.

Note: This model was adopted as the standard service pistol of the German Military in 1938. The P.38 was manufactured by Walther - code "ac" (mfg. 1939-1945), Mauser - code "byf" (mfg. Nov. of 1942-1945), and Spreewerke - code "cyq." (mfg. 1943-1945). The finish on most WWII 1942 and later P.38's is not of the same quality as the pre and early war Walther guns with the Spreewerke (cyq) models being the poorest. Pre-war Walther commercial manufactured P.38's command a 10-35% premium (models MP, AP, and Walther Banner HP's) over Zero-series prices listed below.

ZERO-SERIES HP — "Heeres Pistole", with Mauser banner, high polish finish. Mfg. 1939 and 1940. 5-digit number without suffix. Add 10% for matching mag.

Zero Series - 1st Issue — internal extractor, square firing pin.

	$3,500	$3,000	$2,250	$1,800	$1,500	$1,200	$1,000

Zero Series - 2nd Issue — external extractor, square firing pin.

	$2,750	$2,200	$2,000	$1,700	$1,400	$1,100	$900

Zero Series - 3rd Issue — external extractor, round firing pin.

	$1,800	$1,400	$1,000	$800	$700	$600	$500

480 code — "480" appears on slide.

	$1,850	$1,400	$1,100	$850	$725	$625	$525

Grading	100%	98%	95%	90%	80%	70%	60%

ac-40 CODE — indicates 1940 mfg., the 480 code was dropped in October of 1940, and the "ac" code was started.

	$1,100	$800	$700	$600	$500	$430	$380

Add 20% for matching mag.

ac-41 OR ac-42 CODE — indicates 1941 or 1942 mfg.

	$650	$500	$425	$380	$340	$300	$275

Add 20% for matching mag.

"ac" OR "byf" CODED 43-45 — letters are followed by two digit code corresponding to year of mfg. 1943-1945. Two line codes are more desirable than single line models. Highest P.38 production occurred in 1943 and 1944.

	$450	$375	$300	$250	$225	$200	$175

Add 20% for "dual tone" (phosphate finish — byf-44 date).

cyq CODE AND ac-45 MISMATCH — found in "c" serial suffix range, mismatched slide and frame on ac-45 model.

	$400	$350	$275	$240	$210	$190	$165

Deduct 20% for ac-45 mismatch.

LATE WAR (1945) — Zero Series with rough milled finish.

	$700	$600	$500	$425	$350	$300	$250

1945 svw CODE — Mauser mfg. after January, 1945.

	$350	$300	$260	$230	$200	$180	$165

Recent importation has decreased values substantially in the last several years.

1946 svw CODE — Mauser mfg. 1946.

	$425	$365	$285	$250	$210	$190	$165

GEVARM
Ste. Etienne, France.

E-1 AUTOLOADING RIFLE — .22 LR, 19 in. barrel, open sights, walnut pistol grip stock.

	$165	$130	$110	$100	$85	$65	$55

GIB

10 GAUGE MAGNUM SHOTGUN — 10 ga., 3½ in. chambers, 32 in. full choke barrel, case hardened receiver, matted rib, rubber pad, checkered pistol grip walnut stock. Disc.

	$275	$250	$235	$220	$200	$175	$150

GIBBS GUNS, INC.
Previously manufactured by Volunteer Enterprises in Knoxville, TN and previously distributed by Gibbs Guns, Inc. located in Greenback,TN.

MARK 45 CARBINE — .45 ACP only, based on TS M6 Thompson machine gun, 16½ in. barrel, 5, 15, 30, or 90 shot clip, U.S. mfg. Disc. 1988.

	$315	$275	$225	$180	$165	$155	$145

Add $60 minimum for nickel plating.
Last Mfg.'s Sug. Retail was $279.

GLOCK
Manufactured by Glock Ges.m.b.H. in Austria since 1983. Exclusively imported and distributed by Glock, Inc., located in Smyrna, GA.

All Glock pistols have a "safe action" safety system which includes trigger safety, firing pin safety, and drop safety. Glock pistols have only 33 parts for reliability and simplicity in operation.

Grading	100%	98%	95%	90%	80%	70%	60%

MODEL 17 SPORT/SERVICE — 9mm, double action, unique polymer frame, mag., trigger and other pistol parts. Steel barrel, slide, and springs, 17 or 19 shot mag., 4.49 in. barrel with hexagonal rifling, adj. (Sport Model) or fixed (Service Model) rear sight, hammerless, includes extra mag., case, and spare rear sight, 24 oz. empty. Importation began late 1985.

Mfg.'s Sug. Retail	$580	$490	$385	$300			

Add $110 for factory installed fixed night sights.

Adj. rear sight available at no extra charge (Sport Model).

In some areas, dealers are asking a small premium for the adj. sight.

Model 17L Competition Model — competition version of the Model 17, includes internally compensated 6.02 in. barrel, recalibrated trigger pull (3½ lb. pull), adj. rear sight, 25.4 oz. New 1988.

Mfg.'s Sug. Retail	$963	$775	$650	$500			

MODEL 19 COMPACT SPORT/SERVICE — similar to Model 17, except has scaled down dimensions with 4.02 in. barrel and serrated grip straps, 15 or 17 shot mag, fixed (Service Model) or adj. (Sport Model) rear sight, 23 oz. New 1988.

Mfg.'s Sug. Retail	$580	$490	$385	$300			

MODEL 20 SPORT/SERVICE — 10mm Norma cal., similar action to Model 17, features 4.6 in. barrel, 15 shot mag., thicker trigger guard, fixed (Service Model) or adj. (Sport Model) rear sight, approx. 30 oz. New 1990.

Mfg.'s Sug. Retail	$639	$560	$485	$425			

MODEL 21 SPORT/SERVICE — .45 ACP cal., otherwise similar to Model 20, 13 shot mag., approx. 30 oz. New mid-1990.

Mfg.'s Sug. Retail	$639	$560	$485	$425			

The Sport Model has adj. sights and the Service Model has fixed sights.

MODEL 22 SPORT/SERVICE — .40 S&W cal., similar to Model 20, except has 4½ in. barrel, 15 shot mag., 24 oz. New 1991.

Mfg.'s Sug. Retail	$580	$490	$385	$300			

The Sport Model has adj. sights and the Service Model has fixed sights.

MODEL 23 COMPACT SPORT/SERVICE — compact variation of the Model 22 with 4 in. barrel and 13 shot mag., 22.4 oz. New 1991.

Mfg.'s Sug. Retail	$580	$490	$385	$300			

The Sport Model has adj. sights and the Service Model has fixed sights.

GOLDEN EAGLE
Nikko Limited, Tochigi, Japan.

More research is under way on this trademark. For more information regarding this label or individual Golden Eagle models not listed, please contact the Golden Eagle Collector's Assoc. located at P.O. Box 62213, Sunnyvale, CA 94086-2213.

RIFLES

MODEL 7000 GRADE I — bolt action, all popular American calibers, including .270, and .300 Wby., 24 or 26 in. barrels, select skipline checkered walnut stock, rosewood pistol grip and forearm tip, recoil pad. Mfg. 1976. Disc.

	$495	$440	$360	$305	$275	$220	$195

MODEL 7000 GRADE I AFRICAN — same as 7000, except .375 H&H and .458 Win. Mag., open sights.

	$535	$470	$385	$330	$255	$230	$210

MODEL 7000 GRADE II — scroll engraving, better grade wood.

	$605	$495	$415	$330	$275	$220	$200

SHOTGUNS

Grading	100%	98%	95%	90%	80%	70%	60%

MODEL 5000 GRADE I — O/U shotgun, 12 or 20 ga., 26, 28, or 30 in. barrels, various chokes, vent rib, engraved receiver, gold eagle head inlay, auto ejectors, SST, checkered pistol grip beavertail stock. Mfg. 1975. Disc.

	$880	$855	$715	$635	$525	$470	$415

MODEL 5000 GRADE I SKEET — same as 5000, except 26 or 28 in. skeet bored, wide rib.

	$935	$880	$745	$660	$550	$495	$385

MODEL 5000 GRADE I TRAP — same as Field, except 30 or 32 in. barrel, mod. and full, imp. mod. and full, or full and full choke, wide rib, trap stock with pad.

	$965	$910	$770	$690	$605	$525	$440

MODEL 5000 GRADE II — available in Field, Trap, and Skeet, more engraving, better grade wood, with or without screaming eagle on receiver in gold.

	100%	98%	95%	90%	80%	70%	60%
	$990	$965	$825	$635	$550	$470	$385
Skeet	$1,020	$980	$880	$800	$715	$660	$550
Trap	$1,045	$1,020	$935	$855	$770	$715	$605

GRANDEE GRADE III — same as 5000 Grade II, except elaborate engraving, inlays, and better grade wood.

	$2,500	$2,150	$1,750	$1,300	$1,125	$1,000	$850

GONCZ ARMAMENT INC.

Previous manufacturer located in North Hollywood, CA 1984-1990.

While advertised, records indicate fewer than 150 Goncz pistols and carbines were actually manufactured. Most of these guns were prototypes or individually hand-built and none were ever mass produced through normal fabrication techniques.

In 1990, Claridge Hi-Tec, Inc. assumed control over Goncz Armament, Inc. Claridge Hi-Tec, Inc. is currently manufacturing these older models which may be located under their own section in this text. Although all warranties for Goncz pistols/carbines are now void, Claridge Hi-Tec does offer parts and service for these older weapons (please see information in Trademark Index).

The Goncz action is unique since it is not a copy of any other major design.

MODEL GA SERIES PISTOL — 9mm cal., 9½ in. shrouded barrel, black matte finish, one piece grip, 16 or 18 shot mag., except in .45 ACP cal. (10 or 20 shot), 3 lbs. 2 oz. New 1985.

	$495	$375	$295	$250	$220	$200	$185

Last Mfg.'s Sug. Retail was $595.

While advertised, 7.63 Mauser, .38 Super, and .45 ACP cal.'s were never mfg.

MODEL GAT SERIES PISTOL — similar to GA Series, except has adj. trigger and hand polished parts.

	$1,300	$900	$800	$700	$625	$550	$495

Last Mfg.'s Sug. Retail was $1,525.

MODEL GS SERIES PISTOL — similar to GA Series, except has 5 in. non-shrouded barrel, 2 lbs. 10 oz.

	$350	$280	$250	$220	$200	$185	$170

Stainless steel frame became standard in 1987. Last Mfg.'s Suggested Retail on the steel model was $340.

Model GS Stainless — similar to GS Series, except is 100% stainless steel. New 1987.

	$475	$340	$295

Last Mfg.'s Sug. Retail was $550.

GC CARBINE — same cal.'s as GA Series pistols, 16.1 in. barrel, uncheckered walnut stock, 4 lbs. 10 oz.

	$550	$425	$350	$285	$260	$240	$220

Last Mfg.'s Sug. Retail was $650.

Grading	100%	98%	95%	90%	80%	70%	60%

Model GC Stainless — similar to GC Carbine, except is 100% stainless steel. New 1987.

	$550	$425	$350				

Last Mfg.'s Sug. Retail was $650.

Halogen Carbine — 9mm or .45 ACP only, similar to carbine, except is supplied with halogen lighting unit underneath barrel, can be trigger activated. New 1986.

	$750	$575	$500	$460	$430	$400	$375

Last Mfg.'s Sug. Retail was $875.

Laser Carbine — similar to Halogen Carbine, except sophisticated laser sighting system replaces halogen light - accuracy to 400 yds. New 1986.

	$1,375	$1,100	$935	$825	$770	$700	$650

Last Mfg.'s Sug. Retail was $1,500.

GRANGER, G.

Manufacturer located in Saint Etienne, France since 1902.

G. Granger manufactures high quality, limited production side-by-side boxlock and sidelock shotguns in 12, 16, or 20 ga. All guns are made on a custom order basis with prices ranging between $20,000 - $37,800. Prices will vary per customer specifications and appointments.

G. Granger should be contacted directly (see Trademark Index) regarding up-to-date model information (including current pricing).

GRANT, STEPHEN

Previously manufactured in London, England.

Manufacturer specializing in custom order only SxS rifles and shotguns. Shotguns (12, 16, or 20 ga.) can be top or side lever and are equipped with sidelocks and a self-opening mechanism. Very limited production making values hard to establish. Prices are at par with similar quality H&H firearms.

GREAT WESTERN ARMS CO.

Previous manufacturer located in CA 1954-1964.

SA REVOLVERS

More research is underway to find out more information about this manufacturer that produced over 10,000 SA revolvers. Earlier specimens do not exhibit the top quality control found on the later models. The most commmon variety was a .22 LR in a 5½ in. barrel. Cal.'s included .22 LR, .357 Mag., .38 Spl., .44 Spl., and .45 LC. Collector interest is increasing on this trademark and currently, most common variations are selling between $225-$395.

DERRINGERS

These models were of an O/U design. Cal.'s included .38 S&W or .38 Spl. Current prices range from approx. $125-$200 with not much collector interest.

GREENER, W.W., LIMITED

Manufacturer located in Birmingham, England since 1829.

W.W. Greener manufactures best quality rifles and shotguns only. Approximately 20-50 guns are made annually.

W.W. Greener should be contacted directly (see Trademark Index) for up-to-date model information and current pricing.

RIFLES: SxS - CURRENT MFG.

Boxlock and sidelock rifle quotations may be obtained by writing the company directly (see Trademark Index). A complete choice of calibers, engraving options, and walnut selection are available on a special order basis only.

Grading	100%	98%	95%	90%	80%	70%	60%

SHOTGUNS: SxS - CURRENT MFG.

NO. 5 NEEDHAM EJECTOR—12, 16, 20, or .410 ga., scalloped boxlock action, DT, any barrel length.

Mfg.'s Sug. Retail	$5,760	$5,760	$4,950	$4,250	$3,500	$2,750	$2,250	$1,825

This model has been re-introduced to commemorate the takeover of J. V. Needham by W.W. Greener in 1874.

DH 40 —similar to No. 5 Needham Ejector, except has better engraving and deluxe walnut stock and forearm.

Mfg.'s Sug. Retail	$8,640	$8,640	$7,750	$6,875	$5,900	$5,000	$4,250	$3,500

DH 75—12 ga. only, 2¾ in. chambers, Greener "Facile Princeps" scalloped boxlock action 27, 28, or 30 in. barrels, case hardened receiver, choice of engraving (game scene or fine scroll work).

Mfg.'s Sug. Retail	$14,880	$14,880	$12,000	$9,950	$8,450	$7,250	$6,000	$4,950

DOH 90—12, 16, 20, or .410 ga., 2½, 2¾ or 3 in. Mag. chambers, Anson & Deeley scalloped boxlock action with Greener easy-opening device, French walnut stock, DT.

Mfg.'s Sug. Retail	$17,280	$17,280	$14,500	$11,750	$9,500	$8,250	$7,000	$5,850

L 120 —12, 16, 20, or .410 ga., best sidelock ejector model with dovetail lump barrels, fine scroll engraving with choice of bright or color case hardened frame finish.

Mfg.'s Sug. Retail	$28,800	$28,800	$24,500	$19,500	$16,000	$13,000	$10,000	$7,850

L 150 —12, 16, 20, or .410 ga., 2½ or 3 in. chambers, very best sidelock ejector model with chopper lump barrels and easy-opening device, bright or color case hardened frame finish.

Mfg.'s Sug. Retail	$35,525	$35,525	$30,250	$26,000	$22,000	$18,000	$14,000	$10,000

L 500 —12, 16, 20, or .410 ga., new St. George sidelock ejector model incorporating top-of-the-line engraving, walnut, and worksmanship.

Because this model is entirely custom ordered per individual choice, a price quotation is necessary on every order.

SHOTGUNS: DISCONTINUED

FARKILLER GRADE F35 — double barrel, 12 ga., 28, 30, or 32 in. barrels, hammerless boxlock, checkered straight or semi-pistol grip stock.

	$2,420	$2,200	$2,090	$1,870	$1,760	$1,650	$1,540
Auto ejectors	$3,300	$3,025	$2,750	$2,475	$2,035	$1,925	$1,650

FARKILLER GRADE F35 LARGE BORE — same as F35 above, except 8 or 10 ga.

	$2,750	$2,585	$2,310	$2,090	$1,980	$1,815	$1,650
Auto ejectors	$3,575	$3,300	$3,080	$2,860	$2,640	$2,090	$1,925

HAMMERLESS EJECTOR MODELS — 12, 16, 20, 28, or .410 ga., 26, 28, or 30 in. barrels supplied with any choke combination, auto ejectors, single or double triggers, straight or semi-pistol grip stock, grades differ as follows:

Jubilee Grade DH35

	$2,420	$2,255	$2,090	$1,925	$1,650	$1,540	$1,375

Sovereign Grade DH40

	$2,860	$2,695	$2,420	$2,200	$1,980	$1,815	$1,595

Crown Grade DH55

	$3,300	$3,080	$2,915	$2,750	$2,420	$2,035	$1,760

Royal Grade DH75

	$4,400	$4,180	$3,850	$3,300	$3,080	$2,915	$2,640

Add $400 for SST.

Note: Degree of engraving and grade of wood are the basic differences between models.

Grading	100%	98%	95%	90%	80%	70%	60%

EMPIRE — double barrel, 12 ga. only, 2¾ or 3 in., any choke, 28, 30, or 32 in. barrel, hammerless, boxlock, straight stock or semi pistol grip.

	100%	98%	95%	90%	80%	70%	60%
	$1,760	$1,540	$1,320	$1,100	$935	$825	$770
Auto ejectors	$1,980	$1,760	$1,540	$1,320	$1,155	$1,045	$990

EMPIRE DELUXE — double barrel, same as Empire, only better grade wood.

	100%	98%	95%	90%	80%	70%	60%
	$1,980	$1,760	$1,540	$1,320	$1,155	$1,045	$990
Auto ejectors	$2,200	$1,980	$1,760	$1,540	$1,375	$1,265	$1,100

GENERAL PURPOSE — 12 ga., improved Martini action, single shot, 26, 30, or 32 in. barrel, full or mod., auto ejectors, straight checkered stock.

100%	98%	95%	90%	80%	70%	60%
$330	$305	$275	$220	$195	$165	$160

GREIFELT AND COMPANY
Suhl, Germany.
SHOTGUNS: SIDE-BY-SIDE

MODEL 22 — 12 or 20 ga., 28 or 30 in. mod. and full, hammerless, boxlock, false sideplates, extractors, checkered pistol grip or English style stock, post-WWII.

100%	98%	95%	90%	80%	70%	60%
$2,200	$1,760	$1,595	$1,320	$1,100	$990	$825

MODEL 22E — same as 22, except auto ejectors.

100%	98%	95%	90%	80%	70%	60%
$2,750	$2,200	$1,980	$1,760	$1,540	$1,430	$1,265

MODEL 103 — 12 or 16 ga., 28 or 30 in. mod. and full, extractors, double triggers, checkered pistol grip or English stock, post-war.

100%	98%	95%	90%	80%	70%	60%
$1,980	$1,650	$1,485	$1,210	$990	$880	$715

MODEL 103E — same as model 103, except auto ejectors.

100%	98%	95%	90%	80%	70%	60%
$2,200	$1,760	$1,595	$1,320	$1,100	$990	$825

SHOTGUNS: OVER/UNDER & DRILLING

GRADE NO. 1 — O/U, 12, 16, 20, 28, or .410 ga., any barrel 26-32 in., choke, vent or solid rib, Anson & Deeley boxlock, auto ejectors, checkered pistol grip or English stock, pre-war.

12 or 20 ga.	100%	98%	95%	90%	80%	70%	60%
	$3,600	$3,200	$2,850	$2,500	$2,100	$1,750	$1,500

Deduct 10% for 16 ga.
Add 30% for 28 or .410 ga.
Add $300 for vent rib.
Add $400 for SST.

GRADE NO. 3 — same as No. 1, except less elaborate engraving, pre-WWII.

12 ga.	100%	98%	95%	90%	80%	70%	60%
	$2,850	$2,500	$2,200	$2,000	$1,650	$1,350	$1,200

Deduct 10% for 16 ga.
Add 20% for 28 or .410 ga.
Add $300 for vent rib.
Add $400 for SST.

MODEL 143E — O/U, similar to model 1, except not as high quality as pre-war model, not available in 28 or .410 ga. Mfg. post-WWII.

100%	98%	95%	90%	80%	70%	60%
$2,400	$2,150	$1,850	$1,550	$1,350	$1,175	$1,000

Add 10% for vent rib and SST.

Grading	100%	98%	95%	90%	80%	70%	60%

O/U COMBINATION GUN — 12, 16, 20, 28, or .410 ga., shotgun barrel, rifle in any rimmed caliber, 24 or 26 in. solid rib barrel, pre-WWII.

	$5,200	$4,800	$4,400	$4,000	$3,600	$3,150	$2,800

Add $700 for auto ejectors.

Deduct 10% for 16 ga.

Add 20% for 28 or .410 ga.

Deduct 40-50% for obsolete rifle caliber.

Above values for 12 or 20 ga. over obtainable rifle cartridge.

DRILLING — 12, 16, or 20 ga., SxS over any rimmed rifle caliber, 26 in. barrels, boxlock, extractors, double triggers, rifle sight activated by barrel selector, pre-WWII.

	$3,500	$3,000	$2,750	$2,550	$2,300	$2,000	$1,750

Deduct 10% for 16 ga.

Deduct 40-50% for obsolete cal.'s.

Previous values for 12 and 20 ga. over available caliber.

GRENDEL, INC.

Manufacturer located in Rockledge, FL since 1984.

Grendel firearms are noted for their precision manufacture, outstanding accuracy, and lightweight characteristics.

PISTOLS

MODEL P-10 SERIES — .380 ACP, semi-auto, double action, 10 shot mag., small dimensions, hammerless, matte blue finish, 15 oz.

Mfg.'s Sug. Retail	$155	$140	$125	$115	$105	$95	$90	$85

Add $15 for electroless nickel finish.

Add $15 for nickel green finish.

Green finish is available at no extra charge.

MODEL P-30 — .22 Mag. cal., similar action to P-10, 30 shot mag., 21 oz. New 1990.

Mfg.'s Sug. Retail	$225	$200	$175	$155	$140	$125	$115	$105

Add $25 for electroless nickel finish.

Model P-30M — similar to Model P-30, except has long barrel with muzzle brake. New 1990.

Mfg.'s Sug. Retail	$235	$205	$180	$160	$140	$125	$115	$105

Add $25 for electroless nickel finish.

MODEL P-30L — .22 Mag., semi-auto double action, hammerless, 5, 5.6, or 8 in. barrel, 30 shot mag., all steel construction with Zytel synthetic grips, approx. 22 oz. New 1991.

Mfg.'s Sug. Retail	$280	$240	$200	$180	$160	$140	$125	$110

Add $15 for 8 in. barrel (Model P-30LM).

MODEL P-31 — .22 Mag., same action as P-30L, except has 11 in. barrel, enclosed synthetic barrel shroud and flash hider, 48 oz. New 1991.

Mfg.'s Sug. Retail	$345	$285	$240	$215	$185	$160	$145	$130

RIFLES/CARBINES

MODEL R-31 — similar design to Model P-31, except has 16 in. barrel and telescoping stock, 64 oz. New 1991.

Mfg.'s Sug. Retail	$385	$315	$260	$235	$210	$185	$165	$150

SRT-20F COMPACT — .243 Win. or .308 cal., bolt action based on the Sako A-2 action, 20 in. match grade finned barrel with muzzle brake, folding synthetic stock, integrated bipod rest, no sights, 9 shot mag., 6.7 lbs. Disc. 1989.

	$575	$525	$475	$395	$365	$340	$320

Grendel previously manufactured the SRT-16F, SRT-20L, and SRT-24 - all were disc. 1988. Values are approx. the same as the SRT-20F.

Last Mfg.'s Sug. Retail was $525.

Grading	100%	98%	95%	90%	80%	70%	60%

GRIFFIN & HOWE

U.S. Custom Gunsmith/manufacturer that started in 1923 - located in New York, NY.

Griffin & Howe are custom gunsmiths who do a variety of gunsmithing services (including building custom rifles), almost totally by individual customer order. Prices vary greatly depending on configuration desirability, condition, and special orders/features. Most Griffin & Howe custom rifles (in average condition) start in the $1,200+ range and rise according to the nature of the gun. Less than 2,700 custom rifles have been manufactured between 1923 and 1966. In 1930 G & H became a subsidiary of Abercrombie & Fitch. Because all G & H rifles are essentially special ordered, accurate pricing can only be ascertained by examining one specimen at a time. Elaborate specimens in this trademark will command $4,000 and higher. Engraving by Joseph Fugger (employed by G & H) will add considerably to the value.

.30-06 SPRINGFIELD BOLT ACTION — a classic sporter based on the U.S. 1903 Springfield military rifle.

$1,900	$1,675	$1,300	$1,200	$1,050	$975	$850

G&H rifles with Mauser actions will command premiums over standard actions.
Above values represent a base gun with normal wood and no options.

GRULLA ARMAS

Manufacturer located in Eibar, Spain.

Grulla Armas has had limited U.S. importation to date. To obtain more information about this manufacturer's quality SxS shotguns, please contact per address/FAX number listed under the Grulla heading in the "Trademark Index" located in the back of this text.

GUNWORKS, LTD.

Previously manufactured and distributed in Buffalo, NY. Early Guns Were Made In Tonawanda, NY.

MODEL 9 — O/U derringer, .357 Mag., 9mm or .38 Super, or .38 Spl. cal., electroless nickel finish, 2½ in. barrel, wood grips, Millett sights, 15 oz. Disc. 1986.

$135	$120	$105	$95	$65	$55	$50

Last Mfg.'s Sug. Retail was $149.

GUSTAF, CARL

Manufacturer located in Eskilstuna, Sweden.

Carl Gustaf rifles are not currently imported into the U.S. More information on this famous trademark can be obtained by contacting the factory directly (see Trademark Index).

MODEL CG 2000 — 6.5 x 55, .243, .270, .30-06, or .308 cal., bolt action, Monte Carlo walnut stock with checkering, open sights, cold-swaged barrel and receiver, 60 degree bolt. Importation stopped in 1985.

$595	$550	$495	$450	$400	$350	$325

Last Mfg.'s Sug. Retail was $750.

This model is currently being manufactured in Sweden with a 1991 export price of $1,125 for the Standard Grade, add $380 for Luxe Model, add $2,675 for Super Luxe Model. Current cal.'s include 6.5 x 55mm, .308 Win., .30-06, 9.3 x 62mm.

STANDARD BOLT ACTION RIFLE — 6.5 x 55, 7 x 64, .270, 7mm Mag., .308, .30-06, or 9.3 x 62 cal., 24 in. barrel, folding rear sight, checkered classic style stock. Mfg. 1970-1977.

$375	$325	$300	$275	$250	$225	$200

Monte Carlo stock

$450	$395	$350	$300	$275	$250	$225

GRADE II — same as Monte Carlo Standard, in .22-250, .25-06, 6.5 x 55, .270, 7mm Mag., .308, .30-06, or .300 Win. Mag. cal., select stock and rosewood pistol grip cap, and forearm tip.

$500	$425	$375	$325	$295	$275	$250

Grading	100%	98%	95%	90%	80%	70%	60%

GRADE III — same as Grade II, except fancy wood, deluxe high gloss finish.

	100%	98%	95%	90%	80%	70%	60%
	$575	$475	$425	$350	$325	$300	$275

DELUXE — same as Grade III, except engraved floorplate and trigger guard, Deluxe French walnut, and jeweled bolt.

	100%	98%	95%	90%	80%	70%	60%
	$675	$575	$475	$400	$375	$350	$325

VARMINT TARGET MODEL — bolt action, fast lock time, .222, .22-250, .243, or 6.5 x 55 cal., 27 in. barrel, no sights, large bakelite bolt knob, target type stock. Mfg. 1970. Disc.

	100%	98%	95%	90%	80%	70%	60%
	$550	$495	$440	$385	$360	$320	$290

GRAND PRIX SINGLE SHOT TARGET — fastest lock time bolt action, .22 LR, 27 in. heavy barrel with adj. weight, no sights, target stock, adj. butt plate. Mfg. 1970. Disc.

	100%	98%	95%	90%	80%	70%	60%
	$550	$495	$440	$385	$360	$320	$290

H

H.J.S. INDUSTRIES, INC.
Brownsville, TX.

Grading	100%	98%	95%	90%	80%	70%	60%

FRONTIER FOUR DERRINGER — 4 shot derringer, .22 LR only, stainless steel construction, 5½ oz.

$115 $90 $80

LONE STAR DERRINGER — single shot derringer, .38 S&W only, stainless steel construction, 6 oz.

$137 $105 $95

H-S PRECISION, INC.
Custom rifle manufacturer located in Rapid City, SD. H-S Precision, Inc. also manufactures synthetic stocks and custom machines barrels as well.

RIFLES: CUSTOM MFG. BOLT ACTION

In addition to the models listed below, H-S Precision, Inc. will also build rifles using a customer's action (Remington 700 ADL or 700 BDL, Sako, Weatherby, or Winchester). These models will be approx. ⅓ less expensive than values listed below (not available in Sniper Model).

SPORTER/VARMINT STANDARD MODEL — .223 Rem., .22 PPC, .22-250 Rem., .243 Win., 6mm PPC, 7mm-08 Rem., or .308 Win. cal. are available in short action, .270 Win., .30-06, 7mm Rem. Mag., .300 Win. Mag., or .338 Win. Mag. cal. are available in long action, Remington action only, each rifle is built per individual specifications. New 1990.

Mfg.'s Sug. Retail	$1,420	$1,420	$1,150	$895	$750	$650	$575	$500

Add $150 for left hand action.

STANDARD SNIPER MODEL — .223 Rem., .243 Win., .30-06, .308, 7mm Rem. Mag., or .300 Win. Mag. cal., fluted barrel standard. New 1990.

Mfg.'s Sug. Retail	$1,570	$1,570	$1,225	$900	$800	$700	$600	$525

Add $150 for left hand action.

SPORTER/VARMINT TAKEDOWN MODEL — .22-250, .243 Win., 7mm-08 Rem., or .308 Win. cal. in short action, .25-06 Rem., .270 Win., .30-06, 7mm Rem. Mag., .300 Win. Mag., or .338 Win. Mag. cal. in long action, takedown action. New 1990.

Mfg.'s Sug. Retail	$2,400	$2,400	$1,900	$1,570	$1,225	$900	$800	$700

Add $1,000 for extra barrel.

SNIPER TAKEDOWN MODEL — .223 Rem., .243 Win., .30-06, .308 Win., 7mm Rem. Mag., .300 Win. Mag., or .338 Win. Mag. cal., includes "kwik klip" and fluted barrel. New 1990.

Mfg.'s Sug. Retail	$2,600	$2,600	$2,000	$1,650	$1,350	$950	$850	$750

A complete rifle package consisting of 2 calibers (.308 Win. and .300 Win. Mag.), scope and fitted case is available for $5,200 retail.

HWP INDUSTRIES
Previous manufacturer located in Milwaukee, WI.

THE SLEDGEHAMMER — .500 HWP Mag. cal., 5 shot revolver, double action, stainless steel, full shrouded 4 in. barrel (quick change), pachmayr grips. Limited mfg. 1989 only.

$1,150 $895 $750

Last Mfg.'s Sug. Retail was $1,295.

Grading	100%	98%	95%	90%	80%	70%	60%

HAENEL, C.G.

Previous manufacturer located in Suhl, Germany. Mfg. between 1925-1940.

RIFLES

MAUSER-MANNLICHER SPORTING RIFLE — M/88 Mauser type action, 7 x 57, 8 x 57, or 9 x 57 cal., 22 or 24 in. octagon barrel, Mannlicher box mag., double set triggers, raised rib on barrel leaf sight, sporter stock.

	100%	98%	95%	90%	80%	70%	60%
	$440	$360	$330	$275	$250	$220	$165

88 MAUSER SPORTER — same as Mauser-Mannlicher, with Mauser 5 shot mag.

	100%	98%	95%	90%	80%	70%	60%
	$525	$450	$375	$325	$275	$240	$200

PISTOLS

SCHMEISSER MODEL 1 & 2 — .25 ACP, similar to Baby Browning.

	100%	98%	95%	90%	80%	70%	60%
	$385	$340	$300	$275	$230	$200	$180

MODELS 200-205 — See Hammerli-Walther

HAMBRUSCH, JOSEF

Manufacturer located in Ferlach, Austria.

SHOTGUN — boxlock or sidelock SxS, various ga.'s, most specimens exhibit game scene engraving, ejectors, SST or DT. Not many specimens are encountered in this trademark - please contact Mr. Hambush directly (see Trademark Index) for current model information and price quotations. Please allow 4-6 weeks for a reply.

HAMMERLI

Manufacturer located in Lenzburg, Switzerland. Currently imported and distributed by Mandall Shooting Supplies, Inc. located in Scottsdale, AZ and Beeman Precision Arms located in Santa Rosa, CA. Previously imported by Osborne's located in Cheboygan, MI.

PISTOLS

MODEL 100 FREE PISTOL — .22 LR, 11½ in. octagon barrel, blue, martini action single shot, set trigger, micro rear sight, walnut stock and forearm. Mfg. 1933-1949.

	100%	98%	95%	90%	80%	70%	60%
	$880	$660	$605	$550	$470	$440	$385

Deluxe model — carved stock.

	100%	98%	95%	90%	80%	70%	60%
	$990	$770	$715	$660	$580	$550	$495

MODEL 101 — similar to 100, but heavy round barrel, improved action and sights, matte finish. Mfg. 1956-1960.

	100%	98%	95%	90%	80%	70%	60%
	$880	$660	$605	$550	$470	$440	$385

MODEL 102 — same as 101, except high polished finish. Mfg. 1956-1960.

	100%	98%	95%	90%	80%	70%	60%
	$880	$660	$605	$550	$470	$440	$385
Deluxe model.	$990	$770	$715	$660	$580	$550	$495

MODEL 103 FREE PISTOL — same as model 101, except lighter octagon polished barrel. Mfg. 1956-1960.

	100%	98%	95%	90%	80%	70%	60%
	$935	$715	$660	$605	$580	$550	$495

MODEL 104 MATCH PISTOL — similar to 103, except lighter round barrel, redesigned stock, mfg. 1961-1965.

	100%	98%	95%	90%	80%	70%	60%
	$760	$660	$550	$495	$470	$440	$385

MODEL 105 MATCH PISTOL — similar to 103, except redesigned action and stock. Mfg. 1962-1965.

	100%	98%	95%	90%	80%	70%	60%
	$935	$715	$660	$605	$580	$550	$495

Grading	100%	98%	95%	90%	80%	70%	60%

MATCH PISTOL — similar to 105, except improved trigger.

| | $910 | $690 | $580 | $525 | $495 | $470 | $415 |

MODEL 107 MATCH PISTOL — similar to 105, except improved trigger.

| | $990 | $770 | $660 | $550 | $525 | $495 | $440 |

Deluxe model — engraved and carved wood.

| | $1,320 | $990 | $880 | $660 | $635 | $605 | $550 |

MODEL 120-1 SINGLE SHOT FREE PISTOL — .22 LR, bolt action, 9.9 in. barrel, blue barrel and receiver, side lever operated, anodized aluminum lever and frame, walnut checkered grips.

| | $440 | $360 | $305 | $275 | $220 | $200 | $175 |

MODEL 120-2 — same as 120-1, except stocks hand contoured.

| | $470 | $385 | $330 | $305 | $250 | $220 | $195 |

MODEL 120 HEAVY BARREL — same as 120-1, with 5.7 in. bull barrel.

MODEL 150 FREE PISTOL — .22 LR cal., 11.3 in. barrel, improved Martini-type action, set trigger, innovative design incorporating many unusual features. Disc. 1989.

| Mfg.'s Sug. Retail | $1,980 | $1,850 | $1,495 | $1,275 | $1,120 | $980 | $900 | $850 |

Add $113 for left-hand variation.

While this model has been disc. 1989, above values reflect remaining inventory with importers. The Model 150 has been replaced by the Model 151.

MODEL 151 FREE PISTOL — replacement for the Model 150 Free Pistol. New 1990.

| Mfg.'s Sug. Retail | $1,980 | $1,850 | $1,495 | $1,275 | $1,120 | $980 | $900 | $850 |

MODEL 152 FREE PISTOL — .22 LR cal., 11.3 in. barrel. improved Martini-type action, electronic trigger release, innovative design incorporating many unusual features. State of the art target pistol.

| Mfg.'s Sug. Retail | $2,105 | $1,995 | $1,600 | $1,350 | $1,195 | $1,090 | $990 | $895 |

Add $57 for left-hand variation.

MODELS 200-205 — See Hammerli-Walther

| | $440 | $360 | $305 | $275 | $220 | $200 | $175 |

INTERNATIONAL MODEL 206 — .22 LR, .22 S, semi-auto, $7\frac{1}{16}$ in. barrel with muzzle brake, adj. sights, walnut grips, blue. Mfg. 1962-1969.

| | $690 | $605 | $495 | $470 | $385 | $360 | $330 |

INTERNATIONAL MODEL 207 — same as 206, except adj. grip heel.

| | $705 | $635 | $505 | $480 | $395 | $370 | $340 |

INTERNATIONAL MODEL 208 — .22 LR, semi-auto, 9 shot, 6 in. barrel, blue, adj. sights, checkered walnut grips with adj. heel. Mfg. 1966-1988.

| Mfg.'s Sug. Retail | $1,755 | $1,600 | $1,300 | $1,050 | $950 | $880 | $835 | $770 |

Limited quantities of this model are still available. This model was replaced by the Model 208S.

Model 208S — similar to Model 208, except has redesigned trigger guard and interchangeable rear sight element. Importation started 1988.

| Mfg.'s Sug. Retail | $1,755 | $1,600 | $1,300 | $1,050 | $950 | $880 | $835 | $770 |

This model is distributed by Mandall Shooting Supplies located in Scottsdale, AZ.

Model 208 Deluxe — similar to Model 208, except has carved grips and elaborate engraving. Importation disc. 1988.

| | $2,995 | $2,500 | $1,995 |

Last Mfg.'s Sug. Retail was $3,250.

Model 208C (Commemorative) — limited edition commemorative. Disc. 1987.

| | $2,100 | $1,750 | $1,400 |

Last Mfg.'s Sug. Retail was $2,225.

Grading	100%	98%	95%	90%	80%	70%	60%

INTERNATIONAL MODEL 209 — .22 Short, semi-auto, 5 shot, 4¾ in. barrel, muzzle brake, adj. sights, blue, walnut stock. Mfg. 1966-1970.

	$800	$690	$635	$550	$525	$485	$440

INTERNATIONAL MODEL 210 — same as 209, but grips have adj. heel. Mfg. 1966-1970.

	$800	$715	$660	$590	$540	$525	$495

MODEL 211 — .22 LR, semi-auto, 9 shot, 6 in. barrel, adj. sights, blue, similar to Model 208 except non-adj. walnut stocks. Importation disc. 1990.

Mfg.'s Sug. Retail	$1,669	$1,550	$1,275	$1,050	$950	$880	$835	$770

MODEL 212 HUNTER — .22 LR, semi-auto, hunter's pistol, 9 shot, 5 in. barrel, adj. sights, blue, walnut stocks.

	$1,500	$1,250	$975	$875	$820	$760	$600

Last Mfg.'s Sug. Retail was $1,650.

MODEL 215 — .22 LR, semi-auto, Model 208 specs on commercial target model, 9 shot, 5 in. barrel, adj. sights, blue, walnut stocks. Importation disc. 1990.

	$1,395	$1,050	$895	$775	$695	$650	$600

Last Mfg.'s Sug. Retail was $1,505.

MODEL 230 RAPID FIRE PISTOL — .22 S, semi-auto, 5 shot, 6.3 in. barrel, blue, adj. sights, smooth walnut grips. Mfg. 1970-1983.

	$705	$635	$580	$530	$485	$450	$415

MODEL 230-2 — same as 230, except checkered grips with adj. heel. Mfg. 1970-1983.

	$735	$655	$605	$570	$515	$485	$470

MODEL 232-1 RAPID FIRE PISTOL — .22 S, semi-auto, 6 shot, 5.1 in. barrel, blue, adj. sights, contoured walnut grips.

Mfg.'s Sug. Retail	$1,505	$1,395	$1,125	$950	$850	$750	$700	$650

Add $25 for wrap-around grips sizes S-M-LG (Model 232-2).

MODEL 280 — .22 LR or .32 Wadcutter, new modular pistol design utilizing carbon fiber synthetic material to replace frame and other critical parts, adj. grips, trigger, and rear sight, 4.6 in. barrel, 5 or 6 shot mag., approx. 2.2 lbs. New 1988.

Mfg.'s Sug. Retail	$1,895	$1,675	$1,350	$1,100	$950	$850	$750	$700

Add $1,195 for .22 LR or .32 Wadcutter conversion.

A package is also available with both calibers, magazines, and hard case for $3,000.

MODEL P-240 — see S.I.G.- HAMMERLI for this model.

RIFLES: TARGET

OLYMPIC 300 METER — .30-06 or .300 H&H Mag., bolt action, single shot free rifle, U.S.A. import, 7 x 57mm overseas, 20½ in. heavy barrel, double set trigger, aperture rear sight, globe front, free rifle stock with thumbhole pistol grip, beavertail forearm, Swiss style target butt. Mfg. 1945-1959.

	$880	$745	$605	$550	$470	$440	$415

HAMMERLI-TANNER 300 METER FREE RIFLE — similar to Olympic 300 , except 7.5mm standard, can be ordered in other calibers. Mfg. 1962-disc.

	$895	$825	$770	$715	$660	$580	$520

Last Mfg.'s Sug. Retail was $935.

MODEL 45 SMALLBORE MATCH RIFLE — .22 LR, bolt action, single shot, 27½ in. heavy barrel, same sights and stock type as Hammerli-Tanner. Mfg. 1945-1957.

	$660	$550	$470	$440	$385	$360	$330

MODEL 54 SMALLBORE MATCH RIFLE — similar to 45 Smallbore, except adj. butt. Mfg. 1954-1957.

	$670	$560	$480	$450	$395	$370	$340

Grading	100%	98%	95%	90%	80%	70%	60%
MODEL 503 SMALLBORE FREE RIFLE — similar to 54 Smallbore, except free style stock.							
	$660	$550	$470	$440	$385	$360	$330
MODEL 505 MATCH RIFLE — match stock with aperture sights.							
	$690	$580	$495	$470	$415	$385	$360
MODEL 506 SMALLBORE MATCH RIFLE — similar to 503 Smallbore. Mfg. 1963-1966.							
	$690	$580	$495	$470	$415	$385	$360
SPORTING RIFLE — various calibers, set triggers. Hunting Model-single shot.							
	$725	$650	$490	$425	$360	$325	$300

HAMMERLI-WALTHER

Target Pistols manufactured under joint effort.

PISTOLS: SEMI-AUTO

MODEL 200 OLYMPIA — .22 Short or LR, 7½ in. barrel, 1952 type, adj. sights, barrel weight, blue, checkered walnut grips. Mfg. 1952-1958.

	100%	98%	95%	90%	80%	70%	60%
	$660	$605	$550	$440	$415	$385	$360

MODEL 200 OLYMPIA — 1958 type, same as 1952 type, except has muzzle brake. Mfg. 1958-1963.

	$715	$605	$550	$495	$470	$415	$385

MODEL 201 — same as 200, 1952 type, except 9½ in. barrel. Mfg. 1955-1957.

	$660	$605	$550	$440	$415	$385	$360

MODEL 202 — same as 201, except adj. heel grips. Mfg. 1955-1957.

	$715	$605	$550	$495	$470	$415	$385

MODEL 203 — same as 200, except has adj. heel grip.

1955 Type — no muzzle brake.

	$715	$605	$550	$495	$470	$415	$385

1958 Type — muzzle brake.

	$770	$660	$605	$550	$525	$470	$440

MODEL 204 — similar to 200, except .22 LR only.

1956 Type — no muzzle brake.

	$745	$635	$580	$525	$495	$470	$440

1958 Type — muzzle brake.

	$800	$690	$635	$550	$525	$495	$470

MODEL 205 — .22 LR, same as 204, except adj. heel grips.

1956 type	$800	$690	$635	$550	$525	$495	$470
1958 type, M.B.	$855	$745	$715	$635	$580	$525	$495

HARRINGTON & RICHARDSON, INC.

Previous manufacturer located in Gardner, MA - formerly from Worchester, MA. Successors to Wesson & Harrington, manufactured from 1871 until January 24, 1986.

A manufacturer of utilitarian firearms for over 115 years, H & R ceased operation on January 24, 1986. The discontinuance of this trademark may produce premiums on the older, discontinued models in either N.I.B. or mint condition, but probably will not affect values on those handguns only recently discontinued.

Even though this trademark has been discontinued for over 4 years, collector interest to date has been mimimal. Most H & R firearms are still purchased for their shooting value rather than collecting potential.

Grading	100%	98%	95%	90%	80%	70%	60%

PISTOLS: PRE-1942

MODEL 4 — .32 S&W Long 6 shot, or .38 S&W Long 5 shot, (1904), double action, 2½, 4½, and 6 in. barrels, blued or nickel, hard rubber grips, solid frame, fixed sights.

	$95	$85	$70	$55	$45	$35	$30

MODEL 5 — .32 S&W Long, 5 shot only, (1905), double action, same as Model 4.

	$95	$85	$70	$55	$45	$35	$30

MODEL 6 — .22 LR, 7 shot only, (1906), double action, same as Model 4.

	$95	$85	$70	$55	$45	$35	$30

AMERICAN — .32 S&W, 6 shot, .38 S&W, 5 shot, double action, 2½, 4, or 6 in. barrels, fixed sights, blue or nickel.

	$95	$85	$70	$55	$45	$35	$30

YOUNG AMERICAN — .22 Long, 7 shot, .32 S&W, 5 shot, double action, 2, 4½, or 6 in. barrel, fixed sights, blue or nickel.

	$95	$85	$70	$55	$45	$35	$30

VEST POCKET — double action, 1⅛ in. barrel, blue or nickel, solid frame, spurless hammer.

	$95	$85	$70	$55	$45	$35	$30

HUNTER — .22 LR, double action, 10 in. octagon barrel, 9 shot, checkered walnut grips.

	$140	$110	$100	$85	$65	$55	$45

TRAPPER — .22 LR, double action, 7 shot, 6 in. octagon barrel, checkered walnut stocks.

	$140	$120	$100	$85	$65	$55	$45

MODEL 922 — .22 LR, first issue, 9 shot, 10 in. octagon barrel on early models, 6 in. round barrel on later models, checkered walnut grips.

	$140	$120	$100	$85	$65	$55	$45

AUTOMATIC EJECTING — .32 S&W, 6 shot, .38 S&W, 5 shot, double action, 3¼, 4, 5, or 6 in. barrels, hinged break open, fixed sights, black rubber grips.

	$160	$150	$105	$90	$75	$65	$55

PREMIER — .22 LR, 7 shot, .32 S&W, 5 shot, double action, break open, small frame.

	$95	$85	$70	$55	$45	$35	$30

HAMMERLESS — .22 LR, 7 shot, .32 S&W, 5 shot, double action, 2, 3, 4, 5, or 6 in. barrels, small frame, break open, blue or nickel, black rubber grips.

	$125	$110	$100	$85	$65	$55	$45

HAMMERLESS — .32 S&W, 6 shot, .38 S&W, 5 shot, double action, 3¼, 4, 5, or 6 in. barrels, large frame, break open.

	$125	$110	$100	$85	$65	$55	$45

TARGET MODEL — .22 LR, .22 WRF, 7 shot, double action, 6 in. barrel, fixed sights, break open, small frame, blue only, walnut grips.

	$140	$120	$100	$85	$70	$60	$50

.22 SPECIAL — .22 LR, .22 WRF, 7 shot, double action, 6 in. barrel, break open, large frame, blue only, gold plated front sight, walnut grips.

	$165	$140	$120	$100	$85	$70	$60

EXPERT — double action, same as .22 Special, except 10 in. barrel.

	$150	$140	$120	$100	$85	$70	$60

SPORTSMAN NO. 199 — .22 LR, 9 shot, single action, 6 in. barrel, adj. target sights, break open, blue only, checkered walnut grips.

	$195	$165	$140	$110	$90	$75	$65

Grading	100%	98%	95%	90%	80%	70%	60%

DEFENDER — .38 S&W, double action, 4 or 6 in. barrel, fixed sights, blue, break open, black plastic grips, made during WWII for police reserves and major corporation guards.

	$140	$120	$110	$100	$85	$65	$55

ULTRA SPORTSMAN — .22 LR, 9 shot, single action, 6 in. barrel, blue, break open, adj. sights, walnut grips, short cylinder action, wide hammer spur.

	$220	$200	$180	$150	$120	$100	$85

NEW DEFENDER — .22 LR, 9 shot, double action, 2 in. barrel, break open, adj. sights, blue, round butt, checkered walnut grip.

	$220	$200	$180	$150	$120	$100	$85

USRA SINGLE SHOT TARGET — .22 LR, 7, 8, or 10 in. barrel, blue, hinged break open, adj. sights, walnut grips. Mfg. 1928-1941.

	$440	$415	$385	$330	$290	$250	$195

Add 10% for nickel finish.

.25 CAL. SELF LOADING PISTOL — .25 ACP, 6 shot, 2 in. barrel, blue, black rubber grips.

	$330	$305	$250	$195	$165	$140	$110

.32 CAL. SELF LOADING PISTOL — .32 ACP, 8 shot, 3½ in. barrel, fixed sights, black rubber grips.

	$330	$305	$250	$195	$165	$140	$110

Add 20% for type I models if in 90%+ original condition.
Type I models with 12 slide pull grooves are serialized 1-3,025. Type II (more common) are serialized 3,026 - 35,000.

HANDY GUN — shotgun (mfg. 1924-1935) or rifle (mfg. 1931-1933) pistol mfg. between 1921-1933, available in either 8 (shotgun only) or 12¼ (shotgun or rifle) in. barrel, either .410 or 28 ga. in shotgun configuration, rifle cal.'s (.22 LR or .32-20) also were available, although not as common. Guns were either case hardened (in Tiger stripe colors), or blued. Case hardened frames have "Handy Gun" stamped on side. Serial numbers on barrel lug and back of frame-numbers should match. .410 ga in 12¼ in. barrel length is most common. These guns had to be registered during the Amnesty period pre-1968. Guns that are not cannot be bought or sold legally. Purchasing a Handy Gun requires a $5 treasury stamp necessary for class 6 registration. Centerfire Handy Guns do not need the $5 stamp. Add $50 for original box or H & R holster.
Shotgun

	$675	$575	$475	$425	$375	$300	$250

A detachable wire stock was available on the rifles and optional on the shotguns. Most shotgun models were not drilled for a shoulder stock.
Rifle

	$475	$400	$350	$300	$325	$275	$250

REVOLVERS: RECENT PRODUCTION

MODEL 504 SQUARE BUTT — .32 H&R Mag., 5 shot, 4 or 6 in. bull barrels, adj. rear sight, swing out cylinder, blue, black plastic and walnut grips. Mfg. 1984 and 1985.

	$165	$145	$135	$120	$110	$100	$90

Last Mfg.'s Sug. Retail was $185.

Model 504 Round Butt — compact design available with 3 or 4 in. barrel only. Disc. 1985.

	$165	$145	$135	$120	$110	$100	$90

Last Mfg.'s Sug. Retail was $185.

MODEL 532 — .32 H&R Mag., 5 shot, 2½ and 4 in. barrels, solid frame revolver, blue, pull pin cylinder, black plastic and walnut grips. Mfg. 1984 and 1985.

	$100	$90	$80	$70	$60	$50	$45

Last Mfg.'s Sug. Retail was $115.

Grading	100%	98%	95%	90%	80%	70%	60%

MODEL 586 — .32 H&R Mag., 5 shot, Western-style revolver, double action, 4½, 5½, 7½, or 10 in. barrels, adj. rear sight, fixed cylinder, antique finish, black plastic or walnut grips. Made 1984 and 1985.

	$175	$155	$135	$120	$110	$100	$90

Last Mfg.'s Sug. Retail was $195.

MODEL 603 — .22 Mag. cal., 6 in. barrel, double action. Disc.

	$159	$120	$110	$95	$90	$80	$70

MODEL 604 — same specifications as the Model 603, only has 6 in. bull barrel.

	$170	$130	$115	$95	$90	$80	$70

MODEL 622 — .22 Short, long, or LR, solid frame, 6 shot, 2½, 4, or 6 in. barrels, blue, plastic grips. Mfg. 1957-1985.

	$95	$82	$70	$60	$55	$50	$45

Last Mfg.'s Sug. Retail was $104.

MODEL 623 — same basic specifications as the Model 622, only nickel finish. Disc.

	$115	$95	$75	$60	$55	$50	$45

MODEL 632 GUARDSMAN — .32 S&W, 6 shot, 2½ or 4 in. barrel, solid frame, checkered tenite grips, blue, model 633 chrome. Mfg. 1953-1984.

	$104	$82	$70	$60	$55	$50	$45

MODEL 633 — same basic specifications as the Model 632, only nickel finish. Disc.

	$115	$95	$75	$60	$55	$50	$45

MODEL 642 — .22 Mag cal., 2½ or 4 in. barrel. Disc.

	$95	$70	$65	$60	$50	$45	$40

MODEL 649 CONVERTIBLE — .22 LR or .22 Mag. cal., furnished with extra cylinder, Western style, double action, side loading, 5½ or 7½ in. barrel, 6 shot, walnut grips, blued finish. Mfg. 1976-1985.

	$140	$120	$110	$95	$90	$80	$70

Last Mfg.'s Sug. Retail was $160.

MODEL 650 CONVERTIBLE — same as Model 649, except with nickel finish and only available with 5½ in. barrel. Disc. 1985.

	$150	$130	$115	$100	$90	$80	$70

Last Mfg.'s Sug. Retail was $175.

MODEL 666 — .22 LR, or .22 Win. Mag. cal., 6 shot, 6 in. barrel, blue, plastic grips, convertible. Mfg. 1976-1982.

	$100	$90	$70	$50	$45	$35	$30

MODEL 676 — .22 LR or .22 Win. Mag. cal., 6 shot, 4½, 5½, 7½, or 12 in. barrel, side load and eject, convertible, blue, case hardened frame, one piece walnut stock. Mfg. 1976-1982.

	$140	$120	$100	$85	$60	$45	$35

MODEL 686 CONVERTIBLE — .22 LR or .22 Mag. cal., furnished with extra cylinder, Western style, double action, side loading, 5½, 7½, 10 or 12 in. barrel, 6 shot, walnut grips, color case hardened frame, adj. rear sight, 12 in. barrel. Disc. 1984.

	$185	$160	$140	$125	$110	$90	$80

MODEL 732 — .32 S&W or .32 H&R Mag. cal., 6 shot, 2½ and 4 in. barrels, fixed sights, swing out cylinder, blue, black plastic grips. Add $15 for .32 H&R Mag. cal. Mfg. 1958-disc.

	$127	$100	$85	$75	$65	$55	$45

MODEL 733 — same specifications as the Model 732, only nickel finish and available only with 2½ in. barrel. Add $15 for .32 H&R Mag. cal.

	$140	$125	$110	$85	$75	$60	$50

Grading	100%	98%	95%	90%	80%	70%	60%

MODEL 900 — .22 S, L, or LR, 9 shot, 2½, 4, or 6 in. barrels, snap out cylinder, blue, black plastic grips. Mfg. 1962-1973.

	$90	$85	$70	$55	$50	$40	$30

MODEL 901 — same as 900, but chrome with white tenite grips. Mfg. 1962-1963.

	$110	$100	$90	$70	$50	$40	$30

MODEL 904 — .22 cal., double action, 4 or 6 in. bull barrel, target grade, 9 shot. Disc. 1985.

	$150	$135	$120	$105	$95	$80	$70

Last Mfg.'s Sug. Retail was $168.

MODEL 905 — same as Model 904, except with nickel finish and 4 in. barrel only. Disc. 1985.

	$160	$140	$125	$105	$95	$80	$70

Last Mfg.'s Sug. Retail was $185.

MODEL 922 — Second Issue, .22 LR cal., 9 shot, 2½, 4, or 6 in. barrels, solid frame, blue, plastic grips. Mfg. 1950-1982.

	$85	$70	$60	$45	$40	$30	$25

MODEL 923 — same as 922, only nickel.

	$90	$75	$65	$50	$45	$35	$30

MODEL 925 DEFENDER — .38 S&W cal., 5 shot, 2½ in. barrel, blue, break open, adj. sight, wrap-around one piece grip. Mfg. 1964-1984.

	$130	$120	$100	$85	$70	$60	$50

Model 935 — same as Model 925, except with nickel finish.

	$145	$135	$115	$100	$70	$60	$50

MODEL 926 — .22 LR cal., 9 shot, or .38 S&W, 5 shot, 4 in. barrel, blue, adj. rear sight, break open, walnut grips. Mfg. 1968-1982.

	$130	$120	$100	$85	$70	$60	$50

MODEL 929 SIDEKICK — .22 LR cal., 9 shot, 2½, 4, or 6 in. barrels, swing out cylinder, plastic grips, blue. Mfg. 1956-1985.

	$115	$100	$70	$55	$45	$35	$30

Last Mfg.'s Sug. Retail was $127.

MODEL 930 SIDEKICK — same as 929 Sidekick, only nickel finish and not available with 6 in. barrel. Disc. 1985.

	$125	$110	$80	$65	$55	$45	$40

Last Mfg.'s Sug. Retail was $140.

MODEL 939 ULTRA SIDEKICK — .22 S, L, or LR, 9 shot, 6 in. barrel, swing out cylinder, vent rib, adj. sights, blue. Mfg. 1958-1982.

	$110	$100	$85	$70	$55	$45	$30

MODEL 940 ULTRA SIDEKICK — same as 939, only round barrel. Disc.

	$105	$95	$75	$65	$50	$40	$30

MODEL 949 "FORTY NINER" — .22 S, L, or LR, 5½ in. barrel, double action, solid frame, 9 shot, side load and Western style ejection, adj. rear sight, walnut grips. Mfg. 1960-1985.

	$115	$100	$85	$70	$55	$50	$45

Last Mfg.'s Sug. Retail was $127.

MODEL 950 — same as Model 949, except with nickel finish. Disc. 1985.

	$125	$105	$90	$70	$55	$50	$45

Last Mfg.'s Sug. Retail was $145.

MODEL 976 — same as 949, only color case hardened frame. Disc.

	$100	$90	$85	$70	$60	$50	$35

Grading	100%	98%	95%	90%	80%	70%	60%

MODEL 999 SPORTSMAN — Second Issue, .22 LR cal., 9 shot, 4 or 6 in. vent rib barrel, break open, adj. sights, walnut grips. Mfg. 1950-1985.

	$195	$170	$155	$145	$130	$120	$110

Last Mfg.'s Sug. Retail was $215.

This model was also made in a Sportsman Centennial Commemorative. Add 15%-25% if NIB.

MODEL 999 ENGRAVED — same as 999, only engraved throughout, 6 in. barrel only. Disc. 1985.

	$425	$375	$300	$260	$225	$190	$175

Last Mfg.'s Sug. Retail was $525.

RIFLES

REISING MODEL 60 — semi-auto, .45 ACP cal., 12 or 20 shot, 18¼ in. barrel, detachable mag. Mfg. 1944-1946.

	$360	$340	$310	$275	$220	$200	$175

MODEL 65 MILITARY — .22 LR cal., 10 shot mag., 23 in. barrel, Redfield aperture rear sight. Mfg. 1944-1946 for USMC.

	$250	$230	$200	$165	$145	$130	$110

MODEL 150 — semi-auto, .22 LR cal., 5 shot. Mfg. 1949-1953.

	$95	$85	$70	$55	$40	$35	$30

MODEL 155 — single shot, .44 Mag. or .45-70 cal., break open. Mfg. 1972-disc.

	$120	$110	$100	$85	$65	$45	$30

MODEL 157 — single shot, .22 Mag., .22 Hornet, or .30-30 cal., break open. Mfg. 1976-disc.

	$122	$100	$90	$70	$60	$40	$30

MODEL 158 — .30-30, .22 Hornet, .357 Mag or .44 Mag. cal., single shot break open, 22 in. barrel, side lever action release, ejector, case hardened frame. Disc. 1985.

	$105	$90	$80	$60	$50	$40	$30

Last Mfg.'s Sug. Retail was $115.

Model 158 Combination — supplied with rifle barrel and 20 ga., 26 in. barrel. Disc. 1985.

	$130	$110	$95	$85	$75	$70	$65

Last Mfg.'s Sug. Retail was $145.

MODEL 165 — .22 LR, 10 shot. Mfg. 1945-1961.

	$120	$110	$95	$85	$70	$55	$50

MODEL 171 — .45-70 Model 1873 Trap door copy, 22 in. barrel, Model 174 is the deluxe model. Disc.

	$295	$260	$230	$210	$190	$175	$160

MODEL 171-DL — single shot, .45-70 gov't cal., Springfield copy, 22 in. barrel. Mfg. 1984 and 1985.

	$345	$305	$265	$225	$205	$190	$170

Last Mfg.'s Sug. Retail was $385.

MODEL 174 — Little Big Horn commercial carbine. Mfg. 1972.

	$395	$350	$310	$280	$240	$220	$200

MODEL 300 ULTRA — bolt action, .22-250, .243 Win., .270 Win., .30-06, .308 Win., 7mm Mag., or .300 Win. Mag. cal., 22 or 24 in. barrel. Mfg. 1965-1978.

	$440	$415	$360	$305	$250	$210	$195

MODEL 301 CARBINE — same as 300, but 18 in. barrel, full length Mannlicher stock, N/A .22-250.

	$440	$415	$360	$305	$250	$220	$195

Grading	100%	98%	95%	90%	80%	70%	60%

MODEL 317 ULTRA WILDCAT — short action Sako, .17 Rem., .17-223, .222 Rem., or .223 Rem. cal., 20 in. barrel, no sights. Mfg. 1968-1976.

	$440	$415	$360	$305	$275	$220	$195

MODEL 317P PRESENTATION — same as 317, but deluxe wood basketweave checkering. Mfg. 1968-1976.

	$550	$525	$495	$440	$400	$360	$305

MODEL 333 — same as 300, in 7mm Mag. cal., plainer version. Mfg. 1974 only.

	$250	$230	$215	$180	$160	$140	$120

MODEL 340 — bolt action in .243 Win. Mag., .270 Win. Mag., .30-06, .308 Win. Mag., 7mm Mauser cal., 5 shot, 22 in. barrel, checkered walnut. Disc.

	$395	$300	$275	$240	$220	$200	$180

MODEL 360 ULTRA AUTOMATIC — .243 Win. or .308 Win. cal., 3 shot, 22 in. barrel. Mfg. 1965-1978.

	$350	$330	$315	$275	$240	$220	$200

MODEL 370 ULTRA MEDALIST TARGET — Varmint Rifle, .22-250, .243 Win., or 6mm Rem. cal., 24 in. varmint weight barrel, semi-beavertail forearm. Mfg. 1968-1973.

	$440	$415	$360	$305	$275	$220	$195

MODEL 422 — slide action, .22 S, L, or LR cal. Mfg. 1956-1958.

	$110	$100	$85	$65	$45	$40	$30

MODEL 451 MEDALIST — bolt action, .22 LR cal., 5 shot, 26 in. barrel. Mfg. 1948-1961.

	$165	$150	$140	$110	$100	$85	$55

Model 450 — same as Model 451, only no sights.

	$150	$140	$120	$110	$95	$70	$55

MODEL 700 — .22 Win. Mag. cal., semi-auto, 5 shot, clip mag., 22 in. barrel. Mfg. 1977-1985.

	$185	$165	$140	$120	$100	$80	$65

Last Mfg.'s Sug. Retail was $210.

MODEL 700DL — same as Model 700, except deluxe checkered walnut. 4-power scope is standard, recoil pad. Disc. 1985.

	$315	$270	$230	$195	$175	$150	$135

Last Mfg.'s Sug. Retail was $360.

MODEL 750 — .22 cal. single shot bolt action, 22 in. barrel, open sights, youth stock dimensions. Disc. 1985.

	$85	$75	$60	$50	$45	$40	$35

Last Mfg.'s Sug. Retail was $95.

MODEL 865 — .22 cal. bolt action. 5 shot mag., 22 in. barrel. Disc. 1985.

	$90	$80	$65	$55	$50	$45	$40

Last Mfg.'s Sug. Retail was $105.

MODEL 5200 — .22 cal. target rifle, heavy 28 in. barrel, adj. trigger, no sights, single shot. 11 lbs. Disc. 1985.

	$395	$350	$295	$260	$230	$200	$175

Last Mfg.'s Sug. Retail was $450.

MODEL 5200 SPORTER — .22 cal., bolt action, 5 shot, 24 in. barrel, adj. sights, checkered walnut. Disc. 1983.

	$440	$385	$330	$295	$260	$230	$200

Grading	100%	98%	95%	90%	80%	70%	60%

SHOTGUNS

HARRICH NO. 1 — single barrel Trap Gun, 12 ga., 32 or 34 in. full choke, high quality, engraved, vent rib. Mfg. by Ferlach of Austria from 1971-1975.

	100%	98%	95%	90%	80%	70%	60%
	$1,650	$1,595	$1,485	$1,320	$1,100	$880	$770

MODEL 3 HAMMERLESS — same as 8, but no visible external hammer. Mfg. 1908-1942.

	$85	$75	$70	$55	$45	$40	$30

MODEL 5 LIGHTWEIGHT — 24, 28, or .410 ga. only. Mfg. 1908-1942.

	$95	$90	$75	$65	$55	$40	$35

MODEL 6 HEAVY BREECH — same as 8, only 10 ga. - 20 ga., heavier barrels. Mfg. 1908-1942.

	$95	$85	$75	$60	$50	$45	$35

MODEL 7 OR 9 BAY STATE — same as 8, only 12, 16, 20 or .410 ga., rounded pistol grip. Mfg. 1908-1942.

	$85	$75	$70	$55	$45	$40	$30

MODEL 8 STANDARD — single shot, 12, 16, 20, 24, 28, or .410 ga., 26-32 in. barrels, plain pistol grip stock, auto ejector, break open. Mfg. 1908-1942.

	$85	$75	$70	$55	$45	$40	$30

FOLDING GUN — hinged frame, barrel folds against stock. Mfg. 1908-1942.

	$95	$90	$75	$65	$55	$40	$35

TOPPER — single shot, break open, 10 different models of this pistol, all are very similar and values run too close to differentiate. Mfg. 1946-disc.

	$145	$125	$100	$85	$70	$55	$45

MODEL 088 — 12, 16, 20, 28, or .410 ga., single shot, hammer model, ejector, blue barrel finish with case hardened frame. Disc. 1985.

	$85	$75	$55	$50	$45	$40	$35

Last Mfg.'s Sug. Retail was $95.

MODEL 099 — 12, 16, 20, or .410 ga., similar to Model 088, only electroless nickel finish, ejector. Disc. 1984.

	$95	$80	$60	$55	$50	$45	$40

MODEL 162 — 12 or 20 ga., single shot, 24 in. slug barrel with rifle sights, case hardened frame, 20 ga. Disc. 1984.

	$115	$105	$90	$80	$65	$55	$45

MODEL 176 — 3½ in. 10 ga. Mag., single shot, 36 in. heavy barrel, break open. Mfg. 1977-1985.

	$110	$95	$80	$70	$60	$50	$45

Last Mfg.'s Sug. Retail was $125.

MODEL 400 PUMP ACTION — 12, 16, or 20 ga., 28 in. full choke. Mfg. 1955-1967.

	$155	$145	$125	$110	$90	$75	$55

MODEL 401 PUMP — same as 400, but H&R variable choke. Mfg. 1956-1963.

	$165	$155	$140	$120	$100	$90	$65

MODEL 402 PUMP — same as 400, only .410 ga., lightweight. Mfg. 1959-1967.

	$175	$165	$150	$140	$110	$100	$85

MODEL 403 AUTOLOADER — .410 ga., 26 in. full choke, takedown. Mfg. 1964 only.

	$195	$180	$165	$155	$120	$100	$85

MODEL 404 — double barrel, s x s, 12, 20, or .410 ga., 26 or 28 in. barrel, boxlock, extractors, double triggers. Mfg. by Rossi of Brazil 1969-1972.

	$185	$175	$165	$145	$110	$90	$70

Grading	100%	98%	95%	90%	80%	70%	60%

MODEL 404C — same as 404, only checkered stock.

	100%	98%	95%	90%	80%	70%	60%
	$200	$185	$175	$155	$120	$100	$85

MODEL 440 — pump action, 12, 16, or 20 ga., 26, 28, or 30 in. barrels, available in various chokes, plain pistol grip and slide. Mfg. 1968-1973.

	$145	$130	$110	$100	$85	$70	$55

MODEL 442 — pump action, same as 440, only vent rib, checkered stock. Mfg. 1969-1973.

	$175	$165	$155	$140	$100	$85	$65

MODEL 490 — 20 or .410 ga., made for junior shooters, Greenwing finish — add $10. Disc. 1984.

	$85	$65	$60	$50	$45	$40	$40

MODEL 1212 — O/U, Field, 12 ga., 2¾ in., 28 in. vent rib barrels, various chokes, checkered walnut stocks. Mfg. by Landbar Arms, Spain, from 1976-disc.

	$310	$295	$275	$250	$200	$175	$155

MODEL 1212 WATERFOWL — same as 1212, except 3 in. 12 ga., 30 in. barrel.

	$320	$310	$285	$260	$210	$185	$165

SINGLE SHOT COMBINATION GUNS

MODEL 058 — 20 ga./.30-30, .22 Hornet, .44 Mag., .357 Mag. combination — 2 separate barrels supplied, blue only. Disc. 1985.

	$130	$110	$95	$85	$75	$65	$60

Last Mfg.'s Sug. Retail was $145.

MODEL 258 COMBINATION HANDY GUN II — supplied with 20 ga., 22 in. barrel and 22 in. rifle barrel in .22 Hornet, .30-30 Win., or .357 Mag. cal., electroless, matte nickel finish, side lever action release, cased, 6½ lbs. Disc. 1985.

	$175	$155	$140	$130	$120	$100	$95

Last Mfg.'s Sug. Retail was $195.

COMMEMORATIVES & REPLICAS

H&R 100TH ANNIVERSARY — 1871-1971, Commemorative Officer's Model, Springfield 1873 Replica, trap door, .45-70 cal., engraved metal work, 26 in. barrel, anniversary plaque on stock, 10,000 mfg. in 1971.

	$350	$295	$250

Last Mfg.'s Sug. Retail was $250 (1971).

MODEL 171 AND 171 DELUXE — listed in previous rifle section.

MODEL 173 — .45-70, same as Officer's Model, no plaque on stock. Mfg. 1972-1983.

	$250	$200	$165

MODEL 174 — .45-70, Little Big Horn Commercial Carbine. Quantity unknown.

	$295	$250	$195

Last Mfg.'s Sug. Retail was $220 (1972).

MODEL 178 — .45-70, Infantry Musket Replica, 32 in. barrel. Mfg. 1973-1984.

	$295	$250	$195

CUSTER MEMORIAL ISSUE — .45-70 cal., limited production, deluxe walnut stock, highly engraved, gold inlaid, mahogany display case and two volumes on Custer history. Each weapon bears the name of one who fell at Little Big Horn.

Officer's Model — 25 made new with original box/accessories.

	$3,350	$2,400	$1,650

Last Mfg.'s Sug. Retail was $3,000 (1973).

Enlisted Men's Model — 243 made new with original box/accessories.

	$1,850	$1,350	$900

Last Mfg.'s Sug. Retail was $2,000 (1973).

Grading	100%	98%	95%	90%	80%	70%	60%

HK4 COMMEMORATIVE — .22 LR and .380 ACP cal.'s with conversion kits, mfg. by H & K of West Germany, cased, limited mfg. in 1971 only.

	$495	$375	$295				

HARTFORD ARMS & EQUIPMENT COMPANY

Hartford Arms was the forerunner of High Standard Arms Co., who acquired them in 1932.

HARTFORD AUTOMATIC TARGET — .22 LR, 10 shot, 6¾ in. barrel, blue, black rubber grips. Mfg. 1929-1930.

	$650	$575	$500	$450	$375	$300	$275

HARTFORD REPEATING PISTOL — .22 cal., similar in appearance to Automatic, except a hand operated repeater. Mfg. 1929-1930.

	$495	$425	$360	$310	$260	$250	$225

HARTFORD SINGLE SHOT TARGET — similar in appearance to Automatic, .22 LR cal., 6¾ in. barrel, target sights, case colored frame and slide, blue barrel, rubber or wood grips. Mfg. 1929-1930.

	$475	$390	$350	$310	$260	$250	$225

HASKELL MANUFACTURING

Manufacturer located in Lima, OH.

JS-9mm — 9mm Para. cal., semi-auto single action, 4½ in. barrel, thumb safety, fixed sights, 8 shot mag., non-glare military blue finish, copolymer synthetic grips, 41 oz. New 1990.

Mfg.'s Sug. Retail	$140	$125	$105	$95	$85	$75	$70	$65

Add $10 for nickel finish.

JS-.45 — .45 ACP cal., similar to JS-9mm, except has 7 shot mag. and 4.6 in. barrel, 44 oz. New 1991.

Mfg.'s Sug. Retail	$150	$135	$110	$100	$90	$80	$75	$70

Add $10 for nickel finish.

HATFIELD INTERNATIONAL INC.

Manufactured by Hatfield International Inc. (designated Hatfield Rifle Works until 1986) located in St. Joseph, MO.

Hatfield also manufactures flintlock and percussion black powder rifles which can be located in the Modern Black Powder Guns section of this text.

Values and information below reflect 1990 data as this publication was not afforded 1991 information by press time.

SHOTGUNS: UPLANDER SERIES S X S

GRADE I — 20 or 28 ga., 3 in. chambers, 26 in. IC/M, matted rib barrels, case hardened boxlock action, single trigger, ejectors, deluxe checkered straight grip maple stock and forearm, 5¾ lbs., cased. New 1987.

Mfg.'s Sug. Retail	$1,295	$1,135	$875	$700	$550	$475	$425	$400

Add $400 for extra 28 ga. barrel.

Collector's Grade I — new 1990.

Mfg.'s Sug. Retail	$1,625	$1,475	$1,200	$1,000	$875	$700	$550	$475

Add $400 for extra 28 ga. barrel.

GRADE II PIGEON — similar to Grade I, except has scroll engraving on top lever, sides, floor plate, and trigger guard, cased. New 1987.

Mfg.'s Sug. Retail	$2,495	$2,175	$1,625	$1,325	$1,050	$900	$775	$675

Add $400 for extra 28 ga. barrel.

Collector's Grade II — new 1990.

Mfg.'s Sug. Retail	$3,025	$2,675	$2,000	$1,600	$1,250	$1,050	$875	$775

Add $400 for extra 28 ga. barrel.

Grading	100%	98%	95%	90%	80%	70%	60%

GRADE III SUPER PIGEON — includes heavy relief scroll engraving (total coverage) on frame, top lever, floor plate, and trigger guard, leather cased. New 1987.

Mfg.'s Sug. Retail	$3,500	$3,100	$2,350	$1,900	$1,495	$1,200	$1,025	$900

Add $900 for extra 28 ga. barrel.

Collector's Grade III — new 1990.

Mfg.'s Sug. Retail	$4,375	$3,800	$3,000	$2,500	$2,000	$1,750	$1,400	$1,175

Add $900 for extra 28 ga. barrel.

GRADE IV GOLDEN QUAIL — more extensive engraving including six 24 Kt. gold inlays on frame and floor plate, 2 gold barrel bands, leather cased. New 1987.

Mfg.'s Sug. Retail	$5,500	$4,800	$3,995	$3,575	$2,900	$2,350	$1,900	$1,600

Add $900 for extra 28 ga. barrel.

Collector's Grade IV — new 1990.

Mfg.'s Sug. Retail	$6,625	$5,700	$4,475	$3,900	$3,300	$2,650	$2,175	$1,800

Add $1,350 for extra 28 ga. barrel.

GRADE V WOODCOCK — previous top-of-the-line model with best quality engraving and multiple gold inlays, leather cased. New 1987.

Mfg.'s Sug. Retail	$6,900	$5,875	$4,600	$4,400	$3,350	$2,700	$2,175	$1,800

Add $1,500 for extra 28 ga. barrel.

Collector's Grade V — new 1990.

Mfg.'s Sug. Retail	$8,500	$7,400	$6,200	$5,700	$4,475	$3,900	$3,300	$2,650

Add $2,000 for extra 28 ga. barrel.

GRADE VI BLACK WIDOW — new 1990.

Mfg.'s Sug. Retail	$7,900	$6,475	$5,200	$4,875	$3,700	$3,000	$2,500	$2,100

Collector's Grade VI — new 1990.

Mfg.'s Sug. Retail	$8,900	$7,600	$6,300	$5,750	$4,500	$3,900	$3,300	$2,650

GRADE VII ROYALE — new 1990.

Mfg.'s Sug. Retail	$7,900	$6,475	$5,200	$4,875	$3,700	$3,000	$2,500	$2,100

Collector's Grade VII — new 1990.

Mfg.'s Sug. Retail	$8,900	$7,600	$6,300	$5,750	$4,500	$3,900	$3,300	$2,650

GRADE VIII TOP HAT — top-of-the-line model with best quality wood and extensive engraving with gold inlays. Built to individual customer specifications. New 1990.

Mfg.'s Sug. Retail	$17,500	$15,750	$12,950	$9,995	$8,750	$7,500	$6,500	$5,500

HAWES FIREARMS

Manufactured by J.P. Sauer & Sohn in Eckernforde, W. Germany. Imported by Hawes Firearms in Van Nuys, CA.

Rather than give an individual listing of the various single action revolvers that have been imported, a generalized price range is as follows: centerfire single actions usually are in the $130 - $250 range while .22 rimfire models are typically valued between $60 - $140.

HECKLER & KOCH

Manufacturer located in Oberndorf/Neckar, Germany. Imported and distributed by Heckler & Koch, Inc. (U.S. headquarters) located in Sterling, VA. In early 1991, H & K was absorbed by Royal Ordnance, a division of British Aerospace located in England.

PISTOLS: SEMI-AUTO, RECENT MANUFACTURE

HK4 — double action auto, .380, .32 auto, .25 auto, and .22 LR, available with all caliber conversion units, 3⅓ in. barrel, blue, plastic grips. In recent years, used HK 4's have been imported into the U.S. at discount prices - thus affecting used HK 4 prices. Disc. 1984.

.25 or .32 ACP cal.	$295	$260	$230	$215	$180	$150	$130
.22 or .380 cal.	$430	$345	$300	$250	$195	$160	$140

Grading	100%	98%	95%	90%	80%	70%	60%

.380 with .22 conversion

	$480	$385	$350	$325	$310	$290	$280

.380 with all conversions

	$590	$475	$450	$420	$390	$375	$360

This model was also mfg. in a French model in .22 LR and/or .32 ACP (about 500 imported).

P9S — .45 ACP or 9mm Para., double action combat model, 4 in. barrel, parkerized finish, sculptured plastic grips, fixed sights. Although production ceased in 1984, limited quantities were available until 1989.

	$600	$480	$400	$360	$320	$290	$265

Last Mfg.'s Sug. Retail was $1,299.

P9S TARGET — .45 ACP or 9mm Para., 5½ in. barrel, blue, adj. sights and trigger. Although production ceased in 1984, limited quantities were available until 1989.

	$850	$700	$600	$540	$500	$465	$430

Last Mfg.'s Sug. Retail was $1,382.

P9S COMPETITION KIT — same as Target, except extra 5½ in. barrel and weight, competition walnut grip, 2 slides. Disc. 1984.

	$1,150	$950	$875	$800	$720	$640	$550

Last Mfg.'s Sug. Retail was $2,250.

P7 PSP — 9mm Para., older variation of the P7 M8, without extended trigger guard, ambidextrous mag. release, or heat shield. Disc. 1986.

Mfg.'s Sug. Retail	$949	$700	$575	$495	$450	$410	$390	$370

This model is available in limited quantities only.

P7 M8 — 9mm Para., unique squeeze cocking single action, extended square combat type trigger guard with heat shield, 4.13 in. fixed barrel with polygonal rifling, 8 shot mag., ambidextrous mag. release, fixed 3-dot sighting system, stippled black plastic grips, black phosphate finish, includes 2 mags., 28 oz.

Mfg.'s Sug. Retail	$949	$725	$625	$550	$495	$450	$410	$390

P7 M10 — .40 S&W cal., similar specifications as P7 M13, except has 10 shot mag., 1.8 lbs. New 1991.

Mfg.'s Sug. Retail	$1,199	$895	$775	$680	$630	$580	$530	$480

P7 M13 — similar to P7 M8, only with staggered 13 shot mag., 40 oz.

Mfg.'s Sug. Retail	$1,159	$875	$750	$680	$630	$580	$530	$480

P7 K3 — .22 LR or .380 ACP cal., uses unique oil-filled buffer to decrease recoil, 3.8 in. barrel, 8 shot mag. (includes 2), 1.65 lbs. New 1988.

Mfg.'s Sug. Retail	$949	$700	$575	$495	$450	$410	$390	$370

Add $499 for .22 LR conversion kit.
A .32 ACP conversion unit is also available for this model.

SP 89 — 9mm Para., semi-auto, recoil operated delayed roller-locked bolt system, 4.5 in. barrel, 15 shot mag., rotated aperature adj. rear sight (accepts HK claw-lock scope mounts), 4.4 lbs. New 1990.

Mfg.'s Sug. Retail	$1,259	$950	$800	$725	$650	$600	$550	$500

Add $119 for adj. target grip.

VP 70Z — 9mm, 18 shot, double action only, 4½ in. barrel, parkerized finish, plastic receiver/grip assembly. Disc. 1984.

	$375	$320	$275	$250	$230	$210	$195

RIFLES: SEMI-AUTO

The models listed below, being of a paramilitary design, were disc. 1989 due to Federal legislation as a result of the controversy with this type of firearms configuration.

Currently, the HK-91 Series, HK-93 Series, and HK-94 Series are available to Law Enforcement Agencies only. Retail prices are $999 for fixed stock models and $1,199 for retractable stock models. Most models below have been discontinued as importation to consumers was banned due to 1989 Federal legislation.

Grading	100%	98%	95%	90%	80%	70%	60%

In the early 70's, S.A.C.O. importers located in Virginia sold the Models 41 and 43 which were the predecessors to the Model 91 and 93, respectively. Values for these earlier variations will be higher than values listed below.

SR-9 — .308 cal. (7.62mm), semi-auto sporting rifle, 19½ in. barrel, Kevlar reinforced fiberglass thumbhole stock and forearm, 5 shot mag., Diopter adj. rear sight, accepts HK claw-lock scope mounts. New 1990.

Mfg.'s Sug. Retail	$1,299	$1,100	$975	$850	$725	$650	$575	$500

MODEL 91 A-2 — .308 cal. (7.62mm), semi-auto paramilitary design rifle, delayed roller lock bolt system, antennuated recoil, black cycolac stock, 17.7 in. barrel, 20 shot mag., 9.7 lbs. Importation disc. 1989.

Fixed stock model

	$1,275	$1,100	$995	$895	$795	$695	$600

Add $200 for desert camo finish.
Add $275 for NATO black finish.
Last Mfg.'s Sug. Retail was $999.

Model 91 A-3 — with retractable metal stock.

	$1,750	$1,500	$1,300	$1,100	$950	$850	$725

Add $400 for .22 LR conversion kit.
Last Mfg.'s Sug. Retail was $1,114.

Model 91 A-2 Package — includes A.R.M.S. mount, B-Square rings, Leupold 3 x 9 compact scope with matte finish. Importation disc. 1988.

	$1,850	$1,575	$1,375	$1,175	$995	$875	$750

Add $150 for retractable stock.
Last Mfg.'s Sug. Retail was $1,285.

MODEL 93 A-2 — .223 cal. (5.56mm), otherwise same as H&K 91, 25 shot mag., 16.14 in. barrel, 8 lbs.

Fixed stock model

	$1,100	$995	$900	$800	$700	$625	$550

Add $200 for desert camo finish.
Add $275 for NATO black finish.
Last Mfg.'s Sug. Retail was $946.

Model 93 A-3 — with retractable metal stock.

	$1,250	$1,075	$975	$850	$750	$675	$595

Last Mfg.'s Sug. Retail was $1,114.

Model 93 A-2 Package — includes A.R.M.S. mount, B-Square rings, Leupold 3 x 9 compact scope with matte finish. Importation disc. 1988.

	$1,850	$1,575	$1,375	$1,175	$995	$875	$750

Add $150 for retractable stock.
Last Mfg.'s Sug. Retail was $1,285.

MODEL 94 CARBINE A-2 — 9mm, semi-auto carbine, 16.54 in. barrel, aperture rear sight, 15 shot mag. New 1983.

Fixed stock model

	$1,450	$1,250	$1,075	$925	$800	$725	$625

Last Mfg.'s Sug. Retail was $946.

Model 94 Carbine A-3 — retractable metal stock.

	$1,595	$1,375	$1,100	$975	$875	$795	$675

Last Mfg.'s Sug. Retail was $1,114.

Model 94 A-2 Package — includes A.R.M.S. mount, B-Square rings, Leupold 3 x 9 compact scope with matte finish. Importation disc. 1988.

	$1,850	$1,575	$1,375	$1,175	$995	$875	$750

Add $150 for retractable stock.
Last Mfg.'s Sug. Retail was $1,285.

Grading	100%	98%	95%	90%	80%	70%	60%

Model 94 SGI — 9mm, semi-auto, target rifle, aluminum alloy bipod, Leupold 6X scope, 15 or 30 shot mag. Imported 1986 only.

	$2,150	$1,750	$1,475	$1,250	$1,075	$900	$795

Last Mfg.'s Sug. Retail was $1,340.

MODEL 270 — .22 LR cal. semi-auto, sporting rifle, 19.7 in. barrel with standard or polygonal rifling, 5 or 20 shot mag., high luster blue, checkered walnut stock, approx. 5.7 lbs. Disc. 1985.

	$400	$350	$300	$275	$250	$225	$200

Last Mfg.'s Sug. Retail was $200.

MODEL 300 — .22 Mag. cal., semi-auto, 5 or 15 shot, polygonal rifling standard, otherwise same as H&K 270. Importation disc. 1989.

	$575	$525	$450	$400	$375	$350	$325

Add $150-$175 for factory H&K scope mount system.
Last Mfg.'s Sug. Retail was $608.

Model 300 Package — includes A.R.M.S. mount, B-Square rings, Leupold 3 x 9 compact scope with matte finish. Importation disc. 1988.

	$750	$700	$650	$600	$550	$500	$460

Last Mfg.'s Sug. Retail was $689.

MODEL 630 — .223 cal., semi-auto, delayed roller lock bolt system, 17.7 in. barrel, reduced recoil, checkered walnut, 4 or 10 shot mag., 7.04 lbs. Importation disc. 1986.

	$725	$650	$550	$495	$460	$430	$400

Add $150-$175 for factory H&K scope mount system.
Last Mfg.'s Sug. Retail was $784.

Because of the significant price increases since 1986 triggered by the devaluation of the American dollar, the importation of this model was stopped. Above values are indicative of current market prices, which could fluctuate due to regional supply and demand.

MODEL 770 — .308 cal., 3 or 10 shot mag., 19.7 in. barrel, 7.92 lbs., otherwise same as model 630. Importation disc. 1986.

	$750	$675	$600	$560	$530	$500	$485

Add $150-$175 for factory H&K scope mount system.
Last Mfg.'s Sug. Retail was $797.

Because of the significant price increases since 1986 triggered by the devaluation of the American dollar, the importation of this model was stopped. Above values are indicative of current market prices, which could fluctuate due to regional supply and demand.

Approx. 10 Model 770's were imported in .243 Win. Values for the .243 cal. will be considerably higher than listed above for the .308 cal.

MODEL 940 — .30-06 cal., 21.6 in. barrel, 8.62 lbs., otherwise same as model 770. Importation disc. 1986.

	$800	$695	$625	$565	$500	$465	$430

Add $150-$175 for factory H&K scope mount system.
Last Mfg.'s Sug. Retail was $917.

Because of the significant price increases since 1986 triggered by the devaluation of the American dollar, the importation of this model was stopped. Above values are indicative of current market prices, which could fluctuate due to regional supply and demand.

MODELS SL6 & SL7 CARBINE — .223 or .308 cal., 17.71 in. barrel, semi-auto, delayed roller lock bolt system, reduced recoil, vent wooden hand guard, 3 or 4 shot mag, 8.36 lbs., matte black metal finish, HK-SL6 is .223 cal., HK-SL7 is .308 cal. Disc. in 1986.

	$675	$595	$550	$495	$460	$430	$400

PSG-1 — .308 cal. only, high precision marksman's rifle, 5 shot mag., adj. buttstock, includes accessories (Hensholdt illuminated 6 x 42 power scope), 17.8 lbs.

Mfg.'s Sug. Retail	$8,859	$7,250	$6,500	$5,750	$5,000	$4,500	$3,850	$3,400

Grading	100%	98%	95%	90%	80%	70%	60%

RIFLES: BOLT ACTION

BASR — .22, .22-250, 6mm PPC, 300 Win. Mag., .30-06, or .308 cal., Kevlar stock, stainless steel barrel, limited production. Special order only. Mfg. 1986 only.

	$8,500	$7,500	$6,500	$5,750	$5,000	$4,500	$4,000

Less than 135 of this variation were manufactured and they are extremely rare. Contractual disputes with the U.S. supplier stopped H&K from receiving any BASR models.

SHOTGUNS

H & K imported Benelli shotguns can be found under their own heading.

HENRY RIFLE

Please refer to the Winchester section in this text.

HEROLD RIFLE

Franz Jaeger, Suhl, Germany.

BOLT ACTION SPORTING RIFLE — miniature Mauser action, .22 Hornet, 24 in. barrel, leaf sight, double set trigger, select checkered stock, imported by Daly & Stoeger, pre-WWII.

	$990	$880	$825	$770	$660	$550	$495

HERTERS

Previous importer/distributor/retailer headquartered in Waseca, MN from early 1960's - 1979.

Herters subcontracted various manufacturers (mostly European) to fabricate revolvers, rifles, and shotguns which were mostly patterned after more famous original models. Most of these copies were designed to undersell the competition at the time and while quality in most cases was quite good, consumer sales were not strong enough to continue production. While many Herters models are relatively rare, collectability to date has been minimal. Herters model values are usually under the original trademarks from which they were derived and to date have been based more on the shooting utility than the collector potential.

HEYM, FRIEDRICH WILH.

Originally founded in 1865 by F.H. Heym with location in Suhl. Currently manufactured in Muennerstadt, W. Germany. Currently imported and distributed by Heckler & Koch, Inc. located in Sterling, VA. Previously imported and distributed by Heym America, Inc. (subsidiary of F.W. Heym of W. Germany) located in Fort Wayne, IN.

OVER AND UNDERS

MODEL 22 S2 — rifle/shotgun combination, 12, 16, or 20 ga. (3 in.), under rifle (17 cal.'s available), single set trigger, takedown feature (standard 1990), coin finish, 5½ lbs.

Mfg.'s Sug. Retail	$2,860	$2,400	$2,100	$1,760	$1,525	$1,325	$1,100	$990

This model features a dampened rifle barrel which prevents the "climbing" of groups, thereby enhancing accuracy.

MODEL 55 BF — rifle/shotgun combination, popular U.S. and European cal.'s, shotgun barrels interchangeable in 12, 16, or 20 ga., 25 or 28 in. barrels, boxlock, auto ejectors, silver finish, fine German engraving, folding leaf sight, checkered pistol grip stock. Extra barrels — add $3,250 for O/U rifle and $2,250 for O/U shotgun or shotgun/rifle combination.

Mfg.'s Sug. Retail	$6,000	$5,400	$4,950	$4,525	$3,950	$3,615	$3,210	$2,775

Model 55 B — O/U rifle only, various cal.'s, engraving similar to Model 55 BF.

Mfg.'s Sug. Retail	$8,200	$7,600	$6,875	$5,925	$5,100	$4,650	$3,975	$3,300

Model 55 BS — O/U rifle only with different caliber for each barrel, double set triggers, "Bergstutzen" design.

Mfg.'s Sug. Retail	$8,475	$7,750	$6,950	$5,950	$5,125	$4,650	$3,975	$3,300

Model 55 F — O/U shotgun, ejectors, 20 or 16 ga., engraved, 6.6 lbs.

Mfg.'s Sug. Retail	$5,500	$5,100	$4,525	$3,950	$3,615	$3,200	$2,775	$2,300

Grading	100%	98%	95%	90%	80%	70%	60%

Model 55 SS — sidelock version of Model 55 F, large engraved hunting scenes.

Mfg.'s Sug. Retail	$4,550	$4,250	$3,700	$3,250	$2,850	$2,400	$2,000	$1,700

MODEL 200 — 20 ga., 3 in. chambers, boxlock action, DT's, 28 in. VR barrels, light engraving, previous importation.

	$895	$795	$700	$650	$600	$550	$500

DRILLINGS

MODEL 33 BOXLOCK STANDARD — 16 or 20 ga., boxlock, Arabesque engraving, shotgun barrels over popular European cal.'s, and .222, .243, .270, .308, and .30-06 rifle barrel, 25 in. full and mod. barrels, set trigger on rifle, checkered pistol grip stock.

Mfg.'s Sug. Retail	$7,760	$6,800	$5,600	$4,950	$4,525	$3,950	$3,615	$3,210

Model 33 Deluxe — same specifications as Standard Model, only hunting scene engraved.

Mfg.'s Sug. Retail	$8,300	$7,500	$5,950	$5,150	$4,650	$4,025	$3,700	$3,300

MODEL 37 SIDELOCK STANDARD — shotgun barrels (12, 16, or 20 ga.) over rifle, detachable sidelocks, select French walnut, border engraving, 8 lbs.

Mfg.'s Sug. Retail	$10,300	$9,400	$8,800	$7,750	$6,650	$5,900	$5,300	$4,750

Model 37 Deluxe — same as Model 37 Standard, except has large engraved hunting scenes.

Mfg.'s Sug. Retail	$12,275	$11,000	$9,950	$8,200	$7,475	$6,500	$5,650	$4,875

MODEL 37 B STANDARD — rifle barrels over shotgun (20 ga.), sidelock, border engraved, about 8.6 lbs.

Mfg.'s Sug. Retail	$13,380	$12,000	$10,875	$9,500	$8,400	$7,550	$6,500	$5,650

Model 37 B Deluxe — similar to Model 37 B Standard, except has large hunting scene engraving.

Mfg.'s Sug. Retail	$15,500	$14,000	$12,000	$10,700	$9,450	$8,200	$7,050	$5,750

RIFLES: BOLT ACTION

MODEL SR 20N — available in 18 cal.'s, Mauser type bolt action, single trigger, French walnut, 24 in. Krupp steel barrel except Mag. (25 in.).

Mfg.'s Sug. Retail	$2,120	$1,825	$1,425	$1,100	$900	$800	$700	$600

Add $350 for left-hand variation.

Add $115 for Mag. cal.'s (G suffix).

Model SR 20 Hunter — similar to Model SR 20N, except has classic style fiberglass stock with either matte blue or parkerized metal finish. Imported 1988-90.

	$1,500	$1,225	$1,050	$900	$800	$700	$600

Last Mfg.'s Sug. Retail was $1,750.

Model SR 20L — Mannlicher style stock, 18 in. barrel, 7 lbs.

Mfg.'s Sug. Retail	$1,700	$1,475	$1,225	$985	$895	$785	$720	$650

SR 20 TROPHY — available in 8 cal.'s between 7 X 57mm and .375 H&H, bolt action, 22 or 24 (Mag. cal.'s only) in. octagonal barrel, classic stock configuration with cheek piece and recoil pad. Importation began 1989.

Mfg.'s Sug. Retail	$2,815	$2,550	$2,100	$1,800	$1,500	$1,250	$985	$895

Add $120 for Mag. cal's.

This model is available with either right hand or left hand action.

SR 20G CLASSIC SPORTER — available in 8 cal.'s between .243 Win. and .375 H&H, bolt action, 22 or 24 in. round barrel, steel grip cap. Importation began 1989.

Mfg.'s Sug. Retail	$2,235	$1,875	$1,600	$1,300	$1,050	$900	$785	$720

Subtract $70 without iron sights.

This model is available with either right hand or left hand action.

SR 20 ALPINE — available in 8 cal.'s between .243 Win. and 8 X 57JS, mountain style rifle with full stock, schnabel forend cap, supplied with mounted open sights. Importation began 1989.

Mfg.'s Sug. Retail	$2,165	$1,900	$1,650	$1,325	$1,075	$925	$800	$750

This model is available with either right hand or left hand action.

Grading	100%	98%	95%	90%	80%	70%	60%

SR 20 MATCH — .308 cal. only, 24 in. heavy barrel, target stock with accessory rail, large bolt handle, supplied without sights, 9 lbs. New 1991.

Mfg.'s Sug. Retail	$2,200	$1,860	$1,600	$1,300	$1,050	$900	$785	$720

SR 20 CLASSIC SAFARI — .404 Jeffrey, .425 Express, or .458 Win. Mag., 24 in. barrel only, express rear sight and large front post sights, extra fancy walnut. Importation began 1989.

Mfg.'s Sug. Retail	$2,500	$2,150	$1,650	$1,250	$1,050	$875	$800	$700

This model is available with either right hand or left hand action.

EXPRESS SERIES RIFLE — available in most Mag. cal.'s including .375 H&H, .404 Jeffrey, .416 Rigby, or .500 A-Square, express sights, Timney single trigger. Importation began 1989.

Mfg.'s Sug. Retail	$5,700	$5,150	$4,250	$3,750	$3,000	$2,350	$2,000	$1,750

Add $535 for left-hand action.

.600 NE Rifle — .600 NE cal., 24 in. barrel, reinforced action, 3 shot mag., importation began 1991.

This model is available through customer special order only. Prices start at approx. $14,000. Please contact the importer for an up-to-date quotation.

RIFLES: SINGLE SHOT

MODEL HR 30N SINGLE SHOT — available in many cal.'s, Ruger No. 1 falling block action, 24 in. barrel, French walnut with Bavarian cheek piece, round barrel, Sporter or full length carbine style French walnut stock, engraved coin finished receiver, 6.6 lbs.

Mfg.'s Sug. Retail	$3,675	$3,175	$2,750	$2,225	$1,950	$1,675	$1,350	$1,175

Add $325 for Mannlicher stocked Carbine Model.

Add $2,000 for sideplates with hunting scenes.

Add $175 for Mag. cal.'s.

MODEL HR 38 N — available in many cal.'s, Ruger No. 1 falling block action 24 in. barrel, octagon barrel, French walnut with Bavarian cheek piece, Sporter or full length carbine style French walnut stock, engraved coin finished receiver, 6.6 lbs.

Mfg.'s Sug. Retail	$4,200	$3,725	$3,200	$2,750	$2,225	$1,950	$1,675	$1,350

Add $200 for Mag. cal's.

SIDELOCK RIFLE SHOTGUN

MODEL 35 STANDARD — 3 barrels, (two rifle and one shotgun), choice of cal's with top barrel either 16 or 20 ga., light border engraving, 8#4 lbs.

Mfg.'s Sug. Retail	$13,900	$12,800	$11,000	$10,000	$9,000	$8,000	$6,950	$5,800

Add $2,100 for hunting scene engraving.

RIFLES: SIDE-BY-SIDE

MODEL 88 B — available in various cal.'s between 7mm and .375 H&H, sxs double rifle, boxlock action, Krupp steel barrels, double underlocking lugs with greener crossbolt, ejectors, checkered circassian walnut, built to customer specifications, 7½ lbs.

Mfg.'s Sug. Retail	$10,700	$9,550	$8,450	$6,950	$6,225	$5,420	$4,575	$3,975

Model 88 BSS — sidelock model with interceptor sears.

Mfg.'s Sug. Retail	$15,400	$13,800	$11,750	$10,550	$9,550	$8,150	$7,025	$6,000

Model 88 B Safari — available in .375 H&H, .458 Win. Mag., .470 Nitro Express, or .500 Nitro Express cal., 24 in. barrels, 9.9 lbs.

Mfg.'s Sug. Retail	$14,500	$13,200	$11,250	$10,100	$9,400	$8,000	$6,950	$5,800

MODEL 88 BF RIFLE-SHOTGUN — 2 barrel set with 12 ga. barrels and an extra set of rifle barrels available in cal.'s .375 H&H Mag., .458 Win. Mag., .470 N.E., or .500 N.E.

Mfg.'s Sug. Retail	$14,500	$13,200	$11,250	$10,100	$9,400	$8,000	$6,950	$5,800

Model 88B/S Safari — includes set of rifle and shotgun barrels, choice of .375 H&H, .458 Win. Mag., .470 NE, or .500 NE cal. and extra set of 12 ga. 2¾ in. chamber barrels.

Mfg.'s Sug. Retail	$17,560	$15,400	$13,800	$11,750	$10,550	$9,550	$8,150	$7,025

Grading	100%	98%	95%	90%	80%	70%	60%

MODEL 88 F SIDE-BY-SIDE SHOTGUN — available in cal.'s 20 ga. with 2¾ or 3 in. chambers.

Mfg.'s Sug. Retail	$14,500	$13,200	$11,250	$10,100	$9,400	$8,000	$6,950	$5,800

HIGGINS, J.C.

Trademark used on Sears & Roebuck rifles and shotguns manufactured between 1946-1962.

The J.C. Higgins trademark has appeared literally on hundreds of various models (shotguns and rifles) sold through the Sears & Roebuck retail network. Most of these models were manufactured through subcontracts with both domestic and international firearms manufacturers. Typically, they were "spec." guns made to sell at a specific price to undersell the competition. Most of these models were derivatives of existing factory models with less expensive wood and perhaps missing the features found on those models from which they were derived.

To date, there has been very little interest in collecting J.C. Higgins guns, regardless of rarity. Rather than list J.C. Higgins' models, a general guideline is that values generally are under those of their "1st generation relatives". The Ranger trademark was also used by Sears & Roebuck - it is not any more desirable than those guns marked J.C. Higgins. As a result, prices are ascertained by the shooting value of the gun, rather than its' collector value.

HIGH STANDARD

High Standard Mfg. Co. was founded in 1926. They purchased Hartford Arms and Equipment Co. in 1932. The original plant was located in New Haven, CT from 1932-1950 until they moved to a larger facility at Hamden, CT from 1951-1977. A final move was made to East Hartford, CT in 1978 where they remained until the doors were closed in January, 1984.

Please refer to the High Standard serialization section in the back of this text for ascertaining year of manufacture by serial number on the semi-auto pistols models listed below.

The High Standard section in this edition has changed extensively to reflect the chronological groupings of the various models.

The approximate serial number cut-off for Hamden, CT manufacture is 2,300,000.

High Standard values have risen dramatically over the past several years. Many collectors have realized the rarity and quality factors this trademark has earned (Models C, A, D, E, H-D, H-E, H-A, H-B First Model, G-380, GB, GD, GE, GO - 13 different variations had a total production of less than 48,000 pistols). For these reasons, top condition High Standard pistols are getting more difficult to find each year.

SEMI-AUTO PISTOLS

PRE-WAR HIGH STANDARD SEMI-AUTOMATIC PISTOLS HAD 3 DIFFERENT TAKE-DOWN TYPES.

I-A TYPE MFG. 1932-38. Takedown lever on left side of frame next to safety. Round retracting rod on rear of slide. This takedown was used on Models B & C.

I-B TYPE MFG. 1938. Same as I-A Type except has strengthened rectangular rod on rear of slide.

TYPE II MFG. 1939. Takedown lever located on right side of frame. Round pick-up rod on top of slide.

HAMMERLESS FIXED BARREL SERIES

This series consists of the 5 original pistols mfg. in 1932-1942. All serial numbers are located on forestrap of frame.

Grading	100%	98%	95%	90%	80%	70%	60%

MODEL B — original High Standard pistol, basically the same gun as Hartford Arms 1925 Automatic, .22 LR, small frame, 4½ or 6¾ in. light weight barrel, fixed rear sight, checkered hard rubber grips with or without H.S. monogram. Beginning ser. no. 5,000. Approx. 65,000 mfg. 1932-42.

	$475	$400	$325	$285	$235	$200	$180

Add $50 for I-B Type takedown.
Less than 14,000 pistols with this takedown were mfg.

MODEL C — identical to Model B in appearance, except .22 Short only, small frame, 4½ or 6¾ in. light weight barrel, fixed rear sight, checkered hard rubber grips with or without H.S. monogram. Beginning ser. no. 500 to 31XX, later beginning ser. no. 42XXX. Approx. 4,700 mfg. 1936-42.

	$600	$475	$375	$300	$250	$210	$185

MODEL A — similar to Model B, except enlarged frame, squared-off butt, .22LR, 4½ or 6¾ in. light weight barrel, adj. rear sight, checkered walnut grips, slide lock, trigger stop. Beginning ser. no. 33XXX. Approx. 7,300 mfg. 1938-42.

	$550	$475	$375	$300	$235	$200	$180

MODEL D — identical to Model A except 4½ or 6¾ in. medium weight barrel, .22 LR, adj. sights, walnut grips, slide lock trigger stop. Beginning ser. no. 33XXX. Approx. 2,500 mfg. 1938-42.

	$575	$425	$325	$295	$240	$225	$195

MODEL E — high quality, deluxe model of the hammerless series, .22 LR, adj. sight, 4½ or 6¾ in. heavy barrel, checkered walnut target grips with thumbrest. Beginning ser. no. 34XXX. Approx. 2,600 mfg. 1938-42.

	$725	$575	$450	$375	$300	$270	$230

EXPOSED HAMMER—FIXED BARREL SERIES

This series consists of 4 pistols that were introduced in 1940. Frame and slide modified to accommodate external hammer. All ser. no.'s located on forestrap of frame. Prefix "H" added to standard model designation with the exception of Model C. Mfg. 1940-42.

MODEL H-D — first exposed hammer model, similar to Model D, .22 LR, 4½ or 6¾ in. medium weight barrel, adj. sight, target or standard walnut grips, no external safety. High quality pistol. Beginning ser. no. 51XXX. Approx. 6,900 mfg. 1940-42.

	$575	$440	$345	$285	$250	$225	$200

MODEL H-E — high quality, deluxe model of exposed hammer series, .22 LR, 4½ or 6¾ in. heavy barrel, adj. sight, deluxe hand checkered walnut grips with thumbrests, no external safety. Rarest of the H.S. pistols. Beginning ser. no. 51XXX. Approx 1,000 mfg. 1941-42.

	$995	$795	$625	$500	$375	$315	$275

MODEL H-A — similar to Model A, .22 LR, 4½ or 6¾ in. light weight barrel, adj. sight, plain checkered walnut grips, no external safety. Very rare gun. Beginning ser. no. 53XXX. Approx. 1,000 mfg. 1940-42.

	$625	$475	$400	$350	$260	$225	$195

MODEL H-B — duplicate of Model B with external hammer, .22 LR, 4½ or 6¾ in. light weight barrel, fixed sight, checkered hard rubber grips with our without H.S. monogram, no external safety. This first Model H-B had beginning ser. no. 52XXX. Approx. 2,200 mfg. 1940-42.

	$575	$450	$325	$285	$240	$225	$195

Model H-B Second Model — H.S. reintroduced a H-B second model similar to first model, except with external safety. Beginning ser. no. 308XXX. Approx. 25,000 mfg. 1949-1954.

	$525	$425	$310	$285	$220	$195	$175

Grading	100%	98%	95%	90%	80%	70%	60%

U.S. MILITARY SERIES

These models are earlier H.S. pistols adapted as training guns during WWII. They were the sole suppliers of the .22 cal. pistol for military training. Ser. no.'s located on forestrap of frame.

MODEL B-US — adapted Model B with minor changes, .22 LR, available in 4½ in. barrel only, checkered hard rubber grips, fixed sight, marked "Property of U.S." on right side of frame and on top of barrel. Ordnance acceptance crossed cannon stamped on right side of frame above trigger guard. Beginning ser. no. 95XXX. Approx. 14,000 mfg. 1942-43.

	$575	$450	$350	$285	$240	$225	$195

U.S.A. MODEL H-D — the government needed a training pistol similar to the Colt Model 1911 .45 ACP. The result was a Model HD with external safety and fixed sight, 4½ in. medium weight barrel, .22 LR only. The barrel is marked "Property of USA", black checkered hard rubber grips. First models mfg. had high gloss blue finish, changed to a Parkerized finish near ser. no. 130XXX. Beginning ser. no. 109XXX-153XXX. Approx. 44,000 mfg. 1943-46.

	$525	$440	$325	$275	$210	$190	$165

Add 20% for early blue finish.

This model was also produced for the O.S.S. called the USA-HD-MS, requires N.F.A. transfer. Prices can range from $1,500-$3,000, depending on condition.

MODEL H-D MILITARY — though called H-D Military, this model was not mfg. for the government. Essentially a USA-HD with the addition of adj. sights, .22 LR, 4½ or 6¾ in. barrel, checkered walnut grips, external safety. Beginning ser. no. 147XXX. Approx. 150,000 mfg. 1946-55.

	$475	$375	$285	$250	$210	$190	$160

MODEL G-380 — this is H.S.'s only in-house production of a center-fire pistol other than a .22 cal. A transition model to the G-series using a lever takedown. Has exposed hammer, fixed sights, .380 cal., checkered black plastic grips, external safety, 5 in. barrel only. Beginning ser. no. 100. Approx. 7,400 mfg. 1947-50.

	$600	$475	$400	$350	$275	$240	$210

THE G-SERIES

This series is hammerless with interchangeable target barrel, 6¾ in. and plinking barrel, 4½ in., consists of 4 pistols, all using lever takedown. An adaptation of the G-380 design. Ser. no.'s on right side of slide and rear right side of frame. Mfg. 1948-50.

MODEL GB — similar to Model B with light barrel, small frame, .22 LR, external safety, fixed sight, checkered brown plastic grips, interchangeable 4½ or 6¾ in. barrel with lever takedown. Beginning ser. no. 311XXX. Approx. 4,900 mfg. 1949-50.

	$495	$425	$325	$275	$225	$200	$180

Add 15-20% for both barrels.

MODEL GD — large frame with medium weight with interchangeable 4½ or 6¾ in. barrel with lever takedown, .22 LR, featured new adj. "Davis" sight, named for designer G.F. Davis. Grips avail. in plain checkered walnut or deluxe with thumbrest grips. Beginning ser. no. 311XXX. Approx. 3,300 mfg. 1949-50.

	$495	$425	$325	$275	$225	$200	$180

Add 15-20% for both barrels.

MODEL GE — deluxe top of the line quality .22 LR pistol, large frame with interchangeable 4½ or 6¾ in. heavy "bull" barrel with lever takedown, "Davis" sight adj. sight, deluxe walnut hand checkered grips with thumbrest. Beginning ser. no. 312XXX. Approx. 2,900 mfg. 1949-50.

	$750	$575	$450	$350	$275	$240	$210

Add 15-20% for both barrels.

This model has a grooved fore and rear strap.

Grading	100%	98%	95%	90%	80%	70%	60%

MODEL G-O — also known as First Model Olympic. First fired in Olympic competition in 1948. Adaptation of Model GE in .22 cal. short. Deluxe top-of-the-line quality, interchangeable 4½ or 6¾ heavy "bull" barrel with lever takedown, "Davis" adj. sight, deluxe hand checkered walnut grips with thumbrests. First High Standard large production gun with aluminum slide. Has unique curved magazine. Rare. Beginning ser. no. 307XXX. Approx. 1,200 mfg. 1949-50.

	$850	$675	$525	$450	$375	$325	$285

Add 15-20% for both barrels.
This model has a grooved fore and rear strap.

THE SUPERMATIC SERIES

All of this series was mfg. at the Hamden, CT plant from 1951-53. Consisted of 4 guns, featuring the lever takedown introduced in the G-Series. Hammerless, new positive lock safety, use of one screw to attach grips, no production figures available.

SUPERMATIC (FIRST MODEL) — .22 LR, 10 shot mag., 4½ or 6¾ in. interchangeable barrel with lever takedown, "Davis" adj. sight, slide lock, front and back straps grooved, serated rib between front and rear sight, adj. 2 oz. and 3 oz. weights which dovetail into and beneath barrel.

	$550	$425	$350	$300	$250	$200	$180

Add 15-20% for both barrels.

OLYMPIC (SECOND MODEL) — .22 cal. short, identical in all respects to the Supermatic, except has aluminum slide for rapid recoil, interchangeable 4½ or 6¾ in. barrel with lever takedown, "Davis" adj. sight, adj. 2 oz. and 3 oz. weights, 10 shot mag.

	$600	$475	$395	$300	$250	$200	$180

Add 15-20% for both barrels.

FIELD-KING (FIRST MODEL) — plain version of Supermatic, .22 LR, 10 shot mag., interchangeable 4½ or 6¾ in. barrels with lever takedown, "Davis" adj. sight, 10 shot mag.

	$495	$375	$300	$250	$200	$185	$165

Add 10-15% for both barrels.

SPORT-KING (FIRST MODEL) — .22 LR, 10 shot mag., similar to Field-King but has fixed sight and light weight interchangeable 4½ or 6¾ in. barrel featuring lever takedown.

	$475	$375	$275	$225	$200	$185	$165

Add 10-15% for extra barrel.
This model was available with or without slide lock.

QUICK CHANGE CONVERSION KIT — avail. in 1951 to let you shoot both .22 LR or .22 Short in the Supermatic, Olympic, or Field-King models. Featured factory fitted barrel, slide, barrel weights and magazine included in this kit.

	$375	$300	$275

THE M-100 AND M-101 SERIES

All of this series was mfg. at the Hamden, CT plant from 1954-58. Hammerless design consisting of 5 pistols featuring a new push-button type takedown. The beginning ser. no. for .22 LR pistols only in this series was 443,611.

SUPERMATIC (SECOND MODEL) — S 100 or S 101 stamped on right side of slide, .22 LR, 10 shot mag., 4½ or 6¾ in. interchangeable barrel with push-button takedown, adj. 2 oz. or 3 oz. weights. Slotted stabilizer 6¾ in. target barrel was an option. Adj. rear sight.

	$475	$400	$325	$250	$200	$180	$150

OLYMPIC (THIRD MODEL) — 0-100 or 0-101 stamped on right side of slide, .22 Short, 10 shot mag., 4½ or 6¾ in. interchangeable barrel with push-button takedown, adj. 2 oz. or 3 oz. weights. Slotted stabilizer 6¾ in. target barrel was an option. Adj. rear sight.

	$550	$450	$350	$295	$240	$220	$190

Grading	100%	98%	95%	90%	80%	70%	60%

FIELD-KING (SECOND MODEL) — FK 100 or Fk 101 stamped on right sidse of slide, .22 LR, 10 shot mag. 4½ or 6¾ in. interchangeable barrel with push-button takedown. Slotted stabilizer 6¾ in. target barrel was an option. Adj. rear sight.

	$450	$350	$275	$225	$195	$175	$150

FLITE-KING (FIRST MODEL) — LW 100 or LW 101 stamped on right side of slide, .22 Short, 10 shot mag., 4½ or 6¾ in. interchangeable light weight barrel with push- button takedown, alloy slide. First commercial use of aluminum alloy for frame. Fixed rear sight.

	$450	$350	$275	$225	$195	$175	$150

Add 15-20% for both barrels.

SPORT-KING (SECOND MODEL) — SK 100 or SK 101 stamped on right side of slide, .22 LR, similar to Flite-King but with steel slide and frame. This model was also avail. in nickel. Fixed rear sight.

	$425	$340	$250	$200	$180	$160	$140

Add 15-20% for both barrels.
Add 20% for nickel finish.

SPORT-KING LIGHTWEIGHT — .22 LR, similar to standard Sport-King, except has forged aluminum alloy frame. The word "Lightweight" is inscribed in script on the left side of frame. Also avail. in nickel, 1954-70.

	$425	$340	$250	$200	$180	$160	$140

Add 20% for nickel finish.

DURAMATIC — .22 LR, 4½ or 6¾ in. barrels, fixed sight, large plastic grips. M-100 or M-101 stamped on right side of slide. Mfg. 1954-70. The Duramatic was sold by Sears Roebuck & Co. as the J. C. Higgins Model 80. This Sears variation had some minor exterior differences, but mechanically it was the same. Unique thumb screw takedown.

	$450	$350	$275	$225	$200	$185	$165

Add 20% for extra barrel.

MODEL 102 AND 103 SERIES

This series included the following and were mfg. in Hamden, CT between 1958-1963. The words "Model 102" or "Model 103" were inscribed on the right side of slide. This series introduced an improved push-button takedown.

SPORT-KING — same as previous Sport-King, but inscribed Model 103 on slide.

	$395	$295	$225	$195	$175	$150	$125

Add 10% for nickel finish.

SUPERMATIC TOURNAMENT — .22 LR, 10 shot, 4½ in. bull barrel or 6¾ straight barrel, diamond checkered plastic slant grips, adj. sight, push-button takedown. Mfg. 1961-66. The gov.'t ordered a quantity of Mod. 102 Tournament for training. These were marked "US" on right side of frame.

	$550	$450	$350	$285	$240	$220	$195

SUPERMATIC CITATION — .22 LR, 10 shot, 6¾ in., 8 in. and 10 in. tapered barrels, diamond checkered plastic slant grips, adj. sight, push-button takedown, one grade above Tournament. Barrel weights. Sight located on 8 and 10 in. barrel. Detachable stabilizer available. Mfg. 1961-66.

	$550	$475	$375	$285	$240	$220	$195

SUPERMATIC TROPHY — .22 LR, 10 shot, 6¾ in., 8 in. and 10 in. tapered barrels. Same grips as Tournament and Citation. Features gold trigger, gold safety button, gold inlaid lettering, adj. sight, push-button takedown. Mfg. 1961-66.

	$575	$495	$375	$295	$240	$220	$195

ISU OLYMPIC — this is the model which brought the 33rd Gold Medal in the Rome Olympics in 1960. .22 Short, 10 shot, 6¾ in. barrel with integral stabilizer. Same grips as Tournament and Citation. High luster finish. Top-of-the-line Olympic model. Complies with all rapid-fire International Shooting Union regulations.

	$600	$500	$375	$300	$250	$225	$195

Grading	100%	98%	95%	90%	80%	70%	60%

OLYMPIC — same basic gun as ISU Olympic, but it is of lesser quality finish. Adj. sight located on 8 in. barrel.

	$600	$525	$400	$295	$240	$225	$195

This model has also been observed with markings "OLYMPIC CITATION" or "OLYMPIC TROPHY".

SPORT KING "M" — standard Sport-King with military type grips.

	$375	$275	$215	$195	$175	$150	$125

PLINKER — similar to Duramatic, thumb screw takedown. Mfg. 1971-73.

	$450	$325	$275	$225	$200	$185	$165

Add 20% for extra barrel.

MODEL 104 SERIES

This series was mfg. 1964 only. Models include a Supermatic Citation model and ISU Olympic model.

SUPERMATIC CITATION — same as 102 and 103 series, 5½ in. bull barrel with 2 oz. or 3 oz. round type weights.

	$550	$450	$350	$285	$240	$220	$195

ISU OLYMPIC — same as 102 and 103 Olympic, 6¾ in. tapered barrel with integral stabilizer and barrel weights avail.

	$600	$500	$375	$295	$240	$225	$195

MILITARY MODEL 106 SERIES

This series was mfg. 1965-1967. Models include Supermatic Tournament, Supermatic Citation, Supermatic Trophy, Olympic, and Olympic ISU. This included a military model available on all. The military model features a grip that had the exact heft and feel of the famous military .45. The military models featured a new rear bridge or saddle type sight, permanently fixed to frame.

SUPERMATIC TOURNAMENT MILITARY — same as standard Military Model 106 Series with 5½ bull or 6¾ in. straight barrel with military grips.

	$525	$450	$350	$285	$240	$220	$195

SUPERMATIC CITATION MILITARY — same as standard Military Model 106 Series with 5½ bull or 7¼ in. fluted barrel with military grips. New rear bridge or saddle type sight.

	$575	$450	$350	$295	$240	$225	$195

A Supermatic Trophy also was mfg. in the 104 Series.

SUPERMATIC TROPHY MILITARY — same as standard Military Model 106 Series with 5½ bull or 7¼ in. fluted barrel with military grips. New rear bridge or saddle type sight.

	$600	$525	$400	$300	$250	$225	$195

OLYMPIC MILITARY — same as standard Military Model 106 Series with 5½ in. bull barrel with military grips. New rear bridge or saddle type sight.

	$600	$525	$400	$300	$250	$225	$200

OLYMPIC/ISU MILITARY — same as standard Military Model 106 Series with 6¾ in. tapered barrel, built-in stabilizer, and military grips. New rear bridge or saddle type sight.

	$600	$525	$375	$295	$240	$225	$200

SHARPSHOOTER — .22 LR, 5½ in. bull barrel, adj. rear sight, push-button takedown, brown plastic grips. Mfg. 1971-81.

	$395	$350	$250	$225	$200	$150	$125

MILITARY MODEL 107 SERIES

The Military 107 Series was mfg. during 1968 only. Models include Supermatic Tournament, Citation, and Trophy, also the Olympic ISU and Victor models.

Grading	100%	98%	95%	90%	80%	70%	60%

VICTOR — introduced in 1972-77, made in Hamden, CT. Available in 4½ or 5½ in. vent rib, rear sight mounted on vent rib, 22 LR, 10 shot mag., 4½ in. solid rib also available, push-button takedown.

	$650	$500	$375	$300	$250	$225	$200

Add $50 for solid rib.

This model was available in either Military (normal grip - mfg. 1971-77) or G.I. configuration (slant grip - rare).

1972 OLYMPIC COMMEMORATIVE — a highly engraved version of a Supermatic Trophy Military, Model 107, in .22 LR. Original advertising indicated 1,000 guns, only 200 were mfg., has 5 Olympic rings on right side of receiver. Ser. no. has a "T" prefix, blue finish, lined presentation case avail. Mfg. 1972 only.

	$1,150	$875	$650

1980 OLYMPIC COMMEMORATIVE — .22 Short, an ISU Olympic Military with integral stabilizer on barrel, supplied with weights. Has 5 Olympic rings on right side of receiver. Produced in a limited edition of 1,000 guns. Ser. no. has a "USA" prefix, blue finish, lined presentation case avail. Mfg. 1980 only.

	$725	$550	$450

10-X — specifically designed for top flight match shooting, blue finish, 5½ in. barrel, push-button or allen screw (late mfg.) barrel release. Mfg. 1982-84. This model used hand-picked parts and was precisely assembled by a High Standard Master Gunsmith (with his initials on the gun).

Push button barrel release

	$1,050	$875	$725	$600	$500	$400	$350

Allen screw barrel release

	$875	$700	$600	$500	$475	$400	$350

CITATION II — .22 LR, 10 shot, 5½ or 7¼ in. bull barrel, 45 oz., blue, checkered military-type wood grips, allen screw takedown. Ser. no.'s are prefixed with "SH". Mfg. 1982-84. Slabbed barrel also avail.

	$575	$475	$350	$295	$240	$225	$195

VICTOR — .22 LR, 10 shot, 4½ or 5½ in. vent rib, target sights, push-button takedown, 1978-81. Checkered walnut grips. Allen screw takedown, 1982-84. Ser. no.'s are prefixed with "SH". Mfg. E. Hartford, CT.

	$550	$425	$350	$275	$250	$225	$200

SHARPSHOOTER "M" — .22 LR, 5½ in. bull barrel, adj. rear sight, military-type grips, push-button or allen screw takedown. Mfg. 1982-84.

	$400	$350	$275	$230	$200	$180	$160

Add $50 for push-button takedown.

SURVIVAL PACK — Sharpshooter "M" Model with electroless nickel finish, allen screw takedown, included canvas carrying case and extra nickel magazine. Mfg. 1982-84.

	$495	$425	$350	$295	$240	$220	$195

CONVERSION KITS

These kits convert .22 LR to .22 Short, contain an alloy slide with vent rib, barrel weight, and two Short mag.'s, kit comes in "gun size box" set in styrofoam. This model was designated #9370-71 when in mfg.

VICTOR KIT — this model was designated #9370 when in mfg.

	$350	$300	$225

TROPHY/CITATION KIT — this kit also includes a stabilizer. This model was designated #9371 when in mfg.

	$350	$300	$225

Grading	100%	98%	95%	90%	80%	70%	60%

DERRINGERS

FIRST MODEL — double action only O/U, .22 S, L, or LR, or .22 WMR, 2 shot, 3½in. barrels, blue or nickel. Black or white grips. D-100, D-101, DM-101 appearson left side of gun. The first derringer was mfg. about 1962 in Hamden, CT.

	$185	$150	$130	$110	$95	$80	$65

Add $20 for nickel finish.

LATE MODELS — double action only O/U, .22 S, L, or LR, or .22 WMR 2 shot, 3½ in. barrels, blue or nickel, plastic grips. Mfg. in E. Hartford 1978-84.

Blue Finish — .22 LR of .22 Mag. This model was designated #9194 when in mfg.

	$185	$150	$130	$110	$95	$80	$65

Nickel Finish — .22 Mag.

	$205	$175	$150	$130	$95	$80	$65

Electroless Nickel — included walnut grips. This model was designated #9420-21.

	$225	$175	$160

Silver plated — includes presentation case. 500 mfg. This model was designated #9341. Ser. no. has "SP" prefix.

	$325	$250	$200

Gold plated — introduced in 1965. Includes presentation case. This model was designated #9196. Ser. No. has "GP" prefix.

	$375	$275	$200

Add 120% for a cased, matched set with consecutive serial numbers.

REVOLVERS

SENTINEL — .22 LR, 9 shot, swing out cylinder, 3, 4, or 6 in. barrel, aluminum frame, made 1955-1956.

	100%	98%	95%	90%	80%	70%	60%
Blue finish	$120	$110	$100	$95	$85	$70	$55
Nickel finish	$130	$120	$110	$105	$95	$85	$65
Pink finish	$150	$135	$120	$110	$100	$95	$85
Yellow finish	$150	$135	$120	$110	$105	$95	$85

SENTINEL IMPERIAL — same as Sentinel, with adj. sights, walnut grips, made 1962-1965.

Blue finish	$140	$125	$115	$110	$100	$90	$75
Nickel finish	$150	$140	$125	$120	$110	$100	$90

SENTINEL DELUXE — same as Sentinel, except adj. sights, wide trigger, 4 and 6 in. barrel, square butt, made 1957-1974.

Blue finish	$140	$125	$115	$110	$100	$90	$75
Nickel finish	$150	$140	$115	$120	$110	$100	$90

SENTINEL SNUB — same as Deluxe, except checkered bird's-head grip, 2⅜ in. barrel.

Blue finish	$145	$140	$130	$120	$110	$90	$85
Nickel finish	$155	$150	$145	$130	$120	$100	$95

DURANGO — .22 LR, double action, steel frame, 4½ and 5½ in. barrel, wood grips, made 1971-1973.

Blue finish	$145	$130	$120	$95	$85	$70	$55
Nickel finish	$150	$140	$125	$105	$95	$85	$65

HOMBRE DOUBLE ACTION — similar to Double Nine steel frame, but no ejector rod housing, 4½ in. barrel, made 1971-1973.

Blue finish	$125	$120	$110	$105	$95	$85	$65
Nickel finish	$140	$130	$120	$115	$105	$95	$75

LONGHORN STEEL FRAME — similar to Double Nine, except 9½ in. barrel.

Fixed sights	$210	$170	$150	$120	$110	$105	$85
Adj. sights	$165	$155	$150	$130	$120	$115	$95

Grading	100%	98%	95%	90%	80%	70%	60%

HIGH SIERRA — similar to Double Nine steel frame, except 7 in. octagon barrel, gold plated grip frame. Discontinued in 1984. Add $10 for adj. sights.

Fixed sights	$235	$175	$150	$130	$120	$105	$90

KIT GUN — .22 LR, swing out cylinder, 9 shot, 4 in. barrel, adj. sights, blue, walnut grips, made 1970-1973.

	$155	$145	$140	$125	$115	$105	$85

DOUBLE NINE — .22 LR, Western style double action, 5½ in. barrel, aluminum frame, simulated stag, ebony or ivory grips, made 1959-1984.

Blue finish	$235	$180	$160	$140	$120	$105	$90
Nickel finish (disc. in 1982)	$245	$190	$170	$150	$130	$115	$100

POSSE — similar to Double Nine aluminum, except 3½ in. barrel, blue, brass grip frame, walnut grips, made 1961-1966.

	$120	$110	$95	$90	$85	$70	$55

NATCHEZ — similar to Double Nine aluminum, except has bird's-head grip, made 1961-1966.

	$120	$110	$100	$90	$85	$70	$55

LONGHORN ALUMINUM FRAME — similar to Natchez, but 4½, 5½, and 9½ in. barrel, longhorn hammer spur, made 1961-1966.

	$145	$130	$110	$100	$85	$70	$55

9½ in. model — Discontinued in 1984.

	$250	$190	$160	$140	$120	$100	$90

CAMP GUN DOUBLE ACTION — .22 LR or .22 Win. Mag., 6 in. barrel, blue, adj. rear sight, checkered walnut grips, made 1976-1984.

	$250	$185	$165	$145	$125	$110	$100

SENTINEL 1 DOUBLE ACTION — .22 LR, 2, 3, and 4 in. barrel, 9 shot, smooth walnut grips, made 1974-present.

Blue finish	$235	$180	$160	$140	$120	$105	$90
Nickel finish	$250	$195	$175	$150	$130	$110	$95

Blue w/adj. sights — add $15 to above prices.

SENTINEL MARK IV DOUBLE ACTION — same as Sentinel 1, except .22 WRM.

Blue finish	$145	$140	$125	$120	$115	$95	$90
Nickel finish	$155	$150	$140	$130	$125	$105	$100

Adj. sights

	$160	$155	$150	$145	$125	$115	$100

SENTINEL MARK II DOUBLE ACTION — .357 Mag., 6 shot, double action, 2½, 4, and 6 in. barrel, blue, fixed sights, wood grips, made 1974-1976.

	$225	$190	$165	$155	$150	$140	$130

SENTINEL MARK III DOUBLE ACTION — same as Mark II, except adj. sights.

	$250	$220	$185	$175	$170	$160	$150

CRUSADER — .357 Mag., .44 Mag. or .45 LC, double action employing gear assembly, swing-out cylinder, unique action, adj. sights, limited mfg. starting 1976 because of expensive fabrication.

	$575	$495	$440	$395	$360	$320	$295

Add 10% for NIB condition.

LIMITED EDITIONS

GRISWOLD & GUNNISON — copy of Confederate Revolver, 7½ in. barrel, 500 mfg. in 1974.

	$250	$195	$150

Last Mfg.'s Sug. Retail was $175.

Grading	100%	98%	95%	90%	80%	70%	60%

LEECH & RIGDON — black powder commemorative, 500 mfg. in 1974.

	$250	$195	$150

Last Mfg.'s Sug. Retail was $175.

PRESIDENTIAL DERRINGER — limited mfg. in 1974 only.

	$250	$195	$150

Last Mfg.'s Sug. Retail was $150.

CRUSADER 50TH ANNIVERSARY — .44 Mag. or .45 LC cal., approx. 50 mfg. for each cal. in 1977 only.

	$1,250	$995	$775

Limited availability might affect asking prices considerably. Two gun sets with matching serial numbers were also available - current asking prices are over $3,250.

RIFLES

SPORT KING FIELD MODEL — .22 S (hi-speed), .22 L, .22 LR, semi-auto, tube mag., 22 in. barrel, open sight, plain pistol grip stock, made 1960-1966.

$100	$90	$85	$75	$65	$55	$45

SPORT KING SPECIAL — same as Field, except beavertail forearm and Monte Carlo stock.

$140	$120	$95	$90	$75	$65	$55

SPORT KING CARBINE — same as Field, except 18 in. barrel, straight grip, barrel band and sling, made 1964-1973.

$170	$150	$120	$110	$100	$90	$85

SPORT KING DELUXE — same as Special, but stock checkered, made 1966-1975.

$185	$160	$140	$115	$90	$75	$65

HI-POWER FIELD BOLT ACTION — Mauser type action, .270, .30-06, 4 shot mag., 22 in. barrel, folding rear sight, plain stock, made 1962-1966.

$295	$230	$210	$195	$180	$165	$150

HI-POWER DELUXE — same as Field, except checkered Monte Carlo stock, swivels, made 1962-1966.

$350	$285	$240	$220	$205	$195	$165

FLITE KING SLIDE ACTION — .22 S, L, or LR, 24 in. barrel, tube mag., hammerless, partridge sight, Monte Carlo stock with pistol grip, semi beavertail forearm, made 1962-1975.

$120	$105	$95	$85	$65	$60	$50

SHOTGUNS

SUPERMATIC FIELD GRADE — 12 ga., 28 and 30 in. barrel, mod. or full, gas operated semi-auto, plain pistol grip stock, made 1960-1966.

$205	$185	$175	$160	$145	$140	$120

SUPERMATIC SPECIAL — 12 ga., same as Field, 27 in. barrel, adj. choke, made 1960-1966.

$210	$195	$180	$165	$150	$145	$125

SUPERMATIC DELUXE — same as Field, except vent rib, checkered stock and forearm, made 1961-1966.

$265	$225	$200	$175	$160	$155	$140

SUPERMATIC TROPHY — same as Deluxe, except 27 in. barrel, adj. choke.

$235	$215	$205	$180	$165	$160	$145

SUPERMATIC DUCK — same as Field, except 3 in. Mag., 30 in. full barrel, recoil pad, made 1961-1966.

$275	$235	$190	$160	$145	$125	$110

Grading	100%	98%	95%	90%	80%	70%	60%

SUPERMATIC DUCK VENT RIB — same as Duck, vent rib, checkered stock and forearm, made 1961-1966.

	$295	$250	$210	$175	$150	$130	$115

SUPERMATIC DEER GUN — same as Field, except 22 in. cylinder bore barrel, rifle sights, checkered stock and forearm, recoil pad, made 1965.

	$230	$210	$200	$185	$165	$155	$140

SUPERMATIC SKEET — same as Deluxe Rib, except 26 in. barrel, skeet bore, made 1962-1966.

	$300	$260	$225	$195	$175	$160	$150

SUPERMATIC TRAP — same as Skeet, except 30 in. full barrel, trap stock with pad, made 1962-1966.

	$245	$230	$220	$205	$185	$170	$160

Note: All preceding models, except Deer and Trap, chambered only for 20 ga., 3 in. Mag. values are $10 higher.

High Standard restyled the Supermatic Autoloader in 1966. The new model Supermatics are recognized by the new checkering pattern and jeweled bolt. All models previously listed are offered, 12 and 20 ga. values are $25 higher per model. All are considered deluxe models. They were discontinued in 1975.

FLITE KING PUMP FIELD GRADE — 12 or 20 ga., slide action, 26, 28, or 30 in. barrel, imp. cyl., mod., or full choke, plain pistol grip stock and slide, made 1960-1966.

	$165	$150	$140	$130	$120	$110	$100

FLITE KING SPECIAL — 12 and 20 ga., same as Pump Field, except 27 in. barrel, adj. choke, made 1960-1966.

	$185	$160	$150	$145	$130	$120	$110

FLITE KING DELUXE RIB — 12 or 20 ga., same as Pump Special, except vent rib, checkered stock, made 1961-1966.

	$195	$175	$170	$165	$155	$140	$125

FLITE KING TROPHY — same as Deluxe Rib, except 27 in. vent rib barrel, adj. choke, made 1960-1966.

	$200	$180	$175	$170	$160	$145	$130

FLITE KING BRUSH — 12 ga. only, same as Field, except 18 or 20 in. cylinder bore barrel, rifle sights, made 1962-1964.

	$185	$170	$165	$160	$150	$140	$120

FLITE KING BRUSH DELUXE — 12 ga. only, same as Brush, except adj. aperture rear sight, checkered stock, recoil pad, swivels and sling, 20 in. barrel only, made 1964-1966.

	$265	$230	$195	$170	$155	$145	$130

FLITE KING SKEET — 12 ga. only, same as Deluxe Rib, except 26 in. vent rib, skeet bore, made 1962-1966.

	$265	$230	$195	$170	$155	$145	$130

FLITE KING TRAP — 12 ga. only, same as Deluxe Rib, except 30 in. vent rib, full choke and pad, made 1962-1966.

	$250	$220	$195	$165	$150	$140	$125

Note: Flite King is available in 16 ga. also, except for the Brush, Skeet, and Trap models. Values are about $20 less per model. A .410 bore was offered in all models that were offered in 20 ga., except the Special and Trophy models. Values are generally the same per model.

High Standard restyled the Flite King in 1966. The new models have a jeweled bolt and new checkering pattern. These new guns were available as Deluxe, Deluxe Rib, Brush, Brush Deluxe, Skeet Deluxe, and Trap Deluxe. Their values are about $20 higher per model.

The new redesigned Flite King was also offered in Deluxe, Deluxe Rib, and Deluxe Skeet, in 20, 28, and .410 ga.'s. The 28 and .410 ga.'s will bring an additional 10-40%.

Grading	100%	98%	95%	90%	80%	70%	60%

MODEL 10B — 12 ga. combat shotgun, 18 in. barrel, semi-auto, unique design incorporates raked pistol grip in front of receiver and metal shoulder pad attached directly to rear of receiver, black cycolic plastic shroud and pistol grip, folding carrying handle, provisions made for attaching a small flashlight to receiver top, extended blade front sight, very compact size (28 in. overall). Discontinued.

	$650	$575	$500	$425	$375	$325	$275

The predecessor to this model was the 10A. This variation had the flashlight built in.

RIOT SHOTGUN — 18 or 20 in. barrel, police riot gun was also offered until 1975. This was a reliable weapon available with or without rifle sights, 12 ga. only on the Flite King Action.

	$195	$165	$155	$140	$130	$120	$115

SUPERMATIC INDY O/U — This model was made in Japan and imported in 1974 and 1975, boxlock, fully engraved receiver, selective auto ejectors and single trigger, 12 ga., 27½ sk & sk, 29½ imp. mod. and full, or full and full, air flow vent rib, checkered (skipline) pistol grip stock with pad and vent forearm.

	$815	$720	$635	$590	$550	$495	$440

SUPERMATIC SHADOW SEVEN O/U — same as Indy O/U, except less elaborate engraving, unvented forearm, standard vent rib, regular checkering, no recoil pad, imported 1974-1975.

	$670	$590	$540	$495	$470	$425	$385

SUPERMATIC SHADOW AUTO — 12 and 20 ga., 2¾ or 3 in. chambers in 12 ga., air flow rib, 26 in. imp. cyl. or skeet, 28 in. mod., imp. mod. or full and 30 in. full or trap, checkered walnut stock, gas operated, imported 1974-1975.

	$340	$285	$240	$210	$180	$165	$155

HOFER-JAGDWAFFEN, PETER

Master gunsmith located in Ferlach, Austria. Custom order only, best quality rifles (over 100 cal.'s available) and shotguns (O/U and SxS) made per individual order — prices typically start at $20,000+. Information can be obtained by writing to Mr. Hofer directly at: Peter Hofer-Jagdwaffen, Franz-Lang-Strabe 13, A-9170 Ferlach, Austria.

HOLLAND & HOLLAND LTD.

Manufacturer located in London, England since 1835. All H&H long guns are built per individual special order. Orders may be placed directly with the factory in England. Please refer to their listing in the Trademark Index for address, telephone, telex, or FAX information.

Holland & Holland over the years has justly earned the reputation of producing some of the finest firearms ever manufactured. Their Double Rifles chambered for the Large Black Powder Express Cartridges are still among the most powerful rifles ever made, while exhibiting outstanding quality and superior craftsmanship. Most of these fine arms were made to order for the famous, wealthy, or royalty of their day. Because of the individual nature of each firearm, these early guns, as with any high grade item, must be individually appraised.

The early Double Rifles were proofed and regulated with the Black Powder of their day. These exposed hammer rifles were almost exclusively sold cased with accessories by Holland & Holland. They are seldom found on the market, and then not in the best of condition. Purchase of these as well as any high grade firearm should include trusted appraisal.

Due to the recent devaluation of the U.S. dollar, prices may fluctuate rapidly on this trademark. Values below reflect the dollar/pound exchange rates at this writing ($1.92 per pound).

RIFLES: MODERN

BEST QUALITY MAGAZINE RIFLE — Mauser 98 (current mfg.) or Enfield (disc.) action, various cal.'s, incl. .300 H&H Mag., .375 H&H Mag., 4 shot mag., 24 in. barrel, folding leaf sight, checkered French walnut stock available in tradition configuration or with Monte Carlo pattern.

Mfg.'s Sug. Retail	$14,445	$14,445	$10,250	$7,500	$5,300	$4,250	$3,600	$3,250

Grading	100%	98%	95%	90%	80%	70%	60%

The values above represent the standard model without additional options (of which there are a wide array). Mfg. to customer specifications.

DE LUXE MAGAZINE RIFLE — similar to Best Quality, with engraving and exhibition grade wood, very limited mfg.

Mfg.'s Sug. Retail	$22,100	$22,100	$16,000	$12,500	$9,950	$8,000	$6,950	$5,800

NO. 2 MODEL DOUBLE RIFLE S x S — various British and American cal.'s, 24-28 in. barrels, sidelock, folding leaf sight, checkered French walnut stock, auto ejectors.

$15,000	$13,000	$11,000	$10,000	$9,000	$7,000	$6,500

ROYAL DOUBLE S x S RIFLE — available in most popular cal.'s between .300 and .577, similar to No. 2, except has deluxe finish and more engraving.

Mfg.'s Sug. Retail	$69,120	$69,120	$45,000	$31,500	$25,500	$21,000	$18,000	$15,000

ROYAL DE LUXE S x S RIFLE — similar cal.'s as the Royal Double S x S, top-of-the-line model, every refinement, built to individual order only with almost any option possible.

Mfg.'s Sug. Retail	$76,320	$76,320	$49,500	$33,500	$26,000	$22,500	$19,500	$16,000

H&H .700 BORE DOUBLE RIFLE — .700 H&H cal., 1,000 grain jacketed bullet, approx. 19 lbs with 26 in. barrels chambered 3½ in. Delivery of this rifle is expected to commence in 1990. This is the largest caliber rifle available in the world today.
Prices are available by special quotation from Holland & Holland.

SHOTGUNS: SINGLE SHOT AND SIDE BY SIDE

Holland & Holland currently manufactures the Royal De Luxe Game Gun, Royal Game Gun, Badminton Game Gun, and the Dominion Game Gun models in sidelock configuration (and are listed below). In addition to the sidelock models, H&H also manufactures the boxlock models Cavalier De Luxe, Cavalier, Northwood De Luxe, and Northwood. The values below assume standard model without single trigger, vent rib, de luxe walnut, or casing. These special orders will add considerable value to the price of a new custom order.

In 1988, Holland & Holland absorbed W & C Scott and manufactured the Chatsworth, Bowood, and Kinmount boxlock models until they were discontinued in late 1990. H&H has phased this trademark out, and more information can be found in the W & C Scott section of this text.

SINGLE BARREL TRAP GUN — 12 ga., 30 or 32 in. full choke barrel, vent rib, boxlock, auto ejectors, Monte Carlo pistol grip stock, pad.

Mfg.'s Sug. Retail	$28,420	$28,420	$20,000	$15,000	$12,000	$9,500	$8,000	$6,750

Trap Guns - Older Mfg.

Standard Grade		$5,000	$4,500	$4,000	$3,250	$2,500	$2,250	$2,000
De Luxe Grade		$8,250	$7,000	$6,250	$5,000	$4,500	$3,750	$3,000
Exhibition Grade		$10,500	$8,950	$7,500	$6,000	$5,500	$5,000	$4,250

NORTHWOOD S x S BOXLOCK — 12, 16, 20, or 28 ga., 28 or 30 in. barrels, scalloped-case colored receiver, boxlock, auto ejectors, double triggers, checkered pistol grip or straight stock. The values shown below are for standard model.

Mfg.'s Sug. Retail	$8,625	$8,625	$6,200	$5,200	$4,450	$3,850	$3,300	$2,950

Add $715 for 20 or 28 ga.

Northwood De Luxe — 12, 16, 20, or 28 ga., scalloped-case colored receiver with moderate engraving and select walnut, double triggers. Current mfg.

Mfg.'s Sug. Retail	$9,640	$9,640	$7,250	$6,375	$5,000	$4,450	$3,850	$3,300

Add $910 for 20 or 28 ga.

CAVALIER S x S BOXLOCK — 12, 20, or 28 ga., best quality model boxlock with scalloped frame, double triggers, ejectors, and case colored receiver. Current mfg.

Mfg.'s Sug. Retail	$14,715	$14,715	$10,700	$9,250	$7,500	$6,100	$5,500	$4,850

Add $910 for 20 or 28 ga.

Cavalier De Luxe — similar to Cavalier Model, except has de luxe walnut and better engraving. Current mfg.

Mfg.'s Sug. Retail	$16,745	$16,745	$13,750	$10,500	$8,700	$7,000	$6,000	$5,250

Add $1,115 for 20 or 28 ga.

Grading	100%	98%	95%	90%	80%	70%	60%

DOMINION SIDELOCK — 12, 16, or 20 ga., 25-30 in. barrels, any choke, sidelock, auto ejectors, double triggers, checkered straight grip stock.

	$7,500	$6,250	$5,000	$4,000	$3,500	$3,250	$3,000

20 gauge — add 20%.

Above values are for older, previously manufactured specimens.

Dominion Game Gun — 12 ga. only, single or double triggers. Disc. 1989.

	$20,000	$17,000	$14,500	$12,250	$10,000	$8,500	$6,750

Last Mfg.'s Sug. Retail was $28,000.

ROYAL HAMMERLESS EJECTOR SIDELOCK — 12, 16, 20, 28, or .410 ga., customer specifications as to barrel length and chokes, hand detachable sidelocks and a self opening action, stocked in pistol grip or straight style to specifications. Mfg. 1885-disc.

	$14,500	$11,500	$8,750	$7,750	$6,950	$6,350	$5,250

20 gauge — add 20%.

28 gauge — add 40%.

.410 gauge — add 60%.

Without SST — subtract $1,000.

Above values are for older, previously manufactured specimens.

ROYAL GAME GUN — 12, 16, 20, 28 or .410 ga., best quality sidelock game gun. Mfg. per individual customer specifications. Current production.

Mfg.'s Sug. Retail	$51,170	$51,170	$30,500	$21,500	$16,500	$12,750	$10,500	$9,000

Add $3,455 for 28 or .410 ga.

Add $3,995 for ST.

Add $3,100 for VR.

DE LUXE MODEL — similar to Royal Hammerless Ejector, except with more elaborate engraving and exhibition wood, self-opening gun. Older mfg.

	$18,750	$15,500	$13,000	$11,000	$9,000	$7,500	$6,500

20 gauge — add 20%.

28 gauge — add 40%.

.410 gauge — add 60%.

Without SST - subtract $1,000.

Above values are for older, previously manufactured specimens.

ROYAL DE LUXE GAME GUN — 12, 16, 20, 28, or .410 ga., top-of-the-line sidelock shotgun. Mfg. per individual customer specifications. Current production.

Mfg.'s Sug. Retail	$58,850	$58,850	$33,750	$23,500	$17,750	$14,000	$11,250	$9,000

Add $3,455 for 28 or .410 ga.

Add $3,995 for ST.

Add $3,100 for VR.

BADMINTON SIDELOCK — same as Royal model, without self opening action. Mfg. 1902-disc.

	$10,500	$9,000	$8,000	$7,000	$6,000	$5,000	$4,000

20 gauge — add 20%.

28 gauge — add 40%.

.410 gauge — add 60%.

SST — add $1,000.

Above values are for older, previously manufactured specimens.

Badminton Game Gun — 12 or 20 ga., double or single trigger. Disc. 1988.

	$20,000	$17,000	$14,500	$12,250	$10,000	$8,500	$6,750

Last Mfg.'s Sug. Retail was $28,000.

Grading	100%	98%	95%	90%	80%	70%	60%

RIVIERA SIDELOCK — same as Badminton model, with two sets of barrels. Mfg. until 1967.

	$15,000	$11,500	$9,500	$7,950	$7,100	$6,350	$5,600

20 gauge — add 20%.
28 gauge — add 40%.
.410 gauge — add 60%.

CENTENARY SIDELOCK — 12 ga., 2 in. chambers, lightened version of Royal, Badminton, and Dominion grades. The values would be the same as for the standard models, mfg. until 1962.

SHOTGUNS: O/U

ROYAL MODEL O/U SHOTGUN OLD MODEL — 12 ga., customer specifications as to barrel length and choke, hand detachable sidelocks, auto ejectors, checkered straight grip stock. Mfg. until 1951. Rare, fewer than 30 made.

	$32,000	$28,000	$23,500	$20,000	$18,000	$16,500	$15,000

Single trigger — add $1,000.

ROYAL NEW MODEL O/U — same as Old Model, with improved narrow action. Mfg. until 1960.

	$27,500	$24,000	$22,000	$19,500	$18,500	$17,000	$15,500

ROYAL O/U SIDELOCK GAME GUN — H&H is currently in the process of totally redesigning their O/U Game Gun. Prototype testing is currently underway and finished specimens should be available in the near future. Written quotations on this re-released model are available by contacting H&H directly (see Trademark Index).

HOLLOWAY ARMS CO.
Manufactured In Fort Worth, TX.

Holloway firearms did not make many rifles or carbines before operations ceased. While rare, they still are not particularly collectible at this point.

HAC MODEL 7 — 7.62mm NATO (.308), gas operated semi-auto paramilitary design rifle, 20 in. barrel, adj. front and rear sights, 20 shot mag., side folding stock. Mfg. 1984-1985 only. Also available in fully auto (class III dealers only) — add $80. Add $50 for left-hand variation.

	$995	$895	$795	$695	$595	$525	$465

Last Mfg.'s Sug. Retail was $675.

Model 7C — 16 in. carbine, same general specifications as Model 7. Disc. 1985.

	$995	$895	$795	$695	$595	$525	$465

Last Mfg.'s Sug. Retail was $675. Also available from the manufacturer were the models 7S and 7M (Sniper and Match models).

HOLMES FIREARMS
Manufacturer located in Wheeler, AR. Distributed by D.B. Distributing, Fayetteville, AR.

These pistols were mfg. in very limited numbers, most were in prototype configuration and exhibit changes from gun to gun.

MP-83 — 9mm or .45 ACP cal., paramilitary design pistol, 6 in. barrel, walnut stock and forearm, blued finish, 3½ lbs. Add $75 for deluxe package and $220 for conversion kit. Mfg. 1985 only.

	$595	$550	$500	$450	$400	$375	$350

Last Mfg.'s Sug. Retail was $450.

MP-22 — .22 LR cal., 2½ lbs., steel and aluminum construction, 6 in. barrel, similar appearance to MP-83. Mfg. 1985 only.

	$395	$360	$320	$285	$250	$230	$210

Last Mfg.'s Sug. Retail was $400.

Grading	100%	98%	95%	90%	80%	70%	60%

COMBAT 12 — 12 ga., riot configuration, cylinder bore barrel. Disc. 1983.

	$795	$720	$650	$595	$550	$500	$450

Last Mfg.'s Sug. Retail was $750.

HOWA
Manufacturer located in Japan.

Recently, Howa rifles have been imported by both Smith & Wesson (pre-1985) and Mossberg (1986-87). Currently, Howa sporting rifles are being imported by Interarms and this trademark will appear in the Interarms section in this text. Older Howa models will appear in both the S&W and Mossberg sections of this text.

HUNTER ARMS COMPANY
Manufacturer located in Fulton, NY between 1891 and 1945.

The Hunter Arms Company was formed to manufacture L.C. Smith shotguns. Please refer to the L.C. Smith section in this text for further information regarding this manufacturer (including Fulton, Fulton Special, and Hunter Special models.)

HUSQVARNA
Previous manufacturer located in Husqvarna, Sweden.

Also see: Lahti Pistols

RIFLE: BOLT ACTION

HI-POWER — Mauser type action, .220 Swift, .270, or .30-06 cal., open sight, checkered beech wood. Mfg. 1946-1951, early models found 6.5 x 55, 8 x 57, 9.3 x 57 cal.'s.

	$330	$265	$250	$220	$195	$175	$165

MODEL 1951 — same as Hi-Power, except high combination stock.

	$340	$275	$260	$230	$205	$185	$175

SERIES 1100 DELUXE — same as 1951, except has European walnut and jeweled bolt. Mfg. 1952-1956.

	$440	$360	$330	$310	$290	$275	$250

SERIES 1000 SUPER GRADE — same as 1951, has walnut Monte Carlo stock. Mfg. 1952-1956.

	$440	$360	$330	$310	$290	$275	$250

SERIES 3100 CROWN GRADE — improved HVA Mauser action, .243, .270, .30-06, 7mm, or .308 cal., 24 in. barrel, walnut stock, black forend tip and pistol grip cap. Mfg. 1954-1972.

	$470	$385	$360	$330	$315	$305	$275

SERIES 3000 CROWN GRADE — same as 3100, except has Monte Carlo stock.

	$470	$385	$360	$330	$315	$305	$275

SERIES 4100 LIGHTWEIGHT — HVA Mauser action, calibers same as 3100, 20½ in. barrel, open sights, lightweight walnut stock, pistol grip, Schnabel forend. Mfg. 1954-1972.

	$470	$385	$360	$330	$315	$305	$275

SERIES 4000 LIGHTWEIGHT — same as 4100, except has Monte Carlo stock, no sights.

	$470	$385	$360	$330	$315	$305	$275

MODEL 456 LIGHTWEIGHT — same as 4000/4100, except full length stock. Mfg. 1959-1970.

	$495	$415	$385	$360	$330	$310	$290

SERIES 6000 IMPERIAL GRADE — same as 3100, except has select wood, 3 leaf folding sight. Mfg. 1968-1970.

	$580	$495	$470	$440	$395	$365	$330

Grading	100%	98%	95%	90%	80%	70%	60%

SERIES 6000 IMPERIAL LIGHTWEIGHT — same as 6000 Imperial, except 20½ in. barrel, lightweight stock.

	$580	$495	$470	$440	$395	$365	$330

SERIES P-3000 PRESENTATION — same as Crown, except engraved action, special wood. Mfg. 1968-1970.

	$770	$660	$635	$605	$550	$510	$485

MODEL 9000 CROWN GRADE — Husqvarna action, .300 Win. Mag. added to line, 23½ in. barrel, adj. trigger, adj. sight, walnut stock. Mfg. 1971-1972.

	$470	$385	$360	$330	$315	$305	$275

MODEL 8000 IMPERIAL — same as 9000, but jeweled bolt, engraved floor plate, no sights and deluxe stock. Mfg. 1971-1972.

	$605	$525	$495	$470	$415	$385	$350

HY-HUNTER INC. FIREARMS MANUFACTURING CO.

Previous manufacturer located in W. Germany, imported by Hy-Hunter Inc.

Previous importer of single action revolvers in various calibers. Typically, prices are determined by their shooting value rather than their collector value. Prices generally range from $100-$175 depending on caliber and finish.

HYPER

Previous manufacturer located in Jenks, OK.

SINGLE SHOT RIFLE — all calibers, all standard lengths and contours, falling block trigger guard lever activated, adj. trigger, no sights, stocked to customer specifications, in AA grade walnut. Disc. 1984.

	$2,200	$1,980	$1,925	$1,870	$1,650	$1,540	$1,375

Add $75 for stainless barrel.
Add $85 for octagon barrel.

I

I A B SHOTGUNS

Manufactured by Industria Armi Bresciane, Italy. Previously distributed by Sporting Arms International,Inc. located in Indianola, MS.

I A B manufactures high quality competition (O/U and single barrel trap or skeet) shotguns in various styles and configurations including combo sets. These guns employ a boxlock action, have ejectors, and various amounts of engraving. Prices for 100% condition usually start in the $550-$900 price range. I A B shotguns are not being imported currently — values for older models will be determined by the prices shooters, not collectors, are willing to pay for them.

I A I

Please refer to the Irwindale Arms, Inc. heading in this section.

I G A SHOTGUNS

Manufacturer located in Veranopolis, Brazil By IGA. Currently imported by Stoeger Industries located in South Hackensack, NJ.

Grading		100%	98%	95%	90%	80%	70%	60%

UPLANDER S X S — 12, 20, 28, or .410 ga., 3 in. chambers, underlug lockup, double triggers, extractors.

Mfg.'s Sug. Retail	$357	$270	$200	$170	$145	$130	$115	$100

COACH GUN S X S — 12, 20, or .410 (new 1991) ga., same as standard grade, only 20 in. barrels.

Mfg.'s Sug. Retail	$340	$255	$190	$165	$140	$125	$110	$100

DOUBLE TRIGGER O & U — 12 or 20 (disc.) ga., sliding underlug action, vent rib, checkered walnut, separated barrels.

Mfg.'s Sug. Retail	$390	$330	$285	$260	$240	$220	$195	$170

SINGLE TRIGGER O & U — 12 or 20 ga., 3 in. chambers, sliding underlug action, vent rib, deluxe checkered walnut, separated barrels.

Mfg.'s Sug. Retail	$495	$375	$285	$250	$225	$210	$195	$180

CONDOR O & U — 12 ga. only, single trigger, ejectors, presentation walnut, chrome lined bores. Disc. 1985.

		$580	$500	$450	$410	$375	$350	$325

Last Mfg.'s Sug. Retail was $667.

SINGLE BARREL — 12, 20, or .410 ga., exposed hammer with half-cock, extractor.

Mfg.'s Sug. Retail	$105	$80	$70	$60	$50	$45	$40	$35

INDIAN ARMS

Previously manufactured by Indian Arms Corporation located in Detroit, MI.

INDIAN ARMS .380 SEMI-AUTO — .380 ACP, patterned after Walther PPK, stainless steel, 3¼ in. barrel, 6 shot mag., natural or blue finish, with (early specimens) or without key lock safety, with or without VR barrel, walnut grips, 20 oz. Mfg. 1975-1977.

	$350	$275	$225

This model had limited manufacture with approx. 1,000 guns being made.

Grading	100%	98%	95%	90%	80%	70%	60%

INDUSTRIA ARMI GALESI

Previous manufacturer located in Brescia, Italy.

PISTOL: SEMI-AUTO

GALESI MODEL 6 POCKET AUTO — .22 long, .25 auto, 6 shot, 2¼ in. barrel blue, fixed sights, plastic grips. Mfg. 1930-disc.

	100%	98%	95%	90%	80%	70%	60%
	$130	$120	$105	$90	$75	$65	$55

GALESI MODEL 9 POCKET AUTO — .22 LR, .32 auto, .380 auto, 8 shot, 3¼ in. barrel, blue, fixed sights, plastic grips. Mfg. 1930-disc.

	100%	98%	95%	90%	80%	70%	60%
	$140	$125	$110	$100	$85	$65	$55

INFALLIBLE

Mfg. by Warner Arms Corp. located in Norwich, CT and Davis-Warner Arms Corp. located in Assonet, MA.

INFALLIBLE PISTOL — .32 ACP cal., 3.2 in. barrel, 7 shot mag., 24.7 oz.

Type I — mfg. and marked "Warner Arms Corp., Norwich, Conn.", serial range is 501-2,299.

	100%	98%	95%	90%	80%	70%	60%
	$325	$295	$270	$250	$225	$200	$180

Type II — marked "Davis-Warner Arms Corporation, Assonet, Massachusetts ", serial range is 2,300-5,299.

	100%	98%	95%	90%	80%	70%	60%
	$295	$270	$250	$225	$195	$170	$150

Type III — marked "Warner Arms Corporation, Norwich, Connecticut", serial range is 5,300-7,400.

	100%	98%	95%	90%	80%	70%	60%
	$295	$270	$250	$225	$195	$170	$150

INGLIS HI-POWERS

Manufactured by John Inglis Co. Limited of Toronto, Canada. Over 151,000 Inglis hi-powers were manufactured between February 1944 and September 1945 under military contractual agreement.

CHINESE CONTRACT PATTERN 35

Chinese No. 1 — with markings, slotted for stock and tangent sights.

	100%	98%	95%	90%	80%	70%	60%
	$1,775	$1,475	$1,100	$995	$900	$800	$700

Add $200 for wooden holster stock.

CH SERIES CHINESE CONTRACT — recently being imported again, market is currently somewhat flooded.

MK 1-slotted — tangent sights.

	100%	98%	95%	90%	80%	70%	60%
	$1,200	$1,000	$900	$800	$700	$600	$500

CANADIAN MILITARY

MK 1-No. 1 Inglis — tangent sight, slotted.

	100%	98%	95%	90%	80%	70%	60%
	$1,150	$975	$850	$725	$650	$550	$450

Add $200 for wooden holster stock.

MK 1-No. 2 Inglis — fixed sight, no slot.

	100%	98%	95%	90%	80%	70%	60%
	$550	$475	$450	$425	$400	$350	$275

MK 1-No. 2 Inglis — fixed sight, slotted. Inspect slot carefully.

	100%	98%	95%	90%	80%	70%	60%
	$1,150	$975	$850	$725	$650	$550	$450

Add $200 for wooden holster stock.

T SERIES CANADIAN MILITARY

	100%	98%	95%	90%	80%	70%	60%
1 T	$725	$600	$550	$500	$450	$400	$350
2 T	$600	$500	$450	$395	$345	$295	$275
3 T	$550	$450	$400	$350	$300	$260	$240
4 T	$550	$450	$400	$350	$300	$260	$240
5 T	$550	$450	$400	$350	$300	$260	$240

Grading	100%	98%	95%	90%	80%	70%	60%
6 T	$550	$450	$400	$350	$300	$260	$240
7 T	$550	$450	$400	$350	$300	$260	$240
8 T	$800	$695	$595	$550	$530	$460	$395
9 T	$860	$750	$650	$550	$530	$460	$395

INGRAM

Military Armament Corp. (Mac), previously located in Atlanta, GA. Disc. late 1982.

MAC 10 — .45 ACP or 9mm cal., semi-auto, open bolt, pistol version of the sub machine gun, 16 and 32 shot mag., compact construction, all metal construction, rear aperture and front blade sight. Disc. 1982.

$850	$775	$700	$650	$600	$550	$495

Add approx. $160 for accessories (barrel extension, case, and extra mag).

MAC 10A1 — similar to MAC 10 except fires from a closed bolt.

$295	$275	$250	$230	$215	$200	$190

MAC 11 — same as MAC 10 except in .380 ACP cal.

$650	$595	$550	$525	$500	$480	$460

INTERARMS

Manufacturer/importer/distributor located in Alexandria, VA.

Interarms has imported a multitude of trademarks and models since the early 1960's. Most of the models shown below are recent imports, and specific information on older, limited import models can be obtained by contacting Interarms directly. The Astra, Rossi, Star, and Walther trademarks will be found in their own sections listed alphabetically in this text.

FEG PISTOLS

FEG pistols were imported from Hungary during 1986-87 only.

FEG MODEL R-9 — 9mm Para., patterned after Browning Hi-Power, double action, 13 shot mag., blued finish, steel construction, checkered wood grips. Imported 1986-87 only.

$275	$230	$200	$180	$165	$155	$145

Last Mfg.'s Sug. Retail was $375.

FEG MODEL PPH — .380 ACP, patterned after Walther PP, alloy frame, double action, plastic grips with thumbrest, blued finish. Imported 1986-87 only.

$200	$170	$140	$125	$115	$105	$95

Last Mfg.'s Sug. Retail was $225.

HELWAN PISTOLS

BRIGADIER — 9mm Para., single action, 4.5 in. barrel, all steel construction, 8 shot mag. with finger extension, black plastic grips, 32.6 oz. Importation began 1988.

Mfg.'s Sug. Retail	$275	$180	$160	$140	$125	$115	$105	$95

This design was originally initiated and produced by Pietro Beretta.

VIRGINIAN REVOLVERS: SINGLE ACTION

Virginian Revolvers were previously imported from Europe by various manufacturers (including Hammerli of Switzerland). They were also manufactured in Midland, VA from 1976-1984. Older models with exceptional quality (including Hammerli guns) are worth a premium over values listed below.

VIRGINIAN DRAGOON STANDARD — improved action patterned after Colt S.A. design, 6 shot, .44 Mag. cal. only, 6, 7½, 8⅜, or 12 (Buntline) in. barrel, blue finish, smooth walnut grips, adj. rear sight, 51 oz. with 7½ in. barrel.

$255	$225	$205	$190	$180	$170	$160

Add 15% for Buntline Model.
Last Mfg.'s Sug. Retail was $315.

Grading	100%	98%	95%	90%	80%	70%	60%

Dragoon Standard Stainless — .44 Mag., 6 (disc.), 7½ (disc.), or 8⅜ in. barrel, same general specifications as Standard Dragoon.

	$265	$230	$210				

Last Mfg.'s Sug. Retail was $315.

DRAGOON SILHOUETTE — .357 or .44 Mag. cal., stainless steel, 7½, 8⅜, or 10½ in. (standard on .357 Mag.) barrel, special sights and grips.

	$365	$320	$275				

Last Mfg.'s Sug. Retail was $425.

DRAGOON ENGRAVED — .44 Mag. only, choice of stainless steel or blue finish, 6 or 7½ in. barrel.

	$545	$470	$430	$395	$360	$320	$285

Add $75 for presentation case.
Last Mfg.'s Sug. Retail was $625.

DRAGOON "DEPUTY" — .357 or .44 Mag. cal., blued barrel, case hardened frame, 5 in. barrel only.

	$250	$215	$195	$180	$165	$155	$145

Last Mfg.'s Sug. Retail was $295.

Stainless Deputy — same as above, except .44 Mag. available in 6 in. barrel only, stainless steel.

	$255	$225	$205				

Last Mfg.'s Sug. Retail was $295.

VIRGINIAN .22 CONVERTIBLE — .22 LR/.22 Mag. cylinders, 5½ in. barrel only, adj. rear sight, 38 oz.

	$185	$155	$145	$135	$125	$115	$105

Last Mfg.'s Sug. Retail was $219.

Virginian .22 Convertible Stainless — stainless steel fabrication, otherwise same as above.

	$200	$170	$155				

Last Mfg.'s Sug. Retail was $239.

RIFLES: HOWA MFG.

MODEL 1500 HUNTER — .22-250, .223, .243, .270, .308, .30-06, .300 Win. Mag., or 7mm Rem. Mag. cal., 3 (Mag. cal.'s only) or 5 shot, 22 or 24 in. barrel, adj. rear sight and trigger, checkered walnut stock. Importation with Interarms 1988 only.

	$360	$310	$285	$260	$240	$225	$205

Add $15 for 7mm Rem. Mag./.300 Win. Mag. cal.
Last Mfg.'s Sug. Retail was $440.

Model 1500 Lightning — .270, .30-06, .300 Win. Mag., or 7mm Rem. Mag. cal., lightweight variation of the Model 1500 Hunter featuring lightweight Carbolite (synthetic) stock, 7 lbs. Importation began 1988.

Mfg.'s Sug. Retail	$539	$415	$335	$290	$260	$240	$225	$205

Add $20 for Mag. cal.'s.

MODEL 1500 TROPHY — .22-250, .223, .243, .270, .308, .30-06, .300 Win. Mag., .338 Win. Mag. or 7mm Rem. Mag. cal., 3 (Mag. cal.'s only) or 5 shot, 22 or 24 in. barrel, adj. rear sight and trigger, select Monte Carlo stock with skipline checkering. Importation with Interarms began 1988.

Mfg.'s Sug. Retail	$539	$415	$335	$290	$260	$240	$225	$205

Add $20 for Mag. cal.'s.

Model 1500 Varmint — .22-250, .223, or .308 (new 1990) cal., 24 in. heavy barrel without sights, 5 shot mag., 7 lbs. 1 oz. Importation began 1988.

Mfg.'s Sug. Retail	$579	$445	$350	$300	$275	$255	$230	$210

RIFLES: MAUSER ACTIONS

Whitworth rifles are mfg. in England. Mark X rifles are currently mfg. in Yugoslavia by Zastava Arms.

Grading	100%	98%	95%	90%	80%	70%	60%

MARK X VISCOUNT — .22-250, .243, .25-06, .270, 7 x 57mm, 7mm Mag., .308, .30-06, or .300 Win. Mag. cal., 5 shot, 3 shot mag., 24 in. barrel, adj. rear sight and trigger, classic style Monte Carlo stock. Disc. 1983, re-introduced 1985.

Mfg.'s Sug. Retail	$539	$420	$335	$295	$265	$240	$225	$205

Add $20 for 7mm Rem. Mag./.300 Win. Mag. cal.

This model is often referred to as the Viscount. Early manufacture was done in Manchester, England. Recent manufacture is in Yugoslavia. Earlier Manchester guns (before approx. 1980) will bring a slight premium over the values listed above.

Mini Mark X — .223 or 7.62 X 39mm (new in 1990) cal., miniature M98 Mauser System action, 20 in. barrel with iron sights, checkered hardwood stock, 5 shot mag., adj. trigger, 6.35 lbs. New 1987.

Mfg.'s Sug. Retail	$500	$400	$350	$300	$250	$225	$200	$185

Lightweight Mark X — .270, .30-06, or 7mm Rem. Mag. cal., similar to Mark X Viscount, except has Carbolite (synthetic) stock and 20 in. barrel, 7 lbs. Mfg. in 1988-90.

	$435	$385	$340	$300	$270	$240	$215

Last Mfg.'s Sug. Retail was $519.

MARK X AMERICAN FIELD — same cal.'s as Mark X Rifle, Mauser action, 24 in. barrel, open sights, 5 shot Mag.(.300 Win. Mag. is only 3), checkered deluxe walnut with ebony forearm tip, thumb safety with sling swivels, adj. trigger, rubber recoil butt plate, 7 lbs. Imported since 1984.

Mfg.'s Sug. Retail	$665	$510	$415	$355	$315	$275	$250	$225

Add $20 for 7mm Rem. Mag./.300 Win. Mag. cal.

This model was the Whitworth American Field Series until 1987. Early manufacture was done in Manchester, England. Recent manufacture is in Yugoslavia. Earlier Manchester guns (before approx. 1980) will bring a slight premium over the values listed above.

WHITWORTH MANNLICHER STYLE CARBINE — .243, .270, .308, 7 x 57mm, or .30-06 cal., bolt action with full length walnut Mannlicher style stock, open sights, sling swivels, thumb safety, 20 in. barrel, 5 shot mag., 7 lbs. Imported 1984-87.

	$570	$495	$455	$410	$375	$340	$310

Last Mfg.'s Sug. Retail was $675.

WHITWORTH EXPRESS RIFLE — .375 H&H or .458 Win. Mag. cal., 3 shot, 24 in. barrel, 3 leaf express sight, English style stock of walnut, checkered pistol grip forearm, 8½ lbs. Mfg. 1974-present.

Mfg.'s Sug. Retail	$825	$675	$600	$525	$465	$425	$395	$375

RIFLES: BOLT-ACTION

MODEL JW-15 — .22 LR, 5 shot detachable mag., 23.8 in. barrel, open sights, blued finish, Model 70 style safety, patterned after the Brno Model ZKM, 5.5 lbs. Importation began 1990.

Mfg.'s Sug. Retail	$115	$100	$90	$80	$70	$65	$60	$55

This model is mfg. by Norinco in China.

RIFLES: SEMI-AUTO

22-ATD — .22 LR only, patterned after the Browning Semi-Auto, 19.4 in. barrel, 11 shot mag. in stock, blued finish, checkered hardwood stock, take-down design, adj. rear sight, 4.6 lbs. New 1987.

Mfg.'s Sug. Retail	$165	$145	$115	$110	$105	$100	$95	$90

Add $16 for camo case.

This model is mfg. by Norinco in China.

RIFLES: DISCONTINUED

CAVALIER — same as Viscount, except modern style stock, roll-over cheek piece, rosewood pistol grip cap and forend tip, recoil pad. Disc.

	$365	$330	$305	$290	$265	$230	$195

Grading	100%	98%	95%	90%	80%	70%	60%

MANNLICHER STYLE CARBINE — same as Cavalier, except 20 in. barrel, full length stock, no Magnum or varmint calibers. Disc.

	$365	$330	$305	$290	$265	$230	$195

CONTINENTAL CARBINE — same as Mannlicher Style, except with double set trigger. Disc.

	$395	$365	$330	$310	$285	$255	$220

THE MARQUIS — .243, .270, .308, 7x51mm, or .30-06 cal., 20 in. barrel, adj. trigger. Mannlicher style carbine. Disc. 1984.

	$430	$325	$300	$275	$250	$230	$215

ALASKAN — same as Mark X, except .375 H&H or .458 Win. Mag. cal., recoil pad and extra stock crossbolt. Disc. 1984.

	$460	$350	$330	$310	$290	$250	$210

INTERDYNAMIC OF AMERICA, INC.
Previously distributed 1981-84 under the above heading out of Miami, FL.

KG-9 — 9mm Para., 3 in. barrel, open bolt, semi-auto paramilitary design pistol. Disc. approx. 1983.

	$750	$700	$650	$600	$575	$550	$525

KG-99 — 9mm Para., 3 in. barrel, semi-auto paramilitary design pistol, closed bolt, 36 shot mag., 5 in. vent shroud barrel, blue only, also available in fully auto version (Class III only — add $140), a stainless steel version of the KG 99. Mfg. by Interdynamic 1984 only.

	$260	$200	$180	$160	$145	$130	$120
KG-99M, mini pistol	$213	$165	$155	$145	$135	$125	$115

INTRATEC
Manufacturer located in Miami, FL.

PROTECTOR SERIES PISTOLS

PROTEC-22 — .22 LR cal., double action only semi-auto, 2½ in. barrel, 10 shot mag., fixed sights, choice of black, satin, or Tec-Kote finish, wrap around grips, 13 oz. New 1991.

Mfg.'s Sug. Retail	$89	$75	$60	$50	$40	$35	$30	$25

Add $6 for satin or Tec-Kote finish.

PROTEC-25 — .25 ACP., double action only semi-auto, 2½ in. barrel, 8 shot mag., fixed sights, choice of black, satin, or Tec-Kote finish, wrap around grips, 13 oz. New 1991.

Mfg.'s Sug. Retail	$89	$75	$60	$50	$40	$35	$30	$25

Add $6 for satin or Tec-Kote finish.

TEC-SERIES Pistols

TEC-9 — 9mm Para., semi-auto paramilitary design pistol, 5 in. shrouded barrel, matte black finish, 32 shot mag. New 1985.

Mfg.'s Sug. Retail	$267	$225	$175	$155	$140	$130	$120	$110

TEC-9K — similar to TEC-9, except has new durable Tec-Kote finish with better protection than hard chrome. New 1991.

Mfg.'s Sug. Retail	$300	$245	$185	$160	$140	$130	$120	$110

TEC-9S — matte stainless version of the TEC-9.

Mfg.'s Sug. Retail	$362	$295	$240	$185				

For above TEC-9 with accessory package (deluxe case, 3-36 shot mag.'s, paramilitary design grip, and recoil compensator), add $178.

TEC-9M — mini version of the Model TEC-9, including 3 in. barrel and 20 shot mag.

Mfg.'s Sug. Retail	$245	$200	$165	$150	$140	$130	$120	$110

TEC-9MK — similar to Tec-9M, except has Tec-Kote rust resistant finish. New 1991.

Mfg.'s Sug. Retail	$280	$235	$180	$155	$140	$130	$120	$110

Grading	100%	98%	95%	90%	80%	70%	60%

TEC-9MS — matte stainless version of the TEC-9M.

    Mfg.'s Sug. Retail $338 $270 $220 $180

TEC-9C — 9mm, carbine variation with 16½ in. barrel, 36 shot mag. Only 1 gun mfg. 1987 - extreme rarity precludes pricing.

TEC-22 "SCORPION" — .22 LR, semi-auto pistol, paramilitary design, 4 in. barrel, ambidextrous safety, military matte finish, or electroless nickel, 30 shot mag., adj. sights, 30 oz.

    Mfg.'s Sug. Retail $202 $190 $170 $150 $135 $120 $100 $90

    Add $16 for threaded barrel (Model Tec-22T).

TEC-22TK — similar to Tec-22, except has Tec-Kote rust resistant finish. New 1991.

    Mfg.'s Sug. Retail $226 $200 $175 $150 $135 $120 $100 $90

TEC-22N — similar to TEC-22, except has nickel finish. MFg. 1990 only.

                              $200 $175 $160 $140 $125 $105 $95

    Add $16 for threaded barrel (Model Tec-22TN).

    Last Mfg.'s Sug. Retail was $226.

TEC-38 DERRINGER — .38 Spl., O/U, derringer, 3 in. barrel, blue frame, double action, 13 oz. Mfg. 1986-1988.

                              $110 $95 $85 $75 $65 $60 $55

    Last Mfg.'s Sug. Retail was $125.

IRWINDALE ARMS, INC. (IAI)

Manufacturer located in Irwindale, CA. Manufacture began in 1988.

PISTOLS

AUTOMAG III — .30 Carbine or 9mm Win. Mag. (new 1990), stainless steel only, 6⅜ in. barrel, patterned after Colt Gov.'t Model, Millett adj. sights with white outline, grooved Lexan grips, 8 shot mag., 43 oz. New 1989.

    Mfg.'s Sug. Retail $606 $550 $475 $395

AUTOMAG IV — .45 Win. Mag. cal., semi-auto, 6½ or 8⅜ (new 1991) in. barrel, 7 shot mag., Millett adj. sights, stainless steel only, 46 oz. New 1990.

    Mfg.'s Sug. Retail $630 $565 $485 $500

JAVELINA — 10mm Norma, semi-auto, 5 or 7 in. barrel, 8 shot mag., Millett adj. sights, wraparound Neoprene grips, stainless steel, wide adj. trigger, long grip safety, 48 oz. New 1990.

    Mfg.'s Sug. Retail $570 $525 $450 $375

BACKUP PISTOL — .380 ACP cal., semi-auto action, 2½ in. barrel, stainless steel, Lexan grips, 5 shot mag. in 380, 18 oz. Older disc. walnut grip models are worth a slight premium. Disc. 1989.

                              $200 $165 $135

    In January of 1990 AMT retained mfg. of this model.

    Last Mfg.'s Sug. Retail was $243.

ISRAELI MILITARY INDUSTRIES (IMI)

Manufacturer located in Israel.

IMI manufactured guns (Galil, Magnum Research, Uzi, and others) can be located in their respective sections of this text.

ITALIAN MILITARY ARMS

MODEL 1891 MANNLICHER-CARCANO — bolt action, 6.5mm, 6 shot, 31 in. barrel, straight handle, adj. sight, military stock.

                              $120 $100 $85 $70 $55 $40 $30

Grading	100%	98%	95%	90%	80%	70%	60%

MODEL 38 TERNI MILITARY RIFLE — 7.35mm, similar to 1891, except turned down bolt handle, 21 in. barrel and folding bayonet.

	$120	$100	$85	$70	$55	$40	$30

Gilisenti Model 1910 — 9mm Gilisenti cal., 4 in. barrel, 7 shot mag., checkered wooden grips, official Italian service pistol of both WWI and WWII, 32 oz.

	$550	$400	$285	$250	$225	$200	$185

Warning: 9mm Parabellum ammunition cannot be used in this pistol - only 9mm Gilisenti, as it is approx. 25% less powerful than the 9mm Para.

Brixia — similar to Gilisenti Model 1910, except utilizes simplified mfg. techniques, mostly sold to civilians.

	$500	$400	$275	$240	$215	$190	$175

ITHACA GUN

Manufactured in Ithaca, NY, 1886 to Nov. of 1986. Re-opened in early 1987 as Ithaca Acquisition Corp. using the old trademark. In the past, Ithaca also absorbed companies including Syracuse Arms Co., Lefever Arms Co., Union Fire Arms Co., Wilkes-Barre Gun Co., as well as others.

On March 6, 1987 the Ithaca Gun Company was sold to Ithaca Acquisition Corporation doing business as Ithaca Gun Company. Currently, Ithaca is manufacturing the Model 87 slide action shotgun (previously designated the Model 37).

HANDGUNS

X-CALIBER SINGLE SHOT — .22 LR or .44 Mag. cal., break open action with contoured wooden grip and forearm, 10 or 15 in. barrel, unique dual firing pin detonates both rimfire and centerfire cartridges. Model 20 is target model (blued finish with Goncalo Alves wood grips), or Model 30 Hunting (sandblasted teflon finish with American walnut grips). Frames and barrels can be purchased separately. While advertised in 1988, this gun was never mfg. due to unsolveable production problems. Mfg.'s Sug. Retail was $270.

RIFLES: BOLT ACTION

LSA-55 STANDARD — Mauser type action, .222, .22-250, 6mm, .243, or .308 cal., 22 in. barrel, leaf sight, 3 shot clip mag., checkered Monte Carlo stock. Mfg. in Finland by Tikka from 1969 to 1977.

	$375	$350	$330	$290	$255	$230	$210

LSA-55 DELUXE — same as Standard, except rollover cheek, rosewood pistol grip cap and forend tip, skipline checkering, no sights, scope mounts furnished.

	$415	$385	$365	$330	$285	$260	$240

LSA-55 HEAVY BARREL — same as LSA-55, except .222 or .22-250 only, target heavy barrel, special beavertail stock 8½ lbs.

	$440	$420	$390	$360	$310	$275	$255

LSA-65 — same as LSA-55, except long action for calibers .25-06, .270, or .30-06. Mfg. 1969 to 1977.

	$375	$350	$330	$290	$255	$230	$210

LSA-65 DELUXE — same as LSA-55 Deluxe, except .25-06, .270, or .30-06.

	$415	$385	$365	$330	$285	$260	$240

COMBINATION GUNS

LSA-55 TURKEY GUN — O/U shotgun-rifle combo, 12 ga., .222 Rem., 24½ in. ribbed barrel, exposed hammer, folding rear sight, checkered Monte Carlo stock. Mfg. by Tikka, Finland 1970-1981.

	$605	$550	$415	$495	$425	$385	$330

Grading	100%	98%	95%	90%	80%	70%	60%

RIFLES: SEMI-AUTO

MODEL X5-C — .22LR cal., 7 shot Mag., semi-auto action. Mfg. 1958-1964. Model X5-T has tube mag.

	100%	98%	95%	90%	80%	70%	60%
	$95	$70	$65	$60	$55	$50	$35

MODEL X-15 — .22 LR cal., same as X5-C only forearm is not grooved. Mfg. 1964-1967.

	100%	98%	95%	90%	80%	70%	60%
	$95	$70	$65	$60	$55	$50	$35

RIFLES: LEVER ACTION

MODEL 49 SADDLEGUN — .22 LR cal., lever action, single shot. Mfg. 1961-1978. Martini-style action Mag. — add $15, deluxe model — add $45.

	100%	98%	95%	90%	80%	70%	60%
	$65	$50	$45	$40	$35	$30	$30

MODEL 49 PRESENTATION — like model 49, except gold-plated trigger, hammer, engraved receiver, fancy walnut. Mfg. 1962-1974.

	100%	98%	95%	90%	80%	70%	60%
	$220	$165	$155	$130	$120	$110	$100

MODEL 149 ST. LOUIS BICENTENNIAL — like deluxe model 149, except inscription on receiver, 200 mfg. 1964.

	100%	98%	95%	90%	80%	70%	60%
	$210	$160	$150	$125	$115	$105	$95

MODEL 72 SADDLEGUN — .22 or .22 mag., lever action, 18½ in. barrel, hooded front sight. Mfg. 1973-1978 by Erma Werke, W. Germany.

	100%	98%	95%	90%	80%	70%	60%
	$185	$140	$130	$110	$100	$90	$85

MODEL 72 DELUXE — same as Model 72, except has silver finished engraved receiver, deluxe walnut, octagon barrel. Mfg. 1974-1976.

	100%	98%	95%	90%	80%	70%	60%
	$260	$195	$185	$155	$145	$130	$120

SHOTGUNS: SIDE X SIDE - EARLY PRODUCTION

ITHACA HAMMERLESS DOUBLE BARREL — 12, 16, 20, 28 or .410 ga., 26-32 in. barrels, boxlock, extractors, double triggers, any standard choke, checkered pistol grip stock and forearm, grades shown differ in overall quality, ornamentation, grade of wood, and style of checkering.

Values below are for guns mfg. between 1925-1948. Newer models can be found later in this section.

SST — add $200.   Non-SST — add $150.

Vent rib on grades 4, 5, 7, and $2,000 Grade — add $350.

Vent rib - lower grades — add $200.

Beavertail forearm — add $175.

Auto ejectors - for grades No. 1, 2, and 3 — add 33%.

Without ejectors on grades 4E-7E — subtract 33%.

NOTE: Shotguns mfg. before 1925 have less value (ser. no.'s before 400,000 with underbolt - rib extension locking system) because modern ammunition cannot be shot safely in these earlier models. In 1925 the rotary bolt and stronger frame were adapted (ser. no.'s after 400,000). Once again, it is recommended that these guns (pre-400,000 ser. range) are not shot with modern ammo.

100%	98%	95%	90%	80%	70%	60%	50%	40%	30%	20%	10%

Early hammer doubles in average condition are approx. valued between $175-$450. However, if 60% condition remains (including original case colors), values can approximate those listed below.

FIELD GRADE

10 ga. Mag.

100%	98%	95%	90%	80%	70%	60%	50%	40%	30%	20%	10%
$2,000	$1,800	$1,500	$1,400	$1,300	$1,200	$1,100	$950	$825	$700	$575	$495

3½ in. chambered 10 ga. Mag.'s are serial numbered over 500,000. Total production was approx. 850 guns. 2⅞ in. chambered 10 ga.'s are priced the same as a 12 ga. A 12 ga., 3 in.

100%	98%	95%	90%	80%	70%	60%	50%	40%	30%	20%	10%

model was also made on the 10 ga. frame - only 87 were mfg. and specimens are noted in the 500,000 serial range.

12 ga.

| $1,000 | $800 | $600 | $550 | $500 | $450 | $415 | $380 | $350 | $325 | $300 | $265 |

16 ga.

| $1,000 | $800 | $600 | $550 | $500 | $450 | $415 | $380 | $350 | $325 | $300 | $265 |

20 ga.

| $1,200 | $1,000 | $800 | $675 | $575 | $500 | $450 | $415 | $380 | $350 | $325 | $300 |

28 ga.

| $2,000 | $1,800 | $1,500 | $1,400 | $1,300 | $1,200 | $1,100 | $1,000 | $925 | $850 | $775 | $695 |

.410 ga.

| $2,000 | $1,800 | $1,500 | $1,400 | $1,300 | $1,200 | $1,100 | $1,000 | $925 | $850 | $795 | $750 |

GRADE NO. 2

10 ga. Mag.

| $2,400 | $2,000 | $1,800 | $1,600 | $1,400 | $1,300 | $1,200 | $1,100 | $950 | $825 | $700 | $575 |

3½ in. chambered 10 ga. Mag.'s are serial numbered over 500,000. Total production was approx. 850 guns. 2⅞ in. chambered 10 ga.'s are priced the same as a 12 ga.

12 ga.

| $1,500 | $1,200 | $1,000 | $800 | $600 | $550 | $500 | $450 | $415 | $380 | $350 | $325 |

16 ga.

| $1,500 | $1,200 | $1,000 | $800 | $600 | $550 | $500 | $450 | $415 | $380 | $350 | $325 |

20 ga.

| $1,800 | $1,500 | $1,200 | $1,000 | $800 | $600 | $550 | $500 | $450 | $415 | $380 | $350 |

28 ga.

| $2,500 | $2,000 | $1,800 | $1,500 | $1,400 | $1,300 | $1,200 | $1,100 | $1,000 | $925 | $850 | $775 |

.410 ga.

| $2,500 | $2,000 | $1,800 | $1,500 | $1,400 | $1,300 | $1,200 | $1,100 | $1,000 | $925 | $850 | $795 |

GRADE NO. 3

10 ga. Mag.

| $3,000 | $2,500 | $2,100 | $1,800 | $1,600 | $1,400 | $1,300 | $1,200 | $1,100 | $950 | $825 | $700 |

3½ in. chambered 10 ga. Mag.'s are serial numbered over 500,000. Total production was approx. 850 guns. 2⅞ in. chambered 10 ga.'s are priced the same as a 12 ga.

12 ga.

| $1,850 | $1,500 | $1,200 | $1,000 | $800 | $600 | $550 | $500 | $450 | $415 | $380 | $350 |

16 ga.

| $1,850 | $1,500 | $1,200 | $1,000 | $800 | $600 | $550 | $500 | $450 | $415 | $380 | $350 |

20 ga.

| $1,800 | $1,500 | $1,200 | $1,000 | $800 | $600 | $550 | $500 | $450 | $415 | $380 | $350 |

28 ga.

| $3,200 | $2,800 | $2,400 | $2,100 | $1,800 | $1,500 | $1,400 | $1,300 | $1,200 | $1,100 | $1,000 | $925 |

.410 ga.

| $3,400 | $2,950 | $2,500 | $2,150 | $1,800 | $1,500 | $1,400 | $1,300 | $1,200 | $1,100 | $1,000 | $925 |

GRADE NO. 4E — auto ejectors.

10 ga. Mag.

| $4,000 | $3,500 | $3,000 | $2,500 | $2,100 | $1,800 | $1,600 | $1,400 | $1,300 | $1,200 | $1,100 | $950 |

3½ in. chambered 10 ga. Mag.'s are serial numbered over 500,000. Total production was approx. 850 guns. 2⅞ in. chambered 10 ga.'s are priced the same as a 12 ga.

12 ga.

| $3,000 | $2,500 | $2,200 | $1,850 | $1,500 | $1,200 | $1,000 | $800 | $600 | $550 | $500 | $450 |

16 ga.

| $3,000 | $2,500 | $2,200 | $1,850 | $1,500 | $1,200 | $1,000 | $800 | $600 | $550 | $500 | $450 |

100%	98%	95%	90%	80%	70%	60%	50%	40%	30%	20%	10%

20 ga.

| $4,000 | $3,500 | $3,000 | $2,500 | $2,200 | $1,850 | $1,500 | $1,200 | $1,000 | $800 | $600 | $550 |

28 ga.

Extreme rarity factor precludes accurate pricing evaluation.

.410 ga.

Extreme rarity factor precludes accurate pricing evaluation.

GRADE NO. 5E — auto ejectors.

10 ga. Mag.

| $5,000 | $4,500 | $4,000 | $3,500 | $3,000 | $2,500 | $2,100 | $1,800 | $1,600 | $1,400 | $1,200 | $1,000 |

$3\frac{1}{2}$ in. chambered 10 ga. Mag.'s are serial numbered over 500,000. Total production was approx. 850 guns. $2\frac{7}{8}$ in. chambered 10 ga.'s are priced the same as a 12 ga.

12 ga.

| $4,250 | $3,250 | $2,600 | $2,200 | $1,850 | $1,500 | $1,200 | $1,000 | $800 | $600 | $550 | $500 |

16 ga.

| $4,250 | $3,250 | $2,600 | $2,200 | $1,850 | $1,500 | $1,200 | $1,000 | $800 | $600 | $550 | $500 |

20 ga.

| $4,800 | $4,100 | $3,500 | $3,000 | $2,500 | $2,200 | $1,850 | $1,600 | $1,400 | $1,200 | $1,000 | $895 |

28 ga.

Extreme rarity factor precludes accurate pricing evaluation.

.410 ga.

Extreme rarity factor precludes accurate pricing evaluation.

GRADE NO. 6E — auto ejectors.

10 ga. Mag.

| $5,600 | $5,000 | $4,500 | $4,000 | $3,500 | $3,000 | $2,500 | $2,100 | $1,800 | $1,600 | $1,400 | $1,200 |

$3\frac{1}{2}$ in. chambered 10 ga. Mag.'s are serial numbered over 500,000. Total production was approx. 850 guns. $2\frac{7}{8}$ in. chambered 10 ga.'s are priced the same as a 12 ga.

12 ga.

| $4,750 | $4,000 | $3,250 | $2,600 | $2,200 | $1,850 | $1,500 | $1,200 | $1,000 | $800 | $600 | $550 |

16 ga.

| $4,750 | $4,250 | $3,250 | $2,600 | $2,200 | $1,850 | $1,500 | $1,200 | $1,000 | $800 | $600 | $550 |

20 ga.

| $5,350 | $4,675 | $4,100 | $3,500 | $3,000 | $2,500 | $2,200 | $1,850 | $1,600 | $1,400 | $1,200 | $995 |

28 ga.

Extreme rarity factor precludes accurate pricing evaluation.

.410 ga.

Extreme rarity factor precludes accurate pricing evaluation.

GRADE NO. 7E — auto ejectors.

10 ga. Mag. — extreme rarity factor precludes accurate pricing evaluation.

$3\frac{1}{2}$ in. chambered 10 ga. Mag.'s are serial numbered over 500,000. Total production was approx. 850 guns. $2\frac{7}{8}$ in. chambered 10 ga.'s are priced the same as a 12 ga.

12 ga.

| $9,250 | $8,300 | $7,400 | $6,500 | $5,650 | $4,750 | $4,000 | $3,250 | $2,600 | $2,100 | $1,600 | $1,150 |

16 ga.

| $9,250 | $8,300 | $7,400 | $6,500 | $5,650 | $4,750 | $4,000 | $3,250 | $2,600 | $2,100 | $1,600 | $1,150 |

20 ga.

| $10,400 | $9,250 | $8,300 | $7,400 | $6,500 | $5,650 | $4,750 | $4,000 | $3,250 | $2,600 | $2,100 | $1,600 |

28 ga.

Extreme rarity factor precludes accurate pricing evaluation.

.410 ga.

Extreme rarity factor precludes accurate pricing evaluation.

$2,000 GRADE — 12 ga., top-of-the-line model, auto ejectors, single selective trigger.

| $11,000 | $9,500 | $8,450 | $7,400 | $6,500 | $5,650 | $4,750 | $4,000 | $3,250 | $2,600 | $2,100 | $1,600 |

Rarity on 16 or 20 ga. precludes accurate pricing.

100%	98%	95%	90%	80%	70%	60%	50%	40%	30%	20%	10%

PRE-WAR $1,000 GRADE — 12 ga., top-of-the-line models, auto ejectors, single selective trigger.

$13,000	$11,000	$9,500	$8,450	$7,400	$6,500	$5,650	$4,750	$4,000	$3,250	$2,600	$2,100

Rarity on 16 or 20 ga. precludes accurate pricing.

SOUSA GRADE — has mermaids on trigger guard in gold, only 11 manufactured (including one .410 ga.). This model is very rare and prices are hard to establish. Recently, the price range has been approx. $15,000-$40,000, depending on original condition.

This model had help in development by the famous band director and composer, John Phillip Sousa.

TRAP GUNS

Grading	100%	98%	95%	90%	80%	70%	60%

SINGLE BARREL TRAP — 12 ga., 30, 32, or 34 in. barrels, vent rib, boxlock, auto ejector, checkered pistol grip and forearm, grades differ in engraving, overall workmanship, and grade or wood and checkering. Values on these models sometimes vary greatly depending on originality of finish, customer alterations, and other variations trap shooters might use to alter dimensions for their particular shooting requirements. Below values represent trap guns in original, unaltered condition.

Note: Flues model mfg. prior to 1921 with serial numbers under 400,000 have less value than those models mfg. afterward as pre-400,000 serial no. shotguns cannot be fired safely with modern ammumition.

Trap guns under 60% original condition will be within 25% of the value shown in the 60% column.

Knick Model — mfg. 1921-disc. Serial numbered above 400,000. Can be distinguished by triple underbolt locking.

				$1,395	$1,000	$900	$800	$675	$600	$550

Victory Grade — disc. 1938.

				$995	$850	$775	$675	$575	$495	$440

No. 4E — disc. 1976.

				$1,500	$1,200	$1,000	$875	$750	$650	$595

No. 5E — pre-1986 mfg.

				$2,950	$2,600	$2,300	$1,950	$1,650	$1,400	$1,000

Currently manufactured No. 5E's may be found under a different heading (Single Barrel Trap Shot Guns: Recent Mfg.) in this section.

No. 6E — this model was available by special order only. Rarity factor precludes accurate pricing.

No. 7E — disc. 1964.

				$3,950	$3,450	$3,000	$2,750	$2,475	$2,225	$1,995

$5,000 Grade — same as Pre-War $1,000 grade.

				$9,500	$8,900	$8,175	$7,650	$6,725	$5,825	$4,950

Sousa Grade — extremely rare.

Extreme rarity factor precludes accurate pricing evaluation. Prices will be higher than the $5,000 Grade.

AUTO & BURGLAR S X S — 20 ga., 10 or 14 in. barrels, with or without cocking indicators, blue finish, pistol grip, classified as Curio (short barreled shotgun status) in 1977 - must be registered, offered in Model A (has grip spur on back of pistol grip) or B (squared grips). Approx. 4,500 mfg. 1922-1933.

				$1,050	$925	$775	$725	$675	$650	$575

This model was manufactured in production lots of approx. 100 (as demand dictated).

MODEL 66 LEVER ACTION — 20 or .410 ga. single shot lever action, field gun only. Mfg. 1963-1978. Add 33% to .410 ga.

				$125	$95	$90	$75	$70	$65	$55

Model 66 RS — 20 ga. slug gun with 22 in. barrel and rifle type sights, recoil pad.

				$150	$130	$110	$90	$80	$70	$60

Note: Ventilated ribs were also available on special order in the 20 ga. only — add 25%.

Grading	100%	98%	95%	90%	80%	70%	60%

SKB SHOTGUNS: PREVIOUSLY IMPORTED BY ITHACA

Note: Can be found under SKB heading.

SINGLE BARREL TRAP SHOTGUNS: RECENT MFG.

CENTURY TRAP GRADE SINGLE BARREL — 12 ga., 32 or 34 in. vent rib barrel, engraved, auto ejector, full choke, checkered walnut stock. Mfg. 1973 and 1976 by SKB.

	$550	$525	$470	$440	$385	$360	$320

CENTURY II — improved trap stock version of Century, Monte Carlo stock.

	$600	$550	$495	$470	$415	$385	$350

5E GRADE — 12 ga., 32 or 34 in. barrel, custom order only, elaborate engraving, quality worksmanship throughout. Originally mfg. 1925-1986, mfg. resumed again 1988.

Mfg.'s Sug. Retail	$7,500	$7,500	$2,950	$2,550	$2,175	$1,900	$1,725	$1,495

DOLLAR GRADE — 12 ga., 32 or 34 in. barrel. Top-of-the-line model custom built to customer specifications. Original mfg. was stopped 1986 and resumed again 1988.

Mfg.'s Sug. Retail	$10,000	$10,000	$5,800	$5,000	$4,400	$3,850	$3,250	$2,775

SHOTGUNS: SLIDE ACTION

In 1987, Ithaca Acquisition Corp. reintroduced the Model 37 as the Model 87. New Model 87's are listed below and also include pre-1986 mfg. (Model 37's). Unless a particular Model 37 specimen has rare features, special wood, or was a deluxe order, values will approximate most older models as well.

MODEL 37 FEATHERLIGHT STANDARD — 12, 16, or 20 ga., bottom ejection, 4 shot mag., 26, 28, or 30 in. barrel, hammerless, take down, any standard choke. Mfg. 1937-disc.

	$260	$225	$205	$185	$165	$150	$135

MODEL 37V — same as 37, except vent rib. Mfg. 1962-disc.

	$315	$260	$240	$195	$180	$170	$165

All currently manufactured Model 37's have the Featherlight designation. Prices above are for older manufactured Model 37's.

MODEL 37D — same as 37, except recoil pad, beavertail forearm, checkered. Mfg. 1954-1981.

	$360	$275	$255	$205	$195	$185	$175

MODEL 37DV — same as 37D, except vent rib. Mfg. 1962-1981.

	$395	$320	$295	$245	$225	$200	$185

MODEL 37 FIELD GRADE MAGNUM — 12 or 20 ga., 3 in. chambers, vent rib, walnut stock and corncob forearm, supplied with three choke tubes. Mfg. 1984-1986.

	$300	$240	$195	$180	$170	$165	$150

Last Mfg.'s Sug. Retail was $428.

MODEL 87 DELUXE MAGNUM — 12 or 20 ga., 3 in. chambers, vent rib, deluxe wood with checkered forearm. Mfg. 1981-1986, production resumed 1988 only.

	$320	$270	$230	$210	$200	$185	$165

Add $77 for Combo package (extra 28 in. barrel).
Last Mfg.'s Sug. Retail was $395.

New mfg. 20 ga. shotguns were available with a 25 in. barrel only (with choke tubes).

MODEL 37 FIELD GRADE STANDARD — 12 or 20 ga., economy model, corncob forearm, 26, 28, or 30 in. barrel. Mfg. 1983-1985 only.

	$260	$225	$205	$180	$165	$150	$135

Last Mfg.'s Sug. Retail was $298.

Grading	100%	98%	95%	90%	80%	70%	60%

MODEL 87 BASIC FIELD COMBO — 12 or 20 ga., includes 20/25 in. deer barrel with special bore and 28 in. VR multi-choke field barrel, uncheckered walnut stock and corncob forearm, 7 lbs. New 1989.

Mfg.'s Sug. Retail	$427	$340	$280	$240	$200	$175	$160	$145

Add $32 for rifled bore barrel.

Add $136 for laminated wood (includes rifle bored barrel).

MODEL 87 FIELD GRADE — 12 or 20 ga., 3 in. chamber, economy model, walnut stock and forearm with pressed checkering, 26, 28, or 30 in. barrel with 3 choke tubes standard. Reintroduced 1989.

Mfg.'s Sug. Retail	$458	$375	$325	$275	$230	$205	$185	$165

Model 87 Camo Vent — 12 ga. only, 3 in. chamber, 26 or 28 in. vent rib barrel, camo-seal rust resistant finish on exterior parts. Available in either green or brown, includes sling and swivels. Mfg. began 1986, resumed 1988.

Mfg.'s Sug. Retail	$524	$430	$360	$300	$250	$220	$190	$170

Model 87 Turkey Gun — 12 ga. only, 24 in. VR barrel with choice of fixed full choke or full choke tube, camo or matte blue finish. New 1989.

Mfg.'s Sug. Retail	$409	$330	$275	$235	$195	$175	$160	$145

Add $106 for camo finish.

Add $11 for full choke tube.

Model 87 Deluxe — similar to Model 87 Field Grade except has cut checkering, high gloss lacquer finish, and gold trigger. Mfg. 1989-90 only.

	$410	$345	$285	$240	$210	$190	$170

Add $54 for combo package (includes 20 in. special bore deer barrel).

Add $87 for combo package with 20 or 25 in. rifled bore deer barrel.

Last Mfg.'s Sug. Retail was $495.

MODEL 87 ULTRALITE FIELD — 12 or 20 ga., 3 in. chamber, aluminum receiver, 20 (disc. 1988), 24, 25 (disc. 1988), or 26 in. barrel. 20 ga. weighs 5 lbs., 12 ga. weighs 5¾ lbs, multi-chokes (3) became standard in 1989. Originally mfg. 1988-86, reintroduced 1988-90.

	$400	$340	$285	$240	$210	$190	$170

Add $50 for slim grip model (12½ in. stock - disc. 1985).

Subtract $42 if without multiple choke feature.

The 20 and 25 in. barrels were disc. when mfg. was resumed 1988.

Last Mfg.'s Sug. Retail was $481.

Model 87 Ultra Deluxe — similar to Ultralite Field except has cut checkering, high gloss lacquer finish, and gold trigger. New 1989.

Mfg.'s Sug. Retail	$514	$425	$360	$300	$250	$220	$190	$170

ENGLISH 87 — 20 ga. only, 3 in. chamber, 24 or 26 in. VR barrel with 3 choke tubes, steel receiver, checkered walnut stock and forearm, recoil pad, 6¾ lbs. New 1991.

Mfg.'s Sug. Retail	$395	$335	$275	$235	$195	$175	$160	$145

MODEL 37 ENGLISH ULTRALITE — 12 or 20 ga., 25 or 26 in. barrels, world's lightest pump, 20 ga. weighs 4¾ lb., 12 ga. weighs 5½ lbs., checkered straight stock. Mfg. 1983-1986.

	$350	$310	$275	$250	$225	$200	$180

Last Mfg.'s Sug. Retail was $522.

MODEL 37R — solid rib. Mfg. 1937-1967.

Plain stock	$340	$200	$175	$145	$130	$110	$90
Checkered stock	$380	$220	$200	$175	$165	$145	$120

MODEL 37R DELUXE — same as 37R, except fancy wood. Mfg. 1937-1955.

	$440	$275	$255	$230	$210	$195	$165

MODEL 37S SKEET GRADE — similar to 37, except Knicker vent rib, large forearm, fancy wood. Mfg. 1937-1955.

	$450	$400	$360	$310	$290	$270	$230

Grading	100%	98%	95%	90%	80%	70%	60%

MODEL 37T TRAP GRADE — similar to 37S, except trap stock, select walnut, recoil pad. Mfg. 1937-1955.

| | $425 | $375 | $340 | $295 | $270 | $250 | $235 |

Add 20% for early models with Fleur-de-lis checkering.

MODEL 37T TARGET GRADE — replaced 37S and 37T. Mfg. from 1955-1961.

| | $425 | $375 | $340 | $310 | $285 | $260 | $240 |

MODEL 87 SUPREME GRADE — 12 or 20 ga., presentation walnut, high luster blue, limited production, previously available in either trap, skeet, or field models, fixed chokes. Originally manufactured 1967-86, reintroduced 1988.

| Mfg.'s Sug. Retail | $819 | $695 | $495 | $425 | $395 | $360 | $315 | $280 |

BASIC DEERSLAYER — 12 ga. only, 20 or 25 in. special bore barrel, oil finished stock and corncob forearm with no checkering, iron sights, matte metal finish, 7 lbs. New 1989.

| Mfg.'s Sug. Retail | $391 | $320 | $265 | $230 | $195 | $175 | $160 | $145 |

MODEL 87 FIELD DEERSLAYER — 12 or 20 ga., rifle slug barrel, 20 or 25 in. special bore barrel, open sights. Mfg. 1959-86, reintroduced 1988.

| Mfg.'s Sug. Retail | $407 | $330 | $275 | $235 | $195 | $175 | $160 | $145 |

Model 87 Deluxe Deerslayer — similar to Field Deerslayer except has cut checkering, high gloss lacquer finish, and gold trigger. New 1989.

| Mfg.'s Sug. Retail | $429 | $340 | $280 | $240 | $200 | $175 | $160 | $145 |

Add $33 for rifled bore.

Add $120 for combo package (28 in. multi-choke barrel).

Model 87 Ultra Deerslayer — similar to Deluxe Deerslayer except has aluminum frame. Mfg. 1989-90 only.

| | $350 | $285 | $245 | $200 | $175 | $160 | $145 |

Last Mfg.'s Sug. Retail was $444.

MODEL 37 SUPER DELUXE DEERSLAYER — similar to Model 37 (87) Deerslayer, except fancy wood. Mfg. 1962-1985.

| | $390 | $335 | $300 | $270 | $235 | $210 | $185 |

Last Mfg.'s Sug. Retail was $447.

MONTE CARLO DEERSLAYER II — 12 ga. only, 25 in. barrel with rifling, Monte Carlo stock and forearm with cut checkering, receiver is drilled and tapped for scope mounting, 7 lbs. New 1989.

| Mfg.'s Sug. Retail | $525 | $435 | $360 | $300 | $250 | $220 | $190 | $170 |

MODEL 87 MILITARY & POLICE — 12 or 20 (new 1989) ga., short barrel Model 37 w/normal stock or pistol grip only, 18½ or 20 in. barrel, 5 or 8 shot. Originally disc. 1983, reintroduced 1988.

| Mfg.'s Sug. Retail | $391 | $325 | $265 | $230 | $200 | $180 | $170 | $160 |

Add $103 for nickel finish (new 1991).

Add $16 for normal stock and corncob forearm.

Subtract $35 without parkerizing (disc.).

MODEL 37 BICENTENNIAL — 12 ga., engraved, fancy wood, cased with pewter buckle, 1,776 mfg. 1976, 100% value assumes NIB condition with case and belt buckle.

| | $425 | $375 | $340 | $315 | $295 | $270 | $250 |

MODEL 37 2500 SERIES CENTENNIAL — 12 ga., customized version of the Model 37 commemorating Ithaca's 100th year anniversary, silver plated, etched antique finish receiver, deluxe walnut. Mfg. 1980-1984.

| | $850 | $690 | $600 | $505 | $460 | $415 | $370 |

Last Mfg.'s Sug. Retail was $919.

Grading	100%	98%	95%	90%	80%	70%	60%

MODEL 37 PRESENTATION — 12 ga., blued, engraved, gold mounted receiver with extra-fancy walnut, cased, limited production. Mfg. 1981-86.

	$1,475	$1,245	$1,080	$915	$830	$745	$665

Last Mfg.'s Sug. Retail was $1,658.

MODEL 37 DUCKS UNLIMITED — 12 ga., vent rib.

	$385	$305	$275				

MODEL 37 $1000 GRADE — all gauges, deluxe engraving and checkering, gold inlaid, select figured walnut, hand-finished parts. Mfg. 1937-1940.

	$5,750	$5,200	$4,750	$4,250	$3,750	$3,250	$2,650

MODEL 37 $5000 GRADE — same as $1000 Grade, post-war designation. Mfg. 1947-1967.

	$5,250	$4,850	$4,250	$3,850	$3,250	$2,850	$2,250

SHOTGUNS: SEMI-AUTO

MODEL 51A FEATHERWEIGHT STANDARD — 12 or 20 ga., 30 in. full, 28 in. full or mod., 26 in. imp. cyl., gas operated, autoloading, checkered pistol grip stock. Mfg. 1970-1985. Vent rib became standard during late production.

Older models (no VR)

	$285	$230	$200	$180	$165	$150	$130

Recent production — with vent. rib.

	$350	$300	$275	$250	$225	$195	$165

Last Mfg.'s Sug. Retail with VR was $477.

MODEL 51A MAGNUM — same as 51 Standard, except 3 in. shells only, blue finish, recoil pad, vent rib became standard in 1984. Disc. for 1985.

Older models with no VR	$310	$255	$220	$205	$180	$165	$150
Vent rib	$375	$315	$285	$260	$235	$200	$170

MODEL 51A MAGNUM WATERFOWLER — same as 51 Standard, except 3 in. shells only, matte finished metal & flat finished walnut, recoil pad. Vent rib standard. Mfg. 1984-1986.

	$395	$335	$295	$265	$235	$200	$180

Add $80 for camouflaged exterior finish.
Last Mfg.'s Sug. Retail was $625.

MODEL 51A CAMO VENT — similar to Waterfowler, except has camo-seal rust resistant exterior finish. Mfg. 1986 only.

	$425	$325	$275				

Last Mfg.'s Sug. Retail was $770.

MODEL 51A SUPREME TRAP — same as 51 Standard, except 12 ga. only, 30 in. barrel, 7 post rib, full choke, select wood, pad, trap style stock. Add $36 for Monte Carlo. Mfg. 1970-1986.

	$425	$365	$315	$295	$270	$250	$230

Last Mfg.'s Sug. Retail was $869.

MODEL 51A SUPREME SKEET — same as 51 Standard, except 26 in. vent rib barrel, skeet choke, select wood. Mfg. 1970-present. 20 ga. was available 1983. Disc. 1986.

	$450	$390	$340	$300	$280	$260	$240

Last Mfg.'s Sug. Retail was $858.

MODEL 51A DEERSLAYER — same as 51 Standard, with 24 in. slug barrel, rifle sights, recoil pad, no rib. Mfg. 1972-1983.

	$350	$300	$260	$230	$195	$180	$165

Last Mfg.'s Sug. Retail was $477.

MODEL 51A TURKEY GUN — .12 ga. Mag. only, 26 in. barrel, matte finish, sling and swivels included. Mfg. 1984-1986.

	$360	$305	$275	$265	$250	$230	$210

Last Mfg.'s Sug. Retail was $625.

Grading	100%	98%	95%	90%	80%	70%	60%

MODEL 51 DUCKS UNLIMITED — same as 51 Deluxe, with D/U emblem on receiver.

	100%	98%	95%	90%	80%	70%	60%
	$425	$375	$335	$300	$280	$260	$230

MODEL 51 PRESENTATION — 12 ga., blued, engraved, gold engraved receiver with deluxe walnut. Mfg. 1984-1986.

	100%	98%	95%	90%	80%	70%	60%
	$1,250	$1,000	$875	$700	$575	$450	$325

Last Mfg.'s Sug. Retail was $1,658.

SEMI-AUTO: MAG-10 SEMI-AUTO

All Ithaca Mag-10's were disc. 1986.

MAG-10 — 10 ga., 3½ in. Mag., semi-auto, various barrel lengths, stainless steel breech block assembly, gas operated, various chokes, plain barrel, 11 lb. Mfg. 1975-1986.
100% values assume NIB condition - if without, subtract 10%.

Standard Grade — no checkering, ribless barrel, dull finished wood.

	100%	98%	95%	90%	80%	70%	60%
	$700	$650	$600	$550	$500	$460	$430

Last Mfg.'s Sug. Retail was $726.

Standard Grade with VR — available in 22, 26, 28, or 32 in. barrel lengths - otherwise same as Standard grade. Add $60 for camouflaged exterior finish.

	100%	98%	95%	90%	80%	70%	60%
	$775	$675	$625	$575	$525	$480	$440

Interchangeable choke tubes (3) became available in 1986 — add $60.

Last Mfg.'s Sug. Retail was $781.

Deluxe Vent — select checkered walnut stock and forearm, 22, 26, 28, or 32 in. barrels, high lustre wood finish.

	100%	98%	95%	90%	80%	70%	60%
	$825	$725	$650	$600	$550	$495	$450

Last Mfg.'s Sug. Retail was $924.

Supreme Grade — extra-select checkered walnut stock and forearm, otherwise same as Deluxe Vent.

	100%	98%	95%	90%	80%	70%	60%
	$995	$850	$725	$675	$595	$550	$525

Last Mfg.'s Sug. Retail was $1,124.

Mag. 10 Roadblocker — 22 in. cylinder bored ribless barrel, parkerized finish.

	100%	98%	95%	90%	80%	70%	60%
	$675	$600	$525	$500	$475	$450	$425

Last Mfg.'s Sug. Retail was $741.

National Wild Turkey Fed. Special Edition — mfg. in 1985 only.

	100%	98%	95%
	$950	$795	$625

MAG-10 PRESENTATION OR CENTENNIAL — 10 ga. Mag., blued, engraved, gold inlaid receiver, extra fancy walnut. Limited production. Approx. 200 mfg. in Presentation Grade 1983-1986.

	100%	98%	95%	90%	80%	70%	60%
	$1,875	$1,550	$1,300	$1,050	$915	$830	$745

Last Mfg.'s Sug. Retail was $1,727.

PERAZZI SHOTGUNS

NOTE: Ithaca was sole importer for Perazzi in the 70's. All new and used models will be in the P section under Perazzi. Perazzi today distributes their own firearms.

NOTES

JACKSON HOLE FIREARMS

Previous manufacturer located in Jackson Hole, WY during the mid-70's.

Grading	100%	98%	95%	90%	80%	70%	60%

RIFLES

BOLT ACTION RIFLE — various cal.'s, Mauser 98 action utilizing patented system for interchangeable barrels, checkered walnut stock.

	100%	98%	95%	90%	80%	70%	60%
	$1,050	$875	$800	$725	$650	$575	$495

Jackson Hole Firearms manufactured a limited quantity of their unique interchangeable barrel bolt action rifles. Collectibility to date has been minimal, and values are affected by the J.P. Sauer Models 90 and 200 which also feature the interchangeable barrel design.

JAPANESE MILITARY RIFLES

WWII manufacture in Tokyo, Japan.

NOTE: All Japanese rifles: deduct 20% if National Crest (chrysanthemum flower) has been ground off front receiver ring, deduct 20% if serial numbers are not matching, deduct 10-40% for training rifles of each type.

MODEL 38 ARISAKA RIFLE — Jap. Mauser type action, 6.5mm, 31 in. barrel, adj. sight, adapted 1905.

	100%	98%	95%	90%	80%	70%	60%
	$165	$135	$105	$95	$75	$65	$50

MODEL 38 CAVALRY CARBINE — same as T38 Rifle, except shorter barrel. Mfg. 1911.

	100%	98%	95%	90%	80%	70%	60%
	$175	$140	$110	$100	$80	$70	$55

MODEL 44 CAVALRY ARISAKA CARBINE — same as T38 Carbine, 6.5mm with 19 in. barrel, folding bayonet.

	100%	98%	95%	90%	80%	70%	60%
	$275	$235	$210	$190	$170	$155	$135

MODEL 99 SERVICE RIFLE — WWII version of 38, 7.7mm.

	100%	98%	95%	90%	80%	70%	60%
	$165	$135	$110	$100	$80	$70	$55

Add 20% for monopod.

PARATROOPER TAKEDOWN VERSION — adopted 1940, crossbolt barrel lock.

Type 2	100%	98%	95%	90%	80%	70%	60%
	$395	$325	$265	$220	$190	$165	$135

NAMBU PISTOLS — See Nambu section in this text.

JEFFERY, W.J. & CO. LTD

Previously manufactured in London, England.

In addition to making a complete line of their own shotguns and rifles, W.J. Jeffery also was subcontracted by many other exporters, distributors, and retailers (including Londons' famous Army & Navy department store). Many models were produced and rather than list them individually, a generalized format has been adopted for determining values on both rifles and shotguns.

RIFLES

SINGLE SHOT — various cal.'s, falling block action, checkered walnut stock and forearm, usually multiple folding leave rear sight (also tangent), excellent quality. Prices start in the $600 range for poor condition specimens in obsolete or undesirable cal.'s and can go up to $5,000 for 100% condition in .600 Nitro Express.
Subtract substantially for the Martini action variation.

Grading	100%	98%	95%	90%	80%	70%	60%

BOXLOCK DOUBLE RIFLE — many cal.'s, various engraving patterns, top or under (usually large cal.'s) lever opening, multiple folding leave rear sight, checkered walnut stock and forearm. Prices usually start in the $1,500 range for poor condition in undesirable cal.'s and can exceed $8,000 if encountered with elaborate engraving in .475 Express or larger cal.'s.
Subtract approx. 40% if with hammers, over 50% if with damascus barrels.

SIDELOCK DOUBLE RIFLE — various cal.'s, available in No. 1 or No. 2 grade, top-lever opening, best quality engraving, deluxe checkered walnut stock and forearm, almost any custom order could be filled. Prices start in the $3,250 range for 60% condition in smaller cal.'s and can easily go to $12,000+ when found in excellent condition in the larger cal.'s
Subtract approx. 40% if with hammers, over 50% if with damascus barrels.

SHOTGUNS

BOXLOCK SHOTGUN — most ga.'s, many combinations of options available, top-lever opening, many ranges of engraving, high quality and worksmanship. Values usually start in the $650 range if in poor condition and can go to $4,500+ if in a small ga. in near new condition ($1,750 for 12 ga.).
Subtract approx. 40% if with hammers, over 50% if with damascus barrels.

SIDELOCK SHOTGUN — most ga.'s, many combinations of options available, top-lever opening, many ranges of engraving, high quality and worksmanship. Values usually start in the $1,250 range if in poor condition and can go to $8,500+ if in a small ga. in near new condition ($3,950 for 12 ga.).

JENNINGS FIREARMS, INC.

Manufactured by Bryco Arms located in Irvine, CA. Distributed by Jennings Firearms, Inc. in Carson City, NV. Previously manufactured by Calwestco located in Chino, CA.

PISTOLS: SEMI-AUTO

Bryco Arms will appear under the B section. All pistols below are single action.

MODEL J-22 — .22 LR cal., 6 shot, semi-auto, 2½ in. barrel, satin nickel, bright chrome or black teflon or bright chrome finish, 13 oz.

Mfg.'s Sug. Retail	$75	$65	$50	$40	$35	$30	$30	$30

MODEL J-25 — .25 cal., aluminum alloy frame, 2.5 in. barrel, single action, walnut or black combat grips, positive safety, 11 oz. New 1988.

Mfg.'s Sug. Retail	$70	$60	$50	$40	$35	$30	$30	$30

This model is available in either satin nickel, bright chrome, or black teflon finish.

MODEL M-49 — 9mm Para., locked breech, 8 shot, available late 1991.
Prices have not been established on this model.

MODEL M-59 — similar to Model M-49, except is 13 shot.
Prices have not been established on this model.

JERICHO

Trademark of Israeli Military Industries (I.M.I.) imported exclusively by K.B.I. Inc. located in Harrisburg, PA.

JERICHO 941 — 9mm Para., .41 Action Express (by conversion only), or .40 S&W cal. (new 1991), semi-auto double action or single action, 4.72 in. barrel with polygonal rifling, all steel fabrication, 3 dot Tritium sights, 11 or 16 (9mm) shot mag., ambidextrous safety, polymer grips, decocking lever, 38½ oz. New 1990.

No Mfg.'s Retail	$535	$475	$425	$375	$325	$295	$260

Add $230 for .41 AE conversion kit.

Industrial hard chrome or nickel finishes are also available for all Jericho pistols. Contact K.B.I. for current pricing/availability.

Jericho 941 Pistol Package — includes 9mm Para. and .40 S&W barrels, also includes .41 AE conversion kit, cased with accessories. New 1990.

No Mfg.'s Retail	$775	$695	$625	$550	$495	$450	$400

Grading	100%	98%	95%	90%	80%	70%	60%

JERICHO 945 COMPACT — 9mm Para. or .45 ACP cal., semi-auto double action or single action, 3.62 in. barrel with polygonal rifling, all steel fabrication, 3 dot Tritium sights, 6 or 7 (9mm) shot mag., ambidextrous safety, polymer grips, decocking lever, approx. 32 oz. New 1991.

No Mfg.'s Retail	$535	$475	$425	$375	$325	$295	$260

Add $230 for conversion kit.

JOHNSON AUTOMATICS, INC.

Previous manufacturer located in Providence, RI.

MODEL 1941 — .30-06 or 7mm cal., semi-auto, 22 in. removable air cooled barrel, recoil operated, perforated metal handguard, aperture sight, military stock. Most were made for Dutch military, some used by Marine Paratroopers, during WWII all .30-06 and 7mm were ordered by South American governments.

	$850	$770	$720	$650	$600	$550	$500

7mm caliber — subtract $50 because not original U.S. Military cal. Also deduct 10% if ser. no.'s don't match.

IVER JOHNSON ARMS, INC.

Manufactured in Fitchburg, MA, 1883-1984 and Jacksonville, AR 1984 to date. Formerly Johnson Bye & Co. 1871-1883. Renamed Iver Johnson & Co. in 1871 until 1891. Renamed Iver Johnson's Arms & Cycle Works in 1891 with manufacturing moving to Fitchburg, MA. In 1975 the name changed to Iver Johnson's Arms, Inc. and two years later, company facilities were moved to Middlesex, MA. In 1982, production was moved to Jacksonville, AR under the trade name Iver Johnson Arms, Inc. In 1983 Universal Firearms, Inc. was acquired by Iver Johnson Arms, Inc.

Iver Johnson Arms was sold in March of 1987 and was acquired by American Military Arms Corporation (AMAC). Currently, AMAC has reintroduced some older models, mostly using previously existing parts. In addition, AMAC has also introduced some newly designed models.

REVOLVERS

MODEL 1900 — .22, .32 S&W, or .38 S&W cal., double action, 2½, 4½, or 6 in. barrel, fixed sights, blue or nickel, rubber grips. Mfg. 1900-1947.

	$125	$80	$70	$60	$55	$45	$40

MODEL 1900 TARGET — .22 LR, 6 shot, 6 or 9½ in. barrel, blue, fixed sights. Mfg. 1925-1942.

	$140	$90	$80	$70	$65	$55	$50

TARGET SEALED 8 — .22 LR, 8 shot, 6 or 10 in. barrel, blue, fixed sights, rubber grips. Mfg. 1931-1957.

	$150	$100	$95	$80	$75	$65	$60

TARGET 9 SHOT — same as Target Sealed 8, except 9 shot. Mfg. 1929-1946.

	$145	$90	$80	$70	$65	$55	$50

SAFETY HAMMER MODEL — .22 LR, .32 S&W, or .38 S&W cal., 2 or 3 in. barrel standard, 4, 5, or 6 in. available at extra cost, fixed sights, blue (standard) or nickel, break open. Mfg. 1892-1950.

	$150	$80	$70	$60	$55	$45	$40

SAFETY HAMMERLESS — .32 S&W or .38 S&W cal., 2, 3 (.32 only), or 3¼ in. barrel, double action only, break open, fixed sights, rubber grips, blue or nickel. Mfg. 1895-1950.

	$145	$100	$95	$80	$75	$65	$60

.22 SUPERSHOT — .22 LR, 6 in. barrel, blue, fixed sights, checkered wood grips, break open, no counterbore. Mfg. 1929-1949.

	$150	$80	$70	$60	$55	$45	$40

Grading	100%	98%	95%	90%	80%	70%	60%

TRIGGER COCKING SINGLE ACTION — .22 LR, 8 shot, 6 in. barrel, break open, counterbored, clue, checkered wood grips, first pull on trigger cocks, second fires. Mfg. 1940-1947. Rare in 100% condition.

	$175	$120	$110	$95	$80	$75	$65

.22 TARGET SINGLE ACTION — .22 LR, 8 shot, 6 in. barrel, break open, counterbored, checkered wood, adj. grips and sights. Mfg. 1938-1948.

	$160	$120	$110	$95	$80	$75	$65

SUPERSHOT SEALED 8 — .22 LR, 8 shot, break open, blue, adj. sights, checkered wood grips. Mfg. 1931-1957.

	$175	$130	$120	$110	$90	$85	$75

SUPERSHOT 9 — same as Sealed 8, only 9 shot, not counterbored. Mfg. 1929-1949.

	$135	$90	$80	$75	$60	$50	$40

PROTECTOR SEALED 8 — .22 LR, 8 shot, 2½ in. barrel, break open, fixed sights, blue, wood grips. Mfg. 1933-1949.

	$175	$135	$125	$110	$90	$80	$75

SUPERSHOT MODEL 844 — .22 LR, 8 shot, 4½ or 6 in. barrel, adj. sights, break open, blue, wood grips. Mfg. 1955-1956.

	$100	$90	$85	$80	$75	$60	$50

ARMSWORTH MODEL 855 — .22 LR, single action, 8 shot, 6 in. barrel, break open, blue, adj. sights, wood grips, adj. finger rest. Mfg. 1955-1957.

	$135	$125	$120	$110	$90	$80	$75

MODEL 55A TARGET — .22 LR, 8 shot, 4½ or 6 in. barrel, solid frame, blue, fixed sights, wood grips, loading gate. Mfg. 1955-1984.

	$75	$65	$55	$45	$35	$30	$15

CADET — .22 LR, .22 WRM, .32 S&W, .38 S&W, or .38 Spl. cal., 2½ in. barrel, blue, fixed sights, plastic grips. Mfg. 1955-1984.

	$110	$90	$80	$75	$65	$55	$50

MODEL 57A TARGET — .22 LR, 8 shot, 4½ or 6 in. barrel, solid frame, blue, adj. sights, wood grips. Mfg. 1955-1975.

	$100	$80	$75	$65	$55	$45	$40

MODEL 66 TRAILSMAN — .22 LR, 6 in. barrel, break open, blue, adj. sights, rebounding hammer, wood grips. Mfg. 1958-1975.

	$110	$90	$85	$75	$65	$55	$50

SIDEWINDER — .22 LR, 6 or 8 shot, 4¾ or 6 in. barrel, solid frame, blue, nickel, or case hardened plastic grips, wood on case color model. Mfg. 1961-present, 8 shot pre-1975.

	$110	$90	$85	$75	$65	$55	$50

SIDEWINDER S — same as Sidewinder, except .22 WMR, interchangeable cylinder.

	$125	$100	$95	$85	$75	$65	$60

MODEL 67 VIKING — .22 LR, 8 shot, 4½ or 6 in. barrel, break open, blue, adj. sights, wood grips with thumbrest. Mfg. 1964-1975.

	$135	$110	$100	$95	$85	$75	$65

MODEL 67S VIKING — .22 LR, .32 S&W, or .38 S&W cal., 8 shot in .22, 5 shot in .32 or .38, 2¾ in. barrel, break open, adj. sights, plastic grips. Mfg. 1964-1975.

	$130	$100	$95	$85	$75	$60	$50

AMERICAN BULLDOG — .22 LR, .22 WRM, or .38 Spl. cal., 6 shot in .22, 5 shot in .38, 2½ or 4 in. barrel, blue or nickel, adj. sights, plastic grips. Mfg. 1974-1976.

	$135	$110	$100	$90	$80	$65	$60

Grading	100%	98%	95%	90%	80%	70%	60%

ROOKIE — .38 Spl., 5 shot, 4 in. barrel, solid frame, blue or nickel, plastic grips. Mfg. 1975-1984.

	$100	$80	$75	$65	$55	$45	$35

SPORTSMAN — .22 LR, 6 shot, 4¾ or 6 in. barrel, solid frame, blue, fixed sights, plastic grips. Mfg. 1974-1976.

	$100	$80	$75	$65	$55	$45	$35

DELUXE TARGET — same as Sportsman, adj. sights. Mfg. 1975-1976.

	$110	$90	$85	$75	$65	$55	$40

SWING OUT — .22 LR, .22 WRM, .32 S&W, or .38 S&W cal., 6 shot in .22, 5 shot in .32 or .38, 2, 3, or 4 in. barrel, vent. rib, 4 or 6 in., blue or nickel, fixed or adj. sights. Mfg. 1977-1984.

	$130	$110	$100	$90	$80	$75	$65

VR Barrel — 4 or 6 in. vent. rib barrel, adj. sights.

	$170	$150	$140	$130	$125	$120	$100

PISTOLS: SEMI-AUTO

AMAC also manufactures a Super Enforcer .30 cal., Delta 786 9mm (disc. 1989), and a M-2 machine gun which are not listed in this text.

MODEL 9 — 9mm, double action, 6 shot mag., 3 in. barrel, blue or matte blue only, ambidextrous safety, smooth hardwood grips, 26 oz. Has not been released to date.

TRAILSMEN PISTOL — .22 LR only, semi-auto, all steel construction, 4½ or 6 in. barrel, blue finish, black checkered composition grips, 10 shot mag., approx. 30 oz. Mfg. 1985-86 and reintroduced 1990 only.

	$200	$165	$145	$130	$120	$110	$100

Add $20 for hardwood stocks and high polish blue (disc. 1990).
Last Mfg.'s Sug. Retail was $230.

PONY PISTOL (PO380 SERIES) — .380 ACP only, semi-auto single action, 3 in. barrel, 6 shot mag., all steel construction, blue or matte blue finish, 20 oz. Mfg. 1985-1986 (by Firearms International) and reintroduced 1990 only.

	$290	$245	$210	$185	$170	$155	$140

Last Mfg.'s Sug. Retail was $330.

Pony .380 Stainless — similar to Pony Pistol, except is stainless steel construction. New 1990 only.

	$315	$280	$240

Last Mfg.'s Sug. Retail was $365.

Nickel Pony — with nickel finish. Mfg. 1985 only.

	$260	$230	$215	$200	$185	$170	$160

Last Mfg.'s Sug. Retail was $290 for nickel finish.

POCKET PISTOL (TP SERIES) — .22 LR or .25 ACP cal., semi-auto, double action, 3 in. barrel, 7 shot finger tip extension mag., black plastic grips, fixed sights, blue or matte finish, 15 oz. Previously mfg. 1985-86, reintroduced 1988-90.

	$145	$125	$110	$100	$90	$80	$70

Add $15 for nickel finish (disc. 1989).
Last Mfg.'s Sug. Retail was $165.

AMAC-22/25 COMPACT — .22 Short (disc.) or .25 ACP cal., semi-auto, single action, 5 shot mag., 2 in. barrel, all steel construction, plastic grips, 9.3 oz.

Mfg.'s Sug. Retail	$200	$165	$135	$115	$100	$90	$80	$70

Add $10 for nickel finish (disc. 1990).

Compact Elite Engraved — similar to .25 ACP Compact, except has extensive engraving. New 1991.

Mfg.'s Sug. Retail	$1,000	$850	$600	$475

SILVER HAWK — .22 LR or .25 ACP cal., double action semi-auto, similar to TP-22 Series, except is stainless steel. New 1990.

Mfg.'s Sug. Retail	$250	$215	$185	$160

Grading	100%	98%	95%	90%	80%	70%	60%

SUPER ENFORCER (MODEL 3000) — .30 cal. only, pistol version of the Carbine with 11 in. shrouded barrel. Add $40 for stainless steel (disc. for 1986). Mfg. 1985-1986 only.

	$285	$250	$225	$200	$175	$160	$145

Last Mfg.'s Sug. Retail was $255.

Enforcer — similar to Super Enforcer model, except has 10½ in. barrel. Reintroduced 1988.

Mfg.'s Sug. Retail	$417	$325	$275	$240	$200	$175	$160	$145

CATTLEMAN MAGNUM — .357 Mag., .44 Mag., or .45 Colt, single action, 6 shot, Colt replica, 4¾, 5½, or 7½ in. barrel, case color frame, blue barrel, and brass grip frame, smooth walnut grips, fixed sights. Disc. 1984.

	$190	$175	$150	$140	$130	$125	$110
.44 Mag.	$220	$190	$175	$165	$145	$135	$125

BUCKHORN MAGNUM — same as Cattleman, except flat top, adj. sights.

	$210	$190	$175	$165	$145	$140	$125

BUNTLINE BUCKHORN MAGNUM — same as Buckhorn, only 18 in. barrel, detachable stock.

	$345	$310	$295	$275	$260	$250	$225
.44 Mag.	$375	$325	$310	$295	$280	$275	$250

TRAIL BLAZER — .22 LR, or .22 Mag. cal., interchangeable cylinder, 5½ or 6½ in. barrel, blue.

	$175	$145	$130	$120	$110	$100	$80

RIFLES

AMAC also manufactures a full-auto M2 Carbine that is not listed in this text.

MODEL X — .22 Short, Long, or LR, bolt action, single shot, 22 in. barrel, open sight, pistol grip with knob forend. Mfg. 1928-1932.

	$90	$60	$50	$40	$35	$30	$25

MODEL 2X — improved Model X, 24 in. heavy barrel larger stock, adj. sights. Mfg. 1932-1955.

	$120	$95	$75	$50	$40	$35	$30

LI'L CHAMP — .22 LR only, single shot bolt action, 16¼ in. barrel, black molded stock, nickel plated bolt, youth dimensions, (32½ in. overall length), 3 lbs. Introduced 1986, reintroduced 1988 only.

	$75	$60	$50	$45	$40	$35	$35

Last Mfg.'s Sug. Retail was $92.

LONG RANGE RIFLE — .308 (new 1991) or .50 BMG cal., bolt action design, single shot, 29 in. stainless steel fluted barrel with muzzle brake, adj. trigger pull, built in bipod, adj. rail stock, includes Leupold M-1 Ultra 20X scope, 36 lbs. New 1988.

Mfg.'s Sug. Retail	$5,000	$4,350	$3,500	$3,150	$2,750	$2,400	$2,100	$1,800

Custom rifles in either military or sporting configuration are also available in the AMAC 338/416 cal.

9MM CARBINE (JJ9MM SERIES) — 9mm only, copy of U.S. military M1, 16 in. barrel, blue finish only, 20 shot mag. Mfg. 1985-86 only.

Hardwood Stock Model — disc. 1986.

	$230	$200	$180	$170	$160	$150	$140

Last Mfg.'s Sug. Retail was $255.

Standard Model — with plastic stock. Disc. 1985.

	$225	$200	$180	$170	$160	$150	$140

Last Mfg.'s Sug. Retail was $250.

Folding Plastic Stock Model — disc. 1985.

	$255	$225	$200	$180	$170	$160	$150

Last Mfg.'s Sug. Retail was $281.

Grading	100%	98%	95%	90%	80%	70%	60%

DELTA-786 — 9mm Para., semi-auto, patterned after the U.S. military M1, 16 in. barrel, matte black finish. Mfg. 1989 only.

	100%	98%	95%	90%	80%	70%	60%
	$575	$425	$360	$325	$295	$260	$230

Last Mfg.'s Sug. Retail was $665.

.30 CAL. CARBINE — .30 M1 or 9mm Para. (new 1991) cal., semi-auto, 18 or 20 (new 1991) in. barrel, available in various stock configurations, hardwood stock. Mfg. 1985-1986, reintroduced 1988.

	100%	98%	95%	90%	80%	70%	60%
Mfg.'s Sug. Retail	$350	$285	$215	$190	$165	$150	$140	$130

Add $16 for 9mm Para. cal.

Add $35 for walnut stock, Parkerized finish (disc. 1990), or 20 in. barrel (new 1991).

Paratrooper Model — similar to standard model, except has folding synthetic stock.

	100%	98%	95%	90%	80%	70%	60%
Mfg.'s Sug. Retail	$433	$345	$270	$225	$195	$165	$150	$140

Stainless Steel Variation — disc. 1985.

	100%	98%	95%
	$230	$200	$180

Last Mfg.'s Sug. Retail was $250.

5.7mm Johnson (Spitfire) Cal. — remilled, add $30 for stainless steel.

	98%	95%	90%	80%	70%	60%
	$195	$175	$165	$155	$145	$135	$125

Last Mfg.'s Sug. Retail was $219.

.22 CAL. U.S. CARBINE — .22 LR or .22 Mag. cal., 18½ in. barrel, except for Mag. (19.3 in.), 5.8 lbs., 15 shot mag., sling swivels. Mfg. 1985-1986, reintroduced 1988 only.

	100%	98%	95%	90%	80%	70%	60%
	$150	$120	$110	$100	$90	$85	$80

Add $120 for .22 Mag. model (gas operated — disc. 1986).

Last Mfg.'s Sug. Retail was $183 for .22 Mag. cal.

Last Mfg.'s Sug. Retail was $166 for .22 LR cal.

TARGETMASTER SLIDE ACTION — .22 LR or Mag. (disc. 1986) cal., 18½ in. barrel, 12 shot (LR) tube mag., 5¾ lbs. Mfg. 1985 only, reintroduced 1988-90.

	100%	98%	95%	90%	80%	70%	60%
	$175	$140	$125	$115	$100	$90	$80

This model was designated EW.22 HBP previously.

Last Mfg.'s Sug. Retail was $209.

MODEL EW.22 HBL LEVER ACTION (WAGONMASTER) — .22 S, L, and LR or .22 Mag. cal., 18½ in. barrel, walnut finish, hardwood stock, blue finish, 5¾ lbs., grooved for scope mounts. Mfg. 1985-1986, reintroduced 1988-90.

	100%	98%	95%	90%	80%	70%	60%
	$175	$140	$125	$115	$100	$90	$80

Add $23 for .22 Mag. cal. (19 in. barrel).

This model was designated EW.22 HBL previously. It was also available in a Junior model featuring smaller dimensions; values same as listed above.

Last Mfg.'s Sug. Retail was $209.

TRAIL BLAZER SEMI-AUTO (MODEL IJ.22 HB) — .22 LR only, 10 shot clip mag., 18½ in. barrel, 5.8 lbs. Mfg. 1985 only.

	100%	98%	95%	90%	80%	70%	60%
	$115	$100	$90	$85	$80	$75	$70

Last Mfg.'s Sug. Retail was $125.

SHOTGUNS

CHAMPION — 10, 12, 16, 20, 24, 28, 32, or .410 ga., also available in .44, .45, 12mm, or 14mm rifle cal., single barrel shotgun or rifle, 26-32 in. full barrel, exposed hammer, auto ejector, plain pistol grip stock. Mfg. 1909-1956.

	100%	98%	95%	90%	80%	70%	60%
	$145	$100	$80	$60	$40	$35	$25

Values on both smaller gauge shotguns and rifles would be considerably higher than those listed above. A mint .410 ga. might command 400% more than the above values.

Grading	100%	98%	95%	90%	80%	70%	60%

MATTED RIB GRADE — similar to Champion, except in 12, 16, or 20 ga. only, solid rib, checkered stock. Mfg. 1909-1948.

	$165	$115	$95	$70	$50	$45	$40

This model has either a semi-octagon (with top matted) or jacketed breech.

TRAP GRADE — similar to Matted Rib, except 32 in. full barrel, 12 ga., vent rib. Mfg. 1909-1942.

	$275	$165	$140	$120	$100	$90	$80

HERCULES GRADE — 12, 16, 20, or .410 ga., double barrel, 26-32 in. barrel, hammerless, boxlock, various chokes, extractors and double triggers standard, checkered pistol grip or straight stock. Mfg. until 1948.

	$600	$400	$375	$365	$335	$310	$290

Auto ejectors — add $100.

SST — add $100.

16 ga. — deduct 10%.

.410 ga. — add 20%.

SKEETER MODEL — similar to Hercules, except offered in 28 ga. also, super select wood, beavertail forend. Mfg. until 1946.

	$1,095	$800	$600	$525	$450	$410	$390

Auto ejectors — add 20%.

SST — add $20%.

28 and .410 ga.'s — add 50%.

SUPER TRAP — 12 ga. only, 32 in. full vent rib, boxlock, extractors, checkered pistol grip stock, beavertail forend and recoil pad. Mfg. until 1942. Very rare.

	$1,095	$750	$550	$475	$415	$395	$370

Auto ejectors — add $100.

SST — add $100.

SILVER SHADOW — O/U, 12 ga., 26 or 28 in. barrels, various chokes, extractors, vent rib, checkered pistol grip stock, Italian mfg. Disc.

	$375	$325	$300	$275	$225	$185	$175

Single trigger — add $100.

JURRAS

Custom Pistolsmith located in Prescott, AZ. Distributed by J & G Sales located in Prescott, AZ.

Ammunition for Jurras pistols is exclusively manufactured by Robert Davis, Jr. located in Athens, TN.

PISTOLS

Lee E. Jurras manufactures custom pistols in larger calibers. Almost any caliber is available by special order and the below listings represent a few of his more standard items. Special order inquiries may be directed to Mr. Jurras, in Prescott, AZ.

HOWDAH — available in .375, .416, .460, .475, .500, or .577 cal., action based on Thompson/Center Contender receiver, 12 in. bull barrel, nitex finish, adj. rear sights, limited mfg. (100).
Custom Grade

	$1,150	$925	$800	$725	$650	$575	$500

Presentation Grade — .375 Jurras or .460 Jurras, deluxe Claro walnut stock and forearm.

	$2,000	$1,750	$1,500	$1,250	$1,050	$950	$825

.416, .475, .500, or .577 calibers command a premium on this model.

K

KBI INC.
Importer/manufacturer located in Harrisburg, PA.

KBI Inc. imports C.B.C. from Brazil and the Jericho pistol manufactured by I.M.I. from Israel. The Jericho pistol may be found under it's own heading in this text.

Grading	100%	98%	95%	90%	80%	70%	60%

PISTOLS

PSP-25 — .25 ACP, semi-auto, single action, patterned after the Baby Browning, all steel construction with high polish finish, dual safety system. New 1989.

No Mfg.'s Retail	$230	$200	$185	$170	$160	$150	$140

Add $65 for industrial hard chrome finish.

Add $65 for nickel finish (mfg. 1990 only).

This pistol is mfg. in the U.S. under license from Fabrique Nationale.

PSP Signature Editions — similar to above, except has "Michael B. Kassnar" signature on left slide top in gold. New 1989.

No Mfg.'s Retail	$385	$300	$260	$230	$200	$175	$160

Also available in this series is a Limited Edition that is serial numbered 00011-00100 and includes partial engraving and pearlite grips - retail price $900. Also available is a Limited Edition (serial numbers 00001-00010) with full engraving and gold lining around slide sides - retail price is $1,500.

RIFLES

KASSNAR BOLT ACTION GRADE I — available in various cal.'s, thumb safety that locks trigger, with or without deluxe sights, includes swivel posts and oil finished standard grade European walnut with recoil pad. Importation started 1989.

No Mfg.'s Retail	$525	$400	$350	$300	$265	$230	$195

NYLON 66 — .22 LR, patterned after the Remington Nylon 66. Imported until 1990 from C.B.C. in Brazil, South America.

	$125	$110	$95	$85	$75	$70	$65

Last Mfg.'s Sug. Retail was $134.

MODEL 122 — .22 LR, bolt action design with clip mag. Imported from South America until 1990.

	$125	$110	$95	$85	$75	$70	$65

Last Mfg.'s Sug. Retail was $136.

MODEL 522 — .22 LR, bolt action design with tube mag. Imported from South America until 1990.

	$130	$115	$100	$85	$75	$70	$65

Last Mfg.'s Sug. Retail was $142.

BANTAM SINGLE SHOT — .22 LR, youth dimensions. Imported 1989-90 only.

	$110	$90	$85	$75	$70	$65	$60

Last Mfg.'s Sug. Retail was $120.

Grading	100%	98%	95%	90%	80%	70%	60%

SHOTGUNS

KASSNAR GRADE I O/U — 12, 20, 28, or .410 ga., gold plated SST, extractors, vent rib, checkered walnut stock and forearm. Importation started 1989.

No Mfg.'s Retail	$595	$450	$395	$325	$295	$265	$240

Add $75 for 28 or .410 ga.

Add $75 for choke tubes (12 and 20 ga. only).

Add $120 for automatic ejectors (with choke tubes only).

KASSNAR GRADE II SXS — 10, 12, 16, 20, 28, or .410 ga., boxlock action, case hardened receiver, English style checkered European walnut stock with splinter forearm, chrome barrels with concave rib, extractors, double hinged triggers. Imported 1989-90 only.

	$515	$435	$375	$325	$275	$250	$225

Add $95 for 28 or .410 ga.

Add $85 for 10 ga.

Last Mfg.'s Sug. Retail was $575.

KDF INC.

Manufacturer located in Sequin, TX. Previously, KDF rifles were manufactured by Voere (until 1986) in Vohrenbach, W. Germany. Manufacture in 1987 was absorbed by Mauser-Werke in Oberndorf, W. Germany.

Older KDF rifles were private labeled by Voere and were marked KDF. Since Voere was absorbed by Mauser-Werke in 1987, model designations changed. Mauser-Werke does not private label (i.e. newer guns are marked Mauser-Werke), and these rifles can be found under the Mauser-Werke heading in this text.

RIFLES: U.S. MFG.

K15-AMERICAN — .22-250, .243 Win., 6mm Rem., .25-06 Rem., .270 Win., .280 Rem., .30-06 cal. or .308 Win. cal., 60 degree short lift bolt action with 3 lugs, Kevlar composite or laminate walnut stock, adj. single stage competition trigger, box magazine, thumb activated slide safety, satin blue finish, 24 in. match grade barrel, deluxe checkered walnut stock with ebony accents and Pachmayr Decelerator recoil pad, approx. 8 lbs. Mfg. in U.S. starting 1989.

Mfg.'s Sug. Retail	$1,950	$1,750	$1,375	$1,150	$950	$750	$650	$575

The K15-American is a completely redesigned gun with many improvements as noted in the description above.

K15-American Magnum — .270 Wby., .300 Win. Mag., .300 Wby., 7mm Rem. Mag., .338 Win. Mag., .340 Wby., .375 H&H, .411 KDF, .416 Rem. Mag., or .458 Win. Mag. cal., similar to K15-American, except has 26 in. barrel. Mfg. in U.S. starting in 1989.

Mfg.'s Sug. Retail	$2,000	$1,795	$1,400	$1,175	$975	$775	$675	$600

RIFLES: OLDER VOERE MFG. (PRE-1988)

TITAN SPORTER SERIES — various cal.'s, bolt action, 24 or 26 in. barrel length, select walnut, pistol grip stock.

This series is available with either European Monte Carlo high-luster stock or in classic featherweight configuration with Schnabel forend — add $50-$200.

Titan Menor — .222 or .223 cal. Importation disc. 1987.

	$675	$615	$560	$495	$450	$395	$350

Add $100 for Match or Competition model (.223 cal.).

Last Mfg.'s Sug. Retail was $765.

Titan II Standard — many cal.'s, between .243 and .30-06. Disc. 1988.

	$950	$825	$725	$625	$550	$500	$450

Add $100 for Match or Competition model (.308 cal.).

Last Mfg.'s Sug. Retail was $1,075.

Titan II Magnum — available in cal.'s between 7mm Rem. and .375 H&H. Disc. 1988.

	$995	$875	$750	$650	$575	$520	$475

Last Mfg.'s Sug. Retail was $1,125.

Grading	100%	98%	95%	90%	80%	70%	60%

Titan .411 KDF Mag. — .411 KDF cal., 26 in. barrel with recoil arrestor, 3 shot mag., blue or electroless nickel finish, 9¼ lbs. Imported 1986-1988.

	$1,175	$965	$810	$725	$650	$575	$520

Last Mfg.'s Sug. Retail was $1,300.

MODEL 2005 — .22 LR only, semi-auto, 19½ in. barrel, Monte Carlo stock, 5 shot clip mag., iron sights, 6 lbs. Imported 1986 only.

	$135	$115	$100	$90	$85	$80	$75

Last Mfg.'s Sug. Retail was $165.

This model was ruled no longer importable by the BATF.

Model 2005 Deluxe — similar to Model 2005, except has deluxe checkered walnut. Mfg. 1986-87 only.

	$160	$135	$110	$95	$85	$80	$75

Last Mfg.'s Sug. Retail was $185.

MODEL 2107 — .22 LR or .22 Mag. cal., bolt action, 19½ in. barrel, 5 shot clip mag., adj. iron sights, 6 lbs. Imported 1986-87 only.

	$175	$150	$125	$105	$95	$85	$80

Add $42 for .22 Mag. cal.
Last Mfg.'s Sug. Retail was $197.

Model 2107 Deluxe (Mauser 107) — similar to Model 2107, except has deluxe checkered walnut. Imported 1986-1988.

	$185	$165	$140	$125	$110	$105	$100

Add $50 for .22 Mag. cal.
This model has been redesignated KDF-Mauser Model 107 since current distributer/dealer inventories have been depleted.

Last Mfg.'s Sug. Retail was $219.

MODEL 2112 — .22 LR or .22 Mag. cal., similar to Model 2107, except has extra select walnut. Imported 1988 only.

	$235	$200	$180	$160	$145	$135	$125

Add $50 for .22 Mag. cal.
Last Mfg.'s Sug. Retail was $279.

K-14 INSTA FIRE RIFLE — .22-250, .458 Win. Mag., .270, or .300 Wby. Mag. cal., 24 or 26 in. barrel, no sights, ultra fast lock time, hidden detachable mag., checkered Monte Carlo stock, recoil pad.

	$605	$580	$550	$525	$470	$415	$330
K15 (.22 cal.)	$165	$145	$120	$105	$95	$85	$70

K-15 (MODEL 225) — available in 13 cal.'s between .243 Win. and .300 Wby. Mag., bolt action, 60 degree bolt lift with 3 locking lugs, ultra fast lock time, adj. trigger, 24 or 26 (Mag. only) in. barrel, 3 or 5 shot mag., no sights, guaranteed ½ in. accuracy at 100 yards, many stock options available at extra cost. Left-handed action available in certain cal.'s at a $50 charge.

Deluxe Standard Sporter — standard model available in 6 regular cal.'s and 9 Mag. cal.'s. Disc. 1988.

	$1,075	$950	$810	$700	$625	$550	$495

Add $50 for Magnum action.

Add $525 for .411 KDF cal.

In addition to the 15 regular cal.'s, it is also possible to order various other factory cal.'s as a $200 option.

This model has been redesignated KDF-Mauser Model 225 (standard cal.'s) since current distributer/dealer inventories have been depleted.

Last Mfg.'s Sug. Retail was $1,275.

Grading	100%	98%	95%	90%	80%	70%	60%

K-15 Fiberstock Pro-hunter — similar to the K-15, except is supplied with fiberglass stock (various colors), choice of parkerized, matte blue, or electroless nickel metal finish, and recoil arrestor installed. Imported 1986-1988.

	$1,420	$1,200	$950				

Add $50 for Magnum action.

This model has been redesignated KDF-Mauser Model 225 (standard cal.'s) since current distributer/dealer inventories have been depleted.

Last Mfg.'s Sug. Retail was $1,680.

K-15 Dangerous Game — .411 KDF Mag. (new cartridge 1985), choice of finishes, oil finished deluxe American walnut stock. Imported 1986-1988.

	$1,895	$1,500	$1,150				

This model has been redesignated KDF-Mauser Model 225 since current distributer/dealer inventories have been depleted.

Last Mfg.'s Sug. Retail was $2,100.

K-15 Swat Rifle — .308 cal. standard, 24 or 26 in. barrel, parkerized metal, oil finished target walnut stock, 3 or 4 shot detachable mag., 10 lbs. Importation disc. 1988.

	$1,475	$1,250	$1,000	$850	$725	$650	$575

Last Mfg.'s Sug. Retail was $1,725.

K-16 — available in 6 standard cal.'s between .243 Win. and .300 Win. Mag. in addition to optional cal.'s, modified Remington Model 700 action, standard features include KDF accurizing and instant fire ignition, single stage adj. trigger, Dupont Rynite stock (camel or grey), choice of finishes (high-gloss blue standard), recoil pad and quick detachable sling swivels, many options available. Imported 1988 only.

	$765	$675	$615	$560	$495	$450	$395

Add $120 for KDF muzzle brake.

Add $250 for optional cal.'s.

Add $350 for .411 KDF Mag. cal.

Last Mfg.'s Sug. Retail was $876.

K-22 (MAUSER 201) — .22 LR cal., bolt action, free floating 21 in. barrel, clip 5 shot mag., adj. trigger, scale down version of the K-15, unusual action incorporates two front-located locking lugs on bolt face that engage Stellite inserts on the front receiver portion, guaranteed 1 in. groupings at 100 yards, blue only, no sights, select walnut stock with cheek piece, standard model disc. 1987. Add $50 for .22 Mag. cal. on the K-22 models listed below.

	$310	$285	$260	$240	$225	$210	$195

Last Mfg.'s Sug. Retail was $345.

K-22 Deluxe (Mauser 201) — better walnut and stock options. Model notation changed in 1988.

	$410	$360	$295	$275	$250	$235	$210

This model has been redesignated KDF-Mauser Model 201 since current distributer/dealer inventories have been depleted.

Last Mfg.'s Sug. Retail was $495.

K-22 Deluxe Custom — richly layered walnut and stock options. Importation disc. 1987.

	$655	$595	$550	$495	$450	$395	$350

Last Mfg.'s Sug. Retail was $725.

K-22 Deluxe Special Select — top-of-the-line bolt action, double set triggers. Importation disc. 1987.

	$1,060	$950	$850	$750	$695	$650	$595

Last Mfg.'s Sug. Retail was $1,225.

SHOTGUNS

CONDOR O/U — 12 ga., 28 in. barrel, various chokes, selective single trigger, auto ejectors, wide vent rib, boxlock, checkered pistol grip stock, Italian made.

	$660	$635	$605	$580	$525	$470	$415

Grading	100%	98%	95%	90%	80%	70%	60%

BRESCIA S X S — 12 ga., 28 in. barrel, full and mod., double triggers, engraved, checkered pistol grip stock.

	$330	$305	$275	$250	$195	$165	$140

K.F.C.

Formerly manufactured by Kawaguchiya Firearms Co., Ltd. Previously imported and distributed by La Paloma Marketing, Inc. located in Tucson, AZ.

SHOTGUNS

MODEL 250 — 12 ga. only, semi-auto incorporating a patented, cushioned piston assembly, 26, 28, or 30 in. barrel, matte blue finish, vent rib standard, checkered premium walnut, 7 lbs. Manufactured 1980-86.

	$360	$290	$270	$250	$235	$220	$205

Add $60 for multi-chokes.
Last Mfg.'s Sug. Retail was $485.

Model 250 Deluxe — same specifications as Model 250, except has scrolled acid etching panels on both sides of normally black receiver. Disc. 1986.

	$395	$310	$290	$270	$250	$225	$210

Last Mfg.'s Sug. Retail was $520.

FIELD GUN O/U — 12 ga. only, vent rib, premium grade walnut, semi pistol grip stock, F&IC chokes. Disc. 1986.

	$645	$565	$530	$495	$470	$445	$410

Last Mfg.'s Sug. Retail was $748.

E-1 TRAP OR SKEET O/U — 12 ga. only, vent rib, oil finished premium grade walnut, semi pistol grip stock, engraved. Disc. 1986.

	$935	$800	$750	$700	$625	$550	$495

Last Mfg.'s Sug. Retail was $1,070.

E-2 TRAP OR SKEET O/U — 12 ga. only, vent rib, oil finished premium grade walnut, semi pistol grip stock, detailed engraving. Disc. 1986.

	$1,450	$1,250	$1,075	$950	$850	$750	$650

Last Mfg. Sug. Retail was $1,660.

KASSNAR IMPORTS, INC.

Previous importer and distributor (operations ceased April, 1989) located in Harrisburg, Pa.

Kassnar also imported Omega shotguns which can be found in their individual section.

PISTOLS

PJK-9HP — 9mm, single action, patterned after the Browning Hi-Power, 4¾ in. barrel, 13 shot mag., cone hammer, checkered walnut grips, 32 oz.

	$225	$200	$185	$175	$165	$155	$145

Add $15 for Vent Rib barrel.
This pistol was imported from Hungary. Approx. 18,000 (including the MBK-9HP) were imported until importation was disc. because of Federal ramifications.

MBK-9HP — 9mm, double action, patterned after the Browning Hi-Power, 4⅔ in. barrel, spur hammer, blued metal, checkered walnut grips, 14 shot mag., 36 oz. Limited importation was stopped in late 1985.

	$295	$260	$230	$190	$175	$165	$155

PMK-380 — .380 ACP, double action, patterned after the Walther PP, plastic grips with thumbrest, 4 in barrel, 7 shot mag., 21 oz. Limited importation.

	$275	$235	$200	$185	$175	$165	$155

This model was imported in very limited quantities before Interarms began exclusive importation.

Grading	100%	98%	95%	90%	80%	70%	60%

KEBERST INTERNATIONAL

Previously manufactured and distributed by Kendall International located in Paris, KY.

KEBERST MODEL 1A — .338 Lapua Mag., .338-416 Rigby, or .338-06 cal., bolt action, muzzle brake and unique recoil pad, camouflaged synthetic stock, package includes 3-9 power Leupold scope, stainless steel cleaning rod, custom designed case, built to special order only. Mfg. 1987-1988 only.

	100%	98%	95%	90%	80%	70%	60%
	$3,475	$2,850	$2,475	$2,100	$1,750	$1,400	$1,150

Add $275 for 10X Ultra scope.
Last Mfg.'s Sug. Retail was $3,750.

KENDALL INTERNATIONAL

Previous importer/distributor located in Paris, KY. Kendall International also imported Australian Automatic Arms, the Keberst Rifle, and several air rifles that can be found in their respective sections in this text.

KEPPELER, DIETER

Manufacturer located in Langenau, West Germany. No current domestic importer.

Keppeler rifles are typically centerfire and target configured. Both metric and domestic calibers are available as well as a variety of special order options.

Price quotations are available upon request by writing Dieter Keppeler at the following address: DIETER KEPPELER, Postfach 1106, D-7907, Langenau, W. Germany.

KEPPLINGER, ING. HANNES

Manufacturer located in Kufstein, Austria. No current importer.

RIFLES

Kepplinger rifles are essentially built per individual order. In addition to his unique bolt action, he also makes other bolt action designs and O/U rifles as well.

3-S SYSTEM RIFLE — various cal.'s, unique short action allows for staight on cartridge loading, high strength alloy main parts, grip safety on lower pistol grip, unique uncocking device allowing manual cocking/decocking of the firing pin spring, 23.6 in. standard barrel, 3 shot detachable mag., iron sights, receiver drilled for scope mounts, best quality wood, available in either Schnabel forearm or Mannlicher configuration, many styles of engraving are optional, 7.14 lbs.

Price quotations are available upon request by writing Mr. Kepplinger at the following address: ING. HANNES KEPPLINGER, Carl-Wagner-Strabe 1, A-6330 Kufstein, AUSTRIA.

KESSLER ARMS CORPORATION

Manufacturer located in Silver Creen, NY.

LEVERMATIC SHOTGUN — level action, 12, 16, or 20 ga., 26 or 28 in. full choke, takedown, plain pistol grip stock. Disc. 1953.

	100%	98%	95%	90%	80%	70%	60%
	$125	$75	$60	$50	$45	$45	$45

BOLT ACTION SHOTGUN — 12, 16, or 20 ga., 26 or 28 in. full, takedown, plain stock. Mfg. 1951-1953.

	100%	98%	95%	90%	80%	70%	60%
	$90	$65	$50	$45	$35	$35	$35

J. KIMBALL ARMS CO.

Previous manufacturer located in Detroit, MI.

AUTOMATIC PISTOL — .30 U.S. Carbine or .22 Hornet (very rare) cal., semi-auto, 7 shot, 3 in.(Combat Model) or 5 in. (Target Model) barrel, approx. 32 oz. Less than 300 mfg. in 1958 only.

	100%	98%	95%	90%	80%	70%	60%
	$950	$850	$725	$600	$500	$395	$300

Grading	100%	98%	95%	90%	80%	70%	60%

Functional weaknesses of this pistol caused discontinuance. Surviving specimens should be checked carefully for slide failures and other potential problems. Values above assume no operational damage to the pistol. .22 Hornet cal. rarity factor precludes accurate price evaluation.

KIMBER OF OREGON, INC.
Manufacturer located in Clackamas, OR Since 1980.

RIFLES: BOLT ACTION

Note: No suffix in Kimber models denotes pre-1986 action design, "A" suffix models refer to the new action in right or left-hand, "B" suffix models also incorporate the new action with improved cocking system, faster lock time, swept-back bolt design, improved recoil lug, and are right handed.

Add $150 for skeleton grip cap on models listed below.

Add $250 for skeleton buttplate on models listed below.

Add $80 for checkered bolt handle on models listed below.

MODEL 82 RIMFIRE SERIES

STANDARD MODEL 82 — .22 LR, .22 Mag., or .22 Hornet cal., Mauser type rear locking bolt action, 3(.22 Hornet), 4(.22 Mag.), or 5(.22 LR) shot mag., 22 in. (Sporter) or 24 in. (Varmint) barrel, deluxe claro walnut, steel butt plate, rocker style safety, 6½ lbs. Add $45 for .22 Hornet or .22 Mag. cal. for all variations of this model.

Classic Model — disc. 1988.

	100%	98%	95%	90%	80%	70%	60%
	$600	$500	$400	$350	$295	$250	$225

Add $55 for disc. Cascade Model (Monte Carlo cheek piece).

Last Mfg.'s Sug. Retail was $750.

Custom Classic Model — higher grade claro walnut, ebony forearm tip, Niedner style steel butt plate. Disc. 1988.

	$795	$675	$550	$475	$395	$340	$295

Also previously available in the .218 Bee or .25-20 (single shot only) cal.'s. These cal.'s may bring a slight premium. Mfg. 1985 only (retail price was $695).

Last Mfg.'s Sug. Retail was $995.

Deluxe Grade — .22 LR only, similar to Custom Classic Model, AA walnut, 5 or 10 (optional) shot mag., 6½ lbs. Mfg. 1989-90 only.

	$995	$895	$700	$595	$525	$450	$395

A left-hand variation is also available at no extra charge, but will have limited mfg. in 1990.

Last Mfg.'s Sug. Retail was $1,195.

SPORTER MODEL — .22 LR, includes Model 82A action, 22 in. sporter weight barrel, 4 shot mag., round top receiver with bases, checkered stock and forend, 6½ lbs. New 1991.

Mfg.'s Sug. Retail	$995	$895	$750	$650	$550	$495	$450	$395

RIMFIRE VARMINTER — .22 LR only, Model 82A action, free floating 25 in. medium heavy barrel, laminated stock, 5 or optional 10 shot mag., rubber butt pad, 8¼ lbs. New 1990.

Mfg.'s Sug. Retail	$795	$675	$550	$475	$425	$375	$325	$280

HUNTER GRADE — .22 LR only, similar to Rimfire Varminter with Super America configured barrel and action with low glare metal finish. Mfg. 1990 only.

	$750	$600	$525	$450	$395	$340	$295

Last Mfg.'s Sug. Retail was $895.

MINI CLASSIC — .22 LR only, Model 82 action, 18 in. barrel, steel butt plate, sling swivels. Mfg. 1988 only.

	$550	$475	$415	$375	$340	$300	$275

Last Mfg.'s Sug. Retail was $795.

Grading	100%	98%	95%	90%	80%	70%	60%

GOVERNMENT MODEL 82A TARGET — .22 LR only, specifically designed for U.S. Army training, 25 in. heavy target barrel including scope blocks, oversized stock, 10¾ lbs. Production began late 1987.

Mfg.'s Sug. Retail	$595	$540	$480	$440	$400	$365	$325	$295

20,000 rifles were mfg. 1987-1989 to fill the initial U.S. government contract. Commercial guns are now being manufactured for the private sector with values listed above.

ALL AMERICAN MATCH — .22 LR only, precision rifled 25 in. free floating target grade barrel, stock is adj. both vertically and for length of pull, fully adj. single stage trigger, approx. 9 lbs. New 1990.

Mfg.'s Sug. Retail	$895	$750	$600	$525	$450	$395	$340	$295

CONTINENTAL — .22 LR, .22 Mag., or .22 Hornet cal., Sporter action only, full length Mannlicher stock, open sights, deluxe walnut. New 1987.

This model is now only available as a special order with prices on request from the factory.

Super Continental — similar to Continental, except has AAA claro walnut with 22 lines/in. checkering. Mfg. 1987-1988.

	$1,250	$1,000	$875	$795	$740	$680	$620

Last Mfg.'s Sug. Retail was $1,465.

SUPER AMERICA — top-of-the-line model, includes detachable scope mounts, Niedner checkered steel butt plate and best quality walnut, available in Sporter configuration only. This model was disc. 1988, and reintroduced 1990.

Mfg.'s Sug. Retail	$1,295	$1,075	$950	$775	$625	$550	$475	$425

Super Grade — similar to Super America, AAA walnut, beaded cheek piece, 5 or 10 (optional) shot mag., 6½ lbs. Mfg. 1989 only.

	$950	$775	$625	$550	$475	$425	$375

Last Mfg.'s Sug. Retail was $1,095.

BROWNELL — .22 LR, only 500 mfg. to commemorate the late Leonard Brownell, Mannlicher style extra deluxe claro walnut stock. Mfg. 1986 only.

	$1,250	$1,000	$800

Last Mfg.'s Sug. Retail was $1,500.

CENTENNIAL — .22 LR only, limited edition (100 rifles) to commemorate centennial of .22 LR cal., includes hand-picked checkered walnut, moderate engraving, special Wilson Arms match barrel, skeleton butt plate and other refinements, serial numbered C1-C100. Mfg. 1987 only.

	$2,600	$2,350	$1,900

Last Mfg.'s Sug. Retail was $2,950.

MODEL 84 CENTERFIRE SERIES

Add $250-$300 for 3-position safety in this series.

STANDARD MODEL 84 — .17 Rem., .17 Mach IV (disc. 1987), 6 x 45 or 47mm (disc. 1987), 5.6 x 50mm (disc. 1987), .221 Fireball, .222 Rem., .222 Rem. Mag. (disc. 1987), or .223 Rem. cal., "Mini-Mauser" type head locking bolt action, 5 shot mag., 22 (Sporter) or 24 (Varmint) in. barrel, deluxe claro walnut, steel butt plate, rocker style safety, 6½ lbs.

Classic Model — disc. 1988.

	$705	$625	$540	$450	$375	$300	$260

Add $55 for disc. Cascade Model (Monte Carlo cheek piece).
Last Mfg.'s Sug. Retail was $885.

CUSTOM CLASSIC MODEL — higher grade claro walnut, ebony forearm tip, Niedner style steel butt plate. Disc. 1988.

	$970	$825	$720	$595	$500	$440	$365

Last Mfg.'s Sug. Retail was $1,130.

Deluxe Grade Sporter — .17 Rem., .221 Rem., or .223 Rem. cal., Mauser action, AA walnut, similar to Custom Classic Model, 6¼ lbs. New 1989.

Mfg.'s Sug. Retail	$1,295	$1,075	$950	$775	$625	$550	$475	$425

Also available in left-hand action (.223 cal. only), limited mfg.

Grading	100%	98%	95%	90%	80%	70%	60%

CONTINENTAL — .221 Fireball (new 1988), .222 Rem. or .223 Rem. cal., Sporter action only, full length Mannlicher stock, open sights, deluxe walnut. New 1987.
This model is now only available as a special order with prices on request from the factory.
Super Continental — similar to Continental (same cal.'s), except has AAA claro walnut with 22 lines/in. checkering. Mfg. 1987-1988.

	$1,325	$1,060	$920	$830	$740	$680	$620

Last Mfg.'s Sug. Retail was $1,600.

HUNTER GRADE — .17 Rem., .222 Rem., or .223 Rem. cal., laminated stock, Super America configured action and barrel with low glare metal finish. Mfg. 1990 only.

	$825	$650	$550	$475	$425	$375	$325

Last Mfg.'s Sug. Retail was $995.

SPORTER — .17 Rem., .22 Hornet, .222 Rem., .22-250 Rem., or .223 cal., 22 in. sporter weight barrel, "A" grade Claro walnut, round top receiver with bases, 4 shot mag., hand checkering. New 1991.

Mfg.'s Sug. Retail	$1,095	$975	$800	$700	$600	$550	$500	$495

This model is available in either right or left hand action.
Big Bore Sporter — .250 Savage or .35 Rem. cal., similar action to Sporter Model, except has ¾ in. red Pachmayr Decelerator recoil pad. New 1991.

Mfg.'s Sug. Retail	$1,095	$975	$800	$700	$600	$550	$500	$495

This model is available in either right or left hand action.

SUPER AMERICA — .17 Rem., .22 Hornet, .222 Rem., .22-250 Rem., or .223 Rem. cal., 22 in. sporter weight barrel, top-of-the-line, with detachable scope mounts, available in Sporter configuration only, 4 shot mag., right or left hand action. Disc. 1988, reintroduced 1990.

Mfg.'s Sug. Retail	$1,495	$1,250	$975	$850	$725	$600	$500	$450

Big Bore Super America — .250 Savage or .35 Rem., similar action to Super America Model, except has ¾ in. red Pachmayr Decelerator recoil pad. New 1991.

Mfg.'s Sug. Retail	$1,495	$1,250	$975	$850	$725	$600	$500	$450

SUPER GRADE — .17 Rem., .221 Rem., or .223 Rem. cal., Mauser action, AAA walnut, similar to Super America, 6¼ lbs. Mfg. 1989 only.

	$995	$850	$695	$600	$500	$450	$395

Last Mfg.'s Sug. Retail was $1,250.

ULTRA VARMINTER — .17 Rem., .22 Hornet (new 1991), .221 Rem. (disc. 1990), .222 Rem., .22-250 Rem., or .223 Rem. cal., 24 in. medium weight stainless steel barrel, laminated birch stock, plain butt stock, right or left hand action, 7¾lbs. New 1989.

Mfg.'s Sug. Retail	$1,295	$1,075	$950	$775	$625	$550	$475	$425

Super Varminter — similar to Ultra Varminter except has steel barrel, AAA walnut stock with beaded cheek piece, 7¼ lbs. New 1989.

Mfg.'s Sug. Retail	$1,495	$1,250	$975	$850	$725	$600	$500	$450

MODEL 89 BIG GAME RIFLE SERIES

MODEL 89 BGR — .270 Win., .280 Rem., 7mm Rem. Mag., .30-06, .300 Win. Mag., .338 Win. Mag., or 375 H&H cal., new action incorporates features from both Mauser 98 and Win. pre-64 Model 70, three position safety, 22 or 24 in. barrel. While advertised in 1987, this model was not mfg. until 1989.
Classic Model — deluxe claro walnut checkered 18 lines/in. with steel butt plate. Disc. 1988.

	$790	$675	$550	$475	$395	$340	$295

Add $200 for .375 H&H cal.
Last Mfg.'s Sug. Retail was $985.
Custom Classic Model — higher grade claro walnut, ebony forearm tip, Niedner style steel butt plate. Disc. 1988.

	$1,025	$865	$750	$625	$500	$440	$365

Add $200 for .375 H&H cal.
Last Mfg.'s Sug. Retail was $1,230.

Grading	100%	98%	95%	90%	80%	70%	60%

DELUXE GRADE — similar to Custom Classic Model, round top receiver with Model 70 hole space configuration, AA walnut stock with ebony forend tip and rubber recoil pad (no cheek piece), 22 or 24 in. barrel, 7½-8½ lbs. New 1989.

Featherweight Barrel Model — .257 Roberts, .25-06 Rem., 7 x 57mm (disc. 1990), .270 Win., .280 Rem., or .30-06 cal., 5 shot mag., 22 in. Featherweight barrel, right hand action only, 7½ lbs. Disc. 1990.

	$1,525	$1,175	$975	$825	$700	$600	$525

Add $470 for Super America Grade with square bridge, dovetail receiver (current mfg.). The Super America Grade will accept Kimber double lever scope mounts and has one grade better wood than the Deluxe Grade with beaded cheek piece.

Last Mfg.'s Sug. Retail was $1,795.

Medium-weight Barrel Model — .300 Win. Mag., .300 H&H (disc. 1990), .300 Wby. (new 1991), .338 Win. Mag., .35 Whelen (disc. 1990), or 7mm Rem. Mag. cal., 3 shot mag., 24 in. medium-weight barrel, right hand action only, 7¾-8½ lbs. Disc. 1990.

	$1,600	$1,225	$1,000	$850	$725	$625	$550

Add $495 for Super America Grade with square bridge, dovetail receiver (current mfg.). The Super America Grade will accept Kimber double lever scope mounts and has one grade better wood than the Deluxe Grade with beaded cheek piece.

Last Mfg.'s Sug. Retail was $1,895.

Heavy-weight Barrel Model — .375 H&H Mag. or .458 Win. Mag. (new 1991) cal., 3 shot mag., 24 in. heavy-weight barrel, right hand action only, 9 lbs. Disc. 1990.

	$1,700	$1,275	$1,050	$900	$775	$700	$650

Add $495 for Super America Grade with square bridge, dovetail receiver (current mfg.). The Super America Grade will accept Kimber double lever scope mounts and has one grade better wood than the Deluxe Grade with beaded cheek piece.

Last Mfg.'s Sug. Retail was $1,995.

SPORTER MODEL — same cal.'s as Deluxe/Super America Models, 22 in. featherweight or 24 in. medium or heavy barrel, double square bridge dovetail receiver, "A" grade Claro walnut stock with ¾ red Pachmayr Decelerator recoil pad. New 1991.

Mfg.'s Sug. Retail	$1,595	$1,325	$1,000	$875	$750	$625	$500	$450

Add $100 for medium magnum action.

Add $200 for heavy magnum action (.375 H&H and .458 Win. Mag. cal.'s).

HUNTER GRADE — .270 Win., .30-06, .300 Win. Mag., .338 Win. Mag., or 7mm Rem. Mag. cal., laminated stock, Super America configured action and barrel with low glare metal finish. New 1990.

Mfg.'s Sug. Retail	$1,495	$1,250	$975	$850	$725	$600	$500	$450

Add $100 for Mag. cal.'s.

SUPER GRADE — similar to Super America Model, square top frame, AAA walnut, 22 or 24 in. barrel, plain butt stock, 7½-8½ lbs. Mfg. 1989 only.

	$1,500	$1,275	$995	$825	$695	$550	$500

Add $100 for .375 H&H cal.

Add $100 for matte blue metal finish.

Last Mfg.'s Sug. Retail was $1,495.

The 24 in. barrel is available in Mag. cal.'s only.

LIMITED WILDLIFE EDITION SERIES — series of 5 guns, includes .257 Roberts (Whitetail Deer Edition), .270 Win. (Mule Deer Edition), .338 Win. Mag. (Rocky Mt. Elk Edition), 7mm Rem. Mag. (Big Horn Sheep Edition), and .375 H&H (Grizzly Bear Edition) cal.'s included, hand select walnut, special Shilen Rifle barrel, gold plated trigger, receivers are stamped "Wildlife Edition", special prefix serialization, only 25 sets are to be manufactured in 1991 only, includes rings, swivels, and hard case.

Mfg.'s Sug. Retail	$3,595	$3,295	$2,750	$2,150

This series is being offered at $16,000 total if all guns are ordered at the same time (a savings of $1,975).

Grading	100%	98%	95%	90%	80%	70%	60%

MODEL 89 AFRICAN SERIES

MODEL 89 AFRICAN — .375 H&H, .404 Jeffery (disc. 1990), .416 Rigby, .460 Wby. (disc. 1990), or .505 Gibbs cal., magnum action, 24 in. heavy barrel, AA English walnut stock with beaded cheek piece and rubber recoil pad, includes twin recoil cross bolts, express sights on quarter rib, drop box magazine, 10-10½ lbs. New 1990.

Mfg.'s Sug. Retail	$3,595	$3,100	$2,575	$2,050	$1,725	$1,525	$1,275	$1,100

PISTOLS

PREDATOR MODEL — .221 Fireball, .223 Rem., 6mm TCU (disc. 1987), 7mm TCU, or 6 x 45mm (disc. 1987) cal., single shot Model 84 action with shortened 14⅞ in. barrel, scope use only, one piece deluxe walnut stock with contoured pistol grip, 5¼ lbs. Approx. 200 mfg. 1987-1988 only.

Hunter Grade — AA claro walnut without checkering. Disc. 1988.

	$1,500	$1,250	$1,000	$875	$750	$675	$600

Last Mfg.'s Sug. Retail was $995.

Super Grade — similar to Hunter Grade, except has select French walnut with ebony forend tip and 22 lines/in. checkering. Disc. 1988.

	$1,950	$1,750	$1,500	$1,300	$1,100	$950	$800

Last Mfg.'s Sug. Retail was $1,195.

KIMEL

Manufactured by AAArms located in Mint Hill, NC. Distributed by Kimel Industries, Inc. located in Matthews, NC.

AP-9 PISTOL — 9mm Para., semi-auto paramilitary design, blowback action with bolt knob on left side of receiver, 5 in. barrel with vent. shroud, front mounted 20 shot detachable mag., black matte finish, adj. front sight, 3 lbs. 7 oz. New 1989.

Mfg.'s Sug. Retail	$250	$225	$175	$155	$135	$120	$110	$100

Add $20 for nickel finish.

P-95 — similar to AP-9, except without barrel shroud and is supplied with 5 shot mag., parts are interchangeable with AP-9. New 1990.

Mfg.'s Sug. Retail	$250	$225	$175	$155	$135	$120	$110	$100

AR-9 Carbine — 9mm Para., carbine variation of the AP-9. New 1991.

Mfg.'s Sug. Retail	$250	$225	$175	$155	$135	$120	$110	$100

KLEINGUENTHER FIREARMS CO.

Manufacturer located in Seguin, TX. The original KDF Co. was started by Mr. Robert Kleinguenther and sold in the early 1980's. At this juncture, Mr. Kleinguenther started a new company called Kleinguenther Firearms Co.

RIFLES: BOLT ACTION

Values listed below are for base model only with no additional customer special order options.

BOLT ACTION RIFLE — various cal.'s, individual customer special order rifle with a variety of options, guns are guaranteed to shoot ½ M.O.A., choice of actions, various weights.

Winchester Model 70 Custom

Mfg.'s Sug. Retail	$975	$975	$800	$675	$575	$500	$450	$400

Sako Action

Mfg.'s Sug. Retail	$1,100	$1,100	$950	$800	$675	$575	$500	$450

K-15

Mfg.'s Sug. Retail	$1,375	$1,375	$1,100	$950	$800	$675	$575	$500

Grading	100%	98%	95%	90%	80%	70%	60%

KODIAK CO.
Previous manufacture located in North Haven, CT - circa 1965.

Kodiak Co. was in business for only a short time in the mid-1960's. They produced the first .22 Mag. semi-auto rifle (Model 260), as well as a center fire bolt action (Model 158 Deluxe), and a slide action shotgun (Model 458). While Kodiak long guns are rare and extremely well made, collectibility to date has been minimal with most specimens selling at a slight premium over similar quality trade name counterparts of that circa.

KOLIBRI
Manufactured 1914-1925 by H. Grabner located in Krems/Donau, Austria.

KOLIBRI SEMI-AUTO PISTOL — 2.7 or 3mm centerfire, unrifled barrel, 5 shot box mag., world's smallest semi-auto centerfire pistol.

	$1,200	$1,000	$875	$740	$600	$520	$440

Individual rounds of 2.7 or 3mm (rarer) ammunition are currently trading in the $75 range as it has the distinction of being the world's smallest centerfire shell (shooting a 3 grain bullet).

KORRIPHILA
Manufacturer located in West Germany. Previously imported and distributed by Osborne's located in Cheboygan, MI.

Currently, this trademark has very limited U.S. distribution. Values below reflect 1988 price information.

HSP 701 TYPE I — 7.65 Luger, .38 Spl., 9mm Luger, 9mm Police, 9mm Steyr, .45 ACP, or 10mm auto cal., semi-auto, double action, 40% stainless steel parts, 4 in. barrel, blue or satin finish, very limited production.

Mfg.'s Sug. Retail	$2,395	$2,000	$1,675	$1,375	$1,100	$995	$820	$740

Type II — similar to Type I, except has 5 in. barrel.

Mfg.'s Sug. Retail	$2,615	$2,150	$1,750	$1,475	$1,200	$1,075	$850	$760

Type III — similar to Type II, except single action trigger.

Mfg.'s Sug. Retail	$2,785	$2,200	$1,800	$1,550	$1,200	$1,075	$850	$760

KORTH
Manufacturer located in Ratzeburg, W. Germany. Currently imported by various companies, including Mandall Shooting Supplies, Inc. located in Scottsdale, AZ, H & S, Inc. located in Middlefield, CT, and Executive Arms located in Quogue, NY. Previously imported by Beeman Precision Arms, located in Santa Rosa, CA and by Osborne's in Cheboygan, MI.

Korth handguns are very high quality and are literally manufactured one-at-a-time, resulting in limited mfg. and importation.

REVOLVERS
Currently, Mandall Shooting Supplies, Inc. is stocking these guns with extra cylinders (.22 LR/.22 Mag. or .357 Mag./9mm Para.). This is because both cylinders are cut from the same billet of steel, and for metallurgical reasons, once a gun is made with a single cylinder, the extra convertible cylinder cannot be ordered at a later date.

SPORT/COMBAT RIMFIRE — .22 LR or .22 Mag. cal., 3, 4 (Combat only), 5¼, or 6 in. barrel (VR available on 4 in. or longer barrel only) , 6 shot, micro adj. sights (Sport), Combat sights fully adj., full length shrouded ejector rod, adj. trigger, checkered and oil finished walnut grips, 2.6 lbs. Introduced 1967.

Mfg.'s Sug. Retail	$3,300	$3,300	$2,650	$2,250	$1,850	$1,600	$1,325	$1,050

Add $400 for stainless steel (limited mfg.).

Add $200 for ISU Match Model.

Add $670 for special order 8 in. barrel.

Subtract $475 if without extra .22 LR cylinder.

Grading	100%	98%	95%	90%	80%	70%	60%

SPORT/COMBAT CENTERFIRE — .22 Rem. Jet, .32 S&W Long, .32 H&R Mag., .38 Spl., .357 Mag., or 9mm Para. cal., 3, 4 (Combat only), 5¼ or 6 in. barrel, 6 shot, otherwise similar spec.'s as Sport/Combat Rimfire Model, 2.1-2.6 lbs.

Mfg.'s Sug. Retail	$3,245	$3,100	$2,550	$2,150	$1,775	$1,525	$1,325	$1,050

Add $400 for stainless steel (limited mfg.).

Add $200 for ISU Match Model.

Add $200 for .22 Rem. Jet.

Add $670 for special order 8 in. barrel.

Subtract $475 if without extra 9mm Para. cylinder.

This model is available in additional rimmed and rimless calibers on special order. Most importation has occurred in either .357 Mag. or 9mm Para. cal.

PRESENTATION MODEL — deluxe variation of the Sport/Target Model.

This variation is available with etching, engraving, and other special options that are priced per individual quotation from the importer.

PISTOLS: SEMI-AUTO

KORTH SEMI-AUTO — 9mm Para. or 9 x 21mm IMI (special order only), double action, 4, 5, or 6 in. barrel, all steel construction, 10 shot mag., adj. sights, checkered walnut stocks, very limited production and special order only. Introduced 1986 with first guns shipped 1988.

Mfg.'s Sug. Retail	$3,295	$2,995	$2,250	$1,750

Add $500+ for interchangeable barrels.

KRAG-JORGENSEN

U.S. magazine military rifle. First small caliber (.30-40) military repeating rifle to shoot smokeless powder ammunition. Manufactured 1892-1902.

There have been many conversions of Krag-Jorgensen rifles - many of which are hard to identify. As a rule, these conversions are not as desirable as these specific models listed below.

M1892-DATED 1894, 1895, OR 1896 — Springfield Armory, with cleaning rod. Note: designated Type I, has wide, solid upper barrel band.

$4,180	$3,960	$3,740	$3,575	$3,300	$3,000	$2,600

Dated 1894 or 1895 — designated Type II. Upper band has double strap instead of being solid as in Type I.

$1,870	$1,705	$1,540	$1,210	$880	$720	$595

FACTORY — ALTERED TO M1896 STYLE

$250	$220	$195	$165	$140	$125	$105

M1896 — Dated 1896, 1897, 1898, Springfield Armory.

$470	$440	$330	$250	$220	$185	$155

M1896 CARBINE

$660	$580	$495	$385	$360	$320	$280

M1895 CARBINE — This is a variant that was dated 1895 and 1896 and omits the word "Model".

$880	$800	$660	$550	$440	$385	$330

M1896 CADET RIFLE

$3,025	$2,750	$2,530	$2,200	$1,815	$1,500	$1,200

M1898 RIFLE

$440	$360	$330	$250	$220	$190	$160

M1898 CARBINE

$1,450	$1,225	$950	$800	$660	$580	$525

M1899 CARBINE

$635	$525	$495	$470	$440	$395	$360

Grading	100%	98%	95%	90%	80%	70%	60%

M1899 CARBINE, PHILIPPINE CONSTABULARY

	100%	98%	95%	90%	80%	70%	60%
	$1,100	$990	$825	$715	$550	$480	$400

KRICO

Manufactured in Stuttgart, W. Germany by Sportwaffenfabrik Kriegeskorte Gmbh. Currently imported by Mandall Shooting Supplies, Inc. located in Scottsdale, AZ. Previously imported (until 1988) by Beeman Precision Firearms Inc. located in Santa Rosa, CA.

Between 1983-86, Krico was imported/distributed by over ten U.S. companies/individuals. Beeman Precision Arms imported these rifles 1986-1988 in limited quantities. Krico manufactures a high quality rifle and to date, has had limited domestic distribution.

RIFLES: BOLT ACTION

SPORTING RIFLE — .22 Hornet or .222 Rem. cal., miniature Mauser action, 4 shot, 22, 24, or 26 in. barrel, single or double set triggers, open sights, checkered walnut stock, pistol grip. Mfg. 1956-1962.

	$605	$550	$495	$440	$400	$360	$305

CARBINE — same as Sporting Rifle, except 20 or 22 in. barrel, full length stock.

	$635	$580	$415	$470	$420	$375	$320

SPECIAL VARMINT RIFLE — same as Sporting Rifle, except heavy barrel, no sights.

	$605	$550	$495	$440	$400	$360	$300

MODEL 300 SPORTER — .22 LR, .22 Mag., or .22 Hornet cal., select walnut with straight, checkered stock and fuller forearm, 23½ in. barrel, 5 shot mag., grooved receiver, 6½ lbs.

Mfg.'s Sug. Retail	$595	$550	$495	$450	$410	$380	$350	$320

Add $30 for .22 Mag. cal.

Add $155 for .22 Hornet cal.

This model was designated Model 302 Sporter until 1986.

Model 300 Deluxe — similar to Model 300 Standard, except has deluxe wood and checkering. Importation began 1991.

Mfg.'s Sug. Retail	$695	$625	$550	$480	$430	$385	$350	$320

Add $25 for .22 Mag. cal.

Add $200 for .22 Hornet cal.

MODEL 311 SMALL BORE RIFLE — .22 LR only, bolt action, 5 or 10 shot, 22 in. barrel, single or double set trigger, open sights, checkered stock. Disc.

	$330	$275	$250	$220	$195	$165	$155

Add 30% for Kaps 2½ power scope.

MODEL 320 MANNLICHER SPORTER — .22 LR, .22 Mag., or .22 Hornet cal., full stock sporter, 19½ in. barrel, 5 shot mag., double set triggers, 6 lbs.

Mfg.'s Sug. Retail	$750	$650	$575	$500	$460	$430	$395	$370

Add $25 for .22 Mag. cal.

Add $150 for .22 Hornet cal.

This model was designated Model 304 Mannlicher Sporter until 1986. In 1991 it was redesignated the Model 320 Stutzen.

MODEL 340 S ST — .22 LR only, silhouette model, 21 in. bull barrel, match trigger, no sights, 5 shot mag., stippled pistol grip and forearm, 7½ lbs.

Mfg.'s Sug. Retail	$795	$750	$625	$550	$500	$450	$375	$325

Model 340 Kricotronic — same as above, except with Krico electronic trigger. Importation disc. 1988.

	$1,295	$995	$900	$800	$690	$600	$550

Last Mfg.'s Sug. Retail was $1,450.

Grading	100%	98%	95%	90%	80%	70%	60%

Model 340 Mini-Sniper — non-glare wood and metal finish, military style barrel with muzzle brake, vent forearm, no sights, match trigger (interchangeable), 5 shot, raised cheek piece. Importation disc. 1988.

	100%	98%	95%	90%	80%	70%	60%
	$1,050	$825	$725	$600	$550	$500	$450

Last Mfg.'s Sug. Retail was $1,200.

BIATHLON MODEL 360 S — .22 LR cal., standard biathlon configuration with conventional straight pull bolt.

Mfg.'s Sug. Retail	$1,695	$1,375	$1,075	$925	$750	$625	$550	$500

BIATHLON MODEL 360 S2 — .22 LR cal., biathlon competition rifle featuring unique pistol grip operated rapid fire action, includes 5 mag.'s, aperture sights, snow guards, and black stock.

Mfg.'s Sug. Retail	$1,595	$1,300	$1,050	$900	$750	$625	$550	$500

MODEL 400 SPORTER — .22 LR or .22 Hornet cal., 23½ in. barrel, select checkered walnut with European style curved cheek piece, 5 shot mag., open sights, 6.8 lbs.

Mfg.'s Sug. Retail	$895	$840	$750	$625	$550	$500	$450	$375

Add $55 for .22 Hornet cal.

Model 400 Match Single Shot — .22 LR only, match rifle configuration.

Mfg.'s Sug. Retail	$950	$875	$750	$625	$550	$500	$450	$375

Model 400 Silhouette — .22 LR only, designed for silhouette shooting, no sights.

Mfg.'s Sug. Retail	$775	$725	$615	$550	$500	$450	$375	$325

MODEL 420 L ST MANNLICHER SPORTER — .22 Hornet only, full stock sporter, 19½ in. barrel, double set triggers, 5 shot, 6½ lbs.

	$875	$750	$625	$550	$500	$450	$375

MODEL 440 — .22 Hornet, otherwise same as Model 340. Importation disc. 1988.

	$900	$725	$575	$525	$450	$400	$360

Last Mfg.'s Sug. Retail was $1,025.

MODEL 600 HUNTING — .222 Rem., .223 Rem., .22-250 Rem., .243 Win., .308 Win., or 5.6 x 50 Mag. cal., 23½ in. barrel, select checkered walnut with curved European style cheek piece and vent forend, 3 or 4 shot mag., open sights, single set trigger, 7 lbs.

Mfg.'s Sug. Retail	$1,295	$1,100	$975	$850	$750	$625	$550	$500

Add $55 for Model 600 SC.

Add $300 for Model 600 Benchrest.

Add $355 for Model 600 in sniper configuration.

This model is also available in single shot configuration at at no extra charge as well as in a Match Model Group I & II - add $100 for Group II.

MODEL 620 MANNLICHER SPORTER — same cal.'s as Model 600, full stock sporter, 20¾ in. barrel, double set triggers, 3 shot mag., 6.8 lbs. Importation disc. 1988.

	$1,165	$965	$875	$760	$695	$650	$590

Last Mfg.'s Sug. Retail was $1,300.

MODEL 640 S ST VARMINT — .22-250, .222 Rem., or .223 Rem. cal., 23¾ in. heavy barrel, high Monte Carlo comb and full cheek piece, rosewood forearm tip and grip cap, Wundhammer hand swell, double set triggers, 4 shot mag., 9.6 lbs. Importation disc. 1990

	$875	$750	$625	$550	$500	$450	$375

Last Mfg.'s Sug. Retail was $950.

Model 640 Sniper — same as Model 640, except has non-adj. cheek piece. Importation disc. 1988.

	$1,325	$1,075	$965	$875	$760	$695	$650

Last Mfg.'s Sug. Retail was $1,500.

Grading	100%	98%	95%	90%	80%	70%	60%

MODEL 640 DELUXE/SUPER SNIPER — .223 Rem. or .308 Win., 23 in. barrel, select walnut stock has stippled hand grip, adj. cheek piece and vent forearm, engine turned bolt assembly, 3 shot mag., match trigger, 10 lbs. Importation disc. 1988.

	$1,495	$1,175	$1,025	$875	$760	$695	$650

This model was known as the 650 Sniper/Match until 1986.

Last Mfg.'s Sug. Retail was $1,725.

MODEL 700A ECONOMY — .222 Rem., .243 Win., or .308 Win. cal. (Group I) or 6.5 x 55mm, 7 x 64mm, .270 Win., or .30-06 cal. (Group II), without sights, single trigger. Importation began 1991.

Mfg.'s Sug. Retail	$995	$900	$775	$650	$550	$500	$450	$375

Add $70 for Group II cal.'s.

MODEL 700 SERIES — .17 Rem., .22-250 Rem., .222 Rem., .222 Rem. Mag., .223 Rem., 5.6 x 50mm Mag., .243 Win., .308 Win., or 5.6 x 57 RWS cal. (Group I), 6.5 x 55mm, 7 x 57mm, .270 Win., 7 x 64mm, .30-06, or 9.3 x 72 cal. (Group II), or 6.5 x 68mm, 7mm Rem. Mag., .300 Win. Mag., 8 x 68S, 7.5mm Swiss, or 6 x 62mm Freres (Group III), matte black metal finish, open sights, approx. 7 lbs. Importation began 1991.

Model 700 Hunting — available in Group I or II cal.'s only, walnut hunting stock with Bavarian cheek piece, recoil pad, and palm swell grip.

Mfg.'s Sug. Retail	$1,249	$1,075	$950	$850	$750	$625	$550	$500

Add $50 for Group II cal.'s.

Model 700 DeLuxe — similar to Model 700 Hunting, except has better grade walnut and is available in Group III cal's also.

Mfg.'s Sug. Retail	$1,379	$1,150	$1,000	$875	$750	$625	$550	$500

Add $20 for Group II cal.'s.

Add $71 for Group III cal.'s.

Add $150 for left-hand action.

Model 700 Stutzen — full stock variation (Mannlicher) of the Model 700 DeLuxe.

Mfg.'s Sug. Retail	$1,450	$1,200	$1,025	$895	$750	$625	$550	$500

Add $39 for Group II cal.'s.

Add $160 for Group III cal.'s.

Add $275 for DeLuxe variation (includes better wood and finish).

MODEL 700 DL R SPORTER — .270 or .30-06 cal., 23½ in. barrel, curved European cheek piece, select walnut, 3 shot Mag., single set trigger, open sights, 7 lbs. Importation disc. 1990.

	$925	$800	$650	$575	$500	$450	$375

Subtract $30 for Model 700 DM ST.

Add $470 for Model 700 DLM.

Last Mfg.'s Sug. Retail was $1,025.

MODEL 720 MANNLICHER SPORTER — same as Model 700, only has 20¾ in. barrel, double set triggers, 6.8 lbs. Importation disc. 1990.

	$1,100	$975	$850	$750	$625	$550	$500

Last Mfg.'s Sug. Retail was $1,295.

Model 720 Limited Edition — .270 cal. only, 24Kt. gold scroll work on bolt handle, receiver, barrel and mounts. Trigger and front side are gold plated. Serial numbered in gold. Disc. 1986.

	$2,310	$1,990	$1,700	$1,450	$1,200	$1,050	$950

Last Mfg.'s Sug. Retail was $2,659.

RIFLES: SEMI-AUTO

MODEL 260 SPORTER — .22 LR only, semi-auto action, standard features. Importation began 1991.

Mfg.'s Sug. Retail	$595	$550	$495	$450	$410	$380	$350	$320

Grading	100%	98%	95%	90%	80%	70%	60%

H. KRIEGHOFF GUN CO. (SHOTGUNS OF ULM)

Current manufacturer located in Ulm, W. Germany. Previous manufacture was in Suhl, Germany, 1886-1948. Currently imported and distributed by Krieghoff International Inc. located in Ottsville, PA.

WWII Krieghoff Lugers Appear In The Luger Section Of This Text.

SHOTGUNS: OVER AND UNDER

MODEL 32 STANDARD — O/U, 12, 20, 28, or .410 ga., 26½ - 32 in. barrels, auto ejector, boxlock, single trigger, select wood. Disc. 1980.

	$1,995	$1,795	$1,600	$1,450	$1,300	$1,175	$1,000

Low Rib — 28 or .410 ga., two-barrel set, 50% premium.

	$3,520	$2,860	$2,640	$2,200	$1,980	$1,870	$1,540

MODEL 32 4-BARREL SKEET SET — O/U, 12, 20, 28, or .410 ga., matched barrels in case, grades differ in engraving and wood quality, available as follows:

Standard	$5,500	$4,400	$3,960	$3,300	$3,080	$2,970	$2,750
Munchen Grade	$7,920	$6,820	$6,050	$5,720	$5,500	$5,225	$4,950
San Remo Grade	$9,020	$7,920	$7,150	$6,820	$6,600	$6,325	$6,050
Monte Carlo Grade							
	$16,500	$14,300	$12,650	$11,000	$9,900	$9,350	$8,800
Crown Grade	$19,800	$16,500	$14,300	$13,200	$12,100	$10,340	$9,680
Super Crown Grade							
	$24,200	$19,800	$16,500	$15,400	$14,300	$12,650	$11,000
Exhibition Grade	$39,500	$33,000	$27,500	$24,750	$22,000	$19,800	$16,500

MODEL 32 SINGLE BARREL TRAP — same action as O/U, 12 ga., 32-34 in. barrel, vent rib, mod., imp. mod., or full choke.

	$1,850	$1,400	$1,200	$1,000	$895	$795	$695

KS-5 SINGLE BARREL TRAP — 12 ga. only, adj. point of impact, innovative trigger configuration, optional choke tubes. New 1985.

Mfg.'s Sug. Retail	$3,250	$2,900	$2,100	$1,650	$1,350	$1,100	$925	$850

Add $380 for screw-in choke option.

Add $370 for hard case.

Adj. point of impact on this model is achieved by means of different, optional fronthangers.

KS-5 Special — 12 ga. only, 32 or 34 in. barrel, features adj. rib and comb stock, cased. New 1990.

Mfg.'s Sug. Retail	$4,150	$3,600	$2,850	$2,400	$1,875	$1,575	$1,275	$1,075

Adj. point of impact on this model is achieved by an adj. rib and comb stock at no extra charge.

K-80 TRAP — 12 ga. only, available in O/U, Unsingle, Top Single (single top barrel), and Combo (O/U with extra trap barrel) configurations, standard model has silver finished receiver. In O/U configuration the barrels are separated, about 8½ lbs. A wide variety of custom order options can be ordered on this model.

For the Model K-80, extra barrels cost $2,150 for O/U's, $2,795 for top single, and $2,950 for unsingle barrel. Add $350 for single release trigger, $575 for double release trigger. Add $380 for 3 screw-in chokes (single barrel guns only), $550 for O/U screw-in chokes (5 tubes).

Standard Model O/U — add 9% for Top Single, 19% for Unsingle, and 45% for Combo Standard K-80 variations.

Mfg.'s Sug. Retail	$5,950	$5,250	$4,600	$4,200	$3,550	$3,000	$2,600	$2,295

Add $550 for screw-in chokes (5 tubes).

Bavaria Model O/U — game scene engraved silver receiver with light scroll perimeter scroll work, select walnut. Add 6% for Top Single, 7% for Unsingle, and 28% for Combo Bavaria variations.

Mfg.'s Sug. Retail	$9,775	$8,700	$6,950	$5,975	$5,000	$4,375	$3,950	$3,300

Add $550 for screw-in chokes (5 tubes).

Grading	100%	98%	95%	90%	80%	70%	60%

Danube Model O/U — fine English scrollwork on receiver sides and floorplate. Add 5% for Top Single, 7% for Unsingle, and 23% for Combo Danube variations.

Mfg.'s Sug. Retail	$12,100	$10,875	$8,800	$7,675	$6,950	$6,000	$5,250	$4,800

Add $550 for screw-in chokes (5 tubes).

Gold Target Model — deep chiseled scroll engraving with gold line accents, 100% coverage finest quality walnut. Add 3% for Top Single, 4% for Unsingle, and 18% for Combo Gold Target variations.

Mfg.'s Sug. Retail	$15,870	$13,700	$11,500	$9,995	$8,700	$5,675	$6,570	$5,850

Add $550 for screw-in chokes (5 tubes).

Centennial Model — 12 ga. only, available in combo configuration only, 100 only mfg. 1986 to commemorate Krieghoff's centennial year, ser. no. 14501-14600. H. Krieghoff's signature inlaid in gold on frame sides. Add $150 for screw-in interchangeable chokes, $1,755 for 4-barrel set.

	$6,000	$5,000	$4,400

Last Mfg.'s Sug. Retail was $5,995.

K-80 SKEET O/U — 12 ga. only, available in Lightweight (8mm rib), Standardweight (8mm rib), or International (12mm rib) configurations, factory porting on both barrels, 28 in. barrels only, 8.2 lbs.

International Skeet models are supplied with hard case. Standardweight and Lightweight models include soft case.

Standard Model — available with either lightweight (Dural aluminum) or standardweight frame. Hard case optional.

Mfg.'s Sug. Retail	$5,650	$4,850	$3,995	$3,150	$2,875	$2,450	$2,125	$1,900

Add $345 for Skeet Special (includes 2 choke tubes & tapered flat rib).

Add $600 for International Model.

Add $230 for Tula choking (even patterning).

Bavaria Model O/U — game scene engraved silver receiver with light perimeter scroll work, select walnut. Available in either Standardweight or Lightweight configuration.

Mfg.'s Sug. Retail	$9,790	$8,600	$6,000	$5,450	$4,950	$4,375	$3,950	$3,300

Add $460 for Skeet Special (choke tubes & tapered flat rib).

Add $710 for International Model.

Add $200 for Tula choking (even patterning).

Danube Model O/U — fine English scrollwork on receiver sides and floorplate. Available in either Standardweight or Lightweight configuration.

Mfg.'s Sug. Retail	$11,950	$10,250	$8,700	$7,700	$7,000	$6,100	$5,250	$4,800

Add $450 for Skeet Special (choke tubes & tapered flat rib).

Add $700 for International Model.

Add $200 for Tula choking (even patterning).

Gold Target Model — deep chiseled scroll engraving with gold line accents, 100% coverage finest quality walnut. This model is available in Standardweight frame only.

Mfg.'s Sug. Retail	$15,950	$12,875	$11,000	$9,450	$8,000	$6,800	$5,850	$4,850

Add $450 for Skeet Special (choke tubes & tapered flat rib).

Add $700 for International Model.

Add $200 for Tula choking (even patterning).

Centennial Skeet — available in skeet configuration — special features as noted above on Centennial Model description listed under K-80 Trap. Mfg. 1986 only.

	$3,675	$3,150	$2,700

Last Mfg.'s Sug. Retail was $3,980.

K-80 2-BARREL LIGHTWEIGHT SKEET SET — 12 ga. Tula and tubing barrel, 8mm rib, hard case standard. New 1988.

Standard Grade

Mfg.'s Sug. Retail	$9,990	$8,250	$6,350	$4,900	$4,275	$3,875	$3,300	$3,000

Subtract $1,695 for heavy barrel concept, which does not include sub-gauge tubes.
Retail price for 2 barrel heavy set with choke tubes is $8,650.

Grading	100%	98%	95%	90%	80%	70%	60%

Bavaria Model O/U — game scene engraved silver receiver with light perimeter scroll work, select walnut. Importation began 1988.

Mfg.'s Sug. Retail	$14,250	$12,900	$9,900	$8,000	$7,000	$6,200	$5,250	$4,800

Subtract $2,090 for heavy barrel concept, which does not include sub-gauge tubes.
Retail price for 2 barrel heavy set with choke tubes is $12,750.

Danube Model O/U — fine English scroll work on receiver sides and floorplate. Importation began 1988.

Mfg.'s Sug. Retail	$16,780	$13,500	$10,850	$9,200	$7,750	$6,700	$5,850	$5,450

Subtract $2,090 for heavy barrel concept, which does not include sub-gauge tubes.
Retail price for 2 barrel heavy set with choke tubes is $15,150.

Gold Target Model — deep chiseled scroll engraving with gold line accents, 100% coverage finest quality walnut.

Mfg.'s Sug. Retail	$20,500	$17,000	$12,950	$10,500	$9,100	$7,750	$7,000	$6,650

Subtract $1,950 for heavy barrel concept.
Retail price for 2 barrel heavy set with choke tubes is $18,990.

K-80 4-BARREL SKEET SET — 1 barrel each of 12, 20, 28, and .410 ga., 12 ga. is Tula choked (even patterning), 8mm vent rib., includes hard case.

Standard Grade — satin finished receiver with skeet scroll engraving.

Mfg.'s Sug. Retail	$12,890	$10,250	$9,050	$8,050	$7,100	$6,100	$5,250	$4,500

Bavaria Model O/U — game scene engraved silver receiver with light perimeter scrollwork, select walnut.

Mfg.'s Sug. Retail	$16,500	$14,250	$12,150	$10,650	$9,250	$7,975	$6,900	$5,400

Danube Model O/U — fine English scroll work on receiver sides and floorplate.

Mfg.'s Sug. Retail	$18,500	$15,950	$13,500	$11,850	$9,950	$8,600	$7,725	$6,900

Gold Target Model — deep chiseled scroll engraving with gold line accents, 100% coverage finest quality walnut.

Mfg.'s Sug. Retail	$23,950	$20,500	$17,900	$15,250	$12,250	$9,950	$8,700	$7,500

K-80 PIGEON O/U — 12 ga. only, available with 28, 29, or 30 in. barrels, standard tapered step rib, IM/SF choking, available in Lightweight or Standardweight configuration (no extra charge).

Standard Grade — satin finished receiver with no engraving.

Mfg.'s Sug. Retail	$5,950	$5,250	$4,600	$4,200	$3,550	$3,000	$2,600	$2,295

Bavaria Model O/U — game scene engraved silver receiver with light scroll perimeter scroll work, select walnut.

Mfg.'s Sug. Retail	$9,775	$8,700	$6,950	$5,975	$5,000	$4,375	$3,950	$3,300

Danube Model O/U — fine English scroll work on receiver sides and floorplate.

Mfg.'s Sug. Retail	$12,100	$10,875	$8,800	$7,675	$6,950	$6,000	$5,250	$4,800

Gold Target Model — deep chiseled scroll engraving with gold line accents, 100% coverage finest quality walnut.

Mfg.'s Sug. Retail	$15,870	$13,700	$11,500	$9,995	$8,700	$5,675	$6,570	$5,850

K-80 SPORTING CLAYS O/U — 12 ga. only, 28 or 30 (new 1991) in. barrels with 5 choke tubes, choice of 8mm VR Skeet, tapered flat or step rib, sporting clay stock dimensions. New 1988.

Standard Grade — satin finished receiver with sporting scroll engraving.

Mfg.'s Sug. Retail	$6,350	$5,500	$4,750	$4,175	$3,650	$3,000	$2,600	$2,100

Bavaria Model O/U — game scene engraved silver receiver with light scroll perimeter scroll work, select walnut.

Mfg.'s Sug. Retail	$10,375	$8,850	$7,350	$6,250	$5,350	$4,450	$3,950	$3,300

Danube Model O/U — fine English scroll work on receiver sides and floorplate.

Mfg.'s Sug. Retail	$12,800	$10,750	$9,100	$7,950	$7,150	$6,200	$5,250	$4,400

Gold Target Model — deep chiseled scroll engraving with gold line accents, 100% coverage finest quality walnut.

Mfg.'s Sug. Retail	$16,500	$13,450	$11,150	$9,500	$8,000	$6,950	$5,950	$4,950

Grading	100%	98%	95%	90%	80%	70%	60%

VANDALIA TRAP — high rib, two barrel combination.

	100%	98%	95%	90%	80%	70%	60%
	$4,180	$3,520	$3,300	$2,860	$2,640	$2,530	$2,200

O/U SHOTGUN OR COMBINATION GUN

Add $500 for hand detachable sidelocks (Ulm only).

Add $950 for 4-claw scope mount system.

TECK MODEL — O/U shotgun or rifle/shotgun combo., 12 and 16 ga., various cal.'s (7 x 57R, 7 x 64mm, 7 x 65R, .30-06, or .308 Win.), boxlock action, Kersten double crossbolt, auto ejectors, 7½ lbs.

	100%	98%	95%	90%	80%	70%	60%
Mfg.'s Sug. Retail	$5,900	$5,300	$4,700	$4,225	$3,550	$3,000	$2,600	$2,295

Teck Dural — Dural aluminum frame variation of the Teck, 6.8 lbs.

Mfg.'s Sug. Retail	$5,900	$5,300	$4,700	$4,225	$3,550	$3,000	$2,600	$2,295

ULM — same as Teck, except sidelock and fully engraved with leaf arabesques.

Mfg.'s Sug. Retail	$11,500	$9,600	$8,150	$7,200	$6,250	$5,250	$4,400	$3,500

Ulm Dural — Dural aluminum frame variation of the Ulm.

Mfg.'s Sug. Retail	$11,500	$9,600	$8,150	$7,200	$6,250	$5,250	$4,400	$3,500

ULM PRIMUS — same as Ulm, except game scene engraved with English arabesques.

Mfg.'s Sug. Retail	$15,295	$12,350	$10,100	$8,250	$6,850	$5,975	$5,450	$4,995

Ulm Primus Dural — Dural aluminum frame variation of the Ulm Primus.

Mfg.'s Sug. Retail	$15,295	$12,350	$10,100	$8,250	$6,850	$5,975	$5,450	$4,995

ULTRA — combination O/U, 12 ga. only, various calibers (lower barrel), 25 in. barrels, "Kick-spannar" mechanism allows manual cocking from thumb safety, satin finish receiver, vent rib, 6 lbs. New 1985.

Mfg.'s Sug. Retail	$3,350	$2,775	$2,050	$1,675	$1,400	$1,200	$1,050	$900

Ultra-B — same as Ultra, except features a selector to switch the front set trigger to the top shotgun barrel.

Mfg.'s Sug. Retail	$3,750	$3,100	$2,150	$1,775	$1,500	$1,300	$1,050	$900

SHOTGUNS: O/U

ULM-P — 12 ga. only, live pigeon gun with hand detachable sidelocks, standard grade has light scrollwork engraving.

Mfg.'s Sug. Retail	$14,500	$11,700	$9,675	$8,150	$7,000	$5,850	$5,450	$4,995

Bavaria Grade — same as Ulm-P, only with elaborate game scene engraving.

Mfg.'s Sug. Retail	$17,900	$14,100	$11,250	$9,350	$8,000	$6,600	$5,700	$5,300

KS-2 SERIES — any ga., full H&H type sidelocks, priced by individual special order. Prices start at $24,000. Custom order only with substantial wait.

DOUBLE RIFLES

Various grades differ in style and amount of engraving, choice of walnut and various options that can be special ordered.

TECK O/U — .30-06, .300 Win. Mag., .308 Win., 7 X 65R, 8 X 57JRS, or 9.3 X 74R cal., 25 in. barrel, boxlock action, cocking indicators.

Mfg.'s Sug. Retail	$7,995	$6,950	$5,750	$4,875	$4,100	$3,650	$3,300	$3,000

Add $1,000 for .375 H&H (disc. 1988) or .458 Win. Mag. cal.

Add $850 for DT's with front set trigger.

Teck-Handspanner — manual cocking, 7 x 65R, .30-06, or .308 Win. on 16 ga. receiver frame.

Mfg.'s Sug. Retail	$9,500	$8,200	$7,000	$6,150	$5,100	$4,375	$3,950	$3,200

ULM O/U — same as Teck Double Rifle, with sidelocks and more elaborate engraving.

Mfg.'s Sug. Retail	$13,500	$11,500	$8,900	$7,900	$6,775	$6,100	$5,500	$4,950

Add $500 for hand detachable sidelocks.

Add $1,550 with single/double trigger.

Grading	100%	98%	95%	90%	80%	70%	60%
Ulm Dekor — sidelock with light scroll engraving.							
Mfg.'s Sug. Retail	$12,500	$10,450	$9,150	$8,000	$6,750	$5,600	$5,000	$4,400
Ulm Primus — deluxe sidelock.							
Mfg.'s Sug. Retail	$16,985	$13,350	$11,000	$9,225	$7,700	$6,450	$5,700	$5,300

TRUMPF SxS — boxlock action, similar to Teck model, except in .30-06, 8 x 57JRS, or 9.3 X 74R cal.

Mfg.'s Sug. Retail	$11,995	$9,950	$8,950	$7,950	$7,000	$6,100	$5,300	$4,800

NEPTUN SxS — sidelock double rifle, same features as the Ulm model.

Mfg.'s Sug. Retail	$15,500	$12,750	$10,400	$8,700	$7,350	$6,000	$5,450	$4,995

DRILLINGS

H. Krieghoff drillings can be ordered with a variety of cal.'s (.222 Rem., .243 Win., .270 Win., or .30-06) and special order features. Prices shown below are for standard guns with no options. Better models will have a finer grade walnut and exhibit more elaborate deep relief engraving.

Add $395 for free floating rifle barrels on Trumpf and Neptun Models listed below (both regular steel frame and Dural variations).

PLUS MODEL — 12 or 20 ga. over rifle barrel (.222 Rem., 243 Win., 270, or .30-06 cal.), boxlock action, light engraving. New 1988.

Mfg.'s Sug. Retail	$4,495	$3,800	$3,175	$2,600	$2,150	$1,825	$1,525	$1,200

TRUMPF MODEL — 12, 16, or 20 ga. O/U, or rifle shotgun combo., various cal.'s, boxlock, 25 in. barrels, 7½ lbs.

Mfg.'s Sug. Retail	$8,200	$7,100	$5,750	$5,000	$4,150	$3,300	$2,750	$2,200

Add $1,200 for single trigger.

Trumpf Dural — Dural aluminum frame variation of the Trumpf, 6.8 lbs., cased.

Mfg.'s Sug. Retail	$8,200	$7,100	$5,750	$5,000	$4,150	$3,300	$2,750	$2,200

Add $1,200 for single trigger.

NEPTUN MODEL — 12 or 20 ga., variety of cal.'s, elaborate engraving, sidelocks.

Mfg.'s Sug. Retail	$13,500	$11,250	$9,400	$8,250	$7,100	$6,100	$5,100	$4,150

Neptun Dural — Dural aluminum frame variation of the Neptun, cased.

Mfg.'s Sug. Retail	$13,500	$11,250	$9,400	$8,250	$7,100	$6,100	$5,100	$4,150

NEPTUN PRIMUS MODEL — same as Neptun Model, only hand detachable sidelocks and elaborate deep relief engraving.

Mfg.'s Sug. Retail	$16,950	$13,650	$11,450	$9,650	$8,100	$7,000	$5,850	$4,950

Neptun Primus Dural — Dural aluminum frame variation available at no extra charge.

Mfg.'s Sug. Retail	$16,950	$13,650	$11,450	$9,650	$8,100	$7,000	$5,850	$4,950

NOTES

L

L.A.R. MANUFACTURING, INC.
Manufacturer located in West Jordan, UT.

Grading	100%	98%	95%	90%	80%	70%	60%

GRIZZLY WIN. MAG. MARK I — .357 Mag., 357/45 Grizzly Win. Mag. (new 1990), .45 ACP, 10mm, or .45 Win. Mag., single action, semi-auto based on the Colt 1911 design, 5.4 in. (new 1986), 6½ in., 8 in. (new 1987), or 10 in. (new 1987) barrel, parkerized finish, 7 shot mag., ambidextrous safeties, checkered rubber grips, adj. sights, 48 oz. empty. Also can be converted to .45 ACP, 10mm (new 1988), .357 Mag., or .30 Mauser (disc.). New 1984.

Short Barrel Lengths — 5.4 or 6.5 in. barrel.

Mfg.'s Sug. Retail	$893	$775	$650	$600	$525	$495	$475	$450

Add $27 if purchased in .357 Mag.

Add $135 for hard chrome frame.

Add $228 for full hard chrome.

Add $207 - $221 for cal. conversion units.
Conversion units include .357 Mag., 10mm, .40 S&W (new 1991), and .45 ACP cal.'s.

Long Barrel Lengths — .357 Mag., .45 Win. Mag., or 357/45 Grizzly Win. Mag. (new 1990), 8 or 10 in. barrel, extended slides.

Mfg.'s Sug. Retail	$1,313	$1,195	$975	$895	$800	$725	$650	$575

Add $62 for 10 in. barrel.

Add $25 if purchased in .357 Mag.

Add $143 for scope mounts.

Add $107 for muzzle compensator.

GRIZZLY .44 MAG. MARK 4 — .44 Mag., choice of lusterless blue or parkerized finish, 5.4 or 6.5 in. barrel, adj. sights. New 1991.

Mfg.'s Sug. Retail	$920	$795	$665	$600	$525	$495	$475	$450

GRIZZLY WIN. MAG. MARK II — similar to Mark I, except has fixed sights, standard safeties, and different metal finish. Mfg. 1986 only.

$625	$550	$525	$495	$475	$450	$425

Add $25 for .357 Mag.
Last Mfg.'s Sug. Retail was $550.

L E S INCORPORATED
Previous manufacturer located in Morton Grove, IL.

PISTOL: SEMI-AUTO
The Steyr Model GB is patterned after this action.

P-18 ROGAK DOUBLE ACTION — 9mm Para., double action, 18 shot, 5½ in. barrel, stainless steel, black plastic grips with partial thumb rest. Disc.

$350	$295	$265

High polish finish

$395	$330	$295

Approx. 2,300 P-18's were mfg. before being disc.

LAHTI PISTOL
Previous manufacturer located in Husqvarna, Sweden & Vkt (state rifle factory in Jyvaskyla), Finland.

Grading	100%	98%	95%	90%	80%	70%	60%

SWEDISH MODEL 40 — 9mm Para., 4¾ in. barrel, blued finish, fixed sights, plastic grips, mfg. 1940-1944.

	$395	$350	$300	$275	$260	$250	$240

Add 10% for Holster-Rig.

FINNISH L-35 — mfg. 1935-1944.

	$1,250	$1,050	$900	$760	$680	$620	$575

Note: It is important to note that there are diversely marked variations of this pistol, such as RPLT (Danish State Police); such police markings reduce value by about 10%.

LAKE FIELD ARMS LTD.

Manufacturer located in Ontario, Canada. Imported and distributed by Ellett Brothers located in Chapin, SC.

MARK I — .22 LR, single shot bolt action, 20½ in. barrel, adj. rear sight, thumb rotary safety, walnut finish hardwood stock, 5½ lbs.

Mfg.'s Sug. Retail	$105	$95	$75	$65	$55	$50	$40	$30

This model is also available in youth dimensions at no extra charge (Model Mark I-Y).

MARK II — .22 LR, bolt action, 10 shot clip mag., 20½ in. barrel, adj. rear sight, thumb rotary safety, walnut finish hardwood stock, 5½ lbs.

Mfg.'s Sug. Retail	$120	$105	$80	$70	$60	$50	$40	$30

This model is also available in youth dimensions at no extra charge (Model Mark II-Y).

MODEL 64B — .22 LR, semi-auto, sight ejection, 10 shot clip mag., 20½ in. barrel, adj. rear sight, thumb rotary safety, walnut finish hardwood stock, 5½ lbs.

Mfg.'s Sug. Retail	$125	$110	$85	$75	$65	$55	$45	$40

MODEL 90B — .22 LR, biathlon rifle, includes five 5-shot mag.'s, 21 in. barrel, aperture sights, one piece natural finish hardwood stock, 8¼ lbs. New 1991.

Mfg.'s Sug. Retail	$480	$360	$275	$225	$195	$170	$150	$130

MODEL 91T — .22 LR, target rifle available as either single shot or 5-shot repeater, 25 in. barrel with aperture sights, dark hardwood finished stock, 8 lbs. New 1991.

Mfg.'s Sug. Retail	$390	$290	$225	$195	$170	$150	$135	$115

Add $25 for 5-shot repeater action (Model 91TR, designed for summer biathlon variation).

LAMES

Previous manufacturer located In Italy.

SHOTGUNS

FIELD MODEL O/U — 12 ga., 26, 28, or 30 in. barrels, various chokes, VR, engraving, SST, auto ejectors, checkered pistol grip stock with pad.

	$400	$380	$365	$350	$325	$300	$275

Separated barrels

	$500	$480	$465	$450	$425	$400	$375

STANDARD TRAP O/U — same as Field, 30 or 32 in. various trap bore barrels, with wide vent rib, trap style Monte Carlo stock.

	$600	$575	$550	$525	$425	$400	$450

CALIFORNIA TRAP O/U — same as Standard Trap, with separated barrels.

	$700	$675	$650	$625	$525	$500	$450

SKEET MODEL — same as Field, with 26 in. skeet bore barrels, skeet stock and separated barrels.

	$600	$575	$550	$525	$425	$400	$350

Grading	100%	98%	95%	90%	80%	70%	60%

LANBER SHOTGUNS

Manufacturer located in Zaldbar, Spain. Previously imported by Exel Arms of America, Inc., located in Gardener, MA. And by Lanber Arms of America located in Adrian, MI.

SHOTGUNS: O/U RECENT MANUFACTURE

Please refer to discontinued Exel Models 101-104 and 105-107 in the "E" section of this text.

SHOTGUNS: O/U DISCONTINUED MANUFACTURE

The following models were imported by Lanber Arms of America, Inc. located in Adrian, MI until business ceased in late 1986.

844 ST — 12 ga. only, boxlock, 26 or 28 in. barrels, choked IC/IM, extractors, SST, automatic safety, vent rib, European walnut with hand checkering, blued finish with engraved receiver, 7⅛ lbs. Importation disc. 1986.

	100%	98%	95%	90%	80%	70%	60%
	$395	$340	$320	$300	$285	$270	$255

Last Mfg.'s Sug. Retail was $450.

844 MST — 12 ga. only, 3 in. chambers, 30 in. F & M barrels, otherwise same as 844 ST. Importation disc. 1986.

	100%	98%	95%	90%	80%	70%	60%
	$405	$350	$335	$320	$310	$300	$295

Last Mfg.'s Sug. Retail was $470.

2004 LCH — 12 ga. only, boxlock action, 28 in. barrels, SST, ejectors, supplied with 5 screw-in choke tubes, engraved satin finish receiver, checkered European walnut, 7⅜ lbs. Importation disc. 1986.

	100%	98%	95%	90%	80%	70%	60%
	$575	$485	$460	$440	$420	$395	$380

Last Mfg.'s Sug. Retail was $650.

2004 LCH SKEET — 12 ga. only, 28 in. barrels supplied with 5 choke tubes, blued finish, moderately engraved, select checkered walnut, 7⅜ lbs. Importation disc. 1986.

	100%	98%	95%	90%	80%	70%	60%
	$740	$635	$585	$560	$540	$520	$495

Last Mfg.'s Sug. Retail was $845.

2004 LCH TRAP — 12 ga. only, 30 in. barrels supplied with 3 choke tubes, European walnut has trap dimensions, blued finish. Importation disc. 1986.

	100%	98%	95%	90%	80%	70%	60%
	$675	$625	$585	$560	$540	$520	$495

Last Mfg.'s Sug. Retail was $845.

LASALLE

Previous manufacturer located in France.

SLIDE ACTION SHOTGUN — 12 or 20 ga., 26, 28, or 30 in. barrels, various chokes, alloy frame, checkered pistol grip stock.

	100%	98%	95%	90%	80%	70%	60%
	$250	$225	$200	$175	$150	$125	$100

AUTOMATIC SHOTGUN — 12 ga., 26, 28, or 30 in. barrels, various chokes, gas operated, checkered pistol grip stock.

	100%	98%	95%	90%	80%	70%	60%
	$300	$275	$250	$225	$200	$175	$150

LAURONA

Manufacturer located in Eibar, Spain. Currently imported and distributed by Galaxy Imports located in Victoria, TX.

SHOTGUNS: O/U DISC. MANUFACTURE

Please refer to the Exel 300 Series in the "E" section.

Grading	100%	98%	95%	90%	80%	70%	60%

SHOTGUNS: O/U RECENT MANUFACTURE

Laurona shotguns come standard with a black chrome metal finish that is extremely resistant to oxidation. Left hand stocks are available for the 83 MG Super Game, 85 MS Super Game, Trap, and Super Skeet, Silhouette Trap models, and Silhouette Sporting Clays.

Suffix designations on Laurona shotguns refer to the following: G - twin single triggers, S - selective single trigger, M - multi-chokes, T - Tulip, BV - beavertail.

All Super Game Models are available with a deluxe package which includes a recoil pad, mid-bead sight, and select wood for an additional $250. Special order dull matte finished barrels (with multi-chokes) are available by special order for an additional $200 - extra barrels are priced between $635 (20 ga.) or $800 (12 ga.) per set. All Laurona models are also available with special order Imperial engraving and wood (add $3,000) or Supreme engraving and wood (add $6,500).

If more information is required on an older Laurona model not listed in this publication, it is adviseable to do the following. Please send/FAX an accurate description of your specimen (including Laurona model name, serial number, and other pertinent data - include photos if possible) to Galaxy Imports (see Trademark Index for address and FAX number). The charge for this service is $25 per serial number.

MODEL 82 — double selective trigger system, ejectors, pistol grip, vent rib, various chokes and barrel lengths. Disc.

	$549	$410	$380	$340	$300	$275	$250

This model was imported by Exel Arms of America, Inc.

SUPER GAME MODELS — 12 or 20 ga., boxlock, 28 in. barrels, unique twin single triggers, ejectors, extensive fine scroll engraving on a satin finished receiver, anti-rust black chrome barrel finish, vent. rib, elongated forcing cones, checkered walnut stock and forearm.

Twin single triggers can function as conventional double triggers in addition to either trigger functioning as a non-selective single trigger. By example, each trigger can fire both barrels - the back trigger fires from top to bottom and the front trigger uses the bottom to top sequence.

82 G Super Game — new designation for 82 Super Game, with T forend, 2¾ in. chambers, 28 in. separated barrels choked F/M or IC/IM with 8mm VR, twin single triggers. Importation disc. 1989.

	$975	$875	$795	$675	$625	$550	$495

This model was previously designated 82 Super Game.

Last Mfg.'s Sug. Retail was $1,100.

82 Pigeon Competition — same as 82 Trap Competition, except 28 in. barrels with different chokings. Importation disc. 1986.

	$545	$465	$440	$420	$405	$390	$375

Last Mfg.'s Sug. Retail was $630.

82 Trap Combo — trap model, 8mm vent rib, non-selective single trigger. Importation disc. 1986.

	$485	$390	$375	$360	$350	$340	$330

Last Mfg.'s Sug. Retail was $566.

82 Trap Competition — 29 in. barrels, oil finished Monte Carlo stock, 13mm VR, non-selective single trigger, motif engraving, rubber recoil pad, 8.1 lbs. Importation disc. 1986.

	$540	$460	$435	$420	$405	$390	$375

Last Mfg.'s Sug. Retail was $625.

83 MG SUPER GAME — 12 or 20 ga., similar to 82 G Super Game except has multi-chokes, 2¾ or 3 in. Mag. chambers.

Mfg.'s Sug. Retail	$1,540	$1,275	$1,025	$895	$795	$675	$625	$550

83 MG Super Game 2 Barrel Set — includes 2 sets of barrels (12 and 20 ga.).

Mfg.'s Sug. Retail	$2,180	$1,775	$1,500	$1,275	$1,000	$875	$775	$700

83 M Puma Hunting — importation disc. 1986.

	$485	$445	$425	$410	$395	$380	$375

Last Mfg.'s Sug. Retail was $529.

Grading	100%	98%	95%	90%	80%	70%	60%

84 S SUPER GAME — similar to 82 G Super Game except has SST and available with 3 in. Mag. chambers. Importation disc. 1989.

	$925	$840	$775	$675	$625	$550	$495

Last Mfg.'s Sug. Retail was $1,100.

84 S SUPER TRAP — 29 in. barrels, extensive fine scroll engraving, separated barrels with 13mm aluminum VR, rubber recoil pad, full pistol grip stock with orthopedic grip, beavertail forearm, single selective trigger, elongated forcing cones, choked IM/F or M/F, 7¾ lbs.

Mfg.'s Sug. Retail	$1,920	$1,650	$1,250	$995	$875	$750	$625	$495

85 MS SUPER GAME — available in 12 or 20 ga., similar to 83 MG Super Game, except has SST.

Mfg.'s Sug. Retail	$1,575	$1,295	$1,025	$895	$795	$675	$625	$550

85 MS Super Game 2 Barrel Set — includes 2 sets of barrels (12 and 20 ga.).

Mfg.'s Sug. Retail	$2,215	$1,800	$1,500	$1,275	$1,000	$875	$775	$700

85 MS SUPER TRAP — similar to 84 S Super Trap except chokes are full over multi-choke.

Mfg.'s Sug. Retail	$1,970	$1,675	$1,250	$995	$875	$750	$625	$495

85 MS Super Pigeon — similar to 85 Super Trap, except choked IM/choke tube with 28 in. barrels and 13mm aluminum rib, stocked for live pigeon shooting, 7¼ lbs.

Mfg.'s Sug. Retail	$1,890	$1,625	$1,250	$995	$875	$750	$625	$495

Add $60 for left hand stock.

GTO/GTU TRAP COMBO SILHOUETTE SERIES — 12 ga. only, 2¾ in. chamber, features black and silver striped receiver, 29 in. O/U barrels with multi-F chokes and 34 in. top single barrel with multi-F chokes. Importation began 1990.

Mfg.'s Sug. Retail	$2,660	$2,175	$1,650	$1,300	$1,050	$900	$800	$725

Add $110 for GTU Model (bottom single barrel).

SILHOUETTE GAME — 12 ga. only, 3 in. chambers, 28 in. barrels, multi-K chokes. Although advertised, this model was never imported (similar specifications as the Model 85 MS Super Game).

85 S SUPER SKEET — 12 ga. only, 28 in. barrels, 2¾ in. chambers with elongated forcing cones, extensive fine scroll engraving, rust resistant black chrome finish, separated barrels, 13mm aluminum VR, mechanical triggers with 5 lb. pull, 7¼ lbs.

Mfg.'s Sug. Retail	$1,810	$1,550	$1,225	$995	$875	$750	$625	$495

85 MS Special Sporting — 12 ga. only, similar to 85 MS Super Pigeon except with field stock designed for upland game, SST, 28 in. barrels choked IM over multi-choke, 7¼ lbs. Importation began 1988-90.

	$1,575	$1,225	$995	$875	$750	$625	$500

Last Mfg.'s Sug. Retail was $1,850.

SILHOUETTE 300 SPORTING CLAYS — 12 ga. only, 3 in. chambers, 28 in. barrels with 11mm VR, field stock with special recoil pad designed for dropped stock style shooting, 7¼ lbs. New 1988.

Mfg.'s Sug. Retail	$1,760	$1,495	$1,200	$975	$875	$750	$625	$500

Available with either flush or knurled multi-chokes.

SILHOUETTE 300 TRAP — 12 ga. only, same as 85 MS Super Trap except has 29 in. steel barrels with 11mm VR, flush or knurled multi-chokes, black chrome finish, distinctive silver striped receiver (similar to Silver Sporting Clays), 8 lbs. New 1988.

Mfg.'s Sug. Retail	$1,790	$1,525	$1,200	$975	$875	$750	$625	$500

SILHOUETTE SINGLE BARREL TRAP — 34 in. barrel only with 7/16 in. VR, choice of either top single or bottom single barrel. Importation began 1991.

Mfg.'s Sug. Retail	$2,030	$1,725	$1,275	$995	$875	$750	$625	$495

Add $110 for bottom single barrel.

SILHOUETTE ULTRA-MAGNUM — 12 ga., 3½ in. chamber, 28 in. barrels, single trigger, ejectors, checkered walnut stock and forearm. Importation began 1990.

Mfg.'s Sug. Retail	$1,760	$1,495	$1,200	$975	$875	$750	$625	$500

Grading	100%	98%	95%	90%	80%	70%	60%

Waterfowler Ultra-Magnum — similar to Silhouette Ultra-Magnum, except has non-glare finish and 29 in. barrels. New 1990.

Mfg.'s Sug. Retail	$1,760	$1,495	$1,200	$975	$875	$750	$625	$500

LAW ENFORCEMENT ORDNANCE CORPORATION

Previous manufacturer located in Ridgway, PA until 1990.

STRIKER-12 — 12 ga. only, paramilitary design shotgun featuring 12 shot rotary mag., 12 or 18¼ in. barrel, semi-auto, alloy shrouded barrel with PG extension, folding or fixed paramilitary design stock, 9.2 lbs. Mfg. 1986-1990.

	$725	$650	$575	$500	$475	$450	$425

Add $100 for Marine variation ("Metal Life" finish).

Earlier variations were imported and available to law enforcement agencies only. In 1987, manufacture was started in PA and these firearms could be sold to individuals (18 in. barrel only).

Last Mfg.'s Sug. Retail was $725.

LEBEAU-COURALLY

Manufactured since 1865 in Liege, Belgium. Currently imported by New England Arms Co. located in Kittery Point, ME and Midwest Gun Sport in Zebulon, NC. Previously imported by W.L. Moore & Co. in West Lake Village, CA.

Lebeau-Courally manufactures only best quality rifles and shotguns. Approximately 50 are manufactured annually.

Prices could differ from values shown below because of the fluctuating U.S. dollar.

RIFLES: SINGLE SHOT

SINGLE SHOT — 6.5 x 68 R or 9.3 x 74 R cal., best quality, boxlock or sidelock action.

The importers should be contacted directly (see Trademark Index) for current information and prices regarding this model.

RIFLES: SIDE-BY-SIDE

BOXLOCK EJECTOR — 8 x 57 JRS or 9.3 x 74 R cal., Anson & Deeley boxlock, ejectors, select French walnut stock, quarter rib with ramp front sight, about 8 lbs. Importation disc. 1988.

	$9,200	$7,950	$7,250	$6,500	$5,500	$4,500	$3,750

Add $1,400 for standard cal.'s.

This model was imported by W.L. Moore & Co. only.

Last Mfg.'s Sug. Retail was $10,200.

SIDELOCK EJECTOR — 8 x 57 JRS, 9.3 x 74 R, .375 H&H, .458 Win. Mag., .470 NE (new 1991), or .577 NE (new 1991), chopper lump barrels, reinforced action, select French walnut stock, quarter rib with ramp front sight, approx. 8 lbs.

Mfg.'s Sug. Retail	$22,500	$19,950	$16,600	$14,000	$11,850	$10,250	$8,900	$7,000

SHOTGUNS

For currently manufactured shotguns — add $1,500 for single trigger, and $700 for false sideplates.

SOLOGNE SXS — 12, 16, 20, 28, or .410 ga., Anson & Deeley boxlock action, various chokes and barrel lengths, select walnut, no engraving. Add $530 for false sideplates.

Mfg.'s Sug. Retail	$7,320	$6,725	$5,950	$5,475	$4,950	$4,620	$4,400	$4,125

GRAND RUSSE MODEL — grade up from Sologne Model.

Mfg.'s Sug. Retail	$8,480	$7,625	$7,000	$6,750	$5,500	$4,950	$4,400	$4,125

Grading	100%	98%	95%	90%	80%	70%	60%

BOXLOCK EJECTOR SXS — 12, 16, 20, 28, or .410 ga., choice of classic or rounded action, with or without sideplates, select French walnut stock, choice of numerous engraving patterns (optional), 26, 28, or 30 in. barrels, double trigger. Add 10% for 28 or .410 ga. Importation disc. 1986.

	$8,450	$7,500	$6,500	$5,500	$4,500	$3,750	$3,000

Last Mfg.'s Sug. Retail was $9,400.

Boxlock with sideplates.

	$8,950	$7,900	$6,750	$5,600	$4,500	$3,750	$3,000

Last Mfg.'s Sug. Retail was $10,000.

SIDELOCK EJECTOR SXS — 12, 16, 20, or 28 ga., choice of classic or rounded action, chopper lump barrels, select French walnut stock, choice of numerous engraving patterns (optional), 26, 28, or 30 in. barrels, double triggers. Add 10% for 28 or .410 ga.

Mfg.'s Sug. Retail	$20,600	$18,250	$14,000	$12,000	$9,995	$8,750	$7,500	$6,350

SIDELOCK O/U — similar to Boss Model, except less engraving, and different quality wood.

Mfg.'s Sug. Retail	$19,600	$17,000	$13,725	$11,400	$9,995	$8,750	$7,500	$6,350

BOSS MODEL O/U — 12 only, Boss pattern sidelock with low profile action, top of the line O/U individually made to customer specifications.

Mfg.'s Sug. Retail	$28,000	$24,800	$21,750	$19,000	$16,000	$13,000	$10,750	$9,700

LEFEVER ARMS COMPANY

Previous manufacturer located in Syracuse, NY.

SHOTGUNS

The Lefever was the first commercially successful hammerless double barrel shotgun made in America. They were made in Syracuse, NY from 1885-1916, at which time the company was acquired by Ithaca Gun Company. Ithaca made the Lefever until 1916. In 1921 the Box Lock Nitro Special was introduced and in 1934 the Lefever Grade A was introduced. Production of Lefever guns ceased in 1948.

The following is a percentage breakdown of gauges made between 1885-1916 (totaling 100%): 8 ga.—½%, 10 ga.—25%, 12 ga.—60%, 14 ga.—½%, 16 ga.—8%, 20 ga.—6%. Total manufacture was approx. 72,000 during this period. Damascus specimens of this trademark are worth approximately the same as their fluid steel barrel counterparts because of the rarity and desirability factors. Prices shown below for 90% and up condition are very difficult to evaluate and are meant as a guide only - any Lefever shotgun is rare and hard to evaluate if in over 95%.

SIDELOCK DOUBLE BARREL SHOTGUN — 10, 12, 16, or 20 ga., 26-32 in. barrels, any choke, cocking indicators on all but DS and DSE grades, double triggers standard, checkered straight or pistol grip stock, auto ejectors designated by letter E after grade. Mfg. 1885-1919.

16 ga. — deduct 10%.

20 ga. — add 20%.

SST — add 10%.

DS grade	$1,250	$1,000	$800	$700	$525	$470	$415
DSE grade	$1,650	$1,300	$1,100	$950	$700	$575	$500
H grade	$1,400	$1,100	$950	$800	$625	$580	$525
HE grade	$1,825	$1,650	$1,450	$1,200	$900	$775	$625
G grade	$1,550	$1,425	$1,200	$1,000	$800	$700	$595
GE grade	$1,950	$1,800	$1,575	$1,325	$1,175	$1,000	$800
F grade	$1,700	$1,550	$1,325	$1,125	$925	$800	$750
FE grade	$2,200	$1,950	$1,750	$1,475	$1,250	$1,100	$1,045
E grade	$2,000	$1,675	$1,500	$1,325	$1,100	$975	$950
EE grade	$2,700	$2,200	$1,875	$1,600	$1,400	$1,250	$1,155
D grade	$2,400	$2,000	$1,750	$1,500	$1,430	$1,375	$1,265
DE grade	$3,200	$2,750	$2,400	$2,000	$1,750	$1,595	$1,485

Grading	100%	98%	95%	90%	80%	70%	60%
C grade	$4,000	$3,400	$2,950	$2,400	$2,000	$1,815	$1,705
CE grade	$6,000	$5,500	$5,000	$4,200	$3,200	$2,200	$1,750
B grade	$5,750	$5,100	$4,600	$3,850	$2,750	$2,300	$1,900
BE grade	$10,000	$9,000	$7,500	$5,500	$3,500	$2,875	$2,310

A grade — auto ejectors standard.

	100%	98%	95%	90%	80%	70%	60%
	$20,000	$15,000	$11,000	$8,000	$5,000	$3,650	$2,530

AA grade — auto ejectors standard.

	100%	98%	95%	90%	80%	70%	60%
	$30,000	$20,000	$15,000	$11,000	$7,750	$5,500	$3,500

Optimus Grade — auto ejectors standard. Extreme rarity precludes accurate percentage pricing.

Thousand Dollar Grade — auto ejectors standard. Extreme rarity precludes accurate percentage pricing.

NITRO SPECIAL DOUBLE BARREL SHOTGUN — 12, 16, 20, or .410 ga., 26-32 in. barrels, various chokes, boxlock, extractors, checkered pistol grip stock. Mfg. 1921-1948.

100%	98%	95%	90%	80%	70%	60%
$400	$375	$350	$300	$250	$225	$200

Single trigger — add $75.

16 ga. — deduct 10%.

20 ga. — add 20%.

.410 ga. — add 100%.

GRADE A DOUBLE BARREL SHOTGUN — 12, 16, 20, or .410 ga., 26-32 in. barrels, various chokes, boxlock, checkered pistol grip stock. Mfg. 1934-1942.

100%	98%	95%	90%	80%	70%	60%
$880	$770	$715	$660	$550	$495	$440

Auto ejectors — add 33%.

Single trigger — add $75.

Beavertail forearm — add $75.

16 ga. — deduct 10%.

20 ga. — add 20%.

.410 — add 100%.

GRADE A SKEET MODEL — same as Grade A, with 26 in. skeet bore barrels, auto ejector, single trigger and beavertail forearm standard.

100%	98%	95%	90%	80%	70%	60%
$1,155	$1,045	$990	$935	$825	$770	$715

16 ga. — deduct 10%.

20 ga. — add 20%.

.410 — add 100%.

SINGLE BARREL TRAP GUN — 12 ga. only, 30 or 32 in. VR barrel, full choke, boxlock, auto ejector, checkered pistol grip stock. Mfg. 1972-1942.

100%	98%	95%	90%	80%	70%	60%
$550	$440	$385	$330	$275	$250	$195

LONG RANGE SINGLE BARREL FIELD — 12, 16, 20, or .410 ga., 26-32 in. barrel, boxlock, extractor, checkered pistol grip stock. Mfg. 1972-1942.

100%	98%	95%	90%	80%	70%	60%
$330	$275	$250	$220	$165	$140	$120

LEFEVER, D.M. & SON

Previous manufacturer located in Bowling Green, OH.

SHOTGUNS

"Uncle Dan" Lefever, founder of Lefever Arms, designed and manufactured the first breech loading double hammerless shotgun made in the U.S. Production started in 1872 and continued in the Syracuse, NY plant until he sold his interest in the Lefever Arms Company during the early 1900's. He then moved to Ohio and started another factory under the name D.M. Lefever & Son. After his death a few years later the Ohio factory was closed, while his old company (Lefever Arms Co.) continued manufacturing Lefever's until being sold to Ithaca Gun Company in the early 20's. From that point, Lefever Arms Co. was a branch of Ithaca and continued to make shotguns until shortly after WWII.

Grading	80%	70%	60%	50%	40%	30%	20%	10%

Total production on D.M. Lefever shotguns between 1901-1904 totaled less than 1,200. Because of their inherent rarity, values listed below show only 10%-80% condition specimens. D.M. Lefever specimens are so rare in 80%+ condition that prices cannot be accurately ascertained.

NEW LEFEVER DOUBLE BARREL SHOTGUN — 12, 16, or 20 ga., any length barrel and choke on order, auto ejectors standard on all grades except O Excelsior, double triggers standard on all except Uncle Dan grade, optional single triggers available, checkered walnut pistol grip or straight stock, grades differ as to engraving, wood, checkering and overall quality. Mfg. 1904-1906.

16 ga. — deduct 10%.

20 ga. — add 20%.

SST — add 10%.

O Excelsior Grade

	$2,365	$1,925	$1,650	$1,430	$1,210	$990	$770	$605

Excelsior Grade w/ejectors

	$2,640	$2,310	$1,925	$1,595	$1,320	$1,045	$825	$660

F Grade, No. 9

	$3,000	$2,640	$2,310	$1,925	$1,595	$1,320	$1,045	$825

G Grade — 10 ga., sidelock, damascus barrels.

	$3,450	$2,950	$2,500	$2,000	$1,650	$1,375	$1,100	$875

E Grade, No. 8

	$4,000	$3,350	$2,875	$2,300	$1,980	$1,650	$1,320	$990

D Grade, No. 7

	$4,400	$4,125	$3,850	$3,300	$2,750	$2,475	$2,200	$1,650

C Grade, No. 6

	$4,950	$4,400	$4,125	$3,850	$3,300	$2,750	$2,420	$2,050

B Grade, No. 5

	$6,600	$5,500	$4,400	$4,125	$3,850	$3,300	$3,000	$2,600

AA Grade, No. 4

	$8,800	$7,700	$6,600	$5,500	$4,400	$3,630	$3,250	$2,850

UNCLE DAN GRADE — too rare to accurately determine values.

SINGLE BARREL TRAP GUN — 12 ga., 26-32 in. full choke, auto ejector, boxlock, checkered pistol grip stock. Mfg. 1904-1906. Too rare to accurately determine values.

LE FORGERON

Manufacturer located in Belgium. Currently imported and distributed by Midwest Gun Sport in Zebulon, NC.

Grading	100%	98%	95%	90%	80%	70%	60%

SHOTGUNS

Prices could differ from values shown below because of the fluctuating U.S. dollar.

BOXLOCK EJECTOR SXS — 20 or 28 ga. only, with or without sideplates, select French walnut stock, choice of engraving patterns (optional), single trigger.

Mfg.'s Sug. Retail	$4,400	$3,975	$3,650	$3,325	$2,995	$2,600	$2,250	$1,900

Add $1,000 for sideplates.

SIDELOCK EJECTOR SXS — 20 or 28 ga. only, select French walnut stock, choice of engraving patterns (optional), rounded action, single trigger.

Mfg.'s Sug. Retail	$11,600	$10,200	$9,250	$8,500	$7,900	$7,100	$6,300	$5,500

RIFLES

MODEL 6020 — 9.3 x 74R cal., boxlock action, beavertail forearm, pistol grip stock.

Mfg.'s Sug. Retail	$4,900	$4,450	$4,025	$3,750	$3,475	$3,100	$2,800	$2,550

Add $700 for sideplates (Model 6040).

Grading	100%	98%	95%	90%	80%	70%	60%

LE FRANCAIS PISTOLS
Manufactured in Francais D'armes Et Cycles, Ste. Etienne, France.

STAFF OFFICER MODEL AUTOMATIC — .25 auto, 2½ in. barrel, blue, fixed sights, rubber grips, no visible cocking piece. Mfg. 1914-disc.

	$275	$230	$200	$165	$140	$115	$80

POLICEMAN MODEL AUTOMATIC — .32 auto, double action, 7 shot, 3½ in. barrel, hinged finned barrel, blue, fixed sights, rubber grips. Mfg. 1950's.

	$850	$800	$700	$575	$435	$350	$275

ARMY MODEL AUTOMATIC — 9mm Browning, 8 shot, 5 in. barrel, blue, fixed sights, checkered walnut grips. Mfg. 1928-1938. Early model with tapered barrel, later model with finned barel.

	$1,400	$1,100	$850	$700	$550	$425	$350

LIBERATOR
Mfg. by the Guide Lamp Corporation (division of General Motors) in 1942 Only.

LIBERATOR PISTOL — .45 ACP cal., single shot, simplistic design and action utilizing nonstrategic WWII materials, mfg. for European resistance movement during WWII (most were issued or air-dropped in Europe), each gun was individually packaged in a paraffin-coated cardboard box which included the gun, a graphics only (no English) instruction sheet, wooden ram rod, and 10 rounds of .45 ACP ammo stored in the guns butt, 4 in. smooth bore barrel, sheet steel stamping mfg. with welds, 1 million mfg. 1942 only.

	$595	$525	$465	$415	$380	$340	$300

Even though 1 million of these pistols were mfg., remaining specimens brought into the U.S. with the above listed accessories are rare since all were delivered overseas. While the Liberator's appearance is crude, remember that the entire production run (1 million) was mfg. and ready for overseas shipment in 13 weeks.

LIEGEOISE D'ARMES
Manufacturer located in Belgium.

Small manufacturer specializing in boxlock shotguns, normally engraved and with ejectors. Prices usually start in the $600+ range.

LIGNOSE (BERGMAN)
Manufacturer located in Suhl, Germany.

EINHAND MODEL 2A POCKET AUTOMATIC — .25 auto, 6 shot, 2 in. barrel, blue, rubber grips, can be cocked by rearward pressure on trigger guard.

	$220	$205	$195	$165	$140	$110	$85

MODEL 3 POCKET AUTOMATIC — similar to 3A, except without one hand cocking trigger guard.

	$220	$205	$195	$165	$140	$110	$85

MODEL 3A POCKET AUTOMATIC — same as 2A, except longer grip, 9 shot capacity.

	$220	$205	$195	$165	$140	$110	$85

MODEL 2 POCKET AUTOMATIC — similar to 2A, without one hand cocking trigger guard.

	$165	$155	$140	$110	$90	$75	$55

LILIPUT
Previous mfg. by August Menz, located in Suhl, Germany.

PISTOLS: SEMI-AUTO

4.25mm CAL. — 4.25mm centerfire Liliput cal. (shoots 12 grain bullet), blue or nickel finish, limited 1920's mfg.

	$550	$495	$425	$385	$340	$300	$280

Grading	100%	98%	95%	90%	80%	70%	60%

6.35mm CAL. — .25 ACP cal., mfg. in large quantities pre-WWII.

	100%	98%	95%	90%	80%	70%	60%
	$165	$155	$140	$110	$90	$75	$55

LJUNGMAN
Previous manufacture by Carl Gustaf, located in Eskilstuna, Sweden.

AG 42 — semi-auto rifle, 6.5mm, 10 shot mag., wood stock, tangent rear sight, hooded front, bayonet lug, designed in 1941. This was the first mass produced, direct gas operated rifle. This weapon was also used by the Egyptian armed forces and was known as the Hakim.

	100%	98%	95%	90%	80%	70%	60%
	$925	$850	$715	$660	$580	$525	$440

LJUTIC INDUSTRIES, INC.
Manufacturer located in Yakima, WA.

Prior to 1960, Ljutic was doing business as Ljutic Gun Co.

TRAP SHOTGUNS

To date approx. 12,500 target shotguns have been manufactured total (all models).
ALL CURRENT LJUTIC SHOTGUNS LISTED BELOW ARE SUBJECT TO 11% FEDERAL EXCISE TAX.

DYNATRAP SINGLE BARREL SHOTGUN — 12 ga., 33 in. barrel, full choke, push button opening, extractor, trap stock.

	100%	98%	95%	90%	80%	70%	60%
	$2,000	$1,800	$1,600	$1,475	$1,300	$1,200	$1,100

Release trigger — add $400.

Custom stock — add $500.

Extra release trigger — add $750.

Extra pull trigger — add $550.

MODEL X-73 SINGLE BARREL — 12 ga., 33 in. full, push button opening, high rib fancy Monte Carlo stock.

	100%	98%	95%	90%	80%	70%	60%
	$2,500	$2,250	$2,000	$1,850	$1,700	$1,600	$1,500

Extra barrel — add $1,995.

Extra pull trigger — add $550.

Extra release trigger — add $750.

MONO GUN SINGLE BARREL — 12 ga., 34 in. barrel, custom choked, custom stocked, pull or release trigger, a "built to customers specifications" trap gun. Also known as Standard Rib or Medium Rib.

Standard or Medium Rib Model

	100%	98%	95%	90%	80%	70%	60%
Mfg.'s Sug. Retail	$3,895	$3,895	$3,200	$2,950	$2,775	$2,500	$2,200	$1,900

Add $100 for medium rib.

Add $200 for screw-in choke tubes.

Approximately 3,000 Mono Guns have been manufactured to date.

LTX (Deluxe Mono Trap) — similar to Mono Gun except has 33 in. medium rib barrel and exhibition wood and checkering.

	100%	98%	95%	90%	80%	70%	60%
Mfg.'s Sug. Retail	$4,995	$4,995	$4,250	$3,750	$3,300	$2,950	$2,500	$2,250

Add $500 for pull trigger.

Add $200 for choke tube option.

Add $400 if with release trigger.

Extra release trigger — add $750.

Extra barrel — add $2,195 for standard rib.

SPACE GUN — 12 ga. only, single barrel, unusual design permits in-line round stock with recoil pad, circular forearm wraps around barrel, high post rib on muzzle half of barrel.

	100%	98%	95%	90%	80%	70%	60%
Mfg.'s Sug. Retail	$3,995	$3,995	$3,200	$2,950	$2,575	$2,200	$2,000	$1,850

BI GUN COMBO — 12 ga. only, supplied with one set of O/U barrels in addition to a high rib single barrel, deluxe wood and checkering, separated barrels on O/U.

	100%	98%	95%	90%	80%	70%	60%
Mfg.'s Sug. Retail	$16,995	$16,950	$13,250	$11,000	$9,450	$8,600	$8,000	$7,450

Grading	100%	98%	95%	90%	80%	70%	60%

BI Gun - O/U Only — supplied with O/U barrels only.

Mfg.'s Sug. Retail $9,995 $9,995 $8,500 $7,700 $6,950 $6,250 $5,600 $4,950

BI MATIC AUTO LOADER — 12 ga., 2 shot, 26-32 in. barrels, low recoil, trap or skeet models available, stock and choking to customer specifications.

$2,000 $1,850 $1,650 $1,500 $1,375 $1,225 $1,075

Extra barrel — add $2,000.

Extra release trigger — add $750.

LLAMA HANDGUNS

Manufacturer located in Gabilondo Y Cia, Victoria, Spain. Currently imported and distributed by Stoeger Industries located in South Hackensack, NJ.

PISTOLS: SEMI-AUTO

MODEL IIIA — .380 auto, 7 shot, 3 in. barrel, adj. sights, blue, plastic grips. Mfg. 1951-disc.

$235 $200 $180 $160 $140 $120 $110

MODEL XA — same as model IIIA, except .32 auto.

$235 $200 $180 $160 $140 $120 $110

MODEL XV — same as model XA, except .22 LR.

$235 $200 $180 $160 $140 $120 $110

MODELS C-IIIA, C-XA, C-XV — same as model C, except engraved chrome.

$305 $260 $230 $205 $180 $155 $140

MODELS BE-IIIA, BE-XA, BE-XV — same as model CE, except engraved, blue.

$290 $250 $220 $195 $165 $140 $125

Deluxe Models, all blue or chrome engraved with simulated pearl grips, add $20.

MODEL G-IIIA — same as IIIA, except gold engraved, simulated pearl grips.

$1,515 $880 $825 $660 $550 $440 $330

MODEL VIII — .38 Super, 9 shot, 5 in. barrel, fixed sights, wood grips. Mfg. 1952-disc.

$305 $255 $220 $195 $180 $165 $140

MODEL IXA — same as model VIII, except .45 ACP.

$305 $255 $220 $195 $180 $165 $140

MODEL XI — same as model IXA, except 9mm.

$305 $255 $220 $195 $180 $165 $140

MODELS C-VIII, C-IXA, C-XI — same as VIII, except satin chrome.

$360 $315 $285 $260 $220 $195 $165

MODELS CE-VIII, CE-IXA, CE-XI

$425 $350 $310 $285 $265 $220 $195

MODELS BE-VIII, BE-IXA, BE-XI — same as model CE, except blue, engraving.

$425 $350 $295 $275 $250 $210 $180

Deluxe Models, same as above, except simulated pearl grips - add $20.

OMNI — .45 ACP or 9mm, double action, all steel construction, 2 sear bars, 3 safeties, 4¼ in. barrel, 7 shot mag. in .45 cal., 13 shot mag. in 9mm, blue finish. Importation disc. 1986.

9mm Caliber

$440 $380 $330 $295 $260 $225 $200

Last Mfg.'s Sug. Retail was $546.

.45 ACP Caliber

$395 $360 $320 $285 $250 $220 $195

Last Mfg.'s Sug. Retail was $500.

Grading	100%	98%	95%	90%	80%	70%	60%

SMALL FRAME MODEL — .22 LR, .32 ACP, or .380 ACP cal., Colt 1911 A1 design, semi-auto, single action, 3¹¹⁄₁₆ in. barrel, 7 shot mag, 23 oz. Also available in satin chrome, optional engraving patterns.

	100%	98%	95%	90%	80%	70%	60%
Mfg.'s Sug. Retail	$325	$250	$200	$155	$130	$120	$110	$100

Add $60 for duo-tone finish (.380 ACP only, new 1991).

Add $74 for chrome finish (not avail. in .32 ACP cal.).

COMPACT FRAME MODEL — 9mm or .45 ACP cal., scaled down variation of the Large Frame Model, 4¼ in. barrel, 7 or 9 shot mag., 34 or 37 oz. New 1986.

Mfg.'s Sug. Retail	$385	$280	$235	$190	$170	$160	$155	$150

Add $114 for satin chrome finish.

Add $90 for duo-tone finish (new in 1990).

LARGE FRAME MODEL — 9mm (disc.), .38 Super (new 1988), or .45 ACP cal., similar to small-frame model, 5⅛ in. barrel, 36 oz., 9 shot mag. in 9mm, 7 shot mag. in .45 ACP. Engraved and deluxe models available also.

Mfg.'s Sug. Retail	$385	$280	$235	$190	$170	$160	$155	$150

Add $114 for satin chrome finish (.45 ACP only).

Add $90 for duo-tone finish (.45 ACP only, new 1991).

MODEL 82 — 9mm Para., double action, 4¼ in. barrel, blue finish, 3-dot sighting system, 15 shot mag., ambidextrous safety, loaded chamber indicator, black polymer grips, 39 oz. New 1988.

Mfg.'s Sug. Retail	$975	$850	$675	$550	$495	$450	$395	$365

MODEL 87 COMPETITION — 9mm Para., competition variation of the Model 82, includes built in ported compensator, oversize magazine and safety release, fixed barrel bushing, bevelled rapid load magazine well, 14 shot mag., extended and serrated trigger guard, and adj. trigger. New 1989.

Mfg.'s Sug. Retail	$1,450	$1,275	$995	$850	$750	$650	$575	$500

REVOLVERS

MARTIAL DOUBLE ACTION REVOLVER — .22 LR, .38 Spl., 6 shot, 4 and 6 in. barrels, target sights, blue, checkered wood grips. Mfg. 1969-1976.

		$220	$200	$180	$165	$140	$120	$100

DELUXE MARTIAL — same as Martial, except finish as follows:

	100%	98%	95%	90%	80%	70%	60%
Satin chrome	$275	$250	$220	$195	$165	$140	$120
Chrome, engraved	$305	$275	$250	$220	$195	$165	$140
Blue, engraved	$290	$265	$235	$210	$180	$155	$120
Gold, engraved	$1,430	$880	$770	$660	$550	$495	$415

COMANCHE I — same as Martial .22, double action. Mfg. 1977-1982.

		$255	$220	$195	$165	$155	$140	$110

COMANCHE II — same as Martial .38, double action. Mfg. 1977-1982 and 1986 in .22 LR and .22 Mag. only.

		$240	$220	$195	$165	$155	$140	$110

Last Mfg.'s Sug. Retail was $272.

COMANCHE III — .22 LR (disc.) or .357 Mag., double action, 6 shot, 4, 6, or 8½ (disc. 1986) in. barrel, blue, adj. sights, checkered walnut grips. Mfg. 1975-present. Before 1977, it was called "Comanche".

Mfg.'s Sug. Retail	$339	$280	$245	$200	$165	$155	$140	$130

Satin Chrome Finish

Mfg.'s Sug. Retail	$395	$330	$270	$230	$205	$185	$170	$160

Gold Finish (disc.)

		$1,100	$880	$825	$660	$550	$440	$330

Grading	100%	98%	95%	90%	80%	70%	60%

SUPER COMANCHE IV — .44 Mag., double action, 6 or 8½ in. vent rib barrel, adj. sights, blue only.

Mfg.'s Sug. Retail	$440	$350	$285	$235	$220	$205	$185	$175

SUPER COMANCHE V — .357 Mag., double action, 6 shot, 4, 6, or 8½ in. vent rib barrel, adj. sights, blue only. Importation disc. 1988.

	$335	$275	$230	$210	$200	$190	$180

Last Mfg.'s Sug. Retail was $414.

LORCIN ENGINEERING CO., INC.
Manufacturer located in Riverside, CA.

L-25 MODEL — .25 ACP, semi-auto single action, 6 shot mag., 2.4 in. barrel, anatomically designed grips to fit hand better, choice of black and gold, chrome and pearl, satin chrome and pearl, or black and pearl finish, 13.5 oz. New 1989.

Mfg.'s Sug. Retail	$80	$70	$60	$50	$45	$40	$35	$35

Add $20 for lightweight frame (Model L—25 LT, new in 1990).

Lady Lorcin — same specifications as the L-25 Model, except is available in chrome, satin chrome, or black exterior finish with pink grips. Values are the same as the L-25 Model. New 1990.

LUGERS WITH VARIATIONS
Note: The Luger section in this book is arranged chronologically by year of manufacture (1900 models to Post-War production), under individual manufacturer headings.

Often times, year of production can be hard to nail down, especially on commercial models. An easier way to initially identify your Luger is to categorize by toggle marking first - then by chamber marking within groups (chronologically for dated chambers). Once you know period of manufacture, simply refer to the appropriate subheading in this section. While some rare variations will be excluded in this generalized overview, it will be very helpful to establish correct, basic knowledge about your particular Luger.

While many recently imported Lugers would make workable shooters, they have in no way lowered prices on 90%+ condition specimens due to normal collector activity in top quality only pistols. Recently imported Lugers should have the importer's name visibly stamped on an exterior surface. Most of these imports are in the 9mm - 4 in. barrel configuration.

Every year more and more reblued, restrawed, regripped, reframed, rebarreled Lugers are sold to unknowing military handgun collectors as rare variations. On any expensive contract variation, careful inspection on all parts must be made before potentially purchasing. If in doubt, secure 2 or 3 additional appraisals/observations from qualified individuals. Lugers are a field in themselves and an experienced Winchester dealer would not be qualified to guestimate the originality of these German handguns.

A final note on Lugers: Original pistols in 98%-100% condition have not been affected by the influx of recent imports as these newly imported guns are usually in 80% and lower condition or have been reblued. Top quality original Lugers have never been in more demand and some dealers are reporting that mint specimens are not as frequently encountered as in the past. Because of this, pristine examples could even exceed values listed below.

REFERENCE GUIDE BY TOGGLE MARKING

DWM TOGGLE IDENTIFICATION

DWM MODELS — mfg. from 1900 to 1930 in Berlin, Germany.

1900 Models — grip safety and "Dished" Toggles, ser. no.'s 1-24,999.

1906 Models — grip safety, many chamber markings, ser. no.'s 25,000-74,000.

1908 Commercial Models — no grip safety, 9mm, ser. no.'s 39,000-74,000.

1908 Military Models — no stock lug.

1914 Military Models — stock lug, dated 1913-1918.

1920 Commercial Models — no grip safety, usually 3⅞ in. barrel. Most common Luger, undated chamber, 7.65 mm or 9mm.

Note: Lugers with 4 inch barrels are most frequently encountered in military and commercial models. 6 in. barrels usually denote "Navy" models. 8 in. barrels usually denote "Artillery" models. Guns with barrels over 8 inches are rare and should be checked carefully for originality.

DWM COMMERCIAL LUGERS

DWM MEANS DEUTSCHE WAFFEN & MUNITIONS FABRIKEN

These are models manufactured from 1900-1923 found in the five digit serial range.

MODEL 1900 — Serial range 1-20,000. Configuration: 4¾ in. x .30 Commercial, American Eagle, Swiss.

MODEL 1900 — Serial range 20,001-21,000. Configuration: 4¾ in. x .30 Bulgarian.

MODEL 1902 — Serial range 21,001-25,000. Configuration: 9 mm x 4 in. "fat barrels" and 11¾ in. x .30 Carbine models, intermixed with 4¾ x .30 American Eagles and Commercials.

MODEL 1906 — Serial range 25,001-39,000. Configuration: Commercial American Eagle, Navy Commercial and Swiss, both 4¾ in. x .30 and 9 mm x 4 in. grip safety models.

MODEL 1908 — Serial range 39,001-71,000. Configuration: First 9 mm x 4 in. without grip safety, M1908 Commercials were interspersed with .30 and 9 mm Eagles, Commercials, Navy Commercials, and a few Carbines and Swiss.

MODEL 1914 — Serial range 71,001-74,000. Configuration: Last pre-WWI Commercial Lugers, made with stock lug, with a few 9mm Commercials mixed in.

MODEL 1923 — Serial range 74,001-89,000. Configuration: Post-WWI Commercials, mostly 3⅞ in. x .30 cal.

MODEL 1923 — Serial range 89,001-91,000. Configuration: The last thousand or so made have "safe" on lever and "loaded" on the extractor, 3⅞ in. x .30 barrels.

ERFURT TOGGLE IDENTIFICATION

ERFURT MODELS

Produced from 1911-1914 and 1916-1918 in Erfurt, Germany. Military Model - Chamber dated 1911-1914 and 1916-1918. Erfurt models exhibit the most proof marks and individual parts numbering. Walnut grips.

SIMSON & CO. TOGGLE IDENTIFICATION

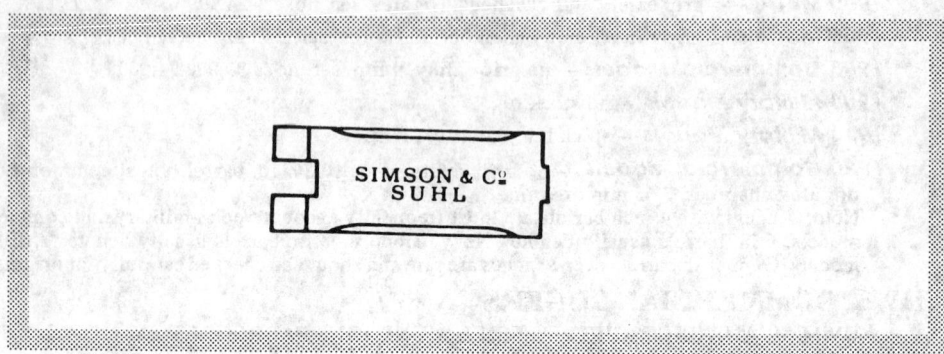

SIMSON & CO.

Manufactured 1922 to 1934 in Suhl, Germany. Most Simson Lugers are military models (9mm - 4 in. barrels). During this 10 year period, Simson supplied the German Army Lugers exclusively. Can be dated 1925-1928. Many reworks of WWI DWM Military Lugers were refurbished by Simson, and can be detected by the Simson "Eagle-over-6" proof on repaired parts. A very few Simsons made in 1934 have just an "S" on the toggle (very rare).

SWISS TOGGLE IDENTIFICATION

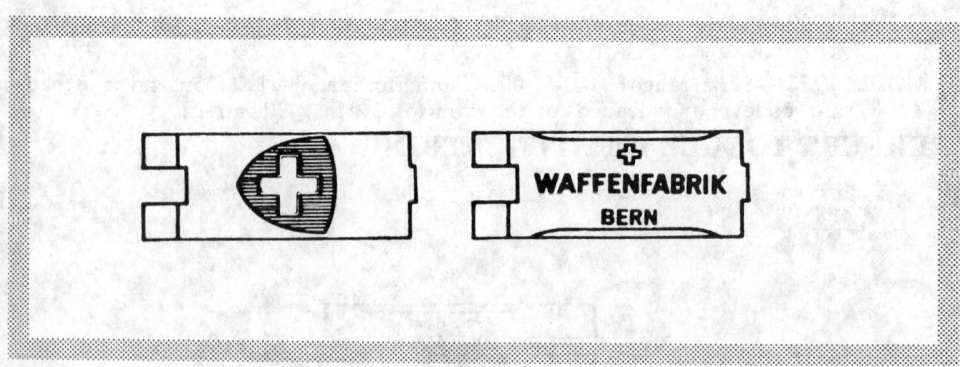

SWISS BERN MODELS

Manufactured 1924 to 1929 by WAFFENFABRIK Bern, Switzerland. Relatively rare - these Swiss models have "improved" changes (flat and curved front grip strap), 4¾ in. barrels, walnut or plastic grips, grip safety. 1929 model has Geneva Cross in shield on front link.

MAUSER TOGGLE IDENTIFICATION

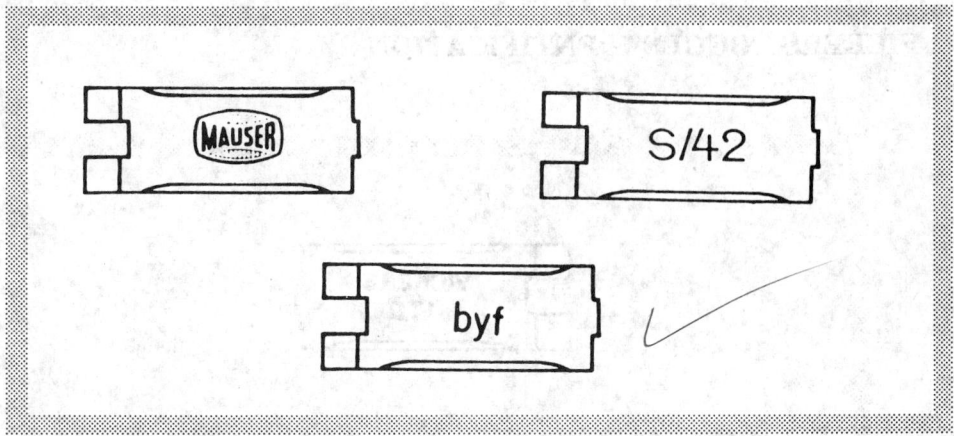

MAUSER VARIATIONS

Manufactured 1934-1942 in Obendorf, Germany. Between 1930 and 1934 Mauser Werke was primarily engaged in reworking older Lugers, since transfer of machinery and personnel to the DWM plant in Berlin was completed in 1931. Mauser "Banner" models were made from 1934 to 1942, many are dated from 1939-1942 on the chamber. S/42 models are MOSTLY MILITARY contract guns manufactured between 1934 and 1940, usually chamber marked. "42" toggle marked guns (Mauser code) were mfg. 1939 and 1940 and are dated. "byf" marked toggles indicate guns made for german military use after 1940 and are more common than other military models. The Mauser Werke trademark also appears on those Lugers made in the 1970's.

KRIEGHOFF TOGGLE IDENTIFICATION

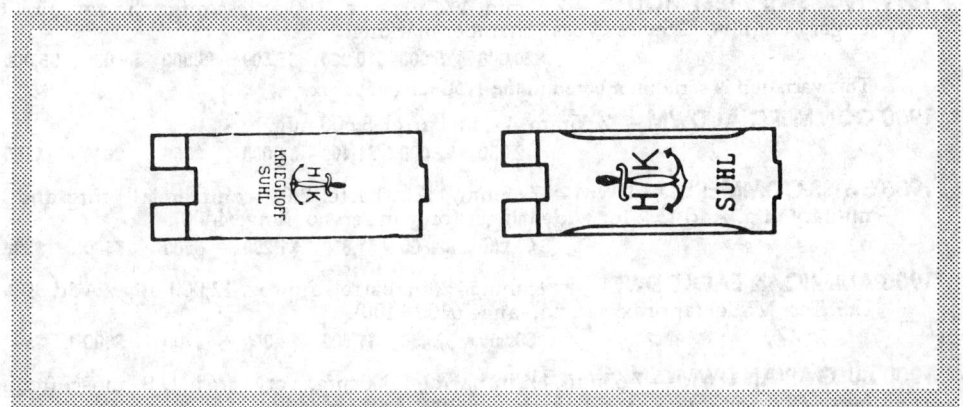

KRIEGHOFF MODELS

Manufactured between 1934-1946 in Suhl, Germany. Early Krieghoffs are side frame inscribed. The German Luftwaffe contracted Kreighoff for military guns in 1935. Early military Krieghoffs have "S" marked chambers, most are chamber dated between 1936 and 1945. Krieghoff Lugers are prized for their quality fit and finish and command higher prices because of their rarity factor.

Grading		100%	98%	95%	90%	80%	70%	60%

VICKERS TOGGLE IDENTIFICATION

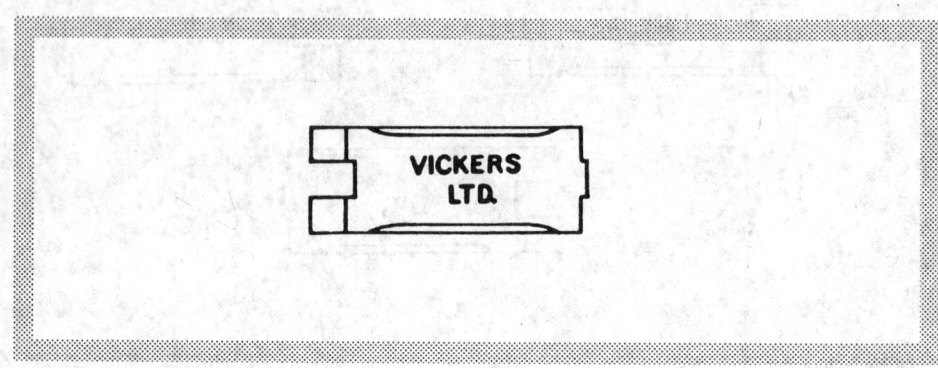

VICKERS

Manufactured by Vickers, Ltd., circa 1921, in England from DWM parts for military contract sale to the Netherlands. Added barrel date is a date of arsenal refinish or refurbishing. Distinguishable by Vickers toggle and "rust" marked safety. Serial range is 1-10,100. Grips can be finely checkered with shallow contour or very coarsely checkered. Configuration is 9mm, 4 in. barrel, and grip safety.

PRE-1900 AND 1900 DWM MANUFACTURED LUGERS

1898/99 BORCHARDT LUGER TRANSITIONAL — 7.65mm, 5 in. barrel, this is perhaps one of the most desirable Lugers, only few mfg. Examples scarce, no reported sales, an original example would command in the 5-figure range.

1899/1900 SWISS TEST MODEL — 7.65mm, 4¾ in. barrel, 100 or less mfg., the very first true Luger. Engraved "Swiss Cross" chamber marking.

		$20,000	$15,000	$10,000	$7,500	$6,500	$6,000	$5,000

This variation is serial numbered in the 1-50 range approx.

1900 COMMERCIAL DWM — 7.65mm, 4¾ in. barrel, 5,500 mfg.

		$2,850	$2,000	$1,400	$1,000	$750	$600	$500

1900 SWISS COMMERCIAL DWM — 7.65mm, 4¾ in. barrel, 2,000 commercially mfg. and 3000 military mfg. Add 15% for wide trigger (only in ser. no. range 4000).

		$3,250	$2,600	$1,800	$1,200	$800	$600	$500

1900 AMERICAN EAGLE DWM — 7.65mm, 4¾ in. barrel, approx. 12,000 mfg. Add 30% for U.S. Test Model (approx. ser. no. range 6200-7400).

		$3,500	$2,450	$1,500	$1,000	$700	$600	$500

1900 BULGARIAN DWM — 7.65mm, 4¾ in. barrel, 1,000 mfg., very rare in U.S., most often seen in the 60% and lower condition, deduct 30% if rebarreled.

		$8,500	$5,500	$4,500	$3,500	$2,700	$2,200	$1,800

LUGERS: 1902-DWM MANUFACTURE

1902 COMMERCIAL — 9mm, 4 in. barrel, serial number range 22,300-22,400 and 22,900-23,500 (500-600 mfg.). Commonly called "Fat Barrel" model.

		$6,500	$5,500	$4,250	$3,400	$3,000	$2,500	$2,000

Grading	100%	98%	95%	90%	80%	70%	60%

1902 AMERICAN EAGLE — 9mm, 4 in. barrel, 600-700 mfg., commonly called the "fat barrel". Same ser. range as 1902 Commercial Model.

	$6,500	$5,500	$4,250	$3,400	$3,000	$2,500	$2,000

1902 CARTRIDGE COUNTER AMERICAN EAGLE — 9mm, only 50 mfg. with the Powell Indication Device; be extremely wary of fakes. ser. no. range 22,401-22,450.

	$16,500	$12,000	$8,500	$6,500	$4,500	$3,850	$3,000

1902 DANZIG TEST — 7.65 or 9mm, blank toggle, 4 in. barrel, Crown D proofs.

	$8,000	$4,600	$3,700	$3,000	$2,200	$1,800	$1,500

1902 CARBINE — 7.65mm, 11¾ in. barrel, approx. 2500 mfg.

Gun w/matching stock	$11,500	$8,000	$6,500	$5,000	$3,500	$3,000	$2,000
Gun only	$6,000	$4,500	$4,000	$3,200	$2,700	$2,200	$1,800

1902/06 TRANSITIONAL CARBINE — 11¾ in. barrel, 50-100 mfg., may have new model frame. Ser. #'s start at 50,000, deduct 20% if no matching stock.

	$12,000	$7,500	$5,500	$4,500	$4,200	$4,000	$3,800

1903 COMMERCIAL — 7.65mm, 4 in. barrel, 50 mfg., extractor marked "charge". Ser. No. Range (25,000-25,050).

	$10,000	$6,500	$6,000	$5,500	$5,000	$3,000	$2,500

LUGERS: 1904-DWM MANUFACTURE

1904 NAVY DWM — 9mm, 6 in. barrel, 1200-1500 mfg., a Transitional Navy.

	$15,000	$11,000	$8,000	$6,000	$4,600	$3,800	$3,200

LUGERS: 1906-DWM MANUFACTURE

1906 COMMERCIAL — 7.65mm, 4¾ in. barrel, "GESICHERT" marked safety, long frame. Approx. 750 mfg.

	$2,400	$1,700	$1,300	$1,100	$900	$750	$600

1906 COMMERCIAL — 9mm, 4 in. barrel, 3500-4000 mfg. Scarcer than 7.65mm.

	$2,500	$1,900	$1,400	$1,000	$800	$650	$500

1906 COMMERCIAL — 7.65mm, 4¾ in. barrel, area under safety polished bright, 5000 mfg.

	$2,200	$1,700	$1,250	$800	$600	$500	$400

1906 AMERICAN EAGLE - 9MM — 9mm, 4 in. barrel, American Eagle stamped in front of breech, 3000 mfg.

	$2,750	$2,250	$1,500	$1,100	$700	$550	$450

1906 AMERICAN EAGLE - 7.65MM — 7.65mm, 4¾ in. barrel, 7,500-8,000 mfg. Add 40% for long frame.

	$2,500	$1,900	$1,400	$750	$600	$475	$400

1906 NAVY COMMERCIAL — 9mm, 6 in. barrel, approx. 2,500 mfg. Add 50% for 7.65 cal. with 6 in. barrel.

	$3,800	$3,000	$2,400	$1,800	$1,600	$1,200	$950

1906 NAVY MILITARY — 9mm, 6 in. barrel, first issue, 19,000 mfg., mostly altered safety marking - "GESICHERT" in lower position. Ser. no. range 1-9,000a.

	$3,500	$2,750	$2,000	$1,600	$1,200	$875	$600

Add 25% for unaltered safety variation.

1906 NAVY MILITARY — 9mm, 6 in. barrel, second issue, 2,000 mfg. Ser. range 9,000a-1,000b.

	$3,250	$2,500	$1,800	$1,600	$1,300	$1,075	$900

Grading	100%	98%	95%	90%	80%	70%	60%

LUGERS: 1906-1918 DWM AND ERFURT MANUFACTURE

Most common variations in good supply within this section in 50% or less condition will approximate the 60% value. This reflects its value as a representative shooter rather than a higher priced collector's gun.

1906 SWISS COMMERCIAL — 7.65 or 9mm, 4¾ in. barrel, less than 1,000 mfg., Swiss "Cross in Sunburst," short frame.

	$2,800	$2,000	$1,750	$1,500	$1,350	$1,200	$1,100

1906 SWISS MILITARY — 7.65mm, 4¾ in. barrel, long frame, Swiss Police has Cross in Shield. Either "Cross in Shield" or "Cross in Sunburst".

	$2,500	$2,000	$1,600	$1,200	$900	$800	$700

1906/23 DUTCH — 9mm, 4 in. barrel, approx. 4,000 mfg., often seen as arsenal rework. Deduct 30% if arsenal reblued and/or rebarreled.

	$1,850	$1,600	$1,400	$900	$750	$600	$525

1906 BRAZILIAN — 7.65mm, 4¾ in. barrel, 5,000 mfg., extremely rare in fine condition.

	$2,350	$1,650	$1,000	$900	$850	$700	$650

1906 BULGARIAN — 7.65mm, 4¾ in. barrel, 1,500 mfg., most rebarrelled to 9mm (deduct 30%).

	$4,800	$4,200	$3,500	$3,500	$2,000	$1,850	$1,450

1908 BULGARIAN — 9mm, 4 in. barrel, DWM on chamber, 10,000 mfg., extremely rare in mint condition.

	$2,400	$1,500	$1,000	$900	$825	$750	$675

1906 PORTUGUESE ARMY — 7.65mm, 4¾ in. barrel, Manuel II crest on chamber. Approx. 5000 mfg.

	$1,450	$1,100	$825	$600	$525	$450	$350

1906 ROYAL PORTUGUESE NAVY — 9mm, 4 in. barrel, Anchor & Crown on chamber, very rare.

	$8,000	$7,000	$6,500	$6,000	$5,000	$4,500	$4,000

1906 REPUBLIC OF PORTUGAL NAVY — Anchor R.P. on chamber, very rare.

	$8,000	$7,000	$6,500	$6,000	$5,000	$4,500	$4,000

1906 RUSSIAN — 9mm, 4 in. barrel, approx. 1,000 mfg., only 6 reported.

	$10,000	$8,500	$7,000	$4,300	$3,200	$2,600	$2,000

1906 VICKERS DUTCH — 9mm, 4 in. barrel, approx. 10,000 assembled by Vickers Ltd. from DWM supplied parts.

	$2,250	$1,700	$1,200	$750	$650	$600	$495

1906 FRENCH COMMERCIAL — 7.65mm, 4¾ in. barrel. Add 30% if cased with accessories.

	$2,400	$2,150	$1,800	$1,575	$1,400	$1,200	$995

1908 COMMERCIAL AND MILITARY — DWM, 9mm, 4 in. barrel, Test/Acceptance Model, approx. 500 mfg. Ser. # range 69,000-71,200.

	$1,200	$1,000	$800	$700	$575	$475	$400

1908 NAVY COMMERCIAL — 9mm, 6 in. barrel. Add 50% for 7.65mm with 6 in. barrel.

	$4,200	$3,500	$2,700	$2,200	$1,800	$1,500	$1,300

1908 DWM MILITARY — 9mm, 4 in. barrel, approx. 95,000 mfg. Each year, undated 1st issue or dated 1910-1913, no stock lug, except for a few late 1913 mfg. guns.

	$1,000	$700	$600	$450	$400	$350	$300

Add 20% for undated or for 1913 date w/stock lug.

Approx. 25,000 1st issue pistols were mfg., 20,000 dated 1910, 15,000 dated 1911, 10,000 dated 1912, 25,000 dated 1913.

Grading	100%	98%	95%	90%	80%	70%	60%

1908 DWM COMMERCIAL — 9mm, 4 in. barrel, no stock lug or hold open, blank chamber.

	$1,000	$800	$600	$450	$400	$350	$300

1911-1914 DATED 1908 ERFURT MILITARY — 9mm, 4 in. barrel (dated 1911-1914), 1911, 1912, and most 1913 chamber dates do not have stock lugs.

	$1,000	$700	$550	$475	$400	$350	$295

Add 20% for 1913 chamber date with stock lug.

1908 NAVY — 9mm, 6 in. barrel, scarce. Ser. # range 1,000b-10,000b, 9,000 manufactured.

	$3,000	$2,500	$1,700	$1,300	$1,100	$950	$800

1908 BOLIVIAN CONTRACT — 9mm, 4 in. barrel.

	$3,600	$3,000	$2,500	$1,700	$1,300	$1,100	$900

1913 COMMERCIAL DWM — 9mm, 4 in. barrel, grip safety and stock lug, horizontal "N" proof mark, 71,000 ser. range, rare.

	$3,000	$2,250	$1,500	$1,050	$900	$780	$700

1914 COMMERCIAL DWM — 9mm, 4 in. barrel, undated, stock lug, horizontal crown-N proofed.

	$1,400	$1,000	$800	$550	$450	$400	$350

1914 NAVY — 9mm, 6 in. barrel, scarce. Dated 1916 and 1917.

	$3,000	$2,500	$2,000	$1,500	$1,050	$950	$800

1916-1918 DATED ERFURT MILITARY — 9mm, 4 in. barrel, dated 1916-1918 - there are no known 1915 chamber dated Erfurt's.

	$895	$700	$550	$450	$400	$350	$300

Add 20% for 1914 date.

Add $75 for original holster in average+ condition.

Add 10% for matching mag.

Add 30% for 2 matching mag.'s.

Note: Date stamped on top frame is date of production; thus dates could be 1914, 1915, 1916, 1917, or 1918. All are Military P.08's, however. 99%-100% Erfurts are rare.

1914 ERFURT ARTILLERY — 9mm, 1914 date is only one seen, 8 in. barrel.

	$1,850	$1,400	$1,150	$850	$675	$550	$425

1913-1918 DATED WWI DWM MILITARY — 9mm, 4 in. barrel. 1913-1918 dated. Most frequently encountered WWI military Luger, stock lug.

	$1,000	$700	$550	$475	$400	$350	$295

Add $75 for original holster in average+ condition.

Add 10% for matching mag.

Add 30% for 2 matching mag.'s.

Note: Date stamped on top frame is date of production; thus dates could be 1914, 1915, 1916, 1917, or 1918. All are Military P.08's, however.

1914-1918 DATED DWM ARTILLERY — 9mm, 8 in. barrel. Dated 1914-1918.

	$1,850	$1,400	$1,000	$800	$600	$500	$400

Add $350 for matching stock.

Add $200 for proper non-matching stock.

Add $200 for original leather holster with shoulder strap.

Add 40% for rare 1914 chamber date.

LUGERS: 1920-1930 DWM

Most common variations in good supply within this section in 50% or less condition will approximate the 60% value. This reflects its value as a representative shooter rather than a higher priced collector's gun.

Grading	100%	98%	95%	90%	80%	70%	60%

1920 DWM OR ERFURT — 9mm, 4 in. barrel, military and police, reworked and issued to police units, many thousand reworked, double date also, 1920 and 1921 dated.

	$850	$700	$540	$450	$375	$300	$250

1920 COMMERCIAL — 7.65mm or 9mm cal., 3⅞-4 in. barrel, many thousand produced.

	$650	$495	$425	$385	$335	$285	$250

Add 25% for 9mm cal.

1920 NAVY COMMERCIAL — 9mm, 6 in. barrel, very rare rework, Navy rear sight. Add 20% for 7.65mm with 6 in. barrel.

	$2,000	$1,550	$1,250	$1,000	$900	$800	$700

1920 COMMERCIAL ARTILLERY — 9mm, 8 in. barrel, very rare rework.

	$1,500	$1,250	$950	$800	$600	$500	$400

While this variation is undoubtedly rarer than the 1914-1918 military Artillery models, it is less desirable.

1920 "LONG BARREL" COMMERCIAL — 7.65mm or 9mm, 10-20 in. barrel, extremely rare.

	$1,850	$1,400	$1,100	$1,000	$750	$655	$600

Watch for fakes - these guns have to be evaluated one at a time.

1920 NAVY CARBINE — 7.65mm, 11¾ in. barrel, long frame (if short frame, be wary of fakes, very few produced). Navy rear sight, no forearm under barrel.

	$2,500	$2,000	$1,600	$1,100	$1,025	$950	$850

1920 CARBINE — 7.65mm, 11¾ in. barrel, very rare.

	100%	98%	95%	90%	80%	70%	60%
Gun only	$5,000	$4,500	$4,000	$3,000	$2,500	$2,000	$1,750
Gun with stock	$8,500	$6,500	$5,000	$4,000	$3,400	$2,900	$2,500

1920 SWISS REWORK — 7.65mm 3⅝-6 in. barrel, several hundred produced.

	$1,650	$1,400	$1,100	$1,000	$750	$655	$600

ABERCROMBIE & FITCH COMMERCIAL — 7.65mm or 9mm, long frame, 4¾ in. barrel, 100 mfg., total for both cal.'s. A few 6 in. barrels - add 30%.

	$4,800	$4,000	$3,500	$3,000	$2,500	$2,100	$1,850

Inspect barrel legend very carefully (as in beware of fakes).

1920/21-DWM — 9mm, 4 in. barrel. Deduct 20% if arsenal reworked.

	$850	$700	$600	$450	$400	$350	$300

1920/23 STOEGER EAGLE — 7.65mm or 9mm, 3⅝-24 in. barrels, less than 1000 mfg., made by DWM for Stoeger, sold in USA, longer barrel models have higher value.

	100%	98%	95%	90%	80%	70%	60%
3⅞ - 6 in. barrels	$4,000	$2,750	$1,450	$1,200	$1,050	$950	$825
8 in. barrel	$6,500	$4,500	$2,300	$2,000	$1,650	$1,200	$995

Add 50% for Mauser mfg.

Be extremely careful when examining the frame markings on this variation as there are many fakes in the marketplace.

1923 DWM COMMERCIAL — 7.65mm, 3⅝ in. barrel, 14,000 mfg. (Ser No. Range 74,000-89,000).

	$750	$650	$525	$435	$375	$330	$275

1923 DWM "SAFE AND LOADED" COMMERCIAL — "safe and loaded" marked on frame and ejector, 7.65mm, 3⅞ in. barrel, safety and extractor marked in English, 2000 mfg. (Ser. No. Range 89,000-91,000).

	$1,250	$1,000	$850	$600	$500	$420	$350

1923 FINNISH LUGER — 7.65mm, approx. 5,000-7,000 units made for Finnish military contract (Army and Navy), marked "SA" surrounded by a rectangle, most have been recently imported into the U.S.

	$1,000	$700	$550	$450	$400	$350	$300

Grading	100%	98%	95%	90%	80%	70%	60%

LUGERS: KRIEGHOFF

1923 DWM/KRIEGHOFF COMMERCIAL — 7.65mm x 3⅞ in. or 9mm x 4 in. barrels, few made, reworked by Krieghoff, chamber dated 1921 or unmarked, most in "in" range, Kreighoff stamped on back-frame. Be wary of fakes.

	$1,950	$1,425	$1,210	$1,100	$880	$770	$660

DWM/KRIEGHOFF COMMERCIAL — 7.65mm or 9mm, 4 in. barrel, a few hundred made, side frame marked Kreighoff. Be wary of fakes.

	$2,800	$2,400	$2,000	$1,650	$1,300	$1,000	$800

KRIEGHOFF COMMERCIAL SIDE FRAME — 7.65mm or 9mm, 4 or 6 in. barrel, 1500 mfg., 1000 with side frame marked, and 500 without. "P" prefix ser. no.'s. Add 30% for side frame marked 7.65mm.

	$3,000	$1,975	$1,775	$1,200	$995	$800	$700

KRIEGHOFF S CODE EARLY — 9mm, 4 in. barrel, 1800 mfg., German Luftwaffe. Has fat walnut grips, "H-K Suhl" toggle.

	$2,400	$1,700	$1,450	$1,200	$995	$895	$775

KRIEGHOFF S CODE MID SERIES — 9mm, 4 in. barrel, 500-700 mfg., Luftwaffe, ser. no. range 1600-2500, fine-checkered plastic grips.

	$3,000	$1,975	$1,775	$1,200	$995	$800	$700

KRIEGHOFF S CODE LATE — 9mm, 4 in. barrel, 1800 mfg., Luftwaffe, ser. no. range 2300-4200.

	$2,250	$1,650	$1,225	$950	$750	$600	$500

KRIEGHOFF 36 DATE — 9mm, 4 in. barrel, 500-700 made, Luftwaffe military, 2 digit date, coarse checkered plastic grips.

	$3,250	$2,650	$2,000	$1,650	$1,300	$1,000	$800

KRIEGHOFF 1936-1945 DATED — 9mm, 4 in. barrel, approx. 9,000 mfg., 4 digit chamber date, 1936, 1937 and 1940 most common; 1938 and 1941 through 1945 dates command 70-200% premiums. 1945 is extremely rare - add 500%.

	$2,750	$2,250	$1,825	$1,550	$1,320	$1,225	$1,100

POST-WAR KRIEGHOFF TYPE I — 9mm, 4 in. barrel, 150 mfg. for occupation forces, H-K marked toggle link.

	$1,800	$1,550	$1,300	$1,200	$1,100	$995	$875

POST-WAR KRIEGHOFF TYPE II — 9mm, 4 in. barrel, 150 mfg., unmarked toggle link, many parts proofed "Eagle-over-2".

	$1,450	$1,200	$1,100	$1,000	$900	$800	$775

POST-WAR KRIEGHOFF COMMERCIAL — 7.65mm, 4 in. barrel, 100-200 mfg., unmarked toggle, many parts proofed "Eagle-over-2".

	$1,450	$1,200	$1,100	$1,000	$900	$800	$775

LUGERS: MAUSER

Most common variations in good supply within this section in 50% or less condition will approximate the 60% value. This reflects its value as a representative shooter rather than a higher priced collector's gun.

1935-06 PORTUGUESE GNR — 7.65mm, 4¾ in. barrel, 564 mfg., GNR on chamber, Portuguese marked safety and extractor.

	$2,200	$1,500	$1,200	$900	$700	$650	$425

1934/06 MAUSER SWISS COMMERCIAL — 7.65mm, 4¾ in. barrel, a few hundred produced, cross in sunburst or blank chamber, grip safety.

	$4,800	$2,800	$2,400	$2,000	$1,500	$1,250	$850

Grading	100%	98%	95%	90%	80%	70%	60%

1934 MAUSER BANNER COMMERCIAL — 7.65mm or 9mm, 4 in. barrel, hundreds produced, unmarked chamber, "v" suffix to ser. no. Add 15% for "Kal. 7.65" barrel marked.

	$2,800	$1,800	$1,600	$1,400	$1,150	$950	$725

S/42 K DATE — mfg. 1934 only, 9mm, 4 in. barrel, approx. 10,000 mfg., military. Add 50% for "large eagle over M Navy" proofed.

	$3,000	$1,850	$1,400	$900	$800	$700	$550

S/42 G DATE — mfg. 1935 only, 9mm, 4 in. barrel, many thousand produced. Add 20% for Navy markings.

	$1,200	$700	$595	$500	$450	$400	$375

S/42 DATED CHAMBER — 9mm, 4 in. barrel, many thousands produced, "S/42" stamped rear toggle, chamber dated 1936-1939. One of the most frequently encountered WWII military Lugers.

	$895	$725	$625	$500	$425	$375	$350

Add $75 for original holster in average+ condition.
Add 10% for matching mag.
Add 25% for 2 matching mag.'s.
Add 20% for Navy markings.
The last regular production S/42 Models were mfg. approx. April of 1939.

MAUSER PERSIAN (IRANIAN) CONTRACT — 9mm, 4 and 8 in. barrels, 1,000 — 8 in. mfg., and 1,000 — 4 in. mfg., Farsi numerals.

	100%	98%	95%	90%	80%	70%	60%
4 in. barrel	$5,000	$3,750	$3,200	$2,750	$2,250	$2,000	$1,750
Artillery (8 in.)	$2,850	$2,400	$2,000	$1,800	$1,650	$1,475	$1,200

This variation became less desirable after the U.S. hostage situation occurred in Iran.

1936-1942 DATED MAUSER BANNER — 9mm, 4 in. barrel, over 1,000 mfg., commercial and contract sales. No sear safety, often have strawed small parts.

	$1,800	$1,350	$1,050	$800	$700	$600	$500

MAUSER BANNER DUTCH CONTRACT — 9mm, 4 in. barrel, 1,000 mfg., safety marked "Rust". Dated 1936-1940. 10% premium on 1936-1838 dates.

	$1,695	$1,300	$750	$695	$600	$500	$400

MAUSER BANNER SWEDISH CONTRACT — 275 mfg. in 9mm, 4¾ in. barrels, dated 1938, 25 mfg. in 9mm, dated 1939, and 30 mfg. in 7.65mm, dated 1939. Add 15% for 7.65mm.

	$2,000	$1,750	$1,300	$750	$695	$600	$500

CODE "S/42" COMMERCIAL CONTRACT — 9mm, 4 in. barrel, a few hundred produced, dated 1938. Commercial proof marks only.

	$1,600	$1,200	$975	$750	$650	$550	$500

CODE "42" — 9mm, 4 in. barrels, dated 1939-1940, rear toggle marked "42". One of the most frequently encountered WWII military Lugers. Add 40% for Navy markings.

	$900	$650	$495	$375	$325	$275	$250

Add $75 for original holster in average+ condition.

MAUSER BANNER POLICE — approx. 30 thousand mfg., dated 1939-1942, police contract, have sear safeties, blued small parts. A few observed dated 1938 — add 30%.

	$1,650	$1,250	$875	$600	$500	$400	$350

CODE "41-42" — 9mm, 4 in. barrel, 2-digit date, approx. 7,000 mfg. in January of 1941, "41" dated chamber, "42" code, most 42 dates are reworks.

	$1,250	$1,000	$750	$500	$425	$375	$350

Add $75 for original holster in average+ condition.

Grading	100%	98%	95%	90%	80%	70%	60%

CODE "byf" — 9mm, 4 in. barrel, thousands made, chamber dated 41 and 42. Rear toggle is stamped "byf", standard magazine was "fxo" marked and had an un-numbered plastic bottom. One of the most frequently encountered WWII military Lugers.

	$1,000	$850	$700	$500	$425	$375	$350

Add 10% for original black bakelite grips.

Add $75 for original holster in average+ condition.

Code "byf" Lugers with black bakelite grips are referred to as the "Black Widow" variation.

AUSTRIAN BUNDES HEER — 9mm, 4 in. barrel, several hundred produced, Austrian Federal Army, no serial letter suffix-same ser. placement as KU. Rarely encountered in mint condition.

	$1,600	$1,400	$1,000	$950	$825	$750	$650

MAUSER 1934 CODE BYF, S/42 AND 42 KU — 3,500 mfg. Post-1942 Luftwaffe subcontract.

	$2,000	$1,700	$1,300	$950	$825	$750	$650

LUGER: REWORKS

DEATH'S HEAD REWORK — 9mm, 4 in. barrel, very rare, possible early SS unit issue. Watch for fakes.

	$1,000	$800	$700	$600	$500	$450	$400

SIMSON REWORK — 9mm, 4 in. barrel, DWM toggles, Simpson Eagle proofs on reworked parts.

	$775	$650	$550	$450	$375	$325	$295

DOUBLE DATED DWM/ERFERT — 9mm, 4 in. barrel, very scarce. 1920 over 1910-1918 chamber dates. Often with sear safety and mag. safety remnant. Add 30% for intact mag. safety.

	$650	$550	$420	$300	$275	$250	$225

KONZENTRATION LUGER REWORK — 9mm, 4 in. barrel, 200-300 marked "KI 1933" and issued to guards working in the first concentration camps - most went to Dachau.

	$1,350	$1,100	$850	$600	$475	$400	$350

LUGERS: SIMSON

SIMSON & COMPANY — 7.65mm or 9mm, 3⅞ or 4 in. barrel, military and limited commercial sales, many thousands produced, but rarely found.

	$1,800	$1,300	$800	$650	$500	$450	$375

SIMSON GRIP SAFETY — 9mm, 3⅞ in. barrel, very rare, production unknown. Be wary of fakes.

	$2,450	$1,800	$1,600	$1,200	$975	$675	$475

SIMSON MILITARY DATED — 9mm, 4 in. barrel, 2,000 mfg., dated 1925-1928.

	$2,500	$2,000	$1,500	$1,000	$800	$675	$550

This model is most commonly encountered with a 1925 chamber date.

SIMSON S CODE — 9mm, 4 in. barrel, less than 1,000 mfg. Rare.

	$2,800	$1,600	$1,200	$975	$675	$550	$475

LUGERS: SWISS BERN

1906 BERN — 7.65mm, 4¾ in. barrel, "Waffenfabrik Bern" on toggle, Swiss military, bordered checkered walnut grips, exactly 17,874 mfg.

	$2,250	$1,750	$1,400	$1,000	$800	$600	$500

1929 SWISS BERN — 7.65mm, 4¾ in. barrel, 29,857 mfg., many machining changes to simplify production, straight front grip strap, P prefix designates commercial model, brown or black plastic grips.

	$1,950	$1,500	$1,100	$900	$800	$600	$500

Grading	100%	98%	95%	90%	80%	70%	60%

LUGERS: KDF, INTERARMS, STOEGER, & RECENT IMPORTATION

Note: These Lugers have been manufactured by Mauser Werke in Oberndorf, W. Germany in the 1970's and again recently. Earlier importation was by Interarms of Alexandria, VA (and so marked on these guns). Currently, Mauser Werke 7.65 and 9mm Lugers are available in various configurations - including the Karabiner (Carbine), Cartridge Counter, and special order variations (4 in. standard barrel and Artillery).

Currently, only Precision Imports, Inc. located in San Antonio, TX, is importing the Mauser manufactured P.08 (on a special order basis only). Prices start at $3,210 for the standard model. Engraved or limited production models typically start at approx. $7,200 and go up according to the amount of workmanship needed to complete the fabrication.

Prices below for 100% condition Lugers assume N.I.B. status. If without box and accessories, deduct 10-15%.

Prices below reflect the recent devaluation of the U.S. dollar against some foreign currencies. While the manufacturer's suggested retails have gone up considerably, prices for used specimens (98% or less original condition) have not increased proportionately, and in some cases, have changed very little.

MAUSER P.O8 — imported by KDF in various configurations including engraved models. Prices start in the $3,210 range (4 in. barrel) and vary substantially depending on model, type(s) of finish, and amount of engraving.

INTERARMS MAUSER P.O8 — 7.65 and 9mm, 4 or 6 in. barrel, fully-contoured front grip strap.

	100%	98%	95%	90%	80%	70%	60%
	$750	$600	$450	$400	$375	$350	$300

INTERARMS "SWISS-STYLE" MAUSER EAGLE — 9mm or 7.65mm, "straight" front grip strap, American eagle logo on top of frame. Add 10% for 6 in. barrel in 9mm.

	100%	98%	95%	90%	80%	70%	60%
	$625	$550	$475	$400	$375	$350	$325

STOEGER .22 CAL. LUGER — .22 LR cal., toggle action, all steel construction, 4½ in. barrel, 10 shot mag. capacity, previously mfg. in the U.S. until 1985.

	100%	98%	95%	90%	80%	70%	60%
	$200	$175	$150	$135	$125	$100	$85

Last Mfg.'s Sug. Retail was $200.

"1 of 1,000" — 1,000 mfg. in 1984-85, includes wooden box and extra mag.

	100%	98%	95%
	$295	$225	$175

NEW MODEL CARBINE WITH STOCK — 9mm Para., authentic reproduction of the original Luger Carbine complete with matching stock, accessories, and case.

Mfg.'s Sug. Retail	$7,500	$4,800	$3,250	$2,500

Manufacture has been disc. but limited quanities are still available through Interarms.

CARTRIDGE COUNTER — left grip is slotted and contains a numbered metal strip. Introduced 1983.

Mfg.'s Sug. Retail	$3,900	$2,600	$1,950	$1,350

Manufacture has been disc. but limited quanities are still available through Interarms.

COMMEMORATIVE BULGARIAN — 100 available on U.S. market.

	100%	98%	95%	90%	80%	70%	60%
	$1,800	$1,600	$1,400	$1,000	$750	$600	$500

COMMEMORATIVE RUSSIAN — 100 available on U.S. market.

	100%	98%	95%	90%	80%	70%	60%
	$1,800	$1,600	$1,400	$1,000	$750	$600	$500

Matched pair of each

	$4,000	$3,175	$1,950

MAUSER SPORT PARABELLUM — 10 each, 7.65mm and 9mm, imported target barrel and adj. sights.

	$2,500	$2,000	$1,250

Grading	100%	98%	95%	90%	80%	70%	60%

MAUSER SPORT PARABELLUM
Consecutive pair — 7.65mm or 9mm.

$4,250 $3,175 $1,950

LUGERS: SPECIAL INTEREST

SPANDAU LUGER — 200 mfg. as prototype in 1918, 10 known. Controversial. Prices vary substantially on this "variation" and are not predictable.

1945 CHAMBER DATED KREIGHOFF — 100 mfg., 3 known.

$10,000 $7,500 $5,500 $4,000 $2,900 $2,400 $1,850

1900 SWISS LUGER NO. 33 — pre-production, 1898-1900.

MO4/05 G.L. BABY LUGER — 7.65mm or 9 mm, 3¼ in. barrel, G.L. proofed, hand-made under Georg Luger's supervision, two known to exist. Made with shortened barrel, mag., and grip frame.

BABY LUGER 1925/26 — Prototype, 380/32 ACP, 4 mfg., only 1 known is .380. Only Luger documented by the manufacturer.

VONO REWORK — 7.54mm or 9mm, 4 in. barrel, commercial, rework by W.P. Von Nordheim, extremely rare variation.

$1,500 $1,275 $1,050 $900 $800 $700 $600

1900 DWM CARBINE — 7.65mm, 11¾ in. barrel, 100 mfg., only one known to exist. Characterized by "Ski slope" sight on rear toggle.

1907 U.S. ARMY TEST TRIAL — .45 cal., at least three mfg., three known to exist.

KRIEGHOFF GRIP SAFETY — 9mm, 4 in. barrel, extremely rare, test trial gun.

$3,800 $3,500 $3,000

1906/29 SWISS SPECIAL ASSEMBLY — 7.65mm, 4¾ in. barrel.

$2,200 $1,650 $1,200

1929 SWISS 9MM PROTOTYPE — 4¾ in. barrel.

$4,200 $3,000 $2,100

CONVERSIONS: JOHN MARTZ — John Martz of CA has converted P.38's and WWI or WWII Lugers into various configurations since 1968. These conversions are known for their quality workmanship and functional accuracy. Below is a generalized listing of variations he has fabricated and their values to date with production totals.

.380 ACP Baby Luger — 6 mfg. (disc.).

$3,500 $3,000 $2,400

7.65mm Baby Luger — 10 mfg.

$4,500 $3,750 $3,000

9mm Baby Luger — 105 mfg., 2 to 3 in. barrel.

$2,500 $2,000 $1,500

Navy Model — .45 ACP, 4 or 8 in. barrel, adj. rear Navy sight, 27 mfg.

$4,500 $3,750 $3,000

Add 10% for Navy Model with 100-200 meter rear sight. @SN = Navy Model Ltd. Edition — .38 Super, 6 in. barrel, adj. rear Navy sight, 10 mfg. (disc.).

$5,000 $3,950 $3,250

Subtract 10% for fixed rear sight (standard model with 4 in. barrel).

Standard Model — .38 Super, 4 to 8 in. barrel, fixed sight, 2 mfg.

$4,500 $3,750 $3,000

Target Luger — .22 Mag., 6 or 8 in. barrel, fixed sight, 5 mfg. (disc.).

$5,000 $3,950 $3,250

Grading	100%	98%	95%	90%	80%	70%	60%

Luger Carbines (with shoulder stock)
.22 Magnum cal.

	$6,000	$4,950	$4,250				

11 to 16 in. barrel, adj. rear sight, 5 mfg. (disc.).
7.65mm Para. cal. - 12 in. barrel

	$5,000	$3,950	$3,250				

Adj. rear sight, 4 mfg.
7.65mm Para. cal. - 18 in. barrel

	$5,000	$3,950	$3,250				

Adj. rear sight, 1 mfg.
9mm Para. - 12 in. barrel

	$5,000	$3,950	$3,250				

12 in. barrel, adj. rear sight, 20 mfg.
9mm Para. - 16 in. barrel

	$5,000	$3,950	$3,250				

12 in. barrel, adj. rear sight, 65 mfg.
.38 Super

	$5,500	$4,400	$3,000				

16 in. barrel, adj. rear sight, 1 mfg.

Baby P.38 — 9mm Para., shortened barrel (3 in.), grip, and 7-shot mag., 43 mfg.

	$2,500	$2,000	$1,500				

P.38 - .38 Super — .38 Super, 4 or 6 in. barrel, 3 mfg.

	$4,500	$3,250	$2,500				

P.38 - .45 ACP — .45 ACP, 4 to 8 in. barrel, 14 mfg.

	$4,500	$3,250	$2,500				

P.38 Carbine — 9mm, 16 in. barrel, adj. rear sight, 26 mfg.

	$5,000	$3,950	$3,250				

Experimental Lugers — experimental pistols have been made in .40 S&W, .41 AE, and .357 Mag. Most have 8 in. barrels (except for .40 S&W cal.). Extreme rarity (and not for sale status) precludes accurate price evaluation.

LUGERS: ACCESSORIES

.22 CALIBER CONVERSION UNITS:

ERMA — (POSTWAR-GREEN CARD BOARD BOX)

	$350	$320	$295	$275	$250	$225	$200

ERMA-PREWAR IN WOODEN BOX — Pre-war in wooden box - deduct 20% for mismatched. Add 20% for Nazi Navy property numbered.

	$650	$600	$550	$550	$430	$400	$360

DETACHABLE STOCKS:

ARTILLERY TYPE FLAT BOARD

	$250	$200	$165	$135	$120	$110	$100

NAVAL-TYPE FLAT BOARD

	$750	$625	$550	$500	$450	$410	$350

CARBINE CONTOURED

	$1,200	$1,000	$900	$850	$750	$700	$600

HOLLOW ARTILLERY HOLSTER TYPE — hollow wood broomhandle type-very rare (watch for fakes).

	$6,000	$5,500	$5,000	$4,500	$4,000	$3,500	$3,000

IDEAL TELESCOPING WITH GRIPS — mfg. U.S. by Ideal Corp.

	$1,200	$750	$675	$625	$575	$530	$500

Grading	100%	98%	95%	90%	80%	70%	60%

"SNAIL" DRUM MAGAZINE:

1ST ISSUE

	$550	$500	$450				

2ND ISSUE

	$450	$400	$350				

LOADING TOOL OR UNLOADING TOOL (2 TYPES)

	$425	$375	$350				

ARTILLERY HOLSTER RIG, COMPLETE

	$450	$400	$350				

If shoulder strap is missing — deduct 20%.

NAVAL HOLSTER RIG, COMPLETE

	$1,500	$1,200	$900	$750	$700	$650	$600

LUNA
Germany.

SINGLE SHOT

SINGLE SHOT TARGET RIFLE — falling block action, .22 LR and .22 Hornet, 20 in. barrel, adj. sights, target type stocks, pre-WWII.

	$990	$880	$800	$690	$605	$550	$495

MODEL 200 FREE PISTOL — .22 LR, 11 in. barrel, blue, target sights, checkered target grips, pre-WWII.

	$1,100	$990	$855	$770	$660	$605	$525

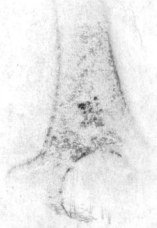

NOTES

MAC (MILITARY ARMAMENT CORP.)
Please refer to the Ingram section in this text.

MAS
Manufacture D'Armes St. Etienne (MAS) located in France.

MODEL 1935S — 7.65mm French Long cal., $4\frac{1}{3}$ in. barrel, enamel finish, Colt Gov.'t Model locking system, 26 oz.

$325	$295	$260	$225	$195	$170	$150

MBA GYROJET
Previous manufacturer (1966-1969) located in San Ramon, CA.

Grading	100%	98%	95%	90%	80%	70%	60%

MARK I GYROJET PISTOL — 12 or 13mm (no cartridge case), uses spin-stabilized rocket projectiles that accelerate to 1,250 FPS in .12 seconds, 2 in. (rare) or 5 in. barrel, 6-shot semi-auto action drives rocket projectile (primer activated) into fixed firing pin, smooth walnut grips, black or antique nickel finish, 13 or 16 oz. Not particularly accurate.

$550	$495	$450	$400	$360	$330	$300

The rocket ammunition for this model is rare and reports of $20+/round are not uncommon. Plans are underway to manufacture a new batch of rocket ammunition in 1991.

Mark I Presentation Model — cased with 10 dummy rounds and bronze medal honoring rocket pioneer Robert H. Goddard.

$2,250	$1,600	$995

MARK I CARBINE — 13mm, same action as Mark I pistol, full stock with pistol grip extension, 18 in. barrel, nickel finish, $4\frac{1}{2}$ lbs. Limited mfg.

$1,050	$850	$750	$650	$595	$550	$500

MK ARMS INC.
Manufacturer located in Irvine, CA.

MK 760 — 9mm Para., semi-auto, paramilitary design carbine configuration, steel frame, 16 in. shrouded barrel, fires from closed bolt, 14, 24, or 36 shot mag., parkerized finish, folding metal stock, fixed sights. Mfg. in CA since 1983.

Mfg.'s Sug. Retail							
$575	$525	$450	$375	$340	$310	$280	$250

MKE
Manufacturer located in Ankara, Turkey. Currently distributed by Mandall Shooting Supplies, Inc., located in Scottsdale, AZ.

KIRIKKALE DOUBLE ACTION AUTOMATIC — 7.65mm (disc.), or .380 ACP, 7 shot, blue, fixed sights, checkered plastic grips, this is a close copy of Walther's PP and the Turkish Army's standard service pistol. Disc. 1987.

$365	$295	$240	$215	$185	$170	$155

Last Mfg.'s Sug. Retail was $395.

This model was disc. by the Turkish Government in 1987.

Grading	100%	98%	95%	90%	80%	70%	60%

M.O.A. CORPORATION
Manufacturer located in Brookville, OH.

PISTOLS

MAXIMUM — available in 26 standard chamberings between .22 Rimfire and .44 Mag., addition custom calibers are also available upon special order, single shot lever action pistol, falling block action, chromoly (disc. 1990), Armoloy (new 1991), or stainless steel (new 1991) receiver, 8¾ (new 1989), 10¾, or 14 in. interchangeable barrel, transfer bar safety, adj. open sights, walnut grips and forearm. New 1986.

Mfg.'s Sug. Retail	$534	$470	$385	$340	$310	$280	$250	$225

Add $52 for scope mount.

Add $32 for stainless steel receiver.

Add $50 for stainless steel barrel.

Add $149 per extra steel barrel.

Add $202 per extra stainless steel barrel.

Barrels must be fitted to individual receivers at the factory initially. Afterwards, they can be changed by the customer with the spanner wrench (included with extra barrels).

Carbine Model — similar to Maximum, except has 18 in. barrel. Mfg. 1986-87 only. This model will be reintroduced shortly.

$495	$430	$365	$330	$300	$275	$250

Last Mfg.'s Sug. Retail was $575.

MAGNUM RESEARCH, INC.
Manufactured by Israel Military Industries. Exclusively imported and distributed by Magnum Research, Inc., in Minneapolis, MN.

In addition to the models listed below, Magnum Research can also provide a variety of special order options through their custom shop. Prices can be obtained by contacting Magnum Research directly.

Magnum Research also offers a Collector's Edition Presentation Series. Special models include a Gold Edition (serial numbered 1-100), a Silver Edition (serial numbered 101-500), and a Bronze Edition (serial numbered 501-1,000). Each pistol from this series is supplied with a walnut presentation case, 2 sided medallion, and certificate of authenticity. Prices are available upon request by contacting Magnum Research directly.

PISTOLS: DESERT EAGLE SERIES

MARK VII .357 MAG. DESERT EAGLE — .357 Mag., gas operated, semi-auto pistol, 6, 10, or 14 in. barrel lengths, steel (58.3 oz.) or alloy (47.8 oz.) frame, adaptable to .44 Mag with optional kit, 9 shot mag. (8 for .44 Mag.). New 1983.

Mfg.'s Sug. Retail	$789	$685	$575	$500	$455	$415	$380	$355

Add $149 for choice of finishes.

Add approx. $150 for 10 or 14 in. barrel.

Subtract $160 for Mark I alloy frame model.

Add $495 for .357 Mag. to .44 Mag. conversion kit (6 in. barrel).

Add $685 for .357 Mag. to .44 Mag. conversion kit (10 or 14 in. barrel).

Choice of finishes includes nickel, polished blue, or hardchrome (matte, polished, or brushed).

Whitetail Special .357 Mag. 14 in. barrel, includes scope mount target walnut grips, and Desert Eagle premiums. New in 1990.

Mfg.'s Sug. Retail	$1,088	$925	$750	$650	$550	$450	$400	$375

Add $50 for stainless steel frame.

Stainless Steel .357 Mag. — similar to .357 Mag. Desert Eagle, except has stainless steel frame, 58.3 oz. New 1987.

Mfg.'s Sug. Retail	$839	$750	$650	$550

Add approx. $150 for 10 or 14 in. barrel.

Grading	100%	98%	95%	90%	80%	70%	60%

MARK VII .41 MAG. DESERT EAGLE — .41 Mag., similar to .357 Desert Eagle, 6 in. barrel only, 8 shot mag., steel (62.8 oz.) or alloy (52.3 oz.) frame. New late 1988.

Mfg.'s Sug. Retail	$799	$690	$575	$510	$460	$415	$390	$365

Subtract $60 for Mark I alloy frame model.

Add $139 for choice of finishes.

Choice of finishes includes nickel, polished blue, or hardchrome (matte, polished, or brushed).

Stainless Steel .41 Mag. — similar to .41 Mag. Desert Eagle, except has stainless steel frame, 58.3 oz. New late 1988.

Mfg.'s Sug. Retail	$849	$755	$650	$550

MARK VII .44 MAG. DESERT EAGLE — .44 Mag., similar to .357 Desert Eagle, 8 shot mag., steel (62.8 oz.) or alloy (52.3 oz.) frame. Introduced late 1986.

Mfg.'s Sug. Retail	$839	$750	$650	$550	$500	$465	$420	$390

Add $139 for choice of finishes.

Add approx. $150 for 10 or 14 in. barrel.

Subtract $90 for Mark I alloy frame model.

Add $475 for .44 Mag. to .357 Mag. conversion kit (6 in. barrel).

Add $675 for .44 Mag. to .357 Mag. conversion kit (14 in. barrel only).

Add $395 for .44 Mag. to .41 Mag. conversion kit (6 in. barrel) - disc.

Choice of finishes includes nickel, polished blue, or hardchrome (matte, polished, or brushed).

Stainless Steel .44 Mag. — similar to .44 Mag. Desert Eagle, except has stainless steel frame, 58.3 oz. New 1987.

Mfg.'s Sug. Retail	$889	$780	$675	$550

Add approx. $130 for 10 or 14 in. barrel.

HUNTER EDITION MARK VII — .357 or .44 Mag., 6 in. barrel with extra 14 in. hunting barrel, includes Simmons 2X x 20 compact scope, scope mount, cherry hardwood presentation case. New late 1987.

Mfg.'s Sug. Retail	$1,239	$1,125	$925	$800	$675	$550	$475	$425

Add $62 for .44 Mag. cal.

Add $159 for choice of finishes.

Choice of finishes includes nickel, polished blue, or hardchrome (matte, polished, or brushed).

MARK VII .50 MAG. DESERT EAGLE — .50 AE cal., 6 in. barrel only, steel only, 7-shot mag., 72.4 oz. New 1991.

Mfg.'s Sug. Retail	$1,189	$1,075	$925	$800	$675	$550	$475	$425

This new cartridge utilizes the same rim dimensions as the .45 ACP. Currently there is a choice between a 300 and 350 grain (both are available in either soft or hollow point) bullet. The .50 Mag. Action Express cal. has 60% more stopping power than the .44 Mag., with a minimal increase in felt recoil.

PISTOLS: SINGLE SHOT

MODEL SSP-91 — .22 LR, .22 Win. Mag., .22 Hornet, .22-250, .223, .243, .30-30, 30-06, .308, 6mmBR, 7mm-08, 7mmBR, .35 Rem., .357 Mag., .358 Win., .44 Mag., or .444 Marlin cal., circular rear breech action, quick change 14 in. barrels (drilled and tapped), synthetic stock with pistol grip. New in 1991.

Mfg.'s Sug. Retail	$299	$270	$230	$195	$170	$150	$135	$120

This model is designed and manufactured by Ordnance Technology, Inc.

MALIN, F.E.

Manufacturer located in England. Currently sold on a limited basis by Cape Horn Outfitters located in Charlotte, NC. Previously imported by Saxon Arms, Inc. located in Clearwater, FL.

Grading	100%	98%	95%	90%	80%	70%	60%

SHOTGUNS: OVER-AND-UNDER AND SIDE-BY-SIDE

BOXLOCK — made to individual order, choice of game scene engraving, Anson & Deeley boxlock actions, select European hybrid walnut, double triggers, leather cased, current manufacture. Prices start at $3,750 and each shotgun is priced per individual special order.

SIDELOCK — made to individual order, choice of game scene engraving, H&H sidelock action, select European hybrid walnut, double triggers, leather cased, current manufacture. Prices start at $5,000 and each shotgun is priced per individual special order.

MAMBA

Previously mfg. by Viper Mfg. Co. (a division of Sandock Austral Boksburg) located in South Africa.

AUTO PISTOL — 9mm Para., less than 80 imported into the U.S.

Rarity factor precludes accurate pricing.

MANDALL SHOOTING SUPPLIES, INC.

Importer/distributor/retailer located in Scottsdale, AZ.

Mandall Shooting Supplies distributes/imports various firearms including pistols, revolvers, rifles, shotguns, as well as other models. Most of these firearms can be located under their individual trademark headings and include Bretton, Britarms, Cabanas, Erma-Werke, FAS, Gaucher, Hammerli, Domino, Korth, Krico rifles, Mandall private label shotguns, Sig, Sig-Hammerli, Tanner rifles, Techni-Mec, Zanardini, and A. Zoli shotguns and rifles.

Due to the fluctuation of the U.S. dollar against the currencies of other countries, the above trademarks can change price during the course of a year. For this reason, Mandall Shooting Supplies, Inc. should be contacted directly for current pricing and special order questions.

COACH SHOTGUN — 12, 16, or 20 ga., SxS sidelock shotgun with either external hammers or hammerless, 18, 26, 28, or 30 in. barrels, DT, sling swivels, mfg. in Spain.

	100%	98%	95%	90%	80%	70%	60%
Mfg.'s Sug. Retail	$500	465	$390	$365	$330	$300	$270	$240

MANNLICHER SCHOENAUER SPORTING RIFLES

Manufactured by Steyr, Daimler, Puch, in Austria from 1850's - present. Please refer to Steyr-Mannlicher in this text for current manufactured rifles.

PRE-WAR

MODEL 1903 CARBINE — bolt action, 6.5 x 53mm, 5 shot, 17.7 in. barrel, rotary mag., two leaf rear sight, double set trigger, full length stock.

	100%	98%	95%	90%	80%	70%	60%
	$1,050	$875	$770	$550	$470	$385	$330

MODEL 1905 CARBINE — same as 1903, except 9 x 56mm, 19.7 in. barrel.

	100%	98%	95%	90%	80%	70%	60%
	$1,200	$950	$825	$660	$580	$495	$415

MODEL 1908 CARBINE — same as 1905, except 7 x 57mm and 8 x 56mm.

	100%	98%	95%	90%	80%	70%	60%
	$1,050	$875	$770	$550	$470	$385	$330

MODEL 1910 CARBINE — same as 1905, except 9.5 x 57mm.

	100%	98%	95%	90%	80%	70%	60%
	$1,050	$875	$770	$550	$470	$385	$330

MODEL 1924 CARBINE — same as 1905, except .30-06.

	100%	98%	95%	90%	80%	70%	60%
	$1,200	$1,050	$990	$770	$715	$605	$525

Grading	100%	98%	95%	90%	80%	70%	60%

HIGH VELOCITY SPORTING RIFLE — bolt action, 7 x 64 Brenneke, .30-06, 8 x 60 Mag., 9.3 x 62mm, 10.75 x 68mm, 23.6 in. barrel, 3 leaf sight, half stock.

	$1,320	$1,100	$825	$660	$580	$495	$415

Takedown Model

	$2,200	$1,980	$1,650	$1,320	$880	$715	$635

RIFLES: POST-WAR

MODEL 1950 — .257 Roberts, .270 Win., and .30-06 cal.'s, bolt action, 5 shot rotary mag., 24 in. barrel, low bolt handle, half length stock, ebony forearm. Mfg. 1950-1952.

MODEL 1950 CARBINE — same as 1950, except 20 in. barrel, full length stock. Mfg. 1950-1952.

	$1,000	$875	$770	$675	$580	$525	$440

MODEL 1950 CARBINE 6.5 — same as 1950 Carbine, except 6.5 x 54mm cal., 18½ in. barrel. Mfg. 1950-1952.

	$1,000	$875	$770	$675	$580	$525	$440

IMPROVED MODEL 1952 — same specifications as 1950, except swept back bolt handle. Mfg. 1952-1956.

	$795	$725	$650	$575	$500	$460	$420

IMPROVED MODEL 1952 CARBINE — .257 Roberts, .270 Win., 7 x 57mm, or .30-06 cal., swept back handle, otherwise same as 1950 Carbine.

	$1,000	$875	$770	$675	$580	$525	$440

IMPROVED MODEL 1952 6.5 CARBINE — same as 1952 Carbine, except 6.5mm, 18½ in. barrel. Mfg. 1952-1956.

	$1,000	$875	$770	$675	$580	$525	$440

MODEL 1956 RIFLE — similar to 1952, except .243 and .30-06 cal.'s, new high comb. stock design, 22 in. barrel, half length stock. Mfg. 1956-1960.

	$795	$725	$650	$575	$500	$460	$420

MODEL 1956 CARBINE — similar to 1956 Rifle, except .243, 6.5 x 53mm, .257 Roberts, .270, 7mm, .30-06, or .308 cal., 20 in. barrel, full length stock. Mfg. 1956-1960.

	$1,000	$875	$770	$675	$580	$525	$440

MODEL 1961 MCA RIFLE — same as Model 1956, except Monte Carlo stock. Mfg. 1961-1971.

	$795	$725	$650	$575	$500	$460	$420

MODEL 1961 MCA CARBINE — same as 1956 Carbine, except Monte Carlo stock. Mfg. 1961-1971.

	$1,000	$875	$770	$675	$580	$525	$440

MODEL M72 L/M RIFLE — M72 bolt action, .243, .308, .270, .30-06, 7 x 57, or 7 x 64 cal., 23 in. barrel, single or double set triggers. Mfg. 1972-1980.

	$795	$725	$650	$575	$500	$460	$420

RIFLES: CURRENT MANUFACTURE

Current production guns are now called Steyr-Mannlicher models and can be located under this trademark in the S section.

MANUFRANCE

Manufacturer located in St. Etienne, France since 1902.

Manufrance currently manufactures many models in both rifles and shotguns that are not being imported in the U.S. at this time. These models are not covered in this book.

AUTO SHOTGUN — 12 ga., 26, 28, or 30 in. imp. cyl., mod. and full, 2¾ or 3 in. chamber, gas operated, walnut stock, black matte receiver, vent rib.

	$330	$305	$290	$275	$255	$240	$220

Grading	100%	98%	95%	90%	80%	70%	60%

FALCOR — O/U, 12 ga., vent rib, 26 in. imp. cyl. and mod., 28 in. mod. and full, SST, auto ejector, chrome lined barrel, walnut checkered stock.

	100%	98%	95%	90%	80%	70%	60%
	$715	$665	$635	$605	$550	$495	$470

MANURHIN

Manufacturer located in Mulhouse, France by Matra Manurhin Defense. Currently imported and distributed exclusively in the U.S. by Atlantic Business Organizations, Inc., located in New York, NY. Previously imported (1984-86) directly by Matra-Manurhin International, Inc., located in Fort Lauderdale, FL.

Manurhin in France has been manufacturing models PP, PPK, and PPK/S since 1952. Previously, they were imported by Interarms out of Alexandria, VA. In 1984, Manurhin imported their new models directly and they were marked Manurhin on the left front slide assembly. This differs from the previous Walther stamped guns. Also, no Interarms logo appears on the right side.

HANDGUNS: CURRENT IMPORTATION

All models listed below are imported exclusively through Atlantic Business Organizations, Inc., located in New York, NY.

MODEL PP — .380 ACP cal., 3⅞ in. barrel, 7 shot mag. blue only, 24 oz., all steel construction, double action with positive steel block safety. Imported resumed 1988.

Mfg.'s Sug. Retail	$415	$360	$320	$275	$230	$205	$185	$170

MODEL PPK/S — .380 ACP cal., 3¼ in. barrel, 7 shot mag. blue only, all steel construction, double action with positive steel block safety, 23 oz. Importation resumed 1988.

Mfg.'s Sug. Retail	$415	$360	$320	$275	$230	$205	$185	$170

MODEL 73 DEFENSE REVOLVER — .357 Mag./.38 Special, 6 shot, 2½, 3, or 4 in. barrel, checkered wood stocks, mfg. to precise tolerances, 31-33½ oz. Importation began 1988.

Mfg.'s Sug. Retail	$1,122	$1,000	$850	$725	$600	$500	$425	$350

MODEL 73 GENDARMERIE — .357 Mag./.38 Special, 6 shot, similar to Model 73 Defense except has adj. sighting components and also is offered in 5¼, 6, or 8 in. barrel lengths. Manufactured for police requirements. Importation began 1988.

Mfg.'s Sug. Retail	$1,220	$1,075	$900	$750	$625	$525	$450	$375

MODEL 73 SPORT — .357 Mag./.38 Special, 6 shot, sport shooting feaures include minimized hammer stroke, micrometer rear sight, and free release trigger with fitted adj. Importation began 1988.

Mfg.'s Sug. Retail	$1,220	$1,075	$900	$750	$625	$525	$450	$375

MODEL 73 CONVERTIBLE — includes choice of .22 LR/.38 Special or .22 LR/.32 cal. cylinders and barrels (5¾ in. for .38 Spl. and 6 in. for .22 LR/.32). Importation began 1988.

Mfg.'s Sug. Retail	$1,847	$1,675	$1,325	$1,125	$950	$800	$700	$600

3 Cylinder Model 73 Convertible — similar to Model 73 Convertible except includes 3 calibers (.22 LR, .32, and .38 Special). Importation began 1988.

Mfg.'s Sug. Retail	$2,230	$1,950	$1,700	$1,375	$1,150	$975	$850	$750

MODEL 73 SILHOUETTE — .22 LR or .357 Mag. cal., Silhouette variation with fully adj. rear sight and either 10 (.22 LR) or 10¾ (.357 Mag.) in. heavy barrel with full shroud, contoured wooden target grips, approx. 4 lbs. Importation began 1988.

Mfg.'s Sug. Retail	$1,189	$1,050	$875	$735	$615	$525	$450	$375

Add $13 for .357 Mag. cal.

PISTOLS: PREVIOUS IMPORTATION

P-1 — 9mm, similar to W. German P-38, double action, 5 in. barrel.

	100%	98%	95%	90%	80%	70%	60%
	$440	$380	$325	$275	$230	$205	$185

Grading	100%	98%	95%	90%	80%	70%	60%

MODEL P4 — 9mm, P.38 variation issued to the French Police when in Berlin during post-WWII.

	$495	$440	$380	$325	$275	$230	$200

MODEL PP — .22 LR, .32 ACP, or .380 ACP cal., 3⅞ in. barrel, 10 shot mag.-.22 LR, 8 shot mag.-.32 ACP, 7 shot mag.-.380 ACP, blue only, all steel construction, double action with positive steel block safety, 24 oz. Add $10 for .22 LR cal., $46 for durgarde finish. Imported 1984-86.

	$360	$320	$275	$230	$205	$185	$170

Last Mfg.'s Sug. Retail was $419.

Collector Model — blue finish, special engraving. Imported 1986 only.

	$465	$415	$350

Last Mfg.'s Sug. Retail was $529.

Presentation Model — blue finish, special ornamentation. Imported 1986 only.

	$720	$650	$500

Last Mfg.'s Sug. Retail was $819.

Also available with various engraving options in either blue, nickel, or gold finish - prices range from $222 - $540.

MODEL PPK/S — .22 LR, .32 ACP, or .380 ACP cal., 3¼ in. barrel, 10 shot mag.-.22 LR, 8 shot mag.-.32 ACP, 7 shot mag.-.380 ACP, blue only, all steel construction, double action with positive steel block safety, 23 oz. Add $10 for .22 LR cal. Imported 1984-86.

	$360	$320	$275	$230	$205	$185	$170

Last Mfg.'s Sug. Retail was $419.

PPK/S Durgarde — same as above, only with bonded brushed chrome finish. Add $14 for .22 LR cal.

	$410	$365	$325	$290	$265	$250	$240

Last Mfg.'s Sug. Retail was $465.

Collector Model — blue finish, special engraving. Imported 1986 only.

	$465	$415	$350

Last Mfg.'s Sug. Retail was $529.

Presentation Model — blue finish, special ornamentation. Imported 1986 only.

	$720	$650	$500

Last Mfg.'s Sug. Retail was $819.

Also available with various engraving options in either blue, nickel, or gold finish - prices range from $222 - $540.

PP SPORT — .22 LR cal. only, double action, 6.1 or 8.1 in. barrel, blue finish only, precision adj. sights, contoured plastic grips with thumb rest, 25 oz. New Manurhin design for 1985. Imported 1984-86.

	$545	$485	$430	$385	$325	$290	$270

Last Mfg.'s Sug. Retail was $635.

PP Sport-C — same as PP Sport, except has single action with softened trigger.

	$540	$475	$415	$370	$310	$280	$260

Last Mfg.'s Sug. Retail was $635.

MARATHON PRODUCTS, INC.

Previously manufactured by Santa Barbara Armaments exclusively for Marathon Products, Inc. Most of the below listed models were also available in kit form but are not shown in this book.

.22 FIRST SHOT — .22 cal., single shot bolt action, 16½ in. barrel, hardwood stock, open sights, 31 in. total length, 3.8 lbs. Mfg. 1985-87.

	$55	$45	$40	$35	$35	$30	$30

Last Mfg.'s Sug. Retail was $60.

Grading	100%	98%	95%	90%	80%	70%	60%

.22 Super Shot — same as First Shot, except with 24 in. barrel and regular dimension stock. Mfg. 1985-87.

	$55	$45	$40	$35	$35	$30	$30

Last Mfg.'s Sug. Retail was $60.

.22 Hot Shot Pistol — .22 LR only, bolt action, single shot, fixed sights, 14¾ in. barrel, hardwood stock with target grip configuration. Mfg. 1986-87.

	$55	$45	$40	$35	$35	$30	$30

Last Mfg.'s Sug. Retail was $60.

CENTERFIRE MODEL — .243, .270 Win., 7 x 57, 7mm Rem. Mag., .30-06, .300 Win. Mag., or .308 Mag. cal., Mauser type bolt action, 5 shot fixed box mag., 24 in. barrel, select walnut with recoil pad, adj. trigger, open sights, 7.9 lbs. Available 1985-86 only.

	$295	$240	$215	$195	$180	$170	$160

Last Mfg.'s Sug. Retail was $320.

MARBLE'S GAME GETTER

Manufacturer located in Lansing, MI.

In addition to axes and compasses, Marble's also manufactured their Game Getter O/U combination gun from approx. 1907 to the late 1920's. During this period of production, the gun underwent quite a few changes including sights (an aperture sight mounted on the rear backstrap was standard until changed to a top frame sight), different configuration folding metal stock, and other changes.

GAME GETTER MODEL — .22 S, L, or LR cal., upper rifled barrel over choice of .44-40 Game Getter/.410 ga. (2 in.) or .410 ga. (2½ in.) smooth bore lower barrel, choice of 12, 15, or 18 in. separated barrels, folding steel skeleton attached stock, pivoting hammer striker mechanically selects upper or lower barrel, tip-up barrels are opened by pulling trigger guard back, gutta percha or walnut stocks, approx. 3½ lbs.

	$795	$725	$650	$600	$550	$520	$480

Add $100 for original leather holster in good condition.

Above values assume 18 in. barrels or correct registration on 12 or 15 in. models. Those 12 or 15 in. barreled Game Getter's not registered during the 1968 BATF ammnesty program are not legally transferable today. If not a legal configuration, values will drop considerably.

The lower barrel of this model was capable of shooting .410 ga. 2 in. paper or brass shotshells, .410 ga. 2½ in. paper shotshell (standard configuration), and .410 or .44 cal. round ball cartridges.

MARGOLIN

Russian Target Pistol manufacturer located in the U.S.S.R.

TARGET MODEL — .22 LR, semi-auto, manufactured to precise tolerances, used by some members of the Russian shooting team, basically individually made to shooters specifications, seldomly encountered in the U.S.A., while rare, desirablity to date has been limited, current mfg.

Margolin pistols are typically priced in the $475-$750 range, depending on features and assuming 95%+ original condition. While currently imported Chinese copies are considerably less expensive, they do not have the quality (or accuracy) of the Russian Margolins.

MARLIN FIREARMS COMPANY

Previous manufacturer 1870-1969 located in New Haven, CT. Manufacturer 1969-present located in North Haven, CT.

Research is underway to include the Ballard rifles — forerunners of the Marlin, mfg. 1875-1881 by John M. Marlin and 1881-1891 by Marlin Fiearms Company. Approx. total is 40,000 rifles.

Grading	100%	98%	95%	90%	80%	70%	60%

PISTOLS: DERRINGERS AND REVOLVERS

Research is underway to gather more information on the variety of derringers and revolvers that Marlin mfg. between 1863-1901. While many of these variations sell in the $150-$250 range (average condition), rarer specimens with 90% original condition will be priced higher.

RIFLES: ANTIQUE MANUFACTURE

Values below are for standard models only without special order features.

MODEL 1881 LEVER ACTION — .32-40, .38-55, .40-60, .45-70, or .45-85 cal., tube mag., 28 in. octagonal barrel standard, top ejection, blued finish with case hardened hammer, lever, and butt plate. First models (pre ser. no. 600) are rare, add 200-300% premium. Approx. 20,000 mfg. between 1881-1892.

	$2,150	$1,850	$1,350	$1,000	$900	$800	$700

This model came in 2 or 3 frame thicknesses for various caibers

MODEL 1888 LEVER ACTION — .32-20, .38-40, or .44-40 cal., 24 in. octagonal barrel most frequently encountered, top ejection, blued finish with case hardened hammer, lever, and butt plate, short throw lever action principle. Approx. 4,800 mfg. between 1888-1889. Ser. range approx. 19,560 - 27,850.

	$2,400	$1,950	$1,650	$1,350	$1,100	$950	$750

MODEL 1889 LEVER ACTION — .25-20 (very rare), .32-20, .38-40, or .44-40 cal., 24 in. octagonal barrel most frequently encountered, side ejection with solid top frame, blued finish with case hardened hammer, lever, and butt plate, short throw lever action principle. Approx. 55,000 mfg. between 1889-1899. Ser. range approx. 25,000-100,000. Also available as Carbine (15 in. barrel-add 50%) or Musket (30 in. barrel-add 300-500%, very rare).

	$875	$775	$675	$575	$500	$400	$395

MODEL 1891 LEVER ACTION — .22 Rimfire and .32 Rimfire/Centerfire, 24 in. octagonal barrel most often encountered, blued finish with case hardened hammer, lever, and butt plate, sear safety system on lever action. Approx. 18,650 mfg. between 1891-1897. Ser. No. range is approx. 37,500-118,000.

	$1,600	$1,300	$950	$775	$600	$475	$400

MODEL 1892 LEVER ACTION — .22 S, L, or LR, .32 S or L, 16, 24, 26, or 28 in. barrel, tubular mag., open sight, plain straight stock. Mfg. 1892-1916.

	$1,050	$900	$750	$650	$550	$475	$395

.22 cal.'s will bring a premium in this model.

MODEL 1893 LEVER ACTION — .25-36 Marlin, .30-30, .32 Spl., .32-40, or .38-55 cal., 28-32 in. round or octagonal barrels, 10 shot tube mag., straight or pistol grip stock. Mfg. 1893-1936. Musket model also mfg. - 30 in. barrel and military style forearm.

	$1,100	$950	$850	$750	$600	$500	$375

MODEL 1893 CARBINE — .30-30 or .32 Spl. cal., 20 in. round barrel, 7 shot tube mag., straight or pistol grip stock. Mfg. 1893-1936.

	1,100	$950	$850	$750	$600	$500	$375

MODEL 1894 LEVER ACTION — .25-20, .32-20, .38-40, or .44-40 cal., 10 shot tube mag., 24 in. round or octagon barrel, straight or pistol grip stock. Mfg. 1894-1934.

	1,100	$950	$850	$750	$600	$500	$375

MODEL 1895 LEVER ACTION — .33 WCF, .38-56, .40-65, .40-70, .40-82, or .45-70 cal., 9 shot tube mag., 24 in. round or octagon barrel standard, other lengths were available, open sights, plain straight or pistol grip stock. Mfg. 1895-1915.

	$1,450	$1,175	$900	$750	$600	$500	$395

MODEL 1897 LEVER ACTION — .22 S, L, or LR, tube mag., 16, 24, 26, or 28 in. barrel, takedown, open sights, plain straight or pistol grip stock. Mfg. 1897-1922.

	$2,500	$1,450	$995	$795	$650	$450	$295

Grading	100%	98%	95%	90%	80%	70%	60%

RIFLES: MODERN PRODUCTION

Year of manufacture can be determined from 1946-1968 by the following letter prefix: 1946-C, 1947-D, 1948-E, 1949-F, 1950-G, 1951-H, 1952-J, 1953-K, 1954-L, 1955-M, 1956-N, 1957-P, 1958-R, 1959-S, 1960-T, 1961-U, 1962-V, 1963-W, 1964-Y,Z, 1965-AA, 1966-AB, 1967-AC, 1968-AD.

MODEL 18 SLIDE ACTION — .22 S, L, or LR, tube mag., 20 in. round or octagon barrel, open sight, exposed hammer, plain straight grip stock. Mfg. 1906-1909.

	$330	$250	$195	$140	$110	$100	$85

MODEL 20 SLIDE ACTION — .22 S, L, or LR, 24 in. octagon barrel, open sight, exposed hammer, takedown, plain straight grip stock. Mfg. 1907-1922.

	$330	$250	$195	$140	$110	$100	$85

MODEL 25 SLIDE ACTION — .22 Short, tube mag., 23 in. barrel, open sight, exposed hammer, takedown, plain straight grip stock. Mfg. 1909-1910.

	$360	$275	$220	$165	$140	$120	$95

MODEL 27 SLIDE ACTION — .25-20 or .32-20 cal., ⅔ tube mag., 7 shot, 24 in. octagon barrel, open sight, plain straight grip stock. Mfg. 1910-1916.

	$330	$250	$195	$140	$110	$100	$85

MODEL 27S — same as 27, with round or octagonal barrel.

	$330	$250	$195	$140	$110	$100	$85

MODEL 29 SLIDE ACTION — similar to 20, with 23 in. round barrel, ½ tube mag. Mfg. 1913-1916.

	$330	$250	$195	$140	$110	$100	$85

MODEL 32 SLIDE ACTION — .22 S, L, or LR, ⅔ tube mag., 24 in. octagon barrel, open sight, plain pistol grip stock, hammerless. Mfg. 1914-1915.

	$330	$250	$195	$140	$110	$100	$85

MODEL 1936 CARBINE LEVER ACTION — .30-30 or .32 Spl. cal., 6 shot, 20 in. barrel, tubular mag., open sights, pistol grip stock, barrel band. Mfg. 1936-1948.

	$275	$220	$195	$165	$140	$110	$95

MODEL 36A — same as 36 Carbine, with 24 in. barrel, ⅔ tube mag.

	$275	$220	$195	$165	$140	$110	$95

MODEL 36A-DL — same as 36A, with deluxe checkered stock, sling and swivels.

	$305	$250	$220	$195	$165	$140	$110

MODEL 37 SLIDE ACTION — same as 29, with 24 in. barrel, full length tube mag. Mfg. 1913-1916.

	$330	$250	$195	$140	$110	$100	$85

MODEL 38 SLIDE ACTION — .22 S, L, or LR, ⅔ tube mag., 24 in. octagon barrel, open sights, hammerless, takedown, plain pistol grip stock. Mfg. 1920-1930.

	$330	$250	$195	$140	$110	$100	$85

MODEL 39 LEVER ACTION — .22 S, L, or LR, tube mag., 24 in. octagon barrel, open sight, takedown, case hardened receiver, plain pistol grip stock. Mfg. 1922-1947.

	$750	$650	$500	$400	$300	$200	$150

MODEL 39A — same as 39, with blued or color case hardened receiver, round barrel. Mfg. 1938-1960.

	$225	$175	$150	$130	$110	$95	$85

GOLDEN 39A — same as 39A, with gold plated trigger, sling swivels. Mfg. 1960-1983.

	$170	$155	$140	$110	$95	$85	$70

Grading	100%	98%	95%	90%	80%	70%	60%

MODEL 39A "MOUNTIE" — straight grip stock, slim forearm, otherwise same as 39A. Mfg. 1953-1960.

	$165	$150	$130	$110	$90	$75	$70

90TH ANNIVERSARY 39A — same as 39A, with chrome barrel and action, select checkered walnut stock, carved squirrel on side of butt stock. Mfg. 500 in 1960.

	$550	$385	$330	$275	$220	$165	$110

90TH ANNIVERSARY MODEL 90 CARBINE — same as 90th Anniversary 39A, except 20 in. barrel, straight stock. Mfg. 500 in 1960.

	$550	$385	$330	$275	$220	$165	$110

MODEL 39A-DL — same as 90th Anniversary, with blue barrel and action, regular production. Mfg. 1960-1963.

	$250	$195	$165	$140	$110	$100	$85

MODEL 39A OCTAGON — same as Golden 39A, with octagon barrel, no pistol grip cap. Mfg. 1972-73.

	$195	$165	$150	$130	$110	$90	$85

MODEL 39M "MOUNTIE" CARBINE — same as "Mountie", with 20 in. barrel. Mfg. 1954-1960.

	$165	$150	$130	$110	$90	$75	$70

MODEL 39 CARBINE — same as 39M, with light barrel, ¾ tube mag. Mfg. 1963-1967.

	$165	$150	$130	$110	$90	$75	$70

MODEL 39D — same as 39M, with pistol grip stock. Mfg. 1970-1974.

	$175	$155	$140	$120	$100	$85	$70

MODEL 39AS — .22 LR cal., current production model, lever action, tube mag., 19 shot, 24 in. barrel, walnut stock, open sights, gold trigger, takedown, 6½ lbs.

Mfg.'s Sug. Retail	$376	$285	$200	$160	$145	$130	$110	$100

This model was previously designated the Model 39A. In 1988, the Model 39AS became the standard production model and included a rebounding hammer and hammer block safety.

MODEL 39TDS — .22 LR cal., carbine variation of the Model 39AS, 16½ in. barrel with open sights, 5¼ lbs. New 1988.

Mfg.'s Sug. Retail	$419	$325	$230	$175	$155	$135	$120	$110

MODEL 39M — carbine version of Model 39A, 20 in. lightweight barrel, 16 shot tube mag., squared finger lever, 6 lbs. Disc. 1987.

	$225	$180	$155	$145	$130	$110	$100

Last Mfg.'s Sug. Retail was $304.

MODEL 39M OCTAGON — same as 39M, with octagon barrel. Mfg. 1973.

	$225	$175	$165	$150	$135	$115	$105

MODEL GOLDEN 39M CARBINE — same as 39M, with gold plated trigger, sling swivels. Mfg. 1960-1982.

	$170	$155	$140	$110	$95	$85	$70

MODEL 39 CENTURY LTD — Marlin Centennial 1870-1970 Commemorative, 20 in. octagon barrel, select walnut straight stock, brass forearm cap and butt plate, name plate in butt. 35,388 mfg. 1970.

	$275	$195	$180	$155	$140	$110	$95

MODEL 39A ARTICLE II — NRA Centennial Commemorative 1871-1971, "Right to Bear Arms" medallion in receiver, 24 in. octagon barrel, fancy pistol grip stock, brass butt plate and forearm cap. Mfg. 6,244 1971.

	$265	$180	$165	$150	$120	$100	$85

Grading	100%	98%	95%	90%	80%	70%	60%

MODEL 39M ARTICLE II CARBINE — same as 39A Article II, with 20 in. barrel, straight grip stock. Mfg. 3,824.

	100%	98%	95%	90%	80%	70%	60%
	$275	$195	$175	$160	$130	$110	$95

MODEL 56 — same as 57, with clip mag. Mfg. 1955-1964.

	$130	$100	$85	$70	$55	$40	$30

MODEL 57 LEVERMATIC — .22 S, L, or LR, tube mag., 22 in. barrel, open sight, Monte Carlo pistol grip stock. Mfg. 1959-1965.

	$130	$100	$85	$70	$55	$40	$30

MODEL 57M — Mag. version of Model 57 Levermatic.

	$195	$180	$165	$155	$140	$120	$110

MODEL 62 LEVERMATIC — .256 Mag. or .30 Carbine cal., 4 shot clip mag., 23 in. barrel, open sight, pistol grip Monte Carlo stock. Mfg. 1963-1969.

	$165	$140	$120	$100	$85	$70	$55

MODEL 322 BOLT ACTION VARMINT — Sako Mauser type action, .222 Rem., 3 shot clip mag., 24 in. medium weight barrel, 2 position aperture sight, checkered stock. Mfg. 1954-1957.

	$385	$305	$275	$220	$195	$165	$140

MODEL 336 — .219 Zipper, 20 in. carbine barrel, ⅔ magazine, 5 shot.

	$275	$225	$190	$150	$130	$110	$95

MODEL 336A — improved 36A, .30-30, .35 Rem., or .32 Spl. cal., round breech bolt, 24 in. barrel with ⅔ mag. Mfg. 1948-1963, re-introduced 1973-1983.

	$210	$180	$165	$150	$130	$110	$95

MODEL 336 CS CARBINE LEVER ACTION — .30-30 Win., .35 Rem., or .375 Win. (disc. 1988) cal., 6 shot tube mag., 20 in. barrel, hammer block safety, American black walnut pistol grip stock, 7 lbs. Introduced 1983.

Mfg.'s Sug. Retail	$375	$285	$200	$160	$145	$130	$110	$100

Add $5 for Model 336C (without hammer block safety - disc. 1984)

MODEL 375 — same as 336 CS, except is .375 Win. cal. Disc. 1983.

	$230	$175	$165	$150	$140	$130	$120

MODEL 336 TS TEXAN — same as 336 CS, except is .30-30 cal., 18½ in. barrel, straight grip stock and squared finger lever. Disc. 1987.

	$240	$185	$160	$150	$140	$130	$120

Add $5 for Model 336T (disc. 1984).
Last Mfg.'s Sug. Retail was $314.

MODEL 336 LTS CARBINE — .30-30 cal. only, 16¼ in. barrel, 5 shot tube mag., 6½ lbs. Mfg. 1988-89 only.

	$275	$215	$175	$150	$140	$130	$120

Last Mfg.'s Sug. Retail was $346.

MODEL 30 AS LEVER ACTION — .30-30 cal. only, 20 in. barrel, walnut finish hardwood, open sights, no frills version of the 336 CS, 7 lbs. New 1985.

Mfg.'s Sug. Retail	$319	$240	$190	$145	$130	$125	$120	$115

Add $53 for 4X scope.

MODEL 336 ER — .307 (disc. 1984) or .356 Win. cal., 5 shot tube mag., 20 in. barrel, walnut pistol grip stock, open sights, 7 lbs. Mfg. 1983-87.

	$270	$210	$190	$175	$165	$155	$140

Last Mfg.'s Sug. Retail was $350.

MODEL 336A CARBINE — same as 336A, with 20 in. barrel. Mfg. 1948-1963.

	$200	$180	$165	$150	$130	$110	$95

Grading	100%	98%	95%	90%	80%	70%	60%

MODEL 336 MICRO GROOVE ZIPPER — same as 336A Carbine, in caliber .219 Zipper. Mfg. 1955-1961.

	$495	$415	$360	$330	$275	$250	$220

MODEL 336T CARBINE "TEXAN" — same as 336A Carbine, with straight stock, .44 Mag. also available. Mfg. 1963-1967.

	$185	$170	$160	$145	$130	$120	$100

MODEL 336DT CARBINE "TEXAN" — select stock version of 336T, longhorn and map of Texas carved on butt stock. Mfg. 1962-1964.

	$275	$220	$195	$165	$155	$140	$120

MODEL 336 RC — carbine.

	$275	$220	$195	$165	$155	$140	$120

MODEL 336 SC — .35 Rem., carbine variation, disc.

	$265	$215	$190	$165	$155	$140	$120

MARLIN CENTENNIAL MATCHED PAIR — Model 336 and Model 339 serial numbered the same, .30-30 or .22 LR cal., engraved, deluxe wood, inlaid medallions, cased. Mfg. 1,000 sets in 197C.

	$955	$750	$500				

MODEL 336 ZANE GREY CENTURY — same as 336A, with .30-30 cal., 22 in. octagon barrel, Zane Grey medallion inlaid in receiver, select walnut stock, pistol grip, brass butt plate and forearm cap. Mfg. 10,000 in 1972.

	$330	$250	$195	$165	$150	$130	$110

MODEL 336 OCTAGON — same as 336T, .30-30 cal. only, with 22 in. octagon barrel. Mfg. 1973.

	$205	$175	$165	$155	$140	$120	$100

MODEL 336 MARAUDER — same as 336T Carbine, with 16¼ in. barrel. Mfg. 1963-1964.

	$250	$200	$180	$165	$155	$140	$120

MODEL 444 LEVER ACTION — .444 Marlin cal., 4 shot tube mag., 24 in. barrel, open sights, straight grip, Monte Carlo stock, recoil pad, swivels, sling. Mfg. 1965-1971.

	$180	$160	$140	$120	$110	$100	$85

MODEL 444 SS SPORTER — same as 444 Rifle, with 22 in. barrel, pistol grip stock without Monte Carlo configuration, 7½ lbs. Mfg. 1972-present.

Mfg.'s Sug. Retail	$454	$380	$320	$275	$230	$195	$180	$170

Add $10 for Model 444S (without hammer block safety - disc. 1984).

MODEL 455 BOLT ACTION SPORTER — FN Mauser action with Sako trigger, .270, .30-06, or .308 cal., 24 in. barrel, stainless steel barrel, Lyman aperture sight, checkered Monte Carlo pistol grip stock. Mfg. 1957-1959.

	$415	$330	$305	$250	$220	$195	$165

MODELS 780, 781, 782, and 783 BOLT ACTION — .22 LR or .22 Mag. (Models 782 and 783) cal., tube or clip mag., 22 in. barrel. Disc. 1988.

	$110	$85	$75	$70	$65	$55	$50

Add $17-$25 for Models 782 and 783.
Last Mfg.'s Sug. Retail was $162.

MODELS 880/881 BOLT ACTION — .22 LR or .22 Mag. cal., replacements for Models 780, 781, Model 880 is .22 LR with 7 shot clip mag. and 22 in. barrel, Model 881 is .22 LR with 17 shot tube mag. and 22 in. barrel, 6 lbs. New 1989.

Mfg.'s Sug. Retail	$202	$160	$125	$100	$85	$75	$70	$65

Add $8 for Model 881.

Grading	100%	98%	95%	90%	80%	70%	60%

MODELS 882/883 BOLT ACTION

— .22 Win. Mag., 7 shot clip (Model 882) or 12 shot tube mag. (Model 883), checkered black walnut Monte Carlo stock with Mar-Shield finish, adj. semi-buckhorn rear sight and hooded front, thumb safety, 6 lbs. New 1989.

Mfg.'s Sug. Retail	$222	$175	$140	$110	$95	$85	$75	$70

Add $9 for Model 883.

Add $33 for nickel finish on Model 883 (883N).

The Models 882 and 883 are the replacements for Models 782 and 783.

MODEL 2000 TARGET BOLT ACTION — .22 LR Cal., single shot (can be converted), 22 in. heavy barrel with Lyman adj. sights, 2 stage target trigger, molded synthetic stock made from fiberglass and Kevlar with twice baked blue enamel, adj. buttplate, aluminum forearm rail, 8 lbs. New 1991.

Mfg.'s Sug. Retail	$510	$440	$375	$340	$300	$275	$250	$225

Add $30 for 5-shot clip conversion unit (for summer biathlon competition).

MODEL 25MB — .22 Mag. cal., bolt action, 16¼ in. micro-groove barrel, 7 shot clip mag., hardwood stock, takedown action, 6 lbs. Mfg. 1987-88 only.

		$145	$115	$95	$85	$75	$70	$65

This model included both a scope and gun case.

Last Mfg.'s Sug. Retail was $173.

MODEL 25MN — .22 Mag. cal., bolt action, 7 shot clip mag., 22 in. barrel, walnut finished hardwood stock, grooved receiver, 6 lbs. New 1989.

Mfg.'s Sug. Retail	$167	$125	$105	$90	$80	$75	$70	$65

MODEL 9 CAMP CARBINE SEMI-AUTO — 9mm only, 16½ in. barrel, 12 and 20 shot mag. disc. 1989, 4 shot clip mag. became standard in 1990, sand blasted steel receiver, open sights, last shot automatic hold-open, 6¾ lbs. New 1985.

Mfg.'s Sug. Retail	$347	$275	$200	$170	$150	$140	$130	$125

Add $44 for nickel plating (new 1991, Model 9N).

A new high visibility orange front sight post with cutaway hood was added in 1989.

MODEL 45 CARBINE — .45 ACP only, 7 shot clip mag., sandblasted steel receiver, 16½ in. barrel, last shot hold open device, adj. rear sight, 6¾ lbs. New 1986.

Mfg.'s Sug. Retail	$347	$275	$200	$170	$150	$140	$130	$125

A new high visibility orange front sight post with cutaway hood was added in 1989.

MODEL 990 SEMI-AUTO — .22 LR cal. only, 18 shot tube mag., 22 in. barrel, last shot automatic bolt hold-open, Monte Carlo American black walnut stock with pistol grip, 5½ lbs. Disc. 1987.

		$115	$90	$75	$65	$60	$55	$50

Last Mfg.'s Sug. Retail was $159.

MODEL 995 SEMI-AUTO — .22 LR cal. only, 7 shot clip mag., 18 in. barrel, Monte Carlo walnut stock, 5 lbs.

Mfg.'s Sug. Retail	$184	$140	$110	$85	$70	$65	$60	$55

MODEL 70P (PAPOOSE) — .22 LR cal. only, semi-auto, takedown carbine with 16¼ in. barrel, 7 shot clip mag., rustproof receiver, bolt hold open, is supplied with floating nylon carrying case. New 1986.

Mfg.'s Sug. Retail	$173	$135	$100	$80	$70	$65	$60	$55

Add $20 for 4X scope.

This model was supplied with a 4X scope until 1989.

MODEL 1894 CS (CARBINE) — copy of original Model 1894, .357 Mag./.38 Spl., 9 shot mag., 18½ in. round barrel, open sights, straight grip stock, squared finger lever, 6 lbs. Mfg. 1969-present.

Mfg.'s Sug. Retail	$421	$330	$240	$190	$170	$150	$140	$130

Subtract $20 for Model 1894 C (without hammer block safety).

Grading	100%	98%	95%	90%	80%	70%	60%

MODEL 1894 S (SPORTER) — .41 Mag., .44 Mag./.44 Spl., or .45 LC (new 1988) cal., 20 in. barrel, 10 shot tube mag., adj. sights, 6 lbs., straight grip walnut stock and forearm.

Mfg.'s Sug. Retail	$421	$330	$240	$190	$170	$150	$140	$130

MODEL 1894 M (.22 MAG.) — .22 Mag. cal., with 20 in. barrel, 11 shot tube mag., straight grip walnut stock and forearm, 6¼ lbs. Disc. 1989.

	$275	$210	$180	$150	$135	$125	$115

Last Mfg.'s Sug. Retail was $358.

MODEL 1894 CL — .218 Bee (new 1990), .25-20 or .32-20 cal., 6 shot (two-thirds length) tube mag., 22 in. barrel, 6¼ lbs. New 1988.

Mfg.'s Sug. Retail	$452	$345	$260	$200	$175	$155	$140	$130

MODEL 1894 OCTAGON — same as 1894 Carbine, with octagon barrel. Mfg. 1973.

	$260	$195	$175	$165	$150	$130	$120

MODEL 1895 LEVER ACTION — .45-70 Gov't., 4 shot tube mag., 22 in. barrel, open sights, straight grip stock with curved buttplate, forearm cap, sling and swivels. Mfg. 1972-1984.

	$265	$210	$185	$175	$165	$150	$140

Model 1895 S — similar to Model 1895, except has pistol grip stock and straight buttplate.

	$265	$210	$185	$175	$165	$150	$140

MODEL 1895 SS — same as Model 1895 S only with hammer block safety. New 1983.

Mfg.'s Sug. Retail	$454	$345	$260	$200	$175	$155	$140	$130

MARLIN PROMOTIONAL MODELS — Models 15, 15Y, 15YN (new 1989), 25, 25M, 25N (new 1989), 60, 70, 70HC (new 1989), and 75C are inexpensive, utilitarian .22 LR or .22 Mag. cal. (Model 25M only), rifles meant for shooting, not for collecting. All the above models retail for approx. $140-$155, but can be purchased for less, depending on discounting. Series 15 and 25 Models designate bolt action, Series 60 and 70 designate semi-auto design.

RIFLES: BOLT ACTION, SINGLE SHOT

Between 1930 and the present, Marlin made a number of .22 cal. rimfire rifles, bolt action single shots, bolt action repeaters and auto loaders. These were good quality, low priced weapons. In 1960 the name Glenfield was also used in connection with these guns. They are valued from a high of about $100 for a 100% gun to about $25 for a 60% or less gun that is still in working order. We will list these models for reference purposes.

Model 65 — 1932-1938.

Model 65E — 1932-1938.

Model 100 — 1936-1941.

Model 100S Tom Mix Special — disc. ($250 if N.I.B.).

Model 100SB — 1936-1941.

Model 101 — 1951-disc.

Model 101 DL — disc.

Model 101G — 1960-1965, Marlin Glenfield.

Model 10 — 1966-disc., Marlin Glenfield.

Model 122 — 1966-disc.

BOLT ACTION: REPEATING RIFLES

Model 80 — 1934-1939.

Model 80E — 1934-1940.

Model 80C — 1940-1970.

Model 80DL — 1940-1965.

Model 80G — 1960-1965, Marlin Glenfield.

Model 20 — 1966-disc., Marlin Glenfield.

Model 780 — 1971-1988.

Model 781 — 1971-1988.

Model 782 — 1971-1988, .22 WRM.

Grading	100%	98%	95%	90%	80%	70%	60%

Model 783 — 1971-1988, .22 WRM.

Model 980 — 1962-1970, .22 WRM.

Model 81 — 1937-1940.

Model 81E — 1937-1940.

Model 81C — 1940-1970.

Model 81DL — 1940-1965.

Model 81G — 1960-1965 Marlin Glenfield.

AUTOLOADING RIFLES

Model 50 — 1931-1934.

Model 50E — 1931-1934.

Model A-1 — 1935-1946.

Model A-1E — 1935-1946.

Model A-1C — 1940-1946.

Model A-1DL — 1940-1946.

Model 88-C — 1947-1956.

Model 88-DL — 1953-1956.

Model 89-C — 1950-1961.

Model 89-DL — 1950-1961.

Model 98 — 1950-1961.

Model 99 — 1959-1961.

Model 99C — 1962-disc.

Model 99G — 1960-1965, Marlin Glenfield.

Model 60 — 1960-present, Marlin Glenfield.

Model 99DL — 1960-1965.

Model 49 — 1968-1971.

Model 49DL — 1971-disc.

Model 99M1 — 1966-disc.

Model 99M2 — 1966-disc.

Model 989 — 1962-1966.

Model 70 — 1966-1969, Marlin Glenfield.

Model 989G — 1962-1964, Marlin Glenfield.

Model 990 — disc.

Model 995 — disc.

SHOTGUNS

MODEL 1898 SLIDE ACTION — 12 ga., 5 shot tube mag., 26-32 in. barrels, various chokes, exposed hammer, pistol grip stock, grades differ in quality of wood and engraving on C and D. Mfg. 1898-1905.

	100%	98%	95%	90%	80%	70%	60%
Grade A	$495	$385	$330	$305	$250	$195	$165
Grade B	$580	$495	$440	$415	$360	$305	$275
Grade C	$880	$715	$635	$580	$525	$495	$440
Grade D	$1,760	$1,540	$1,320	$1,210	$1,045	$965	$880

MODEL 16 — 16 ga. only, 26 or 28 in. barrel, various chokes, takedown, pistol grip stock. Mfg. 1904-1910.

	100%	98%	95%	90%	80%	70%	60%
Grade A	$385	$305	$250	$220	$195	$165	$140
Grade B	$495	$415	$360	$330	$305	$275	$250
Grade C	$635	$525	$495	$440	$415	$385	$330
Grade D	$1,320	$1,100	$990	$825	$715	$635	$550

MODEL 17 SLIDE ACTION — 12 ga., 30 or 32 in. full choke barrel, solid frame, straight stock. Mfg. 1906-1908.

100%	98%	95%	90%	80%	70%	60%
$440	$330	$305	$250	$220	$180	$150

Grading	100%	98%	95%	90%	80%	70%	60%

MODEL 17 BRUSH GUN — same as 17, with 26 in. cylinder bore barrel. Mfg. 1906-1908.

	100%	98%	95%	90%	80%	70%	60%
	$470	$360	$330	$275	$250	$220	$165

MODEL 17 RIOT GUN — same as 17, with 20 in. barrel. Mfg. 1906-1908.

	$415	$330	$275	$250	$195	$180	$160

MODEL 19 SLIDE ACTION — improved lightened version of 1898, matte top surface on barrel. Mfg. 1906-1907.

Grade A	$385	$305	$250	$220	$195	$165	$140
Grade B	$495	$415	$360	$330	$305	$275	$250
Grade C	$635	$525	$495	$440	$415	$385	$330
Grade D	$1,320	$1,100	$990	$825	$715	$635	$550

MODEL 21 SLIDE ACTION — straight grip version of 19.

Grade A	$385	$305	$250	$220	$195	$165	$140
Grade B	$495	$415	$360	$330	$305	$275	$250
Grade C	$635	$525	$495	$440	$415	$385	$330
Grade D	$1,320	$1,100	$990	$825	$715	$635	$550

MODEL 24 — improved 21, takedown, automatic recoil lock on slide, solid matte rib. Mfg. 1908-1915.

Grade A	$330	$305	$275	$250	$220	$195	$165
Grade B	$525	$440	$385	$360	$330	$305	$275
Grade C	$660	$550	$525	$470	$440	$415	$360
Grade D	$1,375	$1,155	$1,045	$880	$770	$660	$580

MODEL 26 — same as 24 Grade A, with solid frame, 30 or 32 in. full choke barrel. Mfg. 1909-1915.

	$275	$230	$210	$195	$165	$150	$140

MODEL 26 BRUSH GUN — 26 in. cylinder bore barrel. Mfg. 1909-1915.

	$305	$275	$250	$220	$195	$165	$150

MODEL 26 RIOT GUN — 20 in. cylinder bore barrel. Mfg. 1909-1915.

	$250	$195	$180	$165	$150	$140	$120

MODEL 28 HAMMERLESS — 12 ga., 26-32 in. barrels, various chokes, takedown, matte top barrel, pistol grip stock. Mfg. 1913-1922.

Grade A	$385	$305	$250	$220	$195	$165	$140
Grade B	$495	$415	$360	$330	$305	$275	$250
Grade C	$635	$525	$495	$440	$415	$385	$330
Grade D	$1,320	$1,100	$990	$825	$715	$635	$550

MODEL 28TS TRAP GUN — same as 28, with 30 in. matte rib barrel, full choke, high combination straight grip stock. Mfg. 1915.

	$415	$330	$275	$250	$220	$195	$165

MODEL 28T — same as 28TS, with fancy wood, checkering, better finish. Mfg. 1915.

	$605	$525	$495	$470	$415	$360	$305

MODEL 30 — same as 16, with automatic recoil lock on slide. Mfg. 1910-1914.

Grade A	$385	$305	$250	$220	$195	$165	$140
Grade B	$495	$415	$360	$330	$305	$275	$250
Grade C	$635	$525	$495	$440	$415	$385	$330
Grade D	$1,320	$1,100	$990	$825	$715	$635	$550

MODEL 30 FIELD GRADE — same as 30 Grade B, with 25 in. mod. barrel, straight stock. Mfg. 1913-1914.

	$360	$275	$220	$180	$160	$130	$115

Grading	100%	98%	95%	90%	80%	70%	60%

MODEL 31 — scaled down small ga. (16 and 20 ga.) version of the Model 28, has 26 and 28 in. barrels, various chokes. Mfg. 1915-1922.

Grade A	$385	$305	$250	$220	$195	$165	$140
Grade B	$495	$415	$360	$330	$305	$275	$250
Grade C	$636	$525	$495	$440	$415	$385	$330
Grade D	$1,320	$1,100	$990	$825	$715	$635	$550

MODEL 31F FIELD GUN — 25 in. mod. barrel. Mfg. 1915-1917.

	$495	$415	$360	$330	$305	$275	$250

MODEL 42A — similar to 24, but less quality finishing. Mfg. 1922-1934.

	$250	$220	$195	$165	$140	$120	$100

MODEL 43 HAMMERLESS — similar to 28, with less quality finish. Mfg. 1923-1930.

	$330	$250	$220	$195	$165	$140	$110

MODEL 43TS — same as 28T, lower quality.

	$525	$440	$415	$385	$360	$305	$275

MODEL 44A — similar to 31A, 20 ga. only. Mfg. 1923-1935.

	$360	$275	$250	$220	$195	$165	$140

MODEL 44S — select checkered stock.

	$470	$385	$360	$330	$195	$165	$140

MODEL 49 — lower priced version of 42A. They were given to purchasers of 4 shares of Marlin stock. 3,000 mfg. in 1925-1928.

	$440	$360	$305	$275	$220	$195	$165

MODEL 53 — similar to 43A. Mfg. 1929-1930.

	$330	$275	$250	$220	$195	$165	$140

MODEL 63 — same as 43, later model. Mfg. 1931-1935.

	$330	$250	$220	$195	$165	$140	$110

MODEL 63TS — similar to 43TS, with trap style stock.

	$385	$305	$250	$220	$195	$165	$140

MODEL .410 LEVER ACTION — .410 ga., 22 or 26 in. barrel, full choke, lever action, similar to 1893, exposed hammer, plain pistol grip stock. Mfg. 1929-1932 as a stockholders promotional firearm.

	$495	$420	$375	$335	$290	$260	$230

Model .410 Deluxe — includes deluxe checkered walnut stock and forearm.

	$675	$595	$500	$425	$350	$300	$275

MODEL 60 SINGLE BARREL — 12 ga., 30 or 32 in. barrel, full choke, top lever, break open, exposed hammer, pistol grip stock. Mfg. 60 in 1923.

	$220	$195	$165	$140	$120	$110	$100

MODEL 90 O/U — 12, 16, 20, or .410 ga., 26, 28, or 30 in. barrels, boxlock, extractors, checkered pistol grip stock. Mfg. 1937-1958. Guns made from 1937-1949 had vent separated barrels, after 1949, solid barrels.

	$495	$385	$360	$330	$290	$265	$230

With single trigger

	$605	$495	$470	$440	$400	$375	$340

MODEL 120 MAGNUM — slide action, 12 ga., 3 in. chamber, 26-38 in. barrel, takedown, various chokes, checkered pistol grip stock. Mfg. 1971-1985.

	$290	$225	$215	$205	$195	$180	$165

Subtract $35 if without vent rib.
Last Mfg.'s Sug. Retail was $370.

Grading	100%	98%	95%	90%	80%	70%	60%

MODEL 778 — 12 ga. Mag. slide action, 20-38 in. barrels, 7¾ lbs. Disc. 1984.

	$225	$190	$175	$155	$140	$125	$110

PREMIER MARK I SLIDE ACTION — 12 ga. only, aluminum receiver, takedown, manufactured in France for Marlin.

	$200	$180	$160	$150	$140	$120	$95

PREMIER MARK II — same as Mark I, except with engraved receiver and checkering. Mfg. 1960-1963 in France.

	$260	$205	$170	$155	$145	$125	$100

PREMIER MARK IV — same as Mark II, only deluxe grade with better wood, more engraving. Mfg. 1960-1963 in France.

	$305	$250	$220	$195	$165	$140	$110
With vent rib	$330	$275	$250	$220	$195	$165	$140

SHOTGUNS: BOLT ACTION

MODEL 55 — 12, 16, or 20 ga., 2 shot detachable mag., 26 and 28 in. full choke barrel, plain pistol grip stock. Mfg. 1950-1965.

	$90	$70	$55	$40	$35	$30	$25

With adj. choke

	$100	$85	$65	$50	$45	$40	$30

MODEL 55 GOOSE GUN — same as 55, except 12 ga. only, 36 in. full choke barrel, 3 in. chamber, 2 shot clip mag., leather carrying strap and detachable swivels, rubber recoil pad, 8 lbs. Mfg. 1962-present.

Mfg.'s Sug. Retail	$255	$195	$165	$135	$110	$95	$85	$80

MODEL 55 SWAMP GUN — same as 55, 12 ga., 20 in. adj. choke barrel, 3 in. mag. Mfg. 1963-1965.

	$105	$90	$70	$55	$50	$45	$35

MODEL 55S SLUG GUN — 24 in. barrel, cylinder bore, rifle sights. Mfg. 1974-1983.

	$140	$120	$110	$95	$85	$55	$40

MODEL 5510 — 10 ga., 3½ in. mag., 2 shot clip mag., 34 in. barrel, leather carrying strap and detachable swivels, rubber recoil pad, 10½ lbs. Mfg. 1976-1985.

	$220	$170	$160	$150	$140	$130	$120

Last Mfg.'s Sug. Retail was $282.

MAROCCHI

Manufactured since 1922 by Armi Marocchi in Brescia, Italy. Currently imported and distributed by Precision Sales International, Inc. located in Westfield, MA and Sile Distributors Inc., located in New York, NY.

Marocchi makes a wide variety of quality shotguns and O/U rifles. Many of their models however, are not being imported currently. Frigon guns (manufactured by Marocchi) appear under the F section in this text.

SHOTGUNS

AVANZA — 12 or 20 ga., 3 in. chambers, mono-block boxlock action, 26 or 28 in. vent barrels with VR (with or without choke tubes), SST, ejectors, deluxe checkered walnut stock and forearm with vent recoil pad, high polish bluing with gold accents, all steel lightweight mfg., 6 lbs. 5 oz. - 6 lbs. 13 oz. Importation began 1990.

Mfg.'s Sug. Retail	$999	$895	$795	$675	$575	$500	$450	$420
Add $20 for 20 ga.								
Add $100 for choke tubes (3).								

This model is imported exclusively by Precision Sales International, Inc.

Grading	100%	98%	95%	90%	80%	70%	60%

Avanza Sporting Clays — 12 ga. only, 3 in. chambers, built on 20 ga. frame, 28 in. vent. barrels with VR and choke tubes, select checkered walnut stock with deluxe recoil pad and forearm, gold plated trigger, 7 lbs. New 1991.

Mfg.'s Sug. Retail	$1,189	$1,075	$925	$825	$725	$650	$575	$495

Add $140 for Premier Grade (includes select walnut and gold etched trigger guard).
This model features a trigger that is adjustable for length and pull without special tools.

FIELD MASTER I O/U — 12 ga. only, 26 or 28 in. VR barrels and rib with choke tubes, engraved coin finished receiver, extractors, SNT, checkered walnut stock and forearm.

Mfg.'s Sug. Retail	$400	$340	$300	$275	$240	$215	$200	$185

The model is imported exclusively by Sile Distributors.

Field Master II — similar to Field Master I except has SST and choke tubes.

Mfg.'s Sug. Retail	$476	$385	$340	$300	$275	$240	$215	$200

SKEET MODEL — 12 ga. only, 26 in. barrels bored SK/SK.

Mfg.'s Sug. Retail	$392	$340	$300	$275	$240	$215	$200	$185

The model is imported exclusively by Sile Distributors.

TRAP MODEL — 12 ga. only, 30 in. barrels bored M/F, ejectors.

Mfg.'s Sug. Retail	$560	$475	$385	$340	$300	$275	$240	$215

The model is imported exclusively by Sile Distributors.

MODEL 2000 SINGLE SHOT — 12 ga. only, 3 in. chamber, hammer, 28 in. barrel, ejector, lightly engraved receiver.

Mfg.'s Sug. Retail	$94	$80	$70	$60	$50	$45	$40	$35

The model is imported exclusively by Sile Distributors.

COMBINATION GUNS

VALLEY COMBO — 12 ga. over .222 Rem. cal., 23½ in. separated barrels with VR, 3 in. chamber, fold down rear sight and will accept claw scope mounts, fixed cylinder choke, DT's, engraved silver receiver, satin finish walnut Monte Carlo stock with checkering and recoil pad, 8¼ lbs.

Mfg.'s Sug. Retail	$680	$575	$475	$415	$375	$325	$295	$275

The model is imported exclusively by Sile Distributors.

MASQUELIER S.A.

Manufacturer located in Belgium. Previously distributed (until 1986) by Ambel Ltd., Inc. located in Sugar Land, TX.

SHOTGUNS

BOXLOCK SxS — 12 ga. only, 2¾ in. chambers, Anson & Deeley boxlock action, ejectors, fine scroll engraving with French walnut. Importation disc. 1986.

	$4,400	$4,000	$3,650	$3,300	$2,995	$2,600	$2,200

Last Mfg.'s Sug. Retail was $4,780.

SIDELOCK SxS — 12 ga. only, 2¾ in. chambers, H&H style sidelocks, auto ejectors, English style fine scroll engraving with French walnut. Importation disc. 1986.

	$12,500	$10,000	$8,750	$7,600	$6,700	$5,800	$5,000

Last Mfg.'s Sug. Retail was $15,850.

RIFLES

CARPATHE — .243, .270, .30-06, 7 x 57R, or 7 x 65R cal., single shot, hair trigger, push-down cocking system. Importation disc. 1986.

	$3,500	$3,200	$2,900	$2,600	$2,300	$2,100	$1,850

Last Mfg.'s Sug. Retail was $3,850.

Grading	100%	98%	95%	90%	80%	70%	60%

EXPRESS — .270, .30-06, 8 x 57JRS, or 9.3 x 74R cal., O/U configuration, SST, ejectors. Add $800 for extra set of 20 ga. barrels. Importation disc. 1986.

	100%	98%	95%	90%	80%	70%	60%
	$3,300	$3,000	$2,800	$2,600	$2,300	$2,100	$1,850

Last Mfg.'s Sug. Retail was $3,600.

ARDENNES MODEL — top-of-the-line model, custom order only. Importation disc. 1986.

	100%	98%	95%	90%	80%	70%	60%
	$6,600	$6,000	$5,400	$4,800	$4,300	$3,900	$3,450

Last Mfg.'s Sug. Retail was $7,250.

MATRA MANURHIN DEFENSE
Please refer to the Manurhin heading in this section.

MAUSER-WERKE
Manufacturer located in Oberndorf, W. Germany 1812 to date. Rifles are currently imported by Precision Imports, Inc. located in San Antonio, TX. Previously imported by KDF located in Seguin, TX (1987-89). Luger pistols are also imported by Precision Imports, Inc. on a custom order basis and may be found in the back of the Luger section in this text.

PISTOLS: SEMI-AUTO

WTP MODEL I VEST POCKET AUTOMATIC — 6.35mm, 6 shot, 2½ in. barrel, blue, rubber grips. Mfg. 1922-1937.

	100%	98%	95%	90%	80%	70%	60%
	$375	$280	$250	$200	$160	$140	$100

WTP MODEL II — similar to Model I, but 2 in. barrel. Mfg. 1938-1940.

	100%	98%	95%	90%	80%	70%	60%
	$400	$300	$250	$200	$150	$140	$130

POCKET MODEL 1910 — 6.35mm, 9 shot, 3 in. barrel, blue fixed sights, checkered walnut or hard rubber grips. Mfg. 1910-1934.

	100%	98%	95%	90%	80%	70%	60%
	$350	$265	$180	$165	$150	$140	$130

POCKET MODEL 1914 — similar to 1910, but 7.65mm, 3.4 in. barrel. Mfg. 1914-1934.

	100%	98%	95%	90%	80%	70%	60%
	$350	$265	$175	$165	$150	$145	$135

Add 10% for Eagle WWI proofs.
Add 500% for the "humpback" model.

POCKET MODEL 1934 — similar to 1914, but one piece grip. Mfg. 1934-1939.

	100%	98%	95%	90%	80%	70%	60%
	$375	$285	$210	$175	$160	$150	$140

Add 15% for Waffenamt.
Add 100% for Nazi Navy marked.

MODEL HSC DOUBLE ACTION — 7.65mm (8 shot) or .380 ACP (7 shot), 3.4 in. barrel, blue or nickel, fixed sights, checkered walnut grips. Mfg. 1938-present (current mfg. is by R. Gamba in Italy).

Early Commercial — standard pre-war Commercial Model. Most frequently encountered variation.

	100%	98%	95%	90%	80%	70%	60%
	$450	$340	$300	$265	$225	$200	$185

Transitional — exhibits features of both early and late models.

	100%	98%	95%	90%	80%	70%	60%
	$425	$320	$290	$250	$215	$195	$175

WWII MILITARY VARIATIONS
Early Nazi Army — proofed 655 and 135.

	100%	98%	95%	90%	80%	70%	60%
	$400	$340	$300	$265	$225	$200	$185

Early Nazi Navy — marked on front grip strap.

	100%	98%	95%	90%	80%	70%	60%
	$750	$595	$540	$500	$440	$395	$350

Grading	100%	98%	95%	90%	80%	70%	60%
Early Nazi Police — Eagle L proof only.							
	$450	$395	$360	$320	$285	$245	$200
Wartime Nazi Army — proof 135 and WaA 135. Eagle N proofed also							
	$375	$325	$290	$250	$200	$180	$150
Wartime Nazi Navy — proofed on left side of trigger guard.							
	$500	$450	$400	$340	$295	$260	$230
Wartime Nazi Police — proofed Eagle L. Add 10% if Eagle F.							
	$450	$395	$360	$320	$285	$245	$200
Wartime Commercial — standard WWII Commercial Model.							
	$375	$325	$290	$265	$200	$180	$150
Swiss Commercial — ser. range 800,000-900,000. Very rare.							
	$1,400	$1,250	$1,125	$995	$900	$850	$600
Low Grip Screw — very rare, less than 2,000 mfg.							
	$2,175	$1,700	$1,350	$995	$875	$775	$650

Add 20% if Navy marked.

Cutaways — mfg. to visibly show mechanism. Should not be proofed.

	$1,495	$1,000	$900	$850	$800	$750	$700

POST-WWII VARIATIONS

French Manufacture — frequently encountered in poor condition — post-WWII production.

	$325	$275	$245	$220	$180	$155	$130

Mauser Production — .32 or .380 cal., 15 shot, mfg. 1968-1981.

	$350	$295	$260	$225	$180	$150	$130

Deduct 20% if not boxed or in .32 cal.

Interarms Import — imported by Interarms from 1983-1985 (Italian mfg. by Gamba).

	$300	$275	$250	$220	$180	$150	$125

Last Mfg.'s Sug. Retail was $415.

One of Five Thousand Edition — American Eagle edition (marked on gun), 5,000 total mfg. (serial numbered 1-5000).

	$375	$300	$250

Armes de Chasse Import — previously imported by Armes De Chasse located in Chadds Ford, PA on a limited basis. For G15 variation (9 shot) add $58.

	$475	$425	$330	$300	$260	$240	$220

Add $195 for Limited Series.
Last Mfg.'s Sug. Retail was $695.

MAUSER LUGERS

Both pre-war and post-war Mauser manufactured Lugers will be found in the Luger section of this book (including those variations currently imported by Precision Imports, Inc. located in San Antonio, TX).

1896 BROOMHANDLE

Note: Manufactured in Oberndorf, Germany between 1897 & 1938.

While many variations of the famous 1896 Broomhandle exist, most common Broomhandles are pre-war Commercials, Model 1930 Commercials, Red 9's, and Bolo's. They can be found in chronological order in this section. Holster stocks are a very popular accessory in this model. Commercial stocks may be matching or may not be serial numbered to gun (proper stock). Add $300+ for stock depending on overall original condition and if matching/non-matching.

In 1984, Federal legislation once again allowed importation of non-domestic WWI and WWII military handguns. As a result, many Bolo and various commercial Banner models have been seen at gun shows in some quantity. Condition on most of these recent imports is 25% or lower (with pitting on many) and prices typically start in the $150 range. While many of these newer imports would make workable shooters, they have in no way lowered prices on 90%+ condition specimens due to normal collector activity in top quality only pistols. Recently imported Broomhandles should have the importer's name visibly stamped on an exterior surface.

Grading	100%	98%	95%	90%	80%	70%	60%

CONEHAMMER VARIATIONS

STANDARD CONEHAMMER — 7.63 Mauser, distinguishable by circular machined upper hammer with concentric rings. 5.5 in. barrel, 23 groove wooden grips, rear adjustable sight available in 1-10, 50-500, 100-300, 50-300, 50-700 meter configurations, 10 shot mag.

	100%	98%	95%	90%	80%	70%	60%
	$3,000	$2,200	$1,600	$1,200	$1,050	$925	$700

Add 40% for matching stock.

FIXED SIGHT CONEHAMMER — 7.63 Mauser, similar to Standard Conehammer, except has fixed rear sight.

	100%	98%	95%	90%	80%	70%	60%
	$3,500	$2,600	$1,600	$1,300	$1,100	$925	$700

6 SHOT CONEHAMMER - FIXED SIGHT — 7.63 Mauser, 4¾ in. barrel, 6 shot mag., rare.

	100%	98%	95%	90%	80%	70%	60%
	$6,000	$5,200	$4,200	$3,500	$3,000	$2,500	$2,000

6 Shot Conehammer w/adjustable sight — 7.63 Mauser, 5.5 in. barrel, very rare.

	100%	98%	95%	90%	80%	70%	60%
	$11,000	$8,500	$6,000	$5,000	$4,000	$3,000	$2,500

Sales of this variation are extremely limited.

TURKISH CONEHAMMER — 7.63 Mauser, 5.5 in. barrel, 10 shot mag. Approx. 1,000 mfg. for Turkey in 1898, Farsi serial numbers.

	100%	98%	95%	90%	80%	70%	60%
	$4,500	$3,600	$2,800	$2,400	$2,100	$1,800	$1,500

"SYSTEM MAUSER" CONEHAMMER — 7.63 Mauser, "SYSTEM MAUSER" marked on top of chamber, improved 5.5 in. tapered barrel, 10 shot mag.

	100%	98%	95%	90%	80%	70%	60%
	$12,500	$9,500	$6,000	$5,000	$4,000	$3,500	$3,000

Add 40% for "SYSTEM MAUSER" stock.

Stepped barrel variation — Similar to System Mauser variation, except has older 5.5 in. stepped barrel with no taper.

	100%	98%	95%	90%	80%	70%	60%
	$18,000	$13,500	$9,000	$8,000	$7,000	$6,000	$5,000

20 SHOT CONEHAMMER — 7.63 Mauser, 20 shot non-detachable mag., frame can either be flatside or have milled panels, 5.5 in. tapered barrel, extremely rare.

	100%	98%	95%	90%	80%	70%	60%
	$27,500	$22,000	$15,000	$12,000	$9,000	$8,000	$7,000

Add 20% for milled panel variation.
Add 40% for matching 20 shot stock.

EARLY TRANSITIONAL LARGE RING HAMMER — 7.63 Mauser, distinguishable by large, open centered ring, 10 shot mag., 5.5 in. barrel.

	100%	98%	95%	90%	80%	70%	60%
	$2,850	$2,100	$1,550	$1,200	$1,050	$925	$700

This variation is normally found in the 12,000-15,000 serial range only.

FLATSIDE VARIATIONS

Add approximately $500 for a matching shoulder stock on the following models, $350 for non-matching.

ITALIAN CONTRACT FLATSIDE — 7.63 Mauser, distinguishable by flatside frame and DV/AV proofmarks, 10 shot mag., 5.5 in. barrel.

	100%	98%	95%	90%	80%	70%	60%
	$3,000	$2,200	$1,600	$1,300	$1,100	$900	$700

This variation is found in the 1-5,000 serial range only.

FLATSIDE COMMERCIAL — 7.63 Mauser, 5.5 in. barrel, 23 groove walnut grips, adj. rear sight typically marked 1-10 or 50-1000.

	100%	98%	95%	90%	80%	70%	60%
	$2,500	$1,750	$1,250	$1,000	$800	$600	$400

Early specimens may have pinned rear sights. Found in serial range 20,000-30,000.

POST 1900 VARIATIONS

Add approximately $400 for a matching shoulder stock on the following models, $325 for non-matching.

Grading	100%	98%	95%	90%	80%	70%	60%

PRE-WAR LARGE RING BOLO — 7.63 Mauser, 3.9 in. barrel, floral grips, usually found in 29,000 and 40,000 serial range.

	$4,000	$3,000	$2,000	$1,450	$1,000	$700	$450

Add $850 for short pre-war bolo stock.

LARGE RING SHALLOW MILLING — 7.63 Mauser, 5.5 in. barrel, 23 groove walnut or hard rubber grips, normally found in the 30,000-33,000 ser. range.

	$2,250	$1,600	$950	$750	$625	$500	$400

LARGE RING DEEP MILLING — 7.63 Mauser, 5.5 in. barrel, 35 groove walnut or hard rubber grips, normally found in the 34,000 ser. range.

	$2,250	$1,650	$950	$750	$625	$500	$400

PRE-WAR SMALL RING BOLO — 7.63 Mauser, 3.9 in. barrel, floral/checkered rubber or 31-36 groove walnut grips, usually found in 40,000-44,000 serial range.

	$3,000	$2,200	$1,600	$1,200	$800	$575	$400

6-SHOT BOLO — 7.63 Mauser, distinctive 6 shot mag., 3.9 in. barrel, either fixed rear sight (more common) or adjustable, could have either large ring or small ring hammer.

	$6,500	$5,000	$3,500	$3,000	$2,600	$2,200	$1,500

STANDARD PRE-WAR COMMERCIAL — 7.63 Mauser, 5.5 in. barrel, 10 shot mag., 34 groove walnut or checkered black rubber grips, typically 50-1,000 adjustable rear sight.

	$1,500	$1,200	$850	$725	$600	$500	$400

This variation is the most commonly encountered of all M1896 broomhandles. It can be encountered in the 39,000-274,000 serial range. Early guns below serial no. 100,000 are often Von Lengerke and Detmold marked and can be encountered with hard rubber grips. Rifling changed from 4 groove to 6 groove at approx. serial no. 100,000.

Note: This model is once again being imported by domestic distributors/dealers. Condition is somewhat poor, and prices usually start in the $250 range. These specimens usually have been reblued in addition to other reworking because the original condition has generally been very poor.

MAUSER BANNER CHAMBER MARKED — 7.63 Mauser or 9mm export (rare), 5.5 in. barrel, distinguishable by Mauser banner trademark on top of chamber, 32 groove walnut grips. Approx. 10,000 mfg. in serial range 84,000-94,000.

	$2,500	$1,750	$1,250	$850	$725	$600	$500

This model is very similar in appearance to the Pre-War Commercial.

PERSIAN CONTRACT — 7.63 Mauser, 5.5 in. barrel, distinguished by Persian lion crest in left rear frame panel, must be in the 154,000 serial range, 50-1,000 meter adj. rear sight.

	$3,500	$2,800	$2,200	$1,600	$1,100	$850	$700

This variation is frequently faked - pay close attention to serial no. and Persian crest.

STANDARD WARTIME COMMERCIAL — 7.63 Mauser, 5.5 in. barrel, 10 shot mag., 30 groove walnut grips, adj. 50-1,000 meter rear sight.

	$1,300	$1,000	$750	$650	$550	$450	$350

This variation is encountered almost as frequently as the Standard Pre-War Commercial. It is usually found in the 290,000-440,000 serial range. It was the first model to utilize the "new safety" design, and can be noticed by the "NS" marking on the back of hammer. Similar features as the Pre-War Commercial, except finish and polishing exhibit more machine and tooling marks.

Note: This model is once again being imported by domestic distributors/dealers. Condition is somewhat poor, and prices usually start in the $250 range. These specimens usually have been reblued in addition to other reworking because the original condition has generally been very poor.

Grading	100%	98%	95%	90%	80%	70%	60%

RED-9 ADJ. SIGHT — 9mm P, 5.5 in. barrel, 10 shot mag., 24 groove walnut grips usually marked with large red no. 9, adj. 50-500 meter rear sight, standard WWI military contract model with separate serial range 1-150,000, generally poorly finished. Mfg. 1916-1918.

	100%	98%	95%	90%	80%	70%	60%
	$1,650	$1,250	$1,000	$850	$750	$650	$550

Add $600 for matching stock.

Add $350 for non-matching stock.

Add $200 for original leather.

Add 10% if Prussian Eagle proofed on front of magazine well.

Note: Be cautious for originality since metal refinishing is prevalent in this model. The last 10,000 guns of this German military contract are not military proofed, are better polished, and will command a slight premium.

RED-9 FIXED SIGHT — 9mm P, 3.9 in. barrel, this is a 1920 commercial rework of the Red-9 military, may be dated 1920 and/or have police markings on front grip strap.

	$925	$750	$650	$550	$475	$400	$350

Because of the Treaty of Versailles following WWI, barrels had to be shortened to less than 4 inches and the adj. rear sight removed.

FRENCH GENDARME — 7.63 Mauser, 3.9 in. barrel, distinguished by Bolo barrel length on large frame, hard rubber or walnut (rare) grips, found in the serial range 431,000-434,000, adj. 50-500 meter rear sight.

	$2,750	$2,000	$1,250	$850	$700	$550	$400

EARLY POST-WAR BOLO — 7.63 Mauser, 3.9 in. barrel, shot extractor, small ring hammer, usually found in the 440,000-500,000 serial range.

	$2,200	$1,600	$925	$725	$600	$500	$375

Add 50% for long barrel Bolo's in approx. the 475,000 serial range.

LATE POST-WAR BOLO — 7.63 Mauser, 3.9 in. barrel, similar features of Early Post-War Bolo except has Mauser banner trademark on left rear frame panel, usually encountered in the 500,000-700,000+ serial range.

	$2,600	$1,750	$1,250	$800	$625	$500	$375

POST 1930 VARIATIONS

Add approximately $500 for a matching shoulder stock on the following models, $350 for non-matching.

EARLY MODEL 1930 COMMERCIAL — 7.63 Mauser, 5.2 (common) or 5.5 in. stepped barrel, 12 groove walnut grips, adj. 50-1,000 meter rear sight, usually found in the 800,000-890,000 serial range.

	$2,000	$1,450	$950	$750	$625	$500	$375

This was the first broomhandle variation to have a high polish, salt blue finish. Small parts are still fire blued and milling grooves were machined in receiver rails.

LATE MODEL 1930 COMMERCIAL — 7.63 Mauser, 5.5 in. stepped barrel, similar appearance to early 1930 Commercial except has solid receiver rails and various small parts are salt blued. Serial range 890,000-921,000 with production ending in late 1930's.

	$1,900	$1,400	$950	$750	$625	$500	$375

This model is serial numbered on rear top of breech bolt assembly.

MODEL 1930 REMOVABLE MAG. — 7.63 Mauser, 5.5 in. stepped barrel, 12 groove walnut grips, adj. 50-1,000 meter rear sight, very rare.

	$11,000	$8,500	$7,000	$5,000	$4,000	$3,200	$2,500

Original specimens of this variation have frames without the extra cuts required for the selector switch. Fakes are usually welded up Schnellfeuers made to look original. Only a very few are known in the 84,000-88,000 serial range. They are not slotted for the shoulder stock. Also known as the Model 711.

Grading	100%	98%	95%	90%	80%	70%	60%

SCHNELLFEUER (MODEL 712) — 7.63 Mauser, 5.5 in. stepped barrel, 12 groove walnut grips, adj. 50-1,000 meter rear sight, switchable full auto variation generally with selector switch, separate serial range 1-100,000, 10 or 20 shot detachable mag. 712 stock is internally grooved for selector switch.

		$3,750	$3,150	$2,600	$2,200	$1,800	$1,500	$1,200

Add $750 for correct stock.

Deduct 60% if Class III transferable only (dealer sample).

The Model 712 is classified as a machine gun and is subject to registration and payment of a $200 transfer tax.

CARBINES: SEMI-AUTO

FLUTED BARREL MODEL — marked "July 1897".

	$20,000	$16,000	$12,000	$8,000	$6,000	$5,000	$4,000

FLATSIDE CONE HAMMER — 7.63mm, 11¾ in. barrel, experimental variation.

	$15,000	$13,000	$10,000	$7,000	$6,000	$5,000	$4,000

FLATSIDE TRANSITIONAL — 7.63mm, 11¾ in. barrel.

	$13,000	$11,000	$8,000	$7,000	$6,000	$5,000	$4,000

LARGE RING HAMMER TRANSITIONAL — 7.63mm, 11¾ in. barrel.

	$13,000	$11,000	$8,000	$7,000	$6,000	$5,000	$4,000

LARGE RING HAMMER — 7.63mm, 14½ in. barrel.

	$13,000	$11,000	$8,000	$7,000	$6,000	$5,000	$4,000

SMALL RING HAMMER — 7.63mm, 14½ in. barrel.

	$10,000	$7,000	$6,000	$5,500	$5,000	$4,500	$4,000

BROOMHANDLE COPIES FROM OTHER COUNTRIES

These pistols are Chinese manufactured copies of the original German design.

HAND-MADE MAUSER CHINESE MARKED AND OTHERS — very poorly made Mauser copies, many thousands made.

	$650	$550	$475	$400	$300	$250	$235

HAND-MADE UNMARKED — poor quality.

	$650	$550	$475	$400	$300	$250	$235

ASIATIC FLATSIDE UNMARKED — better quality, not exceedingly rare.

	$1,200	$950	$740	$680	$600	$500	$400

TAKU-NAVAL DOCKYARD FLATSIDE — machine-made, better quality, not exceedingly rare, approx. 6,000 mfg.

	$1,500	$1,100	$740	$680	$600	$500	$400

Add 30% with correct stock.

Add 5% if with holster.

SHANSI ARSENAL .45 CAL. — .45 ACP cal., approx. 8,500 mfg., scarce and desirable in excellent condition.

	$5,000	$4,250	$3,500	$2,100	$1,700	$1,600	$1,475

SPANISH COPIES OF MAUSER BROOMHANDLES

VERY EARLY ASTRA-900 — Bolo grips, frame has single-line address, approx. 1,200 mfg.

	$2,750	$2,500	$2,200	$2,000	$1,750	$1,600	$1,475

EARLY ASTRA-900 — single-line address, approx. ser. range 1,200-12,000.

	$2,500	$2,000	$1,350	$850	$700	$525	$425

Grading	100%	98%	95%	90%	80%	70%	60%

LATE ASTRA-900 — two and three-line address, two-line address ser. range is approx. 12,000-20,000, three-line address ser. range is approx. 20,000-34,400.

	$2,500	$1,850	$1,350	$850	$700	$525	$425

Add 20% for Japanese character variation in the 27,000 serial range or if in Nazi procurement range.

ROYAL SEMI-AUTO — early Royals are mostly seen in semi-auto with round bolts.

	$3,000	$2,450	$1,900	$1,300	$850	$700	$600

There were many variations of the Royal's and above values assume standard variation.

ROYAL SELECTIVE FIRE — 7.63mm, most of approx. 25,000 Royal's manufactured were selective fire, several variations, transferable only. Add 20% if detachable mag., 100% if equipped with pneumatic rate retarder.

Class III	$2,500	$2,200	$2,000	$1,800	$1,700	$1,600	$1,475

This model had either a fixed mag., detachable mag., or pneumatic rate retarder.

MILITARY RIFLES

Deduct 30% if bolt is not matching or contract crests have been removed.

CZECH MODEL 1924 SHORT — 7.92mm, 23.23 in. barrel.

	$395	$350	$275	$250	$195	$165	$140

MODEL 1935 FN

	$440	$375	$300	$220	$160	$140	$120

KAR 98 POLISH CREST — 7.92mm.

	$325	$260	$200	$150	$125	$100	$80

SWISS CALVARY CARBINE — K31.

	$1,150	$950	$800	$675	$525	$450	$350

GREEK FN

	$395	$320	$275	$220	$190	$175	$140

GERMAN G 33/40-MOUNTAIN CARBINE, 1940-1943 DATES

	$750	$575	$475	$400	$350	$300	$260

GERMAN G 98/40-MOUNTAIN CARBINE

	$950	$875	$750	$650	$575	$500	$425

G 41 SEMI-AUTO
Mauser mfg. (G 41M)

	$1,400	$1,200	$900	$700	$650	$600	$550

Walther mfg. (G 41W)

	$950	$900	$850	$700	$600	$500	$450

G 43 OR K 43 SNIPER RIFLE — add $500 if with scope, Nazi issue.

	$990	$880	$770	$650	$600	$485	$400

KAR 98 ERFURT ROYAL ARSENAL

	$180	$140	$120	$100	$90	$85	$65

GERMAN M98 — WWI Gewehr 98 (Mauser, Simson, Danzig, Amberg, Erfut).

	$295	$250	$195	$155	$140	$110	$90

KAR 98 GERMAN WWII — (K 98 K), dated 1936-1945, coded manufacturers, deduct 20% for 1943-1945 dates. Add 100% for K date S/42. Add 50% for G date S/42.

	$395	$325	$250	$165	$145	$120	$100

RADOM MAUSER MODEL 29 — 7.92mm.

	$395	$320	$275	$220	$190	$175	$140

Grading	100%	98%	95%	90%	80%	70%	60%
K98K PORTUGUESE CONTRACT	$525	$440	$330	$275	$250	$220	$165
TURKISH M1888	$185	$140	$115	$90	$70	$55	$40
SWEDISH CONTRACT M98	$200	$175	$135	$110	$90	$75	$60
CZECH M98 VZ24 — 7.92mm.	$340	$275	$240	$210	$170	$140	$110
YUGOSLAVIAN M24	$250	$200	$150	$120	$110	$100	$85
DANISH 1889 - 10	$250	$200	$165	$155	$140	$110	$90
CHILEAN MODEL 1895 RIFLE — 7mm, 29.06 in. barrel.	$285	$220	$185	$165	$140	$110	$100
CHILEAN MODEL 1898 CARBINE	$350	$325	$280	$250	$220	$185	$165
98K FRENCH OCCUPATION	$285	$220	$180	$165	$140	$110	$100
MODEL 98 COLUMBIAN — .30-06.	$285	$220	$175	$155	$110	$90	$85
SIAMESE MAUSER RIFLE — 29.13 in. barrel, 8 x 50R.	$165	$125	$110	$90	$75	$60	$50
SIAMESE MAUSER CARBINE — 8 x 50R.	$165	$125	$110	$90	$75	$60	$50
SPANDAU MODEL 1915 — 8 X 57mm, mfg. in Spandau, Germany.	$250	$210	$165	$140	$120	$100	$85
SCHILLING MODEL 1916 — 8 x 57mm, mfg. in Suhl, Germany.	$225	$190	$155	$130	$110	$100	$95
IRANIAN MODEL 98/29 — long rifle.	$250	$210	$165	$140	$120	$100	$85
IRANIAN MODEL 98/29 — 7.92mm, 17.91 in. barrel, short.	$270	$220	$195	$165	$145	$120	$100
SWEDISH MODEL 94 — 6.5mm, 17.38 in. barrel carbine.	$225	$190	$155	$130	$110	$100	$95
SPANISH MODEL 93 — 7mm, 29.06 in. barrel.	$185	$150	$120	$110	$90	$85	$65
SPANISH MODEL 43 SHORT — 7.9mm, 23.62 in. barrel.	$200	$160	$125	$100	$90	$85	$75
SOUTH AMERICAN G.E.W. M98 — 7.92mm.	$175	$145	$100	$90	$85	$70	$55
VZ24 ROMANIAN CREST	$325	$250	$220	$200	$180	$165	$140

Grading	100%	98%	95%	90%	80%	70%	60%
BRAZILIAN M1908 — 7 x 57mm.	$350	$300	$240	$180	$110	$95	$65
ARGENTINE M1909 — 7.65mm.	$275	$225	$165	$140	$110	$95	$85
ARGENTINE M1891 — 7.65mm.	$300	$225	$165	$140	$110	$95	$85
PERUVIAN M1935 SHORT — .30-06, 23 in. barrel.	$225	$190	$150	$120	$110	$100	$85
PERUVIAN CREST M98	$250	$185	$120	$110	$100	$90	$85
1934 MAUSER BANNER — 7.92mm. Characterized by side sling and turn down bolt handle.	$375	$280	$250	$220	$195	$165	$140
ITALIAN MAUSER — 7.92mm, 1,000 mfg. for Germany.	$250	$210	$160	$120	$110	$95	$85
GERMAN M71/84 — 11mm, 33.56 in. barrel. Add 60% if M 71 (without tubular mag.).	$250	$225	$200	$180	$160	$140	$125

SPORTING RIFLES

BOLT ACTION SPORTING RIFLE — 6.5 x 55, 6.5 x 58, 7 x 57, 8 x 57, 9 x 57, 9.3 x 63, or 10.75 x 68 cal., 5 shot mag., 23½ in. barrel, double set trigger, adj. sight, rounded (not capped) pistol grip, Schnabel forearm, sling swivels.

	100%	98%	95%	90%	80%	70%	60%
	$650	$550	$495	$450	$395	$350	$300

BOLT ACTION SPORTING RIFLE SHORT MOD. — 6.5 x 54 or 8 x 51 cal., 20 in. barrel, same as Standard for other specifications.

	$650	$550	$495	$450	$395	$350	$300

BOLT ACTION SPORTING RIFLE MILITARY TYPE — same as Standard, except stepped military type barrel and military style sights and trigger, 7 x 57, 8 x 57, or 9 x 57 cal.

	$650	$550	$495	$450	$395	$350	$300

BOLT ACTION SPORTING CARBINE — same as Standard, except Mannlicher style full stock, 6.5 x 54, 6.5 x 58, 7 x 57, or 9 x 57 cal., 19¾ in. barrel.

	$725	$625	$550	$495	$460	$430	$400

TYPE A BOLT ACTION — 7 x 57, .30-06, 8 x 60, 9 x 57, or 9.3 x 62 cal., 23½ in. barrel, 5 shot, express sights, single trigger, Buffalo Horn forearm tip and pistol grip cap.

	$725	$625	$550	$495	$460	$430	$400

TYPE A SHORT ACTION — same as Bolt Action, .250-3000 or 6.5 x 54 cal., and 8½ x 51.

	$725	$625	$550	$495	$460	$430	$400

TYPE A MAGNUM MODEL — same as Short Action, except Mag. cal. .280 Ross, .318 W.R. Express, 10¾ x 68, or .404 Nitro Express.

	$750	$650	$575	$500	$460	$430	$400

Note: Type B, Type K, Type M, and Type S, and the above rifles have great similarity and for the purpose of price evaluation are extremely close to the Type A rifles.

MAUSER STANDARD MODEL RIFLE — refined Kar 98K, 7 x 57 or 8 x 57 cal. Mfg. for commercial sale and possesses quality of Oberndorf Sporters.

	$650	$550	$495	$450	$395	$350	$300

Grading	100%	98%	95%	90%	80%	70%	60%

RIFLES: RECENT MANUFACTURE

All long arms manufactured by Mauser-Werke are currently being imported exclusively by Precision Imports, Inc. located in San Antonio, TX. More information pertaining to current Mauser-Werke long arms can be obtained by contacting Precision Imports, Inc. directly.

Previous importation of Mauser-Werke rifles was by KDF, Inc. located in Seguin, TX until 1989.

MODEL 225 — available in 13 cal.'s between .243 Win. and .300 Wby. Mag., bolt action, 60 degree bolt lift with 3 locking lugs, ultra fast lock time, adj. trigger, 24 or 26 (Mag. only) in. barrel, 3 or 5 shot mag., no sights, guaranteed ½ in. accuracy at 100 yards, many stock options available at extra cost. Left-handed action available in certain cal.'s at the same price as Mag. cal.'s (Model 226).

Deluxe Standard Sporter — standard model available in 6 regular cal.'s and 9 Mag. cal.'s. Importation disc. 1989.

	100%	98%	95%	90%	80%	70%	60%
	$1,275	$1,000	$875	$750	$625	$550	$495

Add $90 for Mag. cal.'s.

This model was formerly the KDF Model K-15.

Last Mfg.'s Sug. Retail was $1,400.

MODEL 66A — similar to Model 66S except has American configured laminate stock (wood grain), cal.'s, action, and features are the same as the Model 66S. Imported 1988-89 only.

Standard Calibers

	100%	98%	95%	90%	80%	70%	60%
	$1,900	$1,425	$1,150	$925	$800	$700	$650

Add $630 per interchangeable barrel.

The A suffix on this model denotes American.

Last Mfg.'s Sug. Retail was $2,100.

Magnum Calibers — includes Weatherby Mag. cal.'s also.

	100%	98%	95%	90%	80%	70%	60%
	$2,050	$1,500	$1,200	$975	$825	$700	$650

Add $670 per interchangeable barrel.

Last Mfg.'s Sug. Retail was $2,270.

Big Game Calibers — includes most popular Mag. cal.'s up to .458 Win. Mag.

	100%	98%	95%	90%	80%	70%	60%
	$2,350	$1,900	$1,425	$1,150	$950	$825	$750

Last Mfg.'s Sug. Retail was $2,700.

MODEL 66S — telescoping short action, 5.6 x 57mm, 6.5 x 57mm, 7 x 64mm, 9.3 x 62mm, .243 Win., .270 Win., .30-06, or .308 Win. cal., 24 in. barrel, standard interchangeable barrels, single or double set triggers, adj. and detachable sights, Monte Carlo walnut stock with checkering, swivels, new safety, rosewood tipped forearm and pistol grip, rubber recoil pad, 7½ lbs. Mfg. 1974-present.

Mfg.'s Sug. Retail	$1,998	$1,700	$1,250	$995	$895	$795	$725	$650

Magnum Model — 28 in. barrel, 6.5 x 68mm, 8 x 68mm S, 9.3 x 64 mm, 7 Rem. Mag., .300 Win. Mag., or .300 Wby. Mag. cal., 7.9 lbs.

Mfg.'s Sug. Retail	$2,104	$1,750	$1,300	$1,025	$925	$825	$750	$675

Stutzen-Mannlicher Model — 21 in. barrel, full-stock (Mannlicher only) and half-stock (disc. in 1989), double or single triggers, same cal.'s as Model 66S, 7.5 lbs.

Mfg.'s Sug. Retail	$2,104	$1,750	$1,300	$1,025	$925	$825	$750	$675

This model was available in a half-stock "Ultra" variation until 1989. Values are similar to those listed above.

Safari Model — .375 H&H Mag. or .458 Win. Mag. cal., single trigger, 9.3 lbs.

Mfg.'s Sug. Retail	$2,332	$1,975	$1,550	$1,275	$1,050	$895	$775	$650

Model 66 prices above reflect the recent devaluation of the U.S. dollar against the Deutschmarke. While the manufacturer's suggested retails have gone up considerably, prices for used specimens (98% or less original condition) have not increased proportionately, and in some cases, have changed very little.

Grading	100%	98%	95%	90%	80%	70%	60%

MODEL 66 SM — telescoping short action, .243 Win., .270 Win., 7 x 64, .308 Win., .30-06, or 6.5 x 57 cal., 24 in. barrel, standard interchangeable barrels, set trigger on tang, adj. and detachable sights, Monte Carlo walnut stock with checkering, swivels, new safety, anatomical gripped select walnut stock with Mauser-nose, cocking lever on tang, rubber recoil pad, 7¼ lbs. Imported 1981-89.

	$1,550	$1,260	$1,075	$875	$730	$620	$520

Last Mfg.'s Sug. Retail was $1,801.

Model 66 SM Ultra — all standard cal.'s, 21 in. barrel, 7¼ lbs.

	$1,625	$1,325	$1,140	$920	$760	$650	$550

Last Mfg.'s Sug. Retail was $1,903.

Magnum Calibers — same as Model 66 S, 26 in. barrel, 8.4 lbs.

	$1,625	$1,325	$1,140	$920	$760	$650	$550

Last Mfg.'s Sug. Retail was $1,903.

Mannlicher type full stock — all standard cal.'s, 21 in. barrel, 7 lbs.

	$1,625	$1,325	$1,140	$920	$760	$650	$550

Last Mfg.'s Sug. Retail was $1,903.

These models were previously available on a custom order only basis through KDF, Inc. located in Seguin, TX.

MODEL 66 SL — same as Model 66 SM, except features extra select walnut with special graining, 7¼ lbs. Disc. 1985.

	$1,370	$1,275	$890	$720	$580	$475	$420

Last Mfg.'s Sug. Retail was $1,470.

Model 66 SL Ultra — 7 x 64 or .30-06 cal., 21 in. barrel, 7¼ lbs. Disc. 1985.

	$1,475	$1,325	$940	$750	$600	$450	$400

Last Mfg.'s Sug. Retail was $1,520.

Magnum Calibers — same as Model 66 S, 8.4 lbs. Disc. 1985.

	$1,475	$1,325	$940	$750	$600	$450	$400

Last Mfg.'s Sug. Retail was $1,520.

Mannlicher Type Full Stock — 21 in. barrel, 7 lbs. Disc. 1985.

	$1,475	$1,325	$940	$750	$600	$450	$400

Last Mfg.'s Sug. Retail was $1,520.

MODEL 66SL DIPLOMAT — same specifications as Model 66 SM, except includes selected walnut and special engraving including deer and wild bore game scenes.
Add $93 for Mannlicher full-stock (21 in. barrel).

Add $387 for Mag. Cal.'s.
This model was available on an individual custom order basis only. The last published retail price (1988) for a standard model without options was $3,167.

MODEL 660 — U.S. designation of 66S. Imported 1971-1973.

	$925	$820	$720	$600	$500	$450	$400

MODEL 66S DELUXE — special order engraved and inlaid, select wood. Priced per individual customer order. All guns are custom made only. Prices usually start in the $2,500 range.

MODEL 66SP SUPER MATCH — telescoping short action, .308 Win., 27½ in. heavy barrel with muzzle brake, no sights match trigger, 3 shot mag., select European walnut stock with stippling and thumbhole, adj. cheek piece and butt plate, includes premium scope, 12 lbs. Disc. 1990.

	$7,375	$6,200	$5,500	$4,800	$4,300	$3,900	$3,500

Last Mfg.'s Sug. Retail was $8,160.

Grading	100%	98%	95%	90%	80%	70%	60%

MODEL 77 — .243 Win., .270 Win., 6.5 x 57, 7 x 64, .308 Win., or .30-06 cal., 24 in. barrel, set trigger on tang, adj. and detachable sights, walnut stock with European cheek piece and hand checkering, swivels, new safety, steel detachable box mag., rubber recoil pad, 7¼ lbs. Disc.

	$1,130	$950	$875	$810	$750	$675	$595

Last Mfg.'s Sug. Retail was $1,331.

Model 77 Ultra — 6.5 x 57, 7 x 64 or .30-06 cal., 20 in. barrel, 7.7 lbs. Disc.

	$1,175	$975	$895	$835	$760	$675	$595

Last Mfg.'s Sug. Retail was $1,394.

Magnum Calibers — same as Model 66S, 8⅛ lbs. Disc.

	$1,175	$975	$895	$835	$760	$675	$595

Last Mfg.'s Sug. Retail was $1,394.

Mannlicher type full stock — 20 in. barrel, Mauser-set trigger, 7.7 lbs. Disc.

	$1,175	$975	$895	$835	$760	$675	$595

Last Mfg.'s Sug. Retail was $1,394.

Big Game Model — .375 H&H Mag. cal., 26 in. barrel, 8⅛ lbs. Disc.

	$1,075	$1,000	$900	$795	$675	$575	$475

Last Mfg.'s Sug. Retail was $1,150.

MODEL 77 SPORTSMAN — .243 or .308 Win. cal., sports version of the Model 77, set trigger on the tang, no sights, 24 in. barrel, 9 lbs. Disc.

	$1,495	$1,230	$1,075	$985	$895	$820	$740

Add $430 for Zeiss 2½-10X scope and mounts.
Last Mfg.'s Sug. Retail was $1,754.

MODEL 83 MATCH SINGLE SHOT — .308 Win. cal.'s only, cylinder locking action with 3 locking lugs in rear, match trigger, anatomical match stock with select walnut, adj. comb and butt plate. Disc.

	$2,170	$1,815	$1,660	$1,545	$1,400	$1,195	$925

This model is a UIT standard rifle at 300 meters.
Last Mfg.'s Sug. Retail was $2,594.

MODEL 83 MATCH UIT FREE RIFLE — .308 Win. cal.'s only, cylinder locking action with 3 locking lugs in rear, match trigger, anatomical match stock with select walnut, adj. comb and butt plate. Disc.

	$2,320	$1,940	$1,760	$1,600	$1,430	$1,195	$925

Last Mfg.'s Sug. Retail was $2,771.

MODEL 83 STANDARD RIFLE — similar to Model 83 Match, except has removable 10 shot steel mag., 26 in. barrel. Disc.

	$2,320	$1,950	$1,800	$1,625	$1,460	$1,250	$1,000

Last Mfg.'s Sug. Retail was $2,766.

MODEL 86-SR — .308 cal., updated version of the Model 83 action, 25.6 in. fluted barrel with muzzle brake, laminate wood stock with rail in forearm, adj. trigger, 9 shot detachable mag., cased, 10.8 lbs. Importation began 1989.

Mfg.'s Sug. Retail	$4,400	$3,900	$3,250	$2,750	$2,175	$1,800	$1,500	$1,250

Add $250 for match thumbhole wood stock.
Many other special order options are available on this model. Contact Precision Imports, Inc. directly for pricing information.

MODEL 99 — 5.6 x 57mm, 6.5 x 57mm, 7 x 57mm, 7 x 64mm, .243 Win., .25-06, .270 Win., .30-06 or .308 Win. cal., bolt action with 60 degree throw, 24 in. free-floating barrel, jeweled bolt, available in either hand-rubbed oil or high-luster lacquer finish for stock, mini-claw extractor, adj. single stage trigger, 4 shot detachable mag., no sights, 8 lbs. Importation began 1989.
This model is available with either a Schnabel forearm with regular stock or rosewood capped forearm with American Monte Carlo stock.

Classic Lacquer Finish — high-luster lacquer finish for stock.

Mfg.'s Sug. Retail	$1,426	$1,250	$1,000	$875	$795	$700	$625	$550

Grading	100%	98%	95%	90%	80%	70%	60%
Classic Oil Finish — hand-rubbed oil finish for stock.							
Mfg.'s Sug. Retail	$1,267	$1,100	$925	$850	$775	$700	$625	$550

MODEL 99 MAGNUM — 8 x 68S, 9.3 x 64mm, 7mm Rem. Mag., .257 Wby., .270 Wby., .300 Wby., .300 Win. Mag., .338 Win. Mag., or .375 H&H cal., similar specifications as Model 99, except has 26 in. barrel and 3 shot mag. Importation began 1989.

This model is available with either a Schnabel forearm with regular stock or rosewood capped forearm with American Monte Carlo stock.

Classic Lacquer Finish — high-luster lacquer finish for stock.

Mfg.'s Sug. Retail	$1,479	$1,295	$1,025	$900	$800	$700	$625	$550

Classic Oil Finish — hand-rubbed oil finish for stock.

Mfg.'s Sug. Retail	$1,320	$1,150	$940	$850	$775	$700	$625	$550

MODEL 2000 BOLT ACTION — .270 Win., .308 Win., or .30-06 cal., 5 shot mag., 24 in. barrel, leaf rear sight, checkered walnut stock. Mfg. by F.W. Heym for Mauser, 1969-1971.

	$305	$290	$275	$220	$175	$155	$140

MODEL 3000 — bolt action, .243 Win., .270 Win., .308 Win., or .30-06 cal., 5 shot mag., 22 in. barrel, no sights, walnut Monte Carlo style stock, rosewood forearm and pistol grip, skipline checkering, recoil pad and swivels. Mfg. 1971-1974.

	$500	$450	$425	$400	$375	$325	$275

MODEL 3000 MAGNUM — same as 3000, except 7mm Rem. Mag., .300 Win. Mag., or .375 H&H Mag. cal., 3 shot mag., 26 in. barrel.

	$550	$500	$450	$425	$375	$350	$325

This model was mfg. by Heym for Mauser.

MODEL 4000 VARMINT RIFLE — same as 3000, except smaller action, .222 Rem. or .223 Rem. cal., folding leaf rear sight, rubber butt plate.

	$425	$400	$375	$350	$300	$260	$225

This model was mfg. by Heym for Mauser.

RIFLES: .22 CAL. SPORTING

MODEL 107 — .22 LR only, bolt action, 19½ in. barrel, 5 shot clip mag., adj. iron sights, 6 lbs. Imported 1988-89 only.

	$265	$215	$175	$150	$135	$120	$110

Last Mfg.'s Sug. Retail was $280

This model is the same as KDF's previous Model 2107 mfg. by Voere.

Model 107 Deluxe — .22 LR or .22 Mag. cal., similar to Model 2107, except has deluxe checkered walnut. Imported 1988-89 only.

	$290	$240	$210	$175	$150	$135	$120

Add $90 for .22 Mag. cal.

Last Mfg.'s Sug. Retail was $320.

This model is the same as KDF's previous Model 2107 Deluxe mfg. by Voere.

MODEL 201 — .22 LR or .22 Mag. cal., bolt action, free-floating 21 in. barrel, clip 5 shot mag., adj. trigger, scaled-down version of the K-15, unusual action incorporates two front-located locking lugs on bolt face that engage Stellite inserts on the front receiver portion, guaranteed 1 in. groupings at 100 yards, blue only, no sights, beechwood stock with cheek piece, 6½ lbs.

Mfg.'s Sug. Retail	$445	$395	$330	$260	$230	$195	$175	$150

Add $27 for sights.

Add $48 for .22 Mag. cal.

This model is the same as KDF's disc. Model K-22 mfg. by Voere. Before 1989, this model came standard with a walnut stock.

Grading	100%	98%	95%	90%	80%	70%	60%

Model 201 Luxus — similar to the Model 201 except has walnut stock with rosewood forend.

Mfg.'s Sug. Retail	$604	$525	$440	$375	$315	$270	$240	$200

Add $27 for sights.

Add $48 for .22 Mag. cal.

This model is the same as KDF's previous Model K-22 Deluxe mfg. by Voere.

MODEL DSM34 — .22 LR, 25 in. barrel. "Deutches Sportmodell" lightweight trainer, side sling, no bayonet lug.

	$425	$375	$325	$300	$260	$225	$200

MODEL MS 420B — .22 LR Sporter, pre-war, 5 shot clip mag.

	$850	$725	$650	$550	$495	$450	$395

Add 15%-25% for double set triggers (rare).

MODEL ES340 — .22 LR, single shot, bolt action, 25½ in. barrel, adj. sights, checkered pistol grip, grooved forearm, pre-1935.

	$500	$425	$350	$325	$295	$260	$230

MODEL ES350 — .22 LR, single shot, bolt action, 27½ in. barrel, championship rifle, micrometer rear sight, ramp front sight, checkered full target stock, swivels, pre-1935.

	$625	$550	$500	$460	$430	$400	$375

Add 15%-25% for double set triggers (rare).

MODEL M410 — .22 LR, bolt action, repeating, 5 shot detachable mag., 23½ in. barrel, adj. sights, sporter stock, checkered pistol grip, swivels, pre-1935.

	$850	$725	$650	$550	$495	$450	$395

Add 15%-25% for double set triggers (rare).

MODEL M420 — .22 LR, bolt action, repeating, 5 shot detachable mag., 25½ in. barrel, adj. sights, sporter stock, checkered pistol grip, swivels, pre-1935.

	$850	$725	$650	$550	$495	$450	$395

Add 15%-25% for double set triggers (rare).

MODEL EN310 — .22 LR, single shot, bolt action, 19¾ in. barrel, fixed sights, plain pistol grip stock, pre-1935.

	$425	$365	$315	$280	$260	$225	$200

MODEL EL320 — .22 LR, single shot, bolt action, 23½ in. barrel, fixed sights, checkered pistol grip stock.

	$475	$395	$330	$295	$275	$250	$225

MODEL KKW — .22 LR, single shot, bolt action, target, 26 in. barrel, tangent rear sight, military style stock with bayonet lug. This weapon was also pro duced by Walther, Gustloff, and Anschutz. It was used as a training rifle in addition to commercial sales. Deduct 15% for 4mm KKW Models.

	$425	$375	$325	$300	$260	$225	$200

MODEL MS350B — .22 LR, bolt action, repeating, 5 shot mag., 26¾ in. barrel, grooved receiver for scope or sight, micrometer rear sight, ramp front sight, target stock, checkered pistol grip and forearm, swivels.

	$850	$725	$650	$550	$495	$450	$395

MODEL ES350B — .22 LR, bolt action, single shot, 5 shot mag., 26¾ in. barrel, grooved receiver for scope or sight, micrometer rear sight, ramp front sight, target stock, checkered pistol grip and forearm, swivels.

	$500	$425	$350	$325	$295	$260	$230

MODEL ES340B — .22 LR, bolt action, single shot, 26¾ in. barrel, adj. sight, plain pistol grip stock.

	$425	$375	$325	$300	$260	$225	$200

Grading	100%	98%	95%	90%	80%	70%	60%

MODEL MM410BN — .22 LR, bolt action sporter, 5 shot mag., 23½ in. barrel, adj. sights, lightweight stock, checkered pistol grip, swivels.

	$750	$650	$575	$500	$450	$400	$365

MODEL MS420B — .22 LR, bolt action target, 5 shot mag., 26¾ in. barrel, adj. sights, target style stock, checkered pistol grip, swivels.

	$750	$650	$575	$500	$450	$400	$365

SHOTGUNS

Mauser shotguns were sub-contracted to various European firms and were made in field and target configurations. While they are relatively rare (these shotguns were never imported into the U.S.), collectibility to date has been minimal. Values will depend on the grade, configuration, features, engraving, and overall desirability. Most of these shotguns have been priced in the $650-$1,300 range.

MARK X SPORTING RIFLE

Currently imported by Interarms. Consult the Interarms Mark X section.

MAVERICK ARMS, INC.

Manufacturer located in Eagle Pass, TX.

MODEL 88 — 12 ga. only, 3 in. chamber, slide-action, 24 (Deer Model with iron sights), 28, or 30 in. barrel, black synthetic stock and forearm with recoil pad, fixed choke, aluminum alloy receiver, crossbolt safety, approx. 7¼ lbs. New 1989.

Mfg.'s Sug. Retail	$196	$170	$140	$125	$115	$110	$105	$100

Add $22 for vent. rib.

Add $22 for Deer Model (24 in. cyl. bore barrel).

Add $41 for choked tube barrel (full choke supplied).

Model 88 Combo — includes 28 in. plain or VR barrel and extra 18½ in. cyl. bore slug barrel. New in 1990.

Mfg.'s Sug. Retail	$240	$200	$175	$150	$125	$115	$110	$105

Add $26 for VR barrel.

Model 88 Combat — 12 ga. only, combat design featuring pistol grip stock and forearm, black synthetic stock is extension of receiver, 18½ in. cyl. bore barrel with vented shroud with built in carrying handle, open sights. New in 1990.

Mfg.'s Sug. Retail	$313	$275	$225	$200	$180	$165	$155	$145

MODEL 91 — 12 ga. only, 3½ in. chamber, 28 in. plain barrel with choke tube, otherwise similar to Model 88, plain barrel only. New in 1991.

Mfg.'s Sug. Retail	$316	$265	$215	$190	$170	$160	$150	$140

McMILLAN, G. & CO. INC.

Manufacturer located in Phoenix, AZ.

McMillan primarily manufactures fiberglass synthetic stocks in a wide variety of configurations and styles (including many camouflaged models). In addition to these, McMillan also custom manufactures the rifles listed below on an individual order basis. More information can be obtained on McMillan's fiberglass stocks by contacting the company directly.

RIFLES: BOLT ACTION

The models listed below are also available with custom wood stocks at varying prices.
Add $150 for stainless steel receiver on most models listed below.

STANDARD SPORTER — available in most standard cal.'s, incorporates many features found on the more expensive models. New 1991.

Mfg.'s Sug. Retail	$1,250	$1,100	$900	$775	$700	$640	$595	$550

Grading	100%	98%	95%	90%	80%	70%	60%

STAINLESS STEEL TALON SPORTER — various cal.'s available between .25-06 and .416 Rem., all stainless steel fabrication, fiberglass stock. New 1991.

Mfg.'s Sug. Retail	$2,100	$1,875	$1,600	$1,300	$1,000	$895	$800	$700

The Talon action is patterned after the Winchester pre-64 Model 70. It features a cone breech, controlled feed, claw extractor, and 3 position safety.

CLASSIC SPORTER — various cal.'s available between .22-250 and .375 H&H, premium wood stock, matte metal finish, buttoning used on rifling for 22 or 24 in. stainless steel barrel, action made from 4340 chrome moly steel (either left or right-handed), 3 or 4 shot mag. supplied with 5 shot test target. New 1988.

Mfg.'s Sug. Retail	$1,900	$1,750	$1,500	$1,200	$950	$850	$750	$675

SUPER VARMINTER — similar to Signature Model, except is available in 9 cal.'s between .22-250 and .25-06, hand bedded fiberglass stock, adj. trigger, 26 in. heavily contoured barrel. New 1988.

Mfg.'s Sug. Retail	$1,950	$1,775	$1,525	$1,250	$1,000	$895	$800	$700

TITANIUM MOUNTAIN RIFLE — .270 Win., .280 Rem., .30-06, .300 Win. Mag., or 7mm Rem. Mag. cal., lighter weight variation with shorter barrel. New 1990.

Mfg.'s Sug. Retail	$2,495	$2,275	$1,975	$1,725	$1,400	$1,100	$925	$825

Add $500 for titanium alloy light contour match grade barrel.

SIGNATURE ALASKAN — available in 11 cal.'s between .270 Win. and .416 Rem. New 1990.

Mfg.'s Sug. Retail	$2,750	$2,450	$2,050	$1,775	$1,425	$1,100	$925	$825

SIGNATURE/TALON SAFARI — available in 12 cal.'s between .300 Win. Mag. and .460 Weatherby, hand bedded fiberglass stock, 4 shot mag., 24 in. stainless steel barrel, matte black finish. New 1988.

Mfg.'s Sug. Retail	$2,950	$2,600	$2,150	$1,850	$1,500	$1,150	$950	$850

Add $55 for .378 Wby., .416 Wby. or Rigby, or .460 Wby.

The Talon action is patterned after the Winchester pre-64 Model 70. It features a cone breech, controlled feed, claw extractor, and 3 position safety. Older Signature action rifles do not have this new Talon action.

M-40 SNIPER RIFLE — .308 Win., Remington action with McMillan match grade heavy contour barrel, fiberglass stock with recoil pad, 4 shot mag., 9 lbs. New 1990.

Mfg.'s Sug. Retail	$1,495	$1,425	$1,200	$1,000	$895	$800	$700	$600

M-86 SNIPER RIFLE — .30-06 (new 1989), .300 Win. Mag. or .308 cal., fiberglass stock, variety of optical sights. New 1988.

Mfg.'s Sug. Retail	$1,695	$1,575	$1,300	$1,025	$895	$800	$700	$600

M-86 Sniper System — includes Model 86 Sniper Rifle, bipod, Ultra scope, rings, and bases. Cased. New 1988.

Mfg.'s Sug. Retail	$2,665	$2,460	$2,050	$1,825	$1,600	$1,350	$1,100	$950

M-87 LONG RANGE SNIPER RIFLE — .50 BMC, stainless steel bolt action, 29 in. barrel with muzzle brake, single shot, camo synthetic stock, accurate to 1500 meters, 21 lbs. New 1988.

Mfg.'s Sug. Retail	$3,395	$3,000	$2,550	$2,250	$2,000	$1,850	$1,700	$1,575

M-87 Sniper System — includes Model 87 Sniper Rifle, bipod, 20X Ultra scope, rings, and bases. Cased. New 1988.

Mfg.'s Sug. Retail	$4,200	$3,950	$3,400	$3,000	$2,750	$2,450	$2,200	$2,000

M-87R — same specs. as Model 87, except has 5 shot fixed box mag. New 1990.

Mfg.'s Sug. Retail	$3,700	$3,350	$2,800	$2,450	$2,200	$2,000	$1,850	$1,700

Add $180 for Combo option.

M-88 — .50 BMC, single shot bolt action, 29 in. barrel with muzzle brake and quick takedown system, full adj. fiberglass stock with recoil pad, 21 lbs. New 1990.

Mfg.'s Sug. Retail	$3,525	$3,150	$2,675	$2,350	$2,100	$1,925	$1,775	$1,650

Grading	100%	98%	95%	90%	80%	70%	60%

M-89 Sniper Rifle — .308 Win., 28 in. barrel with suppressor (also available without), fiberglass stock adj. for length and recoil pad, 15¼ lbs. New 1990.

	100%	98%	95%	90%	80%	70%	60%
Mfg.'s Sug. Retail	$1,950	$1,795	$1,575	$1,300	$1,025	$895	$800	$700

Add $425 for muzzle suppressor.

COMPETITION MODELS — available in Metallic Silhouette (.308 or 7mm/08 cal. - disc. 1989), National Match (.308 cal. only), Long Range (.300 Win. Mag. only), or Bench Rest (shooter's choice). Each model made specifically for individual competition events. New 1988.

	100%	98%	95%	90%	80%	70%	60%
Mfg.'s Sug. Retail	$2,147	$1,825	$1,625	$1,325	$1,050	$895	$800	$700

Add $163 for Benchrest Model.

Subtract $300 for Metallic Silhouette model (disc. 1989).

MENZ, AUGUST

Previous manufacturer located in Suhl, Germany.

Please refer to listings in the Liliput section of this text.

MERCURY

Previous importer of Spanish mfg. shotguns.

MAGNUM DOUBLE BARREL — 10, 12, or 20 ga. Mag., 28 and 32 in. barrels, full and mod., boxlock, extractors, double triggers, engraved frame, checkered pistol grip stock.

	100%	98%	95%	90%	80%	70%	60%
	$300	$275	$250	$225	$200	$180	$150
10 gauge	$400	$375	$325	$300	$275	$225	$200

MERCURY

Previous manufacturer located in Belgium.

MERCURY SEMI-AUTO — .22 LR, 7 shot mag., steel frame, fixed sights.

	100%	98%	95%	90%	80%	70%	60%
	$400	$375	$325	$300	$275	$225	$200

MERKEL, GEBRUDER

Manufacturer located in Suhl, Germany. Currently imported exclusively by Armes De Chasse located in Chadds Ford, PA, 19317.

SHOTGUNS: DISCONTINUED

MODEL 100 O/U — 12, 16, or 20 ga., various barrel lengths and chokes, boxlock, Greener cross bolt, double triggers, extractors, checkered pistol grip or English style stock, pre-WWII.

	100%	98%	95%	90%	80%	70%	60%
Plain	$1,450	$1,250	$1,000	$925	$850	$675	$550
Ribbed	$1,550	$1,300	$1,050	$950	$875	$700	$575

MODEL 101 — same as 100, except selective extractors, rib barrel, some English style scroll engraving, pre-WWII.

	100%	98%	95%	90%	80%	70%	60%
	$1,600	$1,325	$1,100	$1,000	$900	$750	$600

MODEL 101E — same as 100, except auto ejectors, pre-WWII.

	100%	98%	95%	90%	80%	70%	60%
	$1,750	$1,425	$1,250	$1,150	$1,000	$875	$750

MODEL 400 — similar to 101, except arabesque engraving and Kersten double cross bolt, pre-WWII.

	100%	98%	95%	90%	80%	70%	60%
	$1,650	$1,350	$1,200	$1,100	$975	$825	$675

MODEL 400E — same as 400, except auto ejector, pre-WWII.

	100%	98%	95%	90%	80%	70%	60%
	$1,800	$1,450	$1,325	$1,175	$1,025	$925	$775

Grading	100%	98%	95%	90%	80%	70%	60%

MODEL 410 — same as 400, except more engraving and fancier wood, pre-WWII.

	$1,750	$1,425	$1,250	$1,150	$1,000	$875	$750

MODEL 410E — same as 410, except auto ejectors, pre-WWII.

	$1,900	$1,600	$1,450	$1,225	$1,100	$995	$875

MODEL 200 O/U — 12, 16, 20, 24, 28, or 32 ga., ribbed barrels in various lengths, Kersten double cross bolt, scalloped frame, boxlock, double triggers, extractors, cocking indicators, either pistol grip or English style checkered stock.

	$1,700	$1,350	$1,100	$990	$770	$660	$635

MODEL 210 — same as 200, except engraved and better grade wood, pre-WWII.

	$1,900	$1,500	$1,300	$1,075	$895	$800	$725

MODEL 201 O/U — 12, 16, or 20 ga., Greener crossbolt, hunting engraving or fine arabesque, dark walnut.

	$2,000	$1,600	$1,425	$1,200	$995	$900	$800

MODEL 201E — same as 201, except with auto ejectors, pre-WWII.

	$2,400	$1,825	$1,600	$1,400	$1,200	$1,075	$950

MODEL 202 — same as 201, except with false sideplates, higher quality wood, more profuse engraving, pre-WWII.

	$2,800	$2,400	$2,035	$1,700	$1,450	$1,200	$1,050

MODEL 202E — same as 202, with auto ejectors, pre-WWII.

	$3,200	$2,800	$2,485	$2,050	$1,700	$1,425	$1,200

MODEL 203E O/U — similar to 202E except better engraving and wood.

	$4,000	$3,400	$2,900	$2,500	$2,100	$1,800	$1,425

MODEL 204E O/U — similar to 203E, but fine English scroll engraving and Merkel sidelocks, ejectors, pre-WWII.

	$5,650	$4,900	$4,300	$3,850	$3,300	$2,750	$2,100

MODEL 300 O/U — 12, 16, 20, 24, 28, or 32 ga., various lengths and choke ribbed barrels, Merkel-Anson boxlock, Kersten double cross bolt, two underlugs, scalloped frame, either English or pistol grip style stock, cocking indicators, pre-WWII.

	$2,100	$1,900	$1,700	$1,550	$1,375	$1,200	$1,050

This model is usually encountered without engraving and has standard wood.

MODEL 300E — same as 300, with auto ejectors, pre-WWII.

	$2,500	$2,250	$1,900	$1,750	$1,500	$1,350	$1,175

This model is usually encountered without engraving and has standard wood.

MODEL 301 — same as 300, but more profusely engraved and better grade wood pre-WWII.

	$5,250	$4,250	$3,995	$3,500	$3,000	$2,600	$2,150

MODEL 310E — same as 300, with auto ejectors, pre-WWII.

	$6,250	$5,300	$4,450	$3,900	$3,400	$3,000	$2,550

MODEL 302 — similar to 301, but has auto ejectors and more elaborate ornamentation, false sideplates and better grade wood.

	$10,500	$8,500	$6,500	$5,750	$4,900	$4,150	$3,400

MODEL 304E O/U — special order version of 303E, higher quality and more ornamentation, top of Merkel O/U line.

	$16,500	$12,000	$10,500	$8,750	$7,500	$6,250	$5,000

MODEL 130 SxS — all standard gauges, barrel lengths and chokes, Anson & Deeley action with false side plates, boxlock, auto ejectors, English style or pistol grip stock, elaborate game scenes and arabesque engraving, pre-WWII.

	$12,000	$9,500	$7,500	$6,350	$5,400	$4,600	$3,950

Grading	100%	98%	95%	90%	80%	70%	60%

MODEL 127 SxS — all standard gauges, barrel lengths and chokes, H&H, hand detachable sidelocks, auto ejectors, double triggers, pistol or English style stock elaborately engraved, this is a best grade gun, pre-WWII.

	$21,500	$16,500	$12,500	$10,000	$8,800	$7,000	$5,750

RIFLES AND COMBINATION GUNS

O/U COMBINATION GUN — 12, 16, or 20 ga., over 5.6 x 35 Vierling, 7 x 57R, 8 x 57JR, 8 x 60R Mag., 9.3 x 53R, or 9.3 x 72R cal., various barrel lengths and chokes, models include 210, 210E, 211, and 211E, values range between $5,000-$7,000.

SxS COMBINATION GUN — similar gauges and cal.'s to O/U Combination Gun, boxlock models include 8EI and 9EI, 10EI is a sidelock, boxlock models range in price from $5,500-$7,000 and the Model 10EI is $9,500.

O/U DOUBLE RIFLE — models include 220, 220E, 221, 221E, 223, 223E, and 323E, rifle barrels, calibers same as Combination Gun, plus English Bigbore African cal.'s (up to .375 H&H), boxlock models range in price from $8,300- $10,000, sidelock models (223 and 323) range between $15,000-$21,500.

Most of these models are rare since they were not meant to be exported to the U.S. by Eastern Block countries.

SxS DOUBLE RIFLE — various cal.'s between .22 Hornet and 9.3 x 74 R, choice of boxlock (Models 5EI and 6EI) or sidelock (Model 7EI), ejectors, boxlock values range from $9,000-$11,000, sidelock values start at $14,500.

DRILLINGS

Current importation of this configuration into the U.S. has been limited during the past few decades. New mfg. includes a choice of 12, 16, or 20 ga. for the shotgun barrels with the rifle barrel being bored in most popular U.S. and metric cal.'s between .22 Hornet and 9.3 x 74 R. All current models are boxlocks with extractors featuring barrel selectors and cocking indicators. Models currently being offered for sale are 90, 90S, 90K, 95, 95S, and 95K. Prices range from $5,500-$7,500.

MERKEL ANSON DRILLING — usually 2 shotguns over rifle, although 2 rifles over shotgun have been noted, 12, 16, or 20 ga., calibers 7 x 57R, 8 x 57JR, and 9.3 x 74R cal.'s most common, others noted, 25.6 in. or 21.6 in. barrels, boxlock, Anson & Deeley system, double triggers, extractors, checkered pistol grip stock, pre-WWII.

MODEL 142 — engraved.

	$5,000	$4,000	$3,000	$2,750	$2,500	$2,200	$2,000

MODEL 142 — less ornamentation.

	$4,000	$3,500	$3,000	$2,500	$2,250	$2,100	$2,000

MODEL 145 — least ornamentation.

	$3,000	$2,800	$2,700	$2,600	$2,500	$2,100	$1,900

SHOTGUNS: SxS RECENT IMPORTATION

Imported exclusively by Armes de Chasse located in Chadds Ford, PA, 19317.

In 1990, the reunification of East and West Germany allowed G. Merkel to export their long arms to the U.S. without the previous 65% non-favored nation tax. This has opened up the U.S. to a more aggressive marketing effort by both the manufacturer and importer.

Prices below reflect the recent devaluation of the U.S. dollar against the German Deutschmarke. While the manufacturer's suggested retails have gone up considerably, prices for used specimens (98% or less original condition) have not increased proportionately, and in some cases, have changed very little.

MODEL 8 — 12, 16, or 20 ga., case hardened scalloped boxlock action with light engraving, Greener crossbolt with chopper lump extension, extractors, DT's, standard walnut with checkering, cheekpiece on stock, sling swivels.

Mfg.'s Sug. Retail	$1,500	$1,350	$1,100	$900	$800	$700	$600	$500

Grading	100%	98%	95%	90%	80%	70%	60%

MODEL 47E — 12, 16, or 20 ga., case hardened scalloped boxlock action with chopper lump extension and Greener crossbolt, 26, 26¾, or 28 in. barrels, DT's, ejectors, deluxe checkered walnut, sling swivels, 6-7 lbs.

Mfg.'s Sug. Retail	$2,000	$1,750	$1,525	$1,325	$1,045	$820	$690	$630

MODEL 76E — top-of-the-line boxlock shotgun.

Mfg.'s Sug. Retail	$3,500	$3,150	$2,700	$2,300	$1,950	$1,650	$1,375	$995

MODEL 147E — 12, 16, or 20 ga., 26 in barrels, Anson & Deeley boxlock, any choke, double trigger, auto ejectors, straight or pistol grip stock, hunting scene engraved.

Mfg.'s Sug. Retail	$2,500	$2,250	$1,950	$1,650	$1,375	$995	$875	$780

MODEL 122E — 12, 16, or 20 ga., coin finished sidelock action with Greener crossbolt and chopper lump extension, cocking indicators, ejectors, DT's, deluxe game scene engraving. Importation disc. 1989.

Mfg.'s Sug. Retail	$3,500	$3,200	$2,800	$2,250	$1,950	$1,650	$1,375	$995

MODEL 147S — 12, 16, or 20 ga., coin finished sidelock action with Greener crossbolt and chopper lump extension, 26, 26¾, or 28 in. barrels, ejectors, DT's, deluxe game scene engraving, 6-7 lbs.

Mfg.'s Sug. Retail	$5,500	$5,100	$4,250	$3,500	$3,000	$2,500	$2,200	$1,950

MODEL 247S — 12, 16, or 20 ga., similar to Model 147S, except has deluxe scroll engraving.

Mfg.'s Sug. Retail	$5,500	$5,100	$4,250	$3,500	$3,000	$2,500	$2,200	$1,950

MODEL 347S — 12, 16, or 20 ga., similar to Model 247S, except has more elaborate engraving and better walnut.

Mfg.'s Sug. Retail	$6,500	$6,000	$5,000	$4,350	$3,600	$2,950	$2,425	$2,180

MODEL 447S — similar to Model 347S, except has different type of scroll engraving.

Mfg.'s Sug. Retail	$7,000	$6,650	$5,500	$4,600	$3,200	$2,725	$2,425	$2,180

MODEL 47S — 12, 16, or 20 ga., coin finished sidelock action with scroll engraving, Greener crossbolt, DT's, deluxe walnut stock (with cheek piece) and forearm, sling swivels.

Mfg.'s Sug. Retail	$4,500	$4,000	$3,350	$2,700	$2,250	$1,975	$1,625	$1,475

SHOTGUNS: O/U CURRENT IMPORTATION

Imported exclusively by Armes de Chasse located in Chadds Ford, PA, 19317.

Available in limited quantities, the models listed below include the 65% duty levied on all firearms imported from Warsaw Pact countries.

Prices below reflect the recent devaluation of the U.S. dollar against the E. German Deutschmarke. While the manufacturer's suggested retails have gone up considerably, prices for used specimens (98% or less original condition) have not increased proportionately, and in some cases, have changed very little.

The models listed below are also available in either 28 or .410 ga. for an additional charge of $900 and $1,050, respectively.

MODEL 200E — 12, 16, or 20 ga., case hardened scalloped boxlock action with minor scroll engraving, 26, 26¾, or 28 in. barrels, checkered European walnut stock and forearm, ejectors, DT's, solid rib, 6-7 lbs.

Mfg.'s Sug. Retail	$3,700	$3,300	$2,800	$2,350	$1,950	$1,785	$1,650	$1,525

A vent. rib can be obtained on this model for an additional charge.

MODEL 201E — similar to Model 200E, except has coin finished action with light game scene engraving.

Mfg.'s Sug. Retail	$4,800	$4,300	$3,500	$2,750	$2,300	$1,925	$1,750	$1,600

Grading	100%	98%	95%	90%	80%	70%	60%

MODEL 203E — 12, 16, or 20 ga.(24, 28, and 32 ga.'s were once available but are now disc.), 26, 26¾, or 28 in. barrels, VR, ejectors, DT's, elaborate scroll engraving on coin finished receiver, sidelock screws are H&H style but the sidelocks are not, choice of English or pistol grip stock, 6-7 lbs.

Mfg.'s Sug. Retail	$9,500	$9,000	$7,800	$6,200	$5,000	$4,100	$3,700	$3,350

Add $600 for flat cut game scene engraving.

Add $5,700 for deep relief game scene engraving featuring small animals.

Add $6,500 for deep relief game scene engraving featuring large animals.

MODEL 303E — similar to 203E, except H&H type with hidden thumbnail detachable sidelocks, double underlugs, more ornamentation and better wood.

Mfg.'s Sug. Retail	$16,500	$15,000	$12,000	$9,750	$8,250	$7,000	$5,800	$4,775

MODEL 304E (LUXUS GRADE) — available in SXS, O/U, Drilling, or Combo configuration, top-of-the-line Merkel with extensive engraving and typically stock carving (with or without inlays).

Values generally start at $16,500 and go up according to engraving and stock work.

Luxus variations are also encountered in the 201 and 203 series in addition to older pre-war models.

MERRILL

SPORTSMAN SINGLE-SHOT PISTOL — .22 S, L, or LR, .22 WMR, .22 Rem. Jet., .22 Hornet, 30 Herrett, .38 Spl., .357 Mag., .256 Win. Mag., .45 Colt, .44 Mag., or .30-30 cal., 9 in. barrel, hinged break open available, smooth walnut grips.

	$275	$250	$235	$210	$190	$175	$150

Add $70 for interchangeable barrels.

Add $25 for wrist support.

MERWIN HULBERT & CO.

Headquarters located in New York, NY from 1874-1891. Manufactured by Hopkins & Allen Manufacturing Co.

Merwin Hulbert & Co. were designers and promoters who created a revolver that had such advanced features as an automatic ejection system, streamlined appearance, and ease of shooting. Rather than list the individual variations, each specimen should be examined for originality and condition. Prices have recently escalated and currently these revolvers in average condition start in the $500+ range.

MIIDA

Manufacturer located in Japan.

MODEL 612 — O/U shotgun, 12 ga., 26 or 28 in. barrels, vent rib, various chokes, boxlock, auto ejectors, single selective trigger, checkered pistol grip stock. Mfg. 1972-1974.

$880	$745	$660	$605	$550	$495	$440

MODEL 612 SKEET GUN — same as 612, with 27 in. vent rib, skeet bore barrel, more elaborate engraving. Mfg. 1972-1974.

$990	$855	$770	$715	$660	$605	$550

MODEL 2200T TRAP GUN — same as 612, with 29¾ in. imp. mod. and full choke barrel, wide vent rib, 60% engraved coverage and select wood. Mfg. 1972-1974.

$1,100	$935	$880	$825	$770	$715	$660

MODEL 2200S SKEET GUN — same as 2200T, with 27 in. skeet bore barrel.

$1,100	$935	$880	$825	$770	$715	$660

Grading	100%	98%	95%	90%	80%	70%	60%

MODEL 2300 SERIES TRAP OR SKEET — same as 2200, with more engraving. Mfg. 1972-1974.

	$1,320	$1,100	$990	$935	$880	$825	$715

MODEL GRT GRANDEE TRAP GUN — 12 ga., 29 in. full choke barrels, single selective trigger, auto ejector, boxlock with side plates, receiver fully engraved as well as breech ends of barrel, trigger guard and locking lever, gold inlaid, high grade select walnut stock. Mfg. 1972-1974.

	$2,200	$1,980	$1,760	$1,650	$1,430	$1,320	$1,100

MODEL GRS GRANDEE SKEET GUN — same as GRT, with 27 in. skeet bored barrels.

	$2,200	$1,980	$1,760	$1,650	$1,430	$1,320	$1,100

MIROKU SHOTGUNS
Manufacturer located in Miroku, Japan.

Shotguns marked Miroku only without another trademark listing represent that period of manufacture before Miroku began manufacturing shotguns for other companies (i.e. Charles Daly, SKB, Browning, and others). Most guns marked Miroku only were made on a limited basis and although somewhat rare, collector desirability to date has been minimal. Since model notations were not specified in most instances (many shotguns were made to test market demand), a model rundown is virtually impossible. Values can be approx. ascertained by comparing a Miroku shotgun of similar gauge, features, engraving/wood, and condition to an equivalent Japanese Charles Daly model.

MITCHELL ARMS INC.
Importer and distributor located in Santa Ana, CA.

PISTOLS

AMERICAN EAGLE LUGER — 9mm Para., 4 in. barrel, toggle action.

Mfg.'s Sug. Retail	$625	$540	$475	$400	$350	$300	$260	$230

ROLLING BLOCK PISTOL — .22 LR, .22 Mag., .223, .357 Mag., or .45 LC cal., reproduction of the Remington Rolling Block design, 10 in. barrel. New 1991.

Mfg.'s Sug. Retail	$350	$315	$275	$240	$210	$185	$170	$150

PISTOLS: TOKAREV DESIGN

The models listed below are imported from Yugoslavia.

MODEL 57A — .30 Mauser, single action semi-auto, 9 shot mag., hammer block and mag. safety, all steel construction. Imported 1990 only.

	$240	$215	$180	$160	$145	$135	$120

Last Mfg.'s Sug. Retail was $280.

MODEL 70A — 9mm Para., otherwise similar to Model 57A. Imported 1990 only.

	$240	$215	$180	$160	$145	$135	$120

Last Mfg.'s Sug. Retail was $280.

88A OFFICERS MODEL — 9mm Para., newer slenderized variation issued to the Officers Corps., short slide and frame, finger extension mag. Imported 1990 only.

	$255	$225	$190	$165	$145	$135	$120

Last Mfg.'s Sug. Retail was $300.

SKORPION — .32 ACP only, single action, $4^{5}/_{8}$ in. barrel, 20 or 30 shot mag., blue finish only. Mfg. Yugoslavia. Imported 1990 only.

	$615	$520	$480	$440	$395	$360	$330

Last Mfg.'s Sug. Retail was $740.

Grading	100%	98%	95%	90%	80%	70%	60%

SPECTRE — 9mm, single action, 8 in. shrouded barrel, unique frame/barrel cooling system, 30 or 50 shot mag., approx. 4 lbs. Imported 1987-1988 only.

	100%	98%	95%	90%	80%	70%	60%
	$610	$515	$475	$440	$395	$360	$330

Last Mfg.'s Sug. Retail was $670.

Spectre Carbine — 9mm, carbine model with folding butt stock. Imported 1988 only.

	100%	98%	95%	90%	80%	70%	60%
	$610	$520	$480	$440	$395	$360	$330

Last Mfg.'s Sug. Retail was $680.

REVOLVERS

SINGLE ACTION ARMY — .22 LR, .357 Mag., .44 Mag., .45 ACP, or .45 Long Colt cal., 4¾, 5½, 6, or 7½ in. barrel lengths, hammer block safety mechanism, steel construction, case hardened frame, one piece walnut stock. Add $17 for adj. sight. New 1986.

Rimfire Model — .22 LR cal. Importation disc. 1989.

	100%	98%	95%	90%	80%	70%	60%
	$230	$200	$180	$160	$145	$130	$120

Add $30 for adj. rear sight.
Last Mfg.'s Sug. Retail was $280.

Centerfire Model — .357 Mag., .44 Mag., .45 ACP, or .45 LC cal.

Mfg.'s Sug. Retail	$349	$275	$225	$195	$170	$155	$145	$135

Add $50 for nickel finish.

Add $50 for adj. rear sight.

Add $76 for dual cylinder (includes .45 ACP cal.).

Silhouette Model — available with 10, 12, or 18 in. barrel in .44 Mag. or .45 LC cal.

Mfg.'s Sug. Retail	$450	$395	$325	$260	$220	$195	$170	$155

Add $175 for shoulder stock (available with 18 in. barrel only).
The shoulder stock is available with .44 Mag./.44-40 cal.'s only.

Dual Cylinder — available in either .22 LR/.22 Mag. (disc.), .22 LR/.22 Mag. stainless (disc. 1988), .44 Mag./.44-40, or .45 LC/.45 ACP (new 1990). New 1986.

Mfg.'s Sug. Retail	$425	$345	$280	$235	$200	$180	$165	$150

Add $50 for adj. rear sight.

Add $50 for nickel finish.

Stainless Model — available in .22 LR or .357 Mag. (disc. 1987) only, adj. sights. Imported 1986-1988 only.

	100%	98%	95%
	$260	$225	$195

Add $25 for .357 Mag.
Last Mfg.'s Sug. Retail was $301.

BAT MASTERSON MODEL — .45 LC cal., 4¾ in. barrel with full ejector rod housing, nickel plated, one piece walnut stocks, hammer-block safety, rear sight is square notch in frame, two piece backstrap. Imported 1989-90 only.

Mfg.'s Sug. Retail	$349	$315	$275	$240	$210	$185	$170	$150

MODEL 1875 REMINGTON — .357 Mag. or .45 LC cal., royal blue finish with color case hardened frame, walnut grips. New 1990.

Mfg.'s Sug. Retail	$399	$345	$285	$245	$210	$185	$170	$150

Add $76 for nickel finish.

Add $51 for extra convertible .45 ACP cylinder.

RIFLES: MODERN

M-16 — .22 LR, .22 Mag. (disc. 1987), or .32 ACP cal., patterned after Colt's AR-15. New 1987.

Mfg.'s Sug. Retail	$325	$265	$225	$185	$160	$150	$140	$130

Add $75 for .22 Mag. cal. or .32 ACP (disc. 1988).

CAR-15/22 — .22 LR, carbine variation of M-16 with shorter barrel and collapsible stock. New 1990.

Mfg.'s Sug. Retail	$350	$295	$240	$195	$160	$150	$140	$130

Grading	100%	98%	95%	90%	80%	70%	60%

GALIL — .22 LR or .22 Mag. cal., patterned after Galil semi-auto paramilitary design rifle. New 1987.

Mfg.'s Sug. Retail	$325	$265	$225	$185	$160	$150	$140	$130

Add $25 for .22 Mag. cal.

MAS — .22 LR or .22 Mag. cal., patterned after French MAS rifle. New 1987.

Mfg.'s Sug. Retail	$325	$265	$225	$185	$160	$150	$140	$130

Add $75 for .22 Mag. cal. (disc. 1988).

PPS-50 — .22 LR cal., patterned after the Russian WWII PPS military rifle, full length barrel shroud, 20 shot banana clip, adj. rear sight, walnut stock. New 1989.

Mfg.'s Sug. Retail	$325	$265	$225	$185	$160	$150	$140	$130

Add $50 for 50 shot drum magazine.

AK-22 — .22 LR or .22 Mag. (new 1988) cal., copy of the famous Russian AK-47, fully adj. sights, built in cleaning rod, high quality European walnut stock, 20 shot clip mag. New 1985.

Mfg.'s Sug. Retail	$325	$265	$225	$185	$160	$150	$140	$130

Add $25 for .22 Mag.

AK-47 — 7.62 x 39 cal., copy of the original SKS AK-47, semi-auto, teak stock and forend, 30 shot steel mag., last shot hold open. Mfg. Yugoslavia. Imported 1986-1989.

	$595	$550	$495	$450	$400	$360	$310

Add $23 for steel folding butt stock.

Add $150 for 75 shot steel drum mag.

Last Mfg.'s Sug. Retail was $675.

.308 NATO AK-47 (M77B1) — .308 (7.62 NATO) cal., milled receiver, adj. gas port, otherwise similar to AK-47 except has scope rail, day/night Tritium sights, and 20 shot mag. Imported 1989 only.

	$900	$800	$700	$595	$525	$475	$425

Add $600 for military issue sniper scope and rings.

Last Mfg.'s Sug. Retail was $775.

M76 — similar to AK-47, except is 7.9mm cal. and has longer barrel and frame set up for scope mount, counter sniper design, 10 shot mag., mfg. to mil. spec.'s. Imported 1986-1989.

	$1,725	$1,535	$1,350	$1,100	$900	$820	$760

Last Mfg.'s Sug. Retail was $1,995.

SKS-M59 — 7.62 x 39 cal., copy of the SKS-M59 standard rifle, full walnut stock, fully adj. sights, gas operated. Mfg. in Yugoslavia. Imported 1986-1989.

	$610	$525	$465	$410	$360	$315	$260

Last Mfg.'s Sug. Retail was $699.

R.P.K. — 7.62 X 39mm cal., forged heavy barrel with cooling fins, teak stock, detachable bipod, mil. spec.'s. Imported 1989 only.

	$875	$775	$675	$565	$495	$450	$400

Last Mfg.'s Sug. Retail was $995.

RIFLES: REPRODUCTIONS

HENRY RIFLE — .44-40 cal., polished brass frame, octagonal barrel, original loading system. Importation began 1990.

Mfg.'s Sug. Retail	$875	$750	$650	$585	$520	$465	$415	$375

Iron frame also available at extra charge.

MODEL 1866 — .22 LR (disc.), .38 Spl. (disc.), or .44-40 cal., patterned after the Winchester Model 1866 rifle, solid brass frame, octagon barrel. Importation began 1990.

Mfg.'s Sug. Retail	$699	$610	$525	$465	$415	$375	$335	$295

This model is also available in a carbine variation.

Grading	100%	98%	95%	90%	80%	70%	60%

MODEL 1873 — .22 LR (disc.), .38 Spl.(disc), .44-40, or .45 LC cal., patterned after the Winchester 1873 rifle, octagon barrel, solid steel frame. Importation began 1990.

Mfg.'s Sug. Retail	$795	$700	$625	$550	$515	$465	$415	$375

This model is also available in a carbine variation.

MORINI

Target Pistol Manufacturer located in Italy. Previously imported and distributed by Osborne's, located in Cheboygan, MI.

Morini has limited importation into the U.S. and currently does not have an exclusive domestic distributor.

CM-80 STANDARD — .22 LR only, single shot, adj. grips, frame, and sights. Add $50 for left-hand model. Importation disc. 1989.

	$925	$825	$725	$650	$585	$520	$465

Last Mfg.'s Sug. Retail was $1,015.

CM-80 Super Competition — similar to CM-80 Standard, except has deluxe finish, and unique plexiglass front sighting system. Add $50 for left-hand model. Importation disc. 1989.

	$1,085	$920	$800	$690	$590	$520	$450

Last Mfg.'s Sug. Retail was $1,196.

MOSSBERG, O.F. & SONS, INC.

Manufactured 1892-1919 under Oscar F. Mossberg in Fitchburg & Chicopee Falls, MA. From 1919 to date, manufacturer has been located at North Haven, CT.

PISTOLS: DISCONTINUED

BROWNIE — .22 LR, top break open action, rotating firing pin, 4 barrel derringer, double action, 4 shot, limited production.

	$350	$300	$260	$225	$200	$180	$160

RIFLES: DISCONTINUED

MODEL K PUMP RIFLE — .22 S, L, and LR, tube mag., hammerless, 22 in. barrel, takedown, open sights, plain straight stock. Mfg. 1922-1931.

	$165	$130	$110	$95	$70	$60	$50

MODEL M PUMP RIFLE — same as K, except 24 in. octagon barrel. Mfg. 1928-1931.

	$180	$150	$120	$105	$85	$70	$60

MODEL L — .22 S, L, and LR, falling block action, single shot, 24 in. barrel, takedown, open sights, pistol grip stock. Mfg. 1927-1932.

	$305	$240	$220	$195	$165	$155	$130

Note: From 1930 to present, Mossberg has manufactured 40 bolt action .22 rifles, both single and repeating. These guns are very practical and serviceable. Higher priced rifles are listed separately in many places, our concern being values. They are all in a range from about $125 for 100% to $25 for 60% and under.

Mossberg also manufactured 13 different autoloading .22 rifles in the same category. Values are $135 for 100% to $35 for 60% and under.

MODEL 400 PALOMINO — .22 S, L, and LR, lever action, tube mag., open sights, checkered Monte Carlo stock. Mfg. 1959-1964.

	$140	$110	$100	$90	$65	$55	$40

MODEL 402 PALOMINO CARBINE — same as 400, except 18½ in. or 20 in. barrel. Mfg. 1961-1971.

	$140	$110	$100	$90	$65	$55	$40

Grading	100%	98%	95%	90%	80%	70%	60%

MODEL 800 — .222, .22-250, .243, or .308 cal., bolt action, 22 in. barrel, folding sight, checkered pistol grip stock. Mfg. 1967-disc.

	$220	$195	$165	$110	$85	$55	$45

MODEL 800VT — similar to 800, except .222, .22-250, or .243 cal., 24 in. heavy barrel, no sights. Mfg. 1968-disc.

	$220	$195	$165	$110	$85	$55	$45

MODEL 800M — same as 800, except 20 in. barrel, full length stock, spoon bolt handle. Mfg. 1969-1972.

	$275	$240	$220	$205	$175	$160	$145

MODEL 800D — similar to 800, with roll-over combination and cheek piece, checkered stock with rosewood forearm tip and pistol cap, no .222 available. Mfg. 1970-1973.

	$290	$265	$230	$195	$175	$165	$140

MODEL 810 — .270, .30-06, 8mm Rem. Mag., or .338 Win. Mag. cal., bolt action, 22 or 24 in. barrel, leaf sight, checkered Monte Carlo stock. Mfg. 1970-disc.

	$285	$260	$220	$175	$160	$150	$130

MODEL 472 — .30-30 or .35 Rem. cal., lever action carbine, 20 in. barrel, open sights, pistol grip or straight stock, saddle ring on straight model. Mfg. 1972-disc.

	$180	$155	$145	$130	$120	$110	$90

MODEL 472 RIFLE — same as Carbine, except 24 in. barrel, pistol grip stock. Mfg. 1974-1976.

	$195	$165	$155	$145	$130	$120	$100

MODEL 472 BRUSH GUN — same as Carbine, except 18 in. barrel, straight stock only. Mfg. 1974-1976.

	$195	$165	$155	$145	$130	$120	$100

MODEL 472 ONE IN FIVE THOUSAND — same as Brush Gun, except Indian scene etched on receiver, brass butt plate, saddle ring and barrel bands, select stock, only 5,000 mfg., 1974.

	$415	$210	$195	$175	$165	$145	$120

MODEL 479 PCA — .30-30 lever action, 20 in. barrel, 6 shot capacity.

	$195	$135	$120	$110	$95	$85	$75

MODEL 479 RR — limited edition "Roy Rodgers" signature model, gold trigger, barrel bands, 5,000 total mfg. New 1983.

	$350	$275	$215				

MODEL 144 — .22 cal. only, bolt action, 7 shot detachable mag., 27 in. barrel, target style stock and sights, with swivels, 8½ lbs. Disc. 1985.

	$175	$160	$155	$150	$145	$140	$135

Last Mfg.'s Sug. Retail was $210.

MODEL 479 — .30-30 cal. only, lever action, 6 shot tube mag., 20 in. barrel with adj. sights, 7 lbs. Mfg. 1985 only.

	$190	$175	$160	$150	$145	$140	$135

Last Mfg.'s Sug. Retail was $232.

Mossberg also has made several .22 bolt action and semi-auto sporters that are in the $115 - $130 price range. While they are good shooting models, they are not covered in this section as they are not collectible.

RIFLES: RECENT MANUFACTURE

In 1985, Mossberg purchased the parts inventory and importing rights for those rifles that Smith & Wesson imported from Howa of Japan. These new models were identical to those models which S&W disc.

Grading	100%	98%	95%	90%	80%	70%	60%

MODEL 1500 MOUNTAINEER GRADE I — .223, .243, .270, 30-06, or 7mm Mag. cal., bolt action, 22 or 24 (7mm Mag. only) in. barrel, 5 or 6 shot mag., available with or without sights, hardwood stock is satin finished, blued finish, about 7 lbs. 10 oz. Imported 1986-87 only. Add $15 for 7mm Rem. Mag. cal., $25 for iron sights.

	$285	$250	$225	$195	$180	$165	$150

Last Mfg.'s Sug. Retail was $335.

Model 1500 Varmint — .22-250, .223, or .308 cal., similar to Model 1500 Grade I, except has 24 in. heavy barrel only, Monte Carlo stock. Imported 1986-87 only. Add $10 for parkerized finish (oil finished stock with swivels — not available in .22-250 cal.).

	$360	$300	$270	$235	$205	$190	$175

Last Mfg.'s Sug. Retail was $457.

Blued finish and high gloss wood finish available with .22-250 or .223 cal. only. Parkerized variation is available in .223 or .308 cal. only (matte wood finish, includes swivels).

MODEL 1500 MOUNTAINEER GRADE II — similar to Grade I Mountaineer, except has select checkered American walnut stock. Also available in .300 or .338 Win. Mag. cal. Imported 1986-87 only.

	$315	$270	$235	$205	$190	$175	$160

Add $15 for Mag. cal.'s.
Add $25 for iron sights.
Last Mfg.'s Sug. Retail was $368.

MODEL 1550 — similar to Model 1500, except has detachable mag. and available in standard cal.'s (.243, .270, or .30-06), with or without sights. Imported 1986-87 only. Add $24 for iron sights.

	$330	$280	$245	$210	$190	$175	$160

Last Mfg.'s Sug. Retail was $391.

MODEL 1700 LS — .243, .270, or .30-06 cal., no sights, jeweled bolt body and knurled bolt handle, detachable mag., Schnabel forend, deluxe checkering, 7 lbs. Imported 1986-87 only.

	$405	$365	$310	$275	$240	$205	$190

Last Mfg.'s Sug. Retail was $492.

SHOTGUNS

Note: Mossberg made 12 bolt action shotguns from 1940-present. They are good, serviceable guns valued at $125 for 100% to $25 for 60% and under.

In 1985, Mossberg purchased the parts inventory and manufacturing rights for the shotguns that Smith & Wesson disc. These new models (manufactured in Japan) are identical to those models which S&W disc.

MODEL 200K — slide shotgun, 12 ga., 28 in., select choke, plain pistol grip stock, black nylon slide handle. Mfg. 1955-1959.

	$130	$110	$100	$90	$65	$55	$40

MODEL 200D — same as 200K, except interchangeable choke tubes (2). Mfg. 1955-1959.

	$130	$110	$100	$90	$65	$55	$40

BOLT ACTION MODEL — 12, 20, or .410 ga., 3 shot mag., 26, 28, or 38 in. barrel. Deduct $10 for .410 ga. Disc. 1985.

	$115	$105	$100	$90	$65	$55	$40

Add $20 for 38 in. barrel.
Last Mfg.'s Sug. Retail was $135.

HOME SECURITY .410 — .410 ga. only, 18½ in. barrel with spreader choke, Model 500 slide-action, matte beaded metal finish, synthetic field stock with pistol grip forearm, 6¼ lbs. New 1990.

Mfg.'s Sug. Retail	$388	$325	$285	$250	$225	$200	$185	$165

Grading	100%	98%	95%	90%	80%	70%	60%

Laser Home Security .410 — includes laser sighting device in right front of forearm. New 1990.

Mfg.'s Sug. Retail	$699	$610	$550	$495	$450	$400	$360	$325

MODEL 500 REGAL SERIES — 12 or 20 ga., slide action, 26 or 28 in. barrel, select checkered walnut, vent rib. Add $19 for Accu-choke. Importation disc. 1987.

	$240	$195	$175	$165	$155	$145	$135

Add $39 for Combo pack (includes 1 extra 24 in. slugster barrel).
Last Mfg.'s Sug. Retail was $286.

MODEL 500 FIELD GRADE — 12, 20 or .410 ga., slide action, 20-28 in. barrel, various chokes, upper receiver slide safety, C Lect (disc.) & Accu chokes, or with 24 in. slug barrel, checkered pistol grip stock after 1973. Mfg. 1962-present.

Mfg.'s Sug. Retail	$317	$245	$195	$160	$135	$120	$110	$100

Add $5 for .410 ga.

Subtract $30 if without VR.

Add $10 for C Lect (disc.).

Add $11 for Accu II chokes (VR barrel only).

Add $9 for Bantam Model (20 ga. only with youth dimensions & 22 in. barrel - new 1991).

Model 500 Combo — includes a wide variety of extra barrel combinations including slug barrel options, prices vary slightly depending on the configuration (gauge/barrel/choke set-up).

Mfg.'s Sug. Retail	$355	$295	$235	$200	$175	$155	$145	$135

Subtract approx. $25-$35 if without VR.

Add $70 for rifled bore slug barrel with integral scope base.

Model 500 Quail Unlimited — 20 ga. only, 26 in. VR barrel with Accu-II chokes (3), engraved receiver and hand selected stock and forearm, 3,500 mfg. in 1991 to commemorate the 10th anniversary of Quail Unlimited.

Mfg.'s Sug. Retail	$359	$285	$235	$195				

Model 500 Camo/Speedfeed — 12 ga. only, parkerized camo metal and stock finish, 24-30 in. vent rib barrel (choice of cylinder bore with rifle sights or Accu-II chokes), includes swivels, camo sling, and drilled and tapped receiver, stock holds 4 extra shells. New 1986.

Mfg.'s Sug. Retail	$344	$275	$225	$185				

Add $11 for Accu-II choke system.

Add $30 for speedfeed in synthetic stock (disc. 1990).

Add $46 for Camo Combo (includes extra 24 in. slug barrel).

Add $13 for Turkey Model (24 in. VR barrel with Accu-II chokes).

Model 500 Sporting Steel Shot — 12 ga. only, 3 in. chamber, 28 in. vent rib multi-choke barrel capable of shooting steel shot. Mfg. 1987-90.

	$250	$200	$175	$165	$155	$145	$135

Add $29 for camo stock (disc. 1989).

This model was phased out of production in 1990 since all Mossberg shotguns currently manufactured are capable of shooting steel shot safely. The last mfg.'s sug. retail was $295.

Model 500 Trophy Slugster — 12 or 20 ga., 18½ or 24 in. barrel with iron sights, drilled and tapped receiver.

Mfg.'s Sug. Retail	$312	$260	$220	$185	$160	$150	$140	$130

Add $37 for rifled bore.

Add $67 with integral scope base (rifle sights provided).

MODEL 500 HI-RIB TRAP — 12 ga. only, high post trap rib, 28 or 30 in. barrel. Add $20 for Accu-choke. Disc. 1986.

	$285	$250	$230	$200	$175	$155	$140

Last Mfg.'s Sug. Retail was $334.

MODEL 500 SUPER GRADE — same as Field, except vent rib and checkered, no 16 ga. Mfg. 1965-1976.

	$250	$215	$180	$170	$160	$140	$130

Grading	100%	98%	95%	90%	80%	70%	60%

MODEL 500 ATR SUPER GRADE — same as Field, except 12 ga., vent rib, 30 in. full, checkered Monte Carlo. Mfg. 1968-1971.

	$295	$260	$230	$200	$175	$155	$140

MODEL 500 PIGEON GRADE — same as 500 Super Grade, except etched and scroll engraving, select wood, floating vent rib. Mfg. 1971-1975.

	$385	$330	$305	$250	$210	$185	$165

MODEL 500 APTR PIGEON GRADE TRAP — same as 500 ATR, except trap style stock. Mfg. 1971-1975.

	$440	$415	$330	$250	$220	$200	$175

MODEL 500 DSPR DUCK STAMP COMMERCIAL — same as Pigeon Grade, except wood duck etching. 1,000 mfg. 1975.

	$525	$330	$310	$285	$260	$220	$195

MODEL 500L SERIES — same as 500 Field Grade, except no 16 ga., etched receiver, new style stock and slide. Mfg. 1977-1983.

	$250	$220	$210	$200	$175	$165	$140

MODEL 500 PERSUADER — same as 500L, except 12 ga. only, 6 or 8 shot, 18½ or 20 in. plain barrel, optional rifle sights, parkerized, optional bayonet lug, plain pistol grip wood or synthetic stock.

Mfg.'s Sug. Retail	$286	$235	$190	$160	$145	$130	$115	$100

Add $40 for 8 shot.
Add $15 for rifle sights.
Add $25 for parkerized finish.
Add $15 for pistol grip (disc.).
Add $17 for speedfeed stock (disc. 1990).
Add $40 for combo with pistol grip (disc.).

Night Persuader Special Edition — 12 ga. only, includes synthetic stock and factory installed Mepro light night sight bead sight, only 300 mfg. for Lew Horton Distributing in 1990 only.

	$295	$250	$200	$175	$150	$130	$115

Last Mfg.'s Sug. Retail was $296.

MODEL 500 MARINER — 12 ga. only, 18½ or 20 in. barrel, Marinecote finish on all metal parts (more durable than stainless steel), synthetic stock and forearm, 6 or 8 shot.

Mfg.'s Sug. Retail	$385	$320	$270	$200

Add $17 for 8 shot mag. (disc.).
Add $15 for pistol grip adapter (mini-combo - disc.).
Add $23 for speedfeed stock (mini-combo only - disc.).

MODEL 500 CAMPER — 12, 20, or .410 ga. only, 18½ in. barrel, synthetic pistol grip (no stock), camo carrying case optional, blued finish. Mfg. 1986-90 only.

	$235	$190	$175	$165	$155	$145	$135

Add $25 for .410 ga.
Add $30 for camo case.
Last Mfg.'s Sug. Retail was $276.

MODEL 500 CRUISER — 12 or 20 ga., 18½ in. cylinder bore barrel with shroud, 6 shot mag., pistol grip only. Disc. 1990.

	$235	$190	$175	$165	$155	$145	$135

Last Mfg.'s Sug. Retail was $276.

Grading	100%	98%	95%	90%	80%	70%	60%

MODEL 500 BULLPUP — 12 ga. only, 18½ or 20 in. barrel, bullpup configuration, 6 shot mag., includes shrouded barrel, carrying handle, ejection port in stock, employs high impact materials. Mfg. 1986-90 only.

	$350	$300	$255

Add $15 for 8 shot mag. (disc.).
Last Mfg.'s Sug. Retail was $425.

INTIMIDATOR LASER — 12 ga. only, 3 in. chamber, 18½ or 20 in. cyl. bore barrel, 6 or 9 shot tube mag., blue or parkerized finish, synthetic field stock, includes laser sighting device. New 1990.

Mfg.'s Sug. Retail	$635	$525	$460	$400	$350	$295	$270	$225

Add $53 for parkerized finish.
Add $68 for 9 shot mag. (20 in. barrel only).

GHOST RING SIGHT — 12 ga. only, 3 in. chamber, 18½ or 20 in. cyl. bore barrel, 6 or 9 shot tube mag., blue or parkerized finish, synthetic field stock, includes ghost ring sighting device. New 1990.

Mfg.'s Sug. Retail	$345	$285	$230	$190	$160	$150	$140	$130

Add $53 for parkerized finish.
Add $65 for 9 shot mag. (20 in. barrel only).

MODEL 590 — similar to Model 500, except has 9 shot mag., 20 in. barrel with ¾ shroud, and bayonet lug, blued or parkerized finish. New 1987.

Mfg.'s Sug. Retail	$350	$300	$240	$200	$175	$155	$140	$125

Add $50 for parkerized finish.
Add $17 for speedfeed stock.

Model 590 Mariner — similar to Model 500 Mariner except is 9 shot and has 20 in. barrel. New 1989.

Mfg.'s Sug. Retail	$456	$385	$355	$260	$220	$190	$165	$150

Add $17 for speedfeed stock (disc. 1990).
Add $15 for pistol grip adapter (mini combo - disc.).

Model 590 Bullpup — similar to Model 500 Bullpup except is 9 shot and has 20 in. barrel. Mfg. 1989-90 only.

	$425	$360	$300	$250	$225	$195	$175

Last Mfg.'s Sug. Retail was $497.

MODEL 835 ULTI-MAG — 12 ga. with 3½ in. chamber (new 1988), slide action, 24 (Turkey Model - new 1990) or 28 in. VR barrel with Accu-Mag choke tubes, 6 shot mag., safety on top rear of receiver, choice of camo synthetic or checkered hardwood stock. New late 1988.

Mfg.'s Sug. Retail	$430	$375	$310	$265	$220	$190	$165	$150

Add $30 for synthetic camo field stock.
Various Combo packages are available in this model with prices ranging from $469-$534 depending on barrel chokings and scope base options.

MODEL 835 WILD TURKEY FED. LIMITED EDITION — 12 ga. with 3½ in. chamber, 24 in. VR barrel with Accu-Mag. chokes, camo finish, includes camo sling, medallion in stock, and 10-pack of Federal Turkey loads. Mfg. 1989 only.

	$425	$360	$295

Last Mfg.'s Sug. Retail was $477.

NWTF SPECIAL EDITION — 12 ga. only, 24 in. VR barrel with Accu-Mag chokes, features Realtree camo finish, drilled and tapped receiver, 7½ lbs. Mfg. 1991 only to commemorate the National Wild Turkey Federation.

Mfg.'s Sug. Retail	$498	$430	$370	$325

MODEL 835 WATERFOWL LIMITED EDITION — 12 ga. with 3½ in. chamber, 28 in. VR barrel with Accu-Mag. chokes, camo finish, synthetic stock, camo sling. Mfg. 1990 only.

	$425	$360	$295

Last Mfg.'s Sug. Retail was $480.

Grading	100%	98%	95%	90%	80%	70%	60%

MODEL 3000 — 12 or 20 ga. only, 3 in. chamber, slide action, steel receiver, double action bars, various chokes and vent rib barrel lengths, checkered walnut stock and forearm, vent recoil pad. Add $25 for multi-choke II. This model was introduced in 1986 and the field version was disc. in 1987. Law enforcement variations are still available.

	$325	$275	$250	$220	$200	$185	$170

Last Mfg.'s Sug. Retail was $360.

Model 3000 Waterfowler — 12 ga. only, similar to Model 3000, except has dull matte finish on wood and metal, includes swivels and camouflaged sling, vent rib only. Add $30 for multi-choke II option, $70 for camo/speedfeed stock. Mfg. 1986 only.

	$340	$295	$265				

Last Mfg.'s Sug. Retail was $386.

Model 3000 Law Enforcement — 12 or 20 ga. only, 18½ or 20 in. cylinder bore only, rifle or bead sights. Imported 1986-87 only.

	$325	$275	$250	$220	$200	$185	$170

Add $25 for rifle sights.

Add $33 for black speedfeed stock.

Last Mfg.'s Sug. Retail was $362.

MODEL 1000 — 12 or 20 ga., gas semi-auto, 2¾ in. chamber, scroll engraved aluminum alloy receiver, plain or vent rib barrel, also available in trap and skeet configuration, checkered walnut stock and forearm. Imported 1986-87 only. Vent rib became standard in 1987.

	$410	$345	$300	$270	$245	$220	$200

Add $28 for multi-choke II.

Deduct $50 if without VR.

Last Mfg.'s Sug. Retail was $472.

Model 1000 barrels are not interchangeable with Model 1000 Super barrels.

Model 1000 Junior — similar to Model 1000, except 20 ga. only, shortened stock, and 22 in. VR multi-choke barrel. Imported 1986-87 only.

	$425	$355	$310	$275	$250	$220	$200

Last Mfg.'s Sug. Retail was $499.

Model 1000 Slug — 12 or 20 ga., 22 in. barrel with rifle sights, recoil pad. Imported 1986-87 only.

	$405	$340	$295	$270	$245	$220	$200

Last Mfg.'s Sug. Retail was $464.

Model 1000 Skeet — 12 or 20 ga., steel receiver, 26 in. vent rib barrel bored skeet. Mfg. 1986 only.

	$395	$335	$295	$270	$245	$220	$200

Last Mfg.'s Sug. Retail was $439.

MODEL 1000 SUPER — 12 or 20(Super 20) ga., gas semi-auto, 3 in. chambers, shoots 2¾ and 3 in. shells interchangeably, steel receiver, vent recoil pad, select checkered walnut stock and forearm, multi-choke II is standard (except on slug barrel). Slug models are approx. the same price as values listed directly below. Imported 1986-87 only.

	$495	$405	$365	$330	$295	$270	$245

Last Mfg.'s Sug. Retail was $577.

Model 1000 Super barrels are not interchangeable with Model 1000 barrels.

Model 1000 Super Waterfowler — 12 ga. only, matte finished wood and metal, includes swivels and camouflaged sling, 28 in. multi-choke barrel. Imported 1986-87 only.

	$510	$430	$370				

Last Mfg.'s Sug. Retail was $605.

Model 1000 Super Skeet — 12 or 20 ga., 25 in. barrel, jug choking. Imported 1986-87 only.

	$575	$495	$450	$410	$375	$330	$295

Last Mfg.'s Sug. Retail was $658.

Grading	100%	98%	95%	90%	80%	70%	60%

Model 1000 Super Trap — 12 ga. only, 30 in. multi-choke II barrel with high vent rib, Monte Carlo stock, recoil pad. Mfg. 1986 only.

	$470	$380	$345	$320	$285	$270	$250

Last Mfg.'s Sug. Retail was $560.

MODEL 5500 SEMI-AUTO — 12 ga., 2¾ or 3 in. mag., gas operated, 18½ - 30 in. barrels. Add $20 for vent rib. Disc. 1985.

	$250	$235	$205	$185	$170	$155	$140

Last Mfg.'s Sug. Retail was $307.

Model 5500 Mag. — 12 ga. only, 3 in. chamber, 30 in. vent rib barrel. Disc. 1985.

	$275	$250	$225	$205	$190	$175	$160

Last Mfg.'s Sug. Retail was $325.

MODEL 5500 MKII — 12 ga. only, supplied with 2 VR barrels - 26 in./2¾ in. chamber or 28 in./3 in. chamber VR barrel, includes choice of Accu-II choke tubes (lead shot only) or Accu-Steel choke tubes, blue or camo finish (new 1990), checkered hardwood stock and forearm, top receiver safety, recoil pad, 7½ lbs. New 1989.

Mfg.'s Sug. Retail	$425	$365	$300	$260	$220	$190	$165	$150

Add $10 for 24 in. rifled bore barrel.

Add $43 for camo metal finish and synthetic stock.

Add $30 for Turkey Model (24 in. barrel, camo finish, and synthetic stock).

This model is also available with different Combo options. Prices vary between $463-$484, depending on configuration of barrel choking.

Model 5500 U.S. Shooting Team—2¾ in. chamber, 26 in. non-Mag. barrel with VR and Accu-II chokes, blue finish, checkered walnut stock and forearm, 7½ lbs. New 1991.

Mfg.'s Sug. Retail	$441	$375	$310	$260	$220	$190	$165	$150

MODEL 712 — 12 ga. only, semi-auto, gas operated, shoots 2¾ and 3 in. shells interchangeably, plain barrel or vent rib, top of receiver safety, checkered hardwood stock, rubber recoil pad, fixed or Accu Choke II choking. Imported 1986-1988 only.

	$285	$250	$220	$200	$190	$175	$160

Subtract $25 without Accu II choking.

Add $90 for combo pack (includes 1 extra 24 in. slugster barrel.

Last Mfg.'s Sug. Retail was $345.

Model 712 Steel Shot — similar to Model 712, except has Accu-Steel choking system for steel shot, 28 in. VR barrel. Imported 1988 only.

	$290	$250	$220	$200	$190	$175	$160

Last Mfg.'s Sug. Retail was $349.

Model 712 Camo/Speedfeed — 12 ga. only, similar to Model 712, except has camo finished metal parts, stock, and forearm, 24 or 28 in. barrel. Add $20 for Accu II choke. Imported 1986-87 only.

	$340	$295	$240

Last Mfg.'s Sug. Retail was $390.

MODEL 712 REGAL — 12 or 20 ga., action same as Model 712, special bright bluing, vent rib only, deluxe checkered walnut stock and forearm, gold trigger, inlaid medallion on receiver, top of receiver safety. Add $20 for Accu II choke. Imported 1986-87 only.

	$310	$280	$250	$225	$200	$185	$170

Last Mfg.'s Sug. Retail was $366.

NEW HAVEN BRAND — same as previous models, except plainer finish. Disc.

Values are 20% less per model.

MUSGRAVE

Manufacturer located in the Republic of South Africa since 1951.

Currently, this manufacturer has no importation into the U.S. (due to Federal regulations) and listings below represent older models. Newer models manufactured by Musgrave (imported into Austria and Switzerland) include the Model 90 (features Musgrave action)

Grading	100%	98%	95%	90%	80%	70%	60%

Standard Rifle, Model 90 Light Rifle, Mini-90, Model 90 Varmint, Model 90 De Luxe Rifle, Magnum Rifle in addition to the same series in the Mauser 98 action. More information can be obtained (including prices and availability) by writing this manufacturer directly at: MUSGRAVE MANUFACTURERS & DISTRIBUTORS LTD., P.O. Box 183, Bloemfontein 9300, Jagersfontein Road, Republic of South Africa.

VALIANT BOLT ACTION RIFLE — .243, .270, .30-06, .308, or 7mm Mag. cal., 24 in. barrel, leaf sight, skip checkered straight stock, pistol grip. Mfg. 1971-1976.

	100%	98%	95%	90%	80%	70%	60%
	$375	$325	$275	$250	$220	$195	$175

PREMIER — same as Valiant, with 26 in. barrel, select Monte Carlo stock, rosewood pistol grip cap and forearm tip.

	100%	98%	95%	90%	80%	70%	60%
	$425	$365	$315	$275	$250	$225	$200

RSA SINGLE SHOT TARGET RIFLE — .308 cal. only, 26 in. heavy barrel, target sights and stock. Mfg. 1971-1976.

	100%	98%	95%	90%	80%	70%	60%
	$425	$365	$315	$275	$250	$225	$200

MUSKETEER RIFLES
Firearms International Company, Washington, D.C.

SPORTER — .243, .25-06, .270, .265 Mag., .308, .30-06, 7mm Mag., or .300 Win. Mag. cal., bolt action, FN Mauser action, 24 in. barrel, no sights, checkered Monte Carlo stock. Mfg. 1963-1972.

	100%	98%	95%	90%	80%	70%	60%
	$375	$325	$275	$250	$220	$195	$175

SPORTER DELUXE — adj. trigger, select wood, tear drop pistol grip, skipline checkering.

	100%	98%	95%	90%	80%	70%	60%
	$425	$365	$315	$275	$250	$225	$200

CARBINE — same as Sporter, except 20 in. barrel.

	100%	98%	95%	90%	80%	70%	60%
	$375	$325	$275	$250	$220	$195	$175

NOTES

NAMBU PISTOLS

Manufacturer located in Japan for the Japanese Military between 1902-1945.

Grading	100%	98%	95%	90%	80%	70%	60%

TYPE 14 — 8mm, semi-auto pistol, recoil operated, 4.7 in. barrel, blued, wood grips, 8 shot mag., a simply designed pistol used by Japanese armed forces from 1925-1945.

Type 14 Nambu's have a 3 digit number just forward of the lanyard ring on the right side of frame (on back of grip). To determine year and month of manufacture add "1925" to the first two digits and the last number will indicate the month (i.e. code 13.3 indicates a gun built in March of 1938).

Add 10% for matching mag. on models listed below.

1925-1930 Mfg.

	100%	98%	95%	90%	80%	70%	60%
	$475	$420	$360	$320	$295	$260	$230

1930-1935 Mfg. — small trigger guard.

	100%	98%	95%	90%	80%	70%	60%
	$375	$320	$260	$220	$200	$180	$165

1935-1945 Mfg. — large trigger guard.

	100%	98%	95%	90%	80%	70%	60%
	$295	$260	$215	$195	$180	$165	$150

Add 10% for strawed trigger and safety.

TYPE 94 — 8mm, semi-auto, recoil operated, 3.8 in. barrel, blued, and bakelite wood grips, 6 shot mag. Mfg. 1934-1945.

	100%	98%	95%	90%	80%	70%	60%
	$275	$225	$185	$160	$150	$135	$120

Add 20% for pre-WWII commercial.

BABY NAMBU — 7mm Nambu, semi-auto, 3¼ in. barrel, blued, wood grips, grip safety, one of the most desirable Japanese handguns.

	100%	98%	95%	90%	80%	70%	60%
	$2,300	$2,000	$1,800	$1,600	$1,475	$1,300	$1,050

Add 10% for matching mag.

Add 50% for chamber marked "TGE" (Tokyo Gas & Electric).

PAPA NAMBU (MODEL 1904) — 8mm, semi-auto, 4.7 in. barrel, wood grips, grip safety, 8 shot mag., essentially the same action as the Baby, but a larger version. Mfg. 1904-1925.

	100%	98%	95%	90%	80%	70%	60%
	$1,225	$995	$875	$775	$700	$600	$500

Add 10% for matching mag.

1893 REVOLVER (MODEL 26) — 9mm, double action only, 4.7 in. barrel, blued, wood grips. Mfg. 1893-1925.

	100%	98%	95%	90%	80%	70%	60%
	$300	$250	$210	$170	$150	$135	$120

NAVY ARMS COMPANY

Importers since 1958 located in Ridgefield, NJ. Navy Arms Firearms are fabricated by Various Manufacturers including the Italian companies Davide Pedersoli & Co., Pietta & Co., and Uberti & Co.

REVOLVERS: RECENT MFG.

1873 SINGLE ACTION ARMY — .44-40 or .45 LC cal., reproduction of the Colt SAA, case hardened frame with blue finish, 4¾, 5½, or 7½ in. barrel, approx. 36 oz.

Mfg.'s Sug. Retail	100%	98%	95%	90%	80%	70%	60%
	$320	$275	$230	$200	$180	$160	$145	$130

SAA Cavalry Model — .45 LC only, exact replica of the original U.S. Government issue SAA, 7½ in. barrel, arsenal stampings, inspectors cartouche on walnut stocks.

Mfg.'s Sug. Retail	100%	98%	95%	90%	80%	70%	60%
	$475	$415	$350	$295	$260	$230	$200	$175

Grading	100%	98%	95%	90%	80%	70%	60%

SAA Artillery Model — similar specifications to the Cavalry Model, except has 5½ in barrel.

Mfg.'s Sug. Retail $475	$415	$350	$295	$260	$230	$200	$175

1875 REMINGTON REVOLVER — .44-40 or .45 LC cal., reproduction of the 1875 Remington revolver, 7½ in. barrel, case colored frame, 41 oz.

Mfg.'s Sug. Retail $470	$410	$350	$295	$260	$230	$200	$175

1890 REMINGTON REVOLVER — .44-40 LC cal., reproduction of the 1890 Remington revolver, 5½ in. barrel, brass trigger guard and lanyard loop, 39 oz.

Mfg.'s Sug. Retail $465	$405	$350	$295	$260	$230	$200	$175

RIFLES: REPLICA MANUFACTURE

MODEL 1873 RIFLE — .22 LR, .357 Mag., or .44-40 cal., lever action replica of 1873 Winchester, case hardened receiver, 24 in. barrel. Mfg. 1972-1984.

	$305	$275	$250	$220	$165	$140	$110

Model 1873 1 of 1,000 — only 1,000 mfg., deluxe wood, special engraving.

	$1,000	$775	$550				

MODEL 1873 CARBINE — .44-40 cal., blue receiver, 19 in. round barrel.

	$260	$220	$195	$165	$140	$110	$100

MODEL 1873 TRAPPER — .44-40 cal., same as Carbine, with 16½ in. barrel.

	$260	$220	$195	$165	$140	$110	$100

YELLOWBOY — .38 Spl., or .44-40 cal., lever action replica of Winchester 1866, 24 in. octagon barrel. Mfg. 1966-1984.

	$330	$275	$220	$195	$165	$140	$110

YELLOWBOY CARBINE — .44-40 cal., 19 in. round barrel.

	$215	$180	$165	$150	$140	$110	$85

YELLOWBOY TRAPPER — .44-40 cal., 16½ in. barrel.

	$215	$180	$165	$150	$140	$110	$85

REVOLVING CARBINE — .357 Mag., .44-40, or .45 Colt cal., 6 shot cylinder, 20 in. barrel, case hardened frame, straight stock. Mfg. 1968-1984.

	$250	$210	$180	$160	$150	$140	$120

REMINGTON ROLLING BLOCK BUFFALO RIFLE — .444 Marlin (disc.), .45-70, or .50-70 (disc.), replica of Remington Rolling Block, 26 or 30 in. heavy octagon or ½ round/½ oct. barrel, open sight, straight grip stock. Mfg. 1971-present.

Mfg.'s Sug. Retail $485	$385	$320	$275	$230	$180	$160	$140

Add approx. $36 for long or short Creedmoor sight.

Add $55 for 50 x 3¼ Sharps cal. (disc.).

BUFFALO CARBINE — same as Rifle, with 18 in. barrel. Disc. 1985.

	$325	$280	$230	$180	$160	$140	$120

Last Mfg.'s Sug. Retail was $375.

ROLLING BLOCK BABY CARBINE — .22 LR, .22 Hornet, .357 Mag., or .44-40 cal., replica of small frame Remington, 20 in. octagon or 22 in. round barrel, open sight, straight stock. Mfg. 1968-1984.

	$160	$130	$110	$90	$65	$55	$40

ROLLING BLOCK CREEDMOOR TARGET — same as Buffalo Rifle, in .45-70 or .50-70 (disc.) cal., with Creedmoor tang sight, color case hardened receiver, checkered walnut.

Mfg.'s Sug. Retail $640	$515	$440	$350	$250	$195	$175	$150

SHARPS RIFLE/CARBINE — .45-70 or .54 cal., reproduction of Sharps sporting rifle and carbine, 22 or 28½ (rifle) in. barrel, case colored frame and hammer, fixed rear sight.

Mfg.'s Sug. Retail $650	$525	$440	$350	$250	$195	$175	$150

Grading	100%	98%	95%	90%	80%	70%	60%

MODEL 1866 — .44-40 cal. only, choice of rifle (24 in. octagon barrel) or carbine (19 in. round barrel), replica of the Winchester Model 1866.

Mfg.'s Sug. Retail	$660	$530	$445	$350	$250	$195	$175	$150

Add $15 for rifle variation.

MODEL 1873 — .44-40 or .45 LC cal., choice of rifle (24 in. octagon barrel) or carbine (19 in. round barrel), replica of the Winchester Model 1873.

Mfg.'s Sug. Retail	$800	$675	$550	$425	$300	$250	$220	$180

Add $25 for rifle variation.

HENRY RIFLE — .44-40 or .44 Rem. (disc. 1989) cal., reproduction of Winchester's famous Henry Rifle, brass or iron frame. New for 1985.

Add $370 for "A" pattern engraving (25% coverage).

Add $585 for "B" pattern engraving (35% coverage).

Add $975 for "C" pattern engraving (50% coverage).

The above special order engraving patterns usually require 30-60 days.

Military Rifle — 24 in. barrel, brass frame, blued barrel, walnut stock, original style sling swivels, 9¼ lbs. New for 1985.

Mfg.'s Sug. Retail	$875	$685	$535	$450	$350	$275	$225	$195

Union Pacific Railroad Commemorative — .44-40, only 100 mfg.

	$795	$575	$475				

Last Mfg.'s Sug. Retail was $695.

Engraved Rifle — limited mfg., extensive engraving on brass frame. Disc. 1988.

	$1,510	$1,275	$1,100	$900	$750	$650	$550

Add $100 for steel frame.

Last Mfg.'s Sug. Retail was $1,850.

Carbine — 24 in. barrel, limited edition of 1,000 units including 50 engraved specimens, no swivels, 8¼ lbs.

Mfg.'s Sug. Retail	$875	$685	$535	$450	$350	$275	$225	$195

Engraved Carbine — limited production, only 50 mfg. Disc. 1988.

	$1,450	$1,225	$1,075	$900	$750	$650	$550

Last Mfg.'s Sug. Retail was $1,750.

Trapper Model — 16½ in. barrel, 7¼ lbs., 34¼ in. overall length.

Mfg.'s Sug. Retail	$875	$685	$535	$450	$350	$275	$225	$195

Iron Frame Model — with iron frame and butt plate, 24 in. blued barrel, select walnut, 9¼ lbs.

Mfg.'s Sug. Retail	$885	$700	$625	$540	$480	$430	$360	$295

This model is available with either blued or color case hardened receiver - add $10 for blued receiver.

RIFLES: MODERN MANUFACTURE

In addition to the models listed below, Navy Arms in late 1990 purchased the manufacturing rights to the English firm, Parker-Hale. Navy Arms is in the process of switching mfg. from England to the U.S. Parker-Hale rifles mfg. by Navy Arms will appear in the P section of this text.

MARTINI TARGET RIFLE — .444, or .45-70 cal., single shot, 26 or 30 in. octagon barrel, tang sight, pistol grip stock. Mfg. 1972-1984.

	$480	$420	$350	$250	$195	$175	$150

RPKS-74 — .223 or 7.62 X 39mm (new 1989) cal., semi-automatic version of the Chinese RPK Squad Automatic Weapon, Kalashnikov action, 19 in. barrel, integral folding bipod, 9½ lbs. Imported 1988-1989 only.

	$525	$445	$350	$250	$195	$175	$150

Last Mfg.'s Sug. Retail was $649.

Grading	100%	98%	95%	90%	80%	70%	60%

USED MILITARY FIREARMS

Navy Arms sells a wide variety of original military firearms in used condition. Handguns include the Mauser Broomhandle, Japanese Nambu, Colt 1911 Government Model, Tokarev, Browning Hi-Power, S & W Model 1917, and others. Rifles include Mauser contract models, Japanese Type 38's, Enfield's, FN's, Nagant's, M1 Carbines, M1 Garand's, Chinese SKS's, Egyptian Rashid's, French MAS Model 1936's, among others. Most of these firearms are priced in the $75-$500 price range depending on desirability of model and condition. Navy Arms should be contacted directly regarding specific prices for these models.

PISTOLS: LUGERS

LUGER — .22 LR cal. only, 10 shot mag., Luger toggle type action, available in blued or matte finish, 4, 6, or 8 in. barrel, checkered walnut stocks. Mfg. in U.S. 1986-87 only.

	$140	$120	$95	$85	$75	$70	$65

Last Mfg.'s Sug. Retail was $165.

PISTOLS: REPLICA MANUFACTURE

GRAND PRIX SILHOUETTE — .30-30, 7mm Spl., .44 Mag., or .45-70 cal., 13¾ in. barrel, non-glare matte blue finish, walnut forearm and grips, adj. heat dispersing aluminum rib, adj. target sights, 4 lbs. Mfg. 1985 only.

	$320	$280	$240	$220	$195	$175	$150

Last Mfg.'s Sug. Retail was $375.

SHOTGUNS: RECENT IMPORTATION

Importation of the models listed below was disc. in 1990.

MODEL 83 O/U — 12 or 20 ga., manufactured in Italy by R. Luciano, 3 in. chambers, extractors, double triggers, engraved chrome receiver, vent barrels (bored M/F or IC/M) and rib. New 1985.

	$280	$240	$215	$195	$170	$160	$150

Last Mfg.'s Sug. Retail was $320.

MODEL 93 O/U — 12 or 20 ga., manufactured in Italy by R. Luciano, 3 in. chambers, ejectors, double triggers, engraved chrome receiver, vent barrels (bored M/F or IC/M) and rib. New 1985.

	$325	$285	$250	$220	$200	$185	$160

Last Mfg.'s Sug. Retail was $380.

MODEL 95 O/U — same as Model 93, except with single trigger and multi-chokes (includes 5 tubes), extractors.

	$375	$330	$295	$265	$235	$210	$190

Last Mfg.'s Sug. Retail was $420.

MODEL 96 SPORTSMAN O/U — 12 ga. only, 3 in. chambers, vent barrels and rib, engraved chrome receiver, gold plated receiver, multi-choked with 5 choke tubes, ejectors. New 1985.

	$470	$425	$375	$330	$295	$260	$230

Last Mfg.'s Sug. Retail was $530.

MODEL 100 O/U — 12, 20, 28, or .410 ga., 3 in. chambers, 26 in. VR barrels, photo-engraved hard chrome receiver, single trigger, extractors, checkered walnut stock and forearm, approx. 6¼ lbs. New 1985.

	$225	$205	$190	$170	$160	$150	$140

Last Mfg.'s Sug. Retail was $250.

MODEL 100 SXS — 12 or 20 ga., 3 in. chambers, 27½ in. barrels, checkered European walnut, double triggers, extractors, 6½ or 7 lbs. Imported 1985-1987 only.

	$380	$330	$290	$260	$230	$200	$170

Last Mfg.'s Sug. Retail was $475.

Grading	100%	98%	95%	90%	80%	70%	60%

MODEL 150 SXS — same as Model 100, except with ejectors. Imported 1985-1987 only.

	100%	98%	95%	90%	80%	70%	60%
	$455	$395	$350	$310	$280	$250	$220

Last Mfg.'s Sug. Retail was $574.

MODEL 105 SINGLE BARREL — 12, 20, or .410 ga., 26 or 28 in. full choke barrel only, folding action, engraved chrome receiver, checkered hardwood stock and forearm. New 1985.

	100%	98%	95%	90%	80%	70%	60%
	$80	$70	$65	$60	$55	$50	$45

This model was designated the Model 600 before 1988.

Last Mfg.'s Sug. Retail was $90.

Model 105 Deluxe — same as Model 105, except has European walnut stock and vent rib.

	100%	98%	95%	90%	80%	70%	60%
	$95	$85	$75	$65	$60	$55	$50

This model was designated the Model 600 Deluxe before 1988.

Last Mfg.'s Sug. Retail was $105.

NEW DETONICS MANUFACTURING CORPORATION

Manufacturer located in Phoenix, AZ since 1989. Formerly called Detonics Firearms Industries (previous manufacturer located in Bellevue, WA 1976-1988). Detonics was sold in early 1988 to the New Detonics Manufacturing Corporation, a wholly owned subsidiary of "1045 Investers Group Limited".

Note: All pistols listed below are derivatives of the Colt Model 1911 (except the Pocket 9) and are manufactured from high quality stainless steel.

PISTOLS: STAINLESS STEEL

MARK I — .45 ACP, matte blue. Disc. 1981.

$550	$450	$395

MARK II — .45 ACP, satin nickel finish. Disc. 1979.

$495	$375	$300

MARK III — .45 ACP, hard chrome finish. Disc. 1979.

$520	$390	$325

MARK IV — .45 ACP, polished blue. Disc. 1981.

$539	$410	$360

COMBATMASTER MC1 (FORMERLY MARK I) — .45 ACP, 9mm, or .38 Super cal., 3½ in. barrel, two-tone (slide is non-glare blue and frame is matte stainless) finish, 6 shot mag., fixed sights, 28 oz.

Mfg.'s Sug. Retail	$920	$775	$575	$450

Add $15 for OM-3 model (polished slide - disc. 1983).

Add $100 for 9mm or .38 Super cal. (disc. 1990).

This model was originally the MC1, then changed to the Mark I, then changed back to the MC1.

COMBATMASTER MARK V — .45 ACP, 9mm, or .38 Super cal., matte stainless finish, fixed sights, 6 shot mag. in .45 ACP, 7 shot in 9mm and .38 Super, 3½ in. barrel, 29 oz. empty. This model was disc. 1985.

$620	$550	$495

Add $100 for 9mm or .38 Super cal.

Last Mfg.'s Sug. Retail was $689.

COMBATMASTER MARK VI — .45 ACP, 9mm, or .38 Super cal., 3½ in. barrel, 6 shot mag., adj. sights and polished stainless slide sides. Disc. 1989.

$685	$575	$450

Add $100 for 9mm or .38 Super cal.

Last Mfg.'s Sug. Retail was $795.

Grading	100%	98%	95%	90%	80%	70%	60%

.451 Detonics Mag. Cal. — limited mfg. 1,000. Disc. 1985.

	$1,000	$900	$775

Last Mfg.'s Sug. Retail was $1,165.

COMBATMASTER MARK VII — same as Mark VI, only no sights, special order only, 25 oz.

	$895	$775	$600

Add $100 for 9mm or .38 Super cal.

Add $350 for .451 Detonics Mag., (disc. 1982).

MILITARY COMBAT MC2 — .45 ACP, 9mm, or .38 Super cal., dull, non-glare combat finish, fixed sights. Add $55 for 9mm or .38 Super. Comes with camouflaged pile line wallet, and Pachmayr grips. Disc. 1984.

	$621	$560	$500

O.S. MODEL — .45 ACP only, emergency backup pistol, similar to Combatmaster, 6 shot mag., choice of satin stainless or all black finish. New 1991.

Mfg.'s Sug. Retail $895 $775 $550 $425

SCOREMASTER — .45 ACP or .451 Mag. cal., match gun with closer-tolerances, 5 or 6 in. barrel. Millett adj. sights, grip safety, 7 or 8 shot mag., 42 oz.

Mfg.'s Sug. Retail $1,178 $995 $850 $695

Add $40 for 6 in. barrel.

COMPMASTER — .45 ACP only, similar to Scoremaster, except is fully compensated. New 1988.

Mfg.'s Sug. Retail $1,550 $1,375 $1,200 $950

This model was called the Janus Competition Scoremaster in 1988-1989.

COMPETITION MASTER T.F. — .45 ACP cal., competition model with dual port compensator, rotational tork compensating vents, patented cone barrel system, hand tuned trigger, includes all competition modifications.

Mfg.'s Sug. Retail $1,550 $1,375 $1,200 $950

SERVICEMASTER — .45 ACP only, shortened version of the Scoremaster, non-glare combat finish, 4¼ in. barrel, coned barrel system, 8 shot mag., interchangeable front and adj. rear sights, 39 oz. Disc. 1986.

	$625	$555	$495

Last Mfg.'s Sug. Retail was $686.

Servicemaster II — similar to Servicemaster, except has polished stainless steel finish. New 1986.

Mfg.'s Sug. Retail $998 $810 $685 $595

LADIES ESCORT SERIES

This series is designed specifically to suit a woman's shooting requirements.

MIDNIGHT ESCORT — .45 ACP cal., action similar to Combatmaster, 3½ in. barrel, 6 shot mag., black frame, slide and grips are iridescent purple, hammer and trigger are 24 Kt. gold plated. New 1990.

Mfg.'s Sug. Retail $990 $860 $675 $525

JADE ESCORT — similar to Midnight Escort, except has stainless frame, jade colored slide and grips. Mfg. 1990 only.

	$825	$650	$525

Last Mfg.'s Sug. Retail was $918. Less than 25 of this color were mfg.

ROYAL ESCORT — similar to Midnight Escort, except is stain stainless with a black slide and smooth black grips. New 1990.

Mfg.'s Sug. Retail $1,090 $965 $725 $580

Grading	100%	98%	95%	90%	80%	70%	60%

POCKET 9 — 9mm, double action, 3 in. barrel, 6 shot mag., soft matte sheen finish, 26 oz. Mfg. 1985-86 only.

	$425	$385	$325

Last Mfg.'s Sug. Retail was $458.

The entire Pocket 9 series was disc. 1986.

Pocket 9 LS — similar to Pocket 9, except has 4 in. barrel. Mfg. 1986 only.

	$410	$370	$325

Last Mfg.'s Sug. Retail was $458.

Pocket .380 — similar to Pocket 9, except is .380 ACP cal., 23 oz. Mfg. 1986 only.

	$410	$370	$325

Last Mfg.'s Sug. Retail was $458.

POWER 9 — 9mm, similar to Pocket 9, except has polished slide sides and is supplied with 2 mag.'s. Disc. 1986.

	$455	$410	$350

Last Mfg.'s Sug. Retail was $509.

NEW ENGLAND ARMS, CO.

Importer/distributor/retailer located in Kittery Point, ME.

New England Arms, Co. imports, distributes, or retails the following trademarks: Beretta Premium Grades, Bertuzzi, Carlo Casartelli, Americo Cosmi, Henri Dumoulin, Armi Fabbri, Ferlib, Lebeau Courally, Westley Richards, Rizzini, Fabio Zanotti, and Webley & Scott. These trademarks may be found under their own headings in this text. For further information regarding any one of these manufacturers, please contact New England Arms, Co. directly.

NEW ENGLAND FIREARMS CO., INC.

Manufacturer located in Gardner, MA.

REVOLVERS: D/A

Ultra Models listed below are available in blue finish only.

MODEL R22 — .22 LR cal., 9 shot, swing out cylinder, 2½, 4, or 6 in. barrel, blue or nickel finish, hardwood stocks, fixed rear sight, 25-32 oz. New 1988.

No Mfg.'s Retail	$115	$95	$80	$70	$65	$60	$55

Add $13 for nickel finish (2½ or 4 in. barrel only).

Add $43 for adj. rear sight (Ultra Model - 4 or 6 in. barrel only).

Model R22 - .22 Mag. — .22 Mag. cal., 6 shot, 2½, 4, or 6 (Ultra Model only) in. barrel, blue or nickel finish, 25-28 oz. New 1988.

No Mfg.'s Retail	$115	$100	$85	$75	$70	$65	$60

Add $13 for nickel finish.

Add $43 for adj. rear sight (Ultra Model - 4 or 6 in. barrel only).

Model R22 - .32 H&R Mag. — .32 H&R Mag. cal., 6 shot, 2½, 4, or 6 (Ultra Model only) in. barrel, blue or nickel finish, 23-26 oz. New 1988.

No Mfg.'s Retail	$115	$100	$85	$75	$70	$65	$60

Add $13 for nickel finish.

Add $43 for adj. rear sight (Ultra Model - 4 or 6 in. barrel only).

New England Firearms Co. also manufactures blank starter revolvers (.22 or .32 cal.) which are variation of this model.

Grading	100%	98%	95%	90%	80%	70%	60%

SHOTGUNS/COMBINATION GUNS

PARDNER — 12, 16 (new 1989), 20, or .410 ga., single shot, break open action, safety transfer bar mechanism on hammer, side lever release, color case hardened receiver, 24, 26, or 28 in. barrel, extractor, walnut stock and forearm. New 1987.

| No Mfg.'s Retail | $105 | $90 | $80 | $70 | $60 | $50 | $45 |

Add $4 for Youth Gun (20 or .410 ga. - shorter dimension stock).

Add $27 for rifle sights (12 or 20 ga. - 24 in. cyl. barrel only).

Mini-Pardner — 20 or .410 ga. only, shortened stock, sling swivels, 18½ in. barrel. New 1989.

| No Mfg.'s Retail | $105 | $90 | $80 | $70 | $60 | $50 | $45 |

Pardner Magnum — 10 ga. only, 3½ in. chamber, 32 in. barrel, blue finish, recoil pad, 10 lbs. New 1988.

| No Mfg.'s Retail | $175 | $150 | $125 | $105 | $90 | $80 | $75 |

HANDI-RIFLE — .22 Hornet, .223 Rem., .30-30, or .45-70 cal., 22 in. barrel, blued receiver, ramp front and adj. folding rear sights, sling swivels, 7 lbs. New 1989.

| No Mfg.'s Retail | $175 | $150 | $125 | $100 | $90 | $80 | $75 |

Add $17 for .223 Rem. or .45-70 cal.

This model in .223 Rem. cal. is supplied with scope mount and no sights.

HANDI-GUN — includes 12 or 20 ga. 22 in. barrel and choice of .22 Hornet, .223 Rem., .30-30 Win., or .45-70 cal. extra barrel, blue or electroless matte finish nickel, 6½ lbs. New 1988.

| No Mfg.'s Retail | $220 | $190 | $170 | $145 | $125 | $110 | $100 |

Add $15 for blue finish.

NEWTON ARMS CO.

Previous manufacturer located in Buffalo, NY 1913-1932. Also named Charles Newton Rifle Corp. and Buffalo Newton Rifle Co.

NEWTON-MAUSER RIFLE — Oberndorf bolt action, .256 Newton cal., 24 in. barrel, double set triggers, checkered pistol grip stock. Pre-WWI mfg.

| | $800 | $650 | $550 | $440 | $385 | $330 | $275 |

FIRST TYPE STANDARD RIFLE — Newton bolt action, .22, .256, .280, .30, .33, .35 Newton, and .30-06 cal.'s, 24 in. barrel, double set triggers, open or aperture sights, checkered pistol grip stock. Mfg. 1916-1918 by Newton Arms.

| | $1,150 | $925 | $750 | $625 | $500 | $440 | $385 |

SECOND TYPE STANDARD RIFLE — improved Newton action, has Enfield type bolt handle, .256, .30, .35 Newton, and .30-06 cal.'s, open sights, checkered pistol grip stock. Mfg. post-WWI by Charles Newton Rifle Corporation.

| | $1,000 | $825 | $660 | $600 | $500 | $440 | $385 |

BUFFALO NEWTON RIFLE — same as Second Type. Mfg. 1922-1932 by Buffalo Newton Rifle company.

| | $1,000 | $825 | $660 | $600 | $500 | $440 | $385 |

SPRINGFIELD NEWTON — kit consisting of a Newton barrel and sporter stock, barrels were chambered for Newton calibers, kits were available to adapt Springfield rifles into Newton calibers in the 1920's when the NRA made the Springfields available to its membership.

| | $595 | $540 | $495 | $450 | $410 | $375 | $330 |

NIKKO

Manufacturer located in Japan.

Research is underway to gather more information on the various Nikko shotgun and rifle models. Until this data is compiled, please direct questions regarding this trademark to: Golden Eagle Collectors Assoc. located at P.O. Box 62213, in Sunnyvale, CA. 94086-2213.

Grading	100%	98%	95%	90%	80%	70%	60%

NORINCO

Manufacturer located in China. Imported and distributed by China Sports, Inc. located in Ontario, CA.

Norinco pistols, rifles, and shotguns are manufactured in the People's Republic of China by China North Industries Corp. (Norinco - with over 100 factories). They are currently being imported and distributed by China Sports, Inc. Various other new models will be imported in the near future and China Sports, Inc. should be contacted to find out current availability and prices on these upcoming models.

PISTOLS

MODEL 213 — 9mm Para., single action, satin blue finish. Imported 1988 only.

	100%	98%	95%	90%	80%	70%	60%
	$185	$150	$135	$125	$115	$105	$100

Last Mfg.'s Sug. Retail was $200.

TYPE 54-1 TOKAREV STANDARD — 7.62 X 25mm or .38 Super cal., single action semi-auto, 4.5 in. barrel, 8 shot mag., fixed sights, blue finish, 29 oz. Importation began 1989.

No Mfg.'s Retail	$239	$185	$160	$130	$115	$105	$95

Type 54-1 Double Column — similar to Standard Model, except is also available in 9mm Para. cal. and has 13 shot mag., 35 oz. Importation will begin late 1991.

No Mfg.'s Retail	$279	$225	$185	$160	$140	$120	$100

Type 54-1 Compact — .38 Super, 9mm Para., or 7.62 X 25mm cal., 3.8 in. barrel, 8 shot mag., 27 oz. Importation will begin late 1991.

No Mfg.'s Retail	$279	$225	$185	$160	$140	$120	$100

TYPE 59 MAKAROV — 9 X 18mm Makarov or .380 ACP, double action semi-auto, 3.5 in. barrel, 8 shot bottom release mag., checkered plastic grips, PPK design with additional features, adj. rear sight, 24 oz. Importation began 1989.

No Mfg.'s Retail	$339	$275	$230	$200	$180	$160	$140

TYPE 77B — 9mm Para. cal., semi-auto single action, action patterned after the older German Lignoes (unique design permits one handed operation utilizing "trigger guard cocking" enabling the slide to be moved backward cocking the hammer), 5 in. barrel, 8 shot mag., adj. rear sight, 34 oz. Importation began 1991.

No Mfg.'s Retail	$359	$285	$235	$200	$180	$160	$140

MODEL 1911 A1 — .45 ACP only, patterned after the Colt 1911 A1, 5 in. barrel, 7 shot mag., fixed sights, blue finish, wood grips, 39 oz. Importation began 1991.

No Mfg.'s Retail	$399	$315	$270	$240	$215	$190	$175

PARAMILITARY DESIGN CARBINES & RIFLES

Due to 1989 Federal legislation, values on paramilitary configuration firearms have been volatile. Initially (spring of 1989), prices escalated dramatically (many values doubled literally overnight), but in the past year have gone down and become more stable and predictable. Since this is a specialized market, regional demand could lower the values listed below. If further legislation occurs, prices will probably rise again due to the increased demand created when the potential consumer fears that this could be his/her last chance once again to purchase this configuration of firearm.

TYPE 84S AK RIFLE — .223 cal., semi-auto Kalashnikov action, 16.34 in. barrel, hardwood stock and pistol grip, 30 shot mag., 1,000 meter adj. rear sight, includes bayonet and sheath, 8.87 lbs. Imported 1988-1989 only.

	100%	98%	95%	90%	80%	70%	60%
	$495	$450	$400	$360	$330	$300	$285

Last Mfg.'s Sug. Retail was $350.

Type 84S-1 — similar to Type 84S AK except has under-folding metal stock. Imported 1989 only.

	100%	98%	95%	90%	80%	70%	60%
	$525	$475	$425	$385	$350	$325	$300

Last Mfg.'s Sug. Retail was $350.

Grading	100%	98%	95%	90%	80%	70%	60%

Type 84S-3 — similar to Type 84S AK except has composite fiber stock (1½ in. longer than wood stock). Imported 1989 only.

	$550	$500	$450	$400	$375	$350	$325

Last Mfg.'s Sug. Retail was $365.

Type 84S-5 — similar to Type 84S AK except has side-folding metal stock. Imported 1989 only.

	$525	$475	$425	$385	$350	$325	$300

Last Mfg.'s Sug. Retail was $350.

TYPE SKS — .223 or 7.62 X 39mm cal., SKS action, 20.47 in. barrel, 30 shot clip mag., 1,000 meter adj. rear sight, hardwood stock, new design accepts standard AK mag., folding bayonet included, 8.8 lbs. Imported 1988-1989.

	$350	$315	$275	$250	$220	$190	$170

Last Mfg.'s Sug. Retail was $240.

TYPE 81S AK RIFLE — 7.62 x 39mm cal., semi-auto Kalashnikov action, 17.5 in. barrel, 5, 30, or 40 shot clip mag., 500 meter adj. rear sight, fixed wood stock, hold open devise after last shot, 8 lbs. Imported 1988-1989.

	$495	$450	$400	$360	$330	$300	$285

Last Mfg.'s Sug. Retail was $385.

Type 81S-1 — similar to Type 81S AK except has under-folding metal stock. Imported 1988-1989.

	$525	$475	$425	$385	$350	$325	$300

Last Mfg.'s Sug. Retail was $385.

TYPE 56S-2 — 7.62 X 39mm cal., older Kalashnikov design with side-folding metal stock. Importation disc. 1989.

	$495	$450	$400	$360	$330	$300	$285

Last Mfg.'s Sug. Retail was $350.

TYPE 86S-7 RPK RIFLE — 7.62 X 39mm cal., AK action, 23.27 in. heavy barrel with built-in bipod, in-line butt stock, 11.02 lbs. Imported 1988-1989.

	$850	$775	$700	$640	$595	$550	$500

Last Mfg.'s Sug. Retail was $425.

TYPE 86S BULLPUP RIFLE — 7.62 X 39mm cal., bullpup configuration with AK action, under-folding metal stock, 17¼ in. barrel, ambidextrous cocking design, folding front handle, 7 lbs. Imported 1989 only.

	$725	$650	$575	$525	$460	$410	$350

Last Mfg.'s Sug. Retail was $400.

DRAGONOV (MODEL 350 NDM-86)—7.62 x 39mm, sniper variation of the AK-47, features longer barrel with muzzle brake, special stock, includes scope.

Mfg.'s Sug. Retail	$3,700	$2,500	$1,750	$1,500	$1,250	$1,000	$850	$725

OFFICERS NINE — 9mm, 16.1 in. barrel, action patterned after the IMI Uzi, 32 shot mag., black military finish, 8.4 lbs. Imported 1988-1989.

	$550	$475	$415	$375	$335	$300	$275

This model was imported exclusively by Pacific International Merchandising Corporation located in Sacramento, CA.

Last Mfg.'s Sug. Retail was $450.

SPORTING RIFLES

MODEL EM-321 — .22 LR, slide action, 19.5 in. barrel, 10 shot tube mag., hardwood stock and forearm, fixed sights, 6 lbs. Importation began 1989-90 only.

	$100	$80	$70	$60	$55	$50	$45

Last estimated retail was $125.

Grading	100%	98%	95%	90%	80%	70%	60%

TYPE EM-332 — .22 LR cal., bolt action, 18½ in. barrel with adj. rear sight, mag. holder on stock holds two extra 5 shot mag.'s, Monte Carlo stock with cheek piece and recoil pad, 4½ lbs. Importation began 1991.

No Mfg.'s Retail		$250	$220	$180	$160	$140	$120	$95

NHM-90 SPORT AK — 7.62 X 39K cal., sporterized Kalashnikov action featuring American walnut thumb hole stock, 16.34 in. barrel, 5 shot mag., 9 lbs. Importation began 1990.

No Mfg.'s Retail		$400	$350	$300	$265	$225	$200	$185

Each Model NHM-90 is supplied with three 5 shot mag.'s, sling, and cleaning kit.

SHOTGUNS

TYPE HL12-203 O/U — 12 ga. only, 2¾ in. chambers, boxlock action, ejectors, 30 in. vent. barrels and rib, single trigger, multi-chokes, checkered stock and forearm, 7½ lbs. Importation began 1989.

No Mfg.'s Retail		$400	$350	$300	$265	$225	$200	$185

TYPE HL12-102 PUMP — 12 ga. only, 2¾ in. chamber, 28.4 in. barrel, 3 shot mag., crossbolt safety on rear trigger guard, fixed chokes, 9.3 lbs. Importation began 1989.

No Mfg.'s Retail		$230	$200	$175	$165	$150	$135	$120

NORTH AMERICAN ARMS

Manufactured by North American Arms located in Spanish Fork, UT. This company is owned by Teleflex Defense Systems, also located in Spanish Fork, UT.

MINI REVOLVERS

All mini revolvers are manufactured to highest quality control standards and have half-way notches cut on the front cylinder face allowing the hammer to lock up the cylinder between cartridges. This allows the gun to be carried fully loaded without the danger of accidental discharge.

NAA .22 LR — .22 LR cal., 5 shot, single action, spur trigger, 1⅛, 1⅝, or 2½ (disc.) in. barrel, stainless steel, plastic (disc.) or laminated rosewood grips, approx. 4½ oz. Mfg. 1975-present.

Mfg.'s Sug. Retail		$163	$135	$105	$85

Add $15 for 2½ in. barrel (disc.).

Add $33 for holster grip accessory.

The optional holster grip allows the pistol to fold forward allowing concealability, safety, and a clip which allows it to be attatched to a belt.

Viper Belt Buckle Option — belt buckle with built in 1⅛ in. barrel revolver (LR cal.), disc. 1990.

		$180	$150	$120

Last Mfg.'s Sug. Retail was $189.

NAA .22 MAGNUM — similar to .22 LR, except in .22 Mag. cal.

Mfg.'s Sug. Retail		$183	$160	$125	$100

Add $18 for 2½ in. barrel (disc.).

NAA .22 MAGNUM CONVERTIBLE — same as NAA .22 Mag., except has extra LR cylinder in pouch.

Mfg.'s Sug. Retail		$218	$190	$155	$125

Add $18 for 2½ in. barrel (disc.).

Grading	100%	98%	95%	90%	80%	70%	60%

MINI-MASTER TARGET REVOLVER — .22 LR or .22 Mag., 5 shot, 4 in. heavy vent barrel, unfluted bull cylinder, spur trigger, fixed or adj. white outline rear sight, oversize black rubber Mini-master grip, 10.7 oz. New 1990.

Mfg.'s Sug. Retail	$256	$225	$190	$170

Add $35 for extra combo cylinder.

Add $10 for adj. rear sight (elevation only).
This model is also available in hot fuscia colored oversized grips.

MINI-MASTER BLACK WIDOW — .22 LR or .22 Mag. cal., 2 in. heavy VR barrel, full size black rubber grip, fixed or adj. rear sight, unfluted cylinder, 8.8 oz. New 1991.

Mfg.'s Sug. Retail	$224	$195	$160	$130

Add $55 for extra combo cylinder.

Add $10 for adj. rear sight (elevation only).
This model is also available in hot fuscia colored oversized grips.

NAA STANDARD SET — 3 gun set (.22 Short, .22 LR, and .22 Mag.) in walnut display case with matching serial numbers, high polish finish with matte contours.

Mfg.'s Sug. Retail	$718	$625	$480	$375

NAA DELUXE SET — 3 gun set (.22 Short, .22 LR, and .22 Mag.) in walnut display case with matching serial numbers, high polish finish on entire gun.

Mfg.'s Sug. Retail	$775	$675	$560	$450

CASED .22 MAG. — includes .22 Mag. model in walnut display case with high polish finish with matte contours.

Mfg.'s Sug. Retail	$341	$290	$225	$185

REVOLVERS

NAA SINGLE ACTION REVOLVER — .45 Win. Mag. or .450 Mag. Express, polished stainless steel, transfer bar safety inside the hammer, 5 shot, 7½ in. barrel, walnut grips, includes presentation case. North American Arms might resume production of this model in 1989.

Matte finish	$1,200	$950	$700
High polish finish	$1,400	$1,100	$850
Both cylinders	$1,650	$1,275	$975

Last Mfg.'s Sug. Retail was $650.

Also available by special order with 10½ in. barrel and optional scope. Extra cylinders are also available at $75-$100 extra and must be fitted to the gun. A set including 2 cylinders can also be ordered.

NORTH AMERICAN SAFARI EXPRESS
Trademark for those rifles (side by side) assembled by A. Francotte of Belgium for exclusive importation by Armes De Chasse located in Chadds Ford, PA.

O

O.D.I. (OMEGA DEFENSIVE INDUSTRIES)

Previously manufactured in Midland Park, NJ from approximately 1981-1982. Oak's Wholesale, Inc. located in Rockledge, FL has acquired the remaining O.D.I. Viking Inventory of the Double Action .45 ACP Pistols. Previously, Randco Manufacturing located in Monrovia, CA., was providing service (and had parts) for these older O.D.I. Pistols.

Oak's Trading Post is planning to reintroduce the Viking Model's in 1989. Firm prices have yet to be established - please contact Oak's Trading Post for more current information regarding the current status of this model.

Grading	100%	98%	95%	90%	80%	70%	60%

VIKING & VIKING COMBAT — .45 ACP or 9mm, Viking Model is Government size and the Combat Model is Commander size. All stainless steel construction, the design utilizes the Seecamp double action, teakwood grips. 9mm advertised but never saw production. 5 in. barrel on the Viking Model and 4 1/4 in. barrel on the Viking Combat Model, 7 shot mag., 39 oz. Approx. 200-300 Viking Combat Models were made from kits.

$575 $425 $325

Last Mfg.'s Retail was $579.

OBREGON

Manufactured previously by Fabrica de Armas Mexico located in Mexico City, Mexico.

OBREGON — 11.35mm cal., patterned somewhat after the Colt Model 1911A1, features tubular slide and Savage/Steyr type action, limited mfg. in Mexico for commercial sale during and after WWII, slide marked "Sistema Obregon Cal 11.35mm".

$650 $550 $475 $400 $350 $300 $275

This model is not frequently encountered domestically.

OLD-WEST GUN CO.

Importer and distributor that took over the inventory of Allen Fireams after they went out of business in early 1987. Old-West Gun Co. in late 1987 changed their name to Cimarron Arms. Refer to Cimarron Arms in this text for approximate prices on similar models from Old-West Gun Co.

OLYMPIC ARMS, INC.

Manufacturer located in Olympia, WA.

In late 1987, Olympic Arms, Inc. acquired Safari Arms of Phoenix, AZ and is currently manufacturing/assembling guns from existing parts. Once the parts clean-up is over, the Olympic Arms trademark will appear on their firearms. This company also manufactures barrels (including .38 Super & .45 ACP cal.'s) for the Colt Government Model 1911, Browning Hi-Power, and TZ & CZ 75.

Olympic Arms manufactures single action, semi-auto pistols derived from the Browning M1911 design with modifications.

Grading	100%	98%	95%	90%	80%	70%	60%

DEFENSE PISTOLS

ENFORCER — .45 ACP, 3.8 in. barrel, 6 shot mag., shortened grip, available with max hard finish aluminum frame, parkerized, electroless nickel or lightweight anodized finishes, flat or arched mainspring housing, adj. sights, ambidextrous safety, neoprene or checkered walnut grips, 27 oz. (lightweight model).

Mfg.'s Sug. Retail	$710	$650	$545	$495	$450	$425	$400	$375

MatchMaster — similar to the Enforcer, except has 5 in. barrel and 7 shot mag., 40 oz.

Mfg.'s Sug. Retail	$690	$625	$525	$485	$450	$425	$400	$375

GI SAFARI — .45 ACP cal., patterned after the Colt Model 1911 A1, Safari frame, beavertail grip safety and commander hammer. New 1991.

Mfg.'s Sug. Retail	$425	$375	$315	$275	$250	$230	$210	$190

BLACK WIDOW — .45 ACP, 3.9 in. barrel, hand-contoured front grip strap, schrimshawed ivory Micarta grips with black widow emblem, 6 shot mag., 27 oz. Inventory was depleted 1988.

	$565	$510	$460	$430	$400	$375	$350

Last Mfg.'s Sug. Retail was $595.

BILL OF RIGHTS BICENTENNIAL MATCHED SET—includes the MatchMaster Pistol and ServiceMatch Rifle, features beryllium receivers and special engraving.

Mfg.'s Sug. Retail	$7,400	$6,950	$5,250	$3,950

RIFLES

100% values below reflect the current demand versus supply situation on this configuration of firearm due to Federal legislation in 1989. There will also be regional price differences due to localized supply and demand.

ULTRAMATCH — .223 cal., AR-15 action with modifications, 20 or 24 in. match stainless steel barrel, handle removed, Williams set trigger, scope mounts. New 1988.

Mfg.'s Sug. Retail	$1,153	$1,025	$800	$700	$600	$550	$500	$460

Add $130 for custom aperture sights.

INTERNATIONAL MATCH — .223 cal., similar to Ultramatch, except has custom aperture sights. New 1991.

Mfg.'s Sug. Retail	$1,182	$1,050	$800	$700	$600	$550	$500	$460

SERVICE MATCH RIFLE — .223 cal., AR-15 action with modifications, ultra match barrel, standard trigger, choice of A1 or A2 flash suppressor.

Mfg.'s Sug. Retail	$900	$825	$725	$650	$575	$530	$495	$450

MULTIMATCH — .223 cal., tactical short range rifle, 16 in. Ultramatch barrel, stealth vortex flash suppressor. New 1991.

Mfg.'s Sug. Retail	$916	$835	$725	$650	$575	$530	$495	$450

OMEGA

Maker: Armero Specialistas Reunidas, Eibar, Spain, 1920's.

SEMI AUTOMATIC PISTOL — "Eibar" type, marked, Omega on slide, 6 shot mag.

6.35 cal.	$125	$115	$100	$80	$70	$55	$40
7.65 cal.	$130	$120	$105	$90	$80	$70	$55

OMEGA FIREARMS

Previously manufactured in Flower Mound, TX.

SINGLE SHOT BOLT ACTION RIFLE — various cal.'s, premium walnut. Disc. late 1960's.

$775	$650	$575	$495	$425	$360	$295

Grading	100%	98%	95%	90%	80%	70%	60%

OMEGA PISTOL

Manufactured and distributed by Springfield Armory located in Geneseo, IL.

PISTOLS: SEMI-AUTO

OMEGA — .38 Super, 10mm Norma, or .45 ACP cal., single action, ported slide, 5 or 6 in. interchangeable ported or unported barrel with Polygon rifling, special lock-up system eliminates normal barrel link and bushing, Pachmayr grips, dual extractors, adj. rear sight. New late 1987.

	100%	98%	95%	90%	80%	70%	60%	
Mfg.'s Sug. Retail	$849	$675	$575	$495	$425	$360	$295	$265

Add $663 for interchangeable conversion units.

Each conversion unit includes an entire slide assembly, one mag., 5 or 6 in barrel, recoil spring guide mechanism assembly, and factory fitting.

Add $336 for interchangeable 5 or 6 in. barrel (including factory installation).

OMEGA SHOTGUNS

Omega is the trademark of select shotguns imported by K.B.I., Inc. located in Harrisburg, PA.

Other K.B.I. imported shotguns (Kassnar trademark) can be found under the K.B.I. heading in this text.

SHOTGUNS

STANDARD O/U — 12, 20 (disc.), 28 (disc.), or .410 (disc) ga., boxlock action, folding design, SNT, 26 or 28 in. VR barrels, extractors, checkered walnut stock and forearm, 5½-7 lbs.

	100%	98%	95%	90%	80%	70%	60%
No Mfg.'s Retail	$495	$330	$295	$260	$230	$200	$180

Deluxe O/U — 12 ga. only, similar to Standard Model except has better walnut. Importation disc. 1990.

	$335	$290	$255	$220	$185	$160	$140

Last Mfg.'s Sug. Retail was $379.

STANDARD SXS — 20, 28, or .410 ga., boxlock action, folding design, double triggers, hardwood stock and forearm, 26 in. barrels, extractors, 5½ lbs. Disc. 1989.

	$190	$165	$140	$120	$110	$100	$90

Add $40 for 28 or .410 ga.
Last Mfg.'s Sug. Retail was $229.

Deluxe SXS — .410 ga. only, similar to Standard Model except has better walnut. Disc. 1989.

	$200	$185	$170	$155	$140	$130	$120

Last Mfg.'s Sug. Retail was $249.

SINGLE BARREL — 12, 20, or .410 ga., various barrel lengths, matte blue finish, extractor. Importation disc. 1987.

	$85	$75	$65	$55	$45	$40	$35

Last Mfg.'s Sug. Retail was $95.

STANDARD FOLDING SINGLE BARREL — 12, 16, 20, 28, or .410 ga., 28 or 30 in. barrel, checkered hardwood stock, matte chrome receiver, approx. 5½ lbs. Importation disc. 1987.

	$160	$135	$115	$100	$85	$70	$65

Last Mfg.'s Sug. Retail was $180.

DELUXE FOLDING SINGLE BARREL — 12, 16, 20, 28, or .410 ga., similar to Standard Model, except has checkered walnut stock and forearm, blued receiver. Importation disc. 1987.

	$195	$160	$135	$115	$100	$85	$70

Last Mfg.'s Sug. Retail was $220.

Grading	100%	98%	95%	90%	80%	70%	60%

OPUS SPORTING ARMS, INC.

Previously manufactured by Opus Sporting Arms, Inc. located in Long Beach, CA.

OPUS ONE — .243, .270, or .30-06 cal., U.S.R.A. Co. Model 70 action, 24 in. barrel, deluxe checkered walnut stock with ebony forend cap, guaranteed 100 yard accuracy, 6¾ lbs., Halliburton cased. Mfg. 1987-1988 only.

	$2,350	$1,995	$1,675	$1,250	$1,000	$875	$795

Last Mfg.'s Sug. Retail was $2,700.

OPUS TWO — similar to Opus One, except in 7mm Rem. Mag. or .300 Win. Mag. cal., 7¼ lbs., cased. Mfg. 1987-1988 only.

	$2,350	$2,050	$1,705	$1,300	$1,000	$875	$795

Last Mfg.'s Sug. Retail was $2,700.

OPUS THREE — similar to Opus Two, except in .375 H&H or .458 Win. Mag. cal., 10¼ lbs., cased. Mfg. 1987-1988 only.

	$2,600	$2,275	$1,800	$1,375	$1,050	$900	$825

Last Mfg.'s Sug. Retail was $2,850.

ORTGIES PISTOLS

Previously manufactured by Deutsche Werke A.G. located in Erfurt, Germany.

VEST POCKET AUTOMATIC — .25 auto, 6 shot, 2¾ in. barrel, blue or nickel finish, fixed sights, wood grips, post-WWI.

	$200	$180	$165	$145	$125	$110	$100

POCKET AUTOMATIC — .32 auto, 8 shot, .380 auto, 7 shot, 3¼ in. barrel, blue or nickel finish, fixed sights, wood grips.

	$225	$180	$130	$110	$90	$75	$65

Add 10% for .380.

ORVIS

Retailer/importer of private label subcontracted rifles/shotguns located in Dallas, Houston, TX and many other locations.

Orvis imports various rifles and shotguns under subcontract with various international manufacturers. Most of these private label models will approximate the values of the equivalent model manufactured by the subcontractor unless there are additional features and/or options which will add to the value.

SHOTGUNS: OVER/UNDER

UPLANDER SERIES — 12, 20, or 28 ga., boxlock action, 26 in. barrels with choke tubes (except 28 ga.), SST, straight grip, select European walnut with 24 LPI checkering, 6-7 lbs. Mfg. by P. Beretta of Italy.

Mfg.'s Sug. Retail	$2,600	$2,600	$2,200	$1,850	$1,500	$1,175	$995	$875

WATERFOWLER — 12 ga. only, 3 in. chambers, matte metal finish, 28 in. barrels with choke tubes, 7½ lbs. Mfg. by P. Beretta of Italy.

Mfg.'s Sug. Retail	$2,600	$2,600	$2,200	$1,850	$1,500	$1,175	$995	$875

RUGER/ORVIS MODEL — 12 or 20 ga., 3 in. chambers, Red Label Ruger action with customized Orvis features.

Mfg.'s Sug. Retail	$1,475	$1,475	$1,150	$975	$850	$725	$600	$495

SHOTGUNS: SIDE X SIDE

WATERFOWLER — 12 ga. only, 3 in. chambers, matte metal finish, 28 in. barrels with choke tubes, 7¾ lbs. Mfg. by P. Beretta of Italy.

Mfg.'s Sug. Retail	$2,450	$2,450	$2,050	$1,775	$1,425	$1,125	$950	$825

Grading	100%	98%	95%	90%	80%	70%	60%

CUSTOM UPLANDER — 12 - .410 ga., custom ordered gun, 25 or 27 in. barrels only, boxlock action, DT, mfg. by Arrieta located in Spain.

Mfg.'s Sug. Retail	$3,150	$3,150	$2,600	$2,200	$1,800	$1,400	$995	$725

Add $950 for SNT.

Add $1,200 for extra set of barrels (same ga.).

FINE GRADE — 12 - .410 ga., custom ordered gun, 25 or 28 in. barrels only, boxlock action, DT, mfg. by Arrieta located in Spain.

Mfg.'s Sug. Retail	$4,300	$4,300	$3,650	$3,100	$2,500	$1,995	$1,500	$1,150

Add $950 for SNT.

Add $1,950 for extra set of barrels (same ga.).

ROUND ACTION — similar to Fine Grade, except boxlock action has rounded corners.

Mfg.'s Sug. Retail	$5,695	$5,695	$4,650	$3,850	$3,225	$2,550	$1,995	$1,500

NOTES

P.A.F.

Petoria Arms Company. Previous manufacturer located in S. Africa.

Grading	100%	98%	95%	90%	80%	70%	60%

.25 ACP PISTOL — .25 ACP cal., patterned after the Baby Browning, blued finish. Approx. 10,000 mfg.

	$375	$300	$275	$250	$225	$200	$180

P.A.W.S., INC.

Manufacturer located in the U.S. Distributed by Sile Distributors Inc. located in New York, NY.

ZX8 CARBINE — 9mm Para. or .45 ACP cal., semi-auto paramilitary design carbine, 16 in. barrel, 10 or 30 shot mag., folding metal stock, matte black finish, aperture rear sight, partial barrel shroud, 7½ lbs. New 1989.

Mfg.'s Sug. Retail	$695	$600	$495	$440	$395	$360	$330	$300

P.S.M.G. GUN COMPANY

Previous manufacturer located in Arlington, MA.

SIX IN ONE SUPREME — .22 LR, .30 Luger, .38 Super, .38 Spl., 9mm, or .45 ACP cal., single action semi-auto, 3¼, 5, or 7½ in. barrel with solid cooling rib, adj. rear sight, limited mfg. Mfg. 1988-89.

	$700	$600	$500	$450	$400	$365	$330

Add $20-$55 for caliber options.

Add $25 for 7½ in. barrel.

Add $35 for satin nickel plating.

Add $225 per extra barrel.

Add $450 per individual conversion unit.

Last Mfg.'s Sug. Retail was $895

PTK INTERNATIONAL, INC.

Distributor located in Atlanta, GA.

Please refer to listing under Poly-Technologies in this section.

PARAMOUNT MANUFACTURING LTD.

Manufacturer located in Kent, England.

Paramount manufactures top quality competition rifles utilizing their own action. Each rifle is hand checked before leaving the factory. For more information regarding this trademark, please refer to the Trademark Index in this text.

PARA-ORDNANCE MFG. INC.

Manufacturer located in Scarborough, Ontario, Canada.

Para-Ordnance also manufactures the Model 85 full or semi-auto paint-shell carbine (styled after the Ingram). This model retails for $300.

Grading	100%	98%	95%	90%	80%	70%	60%

P14 — .45 ACP cal., patterned after the Colt Model 1911A1 except has choice of alloy, steel, or stainless steel frame that has been widened slightly for extra shot capacity, single action, 5 in. barrel, loaded weight with 13 shot staggered mag. is the same as loaded Colt Model 1911A1 (2.6 lbs.). Introduced 1990.

Mfg.'s Sug. Retail	$716	$660	$575	$525	$475	$435	$400	$360

P13 — similar to P14, except has 12 shot mag., 4¼ in. barrel, and satin nickel finished slide. New 1991.

Mfg.'s Sug. Retail	$716	$660	$575	$525	$475	$435	$400	$360

P12 — compact variation of the P14 featuring 11 shot mag. and 3½ in. barrel. New 1991.

Mfg.'s Sug. Retail	$716	$660	$575	$525	$475	$435	$400	$360

PARDINI

Manufacturer located in Italy. Imported and distributed by Fiocchi of America, Inc., located in Ozark, MO.

STANDARD PISTOL — .22 LR only, target grips, adj. sights, 4.92 in. barrel, interchangeable grips, detachable mag. New 1986.

Mfg.'s Sug. Retail	$859	$775	$650	$525	$460	$410	$380	$350

LADIES PISTOL — similar to Standard Pistol, except grips are suitable for smaller hands. Imported 1986-90 only.

	$850	$700	$600	$520	$460	$410	$380

This variation is imported in limited quantities only.

Last Mfg.'s Sug. Retail was $955.

RAPID FIRE PISTOL — .22 Short, features enclosed style grip assembly, adj. sights, 5.12 in. barrel. New 1986.

Mfg.'s Sug. Retail	$879	$785	$650	$525	$460	$410	$380	$350

CENTERFIRE PISTOL — .32 S&W Long cal., otherwise similar to Standard Pistol, 4.92 in. barrel. New 1986.

Mfg.'s Sug. Retail	$879	$785	$650	$525	$460	$410	$380	$350

FREE PISTOL — .22 LR, single shot, sliding rotating bolt, 9.06 in. barrel, hilted grip, top-of-the-line match pistol.

Mfg.'s Sug. Retail	$989	$875	$725	$600	$550	$475	$410	$380

PARKER BROTHERS

Originally manufactured in Meriden, CT from 1866-1934. Remington took over production in 1934, and in 1938, the plant was moved to Ilion, NY. Over 4,500 "Transition Guns" (exhibiting Meriden and Ilion characteristics) were produced in Meriden between 1934-1937 and about 4,500 Parkers were manufactured at the Ilion location before production stopped. Total production reached approx. 242,387.

At the 1987 Shot Show, Remington Arms Co. reintroduced the Parker shotgun in an AHE grade - 20 ga., serial numbered 242,502 (consecutively numbered to the last Parker built in Ilion in 1934). These limited manufactured new shotguns have different casecolors and single triggers than the originals, but will once again be manufactured in Ilion, NY to precise quality control standards (see separate listing in this section under the Model AH).

SHOTGUNS: DAMASCUS BARRELS — HAMMER MODELS

Parker damascus or hammer shotguns are very collectible if original condition is high. Specimens in 90% or better condition with strong case colors can approximate values of the steel barrel models if the bores are in excellent condition also (no pitting). Values for under 90% specimens fall off rapidly and are no longer comparable to steel barrel guns. As an example, a steel "D" Grade (without ejectors) might range from $1,500 to $7,000 (10%-100%) with a rather even downward progression of values in between the high and low values. A 100%

Grading	100%	98%	95%	90%	80%	70%	60%

damascus "D" Grade might range from $295 to $3,000 with the 70% and lower conditions being $800 down to $295 — not much of a spread. REMEMBER — THE GUNS ARE NOT RARE BUT THEIR ORIGINAL CONDITION IS.

SHOTGUNS: FLUID STEEL BARRELS

Values listed below in the 95%-100% condition columns can vary immensely as there is almost no supply for these high demand items, always a prerequisite for unpredictable prices. 95% OF THE ORIGINAL PARKERS BOUGHT AND SOLD EACH YEAR ARE IN 60%-70% OR LESS CONDITION (REFERRING TO ORIGINAL CASE COLORS).

Note: Values are for non-ejector guns. Add 15% - 30% for vent ribs. Skeet model has beavertail forearm and single selective trigger valued at approx. 50%-75% higher than values shown. Higher grade guns typically had ejectors, and will not make as much difference percentage-wise in the overall value as those lower grades with ejectors. Ejectors typically will add 50% more value to a Parker. Also, lower condition high grade models sometimes have their values established by the potential gain in refurbishing these specimens.

Due to the extremely high value of Parker Guns, extreme care should be taken in their purchase. There are many upgraded and refinished guns represented as original; expert advice should always be sought. Many collectors would rather own a specimen with 30% original casecolors than a refinished gun that is 100% (regardless who did the work). Many advanced collectors will discount a refinished Parker's value 40%-60% of the price for an original gun. Misrepresentation of refinished or upgraded Parkers is rampant today - especially case colors. In other words, be careful, shop carefully, get a receipt, and if in doubt, utilize Fluroscope technology to know for sure.

Frame size on Parker shotguns is determined by the number on the bottom of the barrel lug on breech. Frame sizes (from largest to smallest) include 7, 6, 5, 4, 3, 2, 1½, 1, 0, 00, and 000. 8 ga. guns typically are framed 5, 6, or 7. 10 ga. guns typically are 3 or 4. 12 ga. guns typically range from 2 through 1. 20 and 16 ga.'s range from 2 through 0. 28 ga. guns are either 0 or 00. .410 ga. shotguns are 0, 00, or 000 (most common and most desirable).

The grade on Parker shotguns is a number or initials located on the water table of the frame. An alphabetical designation would indicate the grade immediately. For numerals, a "2" would indicate a GH, while an "8" would specify an A-1 Special. Interpolate for the others (numbers 3 through 7).

A note about Parker condition: Percentages of condition indicate the amount of original case colors remaining on the frame. A Parker IS NOT 60% if the barrel bluing and stock/forearm varnish are 60% but case colors are only 10%. Typically, a 60% case color Parker shotgun will have 90%+ blue and varnish, yet this does not mean the gun is 90% overall. Similarly, a 20% case color Parker will probably have 90% barrel bluing remaining. Strong, original case colors are the key in determining Parker condition and subsequent values.

PREMIUMS FOR PARKER SHOTGUNS:
Add 50% for ejectors (except AAH).
Add 20% for SST.
Add 20% for beavertail forearm.
Add 20%-50% for vent rib (rare on smaller gauges).
Add 20% for straight English stock.
Add 20% for skeleton steel butt plate.
Add 20% for short barrels (26 in. with open chokes).

100%	98%	95%	90%	80%	70%	60%	50%	40%	30%	20%	10%

TROJAN — Parker's lowest-priced gun, single or double triggers, but no auto ejectors available, very rarely found in mint condition because they were used a lot, a genuine utility gun. Approx. 48,000 mfg.

12 ga.

100%	98%	95%	90%	80%	70%	60%	50%	40%	30%	20%	10%
$2,500	$2,000	$1,625	$1,400	$1,150	$995	$900	$825	$750	$675	$600	$500

16 ga.

$2,500	$2,000	$1,625	$1,400	$1,150	$995	$900	$825	$750	$675	$600	$500

20 ga.

$3,500	$3,000	$2,500	$2,175	$1,850	$1,625	$1,400	$1,150	$995	$900	$825	$750

	100%	98%	95%	90%	80%	70%	60%	50%	40%	30%	20%	10%

VH — Parker's biggest selling model, offered with all options, the most commonly found Parker. Approx. 60,000 mfg. 10 ga. is very rare in this model.
Add 50% for ejectors (VHE Model).

12 ga.

100%	98%	95%	90%	80%	70%	60%	50%	40%	30%	20%	10%
$3,250	$2,750	$2,200	$1,750	$1,450	$1,200	$1,000	$900	$825	$750	$675	$600

16 ga.

$3,250	$2,750	$2,200	$1,750	$1,450	$1,200	$1,000	$900	$825	$750	$675	$600

20 ga.

$3,950	$3,750	$3,500	$3,200	$3,000	$2,800	$2,400	$2,200	$2,000	$1,800	$1,600	$1,400

28 ga.

$6,500	$6,250	$5,750	$5,150	$4,600	$3,900	$3,220	$2,875	$2,645	$2,300	$2,075	$1,900

.410 ga.

$18,500	$16,100	$14,000	$12,250	$10,000	$8,750	$7,900	$6,900	$6,250	$5,750	$5,350	$4,775

PH — offered for a very short time, most had damascus barrels, prices here are for fluid steel barrels only. Approx. 8,500 mfg. A very few .410 ga.'s were mfg.. 10 ga. is very rare in this model.
Add 50% for ejectors (PHE Model).

12 ga.

$3,150	$2,850	$2,600	$2,350	$2,100	$1,850	$1,625	$1,400	$1,150	$995	$900	$825

16 ga.

$3,150	$2,850	$2,600	$2,350	$2,100	$1,850	$1,625	$1,400	$1,150	$995	$900	$825

20 ga.

$4,600	$4,300	$4,000	$3,750	$3,350	$2,950	$2,600	$2,350	$2,175	$1,900	$1,650	$1,400

28 ga.

$8,100	$7,800	$7,400	$7,000	$6,500	$6,000	$5,750	$5,500	$5,000	$4,500	$3,750	$3,000

GH — very popular model, barrels marked Parker, special steel, engraved moderately with all options available. Approx. 28,500 mfg. 10 ga. is very rare in this model.
Add 50% for ejectors (GHE Model).

12 ga.

$3,950	$3,500	$3,150	$2,475	$1,850	$1,625	$1,400	$1,150	$950	$795	$695	$595

16 ga.

$4,250	$3,750	$3,350	$2,600	$2,175	$1,850	$1,575	$1,250	$950	$795	$695	$595

20 ga.

$4,600	$4,000	$3,350	$2,600	$2,175	$1,850	$1,625	$1,400	$1,150	$995	$875	$750

28 ga.

$7,000	$6,375	$5,750	$5,125	$4,550	$3,925	$3,375	$2,875	$2,645	$2,300	$2,075	$1,750

.410 ga.

$20,000	$17,250	$15,350	$12,850	$10,500	$8,525	$7,375	$6,600	$5,950	$5,300	$4,500	$3,850

DH — the most popular higher grade gun, very tastefully engraved and flawlessly finished. Approx. 48,000 mfg. 10 ga. is very rare in this model.
Add 50% for ejectors (DHE Model).

12 ga.

$5,500	$4,850	$4,100	$3,450	$2,675	$2,175	$1,850	$1,625	$1,400	$1,125	$925	$795

16 ga.

$5,800	$4,925	$4,200	$3,500	$2,675	$2,175	$1,850	$1,625	$1,400	$1,125	$925	$795

20 ga.

$6,375	$5,750	$5,125	$4,550	$3,925	$3,375	$2,875	$2,400	$2,075	$1,750	$1,350	$950

28 ga.

$10,500	$9,250	$8,175	$7,000	$6,375	$5,750	$5,125	$4,550	$3,925	$3,375	$2,875	$2,375

.410 ga.

$40,500	$35,250	$28,250	$22,000	$18,950	$16,350	$14,000	$12,750	$10,650	$9,100	$8,000	$7,250

CH — scarce because they were only slightly more decorative than the DHE, Acme steel barrels. Approx. 5,000 mfg. 10 ga. is very rare in this model.
Add 50% for ejectors (CHE Model).

	100%	98%	95%	90%	80%	70%	60%	50%	40%	30%	20%	10%

12 ga.

$6,250	$5,575	$4,775	$4,000	$3,350	$2,600	$2,175	$1,850	$1,450	$1,100	$875	$750

16 ga.

$6,575	$5,700	$4,850	$4,050	$3,350	$2,600	$2,175	$1,850	$1,450	$1,100	$875	$750

20 ga.

$8,450	$7,425	$6,375	$5,550	$4,950	$4,300	$3,750	$3,100	$2,650	$2,175	$1,675	$1,000

28 ga.

$21,000	$17,500	$13,850	$10,500	$9,250	$8,175	$7,000	$6,375	$5,750	$5,125	$4,550	$3,895

.410 ga. — very rare, approx. 6 are known to exist.

$49,500	$40,500	$35,250	$28,250	$23,250	$19,950	$17,250	$14,450	$12,950	$11,000	$9,950	$8,950

BH — quite popular and decorative, 4 styles of engraving available, Acme steel barrels. Approx. 13,000 mfg. 10 ga. is very rare in this model.
   Add 50% for ejectors (BHE Model).

12 ga.

$9,500	$8,450	$7,425	$6,375	$5,550	$4,950	$4,300	$3,750	$3,100	$2,650	$2,075	$1,575

16 ga.

$9,950	$8,650	$7,600	$6,400	$5,550	$4,950	$4,300	$3,750	$3,100	$2,650	$2,075	$1,575

20 ga.

$17,500	$14,500	$12,000	$10,250	$9,300	$8,275	$7,100	$6,375	$5,650	$5,000	$4,550	$3,650

28 ga.

$32,500	$27,650	$21,000	$17,500	$13,850	$10,500	$9,250	$8,175	$7,000	$6,275	$5,350	$4,550

.410 ga. — only 2 guns are known in this gauge, the BHE .410 is also the highest grade .410 ga. known to have been made. Extreme rarity precludes accurate price evaluation, but will be VERY expensive.

AH — a scarce gun, extremely decorative and flawlessly executed, Acme steel barrels. Approx. 5,500 mfg. 10 ga. is very rare in this model.
   Add 50% for ejectors (AHE Model).

12 ga.

$23,000	$19,550	$16,100	$12,250	$9,250	$8,000	$7,150	$6,250	$5,600	$4,950	$4,175	$3,450

16 ga.

$26,000	$21,000	$17,000	$13,000	$9,375	$8,100	$7,150	$6,250	$5,600	$4,950	$4,175	$3,450

20 ga.

$32,500	$27,650	$21,000	$17,500	$13,850	$10,500	$9,250	$8,175	$7,000	$6,400	$5,700	$5,100

28 ga.

$57,500	$49,750	$40,250	$31,500	$23,750	$18,975	$16,000	$14,000	$12,250	$10,750	$9,000	$8,250

.410 ga. — no original guns known to exist.

AHE NEW MODEL — 20 ga. only, 28 in. vent. rib barrels, single selective trigger, metal engraving and checkering are similar to the older AHE Model, limited mfg. (50 guns).
   This new model has a color case hardened receiver and black walnut stock and forearm — mfg. by Remington's Custom Shop. While advertised in 1989, this gun has yet to be manufactured because of engineering delays.

AAH — very elaborate model, early AA's have Whitworth barrels, late ones have Peerless. Approx. 340 mfg.
   Add 25% for ejectors (AAHE Model).

12 ga.

$35,000	$32,000	$28,500	$26,000	$23,000	$21,000	$19,000	$17,000	$15,500	$13,750	$12,000	$10,500

16 ga.

$39,000	$35,000	$32,000	$28,500	$26,000	$23,000	$21,000	$19,000	$17,000	$15,500	$13,750	$12,000

20 ga.

$57,500	$54,000	$50,000	$45,000	$40,250	$35,000	$31,050	$28,000	$24,750	$21,000	$19,550	$17,250

28 ga.

$86,250	$79,000	$74,750	$68,500	$63,250	$58,750	$53,475	$46,000	$39,500	$33,925	$28,175	$25,875

100%	98%	95%	90%	80%	70%	60%	50%	40%	30%	20%	10%

A-1 SPECIAL GRADE — 100% engraved, all were special ordered, each one inspected by the company president before being shipped. Approx. 320 mfg.

12 ga.

| $75,000 | $67,500 | $61,000 | $57,000 | $51,750 | $46,250 | $40,250 | $36,175 | $31,050 | $28,500 | $26,450 | $22,000 |

16 ga.

| $75,000 | $67,500 | $61,000 | $57,000 | $51,750 | $46,250 | $40,250 | $36,175 | $31,050 | $28,500 | $26,450 | $22,000 |

20 ga.

| $125,000 | $112,500 | $100,000 | $90,000 | $82,000 | $76,000 | $70,000 | $64,000 | $57,500 | $53,000 | $46,500 | $40,000 |

28 ga. — extreme rarity and desirability factors preclude accurate price evaluation by condition factors. 70% original condition A-1 Specials HAVE sold for over $90,000.

SINGLE BARREL TRAP GUNS

12 ga. only, 26, 28, 30, 32, and 34 in. barrels, any boring is available, as is stock configuration, boxlock, auto ejector. The grades differ only in engraving, checkering and wood finish.

It should be noted that single barrel trap guns cannot be compared to the SxS models as they are not as desirable even though they are rarer. Most side by side collectors are not that interested in single barrel trap models and very few collectors specialize in single barrels.

S.C. GRADE

| $2,275 | $1,850 | $1,625 | $1,400 | $1,150 | $995 | $900 | $825 | $750 | $675 | $600 | $475 |

S.B. GRADE

| $3,400 | $3,050 | $2,675 | $2,275 | $1,700 | $1,425 | $1,100 | $950 | $850 | $750 | $650 | $500 |

S.A. GRADE

| $4,750 | $3,875 | $3,050 | $2,675 | $2,275 | $1,700 | $1,425 | $1,100 | $950 | $850 | $750 | $650 |

S.A.A. GRADE

| $6,950 | $5,800 | $4,750 | $3,875 | $3,050 | $2,675 | $2,275 | $1,700 | $1,425 | $1,100 | $875 | $750 |

S.A.-1 SPECIAL GRADE

| $20,000 | $18,000 | $15,500 | $13,000 | $10,000 | $9,150 | $8,350 | $7,425 | $6,375 | $5,550 | $4,950 | $4,300 |

PARKER REPRODUCTIONS

Previously imported by the Parker Reproduction Division of Reagent Chemical & Research, Inc., located in Middlesex, NJ. Distributed by Parker Reproductions located in Webb City, MO. These shotguns were manufactured in Japan to original Parker specifications by Winchester until the factory closed in January, 1989.

In 1984 Winchester was contracted by Reagent Chemical & Research, Inc. to manufacture a new Parker shotgun. The new SxS was a DHE model, available in 20 and 28 ga. initially. These models were fabricated in Japan to original Parker specifications, and the reproduction is so authentic that most parts are interchangeable with original Parker guns. Mfg. 1984-89.

SHOTGUNS: SIDE BY SIDE

Models listed below with Mfg.'s Sug. Retail indicates limited existing inventory as this edition goes to press. Because of the high quality and limited mfg. of these reproductions, they are becoming quite collectible.

Grading	100%	98%	95%	90%	80%	70%	60%

DHE GRADE — 12 (new 1986), 20, or 28 (new 1986) ga., boxlock action, ejectors, single selective or double triggers, beavertail or splinter forend, straight or pistol grip stock, skeleton steel butt plate, engraving in original DH style, case hardened frame, rust blued barrels. Supplied with leather trunk case, canvas and leather cover, and snap caps.

| Mfg.'s Sug. Retail | $3,415 | $3,415 | $2,970 | $2,850 | $2,100 | $1,850 | $1,650 | $1,500 |

Add $630 for extra set of barrels.

Add $150 for beavertail forend.

Add $1,000 for internal screw chokes (sold out—original retail was $150 extra).

Grading	100%	98%	95%	90%	80%	70%	60%

DHE SMALL GAUGE COMBO — available as a 28/.410 ga. combo with 2 barrels and 2 forends. Less than 160 mfg.

	$5,400	$4,950	$4,400	$4,000	$3,600	$3,250	$2,950

Last Mfg.'s Sug. Retail was $4,970.

3-Barrel Set — includes 28, and .410 ga. barrels. Cased.

	$6,150	$5,500	$5,000	$4,500	$4,000	$3,600	$3,250

Last Mfg.'s Sug. Retail was $5,970.

DHE STEEL SHOT SPECIAL — similar to 12 ga. D Grade, except has stengthened No. 1½ barrels, 3 in. chambers, and 28 in. chrome lined barrels, 7¼-7½ lbs. Very limited mfg. 1987-89.

	$4,500	$3,900	$3,250	$2,750	$2,350	$2,000	$1,700

Add $100 for beavertail forend.
Last Mfg.'s Sug. Retail was $3,120.

BHE GRADE LIMITED EDITION — 12, 20, or 28 ga., original Parker BH specifications, single selective or double trigger(s), straight or pistol grip stock, engraved skeleton butt plate, bank note scroll engraving around game scenes, cased. Only 100 manufactured in each gauge — mfg. began late 1987-89.

	$4,350	$3,750	$3,100	$2,650	$2,150	$1,800	$1,500

Add $600-$1,000 for 28 or .410 ga.
Add $1,000 for extra set of barrels.
Add $150 for beavertail forend.
Last Mfg.'s Sug. Retail was $3,970.
A 28/.410 ga. combo was also available with 2 forends.

A-1 SPECIAL — 12, 20, or 28 (sold out) ga., original Parker A-1 specifications, single selective or double trigger(s), fine scroll engraving with game scenes, 32 lines/in. checkering, cased with accessories. Limited mfg. 1988-89.

Mfg.'s Sug. Retail	$10,050	$10,050	$8,500	$7,250	$6,000	$5,475	$4,800	$4,350

Add $2,000 for 28 ga.
Add $1,000 for extra set of barrels.
Add $200 for beavertail forend.
A 28/.410 ga. combo was also available with 2 forends.

A-1 Special Custom Engraved — custom (per individual special order) engraving, available with two sets of barrels only, cased with accessories. Limited mfg. 1988-89. Prices start at $10,500 and go up according to individualized special features.

Federal Duck Stamp Collector's Series — available in 12 or 20 ga., A-1 Special specifications, authorized by U.S. Department of Interior. Mfg. was limited to 10 per year in 1988-89 only.

Mfg.'s Sug. Retail	$14,000	$14,000	$10,000	$8,000

This model includes special case and 2 barrels per buyers specifications.

PARKER-HALE LIMITED

Manufacturer located in Birmingham, England. Rifles were manufactured in England until 1991 when Navy Arms purchased the manufacturing rights. Shotguns are mfg. in Spain. Rifles are currently being distributed by Navy Arms located in Ridgefield, NJ and shotguns are currently being imported by Precision Sports, a Division of Cortland Line Company, Inc. located in Cortland, NY.

RIFLES: BOLT ACTION

Parker-Hale bolt action rifles utilize the Mauser K-98 action and are offered in a variety of configurations. A single set trigger option was introduced in 1984 on most models which allows either "hair trigger" or conventional single stage operation - add $85.

Grading	100%	98%	95%	90%	80%	70%	60%

MODEL 81 CLASSIC — available in 11 cal.'s between .22-250 and 7mm Rem. Mag., 24 in. barrel, open sights, 4 shot mag., select checkered walnut with sling swivels, 7¾ lbs. New 1985.

Mfg.'s Sug. Retail	$860	$715	$565	$475	$395	$340	$300	$280

Model 81 African — .375 H&H or 9.3 x 62mm cal., similar specifications as Model 81 Classic and has engraved action. New 1986.

Mfg.'s Sug. Retail	$1,110	$875	$700	$600	$500	$425	$360	$330

MODEL 84 TARGET — 7.62mm, match rifle with special sights, adj. cheek piece on stock. Importation disc. 1990.

	$1,080	$875	$760	$680	$610	$530	$465

Last Mfg.'s Sug. Retail was $1,300.

MODEL 85 SNIPER RIFLE — .308 cal., bolt action, extended heavy barrel, 10 shot mag., camo green synthetic stock with stippling, built in adj. bipod, enlarged contoured bolt, adj. recoil pad. Importation began 1989.

Mfg.'s Sug. Retail	$1,975	$1,750	$1,425	$1,275	$1,050	$875	$750	$625

MODEL 86 TARGET — 7.62mm, 27½ in. barrel, 5 shot mag., stippled stock and forend, aperture front and rear sights, 11¼ lbs. Distributed 1986 only by North American Precision.

	$980	$830	$760	$690	$610	$530	$465

Last Mfg.'s Sug. Retail was $1,149.

MODEL 87 TARGET — .243, 6.5 x 55, .308, .30-06, or .300 Win. Mag. cal., target stock, aperture sights. Importation began 1987.

Mfg.'s Sug. Retail	$1,525	$1,375	$1,100	$900	$775	$650	$550	$495

MODEL 1000 STANDARD — available in 9 cal.'s between .22-250 and .308 Win., 22 in. barrel, 4 shot mag., walnut stock with cheek piece, 7¼ lbs. Disc. 1988.

	$400	$330	$285	$255	$230	$215	$195

Last Mfg.'s Sug. Retail was $500.

MODEL 1100 LIGHTWEIGHT — available in 9 cal.'s between .22-250 and .30-06, 22 in. barrel, open sights, 4 shot mag., 6½ lbs. New 1985.

Mfg.'s Sug. Retail	$595	$495	$400	$350	$325	$285	$270	$255

Model 1100M African — .375 H&H, .404 Jeffery, or .458 Win. Mag. cal., 24 in. barrel, 4 shot mag., 9½ lbs.

Mfg.'s Sug. Retail	$960	$800	$650	$575	$500	$450	$425	$400

MODEL 1200 SUPER — bolt action, Mauser type action, .22-250, .243, 6mm, .25-06, .270, .30-06, .300 Win. Mag., 7mm Rem., or .308 cal., 24 in. barrel, folding sight, skip checkered walnut stock, pad swivels, rosewood pistol grip cap and forend tip. Mfg. 1968-present.

Mfg.'s Sug. Retail	$680	$540	$450	$375	$330	$295	$275	$260

This model in Magnum cal.'s is called the 1200 M Super Magnum.

Model 1200 C (Super Clip) — similar to Model 1200 Super, except has detachable 4 shot box mag.

Mfg.'s Sug. Retail	$740	$590	$500	$400	$350	$300	$280	$265

MODEL 1200P PRESENTATION — same as 1200, except .243 or .30-06 cal., scroll engraved, no sights. Mfg. 1969-1975.

	$495	$425	$395	$340	$315	$305	$275

MODEL 1200 SUPER VARMINT — same as 1200, except .22-250, 6mm, .25-06, or .243 cal., 24 in. heavy barrel, no sights. Disc. 1988.

	$525	$425	$365	$325	$285	$270	$255

Last Mfg.'s Sug. Retail was $660.

MODEL 1300 C SCOUT — shorter barrel variation.

Mfg.'s Sug. Retail	$785	$695	$550	$450	$385	$330	$300	$275

Grading	100%	98%	95%	90%	80%	70%	60%

MODEL 2100 MIDLAND (HYBRID ACTION) — available in 11 cal.'s between .22-250 or .300 Win. Mag. cal., 22 in. barrel, 4 shot mag., open sights, 7 lbs.

Mfg.'s Sug. Retail	$365	$325	$270	$230	$200	$190	$180	$170

Model 2100 Midland Magnum — .300 Win. Mag., or 7mm Rem. Mag. cal., 24 in. barrel, 4 shot mag., 9½ lbs. Imported 1989-90 only.

	$380	$325	$295	$270	$260	$250	$240

Last Mfg.'s Sug. Retail was $430.

MODEL 2600 MIDLAND SPECIAL — .243 Win., .270 Win., .308 Win., or .30-06 cal., Midland Gun Co. action, iron sights. New 1989.

Mfg.'s Sug. Retail	$330	$295	$250	$225	$200	$190	$180	$170

MIDLAND 2700 LIGHTWEIGHT — lightweight variation of the Model 2600.

Mfg.'s Sug. Retail	$390	$340	$285	$240	$200	$190	$180	$170

SHOTGUNS

MODEL 640E (ENGLISH) — 12, 16, or 20 ga., boxlock action, double triggers, straight grip stock, splinter forend, concave rib, extractors, silver finished receiver. New 1986.

Mfg.'s Sug. Retail	$850	$750	$595	$540	$475	$415	$350	$295

Add $90 for 28 or .410 ga.

The "E" suffix in this model designates English configuration.

Model 640A (AMERICAN) — same ga.'s as 640E, except has non-selective single trigger, pistol grip, beavertail forend, and raised matted rib. New 1986.

Mfg.'s Sug. Retail	$965	$840	$700	$630	$560	$475	$400	$350

Add $45 for 28 or .410 ga.

The "A" suffix in this model designates American configuration (pistol grip stock and single trigger).

MODEL 640M (MAGNUM) — 10 ga., 3½ in. chambers, 26, 30, or 32 in. barrels bored full and full, DT's, recoil pad. New 1989.

Mfg.'s Sug. Retail	$1,000	$860	$725	$650	$575	$495	$415	$365

In this model, the 26 in. barrels are referred to as the Turkey Gun, the 30 in. is Big Ten, and the 32 in. is Goose Gun.

MODEL 640 SLUG GUN — 12 ga. only, 25 in. barrels bored IC/IC. New 1991.

Mfg.'s Sug. Retail	$1,230	$1,075	$875	$725	$650	$575	$495	$415

MODEL 645E (ENGLISH) — 12, 16, or 20 ga., boxlock action, double triggers, straight grip stock, moderate engraving, splinter forend, concave rib, ejectors, silver finished receiver. New 1986.

Mfg.'s Sug. Retail	$1,090	$940	$775	$675	$595	$500	$415	$365

Add $30 for 28 or .410 ga.

Model 645E-XXV — available in all ga.'s, 25 in. barrels only, ejectors, Churchill rib, moderately engraved, silver finished receiver. New 1986.

Mfg.'s Sug. Retail	$1,120	$960	$785	$675	$595	$500	$415	$365

Add $130 for 28 or .410 ga.

Model 645E Bi-Gauge — 2 barrel set available in either 20/28 ga. or 28/.410 ga. combination. New 1988.

Mfg.'s Sug. Retail	$1,731	$1,575	$1,250	$950	$800	$700	$600	$550

Add $79 for 28/.410 ga. combo.

MODEL 645A (AMERICAN) — same ga.'s as 645E, except has non-selective single trigger, pistol grip, beavertail forend, and raised matted rib. New 1986.

Mfg.'s Sug. Retail	$1,220	$1,025	$825	$700	$615	$515	$440	$400

Add $170 for 28 or .410 ga.

Model 645A Bi-Gauge — 2 barrel set available in either 20/28 ga. or 28/.410 ga. combination. New 1988.

Mfg.'s Sug. Retail	$1,890	$1,710	$1,350	$995	$850	$750	$625	$575

Add $60 for 28/.410 ga. combo.

Grading	100%	98%	95%	90%	80%	70%	60%

MODEL 670E (ENGLISH) — 12, 16, or 20 ga., sidelock action, 26, 27, or 28 in. barrels, ejectors, engraved silver finished receiver, double triggers, straight grip. New 1986.

Mfg.'s Sug. Retail	$4,270	$3,700	$2,975	$2,450	$1,850	$1,550	$1,375	$1,200

Add $770 for 28 or .410 ga.

This model is available by custom order only.

MODEL 680E-XXV (ENGLISH) — similar to Model 670E, except has color case hardened sideplates and 25 in. barrels only.

Mfg.'s Sug. Retail	$4,070	$3,500	$2,800	$2,300	$1,700	$1,475	$1,300	$1,175

Add $400 for 28 or .410 ga.

This model is available by custom order only.

BILL HANUS BIRDGUN — 16, 20, or 28 ga., boxlock action, 26 in. barrels bored SK1/SK2, Churchill raised rib, SNT, ejectors, case colored receiver, checkered straight grip walnut stock and semi-beavertail forend, oil finish, lifetime warranty, 5¼-6½ lbs. New 1991.

Mfg.'s Sug. Retail	$1,270	$1,060	$835	$700	$615	$515	$440	$400

Add $130 for 28 ga.

PEDERSEN CUSTOM GUNS

Previously a division of O.F. Mossberg, North Haven, CT. Manufactured between 1973-1975.

RIFLES

MODEL 3000 — bolt action rifle, Mossberg Model 810 action, .270, .30-06, 7mm Mag., or .338 Mag. cal., 22 and 24 in. barrel, open sight, checkered Monte Carlo stock.

Grade III — no engraving.

	$550	$495	$470	$440	$420	$385	$330

Grade II — moderately engraved.

	$660	$580	$525	$495	$440	$420	$385

Grade I — heavily engraved and inlaid, with select wood.

	$990	$770	$745	$690	$635	$560	$495

Presentation Model — top-of-the-line model.

	$1,250	$1,000	$895	$800	$745	$690	$635

MODEL 4700 — custom deluxe lever action, (Model 472 Mossberg), .30-30 or .35 Rem. cal., 5 shot, tube mag., 24 in. barrel, open sight, black walnut stock.

	$250	$195	$165	$155	$145	$130	$120

SHOTGUNS

MODEL 4000 SLIDE ACTION SHOTGUN — custom Mossberg Model 500, 12, 20, or .410 ga., 3 in. chamber, 26 in. imp. cyl. or skeet, 28 in. full or mod., 30 in. full, vent rib, floral engraved, checkered select walnut stock. Mfg. 1975.

	$460	$375	$330	$305	$265	$230	$220

MODEL 4000 TRAP — same as 4000, except 12 ga., 30 in. full, Monte Carlo trap stock and pad. Mfg. 1975.

	$485	$395	$350	$325	$285	$255	$240

MODEL 4500 — same as 4000, less engraving.

	$420	$330	$305	$275	$240	$200	$175

MODEL 4500 TRAP — same as 4000 Trap, less engraving.

	$440	$350	$310	$280	$240	$210	$200

MODEL 1500 O/U HUNTING GUN — 12 ga., 2¾ or 3 in. chambers, 26 in. imp. cyl. and mod., 28 in. mod. and full, 30 in. mod. and full, boxlock, auto ejectors, selective or non-selective single trigger, checkered pistol grip stock. Mfg. 1973-1975.

	$700	$575	$500	$440	$415	$385	$365

Grading	100%	98%	95%	90%	80%	70%	60%

MODEL 1500 SKEET — same as Hunting Gun, except 27 in. skeet, skeet stock. Mfg. 1973-1975.

	$725	$600	$525	$450	$425	$400	$385

MODEL 1500 TRAP — same as Hunting Gun, except 30 and 32 in. full barrels, trap Monte Carlo stock. Mfg. 1973-1975.

	$650	$550	$475	$435	$410	$375	$350

MODEL 1000 O/U HUNTING GUN — 12 or 20 ga., 26, 28, or 30 in. barrels, various chokes, boxlock, auto ejectors, SST, checkered select walnut stock, silver inlays, more engraving. Mfg. 1973-1975.

	100%	98%	95%	90%	80%	70%	60%
Grade I	$2,200	$1,980	$1,870	$1,700	$1,540	$1,460	$1,375
Grade II	$1,815	$1,540	$1,430	$1,265	$1,185	$1,100	$1,045

MODEL 1000 TRAP GUN — same as Hunting Gun, but 12 ga., 30 or 32 in. mod. and full barrels, Monte Carlo trap stock. Mfg. 1973-1975.

	100%	98%	95%	90%	80%	70%	60%
Grade I	$2,100	$1,800	$1,650	$1,500	$1,350	$1,200	$995
Grade II	$1,650	$1,500	$1,375	$1,200	$1,050	$900	$725

MODEL 1000 SKEET — same as Hunting Gun, except 26 or 28 in. barrels, bored skeet. Mfg. 1973-1975.

	100%	98%	95%	90%	80%	70%	60%
Grade I	$2,255	$2,145	$2,035	$1,870	$1,705	$1,625	$1,540
Grade II	$1,980	$1,705	$1,595	$1,430	$1,350	$1,265	$1,210

MODEL 200 S X S — 12 or 20 ga., 26 in. imp. cyl. and mod., 28 in. mod. and full, 30 in. mod. and full, boxlock, auto ejectors, SST. Mfg. 1973-1974.

	100%	98%	95%	90%	80%	70%	60%
Grade I	$2,420	$2,175	$2,090	$1,955	$1,790	$1,705	$1,625
Grade II	$2,200	$1,955	$1,815	$1,735	$1,625	$1,540	$1,485

MODEL 2500 DOUBLE BARREL — 12 or 20 ga., 26 in. imp. cyl. and mod., 28 in. mod. and full, auto ejectors, boxlock, checkered pistol grip stock and forearm.

	$470	$385	$360	$305	$275	$260	$240

PENTHENY de PENTHENY, INC

Current manufacturer and gunsmith located in Santa Rosa, CA. established In 1987.

RIFLES

The rifles listed below include ebony forend tips, old English style black recoil pads, steel skeleton grip caps, four panels of 22 LPI checkering, and other custom features. These models are built on aU.S.R.A. company Model 70 action.

THE INVADER — small and medium bore cal.'s, classic styled Claro walnut stock, blued finish, includes Buehler rings and bases.

Mfg.'s Sug. Retail	$3,250	$3,250	$2,800	$2,350	$1,950	$1,500	$1,150	$875

THE NORMAN — Mag. cal.'s, classic styled English walnut stock, blued finish, includes Buehler rings and bases.

Mfg.'s Sug. Retail	$3,250	$3,250	$2,800	$2,350	$1,950	$1,500	$1,150	$875

THE CONQUEROR — large bore cal.'s, classic styled English walnut stock, blued finish, action has secondary recoil lug and dual steel reinforced bolt, express sights including fixed and folding leaves.

Mfg.'s Sug. Retail	$4,000	$4,000	$3,350	$2,850	$2,350	$1,950	$1,500	$1,150

PEDERSOLI, DAVIDE & C.

Manufacturer of blackpowder and older historically significant firearms located in Bresia, Italy.

D. Pedersoli manufactures top quality blackpowder replicas and other high quality reproductions. Most of their production domestically is subcontracted by other U.S. firms.

Grading	100%	98%	95%	90%	80%	70%	60%

PERAZZI

Manufacturer located in Brescia, Italy. Imported and distributed by Perazzi Usa, Inc. located in Monrovia, CA. (previously located in Rome, NY).

Note: Previously, Perazzi shotguns were imported by both Winchester and Ithaca during the 1960's and 1970's. The company now has its own distribution network and its current model line-up is extensive. Perazzi shotguns are well known for their quality control standards and reliability in clay target championships and in-field conditions.

Because of the devaluation of the U.S. dollar since 1984, Perazzi shotguns have gone up in value substantially.

SHOTGUNS: DISCONTINUED

Perazzi shotguns have incorporated many improvements during their manufacture. One of the most important changes has been the modification of the forearm design. Basically, there have been 4 different types: Type 1 has a serial range of 30,000 - 33,250, Type 2 is serial numbered 33,251 - 35,450, Type 3 has a range of 35,451 - 51,242, Type 4 started at 51,243 and is still current as of this writing. Differences include changes in the forearm iron and barrel lug attachment. Because of these forearm changes (and other parts modifications), the desirability factor on a Type 4 forearm shotgun as opposed to a Type 1 is much greater. Competition shooters prefer Types 3 or 4 as they are the current design. If a Type 1 or 2 competition gun develops problems, they are automatically retrofitted to the Type 4 design - and these modifications are expensive. For these reasons, the serial number of a Perazzi competition gun will determine its type. Since Types 1 through 3 are discontinued, Types 1 and 2 will be less desirable (and less expensive) than the values listed below for Type 3.

As a final note on older Perazzi shotguns, the most collectable models will be those specimens which exhibit the highest quality and are equally rare. Older SCO grades on small frames with older style "V" springs are at the top for desirability. Also, any older SPECIAL GUNS were all custom made - usually engraved by master engravers with Angelo Galeazzi being considered the best. These models are exceedingly rare, with prices going over the $40,000 level in today's marketplace.

COMPETITION ONE TRAP GRADE — single shot, 12 ga., auto ejector, vent rib, cased.

| | $2,500 | $2,150 | $1,875 | $1,650 | $1,450 | $1,300 | $1,175 |

COMPETITION ONE O/U TRAP — same as Competition, except O/U double.

| | $3,950 | $3,500 | $3,000 | $2,500 | $2,150 | $1,850 | $1,650 |

COMPETITION ONE SKEET

| | $4,250 | $3,750 | $3,200 | $2,700 | $2,350 | $2,000 | $1,750 |

SINGLE BARREL TRAP — 12 ga., 34 in. vent rib, full choke barrel, boxlock, auto ejector, checkered pistol grip stock, recoil pad. Mfg. 1971-1972.

| | $2,350 | $2,050 | $1,800 | $1,600 | $1,450 | $1,300 | $1,175 |

LIGHT GAME MODEL O/U FIELD — 12 ga., 27½ in. vent rib barrels, mod. and full or imp. cyl. and mod., boxlock, auto ejectors, field stock. Mfg. 1972-1974.

| | $4,500 | $3,900 | $3,300 | $2,800 | $2,400 | $2,050 | $1,800 |

MT-6 GRADE — 12 ga., vent rib, auto ejector, cased, five interchangeable choke tubes. Disc. 1983.

| | $4,250 | $3,750 | $3,250 | $2,800 | $2,500 | $2,200 | $1,900 |

This model was also manufactured in DHO and SHO models as well. Please refer to those models listed in the current manufacture section for approximate values.

CURRENTLY MANUFACTURED TRAP, SKEET, AND HUNTING SHOTGUNS

Not until 1988 did most single barrel trap guns have a "Special" option package which includes an adjustable trigger group (designated P4). This P4 trigger is now standard. Non-adj. trigger is a special order. Values below assume shotguns with the "Special" designation (became standard in 1988).

Models listed in the following sections assume a Type 4 forearm attachment design and are serial numbered 51,243 and above. Models that are serial numbered below 51,243 are an older design and will be priced less than the newer Type 4 models (see explanation under SHOTGUNS: DISCONTINUED).

Rather than describe all the following models individually, descriptions will appear only once and are listed below. Because the various grades have similar features and engraving (i.e.: an SCO Grade Sideplate in American Skeet would appear similar to an American Trap SCO Grade Sideplate, except for stock dimensions of course).

Older SHO (Type 3's) and DHO models with rebounding hammers (disc.) are perhaps the most collectable Perazzi shotguns currently.

PERAZZI GRADES WITH DESCRIPTIONS

Special Model — introductory level model with high polished blue on barrels and receiver, normally listing model name on lower frame sides in gold letters and numerals. Checkered walnut stock (interchangeable) and forearm, most have adjustable trigger assembly.

Gold Outline Model — similar to Standard Model, except has gold line engraving around perimeter of frame, also features better grade of walnut. This configuration is very rare.

SC3 Model — features coined finished receiver with two different styles of scroll engraving and four different patterns of game scene engraving (snipe, grouse, pointing bird dog, or woodcock). Better grade of walnut than the Gold Outline Model.

SCO Model — more elaborate than SC3 Model in that it features two different styles of scroll engraving (deep relief "gargoils" or fine English scroll) and four different game scene engraving patterns (two different styles of ducks, grouse, or woodcock). Again, a better grade of walnut (in addition to finer checkering) is utilized.

SCO Gold Grade Model — differentiated from SCO Model in that it has six engraving patterns featuring multiple gold inlays on receiver sides (including two different duck scenes, two separate grouse scences, one woodcock, and one deep relief "gargoil").

SCO Grade Sideplate Model — includes coined finished receiver with game scene engraved sideplates (with boxlock action). Game scene engraving choices include three different duck scenes, one grouse, one "Chisel" relief scroll, and a Diana Goddess of the Hunt pattern.

SCO Gold Grade Sideplate Model — similar to SCO Grade Sideplate Model, except has game figures on sideplates in relief gold. Patterns include three different grouse scenes, two separate ducks patterns, and dogs flushing upland game. This model can also be ordered with detachment lever for sideplates.

Extra Grade Model — denoted by top-of-the-line fine bank note style game scene engraving with elaborate scroll and relief work on metal perimeters. Game scene choices include two different dog scenes, one grouse, and one duck. Top quality Circassion walnut finely checkered.

Extra Gold Grade Model — top-of-the-line boxlock model that differs from Extra Grade Model in that birds/dogs are in gold relief. This model can also be ordered with detachment lever for sideplates.

SHO Over & Under Model — features sidelock action with coined finished receiver and intricate bank note game scene engraving with choices including three different duck patterns and one pheasant. Top quality walnut and checkering.
This model is individually hand made per customer's specifications. Currently, no orders are being taken for this series.

SHO Gold Over & Under Model — similar to SHO Over & Under Model, except features game scene wildlife in relief gold. This model is the best sidelock special order grade that Perazzi currently offers for sale.
This model is individually hand made per customer's specifications. Currently, no orders are being taken for this series.

Grading	100%	98%	95%	90%	80%	70%	60%

DHO Side-by-Side Models — top-of-the-line sidelock model in 12 ga. only for DHO and DHO Gold grades. DHO Extra and DHO Gold Extra grades have similar engraving to Extra Grade and Extra Gold Grade models and are available in all gauges. The DHO Gold Extra is the most elaborate, highly finished side-by-side shotgun (and expensive - current retail is $82,000) that an individual can currently special order from any company. The DHO model is exceedingly rare, and specimens should be appraised individually.

This model is entirely hand made per customer's specifications. Currently, no orders are being taken for this series.

AMERICAN TRAP SHOTGUNS: SINGLE BARREL

12 ga. only, 32 or 34 in. barrel, high post rib, select walnut, more expensive models vary in the amount of engraving, grade of walnut, and other special order features.

NOTE: Combination guns (Combo Models) listed below include either a 32 or 34 in. single barrel and a set of either 29½ or 31½ barrels.

Subtract $600 for shotguns without the "Special" model designation (pre-1988).

STANDARD GRADE MODELS

Add 45-56% for Combo Models depending on grade.

TM1 Special — features normal trap rib.

Mfg.'s Sug. Retail	$5,100	$4,500	$3,500	$3,100	$2,350	$2,150	$1,850	$1,675

TMX Special — features high post trap rib.

Mfg.'s Sug. Retail	$5,100	$4,500	$3,500	$3,100	$2,350	$2,150	$1,850	$1,675

MX 3 Special — features rib similar to TM1 Special.

Mfg.'s Sug. Retail	$5,650	$4,850	$3,700	$3,250	$2,450	$2,200	$1,900	$1,700

MX 8 Special — has tappered stepped rib and adj. trigger.

Mfg.'s Sug. Retail	$6,400	$5,510	$4,250	$3,600	$3,200	$2,875	$2,600	$2,375

Add $2,750 for Gold Outline engraving.

Grand American 88 Special — features MX3 high ramped rib and grooved forearm. New 1988.

Mfg.'s Sug. Retail	$6,400	$5,510	$4,250	$3,600	$3,200	$2,875	$2,600	$2,375

Add $2,750 for Gold Outline engraving.

DB81 Special — featues ultra high ramped rib.

Mfg.'s Sug. Retail	$6,700	$5,720	$4,400	$3,700	$3,250	$2,900	$2,625	$2,400

Add $2,750 for Gold Outline engraving.

SC3 GRADE MODELS

Add 26-31% for Combo Model depending on grade.

MX 3 Special

Mfg.'s Sug. Retail	$9,550	$8,240	$6,500	$5,200	$4,560	$4,175	$3,800	$3,350

MX 8 Special

Mfg.'s Sug. Retail	$10,850	$9,370	$7,750	$6,300	$5,500	$4,950	$4,200	$3,800

Grand American 88 Special

Mfg.'s Sug. Retail	$10,850	$9,370	$7,750	$6,300	$5,500	$4,950	$4,200	$3,800

DB81 Special

Mfg.'s Sug. Retail	$11,150	$9,625	$7,775	$6,300	$5,500	$4,950	$4,200	$3,800

SC0 GRADE MODELS

Add 21-35% for Combo Model depending on grade.

TM1 Special

Mfg.'s Sug. Retail	$14,750	$13,000	$10,150	$8,400	$7,555	$6,600	$6,100	$5,550

TMX Special

Mfg.'s Sug. Retail	$14,750	$13,000	$10,150	$8,400	$7,555	$6,600	$6,100	$5,550

MX3 Special

Mfg.'s Sug. Retail	$16,950	$15,000	$11,650	$9,300	$8,500	$7,600	$7,000	$6,300

MX8 Special

Mfg.'s Sug. Retail	$18,350	$16,100	$13,500	$10,770	$9,250	$8,500	$7,900	$6,850

Grand American 88 Special

Mfg.'s Sug. Retail	$18,350	$16,100	$13,500	$10,770	$9,250	$8,500	$7,900	$6,850

Grading	100%	98%	95%	90%	80%	70%	60%
DB81 Special							
Mfg.'s Sug. Retail	$18,650	$16,300	$13,625	$10,800	$9,250	$8,500	$7,900	$6,850

GOLD GRADE MODELS
Add 17-20% for Combo Model depending on grade.

	100%	98%	95%	90%	80%	70%	60%
TM1 Special							
Mfg.'s Sug. Retail	$16,450	$14,700	$11,450	$9,200	$8,500	$7,600	$7,000	$6,300
TMX Special							
Mfg.'s Sug. Retail	$16,450	$14,700	$11,450	$9,200	$8,500	$7,600	$7,000	$6,300
MX3 Special							
Mfg.'s Sug. Retail	$19,000	$16,550	$13,750	$10,825	$9,250	$8,500	$7,900	$6,850
MX8 Special							
Mfg.'s Sug. Retail	$20,350	$17,550	$14,250	$11,350	$9,650	$8,700	$8,100	$6,950
Grand American 88 Special							
Mfg.'s Sug. Retail	$20,350	$17,550	$14,250	$11,350	$9,650	$8,700	$8,100	$6,950
DB81 Special							
Mfg.'s Sug. Retail	$20,650	$17,770	$14,375	$11,450	$9,700	$8,725	$8,100	$7,000

SCO GRADE SIDEPLATES MODELS
Add 13-14% for Combo Model depending on grade.

	100%	98%	95%	90%	80%	70%	60%
MX8 Special							
Mfg.'s Sug. Retail	$27,250	$24,250	$18,750	$16,000	$13,250	$11,750	$10,250	$9,000
Grand American 88 Special							
Mfg.'s Sug. Retail	$27,250	$24,250	$18,750	$16,000	$13,250	$11,750	$10,250	$9,000
DB81 Special							
Mfg.'s Sug. Retail	$27,550	$24,450	$18,850	$16,100	$13,300	$11,750	$10,250	$9,000

GOLD GRADE SIDEPLATES MODELS
Add 12% for Combo Model.

	100%	98%	95%	90%	80%	70%	60%
MX8 Special							
Mfg.'s Sug. Retail	$31,350	$27,100	$22,000	$20,000	$17,500	$15,250	$13,000	$11,250
Grand American 88 Special							
Mfg.'s Sug. Retail	$31,350	$27,100	$22,000	$20,000	$17,500	$15,250	$13,000	$11,250
DB81 Special							
Mfg.'s Sug. Retail	$31,650	$27,300	$22,150	$21,050	$17,500	$15,250	$13,000	$11,250

EXTRA GRADE MODELS
Add 12% for Combo Model.

	100%	98%	95%	90%	80%	70%	60%
MX8 Special							
Mfg.'s Sug. Retail	$50,000	$44,750	$34,750	$29,950	$25,000	$20,000	$17,000	$14,500
Grand American 88 Special							
Mfg.'s Sug. Retail	$50,000	$44,750	$34,750	$29,950	$25,000	$20,000	$17,000	$14,500
DB81 Special							
Mfg.'s Sug. Retail	$50,300	$44,950	$34,900	$30,000	$25,000	$20,000	$17,000	$14,500

EXTRA GOLD GRADE MODELS
Add 11% for Combo Model.

	100%	98%	95%	90%	80%	70%	60%
MX8 Special							
Mfg.'s Sug. Retail	$54,000	$47,650	$37,500	$31,750	$26,500	$21,250	$18,000	$15,500
Grand American 88 Special							
Mfg.'s Sug. Retail	$54,000	$47,650	$37,500	$31,750	$26,500	$21,250	$18,000	$15,500
DB81 Special							
Mfg.'s Sug. Retail	$54,300	$47,850	$37,650	$31,850	$26,500	$21,250	$18,000	$15,500

Grading	100%	98%	95%	90%	80%	70%	60%

INTERNATIONAL/OLYMPIC TRAP SHOTGUNS: O/U

12 ga. only.

STANDARD GRADE MODELS

The MX2/MX2L configuration is available mainly for the European marketplace. Values for this model represent recent pricing - Perazzi U.S.A. should be contacted directly for an up-to-date price quotation.

MX3 Special — includes 6.4mm high ramped rib and separated barrels.

Mfg.'s Sug. Retail	$6,000	$5,180	$4,050	$3,400	$2,950	$2,675	$2,350	$1,975

Add $350 for MX3C Model (includes choke tubes).

MX8 — denoted by low profile rib, vent. barrels and grooved forearm.

Mfg.'s Sug. Retail	$6,400	$5,510	$4,250	$3,600	$3,200	$2,875	$2,600	$2,375

Add $2,450 for Gold Outline engraving.
This model is also available with standard triggers.

MX8 Special — similar to MX8, except four position adj. trigger (P4S).

Mfg.'s Sug. Retail	$6,700	$5,720	$4,400	$3,700	$3,250	$2,900	$2,625	$2,400

Add $2,850 for Gold Outline engraving.

Grand American 88 Special — features high ramped rib, separated barrels, and grooved forearm.

Mfg.'s Sug. Retail	$6,700	$5,720	$4,400	$3,700	$3,250	$2,900	$2,625	$2,400

Add $2,850 for Gold Outline engraving.

DB81 — features ultra high ramped rib and vent. barrels.

Mfg.'s Sug. Retail	$7,000	$5,925	$4,550	$3,800	$3,300	$2,950	$2,650	$2,450

Add $2,850 for Gold Outline engraving.

MX2/MX2L — denoted by 8.2mm high rib, Monte Carlo stock, and vented side ribs. Model MX2L designates light weight model and has no side ribs.

Mfg.'s Sug. Retail	$5,510	$4,550	$3,700	$3,400	$3,050	$2,750	$2,500	$2,275

Add $2,750 for Gold Outline engraving.

SC3 GRADE MODELS

MX3 Special

Mfg.'s Sug. Retail	$9,850	$8,440	$6,650	$5,300	$4,560	$4,175	$3,800	$3,350

Add $350 for MX3C Model (includes choke tubes).

MX8

Mfg.'s Sug. Retail	$10,950	$9,450	$7,775	$6,300	$5,500	$4,950	$4,200	$3,800

MX8 Special

Mfg.'s Sug. Retail	$11,150	$9,600	$7,800	$6,300	$5,500	$4,950	$4,200	$3,800

Grand American 88 Special

Mfg.'s Sug. Retail	$11,150	$9,600	$7,800	$6,300	$5,500	$4,950	$4,200	$3,800

DB81 Special

Mfg.'s Sug. Retail	$14,350	$11,350	$9,750	$7,900	$6,300	$5,500	$4,950	$4,200

MX2/MX2L

Mfg.'s Sug. Retail	$9,420	$7,750	$6,300	$5,500	$4,950	$4,200	$3,800	$3,650

SCO GRADE MODELS

MX3 Special

Mfg.'s Sug. Retail	$17,250	$15,250	$11,800	$9,400	$8,500	$7,600	$7,000	$6,300

Add $350 for MX3C Special (includes choke tubes).

MX8

Mfg.'s Sug. Retail	$18,400	$16,125	$13,500	$10,770	$9,250	$8,500	$7,900	$6,850

MX8 Special

Mfg.'s Sug. Retail	$18,650	$16,275	$13,600	$10,800	$9,250	$8,500	$7,900	$6,850

Grand American 88 Special

Mfg.'s Sug. Retail	$18,650	$16,275	$13,600	$10,800	$9,250	$8,500	$7,900	$6,850

DB81

Mfg.'s Sug. Retail	$18,950	$16,475	$13,750	$10,900	$9,250	$8,500	$7,900	$6,850

Grading	100%	98%	95%	90%	80%	70%	60%
MX2/MX2L							
Mfg.'s Sug. Retail	$15,860	$13,500	$10,770	$9,250	$8,500	$8,000	$7,400	$6,750

GOLD GRADE MODELS

	100%	98%	95%	90%	80%	70%	60%
MX3 Special							
Mfg.'s Sug. Retail	$19,350	$16,800	$13,950	$11,000	$9,350	$8,500	$7,900	$6,850
Add $350 for MX3C Special (includes choke tubes).							
MX8							
Mfg.'s Sug. Retail	$20,450	$17,625	$14,250	$11,350	$9,650	$8,700	$7,900	$6,850
MX8 Special							
Mfg.'s Sug. Retail	$20,750	$17,825	$14,400	$11,450	$9,650	$8,700	$8,100	$6,950
Grand American 88 Special							
Mfg.'s Sug. Retail	$20,750	$17,825	$14,400	$11,450	$9,650	$8,700	$8,100	$6,950
DB81 Special							
Mfg.'s Sug. Retail	$21,050	$18,025	$14,550	$11,550	$9,650	$8,700	$8,100	$6,950
MX2/MX2L							
Mfg.'s Sug. Retail	$17,610	$14,145	$11,950	$9,750	$8,500	$8,000	$7,400	$6,750

SCO GRADE SIDEPLATES MODELS

	100%	98%	95%	90%	80%	70%	60%
MX8							
Mfg.'s Sug. Retail	$27,250	$24,250	$18,750	$16,000	$13,250	$11,750	$10,250	$9,000
MX8 Special							
Mfg.'s Sug. Retail	$27,600	$24,500	$18,900	$16,100	$13,250	$11,750	$10,250	$9,000
Grand American 88 Special							
Mfg.'s Sug. Retail	$27,600	$24,500	$18,900	$16,100	$13,250	$11,750	$10,250	$9,000
DB81 Special							
Mfg.'s Sug. Retail	$27,900	$24,700	$19,050	$16,200	$13,250	$11,750	$10,250	$9,000
MX2/MX2L							
Mfg.'s Sug. Retail	$23,480	$20,000	$18,000	$16,000	$13,250	$11,750	$10,500	$9,250

GOLD GRADE SIDEPLATES MODELS

	100%	98%	95%	90%	80%	70%	60%
MX8							
Mfg.'s Sug. Retail	$31,650	$27,300	$22,150	$20,100	$17,500	$15,250	$13,000	$11,250
MX8 Special							
Mfg.'s Sug. Retail	$31,900	$27,500	$22,300	$20,200	$17,500	$15,250	$13,000	$11,250
Grand American 88 Special							
Mfg.'s Sug. Retail	$31,900	$27,500	$22,300	$20,200	$17,500	$15,250	$13,000	$11,250
DB81 Special							
Mfg.'s Sug. Retail	$32,200	$27,700	$22,450	$20,300	$17,500	$15,250	$13,000	$11,250
MX2/MX2L							
Mfg.'s Sug. Retail	$27,300	$23,000	$20,250	$17,500	$15,250	$13,000	$11,800	$10,750

EXTRA GRADE MODELS

	100%	98%	95%	90%	80%	70%	60%
MX8							
Mfg.'s Sug. Retail	$50,650	$45,200	$35,050	$30,100	$25,000	$20,000	$17,000	$14,500
MX8 Special							
Mfg.'s Sug. Retail	$50,900	$44,025	$35,150	$30,150	$25,000	$20,000	$17,000	$14,500
Grand American 88 Special							
Mfg.'s Sug. Retail	$50,900	$44,025	$35,150	$30,150	$25,000	$20,000	$17,000	$14,500
DB81 Special							
Mfg.'s Sug. Retail	$51,200	$44,250	$35,300	$30,250	$25,000	$20,000	$17,000	$14,500
MX2/MX2L							
Mfg.'s Sug. Retail	$43,670	$36,250	$30,000	$25,000	$20,000	$17,000	$14,500	$12,750

Grading	100%	98%	95%	90%	80%	70%	60%

EXTRA GOLD GRADE MODELS
MX8
Mfg.'s Sug. Retail $54,700 $48,150 $37,850 $31,950 $26,500 $21,250 $18,000 $15,500
MX8 Special
Mfg.'s Sug. Retail $54,950 $48,300 $37,950 $31,950 $26,500 $21,250 $18,000 $15,500
Grand American 88 Special
Mfg.'s Sug. Retail $54,950 $48,300 $37,950 $31,950 $26,500 $21,250 $18,000 $15,500
DB81 Special
Mfg.'s Sug. Retail $55,250 $48,500 $38,100 $32,000 $26,500 $21,250 $18,000 $15,500
MX2/MX2L
Mfg.'s Sug. Retail $47,170 $38,500 $31,750 $26,500 $21,250 $18,000 $15,500 $13,750

OVER/UNDER SIDELOCK MODELS — older models without rebounding hammers are not as desirable.
SHO Older Mfg.
$18,000 $15,750 $12,000 $9,500 $8,500 $7,600 $6,800
SHO New Mfg.
Mfg.'s Sug. Retail $37,450 $32,750 $25,550 $22,325 $18,900 $16,500 $13,250 $10,000
SHO Gold Older Mfg.
$18,000 $15,750 $12,000 $9,500 $8,500 $7,600 $6,800
SHO Gold New Mfg.
Mfg.'s Sug. Retail $41,900 $36,100 $28,750 $25,000 $22,000 $18,500 $15,950 $13,750

AMERICAN SKEET SHOTGUNS: O/U

12 ga. only, 26, 27⅝ (standard and most common), or 28⅜ in. separated barrels, select walnut, more expensive models vary in the amount of engraving, grade of walnut, and other special order features.

STANDARD GRADE MODELS
MX3 Special — introductory skeet model, detachable and adj. four position P4S trigger, flat rib. Barrel lockup is same as MX8.
Mfg.'s Sug. Retail $6,000 $5,180 $4,050 $3,400 $2,950 $2,675 $2,350 $1,975
Previous to 1988, this model was designated the MX3. It did not have the P4 adj. selective trigger group.
Mirage Special — evolved from Olympic Skeet Model, features detachable and adj. four position trigger.
Mfg.'s Sug. Retail $6,700 $5,720 $4,400 $3,700 $3,250 $2,900 $2,625 $2,400
Add $2,850 for Gold Outline engraving.

SC3 GRADE MODELS
MX3 Special
Mfg.'s Sug. Retail $9,850 $8,440 $6,650 $5,300 $4,560 $4,175 $3,800 $3,350
Mirage Special
Mfg.'s Sug. Retail $11,150 $9,625 $7,775 $6,300 $5,500 $4,950 $4,200 $3,800

SCO GRADE MODELS
MX3 Special
Mfg.'s Sug. Retail $17,250 $15,250 $11,800 $9,400 $8,500 $7,600 $7,000 $6,300
Mirage Special
Mfg.'s Sug. Retail $18,650 $16,275 $13,600 $10,800 $9,250 $8,500 $7,900 $6,850

GOLD GRADE MODELS
MX3 Special
Mfg.'s Sug. Retail $19,350 $16,800 $13,950 $11,000 $9,350 $8,500 $7,900 $6,850
Mirage Special
Mfg.'s Sug. Retail $20,750 $17,825 $14,400 $11,450 $9,650 $8,700 $8,100 $6,950

Grading	100%	98%	95%	90%	80%	70%	60%

SCO GRADE SIDEPLATES MODELS
Mirage Special

	100%	98%	95%	90%	80%	70%	60%
Mfg.'s Sug. Retail	$27,600	$24,500	$18,900	$16,100	$13,250	$11,750	$10,250	$9,000

GOLD GRADE SIDEPLATES MODELS
Mirage Special

Mfg.'s Sug. Retail	$31,900	$27,500	$22,300	$20,200	$17,500	$15,250	$13,000	$11,250

EXTRA GRADE MODELS
Mirage Special

Mfg.'s Sug. Retail	$50,900	$44,025	$35,150	$30,150	$25,000	$20,000	$17,000	$14,500

EXTRA GOLD GRADE MODELS
Mirage Special

Mfg.'s Sug. Retail	$54,950	$48,300	$37,950	$31,950	$26,500	$21,500	$18,000	$15,500

AMERICAN SKEET O/U SHOTGUNS: 4-GAUGE SETS

STANDARD GRADE MODELS
MX3 Special

Mfg.'s Sug. Retail	$13,900	$11,550	$9,575	$8,500	$7,600	$6,900	$6,100	$5,350

Mirage Special

Mfg.'s Sug. Retail	$15,600	$13,750	$10,500	$9,150	$8,230	$7,500	$6,750	$6,000

Add $6,700 for Gold Outline engraving.

SC3 GRADE MODELS
MX3 Special

Mfg.'s Sug. Retail	$20,350	$17,950	$14,145	$11,950	$9,750	$8,750	$7,850	$6,900

Mirage Special

Mfg.'s Sug. Retail	$21,900	$19,000	$14,650	$12,450	$10,250	$9,000	$8,000	$7,000

SCO GRADE MODELS
MX3 Special

Mfg.'s Sug. Retail	$27,700	$24,250	$18,950	$15,750	$13,000	$11,750	$10,500	$9,250

Mirage Special

Mfg.'s Sug. Retail	$30,650	$26,420	$22,500	$18,000	$15,000	$12,875	$11,500	$10,000

GOLD GRADE MODELS
MX3 Special

Mfg.'s Sug. Retail	$30,450	$26,270	$22,450	$18,000	$15,000	$12,875	$11,500	$10,000

Mirage Special

Mfg.'s Sug. Retail	$33,100	$28,530	$23,800	$19,000	$16,500	$13,750	$12,250	$10,750

SCO GRADE SIDEPLATES MODELS
Mirage Special

Mfg.'s Sug. Retail	$42,300	$36,450	$29,500	$25,500	$21,750	$18,000	$15,000	$11,750

GOLD GRADE SIDEPLATES MODELS
Mirage Special

Mfg.'s Sug. Retail	$46,750	$40,320	$32,000	$27,950	$23,750	$19,250	$16,500	$12,500

EXTRA GRADE MODELS
Mirage Special

Mfg.'s Sug. Retail	$74,700	$64,380	$51,000	$41,000	$31,500	$25,000	$21,500	$17,500

EXTRA GOLD GRADE MODELS
Mirage Special

Mfg.'s Sug. Retail	$78,800	$68,250	$54,950	$43,000	$33,000	$26,000	$22,000	$18,000

Grading	100%	98%	95%	90%	80%	70%	60%

INTERNATIONAL/OLYMPIC SKEET SHOTGUNS: O/U

Available in 12 ga. only. Usually supplied with 29½ in. barrels.

STANDARD GRADE MODELS

MX3 Special — introductory International skeet model, detachable and adj. four position trigger, flat rib. Barrel lockup is same as MX8.

Mfg.'s Sug. Retail	$6,000	$5,180	$4,050	$3,400	$2,950	$2,675	$2,350	$1,975

Previous to 1988, this model was designated the MX3. It did not have the P4 adj. selective trigger group.

Mirage — similar to Mirage Special, except does not have adj. four position trigger.

Mfg.'s Sug. Retail	$6,400	$5,510	$4,250	$3,600	$3,200	$2,875	$2,600	$2,375

Add $2,750 for Gold Outline engraving.

Mirage Special — includes low profile rib, vent. barrels with optional muzzle breaks on sides, ungrooved forearm, and adj. four position trigger.

Mfg.'s Sug. Retail	$6,700	$5,720	$4,400	$3,700	$3,250	$2,900	$2,625	$2,400

Add $2,850 for Gold Outline engraving.

MX8 — developed especially for Olympic Skeet Competition featuring vent. barrels with optional muzzle breaks on sides, grooved forearm, interchangeable trigger groupings with non-adj. trigger.

Mfg.'s Sug. Retail	$6,400	$5,510	$4,250	$3,600	$3,200	$2,875	$2,600	$2,375

Add $2,750 for Gold Outline engraving.

SC3 GRADE MODELS

MX3 Special

Mfg.'s Sug. Retail	$9,850	$8,440	$6,650	$5,300	$4,560	$4,175	$3,800	$3,350

Mirage

Mfg.'s Sug. Retail	$10,950	$9,450	$7,775	$6,300	$5,500	$4,950	$4,200	$3,800

Mirage Special

Mfg.'s Sug. Retail	$11,150	$9,600	$7,800	$6,300	$5,500	$4,950	$4,200	$3,800

MX8

Mfg.'s Sug. Retail	$10,950	$9,450	$7,775	$6,300	$5,500	$4,955	$4,200	$3,800

SCO GRADE MODELS

MX3 Special

Mfg.'s Sug. Retail	$17,250	$15,250	$11,800	$9,400	$8,500	$7,600	$7,000	$6,300

Mirage

Mfg.'s Sug. Retail	$18,400	$16,125	$13,500	$10,770	$9,250	$8,500	$7,900	$6,850

Mirage Special

Mfg.'s Sug. Retail	$18,650	$16,275	$13,600	$10,800	$9,250	$8,500	$7,900	$6,850

MX8

Mfg.'s Sug. Retail	$18,400	$16,125	$13,500	$10,770	$9,250	$8,500	$7,900	$6,850

GOLD GRADE MODELS

MX3 Special

Mfg.'s Sug. Retail	$19,350	$16,800	$13,950	$11,000	$9,350	$8,500	$7,900	$6,850

Mirage

Mfg.'s Sug. Retail	$20,450	$17,625	$14,250	$11,350	$9,650	$8,700	$7,900	$6,850

Mirage Special

Mfg.'s Sug. Retail	$20,750	$17,825	$14,400	$11,450	$9,650	$8,700	$7,900	$6,850

MX8

Mfg.'s Sug. Retail	$20,450	$17,625	$14,250	$11,350	$9,650	$8,700	$7,900	$6,850

SCO GRADE SIDEPLATES MODELS

Mirage

Mfg.'s Sug. Retail	$27,250	$24,250	$18,750	$16,000	$13,250	$11,750	$10,250	$9,000

Add $310 for Mirage Special (includes better stock fit and adj. four position trigger).

Grading	100%	98%	95%	90%	80%	70%	60%	

MX8
Mfg.'s Sug. Retail $27,250 $24,250 $18,750 $16,000 $13,250 $11,750 $10,250 $9,000

GOLD GRADE SIDEPLATES MODELS
Mirage
Mfg.'s Sug. Retail $31,650 $27,300 $22,150 $20,100 $17,500 $15,250 $13,000 $11,250
Add $250 for Mirage Special (includes and adj. four position trigger).
MX8
Mfg.'s Sug. Retail $31,650 $27,300 $22,150 $20,100 $17,500 $15,250 $13,000 $11,250

EXTRA GRADE MODELS
Mirage
Mfg.'s Sug. Retail $50,650 $45,200 $35,050 $30,100 $25,000 $20,000 $17,000 $14,500
Add $250 for Mirage Special (includes and adj. four position trigger).
MX8
Mfg.'s Sug. Retail $50,650 $45,200 $35,050 $30,100 $25,000 $20,000 $17,000 $14,500

EXTRA GOLD GRADE MODELS
Mirage
Mfg.'s Sug. Retail $54,700 $48,150 $37,850 $31,950 $26,500 $21,250 $18,000 $15,500
Add $250 for Mirage Special (includes adj. four position trigger).
MX8
Mfg.'s Sug. Retail $54,700 $48,150 $37,850 $31,950 $26,500 $21,250 $18,000 $15,500

OVER/UNDER SIDELOCK MODELS — older models without rebounding hammers are not as desirable.
SHO Older Mfg.
$18,000 $15,750 $12,000 $9,500 $8,500 $7,600 $6,800
SHO
Mfg.'s Sug. Retail $37,450 $32,750 $25,550 $22,325 $18,900 $16,500 $13,250 $10,000
SHO Gold Older Mfg.
$18,000 $15,750 $12,000 $9,500 $8,500 $7,600 $6,800
SHO Gold
Mfg.'s Sug. Retail $41,900 $36,100 $28,750 $25,000 $22,000 $18,500 $15,950 $13,750

COMPETITION SPORTING SHOTGUNS: O/U

12 ga. only, designed for live pigeon or sporting clays competition.

The Mirage Sporting Classic Models listed below replace the Mirage Special Sporting and incorporate several new improvements.

STANDARD GRADE MODELS

The MX1/MX1B configuration is available mainly for the European marketplace. Values for this model represent recent pricing - Perazzi U.S.A. should be contacted directly for an up-to-date price quotation.

MX3 Special Sporting — features vent. rib and barrels, includes adj. four position trigger.
Mfg.'s Sug. Retail $6,450 $5,535 $4,275 $3,600 $3,200 $2,875 $2,600 $2,375

Mirage Sporting — 28⅜ in. barrels with choke tubes, external SST (non-adj.), special sporting dimension stock and forend, Schnabel forearm.
Mfg.'s Sug. Retail $7,050 $6,050 $4,700 $3,900 $3,325 $2,950 $2,700 $2,450
Add $3,500 for Gold Outline engraving.

Mirage Sporting Classic — similar to Mirage Sporting, except has engraving package, SC3 quality wood, and SST.
Mfg.'s Sug. Retail $8,050 $6,950 $5,375 $4,250 $3,650 $3,150 $2,900 $2,600

MX1/MX1B Sporting
— 12 ga. only, MX1 has high tappered ramped rib and separated barrels. MX1B has lower profile flat rib.
Mfg.'s Sug. Retail $5,510 $4,550 $3,700 $3,400 $3,050 $2,750 $2,500 $2,275

Grading	100%	98%	95%	90%	80%	70%	60%
SC3 GRADE MODELS							
MX3 Special Sporting							
Mfg.'s Sug. Retail	$10,300	$9,000	$7,500	$6,100	$5,300	$4,750	$4,100	$3,600
Mirage Sporting							
Mfg.'s Sug. Retail	$11,350	$9,750	$7,900	$6,350	$5,500	$4,950	$4,200	$3,800
MX1/MX1B Sporting							
Mfg.'s Sug. Retail	$9,420	$7,750	$6,300	$5,500	$4,950	$4,200	$3,800	$3,650
SCO GRADE MODELS							
MX3 Special Sporting							
Mfg.'s Sug. Retail	$17,750	$15,600	$12,000	$9,500	$8,550	$7,600	$7,000	$6,300
Mirage Sporting							
Mfg.'s Sug. Retail	$18,950	$16,475	$13,700	$10,850	$9,250	$8,500	$7,900	$6,850
MX1/MX1B Sporting							
Mfg.'s Sug. Retail	$15,860	$13,500	$10,770	$9,250	$8,500	$8,000	$7,400	$6,750
GOLD GRADE MODELS							
MX3 Special Sporting							
Mfg.'s Sug. Retail	$19,700	$17,125	$14,150	$11,100	$9,350	$8,500	$7,900	$6,850
Mirage Sporting							
Mfg.'s Sug. Retail	$21,050	$18,025	$14,550	$11,550	$9,650	$8,700	$8,100	$6,950
MX1/MX1B Sporting							
Mfg.'s Sug. Retail	$17,610	$14,145	$11,950	$9,750	$8,500	$8,000	$7,400	$6,750
SCO GRADE SIDEPLATES MODELS							
Mirage Sporting							
Mfg.'s Sug. Retail	$27,950	$24,725	$19,050	$16,200	$13,250	$11,750	$10,250	$9,000
MX1/MX1B Sporting							
Mfg.'s Sug. Retail	$23,480	$20,000	$18,000	$16,000	$13,250	$11,750	$10,500	$9,250
GOLD GRADE SIDEPLATES MODELS							
Mirage Sporting							
Mfg.'s Sug. Retail	$32,250	$27,725	$22,450	$20,300	$17,500	$15,250	$13,000	$11,250
MX1/MX1B Sporting							
Mfg.'s Sug. Retail	$27,300	$23,000	$20,250	$17,500	$15,250	$13,000	$11,750	$10,000
EXTRA GRADE MODELS							
Mirage Sporting							
Mfg.'s Sug. Retail	$51,250	$44,275	$35,300	$30,250	$25,000	$20,000	$17,000	$14,500
MX1/MX1B Sporting							
Mfg.'s Sug. Retail	$43,670	$35,950	$29,950	$25,000	$20,000	$17,000	$14,500	$12,750
EXTRA GOLD GRADE MODELS							
Mirage Sporting							
Mfg.'s Sug. Retail	$55,300	$48,525	$38,100	$32,000	$26,500	$21,250	$18,000	$15,500
MX1/MX1B Sporting							
Mfg.'s Sug. Retail	$47,170	$38,000	$31,500	$26,500	$21,250	$18,000	$15,500	$13,750

HUNTING SHOTGUNS: O/U BOXLOCK ACTION

12, 20, 28, or .410 ga., 26, 26 -³⁄₈, or 27-⁵⁄₈ in. barrels only, choice of chokes. These small frame shotguns are available in 20, 28, or .410 ga. but choke tubes (MX20C designation) are optional only in 20 ga.

STANDARD GRADE MODELS

MX12 — 12 ga. only, 2¾ in. chambers only, 26 or 27⁵⁄₈ in. separated barrels with vent. rib, coil springs, SST (fixed trigger group), Schnabel forearm, light receiver border engraving.

	100%	98%	95%	90%	80%	70%	60%
Mfg.'s Sug. Retail	$6,400	$5,510	$4,250	$3,600	$3,200	$2,875	$2,600	$2,375

Add $2,750 for Gold Outline engraving.

Grading	100%	98%	95%	90%	80%	70%	60%

MX12C — 27⅝ in. barrels, supplied with 5 interchangeable choke tubes.

Mfg.'s Sug. Retail $6,750 $5,750 $4,425 $3,700 $3,250 $2,900 $2,625 $2,400

Add $2,750 for Gold Outline engraving.

MX20 — similar to MX12, except 20 ga. only on smaller frame, 2¾ or 3 in. chambers, 26 or 27⅝ in. barrels.

Mfg.'s Sug. Retail $6,800 $5,780 $4,450 $3,700 $3,250 $2,900 $2,625 $2,400

Add $2,950 for Gold Outline engraving.

MX20C — similar to MX20, except 26 in. barrels only supplied with 5 interchangeable choke tubes.

Mfg.'s Sug. Retail $7,150 $6,100 $4,650 $3,800 $3,350 $2,975 $2,675 $2,450

Add $2,950 for Gold Outline engraving.

SC3 GRADE MODELS

MX12

Mfg.'s Sug. Retail $10,950 $9,450 $7,775 $6,300 $5,500 $4,950 $4,200 $3,800

Add $350 for MX12C Model (includes 5 interchangeable choke tubes).

MX20

Mfg.'s Sug. Retail $10,950 $9,450 $7,775 $6,300 $5,500 $4,950 $4,200 $3,800

Add $350 for MX20C Model (includes 5 interchangeable choke tubes).

SCO GRADE MODELS

Add 200% for early smaller frame MX20's.

MX12

Mfg.'s Sug. Retail $18,400 $16,125 $13,500 $10,770 $9,250 $8,500 $7,900 $6,850

Add $350 for MX12C Model (includes 5 interchangeable choke tubes).

MX20

Mfg.'s Sug. Retail $18,400 $16,125 $13,500 $10,770 $9,250 $8,500 $7,900 $6,850

Add $350 for MX20C Model (includes 5 interchangeable choke tubes).

Earlier small frame SCO 20 ga. variations are serialized below 10,100. These guns also have better engraving than later specimens.

GOLD GRADE MODELS

MX12

Mfg.'s Sug. Retail $20,450 $17,625 $14,250 $11,350 $9,650 $8,700 $7,900 $6,850

Add $350 for MX12C Model (includes 5 interchangeable choke tubes).

MX20

Mfg.'s Sug. Retail $20,450 $17,625 $14,250 $11,350 $9,650 $8,700 $7,900 $6,850

Add $350 for MX20C Model (includes 5 interchangeable choke tubes).

SCO GRADE SIDEPLATES MODELS

MX12

Mfg.'s Sug. Retail $27,250 $24,250 $18,750 $16,000 $13,250 $11,750 $10,250 $9,000

Add $350 for MX12C Model (includes 5 interchangeable choke tubes).

MX20

Mfg.'s Sug. Retail $27,250 $24,250 $18,750 $16,000 $13,250 $11,750 $10,250 $9,000

Add $350 for MX20C Model (includes 5 interchangeable choke tubes).

GOLD GRADE SIDEPLATES MODELS

MX12

Mfg.'s Sug. Retail $31,650 $27,300 $22,150 $21,000 $17,500 $15,250 $13,000 $11,250

Add $350 for MX12C Model (includes 5 interchangeable choke tubes).

MX20

Mfg.'s Sug. Retail $31,650 $27,300 $22,150 $21,000 $17,500 $15,250 $13,000 $11,250

Add $350 for MX20C Model (includes 5 interchangeable choke tubes).

EXTRA GRADE MODELS

MX12

Mfg.'s Sug. Retail $50,800 $45,300 $35,150 $30,150 $25,000 $20,000 $17,000 $14,500

Add $350 for MX12C Model (includes 5 interchangeable choke tubes).

Grading	100%	98%	95%	90%	80%	70%	60%

EXTRA GOLD GRADE MODELS

Extra Gold — 12 ga. only.

Mfg.'s Sug. Retail	$54,700	$48,150	$37,850	$31,950	$26,500	$21,250	$18,000	$15,500

Add $350 for Extra C Gold Model (includes 5 interchangeable choke tubes).

Extra Gold Small Gauge — 20, 28, or .410 ga.

Mfg.'s Sug. Retail	$54,700	$48,150	$37,850	$31,950	$26,500	$21,250	$18,000	$15,500

Add $350 for Extra C Gold Model (includes 5 interchangeable choke tubes).

HUNTING SHOTGUNS: O/U SIDELOCK MODELS

All SHO models are available by special order only.

SHO Older Mfg. — older models without rebounding hammers are not as desirable.

	$18,000	$15,750	$12,000	$9,500	$8,500	$7,600	$6,800

SHO Newer Mfg. — 12 ga. only, introductry sidelock O/U model with bank note game scene engraving on coin finished receiver.

Mfg.'s Sug. Retail	$37,450	$32,750	$25,550	$22,325	$18,900	$16,500	$13,250	$10,000

SHO Gold Older Mfg. — older models without rebounding hammers are not as desirable.

	$18,000	$15,750	$12,000	$9,500	$8,500	$7,600	$6,800

SHO Gold Newer Mfg. — similar to SHO, except has game scenes in gold relief.

Mfg.'s Sug. Retail	$41,900	$36,100	$28,750	$25,000	$22,000	$18,500	$15,750	$13,700

HUNTING SHOTGUNS: SIDE-BY-SIDE SIDELOCK MODELS

Deduct 40% without rebounding hammers on older DHO models.

DHO — 12 ga. only, extensive sidelock scroll engraving on coin finished receiver. Limited production-special order only.

Mfg.'s Sug. Retail	$39,200	$34,000	$26,550	$23,000	$19,000	$16,500	$14,000	$12,950

DHO Gold — 12 ga. only, extensive sidelock game scene engraving on coin finished receiver with multiple gold inlays.

Mfg.'s Sug. Retail	$43,800	$38,250	$29,750	$26,000	$22,500	$18,500	$15,950	$13,750

DHO Extra — similar engraving to Extra Grade model.

Mfg.'s Sug. Retail	$77,500	$67,250	$54,500	$42,750	$33,000	$26,000	$22,000	$18,000

DHO Gold Extra — top of the line SXS, special order only, any gauge, rare. Perhaps the most expensive new shotgun in the world.

Mfg.'s Sug. Retail	$82,000	$71,500	$57,500	$45,500	$34,500	$27,000	$23,000	$18,750

PERUGINI-VISINI

Manufacturer located in Brescia, Italy. Rifles are currently imported and distributed by W.L. Moore, located in Westlake Village, CA. All other models listed below were previously imported and distributed by Armes De Chasse located in Chadds Ford, PA, 19317 until 1988.

Due to the recent devaluation of the American dollar against foreign currencies, the values listed below could change substantially if there is further fluctuation in the exchange rate. Perugini-Visini rifles and shotguns are very limited production, and are mostly made on a custom order basis only.

RIFLES

STANDARD MODEL: BOLT ACTION — available in most U.S. and metric cal.'s, Mauser 98K action, 24 or 26 in. barrel, 3 shot mag.(non-detachable), matte finished European walnut, high polish bluing, no sights. Importation disc. 1987.

	$4,250	$3,800	$3,400	$2,950	$2,500	$2,000	$1,800

Last Mfg.'s Sug. Retail was $4,250.

DELUXE MODEL: BOLT ACTION — similar to Standard Model, except has finely checkered oil finished walnut stock, sights, knurled bolt handle, and is cased. Importation disc. 1987.

	$4,250	$3,800	$3,400	$2,950	$2,500	$2,000	$1,800

Last Mfg.'s Sug. Retail was $4,250.

Grading	100%	98%	95%	90%	80%	70%	60%

MODEL EAGLE: SINGLE SHOT—available in most U.S. and metric cal.'s, Anson & Deeley type action, ejector, sights, adj. trigger, oil finished finely checkered European walnut stock, 24 or 26 in. Hammerli barrel. Importation disc. 1987.

	$5,255	$4,500	$3,800	$3,400	$2,950	$2,500	$2,000

Last Mfg.'s Sug. Retail was $5,255.

MODEL VICTORIA M SxS — .30-06 (disc.), 7 x 57R, 7 x 65R, or 9.3 x 74R cal., Anson & Deeley type boxlock action, border engraving, ejectors, folding leaf rear sight, DT's, 24 or 26 in. mono-block barrels with chopper lumps, leather cased.

Mfg.'s Sug. Retail	$7,900	$7,000	$5,700	$4,600	$3,500	$2,950	$2,500	$2,000

Model Victoria D Mag. SxS — similar to Model Victoria, except in .375 H&H, .458 Win., .470 NE, or .500-3 in. NE cal., demi-block barrels, and has elaborate engraving.

Mfg.'s Sug. Retail	$13,750	$10,950	$9,150	$8,200	$7,400	$6,600	$5,800	$5,100

MODEL SELOUS SxS — 9.3 x 74R, 375 H&H, .458 Win. Mag., .470 NE, or .500 3 in. NE cal., H&H style detachable sidelock action, ejectors, folding leaf rear sight, border engraving with best quality checkered walnut, top-of-the-line model, leather cased.

Mfg.'s Sug. Retail	$26,000	$23,000	$18,500	$15,000	$12,000	$10,000	$9,000	$8,150

BOXLOCK EXPRESS SxS — .444 Marlin or 9.3 x 74R cal., Anson & Deeley boxlock action, ejectors, color case hardened frame, iron sights. Importation disc. 1989.

	$3,150	$2,800	$2,500	$2,200	$1,950	$1,700	$1,475

Last Mfg.'s Sug. Retail was $3,500.

BOXLOCK MAGNUM O/U — .270 Win., .375 H&H, or .458 Win. Mag. cal., Anson & Deeley boxlock action, ejectors, monoblock barrels, select walnut. Importation disc. 1989.

	$5,500	$4,900	$4,300	$3,750	$3,100	$2,600	$2,200

Last Mfg.'s Sug. Retail was $6,100.

SIDELOCK SUPER EXPRESS SxS — choice of 9 different cal.'s including .470 Nitro Express, H&H patterned sidelocks, chopper lump barrels, third lever fastener, multi-leaf express sights, coin finished or case hardened receiver, engraving patterns optional. Importation disc. 1989.

	$9,500	$8,400	$7,400	$6,850	$6,100	$5,600	$5,000

Last Mfg.'s Sug. Retail was $10,500.

SHOTGUNS

LIBERTY MODEL — 12, 20, 28, or .410 ga., Anson & Deeley type engraved action, 28 in. chopper lump barrels, double Purdey-type lock, ejectors, leather cased. Importation disc. 1989.

	$5,255	$4,500	$3,800	$3,400	$2,950	$2,500	$2,000

Last Mfg.'s Sug. Retail was $5,255.

CLASSIC MODEL — 12 or 20 ga., H&H style scroll engraved sidelock action, 28 in. chopper lump barrels, double Purdey-type lock, best quality checkered walnut stock and forearm, top-of-the-line model, leather cased. Importation disc. 1989.

	$10,970	$8,650	$7,500	$6,925	$6,200	$5,675	$5,050

Last Mfg.'s Sug. Retail was $10,970.

PETERS STAHL GmbH

Manufacturer located in Paderborn, Germany.

Peters Stahl manufactures high quality semi-auto pistols based on the Model 1911 design. In addition to making the Omega, Peters Stahl also produces handguns for Federal Ordnance and Springfield Armory (see seperate listings).

PHELPS, E.F., & CO.

Previous manufacturer located in Evansville, IN.

Grading	100%	98%	95%	90%	80%	70%	60%

HERITAGE I — .45-70 cal., single action revolver, sand casted carbon steel frame, blue finish, adj. rear sight, 7½ (standard), 10, or 12 in. barrel, 6 lbs.

	$1,000	**$850**	**$700**				

Last Mfg.'s Sug. Retail was $675.

PRESTIGE I — .444 Marlin cal., single action revolver, sand casted carbon steel frame, blue finish, adj. rear sight, 7½ (standard), 10, or 12 in. barrel, 6 lbs.

	$1,000	**$850**	**$700**				

Last Mfg.'s Sug. Retail was $675.

PHOENIX ARMS CO.
Previous importer located in Lowell, MA.

PHOENIX — .25 ACP cal., Belgium semi-auto, previously manufactured by Robar et DeKerkhove located in Liege, Belgium.

This trademark is rarely encountered - values would start at $350 and go up according to original condition.

PIETTA, F.LLI
Manufacturer located in Gussago, Italy.

Pietta manufactures blackpowder and modern firearms reproductions in many configurations. This manufacture should be contacted directly for more information regarding current models and pricing (see Trademark Index).

PIOTTI
Manufacturer located in Brescia, Italy. Currently imported and distributed by W.L. Moore & Co. located in Westlake Village, CA and H & S, Inc. located in Middlefield, CT.

Fratelli Piotti is one of Italy's premier gunmakers. These shotguns meet the highest British standards of craftsmanship and are made to customer specifications. Variety of gauges, engraving, styles, chokes, etc.

For the following models — add $375 for single trigger, $250 for hand-detachable locks, $2,500 for self-opening action, approx. $560 for leather case, $625-$1,250 for 28 or .410 ga. (depending on if boxlock or sidelock).

SHOTGUNS

PIUMA — 12, 16, 20, 28, or .410 ga., Anson & Deeley boxlock ejector double with chopper double barrels, level file-cut rib, light scroll and rosette engraving, scalloped frame.

Mfg.'s Sug. Retail	**$10,500**	**$9,750**	**$8,900**	**$7,800**	**$6,700**	**$5,600**	**$4,500**	**$3,400**

WESTLAKE — 12, 16, 20, 28, or .410 ga., H&H sidelock action, moderate scroll engraving. Importation disc. 1989.

	$7,500	**$6,050**	**$5,300**	**$4,700**	**$4,200**	**$3,750**	**$3,000**

Last Mfg.'s Sug. Retail was $8,400.

MONTE CARLO — 12, 16, 20, 28, or .410 ga., best-quality H&H pattern sidelock ejector double with chopper lump barrels, Purdey style scroll and rosette engraving. Importation disc. 1990.

	$9,100	**$8,000**	**$7,100**	**$6,000**	**$5,000**	**$4,500**	**$4,000**

Last Mfg.'s Sug. Retail was $11,400.

Grading	100%	98%	95%	90%	80%	70%	60%

KING NUMBER 1 — 12, 16, 20, 28, or .410 ga., best-quality H&H pattern sidelock ejector double with chopper lump barrels, level file-cut rib, very fine, full coverage scroll engraving with small floral bouquets, gold crest in forearm, gold crown in top lever, name in gold and finely figured wood.

Mfg.'s Sug. Retail	$17,200	$16,000	$13,500	$10,800	$9,100	$7,650	$6,600	$5,500

LUNIK — 12, 16, 20, 28, or .410 ga., best-quality H&H pattern sidelock ejector double with lump (demi-bloc) barrels, level, file-cut rib, Renaissance style large scroll engraving in relief, gold crown in top lever, gold name, and gold crest in forearm, finely figured wood.

Mfg.'s Sug. Retail	$18,300	$16,800	$14,000	$11,100	$9,400	$8,000	$6,900	$5,850

KING EXTRA — 12, 16, 20, 28, or .410 ga., best-quality H&H pattern sidelock ejector double with chopper lump barrels, level file-cut rib, choice of either bulino game scene engraving or game scene engraving with gold inlays, engraved and signed by a master engraver, exhibition grade wood.

This model ranges in price (retail) between $21,300-$26,800, depending on amount of engraving and other special orders. W.L. Moore should be contacted directly for a price quotation on this model.

MONACO NUMBER 1 OR 2 — 12, 16, 20, 28, or .410 ga., best-quality H&H pattern sidelock ejector double with lump (demi-bloc) barrels, level, file-cut rib, Renaissance style large scroll engraving in relief, gold crown in top lever, gold name, and gold crest in forearm, finely figured wood.

Mfg.'s Sug. Retail	$25,200	$23,000	$19,500	$16,750	$14,000	$11,750	$9,950	$8,450

MONACO NUMBER 4 — top-of-the-line model with every refinement incorporated. Custom order only and extremely rare.

Since this model is available on an individual custom order only basis, specimens have to be evaluated one at a time. The last retail price published was $22,000 in 1988.

Mfg.'s Sug. Retail	$30,000	$26,750	$23,000	$19,500	$16,750	$14,000	$11,750	$9,950

PIRANHA

While manufacture was supposed to be by Amprospec, Inc. (located in Phoenix, AZ.), this trademark was never produced. This handgun was designed to have 85% less recoil, but financial difficulty precluded its manufacture.

POLY TECHNOLOGIES, INC.

Distributed by PTK International, Inc. located in Atlanta, GA. Imported by Keng's Firearms Specialty, Inc., located in Riverdale, GA. Manufactured in China by Poly Technologies, Inc.

Poly Technologies commercial firearms are made to Chinese military specifications and have excellent quality control.

These models have been banned from domestic importation due to 1989 Federal legislation.

POLY TECH AKS-762 — 7.62 x 39mm Soviet military, 16¼ in. barrel, semi-auto version of the Chinese AKM (Type 56) paramilitary design rifle, 8.4 lbs., wood stock. Imported 1988-89.

	$525	$460	$415	$365	$300	$250	$230

Add $25 for side-fold plastic stock.

This model was also available with a downward folding stock at no extra charge.

Last Mfg.'s Sug. Retail was $400.

CHINESE SKS — 7.62 x 39mm Soviet military, 20⁹⁄₂₀ in. barrel, full wood stock, machine steel parts to Chinese military specifications, 7.9 lbs. Imported 1988-89.

	$295	$270	$230	$200	$175	$140	$130

Last Mfg.'s Sug. Retail was $200.

Grading	100%	98%	95%	90%	80%	70%	60%

RUSSIAN AK-47/S (LEGEND) — 7.62 x 39mm Soviet military, 16⅜ in. barrel, semi-auto configuration of the original AK-47, 8.2 lbs. Imported 1988-89.

	$575	$500	$450	$410	$385	$350	$325

The S suffix in this variation designates third model specifications.

Last Mfg.'s Sug. Retail was $550.

National Match Legend — utilizes match parts in fabrication.

	$725	$650	$525	$450	$400	$350	$325

U.S. M-14/S — .308 cal., semi-auto, 22 in. barrel, forged receiver, quality reproduction of the famous M-14, 9.2 lbs. Imported 1988-89.

	$675	$625	$550	$495	$420	$385	$360

Last Mfg.'s Sug. Retail was $700.

POWELL, WILLIAM & SON LTD.

Manufacturer located in Birmingham, England. Limited importation by Jaquas, Located In Findley, OH.

NUMBER 3 BOXLOCK EJECTOR — 12, 16, 20, or .410 ga., chopper lump barrels, extra choice French walnut, many special orders available.

	100%	98%	95%	90%	80%	70%	60%
	$7,500	$6,000	$5,350	$4,900	$4,500	$4,000	$3,600
Model 4	$6,000	$5,000	$4,300	$3,500	$3,200	$2,750	$2,400
Model 6	$2,100	$1,750	$1,625	$1,500	$1,375	$1,250	$1,100

NUMBER 1 SIDELOCK EJECTOR — 12, 16, 20, or .410 ga., chopper lump barrels, extra choice French walnut, many special orders available. Gold inlays, deep relief carved action fences, can be obtained in self opener.

	100%	98%	95%	90%	80%	70%	60%
	$18,000	$13,500	$12,000	$10,800	$9,500	$9,000	$8,500

PRANDELLI-GASPERINI

Previous manufacturer located un Brescia, Italy. Previously imported by Richland Arms located in Blissfield, MI.

Prandelli-Gasperini made both O/U and S X S shotguns in either sidelock or boxlock. Currently, older boxlock models start at approx. $1,250 (assuming 80% or better original condition). Sidelock models in similar condition usually start at $2,500, depending on gauge, embellishments, and condition.

Approx. 250 specimens of this trademark were imported during Richland Arms importation.

PREMIER

Previously manufactured in Italy And Spain.

SHOTGUNS: SIDE-BY-SIDE

REGENT DOUBLE BARREL SHOTGUN — 12, 16, 20, 28, or .410 ga., 26, 28, or 30 in. barrels, various chokes, checkered pistol grip stock and beavertail forearm. Mfg. 1955-disc.

	$275	$250	$220	$195	$140	$110	$100

REGENT MAGNUM EXPRESS — 12 ga., 3 in. chambers only, 30 in. full, recoil pad. Mfg. 1957-disc.

	$305	$275	$250	$220	$165	$140	$110

REGENT 10 GAUGE MAGNUM — same as 12 ga. Mag., but 10 ga., 3½ in. chamber, 32 in. full and full. Mfg. 1975-disc.

	$330	$305	$275	$250	$195	$165	$140

Grading	100%	98%	95%	90%	80%	70%	60%

BRUSH KING — 12 or 20 ga., 22 in. imp. cyl. and mod. barrels, straight grip stock. Mfg. 1959-disc.

	$275	$250	$220	$195	$140	$110	$100

MONARCH SUPREME GRADE — 12 or 20 ga., 26 or 28 in. barrels, various chokes, boxlock, auto ejectors, select stock. Mfg. 1959-disc.

	$440	$385	$360	$330	$275	$250	$200

PRESENTATION CUSTOM GRADE — custom made, gold and silver game scene. Mfg. 1959-disc.

	$1,100	$990	$880	$825	$715	$605	$495

AMBASSADOR MODEL — 12, 16, 20, or .410 ga., 26 or 28 in. barrels, mod. and full choke, checkered pistol grip stock. Mfg. 1957-disc.

	$385	$360	$330	$305	$250	$220	$195

Note: The Premier is a trade name for guns that have been produced in both Spain and Italy for various importers.

PRINZ

Manufacturer of bolt action rifles, single shot rifles, and combination guns. Previously imported and distributed by Helmut Hofmann Inc. located in Placitas, NM.

Prinz rifles are now designated "Bavarian" and are currently imported by H & S, Inc. located in Durham, CT. Prinz rifles were imported 1989 only.

GRADE 1 BOLT ACTION — .243 Win., .30-06, .308 Win., .300 Win. Mag. or 7mm Rem. Mag. cal., single or double set trigger(s), oil finished walnut stock.

	$495	$440	$385	$360	$330	$275	$250

Grade 1 Carbine — similar to Grade 1 except has carbine barrel.

	$570	$495	$435	$390	$360	$330	$275

GRADE 2 BOLT ACTION — similar to Grade 1 except has rosewood forend cap.

	$545	$485	$425	$385	$360	$330	$275

TIP UP RIFLE — available in 8 cal.'s between .222 Rem. and .30-06, high quality and limited mfg. Importation began 1989.

	$2,175	$1,900	$1,675	$1,375	$1,100	$950	$775

PRINCESS MODEL 85 — combination gun available in 12 ga. (2¾ in. chamber) and choice of 8 cal.'s between .222 Rem. and .30-06.

	$1,450	$1,275	$1,100	$925	$800	$775	$650

This model comes standard with a leather case.

PURDEY, JAMES & SONS, LTD.

Manufacturer located in London, England. Purdey has been making top quality firearms since 1814.

Purdey guns have long been regarded as among the finest in the world. They were often custom made to customer specifications and as such should be regarded on an individual basis for purposes of evaluation. Value varies with gauge, barrel length, chamber length and age. We shall list the modern models and approximate values for reference purposes, but strongly recommend professional appraisal if purchase or sale is contemplated.

Values for currently manufactured long guns listed below reflect the dollar/pound exchange rate as this edition goes to press ($1.92 per pound).

Grading	100%	98%	95%	90%	80%	70%	60%

RIFLES

PURDEY DOUBLE RIFLE — various English Nitro Express cal.'s, 25½ in. barrels, folding leaf sight, checkered pistol grip stock, recoil pad, sidelock, auto ejectors. Mfg. pre-WWII and post-war.

Large calibers.

	100%	98%	95%	90%	80%	70%	60%
Mfg.'s Sug. Retail	$76,800	$76,800	$65,000	$52,500	$40,000	$32,000	$27,500	$22,500

Smaller calibers.

Mfg.'s Sug. Retail	$67,200	$67,200	$55,000	$42,500	$36,000	$30,000	$25,000	$21,500

The above values represent guidelines only for this trademark. Since each Purdey is basically a special order, new gun pricing is computed per individual customer work order.

MAGAZINE RIFLE — Mauser type bolt action, 7 x 57mm, .300 H&H Mag., or 10.75 x 73mm cal., 24 in. barrel, folding leaf sight, checkered pistol grip stock.

	$6,875	$5,750	$4,500	$3,800	$3,500	$3,000	$2,500

Add a premium for large cal.'s.

SHOTGUNS

BEST QUALITY SIDE BY SIDE — 12, 16, or 20 ga., 26-30 in. barrels, any choke and style of rib, checkered straight or pistol grip stock. Mfg. 1880-present, auto ejector gun, best quality only.

Mfg.'s Sug. Retail	$48,480	$48,480	$39,000	$31,500	$25,000	$21,500	$17,750	$15,000

Add $3,360 for 28 or .410 ga. on new mfg.

Older mfg.

Game gun	$23,450	$19,000	$15,750	$13,500	$11,000	$9,500	$8,750
Heavy Duck gun	$20,500	$17,000	$14,000	$11,000	$9,500	$8,750	$8,000

Add 50% for 20 ga.

Add 35%-50% for 28 or .410 ga.

Deduct 10% if not cased with accessories.

Add $1,000 for SST.

O/U GUN — 12, 16, 20, or 28 ga., 26-30 in. barrel, any choke, sidelock, auto ejectors, ST, checkered straight or pistol grip stock. Since WWII, Purdey has taken over the Woodward Company, and later guns have the Woodward O/U action. Very few early actions; early guns — ⅓ less.

Mfg.'s Sug. Retail	$56,640	$56,640	$49,000	$44,000	$37,000	$31,000	$25,000	$21,500

Older mfg.

	$33,000	$26,500	$21,500	$17,000	$15,000	$13,500	$11,750

Add $3,000 for Woodward action.

Add 25% for 20 ga.

Add 60%+ for 28 ga.

Add 10% for SST.

SINGLE BARREL TRAP GUN — 12 ga. Purdey action only, same as O/U specifications. Mfg. prior to WWII.

	$11,250	$10,000	$8,750	$7,900	$7,200	$6,750	$5,950

QFI (QUALITY FIREARMS INC.)

Manufacturer located in Opa Locka, FL since December, 1990.

QFI also provides non-warranty service for older firearms imported by F.I.E. (went out of business in 1990).

PISTOLS: SEMI-AUTO

Grading	100%	98%	95%	90%	80%	70%	60%

MODEL LA380 — .380 ACP cal., single action semi-auto, 6-shot, magazine disconnect, hammer, trigger, and firing pin block safety, 3¼ in. barrel, blue or chrome finish. New 1991.

Mfg.'s Sug. Retail	$147	$125	$100	$90	$80	$70	$60	$55

Add $23 for chrome finish.

This model may be offered in .32 ACP cal. in late 1991.

MODEL SA 25 — .25 ACP cal., semi-auto single action, 2½ in. barrel, 6-shot, includes inertial firing pin, external exposed hammer with half cock, and trigger blocking thumb safety, blue, dynachrome, or blue/gold finish, smooth walnut grips. New 1991.

Mfg.'s Sug. Retail	$55	$45	$40	$35	$30	$25	$25	$25

Add $50 for blue/gold finish.

Add $10 for chrome finish with pearlite plastic grips.

TIGRESS MODEL — .25 ACP or .380 ACP cal., semi-auto single action, 2½ (.25 ACP) or 3¼ (.380 ACP) in. barrel, blue frame with gold plated slide, 6-shot with finger extention on mag., white polymer grips with a red rose scrimshawed on both sides, designed for women, supplied with zippered gold pouch, 14 or 25 oz. New 1991.

Mfg.'s Sug. Retail	$155	$130	$100	$90	$80	$70	$60	$55

Add $85 for .380 ACP cal.

REVOLVERS: DOUBLE ACTION

All pistols under this heading are 6-shot.

RP SERIES STANDARD REVOLVER — .22 LR, .22 Mag., .32 S&W Long, .32 Mag. or .38 Spl., 2 or 4 in. barrel, blued or chrome finish, fixed sights, hammer block safety, without ejector assembly, composition grips. Mfg. in U.S. starting 1990.

Mfg.'s Sug. Retail	$105	$85	$70	$65	$60	$55	$50	$45

Add $15-20 for chrome finish.

Add approx. $5 for 4 in. barrel.

MODEL SO 38 — .38 Spl., swing out cylinder, 6-shot, 2 in. SR or 4 in. VR barrel, hammer block safety, composition grips. New 1991.

Mfg.'s Sug. Retail	$175	$135	$115	$95	$80	$75	$65	$60

REVOLVERS: SINGLE ACTION

SAA WESTERN RANGER — .22 LR cal., 6-shot, 3, 4, 6, 7, or 9 in. barrel, blue finish with gold accenting, walnut grips. New 1991.

Mfg.'s Sug. Retail	$105	$85	$70	$65	$60	$55	$50	$45

Add approx. $5 for 7 or 9 in. barrel.

Add approx. $15-30 for .22 Mag. extra cylinder (combo).

SAA PLAINS RIDER — similar to Western Ranger, except has black composition grips. New 1991.

Mfg.'s Sug. Retail	$95	$80	$65	$55	$50	$45	$40	$35

Add approx. $25 for .22 Mag. extra cylinder (combo).

Grading	100%	98%	95%	90%	80%	70%	60%

SAA HORSEMAN SERIES — .357 Mag., .44 Mag., or .45 LC cal., 6-shot, 6½ or 7½ in. barrel, color case hardened or blue (Dark Horseman only) finish, walnut or black composition grips, hammer block safety. New 1991.

Mfg.'s Sug. Retail	$250	$220	$190	$170	$150	$130	$115	$100

The Dark Horseman has an extended grip frame with black composition grips and an adj. rear sight.

QUALITY PARTS CO.

A division of Bushmaster Firearms, Inc. located in Windham, ME that manaufactures Paramilitary rifles patterned after the AR-15.

Add $50 for the EM Series rifles.

XM15-E2 RIFLE — .223 cal., semi-auto patterned after the Colt AR-15, 20, 24, or 26 in. Gov.'n spec. mateh grade chrone lined barrel, manganese phosphate barrel finish, rear sight adj. for windage and elevation, Cage flash suppressor, mfg. started in 1989 in U.S.

Mfg.'s Sug. Retail	$800	$750	$700	$650	$600	$550	$500	$450

Add $40 for 24 or 26 in. barrel.

XM15-E2 Carbine — similar to above, except with telescoping buttstock and 16 in. barrel, mfg. started in 1989.

Mfg.'s Sug. Retail	$750	$700	$650	$600	$550	$500	$450	$395

This model does not have the target rear sight system of the XM15-E2 rifle.

R

R.G. INDUSTRIES

Importers located in Miami, FL. Operations ceased in January of 1986.

HAND GUNS

R.G. Industries manufactured and imported plain utilitarian revolvers and semi-auto pistols. Unfortunately, because of the current product liability situation, R.G. Industries was litigated out of business. Whereas their models represent good values, they are not collectible, and a generalized listing is provided below.

Grading	100%	98%	95%	90%	80%	70%	60%

RG 14 S, RG 23, RG 31 — prices vary from $61 to $100 retail.

RG 40, RG 74, & HIGHNOON S.A. — prices vary from $125 to $150 retail.

RG 26 SEMI-AUTO — .25 auto, 6 shot mag., 2¼ in. barrel, plastic grips, single action, 12 oz.

	100%	98%	95%	90%	80%	70%	60%
	$65	$55	$50	$40	$35	$30	$25

Last Mfg.'s Sug. Retail was $66.

RWS

RWS is a trademark of Dynamit Nobel which has been manufacturing firearms in Nuremberg Stadeln, W. Germany since 1865. RWS is currently being imported by Dynamit Nobel of America, Inc. located in Northvale, NJ. Other trademarks currently being distributed by Dynamit Nobel can be located under individual heading names in this text.

RIFLES: MATCH TARGET

MODEL 820 L — .22 LR only, 24 (disc.) or 26 in. barrel, no. 100 aperture sight, oil polished stock for 3 position match, stippled pistol grip and forearm, recoil pad, adj. trigger, 10.6 lbs.

Mfg.'s Sug. Retail	$1,500	$1,275	$1,000	$850	$700	$575	$475	$400

Previous to 1986 this model was designated the 820 S and was supplied with a no. 75 aperture rear sight.

Model 820 S — with Model 82 aperture sight.

	$1,100	$895	$795	$650	$560	$480	$420

Last Mfg.'s Sug. Retail was $995.

MODEL 820 F MATCH — same as Model 820 L, except has heavy match barrel, 15.4 lbs.

Mfg.'s Sug. Retail	$2,000	$1,750	$1,400	$1,275	$1,000	$850	$700	$575

Model 820 SF — with Model 82 aperture sight. Disc.

	$1,125	$900	$795	$650	$560	$480	$420

Last Mfg.'s Sug. Retail was $1,010.

MODEL 820 K — .22 LR only, made for running boar competition, 24 in. barrel, stock similar to Model 820 SF, no sights, 9½ lbs. without barrel weight or scope. Importation disc. 1986.

	$900	$775	$695	$615	$540	$470	$420

Last Mfg.'s Sug. Retail was $870.

Grading	100%	98%	95%	90%	80%	70%	60%

RADOM

Polish Arsenal, located in Radom, Poland.

P-35 AUTOMATIC — 9mm, 8 shot, 4¾ in. barrel, blue, fixed sights, plastic grips. Mfg. 1935-WWII.

POLISH EAGLE — dated 1936, 1937, 1938, 1939.

	100%	98%	95%	90%	80%	70%	60%
	$1,250	$900	$800	$650	$500	$350	$200

POLISH EAGLE NAZI CAPTURE

	$1,650	$1,200	$900	$800	$700	$600	$500

NAZI TYPE I SLOTTED

	$450	$400	$350	$295	$230	$180	$150

NAZI TYPE II NO SLOT WITH TAKE-DOWN LEVER

	$375	$325	$275	$225	$200	$185	$150

NAZI TYPE III NO SLOT, NO TAKE-DOWN LEVER

	$315	$275	$240	$200	$180	$160	$140

NAZI TYPE III — parkerized with wood grips, small parts blued.

	$500	$425	$350	$295	$230	$200	$175

Note: Certain Radoms with German acceptance marks will bring a premium.

RAM-LINE, INC.

Manufacturer located in Golden, CO.

SYN-TECH PISTOL — .22 LR cal., single action semi-auto, aircraft alloy receiver with 5½ in. polymer VR barrel and steel liner, unique two motion safety featuring blocks on hammer, trigger, and sear, 15 shot mag., matte finish, easy disassembly, injected molded grip, fixed sight, 20.3 oz., supplied with case. New in 1990.

Mfg.'s Sug. Retail	$200	$165	$135	$115

RANDALL FIREARMS COMPANY

Previously manufactured in Sun Valley, CA. Manufactured between June, 1983 and May, 1985.

Before manufacturing ceased in May of 1985, 24 models with 12 variations in 3 different calibers had been produced. In some instances, production on certain models was very limited and premiums for these low volume niches are starting to develop. Between June of 1983 and May of 1985, 9,968 handguns were manufactured with 75% of all 9mm cal.'s being exported to Europe, and 35% of 9mm production employing a 10 groove barrel. Models manufactured after 1984 came equipped with an extended slide stop, long trigger and beavertail grip safety. Production ser. no.'s started at 02000 for right hand models and 02100 for left hand models. All but the first 200 (approx.) serial numbers started with "RF" and ended with "C" or "W". A few rare mis-marks are in circulation. Total mfg. for all models and variations was 9,968. Randall prototype serialization starts with a "T" — less than 45 were manufactured and these specimens command up to a 50% premium. In addition, 78 serial numbers under 2,000 were manufactured by special order.

Models below are generally described with values per specific variations listed afterward.

It is advisable to procure a Randall research & factory letter when buying or selling many of the rarer Randall pistols. To take advantage of this service, call/FAX your name and address, Randall model name, serial number, and contact: KK Manufacturing, Attn: Rick "KK" Kennerknecht, PO Box 1586, Lomita, CA. 90717-5586,phone number: 213-325-0102 or FAX number: 213-325-0298. The charge is $20 per serial number. Please allow adequate time for proper response (FAX will be the fastest).

Grading	100%	98%	95%	90%	80%	70%	60%

COMBAT MODEL — same size as Service Model, ribbed top fixed sight slide, Pachmayr grips on right hand model only, left hand models had Herret walnut grips. While this model was advertised as having a flat mainspring housing, it was never produced. The brochures of the time quoted $549 for mfg.'s sug. retail.

RAIDER/SERVICE MODEL-C — 9mm or .45 ACP cal., Colt Commander Model design, 4¼ in. barrel, 36 oz., total stainless steel construction. Add $130 for adj. sights/ribbed slide, available in either right-hand or left-hand (only 2 mfg.) model. Roll-marked Service Model-C in 1983 and Raider in 1984.
Last Mfg.'s Sug. Retail was $460.

Raider/Service Model-C Featherweight — .45 ACP only, alloy receiver, stainless steel slide, roll-marked Service Model-C, T-type serial numbers, 29 oz. Disc. 1984, only 4 mfg.

FULL SIZE SERVICE MODEL — .38 Super, 9mm, or .45 ACP cal., Colt Model 1911 A1 design, 5 in. barrel, total stainless steel construction, 38 oz. Available in either right-hand or left-hand model. Add $130 for adj. sights and rib top slide.
Last Mfg.'s Sug. Retail was $460.

CURTIS E. LEMAY 4-STAR MODEL — 9mm or .45 ACP cal., Gen. Curtis E. LeMay design, 4¼ in. barrel, 6 (.45 ACP) or 7 (9mm) shot mag., total stainless steel construction, 35 oz. Available in either right-hand or left-hand model, left hand models are a true mirror image with over 17 major parts changes. Add $10 for 9mm. Add $90 for adj. sight/ribbed top slide.
Last Mfg.'s Sug. Retail was $533.

This model was ½ in. shorter in magazine well and had a cast, squared off trigger guard compared to the Colt 1911A1 design.

Curtis E. LeMay Featherweight Model — .45 ACP only, alloy receiver, stainless steel slide, T-type serial numbers, 28 oz. Disc. 1984 (only one mfg.).

RANDALL MATCHED SETS — .45 ACP only, each set consisted of a right-hand and a left-hand Service Model with matching serial numbers. Only 4 sets were mfg. on a special order basis. A111/B111 model configuration.
Last Mfg.'s Sug. Retail was $1,250.

RANDALL VARIATIONS

IDENTIFYING RANDALL MODELS:

Randall pistols are denoted by a four-character model notation, starting with an alphabetical prefix followed by three digits. The alphabetical prefix will be either A, B, or C — A designates right-hand configuration only, B designates left-hand configuration only, and C designates right-hand lightweight model. The first digit will be 1, 2, or 3 — 1 denotes Service Model, 2 denotes Service Model-C or Raider, 3 represents the C.E. LeMay Model. The second digit again will be either 1, 2, or 3 — 1 designates round top and fixed sight slide, 2 denotes flat top fixed sight slide, and 3 represents adj. sights, flat top frame. The third digit again, is either 1, 2, or 3 — 1 denotes .45 ACP cal., 2 designates 9mm Para., and 3 represents .38 Super. Hence, if you had a left-hand Randall in the service model size with a flat top adj. sight slide, and in .45 ACP cal., your model would be a B131. These model codes are not marked on the pistols.

The following is a complete listing for Randall Firearms variations including production statistics. Values shown below represent recent aftermarket prices, but it should be noted regional interest can change these prices significantly. After only 6 years of discontinuance, Randall pistols are enjoying good demand.

A111 — 3431 mfg.

	$600	$515	$475				

A112 — 301 mfg.

	$750	$645	$585				

A121 — 1067 mfg.

	$600	$515	$475				

A122 — 18 mfg.

	$1,100	$950	$860				

A131 — 2083 mfg.

	$650	$565	$500				

Grading	100%	98%	95%	90%	80%	70%	60%
A211 — 992 mfg.							
	$625	$545	$485				
A212 — 76 mfg.							
	$750	$675	$600				
A231 — 574 mfg.							
	$675	$575	$525				
A232 — 5 mfg.							
	$1,250	$1,075	$990				
A311 — 361 mfg.							
	$800	$680	$625				

Most LeMay models (4¼ in. barrel) were shipped in gunrugs without a factory box. Original factory LeMay boxes are rare — add 10% premium. Beware of Randall LeMay and service model pistols made from parts kits. There were 226 LeMay receivers and 322 service model receivers (all right hand) sold that could be parts guns. Accordingly, values are less for parts guns.

A312 — 1 mfg.
Too rare to evaluate.

A331 — 293 mfg.

	100%	98%	95%
	$900	$775	$700

The note that appears for the Model A311 also applies to this variation.

A332 — 9 mfg.

	$1,250	$1,075	$975

B111 — 297 mfg.

	$900	$750	$650

B121 — 110 mfg.

	$1,450	$1,225	$1,125

B122 — 2 mfg.

	$2,250	$1,900	$1,750

B123 — 2 mfg.

	$2,250	$1,900	$1,750

B131 — 225 mfg.

	$1,250	$1,075	$975

B311 — 52 mfg.

	$1,250	$1,075	$975

B312 w/.45 ACP factory conversion — 1 mfg.
Rarity precludes accurate price evaluation.

B312 — 9 mfg.

	$2,250,	$1,975	$1,775

B321 — 1 mfg.
Rarity precludes accurate price evaluation. The B321 was the only factory 3-slide set. It was fitted with the 3 different LH LeMay slides available (B311, B321, & B331). This model was mirror polished, engraved, and had ivory grips with the Randall logo.

B331 — 45 mfg.

	$1,475	$1,250	$1,150

B2/321 — 1 mfg.
Rarity precludes accurate price evaluation. This was the only factory model variation to leave Randall Firearms. This was a Left-hand Raider with the C.E. LeMay slide.

C211 — 5 mfg.

	$1,375	$1,175	$1,075

C331 — 1 mfg.
Too rare to evaluate.

C332 — 4 mfg.

	$1,375	$1,175	$1,075

Matched Sets — large premiums exist for different models with the same serial number if NIB condition.
1 set has recently sold for $3,950.

Grading	100%	98%	95%	90%	80%	70%	60%

RAVELL

Manufacturer located in Barcelona, Spain. Currently, Ravell has no single U.S. importer and values below represent guns purchased directly from Spain without import duty/shipping.

MAXIM DOUBLE RIFLE — .375 H & H or 9.3 X 74R cal., H & H type sidelock action with automatic extractor, Purdey scroll engraving, 23 in. barrels, deluxe walnut with full pistol grip and rubber butt plate, double articulated triggers.

Mfg.'s Sug. Retail	$5,410	$5,410	$4,375	$3,750	$3,300	$2,950	$2,600	$2,300

Add $400 for 9.3 X 74R cal.

RAVEN ARMS

Manufacturer located in Industry, CA.

P-25 — .25 cal., single action semi-auto, 2⁷⁄₁₆ in. barrel, 6 shot mag., walnut grips, available in nickel, blue, or chrome finish, 15 oz. Disc. 1984.

$70	$60	$50	$40	$30	$25	$25

MP-25 — same as Model P-25, except die-cast slide serrations are slightly different.

Mfg.'s Sug. Retail	$70	$60	$50	$45	$40	$35	$30	$25

Walnut, slotted plastic, or ivory colored grips are available for this model. In 1987, a new sear-block safety was incorporated into manufacture.

RECORD-MATCH

Manufactured by Anschutz, located in Zella-Mehlis, Germany.

MODEL 210 FREE PISTOL — .22 LR, Martini action, 11 in. barrel, single shot, blue, carved and checkered walnut grips and forearm, set trigger (button release), micrometer rear sight, deluxe target pistol, pre-WWII.

$1,320	$1,265	$1,210	$1,100	$880	$745	$550

MODEL 210A — same as 210, but alloy frame.

$1,265	$1,210	$1,155	$1,045	$825	$690	$495

MODEL 200 FREE PISTOL — similar to 210, but less deluxe features and spur trigger guard, pre-WWII.

$990	$935	$770	$660	$525	$440	$360

REISING ARMS COMPANY

Manufacturer originally located in New York, NY and later in Hartford, CT.

TARGET AUTOMATIC PISTOL — .22 LR, 12 shot, 6½ in. barrel, blue, hard rubber grips, hinged frame, outside hammer. Mfg. 1921-1924.

$385	$370	$340	$315	$265	$220	$195

This model was mfg. in New York, NY from serial number 1,001-4,000. The Hartford, CT address occurs in the serial range 10,000-12,000.

Warning: This pistol may crack the slide if modern high speed .22 ammo is used.

Grading	100%	98%	95%	90%	80%	70%	60%

REMINGTON ARMS COMPANY

Originally E. Remington, Herkimer, NY 1816-1828; moved to Ilion, NY in 1828, manufactured at Ilion, NY to date.

REMINGTON TRADEMARKS - 1816-PRESENT

1816-1840 — Remington (mostly barrel and lock markings)

1840-1852 — E. Remington & Son

1852-1888 — E. Remington & Sons.

1888-1910 — Remington Arms Co.

1910-1925 — Remington Arms U.M.C. Co.

1925 to date — Remington Arms Co.

REMINGTON HANDGUNS: 1857-1945 MFG.

100%	98%	95%	90%	80%	70%	60%	50%	40%	30%	20%	10%

BEALS' FIRST MODEL POCKET REVOLVER — percussion .31 cal., 5 shot, smooth cylinder, 3 in. octagon barrel, blue finish, 1-piece Gutta Percha grips, brass or iron trigger guard. Approx. 5,000 produced, 1857-1858.

$800	$750	$675	$600	$550	$500	$450	$400	$375	$350	$325	$300

BEALS' SECOND MODEL POCKET REVOLVER — percussion .31 cal., 5 shot, smooth cylinder, 3 in. octagon barrel, blue finish, 2-piece Gutta Percha grips, spur trigger. Approx. 1,000 produced 1858-1860.

$4,500	$4,300	$4,150	$4,000	$3,750	$3,500	$3,250	$3,000	$2,750	$2,500	$2,250	$2,000

BEALS' THIRD MODEL POCKET REVOLVER — percussion .31 cal., 5 shot, smooth cylinder, 4 in. octagon barrel, blue finish, 2-piece Gutta Percha grips, spur trigger, first Remington revolver with loading lever. Approx. 1,000 produced.

$1,150	$1,050	$1,000	$950	$900	$850	$800	$700	$650	$600	$500	$425

BEALS' NAVY REVOLVER — percussion .36 cal., 6 shot, smooth cylinder, 7½ in. octagon barrel, blue finish, 2-piece walnut grips, some martially marked with inspectors initials and cartouche on grips. Approx. 15,000 produced, 1860-1862. Barrel address is "Beals' Patent, Sept. 14, 1858 - Manufactured by Remingtons', Ilion, N.Y.".

Commercial Model — single wing base pin (very rare), less than 400 mfg., separate serial range.

$4,000	$3,600	$3,200	$2,900	$2,600	$2,300	$2,000	$1,800	$1,700	$1,500	$1,400	$1,300

Commercial Model — several variations with serialization 1-15,500, most were purchased by military but were not inspected.

$2,500	$2,400	$2,300	$2,100	$1,950	$1,800	$1,600	$1,400	$1,200	$900	$700	$500

Deduct 20% for cartridge conversion.

Martially marked — serial range 13,500-15,500.

$3,500	$3,100	$2,900	$2,600	$2,300	$2,000	$1,800	$1,600	$1,475	$1,300	$1,200	$1,100

BEALS' ARMY REVOLVER — percussion .44 cal., 6 shot, smooth cylinder, 8 in. octagon barrel, blue finish, 2-piece walnut grips. Barrel address is "Beals' Patent, Sept. 14, 1858 - Manufactured by Remingtons', Ilion, N.Y.°.

$3,000	$2,750	$2,500	$2,200	$2,100	$1,950	$1,800	$1,650	$1,500	$1,350	$1,100	$950

Deduct 20% for cartridge conversions.

Martially marked — serial range is 850-1,900 inspected by "WAT" or "CGC".

$6,500	$6,000	$5,500	$5,000	$4,500	$4,000	$3,500	$3,000	$2,600	$2,200	$1,800	$1,375

RIDER'S DOUBLE-ACTION POCKET REVOLVER — percussion .31 cal., 5 shot, unusual "mushroom-shaped" cylinder, 3 in. octagon barrel, blue finish, 2-piece Gutta Percha grips, brass trigger guard, no loading lever. One of the earliest double-action handguns produced. Approx. 20,000 produced, 1860-1888.

$650	$625	$600	$550	$500	$450	$425	$400	$375	$350	$325	$300

Deduct 30% for cartridge conversion.

100%	98%	95%	90%	80%	70%	60%	50%	40%	30%	20%	10%

RIDER'S SINGLE-SHOT DERRINGER — percussion .17 cal., all brass construction, grips included. Less than 1,000 produced, 1860-1863. MANY FAKES, caveat emptor.

100%	98%	95%	90%	80%	70%	60%	50%	40%	30%	20%	10%
$5,500	$5,250	$5,000	$4,500	$4,000	$3,500	$3,250	$3,000	$2,750	$2,500	$2,250	$2,000

MODEL OF 1861 NAVY REVOLVER — percussion .36 cal., 6 shot, unfluted cylinder, 7½ in. octagon barrel, blue finish, 2-piece walnut grips. Loading lever has slot allowing cylinder pin to be pulled forward without lowering lever. Approx. 6,000 produced 1862-1863 in serial range 15,000-21,000. Barrel address "Patented Dec. 17, 1861, 1858 - Manufactured by Remingtons', Ilion, N.Y.".

Commercial Model

100%	98%	95%	90%	80%	70%	60%	50%	40%	30%	20%	10%
$2,000	$1,900	$1,800	$1,700	$1,500	$1,300	$1,100	$900	$800	$700	$600	$500

Deduct 20% for cartridge conversion.

Martially Marked — over 4,000 martially inspected "CGC".

100%	98%	95%	90%	80%	70%	60%	50%	40%	30%	20%	10%
$3,000	$2,750	$2,400	$2,100	$1,800	$1,650	$1,350	$1,100	$950	$800	$650	$500

MODEL OF 1861 ARMY REVOLVER — percussion .44 cal., 6 shot, unfluted cylinder, 8 in. octagon barrel, blue finish, 2-piece walnut grips. Majority are martially inspected "CGC". Loading lever has slot allowing cylinder pin to be pulled forward without lowering lever. Approx. 10,000 produced 1862-1863 in serial range 1,900-12,000. Barrel address "Patented Dec. 17, 1861, 1858 - Manufactured by Remingtons', Ilion, N.Y.".

100%	98%	95%	90%	80%	70%	60%	50%	40%	30%	20%	10%
$3,000	$2,750	$2,400	$2,100	$1,800	$1,650	$1,350	$1,100	$950	$800	$650	$500

Deduct 20% for cartridge conversion.

NEW MODEL ARMY REVOLVER — percussion .44 cal., 6 shot, unfluted cylinder, 8 in. octagon barrel, blue finish, 2-piece walnut grips. Approx. 135,000 produced 1863-1888 in serial range 12,000-148,000. Barrel address "Patented Sept. 14, 1858 - Manufactured by Remingtons', Ilion, N.Y. - New Model". Early models lack "New Model" markings on barrel and have transition features from "1861" model.

100%	98%	95%	90%	80%	70%	60%	50%	40%	30%	20%	10%
$1,500	$1,350	$1,200	$1,050	$950	$850	$775	$675	$600	$500	$400	$350

Deduct 20% for cartridge conversion.

Add 25% for martially inspected.

NEW MODEL NAVY REVOLVER — percussion .36 cal., 6 shot, unfluted cylinder, 7½ in. octagon barrel, blue finish, 2-piece walnut grips. Approx. 18,000 produced in percussion from 1863-1878 with serial range 21,000-48,000. None were martially marked at time of mfg. Approx. 4,000 were purchased by U.S. Navy during 1863-1865 in serial range 21,000-32,000. Barrel address "Patented Sept. 14, 1858 - Manufactured by Remingtons', Ilion, N.Y. - New Model". New models lack "New Model" markings on barrel and have transition features from "1861" model.

100%	98%	95%	90%	80%	70%	60%	50%	40%	30%	20%	10%
$3,000	$2,750	$2,400	$2,100	$1,800	$1,650	$1,350	$1,100	$950	$800	$650	$500

Deduct 50% for cartridge conversion if in 50%+ original condition.

No premium for martial markings.

NEW MODEL BELT REVOLVER, SINGLE ACTION — percussion .36 cal., 6 shot, unfluted or fluted cylinder, 6½ in. octagon barrel, blue or nickel finish, 2-piece walnut grips. Approx. 5,000 produced 1863-1888.

100%	98%	95%	90%	80%	70%	60%	50%	40%	30%	20%	10%
$1,400	$1,300	$1,200	$1,000	$900	$800	$700	$650	$600	$550	$500	$450

Add 50% for fluted cylinder (cylinder numbered to the gun).

Deduct 30% for cartridge conversion.

NEW MODEL BELT REVOLVER, DOUBLE ACTION — percussion .36 cal., 6 shot, smooth or fluted cylinder, 6½ in. octagon barrel, blue or nickel finish, 2-piece walnut grips. Approx. 2,500 produced 1863-1888.

100%	98%	95%	90%	80%	70%	60%	50%	40%	30%	20%	10%
$1,200	$1,150	$1,100	$950	$850	$700	$650	$600	$550	$500	$450	$400

Add 50% for fluted cylinder (most not numbered to the gun).

Deduct 30% for cartridge conversion.

100%	98%	95%	90%	80%	70%	60%	50%	40%	30%	20%	10%

NEW MODEL POLICE REVOLVER — percussion .36 cal., 5 shot, smooth cylinder, 3 to 6½ in. octagon barrels, blue or nickel finish, 2-piece walnut grips. Approx. 18,000 produced 1863-1888.

$1,100	$1,050	$950	$900	$850	$800	$750	$700	$650	$600	$550	$500

Add 10% for 6½ in. barrel.

Deduct 40% for cartridge conversion.

NEW MODEL POCKET REVOLVER — percussion .31 cal., 5 shot, smooth cylinder, spur trigger, 3 to 4½ in. octagon barrel, blue or nickel finish, 2-piece walnut grips. Approx. 25,000 produced, 1863-1888.

$1,200	$1,100	$1,050	$1,000	$950	$900	$850	$800	$700	$600	$500	$400

Add 25%-50% for brass frame and/or trigger sheath.

Deduct 40% for cartridge conversion.

ZIG-ZAG DERRINGER — cartridge .22 cal., 6 shot, 6 barrel cluster (rotating), ring trigger, 3 in. barrel cluster, blue finish, 2-piece hard rubber grips. Less than 1,000 produced, 1861-1863. Reputed to be Remington's first cartridge handgun.

$3,000	$2,850	$2,700	$2,500	$2,250	$2,000	$1,850	$1,600	$1,300	$1,000	$950	$800

ELLIOT'S FIVE SHOT DERRINGER — cartridge .22 cal., 5 shot, 5 barrel cluster (fixed), 3 in. barrel cluster, blue and/or nickel finish, 2-piece hard rubber, walnut, ivory or pearl grips, ring trigger. Approx. 25,000 produced (combined production total with .32 cal.).

$1,500	$1,400	$1,300	$1,200	$1,100	$1,000	$900	$800	$700	$600	$500	$400

ELLIOT'S FOUR SHOT DERRINGER — cartridge .32 cal., 4 shot, 4 barrel cluster (fixed), ring trigger, 3⅜ in. barrel cluster, blue and/or nickel finish, 2-piece hard rubber, walnut, ivory or pearl grips. Approx. 25,000 produced (combined production with .22 cal.).

$1,100	$1,050	$1,000	$950	$900	$850	$800	$700	$600	$500	$400	$350

VEST POCKET DERRINGER — cartridge .22, .30, .32, or .41 cal., single shot, various barrel lengths, blue or nickel finish, 2-piece walnut grips, spur trigger.

.22 Rimfire — approx. 25,000 produced, 1865-1888.

$900	$850	$800	$750	$700	$600	$550	$500	$400	$350	$300	$250

Deduct 25% for guns lacking company name.

.30 or .32 Rimfire — number produced unknown, 1865-1888.

$1,200	$1,150	$1,100	$1,000	$900	$800	$700	$550	$450	$400	$350	$300

.41 Rimfire — approx. 25,000 produced, 1865-1888.

$900	$850	$800	$750	$700	$600	$550	$500	$400	$350	$300	$250

OVER AND UNDER DERRINGER — cartridge .41 Rimfire cal., 2 shot, 3 in. superimposed barrels, oscillating firing pin, spur trigger, blue and/or nickel finish, hard rubber, walnut, ivory or pearl 2-piece grips. Approx. 150,000 produced, 1866-1934. A.K.A. Double Derringer or Model 95.

Type One, Early Variation — maker's name and patent data stamped between the barrels, made without extractor. 1866-1888.

$1,500	$1,400	$1,300	$1,200	$1,100	$900	$800	$700	$650	$600	$500	$450

Type One, Late Variation — maker's name and patent data stamped between the barrels, made with extractor. 1866-1888.

$1,700	$1,600	$1,500	$1,400	$1,300	$1,100	$1,000	$900	$800	$750	$700	$650

Type Two — two line markings atop barrels, maker's name and patent data. 1866-1888.

$1,100	$1,000	$800	$700	$600	$500	$450	$400	$350	$300	$250	$200

Type Three — marked atop barrel, single line, "REMINGTON ARMS CO., ILION, N.Y.". 1888-1911.

$995	$900	$800	$700	$600	$500	$400	$350	$300	$250	$225	$200

Type Four — marked atop barrel, single line, "REMINGTON ARMS-U.M.C. CO. ILION, N.Y.".

$775	$700	$650	$575	$500	$425	$375	$325	$275	$240	$215	$190

100%	98%	95%	90%	80%	70%	60%	50%	40%	30%	20%	10%

MODEL 1866 NAVY ROLLING BLOCK PISTOL — cartridge .50 Rimfire cal., single shot, 8½ in. round barrel, spur trigger, walnut grip and forearm, blue finish. Approx. 6,500 produced, 1866-1875. Erroneously designated as, "Model of 1965 Navy".

Martially Marked

$5,000	$4,150	$3,800	$3,000	$2,500	$2,265	$2,155	$2,000	$1,800	$1,650	$1,500	$1,350

Subtract 40% if not martially marked (Commercial Model mfg. 1866-1875).

Deduct 5% for centerfire breech block.

Less than 150 remain in original condition.

MODEL 1870 NAVY ROLLING BLOCK PISTOL — cartridge .50 Centerfire cal., single shot, 7 in. round barrel, standard trigger with trigger guard, walnut grip and forearm, blue finish. Approx. 6,400 produced 1870-1875. Modified by Remington for the Navy from the Model 1866.

$2,500	$2,250	$2,000	$1,700	$1,500	$1,300	$1,100	$1,000	$900	$800	$700	$600

Add approx. 20% for 8 in. commercial version (approx. 200-400 mfg.) without inspector's marks.

MODEL 1871 ARMY ROLLING BLOCK PISTOL — cartridge .50 Centerfire cal., single shot, 8 in. round barrel, standard trigger with trigger guard, walnut grip and forearm, blue finish. Approx. 5,000 produced, 1871-1872.

$2,250	$2,000	$1,700	$1,500	$1,300	$1,100	$1,000	$900	$800	$700	$600	$500

Deduct 10% for Commercial Model.

Pistols produced between 1871-1872 are martially marked.

MODEL 1887 TARGET ROLLING BLOCK PISTOL — cartridge .22, .25 Rimfire and .32, .50 Centerfire cal.'s, single shot, 8 in. round barrel, standard trigger with trigger guard, walnut grip and forearm, blue finish. Approx. 900 produced 1887-1891. A.K.A. "Plinker" Model of 1887".

$2,250	$2,000	$1,700	$1,500	$1,300	$1,100	$1,000	$900	$800	$700	$600	$500

Add 10% for Navy framed.

Navy framed 1887's are discernable by military proofs on right side of frame, Remington altered from original Navy Model 1870. Estimated mfg. of 100.

MODEL 1891 TARGET MODEL ROLLING BLOCK PISTOL — cartridge .22, .25 Rimfire and .32 Centerfire cal.'s, single shot, 10 in. part octagon, part round barrel, standard trigger with trigger guard, smooth walnut grip and forearm, blue finish. Approx. 100 produced 1891-1900.

$2,500	$2,250	$2,000	$1,700	$1,500	$1,300	$1,100	$1,000	$900	$800	$700	$600

MODEL 1901 TARGET ROLLING BLOCK PISTOL — cartridge .22 S and L, .25 Rimfire, .32 Centerfire, or .44 S&W Russian cal., single shot, 10 in. part octagon, part round barrel, standard trigger with trigger guard, checkered walnut grip and forearm, blue finish. Approx. 800 produced 1900-1909.

$2,500	$2,250	$2,000	$1,700	$1,500	$1,300	$1,100	$1,000	$900	$800	$700	$600

Add $100 for S&W Russian.

RIDER'S MAGAZINE PISTOL — cartridge .32 cal., 5 shot, 3 in. octagon barrel, spur trigger, walnut, rosewood, ivory or pearl grips. Approx. 10,000 produced, 1871-1888.

$1,800	$1,700	$1,600	$1,500	$1,300	$1,100	$1,000	$900	$800	$700	$600	$500

ELLIOT'S SINGLE SHOT DERRINGER — cartridge .41 Rimfire cal., single shot, 2½ in. round barrel, spur trigger, walnut 2-piece grips, blue and/or nickel finish. Approx. 10,000 produced, 1867-1888. A.K.A. "Mississippi Derringer".

$1,500	$1,400	$1,200	$1,000	$900	$800	$700	$550	$500	$450	$400	$350

SMOOT'S NUMBER ONE REVOLVER — cartridge .30 Rimfire cal., 5 shot, 2¾ in. octagon barrel, spur trigger, walnut, hard rubber, pearl or ivory 2-piece grips. Number produced debatable, 1873-1888.

$500	$475	$450	$425	$400	$375	$350	$300	$275	$250	$225	$200

Add 100% on early #1's with revolving recoil shield.

100%	98%	95%	90%	80%	70%	60%	50%	40%	30%	20%	10%

SMOOT'S NUMBER TWO REVOLVER — cartridge .30 or .32 Rimfire cal., 5 shot, 2¾ in. octagon barrel, spur trigger, hard rubber, pearl or ivory 2-piece grips. Number produced debatable, 1873-1888.

$500	$475	$450	$425	$400	$375	$350	$300	$275	$250	$225	$200

SMOOT'S NUMBER THREE REVOLVER — cartridge .38 Rimfire or .38 Centerfire cal., 3¾ in. octagon barrel with or without barrel rib, spur trigger, hard rubber, ivory or pearl 2-piece grips, "bird's head" or "saw-handle" grip frame with Remington logo "R" on the "saw-handle" hard rubber grips. Approx. 30,000 produced, 1875-1888.

$550	$525	$500	$475	$450	$425	$400	$350	$325	$300	$275	$250

Add small premiums on Centerfire Number 3's.

SMOOT'S NUMBER FOUR REVOLVER — cartridge .38 and .41 Rimfire or .38 and .41 Centerfire cal.'s, 5 shot, 2½ in. round barrel, hard rubber, pearl or ivory 2-piece grips. Approx. 25,000 produced, 1877-1888.

$600	$575	$550	$525	$500	$475	$450	$400	$375	$350	$325	$300

Add small premiums on Centerfire Number 4's.

IROQUOS REVOLVER — cartridge .22 Rimfire cal., 7 shot, 2¼ in. round barrel, spur trigger hard rubber, pearl or ivory 2-piece grips, fluted or non-fluted cylinder. Approx. 10,000 produced, 1878-1888.

$600	$575	$550	$525	$500	$475	$450	$400	$375	$350	$325	$300

Deduct 33% if unmarked.

Note: fluted or non-fluted cylinder does not seem to affect valuation.

MODEL 1875 SINGLE ACTION REVOLVER — cartridge .44 or .45 Centerfire cal., 6 shot, 7½ or 53/4 in. round barrel, standard trigger with trigger guard, walnut, ivory or pearl 2-piece grips. Approx. 25,000 produced, 1875-1888.

$3,750	$3,000	$2,800	$2,500	$2,200	$2,000	$1,750	$1,500	$1,250	$1,000	$850	$700

Add 10% for government markings.

Add 50% for .45 cal.

There is some debate over originality of the 5¾ in. barrel.

MODEL 1890 SINGLE ACTION REVOLVER — cartridge .44 Centerfire cal., 6 shot, 7½ or 5¾ in. round barrel, standard trigger with trigger guard, hard rubber 2-piece grips with Remington monogram, ivory or pearl grips on special order, blue or nickel finish. Approx. 2,000 produced, 1891-1894.

$4,500	$4,300	$4,000	$3,700	$3,500	$3,000	$2,500	$2,000	$1,500	$1,000	$800	$700

Subtract 35% for nickel finish.

MODEL 51 SEMI-AUTO — cartridge .32 or .380 Centerfire cal., 8 shot (7 in mag., 1 in chamber), hard rubber 2-piece grips with company's name. Approx. 65,000 produced, 1918-1943.

$600	$525	$500	$475	$450	$425	$400	$350	$325	$300	$275	$250

Note: .380 cal. much more numerous than .32 cal., but valued equally.

MODEL 1911 SEMI-AUTO MILITARY — .45 ACP cal., 8 shot (7 in mag., 1 in chamber), checkered walnut 2-piece grips. 21,676 produced, 1918-1919.

$1,375	$1,075	$800	$625	$550	$495	$450	$430	$410	$390	$375	$350

The serial range for this variation is 1-21,676. The cut-off serial number for 1918 mfg. is 13,152.

Note: Model 1911 is marked Remington-U.M.C.

MARK III SIGNAL PISTOL — 10 ga., single shot, brass frame, 9 in. round steel barrel, spur trigger, walnut 2-piece grips. Approx. 25,000 produced, 1915-1918.

$550	$525	$475	$450	$400	$450	$400	$350	$325	$300	$250	$200

HANDGUNS: POST-WWII MFG.

Grading	100%	98%	95%	90%	80%	70%	60%

MODEL XP22R KS — the Remington Custom Shop should be contacted directly (see Trademark Index) for more information regarding this model.

Mfg.'s Sug. Retail	$432	$375	$300	$265	$225	$200	$185	$165

XP-100 VARMINT SPECIAL — single shot bolt action pistol, .221 Rem. Fireball (disc. 1985-10½ in. barrel) or .223 Rem. (new 1986) cal., 14½ in. barrel, adj. sights (.221 cal. only), drilled and tapped for scope, one piece nylon stock. Mfg. 1963-present.

Mfg.'s Sug. Retail	$418	$335	$295	$230	$195	$165	$150	$140

XP-SILHOUETTE — .35 Rem. (new 1987), 7mm Rem., bench rest model, 14½ in. barrel, comes without sights, nylon stock, drilled and tapped for sight mounts.

Mfg.'s Sug. Retail	$426	$375	$330	$270	$220	$200	$180	$165

Add $14 for .35 Rem. cal.

XP-100R KS .223 Rem., .250 Savage, 7mm-08 Rem., .35 Rem., or .350 Rem. Mag. cal., repeater variation, Kevlar synthetic stock, right hand action only.

Mfg.'s Sug. Retail	$798	$715	$600	$540	$495	$450	$400	$365

XP-100 CUSTOM — .223 Rem. standard or HB (heavy barrel-new 1987), .250 Savage standard or HB (new 1989), 6mm BR standard or HB (new 1989), 7mm BR standard or HB (new 1989), 35 Rem. (standard barrel only), or 7mm-08 Rem. (HB new 1989) cal., available through custom gun shop only, choice of right or left hand action, nylon or wood stock with contoured pistol grip, regular or shrouded barrel, ramp front sight. New 1986.

Mfg.'s Sug. Retail	$943	$825	$735	$660	$575	$525	$450	$400

Also available, on special order only, is the .458 x 2 in. caliber.

RIFLES: DISC. MFG.

100%	98%	95%	90%	80%	70%	60%	50%	40%	30%	20%	10%

REVOLVING PERCUSSION RIFLE — .36 or .44 cal., 6 shot unfluted cylinder, 24 or 28 in. octagon barrel, walnut stock with crescent butt, scroll trigger guard, blue with case hardened frame. Less than 1,000 mfg., 1866-1879.

.36 Caliber

$3,500	$3,200	$2,900	$2,640	$2,475	$2,310	$2,200	$2,090	$1,980	$1,925	$1,815	$1,760

.44 Caliber — very rare.

$4,250	$3,850	$3,400	$3,150	$2,925	$2,650	$2,530	$2,420	$2,310	$2,200	$2,035	$1,925

MODEL 1862 "ZOUAVE RIFLE" — .58 cal., muzzle loading percussion, 33 in. round barrel, two barrel bands, blue barrel, case hardened lock, brass furniture. Mfg. 12,501, 1862-1865.

$3,200	$2,900	$2,650	$2,400	$2,150	$1,800	$1,575	$1,300	$1,050	$850	$650	$450

U.S. NAVY ROLLING BLOCK CARBINE — .50-70 cal., 23¼ in. barrel, open sight, blue with case hardened frame, bar and ring on frame, walnut straight grip stock. Mfg. 5,000, 1868-1869.

$1,400	$1,250	$1,075	$925	$795	$660	$635	$580	$525	$495	$440	$385

LONG RANGE "CREEDMOOR" — rolling block, .44-90, .44-100, .44-70, .50-45, or .50-70 cal., barrel ½ octagon, long range tang sight, globe front sight, checkered pistol grip stock, blue. Approx. 2,000 mfg., 1873-1890.

$3,250	$2,700	$2,400	$1,750	$1,375	$1,100	$990	$880	$770	$715	$605	$550

NO. 1 SPORTING RIFLE — rolling block, .40-50, .40-70, .44-70, .45-70, .50-45, or .50-70 cal., 28 or 30 in. octagon barrels, folding leaf sight, straight grip stock. Several thousand mfg., 1868-1902.

$925	$850	$775	$680	$560	$440	$385	$360	$330	$275	$220	$195

NO. 1½ SPORTING RIFLE — .22, .25 Stevens, .25 Long, .32, and .38 Long & Extra Long rimfire, also in .32-20, .38-40, and .44-40 in centerfire, 24-28 in. octagon medium weight barrel, straight grip walnut stock, standard No. 1 frame - but somewhat lighter than the No. 1 Sporting. Several thousand mfg., 1888-1897.

$850	$775	$680	$560	$440	$385	$360	$330	$275	$220	$195	$175

100%	98%	95%	90%	80%	70%	60%	50%	40%	30%	20%	10%

NO. 2 SPORTING RIFLE — available in many rimfire cal.'s between .22 and .38 as well as centerfire cal.'s between .22 to .38-40, blued finish with case hardened frame, perch belly style walnut stock, many special orders available, smaller size action than the No.1 and rear of frame is curved, mfg. 1873-1909.

| $550 | $515 | $480 | $440 | $400 | $350 | $300 | $260 | $230 | $200 | $165 | $130 |

LIGHT BABY CARBINE — rolling block, .44-40 cal., 20 in. lightweight round barrel with band, straight stock. Few thousand mfg., 1892-1902.

| $3,650 | $3,100 | $2,500 | $2,000 | $1,650 | $1,375 | $1,500 | $895 | $775 | $700 | $640 | $575 |

REMINGTON — HEPBURN NO. 3 — falling block, single shot, side lever actuated, blue barrel, case hardened actions, patented 1879, first introduced 1880, many custom features were offered, variations as follows:

NO. 3 SPORTING & TARGET — various cal.'s from .22 Win. to .50-90 Sharps, 26, 28, or 30 in. round or octagon barrel, open sight, semi-pistol grip stock. Mfg. 1883-1907.

| $1,550 | $1,300 | $1,150 | $1,045 | $935 | $880 | $770 | $660 | $550 | $495 | $440 | $385 |

NO. 3 MATCH RIFLE A QUALITY — same as Sporting and Target, with target match sights (tang), and Schuetzen stock. Less than 1,000 mfg., 1883-1907.

| $1,700 | $1,550 | $1,400 | $1,150 | $1,045 | $960 | $880 | $825 | $715 | $605 | $550 | $495 |

B Quality — select grade wood.

| $2,150 | $1,975 | $1,825 | $1,525 | $1,200 | $1,045 | $935 | $880 | $770 | $715 | $605 | $550 |

NO. 3 LONG RANGE CREEDMOOR — .44 cal., 32 or 34 in. octagon barrel, tang sight, otherwise same as Target Model. A few hundred mfg., 1880-1907.

| $2,500 | $2,225 | $1,950 | $1,675 | $1,400 | $1,225 | $1,100 | $1,045 | $935 | $880 | $770 | $715 |

NO. 3 MID RANGE CREEDMOOR — same as Long Range, in .40-65 cal., 28 in. barrel.

| $2,150 | $1,975 | $1,825 | $1,525 | $1,200 | $1,045 | $935 | $880 | $770 | $715 | $660 | $605 |

NO. 3 LONG RANGE MILITARY — same as Creedmoor, with 34 in. full musket stock, in .44-75-520 Rem. cal., military sights, 1880's.

| $3,375 | $2,950 | $2,625 | $2,250 | $1,925 | $1,700 | $1,540 | $1,430 | $1,320 | $1,100 | $990 | $825 |

NO. 3 SCHUETZEN MATCH — under lever actuated, 30 or 32 in. barrel, tang sight palm rest, target stock, very few known, perhaps the rarest single shot American rifle.

| $5,500 | $5,000 | $4,600 | $4,000 | $3,500 | $2,850 | $2,420 | $2,200 | $2,145 | $2,035 | $1,925 | $1,815 |

With False Muzzle

| $6,100 | $5,400 | $4,900 | $4,300 | $3,875 | $3,200 | $2,850 | $2,600 | $2,300 | $2,100 | $2,000 | $1,900 |

NO. 4 ROLLING BLOCK RIFLE — .22 S-L-LR, .25 Stevens, or .32 Short or Long cal., 22½ octagon barrel standard with round barrels available late in the series, blued finish with case hardened frame, solid frame initially followed by takedown in 2 different types (lever - most common, or knob), this model was Remington's smallest rolling block. Approx. 50,000 mfg. 1890-1933.

| $440 | $400 | $375 | $335 | $300 | $260 | $230 | $200 | $165 | $130 | $100 | $90 |

Solid frame variations will command a premium, especially if over 50% original condition.

Model 4-S "Boy Scout" — .22 S-L-LR, either marked "MILITARY MODEL" (most common) or "AMERICAN BOY SCOUT" (rare), 28 in. round barrel with musket type forend (1 barrel band), thought to have been used by military academies to train their young cadets.

| $750 | $695 | $625 | $550 | $515 | $480 | $440 | $400 | $350 | $300 | $260 | $230 |

Bayonets are an extremely rare accessory for this model.

NO. 6 ROLLING BLOCK RIFLE — .22 S-L-LR or .32 Short or Long rimfire cal., 20 in. round barrel, boy's gun with small dimensions, takedown action, case hardened (early mfg.) or blue finish, also available in smooth bore, many thousands mfg. 1902-1933.

| $350 | $300 | $280 | $260 | $240 | $220 | $200 | $180 | $160 | $140 | $120 | $100 |

Original case colors will bring a premium on this model.

Grading	100%	98%	95%	90%	80%	70%	60%

REMINGTON KEENE MAGAZINE BOLT RIFLE — .45.-70 Gov't, .40, or .43 cal. Mfg. 1880-1888. Approx. 5,000 mfg.,

Frontier Model — made for U.S. Dept. of Interior (Indian Police), marked U.S.I.D.

	$1,325	$950	$800	$600	$500	$400	$350

Carbine Model — 22 in. full stock.

	$1,100	$850	$750	$550	$450	$350	$300

Army Rifle — 32½ in. barrel, full stock.

	$1,100	$850	$750	$550	$450	$350	$300

Sporter Rifle — ½ oct. barrel, full or "BUTTON" mag. Add for pistol grip and select wood variations.

	$1,000	$825	$650	$550	$450	$350	$300

Navy Rifle — 29½ in. barrel, full stock.

	$1,100	$850	$750	$550	$450	$350	$300

RIFLES: MODERN PRODUCTION 1906 TO DATE

MODEL 8 AUTOLOADING RIFLE — .25, .30, .32, or .35 Rem. cal., 22 in. barrel, open sights, 5 shot non-detachable box mag., plain stock. Approx. 60,000 mfg. 1906-1936. Also made in higher grades C through F — add premiums.

	$400	$320	$270	$220	$195	$165	$140

MODEL 81 "WOODSMASTER" — .25, .30, .32, .35 Rem., or .300 Savage cal., semi-auto, 5 shot, non-detachable box mag., 22 in. round barrel, notched elevator rear sight. An improvement of the model 8 is available in 5 grades. Better grades bring higher prices. 55,581 mfg. 1936-1950.

	$400	$350	$300	$250	$200	$175	$150

Add 10% for .25 cal.

The .25 and .32 Rem. calibers were dropped after WWII and the .300 Savage was added in 1941.

MODEL 12A SLIDE ACTION RIFLE — .22 S, L, and LR, hammerless, 22 in. barrel, open sights, tube mag., plain grip stock. Mfg. 1909-1936.

	$350	$300	$250	$200	$120	$95	$85

Originally designated Model 12.

MODEL 12B (GALLERY SPECIAL) — same as 12C, except .22 Short, all had octagon barrels.

	$400	$350	$300	$200	$120	$95	$85

MODEL 12C — same as 12A, except 24 in. octagon barrel. Also mfg. in grades D, E, and F — add premiums.

	$450	$400	$325	$250	$185	$140	$110

MODEL 12C NRA TARGET — limited manufacture.

	$600	$500	$400	$350	$300	$220	$140

MODEL 12CS — same as 12C, chambered for .22 Rem. Spl. (.22 WRF).

	$450	$400	$300	$200	$120	$95	$85

MODEL 121A SLIDE ACTION RIFLE — hammerless, .22 S, L, or LR, 24 in. round barrel, tube mag., plain pistol grip stock. Mfg. 1936-1954.

	$350	$285	$225	$195	$165	$140	$110

Originally designated Model 121.

MODEL 121S — same as 121A, except chambered for .22 Rem. Spl. (rare).

	$450	$375	$315	$260	$215	$175	$140

MODEL 121SB — same as 121A, except smooth bore for .22 shot. 5 different chamberings and barrel markings.

	$500	$400	$350	$275	$240	$200	$165

MODEL 14/14A SLIDE ACTION — .25, .30, .32, or .35 cal., 22 in. barrel, open sight, plain pistol grip stock. Mfg. 1912-1935.

	$350	$285	$230	$195	$165	$130	$110

Grading	100%	98%	95%	90%	80%	70%	60%

MODEL 14R CARBINE — same as 14A, with 18½ in. barrel, straight grip stock.

	$400	$325	$285	$260	$220	$195	$165

MODEL 14½ RIFLE — same as 14A, with 22½ in. barrel, .38-40 or .44-40 cal. Mfg. 1912-1934.

	$550	$475	$425	$350	$300	$275	$250

Quantities mfg. of this model are unknown as serial numbers were intermixed with the Model 14.

MODEL 14½R CARBINE — same as 14½, with 18½ in. barrel.

	$600	$525	$475	$425	$375	$325	$300

MODEL 141/141A SLIDE ACTION — .30, .32, or .35 Rem. cal., 24 in. barrel, takedown, open sight, plain pistol grip stock. Mfg. 1936-1950.

	$395	$305	$250	$220	$195	$165	$140

MODEL 16/16A AUTOLOADING RIFLE — .22 autoloading cal., 22 in. barrel, open sight, tube mag. in butt stock, straight stock. Mfg. 1914-1928. Also mfg. in grades C, D, and F — add premiums.

	$295	$230	$195	$170	$140	$110	$90

MODEL 24/24A AUTOLOADING RIFLE — .22 S or LR, 19 in. barrel, open sights, Browning semi-auto design, bottom ejection, tube mag. through butt stock, takedown, plain pistol grip stock. Mfg. 1922-1935.

	$325	$240	$210	$170	$140	$110	$90

MODEL 241/241A SPEEDMASTER — .22 S or LR, 24 in. barrel, replaced the Model 24, open sights, takedown, tube mag. through stock, non-checkered walnut stock and forearm. Approx. 56,000 mfg. 1935-1949.

	$360	$275	$250	$195	$150	$120	$100

This model was also available in a Special, Peerless, Expert, and Premier Grade - add premiums.

MODEL 25/25A SLIDE ACTION — .25-20 or .32-20 cal., 24 in. barrel, open sight, tube mag., plain pistol grip stock. Mfg. 1923-1936.

	$350	$300	$275	$250	$200	$175	$150

MODEL 25R CARBINE — same as 25A, with 18 in. barrel and straight stock.

	$450	$400	$350	$275	$225	$200	$175

MODEL 550A AUTOLOADER — .22 S, L, or LR interchangeably, 24 in. barrel, open sight, shell deflector, tube mag., plain one piece pistol stock. Approx. 220,000 mfg., 1941-1971.

	$150	$125	$110	$90	$80	$70	$60

This model replaced the Model 241.

MODEL 550P — same as 550A, with aperture sight.

	$190	$150	$125	$105	$85	$75	$65

MODEL 550-2G — same as 550A, except 22 in. barrel and eye screw for counter chain in shooting gallery.

	$200	$175	$150	$130	$110	$100	$85

MODEL 760 SLIDE ACTION "GAMEMASTER" RIFLE — .222, .223, 6mm, .243, .257 Roberts, .270, .280, .30-06, .300 Sav., .308 or .35 Rem. cal., 22 in. barrel, detachable mag., checkered pistol grip stock. Mfg. 1952-1982.

	100%	98%	95%	90%	80%	70%	60%
	$375	$325	$275	$250	$225	$200	$175
.222 cal.	$1,150	$900	$800	$725	$650	$575	$500
.223 cal.	$1,350	$995	$850	$775	$700	$625	$575
.257 R cal.	$925	$800	$700	$600	$500	$400	$300

The Model 760 seems to have regional pricing differences in the rare calibers. Values in the Eastern U.S. seem to be quite a bit higher than prices encountered in the Midwest and West. Hence, values on the .222, .223, and .257 R cal.'s reflect a nationalized average rather than one region's high or another's low. A few Model 760's were also mfg. in .244 cal. (before going to 6mm) — very rare with pricing unpredictable.

Grading	100%	98%	95%	90%	80%	70%	60%

MODEL 760 CARBINE — .270, .280, .30-06, .308, or .35 Rem. cal., 18½ in. barrel.

	$350	$300	$275	$240	$225	$200	$185

MODEL 760D PEERLESS GRADE — same as 760, with engraving and fancy wood. Mfg. 1953-1982.

	$1,100	$935	$825	$770	$690	$605	$525

MODEL 760F — same as 760, with extensive engraved game scenes, best grade wood.

	$2,420	$1,980	$1,760	$1,650	$1,485	$1,375	$1,100

Gold Inlaid Model

	$5,500	$4,675	$4,180	$3,960	$3,300	$2,750	$2,200

MODEL 760 150 YEAR ANNIVERSARY — .30-06 only. Mfg. 1966 only.

	$375	$340	$300	$275	$225	$200	$185

MODEL 760 BICENTENNIAL — same as 760, with commemorative inscription engraved on receiver. Mfg. 1976 only.

	$375	$340	$300	$275	$225	$200	$185

MODEL 760ADL — same as 760, with pistol grip and sling swivels. Mfg. 1953-1963.

	$350	$325	$300	$275	$250	$225	$200

MODEL 760BDL — same as 760, except .270, .30-06, or .308 cal. only, with basket weave checkering, Monte Carlo stock, black pistol grip and forend tip. Mfg. 1953-1982.

	$300	$275	$250	$225	$210	$200	$175

MODEL 76 SPORTSMAN SLIDE ACTION — .30-06 cal. only, 22 in. barrel, 4 shot mag., unchecked-ered hardwood stock and forearm, open sights, 7½ lbs. Mfg. 1985-1987.

	$255	$225	$195	$180	$170	$160	$150

Last Mfg.'s Sug. Retail was $319.

MODEL 7600 SLIDE ACTION RIFLE — 6mm Rem. (disc. 1984), .243 Win., .270 Win., .280 Rem. (new 1988), .30-06, .308 Win., or .35 Whelen (new 1988) cal., modified 760 action, 22 in. barrel, detachable mag., pressed checkered pistol grip stock and forearm, 7½ lbs. Mfg. 1981 to date.

Mfg.'s Sug. Retail	$484	$410	$355	$280	$230	$205	$185	$165

Starting in 1990, a high gloss wood finish became available in cal.'s .270 and .30-06.

Model 7600 Carbine — .30-06 cal. only, similar to Model 7600 Rifle, except has 18½ in. barrel, 7¼ lbs.

Mfg.'s Sug. Retail	$484	$410	$355	$280	$230	$205	$185	$165

Model 7600 Engraved — the below listed engraved Model 7600's were introduced 1988.

D Peerless Grade

Mfg.'s Sug. Retail	$2,383	$1,995	$1,600	$1,200

F Premier Grade

Mfg.'s Sug. Retail	$4,910	$4,275	$3,450	$2,500

F Premier Gold Grade — with gold inlays.

Mfg.'s Sug. Retail	$7,364	$6,600	$3,850	$2,950

MODEL SIX SLIDE ACTION — 6mm Rem. (disc. 1984), 243 Win., 270 Win., .30-06, or 308 Win. (disc. 1984) cal., pump action, detachable sights, 4 shot mag. Mfg. 1981-1987.

	$400	$360	$290	$265	$235	$215	$195

Last Mfg.'s Sug. Retail was $439.

D Peerless Grade

	$1,975	$1,870	$1,200

Last Mfg.'s Sug. Retail was $2,291.

F Premier Grade

	$4,150	$3,835	$2,650

Last Mfg.'s Sug. Retail was $4,720.

Grading	100%	98%	95%	90%	80%	70%	60%

F Premier Gold Grade — with gold inlays.

	$6,420	$5,735	$4,000				

Last Mfg.'s Sug. Retail was $7,079.

MODEL 740 & 740A AUTOLOADER — .30-06 or .308 cal., 22 in. barrel, open sight, box mag., gas operated, plain pistol grip stock. Mfg. 1955-1960.

	100%	98%	95%	90%	80%	70%	60%
.30-06 cal	$335	$295	$275	$250	$225	$200	$180
.308 cal.	$425	$375	$325	$295	$275	$250	$225

Add 15% for carbine version.

MODEL 740ADL — same as 740A, with checkered stock, grip cap and swivels. Mfg. 1955-1960.

	100%	98%	95%	90%	80%	70%	60%
.30-06 cal.	$375	$325	$280	$250	$225	$200	$180
.308 cal.	$450	$400	$350	$300	$275	$250	$225

Add 15% for carbine version.

MODEL 740BDL — same as 740ADL, with select wood.

	100%	98%	95%	90%	80%	70%	60%
.30-06 cal.	$395	$340	$295	$250	$225	$200	$180
.308 cal.	$475	$415	$350	$300	$275	$250	$225

Add 15% for carbine version.

MODEL 742A "WOODSMASTER" SEMI-AUTO — 6mm Rem., .243, .280, .30-06, or .308 cal., 22 in. barrel, open sights, 4 shot box mag., gas operated, checkered pistol grip stock. Mfg. 1960-1980.

100%	98%	95%	90%	80%	70%	60%
$325	$290	$275	$250	$235	$210	$185

Add 10% for .280 Rem. cal.

MODEL 742ADL DELUXE — similar to the Model 742A, except has fine checkering, sling swivels and engraved game scenes on receiver.

100%	98%	95%	90%	80%	70%	60%
$350	$310	$285	$265	$250	$225	$210

MODEL 742 CARBINE — same as 742, except .30-06 or .308 cal. only, 18½ in. barrel. Mfg. 1961-1980.

100%	98%	95%	90%	80%	70%	60%
$350	$310	$285	$265	$250	$225	$210

MODEL 742BDL — same as 742, except .30-06 or .308 cal. only, Monte Carlo basket weave stock and forend, black pistol grip cap and forend tip. Mfg. 1966-1980.

100%	98%	95%	90%	80%	70%	60%
$375	$325	$300	$275	$260	$235	$215

MODEL 742D PEERLESS GRADE — same as 742, with scroll engraving and fancy wood. Mfg. 1961-1980.

100%	98%	95%
$2,000	$1,870	$1,200

MODEL 742F PREMIER GRADE — same as 742, with extensive game scenes and scroll engraving, best grade wood.

100%	98%	95%
$4,200	$3,860	$2,650

MODEL 742F PREMIER GRADE (WITH INLAYS) — gold inlaid model.

100%	98%	95%
$6,500	$5,785	$4,180

MODEL 742 150TH YEAR ANNIVERSARY — .30-06 only. Mfg. 1966 only.

100%	98%	95%
$375	$340	$300

MODEL 742 CANADIAN CENTENNIAL — 1,000 mfg. in 1967. Issue price was $200.

100%	98%	95%
$395	$340	$300

MODEL 742 BICENTENNIAL — same as 742, with inscription on receiver. Mfg. 1976 only.

100%	98%	95%	90%	80%	70%	60%
$375	$340	$300	$275	$225	$200	$185

MODEL 74 SPORTSMAN SEMI-AUTO — .30-06 only, 22 in. barrel, 4 shot mag., uncheckered hardwood stock and forearm, open sights, 7½ lbs. Mfg. 1985-1987.

100%	98%	95%	90%	80%	70%	60%
$295	$260	$235	$210	$190	$175	$160

Last Mfg.'s Sug. Retail was $353.

Grading	100%	98%	95%	90%	80%	70%	60%

MODEL 7400 SEMI-AUTO RIFLE — 6mm Rem. (disc. 1987), .243 Win., .270 Win., .280 Rem., .30-06, or .308 Win. cal., same action as 742, gas operation, 22 in. barrel, 4 shot detachable mag., pressed checkered walnut stock, 7½ lbs. Mfg. 1982 to date.

Mfg.'s Sug. Retail	$501	$425	$365	$300	$255	$230	$210	$185

Starting in 1990, a high gloss wood finish became available in cal.'s .270 and .30-06.

Model 7400 Carbine — .30-06 cal. only, similar to Model 7400 Rifle, except has 18½ in. barrel, 7¼ lbs. New 1988.

Model 7400 175th Anniversary — .30-06 cal. only, Anniversary Model with light engraving and high gloss finish. Mfg. in 1991 only.

Mfg.'s Sug. Retail	$515	$435	$365	$300

Model 7400 Engraved — the below listed engraved Model 7400's were introduced 1988.

D Peerless Grade

Mfg.'s Sug. Retail	$2,383	$1,995	$1,600	$1,200

F Premier Grade

Mfg.'s Sug. Retail	$4,910	$4,275	$3,450	$2,500

F Premier Gold Grade — with gold inlays.

Mfg.'s Sug. Retail	$7,364	$6,600	$3,850	$2,950

MODEL FOUR SEMI-AUTO — 6mm Rem., .243 Win., .270 Win., .280 Rem., .30-06, or .308 Win. (disc. 1984) cal., gas operation with metering system, 22 in. barrel, 4 shot detachable mag., deluxe Monte Carlo stock and forend, detachable sights. Mfg. 1982-1987.

	$395	$360	$325	$275	$250	$225	$195

Last Mfg.'s Sug. Retail was $475.

Model Four Diamond Anniversary — .30-06 only, 1,500 mfg. in 1981 to commemorate 75th anniversary of the Model 8, custom shop engraved with premium checkered walnut stock and forearm.

	$950	$795	$600

D Peerless Grade

	$1,975	$1,870	$1,200

Last Mfg.'s Sug. Retail was $2,291.

F Premier Grade

	$4,150	$3,835	$2,650

Last Mfg.'s Sug. Retail was $4,720.

F Premier Gold Grade — with gold inlays.

	$6,420	$5,735	$4,000

Last Mfg.'s Sug. Retail was $7,079.

MODEL 30A BOLT ACTION RIFLE — Enfield M/1917 type action, 7mm, .30-06, .25, .30, .32, or .35 Rem. cal., 22 in. barrel, checkered pistol grip stock. Mfg. 1921-1940.

	$450	$400	$350	$300	$260	$200	$150

MODEL 30R CARBINE — same as 30A, with 20 in. barrel.

	$500	$450	$375	$325	$275	$225	$150

MODEL 30S — deluxe version of Model 30A, .257 Robts., 7mm, or .30-06 cal., 24 in. barrel, Lyman receiver sight, special stock. Mfg. 1930-1940.

	$550	$500	$450	$375	$300	$250	$220

RIFLES: RIMFIRE

From 1930-1960 Remington produced a number of bolt action .22 cal. Rimfire rifles, both single shot and repeaters. They were good quality, serviceable weapons with many slight variations upon a basic design.

Model 33	$135	$120	$90	$80	$70	$60	$50
Model 33 NRA	$195	$150	$110	$95	$85	$75	$65

263,557 of the Model 33 were mfg. 1932-1935.

Grading	100%	98%	95%	90%	80%	70%	60%
Model 34	$135	$120	$90	$80	$70	$60	$50
Model 34 NRA	$195	$150	$110	$95	$85	$75	$65

162,941 of the Model 34 were mfg. 1936-1940.

Model 341 A	$110	$90	$75	$70	$65	$55	$50
Model 341 P	$110	$90	$75	$70	$65	$55	$50
Model 341 SB	$195	$175	$160	$140	$125	$110	$90

131,604 of the Model 341 "Sportsmaster" were mfg. 1936-1939.

Model 41 A	$110	$90	$75	$65	$60	$55	$50
Model 41 AS	$175	$160	$150	$140	$125	$110	$100
Model 41 P	$110	$90	$75	$65	$60	$55	$50
Model 41 SB	$195	$175	$160	$140	$125	$110	$100
Model 411	$350	$300	$250	$210	$200	$185	$175

306,880 of the Model 41 "Targetmaster" were produced 1936-1939.

The Model 411 is similar to the Model 41 single shot, but in CB Cap only, and without safety on rear of bolt. Eye screw for gallery use. 1,316 mfg. 1937- 1939 (although never cataloged). Extreme rarity precludes accurate price evaluation.

Model 510 A	$100	$90	$75	$65	$60	$55	$50
Model 510P	$100	$90	$75	$65	$60	$55	$50
Model 510 SB	$145	$130	$125	$120	$110	$100	$90

These models were mfg. 1939-1962.

Model 511 A	$110	$90	$75	$65	$60	$55	$50
Model 511 P	$110	$90	$75	$65	$60	$55	$50

These models were mfg. 1940-1962.

Model 512 A	$110	$100	$90	$80	$75	$70	$60
Model 512 P	$110	$100	$90	$80	$75	$70	$60

These models were mfg. 1965-1967.

Model 510-X	$125	$110	$90	$80	$70	$60	$50
Model 511-X	$125	$110	$100	$90	$80	$70	$60
Model 512-X	$125	$110	$100	$90	$80	$70	$60

These models were mfg. 1964-1966.

Model 514 — mfg. 1948-1970.

	$110	$90	$75	$65	$55	$40	$30

Model 514 P — mfg. until 1971.

	$135	$120	$100	$85	$75	$65	$50

Model 514 BC — mfg. until 1971.

	$135	$120	$100	$85	$75	$65	$50

MODEL 37 "RANGEMASTER" BOLT ACTION — .22 LR, 5 shot with single shot adapter, 28 in. barrel, target sight and scope bases, target stock. Mfg. 1937-1940.

	$385	$305	$275	$250	$220	$195	$165

MODEL 37 - 1940 — improved trigger and stock design. Mfg. 1940-1954.

	$440	$360	$330	$305	$275	$220	$195

Total manufacture of the Model 37 was 12,198.

NYLON 66 AUTOLOADER — .22 LR, 19⅝ in. barrel, open sights, butt stock tube mag. holds 14 shells, 4 lbs. Stock made from Zytel plastic in black, brown, or green. Mfg. 1959-1987.

	$110	$95	$85	$70	$60	$55	$50

Add 10% for Black Diamond.
Add 20% for Apache black.
Add 50% for Seneca green.
Last Mfg.'s Sug. Retail was $124.

Grading	100%	98%	95%	90%	80%	70%	60%

NYLON 66 150TH ANNIVERSARY — mfg. in 1966 only with 150th Anniversary Remington logo on receiver.

	$175	$150	$125	$90	$85	$80	$75

NYLON 66 BICENTENNIAL — inscription on receiver. Mfg. 1976 only, brown nylon stock only.

	$150	$135	$125	$100	$85	$70	$60

NYLON 77 — same as Nylon 66, except with 5 shot clip mag. Mfg. 1970-1971 only.

	$165	$145	$125	$90	$75	$60	$50

MODEL 10-C — same as Model 77, renamed after changing to a 10 shot mag. Mfg. 1971-1978.

	$125	$100	$70	$65	$60	$55	$50

NYLON APACHE 77 — similar to Model 10-C, but bright green stock. Mfg. for K-Mart in 1987.

	$100	$85	$65	$55	$50	$45	$40

NYLON 76 LEVER ACTION — similar appearance to Nylon 66 with brown or black stock, short throw lever action. Mfg. 1962-1964 only.

	$175	$150	$125	$95	$80	$70	$60

The Nylon 76 "Trail Rider" is the only lever action repeating rifle ever mfg. by Remington.

NYLON 10 SINGLE SHOT — .22 S, L, or LR, bolt action. Mfg. 1962-1964.

	$150	$125	$100	$80	$70	$60	$50

Nylon 10-SB — similar to Nylon 10, except smooth bore barrel used for .22 shot cartridges.

	$250	$200	$175	$150	$145	$140	$125

MODEL 11 NYLON — bolt action repeater, clip fed, 6 or 10 shot mag., 4½ lbs. Mfg. 1962-1964.

	$150	$125	$100	$80	$70	$60	$50

MODEL 12 NYLON — same as 11, with tube mag. Mfg. 1962-1964.

	$150	$125	$100	$80	$70	$60	$50

MODEL 513TR "MATCHMASTER" BOLT ACTION — .22 LR, 27 in. barrel, Redfield aperture sight, target stock, 6 shot, sling swivels. Mfg. 1940-1969.

	$295	$250	$220	$180	$140	$115	$95

MODEL 513S — similar to 513TR, with Marbles open sight and checkered sporter stock. Mfg. 1941-1956.

	$400	$350	$320	$290	$260	$230	$210

MODEL 521TL JR. BOLT ACTION — .22 LR, 25 in. barrel, Lyman target sights, takedown, 6 shot mag., target stock. Mfg. 1947-1969.

	$225	$190	$160	$140	$120	$100	$90

MODEL 552A SPEEDMASTER — .22 S, L, or LR, 23 in. barrel, semi-auto open sight, tube mag., pistol grip stock. Mfg. 1957-disc.

	$160	$135	$120	$100	$85	$75	$65

This model was also mfg. in a 150th Anniversary Model (1966 only). Slight premiums are being asked if condition is 98% or better.

MODEL 552C — same as 552A, with 21 in. barrel. Mfg. 1961-1977.

	$170	$145	$130	$110	$95	$85	$75

Model 552 BDL Deluxe — same as Model 552, except checkered walnut stock and forearm. Mfg. 1966 to date.

Mfg.'s Sug. Retail	$213	$185	$160	$140	$125	$105	$90	$75

MODEL 572 LIGHTWEIGHT — anodized alloy receiver and barrel, steel sleeved, 3 colors: tan, blue, and black. Mfg. 1958-1962.

	$250	$210	$190	$170	$140	$125	$100

Add 50% for black or 100% for blue color receiver if in 98%+ condition.

Grading	100%	98%	95%	90%	80%	70%	60%

MODEL 572SB — same as 572A, except smooth bore.

	$300	$250	$195	$160	$140	$120	$100

MODEL 572 FIELDMASTER — .22 LR only, slide action, 21 in. barrel, walnut stock and forearm, tube mag., 5½ lbs. Mfg. 1955-1988.

	$160	$145	$125	$105	$90	$75	$65

Last Mfg.'s Sug. Retail was $176.

This model was also mfg. in a 150th Anniversary Model (1966 only). Slight premiums are being asked if condition is 98% or better.

Model 572 BDL Deluxe — same as Model 572, except with checkered walnut stock and forearm. Mfg. 1966 to date.

Mfg.'s Sug. Retail	$223	$190	$170	$150	$125	$105	$90	$75

MODEL 580 SINGLE SHOT — .22 S, L or LR, bolt action, 24 in. barrel, open sights, Monte Carlo stock. Mfg. 1968-1978.

	$95	$80	$70	$65	$55	$50	$45

MODEL 580BR — Boy's Model, 1 in. shorter stock. Mfg. 1971-1978.

	$105	$90	$85	$70	$65	$60	$50

MODEL 581 — .22 LR cal., bolt action, 6 shot clip mag., converts to single shot. Mfg. 1967-1983.

	$150	$115	$110	$100	$90	$70	$60

MODEL 581-S — .22 LR cal., bolt action, 5 shot clip mag., 24 in. barrel, hardwood uncheckered stock, 4¾ lbs. New 1986.

Mfg.'s Sug. Retail	$196	$180	$160	$145	$125	$105	$90	$75

MODEL 582 — same as 581, with tube mag. Mfg. 1967-1983.

	$150	$110	$100	$90	$70	$65	$60

MODEL 591 BOLT ACTION — 5mm Rimfire Mag., 24 in. barrel, open sight, 5 shot clip mag., Monte Carlo stock. Approx. 25,000 mfg. 1970-1974.

	$175	$140	$125	$100	$85	$75	$65

5mm Rimfire ammo has been disc. for some time, and as a result, collectability on this model is mostly for 100% condition since there is no shooter utility in lower conditions. Original 5mm ammo is selling for $35-$50 per box.

MODEL 592 — same as 591, with tube mag. Approx. 2,000 mfg. 1970-1974.

	$295	$260	$230	$200	$180	$160	$145

MODEL 541S CUSTOM — .22 S, L, or LR, bolt action, 24 in. barrel, no sights, 5 shot, scroll engraved receiver and trigger guard, checkered walnut stock with rosewood pistol grip cap and forend tip. Mfg. 1972-1984.

	$400	$350	$300	$275	$250	$225	$200

MODEL 541T — .22 LR only, 5 shot clip mag., 24 in. barrel, checkered American walnut stock with satin finish, barrel is drilled and tapped, 5⅞ lbs. New 1986.

Mfg.'s Sug. Retail	$355	$310	$260	$225	$200	$180	$165	$150

RIFLES: BOLT ACTION CENTERFIRE

MODEL 720A BOLT ACTION — Enfield type action, .257 Robts., .270, or .30-06 cal., 22 in. barrel, open sights, 5 shot, checkered pistol grip stock, 2,500 mfg. 1941-1944.

	$1,150	$975	$850	$700	$600	$500	$400

Add 50%+ for .270 Win. cal.

Add 100%+ for .257 Robts. cal.

Most of the Model 720A's were purchased by the military and used as trophies - these are discernable by crossed cannon proofs on wood.

Most of this model was chambered for .30-06 cal. Approx. 100 were chambered for .270 Win. and 20 or less were chambered for the .257 Robts.

Grading	100%	98%	95%	90%	80%	70%	60%

MODEL 720R — similar to 720A, except with 20 in. barrel.

| | $1,250 | $1,050 | $900 | $750 | $650 | $550 | $450 |

This is the rarest variation in the Model 720 Series.

MODEL 720S — similar to 720A, except with 24 in. barrel.

| | $1,200 | $1,000 | $850 | $700 | $600 | $500 | $400 |

MODEL 721(A) BOLT ACTION — .264 Mag., .270 Win., .280 Rem., or .30-06 cal., 24 in. barrel, open sights, 4 shot, plain pistol grip stock. Mfg. 1948-1962.

| | $295 | $260 | $220 | $195 | $165 | $155 | $145 |

Cal.'s .280 Rem. (688 mfg.) and .264 Win. Mag. (1,115 mfg.) are rare in this model. 100% values on these calibers could bring $600+.

MODEL 721ADL — same as Model 721A, except has deluxe checkered stock.

| | $375 | $325 | $300 | $275 | $250 | $200 | $175 |

MODEL 721BDL — same as 721 ADL, except has extra select wood.

| | $500 | $425 | $375 | $325 | $300 | $275 | $250 |

MODEL 721A MAGNUM — .300 H&H, 26 in. heavy barrel, recoil pad, 3 shot mag., 8¼ lbs.

| | $400 | $360 | $320 | $295 | $275 | $260 | $245 |

MODEL 721ADL MAGNUM — same as 721A Mag., checkered.

| | $450 | $400 | $350 | $315 | $290 | $275 | $260 |

MODEL 721BDL MAGNUM — same as 721ADL Mag., select wood.

| | $525 | $460 | $420 | $385 | $360 | $330 | $300 |

MODEL 722(A) — short action version of 721A, .222 Rem. Mag., .243 Win., .257 Roberts, .300 Savage, or .308 cal., 7 lbs. Mfg. 1948-1962.

| | $325 | $265 | $220 | $200 | $165 | $155 | $145 |

Deduct 10% for .300 Savage cal.

Cal.'s .222 Rem. Mag. (3,803 mfg.) and .243 Win. (2,186 mfg.) are rare in this model. Add approx. 25% to above values for these cal.'s.

MODEL 722ADL — same as Model 722A, except with deluxe checkered wood.

| | $350 | $285 | $235 | $210 | $175 | $165 | $155 |

MODEL 722BDL — same as Model 722ADL, except features extra select wood.

| | $425 | $375 | $325 | $280 | $265 | $245 | $225 |

MODEL 722(A) — .222 Rem., 26 in. barrel, 5 shot. Mfg. 1950-1962.

	100%	98%	95%	90%	80%	70%	60%
	$295	$250	$220	$210	$195	$175	$165
.222ADL	$335	$290	$260	$230	$220	$205	$185
.222BDL	$350	$315	$280	$250	$230	$220	$200

Add 10% for .222 Rem. Mag.

MODEL 722A — .244 Rem., 4 shot. Mfg. 1955-1962.

	100%	98%	95%	90%	80%	70%	60%
	$295	$250	$220	$210	$195	$175	$165
.244BDL	$295	$250	$220	$210	$195	$175	$165

MODEL 725ADL BOLT ACTION — .222, .243, .244, .270,, .280, or .30-06 cal., 22 in. barrel, open sights, 4 shot, checkered Monte Carlo stock. 16,635 mfg. 1958-1961.

	100%	98%	95%	90%	80%	70%	60%
.30-06 cal.	$475	$425	$375	$350	$325	$300	$280
.270 Win.		$500	$450	$400	$375	$350	$325	$300
.280 Rem.		$625	$550	$500	$450	$400	$350	$325
.222 Rem.		$625	$525	$475	$425	$375	$350	$325

Grading	100%	98%	95%	90%	80%	70%	60%
.244 Rem.	$500	$450	$400	$375	$350	$325	$300
.243 Win.	$500	$450	$400	$375	$350	$325	$300

Caliber mfg. breakdown is as follows: 7,657 in .30-06; 2,784 in .280 Rem.; 2,818 in .270 Win.; 840 in .244 Rem.; 1,478 in .222 Rem.; 998 in .243 Win.

MODEL 725 KODIAK — .375 H&H Mag. or .458 Win. Mag. cal., 26 in. barrel, 3 shot, recoil reducer in muzzle, deluxe checkered Monte Carlo stock, black pistol grip cap and forend tip. 52 mfg. 1961 only.

	$3,000	$2,700	$2,500	$2,250	$2,000	$1,800	$1,650

Only 24 rifles in .458 Win. Mag. were mfg. and 28 rifles in .375 H&H Mag.

MODEL 600 BOLT ACTION — .222, .223 (very rare), 6mm, .243, .308, or .35 Rem. cal., 18½ in. vent rib barrel, dog leg bolt handle, checkered pistol grip stock. 94,086 were mfg. 1964-1968.

	100%	98%	95%	90%	80%	70%	60%
Reg. cal.'s	$375	$295	$250	$210	$195	$175	$155
.35 Rem.	$450	$395	$350	$320	$295	$270	$250
.222 cal.	$450	$395	$350	$320	$295	$270	$250
.223 cal.	$800	$700	$600	$500	$400	$350	$325

315 Model 600's in .223 cal. were mfg.

Model 600 Montana Centennial — 6mm Rem., 1,020 mfg. in 1964 only.

	$375	$345	$325	$300	$275	$250	$225

MODEL 600 MAGNUM — 6.5mm Rem. Mag. or .350 Rem. Mag. cal., laminated walnut/beech stock with recoil pad. Mfg. 1965-1968.

	$595	$550	$500	$460	$440	$420	$395

MODEL 600 MOHAWK — .222 Rem., .243 Win., or .308 Win. cal., this variation was a promotional model, 18½ in. barrel with no rib. 94,594 were mfg. in 1971-1979.

	$300	$265	$230	$200	$180	$160	$140

MODEL 660 BOLT ACTION — .222, 6mm, .243, or .308 cal., 20 in. barrel, open sight, dog leg bolt handle, checkered pistol grip stock, black pistol grip cap and forend tip. 50,536 were mfg. 1968-1971.

	$595	$550	$500	$460	$440	$420	$395

Add 10% for .222 Rem. cal.

.223 cal. — 227 total mfg. This cal. was never listed in a Remington catalog.

	$1,100	$875	$725	$600	$500	$400	$350

MODEL 660 MAGNUM — 6.5 Mag. or .350 Mag. cal., laminated stock and recoil pad.

	$650	$575	$500	$450	$400	$350	$300

MODEL 78 SPORTSMAN BOLT ACTION — .223 Rem., .243 Win., .270 Win., .30-06, or .308 Win. cal., 22 in. barrel, 4 shot mag., uncheckered hardwood stock, open sights, 7 lbs. Mfg. 1985-89.

	$270	$235	$210	$190	$170	$160	$150

Last Mfg.'s Sug. Retail was $333.

MODEL 700ADL DELUXE BOLT ACTION — .22-250, .222 Rem. Mag. (disc.), .25-06, 6mm (disc.), .243, .270, .30-06, .308, or 7mm Mag. cal., 20 (carbine), 22 and 24 in. barrel, open sights, 4 shot mag., checkered Monte Carlo stock. Mfg. 1962-present.

Mfg.'s Sug. Retail	$431	$355	$310	$260	$210	$175	$165	$155

Add 20% for 20 in. carbine model.

Add 50% for .222 Rem. Mag. or .280 Rem. cal. in carbine variation.

Add 15% for 7mm Rem. Mag., .264 Win. Mag., or .300 Win. Mag. cal. with stainless steel barrel (mfg. 1962-1970).

Grading	100%	98%	95%	90%	80%	70%	60%

7mm Mag.

Mfg.'s Sug. Retail	$458	$380	$320	$270	$220	$195	$170	$160

Remington, in 1987-89, introduced a Model 700 Gun Kit that enabled the owner to assemble the stock to the barreled action. All metal work is completely finished and wood finishing is all that is required. This kit was available in most popular cal.'s - last mfg.'s sug. retail price was $333 (1989). Add $20 for 7mm Rem. Mag. cal.

Model 700ADL/LS — .243 Win. (new 1989), .270 Win. (new 1989), .30-06, or 7mm Rem. Mag. cal., laminate stock with checkering. New 1988.

Mfg.'s Sug. Retail	$484	$400	$345	$275	$230	$210	$195	$165
Add $21 for 7mm Rem. Mag. cal.								

MODEL 700BDL EARLY MFG. — .222 Rem. Mag., .350 Rem. Mag., or 6.5 Rem. Mag. cal.

	$400	$375	$350	$325	$300	$275	$250

MODEL 700BDL CUSTOM DELUXE — similar to 700ADL Deluxe, except with hinged floorplate, cut skipline checkering, black pistol grip cap and forend tip, .17 Rem., .22-250, .222 Rem., .223 Rem., .243 Win., .25-06, .264 Mag. (disc.), .270 Win., .30-06, .308 Win., .35 Whelen (new 1989), 6mm Rem., 7mm Rem. Mag., 7mm-08 Rem., .300 Win. Mag., .338 Win. Mag. (new 1988), or 8mm Mag. (disc.) cal.

Mfg.'s Sug. Retail	$509	$430	$375	$325	$280	$250	$220	$195

Add $59 for left-hand model.

Add $26 for .17 Rem., 7mm Rem. Mag., .300 Win. Mag., .35 Whelen or .338 Win. Mag. cal.

Add 15% for 7mm Rem. Mag., .264 Win. Mag., or .300 Win. Mag. cal. with stainless steel barrel (mfg. 1962-1970).

.350 Rem. Mag.	$595	$495	$425	$350	$325	$300	$275
6.5mm Rem. Mag. $595	$495	$425	$350	$325	$300	$275	

Remington mfg. the Model 700BDL in .350 Rem. Mag. and 6.5mm Rem. Mag. Approx. 1,500 were assembled in 1969 only. The .350 Rem. Mag. mfg. in 1969 is 3 times rarer than the 1985 Model 700 Classic chambered for .350 Rem. Mag.

Model 700BDL Lew Horton Special Edition — .257 Roberts cal., 500 mfg. in 1990 only, first time the 700BDL has been offered in .257 Roberts cal.

	$575	$525	$450	$395	$360	$325	$280

Last Mfg.'s Sug. Retail was $580.

MODEL 700 MOUNTAIN RIFLE — .243 Win. (new 1988), .257 Roberts (new 1991) .270 Win., 7mm-08 Rem. (new 1988), .280 Rem., .30-06, .308 (new 1988), or 7 x 57mm Mauser (new 1990) cal., 22 in. tapered barrel, checkered satin finished American walnut stock with cheek piece and ebony forend, 4 shot mag., without sights, 6¾ lbs. New 1986.

Mfg.'s Sug. Retail	$517	$435	$380	$315	$275	$250	$220	$195

MODEL 700 CUSTOM KS MOUNTAIN RIFLE — .270 Win., .280 Rem., .300 Win. Mag., .300 Wby. Mag. (new 1989), .30-06, .338 Win. Mag. (new 1986), .35 Whelen (new 1989), 7mm Rem. Mag., 8mm Rem. Mag. (new 1986), or .375 H&H Mag. cal., features extra lightweight Kevlar fiber-reinforced stock — available in either right or left-hand action. New 1986.

Mfg.'s Sug. Retail	$947	$795	$695	$550	$460	$415	$385	$350

This model is available from the Custom Shop only (special order).

MODEL 700BDL VARMINT SPECIAL — .22-250, .222, .223, .25-06 (disc.), 6mm, .243, .308 Win., or 7mm-08 cal., 24 in. heavy barrel, no sights. Mfg. 1967-present.

Mfg.'s Sug. Retail	$543	$470	$415	$350	$315	$285	$265	$250

MODEL 700 SAFARI GRADE — heavier 700BDL, in .375 H&H, 8mm Rem. Mag. (new 1986), .416 Rem. Mag. (new 1989), or .458 Mag. cal., 3 shot mag., 24 in. barrel, available with either classic or Monte Carlo stock configuration. Mfg. 1962-present.

Mfg.'s Sug. Retail	$951	$795	$685	$525	$440	$415	$385	$330

Model 700 Custom KS Safari Grade — 8mm Rem. Mag., .375 H&H, .416 Rem. Mag., or .458 Win. Mag., stock made from extra lightweight Kevlar fiber, 24 in. barrel. New 1989.

Mfg.'s Sug. Retail	$1,096	$980	$825	$700	$625	$550	$485	$430

Grading	100%	98%	95%	90%	80%	70%	60%

MODEL 700 CLASSIC — similar to 700BDL, except classic straight stock, high polish bluing, has been offered in .22-250, .250 Savage (250/3000), 6mm, 7 x 57 Mauser, .243, .25-06 Rem., .257 Roberts, .264 Win. Mag., .270, .300 Wby. Mag., .30-06, 7mm Wby. Mag., .338 Win. Mag., .350 Rem. Mag., .35 Whelen, .300 H&H, or .375 H&H cal.

Mfg.'s Sug. Retail	$535	$445	$365	$300	$265	$250	$220	$195

This model is produced in limited quantities of a different caliber each year. Add premiums for several older calibers in N.I.B. condition only (including 7 x 57 Mauser, .257 Roberts, .300 H&H, and .375 H&H).

The following is a partial list of calibers offered previously and year of manufacture: 7 x 57mm (1981), .257 Roberts (1982), .300 H&H (1983), .250 Savage (1984), .350 Rem. Mag. (1985), .264 Win. Mag. (1986), .338 Win. Mag. (1987), .35 Whelen (1988), .300 Wby. Mag. (1989), .25-06 Rem. (1990), and 7mm Wby. Mag. (1991).

MODEL 700C GRADE — from custom shop, no engraving, deluxe checkered wood with rosewood forearm cap.

		$850	$775	$695	$635	$510	$440	$400

MODEL 700D PEERLESS GRADE — scroll engraving, best wood.

		$1,650	$1,400	$1,200	$1,000	$880	$825	$690

MODEL 700F PREMIER GRADE — elaborate engraving, best wood.

		$3,250	$2,750	$2,420	$2,200	$2,035	$1,870	$1,760

MODEL 700 AS — .22-250, .243 Win., .270 Win., .280 Rem., .30-06, .308 Win., 7mm Rem. Mag., or .300 Wby. Mag. cal., synthetic stock is made from Arylon resin, matte black finished stock and metal, 22 or 24 in. barrel, 6½ lbs. New 1989.

Mfg.'s Sug. Retail	$528	$445	$370	$310	$275	$250	$220	$195

Add $21 for 7mm Rem. Mag. or .300 Wby. Mag. cal.

MODEL 700 RS — .270 Win., .280 Rem., or .30-06 cal., 22 in. polished blue barrel, gray or gray camo DuPont Rynite synthetic stock with smooth cheek piece and solid recoil pad, iron sights, 7¼ lbs. Mfg. 1987-1988 only.

		$490	$440	$405	$370	$335	$310	$285

Add 10% for .280 Rem. cal.

In 1987 approx. 1,000 rifles were dual barrel marked - 7mm EXP REM .280 REM. These specimens will command a 20-40% premium.

Last Mfg.'s Sug. Retail was $547.

MODEL 700 FS — .243 Win., .270 Win., .30-06, .308 Win., or 7mm Rem. Mag. cal., 22 in. polished blue barrel, gray or gray camo Kevlar fiberglass stock with solid recoil pad, iron sights, 6¼ lbs. Mfg. 1987-1988 only.

		$530	$460	$415	$375	$335	$310	$285

Add $20 for 7mm Rem. Mag. cal. (24 in. barrel).
Last Mfg.'s Sug. Retail was $613.

MODEL 700 CUSTOM RIFLE — the Remington Custom Shop should be contacted directly (see Trademark Index) for current information regarding this model.

Mfg.'s Sug. Retail	$2,181	$1,850	$1,600	$1,200

MODEL 700 CUSTOM GRADE — special order only, grades differ in amount of engraving and type of walnut. Available as a custom order only through Remington.

Custom Grade Model I

Mfg.'s Sug. Retail	$1,314	$1,100	$925	$795

Custom Grade Model II

Mfg.'s Sug. Retail	$2,335	$1,995	$1,675	$1,295

Custom Grade Model III

Mfg.'s Sug. Retail	$3,650	$2,900	$2,150	$1,750

Custom Grade Model IV

Mfg.'s Sug. Retail	$5,695	$4,875	$4,100	$2,950

Grading	100%	98%	95%	90%	80%	70%	60%

MODEL 788 BOLT ACTION — .222, .22-250, .223, 6mm, .243, .308, .30-30, 7mm-08, or .44 Mag. cal., 22 or 24 in. barrel, open sight, plain pistol grip Monte Carlo stock. Mfg. 1967-1984.

	100%	98%	95%	90%	80%	70%	60%
Rifle	$275	$250	$225	$200	$185	$175	$160
Carbine (18 in. barrel)	$300	$250	$225	$200	$185	$175	$160

Add 10% for .44 Mag. cal.

MODEL SEVEN BOLT ACTION — compact bolt action available in .223 Rem., .243 Win., 6mm Rem., 7mm-08 Rem., or .308 Win. cal., 18½ in. barrel, 6¼ lbs., 4 or 5 shot mag., individually test fired, oil finished American walnut, 1982-present.

	100%	98%	95%	90%	80%	70%	60%
Mfg.'s Sug. Retail	$517	$435	$350	$275	$225	$205	$180	$165

All steel Model Seven's (including floor plate and trigger guard) are currently commanding a small premium.

Model Seven FS — .243 Win., 7mm-08 Rem., or .308 Win. cal., 18½ in. polished blue barrel, gray or gray camo Kevlar fiberglass stock, adj. rear sight, 5¼ lbs. Mfg. 1987-89 only.

	100%	98%	95%	90%	80%	70%	60%
	$525	$455	$415	$375	$335	$310	$285

Last Mfg.'s Sug. Retail was $600.

Model Seven Custom KS — .223 Rem. (new 1989), 7mm BR (new 1989), 7mm-08 Rem. (new 1989), .308 Win. (new 1991), .35 Rem. or .350 Rem. Mag., 20 in. barrel, synthetic Kevlar stock with solid recoil pad. New 1987.

	100%	98%	95%	90%	80%	70%	60%
Mfg.'s Sug. Retail	$947	$840	$675	$530	$475	$425	$385	$340

This model is available from the Custom Shop only (special order).

TARGET RIFLES

MODEL 40X SPORTER — .22 LR only, sporterized version of the 40X Target Rifle, 5 shot clip, custom 700 stock, a special order only gun from the factory. Rare, less than 700 mfg. 1969-1980.

	100%	98%	95%	90%	80%	70%	60%
	$1,495	$1,200	$925	$800	$720	$650	$595

This model was last listed in the 1977 Remington catalog — retail was $525.

MODEL 40X TARGET RIFLE — bolt action single shot, .22 LR, 28 in. heavy barrel, Redfield Olympic sights, scope bases, target stock, rubber butt, 12¾ lbs. Mfg. 1955-1964.

	100%	98%	95%	90%	80%	70%	60%
	$495	$395	$325	$260	$220	$190	$175
No sights	$450	$360	$295	$240	$200	$180	$165

MODEL 40X STANDARD BARREL — same as 40X Target Rifle, with lighter barrel, 10¾ lbs.

	100%	98%	95%	90%	80%	70%	60%
	$475	$380	$310	$250	$220	$190	$175
No sights	$450	$360	$295	$240	$200	$180	$165

MODEL 40X CENTERFIRE — similar to Model 40X Rim Fire, except in .222, .222 Mag., .30-06, or .308 cal. Mfg. 1961-1964.

	100%	98%	95%	90%	80%	70%	60%
	$525	$440	$360	$320	$305	$275	$250
No sights	$495	$400	$330	$290	$275	$250	$220

MODEL 40XB RANGEMASTER RIMFIRE — .22 LR, bolt action single shot, 28 in. light or heavy barrel, no sights, target stock with guide rail, rubber butt. Mfg. 1964-1974.

	100%	98%	95%	90%	80%	70%	60%
	$525	$420	$335	$275	$220	$195	$165

MODEL 40XB RANGEMASTER CENTERFIRE — over 12 cal.'s, custom made, 27½ in. barrel (current model is stainless), walnut stock, test fired. Mfg. 1964-present.

	100%	98%	95%	90%	80%	70%	60%
Mfg.'s Sug. Retail	$1,053	$930	$800	$625	$500	$410	$370	$315

Add $84 for repeater model (disc. 1989).

Add $140 for 2 oz. trigger (disc. 1989).

An International Free Rifle was also offered - only 107 were mfg. with premiums being paid.

Grading	100%	98%	95%	90%	80%	70%	60%

MODEL 40XB KEVLAR STOCKED — .220 Swift, 27¼ in. bright finished stainless steel barrel, single shot, black finish Kevlar stock, no sights, 9¾ lbs. New 1987.

Mfg.'s Sug. Retail	$1,202	$1,050	$850	$680

Add $76 for bench rest model.

Add $88 for repeater model.

Add $146 for 2 oz. trigger.

MODEL 40XB REPEATER — same as 40XB Centerfire, with 5 shot mag. Disc.

	$870	$770	$625	$500	$420	$370	$315

MODEL 40XC — 7.62 Nato, National Match Course rifle, adj. trigger pull, wood (disc. 1989) or Kevlar (standard 1990) stock.

Mfg.'s Sug. Retail	$1,278	$1,100	$910	$700

Subtract $120 for wood stock.

MODEL 40XR RIMFIRE — .22 LR, single shot bolt action, 24 in. heavy barrel, no sights, adj. butt plate and palm stop, target wood (disc. 1989) or Kevlar (standard 1990) stock. Mfg. 1974-present.

Mfg.'s Sug. Retail	$1,202	$1,050	$850	$680

Subtract $120 for wood stock.

MODEL 40XR CUSTOM SPORTER — the Remington Custom Shop should be contacted directly (see Trademark Index) for current information on this model.

Mfg.'s Sug. Retail	$2,181	$1,850	$1,600	$1,200

MODEL 40XR CUSTOM SPORTER — .22 cal. only, single shot, available on special order from Remington's custom shop only, Grades I-IV increase by amount of engraving, quality of wood, and other special order options/features. New 1986.

Custom Grade Model I

Mfg.'s Sug. Retail	$1,314	$1,100	$925	$795

Custom Grade Model II

Mfg.'s Sug. Retail	$2,335	$1,995	$1,675	$1,295

Custom Grade Model III

Mfg.'s Sug. Retail	$3,650	$2,900	$2,150	$1,750

Custom Grade Model IV

Mfg.'s Sug. Retail	$5,695	$4,875	$4,100	$2,950

MODEL 540X RIMFIRE — .22 LR, single shot bolt action, 26 in. heavy barrel, no sights, target stock, adj. butt. Mfg. 1969-1974.

	$325	$285	$250	$225	$200	$175	$150

MODEL 540XR — similar to 540X, with large position style stock with adj. butt plage. Mfg. 1974-1983.

	$350	$300	$275	$225	$200	$185	$175

SHOTGUNS

100%	98%	95%	90%	80%	70%	60%	50%	40%	30%	20%	10%

MODEL 1873 DOUBLE BARREL HAMMER — 10 or 12 ga., 28 or 30 in. decarbonized or damascus barrels, top "thumb-lever" action activated by pushing forward on opening lever, rib top marked "E. REMINGTON & SONS, ILION. N.Y.", patented AUG.8.1871, APRIL 16.1872, made in various grades, pistol grip was optional. Mfg. 1873-1878.

$1,750	$1,500	$1,200	$995	$900	$800	$700	$600	$500	$425	$350	$275

There were also a very few double rifles and combination guns (shotgun/rifle barrel) made in this model - they are very rare. Above values represent standard model without extra options.

MODEL 1882 DOUBLE BARREL — 10, 12, or 16 ga., 28, 30, or 32 in. damascus barrels, exposed "circular" hammers, checkered pistol grip stock. Approx. 7,500 mfg., 1882-1889. Higher grades will bring premiums.

Damascus Barrels

$1,700	$1,400	$1,150	$995	$900	$800	$700	$600	$500	$425	$350	$275

100%	98%	95%	90%	80%	70%	60%	50%	40%	30%	20%	10%

Steel Barrels

100%	98%	95%	90%	80%	70%	60%	50%	40%	30%	20%	10%
$2,750	$2,400	$2,175	$1,950	$1,600	$1,250	$1,100	$975	$875	$775	$675	$575

Auxiliary rifle barrel inserts were also available in this model — add 15%.

Models 1885 and 1887 were slightly improved Model 1882's available in 10, 12, or 16 ga. Sideplates are marked Remington. Values will approximate those listed above.

MODEL 1889 DOUBLE BARREL — 10, 12 or 16 ga., 28, 30, or 32 in. damascus barrels, exposed hammers, checkered pistol grip stock. Approx. 30,000 mfg., 1889-1909. Higher grades bring premium.

Damascus Barrels

100%	98%	95%	90%	80%	70%	60%	50%	40%	30%	20%	10%
$1,400	$1,150	$995	$900	$800	$700	$600	$500	$425	$350	$275	$225

Steel Barrels

100%	98%	95%	90%	80%	70%	60%	50%	40%	30%	20%	10%
$2,250	$2,000	$1,850	$1,650	$1,250	$1,100	$975	$875	$775	$675	$575	$500

Grades range from No. 1 - No. 7, No. 7 being the highest. Values above assume No. 1 or 2 grade.

MODEL NO. 3 RIDER — 10, 12, 16, 20, 24, or 28 ga., single barrel, 30 or 32 in. barrels, top lever break open, plain pistol grip stock. Mfg. 1893-1903.

100%	98%	95%	90%	80%	70%	60%	50%	40%	30%	20%	10%
$325	$290	$260	$230	$200	$170	$140	$110	$85	$65	$50	$35

MODEL NO. 9 RIDER — same as No. 3, with auto ejector. Mfg. 1902-1910.

100%	98%	95%	90%	80%	70%	60%	50%	40%	30%	20%	10%
$375	$325	$290	$260	$230	$200	$170	$140	$110	$85	$65	$50

MODEL 1894 DOUBLE BARREL — 10, 12, or 16 ga., 26-32 in. "Ordnance" steel barrels, auto ejectors, hammerless, boxlock, double triggers, checkered pistol grip stock. Over 100,000 mfg., 1894-1910.

100%	98%	95%	90%	80%	70%	60%	50%	40%	30%	20%	10%
$800	$700	$600	$550	$520	$480	$440	$395	$360	$330	$295	$260

Grades offered range from "A" (lowest) to "E" and "Special" (highest). Large premiums exist for higher grade models in excellent condition. Trap model was named either "F.E." or "C.E.O.". Values above assume "A" model (most frequently encountered specimen).

MODEL 1900 DOUBLE BARREL — improved model 1894. Mfg. 1900-1910.

100%	98%	95%	90%	80%	70%	60%	50%	40%	30%	20%	10%
$875	$750	$650	$600	$550	$520	$480	$440	$395	$360	$330	$295

Grades ranged from "K", "K.E.", or damascus "K.D." or "K.E.D.". Both steel and damascus barrels were guaranteed for nitro powder.

MODERN SHOTGUNS

Grading	100%	98%	95%	90%	80%	70%	60%

MODEL 10A SLIDE ACTION — 12 ga., 26-32 in. barrels, various chokes, takedown, plain pistol grip stock. Mfg. 1907-1929. Add 10% for 32 in. full choke barrel.

	100%	98%	95%	90%	80%	70%	60%
	$400	$330	$300	$275	$220	$165	$140

MODEL 11A AUTOLOADER 5-SHOT — 12, 16, or 20 ga., 26-32 in. barrels, takedown, various chokes, Browning type, checkered pistol stock. Approx. 300,000 mfg., 1911-1948.

	100%	98%	95%	90%	80%	70%	60%
	$330	$250	$220	$195	$165	$150	$120
Solid rib	$440	$330	$250	$220	$195	$165	$140
Vent rib	$440	$360	$335	$305	$275	$220	$165

This model was mfg. under "A - 5" patent agreements (including royalties) with Fabrique Nationale in Herstal, Belgium.

MODEL 11R RIOT GUN — same as Standard 11A, with 20 in. barrel.

	100%	98%	95%	90%	80%	70%	60%
	$330	$250	$220	$195	$165	$150	$120

MODEL 11B SPECIAL — higher grade wood, engraved.

	100%	98%	95%	90%	80%	70%	60%
	$525	$440	$385	$360	$305	$250	$195

MODEL 11D TOURNAMENT

	100%	98%	95%	90%	80%	70%	60%
	$1,100	$880	$715	$550	$495	$470	$440

Grading	100%	98%	95%	90%	80%	70%	60%
MODEL 11E EXPERT							
	$1,540	$1,265	$990	$770	$660	$605	$550
MODEL 11F PREMIER							
	$2,750	$2,200	$1,650	$1,100	$990	$935	$770

Note: Grades differ in quality, grade of wood, and amount of engraving.

SPORTSMAN SKEET MODEL — 12, 16, or 20 ga., 26 in. barrel, skeet choke, beavertail forend. Mfg. 1931-1949.

	100%	98%	95%	90%	80%	70%	60%
	$385	$305	$275	$250	$195	$165	$140
Solid rib	$470	$415	$330	$275	$220	$195	$165
Vent rib	$470	$415	$360	$330	$275	$250	$220

MODEL 17A SLIDE ACTION — 20 ga., 26-32 in. barrels, various chokes, takedown, bottom ejection, 4 shot mag., plain grip stock. Approx. 48,000 mfg., 1917-1933.

	100%	98%	95%	90%	80%	70%	60%
Plain barrel	$330	$250	$220	$195	$165	$140	$110
Vent rib	$495	$440	$380	$335	$290	$250	$210

Grades range from A - F in suffix form, F being the highest. Large premiums are paid for mint condition, higher grade models.

MODEL 29A SLIDE ACTION — 12 ga., 26-32 in. barrels, bottom ejection, various chokes, takedown, 5 shot mag., checkered pistol grip stock. Approx. 24,000 mfg., 1929-1933. Add 15% for solid rib, 25% for vent rib.

	100%	98%	95%	90%	80%	70%	60%
	$305	$220	$195	$165	$150	$120	$100
30 and 32 in. barrels							
	$525	$475	$425	$350	$250	$200	$180

Grades range from A - C and TA - TF, lowest to highest. Premiums exist for finer condition upper grades. The Model 29 was similar in appearance to the Model 10.

MODEL 29S — "Trap Special" with trap style straight grip stock, matted rib.

	100%	98%	95%	90%	80%	70%	60%
	$385	$305	$275	$250	$195	$165	$140

MODEL 31A SLIDE ACTION — 12, 16, or 20 ga., side ejection, 2 or 4 shot mag., 26-32 in. barrels, various chokes, takedown, pistol grip stock. Approx. 160,000 mfg., 1931-1949.

	100%	98%	95%	90%	80%	70%	60%
	$415	$360	$320	$280	$240	$200	$160
Solid rib	$480	$400	$360	$320	$280	$240	$200
Vent rib	$515	$450	$395	$360	$320	$270	$235

Grades range from A - F suffixes. Higher grades will bring considerable premiums in excellent condition. TC suffix is Target Model. A Model 31L (lightweight) was mfg. 1948-1950 and while rare, premiums for this variation are small.

MODEL 31R RIOT GUN — same as 31A, with 20 in. barrel.

	100%	98%	95%	90%	80%	70%	60%
	$330	$250	$200	$175	$150	$130	$110

MODEL 31 SPECIAL — higher grade wood and engraving.

	100%	98%	95%	90%	80%	70%	60%
	$650	$550	$440	$385	$360	$305	$275

MODEL 31 TOURNAMENT

	100%	98%	95%	90%	80%	70%	60%
	$1,100	$880	$715	$580	$525	$495	$470

MODEL 31E EXPERT

	100%	98%	95%	90%	80%	70%	60%
	$1,320	$1,100	$935	$880	$770	$660	$605

MODEL 31F PREMIER

	100%	98%	95%	90%	80%	70%	60%
	$2,420	$1,980	$1,760	$1,540	$1,320	$1,100	$880

Note: Grades differ in quality, grade of wood, and amount of engraving.

MODEL 31TC TRAP — same as 31A, with 12 ga. only, 30 or 32 in. barrel, vent rib, full choke, trap stock and beavertail forend, pad.

	100%	98%	95%	90%	80%	70%	60%
	$660	$550	$495	$470	$415	$385	$305

Grading	100%	98%	95%	90%	80%	70%	60%

MODEL 31S TRAP — solid rib barrel, plainer wood.

	100%	98%	95%	90%	80%	70%	60%
	$495	$415	$385	$330	$275	$250	$220

MODEL 31H HUNTER — same as 31S, with sporter stock.

	100%	98%	95%	90%	80%	70%	60%
	$470	$385	$360	$305	$250	$220	$195

MODEL 31 SKEET — same as 31A, with 26 in. skeet bored barrel, standard solid rib, beavertail forend.

	100%	98%	95%	90%	80%	70%	60%
	$495	$415	$385	$330	$275	$250	$220
Vent rib	$605	$495	$445	$415	$360	$305	$275

SHOTGUNS: MODEL 870 SERIES

3 in. shells (12 or 20 ga.) may be shot in Magnum receivers only regardless of what the barrel markings may indicate (the ejection port is larger in these Magnum models with M suffix serialization).

MODEL 870AP SLIDE ACTION — "Wingmaster", 12, 16, or 20 ga., 26, 28, or 30 in. barrel, 5 shot, various chokes, plain pistol grip stock. Mfg. 1950-1963.

	100%	98%	95%	90%	80%	70%	60%
	$220	$195	$175	$165	$140	$120	$110
Matted top barrel	$230	$205	$185	$175	$150	$130	$120
Vent rib	$250	$220	$200	$195	$165	$150	$140

In 1959 "Sun Grain" blonde wood became an option.

MODEL 870DL — deluxe checkered version of 870AP. Mfg. 1950-1963.

	100%	98%	95%	90%	80%	70%	60%
	$250	$220	$200	$180	$165	$140	$120
Vent rib	$275	$250	$220	$210	$195	$165	$140

MODEL 870BDL — select walnut stock.

	100%	98%	95%	90%	80%	70%	60%
	$275	$250	$220	$200	$180	$165	$140
Vent rib	$305	$275	$250	$220	$210	$195	$165

SPORTSMAN PUMP — 12 ga. only (3 in. chamber), 28 or 30 in. barrel, recoil pad, vent rib standard, hardwood stock and forearm, Model 870 type action, 7½ lbs. Mfg. 1985-86 only.

	100%	98%	95%	90%	80%	70%	60%
	$225	$195	$180	$165	$150	$140	$130

Add $35 for Rem. chokes
Last Mfg.'s Sug. Retail was $270.

MODEL 870 EXPRESS — 12 ga. only (3 in. chamber), 28 in. VR Rem. choked (supplied with Mod. choke) barrel, parkerized metal, matte finished hardwood stock and forearm, solid recoil pad, 7¼ lbs. New 1987.

	100%	98%	95%	90%	80%	70%	60%
Mfg.'s Sug. Retail $263	$225	$190	$165	$150	$140	$130	$125

Add $95 for Combo package (extra 20 in. IC barrel).

Model 870 Express Deer Gun — 12 ga. only, 20 in. IC choked barrel with rifle sights, Monte Carlo stock. Introduced in 1991.

	100%	98%	95%	90%	80%	70%	60%
Mfg.'s Sug. Retail $255	$220	$190	$165	$150	$140	$130	$125

Add $78 for cantilever scope system and IC Rem. choke.

Model 870 Express Home Security — 12 ga. only, 18 in. cyl. choked barrel with bead sights. Introduced in 1991.

	100%	98%	95%	90%	80%	70%	60%
Mfg.'s Sug. Retail $255	$220	$190	$165	$150	$140	$130	$125

MODEL 870 FIELD WINGMASTER — same as 870AP, with checkering, incorporates twin slide rails, 3 in. chambers became standard in 1985, Rem. chokes became standard in 1987, a choice of high gloss or satin wood finish became available in 1991. Mfg. 1964-present.

	100%	98%	95%	90%	80%	70%	60%
Solid rib	$250	$225	$205	$190	$175	$160	$150

Vent rib — became standard in 1985.

	100%	98%	95%	90%	80%	70%	60%
Mfg.'s Sug. Retail $450	$350	$275	$240	$200	$185	$170	$160

Subtract $45 without Rem. chokes.

Add $59 for left-hand model (12 ga. only).

Grading	100%	98%	95%	90%	80%	70%	60%

MODEL 870 MAGNUM DUCK GUN — 3 in. chamber, 12 or 20 ga., 26, 28, or 30 in. full or mod. barrel, recoil pad. Mfg. 1964-present. 3 in. chambers became standard on all Model 870's starting in 1985. Rem. chokes became standard 1987 (introduced 1986 as $40 option).

Mfg.'s Sug. Retail	$450	$350	$275	$240	$200	$185	$170	$160

Subtract $45 without Rem. chokes.

870 Special Purpose Mag. — 12 ga. only, differs only in that metal parts are sand blasted and wood has low lustre finish, 26 or 28 in. VR barrel. Rem. chokes were introduced 1986.

Mfg.'s Sug. Retail	$450	$350	$275	$240	$200	$185	$170	$160

Subtract $45 without Rem. chokes.

SMALL GAUGE MODEL 870 — scaled down 870, in 28 or .410 ga., 25 in. barrel. Mfg. 1969-present. Vent rib became standard 1984.

Mfg.'s Sug. Retail	$497	$395	$340	$285	$240	$200	$185	$170

Subtract $40 without vent rib.

MODEL 870 LIGHTWEIGHT — 20 ga. only, lighter and shorter mahogany stock, 23 in. barrel. Mfg. 1972-1983.

	$270	$230	$210	$190	$175	$165	$155

Add $30 for vent rib.

Model 870 Youth — similar to Model 870 Lightweight, except has 1 in. shorter stock and 21 in. barrel only.

Mfg.'s Sug. Retail	$263	$230	$200	$180	$165	$150	$140	$130

MODEL 870 SPECIAL FIELD — 12 or 20 ga., lighter straight grip stock with solid recoil pad, 21 in. VR barrel. New 1984. Rem. chokes became standard 1987 (introduced 1986 as $40 option). 6¼ or 7 lbs.

Mfg.'s Sug. Retail	$450	$365	$315	$265	$230	$210	$190	$175

Subtract $45 without Rem. chokes.

MODEL 870 LIGHTWEIGHT MAGNUM — 20 ga., 3 in. chamber, 26 or 28 in. barrel, 6 lbs. Mfg. 1972-present. Rem. chokes became standard 1987.

Mfg.'s Sug. Retail	$450	$365	$320	$260	$225	$200	$175	$160

Subtract $45 without Rem. chokes.

Subtract $40 without vent rib.

MODEL 870 SPECIAL PURPOSE SYNTHETIC — 12 ga. only, 21, 26, or 28 in. VR Rem-choke barrel, synthetic stock and forearm. Introduced in 1991.

Mfg.'s Sug. Retail	$344	$290	$265	$225	$200	$170	$150	$130

Add $14 for 21 in. turkey barrel.

MODEL 870 RIOT — 12 ga. only, 18 or 20 in. barrel, choice of blue or parkerized metal finish.

Mfg.'s Sug. Retail	$355	$295	$265	$225	$200	$170	$150	$130

Add $19 for police rifle sights (20 in. barrel only).

MODEL 870 STANDARD DEER GUN — 12 or 20 ga., 20 in. imp. cyl. with rifle sights, 3 in. chamber standard for 1985, normal bluing with satin finished wood.

Mfg.'s Sug. Retail	$438	$350	$300	$260	$225	$195	$180	$165

Subtract $27 for 20 ga.

Add $55 for left-hand model.

Add $31 for 12 ga. with Rem. choke.

Add $58 for cantilever scope mount system, sling, and swivels.

MODEL 870 DEER BRUSHMASTER — 12 or 20 ga., 20 in. barrel, rifle sights, checkered, recoil pad, 3 in. chamber standard for 1985. Disc. 1988.

	$330	$295	$250	$230	$210	$200	$190

Add $40 for left-hand model (disc.).

Subtract $16 for 20 ga.

Last Mfg.'s Sug. Retail was $381.

Grading	100%	98%	95%	90%	80%	70%	60%

MODEL 870 SPECIAL PURPOSE DEER GUN — 12 ga. only, 3 in. chamber, 20 in. Rem. choke barrel, satin finished stock and forearm, matte black metal, rifle sights, 7¼ lbs. New 1989.

Mfg.'s Sug. Retail	$438	$310	$265	$225	$195	$175	$170	$165

Add $58 for cantilever scope mount system.

MODEL 870 D-GRADE (TOURNAMENT) — custom order only, any gauge. Mfg. 1950-present.

Mfg.'s Sug. Retail	$2,383	$1,995	$1,600	$1,200

MODEL 870 F-GRADE (PREMIER) — custom order only, any gauge. Mfg. 1950-present.

Mfg.'s Sug. Retail	$4,910	$4,275	$3,450	$2,500

MODEL 870 F-GRADE W/GOLD (GOLD PREMIER) — with gold inlays, custom order only. Mfg. 1950-present.

Mfg.'s Sug. Retail	$7,364	$6,600	$3,850	$2,950

Note: Grades differ in quality, grade of wood, and amount of engraving.

MODEL 870 DUCKS UNLIMITED — "DU" in serial number, disc.

	$335	$270	$195

Remington has offered many variations of the Model 870 specifically manufactured according to individual DU chapter specifications. The price of a DU 870 varies substantially from the "DU point of purchase" to real market conditions. When contemplating a DU gun it is always important to know how many of that particular variation were manufactured. The Remington factory normally has this information unless the special DU work was subcontracted elsewhere. While most DU guns are good vehicles for fund raising, their collectability to date has been minimal. Actual market conditions indicate that unless production is truly limited, most DU firearms sell very close to the model it was derived from. Also, any collectability that does exist is for 100% guns new in the box with warranty papers. Used DU guns have values comparable to the standard model from which they are derived.

In addition to regular DU guns, Remington has also produced special editions including the 1982 Mississippi Edition (dinner gun) and a 1974 DU (dinner gun — first 500 mfg.). These were rarer DU shotguns, and current values could vary significantly.

MODEL 870 SKEET — 12 ga., 26 in. vent rib skeet bore barrel. Mfg. 1950-1981.

	$295	$260	$230	$215	$200	$185	$170

MODEL 870 SKEET CASED SET — .410 or 28 ga. Mfg. 1,503 sets, 1969 only.

	$995	$850	$700	$650	$620	$575	$530

MODEL 870TA TRAP — 12 ga. trap model, deluxe walnut, vent rib. Add $15 for Monte Carlo stock. Disc. 1986.

	$365	$345	$280	$240	$220	$200	$180

Last Mfg.'s Sug. Retail was $430.

MODEL 870TB TRAP — same as 870, with 28 or 30 in. vent rib full choke barrel, trap stock, recoil pad. Mfg. 1950-1981.

	$395	$355	$285	$245	$220	$200	$185

MODEL 870TC TRAP — higher grade walnut and special VR, Rem. chokes became standard 1987.

Mfg.'s Sug. Retail	$612	$500	$415	$325	$275	$240	$220	$200

Add $14 for Monte Carlo stock.

Subtract $35 if without Rem. chokes.

COMPETITION TRAP — 12 ga. competition model, reduced recoil, special checkered walnut, vent rib. Disc. 1986.

	$575	$545	$390	$320	$280	$240	$210

Last Mfg.'s Sug. Retail was $680.

Grading	100%	98%	95%	90%	80%	70%	60%

MODEL 870 ALL AMERICAN TRAP — 30 in. full choke barrel, engraved receiver, trigger guard and barrel, deluxe trap stock. Approx. 1,000 mfg., 1972-1976.

	100%	98%	95%	90%	80%	70%	60%
	$795	$700	$650	$605	$495	$440	$385

MODEL SPORTSMAN - 48 SEMI-AUTO — 12, 16, or 20 ga., 26, 28, or 32 in. barrels, 3 shot, mechanical (solid breech) ejection system, various chokes, rounded receiver, checkered pistol grip stock. Approx. 275,000 mfg., 1949-1959.

	100%	98%	95%	90%	80%	70%	60%
	$310	$250	$220	$200	$175	$165	$140
Matted top barrel	$320	$265	$240	$220	$200	$175	$150
Vent rib	$360	$305	$275	$255	$230	$195	$165

Differs from Model 11-48 in that forearm sides have longitudinal grooves and also has capped grips.

MODEL 48B SELECT

	100%	98%	95%	90%	80%	70%	60%
	$420	$360	$310	$290	$245	$220	$195

MODEL 48D TOURNAMENT

	100%	98%	95%	90%	80%	70%	60%
	$1,100	$825	$715	$660	$605	$440	$415

MODEL 48F PREMIER

	100%	98%	95%	90%	80%	70%	60%
	$2,420	$2,035	$1,540	$1,210	$990	$770	$715

MODEL 48A RIOT GUN — 12 ga. only, 20 in. plain barrel.

	100%	98%	95%	90%	80%	70%	60%
	$275	$220	$195	$165	$150	$140	$110

MODEL 48SA SKEET — 26 in. barrel, skeet bore, ivory bead. Mfg. 1949-1960.

	100%	98%	95%	90%	80%	70%	60%
	$305	$275	$255	$230	$210	$195	$165
With vent rib	$360	$310	$285	$260	$230	$210	$195

MODEL 48SC TARGET

	100%	98%	95%	90%	80%	70%	60%
	$385	$360	$330	$305	$275	$250	$220

MODEL 48SD TOURNAMENT

	100%	98%	95%	90%	80%	70%	60%
	$1,100	$825	$715	$660	$605	$440	$415

MODEL 48SF PREMIER

	100%	98%	95%	90%	80%	70%	60%
	$2,200	$1,925	$1,650	$1,210	$990	$770	$715

MODEL 11-48 SEMI-AUTO — 12, 16, 20, 28 (introduced 1952), or .410 (introduced 1954) ga., recoil operated action, walnut stock. Approx. 429,000 mfg., 1949-1968.

	100%	98%	95%	90%	80%	70%	60%
	$280	$250	$215	$185	$175	$160	$150

Add 15% - 40% for 28 and .410 ga.'s, $40 for vent rib.

MODEL 58ADL "SPORTSMAN - 58" SEMI-AUTO — 12, 16, or 20 ga., 26, 28, or 30 in. barrel, gas operation, various chokes, 3 shot, checkered pistol grip stock, scroll game scene engraved. Approx. 271,000 mfg., 1956-1963.

	100%	98%	95%	90%	80%	70%	60%
	$305	$275	$250	$220	$195	$140	$120
With vent rib	$360	$305	$275	$250	$220	$165	$140

MODEL 58BDL — same as 58ADL, with select wood.

	100%	98%	95%	90%	80%	70%	60%
	$360	$330	$305	$275	$220	$195	$165
With vent rib	$415	$360	$330	$305	$275	$220	$195

MODEL 58SA SKEET GUN — same as 58ADL, with 26 in. skeet bore vent rib barrel, skeet stock.

	100%	98%	95%	90%	80%	70%	60%
	$360	$330	$305	$275	$220	$195	$165

MODEL 58SC TARGET

	100%	98%	95%	90%	80%	70%	60%
	$495	$440	$415	$385	$330	$305	$275

MODEL 58D TOURNAMENT

	100%	98%	95%	90%	80%	70%	60%
	$825	$715	$635	$580	$525	$470	$440

Grading	100%	98%	95%	90%	80%	70%	60%

MODEL 58SF PREMIER

	100%	98%	95%	90%	80%	70%	60%
	$1,650	$1,375	$1,210	$1,045	$965	$880	$800

Note: Models differ in grade of wood, and amount of engraving.

MODEL 878A "AUTOMASTER" — 12 ga. gas operated semi-auto, 26, 28, or 30 in. barrels, action similar to Model 58. Approx. 62,000 mfg., 1959-1962. Add 15% for vent rib.

	100%	98%	95%	90%	80%	70%	60%
	$250	$220	$195	$170	$160	$150	$135

Barrels on this model are interchangeable with those on the Model 58.

SPORTSMAN SEMI-AUTO — 12 ga. only, 2¾ in. chamber, 28 or 30 in. barrel, Model 1100 style action, vent rib standard, hardwood stock and forearm, 7¾ lbs. Mfg. 1985-86 only. Add $40 for Rem. chokes (new 1986).

	100%	98%	95%	90%	80%	70%	60%
	$300	$260	$220	$195	$170	$160	$150

Last Mfg.'s Sug. Retail was $405.

SHOTGUNS: MODEL 1100 SERIES

3 in. shells (12 or 20 ga.) may be shot in Magnum receivers only regardless of what the barrel markings may indicate (the ejection port is larger in these Magnum models with M suffix serialization).

MODEL 1100 SEMI-AUTO FIELD — 12 (disc. 1987), 16 (disc.), or 20 ga., 26, 28, or 30 in. barrels, various chokes, gas operated, checkered pistol grip stock. Mfg. 1963-1988. Rem. chokes became standard 1987 (introduced 1986 as $40 option). In 1985, vent ribs became standard on this model. Prices below assume vent rib and Rem. chokes.

	100%	98%	95%	90%	80%	70%	60%
	$395	$320	$275	$255	$220	$200	$180

Subtract $40 if without vent rib.
Subtract $45 if without Rem. chokes.
Last Mfg.'s Sug. Retail was $545.

This model is currently produced only in a Lightweight or Mag. 20 (3 in. chamber), 28, or .410 ga., since the release of the Model 11-87.

MODEL 1100 SPECIAL FIELD — 12 or 20 ga., 21 in. VR barrel, various chokes, gas operated, checkered straight grip stock, vent rib standard, a high gloss wood finish option became available in 1991 at N/C. New 1984. Rem. chokes became standard in 1987.

Mfg.'s Sug. Retail	100%	98%	95%	90%	80%	70%	60%
$588	$455	$385	$325	$265	$230	$210	$180

Subtract $45 if without Rem. chokes.

MODEL 1100 SMALL GAUGE — 28 or .410 ga., 25 in. barrel, scaled down receiver, skeet and field chokes, vent rib standard. Mfg. 1969-present.

Mfg.'s Sug. Retail	100%	98%	95%	90%	80%	70%	60%
$632	$500	$400	$350	$285	$250	$225	$200

MODEL 1100 LT-20 (LIGHTWEIGHT) — same as 1100, 20 ga. only, with mahogany stock and lightened receiver, 21, 26, or 28 in. barrel, vent rib became standard 1985, 6½ lbs.

Mfg.'s Sug. Retail	100%	98%	95%	90%	80%	70%	60%
$588	$455	$385	$325	$265	$225	$200	$180

Subtract $40 if without vent rib.

Model 1100 Youth — similar to Model 1100 Lightweight, except stock is 1 in. shorter and 21 in. barrel only.

Mfg.'s Sug. Retail	100%	98%	95%	90%	80%	70%	60%
$575	$440	$365	$300	$255	$220	$200	$180

MODEL 1100 LIGHTWEIGHT MAGNUM — chambered for 3 in. 20 ga. Mag., vent rib standard, Rem. chokes became standard 1987.

Mfg.'s Sug. Retail	100%	98%	95%	90%	80%	70%	60%
$588	$455	$385	$325	$265	$225	$200	$180

Subtract $40 if without vent rib.

Grading	100%	98%	95%	90%	80%	70%	60%

MODEL 1100 MAGNUM DUCK GUN — same as 1100, in 12 (disc. 1987) or 20 ga., 3 in. chamber, recoil pad, vent rib became standard 1984. Mfg. 1963-1988. Rem. chokes became standard 1987.

	$400	$325	$280	$260	$220	$200	$180

Add $80 for left-hand model (disc. 1986).

Subtract $40 if without vent rib.

Subtract $45 if without Rem. chokes.

Last Mfg.'s Sug. Retail was $533.

Model 1100 Magnum Special Purpose (SP) — 12 ga. only, low lustre finish on stock and forearm, sand blasted metal parts. Mfg. 1985-86 only. Add $40 for Rem. chokes (new 1986).

	$365	$300	$275	$255	$220	$200	$180

Last Mfg.'s Sug. Retail was $550.

MODEL 1100 "1 OF 3,000" FIELD — 12 ga. only, limited edition, serial numbered 1-3,000, deluxe walnut, gold washed etched hunting scenes on receiver, 28 in. modified vent rib barrel. Mfg. 1980.

	$1,100	$900	$600	$500	$425	$350	$300

MODEL 1100 DEER GUN — 12 (disc. 1987) or 20 ga., 20 (disc.), 21 in. (20 ga. only) or 22 (disc.) in. imp. cyl. barrel with rifle sights.

Mfg.'s Sug. Retail	$531	$400	$330	$270	$225	$200	$185	$165

Add $80 for left-hand model (disc. 1986).

Model 1100 Special Purpose Deer (SP) — similar to Model 1100 Deer Gun, except has low lustre finish on stock and forearm, sandblasted metal parts. Mfg. 1986 only.

	$335	$295	$275	$255	$220	$200	$180

Last Mfg.'s Sug. Retail was $495.

MODEL 1100 LT-20 (TOURNAMENT SKEET) — 12 (disc. 1987) or 20 ga., 26 in. skeet bored barrel, optional Cutts Compensator. Mfg. 1963-present.

Mfg.'s Sug. Retail	$669	$495	$425	$375	$325	$275	$225	$200

Add $40 for left-hand model (disc.1986).

MODEL 1100 SMALL GAUGE TOURNAMENT SKEET — 20, 28 or .410 ga., 25 in. vent. rib barrel, 6½-7¼ lbs. Mfg. 1969-present.

Mfg.'s Sug. Retail	$669	$495	$425	$375	$325	$275	$225	$200

MODEL 1100 SKEET CASED SET — 28 and .410 ga.'s, walnut stock and forearm. 5,067 cased Skeet sets were mfg. 1969 and 1970 only.

	$1,125	$950	$800	$725	$675	$630	$600

MODEL 1100 150TH ANNIVERSARY — limited mfg. in 1966 only.

	$400	$340	$290	$270	$240	$220	$200

MODEL 1100TA TRAP — 12 ga., 30 in. barrel, recoil pad on regular stock, available in left or right-hand. Mfg. 1979-86.

	$410	$330	$295	$270	$230	$210	$190

Add $15 for Monte Carlo stock.

Add $50 for left-hand model.

Last Mfg.'s Sug. Retail was $570.

MODEL 1100TB TRAP — 12 ga., 30 in. vent rib full choke barrel, special trap stock, select wood. Mfg. 1963-1981.

	$435	$350	$300	$270	$230	$210	$190
Monte Carlo stock	$450	$360	$310	$280	$235	$220	$195

MODEL 1100 TOURNAMENT TRAP — 12 ga., 30 in. vent rib full choke barrel, special trap stock, extra select wood. Mfg. 1979-86.

	$540	$480	$390	$345	$295	$255	$210

Add $15 for Monte Carlo stock.

Last Mfg.'s Sug. Retail was $675.

Grading	100%	98%	95%	90%	80%	70%	60%

MODEL 1100 DUCKS UNLIMITED — "DU" in serial number.

Remington has offered many variations of the Model 1100 specifically manufactured according to individual DU chapter specifications. The price of a DU 1100 varies substantially from the "DU point of purchase" to real market conditions. When contemplating a DU gun it is always important to know how many of that particular variation were manufactured. The Remington factory normally has this information unless the special DU work was subcontracted elsewhere. While most DU guns are good vehicles for fund raising, their collectability to date has been minimal. Actual market conditions indicate that unless production is truly limited, most DU firearms sell very close to the model it was derived from. Also, any collectability that does exist is for 100% guns new in the box with warranty papers. Used DU guns have values comparable to the standard model from which they are derived.

In addition to regular DU guns, Remington has also produced special editions including the 1982 Atlantic Flyway (dinner gun) and a 1981 DU Lt. 20 ga. and 12 ga. (dinner gun — 2,400 mfg. each), and a 1973 dinner gun (600 mfg.). These were rarer DU shotguns, and current values could vary significantly.

MODEL 1100 D-GRADE (TOURNAMENT) — custom order only, any gauge. Mfg. 1963-present.

Mfg.'s Sug. Retail	$2,383	$1,995	$1,600	$1,200			

MODEL 1100 F-GRADE (PREMIER) — custom order only, any gauge. Mfg. 1963-present.

Mfg.'s Sug. Retail	$4,910	$4,275	$3,450	$2,500			

MODEL 1100 F-GRADE W/GOLD (GOLD PREMIER) — with gold inlay, custom order only. Mfg. 1963-present.

Mfg.'s Sug. Retail	$7,364	$6,600	$3,850	$2,950			

Note: Grades differ in quality, grade of wood, and amount of engraving.

MODEL 11-87 PREMIER — 12 ga. only (3 in. chamber), 26, 28, or 32 in. VR Rem. choked barrel, successor to Model 1100, gas compensating action adaptable to all loads, stainless steel magazine tube, polished blue finish, satin finished and checkered walnut stock and forearm, a high gloss wood finish option became available in 1991 at N/C, solid recoil pad, 8⅛-8⅜ lbs. Introduced 1987.

Mfg.'s Sug. Retail	$605	$495	$415	$335	$285	$240	$220	$200

Add $55 for left-hand action.

Note: Model 11-87 Premier barrels are not interchangeable with Model 1100 barrels.

MODEL 11-87 SPECIAL PURPOSE — 12 ga. only (3 in. chamber), 26 or 30 in. VR Rem. choked barrel, parkerized metal with matte finish stock and forearm, vent recoil pad, includes camouflaged nylon sling, 8¼ lbs. New 1987.

Mfg.'s Sug. Retail	$605	$495	$415	$335	$285	$240	$220	$200

MODEL 11-87 SPECIAL PURPOSE SYNTHETIC — 12 ga. only, 21, 26, or 28 in. VR Rem-choke barrel, synthetic stock and forearm. Introduced in 1991.

Mfg.'s Sug. Retail	$605	$495	$415	$335	$285	$240	$220	$200

Add $13 for 21 in. turkey barrel.

MODEL 11-87 SPECIAL PURPOSE DEER GUN — 12 ga. only (3 in. chamber), 21 in. IC or Rem. choked barrel with rifle sights, parkerized metal with matte finished stock and forearm, vent recoil pad, includes camouflaged nylon sling, 7¼ lbs. New 1987.

Mfg.'s Sug. Retail	$585	$475	$390	$320	$270	$240	$220	$200

Add $53 for cantilever scope mount system.

Subtract $40 for fixed choke barrel.

Rem. chokes became standard on this model in 1989.

MODEL 11-87 PREMIER SKEET — 12 ga. only, 26 in. VR Rem. choked barrel, deluxe walnut with quality cut checkering, 7¾ lbs. New 1987.

Mfg.'s Sug. Retail	$661	$525	$440	$350	$295	$250	$225	$200

Add $65 for left-hand action.

Subtract $40 if without Rem. chokes.

Grading	100%	98%	95%	90%	80%	70%	60%

MODEL 11-87 PREMIER TRAP — 12 ga. only, 30 in. raised VR Rem. choked barrel, deluxe walnut with quality cut checkering, 8¼ lbs. New 1987.

Mfg.'s Sug. Retail	$669	$525	$400	$325	$285	$240	$215	$195

Add $66 for left-hand action.

Add $15 for Monte Carlo stock.

Subtract $40 if without Rem. chokes.

MODEL 11-87 175TH ANNIVERSARY — 12 ga. only, 28 in. barrel with Rem-chokes, 175th Anniversary Model (1816-1991) with light engraving and high gloss wood finish. 1991 mfg. only.

Mfg.'s Sug. Retail	$618	$515	$425	$335

MODEL 11-87 D-GRADE (TOURNAMENT) — custom order only, any gauge. Mfg. 1963-present.

Mfg.'s Sug. Retail	$2,383	$1,995	$1,600	$1,200

MODEL 11-87 F-GRADE (PREMIER) — custom order only, any gauge. Mfg. 1963-present.

Mfg.'s Sug. Retail	$4,910	$4,275	$3,450	$2,500

MODEL 11-87 F-GRADE W/GOLD (GOLD PREMIER) — with gold inlay, custom order only. Mfg. 1963-present.

Mfg.'s Sug. Retail	$7,364	$6,600	$3,850	$2,950

Note: Grades differ in quality, grade of wood, and amount of engraving.

MODEL SP-10 — 10 ga., 3½ in. chamber, semi-auto stainless steel gas system operation, lighter recoil than most 12 ga. Mag.'s, 26 or 30 in. barrel with ⅜ in. VR and Rem. chokes (2), checkered stock and forearm with low gloss satin finish, metal is matte finished, crossbolt safety, recoil pad, supplied with camo sling, approx. 11 lbs. Introduced 1989.

Mfg.'s Sug. Retail	$1,265	$1,175	$1,000	$900	$800	$725	$650	$595

The first 5,000 SP-10's were assigned special serialization (LE89 prefix) and will no doubt command premiums shortly.

This model is NOT a re-designed Ithaca Mag-10 and the parts are NOT interchangeable. The SP-10 is a new design.

Model SP-10 Turkey Combo — includes choice of either 26 or 30 VR regular barrel and extra 22 in. deer barrel with rifle sights. New in 1991.

Mfg.'s Sug. Retail	$1,163	$1,050	$950	$850	$750	$675	$625	$575

SHOTGUNS: SIDE-BY-SIDE

Remington's newly mfg. Parker Model AHE may be found in the Parker section of this text.

SHOTGUNS: OVER/UNDER

MODEL 32 — 12 ga., double lock action, SST, separated barrels, 26, 28, or 30 in. barrels with no rib, SR, or VR. Approx. 15,000 mfg., 1932-1942.

	$2,500	$2,150	$1,800	$1,600	$1,400	$1,300	$1,175

Add 15% for SST.

Add 15% for vent or solid rib.

MODEL 32D TOURNAMENT

	$3,600	$3,250	$2,875	$2,400	$2,100	$1,750	$1,400

MODEL 32E EXPERT

	$4,300	$3,750	$3,300	$2,640	$2,200	$1,875	$1,525

MODEL 32F PREMIER

	$7,000	$6,000	$5,000	$4,400	$3,520	$2,750	$2,420

Note: Grades differ in quality, grade of wood, and amount of engraving.

Grading	100%	98%	95%	90%	80%	70%	60%

MODEL 32 SKEET — same as 32A, with 26-28 in. skeet bored barrel, SST. Mfg. 1932-1942.

	$2,800	$2,475	$2,100	$1,900	$1,700	$1,500	$1,325

Add 10% for vent rib.

MODEL 32TC TARGET — same as 32A, with 30-32 in. vent rib, full choke barrels, trap style stock. Mfg. 1932-1942. Add 10% for SST.

	$3,000	$2,575	$2,200	$1,975	$1,750	$1,525	$1,325

MODEL 3200 FIELD — 12 ga., 26, 28, or 30 in. barrels, vent rib, various chokes, boxlock, auto ejectors, single selective trigger, checkered pistol grip stock, separated barrels. Mfg. 1972-1984.

	$995	$900	$825	$750	$680	$640	$560

Model 3200's with shorter barrels (26 or 28 in.) and open choking are more desirable than 30 in. tubes bored F/M.

MODEL 3200 SERIALIZATION IS AS FOLLOWS: 1973 - 4,200-16,667; 1974 - 16,668-27,393; 1975 - 27,394-35,303; 1976 - 35,304-39,216; 1977 - 39,217-41,432; 1978 - 41,433-42,813; 1979 - 42,814-44,278; 1980 - 44,279-45,504; 1981 - 45,505-45,974; 1982 - 45,975-47,200; 1983 - 47,201-47,308.

MODEL 3200 MAGNUM — 12 ga., 3 in. chambers, 30 in. barrels. Mfg. 1975-1980.

	$1,050	$925	$825	$750	$680	$640	$560

MODEL 3200 SKEET — similar to 3200 Field, with 26 or 28 in. skeet bored barrels, skeet style stock. Mfg. 1973-1980.

	$1,100	$995	$900	$825	$750	$680	$640

28 in. barrels will command a slight premium on this model.

This model was also mfg. in a 28 in. IM/F configuration for live pigeon shooting. A slight premium may be asked.

Model 3200 Four Ga. Set — includes 12, 20, 28, or .410 ga., cased.

	$4,850	$4,400	$4,000	$3,650	$3,400	$3,200	$2,950

28 in. barrels will command a slight premium on this model.

MODEL 3200 COMPETITION SKEET — similar to 3200 Skeet, with scroll engraved frame and trigger guard, select wood. Mfg. 1973-1980.

	$1,350	$1,175	$975	$875	$750	$675	$600

MODEL 3200 TRAP — similar as 3200 Field, with 30 or 32 in. barrels, trap stock. Mfg. 1973-1980.

	$1,050	$950	$850	$795	$740	$680	$640

MODEL 3200 SPECIAL TRAP — similar to 3200 Trap, except fancy wood. Mfg. 1973-1981.

	$1,150	$1,000	$900	$825	$775	$700	$650

MODEL 3200 COMPETITION TRAP — same as 3200 Trap, with scroll engraving. Mfg. 1973-1981.

	$1,250	$1,100	$950	$850	$775	$700	$650

MODEL 3200 PREMIER — 12 ga., sold through Remington's International Division, 500 mfg. 1975 only, patterned after "One of 1000" series, regular or Monte Carlo stock, 116 were engraved in Germany — add 25%+.

	$2,650	$2,200	$1,800	$1,600	$1,400	$1,250	$1,100

MODEL 3200 "ONE OF 1000" — limited edition, elaborate engraving, fancy wood, supplied in case, made in both skeet and trap models. Mfg. 1,000 each model mfg. 1973 (Trap) and 1974 (Skeet).

	100%	98%	95%	90%	80%	70%	60%
Trap	$1,800	$1,600	$1,475	$1,300	$1,200	$1,100	$875
Skeet	$1,800	$1,600	$1,475	$1,300	$1,200	$1,100	$875

28 in. barrels will command a slight premium on this model.

Grading	100%	98%	95%	90%	80%	70%	60%

RENETTE, GASTINE
Please refer to the "G" section of this text.

RHODE ISLAND ARMS COMPANY
Previous manufacturer located in Hope Valley, RI.

MORRONE O/U — 12 or 20 ga., 26 or 28 in. plain barrels, boxlock, extractors, single trigger, checkered straight or pistol grip stock. Mfg. 1949-1953, only 500 of these guns were mfg., 450 in 12 ga., and 50 in 20 ga., very few with vent rib, they are quite rare although collector interest is not overwhelming.

$1,100	$880	$770	$660	$550	$495	$440

Add 20% for 20 gauge.
Add 20% for vent rib.

RICHLAND ARMS COMPANY
Previous importer (until 1986) located in Blissfield, MI. Below listed shotguns were Spanish manufactured.

SHOTGUNS

MODEL 80 LS SINGLE SHOT — 12, 20, or .410 ga., 26 or 28 in. full choke barrel. Mfg. 1986 only.

$140	$120	$110	$100	$90	$80	$70

Last Mfg.'s Sug. Retail was $162.

MODEL 711 MAGNUM SXS — 10 ga., 3½ in. chamber, 12 ga., 3 in. chamber, 32 in. full and full, 30 in. full and full, 20, 28, and .410 ga.'s also available on special order, hammerless, boxlock, extractors, checkered, walnut stock, recoil pad. Mfg. 1963-1985 in Spain.

10 gauge	$400	$325	$275	$250	$230	$210	$190
12 gauge	$340	$295	$265	$250	$230	$210	$190
20 gauge	$450	$340	$295	$260	$230	$210	$195

MODEL 707 DELUXE SXS — 12 or 20 ga., 3 in. chambers, 26, 28, or 30 in. barrels, various chokes, boxlock, extractors, double triggers, checkered stock and forend. Mfg. 1963-1972 in Spain.

$330	$305	$290	$275	$250	$230	$210

MODEL 200 FIELD GRADE SXS — 12, 16, 20, 28, or .410 ga., 22, 26, and 28 in. barrels, various chokes, Anson & Deeley boxlock, extractors, double triggers, checkered stock, 6 lbs. 2 oz. - 7 lbs. 4 oz. Mfg. 1963-1985 in Spain.

$320	$285	$255	$225	$195	$175	$150

Last Mfg.'s Sug. Retail was $379.

MODEL 202 ALL PURPOSE — same as Field, except 2 sets of barrels, 12 and 20 ga. only. Mfg. 1963-disc. in Spain.

$305	$260	$230	$220	$195	$165	$150

MODEL 41 ULTRA O/U — 20, 28, or .410 ga., 3 in. chambers (.410 ga. only), single non-selective trigger, 26 or 28 in. barrels, extractors, vent rib, engraved silver finished receiver, select checkered walnut stock and forearm, 6 lbs. 2 oz. Importation disc. 1986.

$265	$220	$210	$200	$190	$180	$170

Last Mfg.'s Sug. Retail was $298.

MODEL 747 O/U — 20 ga. only, 3 in. chambers, boxlock action, vent rib and barrels, SST, extractors. Importation disc. 1986.

$420	$350	$325	$310	$295	$280	$265

Last Mfg.'s Sug. Retail was $464.

Grading	100%	98%	95%	90%	80%	70%	60%

MODEL 757 O/U — 12 ga., 3 in. chambers, boxlock action with Greener crossbolt, vent barrels and rib, double triggers, extractors, walnut stock and forearm, 7 lbs. 4 oz. New 1986. Add $70 for multi-chokes (Model 7570). Importation disc. 1986.

	$290	$260	$230	$215	$200	$185	$170

Last Mfg.'s Sug. Retail was $325.

MODEL 787 O/U — 12 ga. only, 3 in. chambers, boxlock action with silver finish, single trigger, vent barrels and rib, extractors, walnut stock with recoil pad, is supplied with 5 interchangeable choke tubes, 7¼ lbs. Made 1986 only.

	$435	$375	$340	$310	$295	$280	$265

Last Mfg.'s Sug. Retail was $471.

MODEL 808 O/U — 12 ga., 26, 28, or 30 in. barrels, various chokes, boxlock, extractors, checkered stock. Mfg. 1963-1968 in Italy.

	$420	$360	$330	$315	$290	$270	$230

MODEL 810 O/U — 10 ga., 3½ in. chambers, ST, extractors.

	$775	$650	$600	$550	$500	$460	$430

MODEL 828 O/U — 20 ga., single non-selective trigger, extractors, engraved, only 250 imported.

	$695	$635	$575	$510	$460	$400	$350

RIEDL RIFLE COMPANY

SINGLE SHOT RIFLE — available in any caliber, 22-30 in. barrel, rack and pinion action, lever trigger guard activated, fully adj. trigger, select walnut stock, basically custom made.

	$495	$470	$440	$415	$385	$330	$305

Stainless barrel

	$560	$535	$505	$480	$450	$395	$370

RIGBY, JOHN & CO. (GUNMAKERS), LTD.

Manufacture began in Dublin, Ireland in 1735. Hallowell & Co. is the exclusive U.S. agent/importer for J. Rigby (see Trademark Index).

The first London Branch of J. Rigby was opened in 1865 and the Dublin Premises were closed three years later. The firm became a company in 1900, and has been responsible for many of the large caliber developments in both rifles and ammunition.

Rigby is one of the world's finest weapons makers. A good portion of the guns they manufacture were custom built to customer specifications. They were chambered for the large black powder express cartridges used for dangerous game in Africa and Asia. The modern Rigby guns follow this same tradition.

We will list the modern Rigby Guns with approximate values but strongly urge that if purchase or sale is contemplated, professional appraisal be utilized.

Due to the recent devaluation of the U.S. dollar, prices may fluctuate rapidly on this trademark. Current values are based on the exchange rates at this writing ($1.92 per pound).

RIFLES: BOLT ACTION & SIDE BY SIDE

RIGBY MAGAZINE RIFLE — Mauser action (pre-1939), bolt action, various standard cal.'s including .243 Win., .270, .275 Rigby, 7mm x 57mm, .30-06, .300 H&H, .300 Win. Mag., .308, 7mm Rem. Mag., or .375 H&H, 3-5 shot mag., 20-25 in. barrel, checkered half pistol grip stock, includes non-detachable scope mounts.

Mfg.'s Sug. Retail	$6,720	$6,720	$4,750	$4,175	$3,700	$3,275	$2,850	$2,400

Add $350 for .375 H&H, .404 Rigby, or .458 Win. Mag. cal.

Add $1,920 for express sights.

Add approx. $1,825 for Mag. cal.'s.

The .416 Rigby cal. is also available on special order only — prices start at $12,480.

Grading	100%	98%	95%	90%	80%	70%	60%

Above values are minimums for the Standard Rigby bolt action rifle. The factory quotes a price range of $5,760-$11,520 depending on alternate type of action (Brno, Dakota, Dumoulin, Heym, or Ruger), the grade of wood, engraving, telescopic sight, case, or other details.

LIGHTWEIGHT MAGAZINE RIFLE — similar to Standard, with 24 in. barrel.

Mfg.'s Sug. Retail	$6,720	$6,720	$4,750	$4,175	$3,700	$3,275	$2,850	$2,400

Add $350 for .375 H&H, .404 Rigby, or .458 Win. Mag. cal.

.416 RIGBY BIG GAME MAGAZINE RIFLE — similar to Standard Rigby rifle, except is available in .375 H&H, .404 (disc.), .416 Rigby, .416 Rem. Mag., .458 Win. Mag., or .505 cal. only, modified Brno square bridge magnum action, 4 shot mag., 21-24 in. barrel, approx. 10 lbs.

Mfg.'s Sug. Retail	$8,640	$8,640	$6,125	$5,200	$4,300	$3,700	$3,000	$2,500

Add $680 for .505 cal.

.416 Rigby Deluxe Model — same cal.'s as Big Game Rifle, includes extra quality wood and special engraving.

Mfg.'s Sug. Retail	$10,560	$10,560	$8,640	$7,300	$6,125	$5,200	$4,300	$3,700

.350 MAGNUM MAGAZINE RIFLE — .350 Magnum cal.

	$3,995	$3,400	$2,950	$2,600	$2,300	$2,000	$1,700

Values assume out of production models.

SINGLE SHOT FALLING BLOCK — Farquharson lever actuated action, various English and European cal.'s, 24 in. barrel, ejector, checkered pistol grip stock, deluxe finish and engraving.

	$4,100	$3,400	$2,800	$2,400	$2,000	$1,600	$1,250

BEST QUALITY SIDELOCK EJECTOR DOUBLE RIFLE — .22 LR, .275 Mag., .350 Mag., .416, .458 Win. Mag., .465, or .470 Nitro Express cal., 24-28 in. barrels, sidelocks, folding express rear sight, checkered pistol grip stock, deluxe finish and engraving.

Mfg.'s Sug. Retail	$57,600	$57,600	$47,500	$38,000	$29,000	$24,000	$20,000	$17,500

Add $9,600 for .577 cal.

Subtract 35% without ejectors.

Rigby sidelock double rifles can instantly be recognized by their contoured sideplates.

John Rigby & Co. will also build a .600 Nitro Express — price available by quotation only.

SECOND QUALITY BOXLOCK EJECTOR DOUBLE RIFLE — same as Best Quality, with boxlock.

	$16,500	$13,000	$11,500	$9,500	$8,500	$7,500	$6,500

Subtract 35% without ejectors.

Values above are for larger calibers, smaller cal.'s could have less value than listed.

THIRD QUALITY BOXLOCK EJECTOR DOUBLE RIFLE — same as Second Quality, with plainer wood and less engraving.

	$12,750	$10,750	$9,750	$8,750	$7,350	$6,350	$5,000

Subtract 35% without ejectors.

Values above are for larger calibers, smaller cal.'s could have less value than listed.

SHOTGUNS

BOXLOCK DOUBLE BARREL SHOTGUN — all ga.'s, barrel lengths and chokes to order, checkered stock to order, auto ejectors, double triggers.

Chatsworth Grade

	$4,500	$3,500	$3,000	$2,500	$2,000	$1,600	$1,200

Sackville Grade — deluxe engraved.

	$5,900	$5,000	$4,500	$3,750	$3,100	$2,650	$2,200

20 gauge — add 20%.

28 gauge — add 40%.

.410 gauge — add 60%.

Grading	100%	98%	95%	90%	80%	70%	60%

Boxlock Game Gun — 12, 20, or 28 ga., traditional deep scroll engraving, current mfg. This is John Rigby's only current production boxlock shotgun. The factory should be contacted directly (see Trademark Index) for a price quotation on this model.

SIDELOCK DOUBLE BARREL SHOTGUN — all ga.'s, barrel lengths and chokes to specifications, double triggers, auto ejectors stocked to order.
Sandringham Grade

	$9,500	$7,500	$6,000	$5,000	$4,450	$3,775	$2,950

Regal Grade — deluxe engraved.

	$12,500	$10,000	$8,750	$7,500	$6,400	$5,250	$4,250

20 gauge — add 20%.

28 gauge — add 40%.

.410 gauge — add 60%.

Sidelock Game Gun — 12 or 20 ga., engraving similar to Best Quality SxS rifle, current mfg.

Mfg.'s Sug. Retail	$31,680	$31,680	$26,750	$21,000	$16,500	$13,000	$11,500	$9,400

Add $2,880 for self-opening system.

A matched pair of the Sidelock Game Guns starts at $65,280.

RIPAMONTI, GUY

Manufacturer located in Saint Etienne, France. Shotguns previously imported and distributed exclusively by Wes Gilpin located in Dallas, TX. Rifles imported and distributed exclusively by Morton's Limited located in Lexington, KY.

DOUBLE RIFLES

For further information regarding Ripamonti double rifles, Morton's Ltd. should be contacted directly.

MODEL SE VII SIDE BY SIDE — 9.3 X 74R cal., scalloped rounded triple Helix action, 23½ in. barrels, DT's, extensive engraving on coin finished receiver, pistol grip Monte Carlo stock. Importation began 1989.

Mfg.'s Sug. Retail	$12,333	$12,333	$9,450	$8,200	$7,250	$6,500	$5,800	$5,400

MODEL SE VIII SIDE BY SIDE — similar to Model SE IX except has pistol grip stock and more elaborate engraving with gold inlays. Importation began 1989.

Mfg.'s Sug. Retail	$16,733	$16,733	$13,950	$10,500	$9,100	$8,100	$7,250	$6,500

MODEL SE IX SIDE BY SIDE — 9.3 X 74R cal., scalloped boxlock action with triple Purdey locks, iron sights, 23½ in. barrels, extensive engraving on coin finished receiver, DT's, English straight stock. Importation began 1988.

Mfg.'s Sug. Retail	$15,304	$15,304	$12,950	$10,000	$8,750	$7,800	$7,000	$6,400

JAEGER MODEL — specially mfg. for Paul Jaeger Inc. located in Grand Junction, TN.

Mfg.'s Sug. Retail	$10,325	$10,325	$7,500	$6,725	$5,250	$4,000	$3,400	$3,000

MODEL SI IV OVER/UNDER — 9.3 X 74R cal., reinforced boxlock action, 23½ in. barrels, DT's, extensive engraving. Importation began 1989.

Mfg.'s Sug. Retail	$7,817	$7,817	$6,000	$5,200	$4,400	$3,600	$2,900	$2,300

SHOTGUNS

Ripamonti shotguns are available in 12, 16, 20, 28, or .410 ga. in boxlock actions, 12 or 20 ga. in sidelock actions.

SHOTGUNS: SIDE BY SIDE — Ripamonti S X S shotguns started at $8,490 (Model SE V boxlock) and went up to $22,490 (Model JL sidelock) depending on embellishments and other special order features. Other models included Model SE IV and Model SE VI.

Grading	100%	98%	95%	90%	80%	70%	60%

RIZZINI, BATTISTA
Manufacturer located in Marcheno, Italy since 1965.

Battista Rizzini manufactures hunting and shooting shotguns in every gauge. To date, this manufacturer has had limited importation into the U.S. More information can be obtained by writing the company directly (please refer to their listing in the Trademark Index located in the back of this text).

RIZZINI, F.LLI
Manufacturer located in Magno di Gardone V.T., Italy. Currently imported and distributed by W.L. Moore & Co. located in West Lake Village, CA and New England Arms, Co. located in Kittery Point, ME.

Rizzini shotguns are made by individual custom order only (about 25 are made a year). Prices below do not include engraving (prices range from $5,200-$11,000) and are subject to the fluctuation of the U.S. dollar.

Due to the recent devaluation of the U.S. dollar, prices may fluctuate rapidly on this trademark.

SHOTGUNS

BOXLOCK EJECTOR — 12 or 20 ga., select walnut, inspection plate, various barrel lengths.

	100%	98%	95%	90%	80%	70%	60%
Mfg.'s Sug. Retail	$19,900	$18,250	$14,200	$11,800	$9,700	$8,850	$7,100	$6,200

28 or .410 ga. — otherwise same as above.

Mfg.'s Sug. Retail	$22,000	$20,000	$15,750	$12,250	$9,995	$8,950	$7,300	$6,300

SIDELOCK EJECTOR — 12 or 20 ga., H&H patterned sidelocks, select circassian walnut, various barrel lengths.

Mfg.'s Sug. Retail	$31,500	$27,750	$22,500	$18,000	$15,700	$12,500	$10,400	$9,150

28 or .410 ga. — otherwise same as above.

Mfg.'s Sug. Retail	$35,300	$30,500	$25,000	$20,000	$16,750	$13,250	$11,200	$9,875

RIZZINI, ARMI TECNICHE OF EMILIO
Manufacturer located in Brescia, Italy.

Please refer to the Armi Tecniche of Emilio Rizzini in the A section.

ROGAK
Please refer to the L E S Incorporated listing in this text for more information on the Rogak Pistol.

ROHM
Manufacturer located in Sontheim, West Germany. Limited importation into the U.S.

DERRINGER — .22 LR, blued, copy of Remington O/U derringer. Excellently made, but half-cock safety is old design and could fail if dropped. No longer imported.

$150	$115	$95	$85	$75	$65	$55

ROSS RIFLE COMPANY
Quebec, Canada.

CANADIAN 1907 MARK II — .303 Brit. cal., bolt action, straight pull, 28 in. barrel, pre-WWII.

$295	$250	$200	$180	$160	$140	$120

Grading	100%	98%	95%	90%	80%	70%	60%

MODEL 1910 SPORTING RIFLE — similar action as 1907, .280 Ross or .303 Brit. cal., checkered Sporter stock, leaf sights. Mfg. 1910-1920.

	$275	$225	$200	$180	$160	$140	$120

Note: Many experts state this rifle is unsafe to fire.

ROSSI

Manufactured by Amade Rossi S.A., located in S. Leopoldo, Brazil. Currently imported by Interarms, located in Alexandria, VA.

REVOLVERS: DOUBLE ACTION

MODEL 31 — .38 Spl., 5 shot, 4 in. medium barrel, target trigger and hammer, 22 oz. Disc. 1985. Add $5 for nickel.

	$120	$105	$95	$85	$75	$70	$65

Last Mfg.'s Sug. Retail was $139.

MODEL 51 — .22 LR, 6 shot, 6 in. barrel, blue only, adj. sights. Disc. 1985.

	$125	$110	$100	$90	$85	$80	$75

Last Mfg.'s Sug. Retail was $149.

Sportsman 511 Stainless — .22 LR only, stainless steel, 4 in. barrel, with matted rib, adj. rear sight, 6 shot, hardwood stocks, 30 oz. Imported 1986-90 only.

	$190	$160	$125

Last Mfg.'s Sug. Retail was $235.

MODEL 68 — .38 Spl., 5 shot, 2 or 3 in. barrel.

Mfg.'s Sug. Retail	$200	$155	$125	$100	$90	$80	$70	$65

Add $10 for nickel.
Add $5 for 2 in. barrel.

MODEL 69 — .32 S&W, 6 shot, 3 in. barrel, walnut grips. Disc. 1985. Add $5 for nickel.

	$120	$105	$95	$85	$75	$70	$65

Last Mfg.'s Sug. Retail was $139.

MODEL 70 — .22 cal, 6 shot, 3 in. barrel. Disc. 1985. Add $5 for nickel.

	$120	$105	$95	$85	$75	$70	$65

Last Mfg.'s Sug. Retail was $139.

MODEL 84 STAINLESS — .38 Spl., 6 shot, 3 or 4 in. solid raised rib barrel, standard service sights, checkered hardwood grips, 27½ oz. Imported 1985-86 only.

	$190	$155	$125

Last Mfg.'s Sug. Retail was $205.

MODEL 851 STAINLESS — .38 Spl., 3 or 4 in. vent rib barrel, 6 shot, walnut grips, adj. rear sight, 27½ oz. New 1985.

Mfg.'s Sug. Retail	$260	$205	$165	$135

This model was previously the Model 85 Stainless.

MODEL 88 STAINLESS — .38 Spl., 5 shot, stainless steel construction, 2 or 3 in. barrel, hardwood grips, 21 oz.

Mfg.'s Sug. Retail	$235	$185	$140	$110

Add $5 for 2 in. barrel.

MODEL 89 STAINLESS — .32 S&W cal. only, 6 shot, 3 in. barrel. Imported 1985-86. Reintroduced 1989-90.

	$175	$135	$115

Last Mfg.'s Sug. Retail was $215.

Grading	100%	98%	95%	90%	80%	70%	60%

MODEL 94 — .38 Spl., 6 shot, 3 or 4 in. barrel, blued finish only, 27½ oz. Imported 1985-1988.

	$160	$140	$120	$110	$95	$85	$75

Last Mfg.'s Sug. Retail was $185.

MODEL 951 — .38 Spl., 6 shot, 3 or 4 in. vent. rib barrel, blued finish only, 27½ oz. Imported 1985-90.

	$190	$155	$135	$120	$110	$100	$90

Last Mfg.'s Sug. Retail was $233.

This model was previously designated the Model 95.

MODEL 971 — .357 Mag., 4 in. solid rib barrel with internal ejector shroud, 6 shot, adj. rear sight, blue only, hardwood grips, 36 oz. Importation began 1988.

Mfg.'s Sug. Retail	$260	$205	$165	$145	$135	$125	$115	$105

Model 971 Stainless — .357 Mag., 4 or 6 in. solid rib barrel with full shroud, combat style rubber grips, adj. rear sight, 35.4 - 40.5 oz. Importation began 1989.

Mfg.'s Sug. Retail	$285	$220	$185	$160

RIFLES

MODEL 92 SRC LEVER ACTION — .38 Spl./.357 Mag, .44 Mag, or .44-40 cal., copy of Win. Model 92, 16 (Model 92 SRS) or 20 in. round barrel, 5-5¾ lbs. Also available in matte blue finish at no extra charge.

Mfg.'s Sug. Retail	$350	$270	$215	$165	$125	$110	$100	$90

Add $20 for .44 Spl., .44 Mag., or .44-40 (disc.) cal.

.44-40 or .44 Mag. cal. are Model 65 SRC's.

Blue Engraved — with etched engraving and special wood. Disc. 1989.

	$275	$225	$175

Last Mfg.'s Sug. Retail was $327.

Gold or Chrome Engraved — either gold (disc. 1987) or chrome (disc.) finish with special wood.

	$280	$230	$185	$150	$130	$120	$110

Last Mfg.'s Sug. Retail was $330.

MODEL 62 SA SLIDE ACTION — .22 LR cal., copy of Win. 1890 "gallery" model, rifle (23 in. barrel) or carbine (16½ in. barrel) available, takedown action, round or octagonal barrel, 12 or 13 shot tube mag.

Mfg.'s Sug. Retail	$225	$170	$140	$115	$95	$85	$80	$75

Add $15 for nickel finish.

Add $25 for octagonal barrel.

Model 62 SA Carbine (C) — similar to Model 62 SA, except has 16½ in. carbine barrel with full length mag. tube (12 shot), 4¼ lbs. Importation began 1988.

Mfg.'s Sug. Retail	$225	$170	$140	$115	$95	$85	$80	$75

Add $15 for nickel finish.

Model 62 SA Stainless — similar to regular model, except is stainless steel. Imported 1986 only.

	$165	$145	$120

Last Mfg.'s Sug. Retail was $192.

MODEL 59 — .22 Mag. version of Model 62 SA, 10 shot mag., 5.5 lbs.

Mfg.'s Sug. Retail	$275	$205	$165	$130	$120	$110	$100	$90

MODEL 65 SRC — .44 Spl./.44 Mag. cal., lever action carbine, 20 in. barrel, full tube mag. holding 10 rounds, iron sights, 5¾ lbs. Importation began 1989.

Mfg.'s Sug. Retail	$325	$255	$195	$170	$150	$135	$125	$115

Grading	100%	98%	95%	90%	80%	70%	60%

SHOTGUNS

OVERLUND SxS — 12, 20, or .410 ga., exposed hammers, 20 (Coach Model), 26, or 28 in. barrels, double triggers. Importation disc. 1988.

| | $275 | $230 | $185 | $155 | $140 | $125 | $115 |

Add $5 for .410 ga.
Last Mfg.'s Sug. Retail was $332.

SQUIRE SxS — 12, 20, or .410 ga., hammerless, 20, 26 or 28 in. barrels, double triggers, raised matted rib, beavertail forearm, pistol grip, hardwood stock, 3 in. chambers. Imported 1985-90.

| | $300 | $245 | $195 | $160 | $150 | $140 | $130 |

Add $10 for .410 ga.
Last Mfg.'s Sug. Retail was $350.

ROTTWEIL

Manufacturer located in Rottweil, West Germany. Previously imported by Dynamit Nobel of America located in Northvale, NJ.

SHOTGUNS

MODEL 650 FIELD O/U — 12 ga. only, 28 in. barrels with vent rib, ejectors, single trigger, select checkered walnut, multi-choked with 6 choke tubes, lightly engraved, coin finished receiver. Importation disc. 1986.

| | $750 | $650 | $595 | $550 | $500 | $460 | $435 |

Last Mfg.'s Sug. Retail was $850.

MODEL 72 FIELD O/U — 12 ga. only, 28 in. vent barrels and rib, sand blasted receiver, select walnut with checkered stock and forearm, single trigger, ejectors. Importation disc. 1987.

| | $1,850 | $1,650 | $1,450 | $1,200 | $1,000 | $850 | $700 |

Last Mfg.'s Sug. Retail was $2,295.

MODEL 72 AMERICAN SKEET O/U — 12 ga. only, 26¾ in. barrels, vent rib, ejectors, select French walnut, marginal engraving on sand blasted receiver, single trigger, 7½ lbs. Importation disc. 1987.

| | $1,850 | $1,650 | $1,450 | $1,200 | $1,000 | $850 | $700 |

Last Mfg.'s Sug. Retail was $2,295.

This model was distributed exclusively by Paxton Arms, located in Dallas, TX.

MODEL 72 AAT SINGLE BARREL TRAP — 12 ga. only, adj. American trap (AAT), barrel features adj. point of impact, 34 in. barrel bored full, high vent rib. Importation disc. 1986.

| | $1,400 | $1,200 | $1,000 | $850 | $700 | $650 | $600 |

Last Mfg.'s Sug. Retail was $2,295.

MODEL 72 AT O/U — 12 ga. only, 32 in. IM & F barrels, vent rib and barrels, sand blasted receiver, checkered select walnut stock and forearm, non-adj. point of impact, single trigger ejectors. Importation disc. 1987.

| | $1,850 | $1,650 | $1,450 | $1,200 | $1,000 | $850 | $700 |

Last Mfg.'s Sug. Retail was $2,295.

MODEL 72 AAT COMBINATION — 12 ga. only, comes with 2 single barrels (32 and 34 in.) that have adj. impacts. Importation disc. 1986.

| | $2,450 | $2,100 | $1,850 | $1,600 | $1,450 | $1,250 | $995 |

Last Mfg.'s Sug. Retail was $2,850.

72 AAT Combination — supplied with 1 single adj. barrel and 32 in. O/U barrels.

| | $2,450 | $2,100 | $1,850 | $1,600 | $1,450 | $1,250 | $995 |

Last Mfg.'s Sug. Retail was $2,850.

Grading	100%	98%	95%	90%	80%	70%	60%

MODEL 72 AAT 3-BARREL SET — 12 ga. only, supplied with 2 single barrels (32 and 34 in.) with adj. impact and 1 set of 32 in. O/U barrels bored IM & F. Importation disc. 1986.

	$2,850	$2,600	$2,300	$2,000	$1,800	$1,600	$1,400

Last Mfg.'s Sug. Retail was $3,250.

MODEL 72 INTERNATIONAL TRAP — 12 ga. only, O/U 30 in. barrels bored IM & F with extra high rib. Importation disc. 1987.

	$1,850	$1,650	$1,450	$1,200	$1,000	$850	$700

Last Mfg.'s Sug. Retail was $2,295.

MODEL 72 INTERNATIONAL SKEET — 12 ga. only, 26¾ in. barrels, vent rib, select walnut stock and forearm. Importation disc. 1987.

	$1,850	$1,650	$1,450	$1,200	$1,000	$850	$700

Last Mfg.'s Sug. Retail was $2,295.

ROYAL AMERICAN SHOTGUNS
Previously imported by Royal Arms International, located in Woodland Hills, CA.

SHOTGUNS

MODEL 100 O/U — 12 or 20 ga., 2¾ in. chambers, double triggers, extractors, vent rib and barrels. Imported 1985-87 only.

	$325	$265	$240	$220	$200	$180	$170

Last Mfg.'s Sug. Retail was $390.

Add $40 for above model with 3 in. chambers, single trigger, and auto ejectors.

MODEL 600 BOXLOCK SxS — 12, 20, 28, or .410 ga., sideplates, silver finished receiver, 3 in. chambers, single trigger, auto ejectors. Imported 1985-87 only.

	$365	$295	$265	$235	$210	$195	$180

Last Mfg.'s Sug. Retail was $420.

Deduct 25% for double triggers and 2¾ in. chambers.

MODEL 800 SIDELOCK SxS — 12, 20, 28, or .410 ga., sidelocks with sideplates, silver finished receiver, 3 in. chambers, single trigger, checkered straight grip stock with select walnut, auto ejectors. Imported 1985-87 only.

	$775	$650	$595	$550	$500	$460	$435

Last Mfg.'s Sug. Retail was $899.

RUBY
Manufacturer located in Eibar, Spain.

MILITARY TYPE — trade name for Spanish auto pistol fashioned after M1911 Colt's, cal. 7.65mm, mag. release at bottom of grip, fixed sights. No longer mfg.

	$115	$85	$80	$75	$70	$65	$60

RUGER
See Sturm, Ruger, & Co. section in this text.

Grading	100%	98%	95%	90%	80%	70%	60%

RUSSIAN SERVICE PISTOL AND RIFLE
Tula Arsenal.

MODEL TT30 & TT33 TOKAREV AUTOMATIC — design borrowed from Colt 1911 Petter-type unitized trigger/hammer assembly, 7.62mm Russian, 8 shot, 4½ in. barrel, blue. Mfg. 1930-1954. Add 20% for TT30 model.

	100%	98%	95%	90%	80%	70%	60%
	$325	$290	$250	$225	$165	$145	$110
M.244ADL	$295	$250	$200	$150	$120	$95	$80

Values listed above assume original condition - no recent imports.

NAGANT REVOLVER — 7 shot, cylinder comes forward to seal barrel. Add 10% for pre-communist Imperial marked.

	100%	98%	95%	90%	80%	70%	60%
	$260	$225	$185	$165	$135	$115	$100

MAKAROV MD — 9mm, clip fed double action, post-war manufacture.

	100%	98%	95%	90%	80%	70%	60%
	$1,075	$950	$850	$800	$750	$700	$650

TOKAREV M38 & M40 RIFLE — semi-auto Russian issue bolt action. Add 20% for M38, 100% for scoped sniper.

	100%	98%	95%	90%	80%	70%	60%
	$365	$310	$270	$250	$230	$210	$195

NOTES

S

S.A.C.M.
Cholet, France.

Grading	100%	98%	95%	90%	80%	70%	60%

FRENCH MODEL 1935A — semi-auto, 7.65mm long, 8 shot, 4.3 in. barrel, blue, fixed sights, checkered stocks, used by French troops in WWII and Indo-China 1945-1954. Mfg. 1935-1945.

	100%	98%	95%	90%	80%	70%	60%
	$250	$220	$205	$180	$165	$150	$140

Add 50% for Nazi WWII mfg. (Waffenamt proofed).

SAE
Spain America Enterprises Inc. (SAE) Previous importer of Felix Sarasqueta Shotguns from Spain. SAE was located in Miami, FL.

SHOTGUNS: O/U

MODEL 70 — 12 or 20 ga., 3 in. chambers, boxlock action, single trigger, ejectors, 26 in. VR barrel, European checkered walnut stock and forearm, standard finish is blue, Model 70 multi-choke has silver finished action with Florentine engraving and low gloss stock finish. Imported 1988 only.

	$400	$275	$260	$245	$230	$215	$195

Add $120 for multi-chokes (27 in. barrel).
Last Mfg.'s Sug. Retail was $598.

MODEL 66C — 12 ga. only, 26 in. Skeet or 30 in. F&M VR barrels, boxlock with engraved sideplates including 24Kt. inlays, Monte Carlo deluxe stock and beavertail forearm. Imported 1988 only.

	$950	$725	$650	$575	$495	$450	$395

Last Mfg.'s Sug. Retail was $1,544.

SHOTGUNS: SxS

MODEL 210S — 12, 20, or .410 ga., 3 in. chambers, boxlock action, double triggers, extractors, silver finished receiver with light engraving, approx. 7 lbs. Imported 1988 only.

	$420	$280	$260	$245	$230	$215	$195

Last Mfg.'s Sug. Retail was $638.

MODEL 340X — 12 or 20 ga., sidelock action, 26 in. barrels with 2¾ in. chambers, H&H bolt lock action, case hardened finish with moderate scroll engraving, straight grip select walnut stock and forearm with high gloss finish. Imported 1988 only.

	$700	$550	$495	$460	$430	$395	$375

Last Mfg.'s Sug. Retail was $1,170.

MODEL 209E — 12, 20, or .410 ga., H&H type sidelock action, 26 or 28 in. barrels with 2¾ in. chambers, hand engraved coin finished receiver, select checkered walnut stock and forearm, double triggers. Imported 1988 only.

	$925	$700	$650	$575	$495	$450	$395

Last Mfg.'s Sug. Retail was $1,490.

S K B ARMS COMPANY
Manufacturer located in Tokyo, Japan. Currently imported and distributed by G.U. Inc. located in Omaha, NE. SKB has been manufacturing firearms since 1855.

Formerly imported by Ithaca. In 1987, importation resumed on most SKB models. While the model numbers have changed, quality is similar to those models imported previously by Ithaca. In most cases, the newer models are derived closely from their previous counterparts. Listings below will differentiate older disc. models from currently imported models.

Grading	100%	98%	95%	90%	80%	70%	60%

SHOTGUNS: O/U AND SINGLE SHOT

MODEL 500 — 12, 20, 28, or .410 ga., field grade, vent rib, selective ejector, 26 in. imp. cyl. and mod., 28 in. full and mod., and 30 in. full and mod., checkered stock. Mfg. in Japan by SKB 1966-1979.

	100%	98%	95%	90%	80%	70%	60%
	$525	$440	$395	$365	$330	$300	$275

Add 25% for 28 or .410 ga.

Add 15% for 20 ga.

Model 500 Magnum — 12 ga., 3 in. Mag., field grade, same as 500, except 3 in. Mag. chambers.

	$625	$455	$410	$385	$355	$320	$290

MODEL 505 DELUXE FIELD O/U — similar to Model 500, 3 in. chambers, 12 and 20 ga. barrels are supplied with choke tubes, single selective trigger, ejectors, checkered walnut stock with recoil pad and forearm.

Mfg.'s Sug. Retail	$995	$875	$750	$675	$575	$500	$460	$420

Add $500 for combo package.

The combo package includes either 12/20 ga. barrels with inter-chokes or 28/.410 ga. barrels.

Model 505 Trap — 12 ga., 30 or 32 in. fixed choke barrels with or without Monte Carlo stock, high rib.

Mfg.'s Sug. Retail	$995	$875	$725	$650	$525	$475	$430	$395

Add $400 for O/U Trap Combo.

The above Combo includes one set of O/U Trap barrels and a top single Trap barrel.

Model 505 Trap Single Barrel — 12 ga., 32 or 34 in. barrel with multi-chokes, regular or Monte Carlo stock. Importation disc. 1989.

Mfg.'s Sug. Retail	$995	$875	$725	$650	$525	$475	$430	$395

Model 505 Skeet — 12, 20, 28, or .410 ga., 28 in. barrels with multi-chokes.

Mfg.'s Sug. Retail	$995	$875	$725	$650	$525	$475	$430	$395

Model 505 3-Ga. Skeet Set — includes 20, 28, and .410 ga. extra Skeet barrels, aluminum case.

Mfg.'s Sug. Retail	$2,195	$1,925	$1,575	$1,350	$1,200	$1,125	$950	$875

Model 505 Sporting Clay — 28 in. multi-choke barrels, dimensioned for Sporting Clay competition.

Mfg.'s Sug. Retail	$1,045	$885	$725	$650	$525	$475	$430	$395

MODEL 600 FIELD GRADE — same as 500, except silver plated frame and select wood.

	$700	$495	$465	$440	$375	$345	$325

Add 20% for 20 ga.

MODEL 600 MAGNUM — same as 600 Field, except chambered for 3 in. Mag., 12 ga. Mfg. 1969-1972 by SKB.

	$720	$510	$480	$455	$415	$390	$355

MODEL 600 TRAP GRADE — same as 600, except 12 ga. only, trap stock, recoil pad, select wood.

	$675	$555	$520	$485	$445	$410	$385

MODEL 600 DOUBLES GUN — same as 600 Trap, except choked for 21 yd. and 30 yd. targets. Mfg. 1973-1975.

	$675	$555	$520	$485	$445	$410	$385

MODEL 600 SKEET GRADE — 12, 20, 28, or .410 ga., 26 or 28 in. barrels, bored S&S, otherwise same as 600 Trap.

	$700	$540	$510	$475	$430	$400	$370

28 or .410 ga.

	$850	$740	$620	$560	$485	$440	$420

MODEL 600 SKEET GRADE COMBO SET — same as 600 Skeet, except fitted with matched set of 20, 28, and .410 ga. barrels, in fitted case.

	$2,000	$1,430	$1,265	$1,155	$935	$770	$660

Grading	100%	98%	95%	90%	80%	70%	60%

MODEL 605 FIELD O/U — similar to Model 505 except has silver finished engraved receiver with better walnut.

Mfg.'s Sug. Retail	$1,195	$1,075	$850	$750	$675	$575	$500	$450

Add $500 for extra set of barrels (Combo).

Model 605 Trap — 12 ga., 30 or 32 in. fixed choke barrel with or without Monte Carlo stock, high rib.

Mfg.'s Sug. Retail	$1,195	$1,075	$850	$750	$675	$575	$500	$450

Add $400 for O/U Trap Combo.

The above Combo includes one set of O/U Trap barrels and a top single Trap barrel.

Model 605 Trap Single Barrel — 12 ga., 32 or 34 in. barrel with multi-chokes.

Mfg.'s Sug. Retail	$1,195	$1,075	$850	$750	$675	$575	$500	$450

Model 605 Skeet — 12, 20, 28, or .410 ga., 28 in. barrels with multi-chokes.

Mfg.'s Sug. Retail	$1,195	$1,100	$850	$750	$675	$575	$500	$450

Model 605 3-Ga. Skeet Set — includes 20, 28, and .410 ga. extra Skeet barrels, aluminum case.

Mfg.'s Sug. Retail	$2,395	$2,175	$1,650	$1,400	$1,250	$1,125	$950	$875

Model 605 Sporting Clay — 28 in. multi-choke barrels, dimensioned for Sporting Clay competition.

Mfg.'s Sug. Retail	$1,245	$1,110	$850	$750	$675	$575	$500	$450

Model 605 DU Dinner Gun — mfg. for DU chapters - dinner auction gun, 850 mfg. in 12 ga. (1990) and 850 mfg. in 20 ga. (1991).

DU dinner gun values are usually hard to ascertain in the secondary marketplace. Currently, prices seem to range between $1,200-$1,700.

MODEL 680 ENGLISH — same as 600 Field, except English style stock, select walnut and fine scroll engraving. Mfg. 1973-1976.

	$725	$640	$600	$555	$520	$495	$445

Add 20% for 20 ga.

MODEL 700 TRAP GRADE — 12 ga., same as 600 Trap, except more engraving, better grade wood, wide rib. Mfg. 1969-1975.

	$820	$770	$740	$685	$630	$595	$565

MODEL 700 DOUBLES GUN — 12 ga., same as 700 Trap, except choked for 21 yd. and 30 yd. targets. Mfg. 1973-1975.

	$795	$770	$740	$685	$630	$595	$565

MODEL 700 SKEET GRADE — 12 ga., same as 700 Doubles, only bored S&S, available in 12 or 20 ga.

	$840	$770	$740	$685	$620	$585	$555

MODEL 800 TRAP GRADE — 12 ga., same as 700 Trap, except more engraving, better grade wood, wide rib. Mfg. 1969-1975.

	$1,150	$875	$775	$675	$575	$500	$425

MODEL 800 SKEET GRADE — 12 or 20 ga., skeet chokes. Mfg. 1969-1975.

	$1,200	$1,000	$895	$795	$680	$595	$565

MODEL 880 CROWN GRADE — 12, 20, 28, or .410 ga., coin finish receiver, extensively engraved with sideplates, SST, ejectors, select walnut with fleur-de-lis scroll style checkering, double cross bolt action. Disc. 1980.

	$1,650	$1,300	$1,150	$975	$890	$835	$750

Add 25% for 28 or .410 ga.

Grading	100%	98%	95%	90%	80%	70%	60%

MODEL 885 O/U — available in either Field, Skeet, or Trap configuration, coin finished receiver featuring fine scroll engraving with game scenes, boxlock action with sideplates. Importation started 1988.

Model 885 Field — 12, 20, 28, or .410 ga., field dimensions, barrels include choke tubes. Importation started 1989.

Mfg.'s Sug. Retail	$1,595	$1,375	$1,075	$925	$825	$725	$650	$595

Add $600 for combo package.

The combo package includes either 12/20 ga. barrels with inter-chokes or 28/.410 ga. barrels.

Model 885 Trap — 12 ga., 30 or 32 in. barrels with multi-chokes.

Mfg.'s Sug. Retail	$1,595	$1,375	$1,075	$925	$825	$725	$650	$595

Add $600 for O/U Trap Combo.

The above Combo includes one set of O/U Trap barrels and a top single Trap barrel.

Model 885 Skeet — 12, 20, 28, or .410 ga., 28 in. barrels with multi-chokes.

Mfg.'s Sug. Retail	$1,595	$1,375	$1,075	$925	$825	$725	$650	$595

Model 885 3-Ga. Skeet Set — includes 20, 28, and .410 ga. extra Skeet barrels, aluminum case.

Mfg.'s Sug. Retail	$2,995	$2,775	$2,450	$2,150	$1,900	$1,675	$1,475	$1,375

Model 885 Sporting Clay — 28 in. multi-choke barrels, dimensioned for Sporting Clay competition.

Mfg.'s Sug. Retail	$1,645	$1,400	$1,100	$925	$825	$725	$650	$595

MODEL 5600 — 12 ga. only, available as Trap or Skeet model only, vent rib (Trap only) and barrels (Skeet only), no engraving, select walnut. Disc. 1980.

	$575	$495	$450	$420	$390	$360	$330

Model 5700 — available as Trap or Skeet model only, light engraving, select walnut, vent rib. Disc. 1980.

	$750	$625	$540	$495	$460	$430	$400

Model 5800 — available as Trap or Skeet model only, more deluxe engraving, select walnut. Disc. 1980.

	$950	$800	$695	$595	$500	$450	$425

SHOTGUNS: SIDE-BY-SIDE

Models 100, 150, 200, 280, 300, 400, 480 — 12 and 20 ga. only, 25-30 in. barrels, all boxlock actions, more expensive models differ in the amount of engraving, grade of walnut, and style of checkering, beavertail forend, 6¼ - 7 lbs. Disc. 1980.

MODEL 100 — 12 or 20 ga., Mag. model also, SST, AE, blue only.

	$485	$425	$380	$340	$310	$275	$250

MODEL 150 — same as 100, except scroll engraving, beavertail forearm. Mfg. 1972-1974 by SKB.

	$520	$435	$385	$345	$310	$275	$250

MODEL 200 — 12 or 20 ga., Mag. model also, SST, AE, boxlock, scalloped frame, lightly engraved coin finish receiver.

	$550	$475	$410	$375	$340	$310	$280

MODEL 200 (NEW MFG.) — similar to original Model 200, SST, ejectors, recoil pad. Imported 1987-1988 only.

	$725	$525	$425	$420	$375	$345	$325

Last Mfg.'s Sug. Retail was $895.

Model 200E (English) — similar to New Model 200, except has straight grip stock. Importation disc. 1988.

	$725	$525	$425	$420	$375	$345	$325

Last Mfg.'s Sug. Retail was $895.

MODEL 280 ENGLISH — 12 or 20 ga., Mag. model also, SST, AE, lightly engraved blue receiver, straight grip.

	$850	$775	$625	$525	$440	$410	$375

Grading	100%	98%	95%	90%	80%	70%	60%

MODEL 300 — 12 or 20 ga., Mag. model also, SST, AE, lightly engraved coin finish receiver.

| | $750 | $650 | $575 | $485 | $440 | $410 | $375 |

MODEL 400 — 12 or 20 ga., Mag. model also, boxlock, SST, AE, moderately engraved coin finish receiver with sideplates.

| | $695 | $600 | $510 | $460 | $430 | $410 | $385 |

MODEL 400 (NEW MFG.) — similar to original Model 400, SST, ejectors, recoil pad. Imported 1987-1988 only.

| | $975 | $850 | $780 | $690 | $595 | $525 | $475 |

Last Mfg.'s Sug. Retail was $1,195.

Model 400E (English) — similar to New Model 400, except has engraved sideplates and straight grip stock. Importation disc. 1989.

| | $975 | $850 | $780 | $690 | $595 | $525 | $475 |

Last Mfg.'s Sug. Retail was $1,195.

MODEL 480 ENGLISH — 12 or 20 ga., Mag. model also, SST, AE, moderately engraved coin finish receiver, straight grip.

| | $1,250 | $1,000 | $825 | $725 | $625 | $525 | $475 |

SHOTGUNS: SEMI-AUTO

MODEL 300 STANDARD — 12 or 20 ga., 3 in. chamber, 26 in. imp. cyl., 28 in. mod. or full, 30 in. full, recoil operated, autoloading, checkered pistol grip stock. Mfg. 1968-1972.

| | $295 | $255 | $205 | $165 | $155 | $145 | $140 |
| Vent rib model | $320 | $275 | $220 | $195 | $165 | $155 | $150 |

MODEL 1300 UPLAND — 12 or 20 ga., 3 in. chamber, 22, 26, or 28 in. VR barrel with multi-chokes, matte black receiver, checkered walnut stock and forearm. Importation resumed 1988.

| Mfg.'s Sug. Retail | $495 | $450 | $385 | $340 | $300 | $270 | $240 | $210 |

This model was previously designated the Model 300. The new Model 1300 is also available in Slug configuration with 22 in. barrel/iron sights at no extra charge. New Model 1300's have a magazine cutoff system on front left side of frame.

XL 900 MR — 12 ga. only, gas operated semi-auto, 26-30 in. barrels, 5 shot, alloy receiver, etched game bird scroll work on receiver, shoots both 2¾ and 3 in. shells by interchanging barrels. Disc. 1980.

| | $325 | $280 | $260 | $240 | $225 | $190 | $175 |

XL 900 — same as XL 900, only in 20 ga. and no recoil pad, 6¼ lbs.

| | $360 | $315 | $275 | $250 | $230 | $190 | $175 |

XL 900 TRAP GRADE — same as XL 900, 12 ga. only, scroll engraved black chrome receiver, 30 in. imp. mod. or full, trap style stock, straight or Monte Carlo, recoil pad. Mfg. 1972-present.

| | $395 | $350 | $320 | $305 | $275 | $265 | $260 |

XL 900 SKEET GRADE — same as XL 900, except scroll engraved black chrome receiver, 26 in. barrel, skeet stock. Mfg. 1972-disc.

| | $400 | $350 | $320 | $305 | $275 | $265 | $260 |

XL 900 SLUG GUN — same as XL 900, except 24 in. slug barrel, rifle sights, no rib. Mfg. 1972-disc.

| | $350 | $310 | $280 | $265 | $250 | $220 | $200 |

MODEL 1900 — 12 or 20 ga., 3 in. chamber, 22, 26, or 28 in. VR barrel with multi-chokes, deluxe outdoor field scene etched on receiver, gold trigger, approx. 1,000-2,000 mfg. per year.

| Mfg.'s Sug. Retail | $545 | $485 | $430 | $395 | $360 | $330 | $295 | $260 |

This model was previously designated the Model 900. The new Model 1900 is also available in Slug configuration with 22 in. barrel and iron sights or Trap Model at no extra charge. New Model 1900's have a magazine cutoff system on front left side of frame.

Grading	100%	98%	95%	90%	80%	70%	60%

MODEL 3000 — 12 or 20 ga., 3 in. chamber, gas semi-auto (shoots both 2¾ and 3 in. shells interchangeably) with semi-squareback styling, elaborate game scenes etched on both sides of receiver, deluxe checkered walnut stock and forearm. Imported 1988-90.

	$545	$475	$415	$380	$350	$315	$285

Add $125 for Trap model (2¾ in. chamber).

This model has not previously been imported in this configuration.

Last Mfg.'s Sug. Retail was $597.

SHOTGUNS: SLIDE ACTION

MODEL 7300 — 12 or 20 ga., 2¾ or 3 in. chambers, blue only, French walnut stock-hand checkered, twin action slide bars. Disc. 1980.

	$295	$250	$225	$200	$180	$165	$150

MODEL 7900 — trap or skeet variation of the Model 7300.

	$350	$310	$265	$235	$200	$180	$160

SKS

Manufactured in Russia, China, Yugoslavia, and other countries.

Over 600 million SKS models have been manufactured in China alone.

SKS — semi-auto rifle, 7.62 x 39mm Russian, Soviet designed, gas operated weapon, 10 shot fixed mag., wood stock, permanently attached folding bayonet, tangent rear and hooded front sight.

Please refer to this model under those importers/distributors who import this model and are listed in this text. Values typically range between $200-$350.

SSK INDUSTRIES

Manufacturer/customizer located in Bloomingdale, OH.

SSK Industries uses Thompson Center flatside frames and applies an industrial hard chrome finish. Receivers and barrels may be purchased separately—values below are for a complete assembled pistol with no scope rings (add $60).

SSK has also manufactured various limited editions including the Handgun Hunters International (HHI) Models 1, 2, and 3. Issue price on these guns was $1,100 (Model 3), $1,200 (Model 2), and $1,300 (Model 1). Only 50 were mfg. total in 1987. SSK also customizes a Ruger Super Redhawk (.44 Mag. or .45 LC cal.). This variation comes with either a scoped 7½ in. octagon barrel (Beauty Model) or a 6 in. bull barrel with muzzle brake (Beast Model). Prices start at $1,430 - add $245 for .45 LC cal.

HAND CANNONS

SSK-CONTENDER — over 74 cal.'s available from .17 Bee to .588 JDJ, customized Thompson Center TCR 87 action and barrel, scope rings or iron sights are extra, basically a custom order gun.

Mfg.'s Sug. Retail	$800	$700	$625	$550

Add $800 for arrestor muzzle brake.

Add $150 for SSK chrome finish.

This model includes barrel, frame, stocks, and sights as standard equipment.

Contender Models in cal.'s over .50 since BATF ruling have become very expensive. A .577 NE cal. gun starts at $1,800.

SSK-XP100 — various cal.'s between .17 and .50, includes TSOB mount and rings.

Mfg.'s Sug. Retail	$1,200	$1,050	$875	$700

The .50 cal. XP100 (12.9 X 50.8 JDJ) comes with SSK muzzle brake, scope dyes and new reinforced fiberglass stock - retail price is $1,700.

Grading	100%	98%	95%	90%	80%	70%	60%

S.W.D., INC.

Manufactured in Atlanta, GA. Similar models have previously been manufactured by R.P.B. Industries, Inc. (1979-82), and were met with B.A.T.F. disapproval because of convertability into fully automatic operation. "Cobray" is a trademark for the M11/9 semi-automatic pistol.

COBRAY PISTOLS

M-11/NINEmm SEMI-AUTO PISTOL — 9mm, fires from closed bolt, 3rd generation design, stamped steel frame, 32 shot mag., parkerized finish, similar in appearance to Ingram Mac 10.

No Mfg.'s Retail	$215	$175	$160	$150	$140	$135	$125

This model is also available in a fully-auto variation, class III transferable only.

CARBINES

SEMI-AUTO CARBINE — 9mm, same mechanism as M11, 16¼ in. shrouded barrel, telescoping stock, various Mag.'s.

No Mfg.'s Retail	$265	$230	$195	$170	$160	$150	$140

REVOLVERS

LADIES HOME COMPANION — .45-70 cal., double action design utilizing spring wound 12 shot rotary mag., 12 in. barrel, steel barrel and frame, 9 lbs. 6 oz. New 1990.

No Mfg.'s Retail	$525	$400	$360	$335	$310	$290	$270

SHOTGUNS

TERMINATOR — 12 or 20 ga., single shot paramilitary design shotgun with 18 in. cylinder bore barrel, parkerized finish, ejector. Mfg. 1986-1988 only.

	$95	$80	$70	$60	$55	$50	$45

Last Mfg.'s Sug. Retail was $110.

SAFARI ARMS

Manufacturer/customizer located in Phoenix, AZ. M-S Safari Arms was started in 1978 and is a division of M-S Safari Outfitters. In 1987, Safari Arms was absorbed by Olympic Arms located in Olympia, WA. Olympic Arms is currently utilizing existing parts of older Safari Arms and will be manufacturing pistols with their own trademark once existing inventory parts have been depleted.

Safari Arms manufactured single action, semi-auto pistols derived from the Browning M1911 design with modifications. Values below reflect previously mfg. pistols by Safari Arms. New models can be found under the Olympic Arms, Inc. section of this text.

DEFENSE PISTOLS

ENFORCER — .45 ACP, 3.9 in. barrel, 6 shot mag., shortened grip, available in stainless steel, blue, Armaloy, parkerized, electroless nickel or lightweight anodized finishes, flat or arched mainspring housing, adj. sights, neoprene or checkered walnut grips, 27 oz. Disc. 1987.

	$680	$600	$525	$450	$400	$350	$300

Last Mfg.'s Sug. Retail was $745.

Match Master — similar to the Enforcer, except has 5 in. barrel and 7 shot mag., 30 oz. Disc. 1987.

	$680	$600	$525	$450	$400	$350	$300

Last Mfg.'s Sug. Retail was $745.

Safari Arms also has made the Phoenix, Special Forces, Camp Perry, and Royal Order of Jesters commemoratives in various configurations and quantities. Prices average in the $1,500 range except for the Royal Order of Jesters ($2,000).

Grading	100%	98%	95%	90%	80%	70%	60%

BLACK WIDOW— .45 ACP, 3.9 in. barrel, hand-contoured front grip strap, schrimshawed ivory Micarta grips with black widow emblem, 6 shot mag., 27 oz. Disc. 1987.

	$680	$600	$525	$450	$400	$350	$300

Last Mfg.'s Sug. Retail was $745.

TARGET PISTOLS

MODEL 81 — .38 Spl. or .45 ACP, 5 in. barrel, hand-contoured front grip strap, 2 lbs. 10 oz. Disc. 1987.

	$775	$695	$550	$440	$410	$375	$350

Add $50 for Deluxe Model (with Herrett adj. grips).
Last Mfg.'s Sug. Retail was $875.

Model 81L — .38 Spl. or .45 ACP, 6 in. barrel, 2 lbs. 13 oz. Disc. 1987.

	$850	$775	$695	$550	$440	$410	$375

Add $50 for Deluxe Model (with Herrett adj. grips).
Last Mfg.'s Sug. Retail was $975.

Model 81 NM— .38 Spl. or .45 ACP, similar frame as Model 81, except has flat front grip strap, 5 in. barrel, 2 lbs. 5 oz. Disc. 1987.

	$775	$695	$550	$440	$410	$375	$350

Last Mfg.'s Sug. Retail was $875.

Model 81BP — .38 Spl. or .45 ACP, 6 in barrel, contoured front grip strap, faster cycle time, 2 lbs. 9 oz. Disc. 1987.

	$875	$775	$695	$550	$440	$410	$375

Last Mfg.'s Sug. Retail was $995.

Silueta — .45 ACP or .38/.45 Wildcat, 10 in. extended barrel, designed for silhouette shooting, 2 lbs. 14 oz. Disc. 1987.

	$875	$775	$695	$550	$440	$410	$375

Last Mfg.'s Sug. Retail was $1,050.

ULTIMATE/UNLIMITED — various cal.'s, bolt action target pistol, single shot, $14^{15}/_{16}$ in. barrel, black finished metal, laminate stock. Disc. 1987.

	$850	$775	$695	$550	$440	$410	$375

Last Mfg.'s Sug. Retail was $975.

RIFLES

COUNTER SNIPER RIFLE — .308 cal., bolt action utilizing M-14 mag.'s, 26 in. heavy barrel, camo-fiberglass stock, 10½ lbs. Disc. 1987.

	$1,100	$900	$775	$695	$550	$440	$410

Last Mfg.'s Sug. Retail was $1,225.

SURVIVOR I CONVERSION UNIT — .223 or .45 ACP cal., converts M1911 variations into carbine, bolt action, collapsible stock, 16¼ in. barrel, 5 lbs.

	$275	$225	$195

This kit is also available for S&W and Browning High-Power models.

SAKO

Manufacturer located in Riihimaki, Finland. Current models are presently being imported by Stoeger Industries located in South Hackensack, NJ.

Note: Prices below are for pre-1972 rifles unless stated otherwise. Post-1972 models will sell for approx. 25% less.

RIFLES: DISCONTINUED

DELUXE — various cal.'s, Monte Carlo stock, skipline checkering, long, medium, or short actions, contrasting P.G. Cap & Forearm, engraved floorplate.

	$850	$775	$695	$550	$440	$410	$375

STANDARD SPORTER — long, medium, and short actions.

	$695	$625	$550	$475	$440	$410	$375

Grading	100%	98%	95%	90%	80%	70%	60%

HEAVY BARREL MODEL — long, medium, and short actions.

	100%	98%	95%	90%	80%	70%	60%
	$695	$625	$550	$475	$440	$410	$375

FULL STOCK MODELS — 20 in. carbine barrel (all actions), 23½ in. barrel on rifle (short & medium actions).
  Finnbear — long action.

	100%	98%	95%	90%	80%	70%	60%
	$795	$710	$560	$440	$410	$375	$350

  Forester — medium action.

	100%	98%	95%	90%	80%	70%	60%
	$795	$710	$560	$440	$410	$375	$350

  Vixen — short action.

	100%	98%	95%	90%	80%	70%	60%
	$795	$710	$560	$440	$410	$375	$350

MAUSER ACTION (FN) — .270 Win. or .30-06 cal., long action. Mfg. 1950-1957.

	100%	98%	95%	90%	80%	70%	60%
	$550	$500	$400	$345	$310	$280	$260

MAGNUM MAUSER (FN) — 8 x 60S, 8.2 x 57mm, .300 H&H, or .375 H&H cal.

	100%	98%	95%	90%	80%	70%	60%
	$695	$635	$580	$495	$450	$410	$375

MODEL 74 — various cal.'s.

	100%	98%	95%	90%	80%	70%	60%
	$560	$495	$440	$375	$340	$320	$290

FINNWOLF — lever action, various cal.'s, 4 shot clip early model, 3 shot clip later model. Mfg. 1962-1974.

	100%	98%	95%	90%	80%	70%	60%
	$725	$650	$550	$500	$440	$410	$375

ANNIVERSARY MODEL — 7mm Rem. Mag. only, 1,000 made.

	100%	98%	95%
	$1,500	$995	$850

RIFLES: RECENT MFG.

All Sako left-handed models are available in long action only.

HUNTER LIGHTWEIGHT RIFLE — available in short action (AI) in .17 Rem., .222 Rem., or .223 Rem. cal., medium action (AII) in .22-250, .243 Win., .308 Win., or 7mm-08 cal., or long action (AIII) in .25-06 Rem., .270 Win., .280 Rem., .30-06, 7mm Rem. Mag., .300 Win. Mag., .300 Wby. Mag., .338 Win. Mag., .375 H&H, or .416 Rem. Mag. (new 1991) cal., 21¼, 21¾, or 22 in. barrel, classic styled stock with choice of oil or lacquer finish, finely checkered French walnut.

Mfg.'s Sug. Retail	$945	$775	$635	$550	$490	$460	$430	$410

Add $30 for long action.

Add $50-$60 for Mag. cal.'s.

Add $110 for left-hand action.

  Hunter Carbine (Handy) — available in medium action in .22-250 (disc. 1990), .243 Win. (new 1991), .308 (new 1991) cal. or long action in .25-06 (disc. 1990), Rem., 7mm Rem. Mag. (disc. 1990), .338 Win. Mag. cal., or .375 H&H Mag. (new 1990) cal., 18½ in. barrel with iron sights, oil or lacquer finished deluxe walnut stock with checkering, approx. 7 lbs. New 1986.

Mfg.'s Sug. Retail	$945	$775	$635	$550	$490	$460	$430	$410

  Add $50-$65 for long action (Mag. cal.'s).

FIBERCLASS MODEL — available in medium action in .22-250, .243 Win., .308 Win., or 7mm-08 cal., or long action in .25-06 Rem., .270 Win., .280 Rem., .30-06, 7mm Rem. Mag., .300 Win. Mag., .338 Win. Mag., .375 H&H, or .416 Rem. Mag. (new 1991) cal., has black fiberglass stock.

Mfg.'s Sug. Retail	$1,235	$1,075	$875	$775	$725	$630	$560	$510

Add $40 for long action.

Add $55-$65 for Mag. cal.'s.

Add $80 for left-hand action (disc. 1989).

Grading	100%	98%	95%	90%	80%	70%	60%

FiberClass Carbine (Handy) — available in medium action in .243 Win. or .308 Win. cal. and long action in .25-06 Rem. (disc.), .270 Win. (disc.), .30-06, 7mm Rem. Mag. (disc.), .300 Win. Mag. (disc.), .338 Win. Mag., or .375 H&H (new 1991) cal., 18½ in. barrel with fiberglass stock. New 1986.

Mfg.'s Sug. Retail	$1,239 $1,100	$895	$775	$725	$630	$560	$510

Add $50-$65 for Mag. cal.'s.

LAMINATED RIFLE — available in short action (disc. 1989), medium action in .22-250 Rem., .243 Win., .308 Win., or 7mm-08 cal., or long action in .25-06 Rem., .270 Win., .280 Rem., .30-06, 7mm Rem. Mag., .300 Win. Mag., .338 Win. Mag., .375 H&H, or .416 Rem. Mag. (new 1991) cal., features laminated wood stock. New 1988.

Mfg.'s Sug. Retail	$1,080	$900	$740	$600	$540	$490	$460	$430

Add $45 for long action.

Add $60-$75 for Mag. cal.'s.

Add approx. $100 for left-hand action.

The left-handed action is available in .270 Win., .280 Rem., .30-06, 7mm Rem. Mag., 300 Win. Mag., 338 Win. Mag., .375 H&H, or .416 Rem. Mag. cal.

MANNLICHER CARBINE — available in short action (disc. 1989), medium action in .243 Win. or .308 Win. cal., or long action in .25-06 Rem., .270 Win., .30-06, 7mm Rem. Mag., .300 Win. Mag., .338 Win. Mag., or .375 H&H cal., 18½ in. barrel, two-piece full Mannlicher style stock, open sights.

Mfg.'s Sug. Retail	$1,095	$910	$750	$600	$545	$495	$465	$440

Add $35 for long action.

Add $55-$70 for Mag. cal.'s.

PPC MODEL — 22 PPC or 6 PPC cal., 21¾ or 23¾ (Benchrest Model) in. barrel, single shot in Benchrest Model, 4 shot mag. in Hunter or Deluxe Model, checkered walnut stock, Deluxe Model has rosewood pistol grip and forearm caps plus skip line checkering, matte lacquer finish on Hunter and Deluxe, oiled finish on Benchrest, 6¼ or 8¾ (Benchrest Model with heavy barrel) lbs. Importation began 1989.

Mfg.'s Sug. Retail	$1,185	$995	$835	$700	$650	$590	$540	$500

Add $300 for Deluxe Hunter Model.

Add $80 for Benchrest Model.

VARMINT RIFLE — available in short action (AI) in .17 Rem., .222 Rem., or .223 Rem., and medium action (AII) .22-250 Rem., .243 Win., .308 Win., or 7mm-08 (disc.) cal., 22¾ in. heavy barrel, no sights.

Mfg.'s Sug. Retail	$1,080	$900	$740	$600	$545	$475	$430	$400

Also available in single shot configuration (6mm PPC or .22 PPC only) — subtract $110 (disc. 1989).

CLASSIC GRADE — available in short (AI), medium (AII), or long (AIII) action, .17-7mm Mag. cal.'s, classic styled stock, finely checkered French walnut. Disc. 1985.

		$835	$715	$660	$600	$560	$510	$475

Add $50 for Mag. cal.'s.

Last Mfg.'s Sug. Retail was $954.

DELUXE LIGHTWEIGHT RIFLE — available in short action (AI) in .17 Rem., .222 Rem., or .223 Rem. cal., medium action (AII) in .22-250 Rem., .243 Win., .308 Win., or 7mm-08 cal., or long action (AIII) in .25-06 Rem., .270 Win., .280 Rem., .30-06, 7mm Rem. Mag., .300 Win. Mag., .300 Wby. Mag., .338 Win. Mag., .375 H&H, or .416 Rem. Mag. (new 1991) cal., 21¼, 21¾, or 22 in. barrel, deluxe quality skipline checkered walnut stock with rosewood forend tip.

Mfg.'s Sug. Retail	$1,285 $1,065	$895	$725	$650	$595	$540	$500

Add $40 for long action.

Add $55-$70 for Mag. cal.'s.

Add approx. $100 for left-hand action.

Grading	100%	98%	95%	90%	80%	70%	60%

SAFARI GRADE — available in long (AIII) action only, .300 Win. Mag. (disc. 1989), .338 Win. Mag., .375 H&H Mag., or .416 Rem. Mag. (new 1991) cal., deluxe walnut with sculptured cheek piece, 22 in. barrel, 4 shot mag., open sights, sling swivels.

Mfg.'s Sug. Retail	$2,550	$2,075	$1,725	$1,450	$1,250	$1,050	$900	$795

SUPER DELUXE — a limited edition rifle available on special order only, various cal.'s are available in the short (AI), medium (AII), and long (AIII) actions, presentation grade walnut with both checkering and carving, rosewood forend tip.

Mfg.'s Sug. Retail	$2,710	$2,150	$1,725	$1,450	$1,250	$1,050	$900	$795

MODEL 78 — .22 LR and .22 Hornet, clip mag., same size as short action Standard Model. Importation disc. 1986.

	$480	$395	$340	$310	$280	$265	$250

Add $30 for .22 Hornet cal.
Last Mfg.'s Sug. Retail was $647.

FINSPORT MODEL 2700 — available in long (AIII) action only, .270 - .300 Win. Mag. cal.'s, select checkered walnut. Disc. 1985.

	$795	$680	$600	$560	$510	$475	$430

Last Mfg.'s Sug. Retail was $910.

PISTOLS

TRIACE — .22 Short, .22 LR or .32 S&W wadcutter cal.'s, target pistol incorporating unique action, competition walnut grips with thumb rest and adj. heel, blued finish with chrome accents. Imported 1985-86 only.

	$1,300	$1,150	$950	$825	$700	$600	$500

Last Mfg.'s Sug. Retail was $1,395.

Triace Pistol Kit — consists of Triace frame, .22 Short, .22 LR, and .32 S&W barrels. Cased with accessories. Imported 1985-86 only.

	$2,300	$1,975	$1,700	$1,450	$1,300	$1,175	$1,025

Last Mfg.'s Sug. Retail was $2,385.

SAMCO GLOBAL ARMS, INC.

Importer/distributor located in Miami, FL.

Samco Global Arms currently imports a variety of foreign and domestic surplus military rifles (including various contract Mausers, Loewe, Steyr, Hakim, Lee Enfield, etc.). Most of these guns are in the $60-$120 range and while they offer excellent values to the shooter, to date they have not been collectible. Samco also sells newly remanufactured sporting rifles (German or Spanish) in .308 Win. or 7 x 57mm cal. These sporters range in value from approx. $170-$200. Samco also imports BSA rifles which can be located in their own heading of this text.

SARDIUS

Manufacturer located in Israel. Previously imported and distributed by Armscorp of America, Inc. located in Baltimore, MD.

SD-9 — 9mm Para., semi-auto double action, compact design, 3.07 in. barrel, matte black finish, 6 shot mag., 3 dot sighting system, 1.54 lbs. Imported 1988-90 only.

	$315	$280	$260	$240	$220	$200	$185

Last Mfg.'s Sug. Retail was $350.

Grading	100%	98%	95%	90%	80%	70%	60%

SARRIUGARTE, FRANCISO S.A.

Manufacturer located in Elgoibar, Spain. Previously part of the Diarm S.A. Group which was imported and distributed by American Arms, Inc. located in North Kansas City, MO.

SARASQUETA, FELIX

Manufacturer located in Eibar, Spain. Previously imported and distributed by SAE (Spain America Enterprises), Inc. located in Miami, FL.

SHOTGUNS

MODEL MERKE O/U — 12 ga. only, boxlock action, 22 or 27 in. separated barrels, single non-selective trigger, blue only, extractors, recoil pad. Imported 1986 only.

	100%	98%	95%	90%	80%	70%	60%
	$255	$215	$200	$190	$180	$170	$160

Last Mfg.'s Sug. Retail was $291.

SARASQUETA, J.J.

Manufacturer located in Eibar, Spain. Imported until 1984 by American Arms, Inc. located in Overland Park, KS.

SHOTGUNS: SIDE-BY-SIDE

MODEL 107 E — 12, 16, or 20 ga., ejectors, various barrel lengths, checkered walnut stock and forearm, double triggers.

	$360	$290	$270	$255	$240	$215	$200

Last Mfg.'s Sug. Retail was $435.

MODELS 119E-132E-1882E — more deluxe versions of Model 107E.

	$470	$375	$340	$315	$285	$255	$230

Last Mfg.'s Sug. Retail was $570.

MODEL 130 E — more deluxe version of Model 119 E.

	$800	$635	$590	$555	$515	$480	$450

Last Mfg.'s Sug. Retail was $960.

MODEL 131 E — action similar to Model 107 E, except has deluxe engraving.

	$1,050	$845	$770	$710	$665	$620	$585

Last Mfg.'s Sug. Retail was $1,250.

MODEL 1882 E LUXE — double triggers, moderate engraving, otherwise similar to Model 107 E.

	$825	$660	$615	$565	$520	$480	$450

Last Mfg.'s Sug. Retail was $990.

Model 1882 E Luxe w/gold inlays — SST, extensive engraving.

	$1,120	$920	$850	$790	$740	$695	$650

Last Mfg.'s Sug. Retail was $1,320.

Model 1882 E Luxe w/silver inlays — SST, extensive engraving.

	$1,055	$855	$795	$740	$700	$660	$630

Last Mfg.'s Sug. Retail was $1,260.

MODEL 150 E — 12 or 16 ga., single trigger, ejectors, select walnut and extensive engraving.

	$1,285	$1,035	$960	$895	$835	$770	$695

Last Mfg.'s Sug. Retail was $1,500.

Model 150 E Trap — same as Model 150 E, except trap dimensions on stock.

	$1,360	$1,125	$1,010	$940	$875	$790	$720

Last Mfg.'s Sug. Retail was $1,600.

Grading	100%	98%	95%	90%	80%	70%	60%

SARASQUETA, VICTOR

Previous manufacturer located in Eibar, Spain. Trademark is currently owned by Diarm S.A.

SHOTGUNS

MODEL 3 SXS — 12, 16, or 20 ga., all standard barrel lengths and chokes, boxlock, double triggers, checkered English style stock and forend.
Auto ejectors

	100%	98%	95%	90%	80%	70%	60%
	$580	$505	$480	$440	$380	$365	$345

HAMMERLESS SIDELOCK — 12, 16, or 20 ga., s x s, barrel length and choke to order, straight English style stock, models differ as to amount of engraving, grade of wood, and overall quality as follows:

MODEL 4 — extractors.

	100%	98%	95%	90%	80%	70%	60%
	$620	$550	$525	$495	$450	$415	$360

MODEL 4E — auto ejectors.

	$680	$605	$580	$550	$505	$470	$415

MODEL 203 — extractors.

	$650	$570	$545	$515	$475	$435	$380

MODEL 203E — auto ejectors.

	$710	$625	$600	$570	$530	$490	$435

MODEL 6E

	$800	$715	$690	$660	$615	$580	$525

MODEL 7E

	$855	$770	$745	$715	$670	$635	$580

MODEL 10E

	$1,735	$1,595	$1,485	$1,405	$1,320	$1,240	$1,100

MODEL 11E

	$1,870	$1,680	$1,595	$1,515	$1,430	$1,350	$1,265

MODEL 12E

	$2,145	$1,900	$1,790	$1,705	$1,570	$1,430	$1,375

SAUER, J.P. & SOHN

Manufactured since 1751 in Germany (originally Prussia). Previously located in Suhl - currently headquartered in Eckernforde, W. Germany. Bolt action rifles are currently being imported and distributed by G.U. Inc. located in Omaha, NE. In 1972, J.P. Sauer & Sohn formed a cooperation with the Sig Swiss Industrial Company which is presently the parent house of Sauer & Sohn.

PISTOLS

MODEL 1913 POCKET AUTOMATIC — .32 auto, 7 shot, 3 in. barrel, fixed sights, blue, black rubber grips. Mfg. 1913-1930.

	$250	$220	$185	$165	$155	$145	$135

MODEL 1913 25 AUTOMATIC — .25 auto, 7 shot, 2½ in. barrel, fixed sights, blue, black rubber grips. Mfg. 1913-1930.

	$275	$240	$200	$175	$150	$140	$135

MODEL 28 — .25 ACP, 7 shot, 3 in. barrel, fixed sights, blue, black rubber grips. Mfg. 1930-1938.

	$260	$210	$185	$170	$155	$145	$135

Grading	100%	98%	95%	90%	80%	70%	60%

BEHORDEN (SERVICE) MODEL — .32 ACP, 3 in. barrel, blue only, black plastic grips.

	$275	$240	$200	$175	$150	$145	$135

MODEL 38 H DOUBLE ACTION AUTOMATIC — .22 LR (rare), .32 ACP, or .380 ACP (extremely rare) cal., 3¼ in. barrel, fixed sights, blue, plastic grips. Mfg. 1938-1945. Add 10% for Waffenamt, 60% for alloy frame.

	$300	$275	$240	$205	$185	$165	$150

RIFLES: BOLT ACTION

On Models 90 Lux and Supreme add 69% for Grade I engraving, 105% for Grade II, 128% for Grade III, and 164% for Grade IV.

SAUER MAUSER BOLT ACTION RIFLE — most popular European cal.'s and .30-06, 22 or 24 in. barrel, raised solid rib, Krupp steel, double set triggers, folding 3 leaf express sight, checkered sporter stock. Mfg. pre-WWII.

	$715	$550	$495	$440	$360	$330	$305

MODEL 200 BOLT ACTION — available in 9 cal.'s between .243 Win. and 9.3 x 62, short and medium actions only, 23.62 in. unique interchangeable barrels, 6 lug bolt, easily detachable stock and forearm, optional set trigger, detachable mag. with hidden release button, 7.7 lbs. Importation disc. 1987.

	$600	$550	$500	$465	$435	$400	$375

Add $100 for 7mm Rem. Mag. or .300 Win. Mag. cal.

Add $235 for extra interchangeable barrel.

Last Mfg.'s Sug. Retail was $875.

Model 200 Lightweight — same as Model 200, only with alloy receiver, 6.6 lbs. Importation disc. 1987.

	$575	$525	$480	$450	$425	$395	$370

Add $85 for left-hand version.

Last Mfg.'s Sug. Retail was $875.

Model 200 Lux — similar to Model 200, except has deluxe walnut, rosewood forend tip and pistol grip cap, marmorized bolt and gold trigger. Importation disc. 1987.

	$675	$600	$560	$520	$480	$440	$400

Last Mfg.'s Sug. Retail was $1,075.

American 200 Lux — similar to Model 200 Lux, except has high gloss Monte Carlo stock, 24 in. barrel, jeweled bolt, and gold trigger. Imported 1987-1988 only.

	$775	$675	$600	$550	$500	$465	$430

Add $95 for left-hand action.

Last Mfg.'s Sug. Retail was $1,175.

European 200 Lux — similar to Model 200 Lux, except has European configured stock with Schnabel forearm, 26 in. barrel. Importation disc. 1988.

	$775	$675	$600	$550	$500	$465	$430

Add $95 for left-hand action.

Last Mfg.'s Sug. Retail was $1,175.

Model 200 Carbon Fiber — similar to Model 200, except has carbon fiber stock. Imported 1987-88 only.

	$800	$700	$625	$565	$500	$465	$430

Last Mfg.'s Sug. Retail was $1,200.

MODEL 90 BOLT ACTION — available in 17 cal.'s between .222 Rem. and .458 Win. Mag., short, medium and long actions, 22.44 or 26 in. barrel, 3 or 4 shot detachable mag., deluxe checkered walnut stock, approx. 7½ lbs. (except .458 Win. Mag.). Importation disc. 1989.

	$775	$675	$600	$550	$500	$465	$430

Last Mfg.'s Sug. Retail was $1,175.

Model 90 Stutzen — Mannlicher style full stock, not available in European or Mag. cal.'s. Importation disc. 1989.

	$800	$700	$600	$550	$500	$465	$430

Last Mfg.'s Sug. Retail was $1,225.

Grading	100%	98%	95%	90%	80%	70%	60%

Safari Model — .458 Win. Mag, 23.62 in. barrel, 10½ lbs. Imported 1986-1988 only.

	$1,250	$950	$850	$750	$650	$575	$500

Last Mfg.'s Sug. Retail was $1,675.

MODEL 90 LUX — .300 Win. Mag., .300 Wby., .338 Win. Mag, or .375 H&H cal., similar to Model 90, except has deluxe oil finished walnut stock with rosewood forearm tip and pistol grip cap, recoil pad, gold trigger.

Mfg.'s Sug. Retail	$1,495	$1,300	$1,025	$900	$795	$585	$465	$430

Model 90 Stutzen Lux — Mannlicher style full stock, not available in European or Mag. cal.'s. Importation disc. 1990.

	$1,200	$1,020	$900	$795	$585	$465	$430

Last Mfg.'s Sug. Retail was $1,325.

Safari Model Lux — .458 Win. Mag., 23.62 in. barrel, 10½ lbs. Imported 1986-87 only.

	$1,650	$1,400	$1,100	$940	$775	$680	$600

Last Mfg.'s Sug. Retail was $1,825.

Add 45% for grade I engraving, 65% for grade II engraving, 80% for grade III, and 100% for grade IV engraving on this model. A left-handed stock is also available - add $135.

MODEL 90 SUPREME — 25-06, .270 Win., .30-06, .300 Win. Mag., .300 Wby., 7mm Rem. Mag., .338 Win. Mag., or .375 H&H cal., similar to Model 90 Lux, except has high gloss laquer stock with Monte Carlo cheek piece, jeweled bolt, and gold trigger. New 1987.

Mfg.'s Sug. Retail	$1,495	$1,300	$1,025	$900	$795	$585	$465	$430

RIFLES: DRILLINGS — O/U COMBINATION GUNS

SAUER MODEL 3000 DRILLING — available in either 16 ga./.30-06, 6.5 x 57R, 7 x 57R, 7 x 65R or 12 ga./.222 Rem. (disc.), .243 Win., .30-06, 6.5 x 57R, 7 x 57R, 7 x 65R, 9.3 x 74R, Greener cross-bolt and double barrel lug locking, cocking indicators, front set trigger, automatic sight, walnut pistol grip stock with hog-back and cheek piece, grade III scroll engraving, 7¼ lbs.

Mfg.'s Sug. Retail	$6,450	$5,950	$5,200	$4,100	$3,000	$2,200	$1,650	$1,350

Luxury Grade — same as Model 3000 standard, except select root timber and extensive engraving featuring two animals.

Mfg.'s Sug. Retail	$7,350	$6,800	$5,950	$5,200	$4,100	$3,000	$2,200	$1,650

COMBO BBF 54 O/U — standard grade combination gun, 16 ga./.222 Rem., .243 Win., 6.5 x 57R, 7 x 57R, 7 x 65R, and .30-06 cal.'s, ejectors, double triggers with front set trigger, moderate engraving on coin finished receiver, Greener cross-bolt with double barrel lugs, 6 lbs. Importation disc. 1986.

	$2,200	$2,060	$1,760	$1,565	$1,380	$1,250	$1,125

Last Mfg's Sug. Retail was $2,495.

This model is still available in 1987 from the distributor in limited quantities.

Luxury Grade — same as BBF 54, except game scene engraved and deluxe crotch walnut.

	$2,450	$2,200	$2,000	$1,785	$1,600	$1,475	$1,300

Last Mfg.'s Sug. Retail was $2,745.

LUFTWAFFE SURVIVAL DRILLING — 12 or 16 ga. (65mm) SxS over 9.3 x 74 R, 28 in. barrels, large Eagle swastika on stock and breech end of right barrel. Originally mfg. for Luftwaffe pilots during WWII.

	$4,500	$4,000	$3,600	$3,200	$2,600	$2,400	$2,200

Add 20% for original aluminum case and accessories.

SAUER MODEL 3000E DRILLING — see listing under Colt Sauer Drilling.

SNIPER RIFLE — very accurate, special order only Sniper Rifle, built to customer specifications.

	$4,845	$3,655	$3,200	$2,850	$2,500	$2,275	$2,000

Grading	100%	98%	95%	90%	80%	70%	60%

SHOTGUNS

MODEL 60 — various ga.'s, boxlock action, DT, extractors, checkered walnut stock and fore-arm, this model was the standard model of its period.

	100%	98%	95%	90%	80%	70%	60%
	$715	$550	$495	$440	$360	$330	$305

ROYAL DOUBLE BARREL SHOTGUN — 12, 16 or 20 ga., 26, 28, or 30 in. barrels, various chokes, boxlock, scalloped engraved frame, cocking indicators, SST, auto ejectors, Krupp steel barrel, checkered pistol grip stock. Mfg. 1955-1977.

	100%	98%	95%	90%	80%	70%	60%
	$1,650	$1,375	$1,210	$1,100	$880	$770	$660

20 ga. — add 20%.

ARTEMIS — 12 ga., 28 in. barrels, mod. and full choke, H&H type sidelock, SST, auto ejector, Krupp steel, checkered pistol grip stock. Mfg. 1966-1977.
Grade I — fine line engraved.

	100%	98%	95%	90%	80%	70%	60%
	$5,500	$4,620	$3,850	$3,520	$3,080	$2,640	$2,200

Grade II — extensive engraving.

	100%	98%	95%	90%	80%	70%	60%
	$6,600	$5,500	$4,840	$4,235	$3,850	$3,300	$3,080

MODEL 66 O/U FIELD GUN — 12 ga., 28 in. mod. and full, Krupp steel barrels, H&H type sidelocks, SST, auto ejectors, checkered pistol grip stock, available in three grades of engraving. Mfg. 1966-1975.

	100%	98%	95%	90%	80%	70%	60%
Grade I	$2,200	$1,760	$1,540	$1,320	$1,100	$880	$770
Grade II	$3,080	$2,420	$1,980	$1,650	$1,430	$1,210	$990
Grade III	$3,850	$3,300	$2,860	$2,420	$1,980	$1,650	$1,320

MODEL 66 O/U SKEET GUN — same as Field Gun, with 26 in. vent rib skeet bored barrel and vent forearm. Mfg. 1966-1975.

MODEL 66 O/U TRAP GUN — same as 66 Skeet, with 30 in. barrels, full and full, or mod. and full choke, trap style stock.

	100%	98%	95%	90%	80%	70%	60%
Grade I	$2,090	$1,760	$1,540	$1,320	$1,100	$880	$770
Grade II	$3,080	$2,420	$1,980	$1,650	$1,430	$1,210	$880
Grade III	$3,850	$3,300	$2,860	$2,420	$1,980	$1,650	$1,320

SAUER/FRANCHI STANDARD GRADE O/U — 12 ga. only, double triggers, checkered walnut stock and forearm, SST, blued finish only, sling swivels, VR. Importation disc. 1986.

	100%	98%	95%	90%	80%	70%	60%
	$375	$340	$315	$290	$275	$260	$245

Last Mfg.'s Sug. Retail was $785.

Regent Grade — similar to Standard grade, except has single trigger and lightly engraved silver finished receiver. Importation disc. 1986.

	100%	98%	95%	90%	80%	70%	60%
	$475	$395	$350	$310	$290	$275	$265

Last Mfg.'s Sug. Retail was $825.

Favorit Grade — similar to Regent Grade, except has elaborate scroll engraving on coin finished receiver, gold plated trigger. Importation disc. 1986.

	100%	98%	95%	90%	80%	70%	60%
	$550	$495	$450	$420	$385	$350	$300

Last Mfg.'s Sug. Retail was $875.

Diplomat Grade — similar to Favorit Grade, except has more elaborate scroll engraving and with model name gold filled on receiver sides and barrel, extra grain French walnut, cased.

	100%	98%	95%	90%	80%	70%	60%
	$875	$750	$625	$550	$495	$460	$435

Last Mfg.'s Sug. Retail was $1,520.

SAUER/FRANCHI SPORTING S O/U — 12 ga. only, 28 in. barrels, ejectors, SST, select European walnut with checkered stock and forearm, 10mm vent rib, plain silver finished receiver with model name gold filled on both sides. Importation disc. 1986.

	100%	98%	95%	90%	80%	70%	60%
	$800	$700	$600	$500	$450	$420	$395

Last Mfg.'s Sug. Retail was $1,375.

Grading	100%	98%	95%	90%	80%	70%	60%

SAUER/FRANCHI MODEL TRAP O/U — similar to Sporting S, except has 29 in. barrels, trap chokes and stock dimensions. Importation disc. 1986.

| | $875 | $750 | $625 | $550 | $495 | $460 | $435 |

Last Mfg.'s Sug. Retail was $1,375.

SAUER/FRANCHI MODEL SKEET O/U — similar to Sporting S, except has skeet chokes. Importation disc. 1986.

| | $875 | $750 | $625 | $550 | $495 | $460 | $435 |

Last Mfg.'s Sug. Retail was $1,375.

SAVAGE INDUSTRIES, INC.

Initially manufactured in Utica, NY, later manufactured in Chicopee Falls, MA, currently manufactured in Westfield, MA Since 1959.

This company originally started in Utica, NY in 1895. The Model 1895 was initially manufactured by Marlin between 1895-1899. The company was renamed Savage Arms Co. in 1899. After WWI, the name was again changed to the Savage Arms Corporation. Savage moved to Chicopee Falls, MA in the 1946 circa (to it's J. Stevens Arms Co. plants). In the Mid-1960'S the company became The Savage Arms Division of American Hardware Corp., which later became The Emhart Corporation. This division was sold in September 1981, and became Savage Industries, Inc. located in Westfield, MA (since the move in the 1959 circa).

PISTOLS

MODEL 1907 AUTO PISTOL — .32 auto, 10 shot, .380 auto, 9 shot, $3^{13}/_{16}$ (.32 ACP) or $4^{5}/_{16}$ (.380 ACP) in. barrel, blue, fixed sights, hard rubber grips, exposed hammer. Mfg. 1910-1917.

| | $270 | $220 | $175 | $150 | $125 | $115 | $100 |

Add 80% for factory nickel finish (rare).

Add 15% for .380.

MODEL 1915 HAMMERLESS — same as 1907, with grip safety and no visible hammer. Mfg. 1915-1917.

| | $325 | $290 | $210 | $190 | $170 | $150 | $130 |

Add 15% for .380.

MODEL 1917 AUTOMATIC — same as 1907, with spur hammer and trapezoidal grips. Mfg. 1920-1928.

| | $250 | $225 | $175 | $145 | $130 | $110 | $100 |

Add 15 for .380.

U.S. ARMY TEST TRIAL .45 ACP — .45 ACP, large version of 1910, exposed hammer. Approx. 400 mfg. 1907-1910 for military trials.

| | $4,500 | $3,800 | $3,300 | $2,800 | $2,400 | $2,000 | $1,800 |

Some of these models were repurchased from the government, reconditioned (many reblued), and resold to the public as commercial models.

MODEL 101 SINGLE SHOT — single action, .22 cal., $5^{1}/_{2}$ in. barrel, adj. sight, swing out barrel, blue, wood grips. Mfg. 1960-1968.

| | $150 | $120 | $95 | $80 | $70 | $60 | $50 |

RIFLES

Savage Industries announced in early 1988 that they will no longer publish retail prices for currently manufactured firearms.

MODEL 1895 — .303 Savage only, lever action, mfg. in either carbine (22 in.), rifle (26 in.), or musket (30 in.) variations, closed top, solid breech, side ejecting, 5 shot rotating box mag., unfired shots indicator. Originally mfg. by Marlin, marked "Savage Repeating Arms Co. Utica, N.Y. U.S.A. Pat. Feb. 7, 1893.", approx. 6,000 mfg. 1895-1899, early models had hole in top of bolt — latter ones were smooth.

| | $1,500 | $1,250 | $995 | $880 | $770 | $660 | $495 |

Values assume rifle configuration — add premiums for the carbine (rare) and musket.

Grading	100%	98%	95%	90%	80%	70%	60%

MODEL 1899 — .25-35, .30-30, .303 Savage, .32-40, or .38-55 cal., improvement of Model 1895, 20 in. round (carbine), 22 in. (round), or 26 in. (round, half-oct. or full oct.) barrel marked "Savage Arms Company, Utica, N.Y. Pat. Feb. 7.1893.", over 75,000 mfg. 1899-1917, approx. 7½ lbs. Older "perch-belly stocks" and high-gloss bluing will command a 10%-15% premium on this variation.

	$695	$575	$500	$450	$375	$300	$225

Add 25% for takedown (added 1909).

In 1905 Savage broadened the variety of this model and added the 1899A2, CD, BC, AB, Excelsior, Leader, Crescent, Victor, Rival, Premier, and Monarch (top-of-the-line model). Prices at the time ranged from $21 to $250 — quite a range of prices. Any factory engraved Savage 99 is rare (less than 1,000 mfg. to date) with values having to be computed one gun at a time. Above values assume standard rifle with no engraving options (Grades A through G).

MODEL 99A — .30-30, .250-3000, .300 Sav. or .303 Sav. cal., lever action, 24 in. barrel, open sight, hammerless, straight grip stock, crescent butt. Mfg. 1920-1936.

	$550	$440	$330	$275	$180	$165	$150

MODEL 99A RECENT — similar to original, with .243, .250 Sav., .300 Sav., or .308 Sav. cal., 20 or 22 in. barrel, tang. safety, conventional butt. Mfg. 1971-1981.

	$375	$340	$310	$275	$250	$225	$200

MODEL 99B — takedown version of original 99A. Mfg. 1920-1936.

	$880	$770	$660	$495	$330	$250	$195

MODEL 99H CARBINE — .250-3000, .30-30, or .300 Sav. cal., solid frame, carbine type stock. Mfg. 1931-1942.

	$440	$330	$275	$220	$180	$165	$150

MODEL 99E — .22 Hi Power, .250-3000, .30-30, .300 Sav., or .303 Sav. cal., 22 in. barrel. Mfg. 1920-1936.

	$880	$770	$660	$550	$440	$275	$220

MODEL 99E CARBINE — .243, .250 Sav., .300 Sav., or .308 Win. cal., 22 in. barrel, checkered pistol grip stock, 5 shot rotary mag. Mfg. 1960-1982.

	$320	$260	$230	$200	$180	$165	$150

Last Mfg.'s Sug. Retail was $343.

MODEL 99F FEATHERWEIGHT — same as pre-war 99E, except takedown and ½ pound lighter. Mfg. 1920-1942.

	$440	$330	$275	$220	$195	$175	$160

MODEL 99F — .243, .300 Sav., or .308 Win. cal., solid frame, checkered pistol grip stock. Disc. 1970.

	$350	$310	$285	$260	$230	$210	$190

This model had the receiver marked "99M".

MODEL 99G — same as 99E pre-war, with checkered stock and takedown. Mfg. 1920-1942.

	$660	$550	$440	$275	$220	$165	$150

MODEL 99EG — same as 99G, with solid frame and no checkering. Mfg. 1936-1941.

	$550	$440	$330	$260	$230	$210	$190

MODEL 99EG POST-WAR — .243, .250 Sav., .300 Sav., .308, or .358 cal., checkered stock. Mfg. 1946-1960.

	$350	$310	$285	$260	$230	$210	$190

MODEL 99R PRE-WAR — .250-3000 or .300 Sav. cal., 22 or 24 in. barrel, large pistol grip stock and forearm. Mfg. 1936-1942.

	$495	$440	$305	$275	$250	$220	$195

MODEL 99R POST-WAR — same as Pre-War, .300 Sav., .308, .358, or .243 cal., 24 in. barrel only, swivel studs. Mfg. 1946-1960.

	$350	$310	$285	$260	$230	$210	$190

Grading	100%	98%	95%	90%	80%	70%	60%

MODEL 99RS PRE-WAR — same as 99R Pre-War, with Lyman aperture sight, swivels and sling. Mfg. 1936-1942.

	$605	$550	$440	$330	$275	$250	$220

MODEL 99RS POST-WAR — same as 99R Post-War, with Redfield receiver sight. Mfg. 1946-1958.

	$350	$330	$285	$250	$225	$200	$180

MODEL 99T — 20 or 22 in. barrel, solid frame, lightweight, checkered pistol grip stock. Mfg. 1936-1942.

	$440	$330	$275	$205	$180	$165	$150

MODEL 99K — engraved receiver and fancy wood stock, Lyman aperture sight and folding middle sight. Mfg. 1931-1942.

	$2,200	$1,870	$1,210	$880	$770	$550	$440

MODEL 99DL — .243 or .308 cal., Monte Carlo stock and sling swivels. Post-war mfg. 1960-1973.

	$350	$310	$285	$260	$230	$210	$185

MODEL 99C — same as 99F Post-War, available in .22-250 (rare), .243, .284 Win. (disc.), 7mm-08 (disc.), or .308 cal., 22 in. barrel, Monte Carlo stock with cut checkering and recoil pad, top tang safety, cocking indicator, open sights, detachable 4 shot mag., 8 lbs. Mfg. 1965-present.

Mfg.'s Sug. Retail	$616	$525	$430	$365	$300	$260	$230	$200

MODEL 99CD — same as 99C, with Monte Carlo cheek piece stock. Mfg. 1980-1981.

	$525	$450	$375	$325	$295	$260	$230

MODEL 99-358 — .358 Win. cal., recoil pad. Mfg. 1977-1980.

	$450	$400	$350	$325	$295	$260	$230

MODEL 99PE — elaborately engraved and plated receiver, tang. and lever, fancy wood with hand cut checkering. Mfg. 1966-1970.

	$1,320	$990	$740	$500	$375	$300	$260

This model had the receiver marked "99M".

MODEL 99DE CITATION — similar to Model 99PE, except with less engraving and pressed checkering. Mfg. 1968-1970.

	$885	$660	$495	$330	$250	$220	$195

This model had the receiver marked "99M".

MODEL 99M — while the receivers on models 99F, 99PE, and 99DE were marked "99M" this is not a model designation. Rather, the "M" barrel designation indicated Monte Carlo stock.

SAVAGE 1895 ANNIVERSARY — a replica of the original M1895, .308 cal., 24 in. octagon barrel, engraved receiver, brass plated lever, straight stock, Schnabel forend, medallion in stock, brass crescent butt plate. Mfg. 9,999 in 1970 only, to commemorate Savage's 75th year.

	$385	$275	$220	$195	$165	$150	$140

MODEL 1903 SLIDE ACTION — .22 S, L, or LR, 24 in. barrel, open sights, box mag., pistol grip stock. Mfg. 1903-1921.

	$275	$220	$110	$90	$75	$65	$45

MODEL 1909 SLIDE ACTION — similar to 1903, with 20 in. round barrel. Mfg. 1909-1915.

	$220	$140	$110	$90	$75	$65	$45

MODEL 1904 SINGLE SHOT — .22 S, L, or LR, bolt action, 18 in. barrel, straight stock. Mfg. 1904-1917.

	$140	$85	$55	$45	$35	$30	$30

Grading	100%	98%	95%	90%	80%	70%	60%

MODEL 1905 SINGLE SHOT — similar to 1904, except 24 in. barrel, takedown. Mfg. 1905-1919.

	$140	$85	$55	$45	$35	$30	$30

MODEL 1912 AUTOLOADER — .22 LR, 20 in. barrel, takedown, straight stock. Mfg. 1912-1916.

	$330	$275	$195	$110	$90	$75	$65

MODEL 1914 SLIDE ACTION — .22 S, L, and LR, 24 in. octagon barrel, plain pistol grip stock. Mfg. 1914-1924.

	$275	$250	$195	$110	$90	$75	$65

MODEL 19 NRA BOLT ACTION — .22 LR, 25 in. barrel, adj. aperture sight, 5 shot military stock. Approx. 50,000 mfg. 1919-1937.

	$220	$140	$110	$100	$90	$75	$65

Between 1943-1945 approx. 6,000 Model 19's were made under military contract — add 15%.

MODEL 10 BOLT ACTION TARGET — .22 LR, 25 in. barrel, speed lock, adj. aperture sight, target stock. Mfg. 1933-1946.

	$250	$165	$140	$110	$100	$90	$70

MODEL 19L — same as 19, with Lyman receiver sight. Mfg. 1933-1942.

	$330	$275	$195	$140	$120	$110	$100

MODEL 19M — same as 19, with 28 in. heavy barrel and scope bases. Mfg. 1933-1942.

	$330	$275	$195	$165	$140	$120	$110

MODEL 19H — same as 19, except .22 Hornet. Mfg. 1933-1942.

	$550	$495	$330	$220	$175	$165	$155

MODEL 1920 BOLT ACTION — Mauser type action, .250-3000 or .300 Sav. cal., 22 or 24 in. barrel, open sights, 5 shot, checkered pistol grip, Schnabel forend. Mfg. 1920-1926.

	$330	$250	$220	$200	$175	$165	$155

MODEL 1920-1926 — same as 1920, with 24 in. barrel, Lyman aperture sight, Mfg. 1926-1927.

	$330	$250	$220	$200	$175	$165	$155

MODEL 23A BOLT ACTION RIFLE — .22 LR, 23 in. barrel, open sights, plain pistol grip stock, Schnabel forend. Mfg. 1923-1933.

	$220	$165	$140	$110	$95	$85	$70

MODEL 23AA — improved version of 23A, with speedlock and checkered stock. Mfg. 1933-1942.

	$275	$195	$165	$130	$110	$100	$85

MODEL 23B — same configuration as 23A, with .25-20 cal., 25 in. barrel, full forearm. Mfg. 1923-1942.

	$220	$140	$110	$100	$90	$75	$65

MODEL 23C — same as 23B, with .32-20. Mfg. 1923-1942.

	$220	$140	$110	$100	$90	$75	$65

MODEL 23D — same as 23B, with .22 Hornet. Mfg. 1933-1947.

	$305	$250	$220	$195	$165	$140	$110

MODEL 25 SLIDE ACTION — .22 S, L, or LR, 24 in. octagon barrel, open sight, takedown, hammerless, tube mag., plain pistol grip stock. Mfg. 1925-1929.

	$330	$275	$220	$140	$110	$75	$65

MODEL 40 BOLT ACTION RIFLE — .250-3000, .300 Sav., .30-30, or .30-06 cal., 22 or 24 in. barrel, open sight, 4 shot mag., plain pistol grip stock, Schnabel forend. Mfg. 1928-1940.

	$330	$220	$195	$165	$155	$140	$120

Grading	100%	98%	95%	90%	80%	70%	60%

MODEL 45 SUPER — same as 40, with Lyman receiver sight and checkered stock. Mfg. 1928-1940.

	100%	98%	95%	90%	80%	70%	60%
	$385	$275	$250	$200	$175	$165	$140

MODEL 29 SLIDE ACTION — .22 S, L, or LR, 22 in. barrel, octagon until 1940, round on post-WWII, open sights, checkered pistol grip stock on pre-war, plain on late model. Mfg. 1929-1967.

	100%	98%	95%	90%	80%	70%	60%
	$275	$220	$165	$100	$90	$75	$65
Pre-war	$330	$275	$195	$120	$110	$100	$90

MODEL 3 SINGLE SHOT — .22 S, L, or LR, bolt action, 26 in. barrel, 24 in. barrel on post-war, open sights, plain grip stock. Mfg. 1933-1952.

	100%	98%	95%	90%	80%	70%	60%
	$85	$65	$55	$40	$30	$30	$30

MODEL 3S — same as 3, with aperture sight. Mfg. 1933-1942.

	100%	98%	95%	90%	80%	70%	60%
	$100	$85	$70	$55	$40	$30	$30

MODEL 3ST — same as 3S, with swivels and sling. Mfg. 1933-1942.

	100%	98%	95%	90%	80%	70%	60%
	$110	$90	$85	$70	$45	$35	$30

MODEL 4 BOLT ACTION REPEATER — .22 S, L, or LR, 24 in. barrel, open sight, takedown, 5 shot, checkered pistol grip stock on pre-war, plain stock on post-war. Mfg. 1933-1965.

	100%	98%	95%	90%	80%	70%	60%
	$110	$85	$70	$55	$40	$30	$30
Pre-war	$120	$95	$85	$65	$50	$40	$30

MODEL 4S — same as 4, with aperture sight. Mfg. 1933-1942.

	100%	98%	95%	90%	80%	70%	60%
	$120	$90	$75	$65	$55	$40	$30

MODEL 4M — same as 4, except .22 WRM.

	100%	98%	95%	90%	80%	70%	60%
	$110	$85	$70	$55	$45	$30	$30

MODEL 5 — same as 4, with tubular mag. Mfg. 1936-1961.

	100%	98%	95%	90%	80%	70%	60%
	$110	$85	$70	$55	$45	$30	$30

MODEL 5S — same as 5, with aperture sight. Mfg. 1936-1942.

	100%	98%	95%	90%	80%	70%	60%
	$120	$95	$85	$65	$55	$40	$30

MODEL 6 AUTOLOADER — .22 S, L, or LR, 24 in. barrel, tubular mag., takedown, checkered pistol grip stock on pre-war, plain stock on post-war. Mfg. 1938-1968.

	100%	98%	95%	90%	80%	70%	60%
	$140	$110	$95	$85	$65	$55	$40
Pre-war	$150	$120	$105	$95	$75	$65	$50

MODEL 6S — same as 6, with aperture sight. Mfg. 1938-1942.

	100%	98%	95%	90%	80%	70%	60%
	$150	$120	$105	$95	$75	$65	$45

MODEL 7 AUTOLOADER — same as 6, with box mag. Mfg. 1939-1951.

	100%	98%	95%	90%	80%	70%	60%
	$140	$110	$95	$65	$55	$55	$40
Pre-war	$150	$120	$105	$95	$75	$65	$50

MODEL 7S — same as 7, with aperture sight. Mfg. 1938-1942.

	100%	98%	95%	90%	80%	70%	60%
	$150	$120	$105	$95	$75	$65	$45

MODEL 60 AUTOLOADER — .22 LR, 20 in. barrel, leaf sight, tubular mag., checkered Monte Carlo stock. Mfg. 1969-1972.

	100%	98%	95%	90%	80%	70%	60%
	$95	$85	$70	$55	$45	$35	$30

MODEL 90 AUTOLOADING CARBINE — same as 60, with 16½ in. barrel, plain carbine stock, with barrel band.

	100%	98%	95%	90%	80%	70%	60%
	$95	$85	$70	$55	$45	$35	$30

Grading	100%	98%	95%	90%	80%	70%	60%

MODEL 88 AUTOLOADER — same as 60, except has walnut finished hardwood stock. Mfg. 1969-1972.

	$85	$65	$55	$45	$40	$35	$30

MODEL 63K SINGLE SHOT — .22 S, L, or LR, bolt action, 18 in. barrel, open sights, trigger locks with key, full length pistol grip stock. Mfg. 1970-1972.

	$80	$65	$55	$45	$40	$35	$30

MODEL 63KM — same as 63K, except .22 WRM.

	$90	$70	$65	$55	$45	$40	$35

MODEL 219 SINGLE SHOT — .22 Hornet, .25-20, .32-20, or .30-30 cal., 26 in. barrel, open sight, hammerless, break open, top lever, plain pistol grip stock. Mfg. 1938-1965.

	$100	$85	$70	$55	$45	$35	$30

MODEL 219L — same as 219, with side lever. Mfg. 1965-1967.

	$100	$85	$70	$55	$45	$35	$30

MODELS 221, 222, 223, 227, 228, AND 229 — single barrel, same as 219, only supplied with additional shotgun barrel, interchangeable, different model numbers are for different cal.'s, ga.'s, and barrel lengths, all have been disc.

	$130	$100	$85	$65	$55	$45	$30

SAVAGE/STEVENS MODEL 65 — please refer to listing under Stevens section.

MODEL 34M — same as 34, chambered for .22 WRM. Mfg. 1969-1973.

	$90	$70	$55	$45	$35	$30	$30

MODEL 35 — .22 LR, bolt action, 22 in. barrel, 5 shot clip mag., open sights, hardwood Monte Carlo stock. Disc. 1985.

	$90	$80	$65	$50	$35	$30	$30

Last Mfg.'s Sug. Retail was $100.

MODEL 46 — same as 34, with tubular mag. Mfg. 1969-1973.

	$90	$70	$55	$45	$35	$30	$30

MODEL 65M — same as 65, in .22 WRM.

	$95	$75	$65	$55	$45	$35	$30

SAVAGE/STEVENS MODEL 72 "CRACKSHOT" — please refer to listing under Stevens section.

SAVAGE/STEVENS MODEL 89 SINGLE SHOT — please refer to listing under Stevens section.

MODEL 340 BOLT ACTION — .22 Hornet, .222 Rem., .223 Win., or .30-30 cal., 22 and 24 in. barrel, open sights, 4 or 5 shot mag., 7½ lbs., plain pistol grip stock. Mfg. 1950-1985.

	$225	$195	$170	$160	$150	$140	$130

Last Mfg.'s Sug. Retail was $257.

EL 340C — same as 340, with aperture sight, checkered stock and sling swivels. Mfg. 1952-1960.

	$235	$205	$180	$165	$155	$145	$135

MODEL 340V — .225 Win., varmint configuration, 24 in. barrel. Limited mfg. in late 1960's.

	$295	$265	$235	$205	$180	$165	$150

MODEL 340S DELUXE — same as 340, with aperture sight, checkered stock, sling swivels. Mfg. 1952-1960.

	$260	$225	$205	$190	$175	$160	$150

MODEL 342 AND 342S — same as 340, .22 Hornet designation. Mfg. 1950-1955.

	$250	$215	$200	$185	$170	$160	$150

Grading	100%	98%	95%	90%	80%	70%	60%

MODEL 110 SPORTER — .243, .270, .308, or .30-06 cal., 22 in. barrel, open sight, 4 shot, checkered pistol grip stock. Mfg. 1958-1963.

	$175	$145	$120	$110	$95	$85	$55

MODEL 110-MC — same as 110, with Monte Carlo stock. Mfg. 1959-1969.

	$195	$160	$140	$120	$110	$95	$85

MODEL 110-M — same as 110MC, except 7mm Mag., .264 Mag., .300 Win. Mag., or .338 Mag. cal., recoil pad. Mfg. 1963-1969.

	$275	$220	$195	$150	$140	$125	$110

MODEL 110-D — .22-250 (disc.), .223, .243, .25-06 (disc.), .270, .308 (disc.), .30-06, 7mm Mag., .300 Win. Mag. (disc.), or .338 Win. Mag. cal., similar to Model 110B, push button detachable mag., checkered walnut stock, removable and adj. rear sight, 7½ lbs. Mfg. 1966-1988.

	$340	$290	$260	$240	$215	$190	$170

Add $80 for left-hand version.
Last Mfg.'s Sug. Retail was $409.

MODEL 110-E — .22-250, .223, .243, .270, 7mm Rem. Mag., .308 Win., or .30-06 cal., 22 or 24 (Mag. only) in. barrel, open sights, uncheckered hardwood Monte Carlo stock, push button detachable 5 shot mag., 7 lbs. Mfg. 1963-1988.

	$260	$230	$190	$175	$165	$155	$145

Subtract $16 without sights.

Last Mfg.'s Sug. Retail was $325.

MODEL 110-F — .22-250, .223 Rem., .243 Win., .308 Win., .30-06, .270 Win., 7mm Rem. Mag., .300 Win. Mag., .338 Win. Mag. (new 1991) cal., 22 or 24 (Magnum) in. barrel, black DuPont Rynite stock with swivel studs and recoil pad, adj. rear sight, drilled and tapped for scope mounts, 4 or 5 shot mag., 6¾ lbs. New 1989.

Mfg.'s Sug. Retail	$489	$400	$340	$300	$275	$250	$225	$200

Model 110-FNS — same as Model 110-F, except has no sights. New 1991.

Mfg.'s Sug. Retail	$489	$400	$340	$300	$275	$250	$225	$200

Model 110-FXP3 — .243 Win., .270 Win., .30-06, 7mm Rem. Mag., or .300 Win. Mag. cal., similar to Model 110-F except is without sights and has integral Weaver type scope bases. New 1989.

Mfg.'s Sug. Retail	$481	$395	$340	$300	$275	$250	$225	$200

MODEL 110-CY — .243 Win. or .300 Savage cal., youth/ladies variation with shortened classic stock. New 1991.

Mfg.'s Sug. Retail	$400	$335	$275	$230	$215	$200	$190	$180

MODEL 110-WLE — .250-3000 Savage or .300 Savage. New 1991.

Mfg.'s Sug. Retail	$565	$485	$415	$365	$320	$280	$250	$225

MODEL 110-FP POLICE RIFLE — .223 Rem. or .308 Win. cal., 24 in. heavy barrel, all metal parts are non-reflective, 4 shot internal mag., Black Dupont Rynite stock, tapped for scope mounts, 8 lbs. New 1990.

Mfg.'s Sug. Retail	$565	$485	$415	$365	$320	$280	$250	$225

MODEL 110-G — .22-250, .223 Rem., .243 Win., .308 Win., .30-06, .270 Win., 7mm Rem. Mag., or .300 Win. Mag. cal., top loading internal box mag., 22 or 24 in. barrel, adj. iron sights, checkered hardwood stock, approx. 7 lbs. New 1989.

Mfg.'s Sug. Retail	$400	$335	$275	$230	$215	$200	$190	$180

Model 110-GXP3 — similar to Model 110-G except has no sights and includes integral Weaver type scope bases. New 1989.

Mfg.'s Sug. Retail	$392	$330	$275	$230	$215	$200	$190	$180

Model 110-GL — .30-06, .270 Win., or 7mm Rem. Mag. cal., left hand variation of the Model 110-G.

Mfg.'s Sug. Retail	$466	$375	$295	$250	$225	$200	$190	$180

Grading	100%	98%	95%	90%	80%	70%	60%

Model 110-GLNS — same as Model 110-GL, except has no sights. New 1991.

Mfg.'s Sug. Retail	$450	$360	$285	$240	$215	$200	$190	$180

MODEL 110-K — .243, .270, or .30-06 cal., incorporates laminated camouflage stock. Mfg. 1986-1988.

	$335	$280	$240

Last Mfg.'s Sug. Retail was $399.

MODEL 110-S — .308 Win. & 7mm-08 Rem. (disc.) cal.'s, silhouette model, 22 in. heavy barrel, Wundhammer swell pistol grip with stipling, no sights, 4 shot mag., 8 lbs. 10 oz. Disc. 1985.

	$340	$290	$255	$225	$205	$190	$175

Last Mfg.'s Sug. Retail was $385.

MODEL 110-V — .22-250 or .223 cal. only, varmint model, 26 in. heavy barrel, no sights, 5 shot mag., stippled walnut Wundhammer pistol grip stock, 9¼ lbs. Disc. 1989.

	$370	$315	$265	$230	$205	$190	$175

Last Mfg.'s Sug. Retail was $439.

MODEL 110-GV — .22-250 or .223 Rem. cal., 24 in. medium barrel, no sights, checkered hardwood stock with rubber rifle pad, drilled and tapped for scope, 8¼ lbs. New 1989.

Mfg.'s Sug. Retail	$444	$365	$295	$240	$220	$200	$190	$180

MODEL 110-B — same as 110E, select stock and pistol grip cap on previous manufacture. Mfg. 1976-1979. Reintroduced 1989 with laminate stock (Model 110-B Laminate).

	$360	$300	$265	$235	$205	$190	$175

MODEL 110-B LAMINATE — similar to Model 110-B, except is available in .300 Win. Mag. or .338 Win. Mag. also, has brown laminate hardwood stock with iron sights, approx. 7½ lbs. New 1989.

Mfg.'s Sug. Retail	$477	$385	$310	$250	$225	$200	$190	$180

MODEL 110-P PREMIER GRADE — similar to 110B, with select French walnut stock, skip checkered, rosewood forend and pistol grip cap, sling swivels, 7mm Mag. has recoil pad. Mfg. 1964-1970.

	$440	$330	$310	$275	$250	$220	$195
7mm Mag.	$460	$350	$330	$305	$275	$240	$220

MODEL 110-PE PRESENTATION GRADE — same as 110P, with engraved receiver, floorplate and trigger guard. Mfg. 1968-1970.

	$660	$550	$525	$470	$440	$415	$385
7mm Mag.	$690	$580	$550	$495	$470	$440	$415

MODEL 111 CHIEFTAIN ACTION — .243, .270, 7 x 57mm, 7mm Mag., or .30-06 cal., 22 in. barrel, 24 in. barrel on Mag., leaf sight, 4 shot detachable mag., checkered walnut Monte Carlo stock, pistol grip cap, sling swivels. Mfg. 1974-1978.

	$330	$275	$240	$220	$195	$165	$155
Magnum	$315	$285	$265	$240	$220	$195	$165

MODEL 112V VARMINT RIFLE — .220 Swift, .222 Rem., .223 Rem., .22-250, .243, or .25-06 cal., single shot, bolt action, 26 in. heavy barrel, no sights, heavy select walnut stock, checkered, swivels. Mfg. 1975-1978.

	$305	$275	$250	$230	$210	$175	$155

MODEL 112-FV — .22-250 Rem. or .223 Rem. cal., varmint variation with 26 in. heavy barrel, no sights, 4-shot mag., black Rynite synthetic stock with recoil pad, 9 lbs. New 1991.

Mfg.'s Sug. Retail	$489	$400	$340	$300	$275	$250	$225	$200

MODEL 112 R — .22-250, .25-06, or .243 cal., similar to Model 112V, except has 4 shot mag. Disc. 1980.

	$340	$305	$275	$250	$230	$210	$175

Grading	100%	98%	95%	90%	80%	70%	60%

MODEL 114-CU — .270 Win., .30-06, .300 Win. Mag., or 7mm Rem. Mag. cal., 22 or 24 in. barrel, features high gloss classic American black walnut stock with cut checkering, fitted grip cap, and recoil pad, removable 3 or 4 shot staggered box mag., deluxe adj. sights, approx. 7½ lbs. New 1991.

Mfg.'s Sug. Retail	$500	$425	$350	$300	$275	$250	$225	$200

MODEL 116-FSS — .270 Win., .30-06, 7mm Rem. Mag., .300 Win. Mag., or .338 Win. Mag., features black Dupont Rynite synthetic stock, stainless steel metal parts, drilled and tapped for scope mounting, 22 or 24 in. barrel, 3 or 4 shot mag., 7½ lbs. New 1991.

Mfg.'s Sug. Retail	$565	$485	$415	$365	$320	$280	$250	$225

MODEL 170 PUMP RIFLE — .30-30 or .35 Rem. cal., 22 in. barrel, folding leaf sight, 3 shot tube mag., checkered pistol grip stock. Mfg. 1970-1981.

	$180	$155	$140	$110	$90	$65	$55

MODEL 170C — same as 170, .30-30 only, 18½ in. barrel. Mfg. 1974-1981.

COMBINATION GUNS

Savage Industries announced in early 1988 that they will no longer publish retail prices for their currently manufactured firearms.

MODEL 24 O/U COMBINATION GUN — .22 over .410, 24 in. separated barrels, open rifle sight, visible hammer, break open, plain pistol grip stock. Mfg. 1950-1965.

	$130	$110	$100	$85	$70	$55	$40

MODEL 24S — same as 24, with 20 ga. or .410 barrel, sidelever, dovetail for scope. Mfg. 1965-1971.

	$155	$135	$120	$100	$90	$80	$75

MODEL 24MS — same as 24S, with .22 WRM barrel. Mfg. 1965-1971.

	$140	$120	$110	$90	$85	$70	$55

MODEL 24DL — same as 24S, with top lever, satin chrome frame and checkered stock. Mfg. 1965-1969.

	$140	$120	$110	$90	$85	$70	$55

MODEL 24MDL — same as 24DL, with .22 WRM barrel. Mfg. 1965-1969.

	$145	$125	$115	$95	$85	$70	$55

MODEL 24FG — same as 24S, with top lever. Mfg. 1972-disc.

	$130	$110	$90	$85	$65	$55	$40

MODEL 24 FIELD — .22 LR or .22 Mag. over 20 or .410 ga., lightweight field version, 24 in. separated barrels, 3 in. chambers, 6¾ lbs. Disc. 1989.

	$175	$145	$120	$100	$85	$80	$70

Last Mfg.'s Sug. Retail was $209.

MODEL 24F — choice of .22 LR, .22 Hornet, .222 Rem. (disc. 1989), .223 Rem., or .30-30 cal. over 12 or 20 ga., 3 in. chamber, stocked in wood or matte black Dupont Rynite synthetic, hammer block safety, DT's, approx. 8 lbs. New 1989.

Mfg.'s Sug. Retail	$431	$355	$295	$240	$220	$200	$190	$180

Add $19 for shotgun choke tube.

Add $36 for Camo Rynite stock (Model 12-T, Turkey Model-12 ga. only).

The .22 LR cal. is available with 20 ga. barrel only.

MODEL 24V — simiar to 24, with .22 Hornet (disc. 1984), .222, .223, .30-30, .357 Max., or .357 Mag.(disc.), over 24 in. 20 ga. (3 in.) barrel, single trigger, 7 lbs. Mfg. 1971-89.

	$300	$265	$230	$200	$175	$150	$130

MODEL 24D — .22 LR or .22 Mag. over .410 or 20 ga., black or case hardened frame, game scene decoration was eliminated in 1974, forearm not checkered after 1976.

	$250	$220	$185	$150	$130	$115	$105

Grading	100%	98%	95%	90%	80%	70%	60%

MODEL 24C CAMPER'S COMPANION — nickel finish, .22 LR over 20 ga., 20 in. barrel cylinder bore, butt plate stores 11 cartridges, carrying case. Mfg. 1972-1988.

	$200	$165	$130	$115	$105	$95	$80

Last Mfg.'s Sug. Retail was $239.

MODEL 24 VS CAMPER'S COMPANION — same as 24CS, only .357 Mag. over 20 ga., nickel finish.

	$250	$210	$185	$160	$145	$135	$120

MODEL 389 — 12 ga. with 3 in. chamber over choice of .308 Win. or .222 Rem., choke tubes standard, hammerless, double triggers, checkered walnut stock and forearm with recoil pad. Mfg. 1988-90 only.

	$800	$640	$550	$495	$435	$365	$300

Last Mfg.'s Sug. Retail was $919.

SHOTGUNS

MODEL 420 O/U — 12, 16, or 20 ga., 26-30 in. barrel, various chokes, boxlock, double trigger, extractors, plain pistol grip stock. Mfg. 1938-1942.

	$385	$305	$275	$250	$210	$195	$155
Single trigger	$440	$360	$330	$305	$265	$220	$195

MODEL 430 — same as 420, with checkered stock and solid rib, recoil pad.

	$440	$360	$305	$275	$240	$220	$195
Single trigger	$495	$415	$360	$320	$285	$265	$220

MODEL 220 SINGLE BARREL — 12, 16, 20, 28 or .410 ga., 26-32 in. barrel, various chokes, hammerless, plain pistol grip stock. Mfg. 1938-1965.

	$90	$65	$55	$45	$35	$30	$30

MODEL 220P — same as 220, with poly choke, not made in .410.

	$90	$65	$55	$45	$35	$30	$30

MODEL 220 AC — same as 220, with Savage adj. choke.

	$100	$85	$65	$55	$45	$35	$30

MODEL 220L — same as 220, with sidelever. Mfg. 1965-1972.

	$90	$65	$55	$45	$35	$30	$30

MODEL 720 AUTOLOADER STANDARD — 12 or 16 ga., Browning A-5 style action, 26-32 in. barrels, various choke, checkered pistol grip stock. Mfg. 1930-1949.

	$275	$195	$165	$155	$140	$120	$110

MODEL 726 UPLAND SPORTER — same as 720, except 2 shell mag. Mfg. 1931-1949.

	$275	$195	$165	$155	$140	$120	$110

MODEL 740C SKEET GUN — same as 726, with Cutts Compensator and skeet stock, 24½ in. barrel. Mfg. 1936-1949.

	$305	$230	$200	$175	$155	$140	$120

MODEL 745 LIGHTWEIGHT — same as 720, with alloy receiver, 12 ga. only, 28 in. barrel. Mfg. 1940-1949.

	$275	$195	$165	$155	$140	$120	$110

MODEL 755 STANDARD SEMI-AUTO — 12 or 16 ga., 26, 28, or 30 in. barrel, various chokes, rounded off receiver, checkered pistol grip stock. Mfg. 1949-1958.

	$265	$180	$160	$150	$140	$120	$110

MODEL 755SC — same as 755, with Savage Super Choke.

	$275	$195	$165	$155	$140	$120	$110

Grading	100%	98%	95%	90%	80%	70%	60%

MODEL 775 LIGHTWEIGHT — same as 755, with alloy receiver. Mfg. 1950-1965.

	$275	$195	$180	$165	$150	$140	$120

MODEL 775SC — same as 775, with Savage Super Choke.

	$285	$205	$195	$175	$160	$150	$130

MODEL 750 SEMI-AUTO — 12 ga., Browning patterned semi-auto, 26 or 28 in. barrels, various chokes, checkered pistol grip stock. Mfg. 1960-1967.

	$275	$195	$165	$155	$140	$120	$110

MODEL 750SC — same as 750, with Savage Super Choke.

	$285	$205	$175	$165	$150	$130	$120

MODEL 750AC — same as 750, with poly choke.

	$285	$205	$175	$165	$150	$130	$120

MODEL 30 SLIDE ACTION — 12, 16, 20, or .410 ga., 26, 28, or 30 in. barrels, various chokes, VR, plain pistol grip stock. Mfg. 1958-1970.

	$220	$175	$155	$140	$120	$100	$85

Checkered Late Model

	$230	$185	$165	$150	$130	$110	$95

MODEL 30AC — same as 30, with adj. choke, 12 ga. only. Mfg. 1959-1970.

Checkered.

	$240	$200	$175	$160	$145	$120	$100

MODEL 30T TRAP AND DUCK GUN — same as 30, with 30 in. full, 12 ga. only, Monte Carlo stock and pad. Mfg. 1963-1970.

	$230	$185	$165	$150	$130	$110	$90

MODEL 30FG TAKEDOWN ACTION — 12, 20, or .410 ga., 26, 28, or 30 in., barrel, various chokes, checkered pistol grip stock. Mfg. 1970-1975.

	$175	$155	$130	$110	$95	$85	$70

MODEL 30T TAKEDOWN TRAP — 12 ga. only, 30 in. full, Monte Carlo stock with pad. Mfg. 1970-1973.

	$195	$175	$155	$140	$110	$100	$85

MODEL 30AC TAKEDOWN — same as 30FG, with adj. choke, 12 or 20 ga., 26 in. barrel. Mfg. 1971-1972.

	$200	$180	$165	$150	$120	$110	$90

MODEL 30 TAKEDOWN SLUG GUN — same as 30FG, with 32 in. cylinder bore barrel, rifle sights. Mfg. 1971-disc.

	$195	$175	$160	$140	$110	$100	$85

MODEL 30D TAKEDOWN — same as 30FG, with VR, engraved receiver and pad. Mfg. 1971-disc.

	$200	$180	$165	$150	$120	$110	$90

MODEL 67 SLIDE ACTION — see listing under Stevens Section.

FOX MODELS B, B-SE, AND STEVENS 311 — see listing under Stevens Section.

MODEL 242 O/U — .410 ga., single exposed hammer, single trigger, barrel selector lever, full chokes. Mfg. 1977-1981.

	$350	$300	$260	$230	$200	$175	$150

MODEL 440 O/U — 12 or 20 ga., 26, 28, or 30 in. barrels, various chokes, boxlock, SST, extractors, checkered pistol grip stock, vent rib. Imported from Italy 1968-1972.

	$495	$440	$415	$385	$330	$305	$250

Grading	100%	98%	95%	90%	80%	70%	60%

MODEL 440T — same as Model 440, 12 ga., 30 in. only, imp mod. or full choke, wide vent rib, trap style stock, pad. Mfg. 1969-1972.

	$550	$470	$440	$415	$385	$360	$330

MODEL 444 DELUXE — same as Model 440, with auto ejectors, select walnut. Mfg. 1969-1972.

	$550	$470	$440	$415	$385	$360	$330

MODEL 550 SXS — 12 or 20 ga., 26, 28, or 30 in. barrels, various chokes, boxlock, auto ejectors, single trigger, checkered pistol grip stock. Mfg. 1971-1973.

	$275	$220	$195	$165	$150	$130	$110

MODEL 312 SERIES — 12 ga. only, boxlock action, 3 in. chambers, vent barrels, satin chrome finished receiver, checkered walnut stock and forearm, SST, choke tubes, approx. 7 lbs. New 1990.

312 Field — 26 or 28 in. VR barrels with choke tubes.

Mfg.'s Sug. Retail	$780	$680	$520	$495	$435	$400	$365	$300

312 Trap — 30 in. barrels only, Monte Carlo stock with recoil pad.

Mfg.'s Sug. Retail	$828	$725	$550	$515	$470	$415	$365	$300

312 Sporting Clays — 28 in. barrels only with 7 choke tubes provided, recoil pad.

Mfg.'s Sug. Retail	$850	$740	$580	$540	$480	$435	$365	$300

MODEL 320 FIELD — 20 ga., 3 in. chambers, 26 in. VR barrels with choke tubes, same action as Model 312, high gloss wood finish, DT, ejectors, 6¾ lbs. New 1991.

As this addition goes to press, prices have yet to be established on this model.

MODEL 330 O/U — 12 or 20 ga., 26, 28, or 30 in. barrels, various chokes, boxlock, SST, extractors, checkered pistol grip stock. Mfg. by Valmet between 1969-1980.

	$495	$440	$385	$335	$275	$250	$220

MODEL 333T — same as 330, with 30 in. vent rib, imp. mod. and full choke, trap stock with pad. Mfg. by Valmet between 1972-1980.

	$550	$470	$415	$385	$360	$305	$275

MODEL 333 O/U — 12 or 20 ga., 26, 28, or 30 in. barrels, various chokes, boxlock, SST, auto ejectors, checkered pistol grip stock. Mfg. by Valmet between 1973-1980.

	$580	$525	$470	$440	$400	$375	$330

MODEL 2400 O/U COMBINATION GUN — 12 ga. full choke barrel over .222 or .308 rifle barrel, 23½ in. barrels, folding leaf sight, solid rib, dovetailed for scope mount, checkered Monte Carlo stock. Mfg. by Valmet between 1975-1980.

	$605	$550	$525	$495	$440	$415	$385

SCHALL

Previous manufacturer located in Hartford, CT.

REPEATING HANDGUN — .22 LR only, target pistol, mag. fed manual repeating action. Unusual.

	$425	$360	$320	$270	$220	$180	$150

SCHULTZ & LARSEN

Manufacturer located in Otterup, Denmark since 1911.

NO. 47 MATCH RIFLE — .22 LR, bolt action, single shot, 28 in. heavy barrel, target sights, set trigger, free rifle stock.

	$660	$550	$495	$440	$385	$360	$330

M61 MATCH RIFLE — .22 LR, bolt action, single shot, 28 in. heavy barrel, target sights, set trigger, free rifle stock, palm rest.

	$895	$825	$740	$680	$600	$550	$500

M62 MATCH RIFLE — various cal.'s, bolt action, single shot, 28 in. heavy barrel, target sights, set trigger, free rifle stock, palm rest.

	$995	$875	$780	$700	$620	$550	$500

Grading	100%	98%	95%	90%	80%	70%	60%

MODEL 54 FREE RIFLE — any American centerfire standard caliber, plus 6.5 x 55mm, 27 in. heavy barrel, target sights, free rifle stock.

	$825	$745	$690	$605	$550	$495	$440

MODEL 54J SPORTING RIFLE — .270, .30-06, 7 x 61 Sharpe and Hart cal., bolt action, 3 shot, 24 in. barrel, checkered Monte Carlo stock, no sights.

	$650	$550	$470	$415	$360	$330	$300

MODEL 68 DL — .22-250, .243 Win., 6mm Rem., .264 Win. Mag., .270, .30-06, .308 Win., 7 x 61 S&H, 7 mm Rem. Mag., 8 x 57 JS, 300 Win. Mag., .308 Norma Mag., .338 Win. Mag., .358 Norma Mag., or .458 Win. Mag. cal., bolt action, 24 in. barrel, Bofors Steel receiver, bolt has 4 rear locking lugs, select French walnut, adj. trigger, no sights except for .458 Mag.

	$725	$650	$575	$525	$495	$460	$430

SCHUETZEN RIFLES

A Schuetzen Rifle is a special single shot target rifle. During the time span 1875-1945 this target configuration rifle was very popular for competition shooters. Many of these guns had elaborate locking systems, top quality sights, double set triggers, heavy barrels, palm and thumb rests, sculptured cheek piece, Swiss style butt plate, etc. Rather than list all the various domestic and European makers (there are hundreds), it should be noted that since there are so many combinations of options for this configuration that most guns have to be examined and appraised individually. Most non-major trademarks sell in the $550-$1,500 range, depending on features and condition. Schuetzen Rifles are a field in themselves and a knowledgeable dealer/collector should be consulted before buying or selling one of these guns.

SCOTT, W.C., LTD.

Manufactured since 1834 in Birmingham, England. W.C. Scott, Ltd. has been absorbed by Holland & Holland and later guns were sold through the auspices of H&H located in London, England. Previously distributed by L. Joseph Rahn, Inc., Manchester, MI.

SHOTGUNS: SIDE-BY-SIDE

All W.C. Scott Shotguns were discontinued in 1990.

KINMOUNT — 12, 16, 20, or 28 ga., double barrel boxlock action, ejectors, deluxe checkered walnut, scroll engraving.

	$10,500	$9,000	$8,000	$7,000	$6,000	$5,250	$4,500

Add $790 for 28 or .410 ga.
Add $790 for single non-sel. trigger.
Last Mfg.'s Sug. Retail was $11,000.

BOWOOD — 12, 16, 20, or 28 ga., double barrel boxlock action, ejectors, deluxe checkered walnut, extensive scroll engraving.

	$11,950	$10,000	$9,000	$8,000	$7,000	$6,250	$5,500

Add $790 for 28 or .410 ga.
Add $790 for single non-sel. trigger.
Last Mfg.'s Sug. Retail was $12,500.

CHATSWORTH — 12, 16, 20, or 28 ga., top-of-the line boxlock action, ejectors, deluxe checkered walnut, extensive scroll engraving.

	$13,750	$11,250	$10,000	$9,000	$8,000	$7,000	$6,000

Add $790 for 28 or .410 ga.
Add $790 for single non-sel. trigger.
Last Mfg.'s Sug. Retail was $14,000.

BLENHEIM — 12 bore only, upgraded models, custom made to individual specifications, originally priced per individual order.
Specimen rarity precludes percentage grading pricing. Individual appraisals have to be secured on this model.

Grading	100%	98%	95%	90%	80%	70%	60%

SECURITY INDUSTRIES
Previous manufacturer located in Little Ferry, NJ.

MODEL PSS 38 DOUBLE ACTION — .38 Spl. 5 shot cylinder, 2 in. barrel, stainless steel, fixed sights, wood grips. Mfg. 1973-1978.

	$175	$150	$140	$130	$125	$110	$100

MODEL PM357 — similar to PSS 38, except .357 Mag., 2½ in. barrel. Mfg. 1975-disc.

	$225	$175	$165	$150	$140	$125	$110

MODEL PPM 357 — .357 Mag., 5 shot, 2 in. barrel, spurless hammer until 1977, new models have spur. Mfg. 1965-disc.

	$225	$175	$165	$150	$140	$125	$110

SEDCO INDUSTRIES INC.
Previous manufacturer located in Lake Elsinore, CA until 1990.

MODEL SP-22 — .22 LR cal., semi-auto single action, 2½ in. barrel, rotary safety, serrated slide, nickel, satin nickel (new 1990), or black metal finish, simulated pearl grips in white, blue, gray, or pink, 11 oz. Mfg. 1989-90 only..

	$60	$55	$50	$45	$40	$35	$35

Last Mfg.'s Sug. Retail was $69.

SEDGLEY, R.F., INC.
Previous manufacturer located in Philadelphia, PA.

SPRINGFIELD SPORTING RIFLE — '03 Springfield bolt action, .220 Swift, .218 Bee, .22-3000, .22-4000, .22 Hornet, .25-35, .250-3000, .257 Roberts, .270, 7mm, or .30-06 cal., 24 in. barrel, Lyman receiver sight, checkered pistol grip stock, pre-WWII.

	$550	$470	$415	$360	$315	$275	$250

SPRINGFIELD CARBINE SPORTER — same as Rifle, with 20 in. barrel, and full length stock.

	$605	$525	$470	$415	$360	$330	$295

SEECAMP, L.W. CO.,INC.
Manufacturer located in Milford, CT.

All Seecamp pistols are hand machined and hand fitted from stainless steel. Manufacture has always emphasized quality over quantity - this explains why values often exceed the company's retail prices. There is simply more demand than supply. Currently, approx. 100 pistols (LWS 32 Model) per month are being fabricated.

LWS .25 ACP MODEL — .25 ACP, double action, semi-auto, 2 in. barrel, 7 shot mag., stainless steel, matte finish, 12 oz. Approx. 5,000 mfg. 1982-1985.

	$340	$295	$260	$235	$220	$210	$200

Last Mfg.'s Sug. Retail was $275.

LWS 32 MODEL — .32 ACP Silvertip, double action, semi-auto, 2 in. barrel, stainless steel, 6 shot mag., 12½ oz. Limited mfg.

Mfg.'s Sug. Retail	$350	$440	$385	$360	$330	$310	$295	$280

This model is available in either a matte or polished finish. The polished finish carries a slight premium.

MATCHED PAIR — includes both .25 ACP and .32 ACP pistols with the same serial number, approx. 200 sets were mfg. before the BATF stopped this practice.

	$950	$800	$700

This set contains a matte finished .25 ACP and a polished .32 ACP.

Grading	100%	98%	95%	90%	80%	70%	60%

SEITZ

SINGLE BARREL TRAP GUN — 12 ga. only, single barrel, various barrel lengths, pull or release trigger, only 45 guns mfg.

	100%	98%	95%	90%	80%	70%	60%
	$13,000	$10,000	$8,500	$7,700	$6,950	$6,200	$5,400

SEMMERLING

Manufactured by American Derringer Corp. located in Waco, TX.

Less than 600 LM-4 pistols have been mfg. since 1978.

LM-4 PISTOL — 9mm (new 1986) or .45 ACP cal., 2 in. barrel, blue, smallest .45 ACP repeater available, slide is worked manually with thumb on serrated slide-top, extremely high quality, hand fit and finished, a special purpose weapon, very limited production with 14-24 month waiting period.

Mfg.'s Sug. Retail	$1,750	$3,000	$2,650	$2,000	$1,600	$1,250	$1,100	$1,000

Because of the limited supply, used LM-4's are selling for considerably over their retail price. The original U.S. Army contract pistol sold for $5,000. Earlier mfg. (pre-American Derringer Corp.) will also command a premium over values listed above.

Stainless Steel — matte finish stainless steel variation of the LM-4. Limited mfg. (approx. 100 guns per year). New 1986.

Mfg.'s Sug. Retail	$1,875	$3,350	$2,850	$2,200

SHARPS, CHRISTIAN

Manufactured in Windsor, VT under Sharps Rifle Manufacturing Company between 1851-1855. Manufactured in Hartford, CT under same name between 1855-1874. Reorganized as Sharps Rifle Company in 1876 with production resuming in Hartford (1876 only) and Bridgeport, CT. from 1877-1881.

REVOLVER, PERCUSSION — made 1850's in Philadelphia, production about 2000, 3 in. octagonal tip-up barrel with rib, .25 caliber, 6 shot.

	$900	$850	$800	$750	$675	$600	$500

PEPPERBOX PISTOL — also marked Sharps and Hankins, 4-shot breech-loading, .32, .30, or .22 rimfire cal., firing pin rotates, brass frame with silver plating, or case-hardening on iron frame.

First model — 5 variations. Scarcer variations can be worth up to 150% more.

	$375	$350	$300	$250	$200	$175	$125

Second model — 5 variations. Scarcer variations can be worth up to 150% more.

	$425	$400	$375	$325	$250	$200	$150

Third model — Sharps and Hankins markings, .32 rimfire short, 4 variations. Premium for scarcer variations.

	$375	$350	$325	$275	$225	$175	$150

Fourth model — 4 variations, bird's-head grip, .32 rimfire long. Premium for scarcer variations.

	$385	$360	$330	$275	$220	$195	$140

RIFLES: BREECH LOADING

The Model 1863 Carbine was one of the highest production rifles of the Civil War with production totaling over 100,000. During a period after the Civil War, the Model 1874 was loosely dubbed "Buffalo Rifle" because of its involvement on the western plains.

MODEL 1851 CARBINE — .52-caliber percussion, breech-loading, Maynard tape primer, U.S. military markings. Deduct 40% for non-martial sporting rifle version.

	$3,000	$2,650	$2,500	$2,000	$1,500	$1,350	$1,000

Grading	100%	98%	95%	90%	80%	70%	60%

MODEL 1852 CARBINE — slanting Breech, approx. 4500 mfg. 1853-1855, caliber .52 with Sharps' patented pellet primer built into lockplate. Add 50% for U.S. martial markings. Also sporting rifles in .52, .44, or .36 cal.

	100%	98%	95%	90%	80%	70%	60%
	$925	$900	$850	$750	$650	$550	$425

MODEL 1853 CARBINE — mfg. 1854-1858 in quantity of some 10,350, caliber .52 with Sharps' patented pellet primer feed. Deduct 10% for sporting-rifle version.

	$900	$850	$800	$750	$700	$625	$500

MODEL 1855 CARBINE — U.S. martial model in .52 caliber, breech-loading, Maynard tape primer system, sling ring is mounted on left side.

	$1,750	$1,675	$1,600	$1,500	$1,200	$1,000	$800

STRAIGHT-BREECH RIFLES AND CARBINES, 1859, 1863, 1865. — breech-loading caliber .52 with Sharps patented pellet-priming system in lockplate. (Prices listed are for models that are original and have not been converted). The Model 1859 is worth a slight premium.

	$1,200	$1,150	$1,100	$1,000	$800	$650	$400

Over 32,000 carbines (majority) and rifles were converted to .50-70 centerfire. Can be detected by additional "DFC" ribbon cartouche on left center of stock. These converted specimens (mostly Model 1863's) are worth approx. 50% of values listed above.

COFFEE-MILL MODEL — built-in coffee-grinding mill in stock for cavalry use. Easy to fake.

	$8,500	$8,000	$7,500	$6,000	$5,000	$4,500	$4,000

MODEL 1874 RIFLE — mfg. from 1871 until 1881, known as the "Buffalo Rifle" in its day. Many variations, cal.'s, and accessories. Research should be done before purchasing.

SPORTING RIFLE — .50, .45, .44, or .40 cal. Heavier barrels are worth more. Approx. 6,500 mfg.

	$2,000	$1,800	$1,600	$1,250	$1,000	$900	$800

MILITARY RIFLE — mostly in .50-70 or .45-70 cal., 30 in. barrel with three bands. Approx. 1700 mfg.

	$1,400	$1,300	$1,200	$1,000	$850	$750	$650

MILITARY CARBINE — mostly .50-70 cal. Fewer than 500 mfg.

	$1,750	$1,650	$1,500	$1,150	$850	$750	$675

CREEDMOOR, MID-RANGE, LONG-RANGE, AND BUSINESS RIFLE — these have a basically common look, though there are many differences and variations among them. (Price range is quite general).

	$2,500	$2,350	$2,000	$1,600	$1,350	$1,000	$750

SCHUETZEN RIFLE — .40-50 cal., 30 in. octagonal barrel. Only 70 mfg.

	$2,255	$2,000	$1,800	$1,500	$1,250	$1,000	$900

SHERIDAN PRODUCTS INCORPORATED
Racine, WI.

PISTOL

KNOCKABOUT — .22 S or L, single shot, 5 in. barrel, checkered plastic grips, fixed sights. Mfg. 1953-1960.

	$110	$100	$85	$75	$60	$50	$40

SHILEN RIFLES, INCORPORATED
Ennis, TX.

Grading	100%	98%	95%	90%	80%	70%	60%

RIFLES: BOLT ACTION

DGA SPORTER — .17 Rem., .223 Rem., .22-250, .220 Swift, 6mm Rem., .243 Win., .250 Savage, .257 Roberts, .284 Win., .308 Win., or .358 Win. cal., 3 shot mag., 24 in. barrel, no sights, claro walnut stock.

	100%	98%	95%	90%	80%	70%	60%
	$580	$560	$530	$495	$440	$415	$385

DGA VARMINTER — same as Sporter, except 25 in. medium heavy barrel.

	$580	$560	$530	$495	$440	$415	$385

DGA SILHOUETTE RIFLE — same as Varminter, .308 only.

	$580	$560	$530	$495	$440	$415	$385

DGA BENCHREST RIFLE — single shot, choice of cal.'s, 26 in. heavy barrel or medium barrel, no sights, choice of fiberglass or walnut stock, thumbhole available.

	$690	$670	$635	$580	$525	$475	$430

SHILOH RIFLE MFG. CO., INC.

Manufacturer located in Big Timber, MT.

The Shiloh Arms Company is currently manufacturing replicas of Sharps rifles and carbines. They are available as black powder cartridge rifles. Most models are available in the following cal.'s: .40-50, .40-65 Win., .40-70, .40-90, .45-70, .45-90, .45-100, .45-110, .45-120, .50-70, .50-90 (disc.), .50-100, and .50-140 (disc.). Percussion Rifles also are available in .54 cal. and are breech loading. All models are authentically reproduced and are high quality.

RIFLES: BLACK POWDER CARTRIDGE

MODEL 1874 LONG RANGE EXPRESS

Mfg.'s Sug. Retail	$895	$800	$650	$550	$475	$410	$350	$320

MODEL 1874 NO. 1 SPORTING

Mfg.'s Sug. Retail	$860	$775	$625	$525	$450	$395	$325	$300

MODEL 1874 NO. 2 SPORTING

	$605	$520	$440	$380	$320	$285	$270

MODEL 1874 NO. 3 SPORTING

Mfg.'s Sug. Retail	$765	$675	$535	$450	$380	$320	$295	$270

MODEL 1874 BUSINESS RIFLE

Mfg.'s Sug. Retail	$765	$675	$535	$450	$380	$320	$295	$270

MODEL 1874 HUNTER'S RIFLE

	$480	$440	$400	$340	$300	$280	$260

MODEL 1874 HARTFORD — features Hartford collar between receiver and barrel assembly. New 1989.

Mfg.'s Sug. Retail	$925	$815	$660	$550	$475	$410	$350	$320

MODEL 1874 MILITARY RIFLE

Mfg.'s Sug. Retail	$895	$800	$650	$550	$475	$410	$350	$320

MODEL 1874 MILITARY CARBINE

Mfg.'s Sug. Retail	$795	$690	$550	$450	$380	$320	$295	$270

MODEL 1874 SADDLE RIFLE

Mfg.'s Sug. Retail	$830	$715	$565	$450	$380	$320	$295	$270

MODEL 1874 ROUGHRIDER

Mfg.'s Sug. Retail	$765	$675	$535	$450	$380	$320	$295	$270

Add $95 for semi-fancy walnut.

Grading	100%	98%	95%	90%	80%	70%	60%

MODEL 1874 JAEGER HUNTING RIFLE — hunting rifle with lightweight half-octagon/half-round barrel. New 1987.

Mfg.'s Sug. Retail	$835	$720	$570	$450	$380	$320	$295	$270

CUSTOM SHARPS BUFFALO RIFLE — .45/70 or .45/110 cal., 34 in. heavy barrel, military stock with patch box, vernier aperture rear sight with globe front, mfg. for the motion picture "Quigley Down Under", approx. 13 lbs. New 1990.

Mfg.'s Sug. Retail	$2,650	$2,450	$2,000	$1,500

RIFLES: PERCUSSION-BREECH LOADING

MODEL 1863 NO. 1 SPORTING

Mfg.'s Sug. Retail	$785	$685	$550	$450	$380	$320	$295	$270

MODEL 1863 NO. 2 SPORTING

	$550	$470	$415	$360	$300	$275	$250

MODEL 1863 NO. 3 SPORTING

	$525	$440	$385	$340	$290	$270	$250

MODEL 1863 MILITARY RIFLE

Mfg.'s Sug. Retail	$895	$800	$650	$550	$475	$410	$350	$320

MODEL 1863 MILITARY CARBINE

Mfg.'s Sug. Retail	$795	$690	$550	$450	$380	$320	$295	$270

MODEL 1859 MILITARY CARBINE

	$440	$360	$305	$275	$220	$165	$140

MODEL 1862 ROBINSON CONFEDERATE CARBINE

Mfg.'s Sug. Retail	$915	$805	$650	$550	$475	$410	$350	$320

MONTANA CENTENNIAL RIFLE SERIIES — mfg. to commemorate Montana's 100th Centennial (1889-1989), limited manufacture. Mfg. began 1988-90.

Creedmoor Rifle — .45-70 cal., extra fancy rifle with engraving, 32 in. barrel, walnut cased. 100 mfg. only ser. numbered 1-101.

	$3,750	$2,500	$1,950

Last Mfg.'s Sug. Retail was $3,750.

Hartford Rifle — .45-70 cal, 30 in. barrel, case colored receiver, 12 lbs. Serial numbered 102-902.

	$1,375	$995	$750

Last Mfg.'s Sug. Retail was $1,375.

Bridgeport Rifle — .45-70, 30 in. barrel, similar to Hartford rifle without Pewter forearm cap, 12 lbs.

	$1,075	$775	$575

Last Mfg.'s Sug. Retail was $1,075.

SIG

Manufactured by Sig Swiss Industrial Company since 1860 in Neuhausen, Switzerland. Previously imported and distributed by Sigarms Located in Herndon, VA.

PISTOLS

Mandall Shooting Supplies, Inc. located in Scottsdale, AZ still has limited quantities of the 210-1, 210-2, 210-5, and 210-6. 1991 retail prices are as follows: P 210-2 is $2,000, P 210-5 is $2,700, P 210-6 is $2,500, and the P 210 conversion unit (.22 LR) is $1,295.

While SIG announced the discontinuance of the Model P 210 in 1987, Mandall's has been able to continually import small quantities of this sought after semi-auto pistol.

Grading	100%	98%	95%	90%	80%	70%	60%

P 210 — 9mm or 7.65 Para., single action, 4¾ in. barrel, 8 shot mag., standard weapon of the Swiss Army, 2 lbs.

Originally mfg. in 1947, this pistol was first designated the SP 47/8 and became the standard military pistol of the Swiss Army in 1949. Later designated the P 210, this handgun has been mfg. continuously for over 40 years.

P 210-1 — polished finish, walnut grips, special hammer, fixed sights. Importation disc. 1986.

	$1,700	$1,550	$1,375	$1,195	$995	$900	$800

Last Mfg.'s Sug. Retail was $1,861.

P 210-2 — matte finish, field sights, plastic grips. Importation disc. 1987.

	$1,400	$1,150	$975	$860	$750	$625	$550

Last Mfg.'s Sug. Retail was $1,350.

P 210-5 — matte finish, micrometer sights, 150mm or 180mm (rare) extended barrel, hard rubber grips, special order only, very limited mfg. Importation disc. 1987.

	$1,850	$1,475	$1,325	$1,150	$950	$875	$760

Last Mfg.'s Sug. Retail was $1,795.

P 210-6 — matte finish, micrometer sights, 120mm barrel, hard rubber grips. Importation disc. 1987.

	$1,495	$1,310	$1,200	$1,050	$900	$850	$740

Last Mfg.'s Sug. Retail was $1,595.

P 210 Deluxe Models — various models differ in the amount of engraving, gold inlays, carved wooden grips, presentation cases, and other special order features available from the factory. Prices start at $3,500 and can go up to $5,500, depending on the amount of special orders executed.

Conversion kits can be special ordered converting to either 7.65 Luger or .22 LR cal. Add $630 for conversion kit with field sights or $781 for conversion kit with fixed sights standard (adj. by special order).

RIFLES

While SIG rifles have not been imported in quantity since 1988, Mandall's Shooting Supplies Inc. still has these models left in limited quantities. 1991 retail prices are as follows: PE-57 is $4,400, the AMT is $4,400, and the SG 550/551 is $4,000.

PE-57 — 7.5 Swiss cal. only, semi-auto version of the Swiss military rifle, 24 in. barrel, includes 24 shot mag., leather sling, bipod and maintenance kit. Importation disc. 1988.

	$2,000	$1,800	$1,675	$1,445	$1,325	$1,150	$950

The PE-57 was previously distributed in limited quanities by Osborne's located in Cheboygan, MI.

Last Mfg.'s Sug. Retail was $1,745.

SIG-AMT SEMI-AUTO RIFLE — semi-auto version of SG510-4 auto paramilitary design rifle, roller delayed blowback action, .308 Win., 5, 10, or 20 shot mag., 18¾ in. barrel, wood stock, folding bipod. Mfg. 1960-present. Importation disc. 1988.

	$2,500	$2,250	$2,000	$1,850	$1,700	$1,550	$1,400

This model is available in very limited quantities through Osborne's located in Cheboygan, MI.

Last Mfg.'s Sug. Retail was $1,795.

SG 550/551 — .223 cal. with heavier bullet, Swiss Army's semi-auto version of its newest paramilitary design rifle (SIG 90), 20.8 (SG 550) or 16 in. (SG 551 Carbine) barrel, some synthetics used to save weight, 20 shot mag., diopter night sights, built-in folding bipod, 7.7 or 9 lbs.

	$3,250	$2,700	$2,400	$2,150	$1,900	$1,700	$1,500

Add $250 for case.

Last Mfg.'s Sug. Retail was $1,950.

This model has been banned from domestic importation due to 1989 Federal legislation.

SIG-HAMMERLI

Manufactured by Hammerli Ltd. in Lenzburg, Switzerland. Previously imported by Osborne's located in Cheboygan, MI.

Grading	100%	98%	95%	90%	80%	70%	60%

P240 TARGET PISTOL — .32 S&W Long wadcutter or .38 (disc.) cal., single action, 5 shot mag., 5.9 in. barrel, blued finish, thumb rest walnut grips, adj. sights and trigger, 3 lbs. Add $100 for Morini adj. grips. Importation disc. 1986.

	$1,250	$1,100	$985	$870	$770	$715	$660

Last Mfg.'s Sug. Retail was $1,350.

.38 Mid-range cal. is very desirable in this model - healthy premiums (and inconsistent) are being asked currently.

.22 CONVERSION UNIT

	$550	$495	$400				

Last Mfg.'s Sug. Retail was $595.

SIG SAUER

Manufacturer located in W. Germany by Sauer. Currently imported and distributed by Sigarms located in Exeter, NH.

PISTOLS: SEMI-AUTO

MODEL P210 — refer to listing under SIG pistols.

MODEL P220 — double action, .22 LR (disc.), .38 Super, 7.65mm (disc.), 9mm Luger, or .45 ACP cal., 7 (.45 ACP) or 9 shot mag., 4.4 in. barrel, decocking lever safety, matte blue, lightweight alloy frame, black plastic grips, (action is same as Browning BDA), values are for .45 ACP cal. and assume American side mag. release (standard 1986), 28.2 oz. Mfg. 1976-present.

Mfg.'s Sug. Retail	$750	$660	$595	$495	$440	$395	$350	$310

Add $100 for Siglite night sights.

Add $70 for factory K-Kote finish.

Add $70 for electroless nickel finish.

Add $680 for .22 LR conversion kit (disc.).

Subtract $50 for "European" Model (bottom mag. release - includes 9mm and .38 Super cal.'s).

MODEL P225 — 9mm, double action, similar to P220, shorter dimensions, 3.85 in. barrel, 8 shot, thumb actuated button release mag., fully adj. sights, 28.8 oz.

Mfg.'s Sug. Retail	$750	$675	$600	$500	$450	$400	$350	$310

Add $70 for factory K-Kote finish.

Add $100 for Siglite night sights.

Add $70 for electroless nickel finish.

MODEL P226 — 9mm, double action compact model, 15 or 20 shot mag., 4.4 in. barrel, alloy frame, high contrast sights, 29.9 oz. New 1983.

Mfg.'s Sug. Retail	$780	$695	$625	$525	$475	$415	$360	$310

Add $100 for Siglite night sights.

Add $70 for electroless nickel finish.

Add $70 for K-Kote (Polymer) finish.

This model is also available in double action only (all finishes) at no extra charge.

MODEL P228 — 9mm Para., double action semi-auto, compact design, 4.41 in. barrel, 13 shot mag., automatic firing pin lock safety, 3 dot sighting system, alloy frame, blue, nickel (new 1991), or K-Kote finish, 29.3 oz. New 1990.

Mfg.'s Sug. Retail	$780	$695	$625	$525	$475	$415	$360	$310

Add $100 for Siglite night sights.

Add $70 for electroless nickel finish.

Add $70 for K-Kote (Polymer) finish.

This model is also available in double action only (all finishes) at no extra charge.

Grading	100%	98%	95%	90%	80%	70%	60%

MODEL P229 — .40 S&W cal., similar to Model P228, steel black slide with aluminum alloy frame, 12 shot mag., 30½oz. New 1991.

As this edition goes to press, prices have yet to be established on this model.

This model is also available in double action only at no extra charge.

Model P229 SL (Stainless) — similar to Model P229, except has stainless steel slide. New 1991.

As this edition goes to press, prices have yet to be established on this model.

MODEL P230 — double action, .22 LR (disc.)-10 shot, .32 ACP-8 shot (disc.), .380 ACP, and 9mm Ultra (disc.)-7 shot, 3.6 in. barrel, blue, wood grips. Mfg. 1976-present, 17.6 oz.

Mfg.'s Sug. Retail	$495	$415	$365	$300	$270	$240	$215	$190

Model P230 SL Stainless — same as Model P230, except stainless steel construction, 22.4 oz.

Mfg.'s Sug. Retail	$575	$465	$415	$350

RIFLES

MODEL SSG 2000 — available in .223, 7.5mm Swiss, .300 Wby. Mag., or .308 (standard) cal., bolt action, 4 shot mag., no sights, deluxe sniper rifle featuring thumbhole style walnut stock with stippling and thumbwheel adj. cheek piece, 13 lbs. Importation disc. 1986.

	$2,480	$2,260	$1,950	$1,700	$1,500	$1,300	$1,100

This model was available in .223, .300 Wby. Mag., or 7.5mm cal. by special order only.

Last Mfg.'s Sug. Retail was $2,850.

SILE DISTRIBUTORS

Distributor/importer/manufacturer located in New York, NY.

In addition to distributing a wide variety of firearms and related accessories (including the mfg. of stocks and grips), Sile Distributors also has some handguns "private labeled" to their specifications. These pistols may be found under the Sphinx heading in the S section of this text.

SILMA SPORTING GUNS

Manufacturer located in Brescia, Italy since 1949. To date, there has been limited importation into the U.S. All Silma Shotguns are high quality and utilize premium materials in their manufacture.

Rather than list the various shotgun models and options separately, the following information will help you in ascertaining correct values. Models 70 and 80 are O/U hunting models available in either 12, 20, or .410 ga. They are available with double triggers standard, extractors or ejectors (extra cost), with or without sideplates, or in superlight configuration - retail values range between $437-$854. Competition models (including T.J. 70, T.S. 81, Cobra T1, T2, or T3) are also available for trap, skeet, or sporting clays events. Values range between $860-$3,142 (with T.J. 70 being the least expensive, and Cobra T2 the most expensive). Two side by side models (AS/70 N and AS/70 EJ) are also available at $597 or $678, respectively.

For further information regarding any of the models listed above, please contact the Blue Book of Gun Values or the manufacturer directly (please refer to Trademark Index in back of book for address).

SIRKIS INDUSTRIES, LTD.

Manufacturer located in Ramat-Gan, Israel. Previously imported and distributed by Armscorp of America, Inc. located in Baltimore, MD.

Grading	100%	98%	95%	90%	80%	70%	60%

PISTOLS: SEMI-AUTO

S.D. 9 — 9mm Para., double action mechanism, frame is constructed mostly of heavy gauge sheet metal stampings, 3.07 in. barrel, parkerized finish, chamber indicator, 7 shot mag., plastic grips, 24½ oz. Imported under this trademark between 1986-1988.

	$300	$250	$225	$200	$190	$180	$170

Last Mfg.'s Sug. Retail was $330.

This pistol is now listed under the Sardius heading in this section.

RIFLES

MODEL 35 MATCH RIFLE — .22 LR only, single shot bolt action, 26 in. full floating barrel, select walnut, match trigger, micrometer sights. Disc. 1985.

	$650	$625	$595	$550	$510	$460	$420

Last Mfg.'s Sug. Retail was $690.

MODEL 36 SNIPER RIFLE — 7.62mm only, gas operated action, carbon fiber stock, 22 in. barrel, flash supressor, free range sights. Disc. 1985.

	$670	$580	$520	$475	$430	$390	$350

Last Mfg.'s Sug. Retail was $760.

SKORPION

Please refer to Armitage International, Ltd. in the "A" section of this text.

SMITH, L.C.

Manufactured from 1880-1888 in Syracuse, NY. Manufactured in Fulton, NY 1890-1945 by Hunter Arms Company.

The L.C. Smith shotgun was made from 1890-1945 by the Hunter Arms Company in Fulton, New York. In 1946, the company was acquired by Marlin Firearms Company. Production continued until 1951 when it ceased for a period of 17 years. In 1968, Marlin brought the L.C. Smith back to life for a period of 5 years. Production stopped in 1973. The L.C. Smith is one of the finest American made shotguns and collector interest is very high. All values shown are for hammerless shotguns.

HAMMERLESS SHOTGUNS 1890-1913

All prices listed below are for guns with fluid steel barrels (except A-1 grade).

It is important to note that damascus barreled guns in 90% original condition or better are very collectible and values can approximate those of steel barrel models if the bore is excellent with no pitting. damascus specimens below 90% condition are not as collectible, however, and values fall off rapidly if under 90%. Prices shown below for 90% and up condition are very difficult to evaluate and are meant as a guide only. L.C. Smith shotguns are rare and hard to evaluate if over 95% condition in the higher grades.

100%	98%	95%	90%	80%	70%	60%	50%	40%	30%	20%	10%

OO GRADE — 12, 16, or 20 ga. Approx. 60,000 mfg.

100%	98%	95%	90%	80%	70%	60%	50%	40%	30%	20%	10%
$1,500	$1,200	$800	$600	$500	$465	$430	$395	$375	$350	$325	$295

Auto ejectors — add 33%.

20 ga. — add 50%.

O GRADE — 10, 12, 16, or 20 ga. Approx. 30,000 mfg.

100%	98%	95%	90%	80%	70%	60%	50%	40%	30%	20%	10%
$1,600	$1,400	$1,000	$775	$675	$600	$550	$515	$460	$400	$350	$300

20 ga. — add 50%.

Add 50% for 20 ga.

100%	98%	95%	90%	80%	70%	60%	50%	40%	30%	20%	10%

NO. 1 GRADE — 10, 12, 16, or 20 ga. Approx. 10,000 mfg.

100%	98%	95%	90%	80%	70%	60%	50%	40%	30%	20%	10%
$2,400	$1,950	$1,425	$995	$850	$750	$700	$625	$550	$495	$450	$400

Auto ejectors — add 33%.
20 ga. — add 50%.
SST — add $200.

NO. 2 GRADE — 10, 12, 16, or 20 ga. Approx. 13,000 mfg.

100%	98%	95%	90%	80%	70%	60%	50%	40%	30%	20%	10%
$2,900	$2,275	$1,700	$1,400	$1,200	$1,000	$825	$750	$675	$600	$550	$500

Auto ejectors — add 33%.
20 ga. — add 75%.
Add $200 for SST.

NO. 3 GRADE — 10, 12, 16, or 20 ga. Approx. 4,000 mfg.

100%	98%	95%	90%	80%	70%	60%	50%	40%	30%	20%	10%
$3,475	$2,950	$2,400	$1,850	$1,500	$1,300	$1,100	$995	$875	$775	$625	$500

Auto ejectors — add 25%.
20 ga. — add 75%.
SST — add $200.

PIGEON GRADE — 10, 12, 16, or 20 ga. Approx. 1,200 mfg.

100%	98%	95%	90%	80%	70%	60%	50%	40%	30%	20%	10%
$3,475	$2,950	$2,400	$1,850	$1,500	$1,300	$1,100	$995	$875	$775	$625	$500

Auto ejectors — add 25%.
20 ga. — add 75%.
SST — add $200.

NO. 4 GRADE — 10, 12, 16, or 20 ga. Approx. 500 mfg, seldomly encountered.

100%	98%	95%	90%	80%	70%	60%	50%	40%	30%	20%	10%
$10,000	$8,000	$5,750	$4,500	$3,500	$2,650	$2,000	$1,775	$1,500	$1,375	$1,200	$1,095

Auto ejectors — add 25%.
20 ga. — add 75%.
SST — add $200.

A-1 GRADE — 10, 12, or 16 ga. Approx. 700 mfg. Damascus barrels only.

100%	98%	95%	90%	80%	70%	60%	50%	40%	30%	20%	10%
$4,850	$3,700	$3,000	$2,200	$1,850	$1,725	$1,425	$1,175	$995	$800	$700	$600

Auto ejectors — standard.
SST — add $200.

NO. 5 GRADE — 10, 12, 16, or 20 ga. Approx. 500 mfg.

100%	98%	95%	90%	80%	70%	60%	50%	40%	30%	20%	10%
$9,000	$7,000	$4,950	$4,500	$4,000	$3,500	$3,150	$2,700	$2,450	$2,200	$1,995	$1,800

Auto ejectors — standard.
SST — add $200.
20 ga. — add 75%, extremely rare.

MONOGRAM GRADE — 10, 12, 16, or 20 ga. Approx. 100 mfg.

100%	98%	95%	90%	80%	70%	60%	50%	40%	30%	20%	10%
$10,750	$9,475	$7,400	$6,000	$5,500	$5,000	$4,600	$4,100	$3,800	$3,500	$3,250	$3,000

Auto ejectors — standard.
20 ga. — add 50%, extremely rare.

A-2 GRADE — 10, 12, 16, or 20 ga. Approx. 200 mfg.

100%	98%	95%	90%	80%	70%	60%	50%	40%	30%	20%	10%
$15,000	$11,000	$8,000	$7,000	$6,000	$5,200	$4,700	$4,200	$3,850	$3,500	$3,250	$3,000

Auto ejectors — standard.
20 ga. — only 6 mfg.

A-3 GRADE — 10, 12, 16, or 20 ga. Approx. 20 mfg. Rarity precludes accurate pricing on this model.
Auto ejectors — standard.
20 ga. — only 2 mfg.

100%	98%	95%	90%	80%	70%	60%	50%	40%	30%	20%	10%

SHOTGUNS: 1914-1951 MFG.

Fulton trademarked shotguns mfg. by Hunter Arms Co. were inexpensive, utilitarian shotguns designed for a price point rather than quality. Models Fulton and Fulton Special were supplied in 12, 16, 20, or .410 ga. (rare). When encountered today, values usually are in the $100-$300 range. The Hunter Special, although not a L.C. Smith shotgun, did employ the rotary locking bolt system. This was also a low priced gun in its day and prices today are usually in the $125-$350 range. These models had nothing in common with the L.C. Smith shotguns of the circa.

LC. SMITH DOUBLE BARREL SHOTGUN — 12, 16, 20, or .410 ga., any choke, sidelock, auto ejectors standard from Crown Grade up, extractors on lower grades, double or single triggers, straight, ½ pistol grip, or pistol grip stock, grade specifications differ in grade of wood, degree of engraving, and overall quality.

STANDARD FIELD GRADE

100%	98%	95%	90%	80%	70%	60%	50%	40%	30%	20%	10%
$1,250	$1,000	$775	$675	$600	$500	$465	$435	$395	$375	$340	$295

Auto ejectors — add 33%.
SST — add $200.
20 ga. — add 30%.
.410 — add 300%.

IDEAL GRADE STANDARD

100%	98%	95%	90%	80%	70%	60%	50%	40%	30%	20%	10%
$1,600	$1,400	$1,100	$900	$825	$750	$700	$650	$595	$550	$530	$495

Auto ejectors — add 33%.
SST — add $200.
20 ga. — add 30%.
.410 — add 400%.

TRAP GRADE

100%	98%	95%	90%	80%	70%	60%	50%	40%	30%	20%	10%
$2,000	$1,500	$1,200	$1,100	$1,000	$925	$850	$775	$675	$600	$550	$500

Auto ejectors — add 33%.
SST — add $200.
20 ga. — add 50%.
.410 — add 400%.

SPECIALTY GRADE

100%	98%	95%	90%	80%	70%	60%	50%	40%	30%	20%	10%
$2,950	$2,450	$1,800	$1,375	$1,100	$1,000	$925	$875	$825	$775	$695	$625

SST — add $200.
20 ga. — add 50%.
.410 — add 400%.
Auto ejectors — add 33%.

EAGLE GRADE

100%	98%	95%	90%	80%	70%	60%	50%	40%	30%	20%	10%
$4,750	$4,250	$3,500	$2,900	$2,350	$1,850	$1,500	$1,400	$1,300	$1,200	$1,100	$1,000

SST — add $200.
20 ga. — add 50%.

SKEET SPECIAL GRADE

100%	98%	95%	90%	80%	70%	60%	50%	40%	30%	20%	10%
$3,100	$2,600	$1,650	$1,200	$1,100	$925	$875	$825	$775	$725	$675	$600

20 ga. — add 50%.
.410 — add 400%.
Auto ejectors — add 33%.
SST — add $200.

	100%	98%	95%	90%	80%	70%	60%	50%	40%	30%	20%	10%

PREMIER SKEET GRADE

	100%	98%	95%	90%	80%	70%	60%	50%	40%	30%	20%	10%
	$3,100	$2,600	$1,650	$1,200	$1,100	$925	$875	$825	$775	$725	$675	$600

20 ga. — add 50%.
.410 — add 400%.
Auto ejectors — add 33%.
SST — add $200.

CROWN GRADE

	100%	98%	95%	90%	80%	70%	60%	50%	40%	30%	20%	10%
	$5,750	$4,950	$4,250	$4,000	$3,500	$3,100	$2,700	$2,450	$2,225	$2,000	$1,900	$1,800

SST — add $200.
20 gauge — very rare.
.410 — rare and very expensive, only 6 mfg.

MONOGRAM GRADE

	100%	98%	95%	90%	80%	70%	60%	50%	40%	30%	20%	10%
	$12,000	$9,750	$7,750	$6,400	$5,650	$5,100	$4,650	$4,150	$3,775	$3,500	$3,250	$3,000

20 ga. — add 50%.

PREMIER GRADE — very limited mfg., rarity precludes accurate pricing on this model.

DELUXE GRADE — very limited mfg., rarity precludes accurate pricing on this model.

SINGLE BARREL TRAP GUN — 12 ga. only, 32 or 34 in. vent rib barrel, boxlock, auto ejector, checkered pistol grip stock, recoil pad. Approx. 2,650 mfg. 1917-1951.

	100%	98%	95%	90%	80%	70%	60%	50%	40%	30%	20%	10%
Olympic Grade												
	$1,650	$1,400	$1,200	$1,100	$1,000	$900	$800	$725	$675	$625	$575	$550
Specialty Grade												
	$1,950	$1,700	$1,500	$1,400	$1,300	$1,200	$1,125	$1,075	$1,000	$925	$875	$800
Crown Grade												
	$3,450	$3,125	$2,750	$2,350	$2,100	$2,000	$1,900	$1,800	$1,700	$1,600	$1,500	$1,400
Monogram Grade												
	$6,000	$5,000	$4,250	$3,700	$3,150	$2,750	$2,400	$2,150	$2,000	$1,850	$1,700	$1,525
Premier Grade												
	$9,750	$8,350	$6,400	$5,275	$3,850	$3,300	$2,900	$2,600	$2,350	$2,100	$1,900	$1,750
Deluxe Grade												
	$13,950	$12,000	$9,995	$7,850	$6,000	$5,000	$4,500	$3,995	$3,375	$2,900	$2,500	$2,150

1968-1973 MFG.

Grading	100%	98%	95%	90%	80%	70%	60%

1968 SXS MODEL — 12 ga., 28 in. vent rib barrel, full and mod. choke, sidelock, extractors, double triggers, checkered pistol grip stock. Mfg. 1968-1973 by Marlin.

	100%	98%	95%	90%	80%	70%	60%
	$725	$600	$550	$495	$425	$350	$275

1968 SXS DELUXE MODEL — same as Standard, with Simmons floating rib, beavertail forearm. Mfg. 1971-1973 by Marlin.

	100%	98%	95%	90%	80%	70%	60%
	$995	$825	$725	$600	$495	$400	$350

SMITH & WESSON

Manufacturer located in Springfield, MA 1857 to date. S & W became a subsidiary of Bangor-Punta from 1957-1983. Between 1983-1987 Smith & Wesson was owned by the Lear Siegler Co. On May 22, 1987 Smith & Wesson was sold to R.L. Tompkins, an English plumbing Co.

REVOLVERS: EARLY MODELS

100%	98%	95%	90%	80%	70%	60%	50%	40%	30%	20%	10%

MODEL NO. 1 FIRST ISSUE — single action, .22 Short, 7 shot non-fluted cylinder, $3\frac{3}{16}$ in. octagon barrel, bottom break, spur trigger, silver plated brass frame, blue barrel and cylinder, square rosewood grips. Mfg. 11,671, 1857-1860.

First Type — serial range 1-200.

$4,950	$4,400	$4,125	$3,850	$3,575	$3,300	$2,975	$2,600	$2,200	$1,650	$1,375	$990

Second Type — serial range 200-1130.

$3,025	$2,500	$2,200	$1,975	$1,775	$1,575	$1,320	$1,100	$880	$715	$550	$415

Third Type — serial range 1130-3000.

$2,200	$1,825	$1,600	$1,450	$1,300	$1,155	$1,045	$935	$880	$825	$770	$660

Fourth Type — serial range 3000-4200.

$2,200	$1,825	$1,600	$1,450	$1,300	$1,155	$1,045	$935	$880	$825	$770	$660

Fifth Type — serial range 4200-5500.

$2,200	$1,825	$1,600	$1,450	$1,300	$1,155	$1,045	$935	$880	$825	$770	$660

Sixth Type — serial range 5500-11,671.

$1,925	$1,600	$1,425	$1,300	$1,200	$1,100	$990	$880	$770	$715	$660	$495

MODEL NO. 1 SECOND ISSUE — similar to First Issue, except flat sided frame and irregular shaped sideplate. Mfg. 117,000, 1860-1868.

$360	$305	$275	$220	$195	$180	$165	$150	$140	$120	$110	$100

Second Quality — marked, 4402 revolvers.

$715	$605	$550	$495	$440	$415	$385	$360	$330	$275	$250	$225

MODEL NO. 1 THIRD ISSUE — similar to Second Issue, except fluted cylinder and birds head grip. Mfg. 131,163, 1868-1881.

$3\frac{3}{16}$ *in. barrel model*

$305	$250	$220	$195	$165	$150	$140	$120	$110	$100	$90	$80

$2\frac{1}{11}$ *in. barrel model*

$415	$360	$310	$275	$250	$220	$200	$175	$165	$140	$120	$110

MODEL NO. 1½ FIRST ISSUE — .32 rimfire, single action, 3½ and 4 in. octagon barrel, 5 shot non-fluted cylinder, bottom break, spur trigger, blue or nickel, rosewood grips. Mfg. 26,300, 1865-1868.

$440	$360	$330	$275	$250	$220	$200	$180	$165	$150	$120	$110

MODEL NO. 1½ SECOND ISSUE — similar to First Issue, with birds head grips and round barrel. Mfg. 100,700, 1868-1875.

3½ in. barrel model

$385	$330	$275	$220	$200	$175	$165	$150	$140	$120	$110	$100

2½ in. barrel model

$495	$440	$385	$330	$310	$290	$250	$220	$195	$165	$140	$125

Transitional Model — serial range 27,200-28,800.

$1,210	$1,045	$935	$880	$825	$770	$660	$550	$495	$440	$385	$340

MODEL NO. 1½ SINGLE ACTION — .32 S&W, similar to Second Issue, except top break, rebounding hammer, auto extraction. Mfg. 97,574, 1878-1892.

Early Model — without strain screw, serial range 1-6500.

$415	$360	$330	$275	$250	$220	$195	$165	$140	$110	$95	$85

Later Model — with strain screw, remainder of serial range.

$415	$330	$250	$220	$195	$165	$150	$125	$110	$100	$90	$80

8 and 10 in. barrel model.

$770	$550	$440	$330	$310	$305	$290	$275	$265	$250	$220	$200

MODEL NO. 2 ARMY — .32 rimfire long, similar in appearance to No. 1½ First Issue, except 6 shot cylinder, different barrel lengths, used as a sidearm during Civil War. Mfg. 77,155, 1861-1874.

5 or 6 in. Early Model — serial range 1-3000.

$550	$475	$420	$385	$360	$330	$305	$275	$220	$165	$140	$125

100%	98%	95%	90%	80%	70%	60%	50%	40%	30%	20%	10%

5 or 6 in. Standard Model — remainder of serial range.

| $525 | $460 | $395 | $350 | $315 | $275 | $250 | $195 | $165 | $145 | $120 | $115 |

4 in. barrel model

| $1,045 | $935 | $880 | $770 | $715 | $660 | $580 | $495 | $440 | $385 | $330 | $285 |

Note: Watch for fakes on 4 in. model.

FIRST MODEL .32 DOUBLE ACTION — .32 S&W, 5 shot fluted cylinder, 3 in. round barrel, blue or nickel, black rubber grips, one of the rarest of all S&W's. Mfg. only 30, 1880.

| $3,245 | $2,750 | $2,350 | $1,980 | $1,760 | $1,650 | $1,540 | $1,375 | $1,175 | $1,025 | $935 | $865 |

SECOND MODEL .32 DOUBLE ACTION — similar to First Model, except irregular shaped sideplate. Mfg. 22,142, 1880-1882.

| $330 | $280 | $230 | $195 | $180 | $165 | $150 | $140 | $110 | $100 | $90 | $80 |

THIRD MODEL .32 DOUBLE ACTION — similar to Second Model, except no groove around cylinder. Mfg. 22,232, 1882-1883.

| $330 | $280 | $230 | $195 | $180 | $165 | $150 | $140 | $110 | $100 | $90 | $80 |

FOURTH MODEL .32 DOUBLE ACTION — similar to Third Model, except rounded trigger guard. Mfg. 239,600, 1883-1909.

| $250 | $200 | $165 | $140 | $120 | $110 | $100 | $90 | $85 | $80 | $75 | $70 |

FIFTH MODEL .32 DOUBLE ACTION — similar to Fourth Model, except integral front sight. Mfg. 44,641, 1909-1919.

| $275 | $250 | $220 | $195 | $165 | $150 | $140 | $120 | $110 | $95 | $85 | $55 |

MODEL 320 REVOLVING RIFLE — .320 S&W, 6 shot cylinder, 16, 18, or 20 in. round barrel, hard rubber grips, detachable shoulder stock, blue or nickel finish. Mfg. 977, 1879-1887.

16 or 20 in. barrel model — mfg. 239 - 16 in., or 224 - 20 in.

| $8,500 | $6,600 | $5,500 | $4,400 | $3,575 | $3,300 | $3,135 | $2,750 | $2,640 | $2,420 | $2,200 | $1,925 |

18 in. barrel model — 514 mfg.

| $8,500 | $6,600 | $5,500 | $4,400 | $3,300 | $3,025 | $2,750 | $2,585 | $2,310 | $2,145 | $1,925 | $1,650 |

MODEL NO. 3 FIRST MODEL AMERICAN — .44 S&W or .44 rimfire Henry cal., single action, 6 shot fluted cylinder, 8 in. round barrel, blue or nickel, walnut grips. Mfg. 8000, 1870-1872.

Standard Model — vent hole in extractor housing, first 1500 mfg.

| $2,750 | $2,200 | $1,925 | $1,650 | $1,375 | $1,100 | $990 | $880 | $850 | $775 | $675 | $600 |

Standard Model — without hole in extractor.

| $2,475 | $2,000 | $1,705 | $1,430 | $1,100 | $880 | $825 | $770 | $715 | $605 | $525 | $440 |

Transitional Model — shorter cylinder, serial range 6700-8000.

| $3,025 | $2,525 | $2,225 | $1,950 | $1,775 | $1,650 | $1,375 | $1,210 | $990 | $935 | $825 | $660 |

.44 Rim Fire Henry — 100 mfg.

| $3,850 | $3,300 | $2,975 | $2,750 | $2,475 | $2,310 | $2,200 | $1,980 | $1,815 | $1,650 | $1,485 | $1,210 |

U.S. Marked — approx. 1,000 mfg.

| $3,300 | $2,675 | $2,375 | $2,100 | $1,875 | $1,650 | $1,540 | $1,430 | $1,265 | $1,100 | $990 | $825 |

Nashville Police — very rare, only 32 manufactured. Scarcity precludes accurate pricing.

MODEL 3 RUSSIAN FIRST MODEL — .44 S&W Russian, 6, 7, or 8 in. barrels, Russian contract 8 in., blue or nickel, walnut grips, looks similar to First and Second Model American. Mfg. 5,165 for commercial sale and 20,014 Russian Contract, 1871-1874.

Commercial Version — 4,665 mfg.

| $2,200 | $1,725 | $1,430 | $1,100 | $935 | $855 | $825 | $770 | $715 | $580 | $550 | $440 |

Reject Russian Contract — 500 mfg.

| $3,850 | $3,300 | $2,975 | $2,750 | $2,475 | $2,310 | $2,200 | $1,980 | $1,815 | $1,650 | $1,485 | $1,210 |

Russian Contract — 20,000 mfg., rare, most sent to Russia.

| $3,025 | $2,915 | $2,750 | $2,420 | $1,925 | $1,815 | $1,540 | $1,320 | $1,210 | $1,045 | $935 | $770 |

100%	98%	95%	90%	80%	70%	60%	50%	40%	30%	20%	10%

MODEL NO. 3 SECOND MODEL AMERICAN — similar to First Model, except bump on bottom of frame and steel front sight instead of German silver, 20,735 mfg. between 1872-1874.

Standard Model

| $2,475 | $2,000 | $1,675 | $1,485 | $1,275 | $1,100 | $990 | $880 | $770 | $660 | $550 | $500 |

MODEL NO. 3 SECOND MODEL

.44 Rim Fire Henry — 3,014 mfg.

| $3,245 | $2,750 | $2,300 | $1,925 | $1,815 | $1,650 | $1,485 | $1,210 | $1,045 | $825 | $715 | $650 |

MODEL 3 RUSSIAN SECOND MODEL— 85,200 mfg. in all variations between 1873-78.

Commercial Version — 6,200 mfg.

| $2,200 | $1,725 | $1,430 | $1,100 | $935 | $855 | $825 | $770 | $715 | $580 | $550 | $440 |

.44 Rimfire Henry — approx. 500 mfg.

| $3,245 | $2,750 | $2,300 | $1,925 | $1,815 | $1,650 | $1,485 | $1,210 | $1,045 | $825 | $715 | $650 |

Russian Contract — approx. 70,000 mfg., rare in U.S.

| $2,475 | $2,000 | $1,675 | $1,485 | $1,275 | $1,100 | $990 | $880 | $770 | $660 | $550 | $500 |

Turkish Model— 1,000 mfg. in their own serial number range in .44 rimfire. This is probably the rarest and most valuble variation.

| $4,500 | $4,250 | $3,950 | $3,850 | $3,300 | $2,975 | $2,750 | $2,475 | $2,350 | $2,200 | $1,980 | $1,815 |

Japanese Contract — 1,000 mfg., marked with an anchor on butt.

| $3,245 | $2,750 | $2,300 | $1,925 | $1,815 | $1,650 | $1,485 | $1,210 | $1,045 | $825 | $715 | $650 |

MODEL 3 RUSSIAN THIRD MODEL — commonly called the "New Model Russian" and is similar to old model, except has shorter extractor housing, approx. 60,600 mfg. between 1874 and 1878. Values are similar to old model for comparable variations.

Commercial Version — approx. 13,500 mfg.

| $2,500 | $2,200 | $1,725 | $1,430 | $1,100 | $935 | $855 | $825 | $770 | $715 | $580 | $550 |

.44 Rimfire Henry

| $3,245 | $2,750 | $2,300 | $1,925 | $1,815 | $1,650 | $1,485 | $1,210 | $1,045 | $825 | $715 | $650 |

Russian Contract — 41,138 mfg. Cyrillic lettering.

| $3,245 | $2,750 | $2,300 | $1,925 | $1,815 | $1,650 | $1,485 | $1,210 | $1,045 | $825 | $715 | $6500 |

Ludwig & Lowe, & Tula Copies — copies mfg. for the Russian government.

| $1,725 | $1,430 | $1,100 | $935 | $855 | $825 | $770 | $715 | $580 | $550 | $440 | $375 |

Turkish Contract — 5,000 mfg.

| $4,250 | $3,500 | $3,245 | $2,750 | $2,300 | $1,925 | $1,815 | $1,650 | $1,485 | $1,210 | $1,045 | $825 |

Japanese Contract— 1,000 made.

| $2,200 | $1,900 | $1,725 | $1,430 | $1,100 | $935 | $855 | $825 | $770 | $715 | $580 | $550 |

NEW MODEL NO. 3 — features very short extractor housing under the barrel, knuckle on backstrap is less pronounced than 2nd and 3rd models, 35,796 mfg. between 1878-1912.

Commercial Version — 6½in. barrel, .44 Russian cal.

| $2,175 | $1,850 | $1,500 | $1,265 | $1,045 | $935 | $825 | $740 | $660 | $595 | $550 | $500 |

Add $200 if cut shoulder stock.

Japanese Navy Model— anchor on butt.

| $1,850 | $1,500 | $1,265 | $1,045 | $935 | $825 | $740 | $660 | $605 | $550 | $500 | $450 |

Australian Model — 7 in. barrel, detachable stock,for Australian Colonial Police, broad arrow marking, 200 mfg.

| $4,500 | $4,250 | $3,500 | $3,245 | $2,750 | $2,300 | $1,925 | $1,815 | $1,650 | $1,485 | $1,210 | $1,045 |

Argentine Model — 2,000 mfg., marked "Ejercito Argentina".

| $2,900 | $2,700 | $2,300 | $1,925 | $1,815 | $1,650 | $1,485 | $1,210 | $1,045 | $825 | $715 | $650 |

State of Maryland Model — U.S. marked, serial number range 7126-7405.

| $4,000 | $3,700 | $3,500 | $3,245 | $2,750 | $2,300 | $1,925 | $1,815 | $1,650 | $1,485 | $1,210 | $1,045 |

100%	98%	95%	90%	80%	70%	60%	50%	40%	30%	20%	10%

NEW MODEL NO. 3 FRONTIER — .38-40 (74 mfg.), .44-40 cal., single action, 4, 5, or 6½ in. barrel, blue or nickel, walnut or hard rubber grips. Mfg. 2072, 1885-1908.
Standard Model — .44-40.

100%	98%	95%	90%	80%	70%	60%	50%	40%	30%	20%	10%
$1,650	$1,265	$1,045	$935	$825	$740	$660	$605	$550	$495	$440	$385

Add 100% for .38-40 cal.
Japanese Purchase — 786 conv. to .44 Russian.

| $2,200 | $1,650 | $1,100 | $880 | $770 | $715 | $660 | $550 | $495 | $415 | $330 | $275 |

NEW MODEL NO. 3 TARGET MODEL — .32-44 S&W, and .38-44 S&W, 4,333 mfg. between 1887-1910.

| $2,700 | $2,200 | $1,850 | $1,650 | $1,265 | $1,045 | $935 | $825 | $740 | $660 | $605 | $550 |

NEW MODEL NO. 3 TURKISH — .44 rimfire, 5,461 mfg. between 1879-1888.

| $5,500 | $5,150 | $4,900 | $4,750 | $4,200 | $3,750 | $3,200 | $3,000 | $2,250 | $1,500 | $1,000 | $750 |

FIRST MODEL SCHOFIELD — .45 S&W, single action, 7 in. barrel, 6 shot fluted cylinder, blue finish, nickel rare, walnut grips, 3,035 mfg. 1875.
U.S. Issue — 3,000 mfg.

| $2,475 | $2,000 | $1,725 | $1,540 | $1,375 | $1,155 | $1,045 | $990 | $880 | $770 | $715 | $605 |

Commercial Model-35 produced without U.S. markings.

| $3,025 | $2,550 | $2,145 | $1,925 | $1,650 | $1,430 | $1,320 | $1,100 | $1,045 | $990 | $880 | $770 |

Wells Fargo and Company

| $2,750 | $2,175 | $1,800 | $1,540 | $1,375 | $1,210 | $1,100 | $1,045 | $990 | $935 | $825 | $605 |

SECOND MODEL SCHOFIELD — improved version of First Model.
Standard Model — U.S. on butt.

| $2,750 | $2,200 | $1,800 | $1,650 | $1,375 | $1,210 | $1,045 | $990 | $880 | $770 | $660 | $605 |

Commercial Model — 650 mfg.

| $2,200 | $1,750 | $1,525 | $1,375 | $1,155 | $1,045 | $935 | $825 | $715 | $660 | $605 | $495 |

Wells Fargo and Company

| $2,200 | $1,750 | $1,540 | $1,375 | $1,210 | $1,100 | $1,045 | $990 | $935 | $825 | $715 | $650 |

PISTOLS: SINGLE SHOT, EARLY MODELS

FIRST MODEL — .22 LR, .32 S&W, or .38 S&W cal., 6, 8, or 10 in. barrel blue or nickel, hard rubber grips. Mfg. 1251, 1893-1905.
.22 LR — 862 mfg.

| $660 | $550 | $440 | $305 | $275 | $250 | $230 | $220 | $205 | $195 | $165 | $140 |

.32 S&W — 229 mfg.

| $770 | $660 | $550 | $440 | $385 | $360 | $330 | $310 | $290 | $275 | $250 | $220 |

.38 S&W — 160 mfg.

| $880 | $770 | $660 | $440 | $385 | $360 | $330 | $310 | $290 | $275 | $250 | $220 |

SECOND MODEL .22 LR — similar to First Model, but will not accommodate a revolver cylinder, 10 in. barrel only. Mfg. 4,617, 1905-1909.

| $550 | $440 | $385 | $330 | $275 | $250 | $220 | $200 | $175 | $165 | $150 | $140 |

THIRD MODEL .22 LR — similar to Second Model, but trigger is centered in guard. Mfg. 6,949, 1909-1923.

| $550 | $440 | $385 | $330 | $275 | $250 | $220 | $200 | $175 | $165 | $150 | $140 |

REVOLVERS: MODERN, OUT OF PRODUCTION

Grading				100%	98%	95%	90%	80%	70%	60%

MODEL 1 HAND EJECTOR — .32 S&W Long or .32-20 cal., first solid frame swingout cylinder, 3¼, 4¼, or 6 in. barrel, fixed sights, blue or nickel, round butt, rubber grips. Mfg. 1896-1903.

| | | | | $440 | $415 | $385 | $360 | $275 | $220 | $175 |

Grading	100%	98%	95%	90%	80%	70%	60%

LADYSMITH (MODEL M HAND EJECTOR) — originally chambered for .22 S&W (same as .22 Long), 7 shot fluted cyliner, small frame, available in blue or nickel finish, dubbed "Ladysmith" because many women (including Ladies of the night) liked them as a personal defense weapon due to the diminutive size. Over 26,000 mfg. between 1902-1921.

First Model — .22 L, 2¼, 3, or 3½ in. barrel length, serial numbered 1-4,575, checkered hard rubber grips, round butt. Mfg. 1902-1906.

	$1,350	$1,125	$1,025	$875	$725	$600	$475

Besides serialization, First Models are identifiable by frame mounted cylinder release lever.

Second Model — .22 L, 3 or 3½ in. barrel, distinguishable from first model in that cylinder locking device was placed on barrel bottom - locking at both ends. Serial numbered 4,576-13,950, mfg. 1906-1910,

	$1,200	$1,075	$975	$850	$725	$600	$475

Third Model — .22 L, 2½, 3, 3½, or 6 in. barrel lengths, smooth walnut grips with S&W medallion inlays, square butt, ivory or pearl grips will command a premium. Serial numbered 13,951-26,154, mfg. 1910-1921,

	$1,200	$1,075	$975	$850	$725	$600	$475

The 6 in. barrel length will command a premium - this barrel length was also available with target sights.

MODEL 30 HAND EJECTOR — .32 S&W long, 6 shot, 2, 3, 4, or 6 in. barrel, blue or nickel, fixed sights, walnut or rubber grips. Mfg. 1908-1976.

	$275	$220	$165	$140	$110	$105	$100

SAFETY HAMMERLESS MODEL (LEMON SQUEEZER) — .32 or .38 cal., 5 shot revolver, rear grip safety, break open tip up action, either blue or nickel finish, barrel lengths range from 2 to 6 in, black rubber grips. Mfg. 1887-1940.

	$550	$475	$425	$380	$330	$295	$240
Nickel finish	$600	$495	$400	$350	$300	$275	$240

NEW CENTURY "TRIPLE LOCK" — .44 S&W, .450 Eley, or .455 Mark II cal., 6 shot, 4, 5, 6½, or 7½ in. barrel, fixed sights, blue or nickel, walnut grips, has third lock at crane. Mfg. 1907-1915.

	$1,175	$875	$750	$700	$650	$495	$440

.22-32 TARGET-MODEL 35 (BEKEART MODEL) — "Bekeart Model", .22 LR revolver made on .32 hand ejector frame, 6 shot, 6 in. barrel, adj. sights, blue, checkered walnut extended grips, named after San Francisco gun dealer Phillip Bekeart, who originally contracted S&W to manufacture this revolver. Mfg. 1911-1953.

	$500	$425	$400	$230	$210	$180	$165

1911 Production — 292 mfg., Bekeart's original contract.

	$750	$650	$525	$495	$440	$385	$330

.44 HAND EJECTOR SECOND MODEL — similar to new Century, except triple lock feature eliminated, .44 S&W, .44-40, or .45 Colt cal. Mfg. 1915-1937.

	$650	$600	$450	$385	$330	$275	$230

MODEL 1917 ARMY — .45 Auto Rim or .45 ACP in half moon clip, 6 shot, 5½ in. barrel, fixed sights, satin on military, blue gloss on commercial, smooth walnut on military, checkered walnut on commercial.

Military — 175,000 mfg., 1917-1919.

	$360	$340	$320	$275	$220	$195	$165

Commercial — mfg. 1919-1941.

	$440	$420	$395	$370	$320	$285	$230

REGULATION POLICE TARGET — similar to Regulation Police, but target sight, .32 S&W, 6 in. barrel only, blue. Mfg. 1917-1940.

	$300	$250	$195	$165	$130	$110	$90

Grading	100%	98%	95%	90%	80%	70%	60%

MODEL 31 REGULATION POLICE — .32 S&W, 6 shot, .38 S&W, 5 shot, 2, 3, 4, or 6 in. barrel in .32 cal., 4 in. barrel in .38 cal. (Model 33), square butt, walnut grips, fixed sights, blue or nickel. Mfg. 1917-present.

	100%	98%	95%	90%	80%	70%	60%
MODEL 31-1	$275	$220	$180	$160	$130	$110	$85
PRE-1960 Manufacture	$325	$275	$225	$170	$145	$135	$125

MODEL 44 1926 TARGET — target sight, blue only, otherwise same as 1926 Model 44. Mfg. 1926-1941.

	100%	98%	95%	90%	80%	70%	60%
	$1,400	$1,150	$1,000	$850	$700	$585	$475

MODEL 35 TARGET — See .22-.32 Target (Bekeart) Model on previous page.

MODEL 45 M & P — .22 LR only, originally mfg. as training gun between 1948-1957, also mfg. 500 in 1963.

	100%	98%	95%	90%	80%	70%	60%
	$650	$550	$450	$375	$300	$280	$270

38/44 HEAVY DUTY — .38 or .44 cal., 6 shot, 4, 5, or 6½ in. barrel lengths, fixed sights, walnut grips, blue or nickel, walnut grips. Mfg. 1930-1941 and re-introduced 1946 (with S prefix starting at serial 62,940). The 38/44 Heavy Duty became the Model 20 in 1957.

	100%	98%	95%	90%	80%	70%	60%
	$350	$285	$260	$220	$195	$160	$145
Pre-War (.44 cal.)	$595	$490	$450	$415	$385	$340	$300

MODEL 20 — .38 Spl. or .44 cal., 6 shot, 4, 5, or 6½ in. barrel, fixed sights, blue or nickel, checkered walnut grips. Mfg. 1957-1967.

	100%	98%	95%	90%	80%	70%	60%
	$350	$285	$260	$220	$195	$145	$125

MODEL 23 .38-44 OUTDOORSMAN — similar to Model 20 in .38-44 Heavy Duty, but adj. sights, blue only. Mfg. 1930-1967.

	100%	98%	95%	90%	80%	70%	60%
	$650	$550	$450	$375	$300	$280	$270

Add approx. 50% for older 5 screw model.

MODEL 44 1926 MILITARY — .44 S&W, 6 shot, 4, 5, or 6½ in. large frame, blue, walnut grips, fixed sights. Mfg. 1926-1941.

	100%	98%	95%	90%	80%	70%	60%
	$490	$400	$360	$300	$275	$250	$225

MODEL 51 — .22 Mag. only, .22/32 kit gun, 3 in. barrel, 6 shot, adj. rear sight, blue or nickel, walnut stocks. Disc.

	100%	98%	95%	90%	80%	70%	60%
	$400	$350	$300	$275	$250	$225	$200

MODEL 32 TERRIER — .38 S&W, 5 shot, 2 in. barrel, walnut or rubber grips, blue or nickel, fixed sights, built on .32 frame. Mfg. 1936-1974.

	100%	98%	95%	90%	80%	70%	60%
	$330	$220	$175	$150	$135	$125	$115

K-22 OUTDOORSMAN — K frame, .22 LR, 6 shot, 6 in. barrel, blue, adj. target sights, walnut grips. Mfg. 1931-1940.

	100%	98%	95%	90%	80%	70%	60%
	$575	$500	$450	$375	$330	$285	$250

K-22 MASTERPIECE — similar to K-22 Outdoorsman, but improved sight, short action. Approx. 1,000 mfg. in 1940 only.

	100%	98%	95%	90%	80%	70%	60%
	$1,200	$1,050	$875	$750	$675	$600	$550

K-32 MODEL 16 — .32 S&W long, 6 in. barrel, adj. sights, checkered walnut, blue. Only 3630 mfg., 1947-1974.

	100%	98%	95%	90%	80%	70%	60%
	$700	$540	$400	$380	$330	$275	$230

MODEL .22-32 KIT GUN — same as Model 35 1953 .22-32 Target, except 4 in. barrel, round butt. Mfg. 1935-1953.

	100%	98%	95%	90%	80%	70%	60%
	$800	$700	$575	$500	$450	$400	$350

.22-32 KIT GUN MODEL 43, 1955 — 3½ in. barrel, grip butt square, 15-02. alloy frame. Disc. 1974.

	100%	98%	95%	90%	80%	70%	60%
	$400	$350	$260	$230	$180	$165	$150

Grading	100%	98%	95%	90%	80%	70%	60%

MODEL 13 LIGHTWEIGHT, USAF — .38 Spl., aluminum cylinder and frame. Most were destroyed by the Government.

| | $800 | $725 | $675 | $525 | $475 | $425 | $350 |

MODEL 24 1950 .44 TARGET — post-war 1926 Model .44 Target, redesigned hammer, ribbed barrel, micrometer sights. Mfg. 1950-1967.

| | $750 | $625 | $550 | $500 | $430 | $400 | $350 |

MODEL 21 1950 .44 MILITARY — post-war version of Model 1926, same but redesigned hammer. Mfg. 1950-1967.

| | $1,400 | $1,200 | $1,150 | $1,000 | $900 | $800 | $700 |

MODEL 22 — .45 auto rim or ACP, same specifications as 1917 Army, except redesigned hammer, fixed sights. Mfg. 1950-1967.

| | $770 | $660 | $550 | $440 | $275 | $200 | $150 |

MODEL 26 1950 TARGET .45 ACP — adj. sights, thin barrel.

| | $770 | $660 | $550 | $440 | $275 | $200 | $150 |

MODEL 29 S-PREFIX — .44 mag, 4, 6½, or 8⅜ in. barrel. Disc.

| | $650 | $550 | $500 | $400 | $300 | $275 | $250 |

Subtract $40 if without case.

A rare variation in this model is a 5 in. barrel. Only 500 were mfg. in 1956-57 with bright blue finish, diamond target stocks, and wood case. In N.I.B. condition the value is $2,800 - add 25% for nickel finish.

4 in. barrel — 500 mfg. in 1957-58 only.

| | $1,800 | $1,600 | $1,395 | | | | |

MODEL 29-4 SCREW — .44 Mag., 4 screw, 3 exposed screws on right sideplate. Mfg. began 1957 after approx. ser. no. S175,000.

| | $995 | $850 | $750 | $500 | $450 | $400 | $325 |

MODEL 29-5 SCREW — .44 Mag. 5 screw, 4 exposed screws on right sideplate. Approx. 6,500 mfg. during 1956-1957. Disc.

| | $1,500 | $1,250 | $1,050 | $850 | $800 | $650 | $525 |

Subtract $100 if no box.

100% value assumes new gun with box, papers, and tools.

MODEL 31 REGULATION POLICE — .32 S&W, fixed sights, 2, 3, or 4 (disc.) in. barrels, blue only.

| | $275 | $240 | $230 | $225 | $200 | $185 | $160 |

Add 25% for early flatlatch models.

MODEL 40 CENTENNIAL — .38 Spl., 2 in. barrel double action only, hammerless, grip safety, checkered walnut grips, blue or nickel. Mfg. 1953-1974.

| | $475 | $425 | $345 | $290 | $260 | $240 | $220 |

MODEL 42 CENTENNIAL AIRWEIGHT — same as Model 40 Centennial, but alloy frame.

| | $875 | $775 | $675 | $575 | $495 | $440 | $390 |

MODEL 43 KIT GUN — .22 LR, 4 in. barrel, kit gun, aluminum frame, round or square butt, adj. sights.

| | $425 | $340 | $290 | $260 | $240 | $220 | $200 |

MODEL 50 — Chief Special Target, .38 Spl., mfg. from 1955 in 2 or 3 in. barrels, target sights, most were unmarked for model number. Others were Model 36's.

| | $385 | $350 | $300 | $250 | $225 | $200 | $190 |

MODEL 53 .22 REM. JET — .22 S, L, or LR inserts, 6 shot, 4, 6, or 8⅜ in. barrel, blue, walnut grips, adj. sights. Mfg. 1960-1974.

| | $735 | $650 | $550 | $470 | $385 | $360 | $330 |

Add 10% for 8⅜ in. barrel.

Grading	100%	98%	95%	90%	80%	70%	60%

MODEL 58 — .41 Mag, M&P, fixed sights, 4 in. barrel, blue or nickel finish. Disc.

	$385	$340	$315	$290	$260	$220	$200

Add $25 for nickel finish.
Values above assume early "S" frame variation.

MODEL 35 1953 .22-32 TARGET — same as .22-32 Target, except micrometer rear sight, magna target grips. Mfg. 1953-1974.

	$425	$300	$265	$230	$200	$180	$160

MODEL 520 — .357 mag., 4 in. barrel, fixed sights, N frame, originally ordered for N.Y. State Police but never purchased. Approx. 2,000 mfg. with "N.Y.S.P." on frame.

	$325	$275	$240	$210	$185	$175	$165

.357 MAGNUM FACTORY REGISTERED — This model was mfg. 1935-1938. It could be custom ordered with any barrel length from 3½ - 8 in., adj. sights, checkered walnut grips. The gun was hand fitted and registered to the buyer by a number found on the inside of the yoke. This practice was disc. 1938 (approx. 5,500 were mfg.) due to the tremendous demand for the .357 Mag. revolver.

	$1,150	$995	$850	$675	$575	$500	$450

.357 MAGNUM PRE-WAR — same as above, but not registered. 1,142 mfg. 1938-1941.

	$775	$725	$660	$525	$470	$385	$330

ENGRAVING OPTIONS FOR CURRENT MFG. HANDGUNS

The prices listed below are for original factory finished guns with no extra engraving. The listings below show 1989 factory engraving costs. These prices should be added to the cost of each engraved production gun to determine the correct value.

CLASS "C" ENGRAVING—1/3 METAL COVERAGE
Pistols — add $790.
For J Frame — add $624.
10⅝ in. N Frame — add $916.
2-5 in. K,L, or N Frame — add $805.
6-8⅜ in. K,L, or N Frame — add $916.

CLASS "B" ENGRAVING — ⅔ METAL COVERAGE
Pistols — add $1,032.
For J Frame — add $1,019.
10⅝ in. N Frames — add $1,140.
2-5 in. K,L, or N Frame — add $1,053.
6-8⅜ in. K,L, or N Frame — add $1,140.

CLASS "A" ENGRAVING — FULL COVERAGE
Pistols — add $1,255.
For J Frame — add $1.070.
2-5 in. K,L, or N Frame — add $1,293.
6-8⅜ in. K,L, or N Frame — add $1,368.
10⅝ in. N Frame — add $1,368.

Grading	100%	98%	95%	90%	80%	70%	60%

SPECIAL ENGRAVING — Also available: inlays, seals, game scenes, lettering, prices quoted on request. Special engraving lettering is available at $5.25 per character (plus $48 refinishing charge) - 15 character minimum.

LASERSMITH ENGRAVING — laser etching began in 1989. This process involves a digitally controlled laser producing a variety of designs, logos, commemorative messages, or autograph on the metal surface(s). Some of these designs are made exclusively for major firearms distributors. Others are custom designed for clubs or organizations. Retail prices start at just under $18 and can go as high as $150+, depending on the amount and complexity of the laser etching. To date, premiums are not being paid for these "rarer" variations.

REVOLVERS: RECENT PRODUCTION

To determine which variation a particular revolver is in the following section, simply swing the cylinder out to the loading position and notice the model number inside the yoke. A two digit number followed by a dash and another number designates which engineering change was underway when the gun was manufactured. Hence, a 48-3 is a Model 48 in its 3rd improvement (i.e. 3rd engineering update). Usually, earlier variations are the most desirable to collectors unless a particular improvement is rare. The same rule applies to semi-auto pistols and the model designation is usually marked on the outside of the gun.

A NOTE ON S & W COMMEMORATIVES/SPECIAL EDITIONS:

During the course of a year, I receive many phone calls and letters on special editions and limited editions that do not appear in this section. It should be noted that a commemorative issue is a gun that has been manufactured, marketed, and sold through the auspices of the specific trademark (in this case S&W). During the past several decades, hundreds of limited editions have been ordered through various police agencies, state highway patrol units, and other law enforcement organizations. Many of these variations do not have the special suffix serialization (and may not have had a retail price when issued). Since most of these special editions/commemoratives were made for a specific organization, regional demand has a lot to do with determining values (a Model 66 Montana HP Commemorative will not sell for a premium in Alabama). For this reason, most of these guns will not appear in this section and you should contact the factory to learn more about the provenance of these special editions. Remember - values on these models can vary A LOT from one region to another and an averaged "national" single price is almost impossible. While these guns do have special interest, they do not have the collectability or desirability of many of the standard models listed below.

In this section, the stainless steel variations have been placed next to the standard models from which they are derived for convenience. For a sequential numerical listing, please refer to the section: REVOLVERS:STAINLESS STEEL (following this section).
ADD 10%-15% FOR THOSE MODELS LISTED BELOW THAT ARE PINNED AND RE-CESSED (PRE-1978 MFG.).

MODEL 10 M & P — .38 Spl., 6 shot, round or square butt, fixed sights, 2, 3 (disc.), 4, 5 (disc.), or 6 (disc.) in. barrels.

Mfg.'s Sug. Retail	$333	$255	$205	$150	$140	$130	$115	$100

Add $12 for nickel finish (4 in. only).
The Model 10 is currently available in 2 or 4 in. barrel only.

MODEL 12 M & P AIRWEIGHT — same as Model 10, only alloy frame, 2 or 4 in. barrel. Disc. 1986.

	$280	$245	$210	$200	$185	$175	$150

Add $40 for nickel finish (disc.).
Last Mfg.'s Sug. Retail was $320.

MODEL 13 M & P — .357 Mag., heavy barrel, fixed sights, round or square butt, 3 or 4 in. barrel.

Mfg.'s Sug. Retail	$339	$255	$205	$155	$145	$135	$125	$120

Add $20 for nickel finish (disc. 1986).

Model 13 - N.Y. State Police — .357 Mag., 4 in. barrel, blued, fixed sights, 1200 were mfg. for the N.Y. State Police and are so marked. All 1200 were recalled by S&W and exchanged for Model 28's).

	$375	$300	$250	$200	$175	$150	$140

Grading	100%	98%	95%	90%	80%	70%	60%

MODEL 13 LIGHTWEIGHT, USAF — .38 Spl., aluminum cylinder and frame, 6 shot, only 14⅜ oz. Most were destroyed by the Government.

	$800	$750	$675				

This model was purchased in large quantities during 1953 and early 1954 only. While S&W never assigned a model number to this variation, M 13 is marked on the top strap and thus retains the Model 13 designation. In 1954, a conventional steel cylinder replaced the aluminum cylinder because of cracking.

MODEL 14 K-38 — .38 Spl., target model. Disc. 1981.

	$300	$250	$215	$200	$185	$175	$160

Add $20 for 6 in. barrels single action.

Model 14 Full Lug Barrel—.38 Spl., 6 in. full lug barrel, adj. rear sight, combat style Morado wood square butt grips, blue finish, 47 oz. 2,000 mfg. in 1991 only.

Mfg.'s Sug. Retail	$425	$340	$295	$250	$225	$200	$185	$165

MODEL 15 COMBAT MASTERPIECE — .38 Spl., adj. sights, 6 shot, 2 (disc.), 4, 6, or 8⅜ (disc.) in. barrel (6 and 8⅜ new 1986).

Mfg.'s Sug. Retail	$361	$280	$230	$205	$190	$180	$160	$150

Add $31 for TT or TH.

Add $11 for 8⅜ in. barrel (disc.).

Add $20 for nickel finish (disc. 1987).

MODEL 16 — .32 cal./.32 Mag., 6 shot, 4 (new 1990), 6, or 8⅜ in. barrel, square butt, blue finish only, TH and TT. New 1990.

Mfg.'s Sug. Retail	$403	$325	$275	$225	$210	$200	$190	$180

Subtract $35 for 4 in. barrel.

Add $12 for 8⅜ in. barrel.

MODEL 17 K-22 MASTERPIECE — .22 LR, blue only, 4 (new 1986), 6 or 8⅜ in. barrel.

Mfg.'s Sug. Retail	$379	$295	$255	$230	$215	$200	$185	$175

Add $12 for long barrel (8⅜ in.).

Add $36 for TT, TH, and TS (6 or 8⅜ in. barrel only.).

MODEL 617 — .22 LR cal., stainless steel variation of the Model 17, 6 shot, 4, 6, or 8⅜ in. barrel, straight backstrap grip, combat trigger and grips, semi-target. New 1990.

Mfg.'s Sug. Retail	$400	$310	$235	$195				

Add $30 for 6 in. barrel with TT and TH.

Add $40 for 8⅜ in. barrel with TT and TH.

MODEL 18 .22 COMBAT MASTERPIECE — .22 LR, combat style adj. sights, 4 in. barrel, blue only. Disc. 1985.

	$305	$270	$225	$200	$180	$175	$165

Add $30 for TT and TH.

Last Mfg.'s Sug. Retail was $352.

MODEL 19 .357 COMBAT MAGNUM — K frame, .357 Mag., adj. sights, 2½, 4, or 6 in. barrel, bright blue or nickel finish.

Mfg.'s Sug. Retail	$355	$285	$240	$200	$190	$180	$170	$160

Add $8 for 4 or 6 in. barrel.

Add $23 for white outline rear sight.

Add $20 for nickel finish (4 or 6 in. only).

Add $60 for TS, TT, TH, RR, and WO (6 in. barrel only).

This model is supplied with a round butt on 2½ in. barrel. Nickel finish is available with a 4 or 6 in. barrel only.

Model 19 Oregon State Police Commemorative — boxed with belt buckle.

	$895	$750	$650				

Model 19 Texas Ranger Commemorative

	$750	$625	$495				

Grading	100%	98%	95%	90%	80%	70%	60%

MODEL 24 — 44 Spl., 4 or 6½ in. barrel, blue finish only. Mfg. 1983 and 1984 only.

	100%	98%	95%	90%	80%	70%	60%
	$300	$275	$240	$225	$205	$190	$175

Add $30 for TS, TT, and TH.
Last Mfg.'s Sug. Retail was $359.

Model 24-3 Lew Horton Special — .44 Spl., 3 in. barrel, round butt, adj. sights, blue finish, includes special fitted holster.

	100%	98%	95%
	$380	$325	$250

Deduct 10% without holster.

MODEL 25-2 .45 ACP — N frame, blue or nickel, target grips, 4, 6, 6½, or 8⅜ in. barrel. Disc.

	100%	98%	95%	90%	80%	70%	60%
	$450	$400	$350	$300	$235	$200	$190

Add $14 for nickel finish.

Add $150 for 6½ in. barrel (older mfg. with pinned barrel).
Last Mfg.'s Sug. Retail was $347.

Model 25-3 Lew Horton Special — .45 ACP, 3 in. barrel, adj. sights, blue finish, only 100 mfg.

	100%	98%	95%
	$500	$450	$375

MODEL 25-5 — .45 Long Colt cal., 4, 6, or 8⅜ in. barrel, blue or nickel finish (no extra charge - disc. 1987).

		100%	98%	95%	90%	80%	70%	60%
Mfg.'s Sug. Retail	$429	$335	$285	$225	$210	$200	$190	$180

Add $8 for 8⅜ in. barrel.

Model 25-5 125th Anniversary — .45 LC, presentation cased.

	100%	98%	95%
	$450	$300	$250

MODEL 625 — .45 ACP, stainless variation of the Model 25-5, 6 shot, 3, 4, or 5 (new 1990) in. barrel, round butt, full lug barrel, Pachmayr grips. New 1990.

		100%	98%	95%
Mfg.'s Sug. Retail	$535	$450	$375	$300

MODEL 27 — .357 Mag., N frame, 3½ (disc.), 4, 5 (disc.),6, or 8⅜ in. barrel, blue or nickel (disc. 1987) finish.

		100%	98%	95%	90%	80%	70%	60%
Mfg.'s Sug. Retail	$423	$345	$285	$235	$220	$205	$190	$180

Add $28 for outlined sights.

Add $8 for 8⅜ in. barrel.

Add 20% for 3½ or 5 in. barrel (disc.).

3½ and 5 in. barrel — disc.

	100%	98%	95%	90%	80%	70%	60%
	$425	$365	$275	$265	$240	$230	$180

50th Year .357 Mag. Commemorative — presentation cased.

	100%	98%	95%
	$475	$325	$300

MODEL 28 HIGHWAY PATROLMAN — .357 Mag., "Highway Patrol" utility model, dull finish, adj. sights, standard grips, blue only, 4 or 6 in. barrel. Disc. 1986.

	100%	98%	95%	90%	80%	70%	60%
	$270	$235	$210	$200	$190	$180	$150

Add $20 for TS.
Last Mfg.'s Sug. Retail was $306.

MODEL 29 — .44 Mag., 6 shot, same as Model 25-5, except .44 Mag., 4, 6, or 8⅜ in. barrel, blue or nickel finish.

		100%	98%	95%	90%	80%	70%	60%
Mfg.'s Sug. Retail	$482	$340	$310	$285	$265	$255	$245	$210

Add $10 for 8⅜ in. barrel.

Add $11 for nickel finish.

Add $45 for combat grips with scope mount (8⅜ in. barrel only).

Note: It must be noted that collectors will often pay a 50% premium for the older 5 screw versions of these current production guns. First year production of Model 29 can bring $1500 if condition warrants. Original boxes are extremely desirable! When examining S&W's for purchase, be aware of these factors.

Older Model 29 mfg. will appear under the previous subheading: REVOLVERS: MODERN, OUT OF PRODUCTION.

Grading	100%	98%	95%	90%	80%	70%	60%

Model 29-3 Lew Horton Special — similar to Model 29, except has 3 in. barrel, round butt, adj. sights.

	$425	$350	$295				

MODEL 29 CLASSIC — .44 Mag., 5, 6½, or 8⅜ in. full lug barrel, square butt with synthetic grips, interchangeable front sight with white outline rear sight, blue finish only. New in 1990.

Mfg.'s Sug. Retail	$519	$435	$360	$295	$280	$260	$240	$225

MODEL 29 SILHOUETTE — .44 Mag., 10⅝ in. barrel, adj. front and rear sights, bright blue only, Goncalo Alves target stocks. New 1983.

Mfg.'s Sug. Retail	$536	$445	$370	$300	$280	$260	$240	$225

Add $11 for 8⅜ in. barrel.

MODEL 29 MAGNACLASSIC — .44 Mag., 7½ full lug, ported barrel, high bright bluing, round butt, interchangeable front sight, supplied with carrying case, 3,000 mfg. in 1990 only.

	$850	$725	$600	$500	$450	$395	$360

Last Mfg.'s Sug. Retail was $999.

MODEL 629 STAINLESS STEEL — .44 Mag., same as Model 29. Available with 4, 6, or 8⅜ in. barrel.

Mfg.'s Sug. Retail	$510	$435	$370	$300			

Add $17 for 8⅜ in. barrel.

Add $52 for combat grips with scope mount (8⅜ in. barrel only).

Model 629 Classic Stainless — stainless steel variation of the Model 29 Classic. New in 1990.

Mfg.'s Sug. Retail	$547	$460	$390	$315			

Add $18 for 8⅜ in. barrel.

Model 629-3 Lew Horton Special — .44 Mag., 3 in. barrel with round butt, adj. sights.

	$400	$350	$295				

MODEL 31 REGULATION POLICE — .32 S&W long, fixed sights, 2, 3 or 4 (disc.) in. barrel, blue only.

Mfg.'s Sug. Retail	$365	$290	$235	$195	$185	$175	$165	$150

Add 25% for early flatlatch models.

MODEL 34 - 1953 .22/32 KIT GUN — .22 LR or .32 cal. (disc.), adj. sights, J frame, 6 shot, 2 or 4 in. barrel, round or square butt, blue or nickel (disc. 1986).

Mfg.'s Sug. Retail	$366	$300	$235	$195	$185	$175	$165	$150

Add $25 for nickel finish.

Add 25% for early flatlatch models.

MODEL 36 CHIEF'S SPECIAL — .38 Spl., 5 shot, J frame, round or square butt, 2 in. regular or 3 in. (heavy) barrel, blue or nickel finish.

Mfg.'s Sug. Retail	$338	$255	$210	$175	$165	$155	$150	$145

Add $11 for nickel finish (round butt - 2 in. barrel only).

Note: 1st models with high polish blue and diamond grips will bring premiums when mint in original box.

MODEL 36 LADYSMITH — .38 S&W Special, 5 shot, 2 in. regular or 3 in. heavy barrel, blue finish only, grips are anatomically designed for women (round butt on 2 in., wood combat grips on 3 in.), fixed sights, redesigned double action, 20-23 oz. New 1990.

Mfg.'s Sug. Retail	$352	$280	$220	$190	$185	$175	$165	$150

Add $27 for Morocco-grain carrying case.

MODEL 37 CHIEF'S SPECIAL AIRWEIGHT — same as 36 Chief's Special, except alloy frame and 2 in. barrel only.

Mfg.'s Sug. Retail	$358	$265	$225	$195	$185	$175	$165	$150

Add $14 for nickel finish.

Grading	100%	98%	95%	90%	80%	70%	60%

MODEL 38 BODYGUARD AIRWEIGHT — .38 S&W Spl., 5 shot, alloy frame, round butt, shrouded hammer, 2 in. barrel, blue or nickel finish.

Mfg.'s Sug. Retail	$379	$295	$240	$205	$190	$180	$170	$150

Add $13 for nickel finish.

MODEL 40 GRIP SAFETY BODYGUARD — 38 S&W Spl. Disc.

	$475	$425	$395	$325	$300	$265	$240

Add $20 for Airweight.

Model 40 Centennial — 2 in. barrel, blue finish only.

	$500	$400	$275

MODEL 48 K-22 MASTERPIECE — .22 Mag, 4, 6 or 8⅜ in. barrel, blue only. Disc. 1986.

	$275	$245	$200	$185	$175	$165	$150

Add $15 for 8⅜ in. barrel.
Add $15 for TT, TH, and TS (disc.).
Last Mfg.'s Sug. Retail was $320.

MODEL 49 BODYGUARD — same as Model 38, only steel frame, blue or nickel.

Mfg.'s Sug. Retail	$359	$270	$220	$180	$170	$160	$150	$145

Add $25 for nickel finish (disc.).

MODEL 649 STAINLESS BODYGUARD — same as Model 49 Bodyguard, except in stainless steel. New 1986.

Mfg.'s Sug. Retail	$408	$315	$235	$195

MODEL 57 — .41 Mag., same as Model 29, except for cal., 4, 6 or 8⅜ in. barrel, blue or nickel (disc.) finish.

Mfg.'s Sug. Retail	$427	$325	$245	$220	$205	$190	$175	$165

Add 10% for nickel finish if NIB.
Add $15 for 8⅜ in. barrel.

MODEL 657 STAINLESS — .41 Mag., 4 (disc.), 6, or 8⅜ in. barrel. New 1986.

Mfg.'s Sug. Retail	$455	$370	$300	$260

Add $16 for 8⅜ in. barrel.

Model 657-3 Lew Horton Special — .41 Mag., 3 in. barrel with round butt, adj. sights.

	$410	$360	$300

MODEL 58 — .41 Mag., M&P, fixed sights, 4 in. barrel, blue or nickel finish. Disc.

	$350	$315	$290	$260	$220	$200	$180

Add $25 for nickel finish.

MODEL 544 COMMEMORATIVE — .44-40 cal. only, 6 shot, 5 in. barrel, bright blue finish, adj. sights, 7,800 mfg. 1986 to commemorate the Texas Sesquicentennial (1836-1986). Special markings on frame and barrel, smooth Goncalo commemorative grips, ser. no. TWT001 - TWT7800 (estimated). Made 1986 only.

	$495	$375	$350

Last Mfg.'s Sug. Retail was $600.

MODEL 547 M & P — 9mm, 3 or 4 in. heavy barrel, 6 shot, round (3 in. barrel) or square (4 in. barrel) butt, blue only, 32 oz. Disc. 1985.

	$295	$265	$240	$210	$195	$185	$175

Last Mfg.'s Sug. Retail was $317.

MODEL 581 — .357 Mag., L-Frame, 4 in. barrel, 6 shot, blue or nickel finish, 38 oz.

	$275	$225	$180	$170	$160	$150	$145

Add $20 for nickel (disc. 1987).
This model was disc. 1985-86, and reintroduced 1987-1988.
Last Mfg.'s Sug. Retail was $335.

Grading		100%	98%	95%	90%	80%	70%	60%

MODEL 586 — .357 Mag., L-Frame, 4, 6, or 8⅜ in. barrel, fixed or adj. sights, blue or nickel finish.

Mfg.'s Sug. Retail	$401	$315	$260	$210	$195	$185	$175	$165

Add $12 for nickel finish.

Add $4 for white outlined sights.

Add $22 for 8⅜ in. barrel.

Add $35 for adj. front sight (6 in. barrel only — new 1986).

1985 Model 586 Iowa Highway State Patrol — mfg. to commemorate 50th anniversary, gold etching, 4 in. barrel. Mfg. 1985 only.

				$375	$250	$225		

REVOLVERS: STAINLESS STEEL

MODEL 60 CHIEF'S SPECIAL — .38 Spl., stainless version of Chief's Special, 2 in. barrel.

Mfg.'s Sug. Retail	$386	$295	$230	$195

Add $24 for 3 in. full lug barrel and combat grips.

The full lug barrel option began in 1990 with limited mfg. It has been tested for +P+ ammo and features an adj. rear sight - 24½ oz.

MODEL 60 LADYSMITH — .38 S&W Special, 5 shot, 2 in. regular or 3 in. heavy barrel, frosted stainless steel finish, grips are anatomically designed for women (round butt on 2 in., wood combat grips on 3 in.), fixed sights, redesigned double action, 20-23 oz. New 1990.

Mfg.'s Sug. Retail	$400	$315	$230	$195

Add $27 for Morocco-grain carrying case.

MODEL 63 .22/32 KIT GUN — .22 LR/.32, stainless kit gun, 4 in. barrel, 19 oz.

Mfg.'s Sug. Retail	$402	$315	$230	$195

MODEL 64 M & P — .38 S&W, stainless Model 10, has 2, 3, or 4 in. barrel. 3 and 4 in. barrels are heavy.

Mfg.'s Sug. Retail	$417	$325	$240	$200

MODEL 65 — .357 Mag., stainless version of Model 13, has 3 or 4 in. heavy barrels.

Mfg.'s Sug. Retail	$368	$280	$205	$185

Add $35 for TT, TH, and TS (disc.).

MODEL 66 — .357 Mag., stainless version of model 19, has 2½, 4, or 6 in. barrel.

Mfg.'s Sug. Retail	$404	$335	$250	$195

Add $6 for 4 or 6 in. barrel.

Add $5 for white outlined sights.

Add $46 for TT, TH, and TS (4 or 6 in. barrel only).

Note: Several models of the Model 66 were made — such features as an all-stainless steel rear sight and a recessed cylinder will bring a slight premium if N.I.B.

Model 66 Missouri Highway Patrol Commemorative — cased, with Bowie knife and badge. Disc.

		$850	$600	$500

Model 66 Montana Highway Patrol Commemorative — 4 in. barrel, commemorates 44 years of service, 213 mfg.

		$650	$525	$425

Model 66-1 Chicago Police Commemorative — 4 in. barrel, presentation cased.

		$375	$300	$260

Model 66 Border Patrol — .357 Mag., includes Gonsalvo Alves hand carved grips, border patrol badge etched on right side of frame, 50th anniversary (1924-1974), USBP serialization prefix.

		$650	$525	$425

Grading	100%	98%	95%	90%	80%	70%	60%

MODEL 67 COMBAT MASTERPIECE — .38 S&W, stainless version of Model 15, has 4 in. barrel. Disc. 1988.

		$295	$220	$195			

Last Mfg.'s Sug. Retail was $360.

MODEL 617 — .22 LR cal., stainless steel variation of the Model 17, 6 shot, 4, 6, or 8⅜ in. barrel, straight backstrap grip, combat trigger and grips, semi-target. New 1990.

Mfg.'s Sug. Retail	$400	$310	$235	$195			

Add $30 for 6 in. barrel with TT and TH.

Add $40 for 8⅜ in. barrel with TT and TH.

MODEL 624 .44 TARGET — .44 S&W Spl., 6 shot, 4 or 6½ in. barrel, 42 oz. Mfg. 1986-87 only.

		$340	$250	$225			

Add $14 for 6½ in. barrel.
Last Mfg.'s Sug. Retail was $449.

Model 624-2 Lew Horton Special — .44 Spl., 3 in. barrel with round butt, adj. sights, includes special fitted holster.

		$395	$350	$295			

Deduct 10% if without holster.

MODEL 625 — .45 ACP, stainless variation of the Model 25-5, 6 shot, 3 or 4 in. barrel, round butt, full lug barrel, Pachmayr grips. New 1990.

Mfg.'s Sug. Retail	$535	$450	$375	$300			

MODEL 629 — .44 Mag, same action as Model 29, has 4, 6, or 8⅜ in. barrel.

Mfg.'s Sug. Retail	$510	$435	$370	$300			

Add $17 for 8⅜ in. barrel.

Add $52 for combat grips with scope mount (8⅜ in. barrel only).

Model 629 Classic Stainless — stainless steel variation of the Model 29 Classic. New in 1990.

Mfg.'s Sug. Retail	$547	$460	$390	$315			

Add $18 for 8⅜ in. barrel.

MODEL 640 CENTENNIAL — .38 S&W, 5 shot, 3 in. barrel, fully concealed hammer, round butt, tested for +P+ ammo, 22½ oz. New in 1991.

Mfg.'s Sug. Retail	$408	$315	$235	$195			

MODEL 642 AIRWEIGHT — .38 Spl, 5 shot, 2 or 3 in. barrel, alloy frame with stainless steel cylinder and barrel, combat grips, concealed hammer, fixed rear sight, approx. 16 oz. New in 1990.

Mfg.'s Sug. Retail	$410	$315	$235	$195			

MODEL 648 — .22 Mag., 6 in. full lug barrel, combat grips, square butt, combat trigger, semi-target hammer. New in 1990.

Mfg.'s Sug. Retail	$400	$310	$230	$195			

MODEL 649 BODYGUARD — same as Model 49 Bodyguard, except in stainless steel. New 1986.

Mfg.'s Sug. Retail	$408	$315	$235	$195			

MODEL 650 — .22 Mag., service kit gun, 3 in. heavy barrel, J-Frame, fixed sights. Mfg. 1983-87.

		$250	$200	$185			

Last Mfg.'s Sug. Retail was $305.

MODEL 651 — .22 Mag., target kit gun, 4 in. barrel, J-Frame, adj. sights (same as old Model 51). Mfg 1983-87, re-released in late 1990.

Mfg.'s Sug. Retail	$412	$320	$235	$195			

MODEL 657 — .41 Mag., 4 (disc.), 6, or 8⅜ in. barrel. New 1986.

Mfg.'s Sug. Retail	$455	$370	$300	$260			

Add $16 for 8⅜ in. barrel.

Grading	100%	98%	95%	90%	80%	70%	60%

MODEL 681 DISTINGUISHED SERVICE — .357 Mag., distinguished service Magnum, 4 in. barrel, L-Frame. Disc. 1988.

		$285	$200	$185			

Last Mfg.'s Sug. Retail was $362.

MODEL 686 DISTINGUISHED COMBAT — .357 Mag., similar to Model 586, except 2½ (new 1990), 4, 6, or 8⅜ in. barrel, adj. sights, L-Frame.

Mfg.'s Sug. Retail	$422	$340	$250	$225			

Add $9 for 4 or 6 in. barrel.

Add $30 for 8⅜ in. barrel.

Add $13 for white outline sights.

Add $57 for adj. front sight (6 or 8⅜ in. barrel only - new 1986).

1984 Model 686 Lew Horton Edition — 2½ in. barrel only, limited mfg.

		$450	$275	$225			

PISTOLS: SINGLE SHOT

STRAIGHT LINE TARGET SINGLE SHOT — .22 LR, single shot, 10 in. barrel, sideswing barrel, blue, target sights, smooth walnut grips, shaped like an autoloader. Mfg. 1925-1936.

		$635	$560	$495	$440	$415	$365	$350

PISTOLS: SEMI-AUTO - RECENT MFG.

The following models have been arranged in a numerical model format to allow faster indexing.

MODEL 32 — .32 auto, similar to Model 35, very limited production. Mfg. 1924-1937.

	$1,200	$900	$820	$760	$700	$650	$500

MODEL 35 — .35 S&W Auto cal., 7 shot, 3½ in. barrel, blue or nickel, fixed sights, plain walnut grips. Mfg. 1913-1921.

	$625	$420	$370	$330	$275	$250	$225

A slight premium might exist for the first model (up to ser. no. 3,125).

MODEL 39 EARLY STEEL FRAME — 9mm Para., 8 shot, 4 in. barrel, walnut stocks, blue, adj. rear sight, double action M41 without the fine finish and walnut grips. Mfg. 927 pistols, 1954-1966.

	$1,100	$875	$775	$675	$600	$500	$425

First commercially mfg. 9mm double action semi-auto in the U.S.

MODEL 39 ALLOY FRAME — 9mm, double action, 8 shot mag., 4 in. barrel, checkered walnut grips, adj. sight, alloy frame. Disc. 1982.

	$360	$325	$260	$240	$220	$200	$195

Add $35 for nickel finish.

MODEL 46 — .22 LR, 5, 5½, or 7 in. barrel, blue, nylon grips, adj. sights. Mfg. 4000, 1957-1966.

	$450	$335	$300	$260	$225	$200	$195

This model is the same as a Model 41 without high polish bluing.

MODEL 52-A — .38 Spl., similar action to Model 39, 5 in. barrel. Originally mfg. for U.S. Army Marksman Training Unit, less than 90 mfg.

	$3,000	$2,500	$2,200	$1,950	$1,600	$1,300	$1,000

MODEL 52 — .38 Spl. wadcutter only, similar action to Model 39, except incorporates a set screw locking out the double action, 5 in. barrel, 5 shot mag. Approx. 3,500 mfg. 1961-1963.

	$875	$775	$675	$575	$475	$395	$360

Grading	100%	98%	95%	90%	80%	70%	60%

MODEL 52-1 — .38 Spl. wadcutter only, 5 shot mag., 5 in. barrel, single action trigger and hammer, bright blue only. Mfg. 1963-1971.

	$500	$460	$385	$350	$325	$300	$295

MODEL 52-2 — .38 Spl. Mid Range Wad Cutter only, single action semi-auto, 5 in. barrel, adj. sights, checkered walnut grips, 5 shot mag. Mfg. 1971-present.

Mfg.'s Sug. Retail	$885	$660	$550	$450	$400	$350	$295	$265

MODEL 59 — similar to Model 39, except has 14 shot mag., black nylon grips. Disc. 1981.

	$385	$340	$270	$250	$225	$215	$200

Add $35 for nickel finish.

MODEL 61 ESCORT POCKET — .22 LR, 5 shot, semi-auto, blue or nickel, 2½ in. barrel, plastic grips.

Blue finish	$250	$210	$165	$150	$140	$110	$95
Nickel finish	$275	$230	$165	$150	$140	$110	$95

MODEL 147-A — 9mm Para., 14 shot, steel frame, 4 in. barrel, black plastic grips, adj. sights for windage only, similar to Model 59, except has steel frame, 112 mfg. in 1979 only.

	$1,050	$875	$800	$725	$650	$575	$495

MODEL 439 — 9mm, double action, 4 in. barrel, blue or nickel finish, alloy frame, 8 shot mag., checkered walnut grips, 30 oz. Disc. 1988.

	$385	$315	$255	$240	$225	$210	$200

Add $34 for nickel finish (disc. 1986).

Add $26 for adj. sights.

Last Mfg.'s Sug. Retail was $472.

MODEL 459 — 9mm, 14 shot version of Model 439, checkered nylon stocks. Disc. 1988.

	$410	$345	$290	$270	$255	$240	$210

Add $26 for adj. sights.

Add $44 for nickel finish (disc. 1986).

Last Mfg.'s Sug. Retail was $501.

Model 459 "FBI" Variation — 9mm Para., 14 shot, 4 in. barrel, dull finish, fixed sights, special grips made to F.B.I. or Police specs., 803 mfg.

	$650	$600	$550	$440	$385	$330	$300

MODEL 469 "MINI" — 9mm, double action, alloy frame, 12 shot finger extension mag., short frame, bobbed hammer, 3½ in. barrel, sandblast blue finish, amibidextrous safety standard (1986), molded Delrin black grips, 26 oz. Disc. 1988.

	$370	$320	$265	$250	$235	$220	$210

Last Mfg.'s Sug. Retail was $478.

MODEL 539 — 9mm, double action, steel frame, 8 shot, 4 in. barrel, blue or nickel. Disc. 1983.

	$450	$395	$375	$350	$325	$300	$275

Add $35 for nickel finish.

Add $30 for adj. rear sight.

MODEL 559 — 9mm, double action, steel frame, 12 shot, 4 in. barrel, blue or nickel. Disc. 1983.

	$485	$435	$375	$275	$250	$225	$200

Add $35 for nickel finish.

Add $30 for adj. rear sight.

MODEL 639 STAINLESS — 9mm, same as Model 439-only stainless steel, 8 shot mag., ambidextrous safety became standard 1986, 36 oz. Disc. 1988.

	$420	$300	$275

Add $27 for adj. sights.

Last Mfg.'s Sug. Retail was $523.

Grading	100%	98%	95%	90%	80%	70%	60%

MODEL 645 STAINLESS — .45 ACP only, 5 in. barrel, 8 shot mag., squared off trigger guard, black molded nylon grips, ambidextrous safety, fixed sights, 37½ oz. New 1986. Disc. 1988.

$475 $365 $300

Add $27 for adj. sight.

Last Mfg.'s Sug. Retail was $622.

Approx. 150 Model 645 "Interim" pistols were mfg. in 1988 only. Add $120 to values listed above.

MODEL 659 STAINLESS — 9mm, same as Model 459-only stainless steel, 14 shot mag., ambidextrous safety became standard 1986, 39½ oz. Disc. 1988.

$445 $335 $300

Add $27 for adj. sights.

Last Mfg.'s Sug. Retail was $553.

Approx. 150 Model 659 "Interim" pistols were mfg. in 1988 only. Add $150 to values listed above.

MODEL 669 STAINLESS — 9mm, smaller version of Model 659 with 12 shot finger extension mag., 3½ in. barrel, fixed sights, molded Delrin grips, ambidextrous safety standard, 26 oz. Mfg. 1986-1988 only.

$425 $305 $275

Last Mfg.'s Sug. Retail was $522.

Approx. 150 Model 669 "Interim" pistols were mfg. in 1988 only. Add $150 to values listed above.

MODEL 745 IPSC — .45 ACP, single action, 5 in. barrel, stainless steel frame with steel slide hammer and trigger, checkered walnut stocks, fixed rear sight, 38¾ oz. Mfg. 1987-90.

$575 $440 $335

Last Mfg.'s Sug. Retail was $699.

Add $45 for "IPSC" markings on left side of slide (N.I.B. only).

PISTOLS: SEMI-AUTO - 3RD GENERATION CURRENT MFG.

To understand S&W 3rd generation model nomenclature, the following rules apply. The first two digits (of the four digit model number) specify caliber. Numbers 39, 59, and 69 refer to 9mm Para. cal. The third digit refers to the model type. 0 means standard model, 1 is for compact, 2 is for standard model with decocking lever, 3 is for compact variation with decocking lever, 4 is for standard with double action only, 5 designates a compact model in double action only, 6 indicates a non-standard barrel length, 7 is a non standard barrel length with decocking lever, 8 refers to non-standard barrel length in double action only. The fourth digit refers to the material(s) used in the fabrication of the pistol. 3 refers to an alluminum alloy frame with stainless steel slide, 4 designates an alluminum alloy frame with carbon steel slide, 5 is for carbon steel frame and slide, 6 is a stainless steel frame and slide, and 7 refers to a stainless steel frame and carbon steel slide. Hence, a Model 4053 refers to a pistol in .40 S&W cal. configured in compact version with double action only and fabricated with an alluminum alloy frame and stainless steel slide. This model nomenclature does not apply to 2 or 3 digit model numbers (i.e., Rimfire Models and the Model 52).

MODEL 41 RIMFIRE — .22 LR, match target pistol, single action, 10 shot mag., adj. sights, walnut grips, 5½ or 7 in. heavy barrel, blue only. Mfg. 1957-present.

Mfg.'s Sug. Retail	$710	$510	$450	$375	$300	$260	$240	$220

Add $60 for 5 or 5½ in. barrel with extended sight (disc.).

Add $35 for 7⅜ in. barrel with muzzle brake (disc.).

Add 125% for .22 Short cal. with counterweight and muzzle brake.

Earlier variations (A series guns with cocking indicator, Model 41-1, etc.) will command substantial premiums over values listed above.

Note: there are several disc. barrels on the Model 41. They are the 5 in. standard weight w/extended sight, 7⅜ in. with muzzle brake, and 5½ in. heavy barrel with extended sight.

Grading	100%	98%	95%	90%	80%	70%	60%

MODEL 422 RIMFIRE FIELD — .22 LR, single action, 4½ or 6 in. barrel, aluminum frame with steel slide, 10 shot mag., fixed sights, black plastic or wood grips, matte blue finish, 22 oz. New 1987.

Mfg.'s Sug. Retail	$206	$170	$140	$115	$110	$105	$100	$95

Model 422 Target — .22 LR, single action, 4½ or 6 in. barrel, aluminum frame with steel slide, 10 shot mag., adj. rear sight, checkered walnut grips, matte blue finish, 22 oz. New 1987.

Mfg.'s Sug. Retail	$257	$210	$165	$120	$115	$110	$105	$95

MODEL 622 RIMFIRE FIELD — .22 LR, single action, 4½ or 6 in. barrel, stainless/ alloy construction, 10 shot mag., fixed sights, black plastic grips, 21½ or 23½ oz. New 1990.

Mfg.'s Sug. Retail	$266	$210	$185	$160

Model 622 Target — .22 LR, single action, 4½ or 6 in. barrel, stainless steel construction, 10 shot mag., adj. rear sight, checkered walnut grips, 21½ or 23½ oz. New 1990.

Mfg.'s Sug. Retail	$316	$260	$225	$175

MODEL 1006 STAINLESS — 10mm, double action semi-auto, stainless steel construction, 5 in. barrel, exposed hammer, 9 shot mag., fixed or adj. sights, ambidextrous safety. New 1990.

Mfg.'s Sug. Retail	$747	$625	$525	$400

Add $26 for adj. rear sight.

MODEL 1026 STAINLESS — 10mm, 5 in. barrel, features frame mounted decocking lever, 9 shot mag., straight backstrap. New in 1990.

Mfg.'s Sug. Retail	$755	$630	$525	$400

MODEL 1066 STAINLESS — 10mm, 4¼ in. barrel, 9 shot mag., straight backstrap, ambidextrous safety, fixed sights. New in 1990.

Mfg.'s Sug. Retail	$730	$610	$515	$395

Add $40 for Tritium night sights (Model 1066-NS).
Only 1,000 Model 1066-NS's will be manufactured.

MODEL 1076 STAINLESS — similar to Model 1026 Stainless, except has 4¼ in. barrel. New in 1990.

Mfg.'s Sug. Retail	$755	$630	$525	$400

MODEL 1086 STAINLESS — similar to Model 1066 Stainless, except is double action only.

Mfg.'s Sug. Retail	$730	$610	$515	$395

MODEL 2206 STAINLESS RIMFIRE — .22 LR cal., similar to Model 622 Field, except is all stainless steel with black plastic grips, 35 or 39 oz. New 1990.

Mfg.'s Sug. Retail	$299	$230	$195	$165

Add $56 for adj. sights.

MODEL 2214 RIMFIRE "SPORTSMAN" — .22 LR cal., single action, entry level variation with 3 in. barrel and 8 shot mag., blue finish. New in 1991.

Mfg.'s Sug. Retail	$236	$195	$175	$160	$150	$140	$130	$120

MODEL 3904 — 9mm Para., double action semi-auto, aluminum alloy frame, 4 in. barrel with fixed bushing, 8 shot mag., Delrin one piece wraparound grips, exposed hammer, ambidextrous safety, beveled magazine well, extended squared off trigger guard, adj. or fixed rear sight, 3 dotsighting system, 28 oz. New 1989.

Mfg.'s Sug. Retail	$541	$450	$385	$350	$325	$300	$280	$265

Add $25 for adj. rear sight.

MODEL 3906 STAINLESS — stainless steel variation of the Model 3904, 35½ oz. New 1989.

Mfg.'s Sug. Retail	$604	$510	$435	$375

Add $28 for adj. rear sight.

MODEL 3913 STAINLESS — stainless steel variation of the Model 3914, 25 oz. New 1990.

Mfg.'s Sug. Retail	$568	$485	$415	$365

This model is also available with a single side manual safety at no extra charge (Model 3913NL).

Grading	100%	98%	95%	90%	80%	70%	60%

Model 3913 LadySmith — similar to Model 3913 Stainless, except has white Delrin grips and mag. does not have finger extension, 25 oz. New in 1990.

Mfg.'s Sug. Retail $568 $485 $415 $365

MODEL 3914 — 9mm Para., double action semi-auto, aluminum alloy frame, 3½ in. barrel, hammerless, 7 shot finger extension mag., fixed sights only, ambidextrous safety, blue finish, straight backstrap grip, 25 oz. New 1990.

Mfg.'s Sug. Retail $513 $435 $375 $340 $320 $295 $280 $265

This model is also available with a single side manual safety at no extra charge (Model 3914NL).

Model 3914 LadySmith — similar to Model 3914, except has Delrin grips, 25 oz. New in 1990.

Mfg.'s Sug. Retail $568 $485 $415 $365

MODEL 3953 — 9mm Para., double action only, aluminum alloy frame with stainless steel slide, compact model with 3½ in. barrel, 8 shot mag. New in 1990.

Mfg.'s Sug. Retail $568 $485 $415 $365

MODEL 3954 — similar to Model 3953, except has blue steel slide. New in 1990.

Mfg.'s Sug. Retail $513 $435 $375 $340 $320 $295 $280 $265

MODEL 4006 STAINLESS — .40 S&W cal., 4 in. barrel, 11 shot mag., satin stainless finish, exposed hammer, Delrin one piece wraparound grips, 3 dot sights, 38½ oz. New in 1990.

Mfg.'s Sug. Retail $708 $600 $515 $400

Add $20 for adj. rear sight.

MODEL 4013 STAINLESS — .40 S&W cal., semi-auto, standard double action, 3½ in. barrel, 8 shot mag., fixed sights, ambidextrous safety, alloy frame. New 1991.

Mfg.'s Sug. Retail $686 $580 $495 $395

MODEL 4014 — similar to Model 4013, except is steel with blue finish. New 1991.

Mfg.'s Sug. Retail $629 $510 $425 $375

MODEL 4046 STAINLESS — similar to Model 4006 Stainless, except is double action only. New in 1991.

Mfg.'s Sug. Retail $708 $600 $515 $400

MODEL 4053 — double action only variation of the Model 4013. New 1991.

Mfg.'s Sug. Retail $686 $580 $495 $395

MODEL 4054 — double action only variation of the Model 4014. New 1991

Mfg.'s Sug. Retail $629 $510 $425 $375

MODEL 4506 STAINLESS — .45 ACP, 5 in. barrel, 8 shot mag., combat trigger guard, exposed hammer, fixed or adj. rear sight, straight backstrap (curved is optional), Delrin one-piece grips, 38½ oz. New in 1990.

Mfg.'s Sug. Retail $714 $605 $515 $400

Approx. 100 Model 4506's left the factory mismarked Model 645 on the frame. In N.I.B. condition they are worth $700.

MODEL 4516 STAINLESS COMPACT — .45 ACP, hammerless compact variation of the Model 4506, 3¾ in. barrel, 7 shot mag., fixed rear sight only, 34½ oz. New in 1990.

Mfg.'s Sug. Retail $714 $605 $515 $400

MODEL 4526 STAINLESS — similar to Model 4506 Stainless, except has frame mounted decocking lever. New in 1990.

Mfg.'s Sug. Retail $740 $620 $525 $400

MODEL 4536 STAINLESS — similar to Model 4516 Compact, except has frame mounted decocking lever only. New in 1990.

Mfg.'s Sug. Retail $740 $620 $525 $400

Grading	100%	98%	95%	90%	80%	70%	60%

MODEL 4546 STAINLESS — similar to Model 4506, except is double action only. New in 1990.

Mfg.'s Sug. Retail	$714	$605	$515	$400			

MODEL 4556 STAINLESS — .45 ACP, features double action only, 3¾ in. barrel, 7 shot mag., fixed sights. New in 1991.

Mfg.'s Sug. Retail	$714	$605	$515	$400			

MODEL 4566 STAINLESS — .45 ACP, traditional double action with ambidextrous safety, 4¼ in. barrel, 8 shot mag. New in 1990.

Mfg.'s Sug. Retail	$714	$605	$515	$400			

MODEL 4567-NS — similar to Model 4566 Stainless, except has Tritium night sights and stainless/blue finish. 2,500 mfg. in 1991 only.

Mfg.'s Sug. Retail	$735	$615	$520	$400			

MODEL 4576 STAINLESS — .45 ACP, features 4¼ in. barrel, frame mounted decocking lever, fixed sights. New in 1990.

Mfg.'s Sug. Retail	$740	$620	$525	$400			

MODEL 4586 STAINLESS — .45 ACP, 4¼ in. barrel, double action only, 8 shot mag. New in 1990.

Mfg.'s Sug. Retail	$714	$605	$515	$400			

MODEL 5903 STAINLESS — 9mm Para., double action semi-auto, 4 in. barrel, exposed hammer, 15 shot mag., adj. or fixed rear sight, ambidextrous safety. New 1990.

Mfg.'s Sug. Retail	$636	$540	$460	$395			

Add $30 for adj. rear sight.

MODEL 5904 — similar to Model 3904 except has steel slide and blue finish, 26½ oz. New 1989.

Mfg.'s Sug. Retail	$592	$490	$430	$360	$330	$300	$280	$265

Add $28 for adj. rear sight.

MODEL 5906 STAINLESS — stainless steel variation of the Model 5904, 37½ oz. New 1989.

Mfg.'s Sug. Retail	$652	$550	$465	$395			

Add $28 for adj. rear sight.

MODEL 5924 — 9mm Para., 4 in. barrel, features frame mounted decocking lever, 15 shot mag. New in 1990.

Mfg.'s Sug. Retail	$617	$505	$435	$365	$330	$300	$280	$265

MODEL 5926 STAINLESS — stainless variation of the Model 5924.

Mfg.'s Sug. Retail	$677	$565	$475	$395			

MODEL 5943 STAINLESS — 9mm Para., double action only, 4 in. barrel, aluminum alloy frame with stainless steel slide, 15 shot mag. New in 1990.

Mfg.'s Sug. Retail	$636	$540	$460	$390			

Model 5943-SSV — similar to Model 5943 Stainless, except has 3½ in. barrel, stainless/blue finish, and Tritium night sights. New in 1990.

Mfg.'s Sug. Retail	$690	$580	$485	$395			

MODEL 5944 — similar to Model 5943, except has blue finish slide. New in 1990.

Mfg.'s Sug. Retail	$592	$495	$430	$360	$330	$300	$280	$265

MODEL 5946 STAINLESS — all stainless steel variation of the Model 5944. New in 1990.

Mfg.'s Sug. Retail	$652	$550	$465	$390			

MODEL 6904 — compact variation of the Model 5904, 3½ in. barrel, 12 shot finger extension mag., fixed rear sight, 26½ oz. New 1989.

Mfg.'s Sug. Retail	$561	$470	$395	$350	$325	$300	$280	$265

MODEL 6906 STAINLESS — stainless steel variation of the Model 6904, 26½ oz. New 1989.

Mfg.'s Sug. Retail	$618	$515	$440	$375			

Grading	100%	98%	95%	90%	80%	70%	60%

MODEL 6926 — 9mm Para., 3½ in. barrel, standard double action, features frame mounted decocking lever, aluminum alloy frame with stainless slide, 12 shot mag. New in 1990.

Mfg.'s Sug. Retail	$644	$535	$450	$375			

MODEL 6944 — 9mm Para., double action only, 3½ in. barrel, 12 shot mag., aluminum alloy frame with blue steel slide. New in 1990

Mfg.'s Sug. Retail	$561	$470	$395	$350	$325	$300	$280	$265

MODEL 6946 STAINLESS — similar to Model 6944, except has stainless steel slide. New in 1990.

Mfg.'s Sug. Retail	$618	$515	$440	$375			

RIFLES

S&W in 1984 disc. importation of all Howa manufactured rifles. Mossberg continued importation utilizing both leftover S&W parts in addition to fabricating their own.

MODEL A BOLT ACTION RIFLE — .22-250, .243, .270, .308, .30-06, 7mm Mag., or .300 Win. Mag. cal., 23¾ in. barrel, folding leaf sight, checkered Monte Carlo stock with rosewood forend tip and pistol grip cap. Mfg. 1969-1972.

			$385	$330	$305	$275	$220	$195	$165

MODEL B — same as A, in .243, .270, or .30-06 cal., 20¾ in. barrel, Schnabel forend.

			$425	$305	$275	$250	$195	$165	$140

MODEL C — same as B, with cheek piece.

			$425	$305	$275	$250	$195	$165	$140

MODEL D — same as C, with full length stock.

			$550	$385	$360	$305	$250	$220	$195

MODEL E — same as D, with no cheek piece.

			$550	$385	$360	$305	$250	$220	$195

Note: These rifles were made for S&W by Husqvarna in Sweden.

MODEL 1500 MOUNTAINEER — .222 Rem., .22-250, 223 Rem, .243 Win, .25-06 Rem, .270 Win, .30-06, or .308 Win. cal., bolt action, 22 in. barrel 5-6 shot mag., no sights, walnut stock and forend, approx. 7 lbs. 10 oz. New 1983.

			$300	$250	$245	$210	$195	$175	$160

Add $27 for sights.

Model 1500 Mountaineer Magnum --7mm Rem. Mag. or .300 Win. Mag. cal.

			$325	$275	$260	$225	$200	$180	$160

MODEL 1500 DELUXE — same cal.'s as standard 1500, Monte Carlo stock, skip-line checkering, select walnut, no sights. New 1983.

			$350	$300	$260	$220	$200	$180	$160

Add $20 for 7mm Mag. and .300 Win. Mag.

MODEL 1500 DELUXE VARMINT — .222 Rem, .22-250, or .223 Rem-heavy cal., 24 in. barrel, skip-line checkering, no sights. New 1983.

			$350	$275	$315	$275	$215	$195	$170

Add $15 for parkerized finish.

MODEL 1700 LS "CLASSIC HUNTER" — .243 Win, 270 Win, or .30-06 cal., 22 in. barrel, removable 5 shot mag., solid recoil pad, no sights, Schnabel forend, finely checkered. New 1983.

			$400	$350	$315	$265	$240	$220	$195

SHOTGUNS

S&W in 1984 disc. importation of all Howa manufactured shotguns. Mossberg continued importation utilizing both leftover S&W parts in addition to fabricating their own.

MODEL 916 SLIDE ACTION SHOTGUN — 12, 16, or 20 ga., 20, 26, 28, or 30 in. barrels, various chokes, plain pistol grip stock, solid frame. Mfg. 1972-disc.

			$175	$150	$140	$130	$120	$110	$100

Grading	100%	98%	95%	90%	80%	70%	60%
Vent rib and pad							
	$200	$175	$155	$145	$135	$130	$120

MODEL 916T SLIDE ACTION — same as 916, except barrels can be interchanged.

	$195	$170	$155	$145	$135	$130	$125
Vent rib and pad							
	$225	$200	$180	$170	$155	$145	$135

MODEL 96 SLIDE ACTION — various cal.'s, ga.'s, disc.

	$125	$110	$100	$90	$75	$70	$65

MODEL 1000 P SLIDE ACTION — 12 ga, various barrel lengths, chokes, vent rib.

	$350	$305	$270	$230	$210	$190	$170

This model is the same as the Model 3000.

MODEL 3000 SLIDE ACTION — 12 or 20 ga., 3 in. chambers, 22-30 in. barrels, walnut stock and forend, 6¼-7½ lbs.

	$350	$305	$270	$230	$210	$190	$170

Add $30 for multi-choke insertion tubes.

Subtract $40 for slug gun (rifle sights on 22 in. barrel).

This model was also available in a "Waterfowler" variation - values are approx. the same as listed above.

MODEL 3000 POLICE — 12 ga. only, blue or parkerized finish, many combinations of finishes, stock types, and other combat accessories are available for this model, 18 or 20 in. barrel.

	$332	$255	$215	$185	$170	$155	$140

Add $70 for folding stock.

MODEL 1000 AUTOLOADER — 12 or 20 ga., 22-30 in. barrels, various chokes, gas operated, vent rib, engraved alloy receiver, checkered pistol grip stock. Mfg. 1972-1984.

	$350	$325	$295	$260	$240	$220	$200

Add $30 for multi-choke tubes.

12 and 20 gauge — Magnum 28 or 30 in. barrel, multi chokes, steel receiver, "M" suffix.

	$375	$340	$310	$275	$255	$235	$215

Model 1000 Super 12 — handles all loads interchangeably, top-of-the-line model during its circa.

	$500	$450	$400	$360	$330	$300	$280

Add $50 for multi-choke.

MODEL 1100 TARGET — 12 or 20 ga., skeet, super skeet and trap models available. Super skeet has 15 barrel muzzle vents to reduce recoil. Trap model has multi-choke tubes, Monte Carlo select walnut stock and forend. Both alloy and steel receivers available in Skeet model, Trap is steel only.

	100%	98%	95%	90%	80%	70%	60%
Skeet	$400	$390	$335	$260	$235	$215	$190
Super skeet-steel frame	$450	$535	$460	$390	$355	$320	$285
Trap	$450	$460	$370	$310	$285	$255	$225

Note: Shotguns made for S&W by Howa Machinery, Ltd., Japan.

SNAKE CHARMER

Manufactured by Sporting Arms Manufacturing, Inc. located in Littlefield, TX.

SNAKE CHARMER II — .410 ga. only, stainless steel, break open single shot, molded plastic stock and forend, shell holder in stock, 3½ lbs. Also available as Night Charmer (disc. 1988) and Sea Charmer (disc. 1988).

Mfg.'s Sug. Retail	$149	$125	$100	$85

Add $10 for Night Charmer.

Add $18 for Sea Charmer.

Add $10 for black carbon steel barrel (New Generation Model).

Grading	100%	98%	95%	90%	80%	70%	60%

SOCIETA SIDERURGICA GLISENTI
Manufacturer located in Brescia, Italy.

GLISENTI MODEL 1910 — 9mm Glisenti, 7 shot, 4 in. barrel, fixed sights, blue, checkered wood, rubber or plastic grips, Italian service pistol. Mfg. 1910-WWII.
Warning: While some Glisentis may chamber and fire the 9mm Luger cartridge, it is extremely dangerous to do so.

	100%	98%	95%	90%	80%	70%	60%
	$210	$200	$180	$170	$140	$125	$100

SODIA, FRANZ
Manufacturer located in Ferlach, Austria.

Sodia arms are superb and are often excellently engraved and inlaid. Professional appraisal should be sought before purchase, since prices are high. Sodia is famous for double-barrel shotguns as well as two- and three-barrel combinations of rifles and shotguns.

BOCHDRILLING — various cal.'s, top quality worksmanship.

	100%	98%	95%	90%	80%	70%	60%
	$7,000	$6,500	$6,000	$5,000	$4,000	$3,000	$2,500

DOPPLEBUSCHE — various cal.'s, top quality worksmanship.

	$5,000	$4,500	$4,000	$3,000	$2,000	$1,800	$1,600

RIFLE, OVER/UNDER — various cal.'s, top quality worksmanship.

	$4,500	$4,250	$4,000	$3,500	$3,000	$2,000	$1,800

TRAP SHOTGUN — 12 ga. only, boxlock action, various degrees of engraving and ornamentation.

	$2,500	$1,850	$1,475	$1,100	$900	$750	$600

SOKOLOVSKY CORPORATION SPORT ARMS (SCSA)
Manufacturer located in Sunnyvale, CA.

SOKOLOVSKY .45 AUTOMASTER — .45 ACP only, stainless steel, single action, 6 in. barrel, 6 shot mag., adj. millet sights, unique action, is free of external devices, 55 oz. Mfg. since 1984.

Mfg.'s Sug. Retail	$3,300	$2,700	$2,200	$1,850

Total production on this model is 50 pistols.

SPECIAL SERVICE ARMS MFG., INC.
Manufacturer located in Aiken, SC. Because of potential legislative action regarding the Crossfire Model 88P, it was never manufactured. Currently, Special Service Arms Mfg. is manufacturing a fully auto pistol designated The Champ for law enforcement and military sales only. For more information regarding this pistol, please write/Fax them (see Trademark Index for listing).

SPECTRE FIVE
Shotgun revolver mfg. by Mil, Inc. located in Piney Flats, TN. Distributed by C.L. Reedy & Associates, Inc. located in Melbourne, FL. and Specialized Weapons, Inc. located in Smyrna, GA.

SPECTRE FIVE — .45 LC cal./.410 ga. with 3 in. chambers, unique 5 shot revolver design (double action) permits shooting .45 LC or .410 shotshells interchangeably, 2 in. rifled barrel, matte black finish, external ambidextrous hammer block safety, internal draw bar safety, Pachmayr grips includes padded plastic carrying case, 48 oz. New 1991.

Mfg.'s Sug. Retail	$379	$350	$285	$250	$225	$200	$185	$170

Grading	100%	98%	95%	90%	80%	70%	60%

CROSSFIRE MODEL 88P — combination gun (12 ga. over .308 Win.) in paramilitary design featuring independent O/U shotgun/rifle operation, dual gas piston rotating bolts, slide activated, 3 position selector designates rifle, shotgun, or safe operation, twin box magazines (20 shot rifle and 7 shot shotgun), 20 in. barrels, composite construction, 9½ lbs. While this model was advertised in 1989, it never saw production. The 1989 advertised retail was $1,177.

SPHINX

Private label trademark of those pistols imported by Sile Distributors located in New York, NY.

PISTOLS

MODEL AT-380 — .380 ACP cal., semi-auto double action only, 3.27 in. barrel, stainless steel fabrication, 10 shot mag. with finger extension, checkered walnut grips.

Mfg.'s Sug. Retail	$700	$575	$475	$440	$410	$380	$350	$325

MODEL AT-2000 STANDARD — 9mm Para. cal., semi-auto in standard double action or double action only, 4.53 in. barrel, stainless steel fabrication, 15 shot mag., checkered walnut grips, fixed sights.

Mfg.'s Sug. Retail	$800	$700	$575	$475	$440	$410	$380	$350

Model AT-2000 Compact — similar to Model AT-2000 Standard, except has 3.66 in. barrel and 13 shot mag.

Mfg.'s Sug. Retail	$800	$700	$575	$475	$440	$410	$380	$350

Model AT-2000 Sub-Compact — similar to Model AT-2000 Compact, except has 3.34 in. barrel and 11 shot mag.

Mfg.'s Sug. Retail	$800	$700	$575	$475	$440	$410	$380	$350

SPRINGFIELD ARMORY

America's First Federal Armory located in Springfield, MA. Production began in 1795 and an act of congress made it an official federal arsenal in 1872. Not associated with the private firm of the same name located in Geneseo, IL.

In recent years collectors have realized that military specimens in 98%-100% original condition are very rare and desirable in most cases. Since the supply of these guns is so limited, values listed below for these condition factors may not be indicitive of current market conditions. As always, many collectors agree that it is hard to overpay for a mint, original, military specimen.

MODEL 1870 ROLLING-BLOCK RIFLE, U.S.N. — .50 cal. centerfire, 32⅝ in. barrel, not serial numbered, 22,013 mfg.

$1,600	$1,300	$1,050	$900	$775	$650	$600

MODEL 1871 ROLLING-BLOCK RIFLE, U.S.A. — .50 cal. centerfire, 36 in. barrel, not serial numbered, 10,001 mfg.

$1,600	$1,300	$1,050	$900	$775	$650	$600

MODEL 1873 RIFLE "TRAPDOOR" — .45-70, 32⅝ in. barrel, 2 bands. Approx. 73,000 mfg. between 1873-1877. Deduct 20% if stock cartouche faint or absent.

$1,350	$1,100	$900	$775	$650	$495	$395

MODEL 1884 RIFLE "TRAPDOOR" — .45-70, 32⅝ in. barrel, 2 bands. Approx. 232,000 mfg. between 1885-1890. Deduct 20% if stock cartouche faint or absent.

$1,000	$875	$725	$625	$525	$425	$360

MODEL 1873 CARBINE — 22 in. barrel, half stock, single barrel band/stacking swivel, 20,000 made, but semi-scarce. Pre-Custer serial numbers below 43,700 made, add up to 50%. (Pre-1876 mfg.).

$2,350	$1,950	$1,750	$1,595	$1,400	$1,150	$900

Grading	100%	98%	95%	90%	80%	70%	60%

MODEL 1873 CADET RIFLE — 29½ in. barrel, stacking swivel, no sling swivels. Deduct $100 for variation with sling-swivels.

	100%	98%	95%	90%	80%	70%	60%
	$1,600	$1,300	$1,050	$900	$775	$650	$600

Deduct 25-35% if restocked with hole drilled and butt plate for cleaning tools.

MODEL 1875 OFFICER'S RIFLE FIRST TYPE — mfg. 477 between 1875 and 1886, 26 in. barrel, single barrel band. Not serial numbered, some dated, non-issue.

	100%	98%	95%	90%	80%	70%	60%
	$7,750	$6,800	$5,750	$5,500	$5,000	$4,500	$4,000

Deduct 15-20% for types 2 and 3.

MODEL 1877 RIFLE — mfg. 3943.

	100%	98%	95%	90%	80%	70%	60%
	$1,450	$1,200	$900	$800	$700	$600	$550

MODEL 1877 CARBINE — 22 in. barrel, "C" rear sight to 1,200 yards. Mfg. 2946.

	100%	98%	95%	90%	80%	70%	60%
	$2,750	$2,400	$2,000	$1,900	$1,800	$1,600	$1,300

MODEL 1877 CADET RIFLE — 29½ in. barrel. Mfg. 1,050.

	100%	98%	95%	90%	80%	70%	60%
	$1,475	$1,200	$1,000	$950	$900	$800	$700

MODEL 1879 RIFLE — mfg. approx. 140,000.

	100%	98%	95%	90%	80%	70%	60%
	$795	$650	$500	$450	$400	$350	$300

MODEL 1879 CARBINE — no stacking swivel. Approx. 15,000 mfg.

	100%	98%	95%	90%	80%	70%	60%
	$1,100	$900	$800	$700	$650	$550	$500

MODEL 1879 CADET RIFLE — stacking swivel but no sling swivels. Mfg. 5,000.

	100%	98%	95%	90%	80%	70%	60%
	$850	$775	$650	$550	$475	$425	$375

MODEL 1880 — combination triangular, bayonet-ramrod, sliding-type. Mfg. 1,001.

	100%	98%	95%	90%	80%	70%	60%
	$1,400	$1,200	$1,000	$895	$800	$700	$600

MODEL 1881 FORAGER — 20 ga., 1,376 mfg. 1881-1885. Be cautious when purchasing.

	100%	98%	95%	90%	80%	70%	60%
	$2,250	$1,950	$1,700	$1,500	$1,250	$1,000	$875

U.S. MODEL 1892-1895-1896-1898 KRAG JORGENSEN — .30-40 Krag, bolt action. Mfg. until 1904.

	100%	98%	95%	90%	80%	70%	60%
	$650	$550	$450	$395	$320	$280	$240

1898 CARBINE — same as 1898 Krag Jorgensen, with 22 in. barrel.
Add 20% for Model 1899 Carbine.

	100%	98%	95%	90%	80%	70%	60%
	$750	$625	$595	$525	$460	$420	$385

1898 KRAG NRA CARBINE — Carbine stock and hardware, shortened rifle (22 in.) barreled action, identifiable by full band front sight.

	100%	98%	95%	90%	80%	70%	60%
	$725	$600	$525	$450	$360	$330	$250

U.S. MODEL 1903 SPRINGFIELD — .30-06, bolt action, 24 in. barrel. Mfg. 1903-1930.
Pre-WWI Mfg. — values below represent original rifles - deduct 80% if reworked.

	100%	98%	95%	90%	80%	70%	60%
	$1,750	$1,500	$1,250	$995	$750	$675	$600

Serialized 800,000 - 1,275,767 — double heat treated receiver.

	100%	98%	95%	90%	80%	70%	60%
	$395	$350	$275	$220	$195	$165	$140

Serialized 1,275,768+ — nickel steel receiver.

	100%	98%	95%	90%	80%	70%	60%
	$450	$395	$330	$275	$250	$220	$180

U.S. MODEL 1903 MARK I — same as 1903, except altered for the Pedersen device, a slot is milled into the left side of receiver to act as an ejection port for use of the semi-auto bolt insert, value without device.

	100%	98%	95%	90%	80%	70%	60%
	$450	$395	$330	$275	$250	$220	$180

Grading	100%	98%	95%	90%	80%	70%	60%

1903 A1 — same as 1903, except type C pistol grip stock. Mfg. 1930-1939. In 1941 Remington mfg. approx. 350,000.

	100%	98%	95%	90%	80%	70%	60%
	$450	$395	$350	$300	$260	$230	$195

Remington produced

	$395	$350	$295	$250	$210	$180	$155

1903-A3 — similar to 1903, with production modifications, aperture rear sight, no finger groove in forestock, lower quality finish, stamped floorplate and barrel band. Mfg. WWII by Remington and Smith Corona.

	$450	$420	$390	$360	$330	$300	$275

1903-A3 NATIONAL MATCH — 200 mfg., known as the "unmatched" match rifle.

	$1,500	$1,300	$1,000	$850	$750	$675	$600

1903-A4 SNIPER — .30-06 with M73B1 or M84 scope in Redfield mount, no front sight.

	$1,000	$875	$775	$675	$575	$500	$450

1903 NRA NATIONAL MATCH — similar to 1903, with hand selected and custom fit parts, produced for target shooting. "NRA" and flaming bomb proofed on trigger guard. 1915 date.

	$1,000	$875	$775	$675	$575	$500	$450

1903 SPORTER — same as National Match, with sporter stock and Lyman sight.

	$1,200	$1,000	$825	$750	$625	$525	$470

1903 MATCH STYLE T — same as Sporter, with heavy barrel, globe sight, target bases, 26, 28, or 30 in. barrel.

	$1,500	$1,275	$1,000	$825	$725	$635	$580

1903 FREE RIFLE TYPE A — same as Type T, with 28 in. barrel, and Swiss hook butt.

	$1,650	$1,475	$1,300	$1,150	$995	$895	$775

1903 FREE RIFLE TYPE B — same as Type A, with double set triggers, cheek piece stock, modified firing pin.

	$2,250	$1,900	$1,600	$1,300	$1,075	$950	$825

MODEL 1922-M1 — .22 Target Rifle or .22 LR, 5 shot mag., 24 in. barrel, modified 1903, Lyman receiver sight, sporter stock, issued 1927.

	$950	$875	$795	$695	$595	$540	$495

M2 .22 TARGET RIFLE — similar to 1922 M1, except improved lock time, adj. head space, bolt design.

	$1,000	$900	$800	$700	$600	$550	$500

SPRINGFIELD ARMORY, GENESEO, IL.

Private manufacturer/importer located in Geneseo, IL.

The Springfield Armory manufactures commercial reproductions of older military handguns and rifles. Prices shown below are for current manufactured models. In addition to manufacture, Springfield Armory also imports the Galil Sporter rifle and the Uzi pistol (please refer to their respective headings for more information).

Because of Springfield Armory's changes/additions in their model offerings for 1991, some of the information was not available to this publication before it went to press. Also, some of the retail values reflect 1990 information. As a result, Springfield Armory should be contacted directly (see Trademark Index) for an up-to-date listing of currently manufactured/imported models with prices.

Grading	100%	98%	95%	90%	80%	70%	60%

COMBINATION GUNS

M6 SCOUT — .22 LR, .22 Mag. (disc.), or .22 Hornet (disc.)/.410 O/U Survival Gun, 14 (legal transfer needed) or 18 in. barrels.

Mfg.'s Sug. Retail	$226	$200	$185	$165	$150	$135	$120	$110

Add $30 for .22 Hornet cal.

PISTOLS

M6 PISTOL — .22 cal. over .45 LC cal. (also shoots .410 ga. shotshells), 16 in. barrels. Available Aug. 1991.

Mfg.'s Sug. Retail	$226	$200	$185	$165	$150	$135	$120	$110

OMEGA PISTOL — .38 Super, 10mm Norma, or .45 ACP cal., single action, ported slide, 5 or 6 in. interchangeable ported or unported barrel with Polygon rifling, special lock-up system eliminates normal barrel link and bushing, Pachmayr grips, dual extractors, adj. rear sight. Mfg. 1987-90.

	$775	$650	$575	$495	$425	$360	$295

Add $663 for interchangeable conversion units.

Each conversion unit includes an entire slide assembly, one mag., 5 or 6 in barrel, recoil spring guide mechanism assembly, and factory fitting.

Add $336 for interchangeable 5 or 6 in. barrel (including factory installation).

Last Mfg.'s Sug. Retail was $849.

OMEGA MATCH — same cal.'s as Omega, except has low profile combat sights, 8 shot mag., and beveled mag. well. New 1991.

Mfg.'s Sug. Retail	$1,103	$925	$775	$660	$535	$460	$420	$385

MODEL P9 — 9mm Para. (disc. 1990), 9 x 21mm (new 1991), or .40 S&W (new 1991) cal., patterned after the Czech CZ-75, selective double action design, blue, parkerized, or duotone finish, various barrel lengths, checkered walnut grips. Mfg. in U.S. starting 1990.

Standard Model—4.72 in. barrel, 15 shot mag., parkerized finish standard, 35.3 oz.

Mfg.'s Sug. Retail	$493	$325	$290	$265	$245	$225	$200	$180

Add $13 for blue finish.

Add $182 for duotone finish.

Compact Model—3.66 in. barrel, 13 shot mag., shorter slide and frame, 32.1 oz.

Mfg.'s Sug. Retail	$506	$330	$290	$265	$245	$225	$200	$180

Add $13 for blue finish.

Add $187 for duotone finish.

LSP Model — competition model with 5.03 in. barrel, adj. rear sight, extended thumb safety, and rubberized competition grips, 15 shot mag., 38.4 oz.

Mfg.'s Sug. Retail	$545	$500	$450	$395	$350	$300	$270	$250

Add $13 for blue finish.

Add $182 for duotone finish.

P9 World Cup—same cal.s as the P9, features hard chrome finish only. New 1991.

Mfg.'s Sug. Retail	$2,860	$2,450	$2,050	$1,775	$1,500	$1,250	$1,000	$825

MODEL 1911-A1 STANDARD MODEL—.38 Super, 9mm Para., 10mm (new 1990), or .45 ACP cal., patterned after the Colt M1911-A1, 5.04 (Standard) or 3.63 (Commander or Compact Model) in. barrel, 7 shot (Compact), 8 shot (.45 ACP), 9 shot (10mm), or 10 shot (9mm Para. and .38 Super) mag., walnut grips, parkerized, blue, or duotone finish. Mfg. 1985-1990.

	$400	$360	$330	$300	$280	$260	$240

Last Mfg.'s Sug. Retail was $454.

Add $35 for blued finish.

Add $80 for duotone finish.

This model is also available with a .45 ACP to 9mm Para. conversion kit for $170 in parkerized finish, or $175 in blued finish.

Grading	100%	98%	95%	90%	80%	70%	60%

Defender Model—.45 ACP only, similiar to Standard 1911-A1 Model, except has fixed combat sights, bevelled mag. well, extended thumb safety, bobbed hammer, flared ejection port, walnut grips, factory serrated front strap and two stainless steel magazines, parkerized or blued finish. Mfg. 1988-90.

	$485	$435	$375	$340	$300	$280	$260

Add $35 for blued finish.

Last Mfg.'s Sug. Retail was $567.

Commander Model—.45 ACP cal. only, similar to Standard 1911-A1 Model, except has 3.63 in. barrel, shortened slide, Commander hammer, low profile 3-dot sights, walnut grips, parkerized, blued, or duotone finish. Mfg. in 1990 only.

	$450	$415	$350	$325	$285	$260	$245

Add $30 for blued finish.

Add $80 for duotone finish.

Last Mfg.'s Sug. Retail was $514.

Combat Commander Model—.45 ACP cal. only, 4¼ in. barrel, bobbed hammer, walnut grips. Mfg. 1988-89.

	$435	$385	$325	$295	$275	$250	$230

Add $20 for blued finish.

Compact Model—.45 ACP cal. only, compact variation featuring shortened Commander barrel and slide, reduced M1911 straight grip strap frame, checkered walnut grips, low profile 3-dot sights, extended slide stop, combat hammer, parkerized, blued, or duotone finish. Mfg. 1990 only.

	$450	$415	$350	$325	$285	$260	$245

Add $30 for blued finish.

Add $80 for duotone finish.

Last Mfg.'s Sug. Retail was $514.

Custom Carry Gun—.38 Super (special order only), 9mm, 10mm (new 1990), or .45 ACP cal., similiar to Defender Model, except has tuned trigger pull, heavy recoil spring, extended thumb safety, and other features. New 1988.

	$860	$725	$660	$535	$460	$420	$385

Add $130 for .38 Super Ramped, 10mm is POR.

Last Mfg.'s Sug. Retail was $969.

National Match Hardball Model—.38 Super (disc.), 9mm (disc.), or .45 ACP cal., National Match barrel and bushing, specially fitted frame and slide, BoMar adj. rear sight, Herrett walnut grips, plastic cased. Mfg. 1988-90.

	$780	$650	$565	$515	$460	$415	$385

This model is made specifically for DCM competition shooting.

Last Mfg.'s Sug. Retail was $897.

Bullseye Wadcutter Model—.45 ACP cal. only, designed for wadcutter loads only, 5 or 6 (ported or unported) in. barrel, BoMar rib mounted on slide, checkered grip straps, matched trigger, beavertail grip safety, polished feed ramp and throated barrel. New 1989.

	$1,415	$1,200	$1,025	$925	$825	$750	$675

Add $25 for 6 in. barrel.

Add $80 for 6 in. ported barrel.

Last Mfg.'s Sug. Retail was $1,599.

Trophy Master Competition Pistol—.38 Super, 9mm (disc.), 10mm (new 1990), or .45 ACP cal., competition model which includes low profile combat sights, ambidextrous safety, long match trigger, bobbed hammer, Pachmayr wraparound grips. Mfg. 1988-90.

	$1,300	$1,100	$950	$875	$800	$730	$660

Add $130 for .38 Super with supported chamber, 10mm is POR.

Last Mfg.'s Sug. Retail was $1,443.

Grading	100%	98%	95%	90%	80%	70%	60%

Trophy Master Competition Expert Model—.38 Super, 9mm (disc.), 10mm (new 1990), or .45 ACP cal., mfg. for IPSC competition shooting, dual chamber compensator system on match barrel, blued finish, ambidextrous thumb safety, beveled and polished mag. well, lowered and flared ejection port, wraparound Pachmayr grips, shock buffer, includes 2 mag.'s and plastic carrying case. Mfg. 1988-90.

	$1,664	$1,450	$1,225	$1,025	$950	$890	$850

Add $130 for .38 Super with supported chamber, 10mm is POR.

This model is an improved variation of the Master Grade Competition Pistol "A".

Last Mfg.'s Sug. Retail was $1,664.

Trophy Master Competition Distinguished Model—similiar to Expert Model, except has brushed hard chrome finish, checkered grip straps and trigger guard, top-of-the-line competition model. Mfg. 1988-90.

	$2,000	$1,675	$1,450	$1,225	$1,025	$950	$875

Add $130 for .38 Super with supported chamber, 10mm is POR.

Subtract $130 for "B" Model.

This model is an improved variation of the Master Grade Competition Pistol "B-1".

Last Mfg.'s Sug. Retail was $2,275.

1911-A2 S.A.S.S.—various cal.'s, single shot breakopen action featuring interchangeable barrels, Pachmayr grips, adj. front and rear sights, blue finish only, various weights. Mfg. 1990 only.

10.75 in. barrel—.22 LR, 7mm BR, .357 Mag., or .44 Mag. cal.

	$465	$380	$340	$300	$280	$260	$240

Add $130 per interchangeable barrel.

Last Mfg.'s Sug. Retail was $519.

14.9 in. barrel—.22 LR, .223 Rem., 7mm BR, 7mm-08, .308 Win., or .358 Win. cal.

	$465	$380	$340	$300	$280	$260	$240

Add $130 per interchangeable barrel.

Last Mfg.'s Sug. Retail was $519.

MODEL 1911-A1 90's EDITION—.38 Super, 9mm Para., 10mm, .40 S&W, or .45 ACP cal., patterned after the Colt M1911-A1, except has linkless operating system, 5.04 (Standard) or 3.63 (Commander or Compact Model) in. barrel, 7 shot (Compact), 8 shot (.45 ACP), 9 shot (10mm), or 10 shot (9mm Para., .38 Super, and .40 S&W) mag., walnut grips, parkerized, blue, or duotone finish. New 1991.

Mfg.'s Sug. Retail	$623	$550	$450	$375	$330	$300	$260

Add $39 for blued finish.

Add $94 for duotone finish.

Defender Model—.45 ACP only, similiar to Standard 1911-A1 Model, except has fixed combat sights, bevelled mag. well, extended thumb safety, bobbed hammer, flared ejection port, walnut grips, factory serrated front strap and two stainless steel magazines, parkerized or blued finish. Mfg. began 1991.

Springfield Armory should be contacted directly regarding prices for this model.

Commander Model—.45 ACP cal. only, similar to Standard 1911-A1 Model, except has 3.63 in. barrel, shortened slide, Commander hammer, low profile 3-dot sights, walnut grips, parkerized, blued, or duotone finish. Mfg. began 1991.

Springfield Armory should be contacted directly regarding prices for this model.

Combat Commander Model—.45 ACP cal. only, 4¼ in. barrel, bobbed hammer, walnut grips. Mfg. began 1991.

Springfield Armory should be contacted directly regarding prices for this model.

Compact Model—.45 ACP cal. only, compact variation featuring shortened Commander barrel and slide, reduced M1911 straight grip strap frame, checkered walnut grips, low profile 3-dot sights, extended slide stop, combat hammer, parkerized, blued, or duotone finish. New 1991.

Springfield Armory should be contacted directly regarding prices for this model.

Grading	100%	98%	95%	90%	80%	70%	60%

Custom Carry Gun—.38 Super (special order only), 9mm Para., 10mm, .40 S&W, or .45 ACP cal., similiar to Defender Model, except has tuned trigger pull, heavy recoil spring, extended thumb safety, available in blue or phosphate finish. New 1991

Mfg.'s Sug. Retail	$995	$885	$735	$660	$535	$460	$420	$385

Add $204 for 10mm cal.

.40 S&W is POR from the factory.

Add $35 for 9mm Para. or .38 Super cal.

National Match Hardball Model—.45 ACP cal. only, National Match barrel and bushing, specially fitted frame and slide, blue only, BoMar adj. rear sight, Herrett walnut grips, plastic cased. New 1991.

Mfg.'s Sug. Retail	$923	$800	$660	$565	$515	$460	$415	$385

This model is made specifically for DCM competition shooting.

Entry Level Wadcutter—.38 Super or .45 ACP cal., 5 in. barrel, standard competion features. New 1991.

Mfg.'s Sug. Retail	$982	$840	$680	$575	$515	$460	$415	$385

Add $195 for .38 Super cal.

Trophy Master Competition Model Marksman—.38 Super, 9mm, 10mm, .40 S&W, or .45 ACP cal., competition model which includes low profile combat sights, ambidextrous safety, long match trigger, bobbed hammer, Pachmayr wraparound grips.

Mfg.'s Sug. Retail	$1,476	$1,320	$1,110	$950	$875	$800	$730	$660

Add $260 for 10mm cal.

Add $130 for .38 Super cal.

.40 S&W cal. is POR from the factory.

Trophy Master Competition Model Expert—.38 Super, 10mm, .40 S&W, or .45 ACP cal., mfg. for IPSC competition shooting, dual chamber compensator system on match barrel, duotone finish, ambidextrous thumb safety, beveled and polished mag. well, lowered and flared ejection port, wraparound Pachmayr grips, shock buffer, includes 2 mag.'s and plastic carrying case.

Mfg.'s Sug. Retail	$1,703	$1,480	$1,235	$1,025	$950	$890	$850	$800

Add $260 for 10mm cal.

Add $130 for .38 Super cal.

.40 S&W cal. is POR from the factory.

This model is an improved variation of the Trophy Master Competition Model Marksman.

Trophy Master Competition Model Distinguished — similiar to Expert Model, except has brushed hard chrome finish, checkered grip straps and trigger guard, top-of-the-line competition model.

Mfg.'s Sug. Retail	$2,399	$2,080	$1,715	$1,450	$1,225	$1,025	$950	$875

Add $295 for 10mm cal.

Add $175 for .38 Super cal.

.40 S&W cal. is POR from the factory.

Add $130 for .38 Super with supported chamber, 10mm is POR.

This model is an improved variation of the Trophy Master Competition Model Expert.

RIFLES: MILITARY DESIGN

The M1 Garand and variations listed below have been temporarily discontinued in 1991. Retail prices have been left intact and reflect 1989 retail values. Parts and upgrades for older Springfield Garands are still available, however. The factory should contacted directly for prices and availability of parts.

M1 GARAND AND VARIATIONS—.30-06 Springfield (disc.), .270 (disc. 1987), or .308 Win. cal., semi-auto, 24 in. barrel, gas operated, 8 shot mag., adj. sights, 9½ lbs.

Standard Model—supplied standard with camo GI fiberglass stock. Temporarily disc. in 1990.

Mfg.'s Sug. Retail	$761	$725	$650	$575	$525	$485	$450	$425

Subtract $65 if with GI stock.

Grading	100%	98%	95%	90%	80%	70%	60%
National Match—walnut stock, match barrel and sights.							
Mfg.'s Sug. Retail	$897	$850	$775	$700	$650	$600	$550	$495
Add $240 for Kevlar stock (disc.).							
Ultra Match—match barrel and sights, glass bedded stock, walnut stock standard. Temporarily disc. in 1990.							
Mfg.'s Sug. Retail	$1,033	$950	$850	$725	$675	$610	$550	$500
Add $240 for Kevlar stock (disc.).							
M1-D Sniper Rifle—limited quantities, with original M84 scope, prong type flash suppressor, leather cheek pad and slings, .30-06 only.							
Mfg.'s Sug. Retail	$1,033	$950	$850	$725	$675	$610	$550	$500
Tanker Rifle—same as T-26 authorized by Gen. MacArthur at the end of WWII, 18¼ in. barrel, .30-06 or .308 cal., GI stock standard.							
Mfg.'s Sug. Retail	$797	$725	$675	$600	$525	$460	$380	$335
Add $23 for walnut full stock.							

BM 59—.308 Win. cal., mfg. in Italy and machined and assembled in the Springfield Armory factory, 19.32 in. barrel, 20 shot box mag., 9½ lbs.

	100%	98%	95%	90%	80%	70%	60%
Standard Italian Rifle—with grenade launcher, winter trigger, tri-compensator, and bipod.							
Mfg.'s Sug. Retail	$1,950	$1,750	$1,400	$1,200	$1,000	$895	$850	$800
Alpine Rifle—with Beretta pistol grip type stock.							
Mfg.'s Sug. Retail	$2,275	$2,025	$1,625	$1,350	$1,150	$1,000	$925	$850
This model is also available in a Paratrooper configuration with folding stock at no extra charge.							
Nigerian Rifle—same as BM 59, except has Beretta pistol grip type stock.							
Mfg.'s Sug. Retail	$2,340	$2,075	$1,650	$1,375	$1,150	$1,000	$925	$850
E Model Rifle							
Mfg.'s Sug. Retail	$2,210	$1,975	$1,595	$1,325	$1,125	$975	$900	$825

BM 59 M-1 GARAND—with original Beretta M1 receiver, only 200 imported into the U.S.

	100%	98%	95%	90%	80%	70%	60%
Mfg.'s Sug. Retail	$2,080	$1,850	$1,475	$1,250	$1,000	$895	$850	$800

M1A RIFLES—.243 Win., .243 Win., or 7mm08 (new 1991) cal., patterned after the original Springfield M14 - except semi-auto, walnut or fiberglass stock, 22 in. barrel, fiberglass handguard, 9 lbs. Add $75 for walnut stock, $149 for heavy composition stock, $323 for fiberglass stock (disc.), $314 for fancy burl walnut stock (disc.), $75 for folding stock (disc.) on Standard Model.

	100%	98%	95%	90%	80%	70%	60%
Standard Model—above specifications.							
Mfg.'s Sug. Retail	$970	$850	$740	$625	$540	$500	$460	$400
M1A E-2—add $31 for walnut stock, $119 for Shaw stock with Harris bipod, standard stock is birch. Disc.							
		$745	$650	$590	$550	$495	$505	$460

Last Mfg.'s Sug. Retail was $842.

National Match—National Match sights, barrel, mainspring guide, flash suppressor, and gas cylinder, special glass bedded oil finished match stock, tuned trigger, 9 lbs. Add $155 for heavy composition stock, $314 for fiberglass stock, $257 for fancy burle stock (disc.), $34 for Shaw IPSC walnut stock, $50 for Shaw stock with Harris bipod, no extra charge for E-2 (disc.).

	100%	98%	95%	90%	80%	70%	60%
Mfg.'s Sug. Retail	$1,269	$1,125	$900	$800	$725	$650	$575	$525

Add $75 for walnut stock.

Add $155 for heavy composition stock.

Add $34 for Shaw IPSC walnut stock.

.243 Win. and 7mm-08 cal.'s are also available at no extra charge.

Super Match—same as National Match, except has air-gauged Douglas or Hart heavy barrel, oversized walnut super match stock, and modified operating rod guide, approx. 10 lbs. Add $239 for fiberglass stock, add $257 for fancy burle walnut stock (disc.), subtract $31 for Shaw IPSC walnut stock, add $50 for Shaw stock with Harris bipod, no extra charge for E-2 (disc.).

	100%	98%	95%	90%	80%	70%	60%
Mfg.'s Sug. Retail	$1,525	$1,340	$1,100	$925	$800	$700	$625	$575

.243 and 7mm-08 cal.'s are also available at no extra charge.

Grading	100%	98%	95%	90%	80%	70%	60%

Law Enforcement Rifle—.308 Win. cal., law enforcement variation of the M1A mfg. with match grade parts giving superior accuracy. New 1990.

Mfg.'s Sug. Retail	$2,163	$1,875	$1,525	$1,340	$1,100	$925	$800	$700

M1A "GOLD SERIES"—.308 Win. cal., heavy walnut competition stock, gold metal grade heavy Douglas barrel. Add $126 for Kevlar stock, add $390 for special Hart stainless steel barrel, add $516 for Hart stainless steel barrel with Kevlar stock. Mfg. 1987 only.

	$1,944	$1,750	$1,375	$1,150	$975	$850	$740	$650

Last Mfg.'s Sug. Retail was $1,944.

M1A-A1 BUSH RIFLE—7.62mm only, 18¼ in. shrouded barrel, 8 lbs. 12 oz., GI fiberglass stock standard. Add $66 for walnut stock, $68 for folding stock (disc.), $106 for Shaw IPSC walnut stock, $320 for oversize fiberglass competition stocks (disc.), $53 for E-2 (disc.).

Mfg.'s Sug. Retail	$1,000	$900	$750	$675	$600	$550	$500	$450

Add $238 for National Match variation.

Add $525 for Super Match variation.

SAR-8—.308 Win. cal., patterned after the H & K Model 91, recoil operated delayed roller lock action, fluted chamber, rotary adj. rear aperture sight, 18 in. barrel, supplied with walnut thumbhole sporter stock, 20 shot detachable mag., 8.7 lbs. Mfg. in U.S. starting 1990.

Mfg.'s Sug. Retail	$1,164	$995	$825	$750	$675	$600	$550	$500

Add $254 for compact accurizing package (includes retractable stock).

SAR-8 parts are interchangeable with both SAR-3 and HK-91 parts.

SAR-48/SAR-4800 SPORTER MODEL—.308 Win. cal., authentic model of the Browning semi-auto FAL/LAR rifle, 21 in. barrel, adj. gas operation, 20 shot mag., adj. sights, supplied with two 20 shot mag.'s, sling, and mag. loader. New 1985.

Mfg.'s Sug. Retail	$1,286	$1,125	$925	$795	$695	$640	$595	$550

Add $70 for Paratrooper model with folding stock (disc.).

Add $17 for Compact Sporter Model.

The SAR-48 was disc. in 1989 and reintroduced as the Model SAR-4800 in 1990. The SAR-4800 comes standard with a walnut thumbhole sporter stock. All SAR-4800 parts are interchangeable with both SAR-48 and FN/FAL parts.

SAR-48/SAR-4800 Bush Rifle Sporter Model—similiar to standard model, except has 18 in. barrel.

Mfg.'s Sug. Retail	$1,216	$1,085	$900	$795	$695	$640	$595	$550

SAR-48 .22 Cal.—.22 LR variation of the Sporter Model. Disc. 1989.

	$725	$660	$595	$540	$495	$450	$400

Last Mfg.'s Sug. Retail was $760.

DR-200 SPORTER RIFLE—.223 cal., paramilitary design rifle, 18 in. barrel, gas operated rotating bolt assembly, sporter stock with thumbhole, 5 shot mag. Importation began in 1991.

Mfg.'s Sug. Retail	$687	$595	$525	$450	$400	$365	$340	$320

This model is mfg. in Korea by Daewoo. Older listings may be found under the Daewoo heading.

RIFLES: SPORTING

MAUSER M98—7 x 57mm, surplus rifles with standard military dimensions and features. Importation disc. 1989.

Hunting/Utility Grade

	$70	$50	$45	$45	$40	$40	$35

Last Mfg.'s Sug. Retail was $75.

Collector Grade

	$105	$90	$80	$70	$60	$50	$40

Last Mfg.'s Sug. Retail was $116.

Premium Grade

	$170	$150	$130	$115	$100	$90	$80

Last Mfg.'s Sug. Retail was $194.

Grading	100%	98%	95%	90%	80%	70%	60%

M-1 CARBINE, GARAND, ENFIELD, AND OTHERS
See U.S. Military Section in this Book.

STALLARD ARMS
Manufactured and distributed by MKS Inc. located in Mansfield, OH.

JS-9mm — 9mm Para. cal., semi-auto single action, 4½ in. barrel, thumb safety, fixed sights, 8 shot mag., non-glare military blue finish, copolymer synthetic grips, 41 oz. New 1990.

Mfg.'s Sug. Retail	$140	$125	$105	$95	$85	$75	$70	$65

Add $10 for nickel finish.

JS-.45 — .45 ACP cal., similar to JS-9mm, except has 7 shot mag. and 4.6 in. barrel, 44 oz. New 1991.

Mfg.'s Sug. Retail	$150	$135	$110	$100	$90	$80	$75	$70

Add $10 for nickel finish.

STANDARD ARMS COMPANY
Wilmington, DE.

MODEL G AUTOLOADER — .25-35, .30-30, .25 Rem., .30 Rem., or .35 Rem. cal., bottom loading box mag., 22 in. barrel, open sight, straight stock. This was the first gas operated rifle in U.S.A. Gas port can be closed and gun will function as a slide action, mfg. 1910.

$400	$300	$275	$250	$225	$175	$150

A variation that was slide action only (Model M) also was mfg. — subtract 35% from values listed above.

STAR, BONIFACIO ECHEVERRIA
Manufactured in Eibar, Spain. Currently imported by Interarms located in Alexandria, VA.

PISTOLS: SEMI-AUTO

MODEL I — .32 ACP, 9 shot, 4¾ in. barrel, blue, fixed sights, plastic grips. Mfg. 1934-1936.

$235	$200	$160	$120	$100	$85	$70

MODEL IN — .380 ACP, 8 shot, 4¾ in. barrel, blue, same as I.

$250	$215	$170	$125	$105	$90	$75

MODEL M (MILITARY) — a modification of Government Colt, available in 9mm Bergman, 9mm Luger, or .38 Super cal., 8 shot, and .45 ACP, 7 shot, 5 in. barrel, blue, fixed sights, checkered wood grips.

$295	$250	$200	$165	$150	$140	$120

MODEL HN — .380 auto, 6 shot, 2¾ in. barrel, blue, fixed sights, plastic grips. Mfg. 1934-1941.

$225	$180	$140	$120	$100	$90	$75

MODEL H — same as HN, except 7.65mm, 7 shot.

$225	$180	$140	$120	$100	$90	$75

SUPER STAR — improved Model M, .38 Super or 9mm Luger, 8 shot, 5 in. barrel, checkered wood grips, loaded chamber indicator, Spanish service pistol. Mfg. 1946.

$325	$295	$275	$250	$210	$175	$165

SUPER STAR TARGET MODEL — same as Super Star, but target sights, extended trigger guard.

$650	$500	$400	$300	$200	$180	$160

MODEL 1920 — 9mm BB or .38 Super cal., easily identified by unusual safety located on left rear slide.

$375	$315	$295	$240	$185	$150	$120

Grading	100%	98%	95%	90%	80%	70%	60%

MODEL 1921 — 9mm BB or .38 Super cal., predecessor to the later Model A, this model was fit with a grip safety that was later dropped when standardizing the Model A production.

| | $350 | $285 | $240 | $215 | $180 | $145 | $115 |

MODEL 1922 — designation for the early Model A.

| | $325 | $285 | $240 | $215 | $180 | $145 | $115 |

MODEL A — modified Government Colt, .38 Super, 5 in. barrel, no grip safety, blue, checkered wood grips. Mfg. 1934-present but not currently imported.

| | $275 | $230 | $200 | $165 | $145 | $130 | $110 |

MODEL A CARBINE — usually 7.63mm, unusual variation, slotted with tangent rear sight and extended barrel. Add $300 for original stock.

| | $1,500 | $1,250 | $1,050 | $825 | $700 | $575 | $450 |

MODEL B — same as Model A, but 9mm Luger. Mfg. 1934-1975.

| | $295 | $250 | $205 | $170 | $150 | $140 | $115 |

MODEL P — same as Model A, except .45 ACP, 7 shot mag. Mfg. 1934-1975.

| | $325 | $275 | $210 | $175 | $155 | $145 | $120 |

MODELS SUPER A AND P — same as Models A and P, except loaded chamber indicator, mag. safety and easier takedown feature. Mfg. 1946-1989.

| | $275 | $240 | $215 | $180 | $160 | $145 | $125 |

Last Mfg.'s Sug. Retail was $340.
Add 50% for Super P.

MODELS SUPER B — 9mm Para., similiar to Models A/P, except has loaded chamber indicator, mag. safety and easier takedown feature, choice of blue or Starvel finish on Model B. Importation disc. in 1990.

| | $270 | $240 | $210 | $185 | $160 | $140 | $120 |

Add $30 for Starvel finish.
Last Mfg.'s Sug. Retail was $330.

MODEL MB — 9mm Para., late production Model M cut for shoulder stock, mag. safety. Add $300 for shoulder stock.

| | $1,000 | $825 | $675 | $565 | $450 | $365 | $250 |

MODEL MMS — 7.63mm, late production Model M cut for shoulder stock, mag. safety. Add $300 for original stock.

| | $700 | $580 | $460 | $400 | $325 | $260 | $200 |

MODEL SI — .32 ACP, 8 shot, 4 in. barrel, blue, without grip safety, small version of Government .45 in appearance, plastic grips. Mfg. 1941-1965.

| | $200 | $190 | $160 | $135 | $115 | $100 | $80 |

MODEL S — same as S1, except .380 ACP cal., 9 shot, mfg. 1941-1965.

| Mfg.'s Sug. Retail | $237 | $195 | $170 | $145 | $125 | $110 | $95 | $85 |

Add $30 for Starvel finish.
Beginning in 1989, Interarms started importing factory reconditioned used Spanish Police Contract Model S pistols - these guns are available in either blue or Starvel finish and are supplied with a plastic box with accessories.

MODELS SUPER SI AND S — same as S, with Super Star improvements. Mfg. 1946-1972.

| | $240 | $230 | $210 | $195 | $165 | $140 | $120 |

MODEL SUPER SM — same as Super S, except adjustable sight and wood grips. Mfg. 1973-1981.

| | $250 | $235 | $220 | $200 | $175 | $145 | $125 |

MODEL CO POCKET — .25 auto, 2¾ in. barrel, blue, fixed sights, plastic grips. Mfg. 1941-1957.

| | $195 | $180 | $165 | $145 | $120 | $110 | $90 |

Grading	100%	98%	95%	90%	80%	70%	60%

MODEL CU STARLET — .25 auto, 2⅜ in. barrel, alloy frame, fixed sights, plastic grips, blue, or chrome slide, frame anodized in black, blue, green, gray, or gold. Mfg. 1957-present, no longer imported as 1968 GCA.

	$195	$180	$165	$145	$120	$110	$90

MODEL DK (STARFIRE) — .380 auto, 3⅛ in. barrel, fixed sights, plastic stocks, finished in same color availability as Model CU. Mfg. 1957-present, U.S. import ceased with 1968-GCA.

	$400	$350	$295	$255	$225	$180	$155

MODEL HK LANCER — similar to Starfire, except .22 LR. Mfg. 1955-1968.

	$225	$200	$180	$160	$140	$120	$110

MODEL F — .22 LR, 10 shot, 4 in. barrel, fixed sights, blue, plastic grips. Mfg. 1942-1967.

	$200	$170	$140	$110	$95	$85	$55

MODEL FS — same as F, except 6 in. barrel, adj. sights. Mfg. 1942-1967.

	$175	$165	$150	$120	$100	$90	$65

MODEL F OLYMPIC RAPID FIRE — .22 Short, 9 shot, 7 in. barrel, adj. sight, aluminum slide, barrel weights and muzzle brake, blue, plastic grips. Mfg. 1942-1967.

	$250	$230	$210	$175	$155	$140	$130

MODEL FR — restyled Model F, adj. sight and slide stop. Mfg. 1967-1972.

	$175	$165	$150	$120	$100	$90	$65

MODEL FRS — same as FR, only 6 in. barrel, available in chrome. Mfg. 1967-present.

	$175	$165	$150	$120	$100	$90	$65

MODEL FM — same as FR, except heavier frame, web ahead of trigger guard, 4½ in. barrel. Mfg. 1972-present.

	$175	$165	$150	$120	$100	$90	$65

MODEL BKS STARLIGHT — 9mm Para., 8 shot, 4¼ in. barrel, plastic grips. Mfg. 1970-1981.

	100%	98%	95%	90%	80%	70%	60%
Blue	$250	$230	$210	$180	$160	$145	$130
Chrome	$275	$240	$220	$195	$170	$155	$145

MODEL BM SEMI-AUTO — 9mm, single action, 8 shot mag., 4 in. barrel, steel frame, Colt 1911 action, blue, chrome (disc. 1989), or Starvel (new 1990) finish, plastic grips, 35 oz.

Mfg.'s Sug. Retail	$415	$310	$245	$205	$180	$165	$155	$145

Add $30 for Starvel or chrome (disc. 1990) finish.

MODEL BKM — similar to BM, except lightweight duraluminum frame, blued finish only, 26 oz.

Mfg.'s Sug. Retail	$415	$310	$250	$215	$190	$170	$160	$150

MODEL PD — .45 ACP, 6 shot mag., single action, 4 in. barrel, adj. rear sight, blue or Starvel (new 1990) finish only, walnut grips, alloy frame, 25 oz. Mfg. 1975-present.

Mfg.'s Sug. Retail	$475	$345	$290	$250	$215	$195	$170	$160

Add $20 for Starvel finish (new 1990).

MODEL 28 — 9mm, double action, 15 shot mag., 4¼ in. barrel, blue finish only, advanced design, 40 oz. Mfg. 1983 and 1984 only.

	$414	$310	$325	$275	$250	$225	$200

Note: Model 28 is interesting since no screws are used in its manufacture. Hammer assembly (including spring, cocking lever, sear, disconnector and ejector) is housed under removable backstrap.

MODEL 30M — 9mm Para. only, successor to the Model 28, double action, 4.33 in. barrel, 15 shot mag., blued finish only, adj. rear sight, checkered wrap around plastic grips, steel frame, 40 oz. New 1985.

Mfg.'s Sug. Retail	$495	$400	$340	$315	$295	$270	$250	$225

Grading	100%	98%	95%	90%	80%	70%	60%

MODEL 30/31 PK DURAL — similiar to Model 30M, except duraluminum frame, 3.86 in. barrel, 30 oz.

Mfg.'s Sug. Retail	$550	$435	$355	$315	$295	$270	$250	$225

The Model 30 PK was discontinued in 1989 and the Model 31 PK was introduced in 1990.

MODEL 31P — 9mm Para. or .40 S&W (new 1990) cal., compact variation utilizing double action, features Acculine barrel (3.86 in.) similiar to Firestar Model, 14 shot mag., ambidextrous safety with decocking lever, blue or Starvel finish, all steel construction, 39.4 oz. New 1990.

Mfg.'s Sug. Retail	$550	$435	$355	$315	$295	$270	$250	$225

Add $60 for .40 S&W cal.

Add $30 for Starvel finish.

MODEL FIRESTAR — 9mm Para. or .40 S&W (new 1990) cal., single action, 7 shot mag., 3.39 in. Acculine barrel, checkered rubber grips, compact design utilizing all steel construction, 3 dot sighting system with adjustable rear sight, blue or Starvel finish, 30.35 oz. New 1990.

Mfg.'s Sug. Retail	$485	$375	$300	$260	$230	$200	$180	$165

Add $25 for .40 S&W cal.

Add $30 for Starvel finish.

STEEL CITY ARMS, INC.
Previous manufacturer located in Pittsburgh, PA until 1990.

DOUBLE DEUCE — .22 LR only, double action semi-auto, matte finish stainless steel, 2½ in. barrel, 7 shot mag., uncheckered rosewood grips, 18 oz. New 1984.

Mfg.'s Sug. Retail	$290	$265	$230	$200

Various select hardwood stocks are also available at extra cost ($20-100).

STERLING
Previous manufacturer located in Gasport, NY. Disc. 1983.

PISTOLS
Rather than list individual models, the following generalizations will help in ascertaining values for this trademark. Models 300, 302 and 402 will average between $75 and $150 if in 70%+ condition, Models 283, 284, 285 (Husky), and 286 (Trapper) are semi-auto .22 cal. pistols with various barrel lengths — values will range between $90-$150. Models 400 (.380 ACP), PPL (.380 ACP short barrel), and 450 (.45 ACP) usually range in the $150-$275 range.

STERLING ARMAMENT, LTD.
Manufacturer located in England since 1900. Previously imported and distributed by Cassi Inc. located in Colorado Springs, CO until 1990.

CARBINES

STERLING MK 6 — 9mm, blowback semi-auto with floating firing pin, shrouded 16.1 in. barrel, side mounted mag., folding stock, 7½ lbs.

	$565	$495	$450	$410	$375	$340	$310

Last Mfg.'s Sug. Retail was $650.

PISTOLS

PARAPISTOL MK 7 C4 — 9mm, 4 in. barrel, semi-auto paramilitary design pistol, crinkle finish, same action as MK. 6 Carbine, fires from closed bolt, 10, 15, 20, 30, 34 or 68 shot mag., 5 lbs.

	$500	$435	$375	$350	$325	$295	$265

Last Mfg.'s Sug. Retail was $600.

PARAPISTOL MK 7 C8 — 9mm, similar to C4, except has 7.8 in. barrel, 5¼ lbs.

	$525	$450	$390	$365	$330	$300	$275

Last Mfg.'s Sug. Retail was $620.

Grading	100%	98%	95%	90%	80%	70%	60%

STEVENS, J., ARMS COMPANY

J. Stevens Arms Company was founded in 1864 at Chicopee Falls, MA as J. Stevens & Co. In 1866 the name was changed to J. Stevens Arms and Tool Co. In 1916, the plant became New England Westinghouse, and tooled up for both Browning machine guns and Moison-Nagant Rifles. In 1920, the plant was sold to the Savage Arms Corp. and manufactured guns were marked "J. Stevens Arms Co.". This designation was dropped in the late 1940's, and only the name "Stevens" has been used up to the present date.

In 1990, Savage Arms discontinued the manufacture of all firearms (rifles and shotguns) bearing the Stevens trademark. All guns manufactured by Savage Arms now bear the Savage trademark only.

PISTOLS

NO. 10 TARGET SINGLE SHOT — .22 LR, 8 in. barrel, blue, adj. sights, rubber grips, squared off like an automatic pistol, tip up action. Mfg. 1919-1939.

	$220	$200	$185	$165	$140	$120	$100

NO. 35 TARGET SINGLE SHOT — .22 LR, 6, 8, 10, or 12¼ in. barrel, blue, walnut grips. Mfg. 1907-1939.

	$350	$300	$265	$220	$200	$185	$165

NO. 35 "OFFHAND" AUTOSHOT — .410 (actually a pistol-length shotgun). Class Three — must be registered with BATF. Introduced 1931, disc. 1935.

	$300	$250	$200	$150	$100	$75	$60

RIFLES

MODEL 44 IDEAL SINGLE SHOT — .22 LR through .44-40 cal.'s, rolling block, lever action, takedown, 24 or 26 in. barrels, straight grip stock and forearm. Mfg. 1894-1932.

	$850	$775	$675	$575	$500	$425	$350

MODEL 44½ IDEAL SINGLE SHOT — .22 LR through .44-40 cal.'s, falling block, lever action, takedown, 24 or 26 in. barrels, straight grip stock and forearm, action redesigned 1903, otherwise basically same as Model 44. Mfg. 1903-1916.

	$850	$775	$675	$575	$500	$425	$350

MODELS 45-54 SINGLE SHOTS — .22 LR through .44-40 cal.'s, rolling and falling block receivers, lever action, takedown, deluxe versions of the Models 44 and 44½, many special order features, including double set triggers, types of finish, engraving, length and weight of barrels, stock configuration could be special ordered. The higher grade Schuetzens and Stevens-Pope are very collectible and command premiums. These models have to be taken one at a time for determining value. Therefore, no prices are shown. Mfg. 1896-1916.

NO. 414 ARMORY MODEL — .22 LR or .22 Short only, lever action, 26 in. barrel, single shot, Lyman aperture sight. Mfg. 1912-1932.

	$450	$400	$375	$330	$290	$250	$220

MODEL 416 — bolt action, .22 LR, 25 in. medium barrel, 5 shot mag. Disc.

	$140	$120	$110	$100	$90	$80	$70

This model was also mfg. as a U.S. military training rifle. Can be denoted by "U.S. Property" on rear of bolt housing. Healthy premiums exist for this variation.

NO. 417 WALNUT HILL MODEL — .22 LR, .22 Short, and .22 Hornet, lever action, 28 or 29 in. extra heavy barrel, target stock with full pistol grip, beavertail forend, made in 0-3 suffix variations (different sights). Mfg. 1932-1947.

	$700	$600	$525	$475	$440	$395	$360

Grading	100%	98%	95%	90%	80%	70%	60%

NO. 417½ WALNUT HILL MODEL — Same as No. 417, except available in .25 rimfire also. Mfg. 1932-1940.

	$700	$600	$525	$475	$440	$395	$360

NO. 418 WALNUT HILL MODEL — .22 LR or .22 Short only, 26 in. barrel, pistol grip stock, semi beavertail forearm. Mfg. 1932-1940.

	$325	$290	$260	$230	$200	$180	$160

STEVENS' FAVORITE NO.'S 17-29 — .22 LR, .25 RF or .32 RF cal., 24 in. barrel most common, other lengths available, Rocky Mountain front sight, straight grip stock, small tapered forearm. Mfg. 1894-1935. Octagonal barrels command a 33% premium.

	$225	$175	$150	$130	$115	$100	$90

STEVENS' MODEL 65 — bolt action, 20 in. barrel, open sights, 5 shot mag., checkered walnut stock. Mfg. 1969-disc.

	$90	$70	$55	$45	$35	$30	$30

NO. 70 "VISIBLE LOADING" SLIDE ACTION RIFLE — .22 LR-L-S, exposed hammer, 22 in. barrel, open sights, straight grip stock, tube mag., grooved slide handle. Other variations with different barrel lengths and sights will command slight premiums.

	$250	$175	$150	$130	$115	$100	$90

MODEL 71 "STEVENS' FAVORITE" — replica of original, .22 LR, 22 in. octagon barrel, plain straight stock, medallion inlaid, crescent butt. Mfg. 10,000 in 1971.

	$200	$175	$160	$145	$135	$115	$95

MODEL 72 CRACKSHOT — single shot falling block action, .22 cal., 22 in. octagon barrel, open sights, color case hardened frame, straight stock. Mfg. 1972-89.

	$125	$105	$85	$70	$60	$50	$40

Last Mfg.'s Sug. Retail was $165.

MODEL 987 — .22 LR only, semi-auto, 15 shot tube mag., 20 in. barrel, hardwood Monte Carlo stock, adj. rear sight, 6 lbs. Disc. 1989.

	$95	$80	$70	$60	$50	$40	$45

Last Mfg.'s Sug. Retail was $119.

MODEL 89 LEVER ACTION — .22 LR, single shot, 18½ in. barrel, Martini type action, Western style lever, straight stock. Mfg. 1976-disc.

	$85	$65	$60	$50	$45	$40	$35

SHOTGUNS

MODEL 520 PUMP

	$190	$180	$150	$125	$95	$85	$75

MODEL 520 TRENCH GUN — 12 ga., 6 shot, field grade for military use, 20 in.

	$350	$300	$250	$225	$175	$150	$100

MODEL 620 — an improved version of the Model 520 with streamline receiver.

	$325	$290	$250	$225	$175	$150	$100

MODEL 67 SLIDE ACTION — 12, 20, or .410 ga., all are 3 in. chambered, steel receiver, 5 shot, upper receiver safety, 6¼ - 7½ lbs. Recent mfg. by Stevens. Disc. 1989.

	$200	$180	$170	$155	$145	$135	$125

Add $30 for choke tubes (with VR).

Add $10 for VR only.

Last Mfg.'s Sug. Retail was $229.

Model 67 VTR-K Camo — 12 or 20 ga., 28 in. vent rib barrel with choke tubes, laminated camo stock. Mfg. 1986-1988.

	$250	$220	$190	$170	$155	$145	$135

Last Mfg.'s Sug. Retail was $295.

Grading	100%	98%	95%	90%	80%	70%	60%

Slug Model — 12 ga. only, 21 in. barrel, rifle sights. Disc. 1989.

| | $200 | $165 | $140 | $110 | $100 | $90 | $80 |

Last Mfg.'s Sug. Retail was $245.

Model 67 VRT-Y — 20 ga. only, 22 in. vent rib barrel with choke tubes, youth model with smaller stock dimensions. Mfg. 1987-1988.

| | $205 | $170 | $140 | $110 | $100 | $90 | $80 |

Last Mfg.'s Sug. Retail was $259.

MODEL 675 — 12 ga. only, 24 in. vent rib multi-choked barrel with iron sights (including removable rear ramp), hardwood stock with recoil pad, 6½ lbs. Mfg. 1987-1988.

| | $250 | $220 | $190 | $170 | $155 | $145 | $135 |

Last Mfg.'s Sug. Retail was $295.

MODEL 240 O/U — .410 ga.

| | $350 | $300 | $250 | $220 | $190 | $170 | $155 |

MODEL 69-RXL — 12 ga. only, slide action law enforcement version of the Model 67, 18¼ in. cylinder bore barrel with recoil pad, 6½ lbs. Disc. 1989.

| | $200 | $165 | $140 | $110 | $100 | $90 | $80 |

Last Mfg.'s Sug. Retail was $245.

MODEL 311 — 12, 20, or .410 ga., 3 in. chambers, double triggers, extractors, vent rib. Disc. 1989.

| | $245 | $205 | $185 | $150 | $140 | $125 | $115 |

Last Mfg.'s Sug. Retail was $309.

Model 311-R — 12 ga. only, similar to Model 311, except has 18¼ in. cylinder bore barrels for law enforcement use, 3 in. chambers, 6¾ lbs. Disc. 1989.

| | $245 | $205 | $185 | $150 | $140 | $125 | $115 |

Last Mfg.'s Sug. Retail was $309.

FOX/STEVENS MODEL B — 12, 20 or .410 ga., double triggers, VR, extractors, 26, 28, or 30 in. barrels, 7 lbs. Disc. 1986.

| | $315 | $280 | $240 | $220 | $200 | $180 | $160 |

Add 25% for BDE Model (with ejectors).
Last Mfg.'s Sug. Retail was $369.

FOX/STEVENS MODEL B-SE — 12, 20, or .410 ga., single trigger, selective ejectors, vent. rib, beavertail forend, select walnut. Disc. 1989.

| | $415 | $370 | $325 | $280 | $240 | $210 | $180 |

Add 20% for .410 ga.
Last Mfg.'s Sug. Retail was $525.

MODEL 94 — 12, 16, 20, or .410 ga., single shot breakopen, inertia firing pin design, open hammer, 6¼ lbs. Mfg. 1939-1937.

| | $80 | $70 | $65 | $55 | $50 | $45 | $40 |

Last Mfg.'s Sug. Retail was $92.

STEYR AUSTRIAN MILITARY

Manufacturer located in Steyr, Austria.

MODEL 95 RIFLE — straight pull bolt action, 8 x 50R Mannlicher, 30 in. barrel, adj. sights, military full stock.

| | $140 | $110 | $100 | $85 | $65 | $55 | $40 |

MODEL 90 CARBINE — same as Model 95, except 19½ in. barrel.

| | $155 | $125 | $110 | $95 | $85 | $65 | $45 |

Grading	100%	98%	95%	90%	80%	70%	60%

STEYR DAIMLER PUCH A.G.
Steyr, Austria. 1911 to date.

ARGENTINE MODEL 1905 — 7.65mm, Argentine crest on left panel is usually machined off, values assume matching numbers but removed crest.

	$385	$340	$300	$255	$220	$185	$150

POCKET AUTO — .25 ACP or .32 cal., tip up barrel, mag. fed. Disc.

	$220	$180	$165	$150	$140	$130	$120

ROTH STEYR AUTO (MODEL 1907) — 8mm Steyr cal.

	$350	$315	$270	$225	$180	$160	$140

Add 30% for "Budapest" markings.

STEYR-HAHN MODEL 1911 AUTOMATIC — 9mm Steyr, 8 shot, 5.1 in. barrel, fixed magazine top loaded by stripper clip, blue, checkered wood grips. Mfg. 1911-1919. In 1938, the Germans confiscated and converted about 250,000 Steyr Hahns to 9mm Para., "08" was stamped on the left side of these guns.

	$305	$285	$275	$230	$195	$165	$140

Add 50% if marked "Budapest", "08", or with Rumanian Crest.

MODEL SP — .32 ACP, semi-auto, trigger cocking mechanism, very rare - mfg. in 1959 only.

	$650	$595	$540	$495	$450	$400	$350

STEYR MANNLICHER
Manufactured by Steyr-Daimler-Puch in Austria. Founded by Ferdinand Ritter Von Mannlicher and Otto Schoenauer in 1903. Currently imported and distributed by Gun South, Inc. located in Trussville, AL.
Note: also see Mannlicher Schoenauer in the M section for pre-WWII models.

PISTOLS

MODEL GB — 9mm, double action, 18 shot mag, gas delayed blowback action, non-glare checkered plastic grips, 5¼ in. barrel with Polygon rifling, matte finish, steel construction, 2 lbs. 6 oz. Importation disc. 1988.

	100%	98%	95%	90%	80%	70%	60%
Commercial	$525	$475	$425	$375	$335	$300	$280
Military	$450	$395	$350	$300	$280	$260	$240

Last Mfg.'s Sug. Retail was $514.

This model had its action originally derived from the Rogak Pistol. In 1987, Steyr mfg. a military variation of the Model GB - 937 were exported into the U.S.

RIFLES: POST-WW II

MODEL 1950 — .257 Roberts, .270 Win., or .30-06 cal., bolt action, 5 shot rotary mag., 24 in. barrel, low bolt handle, half length stock, ebony forearm. Mfg. 1950-1952.

	$795	$725	$650	$575	$500	$460	$420

MODEL 1950 CARBINE — same as 1950, except 20 in. barrel, full length stock. Mfg. 1950-1952.

	$1,000	$875	$770	$675	$580	$525	$440

MODEL 1950 CARBINE 6.5 — same as 1950 Carbine, except 6.5 x 54mm cal., 18½ in. barrel. Mfg. 1950-1952.

	$1,000	$875	$770	$675	$580	$525	$440

IMPROVED MODEL 1952 — same specifications as 1950, except swept back bolt handle. Mfg. 1952-1956.

	$795	$725	$650	$575	$500	$460	$420

Grading	100%	98%	95%	90%	80%	70%	60%

IMPROVED MODEL 1952 CARBINE — .257 Roberts, .270 Win., 7 x 57mm, or .30-06 cal., swept back handle, otherwise same as 1950 Carbine.

	$1,000	$875	$770	$675	$580	$525	$440

IMPROVED MODEL 1952 6.5 CARBINE — same as 1952 Carbine, except 6.5mm, 18½ in. barrel. Mfg. 1952-1956.

	$1,000	$875	$770	$675	$580	$525	$440

MODEL 1956 RIFLE — similar to 1952, except .243 or .30-06 cal., new high comb. stock design, 22 in. barrel, half length stock. Mfg. 1956-1960.

	$795	$725	$650	$575	$500	$460	$420

MODEL 1956 CARBINE — similar to 1956 Rifle, except .243, 6.5 x 53mm, .257 Roberts, .270, 7mm, .30-06, and .308 cal.'s, 2 in. barrel, full length stock. Mfg. 1956-1960.

	$1,000	$875	$770	$675	$580	$525	$440

MODEL 1961 MCA RIFLE — same as Model 1956, except Monte Carlo stock. Mfg. 1961-1971.

	$795	$725	$650	$575	$500	$460	$420

MODEL 1961 MCA CARBINE — same as 1956 Carbine, except Monte Carlo stock. Mfg. 1961-1971.

	$1,000	$875	$770	$675	$580	$525	$440

MODEL M72 L/M RIFLE — M72 bolt action, .243, .308, .270, .30-06, 7 x 57, and 7 x 64 cal.'s, 23 in. barrel, single or double set triggers. Mfg. 1972-1980.

	$795	$725	$650	$575	$500	$460	$420

RIFLES: CURRENT MANUFACTURE

Current production guns are now called Steyr-Mannlicher models.

Prices below reflect the recent devaluation of the U.S. dollar against some foreign currencies. While the manufacturer's suggested retails have gone up considerably, prices for used specimens (98% or less original condition) have not increased proportionately, and in some cases, have changed very little.

The below listed models have 4 different action lengths and model designations stand for the following: SL=Super Light, L=Light, M=Medium, S=Magnum, S/T=Magnum with heavy barrel. All sporting rifles are available with left-hand stock - add $75 and with either single set or double set triggers - add $108.

MODEL SL — .222 Rem. and Mag., .223 Rem., .22-250 Rem., and 5.6 x 50 Mag. cal.'s, bolt action, 23.6 in. barrel, double set triggers, rotary mag. Available in full-stock (Carbine), half stock (rifle), or varmint version (vent square forearm).

Mfg.'s Sug. Retail	$1,618	$1,475	$1,100	$895	$775	$675	$600	$540

Carbine Model — skip line checkered full stock, 20 in. barrel.

Mfg.'s Sug. Retail	$1,743	$1,575	$1,150	$900	$795	$675	$600	$540

Varmint Rifle — .222 R., .22-250, .243 Win., and .308 Win. cal.'s, 26 in. heavy barrel, stippled pistol grip, vent forearm, no sights.

Mfg.'s Sug. Retail	$1,743	$1,575	$1,150	$900	$795	$675	$600	$540

MODEL L — 5.6 x 57, .243 Win., or .308 Win. cal.'s, available in .22-250 and 6mm Rem. on special order only, otherwise same general specifications as Model SL.

Mfg.'s Sug. Retail	$1,618	$1,475	$1,100	$895	$775	$675	$600	$540

Carbine Model — skip-line checkered full stock, 20 in. barrel.

Mfg.'s Sug. Retail	$1,743	$1,575	$1,150	$900	$795	$675	$600	$540

Varmint Rifle — .222 R., .22-250, .243 Win., and .308 Win. cal.'s, 26 in. heavy barrel, stippled pistol grip, vent forearm, no sights.

Mfg.'s Sug. Retail	$1,743	$1,575	$1,150	$900	$795	$675	$600	$540

Model L Luxus — 5.6 x 57, .243 Win., or .308 Win. cal.'s, full or half stock only, .22-250 and 6mm Rem. available on special order, 3 shot mag.

Mfg.'s Sug. Retail	$2,118	$1,925	$1,400	$1,150	$925	$775	$700	$650

Grading	100%	98%	95%	90%	80%	70%	60%

Model L Luxus Carbine — similar to L Luxus rifle, except has full stock and 20 in. barrel.

Mfg.'s Sug. Retail	$2,243	$2,000	$1,475	$1,175	$950	$800	$725	$660

MODEL M — 6.5 x 57, 7 x 64, .270 Win., .30-06, and 9.3 x 62, cal.'s, bolt action, full stock or half stock, rotary mag., double set triggers.

Mfg.'s Sug. Retail	$1,618	$1,475	$1,100	$895	$775	$675	$600	$540

Carbine Model — skip-line checkered full stock, 20 in. barrel.

Mfg.'s Sug. Retail	$1,743	$1,575	$1,150	$900	$795	$675	$600	$540

Professional Rifle — .270 Win., 7 x 57, 7 x 64, and .30-06 cal.'s, 23.6 in. barrel, Cycolac synthetic stock, 7½ lbs.

Mfg.'s Sug. Retail	$1,368	$1,250	$925	$800	$675	$595	$540	$495

Add $375 for left hand action with half stock (rifle).

Add $500 for left hand action with full stock (carbine).

This variation is also available in .270 Win. or .30-06 cal. with half stock and 20 in. barrel (carbine).

Model M Luxus — 6.5 x 57, 7 x 64, .270 Win., and .30-06 cal.'s, special order in 6.5 x 55 and 7.5 Swiss.

Mfg.'s Sug. Retail	$2,118	$1,925	$1,400	$1,150	$925	$775	$700	$650

Model M Luxus Carbine — same as Model M Luxus, except with full stock and 20 in. barrel.

Mfg.'s Sug. Retail	$2,243	$2,000	$1,475	$1,175	$950	$800	$725	$660

Carbine - 1000 Year Commemorative — 1984 only, .30-06 cal.

	$4,200	$3,620	$2,835					

MODEL S — 6.5 x 68, 8 x 68S, .300 Win. Mag., .338 Win. Mag., 7mm Rem. Mag. cal.'s, half-stock, 26 in. barrel, bolt action.

Mfg.'s Sug. Retail	$1,743	$1,575	$1,150	$900	$795	$675	$600	$540

MODEL S/T — available in 9.3 x 64, .375 H & H or .458 Win. Mag. cal., 26 in. heavy barrel.

Mfg.'s Sug. Retail	$1,868	$1,650	$1,200	$950	$825	$700	$625	$550

Tropical Rifle — .375 H&H and .458 Win. Mag. cal.'s, 26 in. heavy barrel. Disc. 1985.

	$1,150	$900	$810	$730	$660	$600	$550	

Last Mfg.'s Sug. Retail was $1,332.

Luxus S — available in 6.5 x 68, 8 x 68S, 7mm Mag., .300 Win. Mag. cal.'s, 26 in. barrel, half stock only, 3 shot mag., 8 lbs.

Mfg.'s Sug. Retail	$2,243	$2,000	$1,475	$1,175	$950	$800	$725	$660

MODEL SSG — .243 Win. and .308 Win cal.'s, for competition or law-enforcement use. Marksman has regular sights, rotary mag., teflon coated bolt with heavy duty locking lugs, synthetic stock has removeable spacers, parkerized finish. Match version has heavier target barrel and "match" bolt carrier, can be used as single shot. Extremely accurate.

PI Rifle — 26 in. barrel, 3 shot mag., black or green ABS Cycolac synthetic stock.

Mfg.'s Sug. Retail	$1,634	$1,425	$1,000	$850	$700	$625	$565	$525

Add $448 for walnut stock.

PII Sniper Rifle — .243 or .308 Win. cal.'s, 26 in. heavy barrel, no sights, green or black synthetic Cycolac stock, modified bolt handle, choice of single or set triggers.

Mfg.'s Sug. Retail	$1,783	$1,550	$1,050	$950	$800	$675	$600	$540

Add $448 for walnut stock.

PIII Rifle — .308 Win. cal., 26 in. heavy barrel with diopter match sight bases, H-S Precision Pro-Series stock in black only. Importation began 1991.

Mfg.'s Sug. Retail	$2,529	$2,150	$1,600	$1,300	$995	$800	$700	$600

PIV Urban Rifle — .308 Win. cal., carbine variation with 16½ in. heavy barrel and flash hider, ABS Cycolac sythetic stock in green or black. Importation began 1991.

Mfg.'s Sug. Retail	$2,082	$1,775	$1,200	$1,000	$850	$700	$625	$550

Jagd Match — .222 Rem., .243 Win., or .308 Win. cal., hunting rifle that features checkered wood laminate stock, 23.6 in. barrel, Mannlicher sights, double set triggers, supplied with test target. Importation began 1991.

Mfg.'s Sug. Retail	$1,778	$1,550	$1,050	$950	$800	$675	$600	$540

Grading	100%	98%	95%	90%	80%	70%	60%

Match Rifle — .308 Win. only, 26 in. heavy barrel, brown ABS Cycolac stock, Walther Diopter sights, 8.6 lbs.

Mfg.'s Sug. Retail	$2,306	$2,000	$1,500	$1,225	$925	$800	$700	$600

Add $437 for walnut stock.

Match UIT — .308 Win. only, 10 shot steel mag., special single set trigger, free floating barrel, Diopter sights, raked bolt handle, 10.8 lbs.

Mfg.'s Sug. Retail	$4,562	$4,100	$3,500	$3,150	$2,750	$2,400	$2,050	$1,700

UIT stands for Union Internationale de Tir.

AUG S.A. — .223 Rem./5.56mm, semi-auto paramilitary design rifle, design incorporates use of advanced plastics, integral Swarovski scope, 20 in. barrel, bullpup configuration, 7.9 lbs.

Mfg.'s Sug. Retail	$1,375	$1,100	$900	$800	$725	$650	$575	$525

Add $595 for special receiver mfg. with Stanag.

This model is now available in limited quantities only to law enforcement agencies due to 1989 Federal legislation banning the importation for commercial sales.

AUG S.A. Commercial — same as above, except values reflect price increases due to consumer demand after Federal legislation banned the commercial importation in 1989.

	$2,500	$2,150	$1,900	$1,700	$1,500	$1,250	$1,000

Last Mfg.'s Sug. Retail was $1,362 (1989).

MODEL MAADI AKM — 7.62 x 39 Russian, semi-auto, copy of Soviet AKM paramilitary design rifle, 30 shot mag., open sights.

	$1,500	$1,300	$1,150	$995	$850	$775	$700

STOCK, FRANZ
Germany.

SEMI-AUTO PISTOL — .22 LR. Mfg. in Germany 1920-1940.

	$275	$250	$225	$175	$125	$100	$75

SEMI-AUTO PISTOL — .25 ACP, .32 ACP. Mfg. in Germany 1920-1940.

	$220	$200	$175	$150	$100	$90	$80

STOEGER ARMS CORP.
Importer located in New York, NY.

Stoeger has imported a variety of firearms during the past seven decades. Many of these guns were good quality and came from known makers in Europe (private labeled). As a general rule, values for Stoeger rifles and shotguns may be ascertained by comparing them with a known trademark of equal quality and cal./ga. Certain configurations will be more desireable than others (i.e. a Stoeger .22 caliber Mannlicher with double set triggers and detachable mag. will be worth considerably more than a single shot target rifle). Further information regarding this trademark can be obtained by studying older copies of "The Shooter's Bible" (Stoeger's annual catalog).

STREET SWEEPER
Manufactured by Sales of Georgia, Inc. located in Atlanta, GA.

STREET SWEEPER — 12 ga. only, 12 shot rotary mag., paramilitary configuration with 18 in. barrel, double action, folding stock, 9¾ lbs. New 1989.

Mfg.'s Sug. Retail	$595	$475	$420	$375	$325	$300	$275	$250

Grading	100%	98%	95%	90%	80%	70%	60%

STURM, RUGER, & COMPANY

Manufactured in Southport, CT 1949 to date. P-85's are being manufactured at Ruger's new facility in Prescott, AZ (1986).

> NOTE: In 1976, Ruger stamped "Made in the 200th year of American Liberty" on the side of all of the guns they produced for this one year only. These Bicentennial or "Liberty Model" guns will bring a $50 - $75 premium from collectors interested in acquiring them. In most cases this is only true of 100% guns, unfired with the original box and papers.
> ALL VALUES FOR 100% CONDITION RUGERS ASSUME N.I.B. CONDITION — SUBTRACT 5% - 10% WITHOUT BOX AND ACCESSORIES.

PISTOLS: SEMI-AUTO

STANDARD MODEL — .22 LR, 9 shot, 4¾ in. or 6 in. barrel, blue, fixed sights, checkered wood or rubber grips. Mfg. 1951-1982.

	100%	98%	95%	90%	80%	70%	60%
	$140	$125	$115	$105	$95	$85	$75

Variations marked "Hencho En" Mexico are rare. NIB specimens have sold for $750.

Standard Model was also available in a refined version called the Mark I. Barrel lengths were 5¼, 5½, and 6⅞ in. - add 10%.

Stainless Steel 1 of 5,000

	$450	$390	$325

"RED EAGLE" — approx. 25,600 mfg. 1949-1952, most production occurred prior to Alexander Sturm's death (1951).

	$550	$500	$450	$375	$325	$275	$225

Distinguishable by recessed red enamel eagle in grips. Produced until early 1952. Serialized approx. 001 - 30,000 with Mark I Auto occupying blocks from 15,000 - 17,000 and 25,000 - 30,000.

MARK I TARGET — same as Standard, but 5½ in. heavy barrel, or 7 in. heavy tapered barrel, adj. rear sights, target sight. Mfg. 1951-1982.

	$190	$175	$160	$150	$140	$130	$120

Add 200%-300% if U.S. marked.

For factory installed muzzle brake - add $100.

MARK II STANDARD — .22 LR, 4¾ or 6 in. barrel, checkered black Delrin synthetic grips, blue finish, 10 shot mag., approx. 2¼ lbs. Mfg. 1982 to date.

Mfg.'s Sug. Retail	$225	$180	$150	$125	$115	$110	$100	$95

Stainless Steel — otherwise same as Mark II Standard.

Mfg.'s Sug. Retail	$299	$240	$195	$165

Serial numbers start approx. at 18-00001.

MARK II TARGET — .22 LR, 5¼, 5½ bull, 6⅞ standard, or 10 in. bull barrel, single action, 2⅝ - 3¼ lbs. depending on barrel.

Mfg.'s Sug. Retail	$281	$215	$175	$150	$135	$120	$110	$100

Stainless Steel — stainless variation of the Mark II Target, also includes 6⅞ in. bull barrel.

Mfg.'s Sug. Retail	$355	$280	$230	$185

Government Model (MK678G) — commercial variation of the government training model without "U.S." markings, 6⅞ in. bull barrel, adj. rear sight, blue finish, black plastic grips, 46 oz., individually test targeted. New 1987.

Mfg.'s Sug. Retail	$324	$265	$225	$180

P-85 — 9mm Para., double action, 4½ in. barrel, aluminum frame with steel slide, 3-dot fixed sights, 15 shot mag., ambidextrous safety, oversized trigger, synthetic Xenoy grips, matte black finish, 2 lbs. New 1987.

Mfg.'s Sug. Retail	$390	$325	$295	$265	$235	$215	$200	$185

Subtract $30 if without case and extra mag.

This model can be ordered in a decocking or double action only version at no extra charge.

Grading	100%	98%	95%	90%	80%	70%	60%

P-85 Stainless Steel — stainless variation of the P-85. New 1990.

Mfg.'s Sug. Retail $430 $350 $315 $280 $245 $220 $205 $190

Subtract $30 if without case and extra mag.

This model can be ordered in a decocking or double action only version at no extra charge.

REVOLVERS: OLD MODELS - SINGLE ACTION

Note: Some of the following Rugers are known as "Old Models" (mfg. 1963-1973) and are instantly recognized by the three screws through the frame and the four clicks emitted upon cocking. They are now actively sought by collectors and some shooters who desire the smoother operation they afford.

SINGLE SIX REVOLVER — .22 LR, 4⅝, 5½, 6½, or 9½ in. barrel, fixed sights, rubber or wood grips, blue. Mfg. 1953-1972.

$265 $195 $175 $130 $120 $110 $100

This model will command a premium with either a 4⅝ in. or 9½ in. barrel.

Flat loading gate — 5½ in. barrel only, approx. 61,000 mfg. from 1953-1957. Four variations.

$300 $250 $200 $175 $165 $160 $150

.22 Mag. — 6½ in. barrel only, mfg. only three years, serial numbered between 300,000 - 342,000. Frame stamped Mag. only.

$300 $250 $200 $175 $165 $160 $150

Add 40% for extra .22 LR cylinder.

Approx. 250 factory cased, engraved Single Six models have been mfg. Seldomly seen and among the rarest of Ruger revolvers, prices have been reported at over $3,000 - $6,000.

SINGLE SIX CONVERTIBLE — same as Single Six, except .22 LR and .22 WMR interchangeable cylinders, 4⅝, 5½, and 6½ in. barrels with 4⅝ in. being the rarest.

$275 $200 $175 $150 $140 $115 $100

LIGHTWEIGHT SINGLE SIX — same as Single Six, except alloy frame, 4⅝ in. barrel, made 1956-1958. 200,000 - 212,000 serial range, can have alloy or steel cylinder.

$300 $250 $175 $170 $165 $160 $150

Add 100% if all blue with blue alloy cyl.

SUPER SINGLE SIX CONVERTIBLE — same as Single Six Convertible, except adj. sights. Mfg. 1964-1972.

$275 $250 $200 $155 $140 $120 $105

This model in 4⅝ in. barrel is the rarest with prices ranging between $1,500-$1,800 in blue finish, nickel finish specimens are trading for $2,000-$2,500.

BLACKHAWK SINGLE ACTION — .357 Mag., .41 Mag., or .45 LC cal.'s, this model is the 1962 variation, hooded rear sight, 4⅝ or 6½ in barrel.

$350 $300 $250 $215 $180 $160 $140

Add $150 for brass grip frame (rare).

This model was also available in .30 carbine with a 7½ in. barrel — add 10%. Beware of non-factory brass grip frames on this model.

BLACKHAWK SINGLE ACTION "FLAT-TOP" — .357 Mag., 6 shot, 4⅝, 6½, and 10 in. barrel, flat top cylinder strap, adj. sight, blue, black rubber or walnut grips. Approx. 43,000 mfg. between 1955-1963.

$400 $350 $300 $250 $210 $200 $175

6½ in. barrel — add 50%.

10 in. barrel — add 150%.

BLACKHAWK CONVERTIBLE — same as Blackhawk, with extra cylinder, .357 and 9mm, and .45 Colt and .45 ACP cal.'s.

$395 $350 $295 $250 $225 $195 $175

Add $50 for .45 LC/.45 ACP combination.

Buckeye Special — .32-20/.32 H&R Mag., 6½ in. barrel.

$425 $350 $295 $250 $220 $200 $180

Grading	100%	98%	95%	90%	80%	70%	60%

BLACKHAWK FLAT-TOP .44 MAGNUM — similar to Blackhawk Flat-Top, except heavier frame and cylinder, .44 Mag., 6½, 7½, and 10 in. barrels. Approx. 28,000 mfg. between 1956-1963.

	$550	$485	$415	$360	$305	$230	$210

7½ in. barrel — add 25%.

10 in. barrel — add 50%.

Distinguishable by fluted cylinder and rounded trigger guard.

SUPER BLACKHAWK — .44 Mag., 6½ (rare) or 7½ in. barrel, larger frame and improved trigger guard, unfluted cylinder, adj. sights, walnut grips. Mfg. 1959-1972.

	$300	$250	$200	$195	$190	$185	$175

Rare early models in wood case will command 200-300% premium. White cardboard boxed (rarer) Super Blackhawks will command a 300-400% premium. 6½ in. barrel will command a 50%+ premium.

BEARCAT — .22 cal., 6 shot, 4 in. barrel, alloy frame, brass trigger guard, blue, wood grips with medallion, 17 oz. Mfg. 1958-1973.

	$240	$220	$195	$180	$165	$150	$135

Several variations exist within this model incorporating production changes.

SUPER BEARCAT — same as Bearcat, except steel frame, made with brass trigger guard (early model), or blued steel guard, 25 oz. Mfg. 1971-1973.

	$275	$240	$225	$200	$180	$165	$150

HAWKEYE SINGLE SHOT — .256 Mag., single shot, cylinder replaced by rotating breech block, 8½ in. barrel, blue, walnut grips, adj. sight, very rare, approx. 3,300 mfg. Mfg. 1963-1964.

	$1,175	$1,000	$875	$700	$580	$475	$400

REVOLVERS: NEW MODELS - SINGLE ACTION

The following single actions are known as "New Models". They have 2 pins through the frame and cock without the clicks associated with the single action. The change over occurred as a result of desire for safety features. The "New Models" have a transfer bar similar to those found on modern double action revolvers and do not accidentally discharge if dropped. Manufacture started 1973.

During certain years of manufacture, Rugers' changes in production on certain models (cal.'s, barrel markings, barrel lengths, etc.) have created rare variations that are now considered premium niches. These areas of low manufacture will add premiums to the values listed below on standard models.

SUPER SINGLE SIX CONVERTIBLE — .22 LR, includes interchangeable .22 WMR cylinder, 4⅝, 5½, 6½, or 9½ in. barrel, similar to old Super Single Six, except has new interlocking safety mechanism previously described, adj. rear sight. Mfg. 1973-present.

Mfg.'s Sug. Retail	$268	$215	$180	$150	$130	$120	$110	$100

Subtract 15% if without extra .22 Mag. cylinder.

Stainless steel — similar to Super Single Six, except stainless steel construction, 4⅝ (disc.-rare), 5½, 6½ or 9½ (disc.-rare) in. barrel.

Mfg.'s Sug. Retail	$337	$270	$225	$180

Values for 4⅝ or 9½ in. barrel are approx. $575 if N.I.B.

Colorado Centennial Super Single Six — 15,000 mfg. 1975 only, includes walnut case with medallion insert, stainless steel grip frame, 6½ in. barrel, issue price was $250.

	$295	$245	$200

This model also was a U.S. Bicentennial gun as well as the Colorado Centennial Pistol. Most specimens do not have the Bicentennial statement on the barrel and are rarer with that stamping.

SINGLE SIX SSM — .32 H&R Mag. cal., 4⅝, 5½, 6½ or 9½ in. barrel, blue only, 32 oz. with 5½ in. barrel.

Mfg.'s Sug. Retail	$257	$205	$165	$145	$135	$125	$115	$105

Grading	100%	98%	95%	90%	80%	70%	60%

BLACKHAWK — similar to old Model Blackhawk, with new interlocking safety mechanism, 30 Carbine, .357 Mag., .41 Mag., and .45 LC cal.'s available, 4⅝, 6½, or 7½ in. (.30 Carbine and .45 LC only) barrel. Mfg. 1973-present.

Mfg.'s Sug. Retail	$312	$245	$200	$170	$155	$145	$135	$125

Subtract $12 for .30 Carbine cal.

Blackhawk Convertible — same as New Model Blackhawk, except interchangeable cylinders, .357/9mm (current), or .45 Colt/.45 ACP (disc. 1985), 4⅝ or 6½ in. barrel only.

Mfg.'s Sug. Retail	$327	$260	$210	$185	$170	$160	$150	$140

Stainless steel — .357 Mag. only, 4⅝ or 6½ in. barrel.

Mfg.'s Sug. Retail	$385	$320	$250	$210

300 Convertible pistols were made in this model - NIB prices have ranged $750-$850.

New Model Blackhawks are serial numbered 32-00001 on up.

BLACKHAWK-SRM — same as New Model Blackhawk, except is chambered for .357 Rem. maximum, 7½ or 10½ in. barrels available, target sights, 53 oz., 14,000 mfg. 1984 only - production suspended due to unresolvable engineering problems.

	$395	$360	$310	$275	$250	$225	$200

BISLEY MODEL — .22 LR, .32 H&R Mag., .357 Mag., .41 Mag., .44 Mag., and .45 LC cal.'s, incorporates Bisley features (flat-top frame, raked hammer, longer grip frame), 6½ or 7½ in. barrel, fixed or adj. sights, available with fluted/unfluted or roll-marked/unmarked (disc.) cylinders, satin blue finish only, Goncalo Alves smooth grips. New 1986.

Mfg.'s Sug. Retail	$313	$260	$210	$180	$170	$160	$150	$140

Add $59 for .357 Mag.-.45 LC cal.'s (available with 7½ in. barrel only).

SUPER BLACKHAWK — .44 Mag., 5½ (new 1987), 7½ or 10½ in. barrel, blued finish, walnut grips, similar to old model in appearance, but has new action. Mfg. 1973-present. The new model started with serial number 81-00001.

Mfg.'s Sug. Retail	$360	$280	$230	$200	$180	$170	$160	$150

Stainless steel — otherwise same as Super Blackhawk.

Mfg.'s Sug. Retail	$394	$330	$275	$220

OLD ARMY PERCUSSION — .44 cal., black powder, 6 shot, 7½ in. barrel, single action, blued finish, walnut grips.

Mfg.'s Sug. Retail	$319	$260	$210	$170	$150	$135	$120	$110

Add $100 for brass frame.

Stainless Steel

Mfg.'s Sug. Retail	$407	$325	$270	$210

REVOLVERS: DOUBLE ACTION

During certain years of manufacture, Rugers' changes in production on certain models (cal.'s, barrel markings, barrel lengths, etc.) have created rare variations that are now considered premium niches. These areas of low manufacture will add premiums to the values listed below on standard models.

SPEED SIX (MODELS 207, 208 and 209) — .38 Spl., .357 Mag., or 9mm cal.'s, 2¾ or 4 in. barrel, fixed sights, checkered walnut grips, round butt, blued finish, some guns have factory speed hammer (no hammer spur). Mfg. 1973-present. Model 207 and 208 disc. 1988.

	$220	$205	$190	$170	$160	$150	$140

Add $40 for 9mm (Model 209 disc. 1984).
Last Mfg.'s Sug. Retail was $292.

Models 737 and 738 — stainless steel versions of Models 207 and 208, .357 Mag and .38 Spl. cal.'s, 2¾ or 4 in. barrel. Disc. 1988.

	$280	$245	$220

Last Mfg.'s Sug. Retail was $320.

Model 739 — stainless steel, 9mm. Disc. 1984.

	$300	$250	$230

Grading	100%	98%	95%	90%	80%	70%	60%

SECURITY SIX MODEL 117 — .357 Mag. cal., 6 shot, 2¾, 4 (heavy), or 6 in. barrel, adj. sights, checkered walnut grips, square butt. Mfg. 1970-1985.

	$250	$225	$195	$185	$160	$150	$140

Add $15 for target grips.
Last Mfg.'s Sug. Retail was $309.

500 of this model were mfg. for the California Highway Patrol during 1983 (.38 Spl. cal.) in stainless steel only. They are distinguishable by a C.H.P. marking. Premiums might exist in certain regions for this derivative.

Model 717 — stainless steel version of Model 117. Disc. 1985.

	$295	$255	$230				

Last Mfg.'s Sug. Retail was $338.

POLICE SERVICE SIX — .357 Mag, .38 Spl., and 9mm cal.'s, blued finish only, square butt, fixed sights, checkered walnut grips.

Model 107 — .357 Mag, 2¾ or 4 in. barrel, fixed sights. Disc. 1988.

	$250	$220	$200	$190	$180	$170	$165

Last Mfg.'s Sug. Retail was $287.

Model 108 — .38 Spl., 4 in. barrel, fixed sights. Disc. 1988.

	$250	$220	$200	$190	$180	$170	$165

Last Mfg.'s Sug. Retail was $287.

Model 109 — 9mm, 4 in. barrel, fixed sights. Disc. 1984.

	$275	$230	$205	$195	$185	$180	$175

POLICE SERVICE SIX STAINLESS — stainless construction, 4 in. barrel only, fixed sights, checkered walnut grips.

Model 707 — .357 Mag., square butt. Disc. 1988.

	$270	$235	$210				

Last Mfg.'s Sug. Retail was $310.

Model 708 — .38 Spl., square butt. Disc. 1988.

	$270	$235	$210				

Last Mfg.'s Sug. Retail was $310.

GP-100 — .357 Mag. or .38 Spl. cal., 3 (new 1990), 4, or 6 in. standard or heavy barrel, strengthened design intended for constant use with all .357 Mag. ammunition, rubber cushioned grip panels with polished Goncalo Alves wood inserts, fixed or adj. sights with white outlined rear and interchangeable front, 6 shot, 35 - 46 oz. depending on barrel configuration. New 1986.

Mfg.'s Sug. Retail	$378	$325	$270	$240	$220	$200	$185	$170

Add $16 for adj. rear sight (.357 Mag. cal., 4 or 6 in. barrel only).
In .38 Spl. cal., this model is available in 3 or 4 in. barrel only.

GP-100 Stainless — same as GP-100, except is stainless steel. New 1987.

Mfg.'s Sug. Retail	$409	$350	$285	$250			

Add $16 for adj. rear sight (4 or 6 in. barrel only).

SP-101 STAINLESS — .22 LR (6 shot - new 1990), .32 H&R (6 shot - new 1991), .38 Spl. (5 shot), 9 mm Para. (5 shot - new 1991), or .357 Mag. (5 shot - new 1991) cal., small frame variation of the GP-100 Stainless, fixed sights, 2¼, 3¹⁄₁₆, or 4 (new 1990) in. barrel, approx. 27 oz. New 1989.

Mfg.'s Sug. Retail	$388	$325	$265	$240			

SP-101 barrel length are as follows: .22 cal. is available in 2¼ or 4 in. standard or heavy barrel, .32 H&R is available in 3¹⁄₁₆ only, .38 Spl. is available in 2¼ or 3¹⁄₁₆ in. length only, 9mm Para. is available in 3¹⁄₁₆ in. only, and .357 Mag. is available in 2¼ or 3¹⁄₁₆ in. only.

REDHAWK — .357 Mag. (disc. 1985), .41 Mag., or .44 Mag. cal., this is a redesigned stainless steel, large frame handgun, 5½ and 7½ in. barrel only, square butt, smooth hardwood grips, 52 oz.

Mfg.'s Sug. Retail	$437	$375	$315	$285	$240	$215	$180	$165

Add $36 for scope rings.

Grading	100%	98%	95%	90%	80%	70%	60%

Redhawk Stainless — stainless steel construction.

Mfg.'s Sug. Retail $492 $415 $345 $300

Add $39 for stainless scope rings.

SUPER REDHAWK STAINLESS — .44 Mag., 7½ or 9½ barrel, adj. rear sight, cushioned grip panels (GP-100 style), 53 oz. Delivery began in late 1987.

Mfg.'s Sug. Retail $561 $475 $370 $285

This model is supplied with stainless steel scope rings.

RIFLES: SEMI-AUTO

During certain years of manufacture, Rugers' changes in production on certain models (cal.'s, barrel markings, barrel lengths, etc.) have created rare variations that are now considered premium niches. These areas of low manufacture will add premiums to the values listed below on standard models.

The Model 10/22 has been mfg. in several limited production models including a multi-colored or green laminate wood stock variation (1986), a brown laminate stock (1988), a Kittery Trading Post Commemorative (1988), a smoke or tree bark laminate stock (1989), a Chief AJ Model, etc. These limited editions will command premiums over the standard models listed below.

10/22 STANDARD CARBINE — .22 LR, 10 shot rotary mag., 18½ in. barrel, birch or deluxe hand checkered walnut stock, folding rear sight. Mfg. 1964-present.

Mfg.'s Sug. Retail $192 $150 $130 $100 $80 $70 $60 $55

Add $20 for uncheckered walnut stock (mfg. 1987-1989).

Add $51 for deluxe checkered walnut stock.

10/22 SPORTER — same as Standard, except Monte Carlo stock and beavertail forearm. Mfg. 1964-1971.

    $170 $150 $140 $130 $120 $110 $100

10/22 CANADIAN CENTENNIAL — limited production. Disc.

    $375 $350 $325 $275 $250 $225 $180

10/22 INTERNATIONAL — same as Standard, except full stock Mannlicher style. Mfg. 1964-1971.

    $475 $425 $350 $330 $300 $250 $225

MODEL 44 STANDARD CARBINE — .44 Mag., 4 shot mag., 18½ in. barrel, gas operated, folding sight, curved butt. Mfg. 1961-1985.

    $325 $275 $250 $220 $195 $185 $175

Last Mfg.'s Sug. Retail was $332.

Deerstalker Model — approx. 2,000 mfg. with "Deerstalker" marked on rifle until Ithaca lawsuit disc. manufacture (1962).

    $475 $425 $350 $285 $250 $220 $195

25th Year Anniversary Model — mfg. 1985 only, limited production, engraved.

    $400 $350 $310

Last Mfg.'s Sug. Retail was $495.

MODEL 44RS — same as 44, but has aperture sight and swivels.

    $295 $275 $250 $230 $210 $195 $175

MODEL 44 SPORTER DELUXE — stocked version of 44 Standard. Mfg. until 1971.

    $350 $320 $280 $255 $225 $205 $190

MODEL 44 INTERNATIONAL — same as Standard, except full length Mannlicher style stock. Mfg. until 1971.

    $660 $550 $400 $350 $325 $300 $275

Grading		100%	98%	95%	90%	80%	70%	60%

MINI-14 — .223 Rem. or .222 (disc.) cal.'s, 5 (standard mag. starting in 1989), 10, or 20 shot detachable mag., 18½ in. barrel, gas operated, aperture rear sight, military style stock, 6½ lbs. Mfg. 1976-present.

Mfg.'s Sug. Retail	$468	$395	$365	$335	$300	$265	$240	$215

Add $85 for folding stock (disc. 1989).

Due to 1989 Federal legislation and public sentiment, the Mini-14 is now being shipped with a 5 shot detachable mag. only.

Mini 14 Stainless — mini stainless steel version.

Mfg.'s Sug. Retail	$516	$475	$375	$340

Add $85 for folding stock (disc. 1990).

Due to 1989 Federal legislation and public sentiment, the K Mini-14 is now being shipped with a 5 shot detachable mag. only.

MINI-14 RANCH RIFLE — .223 cal., 15⅕ in. barrel, folding rear sight, receiver cut for factory rings, similar to Mini-14, supplied with scope rings, approx. 6 lbs. 5 oz.

Mfg.'s Sug. Retail	$504	$495	$450	$375	$335	$300	$265	$240

Due to 1989 Federal legislation and public sentiment, the Mini-14 Ranch Rifle is now being shipped with a 5 shot detachable mag. only.

Stainless Ranch Rifle — stainless steel construction. New 1986.

Mfg.'s Sug. Retail	$552	$550	$495	$450

Add $85 for folding stock (disc. 1990).

Due to 1989 Federal legislation and public sentiment, the Mini-14 Ranch Rifle is now being shipped with a 5 shot detachable mag. only.

MINI-THIRTY — 7.62 x 39mm Russian, 18½ in. barrel, 5 shot detachable mag., hardwood stock, includes scope rings, 7 lbs. 3 oz. New 1987.

Mfg.'s Sug. Retail	$504	$465	$375	$335	$300	$265	$240	$215

Mini- Thirty Stainless -- Stainless steel variation of the Mini-Thirty, new 1990.

Mfg.'s Sug. Retail	$552	$550	$495	$450

XGI — .243 or .308 Win. cal.'s , similar to Mini 14, 20 in. barrel, 5 shot mag., 8 lbs. Mfg. 1985-86 only.

	$495	$425	$375	$350	$325	$300	$285

Last Mfg.'s Sug. Retail was $425.

RIFLES: SINGLE SHOT

Note: All Ruger Rifles, except Stainless Mini-14, were made 1976 "Liberty" version. Add $50 - $75 when in 100% in the original box condition.

During certain years of manufacture, Rugers' changes in production on certain models (cal.'s, barrel markings, barrel lengths, etc.) have created rare variations that are now considered premium niches. These areas of low manufacture will add premiums to the values listed below on standard models.

NO. 1-A & B STANDARD — falling block action with curved Farquharson lever, popular cal.'s include .22 Hornet (rare), .22-250, .220 Swift, .223, .257 Roberts, .243, 6mm, .25-06, .270, .280, .30-06, 7mm Mag., .270 Wby. Mag. (new 1990), .300 Wby. Mag. (new in 1990), .300 Win. Mag., or .338 Win. Mag., 22 or 26 in. barrel, quarter rib with integral scope bases, supplied with rings and no sights, checkered stock and semi beavertail forearm. Mfg. 1966-present.

Mfg.'s Sug. Retail	$604	$425	$375	$320	$290	$260	$230	$200

The "A" suffix designates an Alexander Henry classic forearm with light barrel and is available in .243, .270, 7 x 57mm, and .30-06 cal.'s only. The "B" suffix designates semi beavertail forearm with medium barrel and is available in all cal.'s under .375 H&H except 7 x 57mm.

NO. 1-RSI — .243 Win., .270 Win., 7 X 57mm, or .30-06 cal., features 20 in. barrel with full length Mannlicher stock, includes swivels and open sights, 7¼ lbs.

Mfg.'s Sug. Retail	$625	$435	$385	$325	$300	$270	$240	$210

Grading	100%	98%	95%	90%	80%	70%	60%

NO. 1-V VARMINT — similar to No. 1-B Standard, except .22-250, 220 Swift, .223, .243 (disc.), .25-06, 6mm (disc.), or .280 (disc.) cal., 24 in. heavy barrel, without rib, target scope blocks, 9 lbs. Mfg. 1966-present.

Mfg.'s Sug. Retail	$604	$425	$385	$325	$300	$275	$245	$215

NO. 1-A LIGHT SPORTER — same as Standard, .243, .270, 7 x 57, .30-06 cal.'s, 22 in. barrel, folding sight on quarter rib, ramp front sight, no rings, Alexander Henry forearm, front swivel in barrel band, 7¼ lbs. Mfg. 1966-present.

Mfg.'s Sug. Retail	$604	$425	$385	$325	$300	$275	$245	$215

NO. 1-S MEDIUM SPORTER — same as Light Sporter, only 7mm, .300 Win. Mag. and .338 Win. Mag. cal.'s, 26 in. medium barrel, open sights, 8 lbs.

Mfg.'s Sug. Retail	$604	$425	$385	$325	$300	$275	$245	$215

.45-70 cal. — with 22 in. barrel, 7¼ lbs.

Mfg.'s Sug. Retail	$604	$425	$385	$325	$300	$275	$245	$215

NO. 1-H TROPICAL RIFLE — similar to Medium Sporter, except 24 in. heavy barrel, open sights .375 H&H, .416 Rigby (new 1991), or .458 Win. Mag. cal., approx. 9 lbs.

Mfg.'s Sug. Retail	$604	$540	$475	$400	$360	$320	$290	$260

NO. 1 INTERNATIONAL — .243 Win., .30-06, .270 Win., and 7 x 57mm cal.'s, lightweight 20 in. barrel, Mannlicher style forearm. Disc.

	$450	$400	$360	$320	$290	$260	$230

NO. 3 CARBINE — same basic action as No. 1, except simpler lever design, stock uncheckered and very similar to .44 Carbine, made in .22 Hornet, .30-40 Krag, .45-70 (only cal. available 1986), .223, .44 Mag., and .375 Win. cal.'s, 22 in. barrel, folding sight. Mfg. 1972-1987.

	$250	$215	$200	$180	$165	$145	$130

Add 25-35% for .223 cal.
Last Mfg.'s Sug. Retail was $284.

RIFLES: BOLT ACTION

Note: All Ruger Rifles, except Stainless Mini-14, were made in 1976 "Liberty" version. Add $50 - $75 when in 100% in the original box condition.

During certain years of manufacture, Rugers' changes in production on certain models (cal.'s, barrel markings, barrel lengths, etc.) have created rare variations that are now considered premium niches. These areas of low manufacture will add premiums to the values listed below on standard models.

Earlier flat-bolt models (pre-1972) are desirable in the rarer cal.'s and will command premiums if 98%+ condition.

MODEL 77/22 — .22 LR only, 10 shot rotary mag., 20 in. barrel, all steel construction, 3 position safety, checkered walnut stock, blue finish, non-adj. trigger, available with either iron sights or plain barrel (no sights) with scope rings, 2.7 millisecond lock time on trigger, 6 lbs. 2 oz. New 1984.

Mfg.'s Sug. Retail	$383	$315	$285	$250	$230	$210	$190	$175

Add $21 for scope rings and iron sights.

Model 77/22 Synthetic Stock — similar to Model 77/22 except has matte black synthetic stock, approx. 6 lbs. New 1989.

Mfg.'s Sug. Retail	$315	$270	$225	$200	$185	$175	$165	$155

Add $21 for scope rings.

Model 77/22 All-Weather Stainless — similar to Model 77/22 except has stainless steel metal with matte black DuPont Zytel synthetic stock affording the lowest shooter maintenance, 5 lbs. 14 oz. New 1989.

Mfg.'s Sug. Retail	$378	$315	$280	$250				

Add $21 for scope rings.

Grading	100%	98%	95%	90%	80%	70%	60%

MODEL 77/22 MAG. — similar to Model 77/22, except in .22 Win. Mag. cal., blue finish, checkered walnut stock. New 1990.

Mfg.'s Sug. Retail	$383	$315	$285	$250	$230	$210	$190	$175

Add $21 for scope rings.

Model 77/22 Mag. All-Weather Stainless — similar to Model 77/22 All-Weather Stainless, except in .22 Win. Mag. cal. New 1990.

Mfg.'s Sug. Retail	$399	$330	$290	$250

Add $20 for scope rings.

MODEL 77R — .22-250, .220 Swift, 6mm (disc.), .243 (disc.), .257 Roberts, .25-06, .270, 7 x 57mm, 7mm-08 (disc.), 7mm Rem. Mag., 280 Rem., .308 (disc.), .30-06, .300 Win. Mag., or .338 Win Mag. cal., long or short action, blue finish, 5 shot mag., 3 shot in Mag. cal.'s, 22 or 24 in. barrel, available with integral bases or round top, some models supplied with sights, stock is checkered walnut with red rubber butt plate, approx. 7 lbs. Mfg. 1968-present.

Mfg.'s Sug. Retail	$531	$400	$350	$295	$265	$245	$200	$200

Add 10-15% for .284 cal.

This model is encountered with or without the "R" suffix.

Model 77 RL — .22-250 (disc.), .257 Roberts, .270, or .30-06 cal., ultra light variation weighing 6 lbs., black forearm tip.

Mfg.'s Sug. Retail	$564	$430	$375	$300	$270	$250	$225	$205

Model 77 RS — .25-06 (disc.), 270, .30-06, 7mm Rem. Mag., 300 Win. Mag., 338 Win. Mag, or .35 Whelen cal., similar to Model 77R, except has open sights.

Mfg.'s Sug. Retail	$587	$440	$390	$315	$285	$265	$230	$210

Model 77V Varmint — .22-250, .220 Swift, .243 (disc.), 6mm (disc.), .25-06, or .308 cal. (disc.), 24 in. heavy barrel (26 in. on .220 Swift), drilled and tapped for target bases, approx. 9 lbs. Mfg. 1968-present.

Mfg.'s Sug. Retail	$546	$420	$365	$300	$265	$245	$210	$200

Model 77 RS African — similar to Model 77R, except in .458 Win. Mag. cal.

Mfg.'s Sug. Retail	$680	$550	$475	$400	$365	$335	$315	$300

This model is supplied standard with a steel trigger guard and steel floor plate.

Model 77 RSC — similar to Model 77 RS African, except has fiddleback walnut stock (C suffix), circa 1982.

	$675	$575	$500	$450	$400	$365	$335

Model 77 RLS — .243 (disc. 1989), .270, .30-06, and .308 cal. (disc. 1989), ultra light, 18½ in. barrel, open sights, 6 lbs. New 1987.

Mfg.'s Sug. Retail	$564	$430	$375	$310	$280	$260	$230	$210

Model 77 RSI — .22-250, .250-3000 (reintroduced 1990), .270, .30-06, or .308 cal., international Mannlicher (full length stock) with 18½ in. barrel and open sights (includes scope rings), approx. 7 lbs.

Mfg.'s Sug. Retail	$594	$450	$390	$315	$285	$265	$230	$210

MODEL 77R MARK II SERIES — various cal.'s as listed below, evolutionary design of the Ruger Model 77R featuring slenderized proportioning, 3 position swing-back safety, new trigger, trigger guard and floor plate latch, stainless steel bolt with Mauser extracter design, 20 in. barrel, integral base receiver, hand checkered American walnut stock, approx. 6 lbs. 7 oz. New 1989.

Model 77R — .243 Win., 6mm, or .308 Win. cal., standard model of the new Mark II Series.

Mfg.'s Sug. Retail	$531	$435	$350	$295	$265	$245	$200	$200

Add $15 for left hand action.

Left hand action is available in .270, .30-06, 7mm, or 300 Win. Mag. only.

Model 77 RL — .223, .243, or .308 cal., ultra light variation weighing approx. 6 lbs., black forearm tip. New 1990.

Mfg.'s Sug. Retail	$564	$460	$375	$300	$270	$250	$225	$205

Model 77 RS — 6mm (disc.), .243, .308 cal., .375 H&H (new 1991), or .416 Rigby (new 1991) cal., similar to Model 77R, except has open sights. New 1990.

Mfg.'s Sug. Retail	$587	$475	$390	$315	$285	$265	$230	$210

Grading	100%	98%	95%	90%	80%	70%	60%
Model 77 RLS — .243 or .308 cal., ultra light, 18½ in. barrel, open sights. Mfg. 1990 only.							
	$460	$375	$310	$280	$260	$230	$210

Last Mfg.'s Sug. Retail was $564.

Model K77 RP All-Weather Stainless — .223, .243, .270, .30-06, .308, 7mm, or .300 Win. Mag. cal., similar to Model 77R Mark II except has stainless steel metal with matte black DuPont Zytel synthetic stock affording the lowest shooter maintenance. New 1990.

Mfg.'s Sug. Retail	$531	$435	$350	$295			

Model 77LR — .270 Win., .30-06, .300 Win. Mag., or 7mm Rem. Mag. cal., left hand variation of the Model 77R. New 1991.

Mfg.'s Sug. Retail	$546	$445	$360	$300	$265	$245	$200	$200

Model 77 RSM — .375 H&H or .416 Rigby cal, premium grade wood with hand cut checkering and ebony forend tip, integral barrel and sighting rib. New 1990.

Mfg.'s Sug. Retail	$1,550	$1,375	$1,100	$950	$825	$750	$675	$595

SHOTGUNS

RED LABEL O/U — 12 or 20 ga., 3 in. chambers, various barrel lengths and choke (including skeet) combinations, boxlock, SST, VR, auto ejectors, checkered pistol grip stock, stainless steel frame became standard on 12 ga. 1985 (not available in 20 ga.). Choke tubes became optional in 1988, standard 1990. Mfg. 1977-present.

Mfg.'s Sug. Retail	$1,102	$875	$725	$650	$595	$550	$500	$450

Subtract 15-20% without choke tubes.

Earlier all-steel 12 ga. models (approx. 500 mfg.) with short field tubes could command 10%-15% premiums over values listed above to collectors interested in acquiring this variation. 20 ga. models are blue only.

SUNDANCE INDUSTRIES, INC.

Manufacturer located in Valencia, CA.

MODEL A-25 SEMI-AUTO PISTOL — .25 ACP cal., semi-auto single action design, $2^7/_{16}$ in. barrel 7 shot mag., rotary safety, lower grip push button mag. release, bright chrome, satin nickel, or black teflon finish, choice of simulated pearl or grooved black grips, serrated slide. Mfg. in the USA. New 1989.

Mfg.'s Sug. Retail	$80	$60	$50	$45	$40	$35	$30	$25

MODEL BOA — similar to Model A-25, except has squeeze grip safety. New in 1990.

Mfg.'s Sug. Retail	$95	$70	$55	$50	$45	$40	$35	$30

MODEL D-22M DERRINGER — although advertised, this gun was never mfg.

NOTES

T

TALON

Manufactured and distributed by Ports of Call located in Minden, NV.

Grading	100%	98%	95%	90%	80%	70%	60%
TALON MKI — 9mm Para., paramilitary design carbine, 18 in. barrel, fires from a closed bolt, compact design, set trigger, military satin black powder coating, uses 13 shot Hi-Power mag., M16 style rear sight, 6½ lbs. Mfg. in U.S. starting 1990.							
Mfg.'s Sug. Retail	$495	$450	$375	$335	$300	$280	$260	$240

This model is also available in 9mm x 18 Police, 9mm x 21 Mini-Mag, or 9mm x 18 Makarov cal. for an additional cost. .22 LR and .45 ACP cal. conversion kits will also be available at a later date.

TANNER, ANDRE'

Manufacturer located in Switzerland. Currently imported and distributed by Mandall Shooting Supplies Inc. located in Scottsdale, AZ. Previously imported by Osborne's located in Cheboygan, MI.

Tanner rifles are noted for their superior accuracy and limited production - less than 150 are mfg. each year.

Prices below reflect the recent devaluation of the U.S. dollar against some foreign currencies. While the manufacturer's suggested retails have gone up considerably, prices for used specimens (98% or less original condition) have not increased proportionately, and in some cases, have changed very little.

300 METER MATCH RIFLE — 7.5 Swiss (special order) or 7.62mm cal. only, single shot, top-of-the-line 300 meter match rifle incorporating all match shooting features including deluxe palm rest, aperture sights. Add $100 for adj. cheek piece.

Mfg.'s Sug. Retail	$4,900	$4,650	$3,995	$3,400	$2,775	$2,250	$1,900	$1,600

Subtract $190 for repeating model with similar features.

300 Meter UIT Standard — similar to Model 300 F, except is without palm rest and adj. Swiss butt plate, 10 shot mag., aperture sights. Add $100 for adj. cheek piece.

Mfg.'s Sug. Retail	$4,700	$4,450	$3,850	$3,350	$2,750	$2,225	$1,925	$1,600

SUPERMATCH MODEL 50 M — .22 LR only, 50 meter free rifle, deluxe palm rest, adj. butt plate, thumbhole stock. Add $100 for adj. cheek piece.

Mfg.'s Sug. Retail	$3,900	$3,600	$3,200	$2,850	$2,450	$2,050	$1,800	$1,600

TAURUS INTERNATIONAL FIREARMS

Manufacturer located in Porto Alegre, Brazil. Currently imported by Taurus International Firearms located in Miami, FL since 1982.

Previous to 1990, this company name was Taurus International Manufacturing, Inc. Taurus products are imported in Canada by Century Arms located in Montreal, Quebec.

REVOLVERS: CURRENT MANUFACTURE

In 1990, certain models became available with a Laser Aim LA1 sighting system that includes mounts, rings (in matching finish), 110 volt AC recharging unit, 9 volt DC field charger, and high impact custom case.

MODEL 65 — .357 Mag./.38 Spl., double action, 6 shot, 3 or 4 in. barrel, checkered walnut grips, 34 oz.

Mfg.'s Sug. Retail	$247	$200	$150	$125	$115	$100	$90	$85

Add $14 for satin nickel finish.

Grading	100%	98%	95%	90%	80%	70%	60%

MODEL 66 — .357 Mag./.38 Spl., double action, 6 shot, 3, 4, or 6 in. barrel, checkered walnut grips, adj. sights, 35 oz.

Mfg.'s Sug. Retail	$270	$215	$160	$135	$125	$115	$100	$90

Add $14 for satin nickel finish.

Model 66 Stainless — similar to Model 66, but in stainless steel. New 1987.

Mfg.'s Sug. Retail	$345	$285	$215	$185

MODEL 669 — similar to Model 66 except has fully shrouded barrel, 4 or 6 in. barrel, 37 oz.

Mfg.'s Sug. Retail	$280	$225	$170	$145	$125	$115	$100	$90

Add $11 for VR barrel (new 1989).

Add $400 for Laser Aim Sight (new 1990).

Model 669 Stainless — similar to Model 669, but in stainless steel.

Mfg.'s Sug. Retail	$355	$295	$225	$190

Add $12 for VR barrel (new 1989).

Add $390 for Laser Aim Sight (new 1990).

MODEL 73 — .32 long only, double action, 6 shot, 3 in. heavy barrel only, checkered walnut grips, 20 oz.

Mfg.'s Sug. Retail	$220	$175	$150	$125	$115	$105	$95	$85

Add $20 for satin nickel finish.

MODEL 76 — .32 H&R cal., double action, 6 shot, 6 in. heavy barrel with solid rib, fully adj. rear sight, transfer bar safety, checkered hard wood grips, blue only, 34 oz. New 1991.

Mfg.'s Sug. Retail	$290	$230	$185	$155	$130	$115	$100	$90

MODEL 80 — .38 Spl. only, double action, 6 shot, 3 or 4 in. barrel, checkered walnut grips, 30 oz.

Mfg.'s Sug. Retail	$215	$170	$135	$115	$105	$95	$85	$80

Add $14 for satin nickel finish.

MODEL 82 — .38 Spl. only, double action, 6 shot, 3 or 4 in. heavy barrel, checkered walnut grips, 34 oz.

Mfg.'s Sug. Retail	$215	$170	$135	$115	$105	$95	$85	$80

Add $14 for satin nickel finish.

MODEL 83 — .38 Spl. only, double action, 6 shot, 4 in. heavy barrel, checkered walnut grips, adj. sights, 34½ oz.

Mfg.'s Sug. Retail	$225	$180	$140	$125	$115	$105	$95	$80

Add $13 for satin nickel finish.

MODEL 85 — .38 Spl. only, double action, 5 shot, 2 or 3 in. heavy barrel, checkered walnut grips, 21 oz.

Mfg.'s Sug. Retail	$235	$190	$145	$125	$115	$105	$95	$85

Add $19 for satin nickel finish (3 in. barrel only).

Model 85 Stainless — stainless construction, otherwise same as Model 85.

Mfg.'s Sug. Retail	$295	$235	$185	$150

MODEL 86 CUSTOM TARGET — .38 Spl. only, double action target model, 6 shot, 6 in. barrel, specially contoured smooth walnut grips, adj. rear sight, blue only, 34 oz.

Mfg.'s Sug. Retail	$305	$240	$190	$160	$150	$140	$130	$120

This model is available in either single or double action with adj. counterweight and interchangeable front sight inserts.

MODEL 94 — .22 LR, double action, 9 shot, 3 (new 1991) or 4 in. barrel, blue finish, adj. rear sight, target featues, 25 oz. New 1989.

Mfg.'s Sug. Retail	$245	$190	$150	$135	$120	$105	$95	$85

Model 94 Stainless — stainless construction, otherwise same as Model 94. New 1990.

Mfg.'s Sug. Retail	$300	$235	$185	$150

Grading	100%	98%	95%	90%	80%	70%	60%

MODEL 96 TARGET SCOUT — .22 LR only, double action, 6 shot, 6 in. barrel, checkered walnut grips, same features as Model 86, 34 oz.

Mfg.'s Sug. Retail	$305	$240	$185	$160	$150	$140	$130	$120

PISTOLS: SEMI-AUTO

In 1990, certain models became available with a Laser Aim LA1 sighting system that includes mounts, rings (in matching finish), 110 volt AC recharging unit, 9 volt DC field charger, and high impact custom case.

PT-58 — .380 ACP, similar to PT-99AF, except in .380 ACP cal., 4 in. barrel, 12 shot mag. New 1988.

Mfg.'s Sug. Retail	$420	$330	$270	$235	$215	$200	$190	$180

Add $28 for satin nickel finish.

PT-91AF — .41 Action Express cal., action similiar to PT-92AF, except is in .41 AE cal., 10 shot mag., 34 oz. Imported 1990 only.

	$365	$300	$250	$225	$200	$190	$180

Add $36 for satin nickel finish.

Add $25 for shooter's pack (includes custom case and extra mag.).

Last Mfg.'s Sug. Retail was $446.

PT-92AF — 9mm Para., semi-auto double action, design similar to Beretta Model 92 SB-F, exposed hammer, 5 in. barrel, 15 shot mag., smooth Brazilian walnut grips, blue or nickel finish, fixed sights, 34 oz.

Mfg.'s Sug. Retail	$470	$385	$300	$250	$225	$200	$190	$180

Add $36 for satin nickel finish.

Add $415 for Laser Aim Sight.

Add $25 for shooter's pack (includes custom case and extra mag.).

PT-92AFC — compact variation of the Model PT-92AF, 4 in. barrel, 13 shot mag., fixed sights.

Mfg.'s Sug. Retail	$470	$385	$300	$250	$225	$200	$190	$180

Add $36 for satin nickel finish.

PT-92AF Lew Horton Special Edition — 9mm Para., matte satin finished frame with high polish stainless steel slide, blue barrel, hammer, trigger, mag. release, safety, and slide release. 250 mfg. in 1990 only.

	$395	$350	$295	$250	$225	$210	$190

Last Mfg.'s Sug. Retail was $454.

PT-99AF — same as Model PT-92AF, except has adj. rear sight.

Mfg.'s Sug. Retail	$510	$400	$325	$270	$235	$210	$200	$190

Add $40 for satin nickel finish.

Add $25 for shooter's pack (includes custom case and extra mag.).

This action is similar to the Beretta Model 92SB-F.

PT-100 — .40 S&W cal., semi-auto, standard double action, 5 in. barrel, 15 shot mag.,safeties include ambidextrous manual, hammer drop, inertia firing pin, and chamber loader indicator, choice of blue, satin nickel or stainless steel finish, smooth Brazilian hard wood stocks, 34 oz. New 1991.

Prices were not released on this model as this publication went to press.

TECHNI-MEC

Manufacturer located in Brescia, Italy (owned by Isidoro Rizzini). Limited current importation and distribution by Mandall's Shooting Supplies, Inc. located in Scottsdale, AZ.

SHOTGUNS

Techni-Mec manufactures a wide variety of shotguns including O/U's and single shots in assorted models. Most models, however, are not being imported into the U.S. at this time. The models listed below are exclusively imported by Mandall's Shooting Supplies, Inc. For

Grading	100%	98%	95%	90%	80%	70%	60%

more information on the complete Techni-Mec model line-up, please contact the factory in Italy directly (please refer to the Trademark Index in the back of this text).

MODEL S 610 — 10 ga., 3½ in. Mag., O/U boxlock action, double underlug blocking, 32 in. VR barrels, SST, ejectors, checkered walnut stock and forearm. Importation began 1991.

Mfg.'s Sug. Retail	$1,050	$950	$875	$800	$750	$695	$640	$585

MODEL SPL 640 — 12, 16, 20, 28, or .410 ga., folding O/U design, DT, 26 in. VR barrels.

Mfg.'s Sug. Retail	$500	$465	$390	$325	$260	$215	$180	$160

TERRIER ONE
Foreign manufacture. Previously distributed (1984-85) by Southern Gun Distributors, Miami, FL.

TERRIER ONE — .32 S&W revolver, double action, 2¼ in. barrel, 5 shot, nickel plated, 17 oz. Mfg. 1984-87.

		$45	$35	$30	$25	$25	$25	$25

Last Mfg.'s Sug. Retail was $55.

TEXAS GUNFIGHTERS
Importer located in Irving, TX.

SHOOTIST EDITION SINGLE ACTION — .45 LC, patterned after the Colt SAA, 4¾ in. barrel, nickel plated blackpowder frame, one piece walnut grips, mfg. by A. Uberti of Italy. New 1988.

Standard Model — 1,000 total mfg., cased.

Mfg.'s Sug. Retail	$649	$649	$525	$440

1 of 100 Edition — 100 total mfg., fully engraved, genuine mother-of-pearl one piece grips, cased.

Mfg.'s Sug. Retail	$1,395	$1,395	$1,050	$775

This model is also supplied with an extra set of walnut grips.

TEXAS LONGHORN ARMS, INC.
Manufacturer located in Richmond, TX.

REVOLVERS

SINGLE-ACTION — various cal.'s, patterned after Colt's S.A.A., except the ejection port has been moved to left side of frame enabling left-hand loading, mfg. from 4140 steel, Pope rifled barrels, 1 piece grips, adj. trigger, case-hardened and blued, entirely hand-made, supplied with lifetime warranty. Mfg. 1,000 of each model.

Texas Border Special — .44 Spl. or .45 LC cal., 3½ in. barrel, 1 piece birdshead grip.

Mfg.'s Sug. Retail	$1,500	$1,500	$1,300	$1,000

South Texas Army — .357 Mag., .44 Spl., or .45 LC cal., 4¾ in. barrel, 1 piece regular walnut stock.

Mfg.'s Sug. Retail	$1,500	$1,500	$1,300	$1,000

West Texas Target — .32-20, .357 Mag., .44 Mag./Spl., or .45 LC cal., flat top frame, 7½ in. barrel.

Mfg.'s Sug. Retail	$1,500	$1,500	$1,300	$1,000

Grover's Improved Number Five — .44 Mag. only, 5½ in. target barrel, 1,200 mfg. serial numbered K1-K1200. This variation incorporates Elmer Keith's 1926 designs including No. 5 lockwork, base pin and latch, and grip straps. New 1988.

Mfg.'s Sug. Retail	$985	$985	$725	$595

Special Edition — includes 10 sets, one of each model listed above, matching cal.'s (.44 Spl. and .45 LC only), matching ser. no.'s divisible by 100 to 1,000 only. Includes carrying case.

Mfg.'s Sug. Retail	$5,750	$5,750	$4,950	$4,200

Grading	100%	98%	95%	90%	80%	70%	60%

Engraved Special Edition — each set includes 3 guns that are factory engraved.
Mfg.'s Sug. Retail $7,650 $7,650 $6,800 $5,950

Texas Sesquicentennial Commemorative — .45 LC, 4¾ in. barrel, one piece elephant ivory grips, 75% engraved in Nimschke style, walnut presentation case. Mfg. 150 1987 only.
Mfg.'s Sug. Retail $2,500 $2,500 $1,950 $1,500

Mason Commemorative — .45 LC, 4¾ in. barrel, one piece extra-grained walnut grips, engraved 18 Kt. Mason insignia, oak presentation case, serial numbered BL-1 on up. New 1987.
Mfg.'s Sug. Retail $1,500 $1,500 $1,300 $1,000

PISTOLS

JEZEBEL MODEL — .22 LR or .22 Mag., single shot, tip-up action, stainless steel, 6 in. barrel, walnut stock and forearm, right or left hand action, 17 oz. New 1987.
Mfg.'s Sug. Retail $200 $200 $160 $135

THOMPSON CARBINES
See Auto Ordnance section of this book.

THOMPSON/CENTER ARMS
Manufacturer located in Rochester, NH 1967 to date.
PISTOL: SINGLE SHOT

Caution: older and newer TC components do not interchange safely. Although parts will fit, they may not function properly. Special ordering of barrels, frames, and calibers started in 1988.

CONTENDER — .22 LR, .22 WMR, 5mm Rem., .218 Bee, .22 Hornet, .22 Jet, .221 Fireball, .222, .25-35, .256 Mag., .30 Carb., .30-30, .38 Spl., .357 Mag., .17 Ackley Bee, .17 Bumblebee, .17 Hornet, .17K Hornet, .17 Rem., .30 Herrett, .357 Herrett, .357-44 B&D, 7 x 30 Waters, .32 H&R Mag., .32-20 Win., 6mm TCU, 6.5mm TCU, or 9mm Para. cal., barrels are interchangeable, 8¾ (disc.), 10, or 14 in. barrel, hinged break open, trigger guard, action lever, blue, .44, .357 Mag., and .45 Colt available with detachable choke for hot shot cartridges, vent rib, 10 in. barrel available, 10 in. bull barrel, adj. sights, checkered walnut grip and forearm.
The Contender action is in its third variation and a wide variety of changes have been made to grips, stocks, sights, etc. since 1967. These production variances do not necessarily add premiums to values listed below.

Octagon barrel — .22 LR, .22 Mag., .22 Hornet, .22K Hornet, .222 Rem., or .357 Mag. cal., 10 in. barrel.
Mfg.'s Sug. Retail $385 $310 $245 $195 $180 $170 $160 $150

Bull barrel — available in 15 cal.'s between .22 LR and .45 Win. Mag., 10 in. round barrel only.
Mfg.'s Sug. Retail $385 $310 $245 $195 $180 $170 $160 $150
Add $5 for .44 Mag/.45 Colt with internal chokes.

Armour Alloy II Bull Barrel — 7 cal.'s between .22 LR and .30-30, similar to regular Bull Barrel, except has Armour Alloy II satin finish which is harder than stainless steel. Mfg. 1986-89.

$320 $285 $230

Add $5 for .45 Colt/.410 ga. internal choke.
Last Mfg.'s Sug. Retail was $415.

Vent Rib — .357 Mag.(disc.), .44 Mag.(disc.) or .45 Colt/.410 cal., 10 in. VR barrel only, adj. front and flip up rear sight, internal choke became standard in 1985.
Mfg.'s Sug. Retail $405 $325 $250 $200 $190 $180 $165 $155
Extra barrels (14 available) without vent rib — $155, or with vent rib — $175.

Grading	100%	98%	95%	90%	80%	70%	60%

Armour Alloy Vent Rib — .45/.410 internal choke, has Armour Alloy II satin finish which is harder than stainless steel. New 1986.

	$350	$295	$230				

Last Mfg.'s Sug. Retail was $435.

CONTENDER SUPER — 13 cal.'s available from .22 LR - .45 Win. Mag. (disc.), 14 or 16 in. bull barrel only, special grips, beavertail forearm, adj. sight, 3½ lbs.

Mfg.'s Sug. Retail	$395	$315	$245	$200	$190	$180	$165	$155

Add $5-$10 for 16 in. barrel.

Add approx. $185 per extra barrel.

Add $30 for 16 in. VR barrel (.45 ACP/.410 ga. only).

Thompson Center will also make special order guns in different cal.'s other than those listed above. If factory work, these pistols will be worth a premium.

Armour Alloy II Super Contender — 5 cal.'s between .22 LR and 7mm, similar to regular Super Contender, except has Armour Alloy II satin finish which is harder than stainless steel. Mfg. 1986-89.

	$355	$295	$240				

Extra Armour Alloy II Bull Barrels were available for $195+.

Last Mfg.'s Sug. Retail was $425.

CONTENDER HUNTER — .223 Rem., 7-30 Waters, .30-30, .35 Rem., .357 Rem. Max., .44 Mag., or .45-70 cal., special 12 in. barrel with muzzle brake, 2.5X power scope with lighted recticle, walnut grip has nonslip rubber insert to cushion recoil, includes studs, swivels, sling, and deluxe carrying case, approx. 4 lbs. New 1990.

Mfg.'s Sug. Retail	$665	$585	$520	$465	$410	$360	$315	$275

RIFLES

CONTENDER CARBINE — available in 14 cal.'s between .22 LR and .44 Rem. Mag., also .410 ga. (3 in.), Contender action with pistol grip full stock and forearm, 21 in. interchangeable barrel, drilled for scope mounts, iron sights standard. New 1986.

Mfg.'s Sug. Retail	$430	$345	$285	$245	$215	$190	$175	$160

Add $30 for .17 Rem. cal.

Add $20 for .410 ga. barrel.

Add approx. $195 per extra barrel.

Subtract $35 for Youth Model (16¼ in. barrel w/o VR).

Rynite Contender Carbine — similar to above, except has Rynite stock and forend. New 1990.

Mfg.'s Sug. Retail	$395	$325	$265	$220	$195	$180	$165	$155

Add $30 for .17 Rem. cal.

Add $25 for 21 in. VR smooth bore .410 ga. barrel.

HUNTER RIFLE MODEL — single shot, top lever break open action w/interchangeable barrels, .22 Hornet, .223, .22-250, .243, .270, 7mm, .30-06, or .308 Win. cal., 23 in. barrel, 6 lbs. 14 oz., checkered walnut stock, choice of medium or light sporter weight barrel. New 1983 and improved in 1987. Available in left-hand at no extra charge.

Mfg.'s Sug. Retail	$550	$475	$390	$340	$295	$265	$240	$220

Hunter Shotgun Model — same action as Hunter Rifle, except is supplied with 12 ga. barrel (field choke with 3½ in. chamber or slug with 3 in. chamber and iron sights) or 10 ga. barrel (3½ in. chamber).

Mfg.'s Sug. Retail	$550	$475	$390	$340	$295	$265	$240	$220

TRC '83 ARISTOCRAT — same as Hunter Model, except stock has cheek piece and forearm is checkered, stainless steel double set triggers. Disc. 1986.

	$425	$370	$345	$320	$300	$280	$260

Add $175 for each additional barrel(s) (including 12 ga. slug).
Last Mfg.'s Sug. Retail was $475.

Grading	100%	98%	95%	90%	80%	70%	60%

TIKKA

Currently manufactured by Armi Marocchi located in Italy. Previously manufactured by Oy Tikkakoski Ab, of Tikkakoski Finland (pre-1989). Currently imported by Stoeger Industries located in South Hackensack, NJ.

Also see listings under Ithaca LSA for older models.

RIFLES: BOLT ACTION

NEW GENERATION RIFLE — .22-250 Rem., .223 Rem., .243 Win., .270 Win., .30-06, .308 Win., 7mm Rem. Mag, .300 Win. Mag., or .338 Win Mag. cal., 22½ (non-Mag.) or 24½ (Mag. cal.'s) in. barrel, detachable 3 (standard) or 5 (optional) shot mag., forged and milled action in two lengths, checkered walnut stock, 7-7 ½ lbs. Sako mfg. began in 1989.

Mfg.'s Sug. Retail	$795	$700	$600	$550	$500	$450	$400	$360

Add $25 for Mag. cal.'s.

Cal.'s .22-250 Rem., .308 Win., and .300 Win. Mag. were introduced in late 1989.

PREMIUM GRADE RIFLE — same cal.'s as New Generation Rifle, stock is select walnut with roll-over cheek-piece and rosewood pistol grip cap and forend tip, high polished barrel blue. Importation began 1989.

Mfg.'s Sug. Retail	$980	$830	$715	$600	$550	$500	$450	$400

Add $35 for Mag. cal.'s.

VARMINT RIFLE — .22-250, .223, .243 Win., or .308 Win. cal., 24½ in. heavy barrel, no sights. New in 1991.

Mfg.'s Sug. Retail	$1,035	$860	$725	$610	$550	$500	$450	$400

WHITETAIL/BATTUE RIFLE — .270 Win., .30-06, .308 Win., 7mm Rem. Mag., .300 Win. Mag., or .338 Win. Mag. cal., 20½ in. barrel, open sights on raised rib. New in 1991.

Mfg.'s Sug. Retail	$820	$715	$615	$560	$500	$450	$400	$360

Add $30 for Mag. cal.'s.

O/U COMBINATIONS (MODEL 412S)

Previously manufactured in Jyvaskyla, Finland. In 1989, under a joint venture agreement made in Italy, the 412 O/U shooting system is now being manufactured in Italy. Older models may be found in the Valmet trademark section of this text.

When current inventory levels are depleted, the Model 412 will no longer be imported.

MODEL 412S O/U SHOOTING SYSTEM — interchangeable barrel assemblies permit a double rifle, shotgun/rifle, and O&U shotgun configuration, user installed interchangeable barrels, monobloc locking, rifle barrel positioning by adjustment, SST, extractors or ejectors, checkered walnut stock and forend, cocking indicators, blued finish.

Model 412S Field Grade — 12 ga. only, 3 in. chambers, auto ejectors, screw-in choke tubes (includes 5), 26 or 28 in. barrels, matte nickel finish. New 1986.

Mfg.'s Sug. Retail	$1,060	$895	$695	$580	$540	$475	$440	$400

Model 412ST Trap — 12 ga., Monte Carlo stock, 30 in. barrels, screw-in chokes standard.

Mfg.'s Sug. Retail	$1,325	$1,125	$925	$725	$650	$580	$540	$475

This variation was made by Valmet in Finland and only small quantities remain.

Model 412ST Premium Grade Trap — similar to Model 412ST Trap, except has better walnut and checkering.

Mfg.'s Sug. Retail	$1,665	$1,425	$1,000	$875	$750	$625	$580	$515

This variation was made by Valmet in Finland and only small quantities remain.

Model 412S Combination Gun — combination rifle/shotgun, 12 ga, 3 in. chambers, 24 in. barrels, under rifle barrel has choice of .222 or .308 cal., extractors.

Mfg.'s Sug. Retail	$1,195	$1,030	$875	$700	$600	$550	$475	$440

Model 412S Double Rifle — 9.3 x 74R cal., 24 in. barrels, extractors.

Mfg.'s Sug. Retail	$1,365	$1,095	$925	$775	$700	$625	$550	$475

Grading	100%	98%	95%	90%	80%	70%	60%

Extra Barrel Assemblies (Model 412S O/U) — $600 each for shotgun (includes screw-in chokes), $685 each for shotgun/rifle combo, $755 each for double rifle.

TIPPMAN ARMS CO.
Previous manufacturer located in Fort Wayne, IN.

Tippman Arms manufactured 1/2 scale semi-auto working models of famous machine guns. All models were available with an optional hardwood case, extra ammo cans, and other accessories. Mfg. 1986-1987 only.

MODEL 1919 A-4 — .22 LR only, copy of Browning 1919 A-4 Model, belt fed, closed bolt operation, 11 in. barrel, includes tripod, 10 lbs.

	100%	98%	95%	90%	80%	70%	60%
	$1,195	$1,045	$950	$870	$800	$750	$695

Last Mfg.'s Sug. Retail was $1,325.

MODEL 1917 — .22 LR only, copy of Browning M1917, watercooled, belt fed, closed bolt operation, 11 in. barrel, includes tripod, 10 lbs.

	100%	98%	95%	90%	80%	70%	60%
	$1,650	$1,445	$1,285	$1,140	$995	$895	$795

Last Mfg.'s Sug. Retail was $1,830.

MODEL .50 HB — .22 Mag. only, copy of Browning .50 cal. machine gun, belt fed, closed bolt operation, 18¼ in. barrel, includes tripod, 13 lbs.

	100%	98%	95%	90%	80%	70%	60%
	$1,750	$1,525	$1,350	$1,200	$1,050	$950	$850

Last Mfg.'s Sug. Retail was $1,929.

TOKAREV
See Russian Military heading.

TRADEWINDS
Tacoma, WA Importers.

HUSKY MODEL 5000 — .22-250, .243, .270, .308, or .30-06 cal., bolt action, 23¾ in. barrel, adj. sight, removable mag., hand checkered walnut stock.

	100%	98%	95%	90%	80%	70%	60%
	$325	$310	$290	$250	$225	$200	$175

MODEL 311-A — .22 LR, bolt action, 5 shot, 22½ in. barrel, folding leaf rear sight, walnut checkered stock.

	100%	98%	95%	90%	80%	70%	60%
	$180	$170	$150	$130	$120	$100	$85

MODEL 260-A — .22 LR, semi-auto, 5 shot, 22½ in. barrel, 3 leaf folding sight, checkered walnut stock.

	100%	98%	95%	90%	80%	70%	60%
	$200	$190	$175	$150	$130	$120	$100

MODEL H-170 — 12 ga., auto shotgun, 2¾ in. chamber, 26 in. mod. or 28 in. full, recoil operated action, alloy receiver, 5 shot, tube mag., vent rib, checkered walnut stock.

	100%	98%	95%	90%	80%	70%	60%
	$275	$265	$250	$225	$200	$180	$150

USAS 12

Currently manufactured in Nashville, TN beginning Oct. 1989. Designed and distributed in the U.S by Gilbert Equipment Co., Inc. located in Mobile, AL. Previously manufactured under license by Daewoo Precision Industries, Ltd. located in South Korea.

Grading	100%	98%	95%	90%	80%	70%	60%

USAS 12 — 12 ga. only, gas operated action available in either semi or fully auto versions, 18¼ in. cylinder bore barrel, synthetic stock, pistol grip, and forearm, carrying handle, 10 round box or 20 drum mag., 2¾ in. chamber only, parkerized finish, 12 lbs. New 1987.

Mfg.'s Sug. Retail	$1,100	$995	$875	$750	$675	$600	$550	$495

Values above are for a semi-auto model. Add $50 for fully auto version (Class III only). This model previously has been saleable to military or law enforcement agencies because of BATF rulings. Potential manufacture in the U.S. would allow this gun to be owned by individual citizens.

U.S. ARMS COMPANY

Previous manufacturer located in Riverhead, NY.

REVOLVERS: SINGLE ACTION

ABILENE .357 MAG. — 6 shot, 4⅝, 5½, or 6½ in. barrel, adj. sights, transfer bar ignition, smooth walnut grips, blue finish only. Mfg. 1976-1983.

	$275	$240	$200	$185	$170	$155	$140

ABILENE .357 MAG. STAINLESS STEEL — same as Abilene, only in stainless steel.

	$325	$275	$225

ABILENE .44 MAG. — 7½ and 8½ in. barrel, unfluted cylinder blue finish only, otherwise similar to .357 Mag.

	$325	$265	$240	$220	$200	$165	$150

ABILENE .44 MAG. STAINLESS STEEL — same as Abilene .44 Mag., only stainless steel.

	$375	$330	$290

UBERTI USA, INC.

Importer and distributor located in Lakeville, CT. Both Black Powder and Modern firearms are imported by Uberti Usa, Inc. and are manufactured by Aldo Uberti of Ponte Zanano, Italy.

A. Uberti also manufactures firearms for Cimarron Arms which are marked differently from those firearms imported by Uberti USA, Inc. These firearms can be located under the "Cimarron Arms" heading in this text.

REVOLVERS & CARBINES: SINGLE ACTION REPRODUCTIONS

These guns can be ordered with either black powder or modern configured frames. Factory engraving and other embellishments can be special ordered by contacting the importer directly.

Add $490 for standard engraving pattern on Cattleman variations.

Grading	100%	98%	95%	90%	80%	70%	60%

CATTLEMAN VARIATIONS — available in .45 LC, .44-40, .44 S&W Spl. (new 1989), .38-40 (new 1989) .38 Spl., .357 Mag., .32-20 (new 1989), .22 LR, or .22 Mag cal., 4¾, 5½, and 7½ in. barrel lengths, brass or steel backstraps and trigger guard.

Quick Draw Model

Mfg.'s Sug. Retail	$350	$310	$240	$195	$175	$160	$150	$135

Add $49 for steel backstrap and trigger guard.

Add $64 for stainless steel construction (disc. 1989).

Sheriff's Model — .44-40 or .45 LC cal., 3 in. barrel, brass backstrap.

Mfg.'s Sug. Retail	$350	$310	$245	$200	$180	$165	$155	$145

Add $49 for steel backstrap and trigger guard.

Target Model — same as standard Cattleman model, only fully adj. rear blade sight, brass backstrap. Imortation disc. 1990.

	$315	$245	$200	$185	$170	$150	$135

Add $25 for steel backstrap and trigger guard.

Add $60 for stainless steel construction (disc.).

Last Mfg.'s Sug. Retail was $335.

CATTLEMAN BUNTLINE — .45 LC or .357 Mag. cal., 18 in. barrel, brass backstrap cut for shoulder stock. Importation disc. 1989.

	$335	$250	$210	$185	$175	$165	$150

Add $23 for target sights.

Add $23 for steel backstrap and trigger guard.

Last Mfg.'s Sug. Retail was $360.

Buntline Carbine — similar cal.'s as Cattleman Buntline, 18 in. barrel, includes non-detachable shoulder stock with brass hardware and lanyard ring. Importation disc. 1989.

	$415	$285	$230	$200	$185	$180	$175

Add $34 for target sights.

Add $34 for .22 LR/.22 Mag. combo.

Add $122 for detachable shoulder stock.

Last Mfg.'s Sug. Retail was $440.

BUCKHORN — .44 Mag., .44 Spl., or .44-40 cal., various barrel lengths, brass backstap, Buntline and revolving carbine models also available in the Buckhorn series — add approx. $32.

Quick Draw Model — importation disc. 1989.

	$300	$210	$205	$190	$180	$170	$160

Add $30 for steel backstrap and trigger guard.

Add $30 for convertible cylinder.

Add $30 for Target Model.

Last Mfg.'s Sug. Retail was $337.

Buckhorn Carbine — .44-40 or .44 Mag. cal., 18 in. barrel, includes non-detachable shoulder stock with brass hardware and lanyard ring. Importation disc. 1989.

	$360	$285	$230	$200	$185	$180	$175

Add $34 for target sights.

Add $38 for extra .44-40 cylinder combo.

Add $122 for detachable shoulder stock.

Last Mfg.'s Sug. Retail was $450.

STALLION 1873 COLT — .22 LR/.22 Mag. combo only, 4¾, 5½, or 6½ in. barrel, case hardened frame, 1-piece walnut grip, 2.4 lbs. Importation disc. 1989.

	$300	$210	$195	$170	$155	$140	$120

Add $27 for steel backstrap and trigger guard.

Add $26 for Target Model.

Last Mfg.'s Sug. Retail was $325.

Stainless Stallion — similar to standard Stallion, except is stainless steel. Importation disc. 1989.

	$370	$275	$225	$200	$185	$180	$175

Last Mfg.'s Sug. Retail was $425.

Grading	100%	98%	95%	90%	80%	70%	60%

"OUTLAW" 1875 REMINGTON — available in .45 LC, .44-40, or .357 Mag. cal., 7½ barrel.

Mfg.'s Sug. Retail	$355	$315	$235	$200	$170	$155	$140	$120

Add $40 for nickel plating (disc.).

Model 1875 Carbine — same cal.'s as Outlaw 1875, 18 in. barrel, includes non-detachable shoulder stock with brass hardware and lanyard ring. Importation disc. 1989.

	$425	$285	$230	$200	$185	$180	$175

Add $110 for nickel plating.
Last Mfg.'s Sug. Retail was $440.

1890 REMINGTON — available in .45 LC, .44-40, or .357 Mag. cal., 5½ barrel.

Mfg.'s Sug. Retail	$375	$330	$245	$205	$175	$155	$140	$120

Add $40 for nickel plating (disc.).

PHANTOM MODEL — .357 or .44 Mag. only, 10½ in. barrel for silhouette use. Imported 1985-89.

	$475	$395	$325	$290	$260	$230	$215

Last Mfg.'s Sug. Retail was $509.

REVOLVERS: DOUBLE ACTION

INSPECTOR MODEL — .32 S&W or .38 Sp. cal., 3, 4, or 6 in. barrels, double action, blued or chrome finish. Imported 1985-89.

	$390	$295	$245	$210	$170	$145	$125

Add $35 for target sights.
Add $25 for chrome plating.
Last Mfg.'s Sug. Retail was $406.

TARGET PISTOLS

1871 ROLLING BLOCK TARGET PISTOL — available in .22 LR, .22 Mag., or .22 Hornet, or .357 Mag. cal., 9½ in. barrel.

Mfg.'s Sug. Retail	$370	$320	$235	$195	$160	$140	$120	$100

Add $60 for carbine model (22 in. barrel).

RIFLES: REPRODUCTIONS

HENRY RIFLE/CARBINE — .44-40 cal., brass frame, 24½ in. barrel on rifle, 22½ in. barrel on carbine.

Mfg.'s Sug. Retail	$899	$810	$625	$515	$425	$360	$320	$260

The carbine was disc. in 1989.

Can also be special ordered with Grade A engraving ($234 extra), Grade B engraving ($412 extra), and Grade 3 (C) engraving ($635 extra). Standard production engraving in 1991 retails for $623.

Henry Trapper — similar to above, except has 16½ or 18½ in. barrel. Importation began 1990.

Mfg.'s Sug. Retail	$899	$810	$625	$515	$425	$360	$320	$260

Henry 1 of 1,000 — disc. several years ago, premiums are slightly higher than a C engraved gun.

1866 CARBINE — .44-40, .38 Spl., .22 Mag., or .22 LR cal., brass receiver, 19 in. round barrel. Importation disc. 1989.

	$545	$420	$340	$285	$260	$235	$210

Add $40 for "Indian" model.
Last Mfg.'s Sug. Retail was $587.

1866 Trapper Carbine — .22 LR, .38 Spl., or .44-40 cal., 16 or 18½ in. barrel. Importation disc. 1989.

	$650	$475	$395	$340	$285	$260	$235

Last Mfg.'s Sug. Retail was $686.

Grading		100%	98%	95%	90%	80%	70%	60%
1866 Yellowboy Indian Carbine — .22 LR, .22 Mag., .38 Spl., or .44-40 cal., 19 in. barrel.								
Mfg.'s Sug. Retail	$685	$615	$500	$415	$360	$310	$275	$240
Subtract $20 without brass tacks.								
Red Cloud Commemorative Carbine — same cal.'s, special engraving and brass tacks in forearm and stock. Importation disc. 1989.								
		$625	$475	$385	$310	$275	$240	$220
Last Mfg.'s Sug. Retail was $660.								
1866 RIFLE — brass receiver, same cal.'s as the carbine, 24¼ in. octagonal barrel.								
Mfg.'s Sug. Retail	$750	$685	$560	$475	$385	$300	$260	$235
Add $420 for standard engraving.								
1866 Yellowboy Indian Rifle — .22 LR, .22 Mag., .38 Spl., or .44-40 cal., 19 in. barrel. Importation disc. 1989.								
		$645	$475	$385	$310	$275	$240	$220
This model comes without brass tacks.								
Last Mfg.'s Sug. Retail was $675.								
1873 CARBINE — .22 LR, .22 Mag., .357 Mag., .38 Spl. or .44-40 cal., steel receiver, 19 in. round barrel.								
Mfg.'s Sug. Retail	$850	$775	$585	$495	$425	$360	$320	$280
Add $95 for nickel plating (disc.).								
1873 Trapper Carbine — .44-40 cal. only, 16⅛ in. barrel. Importation disc. 1990.								
		$695	$550	$475	$400	$360	$320	$280
Last Mfg.'s Sug. Retail was $750.								
1873 RIFLE — case hardened receiver, same cal.'s as the carbine, except also avail. in .45 LC, 20 (new 1990), 24¼, or 30 (new 1990) in. octagonal barrel.								
Mfg.'s Sug. Retail	$899	$810	$625	$515	$425	$360	$320	$260
Add $46 for 30 in. long barrel.								
Add $455 for standard engraving.								
Add $980 for "1 of 1,000" engraving pattern.								
This model with a 20 or 30 in. barrel is available in .44-40 cal. only.								

UGARTECHEA, IGNACIO

Manufacturer located in Eibar, Spain.

Ugartechea manufactures side-by-side shotguns that to date, have had limited and non-exclusive importation into the U.S. For further information (including 1990 retail prices and model descriptions), please contact the manufacturer directly (refer to their listing in the Trademark Index in the back of this text) or the Blue Book of Gun Values.

ULTIMATE

Please refer to Camex-Blaser USA in the C section of this text.

ULTRA LIGHT ARMS, INC.

Manufacturer located in Granville, WV.

RIFLES: BOLT ACTION

ULTRA LIGHT RIFLE — caliber to customer spec.'s, various actions, stock 2 position lever safety, Timney trigger, Douglas 22 or 24 in. barrel, no sights, graphite reinforced stock with recoil pad, matte finish standard, other finishes at extra cost. Many special order features and services are available on these models - contact the manufacturer for prices, 4¾-5¾ lbs. New 1986.

Model 20 — 18 cal.'s available, short action, Kevlar stock.								
Mfg.'s Sug. Retail	$2,400	$2,150	$1,650	$1,225	$950	$800	$700	$640
Add $100 for left-hand action.								

Grading	100%	98%	95%	90%	80%	70%	60%

Model 24 — .25-06, .270 Win., .30-06, and 7mm Exp. cal.'s, long action, Kevlar stock.

	100%	98%	95%	90%	80%	70%	60%
Mfg.'s Sug. Retail	$2,500	$2,250	$1,750	$1,300	$995	$825	$700	$640

Add $100 for left-hand action.

Model 28 Magnum — .264 Win. Mag., .300 Win. Mag., .338 Win. Mag., or 7mm Rem. Mag. cal., Kevlar stock.

	100%	98%	95%	90%	80%	70%	60%
Mfg.'s Sug. Retail	$2,900	$2,625	$1,975	$1,550	$1,225	$950	$700	$600

Add $85 for left-hand action.

PISTOLS: BOLT-ACTION

MODEL 20 HUNTERS PISTOL — various cal.'s, 14 in. Douglas heavy barrel, 5-shot mag., Kevlar graphite reinforced stock in choice of 4 colors, Timney trigger, left-hand or right-hand bolt, approx. 4 lbs. Mfg. 1987-89.

$1,175	$1,000	$900	$800	$700	$640	$575

Last Mfg.'s Sug. Retail was $1,300.

UNIQUE

Manufacturer located in Hendaye, France. Previously imported by Beeman Precision Arms located in Santa Rosa, CA.

PISTOLS: SEMI-AUTO

KREIGS MODEL L — 7.65mm, 9 shot, 3.2 in. barrel, blue, plastic grips, fixed sights. Mfg. 1940-1945, during German occupation of France, has German acceptance marks.

$325	$250	$220	$200	$180	$160	$140

MODEL RR — post-war commercial version of Kreigsmodell, higher quality finish. Mfg. 1951-disc. Add 15% for .22 LR

$180	$170	$155	$130	$120	$110	$90

MODEL B/CF — 7.65mm, 9 shot, or .380 auto cal., 8 shot, 4 in. barrel, blue, plastic thumbrest grips. Mfg. 1954-disc.

$205	$195	$175	$155	$145	$130	$110

MODEL D6 — .22 LR, 10 shot, 6 in. barrel, adj. sights, blue, plastic grips. Mfg. 1954-disc.

$300	$250	$200	$160	$145	$135	$120

MODEL D2 — same as D6, except 4½ in. barrel.

$300	$250	$200	$160	$145	$135	$120

MODEL L — .22 LR, 10 shot, 7.65mm, 7 shot, and .380 auto, 6 shot, 3.3 in. barrel, fixed sights, steel and alloy frame offered, plastic grips. Mfg. 1955-disc.

$250	$200	$150	$130	$115	$100	$90

MODEL MIKROS POCKET — .22 Short and .25 auto, 6 shot, fixed sights, blue, plastic grips, steel or alloy frame. Mfg. 1957-disc.

$200	$155	$140	$120	$100	$90	$75

MODEL DES/69U STANDARD MATCH — .22 LR, 5 shot mag., 5.9 in. barrel, adj. rear sight, adj. target, stippled stocks, blue finish only. Importation began 1969.

Mfg.'s Sug. Retail	$1,242	$1,125	$995	$875	$750	$625	$500	$450

Add $51 for left-hand model.

MODEL DES/823-U RAPID FIRE MATCH — .22 Short, 5 shot, 6 in. barrel, adj. sight, adj. trigger, adj. walnut target grips, squared barrel assembly, dry fire mechanism. Imported 1974-1988.

$1,100	$850	$725	$625	$550	$490	$445

Add $60 for left-hand model.
Last Mfg.'s Sug. Retail was $1,300.

Grading	100%	98%	95%	90%	80%	70%	60%

MODEL DES/2000-U — .22 LR target pistol, wrap around grips, adj. features. Imported 1986-1988.

	$995	$850	$725	$625	$550	$490	$445

Add $62 for left-hand model.
Last Mfg.'s Sug. Retail was $1,198.

RIFLES

T66 MATCH RIFLE — .22 LR, single shot, bolt action, 25½ in. barrel, micro rear globe front, full target stock. Mfg. 1966-disc.

	$425	$410	$390	$350	$300	$280	$250

MODEL F 11 — .22 LR, military trainer, adj. sights, target walnut stock. Limited importation.

	$560	$435	$350	$285	$260	$240	$220

Last Mfg.'s Sug. Retail was $695.

UNITED SPORTING ARMS, INC.

Previous manufacturer located in Tucson, AZ. Manufacture ceased in early 1986. All the below models were disc. in early 1986.

SEVILLE — .357 Mag., .41 Mag., .44 Mag., or .45 Colt cal., single action revolver, 4⅝, 5½, 6½, or 7½ in. barrels, adj. sights, smooth walnut grips.

	$395	$350	$315	$280	$260	$240	$220

Last Mfg.'s Sug. Retail was $435.
Stainless steel — otherwise same as above.

	$395	$350	$315				

Last Mfg.'s Sug. Retail was $435.
Silver Seville — same as Seville, except has blue barrel, and high polish stainless steel grip frame.

	$425	$370	$330				

Last Mfg.'s Sug. Retail was $460.
Stainless .357 Maxi — available in 5½ or 7½ in. barrel only.

	$575	$475	$395				

Last Mfg.'s Sug. Retail was $465.
Stainless .375 USA — only in 7½ in. barrel.

	$625	$525	$425				

Last Mfg.'s Sug. Retail was $490.
Stainless .454 Mag. — only in 7½ in. barrel, 5 shot.

	$700	$600	$500				

Last Mfg.'s Sug. Retail was $595.

Note: In late 1986, some .454 Mag.'s were made up from parts purchased from the manufacturer. Unfortunately, while the exterior appearance might seem normal, they were not involved with any type of factory quality control program. As a result, shooting these non-factory revolvers could be dangerous, and careful inspection should be made before purchasing/shooting this particular specimen.

Eldorado Stainless— .44 Mag., 10 $1/2 in. barrel, adj. sights.

	$700	$600	$500				

SILVER SEVILLE SILHOUETTE — .357 Mag., .41 Mag., or .44 Mag. cal., single action revolver, 10½ in. barrel, adj. sights, Pachmayr grips, blued barrel finish with stainless grip frame.

	$445	$370	$330	$295	$270	$250	$230

Last Mfg.'s Sug. Retail was $485.
Stainless steel — otherwise same as above.

	$425	$370	$330				

Last Mfg.'s Sug. Retail was $460.

Grading	100%	98%	95%	90%	80%	70%	60%

Stainless .357 Maxi — available in 10½ in. barrel only.

	$575	$475	$395				

Last Mfg.'s Sug. Retail was $480.

Stainless .375 USA — available in 10½ in. barrel only.

	$625	$525	$425				

Last Mfg.'s Sug. Retail was $515.

Stainless .454 Mag. — available in 10½ in. barrel only, 5 shot.

	$700	$600	$500				

Last Mfg.'s Sug. Retail was $620.

Note: In late 1986, some .454 Mag.'s were made up from parts purchased from the manufacturer. Unfortunately, while the exterior appearance might seem normal, they were not involved with any type of factory quality control program. As a result, shooting these non-factory revolvers could be dangerous, and careful inspection should be made before purchasing/shooting this particular specimen.

SHERIFF MODEL — .357 Mag., .38 Spl., .44 Spl., .44 Mag., or .45 Colt cal., single action revolver, 3½ in. barrel, adj. sights, smooth walnut grips.

	$395	$350	$315	$280	$260	$240	$220

Last Mfg.'s Sug. Retail was $435.

Stainless steel — otherwise same as Sheriff Model

	$395	$350	$315				

Last Mfg.'s Sug. Retail was $435.

UNITED STATES HISTORICAL SOCIETY

An organization which markets Historically Significant Firearms Reproductions. Located in Richmond, VA. Most firearms are manufactured by the Williamsburg Firearms Manufactory and the Virginia Firearms Manufactory.

PISTOLS

ANDREW JACKSON

Silver Edition — 2,500 mfg.

	$2,100	$1,750	$1,400

Issue price was $2,100.

Gold Edition — 100 mfg.

	$5,500	$3,995	$2,750

Issue price was $5,500.

PITCAIRN — 900 mfg.

	$2,950	$2,300	$1,750

Issue price was $2,950.

THOMAS JEFFERSON — 1,000 mfg., issue price was $1,900.

	$3,500	$2,750	$1,995

HAMILTON — BURR DUALING PISTOLS — 1,200 mfg., issue price was $2,995 in 1981.

	$3,500	$2,750	$1,995

WASHINGTON AND LEE FLINTLOCK PISTOLS — .69 cal., flintlock pistols with 9¹⁵⁄₁₆ in. barrels, burl walnut stocks with sterling silver fittings, engraved silver plated lock plates, trigger guard, and side plate, firing capability, cased with accessories, limited issue of 1,000 in 1989.

Mfg.'s Sug. Retail	$2,700	$2,700	$2,150	$1,650

GEORGE WASHINGTON — 975 mfg., issue price was $2,500.

	$4,250	$3,400	$2,450

Grading	100%	98%	95%	90%	80%	70%	60%

H. DERINGER PISTOL SET — .41 cal., percussion, reproduction of H. Deringer's famous pistol. Available with sterling silver mounts (1,000 pair manufactured — issue price $1,900), 14Kt. gold mounted (100 pair mfg.-$2,700 issue price), precious gem stone mounted (only 5 pair mfg. — $25,000 issue price). Mfg. 1978.

Silver mounted

$2,500 $1,750 $1,000

14Kt. gold mounted

$7,500 $5,000 $3,000

18Kt. jewel mounted — too limited a supply for price evaluation.

TEXAS PATERSON EDITION — reproduction of the famous Colt folding trigger model mfg. in Paterson, NJ, engraved, cased. 1,000 mfg. starting in 1988. Cased with accessories.

Mfg.'s Sug. Retail $2,500 $2,500 $1,900 $1,450

This model is an exact reproduction of the original Colt Paterson ser. no. 755, Model 5.

SAM HOUSTON WALKER — .44 cal., reproduction of the Colt Walker, 9 in. barrel, extensive gold etching on highly polished blued surface, smooth walnut stocks with S. Houston medallions, cased with accessories. 2,500 mfg.

$2,300 $2,000 $1,575

Issue price was $2,300

TEXAS RANGER DRAGOON — .44 cal., features silver plated cylinder, trigger guard, and gripstraps, color case hardened frame and loading lever, multiple 24 Kt. etchings on barrel and frame front, cased with accessories, 66 oz. 1,000 mfg. in 1990 only.

Mfg.'s Sug. Retail $1,585 $1,585 $1,050 $795

TOWER OF LONDON COL. SAM COLT DRAGOON — .44 cal., exact reproduction of the Second Model Dragoon, 7½ in. barrel, hand engraved, Texas ranger cylinder scene, one piece walnut grip with inscribed sterling silver plaque, casehardened frame, hammer, loading lever and rammer, cased with accessories, limited issue of 1,000 in 1989.

Mfg.'s Sug. Retail $2,450 $2,450 $1,950 $1,500

ROBERT E. LEE MODEL 1851 NAVY — .36 cal. only, reproduction of the 1851 Navy Colt, extensive gold etching, cylinder scene portrays historical Civil War events, walnut stocks with Robert E. Lee medallion, cased with accessories, 41 oz. 2,500 mfg.

$2,400 $1,900 $1,450

Issue price is $2,400.

MONITOR AND VIRGINIA MODEL 1851 NAVY REVOLVER — .44 cal., issued to commemorate the Civil War naval battle between the USS Monitor and Confederate Virginia, features gold etchings on barrel, frame, and Monitor/Virginia battle scene on cylinder, cased, 41 oz. 1.000 mfg. in 1991.

Mfg.'s Sug. Retail $1,250 $1,250 $875 $500

STONEWALL JACKSON MODEL 1851 REVOLVER — .36 cal., reproduction of Colt's Model 1851 Navy, elaborate gold etching on frame and barrel, walnut grip with medallion, cased with sterling medallion and silver plated powder flask. 1988 release. 2,500 total mfg.

Mfg.'s Sug. Retail $2,100 $2,100 $1,650 $1,250

JEFFERSON DAVIS 1851 NAVY REVOLVER — .36 cal., extensive Nimsche style engraving on barrel, loading lever, frame, and trigger, case hardened frame with silver plated brass backstrap and trigger guard, includes engraved, silver plated detachable shoulder stock, cased with accessories, 41 oz. 1,000 mfg. in 1990 only.

Mfg.'s Sug. Retail $2,750 $2,750 $1,850 $1,250

MODEL 1851 U.S. NAVY REVOLVER — .36 cal., 7½ in. octogon barrel, features gold etched cylinder and other embellishments, brass trigger guard and backstrap plated with 24 Kt. gold, 41 oz. 1,000 mfg. in 1988 only.

Mfg.'s Sug. Retail $1,250 $1,250 $875 $500

Grading	100%	98%	95%	90%	80%	70%	60%

U.S. CAVALRY MODEL 1860 ARMY — .44 cal., reproduction of the Colt Model 1860, stag grips, gold etched cylinder scene, cased with brass buckle. 975 manufactured starting in 1988.

Mfg.'s Sug. Retail	$1,450	$1,450	$1,050	$800

FREDERIC REMINGTON MODEL 1860 ARMY REVOLVER — .44 cal., issued to commemorate Frederic Remington's 100th anniversary as an associate of the National Academy of Design, features gold etched barrel, cylinder (with 5 panels), trigger, frame, and gripstraps, cased with accessories, 42 oz. 1,000 mfg. in 1990 only.

Mfg.'s Sug. Retail	$1,500	$1,500	$1,000	$775

BUFFALO BILL CENTENNIAL MODEL 1860 ARMY — .44 cal., reproduction of the Colt Model 1860, bonded ivory stocks, extensive gold etchings portraying various wild west scenes, bonded ivory powder flask, brass accessories, cased. 2,500 mfg. 1983.

	$1,950	$1,450	$1,100

Issue price is $1,950.

SECRET SERVICE MUSEUM EDITION — 500 mfg. starting 1988.

Mfg.'s Sug. Retail	$2,750	$2,750	$2,000	$1,600

Secret Service Investigator's Edition — 1,000 mfg. starting 1988.

Mfg.'s Sug. Retail	$1,250	$1,250	$875	$500

ROY ROGERS COWBOY EDITION SAA — .45 LC, SAA revolver, 4¾ in. barrel, features gold plated cylinder and other 24 Kt. etchings on barrel, frame and gripstrap, hand fitted stag grips, made to commemoratate Roy Rogers 50th Anniversary (1940-1990), cased. 2,500 mfg. in 1990 only.

Mfg.'s Sug. Retail	$1,350	$1,350	$900	$550

Roy Premier Edition SAA — similar to Cowboy Edition, except has elaborate inlays and engraving. 250 mfg. in 1990 only.

Mfg.'s Sug. Retail	$4,500	$4,500	$2,950	$1,750

MINIATURE REVOLVER SERIES

1847 WALKER PRESIDENTIAL EDITION — miniature reproduction of 1847 Colt Walker, color case hardened receiver, all parts operational, sterling silver grips, full coverage engraving, cased. 1,500 mfg. starting 1990.

Mfg.'s Sug. Retail	$1,575	$1,575	$1,100	$825

1847 Walker Classic Edition — similar to Presidential Edition, except has walnut grips and frame is not engraved, cased. 1,500 mfg. starting 1990.

Mfg.'s Sug. Retail	$625	$625	$450	$325

1851 NAVY PRESIDENTIAL EDITION — miniature reproduction of 1851 Navy Colt, color case hardened receiver, all parts operational, mother-of-pearl grips, full coverage engraving, cased. 1,500 mfg. starting 1988.

Mfg.'s Sug. Retail	$1,575	$1,575	$1,100	$825

1851 Classic Edition — similar to Presidential Edition, except has walnut grips and cylinder is roll-engraved, cased. 3,500 mfg. starting 1986.

Mfg.'s Sug. Retail	$525	$525	$400	$295

1860 ARMY PRESIDENTIAL EDITION — miniature reproduction of 1860 Army Colt, color case hardened engraved receiver and barrel, roll-engraved cylinder scene, all parts operational, ivory grips, cherry cased. 1,500 mfg. starting 1988.

Mfg.'s Sug. Retail	$1,575	$1,575	$1,200	$875

1860 Classic Edition — similar to Presidential Edition without engraving, except has rosewood grips, cased. 3,500 mfg. starting 1988.

Mfg.'s Sug. Retail	$525	$525	$400	$295

1861 NAVY PRESIDENTIAL EDITION — miniature reproduction of 1861 Navy Colt, color case hardened engraved receiver and barrel, roll-engraved cylinder scene, all parts operational, includes detachable shoulder stock, cased. 1,500 mfg. starting 1990.

Mfg.'s Sug. Retail	$1,500	$1,500	$1,150	$850

Grading	100%	98%	95%	90%	80%	70%	60%

1861 Navy Classic Edition — similar to Presidential Edition without engraving, cased. 1,500 mfg. starting 1990.

Mfg.'s Sug. Retail	$625	$625	$450	$350			

SA ARMY PRESIDENTIAL EDITION — miniature reproduction of 1873 SAA Colt, nickel plated receiver and barrel with scroll engraving, gold plated cylinder, hammer, trigger, and ejector rod housing, one piece ivory grips, cherry cased. 1,500 mfg. starting 1988.

Mfg.'s Sug. Retail	$1,550	$1,550	$1,100	$825			

This miniature is an exact replica of Serial No. 114 SAA (earliest known gold engraved SAA). All features are the same, only on a miniature basis.

SA Army Classic Edition — similar to Presidential Edition without engraving, except has color case hardened receiver and blued metal parts, one piece rosewood grips. 1,500 mfg. starting 1988.

Mfg.'s Sug. Retail	$575	$575	$425	$300			

The Classic Edition is miniaturized, exact reproduction of Colt Serial No. 1 (includes pinched frame, slanted barrel address marking, donut ejector rod head, knurled hammer spur, etc.). All are serial numbered 1.

SHOTGUNS

CHUCK YEAGER SHOTGUN — 12 ga. only, O/U boxlock action with engraved silver finished sideplates depicting Gen. Yeager and his P-51 Mustang, SST, 28 in. VR barrels with choke tubes, cased with accessories. 100 mfg. in 1989 only.

Mfg.'s Sug. Retail	$12,500	$12,500	$9,000	$6,250			

This model was mfg. by Bertuzzi located in Brescia, Italy. Over 120 hours were required to engrave each gun.

ARNOLD PALMER SHOTGUN — 20 ga., SxS boxlock with engraved sideplates depicting Arnold Palmer in 24 Kt. gold as well as other inlays, 26 in. barrels, 6 lbs. 6 oz. 100 mfg. in 1990 only.

Mfg.'s Sug. Retail	$9,750	$9,750	$6,250	$3,995			

UNIVERSAL FIREARMS

Universal Firearms became a division of Iver Johnson's Arms, Inc. in 1982. Formerly imported out of Hialeah, FL. Currently manufactured in Jacksonville, AR.

RIFLES: SEMI-AUTO CARBINE

1000 MILITARY — .30 cal., "G.I." copy, satin blue, birch stock, 18 in. barrel. Disc.

	$229	$180	$170	$160	$150	$135	$125

MODEL 1003 — 16, 18, or 20 in. barrel, .30 M1 copy, blued finish, adj. sight, birch stock, 5½ lbs. Add $45 for 4X scope. See current listing under Iver Johnson. Disc.

	$180	$160	$140	$120	$110	$100	$85

Last Mfg.'s Sug. Retail was $203.

Model 1010 — nickel finish, disc.

	$299	$265	$240	$210	$180	$155	$120

Model 1015 — gold electroplated, disc.

	$325	$275	$250	$215	$185	$160	$130

1005 DELUXE — .30 cal., custom Monte Carlo walnut stock, high polish blue, oil finish on wood.

	$246	$200	$180	$170	$150	$140	$130

1006 STAINLESS — .30 cal., stainless steel construction, birch stock, 18 in. barrel, 6 lbs. Disc.

	$205	$190	$170				

Last Mfg.'s Sug. Retail was $234.

1020 TEFLON — .30 cal., Dupont Teflon-S finish on metal parts, black or grey color, Monte Carlo stock.

	$279	$259	$240				

Grading	100%	98%	95%	90%	80%	70%	60%

1256 "FERRET" — .256 Win. Mag. cal., M1 Action, satin blue, birch stock, 18 in. barrel, 5½ lbs. Disc.

	$200	$175	$165	$155	$145	$135	$125

Last Mfg.'s Sug. Retail was $219.

2200 LEATHERNECK — .22 cal., recoil operated action, birch stock, satin blue, 18 in. barrel, 5½ lbs.

	$240	$190	$180	$170	$160	$145	$135

MODEL 3000 ENFORCER PISTOL — 11¼ in. barrel, .30 M1 Carbine, walnut stock, 17¾ in. overall, 15, and 30 shot. Mfg. 1964-1983. Add $50 for Teflon-S finish. See current listing under Iver Johnson.

	100%	98%	95%	90%	80%	70%	60%
Blued finish	$235	$200	$185	$170	$160	$150	$140
Nickel plated	$289	$235	$220	$200	$185	$165	$145
Gold plated	$328	$235	$220	$200	$185	$165	$145
Stainless	$312	$280	$260				

5000 PARATROOPER — .30 cal., metal folding extension, walnut stock, 16 or 18 in. barrel. Disc. See current listing under Iver Johnson.

	$215	$185	$170	$160	$150	$140	$130

Last Mfg.'s Sug. Retail was $234.

5006 PARATROOPER STAINLESS — same as 5000, only stainless with 18 in. barrel only. Disc.

	$255	$235	$205

Last Mfg.'s Sug. Retail was $281.

1981 COMMEMORATIVE CARBINE — .30 cal., "G.I Military" model, cased with accessories. Mfg. for 40th Anniversary 1941-1981.

	$650	$490	$400

SHOTGUNS

All Universal shotguns were disc. after 1982.

MODEL 7312 O/U — 12 ga., 30 in. full and mod., vent rib barrel, boxlock, vent barrel spacer, SST, auto ejectors, barrels ported to reduce recoil, engraved, color case hardened receiver, trap or skeet style, checkered select stock.

	$1,650	$1,540	$1,485	$1,430	$1,320	$1,210	$1,045

MODEL 7412 O/U — similar to 7312, without ejectors, blue and silver receiver.

	$1,430	$1,210	$1,155	$1,100	$9,900	$880	$825

MODEL 7712 O/U — 12 ga., 26 or 28 in. barrel, vent rib, non-selective single trigger, extractors, light engraving, checkered pistol grip stock.

	$440	$415	$385	$360	$330	$275	$220

MODEL 7812 O/U — same as 7712, with auto ejectors and more engraving.

	$605	$580	$550	$525	$470	$415	$385

MODEL 7912 O/U — same as 7812, with selective single trigger and gold damascene engraving.

	$1,210	$1,155	$1,100	$1,045	$965	$880	$825

MODEL 7112 DOUBLE BARREL — 12 ga., 26 or 28 in. barrels, various chokes, boxlock, extractors, engraved case hardened frame, checkered pistol grip stock.

	$330	$305	$275	$250	$195	$165	$140

DOUBLE WING — 10, 12, 20, or .410 ga., 26, 28, or 30 in. barrels, various chokes, double triggers, boxlock, extractors, checkered pistol grip stock.

	$330	$305	$275	$250	$195	$165	$140
10 gauge.	$385	$360	$330	$305	$250	$220	$165

Grading	100%	98%	95%	90%	80%	70%	60%

MODEL 7212 SINGLE BARREL TRAP — 12 ga., 30 in. full, Simmons type vent rib, engraved case colored frame, vent barrel to reduce recoil, boxlock, auto ejector, select checkered trap style stock.

	100%	98%	95%	90%	80%	70%	60%
	$1,100	$990	$935	$880	$770	$715	$605

U.S. MILITARY
See listings under Colt, Springfield Armory, and Winchester.

U.S. M1 CARBINE
Various makers.

U.S. M1 CARBINE — semi-auto, .30 cal., 18 in. barrel, 15 or 30 shot box mag., wood stocked, two or four position aperture rear, blade front sight with protective ears, with or without bayonet lug. This weapon was designed by Winchester for the U.S. government, over 6 million were produced by 10 different companies. It is a gas operated lightweight carbine that was also used by other countries' armed forces. Makers and values as follows. Values are for original, unmodified carbines, with proper parts makers and stock cartouches. Deduct 10% - 20% if modified for bayonet or adj. rear sight.

Values below are for original mfg. only, not recent imports.

	100%	98%	95%	90%	80%	70%	60%
Underwood	$575	$495	$450	$400	$350	$300	$275
S.G. Saginaw	$575	$495	$450	$400	$350	$300	$275
Quality Hardware	$595	$525	$465	$415	$370	$325	$295
Nat'l Postal Meter	$595	$525	$465	$415	$370	$325	$295
IBM	$595	$525	$465	$415	$370	$325	$295
Standard Products	$595	$525	$465	$415	$370	$325	$295
Inland	$575	$495	$450	$400	$350	$300	$275
SG Grand Rapids	$650	$575	$500	$435	$375	$340	$310
Winchester	$675	$595	$525	$450	$400	$350	$325
Irwin Pedersen	$1,100	$925	$800	$760	$700	$640	$580
Rockola	$600	$540	$485	$430	$395	$340	$300
Plainfield	$775	$675	$550	$450	$395	$360	$330

M1 A1 PARATROOPER CARBINE — .30 cal., mfg. by Inland — WWII production, folding stock, crossed cannon proofed on bottom, 110,000 mfg. between 1942-1945. Stock folds to 26½ in. overall.

	100%	98%	95%	90%	80%	70%	60%
	$675	$600	$525	$450	$400	$350	$300

M1 GARAND — .30-06 cal., semi-auto, 8 shot en bloc clip fed, gas operated, adj. aperture sight, wooden stock. Made 1937-1957 by Springfield, Winchester, H&R, and International Harvester. Add 10% for WWII date, deduct 40% if rewelded, 20% if mismatched.

	100%	98%	95%	90%	80%	70%	60%
	$850	$700	$525	$475	$430	$400	$375

M1-C or M1-D Sniper — with scope and mounts (be wary of fakes and rewelds).

	100%	98%	95%	90%	80%	70%	60%
	$1,650	$1,455	$1,200	$1,060	$900	$780	$650

M1 NATIONAL MATCH — target version of the Garand, using National Match barrel and sights, glass bedding, etc. Should have serialized N.M. paperwork for premium.

	100%	98%	95%	90%	80%	70%	60%
	$1,250	$1,000	$900	$700	$500	$460	$425

U.S. MODEL 1917 ENFIELD RIFLE — .30-06, bolt action, 5 shot, 26 in. barrel, adj. sights, military stock, derived from English P14 Enfield, over two million produced in 1917 and 1918.

	100%	98%	95%	90%	80%	70%	60%
	$450	$400	$350	$300	$275	$250	$225

Grading	100%	98%	95%	90%	80%	70%	60%

UZI

Manufactured by Israel Military Industries (IMI). Currently imported by Action Arms, Ltd., located in Philadelphia, PA, and Springfield Armory, Inc. located in Geneseo, IL.

Serial number prefixes used on Uzi Firearms are as follows: "SA" on all 9mm Para. semi-auto carbines Models A and B; "45 SA" on all .45 ACP Model B carbines; "41 SA" on all .41 AE Model B carbines; "MC" on all 9mm (only cal. made) semi-auto mini-carbines; "UP" on all 9mm Para. semi-auto Uzi pistols; "45 UP" on all .45 semi-auto Uzi pistols (disc. 1989). There are also prototypes or experimental Uzi's with either "AA" or "AAL" prefixes - these are rare and will command premiums over values listed below.

UZI CARBINE MODEL A — 9mm Para., semi-auto, 16.1 in. barrel, parkerized finish, mfg. by IMI 1980-1983 and serial range is SA01001-SA037000.

	$1,050	$950	$825	$725	$650	$600	$550

Approx. 100 Model A's were mfg. with a nickel finish. These are rare and command considerable premiums over values listed above.

UZI CARBINE MODEL B — 9mm, .41 Action Express (new 1987), or .45 ACP (new 1987) cal., semi-auto carbine, 16.1 in. barrel, parkerized finish, 20, 25, 32 shot clip or 50 shot snail drum mag. (9mm), metal folding stock, includes molded case and carrying sling, 8.4 lbs. Mfg. 1983 - until Federal legislation disc. importation 1989 and serial range is 037001-SA073544.

	$925	$875	$825	$725	$650	$600	$550

Last Mfg.'s Sug. Retail was $698.
Add $150 for .22 cal. conversion kit (new 1987).
Add $215 for .45 ACP to 9mm/.41 AE conversion kit.
Add $150 for 9mm to .41 AE (or vice-versa) conversion kit.
Add $215 for 9mm to .45 ACP conversion kit.

UZI MINI-CARBINE 1 — 9mm or .45 ACP cal., similar to Carbine except has 19¾ in. barrel, swing-away metal stock, scaled down version of the regular carbine, 7.2 lbs. New 1987. Federal legislation disc. importation 1989.

	$1,050	$950	$825	$725	$650	$600	$550

Last Mfg.'s Sug. Retail was $698.

UZI PISTOL — 9mm or .45 ACP cal. (disc.), semi-auto pistol, 4½ in. barrel, parkerized finish, 20 shot mag., 3.8 lbs., supplied with molded carrying case.

Mfg.'s Sug. Retail	$585	$500	$425	$390	$360	$330	$300	$280

Add $285 for .45 ACP to 9mm/.41 AE conversion kit.
Add $100 for 9mm to .41 AE conversion kit.

NOTES

VALMET, INC.

Manufacturer located in Jyvaskyla, Finland. Previously imported by Stoeger Industries, Inc. located in South Hackensack, NJ.

The Valmet line was discontinued in 1989 and replaced by Tikka (please refer to the Tikka section in this text) in 1990. All models below have been discontinued and values reflect older mfg.

Grading	100%	98%	95%	90%	80%	70%	60%

LION O/U SHOTGUN — 12 ga., 26, 28, or 30 in. barrels, various chokes, boxlock, SST, checkered stock. Mfg. 1947-1968.

| | $415 | $370 | $340 | $320 | $305 | $275 | $240 |

M-62S PARAMILITARY DESIGN RIFLE — semi-auto version of Finn M-62, 7.62 x 39 Russian, 15 or 30 shot mag., 16⅝ in. barrel, gas operated, rotary bolt, adj. rear sight, tube steel or wood stock. Mfg. 1962-disc.

| | $770 | $715 | $635 | $605 | $550 | $530 | $495 |

Add $50 for wood stock.

M-715 — same as M-625, except .223, reinforced resin or wood stock.

| | $635 | $550 | $415 | $385 | $370 | $340 | $325 |

Add $50 for wood stock.

PRE-1989 MFG.

MODEL 412 O/U SHOOTING SYSTEM — interchangeable barrel assemblies permit a double rifle, shotgun/rifle, and O&U shotgun configuration, user installed interchangeable barrels, monobloc locking, rifle barrel positioning by adjustment, SST, extractors or ejectors checkered walnut stock and forend, cocking indicators, blued finish. Importation on all models was disc. 1989.

Add $100 for synthetic stock on all 412 models.

Model 412S Field Grade — 12 ga. only, auto ejectors, screw-in choke tubes, matte nickel finish. New 1986.

| | $855 | $670 | $580 | $540 | $475 | $440 | $400 |

Last Mfg.'s Sug. Retail was $999.

Model 412S Field and Target — 12 ga. only, 2¾ and 3 in. chambers, ejectors. Disc. 1988.

| | $775 | $660 | $580 | $540 | $475 | $440 | $400 |

Last Mfg.'s Sug. Retail was $874.

Model 412ST Trap and Skeet — 12 ga., Monte Carlo stock on Trap model, 28 in. barrels on Skeet model, screw-in chokes standard.

| | $1,040 | $875 | $695 | $650 | $580 | $540 | $475 |

Last Mfg.'s Sug. Retail was $1,215.

Model 412ST Premium Grade Target — similar to Model 412ST Trap and Skeet, except has better walnut and checkering. New 1987.

| | $1,355 | $1,050 | $865 | $750 | $640 | $580 | $515 |

Last Mfg.'s Sug. Retail was $1,550.

Model 412S Combination Gun — combination, 12 ga, 3 in. chamber over choice of .222, .223, .243, .30-06, or .308 cal., extractors.

| | $1,025 | $850 | $675 | $600 | $550 | $475 | $440 |

Last Mfg.'s Sug. Retail was $1,615.

Grading	100%	98%	95%	90%	80%	70%	60%

Model 412S Double Rifle — .243 (disc. 1987), .30-06, .308 (disc. 1987), .375 H&H (disc. 1987), or 9.3 x 73 R cal., extractors, 24 in. barrels.

	$1,060	$895	$725	$650	$580	$540	$475

Add $100 for 9.3 x 74 R cal. or .375 H&H cal.
This model in .30-06 cal. has extractors only while in 9.3 x 74 R cal. ejectors are standard.

Last Mfg.'s Sug. Retail was $1,275.

Model 412K Double Rifle — .30-06 or .308 cal. only, 24 in. separated barrels, extractors. Importation disc. 1986.

	$800	$660	$580	$540	$475	$440	$400

Last Mfg.'s Sug. Retail was $899.

Model 412 Engraved — satin finish, receiver extensively bank note engraved in choice of 4 patterns, select Triple-X wood hand checkered — choice of field or target, available in any Valmet model. Add $85 for shotgun rifle, $320 for double rifle.
This model has limited availability and prices are on request from the manufacturer. Last Mfg.'s Sug. retail was $2,499.

Extra Barrel Assemblies (Model 412 O/U) — $505 - $605 each for shotgun (includes screw-in chokes), $579 each for shotgun/rifle combo, $660 each for double rifle (add $100 for ejectors).

RIFLES

HUNTER MODEL — .223, .243, or .308 cal., gas operated semi-auto, Kalashnikov action, 20½ in. barrel, checkered walnut stock and forearm, matte finished metal, 5, 9, or 20 shot mag., 8 lbs. New 1986, Federal legislation disc. importation 1989.

	$795	$700	$625	$550	$500	$450	$420

Last Mfg.'s Sug. Retail was $795.

MODEL 76 — .223, 7.62 x 39mm, or .308 cal., gas operated semi-auto paramilitary design rifle, 16¾ in. or 20½ (.308 only) in. barrel, 15 or 30 (7.62 x 39mm only) shot mag., parkerized finish. Federal legislation disc. importation 1989.

	$750	$675	$600	$525	$475	$450	$420

Add $95-$125 for synthetic or folding stock.
Last Mfg.'s Sug. Retail was $740.

MODEL 78 — .308 cal. only, similar to Model 76, except has 24½ in. barrel, wood stock and forearm, and barrel bipod, 11 lbs. New 1987. Federal legislation disc. importation 1989.

	$1,100	$925	$800	$700	$600	$530	$475

Last Mfg.'s Sug. Retail was $1,060.

VARNER SPORTING ARMS, INC.
Manufacturer located in Marietta, GA.

VARNER FAVORITE HUNTER — .22 LR, patterned after J. Stevens Favorite Model, ½ round - ½ octagon 21½ in. takedown barrel, blued frame, walnut stock and forearm, aperture rear sight, 5 lbs. New 1988.

Mfg.'s Sug. Retail	$369	$325	$270	$220	$185	$150	$130	$110

Hunter Deluxe — similar to Field Grade, except has case colored frame and lever, and deluxe walnut. New 1988.

Mfg.'s Sug. Retail	$500	$450	$375	$285	$225	$175	$150	$135

Presentation Grade — includes target hammer and trigger, AAA quality checkered stock and forearm, includes takedown case. New 1988.

Mfg.'s Sug. Retail	$569	$480	$400	$310	$250	$195	$170	$155

PRESENTATION ENGRAVED — available in a No. 1 Grade for $649, a No. 2 for $779, or a No. 3 for $1,099.

Grading	100%	98%	95%	90%	80%	70%	60%

VERNEY-CARRON
Ventura Imports.

O/U SHOTGUN — 12 ga., 26 or 28 in. vent rib barrel, boxlock, auto ejectors, SST, choked to specifications, checkered French walnut straight or pistol grip stock. Mfg. 1978-disc.

	100%	98%	95%	90%	80%	70%	60%
	$990	$880	$825	$770	$715	$660	$605

SKEET GUN — 12 ga., same as Field, with 28 in. skeet and skeet barrel, skeet style pistol grip stock.

	100%	98%	95%	90%	80%	70%
	$1,045	$935	$880	$825	$770	$715	$660

VICKERS LIMITED
Manufacturer located in Crayford/Kent, England.

JUBILEE SINGLE SHOT TARGET RIFLE — Martini type action, .22 LR, 28 in. heavy barrel, target sights, one piece pistol grip, target stock, pre-WWII.

	$440	$330	$305	$275	$250	$220	$165

EMPIRE MODEL — similar to Jubilee, with 27 or 30 in. barrel, straight grip stock.

	$415	$310	$285	$260	$220	$195	$150

VICTORY ARMS CO. LIMITED
Manufactured by Victory Arms Co. Limited located in Phoenix, AZ. Distributed by Magnum Research Inc. located in Minneapolis, MN.

PISTOL: SEMI-AUTO

MODEL MC5 — 9mm Para., .38 Super, .40 S&W (new 1991), .41 AE, 10mm, or .45 ACP cal., double action, 4⅜ (standard), 5⅞, or 7½ in. interchangeable barrel, decocking lever, 10 shot mag. in .45 ACP cal. (17 for 9mm/.38 Super, 12 for 41 AE cal.), stippled wooden grips, 3 dot sighting system, 45 oz. empty weight. While advertised in 1989, this model will be released in 1991.

Mfg.'s Sug. Retail	$499	$440	$385	$350	$300	$275	$255	$240

Add $100 per individual barrel.

Add $59 for adj. Millett sights.

Converting this model from 9mm to .38 Super requires a barrel change only - magazines are interchangeable. Converting from .38 cal. to over .40 also requires a different mag. and vise versa.

VIERLINGS
Four Barrel Long Arm Configuration mostly mfg. previously in Germany or Austria.
This configuration of long arm has four barrels, typically with a .22 caliber barrel incorporated in the center rib or stacked below two SxS shotgun barrels and a lower, larger caliber rifle barrel. Vierlings typically have two triggers, both single set. Barrel selectors are usually on the top tang. This unusual configuration is mostly of German mfg., although there are a few Austrian specimens also (the gunmakers of Ferlach still custom make this model). All Vierlings are mfg. one at a time, with fabrication being very complicated, lengthy, and expensive. As a result, every Vierling must be appraised individually - most specimens, however, are priced approx. $2,750-$6,500+.

VIRGINIAN
This trademark can be located under the Interarms section in this text.

Grading	100%	98%	95%	90%	80%	70%	60%

VOERE

Manufacturer located in Kufstein, Austria since 1964. Voere has had little distribution in the U.S. since Mauser stopped selling this trademark in the U.S.

Voere manufactures a complete line of both semi-auto and bolt-action rifles. Their new caseless ammunition released in 1991 is a bold step and will have to hold up to the performance and reliability of its cased relatives. More information on this trademark can be obtained by writing/ FAX'ing them directly (see Trademark Index for information).

RIFLES

MODEL VEC 91 BOLT ACTION — 5.7 x 26 UCC caseless ammo, unique ignition system requires electrical impulse to activate semi-conducting primer that ignites propellant (2 small batteries are housed in the pistol grip capable of igniting 5,000 shots), 5 shot detachable mag., 20 in. free floating barrel, twin forward locking lugs, 2 stage electrical trigger adj. from ½ oz. to 7 lbs, 55 grain bullet achieves 3,300 fps with no loss in accuracy over normal mechanical primer ignited cartridges, 6 lbs. New 1991.

Please contact the manufacturer directly to obtain pricing and export information on this model.

BOLT-ACTION MODEL — various cal.'s, no longer imported.

	100%	98%	95%	90%	80%	70%	60%
	$325	$250	$225	$200	$175	$125	$100

.22 SEMI-AUTO — .22 LR, open or closed bolt design, clip mag., checkered hardwood stock, adj. rear sight.

	100%	98%	95%	90%	80%	70%	60%
	$225	$195	$165	$145	$130	$120	$95

VOLUNTEER ENTERPRISES

Previous manufacturer located in Knoxville, TN.

Volunteer Enterprizes became Commando Arms after 1978.

COMMANDO MARK III CARBINE — semi-auto, blowback action, .45 ACP, 16½ in. barrel, aperture sight, stock styled after "Tommy Gun". Mfg. 1969-1976.

	100%	98%	95%	90%	80%	70%	60%
	$350	$315	$280	$225	$195	$160	$145

COMMANDO MARK III CARBINE

Vertical grip	$365	$320	$280	$225	$195	$160	$145

COMMANDO MARK 9 — same as Mark III in 9mm.

	100%	98%	95%	90%	80%	70%	60%
	$350	$315	$280	$225	$195	$160	$145
Vertical grip	$365	$320	$280	$225	$195	$160	$145

VOUZELAUD

Manufacturer located in France. Imported by Waverly Arms Co. located in Suffolk, VA 23433.

SHOTGUNS: SIDE-BY-SIDE

MODEL 315 E — 12, 16 or 20 ga., boxlock, 28 in. barrels, auto ejectors, straight grip French walnut stock, double triggers, case colored receiver, light engraving. Importation disc. 1987.

Prices generally range between $4,000-$10,000 and can vary substantially due to the exchange rate.

MODEL 315 EL — same as Model 315 E, except has satin finish receiver engraved with bouquets of fine English scroll work, trigger guard and forearm also engraved. Importation disc. 1987.

Prices on this model are available upon request from importer listed above.

This model was also available by special order in 28 or .410 ga. (Model 315 EL-S) - add $1,100.

Grading	100%	98%	95%	90%	80%	70%	60%

MODEL 315 EGL — 12, 16 or 20 ga., sidelock, 28 in. barrels, selective ejectors, double triggers, extensive scroll engraving on coin finish receiver, English style stock of extra fancy French walnut. Importation disc. 1987.

Prices on this model are available upon request from importer listed above.

MODEL 315 EGL-S — same general features as the Model 315 EGL, except monobloc barrel construction, extensive game scene engraving, and grand deluxe walnut stock and forearm with extra fine hand checkering. Importation disc. 1987.

	$5,350	$4,720	$4,260	$3,850	$3,400	$3,020	$2,680

Last Mfg.'s Sug. Retail was $5,895.

NOTES

WALTHER

Previously manufactured in Zella-Mehlis (now Suhl, E. Germany) 1886 to 1945. Current production is in Ulm, W. Germany, 1953 to date. Currently imported and distributed by Interarms located in Alexandria, VA.

The calibers listed in the Walther Pistol sections are listed in American caliber designations. The German metric conversion is as follows: .22 LR - same, .25 ACP - 6.35mm, .32 ACP - 7.65mm, .380 ACP - 9mm Kurz. The metric caliber designations in most cases will be indicated on the left slide legend for German mfg. pistols listed in the Walther section.

SEMI-AUTO PISTOLS, PRE-WAR

Grading	100%	98%	95%	90%	80%	70%	60%

MODEL 1 — .25 ACP, 2.1 in. barrel, fixed sights, blue, checkered hard rubber grips, pre-WWI. Mfg. 1908.

	100%	98%	95%	90%	80%	70%	60%
	$500	$400	$350	$250	$200	$150	$125

MODEL 2 — .25 ACP, 2.1 in. barrel, fixed sights, blue, rubber grips, pop-up rear sight on early models, fixed on late models. Mfg. 1909.

	$425	$390	$325	$225	$175	$120	$100

This model can usually be distinguished by its knurled barrel ring.

Early Model — differentiated by its pop-up rear sight.

	$1,100	$950	$875	$750	$675	$550	$400

MODEL 3 — .32 ACP, 2.6 in. barrel, blue, fixed sights, rubber grips, ejection port on left side. Mfg. 1910.

	$1,500	$1,250	$1,100	$800	$550	$500	$400

MODEL 4 — .32 ACP, 8 shot, 3½ in. barrel, blue, rubber grips, ejection port on left side. Mfg. 1910-1918.

	$375	$300	$250	$200	$125	$100	$ 80

Add 10% for WWI "Eagle" proofs.

MODEL 5 — better quality version of 2, fixed rear sight. Mfg. 1913.

	$300	$350	$275	$200	$145	$115	$100

MODEL 6 — 9mm Para., 4¾ in. barrel, blue, hard rubber grips, ejection port on right side. Mfg. 1915-1917. Some are Imperial proofed.

	$5,500	$4,500	$3,000	$2,300	$1,500	$1,050	$800

MODEL 7 — .25 ACP, 3 in. barrel, blue, fixed sights, rubber grips, ejector port on right side. Mfg. 1917-1918.

	$625	$475	$400	$325	$250	$200	$125

MODEL 8 — .25 ACP, 2⅞ in. barrel, blue, fixed sights, plastic grips. Mfg. 1920-1945. Add 25% for engraved slide.

	$425	$375	$325	$265	$200	$150	$125

Add 10% for "Eagle N" proofing.

MODEL 9 VEST POCKET — .25 ACP, 2 in. barrel, blue, fixed sights, plastic grips. Mfg. 1921-1945.

	$475	$425	$350	$275	$200	$160	$140

Add 40% for engraved slide, 20% for nickel, 100% for gold engraved.

Grading	100%	98%	95%	90%	80%	70%	60%

MODEL PP DOUBLE ACTION AUTOMATIC "POLICE PISTOL" — .22 LR, .25 ACP, .32 ACP, or
.380 ACP cal., 3⅞ in. barrel, blue, fixed sights, plastic grips. Mfg. 1929-1945. Crown N proof until 1939. Eagle N Nazi commercial proof until 1945.

.22 LR cal.	$850	$750	$675	$625	$525	$385	$320
.25 ACP cal.	$3,200	$3,000	$2,500	$2,000	$1,500	$1,200	$1,000
.32 ACP cal.	$450	$400	$375	$350	$275	$225	$200
.380 ACP cal.	$950	$900	$825	$775	$725	$650	$500

Add 15% for alloy frame.

Original nickel finished Model PP's are very rare and precludes accurate price evaluation.

.32 ACP Bottom Release Magazine — 90 degree safety

	$800	$700	$625	$600	$525	$425	$395

.380 ACP Bottom Release Magazine — 90 degree safety.

	$1,050	$950	$875	$800	$700	$600	$500

Pre-War Persian proofed — 9mm Kurz BMR.

	$2,000	$1,800	$1,600	$1,450	$1,250	$995	$825

Pre-War Verchromt .32 ACP cal. — add 50% for .380 ACP

	$1,450	$1,250	$800	$750	$675	$485	$395

Pre-War Stoeger — .32 ACP cal. only.

	$1,200	$1,050	$925	$800	$600	$425	$325

Nairobi — Chas. Heyer.

	$1,200	$1,000	$850	$725	$575	$400	$300

Aluminum frame — 90 degree safety.

	$650	$600	$500	$400	$275	$235	$200

Allemagne — French Comm.

	$1,050	$950	$825	$720	$600	$425	$325

MODEL PP WARTIME PRODUCTION — mfg. 1940-1945, "Eagle N" Proof (Nazi commercial nitro proof after April 1940) or "Crown N" proof (German commercial proof mark used to April, 1940) found on pre-WWII military production. Variations are listed either by proof marks or frame/slide markings.

"Waffenamt" Proofed — .32 ACP cal., "Eagle N", military acceptance marking.

.32 ACP cal.	$500	$400	$350	$300	$250	$220	$200
.380 ACP cal.	$800	$725	$650	$600	$550	$500	$450

Original nickel finished Model PP's are very rare and precludes accurate price evaluation.

Late war PP's are sometimes encountered with Walther marked walnut grips - add 20% if Waffenamt proofed.

Eagle N Proofed — .22 LR or .32 ACP cal., with lanyard loop.

.32 ACP cal.	$450	$395	$350	$300	$250	$200	$150
.22 LR cal.	$750	$700	$625	$550	$495	$450	$395

After WWII the French added a lanyard to the left side of the grip. Deduct 25% for this alteration.

Eagle C & F Marked (Nazi Police) — .32 ACP cal., "Eagle N or C" proofed on left side of frame.

	$700	$650	$600	$500	$450	$380	$300

Add 50% if Eagle C marked.

RFV Marked — .32 ACP cal., "Crown N". Mfg. for Reich Finance Administration.

	$700	$650	$600	$500	$400	$325	$225

RJ Marked — .32 ACP cal., "Crown N". Mfg. for Reich Justice Ministry.

	$750	$675	$600	$525	$450	$325	$225

SA Marked — .22 LR or .32 ACP cal., "Crown N". Mfg. for SA (storm troops) of the Nazi party.

	$1,450	$1,350	$1,050	$925	$725	$600	$425

Add 10% for .22 LR.

Rare SA markings may bring as much as 50% more over values listed above.

Grading	100%	98%	95%	90%	80%	70%	60%

NSKK Marked — .32 ACP cal., "Crown N or Eagle N" proofed. Mfg. for Nazi Party Transport Corps, rare.

	$1,950	$1,625	$1,350	$1,025	$875	$700	$550

RRZ proofed — .32 ACP cal., "Reich Rundfunk Zenhale", for German Radio Broadcasting - only 3 known.

	$3,500	$3,000	$2,500				

PDM Marked — .32 ACP cal., "Crown N", Munich Police Department.

	$850	$775	$700	$625	$525	$450	$360

AC Marked — .32 ACP cal., replaced Walther Banner during 1945, "Eagle N".

	$300	$275	$250	$225	$175	$150	$125

Czech. Contract — stamped Rampant Lion.

	$950	$850	$825	$700	$600	$500	$400

Panagraphed

	$825	$750	$695	$630	$550	$385	$275

Danish Rplt.

	$975	$925	$825	$775	$700	$625	$400

MODEL PP LIGHTWEIGHT — aluminum alloy version.
Add 20% to Standard Model prices.
Add 20%-40% for original nickel finish (very rare).

MODEL PPK PRE-WAR PRODUCTION — .22 LR, .25 ACP, .32 ACP, or .380 ACP cal., PPK designates Police Pistol Kriminal, 3¼ in. barrel, blue, fixed sights, plastic grips. Mfg. 1931-1940.

	100%	98%	95%	90%	80%	70%	60%
.22 LR cal.	$1,100	$925	$750	$700	$650	$525	$400
.25 ACP cal.	$4,000	$3,600	$3,150	$2,350	$1,600	$1,250	$800
.32 ACP cal.	$550	$500	$425	$350	$300	$250	$225
.380 ACP cal.	$2,000	$1,725	$1,500	$1,100	$800	$600	$500

Add 60% for bottom release Mag (.32 ACP cal.).

MODEL PPK WARTIME PRODUCTION — mfg. 1940-1945, "Eagle N" proofed after April 1940, "Crown N" proofs appear on pre-1940 production with frame/slide markings. Variations are listed either by proof marks, frame/slide markings, or type of finish.

Commercial "Eagle N" Proofed — .22 LR, .32 ACP, or .380 ACP cal., Nazi Eagle over N (standard Nazi commercial acceptance proof).

	100%	98%	95%	90%	80%	70%	60%
.22 LR cal.	$995	$800	$675	$595	$525	$460	$420
.32 ACP cal.	$495	$425	$350	$300	$200	$180	$160
.380 ACP cal.	$1,000	$900	$800	$700	$600	$500	$400

This variation is normally encountered with unpolished exterior metal showing milling marks.

Waffenamt Proofed With High Polish

	$850	$650	$575	$500	$425	$330	$275

Eagle C Marked — .32 ACP cal., "Crown N - Eagle C", mfg. for Nazi Police.

	$575	$525	$450	$400	$315	$260	$200

Add 25% for high polish finish.

Eagle F Marked — .32 ACP cal., "Crown N - Eagle F", Nazi Police.

	$800	$700	$600	$475	$375	$300	$250

RZM Marked — .32 ACP cal., "Crown N", proof marking for Nazi Party Purchasing Office.

	$875	$800	$765	$600	$350	$275	$225

Party Leader — .32 ACP cal., named because grips (brown or black plastic) have the German eagle holding a Swastika, "Crown N" proofed, honor weapon awarded 3rd Reich political leaders, rare. Be very wary of fake grips (especially black color) as reproductions have been made recently. Unfortunately, the grips on a Party Leader (in correct serial range) are the only distinguishing feature on this very desireable configuration.

	$2,600	$2,250	$1,800	$1,500	$1,200	$1,100	$1,000

RZM Party Leader — .32 ACP cal., RZM marked, "Crown N" proofed.

	$3,200	$2,950	$2,650	$2,200	$1,300	$1,200	$1,100

Grading	100%	98%	95%	90%	80%	70%	60%
RFV Marked — .32 ACP cal., "Crown N". Mfg. for Reich Finance Administration.							
	$975	$900	$825	$750	$800	$700	$675
PDM Marked — .32 ACP cal., "Crown N". Mfg. for Police Dept. Munich.							
	$975	$900	$825	$750	$600	$500	$395
POM — aluminum frame — BMR.							
	$900	$825	$750	$650	$525	$500	$475
DRP Marked — .32 ACP cal., "Crown N". Mfg. for Postal Service.							
	$850	$750	$675	$525	$420	$350	$260
Panagraph Slide							
	$850	$750	$675	$525	$450	$375	$300
Verchromt — .32 ACP or 380 ACP cal., differentiated by dull silver satin type finish.							
	$2,000	$1,600	$1,300	$1,000	$800	$650	$500

Add 25% for .380 ACP cal.

	100%	98%	95%	90%	80%	70%	60%
"K" suffix — "K" beneath ser. no.							
	$625	$525	$475	$375	$300	$275	$250
"W" suffix — .32 ACP cal., "Crown N" proofed, W-suffix ser. no.							
	$725	$650	$575	$525	$475	$450	$375
Early 90 degree safety							
	$650	$575	$475	$425	$325	$260	$195
Early bottom release Mag.							
	$950	$850	$750	$650	$500	$475	$375
PPK marked PP							
	$2,500	$2,150	$1,850	$1,600	$1,400	$1,180	$900
7-digit ser. no.							
	$725	$700	$650	$600	$550	$400	$300
Dural frame — .22 LR, .32 ACP, or .380 ACP cal., chrome finish (very rare), "Eagle N".							
	$650	$600	$575	$525	$400	$325	$275

Add 25% for .380 ACP or .22 LR cal.

	100%	98%	95%	90%	80%	70%	60%
Stoeger Contract — .32 ACP cal., marked "A. F. Stoeger Inc. New York" on left center of slide.							
	$1,200	$900	$700	$500	$350	$225	$200
Heyer Contract — .32 ACP cal., marked "Chas. A. Heyer and Co., Nairobi" on top left of slide.							
	$1,200	$1,050	$900	$775	$675	$550	$400
Czech. Contract — Rampant Lion stamped.							
	$950	$875	$750	$625	$550	$425	$325
Danish Rplt.							
	$950	$875	$750	$625	$550	$425	$325
Allemagne — French Commercial — rare.							
	$950	$875	$750	$625	$550	$425	$325

MODEL PPK LIGHTWEIGHT — aluminum alloy version.
Add 20% to Standard Model pricing.

SPORT MODEL 1926 — .22 S and LR (known as Standard Model in Germany) cal.'s.

	100%	98%	95%	90%	80%	70%	60%
	$1,050	$900	$800	$675	$595	$550	$495

1932 OLYMPIA MODEL — .22 S or LR, 10 shot, 6 or 9 in. barrel, target sights, one piece grip, introduced in 1928 and used in 1932 Olympics. Marketed by Stoeger and Chas. Heyer-Nairobi.

	100%	98%	95%	90%	80%	70%	60%
	$1,050	$850	$750	$575	$495	$440	$395

OLYMPIA SPORT MODEL — .22 LR, 4 in. barrel, adj. target sights, blue, wood grips, 4 barrel weights available. Mfg. 1936-1940.

	100%	98%	95%	90%	80%	70%	60%
	$895	$795	$700	$600	$475	$420	$375

Add 20% for weight set.

Grading	100%	98%	95%	90%	80%	70%	60%

1936 OLYMPIA "JAGERSCHAFTS" HUNTING MODEL — same as Sport, with 4 in. barrel. Mfg. 1936-1940. Also seen with Eagle N proofs.

	$850	$750	$675	$550	$495	$440	$360

OLYMPIA RAPID FIRE MODEL — .22 Short only, 7.4 in. barrel, blue, adj. sight, wood grip, has alloy side. Mfg. 1936-1940.

	$950	$850	$785	$600	$520	$460	$380

1936 OLYMPIA FUNFKAMPF MODEL — .22 Short or LR, 9¼ in. barrel, blue, adj. sight, wood grips, barrel weights, circa 1936.

	$1,250	$1,000	$850	$775	$575	$500	$440

MODEL HP COMMERCIAL DOUBLE ACTION — pre-war version of P-38, 9mm, 5 in. barrel, fixed sight, blue, wood or plastic grips. Mfg. 1937-1944. Many variations, including several different finishes.
See German WWII Military Pistols for values on this model.

PISTOLS: SEMI-AUTO, POST-WAR

In 1983, Carl Walther from West Germany announced the discontinuance of models PP and PPK/S from the American market. These guns are attracting more collector interest as their production records are now complete. Manurhin of France no longer imports into the U.S. and guns imported between 1984-86 will not have the Interarms logo or Walther trademark.

Prices below reflect the recent devaluation of the U.S. dollar against some foreign currencies. While the manufacturer's suggested retails have gone up considerably, prices for used specimens (98% or less original condition) have not increased proportionately, and in some cases, have changed very little.

MODEL PP DOUBLE ACTION — .22 LR, .32 ACP, or .380 ACP cal., specifications similar to pre-war PP, 3⅞ in. barrel. Imported 1963-present. W. German manufacture.
.380 ACP cal. — 6 shot mag.

Mfg.'s Sug. Retail	$1,075	$695	$495	$375	$330	$300	$275	$250

.32 ACP cal. — 6 shot mag.

Mfg.'s Sug. Retail	$1,000	$625	$450	$350	$295	$275	$250	$225

.22 LR cal. — 7 shot mag., disc. 1989.

	$600	$425	$375	$350	$325	$230	$275

Last Mfg.'s Sug. Retail was $875.
Blue Engraved — .22 LR (disc.) or .380 ACP cal.

Mfg.'s Sug. Retail	$1,650	$1,350	$1,100	$950

Add 5% for .22 LR cal.
Chrome Engraved — .22 LR or .380 ACP cal. Disc. 1990.

	$1,350	$1,100	$950

Add $50 for .22 LR cal.
Last Mfg.'s Sug. Retail was $1,600.
Silver Engraved — .22 LR or .380 ACP (disc. 1990) cal.

Mfg.'s Sug. Retail	$1,850	$1,525	$1,150	$1,000

Add $50 for .22 LR cal.
Gold Engraved — .22 LR or .380 ACP (disc. 1989) cal.

Mfg.'s Sug. Retail	$1,950	$1,675	$1,350	$1,150

Manurhin PP — .22 LR, .32 ACP, or .380 ACP cal.

	$350	$310	$285	$225	$180	$165	$150

Add 10% for .380 ACP cal.
Model PP 50th Anniversary Commemorative — .22 LR or .380 ACP, gold-plated parts, hand carved grips, presentation case. 500 imported to U.S. 1979.

	$1,350	$1,050	$750

Add $100 for .22 LR cal.
Last Mfg.'s Sug. Retail was $1,700.

Grading	100%	98%	95%	90%	80%	70%	60%

PP SPORT — double action, thumbrest grips, round hammer with spur, adj. rear sight, long barrel. Mfg. 1953-1970.

Manurhin manufacture	$650	$625	$600	$525	$475	$400	$325
Mark II (mfg. 1955-1957)	$725	$680	$625	$575	$520	$480	$425
Walther manufacture	$775	$725	$700	$575	$520	$475	$400

Deduct 10% if not marked.

Note: Add $75 for barrel weight, $100 for factory case, 20% for factory nickel, 5% for single action.

PP Sport "C" Model C — mfg. for competition shooting, single action, 7⅝ in. barrel, spur hammer.

	$750	$725	$675	$625	$525	$475	$400

MODEL PPK — similar to pre-war PPK, .22 LR, .32 ACP, or .380 ACP cal., 3.31 in. barrel. Mfg. 1963-present, U.S. import stopped by GCA 68 on W. German and French production.

.32 ACP cal.	$525	$450	$375	$325	$295	$270	$250
.22 LR cal.	$725	$625	$550	$500	$425	$350	$300
.380 ACP cal.	$650	$575	$500	$450	$400	$325	$275
Blue engraved		$1,600	$1,300	$950			
Silver engraved		$1,850	$1,400	$1,000			
Gold engraved		$2,200	$1,675	$1,250			

100% column assumes NIB condition - deduct 15% if not boxed.

MODEL PPK LIGHTWEIGHT — same as Standard, with dural frame, .22 LR or .32 ACP cal.

	$600	$550	$500	$440	$400	$360	$330

Add 20% for .22 LR cal.

MODEL PPK-1986 U.S. MFG. — .380 ACP cal. only, 3.2 in. barrel, similar specifications as previous W. German and French manufacture, 6 shot finger extension mag., black plastic grips, 21 oz. Made in the U.S. Introduced 1986.

Mfg.'s Sug. Retail	$585	$475	$390	$340	$310	$290	$275	$260

Manufacture in the U.S. is under an exclusive licensing agreement with Walther of W. Germany.

PPK Stainless — stainless steel construction. New 1986.

Mfg.'s Sug. Retail	$585	$475	$390	$340

MODEL PPK/S — .22 LR, .32 ACP, or .380 ACP cal., similar to PPK, except has larger PP frame to meet import requirements of 1968, 3¼ in. barrel, production in W. Germany (now disc.), Manurhin of France (disc. 1986), and in the U.S. (mfg. under license from Walther by Interarms). 7 or 8 shot, double action, fixed sights.

American PPK/S — .380 ACP cal. only, blue finish, 7 shot finger extension mag.

Mfg.'s Sug. Retail	$585	$475	$370	$335	$310	$290	$275	$260

W. German PPK/S — .22 LR, .32 ACP, or .380 ACP cal. Disc. 1982.

.32 ACP cal.	$495	$425	$350	$325	$295	$270	$250
.22 LR cal.	$650	$575	$525	$425	$350	$300	$275
.380 ACP cal.	$600	$525	$475	$375	$300	$275	$250

Stainless PPK/S — .380 ACP cal. only, American manufacture, introduction July of 1983.

Mfg.'s Sug. Retail	$585	$475	$375	$335

American PPK/S — blue engraved. Disc. 1985.

	$875	$850	$800

Last Mfg.'s Sug. Retail was $990.

American PPK/S Gold-Engraved Commemorative — 500 total mfg. Disc. 1987.

	$1,000	$850	$675

Last Mfg.'s Sug. Retail was $1,200.

American PPK/S Gold-Engraved — disc. 1985.

	$975	$800	$675

Last Mfg.'s Sug. Retail was $1,070.

Grading	100%	98%	95%	90%	80%	70%	60%

W. German PPK/S Blue Engraved — all quantities became out of stock in 1990.

	$1,395	$1,050	$850				

Last Mfg.'s Sug. Retail was $1,550.

W. German PPK/S Chrome Engraved

Mfg.'s Sug. Retail $1,700 $1,450 $1,075 $950

Only a limited quantity is still available in .380 ACP cal. only.

W. German PPK/S Silver Engraved — disc. 1988.

	$1,595	$1,150	$975				

Last Mfg.'s Sug. Retail was $1,700.

W. German PPK/S Gold Engraved — disc. 1985.

	$1,850	$1,250	$1,000				

Last Mfg.'s Sug. Retail was $1,800.

PPK/S Durgarde (Manurhin mfg.) — same as above, only with bonded brushed chrome finish.

Under Walther license $395 $310 $290 $265 $245 $210 $195

Add $25 for .22 LR cal.

MANURHIN PPK/S — see listings under Manurhin section.

MODEL PP SUPER — 9 x 18mm, (Police) or .380 ACP cal., 3.6 in. barrel, fixed sights, plastic grips, blue. Mfg. 1975-1981.

	$600	$525	$400	$345	$275	$250	$235

Deduct 25% if in 9 x 18mm cal.

PP Super-Cutaway

	$650	$600	$550				

MODEL TP — .22 LR or .25 ACP cal., updated version of Model 9, concealed hammer. Mfg. 1962-1970.

.22 LR cal.	$675	$600	$435	$350	$300	$260	$210
.25 ACP cal.	$495	$425	$360	$300	$250	$220	$185

MODEL TPH — .22 LR or .25 ACP cal., double action 2.8 in. barrel, alloy frame, blue, fixed sights, plastic grips. Mfg. 1969-present in W. Germany, U.S. import stopped by GCA of 1968.

.22 LR cal.	$625	$560	$495	$425	$300	$275	$220
.25 ACP cal.	$700	$625	$550	$475	$350	$300	$250

Deduct 10% on the 100% values if not boxed with all accessories.

100% price assumes NIB condition.

AMERICAN MODEL TPH — .22 LR only, stainless steel double action, black plastic grips, 6 shot mag., 2¼ in. barrel, 14 oz. Introduced 1987.

Mfg.'s Sug. Retail $445 $375 $320 $250

MODEL P.38 — Post-war version of P.38 Military, .22 LR, .30 Luger (disc.), or 9mm Para. cal., 5 in. barrel, alloy frame, matte black finish, 28 oz. W. German manufacture. See German WWII Military Pistols for wartime listings.

Note: Due to the release of large numbers of W. German Police and Army trade-ins of P.38 9mm and PP .32 ACP cal. models, the actual value of these models has only recently gone down. The two models most affected are the P-1 variation of the P.38, and the German PP in .32 ACP cal.

Mfg.'s Sug. Retail $1,065 $825 $550 $425 $360 $295 $245 $190

Steel Frame P.38 — 9mm Para., similar to regular P.38, except has steel frame, 34 oz. Imported 1987-1989 only.

	$975	$850	$650	$550	$400	$295	$245

Last Mfg.'s Sug. Retail was $1,400.

P.38 in .22 LR cal. — disc. 1989.

	$850	$700	$550	$450	$350	$300	$200

Last Mfg.'s Sug. Retail was $1,050.

Grading	100%	98%	95%	90%	80%	70%	60%

MODEL P.38 SPECIAL EDITIONS/ENGRAVED

P.38 100th Year Commemorative — alloy frame, presentation engraved with deluxe walnut presentation case. New 1987.

Mfg.'s Sug. Retail	$1,065	$825	$650	$500			

Blue Engraved — 9mm Para. cal.

Mfg.'s Sug. Retail	$1,850	$1,325	$1,125	$900			

Chrome Engraved — 9mm Para. cal.

Mfg.'s Sug. Retail	$2,125	$1,475	$1,175	$925			

Silver Engraved — 9mm Para. cal.

Mfg.'s Sug. Retail	$2,100	$1,450	$1,175	$925			

Gold Engraved — 9mm Para. cal. Disc. 1987.

	$1,800	$1,500	$1,000				

Last Mfg.'s Sug. Retail was $2,050.

MODEL P1 — 9mm Para., post-war commercial variation of the P.38 with steel slide and alloy frame, 5 in. barrel, 8 shot mag., black plastic grips, Disc.

	$575	$500	$425	$350	$300	$250	$200

MODEL P.38 IV — 9mm Para. cal., modernized variation of the original P.38, 4½ in. barrel, 8 shot mag., updates include reinforced steel slide and alloy frame, includes decocking lever and automatic safeties, adj. rear sight, 29 oz. Importation disc. 1982.

	$595	$525	$450	$350	$300	$250	$200

MODEL P.38K — 9mm Para. cal., shortened 2.8 in. barrel variation of P.38, front sight on slide. Mfg. 1974-1980.

	$850	$750	$500	$400	$300	$250	$200

MODEL P-5 — 9mm Para. cal., double action, alloy frame, frame mounted decocking lever, 3½ in. barrel, adj. rear sight, blue finish only, 8 shot mag., auto safeties, 28 oz.

Mfg.'s Sug. Retail	$1,085	$875	$650	$550	$495	$465	$425	$380

P-5 Compact — compact variation of P-5.

Mfg.'s Sug. Retail	$1,460	$1,100	$900	$750	$625	$525	$485	$445

P-5 100th Year Commemorative — elaborate engraving with presentation walnut case. New 1987.

Mfg.'s Sug. Retail	$2,890	$2,100	$1,425	$1,025			

MODEL P-88 — 9mm Para. cal., double action, alloy frame, 4 in. barrel, 15 shot side release mag., ambidextrous decocking lever, matte finish, adj. rear sight, internal safeties, loaded chamber indicator, black synthetic grips, 31½ oz. New 1987.

Mfg.'s Sug. Retail	$1,550	$1,250	$950	$750	$625	$575	$490	$450

TARGET PISTOLS

MODEL GSP TARGET — .22 LR cal., 4½ in. barrel, single action, 5 shot mag., adj. sights, blue finish, walnut target grips, supplied with carrying case, 49.4 oz.

Mfg.'s Sug. Retail	$1,750	$1,425	$1,250	$1,000	$750	$600	$500	$425

Model GSP Junior — similar to GSP Target, except has slimmer barrel design, smaller walnut grips, less weight.

Mfg.'s Sug. Retail	$1,810	$1,400	$1,100	$925	$750	$600	$500	$425

Model GSP-C — same as Model GSP Target, except in .32 S&W wadcutter, 42.3 oz.

Mfg.'s Sug. Retail	$2,140	$1,600	$1,200	$995	$800	$650	$550	$475

Add $1,420 for GSP-C .22 Short conversion unit.

Add $1,000 for GSP-C .22 LR cal. conversion unit.

Add $1,250 for GSP-C .32 S&W Wadcutter converison unit.

MODEL OSP RAPID FIRE — similar to GSP, in .22 Short. Mfg. 1968-present, for international competition (meets ISU and NRA reg.'s), 4½ in.barrel, 44.4 oz., supplied with case.

Mfg.'s Sug. Retail	$2,085	$1,575	$1,250	$950	$800	$650	$550	$475

Grading	100%	98%	95%	90%	80%	70%	60%

FREE PISTOL — .22 LR cal., single shot, electronic trigger, 11.7 in. heavy barrel, advanced target design with fully adj. grips and sights, 48 oz.

	100%	98%	95%	90%	80%	70%	60%
Mfg.'s Sug. Retail	$2,140	$1,600	$1,200	$1,000	$850	$675	$575	$500

P.38 WWII MILITARY MFG. — see German Military for breakdown.

HAMMERLI-WALTHER — see Hammerli.

RIFLES: DISCONTINUED

MODEL B — .30-06 bolt action, post-war mfg., 22 in. barrel. Add 20% for double set triggers. Disc.

	$450	$420	$380	$340	$300	$275	$250

OLYMPIC SINGLE SHOT — .22 LR, bolt action, 26 in. heavy barrel, target sights, checkered pistol grip, full beavertail forearm, palm rest, adj. butt, pre-war.

	$935	$825	$770	$715	$605	$550	$440

MODEL 1 — Carbine model, clip fed.

	$395	$350	$310	$295	$270	$250	$200

MODEL 2 AUTOLOADING — may be used as bolt action, autoloader or single shot, .22 LR, 24½ in. barrel, tangent sight, checkered sporter stock, pre-war.

	$495	$440	$385	$330	$275	$220	$165

MODEL 2 LIGHTWEIGHT — 20 in. barrel, lighter stock.

	$495	$440	$385	$330	$275	$220	$165

MODEL V SINGLE SHOT — .22 LR cal., bolt action, 26 in. barrel, open sight, plain pistol grip stock, pre-war.

	$385	$360	$330	$305	$275	$250	$195

MODEL V CHAMPION — same as Standard, with micrometer adj. sight and checkered pistol grip stock.

	$470	$440	$415	$385	$330	$305	$250

MODEL KKM INTERNATIONAL MATCH — .22 LR cal., single shot bolt action, 28 in. heavy barrel, adj. aperture sight, adj. hook butt, thumbhole stock, accessory rail, post-war mfg.

	$880	$770	$715	$660	$550	$495	$440

MODEL KKM-S — same as KKM, with adj. cheek piece.

	$935	$825	$770	$715	$605	$550	$495

MODEL KKJ SPORTER — .22 LR cal., bolt action, 5 shot, 22½ in. barrel, open sight, checkered sporter stock, post-war.

	$550	$500	$450	$385	$330	$250	$200

Add 20% for double set triggers.

MODEL KKW — .22 LR cal., single shot, military stock, tangent sight, pre-war mfg.

	$540	$490	$420	$300	$260	$220	$195

MODEL KKJ-MA — .22 WMR cal.

	$550	$495	$440	$385	$305	$250	$220

MODEL KKJ-HO — .22 Hornet.

	$725	$675	$625	$580	$540	$480	$440

Add 20% for double set triggers.

Grading	100%	98%	95%	90%	80%	70%	60%

MODEL SSV VARMINT — .22 LR cal., single shot bolt action, 25½ in. barrel, no sights, Monte Carlo pistol grip stock, post-war mfg.

	100%	98%	95%	90%	80%	70%	60%
	$605	$550	$525	$495	$415	$360	$330
.22 Hornet	$660	$605	$580	$550	$470	$415	$385

MODEL PRONE 400 — similar to UIT Match, with Prone style competitive stock and no sights. Disc.

	100%	98%	95%	90%	80%	70%	60%
	$750	$635	$580	$525	$415	$360	$305

RIFLES: CURRENT MFG.

Prices below reflect the recent devaluation of the U.S. dollar against some foreign currencies. While the manufacturer's suggested retails have gone up considerably, prices for used specimens (98% or less original condition) have not increased proportionately, and in some cases, have changed very little.

MODEL UIT BV UNIVERSAL — .22 LR cal., single shot bolt action, 25½ in. heavy barrel, adj. aperture sight, target stock with palm rest, adj. butt, meets IUS reg.'s, 16 lbs. Disc. 1990.

	100%	98%	95%	90%	80%	70%	60%
	$1,325	$1,050	$850	$700	$635	$580	$530

Last Mfg.'s Sug. Retail was $1,700. This model was previously known as the Model UIT Special.

MODEL UIT MATCH — same as UIT Special, except with improved stock design which includes fully stippled lower forearm and pistol grip, 13 lbs.

	100%	98%	95%	90%	80%	70%	60%
Mfg.'s Sug. Retail	$1,400	$1,125	$925	$800	$660	$610	$555	$510

Model UIT-E — electronic trigger, 25½ in. barrel, 9 lbs. Disc. 1986.

	100%	98%	95%	90%	80%	70%	60%
	$1,350	$940	$860	$770	$670	$630	$560

Last Mfg.'s Sug. Retail was $1,250.

GX-1 — similar to UIT Match, 25½ in. barrel with fully adj. free rifle stock, all accessories included, 16½ lbs.

	100%	98%	95%	90%	80%	70%	60%
Mfg.'s Sug. Retail	$2,350	$1,895	$1,375	$1,125	$985	$860	$775	$680

MODEL KK/MS SILHOUETTE — .22 LR cal. only, designed for silhouette shooting with no sights, thumbhole stock with adj. butt, fully stippled forend and stock grip, front barrel weight, 25½ in. barrel, 8¾ lbs. New 1984.

	100%	98%	95%	90%	80%	70%	60%
Mfg.'s Sug. Retail	$1,175	$975	$795	$625	$560	$495	$435	$395

RUNNING BOAR MODEL 500 — similar to KK/MS, no sights, thumbhole stock with adj. butt and cheek piece, 23½ in. barrel, 10¼ lbs. Disc. 1990.

	100%	98%	95%	90%	80%	70%	60%
	$1,025	$825	$640	$570	$500	$435	$395

Last Mfg.'s Sug. Retail was $1,300.

MODEL WA-2000 — .300 Win. Mag. or .308 cal., ultra-deluxe bolt action, special order only. Disc. 1988.

	100%	98%	95%	90%	80%	70%	60%
	$6,400	$4,800	$4,500	$4,000	$3,500	$3,000	$2,500

SHOTGUNS: SIDE-BY-SIDE

MODEL SF — 12 or 16 ga., double barrel, checkered walnut stock, double triggers, boxlock, sling swivels. Disc.

	100%	98%	95%	90%	80%	70%	60%
	$500	$450	$395	$325	$275	$240	$200

MODEL SFD — 12 or 16 ga., double barrel, cheek piece, checkered walnut stock, double triggers, boxlock, sling swivels. Disc.

	100%	98%	95%	90%	80%	70%	60%
	$625	$575	$500	$425	$375	$340	$300

Grading	100%	98%	95%	90%	80%	70%	60%

WALTHER, FRENCH-MADE BY MANURHIN
Manufactured in Mulhouse, France. Previously imported 1984-86 by Matra-Manurhin International, Inc., Alexandria, VA.

PISTOLS: SEMI-AUTO

Manufacture of these Walther pistols commenced in France in 1951. They were marked MANURHIN on slide until 1954. Since then they were designated Walther MKII. They were imported into the USA by Interarms up to 1983. In 1984, Manurhin was imported directly with no Interarms logo or Walther trademark appearing on Models PP and PPK/S. Importation disc. 1986.

MODEL PP — .22 LR, .32 ACP, or .380 ACP cal., 3⅞ in. barrel, 10 shot mag.-.22 LR, 8 shot mag.-.32 ACP, 7 shot mag.-.380 ACP, blue only, all steel construction, double action with positive steel block safety, 24 oz. Add $10 for .22 LR cal., $46 for durgarde finish.

$360	$320	$275	$230	$205	$185	$170

Last Mfg.'s Sug. Retail was $419.

Collector Model — blue finish, special engraving. New 1986.

$465	$415	$350

Last Mfg.'s Sug. Retail was $529.

Presentation Model — blue finish, special ornamentation. New 1986.

$720	$650	$500

Last Mfg.'s Sug. Retail was $819.

Also available with various engraving options in either blue, nickel, or gold finish - prices range from $222 - $540.

Interarms import	$350	$325	$285	$230	$205	$180	$160

PP SPORT — .22 LR cal. only, double action, 6.1 or 8.1 in. barrel, blue finish only, precision adj. sights, contoured plastic grips with thumb rest, 25 oz. New Manurhin design for 1985.

$545	$485	$430	$385	$325	$290	$270

Last Mfg.'s Sug. Retail was $635.

PP Sport-C — same as PP Sport, except is single action.

$540	$475	$415	$370	$310	$280	$260

Last Mfg.'s Sug. Retail was $635.

MODEL PPK — .22 LR, .32 ACP, or .380 ACP cal., 3¼ in. barrel, 10 shot mag.-.22 LR, 8 shot mag.-.32 ACP, 7 shot mag.-.380 ACP, blue only, all steel construction, double action with positive steel block safety, 23 oz. Add 10% for .22 LR cal.

$600	$495	$425	$375	$350	$325	$300

MODEL PPK/S — .22 LR, .32 ACP, or .380 ACP cal., 3¼ in. barrel, 10 shot mag.-.22 LR, 8 shot mag.-.32 ACP, 7 shot mag.-.380 ACP, blue only, all steel construction, double action with positive steel block safety, 23 oz. Add $10 for .22 LR cal.

$360	$320	$275	$230	$205	$185	$170

Last Mfg.'s Sug. Retail was $419.

PPK/S Durgarde — same as above, only with bonded brushed chrome finish. Add $14 for .22 LR cal.

$410	$365	$325	$290	$265	$250	$240

Last Mfg.'s Sug. Retail was $465.

Collector Model — blue finish, special engraving. New 1986.

$465	$415	$350

Last Mfg.'s Sug. Retail was $529.

Presentation Model — blue finish, special ornamentation. New 1986.

$720	$650	$500

Last Mfg.'s Sug. Retail was $819.

Grading	100%	98%	95%	90%	80%	70%	60%
Interarms import	$395	$340	$300	$275	$250	$235	$210

Also available with various engraving options in either blue, nickel, or gold finish — prices range from $222 - $540.

WARNER ARMS CORPORATION
Norwich, CT.

INFALLIBLE POCKET AUTO PISTOL — .32 auto, 7 shot, 3 in. barrel, fixed sights, rubber grips. Mfg. 1917-1919.

$450	$350	$250	$150	$125	$100	$90

WEATHERBY
Manufacturer/importer located in South Gate, CA, 1945 to date.

Weatherby is an importer of long arms. Earlier production was from Germany and Italy and German mfg. is usually what is collectible. Current production is from Japan. Workmanship in all instances is quite good. Weatherby is well known for their high-velocity proprietary rifle calibers.

Early Weatherby rifles used a Mathieu Arms action in the 1950's - primarily since it was available in left hand action. Right handed actions were normally mfg. from the FN Mauser type.

SILOUETTE PISTOL

WEATHERBY SILOUETTE PISTOL — .22-250 or .308 cal., mfg. in Japan during late 1970's, 14½ in. barrel, Lyman or Williams sights, fitted case. Only 50 were mfg. in .22-250 and 150 in .308 cal.

$3,750	$3,300	$2,750	$2,450	$2,100	$1,850	$1,650

RIFLES - MARK V BOLT ACTION

For German rifle manufacture, add 15% to 25% for calibers under .35.

MARK V DELUXE — .240 Wby. Mag., .257 Wby. Mag., .270 Wby. Mag., 7mm Wby. Mag., .30-06, or .300 Wby. Mag. cal., bolt action, 3-5 shot mag., 24 or 26 in. barrel, deluxe skip line checkered pistol grip walnut stock with rosewood tipped forearm and pistol grip, no sights, 8 lbs. Left hand actions available at no extra charge.

No Mfg.'s Retail	$995	$750	$625	$525	$475	$450	$410

Add $25 for 26 in. barrel.

Mark V .340 Wby. Mag. — 26 in. barrel only, 8½ lbs.

No Mfg.'s Retail	$1,015	$750	$615	$535	$475	$450	$410

Mark V .378 Wby. Mag. — 26 in. barrel only, 8½ lbs.

No Mfg.'s Retail	$1,165	$900	$795	$675	$580	$520	$480
German mfg.	$2,250	$2,000	$1,750	$1,500	$1,350	$1,100	$950

German mfg. in this model used the .375 Wby. Mag. cal.

Mark V .416 Wby. Mag. — first new caliber (introduced 1989) since the .240 Mag. was released 1965.

No Mfg.'s Retail	$1,270	$1,000	$850	$725	$600	$550	$495

Add $25 for 26 in. barrel (includes muzzle brake).

Mark V .460 Wby. Mag. — 24 or 26 in. barrel, includes custom stock, internal muzzle brake, 10 lbs. No extra charge for left-hand.

No Mfg.'s Retail	$1,340	$1,050	$875	$750	$625	$575	$525

Add $25 for 26 in. barrel.

This model includes custom stock, customized action, and integral muzzle brake.

German mfg.	$2,500	$2,250	$2,000	$1,750	$1,500	$1,350	$1,100

Grading	100%	98%	95%	90%	80%	70%	60%

MARK V ULTRAMARK — .240 Wby. Mag., .257 Wby. Mag., .270 Wby. Mag., .30-06, 7mm Wby. Mag., .300 Wby. Mag., .378 Wby. Mag. (mfg. 1989 only), or .416 Wby. Mag. (mfg. 1989 only) cal., fancy American walnut, individually hand-bedded, high lustre finish, customized action, 24 or 26 in. barrel, basket weave checkering (including pistol grip). Imported 1989-90 only.

| | $1,125 | $925 | $800 | $700 | $630 | $590 | $550 |

Add $25 for 26 in. barrel.

Add $220 for .378 Wby. Mag. cal. (26 in. barrel only).

Add $325 for .416 Wby. Mag. cal. (26 in. barrel only).

Last Mfg.'s Sug. Retail was $1,315.

MARK V VARMINTMASTER — .22-250 or .224 Varmintmaster cal., 24 or 26 in. barrel, 6½ lbs.

| No Mfg.'s Retail | $975 | $740 | $625 | $525 | $475 | $450 | $410 |

Add $25 for 26 in. barrel.

Not available in left-hand action.

MARK V EUROMARK — available in all cal.'s, except .22-250 and .224 Varmintmaster, differs from Mark V in that it has an oil finished, hand checkered, deluxe American claro walnut pistol grip cap stock with ebony forend tip, low lustre bluing, and solid black recoil pad. New 1986.

| No Mfg.'s Retail | $1,040 | $800 | $650 | $560 | $500 | $460 | $425 |

Add $25 for 26 in. barrel.

.340 Wby. Mag. — 26 in. barrel only.

| No Mfg.'s Retail | $1,065 | $810 | $660 | $565 | $500 | $460 | $425 |

.378 Wby. Mag. — 26 in. barrel only.

| No Mfg.'s Retail | $1,215 | $925 | $700 | $600 | $525 | $480 | $450 |

.416 Wby. Mag. — first new caliber (introduced 1989) since the .240 Mag. was released 1965, includes muzzle brake.

| No Mfg.'s Retail | $1,320 | $995 | $750 | $640 | $530 | $495 | $465 |

Add $30 for 26 in. barrel.

.460 Wby. Mag. — 24 or 26 in. barrel, includes custom stock, internal muzzle brake, no extra charge for left-hand.

| No Mfg.'s Retail | $1,390 | $1,050 | $925 | $775 | $625 | $575 | $525 |

Add $25 for 26 in. barrel.

MARK V LAZERMARK — available in the same calibers and barrel lengths as the Mark V Deluxe (including Varmint Model), differs only in that stock and forearm have been laser carved. New 1985.

| No Mfg.'s Retail | $1,110 | $820 | $675 | $575 | $500 | $460 | $425 |

Add $25 for 26 in. barrel.

.340 Wby. Mag. — 26 in. barrel only.

| No Mfg.'s Retail | $1,130 | $840 | $685 | $580 | $500 | $460 | $425 |

.378 Wby. Mag. — 26 in. barrel only.

| No Mfg.'s Retail | $1,280 | $995 | $850 | $725 | $600 | $550 | $495 |

.416 Wby. Mag. — first new caliber (introduced 1989) since the .240 Mag. was released 1965, includes muzzle brake.

| No Mfg.'s Retail | $1,390 | $1,050 | $925 | $775 | $625 | $575 | $525 |

Add $25 for 26 in. barrel.

.460 Wby. Mag. — 24 or 26 in. barrel, includes custom stock, internal muzzle brake, no extra charge for left-hand.

| No Mfg.'s Retail | $1,460 | $1,080 | $950 | $795 | $650 | $600 | $540 |

Add $25 for 26 in. barrel.

Varmintmaster — .22-250 or .224 Varmintmaster cal., 24 or 26 in. barrel.

| No Mfg.'s Retail | $1,085 | $815 | $675 | $575 | $500 | $460 | $425 |

Add $25 for 26 in. barrel.

Not available in left-hand action.

Grading	100%	98%	95%	90%	80%	70%	60%

MARK V FIBERMARK — available in .240 Wby. Mag., .257 Wby. Mag., .270 Wby. Mag., .30-06, 7mm Wby. Mag., .300 Wby. Mag., or .340 Wby. Mag. cal., black non-glare fiberglass with wrinkle finish stock, metal has non-glare matte finish, 24 or 26 in. barrel, 7¼ lbs.

| No Mfg.'s Retail | $1,125 | $840 | $685 | $580 | $500 | $460 | $425 |

Add $25 for 26 in. barrel or .340 Mag. cal.

1976 BICENTENNIAL MARK V — .257 WM, .270 WM, 7mm WM, or .300 WM cal., 1,000 mfg. in 1976 only.

| | $1,495 | $1,150 | $895 | | | | |

Last Mfg.'s Sug. Retail was $2,000.

1984 MARK V OLYMPIC COMMEMORATIVE — .257 WM, .270 WM, 7mm WM, or .300 WM cal., special gold accenting, extra-fancy walnut stock with "star in motion" inlay. Mfg. 1,000 1984 only at $2,000 retail.

| | $1,000 | $895 | $700 | | | | |

MARK V 35TH ANNIVERSARY COMMEMORITIVE — .257 WM, .270 WM, 7mm WM, or .300 WM, limited mfg. 1980, 1,000 produced total.

| | $1,000 | $895 | $700 | | | | |

SAFARI GRADE CUSTOM — .300 Wby. Mag., .340 Wby. Mag., .378 Wby. Mag., .416 Wby Mag., or .460 Wby. Mag. cal., custom order only, various options available, 8-10 month delivery.

| No Mfg.'s Retail | $2,785 | $2,150 | $1,750 | $1,600 | $1,450 | $1,300 | $1,175 |

Add approx. $160 - $240 for .378 and larger cal.'s.

CROWN MODEL CUSTOM — custom order only, engraved barrel receiver and scope mount, top-of-the-line model.

| No Mfg.'s Retail | $4,115 | $3,225 | $2,600 | $2,200 | $1,850 | $1,550 | $1,350 |

Subtract $1,143 without Crown engraving option.

RIFLES - VANGUARD SERIES BOLT ACTION

VANGUARD CLASSIC I — .223 Rem., .243 Win., .270 Win., 7mm/08 Rem., 7mm Rem. Mag., .30-06 or .308 Win. cal., checkered walnut stock with satin finish, black butt pad, 24 in. barrel, 3 (7mm Rem. Mag.) or 5 shot mag., No. 1 barrel contour, approx. 7 lbs. 5 oz. New 1989.

| No Mfg.'s Retail | $465 | $350 | $320 | $290 | $260 | $230 | $200 |

This model is the replacement for the Vanguard VGS and VGL.

VANGUARD CLASSIC II — .22-250, .243 Win., .270 Wby. Mag., .270 Win., 7mm Rem. Mag., .30-06, .300 Win. Mag., .300 Wby. Mag., or .338 Win. Mag. cal., 24 in. barrel, 3 or 5 shot mag., custom checkered deluxe walnut stock with pistol grip cap and black forend cap, solid black recoil pad, matte finished metal, approx. 7¾ lbs. New 1989.

| No Mfg.'s Retail | $605 | $520 | $465 | $425 | $395 | $360 | $330 |

VANGUARD VGX DELUXE — similar to Vanguard Classic II except has Monte Carlo stock, high gloss wood and metal, and 60% cut forend cap. New 1989.

| No Mfg.'s Retail | $605 | $520 | $465 | $425 | $395 | $360 | $330 |

VANGUARD WEATHERGUARD — same cal.'s as Classic I, replacement for Fiberguard, wrinkle black finished synthetic stock, entry level Weatherby, similar spec.'s as Classic I, approx. 8 lbs. New 1989.

| No Mfg.'s Retail | $415 | $350 | $300 | $280 | $265 | $250 | $235 |

VANGUARD VGX — .22-250, .243 Win., .25-06, .270 Win., 7mm Rem. Mag., .30-06, or 300 Win. Mag. cal., bolt action, checkered deluxe walnut stock with rosewood tip forearm and pistol grip, 24 in. barrel, no sights, 5 shot mag.(except 3 shot for .300 Win. Mag.), high luster bluing, about 8 lbs. Disc. 1988.

| | $525 | $425 | $365 | $330 | $300 | $275 | $255 |

Not available in left-hand action.

Last Mfg.'s Sug. Retail was $600.

Grading	100%	98%	95%	90%	80%	70%	60%

VANGUARD VGS — same cal.'s as Vanguard VGX, bolt action, checkered satin finished walnut stock, 24 in. barrel, no sights, approx. 8 lbs. Disc. 1988.

	$415	$355	$295	$265	$245	$220	$200

Not available in left-hand action.

Last Mfg.'s Sug. Retail was $467.

VANGUARD VGL — .223 Rem., .243 Win., .270 Win., 7mm Rem. Mag., .30-06, or 308 Win. cal., lightweight bolt action, checkered walnut stock, 5 shot mag.(6 on .223 Rem.), 20 in. barrel, no sights, 6½ lbs. Disc. 1988.

	$415	$355	$295	$265	$245	$220	$200

Not available in left-hand action.

Last Mfg.'s Sug. Retail was $467.

VANGUARD FIBERGUARD — .223 Rem., .243 Win., .270 Win., 7 mm Rem Mag., .30-06, or 308 Win. cal., 20 in. barrel, green fiberglass stock, 3 to 6 shot mag.'s, no sights, blued metal parts, approx. 6½ lbs. Disc. 1988.

	$500	$450	$395	$355	$285	$255	$220

Not available in left-hand action.

Last Mfg.'s Sug. Retail was $560.

RIFLES - .22 LR BOLT ACTION

ACCUMARK CLASSIC & DELUXE — while these models were advertised in 1990 ($635 retail), they were never manufactured.

RIFLES - .22 LR SEMI-AUTO

MARK XXII CLIP MAG — .22 LR cal., mag. feed, skip line checkered walnut stock with rosewood forearm and pistol grip caps, 10 shot detachable mag., 24 in. barrel, open sights, 6 lbs. Disc. 1989.

	$395	$320	$265	$245	$215	$195	$180

Last Mfg.'s Sug. Retail was $454.

The Mark XXII clip mag. was originally mfg. in Italy - a slight premium might be asked.

MARK XXII TUBE MAG — .22 LR cal., same general specifications as above model, except tube-feed, 15 shot, 6 lbs. Disc. 1989.

	$395	$320	$265	$245	$215	$195	$180

Last Mfg.'s Sug. Retail was $454.

SHOTGUNS: OVER AND UNDER

REGENCY FIELD GRADE — 20 ga. Mag. or 12 ga., checkered stock, vent rib, engraved side plates, SST, early importation beginning in 1972 was from Italy, later mfg. was switched to Japan.

	$900	$800	$700	$600	$550	$500	$475

Add 10-15% for early Italian mfg. (note proof marks).

REGENCY TRAP GRADE — 12 ga., checkered trap stock, engraved, vent rib, SST. Imported from Italy.

	$900	$800	$700	$600	$550	$500	$475

OLYMPIAN STANDARD — 12 and 20 ga., lightly engraved sideplates. Disc. 1980.

	$850	$775	$725	$625	$525	$450	$400

OLYMPIAN SKEET — 26 or 28 in. barrel.

	$885	$775	$725	$625	$525	$450	$400

Grading	100%	98%	95%	90%	80%	70%	60%

OLYMPIAN TRAP — 30 or 32 in. barrel, vent rib.

	100%	98%	95%	90%	80%	70%	60%
	$850	$775	$725	$625	$525	$440	$400

ATHENA GRADE IV — 12, 20, 28 (new 1989), or .410 (new 1989) ga., 3 in. chambers, boxlock with Greener Crossbolt, SST, ejectors, high luster finish on hand checkered claro walnut, engraved sideplates with satin nickel finish, vent barrels and rib, multi-chokes became standard (except 28 and .410 ga.) 1986, 7-8½lbs. Introduced 1982.

No Mfg.'s Retail	$1,600	$1,225	$1,050	$875	$725	$600	$525

Subtract $100 if without choke tubes.

This model was redesignated the Grade IV in 1989.

Skeet & Trap Models — 12 (Trap only) or 20 ga., special stock dimensions, target sights.

No Mfg.'s Retail	$1,615	$1,235	$1,050	$875	$725	$600	$525

Skeet models are available in fixed choke only.

Single Trap Grade IV — 12 ga., 32 or 34 in. barrel with multi-choke feature.

No Mfg.'s Retail	$1,615	$1,235	$1,050	$875	$725	$600	$525

Trap Combo — 12 ga., includes a set of O/U barrels and oversingle barrel with multi-choke feature.

No Mfg.'s Retail	$2,140	$1,725	$1,425	$1,200	$950	$800	$675

Master Skeet Set — 12 ga., includes 6 fitted full length Briley tubes with integral extractors (20, 28, and .410 ga.), cased. New 1988.

No Mfg.'s Retail	$3,200	$2,650	$2,150	$1,900	$1,775	$1,625	$1,525

ATHENA GRADE V — 12 or 20 ga., 3 in. chambers, similar to Grade IV, except has more elaborate engraving and better walnut. New 1989.

No Mfg.'s Retail	$2,000	$1,600	$1,350	$1,150	$900	$775	$675

ORION GRADE I — 12 or 20 ga., 3 in. chambers, 26 or 28 in. VR barrels with multi-chokes, SST, ejectors, entry level O/U with no engraving, checkered walnut stock and forearm. New 1989.

No Mfg.'s Retail	$860	$725	$650	$550	$495	$450	$400

ORION GRADE II — 12, 20, 28, or .410 ga., 3 in. chambers (except 28 ga.), boxlock with Greener Crossbolt, SST, ejectors, walnut with high-gloss finish, blue only, light engraving. Multi-chokes became standard 1986.

No Mfg.'s Retail	$1,005	$825	$700	$595	$540	$475	$435

Add $50 for Trap grade.

Subtract $85 if without choke tubes.

Add $15 for Skeet grade (12 and 20 ga., fixed chokes only).

This model was redesignated Grade II in 1989.

Ducks Unlimited Orion — 12 ga. (sponsor gun in 1986) or 20 ga. (sponsor gun in 1987), deluxe walnut with gold duck scenes, blue receiver, multi-chokes, includes presentation case.

	$1,395	$1,100	$875				

ORION GRADE III — 12 or 20 ga. only, similar to Grade II, except has silver grey receiver with custom engraving including mallard and pheasant game scenes, multi-chokes standard. New 1989.

No Mfg.'s Retail	$1,105	$895	$740	$650	$560	$500	$465

SHOTGUNS: SEMI-AUTO

CENTURION FIELD GRADE — 12 ga., vent rib, checkered stock, gas operation, walnut full pistol grip stock. Mfg. 1972-1981.

	$300	$280	$250	$240	$230	$210	$190

CENTURION TRAP GRADE — 12 ga., checkered stock, vent rib.

	$335	$300	$250	$240	$230	$210	$190

Grading	100%	98%	95%	90%	80%	70%	60%

CENTURION DE LUXE — 12 ga., vent rib, checkered stock, lightly engraved, fancy wood ($200-250).

	$375	$350	$310	$275	$250	$235	$210

Centurion DU — mfg. 1980 for DU chapters.

	$550	$375	$325

MODEL 82 — 12 ga. only, 2¾ or 3 in. chamber, gas operation, alloy receiver, vent rib, deluxe walnut, multi-chokes became standard in 1985, Trap Grade was disc. 1984. Mfg. 1983-89.

	$395	$350	$315	$280	$250	$235	$210

Subtract $30 without multi-chokes.
Subtract $35 for Trap Grade (disc. 1984).
Last Mfg.'s Sug. Retail was $500.

Model 82 Buckmaster — 22 in. barrel choked skeet, rifle sights, 7½ lbs. Disc. 1989.

	$395	$350	$315	$280	$250	$235	$210

Last Mfg.'s Sug. Retail was $500.

SHOTGUNS: SLIDE ACTION

PATRICIAN FIELD GRADE — 12 ga., checkered stock, vent rib. Mfg. 1972-1981.

	$275	$230	$210	$190	$180	$160	$140

PATRICIAN TRAP GRADE — 12 ga., checkered stock, vent rib.

	$295	$250	$225	$200	$185	$175	$165

PATRICIAN DE LUXE — 12 ga., checkered stock, lightly engraved, fancy wood, vent rib.

	$325	$275	$250	$215	$195	$175	$165

MODEL 92 — 12 ga. only, 2¾ and 3 in. chambers, ultra-short slide action w/twin rails, 26-30 in. vent rib barrels, engraved black alloy receiver, checkered pistol grip walnut stock and forearm. New 1983. Subtract $30 for Trap grade (disc. 1984), $20 if fixed choke (multi-chokes became standard 1985) barrel. Disc. 1987.

	$325	$275	$250	$225	$200	$185	$175

Model 92 Buckmaster — 22 in. skeet bore barrel rifle sights, 7½ lbs. Disc. 1987.

	$345	$285	$260	$240	$220	$200	$185

Last Mfg.'s Sug. Retail was $400.

WEAVER ARMS CORPORATION

Previous manufacturer located in Escondido, CA from 1984-1990.

NIGHTHAWK CARBINE — 9mm Para., closed bolt semi-auto paramilitary design carbine, fires from closed bolt, 16.1 in. barrel, retractable shoulder stock, 25, 32, 40, or 50 shot mag. (interchangeable with Uzi), ambidextrous safety, parkerized finish, 6½ lbs.

	$440	$360	$330	$300	$275	$250	$230

Last Mfg.'s Sug. Retail was $575.

NIGHTHAWK PISTOL — 9mm Para., closed bolt semi-auto, 10 or 12 in. barrel, alloy upper receiver, ambidextrous safety, black finish, 5 lbs. New 1987.

	$410	$340	$320	$295	$275	$250	$230

Last Mfg.'s Sug. Retail was $475.

WEBLEY & SCOTT, LIMITED

Manufactured in London and Birmingham, England 1898 to 1981. Shotguns are currently imported by New England Arms Co. located in Kittery Point, ME.

PISTOLS

MARK III M&P REVOLVER — double action, .38 S&W, 6 shot, 3 in. and 4 in. barrel, hinged top break, blue, fixed sights, wood service or competition grips. Mfg. 1897-1945.

	$350	$295	$255	$220	$195	$165	$140

MARK IV M&P REVOLVER — same as Mark III, except 3 in., 4 in., or 5 in. barrel, improved hammer and grip design. Mfg. 1929-1957.

	$350	$295	$255	$220	$195	$165	$140

MARK IV .22 TARGET REVOLVER — same as Mark IV, except .22 LR, 6 in. barrel, target sights, production ceased 1945.

	$450	$385	$330	$285	$235	$200	$165

NO. 1 MARK VI BRITISH SERVICE REVOLVER — .455 Webley, 4 in., 6 in., or 7½ in. barrel, top break, blue, fixed sights, wood service or competition grips. Mfg. 1915-1947.

	$300	$250	$225	$195	$165	$135	$110

MARK VI .22 TARGET REVOLVER — same as Mark VI, except .22 LR, target sights, mfg. until 1945.

	$300	$250	$225	$195	$165	$135	$110

MARK V REVOLVER — .455 calibre. Many were military-modified for .45 Colt or .45 ACP, many were civilian-modified, round butt, top-break.

	$375	$325	$275	$225	$175	$150	$125

BULLDOG OR RIC MODEL — double action, .455 Webley, 5 shot, 2½ in. barrel, solid frame, blue, fixed sights. Mfg. for Royal Irish Constabulary.

	$295	$250	$225	$175	$140	$110	$90

WEBLEY-FOSBERY AUTOMATIC REVOLVER — .455 Webley, 6 shot, top break, recoil revolves cylinder and cocks hammer, walnut or hard rubber grips. Mfg. 1901-1939.
A small number of Webley-Fosbery pistols were chambered for .38 Colt Auto Cartridge, usually found in 13xx range, features 8 shot mag.
Add $1,000 for .38 cal.
1901 Model — large frame, early features.

	$3,500	$3,000	$2,500	$2,250	$1,800	$1,350	$900

Add 20% for Target Model (adj. rear sight).
1902 Model — large frame, late features.

	$2,750	$2,350	$2,000	$1,750	$1,500	$1,200	$900

Add 20% for Target Model (adj. rear sight).
1904 Model — small frame, late features.

	$2,750	$2,350	$2,000	$1,750	$1,500	$1,200	$900

Add 20% for Target Model (adj. rear sight).

HAMMER MODEL .25 AUTOMATIC — .25 auto, 6 shot mag., 2 in. barrel, no sights, blue, composition grips. Mfg. 1906-1940.

	$275	$225	$175	$150	$135	$125	$115

HAMMERLESS MODEL .25 — .25 auto, same as Hammer Model .25, except no exposed hammer and fixed sights. Mfg. 1909-1940.

	$275	$225	$175	$150	$135	$125	$115

SINGLE SHOT TARGET PISTOL — .22 LR, 10 in. barrel, top break, blue, fixed sights on early models. Mfg. 1909-present.

	$250	$195	$120	$110	$100	$90	$75

Grading	100%	98%	95%	90%	80%	70%	60%

METROPOLITAN POLICE AUTOMATIC — .32 auto or .380 auto, 7 or 8 shot, 3½ in. barrel, blue, fixed sights, composition grips. Mfg. 1906-1940.

	$850	$750	$650	$600	$550	$475	$400

SEMI-AUTO SINGLE SHOT — .22 long, 4¼ and 9 in. barrel, adj. sights, blue, composition grips, empty case is ejected and hammer cocked as in a semi-auto, then it is loaded singly and slide closed. Mfg. 1911-1927.

	$330	$275	$165	$120	$110	$100	$85

9MM M&P AUTOMATIC — 9mm Browning Long, 8 shot, 5 in. barrel, blue, fixed sights. Mfg. 1909-1930.

	$950	$850	$750	$650	$550	$475	$400

HAMMERLESS MODEL 1913 — .38 cal., high velocity, approx. 1,000 mfg.

	$1,650	$1,250	$1,000	$800	$700	$600	$500

MARK I .455 AUTO PISTOL — .455 Webley, 7 shot, 5 in. barrel, blue, fixed sights. Mfg. 1912-1945.

	$1,500	$1,150	$900	$750	$600	$500	$400

MARK I NO. 2 — same as Mark I, except adj. sights, modified safety, and cut for shoulder stock.

	$2,750	$2,250	$1,800	$1,500	$1,200	$900	$600

The shoulder stock is an extremely rare accessory for this variation.

SHOTGUNS

MODEL 700 SIDE-BY-SIDE DOUBLE BARREL — 12 or 20 ga.'s, boxlock, case hardened receiver, minimum engraving, single trigger. Deduct $50 for double trigger.

	$1,700	$1,625	$1,500	$1,400	$1,000	$750	$600

MODEL 701 — same as 700 but fanciest walnut, most engraving. Deduct $100 for double trigger.

	$3,150	$2,500	$2,100	$1,800	$1,400	$1,150	$925

MODEL 702 — same as 700 but middle grade. Deduct $75 for double trigger.

	$2,650	$2,200	$1,800	$1,500	$1,250	$950	$750

WEIHRAUCH, HANS-HERMANN

Manufacturer located in Mellrichstadt, Germany. Exclusive factory authorized U.S. distributer is Beeman Precision Arms, Inc. located in Santa Rosa, CA.

MODEL HW 60M — .22 LR, match rifle featuring adj. sights, 26¾ in. barrel, single shot, match walnut stock, and other match features, 10.8 lbs.

Mfg.'s Sug. Retail	$798	$620	$525	$420	$345	$300	$265	$225

Add $135 for lefthand action.

MODEL HW 60J — .22 LR or .222 Rem. cal., sporter model with checkered walnut stock.

Mfg.'s Sug. Retail	$850	$710	$600	$480	$395	$345	$300	$260

Add $265 for .222 Rem. cal.

MODEL HW 66 RIFLE — .22 Hornet or .222 Rem. cal., match grade bolt action rifle. Imported 1989-90 only.

	$575	$495	$395	$325	$285	$250	$215

Add $78 for double set triggers.
Add $55 for stainless steel barrel (.22 Hornet).
Last Mfg.'s Sug. Retail was $688.

MODEL HW 660 MATCH — .22 LR cal., match rifle variation. Importation began 1991.

Mfg.'s Sug. Retail	$889	$775	$615	$525	$465	$415	$340	$300

Grading	100%	98%	95%	90%	80%	70%	60%

WESSON FIREARMS CO. INC.

Manufacturer located in Palmer, MA. In late 1990, ownership of Dan Wesson Arms changed (within the family), and the new company has been renamed Wesson Firearms Co., Inc.

REVOLVERS: DOUBLE ACTION

MODEL 11 — .357 Mag., 6 shot, 2½, 4, or 6 in. interchangeable barrels, fixed sights, blue, interchangeable grips, exposed barrel nut. Mfg. 1970-1971.

		100%	98%	95%	90%	80%	70%	60%
		$200	$175	$160	$150	$140	$130	$120

Add $60 per extra barrel.

MODEL 12 — same as 11, with adj. sights. Mfg. 1970-1971.

	$245	$200	$175	$160	$150	$140	$130

MODEL 14 — same as 11, with recessed barrel nut. Mfg. 1971-1975.

	$225	$185	$170	$160	$150	$140	$130

MODEL 8 — same as 14, except .38 Spl.

	$200	$170	$155	$145	$135	$125	$115

MODEL 15 — same as 14, with adj. sights. Mfg. 1971-1975.

	$245	$200	$155	$145	$135	$125	$115

MODEL 9 — same as 15, except .38 Spl. Mfg. 1971-1975.

	$245	$200	$155	$145	$135	$125	$115

REVOLVERS: CURRENT MANUFACTURE

Dan Wesson revolvers are mfg. with solid rib barrels as standard equipment.

MODEL 22 — .22 LR, double action, 6 shot, adj. sights, 2½, 4, 6, 8, or 10 in. (disc. 1987) barrel, current production. Add $20 for vent rib, $48 for heavy vent rib, $8 for each additional longer barrel length.

Mfg.'s Sug. Retail	$337	$280	$225	$200	$190	$180	$170	$160

Model 22 Pistol Pac — includes 2½, 4, 6, and 8 in. barrel assemblies, extra grip, 4 additional front sight blades, and aluminum case.

Mfg.'s Sug. Retail	$615	$495	$395	$360	$330	$300	$275	$260

Add $100 for full shroud VR barrels.

Add $190 for heavy full shroud VR barrels.

MODEL 22M — .22 Mag., otherwise same as Model 22.

Mfg.'s Sug. Retail	$349	$290	$230	$200	$190	$180	$170	$160

Model 22M Pistol Pac — includes 2½, 4, 6, and 8 in. barrel assemblies, extra grip, 4 additional front sight blades, and aluminum case.

Mfg.'s Sug. Retail	$637	$500	$400	$360	$330	$300	$275	$260

Add $100 for full shroud VR barrels.

Add $190 for heavy full shroud VR barrels.

MODEL 32 — .32 H&R Mag., 2½, 4, 6, or 8 in. barrel, adj. rear sight, interchangeable colored front sight blades, blue finish, checkered target grips. New 1986. Add $20 for VR barrel shroud (Model 32-V), add $43 for VR heavy barrel shroud (Model 32-VH). Also add approx. $8 for each additional barrel length over 2½ in.

Mfg.'s Sug. Retail	$337	$280	$225	$200	$190	$180	$170	$160

Grading	100%	98%	95%	90%	80%	70%	60%

Model 32 Pistol Pac — includes 2½, 4, 6, and 8 in. barrel assemblies, extra grip, 4 additional front sight blades, and aluminum case.

Mfg.'s Sug. Retail	$615	$495	$395	$360	$330	$300	$275	$260

Add $100 for full shroud VR barrels.

Add $190 for heavy full shroud VR barrels.

MODEL 322 — .32-20 cal., 2½, 4, 6, or 8 in. barrel, adj. rear sight, interchangeable colored front sight blades, blue finish, checkered target grips. New 1986. Add $20 for VR barrel shroud (Model 322-V), add $43 for VR heavy barrel shroud (Model 322-VH). Also add approx. $8 for each additional barrel length over 2½ in. New 1991.

Mfg.'s Sug. Retail	$337	$280	$225	$200	$190	$180	$170	$160

Model 322 Pistol Pac — includes 2½, 4, 6, and 8 in. barrel assemblies, extra grip, 4 additional front sight blades, and aluminum case.

Mfg.'s Sug. Retail	$615	$495	$395	$360	$330	$300	$275	$260

Add $100 for full shroud VR barrels.

Add $190 for heavy full shroud VR barrels.

MODEL 14-2 — .357 Mag., 4, 6, or 8 in. interchangeable barrels, fixed sights, blue. Mfg. 1975-present. Add $8 for each additional longer barrel length.

Mfg.'s Sug. Retail	$267	$215	$170	$150	$140	$130	$120	$110

Model 14-2 Pistol Pac — includes 2½, 4, and 6 in. barrel assemblies, extra grip and aluminum case.

Mfg.'s Sug. Retail	$456	$385	$325	$300	$275	$260	$245	$230

MODEL 8-2 — same as 14-2, except .38 Spl. cal.

Mfg.'s Sug. Retail	$267	$215	$170	$150	$140	$130	$120	$110

This model is also available in a Pistol Pac - same specifications and values as the Model 14-2 Pistol Pac.

MODEL 15-2 — same as 14-2, except adj. sights, available with 2, 4, 6, 8, 10, 12, or 15 in. barrels. Add approx. $9 for each additional barrel length over 2 inches, $20 for VR barrel (Model 15-2V), or $44 for VR heavy barrel shroud (Model 15-2HV).

2 in. barrel

Mfg.'s Sug. Retail	$337	$280	$225	$200	$190	$180	$170	$160

Model 15-2 Pistol Pac — includes 2½, 4, 6, and 8 in. barrel assemblies, extra grip, 4 additional front sight blades, and aluminum case.

Mfg.'s Sug. Retail	$615	$495	$395	$360	$330	$300	$275	$260

Add $100 for full shroud VR barrels.

Add $190 for heavy full shroud VR barrels.

MODEL 15 GOLD SERIES — .357 Mag., 6 or 8 in. VR heavy slotted barrel, "Gold" stamped shrould with Dan Wesson signature, smoother action (8 lb. double action pull), 18 kt. gold plated trigger, white triangle rear sight with orange dot patridge front sight, exotic hardwood grips. Mfg. 1989-90 only.

	$475	$420	$380	$340	$300	$260	$225

Last Mfg.'s Sug. Retail was $544.

MODEL 9-2 — same as 15-2, except .38 Spl. Use same add-ons as in Model 15-2.

Mfg.'s Sug. Retail	$337	$280	$225	$200	$190	$180	$170	$160

This model is also available in a Pistol Pac - same specifications and values as the Model 9-2 Pistol Pac.

MODEL 375V SUPERMAG — .375 Super Mag., 6, 8, or 10 in. VR barrel, adj. rear sight, interchangeable front and rear sight blades, bright blue finish, smooth target grips. New 1986. Add approx. $15 for each barrel length after 6 in., $26 for slotted shroud (Model 375-V8S, 8 in. barrel only), $12 for VR heavy shroud (Model 375 -VH).

Mfg.'s Sug. Retail	$508	$410	$335	$285	$260	$240	$230	$225

Grading	100%	98%	95%	90%	80%	70%	60%

MODEL 40V (.357 SUPERMAG) — .357 Super Mag. (.357 Max.), double action, 6 shot, 6, 8, or 10 in. barrel vent rib. Add $26 for slotted barrel shroud (8 in. barrel only), $12 for heavy VR barrel, $15 for each additional barrel length.

Mfg.'s Sug. Retail	$508	$410	$335	$285	$260	$240	$230	$225

MODEL 41V — .41 Mag., double action, 6 shot, 4, 6, 8, or 10 in. barrel vent rib. Add $21 for heavy barrel, $11 for each additional barrel length.

Mfg.'s Sug. Retail	$413	$345	$290	$270	$255	$240	$230	$225

Model 41V Pistol Pac — includes 6 and 8 in. VR barrel assemblies, extra grip, 2 additional front sight blades, and aluminum case.

Mfg.'s Sug. Retail	$624	$495	$395	$360	$330	$300	$275	$260

Add $50 for ventilated shroud VR barrels.

MODEL 44V — .44 Mag., double action, same as Model 41V, adj. sights. Add $21 for heavy barrel, $11 for each additional barrel length.

Mfg.'s Sug. Retail	$431	$365	$300	$265	$250	$230	$215	$200

Model 44V Pac — includes 6 and 8 in. VR barrel assemblies, extra grip, 4 additional front sight blades, and aluminum case.

Mfg.'s Sug. Retail	$707	$585	$425	$380	$330	$300	$275	$260

Add $50 for ventilated shroud VR barrels.

MODEL 45V — .45 Long Colt, 4, 6, 8, or 10 in. VR barrel, same frame as Model 44V, blued finish. Add $11 for each additional barrel length. New 1988.

Mfg.'s Sug. Retail	$431	$365	$300	$265	$250	$230	$215	$200

Model 45V Pistol Pac — includes 6 and 8 in. VR barrel assemblies, extra grip, 2 additional front sight blades, and aluminum case.

Mfg.'s Sug. Retail	$707	$585	$425	$380	$330	$300	$275	$260

Add $50 for ventilated shroud VR barrels.

MODEL 445 SUPERMAG — .445 Super Mag., 6, 8, or 10 in. VR barrel, adj. rear sight, interchangeable front and rear sight blades, bright blue finish, smooth target grips. New 1991. Add approx. $18 for each barrel length after 6 in., $38 for slotted shroud (Model 445-V8S, 8 in. barrel only), $14 for VR heavy shroud (Model 445 -VH).

Mfg.'s Sug. Retail	$548	$440	$350	$300	$275	$250	$230	$225

REVOLVERS: STAINLESS STEEL

MODEL 722 — stainless version of Model 22, use same add-ons for various barrel options.

Mfg.'s Sug. Retail	$366	$315	$250	$205

This model is also available in a Pistol Pac including 2½, 4, 6, and 8 in. solid rib barrel assemblies, extra grip, 4 additional sight blades, and fitted carrying case - Mfg.'s Suggested Retail is $689. Add $100 for VR barrels, $200 for full shroud heavy VR barrels.

MODEL 722M — .22 Mag, otherwise same as Model 722, use same add-ons for various barrel options.

Mfg.'s Sug. Retail	$390	$320	$270	$230

This model is also available in a Pistol Pac including 2½, 4, 6, and 8 in. solid rib barrel assemblies, extra grip, 4 additional sight blades, and fitted carrying case. Mfg.'s Suggested Retail is $724. Add $100 for VR barrels, $200 for full shroud heavy VR barrels.

MODEL 708 — .38 Spl., same as Model 8-2. Add $6 for each additional barrel length.

Mfg.'s Sug. Retail	$311	$260	$200	$170

This model is also available in a Pistol Pac including 2½, 4, and 6 in. solid rib barrel assemblies, extra grip and fitted carrying case. Mfg.'s Suggested Retail is $517.

Grading	100%	98%	95%	90%	80%	70%	60%

MODEL 709 — .38 Spl., target revolver, adj. sights. Add $9 for each additional longer barrel length, $20 for vent rib, $45 for heavy vent rib. Also available in special order 10, 12, or 15 barrel lengths (add approx. $100 for 10 in.).

Mfg.'s Sug. Retail	$366	$305	$250	$205

This model is also available in a Pistol Pac including 2½, 4, 6, and 8 in. solid rib barrel assemblies, extra grip, 4 additional sight blades, and fitted carrying case. Mfg.'s Suggested Retail is $689. Add $100 for VR barrels, $200 for full shroud heavy VR barrels.

MODEL 714 — .357 Mag., same as Model 14-2. Add $6 for each additional barrel length.

Mfg.'s Sug. Retail	$311	$260	$200	$170

This model is also available in a Pistol Pac including 2½, 4, and 6 in. solid rib barrel assemblies, extra grip and fitted carrying case. Mfg.'s Suggested Retail is $517.

MODEL 715 — .357 Mag., target revolver, adj. sights. Add $20 for vent rib, $45 for heavy vent rib.

Mfg.'s Sug. Retail	$366	$305	$250	$205

This model is also available in a Pistol Pac including 2½, 4, 6, and 8 in. solid rib barrel assemblies, extra grip, 4 additional sight blades, and fitted carrying case. Mfg.'s Suggested Retail is $689. Add $100 for VR barrels, $200 for full shroud heavy VR barrels.

MODEL 732 — .32 H&R Mag., same as Model 32, except is stainless steel. New 1986. Add $20 for VR barrel shroud (Model 732-V), $44 for VR heavy barrel shroud (Model 732-VH). Also add approx. $9 for each additional barrel length over 2½ in.

Mfg.'s Sug. Retail	$366	$305	$250	$205

This model is also available in a Pistol Pac including 2½, 4, 6, and 8 in. solid rib barrel assemblies, extra grip, 4 additional sight blades, and fitted carrying case. Mfg.'s Suggested Retail is $689. Add $100 for VR barrels, $200 for full shroud heavy VR barrels.

MODEL 7322 — .32-20 cal., same as Model 322, except is stainless steel. New 1991. Add $20 for VR barrel shroud (Model 7322-V), $44 for VR heavy barrel shroud (Model 7322-VH). Also add approx. $9 for each additional barrel length over 2½ in.

Mfg.'s Sug. Retail	$366	$305	$250	$205

This model is also available in a Pistol Pac including 2½, 4, 6, and 8 in. solid rib barrel assemblies, extra grip, 4 additional sight blades, and fitted carrying case. Mfg.'s Suggested Retail is $615. Add $100 for VR barrels, $190 for full shroud heavy VR barrels.

MODEL 740V - .357 SUPERMAG — .357 Max., 6, 8, or 10 in. barrel, adj. rear sight with interchangeable front and rear blades, high polished finish, smooth target grips. New 1986. Add approx. $20 for each additional barrel length after 6 in., $27 for slotted shroud (only avail. with 8 in. barrel), $15 for VR heavy barrel shroud (Model 740-VH).

Mfg.'s Sug. Retail	$569	$455	$350	$315

MODEL 741V — .41 Mag., same as Model 41V. Add $23 for heavy vent rib, $11 for each barrel length over 4 in.

Mfg.'s Sug. Retail	$462	$385	$315	$270

This model is also available in a Pistol Pac including 6 and 8 in. VR barrel assemblies, extra grip, 2 additional sight blades, and fitted carrying case. Mfg.'s Suggested Retail is $690. Add $49 for ventilated shroud VR barrels.

MODEL 744V — .44 Mag., same as Model 44V. Add $21 for heavy vent rib, $10 for each barrel length over 4 in.

Mfg.'s Sug. Retail	$507	$420	$340	$285

This model is also available in a Pistol Pac including 6 and 8 in. VR barrel assemblies, extra grip, 2 additional sight blades, and fitted carrying case. Mfg.'s Suggested Retail is $814. Add $53 for ventilated shroud VR barrels.

Model 744 Commemorative — limited mfg.

	$595	$475	$325

773

Grading		100%	98%	95%	90%	80%	70%	60%

MODEL 745V — .45 Long Colt, same as Model 45V, except in stainless steel. Add $23 for heavy full shroud VR barrels, $11 for each additional barrel length.

Mfg.'s Sug. Retail	$507	$420	$340	$285

This model is also available in a Pistol Pac including 6 and 8 in. VR barrel assemblies, extra grip, 2 additional sight blades, and fitted carrying case. Mfg.'s Suggested Retail is $814. Add $53 for ventilated shroud VR barrels.

MODEL 7445 - .445 SUPERMAG — .445 Supermag., 6, 8, or 10 in. barrel, adj. rear sight with interchangeable front and rear blades, high polished finish, smooth target grips. New 1986. Add approx. $21 for each additional barrel length after 6 in., $25 for slotted shroud (only avail. with 8 in. barrel), $15 for VR heavy barrel shroud (Model 7445-VH).

Mfg.'s Sug. Retail	$609	$480	$370	$340

WESSON, FRANK
Worcester, MA 1854 to 1865, Springfield, MA 1865-1875.

PISTOLS: SINGLE SHOT

100%	98%	95%	90%	80%	70%	60%	50%	40%	30%	20%	10%

SMALL FRAME FIRST MODEL — .22 cal., tip up action, 3½ in. ½ octagon barrel, brass frame, spur trigger, rosewood grips, round frame, irregular sideplate. Mfg. 2500, 1859-1862.

$605	$550	$495	$440	$385	$330	$275	$220	$195	$165	$140	$110

SMALL FRAME SECOND MODEL — same as First Model, with flat sided frame and circular sideplate. Mfg. 12,000, 1862-1880.

$550	$495	$440	$385	$330	$305	$250	$195	$165	$110	$105	$85

MEDIUM FRAME FIRST MODEL — .30 S or L, .32 S rimfires, 4 in. ½ octagon barrel, iron frame, same as Small Frame in other respects, narrow hinge and short trigger. Mfg. 1000, 1859-1862.

$525	$470	$415	$360	$305	$275	$220	$195	$165	$110	$105	$85

MEDIUM FRAME SECOND MODEL — same as First Model, with wider hinge and longer trigger. Mfg. 1000, 1862-1870.

$495	$440	$385	$330	$275	$250	$220	$195	$165	$110	$105	$85

RIFLES

NO. 1 LONG RANGE — side hammer, falling block lever actuated, .44-100 and .45-100 standard, 34 in. octagon barrel, tang. sight, select checkered pistol grip stock. Less than 50 mfg., circa 1870-1880.

$4,950	$4,675	$4,400	$3,850	$3,575	$3,080	$2,860	$2,475	$2,200	$2,035	$1,760	$1,500

NO. 2 HUNTING RIFLE — similar to No. 1, with finger loop lever. Less than 100 mfg.

$4,400	$4,180	$3,850	$3,520	$3,025	$2,750	$2,420	$2,255	$2,035	$1,925	$1,760	$1,540

NO. 1 SPORTING RIFLE — similar to No. 2, with center hammer, .38-100, .40-100, .45-100. Less than 25 mfg.

$4,400	$4,180	$3,850	$3,520	$3,025	$2,750	$2,420	$2,255	$2,035	$1,925	$1,760	$1,540

POCKET RIFLES

SMALL FRAME TIP UP — .22 rimfire, 6 in. ½ octagon barrel, brass frame, spur trigger, rosewood grips. Approx. 500 mfg., 1865-1875.

$605	$550	$525	$495	$470	$440	$415	$360	$330	$275	$220	$165

If without stock - deduct 25%.

100%	98%	95%	90%	80%	70%	60%	50%	40%	30%	20%	10%

MEDIUM FRAME TIP UP — .22, .30, or .32 rimfire cal.s, 10 or 12 in. barrel, same as small frame, with exceptions noted and larger frame. Approx. 1000 mfg., 1862-1870.

$605	$550	$525	$495	$470	$440	$415	$360	$330	$275	$220	$165

If without stock - deduct 25%.

MODEL 1870 SMALL FRAME FIRST TYPE — similar to Small Frame Tip Up, except barrel rotates on its axis to load, detachable stock. Approx. 3000 mfg., 1870-1890.

$550	$495	$470	$440	$415	$385	$360	$305	$275	$220	$195	$165

If without stock - deduct 25%.

MODEL 1870 SMALL FRAME SECOND TYPE — full octagon barrel.

$525	$470	$440	$415	$385	$360	$330	$275	$250	$195	$165	$140

MODEL 1870 SMALL FRAME THIRD TYPE — iron frame, push button ½ cock.

$495	$440	$415	$385	$360	$330	$305	$250	$220	$165	$140	$110

MODEL 1870 MEDIUM FRAME FIRST TYPE — same as Small Frame, except in size and availability of .32 cal. Approx. 5000 mfg., 1870-1893.

$525	$495	$470	$440	$415	$385	$360	$305	$275	$250	$195	$165

Deduct 25% if without stock.

MODEL 1870 MEDIUM FRAME SECOND TYPE — external push half cock and iron frame.

$440	$415	$385	$330	$305	$275	$220	$195	$165	$140	$110	$90

Deduct 25% if without stock.

MODEL 1870 MEDIUM FRAME THIRD TYPE — has three screws in frame, iron frame.

$440	$415	$385	$330	$305	$275	$220	$195	$165	$140	$110	$90

Deduct 25% if without stock.

MODEL 1870 LARGE FRAME FIRST TYPE — .32, .38, .42, or .44 rimfire cal., 15-24 in. barrels, similar to smaller frame models, auto extractor. Approx. 500 mfg., 1870-1880.

$825	$770	$715	$660	$605	$550	$525	$495	$440	$385	$305	$275

If without stock — deduct 25%.

MODEL 1870 LARGE FRAME SECOND TYPE — same as First Type, with standard sliding extractor.

$825	$770	$715	$660	$605	$550	$525	$495	$440	$385	$305	$275

Deduct 25% if without stock.

WESTERN ARMS COMPANY
Ithaca, NY.

WESTERN LONG RANGE DOUBLE BARREL SHOTGUN — 12, 16, 20, or .410 ga., 26-32 in. barrels, mod. and full choke, boxlock, extractors, double or single trigger, plain pistol grip stock, Western Arms Co. was a division of Ithaca Gun. Mfg. 1929-1946.

$275	$225	$200	$175	$150	$125	$100

Single trigger

$325	$275	$250	$225	$200	$150	$125

WESTERN FIELD
Trademark used on Montgomery Wards rifles and shotguns.

The Western Field trademark has appeared literally on hundreds of various models (shotguns and rifles) sold through the Montgomery Wards retail network. Most of these models were manufactured through subcontracts with both domestic and international firearms manufacturers. Typically, they were "spec." guns made to sell at a specific price to

Grading	100%	98%	95%	90%	80%	70%	60%

undersell the competition. Most of these models were derivatives of existing factory models with less expensive wood and perhaps missing the features found on those models from which they were derived. To date, there has been very little interest in collecting Western Field guns, regardless of rarity. Rather than list J.C. Higgins' models, a general guideline is that values generally are under those of their "1st generation relatives". As a result, prices are ascertained by the shooting value of the gun, rather than its' collector value.

WESTLEY RICHARDS & CO. LTD.

Originally William Westley Richards located in Birmingham, England. Currently manufactured by Westley Richards and Co., Ltd. located on Grange Road, Birmingham, England (B296ar). Manufactured 1821 to date. Currently imported by New England Arms Co. located in Kittery Point, ME, or directly from factory.

Note: Westley Richards guns are essentially custom ordered - only 25-30 guns are made annually. They make many weapons that are impossible to list and evaluate, except on an individual basis. Professional appraisal is necessary upon purchase or sale.

Due to the recent devaluation of the U.S. dollar, prices could fluctuate significantly from values listed below. To obtain a quotation for a new Westley Richards shotgun, an inquiry should be submitted to the manufacturer or importer (see Trademark Index for addresses). Values below have been computed at an exchange rate of $1.92/pound.

SHOTGUNS

OVUNDO O/U — 12 ga., barrel length and choke to order, hand detachable boxlock with dummy sideplates, SST, checkered straight or pistol grip stock, pre-WWII.

	100%	98%	95%	90%	80%	70%	60%
	$18,000	$15,000	$13,000	$11,000	$9,750	$8,500	$7,250

MODEL E SxS — 12, 16, or 20 ga., barrel length and choke to order, boxlock, extractors, double triggers, checkered pistol grip or straight stock.

Mfg.'s Sug. Retail	$3,820	$3,820	$3,300	$2,900	$2,600	$2,300	$1,950	$1,600

20 gauge — add 20%.

Auto ejectors — add 50%.

CONNAUGHT MODEL SxS — 12, 20, or 28 ga., Anson & Deeley scalloped boxlock action, scroll engraving, 26 or 28 in. barrels, ejectors, about 6½ lbs.

Mfg.'s Sug. Retail	$9,165	$9,165	$7,800	$6,600	$5,600	$4,800	$4,000	$3,400

Add $275 for 20 or 28 ga.

BEST QUALITY BOXLOCK SxS — 12, 16, 20, 28, or .410 ga., barrel lengths and chokes to order, detachable locks with hinged cover, checkered straight or pistol grip stock, auto ejectors.

Mfg.'s Sug. Retail	$13,365	$13,365	$10,750	$8,750	$7,000	$5,500	$4,400	$3,700

28 gauge — add 30%-40%.

20 gauge — add 20%.

SST — add $1,000.

Only 6 .410 Best Quality Boxlock's have been mfg. to date - values for mint condition specimens can exceed $30,000.

BEST QUALITY SIDELOCK — 12, 16, 20, 28, or .410 ga., barrel length and choke to order, hand detachable sidelocks, auto ejectors, checkered straight or pistol grip stock.

Mfg.'s Sug. Retail	$19,090	$19,090	$16,000	$13,000	$10,550	$8,750	$7,600	$6,400

20 gauge — add 20%.

28 gauge — add 40%.

.410 gauge — add 60%.

SST — add $1,000.

Most specimens in this model were custom ordered, and as a result, each gun has to be evaluated individually.

Grading	100%	98%	95%	90%	80%	70%	60%

WILLIAM BISHOP SIDELOCK MODEL — current mfg., best quality sidelock, made to individual customer specifications.

Mfg.'s Sug. Retail $25,770 $25,770 $21,000 $17,500 $14,750 $11,750 $9,500 $8,250
Add $120 - $245 for 20 or 28 ga.

CARLTON DETACHABLE SIDELOCK — 12 or 20 ga., current mfg., detachable sidelocks, top of the line shotgun custom made per customer specifications, elaborate game scene engraving. Many options upon request - values below are for base gun only.

Mfg.'s Sug. Retail $28,635 $28,635 $24,000 $20,500 $16,750 $13,750 $10,500 $9,000

RIFLES

BEST QUALITY DOUBLE RIFLE — .300, .375 H&H, .470 NE, .577 NE, or .600 NE cal., auto ejectors, boxlock, hammerless, folding leaf rear sight, hooded front sight, engraved with quality French walnut stock, horn forend tip. Values will vary according to caliber.

Mfg.'s Sug. Retail $38,180 $38,180 $33,200 $29,000 $25,000 $21,000 $18,750 $16,000
Values will vary greatly on this model depending on caliber and type/style of engraving. Values above are for .577 Nitro Express.

DETACHABLE LOCK DOUBLE RIFLE — available in most cal.'s, boxlock with detachable locks, ejectors, colored case hardened frame, cased.

Mfg.'s Sug. Retail $43,910 $43,910 $38,180 $33,750 $29,600 $25,000 $22,000 $18,250

STALKER MAGAZINE RIFLE — .243 Win., .270 Win., .30-06, .300 H&H, .375 H&H, or .458 Win. Mag. cal., bolt action, Mauser action, 22, 24, or 25 in. barrel, leaf rear and hooded front sight, engraved with French walnut stock, horn forend tip. Current mfg.

Mfg.'s Sug. Retail $8,590 $8,590 $7,400 $6,500 $5,500 $4,750 $4,000 $3,300
Add $322 for mag. cal.'s.

WHITNEY FIREARMS COMPANY
Manufactured between 1956-1959 in Hartford, CT.

PISTOL: SEMI-AUTO

WOLVERINE OR LIGHTNING — .22 auto, unique futuristic appearance, 10 shot, 4⅝ in. barrel, plastic grips, aluminum alloy frame and barrel shroud, blue model is more common (approx. 13,000 mfg.), nickel is rare (approx. 900 mfg.). Mfg. 1955-1962.

Blue finish	$425	$350	$300	$260	$230	$200	$175
Nickel finish	$550	$450	$375	$300	$260	$230	$200

WHITWORTH
This trademark can be found in the Interarms section of this text.

WICHITA ARMS, INC.
Manufacturer located in Wichita, KS.

PISTOLS

WICHITA INTERNATIONAL PISTOL (WIP) — available in 8 cal.'s between .22 LR and .357 Mag., single shot, break open action, stainless steel, adj. sights, 10½ or 14 in. barrel, adj. sights or scope mounts, smooth walnut stocks and forearm.

Mfg.'s Sug. Retail $485 $445 $385 $340

Grading	100%	98%	95%	90%	80%	70%	60%

WICHITA CLASSIC PISTOL — assorted cal.'s to .308 Win., 11¼ in. barrel, action has left-hand bolt for shooting with right-hand, deluxe walnut, custom made, 3 lbs. 15 oz.

Mfg.'s Sug. Retail	$2,950	$2,950	$2,400	$2,100	$1,850	$1,575	$1,265	$1,000

Wichita Classic Engraved — similar to Wichita Classic, except is extensively engraved.

Mfg.'s Sug. Retail	$4,850	$4,850	$3,500	$2,750

WICHITA SILHOUETTE PISTOL (WSP) — .308 Win. or 7mm/HMSA cal., adj. trigger and sights, 14¹⁵⁄₁₆ in. barrel, center grip walnut stock, 4½ lbs. Left-hand action for shooting with right-hand.

Mfg.'s Sug. Retail	$1,100	$1,100	$900	$750	$600	$525	$460	$400

WICHITA MK40 — .308 Win. or 7mm/HMSA, fiberthane (disc. 1987) or walnut (new 1988) stock, 13 in. barrel, adj. trigger, multi-range sights, 4½ lbs.

Mfg.'s Sug. Retail	$1,100	$1,100	$900	$750	$600	$525	$460	$400

Add $225 for stainless steel barrel.

RIFLES

WICHITA CLASSIC RIFLE (WCR) — 17-222, 17-222 Mag., .222 Rem, 222 Mag., 223 Rem., 6x47, and other cal.'s up to and including .308 cal., bolt action, single shot, select walnut, 21 in. octagon barrel, Canjar trigger, no sights, 7 lbs.

Mfg.'s Sug. Retail	$2,950	$2,950	$2,400	$2,100	$1,850	$1,575	$1,265	$1,000

Add P.O.R. for blind box mag.

Add $175 for left-hand action.

Wichita Varmint Rifle (WVR) — similar to WCR, except available only in Varmint cal.'s (up to and including .308) and round barrel.

Mfg.'s Sug. Retail	$1,975	$1,975	$1,600	$1,325	$1,100	$950	$800	$750

Add P.O.R. for blind box mag.

Add $175 for left-hand action.

Wichita Silhouette Rifle (WSR) — available in most cal.'s, gray fiberthane stock, 24 in. match grade barrel, 2 oz Canjar trigger, no sights, 9 lbs.

Mfg.'s Sug. Retail	$2,150	$2,150	$1,700	$1,375	$1,140	$975	$825	$750

Add $175 for left-hand action.

Wichita Magnum — Mag. cal.'s. Disc. 1984.

	$1,725	$1,300	$1,175	$1,100	$1,000	$925	$875

WICKLIFFE RIFLES
Previous mfg. by Triple S Development located in Wickliffe, OH.

RIFLES - SINGLE SHOT

MODEL 76 STANDARD — falling block action, most popular cal.'s, 22 or 26 in. barrel, no sights, select walnut pistol grip, 2 piece stock. Mfg. 1976-disc.

	$370	$320	$305	$275	$250	$220	$165

MODEL 76 DELUXE GRADE — same as Standard, in .30-06 only, 22 in. barrel, fancy wood, silver pistol grip cap.

	$460	$415	$385	$360	$320	$290	$250

MODEL 76 COMMEMORATIVE — same as Deluxe, except etched receiver, U.S. silver dollar inlaid in stock, presentation case. Mfg. 100, 1976.

	$1,100	$825	$550	$495	$440	$330	$305

STINGER — similar to 76, .22 in. Hornet or .223, lightweight 22 in. barrel.

	$370	$320	$305	$275	$250	$220	$165

Grading	100%	98%	95%	90%	80%	70%	60%

STINGER DELUXE — same as 76 Deluxe, in .22 Hornet or .223, lightweight 22 in. barrel.

	$460	$415	$385	$360	$325	$290	$250

TRADITIONALIST — same as Standard 76, in .30-06 or .45-70, 24 in. barrel.

	$370	$320	$305	$275	$250	$220	$165

KODIAK COMMEMORATIVE — similar to Deluxe, .338 Mag., 26 in. barrel, etched receiver.

	$650	$550	$475	$425	$375	$325	$275

WILDEY INC.

Originally manufactured in Cheshire, CT. New manufacture is in New Melford, CT.

WILDEY AUTO PISTOL — .45 Win. Mag., .357 Peterbuilt (limited mfg.), or .475 Wildey Mag., gas operated, 5, 6, 7, 8, 10, or 14 in. vent rib barrel, selective single shot or semi-auto, 3 lug rotary bolt, fixed barrel (interchangeable), stainless steel construction, 7 shot, double action, adj. sights, smooth wood grips, designed to fire proprietary new cartridges specifically for this gun including the .45 Win. Mag. cal., 64 oz. with 5 in. barrel.
In late 1990, Wildey announced that they would be introducing 3 new proprietary cartridges. They are the .30 WM, 10mm WM, and 11mm WM based on the .475 Wildey Mag. necked down to respective cartridge dimensions. Norma, located in Sweden, produces the .475 WM brass.
Add $475-$590 per interchangeable barrel.

Survivor Model — .45 Win. Mag. or .475 Wildey Mag. cal., 5, 6, 7, 8, 10, or 12 in. barrel only. New 1990.

Mfg.'s Sug. Retail	$1,175	$1,050	$875	$725

Add $20 for 8 or 10 in. barrel.
Add $50 for new model VR (8, 10, or 12 in. barrel only).
Add $150 for 12 in. barrel (.475 WM, new model rib only).
The .475 Wildey cal. is derived from the .284 Win. case. This cal. is available in 8 or 10 in. barrel only.

Survivor Guardsman — similar to Survivor Model, except has squared off trigger guard. New 1990.

Mfg.'s Sug. Retail	$1,210	$1,075	$885	$725

Add $20 for 8 or 10 in. barrel.
Add $46 for new model VR (8, 10, or 12 in. barrel only).
Add $151 for 12 in. barrel (.475 WM, new model rib only).

Hunter Model — .45 Win. Mag. or .475 Wildey Mag. cal., 8, 10, or 12 in. barrel, matte finish on all metal parts, adj. sights. New 1990.

Mfg.'s Sug. Retail	$1,316	$1,125	$950	$825

Add $30 for 12 in. barrel.

Hunter Guardsman — similar to Hunter Model, except has squared off trigger guard. New 1990.

Mfg.'s Sug. Retail	$1,351	$1,150	$975	$850

Add $30 for 12 in. barrel.

Older Mfg. — .45 Win. Mag. or .475 Wildey Mag. cal., Cheshire, CT addressed, serial numbered 1-2,489 with 3 character prefix, priced by serialization, 7, 8, or 10 in. barrel is most desirable. These pistols are older mfg. and Wildey should be contacted directly to find out which models are still remaining (address can be found in the Trademark Index in the back of this text).
Add $475-$500 per interchangeable barrel.
.475 Wildey Mag. cal. is available in 8 or 10 in. barrel only.
SERIAL NO. 1-200.

Mfg.'s Sug. Retail	$2,180	$1,900	$1,700	$1,550

Add $20 for 8 or 10 in. barrel.

Grading		100%	98%	95%	90%	80%	70%	60%
SERIAL NO. 201-400.								
Mfg.'s Sug. Retail	$1,980	$1,750	$1,550	$1,400				
Add $20 for 8 or 10 in. barrel.								
SERIAL NO. 401-600.								
Mfg.'s Sug. Retail	$1,780	$1,650	$1,375	$1,250				
Add $20 for 8 or 10 in. barrel.								
SERIAL NO. 601-800.								
Mfg.'s Sug. Retail	$1,580	$1,450	$1,200	$1,000				
Add $20 for 8 or 10 in. barrel.								
SERIAL NO. 801-1,000.								
Mfg.'s Sug. Retail	$1,275	$1,100	$925	$800				
Add $25 for 8 or 10 in. barrel.								
SERIAL NO. 1,001-2,489.								
Mfg.'s Sug. Retail	$1,175	$1,025	$850	$750				
Add $20 for 8 or 10 in. barrel.								

Presentation Model — same specifications as above model, except is engraved with hand checkered stocks.

	100%	98%	95%
	$2,500	$2,000	$1,600

Last Mfg.'s Sug. Retail was $2,000.

WILKINSON ARMS

DIANE AUTOMATIC PISTOL — .25 ACP, 6 shot, 2⅛ in. barrel, fixed sight, matte blue, plastic grips.

	100%	98%	95%	90%	80%	70%	60%
	$125	$110	$90	$80	$65	$55	$50

"TERRY" CARBINE — blowback action, 9mm Para., 30 shot mag., 16³⁄₁₆ in. barrel, closed breech, adj. sights.

	100%	98%	95%	90%	80%	70%	60%
With black P.V.C. stock	$325	$310	$300	$275	$230	$210	$180
With maple stock	$350	$340	$325	$300	$260	$230	$200

WINCHESTER

Manufactured in New Haven, Ct from 1866 to date. Also includes U.S. Repeating Arms formed in 1981 with licensing agreement from Olin Corp. to manufacture shotguns and rifles domestically using the Winchester Trademark. Olin Corp. previously manufactured shotguns and rifles bearing the Winchester Hallmark at the Olin Kadensha Plant (closed 1989) located in Tochigi, Japan and also in European Countries.

RIFLES: LEVER ACTIONS — 1860-1895.

Note: Winchester Rifles are a field in themselves. Models Henry, 1866, 1873, 1876, 1885, 1886, 1892, 1894, and 1895 all were produced with a multitude of special order options. Special orders included front and rear special sights, half or ⅔ magazines, takedown, various barrel lengths, configurations, and weights, special metal finishes, deluxe wood (either checkered or carved) in a variety of finishes, an impressive range of engraving options, different butt plates, etc. All of these special orders act independently and interdependently to determine the correct value of a particular Winchester. Some of the finest rifles ever made are special order Winchesters engraved by the Ulrich's, G. Young, L.D. Nimschke, and others. For these reasons a Model 92 Winchester can range in price from $200 to over $250,000 - quite a price range for one model alone! When contemplating a purchase on the higher dollar range, qualified and professional opinions should be secured, preferably from at least 2 sources. Unfortunately many fakes and upgraded (non-original) guns have surfaced in the last 10 years with the sudden increase in prices. Winchesters shown in this section are priced assuming a standard model with no special orders. Any special orders will further add to the prices shown. Caliber rarities must also be considered. Many of the early Winchesters are broken down by year of manufacture. Refer to the "Model Serialization" section in this book.

A factory letter specifying original shipping information by serial number will certainly help solidify values shown on older out of production Winchester rifles and shotguns. A listing has been provided below by model number with serialization range which can be historically researched by the Winchester Museum now located in Cody, WY. To use this outstanding service, make sure the model and its serial number fall within the range listed below. If so, send $25 per serial number needing research payable to the Buffalo Bill Historical Center, P.O. Box 1000 in Cody, WY, 82414. Information received back will include specimen caliber, barrel length, any special orders or finishes, return(s) to the factory, as well as any additional provenance contained within Winchesters' factory shipping ledgers. I would recommend a trip to the Buffalo Bill Historical Center as it contains the most comprehensive collection of projectile arms (including Chinese specimens that date back 2,000 years) and Americana housed under one roof in this country.

A NOTE ON WINCHESTER FINISHES: Values below are for original finish with the percentage of bright blue ascertaining the current price. It is very important to understand that there is a big value difference between a Model 1873 with 90% bright blue as opposed to a gun that has 90% patina finish (turning brown). Even though it is true that both guns are 90%, the bright blue specimen might be worth 50%+ more because it is closer to the way it originally left the factory — with bright bluing. For this reason, the type of finish remaining becomes as important as the amount of finish. "Brown" guns are simply not as desirable as bright guns that show little discoloration. Because of this, much consideration must be given as to what type of finish a specimen has, and if shiny or mostly brown, value has to be taken away from prices listed below accordingly.

PLEASE REFER TO THE 32-PAGE UN-NUMBERED PHOTO PERCENTAGE GRADING SYSTEM IN THE FRONT OF THIS TEXT TO LEARN MORE ABOUT THE VARIOUS CONDITION FACTORS ENCOUNTERED ON WINCHESTER RIFLES AND SHOTGUNS.

Model 1866 Lever Action Rifle — ser. no. range 124,995-170,101.

Model 1873 Lever Action Rifle — ser. no. range 1-720,496.

Model 1876 Lever Action Rifle — ser. no. range 1-63,871.

Model 1883 Bolt Action Rifle (Hotchkiss Repeater) — ser. no. range 1-84,555.

Model 1885 Single Shot Rifle or Shotgun — ser. no. range 1-109,999.

Model 1886 Lever Action Rifle — ser. no. range 1-156,599.

Model 1887 & 1901 Lever Action Shotguns — ser. no. range 1-72,999.

Model 1890 Slide Action Rifle — ser. no. range 1-329,999.

Model 1892 Lever Action Rifle — ser. no. range 1-379,999.

Model 1893 Slide Action Shotgun — ser. no. range 1-34,050.

Model 1894 Lever Action Rifle — ser. no. range 1-353,999.

Model 1895 Lever Action Rifle — ser. no. range 1-59,999.

Model "Lee" Bolt Action Rifle — ser. no. range 1-19,999.

Model 1897 Lever Action Shotgun — ser. no. range 34,051-377,999.

Model 1903 Semi-Auto .22 Cal. Rifle — ser. no. range 1-39,999.

Model 1905 Semi-Auto Rifle — ser. no. range 1-29,078.

Model 1906 Semi-Auto Rifle — ser. no. range 1-79,999.

Model 1907 Semi-Auto Rifle — ser. no. range 1-9,999.

Winchester factory data on models produced between approx. 1907-1961 is almost non-existent (except Custom Shop mfg.) since there was a fire at the Winchester factory in 1961.

100%	98%	95%	90%	80%	70%	60%	50%	40%	30%	20%	10%

HENRY RIFLE — .44 twin rimfire, 15 shot, 24 in. barrel with integral slotted tube mag. and loading, blued barrel, brass frame. Approx. 13,000 total production, mfg. 1860-1866.

Iron Frame Model — frame made of iron, round type butt plate, no lever latch, adj. sporting type rear leaf sight, serial numbers are in three digits only. Total production is believed to be less than 300.

			$25,000	$22,000	$19,000	$17,500	$16,000	$15,000	$14,000	$13,000

Early Model — approx. 1,500 mfg., serialized below 2,500, with or without lever latch.

$25,000	$22,500	$20,000	$17,500	$14,500	$11,000	$9,000	$7,000	$5,500	$4,500	$3,750	$3,250

Martial Marked — contracted by U.S. military for Civil War use, denoted by "C.G.C." inspector markings on upper barrel breech and stock, approx. 1,900 with serialization scattered.

$28,500	$25,000	$22,500	$20,000	$17,500	$14,500	$11,000	$9,000	$7,000	$5,500	$4,500	$3,750

This rifle was the most revolutionary shoulder weapon introduced in the Civil War.

Late Model — similar to early model, except butt plate heel has pointed profile, lever latch became standard, most commonly encountered Henry, over 8,000 mfg.

$17,500	$14,500	$11,750	$9,500	$8,250	$7,250	$5,950	$5,000	$4,250	$3,700	$3,400	$3,150

MODEL 1866 RIFLE — .44 twin rimfire or centerfire (4th Model only), 24 in. barrel, blued barrel with brass frame, differs from Henry in that it has a wood forearm, frame cartridge loading port (King's improvement), and separate tube mag. Total production reached 170,101 for all models, mfg. 1866-1898.

Model 1866 First Model Rifle — "Improved Henry" action, .44 cal. twin rimfire, two screws on upper tang, no forend cap, serialization is concealed on lower tang inside butt stock, serial range is from mid 12,000 to mid 15,000 (which includes a number of Henry's).

$16,000	$14,750	$11,550	$9,900	$7,700	$6,820	$6,270	$5,500	$5,000	$4,675	$3,950	$3,300

Model 1866 Carbine First Model — same action as Rifle, only with 20 in. barrel, 2 barrel bands and saddle ring.

$19,500	$16,000	$14,750	$11,550	$9,900	$7,700	$6,820	$6,270	$5,500	$5,000	$4,675	$3,950

Model 1866 Rifle Second Model — "New Model" with redesigned frame, one screw on upper tang, and serial numbered outside lower tang beneath lever (approx. after serial number 20,000) and outside lower tang beneath lever.

$10,750	$9,250	$7,500	$6,250	$4,675	$3,850	$3,135	$2,640	$2,200	$1,650	$1,100	$825

Model 1866 Carbine Second Model — frame and other changes similar to Second Model Rifle.

$9,250	$8,000	$6,160	$4,840	$4,125	$3,080	$2,200	$1,815	$1,320	$1,100	$825	$550

Model 1866 Rifle Third Model — block style serial numbers usually located behind trigger, improved frame. Serial numbered approx. 25,000-149,000.

$9,250	$8,000	$6,160	$4,840	$4,125	$3,080	$2,200	$1,925	$1,650	$1,430	$1,210	$1,045

Model 1866 Carbine Third Model — same changes as Model 1866 Third Model Rifle, 20 in. barrel with 2 bands.

$8,750	$7,500	$5,720	$4,510	$3,575	$3,025	$2,475	$1,980	$1,540	$1,100	$770	$550

Model 1866 Musket Third Model — 27 in. round barrel, 24 in. magazine, 3 barrel bands.

$6,750	$5,250	$4,125	$3,520	$3,025	$2,530	$2,145	$1,760	$1,375	$990	$715	$495

Model 1866 Rifle Fourth Model — .44 cal., twin rimfire and centerfire, script style serial number on lower tang near lever latch, improved frame, serial range approx. 149,000-170,101.

$8,750	$7,500	$5,830	$4,840	$3,850	$3,080	$2,530	$2,090	$1,705	$1,320	$1,045	$715

Model 1866 Carbine Fourth Model — same changes as Model 1886 Rifle Fourth Model, 20 in. barrel with 2 bands.

$8,400	$7,000	$5,500	$4,400	$3,300	$2,750	$2,090	$1,650	$1,320	$1,045	$770	$605

Model 1866 Musket Fourth Model — same changes as Model 1886 Rifle Fourth Model, 27 in. round barrel with 3 bands.

$6,000	$5,000	$3,950	$3,300	$2,750	$2,310	$1,925	$1,595	$1,265	$990	$715	$495

100%	98%	95%	90%	80%	70%	60%	50%	40%	30%	20%	10%

MODEL 1873 RIFLE — .32-20, .38-40, or .44-40 centerfire cal., iron frame (changed to steel 1884) with sideplates, frame loading port, 24 in. round or octagon barrel, tube mag., blued finish with case hardened parts, oil finished stock, serial numbered on lower tang, 720,610 mfg. between 1873-1919, guns produced after serial number 525,923 are modern firearms.

Deluxe Model 1873's had color case hardened frames and will add at least 50% to the values listed below for standard models.

Model 1873 First Model Rifle — serial numbered approx. 1-28,000, distinguishable by 2 screws in frame above trigger and separate thumbrest affixed to grooved dust cover.

| $5,250 | $4,850 | $4,400 | $3,500 | $3,000 | $2,420 | $1,980 | $1,650 | $1,375 | $1,100 | $880 | $775 |

Model 1873 Carbine First Model — 20 in. round barrel with 2 bands. Distinctive curved butt plate, with saddle ring.

| $5,750 | $5,000 | $4,375 | $3,750 | $3,300 | $2,675 | $2,250 | $1,750 | $1,400 | $1,125 | $950 | $825 |

Late First Model 1873 Rifle — serial numbers from 28,000-31,000. Can be determined by thumbrest checkered on dust cover and trigger pin below the 2 frame screws.

| $5,125 | $4,600 | $4,000 | $3,350 | $2,550 | $2,000 | $1,500 | $1,200 | $875 | $650 | $495 | $395 |

Late First Model 1873 Carbine — same changes as Late First Model Rifle.

| $5,675 | $3,850 | $3,575 | $3,300 | $3,025 | $2,420 | $2,145 | $1,870 | $1,595 | $1,320 | $1,100 | $715 |

Late First Model 1873 Musket — 30 in. round barrel, 27 in. mag. with 3 barrel bands.

| $4,850 | $3,300 | $2,750 | $2,420 | $2,200 | $1,980 | $1,760 | $1,650 | $1,485 | $1,320 | $1,100 | $715 |

Model 1873 Rifle Second Model — improved dust cover featuring slides on center rail on rear section of frame top, serial range 31,000-90,000.

| $4,100 | $3,650 | $3,150 | $2,250 | $1,650 | $1,320 | $1,100 | $880 | $660 | $440 | $330 | $260 |

Model 1873 Carbine Second Model — changes similar to 1873 Second Model Rifle, with 20 in. round barrel and 2 barrel bands.

| $4,850 | $3,300 | $2,750 | $2,420 | $2,200 | $1,980 | $1,760 | $1,650 | $1,485 | $1,320 | $1,100 | $715 |

Model 1873 Musket Second Model — changes similar to 1873 Second Model Rifle, with 30 in. barrel and 3 barrel bands.

| $2,750 | $2,475 | $2,200 | $1,925 | $1,650 | $1,320 | $1,100 | $875 | $725 | $550 | $450 | $325 |

Model 1873 Rifle Third Model — dust cover rail integral with frame, improved action with rear frame screws (2), serial 90,000-end of production.

| $4,250 | $3,250 | $2,350 | $1,925 | $1,650 | $1,325 | $1,100 | $875 | $675 | $450 | $375 | $325 |

Model 1873 Carbine Third Model — changes similar to 1873 Rifle Third Model, with 20 in. barrel and 2 barrel bands.

| $5,150 | $4,250 | $3,750 | $3,150 | $2,675 | $2,200 | $1,815 | $1,595 | $1,000 | $675 | $450 | $375 |

Model 1873 Musket Third Model — changes similar to 1873 Rifle Third Model, with 30 in. round barrel and 3 barrel bands.

| $4,250 | $3,250 | $2,350 | $1,925 | $1,650 | $1,320 | $1,100 | $875 | $725 | $550 | $400 | $300 |

Model 1873 .22 Rim Fire Rifle — .22 short and long, 24 or 26 in. barrel, no loading gate, the first .22 caliber repeater, 19,552 produced, mfg. 1884-1904. Made in rifle configuration only.

| $4,250 | $3,750 | $3,150 | $2,650 | $2,350 | $2,000 | $1,800 | $1,475 | $1,200 | $950 | $750 | $550 |

Model 1873 "1 of 1000" — special care taken in manufacture to guarantee better accuracy, markings on top of breech designate model, deluxe walnut, best model, extremely rare, 136 mfg. Original cost was $100.

Values can range from $12,500 - $65,000, depending on condition. A factory letter is a must for any "1 of 100" Winchester.

Note: Rarity of the "1 of 1,000" and the "1 of 100" models makes upgrading to this model fairly common. Use extreme caution in purchasing.

Model 1873 "1 of 100" — similar to "1 of 1000" only rarer, 8 mfg. Sold new for $20 over the list price of a similarly equipped Model 1873.

Values can range from $20,000 - $250,000, depending on condition. A factory letter is a must for any "1 of 100" Winchester.

100%	98%	95%	90%	80%	70%	60%	50%	40%	30%	20%	10%

MODEL 1876 RIFLE — .40-60, .45-60, .45-75 (first caliber offered), or .50-95 Express cal., 26 or 28 in. round or octagon barrel, similar but larger frame than Model 1873, tube mag., crescent butt, blued finish, straight grip stock, 63,871 mfg. between 1876-1897.
The Model 1876 was also called the Centennial Model since its introduction coincided with the U.S. Centennial Exposition held in Philadelphia, PA in 1876. Popularity for this model decreased ten years later when the more powerful and advanced Model 1886 was introduced.

Deluxe Model 1876's had color case hardened frames and will add at least 50% to the values listed below for standard models. Deluxe Model 1876's with 90%+ original case colors are very rare, desirable, and expensive.

Model 1876 Rifle First Model — serial numbered approx. 1-3,000, distinguishable by no dust cover on frame top.

| $5,450 | $4,850 | $3,950 | $3,050 | $2,650 | $2,150 | $1,650 | $1,375 | $1,100 | $875 | $825 | $625 |

Model 1876 Carbine First Model — 22 in. round barrel, one barrel band, saddle ring, provision for bayonet attachment.

| $6,000 | $5,500 | $4,750 | $3,950 | $3,350 | $2,775 | $2,200 | $1,975 | $1,675 | $1,475 | $1,150 | $750 |

Model 1876 Musket First Model — 32 in. round barrel with 1 band, scarce model because no foreign military contracts.

| $7,600 | $6,050 | $5,500 | $4,400 | $4,125 | $3,575 | $3,300 | $3,025 | $2,750 | $2,475 | $2,035 | $1,650 |

Model 1876 Rifle Early Second Model — "Thumbprint" dust cover with guide screwed to receiver added, serial range 3,000-7,000.

| $5,000 | $4,400 | $3,750 | $3,150 | $2,400 | $1,875 | $1,500 | $1,250 | $1,050 | $900 | $795 | $600 |

Model 1876 Carbine Second Model — changes similar to Model 1876 Rifle Early Second Model, with 22 in. round barrel and distinctive forend cap.

| $5,450 | $4,850 | $3,950 | $3,050 | $2,650 | $2,150 | $1,650 | $1,375 | $1,100 | $875 | $825 | $625 |

Model 1876 Musket Early Second Model — changes similar to Model 1876 Rifle Early Second Model, with 32 in. round barrel and carbine forend tip.

| $7,000 | $6,150 | $5,450 | $4,750 | $3,950 | $3,575 | $3,300 | $3,025 | $2,750 | $2,200 | $1,750 | $1,350 |

Model 1876 Rifle Late Second Model — improved dust cover lacking oval thumbprint, serial range 7,000-30,000.

| $4,550 | $3,700 | $3,250 | $2,700 | $2,100 | $1,650 | $1,425 | $1,250 | $1,050 | $900 | $795 | $600 |

Model 1876 Carbine Late Second Model — frame similar to Model 1876 Rifle Late Second Model, with 22 in. barrel.

| $5,400 | $4,800 | $3,900 | $3,000 | $2,475 | $2,100 | $1,650 | $1,375 | $1,100 | $875 | $775 | $625 |

Model 1876 Musket Late Second Model — frame similar to Model 1876 Rifle Late Second Model, with 32 in. round barrel.

| $7,600 | $6,050 | $5,500 | $4,400 | $4,125 | $3,575 | $3,300 | $3,025 | $2,750 | $2,475 | $2,035 | $1,650 |

Model 1876 Rifle Third Model — dust cover rail integral with frame, serial range 30,000-end of production.

| $4,300 | $3,600 | $3,150 | $2,600 | $2,100 | $1,650 | $1,425 | $1,250 | $1,050 | $900 | $795 | $600 |

Model 1876 Carbine Third Model — frame similar to Model 1876 Rifle Third Model, with 22 in. round barrel.

| $5,100 | $4,500 | $3,600 | $2,950 | $2,350 | $2,000 | $1,575 | $1,325 | $1,025 | $850 | $750 | $600 |

Model 1876 Musket Third Model — frame similar to Model 1876 Rifle Third Model, with 32 in. round barrel.

| $6,500 | $5,500 | $4,750 | $4,000 | $3,500 | $3,000 | $2,625 | $2,300 | $2,000 | $1,650 | $1,400 | $1,200 |

Model 1876 "1 of 1000" — special care taken in manufacture to guarantee better accuracy, markings on top of breech designate model, deluxe walnut, best model, extremely rare, 54 mfg. Original cost was $100.
Values can range from $27,500 - $85,000, depending on condition. A factory letter is a must for any "1 of 100" Winchester.

Values are not listed because too few original specimens are bought or sold to accurately establish pricing. A factory letter is a must for any "1 of 1,000" Winchester.

100%	98%	95%	90%	80%	70%	60%	50%	40%	30%	20%	10%

Note: Rarity of the "1 of 1,000" and the "1 of 100" models makes upgrading to this model fairly common. Use extreme caution in purchasing.

Model 1876 "1 of 100" — similar to "1 of 1000" only rarer, 8 mfg. Sold new for $20 over the list price of a similarly equipped Model 1876.
Values can range from $20,000 - $250,000, depending on condition. A factory letter is a must for any "1 of 100" Winchester.

Values are not listed because too few original specimens are bought or sold to accurately establish pricing. A factory letter is a must for any "1 of 100" Winchester.

Model 1876 Northwest Mounted Police Carbine — .45-75 cal. only, 22 in. barrel, "NWMP" stamped on butt stock, serial range 23,801-24,100 and 43,900-44,400.

| $6,225 | $5,400 | $4,250 | $3,750 | $3,000 | $2,750 | $2,300 | $1,980 | $1,650 | $1,320 | $1,100 | $825 |

MODEL 1886 RIFLE — .33 WCF, .38-56 WCF, .38-70 WCF, .40-65 WCF, .40-70 WCF, .40-82 WCF, .45-70, .45-90, .50-110 Express, or .50-100-450 cal. available, Brownings' first high power lever action design distinguishable by vertical locking bars, .45-70 most popular cal., 26 in. round or octagon barrel, tube mag., steel forend cap, straight grip stock. Approx. 159,990 mfg. between 1886-1935.
The Model 1886 had case hardening standard on the frame, butt plate, and forend cap until 1901 (approx. 122,000 serial range) when the standard finish became blue.

Model 1886 Rifle — same as above.

| $3,750 | $3,250 | $2,750 | $2,250 | $1,675 | $1,375 | $1,100 | $950 | $850 | $750 | $625 | $500 |

Add 20% and more if .45-70 or .50-100/110 cal. Original bright case colors will also bring premiums over values shown above.

Model 1886 Carbine — same general specifications as Rifle, except 22 in. round barrel and saddle ring, solid frame only.

| $9,250 | $7,150 | $6,600 | $5,775 | $4,950 | $4,400 | $3,850 | $3,300 | $2,475 | $1,925 | $1,650 | $1,320 |

Model 1886 Full Stock Carbine — same as regular carbine, except forearm extends almost to end of barrel (similar to Model 1876 Carbine).

| $10,350 | $8,250 | $7,700 | $7,150 | $5,500 | $4,950 | $4,400 | $3,850 | $3,025 | $2,475 | $1,925 | $1,650 |

Model 1886 Musket — 30 in. round barrel, one barrel band, military sights, only 350 mfg., very rare.

| $14,200 | $11,000 | $9,350 | $8,250 | $7,150 | $6,050 | $5,500 | $4,675 | $3,850 | $3,245 | $2,750 | $2,200 |

Model 1886 Lightweight Rifle — .45-70 or .33 WCF cal. only, 22 in. round nickel steel tapered barrel, half mag., rubber shotgun butt plate.

.33 caliber

| $2,650 | $2,250 | $1,850 | $1,475 | $1,200 | $1,000 | $875 | $775 | $700 | $650 | $600 | $500 |

.45-70 caliber

| $4,250 | $3,750 | $3,250 | $2,850 | $2,250 | $1,925 | $1,675 | $1,400 | $1,100 | $875 | $700 | $575 |

Model 1886 Takedown — magazine unscrews from frame allowing disassembly forward of breech.
Add 10% - 15% premium on rifles only.

100%	98%	95%	90%	80%	70%	60%	50%	40%	30%	20%	10%

RIFLES: 1890-1944 MANUFACTURE

MODEL 1890 SLIDE ACTION — See listing under RIFLES - SLIDE ACTION: DISCONTINUED in this section.

MODEL 1892 LEVER ACTION RIFLE — .218 Bee, .25-20, .32-20, .38-40, or .44-40 cal., 24 in. round or octagon barrel, blue, tube mag., forend cap, crescent butt. Mfg. 1,004,067 between 1892-1941.

| $2,650 | $1,775 | $1,300 | $935 | $825 | $675 | $575 | $475 | $395 | $335 | $275 | $225 |

Add 25% for .218 Bee caliber (mfg. 1936-1938, not advertised - special order only). Model 92's are also seen with barrels marked Model 65.

Model 1892 Takedown Rifle — magazine unscrews at frame allowing barrel/magazine takedown.
Add 20%+ premium.

MODEL 1892 CARBINE — 20 in. round barrel, two bands and saddle ring.

| $2,535 | $1,800 | $1,600 | $1,375 | $1,100 | $905 | $785 | $670 | $560 | $450 | $350 | $250 |

Manufactured in 12, 14, 15, 16, 17, 18, and 20 in. barrel lengths in both carbines and rifles for the South American rubber industry.

MODEL 1892 TRAPPER'S CARBINE — same as Carbine, with 14, 15, 16, or 18 in. barrels. So called because was handy for trappers who had to carry a powerful but lightweight repeating rifle.

| $3,250 | $2,420 | $1,980 | $1,870 | $1,650 | $1,375 | $1,125 | $900 | $740 | $600 | $475 | $350 |

14, 15, and 16 in. barrels are rare on this model. Note: Check federal laws on legality of 14 and 15 in. models.

MODEL 1892 MUSKET — 30 in. round barrel, 3 barrel bands, military sights. Modified shotgun style butt plate.

| $4,350 | $3,575 | $3,200 | $2,950 | $2,600 | $2,200 | $1,900 | $1,600 | $1,200 | $900 | $675 | $450 |

MODEL 1894 LEVER ACTION RIFLE — .25-35, .30-30, .32-40, .32 Spl., or .38-55 cal., most common (and popular) is .30-30 cal., tube mag., 26 in. octagon barrel, blue, straight grip stock. Over 5,000,000 produced to date, mfg. 1894-present, currently available - see Modern Section.

Antique Model — ser. no.'s before 111,454.

| $2,500 | $1,400 | $995 | $825 | $700 | $575 | $450 | $400 | $360 | $340 | $320 | $300 |

1899-1936 Mfg. — model 94's built post 1898-1936.

| $1,495 | $1,200 | $850 | $750 | $650 | $525 | $425 | $360 | $325 | $300 | $275 | $250 |

The Model 1894 Winchester has the distinction of being the world's most popular rifle. Add 20% for .25-35 caliber (disc. 1936, reintroduced 1940-1950). Deluxe models or takedown variations will command substantial premiums over values listed above.

Model 1894 Takedown Rifle — magazine unscrews at frame allowing barrel/magazine takedown.
Add 20%+ premium.

MODEL 1894 TRAPPER'S CARBINE — same as Carbine, with 14, 16, or 18 in. barrel.

| $2,970 | $2,500 | $2,200 | $1,975 | $1,760 | $1,475 | $1,100 | $975 | $850 | $750 | $650 | $550 |

Note: Check federal laws on legality of 14 in. barrel. 70%-100% variations are almost never encountered in this model. Shorter barrels than 14 in. have been encountered on this model, but extreme rarity precludes accurate price evaluation.

MODEL 1894 SADDLE RING CARBINE — 20 in. round barrel, deduct 10-20% for .30-30 and .32 Special cal.'s.

| $1,100 | $950 | $800 | $600 | $500 | $475 | $450 | $425 | $400 | $375 | $350 | $325 |

Without saddle ring — mfg. until 1940.

| $875 | $725 | $650 | $550 | $450 | $375 | $350 | $325 | $300 | $275 | $250 | $225 |

100%	98%	95%	90%	80%	70%	60%	50%	40%	30%	20%	10%

MODEL 1894 POST-WAR CARBINE — 1945-1964 mfg. without saddle ring.

| $450 | $395 | $375 | $350 | $325 | $310 | $290 | $270 | $250 | $230 | $210 | $190 |

.32-40, .32 Special, and .38-55 cal.'s will command premiums ($50-$100).

MODEL 1895 LEVER ACTION — .30-03, .30-06, .30-40 Krag, .303 Brit., .35 Win., .38-72, .40-72, .405 Win., or .762 Russian cal., 24-28 in. barrel, blued action, box mag., straight grip stock, 425,881 mfg. from 1896-1931. Add 15% for .30-06 and .405 cal.'s.

| $2,050 | $1,375 | $1,100 | $935 | $825 | $675 | $600 | $525 | $475 | $450 | $425 | $375 |

The Model 1895 was a Browning design incorporating the first box type mag. in a lever action repeating rifle. A large Russian military contract was secured in 1915 with chambering for the 7.62mm Russian cartridge (over 293,000 mfg. or over 66% of total production). A very few were made with color case hardened frames (Winchesters last large frame rifle to have case colors) and are very rare and expensive.

Model 1895 Takedown Rifle — disassembles at breech.
Add 15%+ premium.

MODEL 1895 RIFLE FLATSIDE — early model, distinguishable in that frame does not have fluting or ridge contouring, serial range approx. 1-5000.

| $2,750 | $2,000 | $1,800 | $1,600 | $1,375 | $1,100 | $905 | $785 | $670 | $560 | $475 | $425 |

MODEL 1895 CARBINE — .30-03, .30-06, or .303 Brit. cal., 22 in. round barrel, one barrel band, with or without saddle ring, escalloped frame sides.

| $2,500 | $2,150 | $1,850 | $1,600 | $1,400 | $1,200 | $1,000 | $875 | $750 | $625 | $500 | $375 |

Model 1895 Government Carbine — with government markings.

| $2,800 | $2,300 | $1,975 | $1,650 | $1,400 | $1,200 | $1,000 | $875 | $750 | $625 | $500 | $375 |

MODEL 1895 FLATSIDE MUSKET — early models have serial range under 5000, no flutes on frame, .30-40 Krag only.

| $4,850 | $3,575 | $3,300 | $3,000 | $2,750 | $2,475 | $2,100 | $1,870 | $1,500 | $1,250 | $995 | $600 |

MODEL 1895 MUSKET — .30-03, .30-06, or .30-40 Krag cal., 28 in. round barrel, two bands, hand guard over barrel, military sights.

| $2,500 | $2,150 | $1,850 | $1,600 | $1,400 | $1,200 | $1,000 | $875 | $750 | $625 | $500 | $375 |

U.S. GOVT. MODEL 1895 MUSKET — .30-40 Krag, "U.S." marked on frame.

| $2,950 | $2,500 | $2,150 | $1,850 | $1,600 | $1,400 | $1,200 | $1,000 | $875 | $750 | $625 | $500 |

U.S. ARMY NRA MUSKET 1895 — same as Standard, with 30 in. barrel, 1901 Krag, rear sight. NRA approved for official NRA competition.

| $2,500 | $2,150 | $1,850 | $1,600 | $1,400 | $1,200 | $1,000 | $875 | $750 | $625 | $500 | $375 |

Also available in Models 1903 and 1906 which designated .30-30 and .30-06 cal.'s respectively.

MODEL 1895 RUSSIAN MUSKET — 7.62mm Russian cal., over 293,000 mfg. for Imperial Russian Govt., mfg. 1915-1916, various Russian Ordnance stamps should be present.

| $2,200 | $1,900 | $1,600 | $1,400 | $1,200 | $1,000 | $875 | $750 | $625 | $500 | $375 | $300 |

MODEL 53 LEVER ACTION — .25-20, .32-20, or .44-40 cal., 22 in. round barrel, ½ tube mag. holding 6 cartridges, blued finish, pistol grip or straight grip stock. Mfg. 24,916 between 1924-1932.

| $1,900 | $1,650 | $1,375 | $1,075 | $925 | $775 | $625 | $500 | $450 | $400 | $350 | $300 |

100%	98%	95%	90%	80%	70%	60%	50%	40%	30%	20%	10%

MODEL 53 TAKEDOWN RIFLE — magazine unscrews at frame allowing barrel to come apart at breech.
Add 5-15% premium over standard model.

MODEL 65 LEVER ACTION RIFLE — .218 Bee (introduced 1939), .25-20, or .32-20 cal., 22 in. round barrel (except 218 Bee - 24 in.), ½ tube mag. holding 7 cartridges, blue with pistol grip stock. Mfg. 5704 between 1933-1947.

| $2,500 | $2,200 | $1,875 | $1,500 | $1,175 | $975 | $850 | $775 | $700 | $625 | $550 | $425 |

The Model 65 was a design evolving from the Model 53.

MODEL 55 LEVER ACTION RIFLE — .25-35, .30-30, or .32 Win. Spl. cal., lever action designed, solid frame and takedown, 24 in. round barrel, shotgun style butt stock with checkered steel butt plate, tube mag., holds 3 cartridges. Approx. 20,500 mfg. between 1924-1932. Serial numbered independently to approx. 2,865, then serialized with Model 1894 production on underside of receiver. Simply could not compete with the Model 1894.

| $1,325 | $1,100 | $900 | $825 | $750 | $675 | $600 | $525 | $475 | $425 | $375 | $325 |

MODEL 71 RIFLE STANDARD — .348 Win. cal., ⅔ tube mag. holding 4 cartridges, improved Model 1886 frame, blued metal with pistol grip stock, 20 or 24 in. barrel. Mfg. 47,254 between 1935-1957.

| $850 | $725 | $650 | $600 | $575 | $525 | $475 | $440 | $400 | $360 | $330 | $300 |

Model 71 — 20 in. barrel — barrels mfg. during 1936-1937 only, model mfg. 1937-1947, very rare and desirable.

| $3,600 | $3,150 | $2,650 | $2,250 | $1,950 | $1,700 | $1,475 | $1,200 | $995 | $875 | $750 | $625 |

MODEL 71 RIFLE DELUXE — same as Standard, with higher grade wood and checkering.

| $1,250 | $1,050 | $875 | $775 | $695 | $650 | $600 | $575 | $525 | $475 | $425 | $400 |

MODEL 64 RIFLE — .219 Zipper, .25-35, .30-30, or .32 Win. Spl. cal., 20, 24, or 26 in. round barrel, blued metal, pistol grip stock, revamped Model 55 action with increased mag. capacity, 66,783 mfg. between 1933-1957 and 1972-1973 (over 8,250 mfg. in .30-30 cal. only - these last two years with minor changes). Add 15% for .25-35 cal.

| $1,050 | $900 | $775 | $650 | $575 | $500 | $450 | $400 | $375 | $325 | $300 | $275 |

Add 50% for Deluxe Model.
.219 Zipper cal. — mfg. 1938-1941 only.

| $1,600 | $1,375 | $1,050 | $925 | $800 | $700 | $625 | $550 | $500 | $450 | $425 | $395 |

Model 64 1972-73 mfg. may be found in the post-64 section.

RIFLES: SINGLE SHOT

MODEL 1885 — most popular cal.'s available from .22-.50, falling block trigger guard activated action, John Browning's first high power single shot rifle design, many variations were made and we will list the standard types. Over 139,725 mfg. between 1885-1920.
This design was originally mfg. as the Model 1878 by the Browning Brothers in Ogden, UT in the early 1880's. Fewer than 600 were mfg. - see the Browning section for values.
Sporting Rifle Low Wall — 28 in. round or octagon barrel, open sights, solid frame, standard trigger.

| $2,375 | $2,000 | $1,800 | $1,600 | $1,400 | $1,200 | $1,000 | $825 | $700 | $575 | $450 | $375 |

Sporting Rifle High Wall — 30 in. barrel, standard trigger, open sights, solid frame. Available in various size and weight barrels numbered (in front of forearm) from numeric 1, 2, 3, 3½ (introduced 1910), 4, and 5, lightest to heaviest. Case hardened frames standard until 1901 when bluing became standard, three different frames depending on caliber. Heavier barrels in rare calibers will bring a premium.

| $2,500 | $2,200 | $1,950 | $1,600 | $1,400 | $1,200 | $1,000 | $825 | $700 | $575 | $450 | $375 |

Add 20% for Takedown frame.

100%	98%	95%	90%	80%	70%	60%	50%	40%	30%	20%	10%

20 ga. High Wall Shotgun — chambered for 3 in., 26 in. full choke nickel steel barrel standard, receiver has matting on top. Also available with matted ribs (rare). Solid frame or takedown. Introduced 1914.

| $2,850 | $2,450 | $2,150 | $1,725 | $1,500 | $1,300 | $1,100 | $875 | $750 | $625 | $500 | $450 |

Deluxe Grade High Wall — same as Standard, with fancy walnut and checkering.

| $3,200 | $2,775 | $2,350 | $1,950 | $1,650 | $1,400 | $1,200 | $995 | $825 | $700 | $575 | $450 |

Schuetzen Rifle — high wall, 30 in. octagon barrel, double set triggers, spur lever, aperture sight, Schuetzen style stock, adj. palm rest and butt plate.

| $4,750 | $4,150 | $3,750 | $3,375 | $2,750 | $2,250 | $1,875 | $1,650 | $1,400 | $1,200 | $995 | $775 |

Add 20% for Takedown frame.

Winder Musket — low wall, 3rd model, .22 Short or LR, 28 in. barrel, standard trigger and lever, military style stock and sights, grooved forearm, one barrel band.

| $600 | $550 | $475 | $400 | $375 | $350 | $330 | $310 | $290 | $270 | $250 | $220 |

Add 20% for Takedown frame.

RIFLES: BOLT ACTION

MODEL 1883 (HOTCHKISS REPEATER) — .45-70 cal., designed by Benjamin D. Hotchkiss, unique tube mag. located in butt stock attached to receiver, up-turn/pull-back bolt action, 26 in. round or octagon standard on rifle. Over 84,000 mfg. between 1879-1889. Also available in carbine configuration (24 in. round barrel with one band), and musket (32 in. round barrel with cleaning rod and two barrel bands) — subtract 25%. Carbine extremely rare in Third Model (20 in. barrel).

First Style — approx. 6,419 mfg. with magazine cut off and safety control incorporated into one unit.

| $1,100 | $950 | $800 | $600 | $500 | $450 | $400 | $360 | $330 | $300 | $260 | $220 |

Second Style — approx. 16,102 mfg., magazine cut off on right receiver top, safety on left side.

| $950 | $800 | $600 | $500 | $450 | $400 | $360 | $330 | $300 | $260 | $220 | $200 |

Third Style — most commonly encountered Hotchkiss, approx. 62,034 mfg. 1883-1899.

| $880 | $825 | $575 | $450 | $400 | $360 | $330 | $300 | $260 | $220 | $200 | $180 |

The Model 1883 Hotchkiss was the first bolt action designed for the U.S. military .45-70 cartridge. On the First and Second models inspect wood directly below bolt and left frame side for cracks, breaks or older repairs as it is frequently encountered on these early models with thin wrists.

LEE STRAIGHT PULL RIFLE — 6mm Lee (.236 U.S.N. cal.), 5 shot non-detachable box mag., 24 (Sporting Rifle) or 28 (Musket) in. barrel, folding leaf sight, blue metal, military style full stock, mfg. 1897-1902, Navy Issue Model is the Musket with "236 U.S.N." on barrels. Approx. 20,000 mfg. (including 15,000 Muskets for the U.S. Navy military contract) between 1895-1902 with parts clean up occurring in 1916.

U.S.N. Military Musket

| $880 | $825 | $575 | $450 | $400 | $360 | $330 | $300 | $260 | $220 | $200 | $180 |

Lee Sporting Rifle — same as Musket, with 24 in, barrel, sporter style stock. Approx. 1,700 mfg. 1897-1902.

| $950 | $800 | $600 | $500 | $450 | $400 | $360 | $330 | $300 | $260 | $220 | $200 |

This design was originally patented by James Paris Lee and assigned to the Lee Arms Company. Winchester obtained manufacturing rights to produce this model for the U.S Navy military contract 1895-1902.

MODEL 1900 SINGLE SHOT — .22 S and L cal., 18 in. round barrel, blued metal, open sights, one piece straight grip stock without fitted butt plate, takedown, not serial numbered. Approx. 105,000 mfg. between 1899-1902.

| $400 | $370 | $350 | $330 | $310 | $290 | $270 | $250 | $220 | $185 | $140 | $110 |

100%	98%	95%	90%	80%	70%	60%	50%	40%	30%	20%	10%

MODEL 1902 SINGLE SHOT — same as 1900, with minor improvements. Distinguishable by special shaped extended trigger guard. Not serial numbered. Approx. 640,299 mfg. between 1902-1931.

$175	$125	$110	$100	$90	$80	$70	$60	$55	$50	$45	$40

Chambering included .22 cal. Extra Long in 1914 (interchangeable with S&L).

THUMB TRIGGER MODEL 99 — same as 1902, with button behind cocking piece used to fire with thumb instead of trigger, not serial numbered. Approx. 75,433 were mfg. between 1904-1923.

$650	$575	$500	$400	$325	$290	$270	$250	$220	$185	$140	$110

MODEL 1904 SINGLE SHOT — improved version of 1902, 21 in. round barrel, chambering included .22 Extra Long in 1914, not serial numbered. Approx. 302,859 mfg. between 1904-1931.

$175	$125	$110	$100	$90	$80	$70	$60	$55	$50	$45	$40

Model 1904-A — introduced 1927 with new sear bar and chambered for .22 LR.

$200	$160	$125	$110	$100	$90	$80	$70	$60	$55	$50	$45

MODEL 43 — .218 Bee, .22 Hornet, .25-20, or .32-20 cal., dubbed "Poor Man's Model 70", 24 in. round tapered barrel, box type mag. Approx. 62,617 mfg. between 1949-1957.

$595	$520	$475	$440	$400	$360	$320	$290	$260	$240	$220	$200

Add 10% for Deluxe Model.

Add $50 for Special Grade.

Add $50 for .22 Hornet cal.

Grading		100%	98%	95%	90%	80%	70%	60%

On Models 52, 54, 56, 57, 58, 59, 60, 60A, 67, 677, 68, 69, 69A, 697, and 70 values in 50% or less original condition have been omitted since values in those conditions will approximate the 60% price. This reflects the fact that while these lower condition specimens are not as desirable to collectors, they are still sought after as shooters.

MODEL 47 — .22 S, L, or LR cal., single shot bolt action, 25 in. round barrel, uncheckered walnut stock, 5¼ lbs., approx. 43,000 (not serial numbered) mfg. during 1948-1954.

		$250	$225	$195	$175	$150	$125	$100

MODEL 52 TARGET — .22 LR cal., 5 shot mag., 28 in. standard barrel, target sights and target style stock. Approx. 125,233 Model 52's in all variations were mfg. between 1919-1979.

		$440	$415	$375	$345	$315	$290	$265
With speedlock		$495	$470	$415	$375	$335	$310	$290

Model 52A Target — similar to Model 52, except has slow lock mechanism. Values are similar to above.

MODEL 52 HEAVY BARREL — same as Standard Target, with heavy barrel.

		$660	$605	$550	$525	$470	$415	$330

MODEL 52-B TARGET — extensively redesigned action, improved stock design, offered with a variety of sights. Mfg. 1935-1947.

		$605	$550	$495	$470	$415	$360	$305

MODEL 52-B HEAVY BARREL — same as 52-B, with heavy barrel.

		$660	$605	$550	$525	$470	$415	$330

MODEL 52-B BULL GUN — extra heavy weight barrel.

		$690	$635	$580	$550	$495	$440	$360

Grading	100%	98%	95%	90%	80%	70%	60%

MODEL 52 SPORTER (SPORTING RIFLE) — 24 in. round lightweight barrel with front sight cover, sporting type select walnut stock with cheek piece, hard rubber pistol grip cap, black plastic tipped forearm, checkered steel butt plate, about 7¼ lbs. Mfg. 1934-1958. The Models 52 and 52B are not generally factory drilled for scopes, as the receiver was specially designed for aperture rear sights, be cautious of "factory" drilled and tapped receivers on all model 52's.

Model 52 — introduced 1920, original slowlock time model changed to speedlock 1929.

	$2,350	$1,875	$1,500	$1,400	$1,275	$1,150	$975

Model 52A — introduced 1932, receiver and locking lug were strengthened.

	$2,350	$1,875	$1,500	$1,400	$1,275	$1,150	$950

Model 52B — introduced 1935 with adj. sling swivel assembly and single shot adapter.

	$2,350	$1,700	$1,400	$1,200	$1,100	$1,000	$900

Model 52C — introduced 1947 with adj. micro motion trigger.

	$2,500	$1,875	$1,500	$1,400	$1,275	$1,150	$950

A few Model 52 Sporters & Targets were mfg. with stainless steel barrels (17,XXX serial range) - these guns will command a premium over values shown above.

MODEL 52-C TARGET — "Micro Motion" trigger and "Marksman" stock, otherwise same as 52-B. Mfg. 1947-1961.

	$700	$625	$550	$525	$470	$415	$330

MODEL 52-C STANDARD — same as Target, with standard sporter barrel.

	$625	$550	$490	$470	$415	$360	$305

MODEL 52-C BULL GUN — extra heavy barrel model of Target 52-C. Mfg. 1952-1961.

	$775	$675	$580	$550	$495	$440	$360

MODEL 52-D TARGET — improved version of 52-C with free floating barrel and adj. bedding device. Mfg. 1961-disc.

	$625	$550	$495	$440	$385	$360	$275

MODEL 52 INTERNATIONAL MATCH — same as 52-D, with free rifle stock, accessory rail and lead lapped barrel. Mfg. 1969-disc.

	$750	$675	$605	$550	$495	$470	$385

MODEL 52 INTERNATIONAL PRONE — similar International Match, with prone style stock. Mfg. 1975-disc.

	$750	$675	$605	$550	$495	$470	$385

MODEL 54 HIGH POWER SPORTER — .270, 7 x 57mm, .30-30, or .30-06 cal., 5 shot mag., 24 in. barrel, open sights, checkered pistol grip stock. Mfg. 1925-1930. Approx. 50,145 Model 54's were mfg. in all variations between 1925-1936.

	$675	$595	$525	$450	$385	$330	$305

Rare cal.'s will add premiums to the values listed above. This model was also mfg. with a stainless steel barrel during the late 1920's - early 30's with premiums also being asked.

MODEL 54 CARBINE — introduced 1927, same as Rifle, with 20 in. barrel, plain stock.

	$750	$675	$595	$525	$475	$385	$360

MODEL 54 IMPROVED SPORTER — .22 Hornet, .220 Swift, .250-3000, .257 Robts., .270, 7 x 57mm, or .30-06 cal., 5 shot mag., 24 or 26 in. barrel, one piece firing pin, checkered pistol grip stock. Mfg. 1930-1936.

	$675	$595	$525	$450	$385	$330	$305

Rare cal.'s will add premiums to the values listed above.

MODEL 54 CARBINE IMPROVED — same as Rifle, with 20 in. barrel.

	$750	$675	$595	$525	$475	$385	$360

Grading	100%	98%	95%	90%	80%	70%	60%

MODEL 54 SUPER GRADE — introduced 1934, same as Sporter, with better wood and black forend tip and pistol grip cap.

	$950	$850	$775	$695	$625	$550	$525

Rare calibers will command considerable premiums (i.e. this variation in 7 x 57mm cal. will sell for $2,500 in mint condition).

MODEL 54 SPORTING SNIPER'S RIFLE — introduced 1929, same as Sporter, with 26 in. heavy barrel, .30-06 only, aperture sight.

	$1,000	$875	$775	$695	$625	$550	$525

MODEL 54 NATIONAL MATCH — introduced 1935, same as Standard, with Lyman sights and Marksman stock.

	$1,000	$875	$775	$695	$625	$550	$525

MODEL 56 SPORTER — .22 S or LR cal., 5 or 10 shot box mag., 22 in. round barrel, open sights, plain pistol grip stock. Approx. 8,297 mfg. between 1926-1929.

	$600	$525	$460	$400	$350	$300	$250

The .22 cal. Short was disc. 1929.

MODEL 57 TARGET — similar to Model 56, except with aperture sight and heavier target stock. Approx. 18,600 were mfg. between 1926-1936.

	$595	$525	$450	$375	$300	$260	$220

MODEL 58 SINGLE SHOT — similar to Models 1902 and 1904, .22 LR cal., 18 in. round barrel, open sights, takedown. Approx. 38,992 mfg. between 1928-1931.

	$250	$225	$200	$175	$150	$125	$120

MODEL 59 SINGLE SHOT — improved Model 58 with 23 in. round barrel and pistol grip stock with butt plate. Approx. 9,200 mfg. between 1930-1931.

	$450	$425	$400	$350	$300	$250	$200

This model was disc. due to lack of sales.

MODEL 60 — improved Model 59, 23 in. round barrel increased to 27 in. 1933. Approx. 160,754 mfg. between 1930-1934.

	$175	$130	$95	$80	$70	$60	$50

MODEL 60A TARGET — similar to Model 60 with Lyman 55W aperture rear sight, heavier target stock, and 27 in. round tapered barrel. Approx. 6,118 mfg. between 1932-1939.

	$650	$525	$450	$375	$300	$260	$230

MODEL 67 — .22 LR or .22 WRF (authorized 1935) cal., 20 in. (Junior Rifle), 24 (miniature target boring), and 27 in. (sporting or smooth bore) round barrels, same basic action as the Model 60, not serial numbered. Approx. 383,000 mfg. between 1934-1963.

	$175	$130	$95	$80	$70	$60	$50

MODEL 677 — same basic specifications as Model 67, except no iron sights or sight cuts in barrel, not serial numbered. Approx. 2,240 mfg. between 1937-1939.

	$400	$350	$320	$250	$200	$150	$100
In .22 WRF cal. (rare)	$1,200	$1,000	$800	$600	$400	$300	$250

MODEL 68 — .22 cal, bolt action single shot, similar to Model 67, walnut stock. Approx. 100,000 mfg. between 1934-1946 no ser. no.'s on gun.

	$175	$130	$95	$80	$70	$60	$50

MODEL 69 & 69A — .22 LR or RF cal., 5 or 10 shot repeater, 25 in. barrel, aperture or open rear sight, not serial numbered. Approx. 355,000 mfg. between 1935-1963. Add $50 for Target version.

	$200	$150	$110	$95	$85	$75	$70

The Model 69 was cocked by the closing motion of the bolt, whereas the 69A was cocked by the opening motion of the bolt.

Grading	100%	98%	95%	90%	80%	70%	60%

MODEL 697 — same general specifications as the Model 69, except no iron sights or sight cuts in barrel and no ramp or sight cover. Telescope bases attached to barrel were standard.

	100%	98%	95%	90%	80%	70%	60%
	$175	$80	$70	$60	$55	$50	$45
.22 WRF cal.	$350	$320	$230	$180	$140	$120	$100

MODEL 777 — .30-06 cal., bolt action, 4 shot mag., mfg. by Nikko in Japan during 1979-80 for sale to Winchester subsidiaries in Australia, Germany, Italy, and Scandinavia, only 3 were shipped to the U.S., checkered Monte Carlo stock with Wundhammer swell grip, lightweight barrel, engraved action, "Winchester" is cast on the left side of the receiver near the top, approx. 1,000 mfg. with 250 in .30-06 cal. - 750 mfg. in different cal. and sold elsewhere, 8½ lbs.
Extreme rarity factor precludes accurate price evaluation. Some specimens have been reported as sold in the $1,850+ range.

MODEL 70 STANDARD GRADE BOLT ACTION — .22 Hornet, .220 Swift, .243, .250-3000, .257 Robts., .264 Mag., .270, 7 x 57mm, 300 Sav., .30-06, .308, .300 Mag., 7.65, 338 Mag., 35 Rem., .358, 375 H&H, & 9mm, or .300 H&H cal., 5 shot mag., 4 shot mag. on Magnums, 24, 25, or 26 in. barrels, open sights, checkered walnut pistol grip stock. Mfg. 1937-1963.
Values listed below assume original, unaltered specimens — modifications/alterations to either the metal or wood surfaces can reduce prices by large amounts.
Standard Calibers — .243, .270, .30-06, or .308.

	100%	98%	95%	90%	80%	70%	60%
	$775	$700	$625	$575	$550	$525	$500
Rarer Calibers							
.22 Hornet or Swift	$925	$825	$750	$675	$600	$550	$500
.257 Roberts	$925	$825	$750	$675	$600	$550	$500
.300 Win. Mag.	$1,000	$900	$800	$725	$675	$600	$550
.338 Win. Mag.	$1,200	$1,000	$900	$800	$750	$675	$575
.375 H&H	$1,495	$1,250	$1,100	$995	$925	$850	$795
.250-3000 Savage	$1,750	$1,625	$1,500	$1,300	$1,100	$975	$850
7 x 57mm	$2,950	$2,600	$2,200	$1,800	$1,500	$1,300	$1,100

ADD APPROX. 80% FOR CARBINE VARIATIONS (MFG. 1936-1946 WITH 20 IN. BARREL IN .22 HORNET, .250-3000, .257 ROBERTS, .270, 7MM, and .30-06).
Rare cal.'s such as the .35 Rem., .300 Savage, and 9mm are seldomly encountered and their scarcity precludes accurate price determination.

MODEL 70 SUPER GRADE — same as Standard, with deluxe wood, black pistol grip cap and forend tip. Disc. 1960. A general rule for Super Grades is that if you add 80% to the standard grade in similar calibers, values should be rather close. For large cal.'s, values are listed below.

	100%	98%	95%	90%	80%	70%	60%
.375 H&H	$2,750	$2,350	$1,950	$1,675	$1,450	$1,200	$1,000
.458 Win. Mag.	$3,200	$2,900	$2,500	$2,200	$1,995	$1,750	$1,650

MODEL 70 FEATHERWEIGHT — lightened version of Standard, .243, .264 Mag., .270, .308, .30-06, or .358 cal., 22 in. barrel, aluminum trigger guard and floorplate. Mfg. 1952-1963.
Standard Calibers — .243, .264 Win. Mag., .30-06, .270, or .308 cal.

	100%	98%	95%	90%	80%	70%	60%
	$825	$750	$675	$600	$550	$500	$450
.358 Mag.	$1,595	$1,250	$1,000	$900	$775	$650	$550

Add 150-200% for Super Grade Models.

MODEL 70 NATIONAL MATCH — same as Standard, with target stock and scope bases, .30-06 only. Disc. 1960.

	100%	98%	95%	90%	80%	70%	60%
	$1,100	$825	$770	$715	$660	$550	$525

Grading	100%	98%	95%	90%	80%	70%	60%

MODEL 70 TARGET — same as 70 Standard, in .243 or .30-06 cal., 24 in. medium weight barrel and target stock. Disc. 1963.

	$1,100	$825	$770	$715	$660	$550	$525

MODEL 70 BULL GUN — same as Standard Model 70, with 28 in. heavy barrel, .300 H & H or .30-06 cal. only.

	$1,750	$1,400	$1,000	$800	$660	$550	$525

MODEL 70 VARMINT — same as Standard Model 70, in .220 Swift or .243 cal., 26 in. heavy barrel, scope bases, varmint style stock. Mfg. 1956-1963.

	$900	$770	$715	$605	$550	$440	$385

MODEL 70 WESTERNER — same as Standard Model 70, with 26 in. barrel, .264 Win. Mag.

	$900	$825	$770	$660	$550	$440	$375

MODEL 70 ALASKAN — same as Standard Model 70, in .338 Win. Mag. or .375 H&H Mag. cal., 25 in. barrel, recoil pad. Mfg. 1960-1963.

	$1,450	$1,250	$995	$825	$715	$605	$495

MODEL 72 — .22 LR and Gallery Model (.22 short only), tube mag., bolt action, 25 in. round, tapered barrel, not serial numbered. Over 161,000 mfg. between 1938-1959.

	$225	$180	$160	$140	$115	$100	$90

Add 50% for Gallery Model (mfg. 1939-1942).
The Model 72 has an aperture rear sight and the Model 72A has an open "V" rear sight - values are similar.

MODEL 75 TARGET — .22 LR, 5 or 10 shot mag., 28 in. barrel, target sights, slight variation used by Government in WWII. Approx. 88,715 Model 75 Target and Model 75's were mfg. between 1938-1958.

	$500	$450	$400	$370	$330	$275	$200

MODEL 75 SPORTER — same as Target except 24 in. barrel, non-target sights and select checkered walnut.

	$625	$550	$500	$450	$375	$300	$270

RIFLES: DISCONTINED SEMI-AUTO

On Models 1903, 1905, 1907, 1910, 55, 63, 74, and 77 values in 50% or less original condition have been omitted since values in those conditions will approximate the 60% price. This reflects the fact that while these lower condition specimens are not as desireable to collectors, they tend to bottom out at the 60% price.

MODEL 1903 — .22 Win. Auto rimfire, 10 shot tube mag., 20 in. round barrel, open sights, straight grip stock cut out for partial magazine filling. Approx. 126,000 mfg. between 1903-1932.

	$625	$500	$400	$300	$265	$215	$175

First U.S. semi-auto rifle designed for .22 rimfire cartridges.

MODEL 1905 — .32 Win. or .35 Win. cal., 5 or 10 shot box mag., 22 in. round barrel, open sights, plain pistol grip stock. Approx. 29,113 mfg. between 1905-1920.

	$650	$550	$425	$350	$275	$200	$175

MODEL 1907 — .351 Win., 5 or 10 shot box mag., 20 in. round barrel, open sights, plain pistol grip stock, an improved version of the Model 1905. Approx. 58,490 mfg. between 1907-1957.

	$450	$375	$330	$305	$250	$195	$140

Grading	100%	98%	95%	90%	80%	70%	60%

MODEL 1910 — .401 Win., 4 shot box mag., 20 in. barrel, open sight, plain pistol grip stock. Mfg. 20,786 between 1910-1936.

	100%	98%	95%	90%	80%	70%	60%
	$600	$500	$400	$350	$275	$220	$165

Add 10-15% for Fancy Sporting Rifle (special checkered walnut).

MODEL 55 — .22 cal. only, top loading single shot, bottom ejection, 22 in. round barrel, open sporting sights, not serial numbered. Over 45,000 mfg. between 1958-1961.

	100%	98%	95%	90%	80%	70%	60%
	$275	$225	$175	$140	$120	$100	$80

MODEL 63 — .22 LR, styling similar to Model 1903, 10 shot tube mag., 20 (disc. 1936) or 23 in. barrel, open sights, plain pistol grip stock. Approx. 174,692 mfg. between 1933-1958.

	100%	98%	95%	90%	80%	70%	60%
	$575	$480	$435	$370	$330	$290	$235

Add 50%-100% for 20 in barrel depending on condition.
The Model 63 was introduced to take advantage of the new .22 LR cartridge, which the older Model 1903 couldn't chamber. Add a slight premium for grooved receiver variation.

MODEL 74 — .22 Short or LR, tubular mag. in stock, pop-out bolt assembly. Approx. 406,574 mfg. between 1939-1955. Distinguishable by squared off rear receiver.

	100%	98%	95%	90%	80%	70%	60%
	$200	$175	$150	$120	$100	$85	$75

MODEL 77 — .22 rimfire, detachable box mag. or tubular mag. under barrel. Over 217,000 mfg. between 1955-1962. Add $15 for tubular mag.

	100%	98%	95%	90%	80%	70%	60%
	$150	$125	$100	$85	$75	$60	$50

RIFLES: DISCONTINUED SLIDE ACTION

100%	98%	95%	90%	80%	70%	60%	50%	40%	30%	20%	10%

MODEL 1890 SLIDE ACTION — .22 S, L, LR, or WRF rimfire, cal.'s were non-interchangeable, visible hammer, solid-frame (first 15,000) or takedown, 24 in. octagonal barrel, case hardened receivers until 1901. Approx. 849,000 mfg. between 1890-1932.
Blued Finish — post-1901 manufacture.

100%	98%	95%	90%	80%	70%	60%	50%	40%	30%	20%	10%
$1,200	$775	$600	$495	$450	$400	$360	$330	$300	$260	$220	$195

Add 20% premium for .22 LR cal.

Color casehardened receiver — disc. 1901, takedown feature was added in 1892 after over 15,000 solid frames had been made.

100%	98%	95%	90%	80%	70%	60%	50%	40%	30%	20%	10%
$3,600	$2,750	$2,100	$1,700	$1,000	$675	$495	$390	$350	$300	$275	$250

Deluxe models or solid frames will bring premiums over values listed above. There were also a limited amount of guns mfg. with stainless steel barrels which will add to values of post-1901 mfg.

The Model 1890 was Winchester's first slide action repeating rifle. It replaced the Model 1873 .22 cal. It was an excellent and inexpensive .22 rifle that rapidly became the universal firearm used in shooting galleries. Even though production reached approx. 849,000 units, most guns were heavily used and specimens existing today in 98%+ condition are rare. Check carefully for rebarreling (notice proofmarks on barrel).

MODEL 1906 — .22 S, L, or LR, 20 in. round barrel, tube mag., visible hammer, open sights, straight stock with shotgun butt plate. Approx. 848,000 mfg. between 1906-1932.

100%	98%	95%	90%	80%	70%	60%	50%	40%	30%	20%	10%
$1,000	$800	$600	$495	$450	$400	$360	$330	$300	$260	$210	$165

This model is seldomly encountered in over 90% original condition.

Model 1906 Expert — similar to Model 1906, except has a pistol grip stock and different shaped slide handle, finish choices included blue, nickel trimmed receiver, guard, and bolt, or full nickel trimmed, mfg. 1917-1925.

100%	98%	95%	90%	80%	70%	60%	50%	40%	30%	20%	10%
$1,200	$1,000	$800	$600	$495	$450	$400	$360	$330	$300	$260	$210

Grading	100%	98%	95%	90%	80%	70%	60%

MODEL 61 HAMMERLESS — .22 S, L, or LR, 24 in. round or octagonal barrel, tube mag., open sights, plain grip stock. Approx. 342,000 mfg. between 1932-1963.

	$500	$420	$375	$330	$300	$250	$225

Pre-war manufacture has small forearm. Add 15% for single caliber barrel marking. Pre-war octagon barrel in S or L cal.'s will command a 100% premium. "WRF" marked round barrel is rare - front of receiver must be marked "W.R.F.".

MODEL 61 MAGNUM — same as Standard 61, but chambered for .22 Win. Mag. Mfg. 1960-1963.

	$575	$450	$400	$350	$300	$250	$225

MODEL 62 — 62A VISIBLE HAMMER — modern version of 1890, 23 in. round tappered barrel. Over 409,000 mfg. between 1932-1958.

	$450	$395	$360	$330	$250	$195	$165

Pre-war model is 62, distinguishable by small forearm. Add 30% for pre-war. The Model 62-A was introduced 1940 at serial number 99,200 with minor changes. Model 62A single cal. barrel markings do not add premiums. Gallery variations of these models will command a large premium.

RIFLES: LEVER ACTION - POST 1964 MFG.

MODEL 94 STANDARD RIFLE — lever action, .30-30, 7-30 Water (new 1989), or .44 Mag. (mfg. 1984 and 1985 only) cal., 6 or 7 (24 in. barrel only) shot tube mag., 20 or 24 (mfg. 1987-88 only) in. round barrel, open sights, straight walnut stock, barrel band on forearm. Mfg. 1964-present. Angled ejection became standard 1982, 6½ lbs.

Mfg.'s Sug. Retail	$309	$250	$210	$180	$165	$150	$140	$135

Add $15 for 24 in. barrel (disc. 1990).

Add $16 for .44 Mag. cal. (disc. 1986).

Model 94 Deluxe — .30-30 only, similar to Standard Rifle, except has checkered walnut stock and forearm. New 1988.

Mfg.'s Sug. Retail	$335	$265	$210	$165	$145	$135	$120	$105

Add $53 for 1.5 - 4.5X scope with low mounts.

Model 94 Ranger — .30-30 only, 20 in. barrel, uncheckered hardwood stock and forearm, 5 shot mag., 6½ lbs. New for 1985.

Mfg.'s Sug. Retail	$277	$225	$185	$160	$150	$140	$130	$120

Add $48 for 4x32 scope with see-through mounts.

Win-Tuff Rifle — similar to Model 94 Rifle, except has laminated hardwood stock and forearm with checkering. Drilled and tapped for scope mounts. New 1987.

Mfg.'s Sug. Retail	$335	$265	$210	$160	$145	$135	$120	$105

MODEL 94 XTR — .30-30 or 7-30 Waters (new 1985) cal., 20 or 24 (7-30 Waters only) in. barrel, checkered select walnut, hooded front sight (except 7-30 Waters which has dovetailed front blade), 6½ lbs. Disc. 1988.

	$260	$225	$205	$185	$160	$150	$140

For 7-30 Waters cal. rifle - add $26.

Last Mfg.'s Sug. Retail was $285.

Model 94 XTR Deluxe — .30-30 cal. only, deluxe American walnut stock and lengthened forearm with fancy checkering, 20 in. barrel with deluxe script, rubber butt pad. Mfg. 1987-1988 only.

	$370	$310	$270	$235	$210	$190	$160

Last Mfg.'s Sug. Retail was $426.

MODEL 94 TRAPPER — .30-30, .45 Colt (new 1985), or .44 Mag./.44 Spl. cal., 16 in. barrel, side ejection, walnut stock, 5 or 9 shot tube mag., blue finish, dovetailed front sight, 6 lbs.

Mfg.'s Sug. Retail	$309	$260	$215	$180	$160	$150	$140	$130

Add $19 for .45 Colt or .44 Mag. cal.

The .44 Mag. cal. was introduced 1985.

Grading	100%	98%	95%	90%	80%	70%	60%

MODEL 94 .44 MAG. S.R.C. — .44 Mag., top eject, 20 in. barrel, SRC. Mfg. 1967-72.

	$325	$275	$250	$225	$200	$175	$150

MODEL 94 CLASSIC SERIES — .30-30 cal., 20 or 26 in. barrel. Approx. 47,000 mfg. 1967-70.

	$275	$225	$200	$185	$160	$150	$140

MODEL 94 ANTIQUE CARBINE — same as Standard, with scroll on receiver, case hardened, gold-plated saddle ring. Mfg. 1964-1983.

	$250	$225	$200	$175	$160	$150	$140

MODEL 94 WRANGLER — .32 Win. Special, top ejection, only 7,947 mfg. Disc.

	$350	$310	$270	$235	$210	$190	$160

MODEL 94 WRANGLER II — .32 Win. Special (disc. 1984) or .38-55 Win. cal., angle ejection, 16 in. barrel, oversized hoop-shaped lever, roll-engraved receiver, 5 shot mag., 6⅛ lbs. Made 1983-1985 only.

	$245	$220	$200	$185	$165	$150	$140

Last Mfg.'s Sug. Retail was $275.

MODEL 94 BIG BORE — .307, .356, or .375 (disc. 1987) Win. cal., angled ejection port provides scope mounting, checkered walnut Monte Carlo stock with recoil pad, 20 in. barrel, 6 shot mag., sling swivels, 6½ lbs. New 1983.

Mfg.'s Sug. Retail	$335	$275	$215	$195	$175	$160	$150	$140

Also mfg. in a top eject (pre-USRA).

This model had an "XTR" suffix until 1989.

MODEL 9422 STANDARD — .22 LR or Mag., takedown, 20½ in. round barrel, 15 shot (LR) mag., checkered straight grip, checkered high gloss (disc.) or satin weather resistant finish (new 1988) walnut stock and forearm, 6¼ lbs. Mfg. 1972-present.

Mfg.'s Sug. Retail	$342	$285	$240	$210	$190	$175	$160	$145

This model had an "XTR" suffix until 1989. Earlier mfg. including pre-XTR and early XTR rifles had no checkering - these guns will command slight premiums over values listed above.

.22 Mag. cal. — 11 shot mag., 6¼ lbs.

Mfg.'s Sug. Retail	$357	$295	$250	$220	$200	$180	$170	$160

Model 9422 Win-Cam — .22 Win. Mag. only, similar to 9422 XTR Standard, except has checkered greenish laminated hardwood stock and forearm. New 1987.

Mfg.'s Sug. Retail	$357	$295	$240	$210	$190	$175	$160	$145

Model 9422 Win-Tuff — .22 LR or .22 Mag., checkered laminated brown hardwood stock and forearm. New 1988.

Mfg.'s Sug. Retail	$342	$280	$240	$210	$190	$175	$160	$145

Add $15 for .22 Mag. cal.

MODEL 9422 XTR CLASSIC — same general specifications as Model 9422 XTR Standard, except has 22½ in. barrel and non-checkered, satin finished, pistol grip walnut stock and extended forearm, stock also has fluted comb with crescent steel butt plate, curved finger lever, 6½ lbs. Mfg. 1985-1987.

	$285	$255	$230	$205	$185	$175	$160

Last Mfg.'s Sug. Retail was $301.

MODEL 64 1972-1974 MODEL — .30-30, lever action, 5 shot, ⅔ tube mag., 24 in. barrel, open sight, plain pistol grip stock. Mfg. 1972-1974.

	$220	$195	$165	$140	$110	$90	$70

Grading	100%	98%	95%	90%	80%	70%	60%

RIFLES: BOLT ACTION - POST 1964 MFG.

MODEL 52D BOLT ACTION TARGET RIFLE — .22 LR, single shot, free floating standard or heavy barrel, scope bases, target stock with palm stop. Mfg. 1961-1980. Total production on all variations is approx. 125,233.

	$435	$415	$385	$360	$305	$275	$220

MODEL 52 INTERNATIONAL MATCH — similar to 52-D Heavy Barrel, with special free rifle stock, hooked butt.

	$495	$470	$440	$415	$330	$305	$250

MODEL 52 INTERNATIONAL PRONE — similar to 52-D, with prone stock, removable roll over cheek piece. Mfg. 1975-1980.

	$495	$470	$440	$415	$330	$305	$250

MODEL 70 STANDARD — .22-250, .222, .225, .242, .270, .308, or .30-06 cal., 5 shot, 22 in. barrel, open sight, Monte Carlo stock, swivels. Mfg. 1972-1980.

	$350	$330	$310	$285	$220	$200	$175

MODEL 70 MAGNUM — .264 Win. Mag., 7mm Rem. Mag., .300 H&H Mag., .300 Win. Mag., .338 Win. Mag., .375 H&H Mag., or .458 Win. Mag. cal., 24 in. barrel.

	$400	$350	$330	$310	$285	$220	$200

Add 25-35% for .375 H&H Mag. or .458 Win. Mag. cal.

MODEL 70 FEATHERWEIGHT — .22-250, .223 Rem., .243 Win., .257 Robts. (disc.), .270 Win., .280 Rem., 6.5 x 55mm Swedish (new 1991), 7mm Mauser (disc.), .30-06, .308, 7mm Rem. Mag. (new 1991), or .300 Win. Mag. (new 1991) cal., bolt action, both short and medium action, 5 shot mag., 22 in. barrel (24 in. with .300 Win. Mag.), checkered walnut stock, no sights, approx. 6½ lbs. New 1981.

Mfg.'s Sug. Retail	$510	$405	$365	$325	$300	$280	$260	$240

In 1981 during U.S.R.A. takeover transition guns were built distinguishable by the U.S.R.A. trademark on the recoil pad. Some collectors will pay a premium for Win. marked pads. Cal.'s .257 Robts. and 7mm Mauser were disc. 1985.

This model had an "XTR" suffix until 1989.

Model 70 Win-Tuff Featherweight Rifle — similar to Model 70 Lightweight Rifle, except has wraparound, checkered stock with Schnabel forend, pistol grip cap. Not available in .22-250 cal. Mfg. 1988-89 only.

	$400	$340	$310	$275	$250	$230	$210

Last Mfg.'s Sug. Retail was $476.

MODEL 70 XTR EUROPEAN FEATHERWEIGHT — 6.5 x 55 Swedish Mauser cal., 22 in. barrel, 5 shot mag., rifle sights, 6¾ lbs. Made 1986 only.

	$390	$365	$330	$305	$280	$260	$240

Last Mfg.'s Sug. Retail was $460.

MODEL 70 50TH ANNIVERSARY MODEL — .300 Win. Mag., 24 in. barrel, deluxe walnut stock, engraving and special motifs on metal surfaces, serial numbered 50 ANV 1 - 50 ANV 500, 7¾ lbs. 500 mfg. 1987 only.

	$1,000	$840	$725

Last Mfg.'s Sug. Retail was $939.

MODEL 70 CUSTOM GRADE — various cal.'s, old style Model 70 action, semi-fancy American walnut checkered stock, engine turned bolt and follower, hand honed internal parts. Mfg. 1988-89 only.

	$1,100	$875	$700

Last Mfg.'s Sug. Retail was $1,172.

Grading	100%	98%	95%	90%	80%	70%	60%

MODEL 70 SUPER GRADE — .270 Win. (new 1991), .30-06 (new 1991), 7mm Rem. Mag., .300 Win. Mag., or .338 Win. Mag. cal., 24 in. barrel, 3 shot mag., jeweled bolt, stainless steel extractor for true claw controlled round feeding and ejecting, three-position safety, checkered satin finish walnut stock with wood cheek piece, bases and rings included, 7¾ lbs. New 1990.

Mfg.'s Sug. Retail	$997	$925	$795	$625

MODEL 70 CUSTOM SUPER GRADE — similar to Model 70 Super Grade, but must be special ordered through the Custom Gun Shop and includes many custom features including semi-fancy walnut with satin finish and hand-honed internal parts. New 1990.

Mfg.'s Sug. Retail	$1,695	$1,695	$1,250	$995

A Model 70 Collector Grade is also a variation of this model that is mfg. in the Custom Gun Shop - this model is priced on request only.

MODEL 70 CUSTOM SUPER GRADE EXPRESS — .375 H&H Mag., .416 Rem. Mag., .458 Win. Mag. cal., or .470 Capstick 24 in. (22 in. on .458 Win. Mag.) barrel, features claw controlled ground feeding, deluxe walnut with satin finish and checkering, 3-leaf express rear sight, high luster metal finish, bolt and follower are engine turned, available by special order through the custom gun shop only. New 1990.

Mfg.'s Sug. Retail	$2,125	$2,125	$1,500	$1,175

MODEL 70 EXHIBITION GRADE — various cal.'s, fancy checkered American walnut stock with hardwood forend tip. Mfg. 1988-89 only.

	$1,995	$1,575	$1,000

Last Mfg.'s Sug. Retail was $2,192.

MODEL 70 XTR FEATHERWEIGHT ULTRA GRADE — .270 Win., bolt action, extensively engraved, finely checkered deluxe French walnut, with mahogany presentation case.

	$2,000	$1,500	$950

Last Mfg.'s Sug. Retail was $5,000.

MODEL 70 LIGHTWEIGHT CARBINE — .22-250, .223 Rem., .243 Win., .250 Savage (new 1986), .308 Win., .270 Win., or .30-06 cal., bolt action, 5 shot mag., both short and medium action, 20 in. barrel, checkered walnut stock, no sights, approx. 6 lbs. Mfg. 1984-86. Add $15 for open sights.

	$355	$320	$285	$255	$230	$210	$190

Last Mfg.'s Sug. Retail was $395.

MODEL 70 LIGHTWEIGHT RIFLE — .22-250, .223 Rem., .243 Win., .270 Win., .280 Rem. (new 1988), .30-06, or .308 Win. cal., 22 in. barrel, checkered walnut stock, no sights, 6½ lbs. New 1987.

Mfg.'s Sug. Retail	$447	$380	$325	$285	$255	$230	$210	$190

Model 70 Win-Tuff Lightweight Rifle — .22-250 (mfg. 1988-89), .223 (new 1989), .243 Win. (new 1988), .270 Win. .30-06 or .308 Win. (new 1989) cal., similar to Model 70 Lightweight Rifle, except has laminated brown hardwood stock with checkering. New 1987.

Mfg.'s Sug. Retail	$447	$380	$325	$285	$255	$230	$210	$190

Model 70 Win-Cam Lightweight Rifle — .270 Win. or .30-06 cal., greenish laminated hardwood stock with checkering, 22 in. barrel. New 1987.

Mfg.'s Sug. Retail	$447	$380	$325	$300	$280	$260	$240	$220

This model was previously desigated Featherweight before 1989.

Grading	100%	98%	95%	90%	80%	70%	60%

MODEL 70 SPORTER — .22-250 (new 1989), .223 (new 1989), .243 (new 1989), .25-06 Rem. (mfg. 1985-87 and reintroduced 1990), .270 Win., .30-06 or .308 Win. (mfg. 1986-89) cal., 24 in. barrel, 5 shot mag., custom Sporter styling, Monte Carlo cheek piece, detachable sling swivels, 7¾ lbs.

Mfg.'s Sug. Retail	$510	$420	$365	$320	$295	$275	$255	$235

This model had an "XTR" suffix until 1989. Before 1989, iron sights cost $15 additionally - for 1990, prices became the same for either iron sights or base and rings.

MODEL 70 SPORTER MAGNUM — same general specifications as standard Sporter, 7mm Mag., .264 Mag., .270 Wby. Mag. (new 1988), .300 Wby. Mag. (new 1989), .300 Win. Mag., .300 H&H (new 1989), or .338 Win. Mag. cal., reinforced stock, 3 shot mag., 24 in. barrel, 7¾ lbs. Mfg. 1972-present.

Mfg.'s Sug. Retail	$510	$420	$365	$320	$295	$275	$255	$235

This model had an "XTR" suffix until 1989. Before 1989, iron sights cost $15 additionally - for 1990, prices became the same for either iron sights or base and rings.

Model 70 Super Express Mag. — .375 H&H or .458 Win. Mag. cal., 3 shot mag., 22 or 24 in. (.375 H&H only) barrel, 8½ lbs.

Mfg.'s Sug. Retail	$816	$700	$575	$525	$495	$460	$430	$400

This model had an "XTR" suffix until 1989.

MODEL 70 VARMINT — same general specifications as standard Sporter, .22-250, .223, .243 Win., or .308 cal., 26 in. heavy barrel, no sights, 5 shot mag., target scope bases, 7¾ lbs. Mfg. 1964-present.

Mfg.'s Sug. Retail	$531	$440	$365	$325	$295	$280	$260	$240

This model had an "XTR" suffix 1978-89.

MODEL 70 WINLIGHT — .270, .280 Rem. (new 1987), .30-06, 7mm Rem. Mag., .300 Win. Mag., .300 Wby. Mag., or .338 Win. Mag. cal., McMillan fiberglass stock, thermoplastic receiver bedding, blued metal parts, 22 or 24 (Mag. cal.'s only) in. barrel, 3 or 4 shot mag., no sights, approx. 6½ lbs. Mfg. 1986-90.

	$555	$490	$440	$395	$350	$310	$280

Last Mfg.'s Sug. Retail was $637.

RANGER RIFLE — .243 Win. (new 1991), .270 Win., .30-06, or 7mm Rem. Mag. (disc. 1985) cal., 22 or 24 in. barrel, 3 (7mm Rem. Mag.) or 4 shot mag. plain hardwood stock with no checkering, open sights, 7⅛ lbs.

Mfg.'s Sug. Retail	$414	$325	$265	$215	$200	$180	$165	$155

RANGER YOUTH/LADIES CARBINE — .223 Rem. (disc. 1989), .243 Win., or .308 Win. (new 1991), cal., 20 in. barrel, 4 or 5 (.223 Rem.) shot mag., shorter hardwood stock dimensions, 5¾ lbs.

Mfg.'s Sug. Retail	$423	$335	$275	$220	$185	$170	$160	$150

MODEL 70 DELUXE — .243, .270, .30-06, or .300 Win. Mag. cal., 22 in. barrel, open sight, hand checkered, black forend tip, became standard 1972. Mfg. 1964-1971.

	$475	$415	$360	$320	$285	$220	$180

MODEL 70 TARGET RIFLE 1964-1971 — .308 or .30-06 cal., 24 in. heavy barrel, no sights, target bases, heavy target style stock with hand stop. Mfg. 1972-disc.

	$630	$550	$495	$440	$360	$330	$275

MODEL 70 INTERNATIONAL ARMY MATCH 1971 — .308 cal., 5 shot, 24 in. heavy barrel, no sights, adj.rigger, ISU stock with forearm, accessory rail, adj. butt. Mfg. 1973-disc.

	$715	$660	$605	$550	$470	$440	$385

Grading	100%	98%	95%	90%	80%	70%	60%

MODEL 70 MANNLICHER 1969-1971 — .243, .270, .30-06, or .308 Win. cal., 19 in. barrel, open sight, full length Monte Carlo stock with steel forend cap. Disc. 1972.

	100%	98%	95%	90%	80%	70%	60%
	$550	$440	$385	$360	$305	$275	$250

MODEL 70A — economy version of 1972 type Model 70, same cal.'s, no hinged floorplate or forend tip. Mfg. 1972-1978.

	$325	$285	$265	$230	$200	$165	$140

MODEL 70A MAGNUM — similar to Model 70A, except in Mag. cal.'s but not .375 H&H or .458. Mfg. 1972-1978.

	$340	$310	$275	$250	$220	$195	$165

MODEL 670 BOLT ACTION RIFLE — another economy version of the model 70, .225, .243, .270, .308, or .30-06 cal., 22 in. barrel, open sights, no hinged floorplate, pistol grip stock. Mfg. 1967-1973.

	$300	$250	$220	$195	$175	$165	$140

MODEL 670 CARBINE — same as 670, with 19 in. barrel, not available in .308. Mfg. 1967-1970.

	$300	$250	$220	$195	$175	$165	$140

MODEL 670 MAGNUM — same as 670, with reinforced stock, .264 Mag., 7mm Mag., or .300 Win. Mag. cal. Mfg. 1967-1970.

	$330	$275	$255	$220	$205	$195	$165

MODEL 770 BOLT ACTION — .22-250, .222, .243, .270, or .30-30 cal., 22 in. barrel, open sights, no floorplate or forend tip. Mfg. 1969-1971.

	$325	$285	$275	$260	$250	$220	$195

MODEL 770 MAGNUM — same as Standard, in .264 Mag., 7mm Mag., or .300 Win. Mag. cal., recoil pad. Mfg. 1969-1971.

	$350	$310	$285	$275	$265	$250	$220

MODEL 88 LEVER ACTION CARBINE — .243, .284, or .308 cal., 19 in. barrel, pistol gripped, one piece stock, barrel band. Mfg. 1968-1973.

.308 cal.

	$500	$400	$300	$250	$225	$200	$175

For .243 cal. — add 25%.
For .284 cal. — add 50-75%.

MODEL 88 RIFLE — .243, .284, .308, or .358 cal., 22 in. barrel, basket weave or diamond cut checkering, no barrel band. Approx. 284,000 mfg. 1955-1973.

	100%	98%	95%	90%	80%	70%	60%
.308 cal.	$375	$325	$300	$250	$225	$200	$175
.243 cal.	$450	$380	$350	$325	$275	$250	$225
Pre-1964 production — add $50.							
.284 cal.	$700	$585	$500	$450	$400	$300	$200
Pre-1964 production — add 50%.							
.358 cal.	$850	$775	$700	$500	$400	$300	$250

Available between 1956-1962 only.

MODEL 100 AUTOLOADING RIFLE — .243, .284, or .308 cal., 4 shot detachable mag., 22 in. round barrel with open sights, gas operated, one piece basket weave stock, pistol grip cap. Over 262,000 mfg. 1961-1973.

	$375	$320	$285	$265	$240	$220	$200

Pre-1964 production
For .243 cal. — add $25.
For .284 cal. — add $50.

Grading	100%	98%	95%	90%	80%	70%	60%

MODEL 100 CARBINE — same as rifle, with 19 in. barrel, plain pistol grip stock, barrel band. Mfg. 1967-1973.

	100%	98%	95%	90%	80%	70%	60%
	$475	$375	$300	$260	$235	$215	$200

For .243 cal. — add $25.
For .284 cal. — add $50.

MODEL 121 SINGLE SHOT RIFLE — .22 rimfire, bolt action, 20¾ in. barrel, open sights, plain pistol grip stock. Mfg. 1967-1973.

$115	$85	$70	$55	$45	$35	$30

MODEL 121Y SINGLE SHOT RIFLE — same as 121, with shorter stock.

$115	$85	$70	$55	$45	$35	$30

MODEL 121 DELUXE — same as 121, with ramp front sight and sling swivels.

$125	$90	$75	$60	$50	$40	$35

MODEL 131 REPEATING RIFLE — .22 rimfire, bolt action, 7 shot, 20¾ in. barrel, plain Monte Carlo stock. Mfg. 1967-1973.

$135	$100	$85	$70	$60	$50	$40

MODEL 141 REPEATER — same as 131, with tube mag. in butt stock. Mfg. 1967-1973.

$135	$100	$90	$75	$65	$55	$45

MODEL 190 SEMI-AUTO RIFLE — .22 S, L, or LR cal., semi-auto, 15 shot LR tube mag., alloy receiver, uncheckered walnut finished hardwood stock, 20½ (Carbine Model) or 24 (Rifle Model) in. barrel, approx. 2,150,000 (including the Model 290 listed below also) during 1967-1980.

$150	$125	$100	$85	$75	$65	$55

MODEL 310 SINGLE SHOT — .22 rimfire, bolt action, 22 in. barrel, open sights, checkered pistol grip stock, swivels. Mfg. 1972-1975.

$200	$175	$140	$100	$80	$70	$60

MODEL 320 REPEATING RIFLE — same as 310, with 5 shot clip. Mfg. 1972-1974.

$375	$325	$275	$225	$165	$140	$100

MODEL 250 LEVER ACTION — .22 rimfire, 20½ in. barrel, tube mag., hammerless, checkered pistol grip stock. Mfg. 1963-1973.

$110	$95	$70	$60	$50	$40	$30

MODEL 255 — same as 250, in .22 WMR. Mfg. 1964-1970.

$135	$115	$90	$70	$60	$50	$40

MODEL 250 DELUXE — same as 250, with select wood and sling swivels. Mfg. 1965-1971.

$150	$125	$90	$75	$60	$50	$45

MODEL 255 DELUXE — .22 WMR, with select wood and swivels. Mfg. 1965-1973.

$175	$140	$110	$90	$80	$70	$60

MODEL 270 SLIDE ACTION — .22 rimfire, tube mag., 20½ in. barrel, checkered pistol grip stock. Mfg. 1963-1973.

$115	$90	$75	$60	$50	$40	$35

Plastic stock version

$85	$75	$50	$40	$30	$20	$20

Grading	100%	98%	95%	90%	80%	70%	60%

MODEL 275 — same as 270, in .22 WMR.

	$135	$110	$100	$90	$80	$70	$65

MODEL 270 DELUXE — same as 270, with select wood, Monte Carlo stock. Mfg. 1965-1973.

	$135	$110	$90	$80	$70	$60	$50

MODEL 275 DELUXE — same as 270 Deluxe, in .22 WMR.

	$165	$140	$110	$90	$80	$70	$60

MODEL 290 DELUXE RIFLE — same as 290, with select Monte Carlo stock. Mfg. 1965-1973.

	$185	$160	$135	$115	$100	$90	$80

MODEL 490 AUTOLOADING RIFLE — .22 rimfire, 5 shot clip mag., 22 in. barrel, folding sight, checkered one piece stock. Mfg. 1975-1980.

	$250	$215	$185	$155	$145	$130	$110

DOUBLE EXPRESS RIFLE — .30-06, 7x65R, 9.3x74R, .257 Roberts, or .270 Win. cal., 23½ in. O&U barrels, iron sights with claw scope mounts, ejectors, fully engraved satin finish receiver, walnut specially hand checkered, sling swivels, 8½ lbs. Disc. 1986.

	$1,750	$1,495	$1,250	$1,125	$1,000	$875	$750

Last Mfg.'s Sug. Retail was $2,995.

In 1984, Aero Marine located in Birmingham, AL special ordered 200 deluxe double rifles in 7 x 57mm Mauser cal. They featured better engraving and game scenes with bottom of receiver marked Jaeger. Of the 200, 100 were rifles with 90 being standard grade and 10 being deluxe. The other 100 were supplied with an extra set of O/U shotgun barrels. Sales were slow on these special guns and eventually they were liquidated to another wholesaler. Recently, prices are in the $2,250-$3,000 range for the rifle alone and $3,000-$3,750 for the Combo.

SHOTGUNS: 1879-1964

On Models 1887, 1893, 1897, 1901, 1911, and 36 the values on 50% or less original condition have been omitted since values in those conditions will approximate the 60% price. This reflects the fact that while these lower condition specimens are not as desireable to collectors, they tend to bottom out at the 60% price because of their shooting value.

BREECH LOADING SXS — 10 or 12 ga., imported from England for sales through the Winchester New York City office only, exposed hammers, available in 5 grades ranging from Class D - Class A and Match gun (lowest to highest). Higher grades were mfg. by W.C. Scott & Sons, about 10,000 were imported between 1879-1884. Prices vary greatly due to condition and grade. Prices can range from $300 (poor condition Class D) to over $4,000 (95%+ condition specimen in Class A or Match gun).

This side by side model was the first shotgun bearing the Winchester name sold in the U.S. Identifiable by "Winchester Repeating Arms Co., New Haven, Connecticut, U.S.A." marking on barrel rib top.

MODEL 1887 LEVER ACTION — 10 or 12 ga., 4 shot tube mag., 30 or 32 in. full choke barrels, plain pistol grip stock, first Browning patent shotgun mfg. by Winchester. Mfg. 1887-1901. Approx. 64,855 mfg.

	$1,000	$900	$825	$750	$650	$575	$500

Standard frame finish on this model was color case hardening. Premiums exist for original bright case colored specimens. 10 ga. began production with serial number 22148. Also mfg. in Riot configuration (20 in. cylinder bore barrel). Gauges were chambered for 2⅝ in. (12 ga.) and 2⅞ in. (10 ga.). First lever action repeating shotgun domestically mfg.

Grading	100%	98%	95%	90%	80%	70%	60%

Model 1887 Deluxe — damascus barrel, checkered stock, and other special order features.

	$1,350	$1,100	$850	$700	$600	$500	$450

MODEL 1893 SLIDE ACTION — 12 ga., 30 (standard) and 32 in. barrel, black powder only. First Winchester shotgun with sliding forearm action, first Browning slide action patent, disc. 1897 after run of some 34,050. Note: chambered for $2\frac{5}{8}$ shells only, damascus barrels were available at extra cost, as were fancy stocks.

	$850	$600	$425	$350	$300	$225	$175

This gun had limited sales because mechanical weaknesses developed when shooting smokeless powder.

MODEL 1897 SLIDE ACTION — 12 or 16 ga. (introduced 1900), improved Model 1893 action, 26-32 in. barrels, visible hammer, various chokes, takedown or solid frame, plain pistol grip stock. Over 1,024,700 mfg. between 1897-1957.

	$675	$400	$325	$275	$240	$200	$175

First Winchester shotgun chambered for $2\frac{3}{4}$ in. smokeless ammunition.

MODEL 1897 RIOT GUN — same as Standard, with 20 in. cylinder bore barrel, 12 ga. only. Mfg. 1898-1935.

	$600	$475	$450	$400	$375	$300	$200

MODEL 1897 TRENCH GUN — same as Riot Gun, with hand guard and bayonet, issued for U.S. Army for trench warfare in WWI, also mfg. post-WWI. Mfg. 1916-1935.

	$1,100	$900	$825	$750	$675	$575	$525

This model changed its stock configuration after WWI.

MODEL 1897 TRAP — higher grade version of Standard, sometimes encountered with special order ebony diamond inlay in stock pistol grip. Mfg. 1897-1931.

	$750	$700	$660	$480	$385	$330	$275

MODEL 1897 PIGEON — higher grade version of Standard 97. Mfg. 1897-1939.

	$1,100	$950	$800	$600	$500	$400	$350

MODEL 1901 — 10 ga. only, strengthened Model 1887 action to accept smokeless powder, lever action, standard barrel 32 in., blued barrel and frame, 5 shot mag. 13,500 mfg. between 1901-1920, starting with serial number 64,856. Fancy grade - add 25%.

	$1,300	$950	$750	$600	$500	$450	$400

This shotgun was chambered for $2\frac{7}{8}$ in. smokeless powder ammunition.

MODEL 1911 AUTOLOADER — 12 ga., recoil operated, 26 or 28 in. barrel, various chokes, pistol grip laminated birch stock. Mfg. 1911-1925, 82,774 produced, action had design problems.

	$500	$375	$300	$250	$195	$165	$110

The Model 1911 was Winchester's first semi-auto shotgun. It did not prove to be satisfactory partly because the design had to be exclusive of the patents for Browning's famous A-5 model, interestingly enough a design which Winchester originally had helped Browning patent.

MODEL 36 SINGLE SHOT — 9mm long shot, short shot, and ball, 18 in. round barrel, single shot bolt action, guns were not serial numbered, one piece plain stock and forearm, special shaped trigger guard, $2\frac{3}{4}$ lbs. Approx. 20,000 mfg. between 1920-1927.

	$495	$375	$275	$250	$225	$200	$180

Grading	100%	98%	95%	90%	80%	70%	60%

MODEL 12 STANDARD SLIDE ACTION — 12, 16, 20, or 28 ga., 26-32 in. barrels, 6 shot, various chokes, hammerless, plain pistol grip walnut stock. Mfg. 1912-1976.
The following add-ons do not apply to the 28 ga.
Add $100 if in original unremarked box (N.I.B. only).
Add $75 for Win. special VR (offset barrel proofmark).
Add $150 for Win. solid rib.
Add 75% for Win. milled VR.
Extra barrel(s) — add 50% of specimens value/set.

Special order features on field guns have captured much collector interest in recent years. Combinations of these features can add a considerable percentage to the base values listed below. Rare special orders on rare variations are very desirable and prices can double and more if the combination is right. As is the case with most other collectible shotguns at this time, Model 12's with open choked barrels in shorter lengths are a lot more desireable (and expensive) than a specimen with a 30 in. full choke barrel (most common). Values listed below are for standard configuration (28 or 30 in. full choke barrel with no rib). Premiums must be added for the rarer open choked barrels in shorter length on all gauges.

ORIGINAL GAUGE CAN BE DETERMINED BY REMOVING THE BUTT STOCK AND OBSERVING THE GAUGE MARKING ON THE STOCK SCREW BOSS.

12 ga.

	$595	$500	$415	$365	$330	$295	$250

16 ga.

	$675	$595	$550	$475	$400	$340	$315

20 ga.

	$775	$675	$600	$525	$450	$395	$375

28 ga.

	$3,500	$3,200	$2,750	$2,450	$2,000	$1,750	$1,500

Subtract 40% if with factory Cutts compensator.
In the past several years many non-original, re-stamped 28 ga. barrels have been added to 16 or 20 ga. frames "creating" a more desirable (and expensive) gun to unsuspecting buyers. Roll die markings are getting better and better so be very cautious when considering a non-Cutts 28 ga. (as in get a receipt specifying originality). The last observed ser. no. for an original 28 ga. is 1,586,817.

Editor's Note: The Model 12 Winchester was produced continuously from 1912-1980. Over 2,027,500 were produced both in standard and deluxe (Pigeon) grades. Pigeon grades were first listed in 1914 and disc. during the war (1941). Reintroduced in 1948, they were disc. permanently in 1964, after which the Super Pigeon Grade became available only on a custom order basis from Winchester's Custom Gun Shop. These guns are worth 50-300% premiums depending on gauge, barrel lengths, stock options, engraving patterns, etc. With an attrition rate of 33%, Model 12's with rare features 50 years ago will only be much rarer today (and expensive). 28 ga. guns were built between 1934 and 1960. Gauge rarity in increasing order is 12 ga, 16 ga, 20 ga, .410 (Model 42), and 28 ga. Serialization breakdown by year of manufacture is provided under the "Model Serialization" section of this book. When collecting Model 12's, ser. no.'s on the underside of receiver (forward end), should match ser. no. on bottom rear of Mag. tube. Stainless steel barrel Model 12's were mostly mfg. in the late 1920's - early 1930's (65X,XXX serial range). Values typically range between $1,000-$2,500.
"Y" prefix appears on Model 12's built 1964-1980 — see listing under Post-64 Models.

MODEL 12 FEATHERWEIGHT — same as Standard, with alloy guard. Mfg. 1959-1962. "F" suffix after ser. no.

	$495	$425	$365	$320	$275	$250	$200

MODEL 12 RIOT GUN — 12 ga., 20 in. cylinder bore barrel. Mfg. 1918-1963.

	$525	$450	$395	$350	$300	$250	$225

Grading	100%	98%	95%	90%	80%	70%	60%

MODEL 12 MILITARY TRENCH GUN — 12 ga., vent hand guard on barrel, bayonet lug, takedown or solid frame, must have parkerized finish and flaming bomb proofs on frame and barrel. Disc.

	$1,300	$1,195	$950	$825	$725	$625	$550

Note: barrel must not be drilled for front bead sight.

MODEL 12 HEAVY DUCK GUN — 12 ga., 3 in. chamber, 30 or 32 in. barrel, solid rubber recoil pad, ½ in. shorter pull than regular Model 12. Mfg. 1935-1963.

	$675	$525	$450	$400	$350	$325	$300

Solid rib — add 40%.

Vent. rib — 2 different styles mfg. by Simons, notice barrel proof marking - rare.

32 in. barrel — add 15%.

MODEL 12 SKEET GUN — 12, 16, 20, or 28 ga., 26 in. barrel, skeet choke, checkered pistol grip stock, pre-WWII. Mfg. 1933-1976.

	$895	$795	$700	$600	$550	$500	$450

Solid rib — add 10%.

Win. Special VR — add 15%.

Win. milled VR — add 25%.

Factory-Cutts compensator — subtract 50%.

16 gauge — rarity will command a premium.

20 gauge — add 40%.

28 gauge — add 400%.

MODEL 12 TRAP GUN — various ga.'s, full choke barrel, deluxe trap styled stock, solid recoil pad. Mfg. 1938-1964.

	$895	$795	$695	$650	$500	$435	$400

Add $100 for white or brown plastic Hydrocoil stock. While plain barrelled variation is rare, it is not as desirable.

MODEL 12 PIGEON GRADE — finer and more deluxe version of Model 12, many variations. Mfg. 1914-1941 and 1948-1964, usually with engraved pigeon on bottom rear of mag. tube. Add $500 or more if N.I.B.

	$1,900	$1,500	$1,175	$850	$800	$775	$700

Vent rib — add $150.

Above values are for 12 ga. - smaller gauges with desireable features will command healthy premiums.

MODEL 20 — .410 bore, hammer, boxlock, 26 in. full choke, 6 pounds. Mfg. 23,616 between 1919-1924.

	$400	$300	$250	$175	$140	$110	$85

Winchester Junior Trap Shooting Outfit — includes shotgun, midget hand trap, 150 .410 ga. shells, 100 clay targets and accessories, cased.

	$600	$475	$400	$365	$330	$295	$250

MODEL 21

Approx. 32,000 mfg. since 1931. Approx. 2,000 mfg. in Custom Grade to date.

The Winchester Model 21 is a boxlock side by side double barrelled shotgun. After years in the design stage, production began in 1929 with guns being shipped to the warehouse in 1930 and first offered in Winchester's 1931 price list. Regular production continued for thirty years, through 1959.

Grading	100%	98%	95%	90%	80%	70%	60%

The early guns were plain, standard 12 gauge models with double triggers and extractors. Later in 1931, 16 and 20 gauge chamberings became available as did selective single triggers and automatic ejectors.

By the end of 1933 the Model 21 skeet gun had been introduced as had Tournament, Trap and Custom Built grades. By about this time options included fancier wood, beavertail or semi-beavertail fore-ends, checkered butts (standard on skeet guns) or skeleton steel butt plates, recoil pads and almost any variation the customers might desire. Metal finishes on a Model 21 are unusual in that they have salt blued frames and rust blued barrels — this explains the difference in coloration between these metal surfaces.

The Tournament Grade was dropped in 1936 and the Trap Grade in 1940. A Standard Grade Trap Gun was added in 1941. The early Custom Built Grade was dropped in 1942 and the Deluxe Grade was added. This grade included as standard many of the previously available extra cost options.

Relatively few guns were produced in chamberings smaller than 20 gauge. 28 gauge first appeared in the 1936 catalog, although a few were probably produced before that. Winchester records are unclear as to the total but it is generally believed that fewer than 100 original factory guns were made. In addition, a number of original 20 gauge guns have been modified at the factory or elsewhere with factory 28 gauge barrels. These latter guns are just as valuable if the conversion was done at the Winchester Custom Gun Shop. Authenticity of the original guns should be established by factory letter.

.410 bore guns were first listed in 1955 but again some had been produced earlier, one having been built for John Olin in 1950. Throughout Winchester history all the rules seem to have had exceptions and nowhere is this more apparent than with respect to the Model 21 which, after all, has been pretty much a custom gun from the very beginning. Factory records and tallies among dealers indicate the existence of from 40 to 50 original factory guns. As in the case of the 28 gauge, extra barrels were available and at least some of those have been added to original 20 gauge guns.

The 3 inch Magnum 12 gauge Duck gun (stamped "Duck" on floor plate) was offered in Winchester catalogs from 1940 through 1952. Selective single triggers and automatic ejectors were standard as were the solid red Winchester recoil pads and 30 in. or 32 in. barrels. Some cases of non-factory upgrading of 2¾ or 3 inch Magnum guns have been reported. If authenticity is important to the buyer, a factory letter should be requested.

With respect to such letters, in cases where records may be missing or incomplete, the resultant letters may be less conclusive than desired. In some instances, consultation with, or a written appraisal from an authoritative collector arms dealer might be helpful.

Six standard patterns of engraving and several stock checkering and carving styles evolved during the production years. Values added by these and other embellishments such as precious metal inlays are beyond the scope of this work.

The following retail prices are for a standard field gun with average wood, beavertail forearm, ejectors, and single selective trigger with no alterations.

12 ga.

	$3,250	$3,000	$2,700	$2,450	$2,250	$2,000	$1,800

16 ga.

	$3,500	$3,250	$3,000	$2,700	$2,500	$2,250	$2,100

20 ga.

	$4,750	$4,400	$4,050	$3,700	$3,400	$3,200	$3,000

Add $400-$550 for VR.

Double triggers w/extractors — deduct approx. 50%.

If double triggers with ejectors, subtract 10%-20%. Normally DT, extractor guns have splinter forearms.

Grading	100%	98%	95%	90%	80%	70%	60%

Skeet Gun — available in Standard, Tournament, and Trap grades. Introduced 1933. Add 20-50% depending on grade.

Trap Gun — introduced 1940, Trap Grade disc. same year, unaltered specimens will bring premium — add 10-25%.

3 Inch Duck Gun — introduced 1940, must be so stamped (observe the 3 in. marking very carefully — no premium exists for this variation.

As can be seen, values are partly based on a certain interdependence between options. Higher grade guns, of course, will bring somewhat higher prices although much of their increased value results from many "options" being included as standard features.

Buyers or sellers with limited experience should always seek expert advice or appraisals in dealing with a Model 21. This is especially true with regard to higher grade guns and those with extra ornamentation.

.410 BORE:

Retail prices for original guns may be expected to range between $25,000 and $45,000 for mechanically sound guns depending on quality of finish. These prices take into consideration the reported sale of a plain standard gun in recent years for $37,000. Non-original guns with add-on factory barrels would probably be reduced by one-third.

28 GAUGE:

Factory original guns will probably bring from $11,500 to $17,000 and, as with the 410's, 20 gauge guns modified to 28 gauge with factory barrels would be worth approx. the same if done at the factory.

Refinishing or Restoration: There is disagreement as to the effects of refinishing a Model 21. Many shooters and at least some collectors prefer a well refinished gun to a badly worn one. Higher grade guns restored by a master craftsman may approach factory original guns in value.

MODEL 21: RECENT MFG. — since 1960 Model 21 production has been limited to high grade, built from special order, U. S. Repeating Arms currently offers the Model 21 in 12, 16 or 20 ga. U.S.R.A. has disc. the mfg. of the Model 21 temporarily beginning in 1988 as their Custom Gun Shop is backordered on many other projects. Values below reflect 1989 information. It is important to note that while advertised, U.S. Repeating Arms has not taken an order for approximately 3 years on any Model 21 Winchester.

Standard Custom guns (12 ga.) are currently trading in the $6,500 - $7,000 range if NIB.

Custom Built — standard model with no engraving.

Mfg.'s Sug. Retail $8,100 $8,100 $5,000 $3,750

Custom Grade — includes No. 6 engraved reciever and vent rib.

Mfg.'s Sug. Retail $11,080 $11,080 $7,250 $5,500

Grand American Grade — includes 2 sets of barrels with forearms, No. 6 engraved with gold inlays, cased.

Mfg.'s Sug. Retail $22,745 $22,745 $15,000 $11,500

Grand American Small Gauge — 28 or .410 ga.

Mfg.'s Sug. Retail $34,460 $34,460 $25,000 $17,500

Add 10% for 28/.410 ga. combo.

MODEL 24 DOUBLE-BARREL — 12, 16, or 20 ga., boxlock, hammerless, double triggers. Introduced 1940, disc. 1957 after approx. 116,280 mfg. Add 10% for 20 ga.

	100%	98%	95%	90%	80%	70%	60%
	$595	$525	$475	$400	$325	$250	$190

MODEL 25 SLIDE ACTION — 12 ga. only, non-takedown version of the Model 12, 26 or 28 in. barrel. 87,937 mfg. between 1949-1954.

	100%	98%	95%	90%	80%	70%	60%
	$450	$375	$350	$275	$250	$200	$175

Grading	100%	98%	95%	90%	80%	70%	60%

MODEL 37 SINGLE-SHOT — 12, 16, 20, 28 or .410 ga., .410 bore, top-lever break-open action. Not serial-numbered. Over 1,015,000 mfg. between 1936-1963.

	100%	98%	95%	90%	80%	70%	60%
12 gauge	$175	$145	$125	$100	$85	$75	$55
16 gauge	$175	$145	$125	$100	$85	$75	$55
20 gauge	$200	$150	$125	$105	$85	$75	$55
28 gauge	$325	$260	$230	$200	$175	$150	$125
.410 gauge	$250	$200	$175	$125	$95	$85	$75

"Red Letter" models will bring 10%+ premiums. Subtract 10-15% for post-64 models. 28 ga. is most desirable.

MODEL 40 SEMI-AUTO — 12 ga. only, long recoil action, 28 or 30 in. barrel, walnut stock, skeet model also, poorly designed, many recalled by Winchester. Approx. 12,000 mfg. 1940-1941.

	100%	98%	95%	90%	80%	70%	60%
	$650	$495	$425	$350	$300	$275	$250

MODEL 41 BOLT ACTION — .410 ga., 2½ in. chamber until 1933 when it changed to 3 in., bolt action, single shot, 24 in. round barrel bored F, one-piece plain walnut stock and forearm, not serialized, approx. 22,145 were mfg. 1920-1934.

	100%	98%	95%	90%	80%	70%	60%
	$1,200	$995	$800	$675	$475	$375	$250

This model is rarely encountered with over 80% original condition.

MODEL 42 SLIDE ACTION — the first pump specifically made for the .410 ga., hammerless, 2½ (introduced 1935) or 3 in. chamber, 26 or 28 in. barrel, plain walnut pistol grip stock with circular grooved forearm (modified 1947). Approx. 160,000 mfg. between 1933-1963.

Special order features on field guns have captured much collector interest in recent years. Combinations of these features can add a considerable percentage to the base values listed below. Rare special orders on rare variations are very desirable and prices can double and more if the combination is right.

Standard Grade

	100%	98%	95%	90%	80%	70%	60%
	$900	$800	$700	$625	$550	$500	$450

Add 65% for solid rib.

Skeet or Trap Grade — has solid matted rib, fancy wood.

	100%	98%	95%	90%	80%	70%	60%
	$1,650	$1,450	$1,350	$1,100	$1,000	$900	$800

Deluxe Grade — fanciest grade, value is affected by wood and finish. Factory special orders can bring prices up to $10,000.

	100%	98%	95%	90%	80%	70%	60%
	$1,850	$1,650	$1,600	$1,500	$1,400	$1,200	$1,000

Factory vent rib barrels were never made available on the Model 42. Older catalogs list the Winchester special vent rib which were ribs installed by Simmons.

MODEL 50 SEMI-AUTO — 12 or 20 ga., 3 shot, recoil-operated (non-recoiling barrel), 26-30 in. barrels, vent rib optional, feather weight model introduced 1958, all steel construction. Over 196,000 mfg. between 1954-1961, starting with serial number 1,000.

	100%	98%	95%	90%	80%	70%	60%
	$425	$360	$295	$280	$265	$240	$220

Vent rib (Simmons installed) — add $50.

20 ga. — add $50.

Trap & Skeet Model — add 15%.

Pigeon Grade — add 200-350%.

Grading	100%	98%	95%	90%	80%	70%	60%

MODEL 59 SEMI-AUTO — 12 ga. only, 3 shot, short recoil operation, Win-lite (steel and fiberglass) ribless barrels, 26-30 in. barrel lengths, alloy receiver inscribed with hunting scenes, Versalite (first interchangeable choke tubes) option introduced 1961, 6½ lbs. 82,085 mfg. between 1960-1965.

	$525	$460	$420	$370	$340	$310	$260

Inspect carefully for either cracked receiver (by bolt handle cutout), or separating fiberglass on end of barrel.

Pigeon Grade — mfg. 1962-1965, add 200-350% (rare).

Winchester also mfg. 20 and 14 ga.'s experimentally in this model, extremely rare and expensive.

SHOTGUNS: POST-1964

MODEL 370 SINGLE BARREL — 12, 16, 20, 28 or .410 ga., 28-32 in. full choke plain barrel, replaced the Model 37, top lever break open, exposed hammer, plain pistol grip stock. Approx. 221,578 mfg. between 1968-1973.

	$120	$100	$90	$85	$80	$75	$70

Add 20-60%+ for .28 ga. and .410 ga.

The Model 370 was mfg. in Winchester's Canadian plant in Cobourg, Ontario.

MODEL 370 YOUTH — same as 370, with 26 in. barrel, 12½ in. stock, with recoil pad.

	$145	$110	$95	$85	$80	$75	$70

MODEL 37A SINGLE BARREL — replaced the Model 370, roll engraved receiver, gold trigger. Approx. 391,168 mfg. between 1973-1980 in the Winchester plant in Cobourg, Ontario.

	$140	$110	$95	$85	$75	$65	$55

Add 10% for 36 in. goose barrel.

Add 30% for 28 ga. and 60% for .410 ga.

MODEL 37A YOUTH — same as 37A, except 20 ga. only with 12½ in. pull stock.

	$175	$145	$100	$85	$70	$55	$40

MODEL 12 SUPER PIGEON GRADE — 12 ga., slide action, 26, 28, or 30 in. barrel, vent rib, any choke, hand honed action, engine turned breech block and loading flap, "B" checkering and No. 5 engraving, custom order grade walnut stock. Limited production between 1964-1972.

	$2,995	$2,500	$2,250	$2,100	$1,750	$1,500	$1,300

An additional 380 Super Pigeon Grades were mfg. 1984-85.

MODEL 12 FIELD GRADE — 12 ga., slide action, 26, 28, or 30 in. vent rib barrel, various chokes, jeweled bolt, hand checkered, checkered select walnut stock. Mfg. 1972-1976, "Y" Serial No. Prefix.

	$675	$550	$525	$495	$450	$400	$350

In 1984 Y series Model 12's were once again available through a private contract with U.S.R.A. Co. which included engraving on Grades 1A-1C, and 2-5. These guns were available in either Field, Trap, or Skeet configurations. Since there was no manufacturers' suggested retail, Model 12 values shown below are established by analyzing the sales of the two private contractors - no more of these variations are available.

Grades 1-A, 1-B, & 1-C — light engraving depicting dogs or ducks. Disc.

	$1,300	$1,195	$1,000	$875	$785	$695	$600

Last Mfg.'s Sug. Retail was $1,375.

Grades 2 & 3 — engraving features large duck and dog game scenes on receiver flats. Disc.

	$1,600	$1,495	$1,295	$1,075	$950	$830	$725

Last Mfg.'s Sug. Retail was $1,695.

Grading	100%	98%	95%	90%	80%	70%	60%

Grade 4 — more elaborate game scene engraving than Grades 2 & 3. Disc.

	$1,850	$1,695	$1,450	$1,225	$1,075	$950	$850

Last Mfg.'s Sug. Retail was $1,995.

Grade 5 — elaborate game scene engraving with style B checkering. Disc.

	$2,195	$1,995	$1,725	$1,500	$1,225	$1,095	$950

Also available with gold inlays - add $1,000 to values shown above. Last Mfg.'s Sug. Retail was $2,450.

3 Barrel Set — grade 5 engraving with gold inlays and two extra barrels. Disc.

	$5,500	$4,995	$4,350	$3,750	$3,325	$2,750	$2,300

Last Mfg.'s Sug. Retail was $6,000.

MODEL 12 SKEET GRADE — same as Field Grade, with 26 in. vent rib skeet bore barrel, skeet style stock, with recoil pad. Mfg. 1972-1975.

	$825	$750	$625	$550	$495	$450	$425

See listings under Model 12 Field Grade for engraved values.

MODEL 12 TRAP GRADE — same as Field grade, with 30 in. vent rib full choke barrel, trap style stock, straight or Monte Carlo, recoil pad. Mfg. 1972-1980.

	$750	$675	$575	$525	$495	$450	$425

See listings under Model 12 Field Grade for engraved values.

MODEL 12 DU — limited mfg. for Ducks Unlimited Chapters.

	$1,200	$995	$825				

MODEL 1200 SLIDE ACTION FIELD GRADE — 12, 16, or 20 ga., 26, 28, or 30 in. barrel, alloy receiver, various chokes, checkered pistol grip stock, pad. Mfg. 1964-1981.

	100%	98%	95%	90%	80%	70%	60%
	$220	$200	$180	$165	$140	$110	$100
Vent rib	$240	$220	$205	$195	$165	$140	$110
Win. choke	$260	$240	$215	$200	$190	$180	$160

For Hydro-coil recoil system — add 33%.

MODEL 1200 MAGNUM — same as 1200, chambered for 12 or 20 ga., 3 in. magnum shells. Mfg. 1964-1980.

	100%	98%	95%	90%	80%	70%	60%
	$230	$200	$175	$165	$140	$110	$100
Vent rib	$275	$225	$200	$185	$150	$140	$110

MODEL 1200 SKEET GUN — same as 1200, 12 or 20 ga., 26 in. vent rib barrel, skeet bore, 2 shot mag. and select style stock. Mfg. 1965-1974.

	$300	$275	$250	$220	$195	$165	$140

MODEL 1200 TRAP GUN — same as 1200, with 12 ga., vent rib, 30 in. full choke barrel, select trap style stock. Mfg. 1965-1974.

	100%	98%	95%	90%	80%	70%	60%
	$300	$275	$250	$220	$195	$165	$140
Winchoke	$360	$330	$305	$275	$250	$220	$165

MODEL 1200 DEER GUN — same as 1200, with 22 in. barrel, rifle sights, 12 ga. only. Mfg. 1965-1974.

	$220	$195	$165	$140	$110	$100	$85

Grading	100%	98%	95%	90%	80%	70%	60%

MODEL 1300 FEATHERWEIGHT SLIDE ACTION — 12 or 20 ga., 3 in. chamber, takedown, 22, 26 (new 1991), or 28 in. barrel, 5 shot, plain or vent rib. (became standard 1990), Winchoke tubes, checkered walnut stock and grooved forearm, alloy frame. Mfg. 1978-present.

Mfg.'s Sug. Retail	$355	$295	$260	$230	$195	$175	$160	$145

Subtract $30 without vent rib.

Subtract $17 for Youth Model (20 ga. only - new 1989).

This model had an "XTR" suffix until 1989. Older Model 1300 Featherweights had roll-engraving but no premiums are being asked at this time.

MODEL 1300 CUSTOM HIGH GRADE — 12 ga. only, 28 in. VR Winchoke barrel, special order only through the Custom Gun Shop, features deluxe hand checkered walnut and special engraving. New 1991.

Mfg.'s Sug. Retail	$1,395	$1,395	$900	$650

MODEL 1300 WATERFOWL — 12 ga. only, 3 in. chamber, 28 or 30 (disc.) in. vent rib barrel, matte finished metal, choice of low luster walnut finish or brown Win-Tuff wood, recoil pad, includes camo sling and swivels, Winchokes standard, 7 lbs. New 1984.

Mfg.'s Sug. Retail	$367	$300	$270	$235	$200	$180	$165	$150

MODEL 1300 TURKEY GUN — 12 ga. only, 3 in. chamber, 22 in. vent rib barrel, Winchoked, walnut stock and forearm with low luster finish, metal surfaces have matte finish, supplied with camouflaged fabric sling, 6⅜ lbs. Mfg. 1985-1988 only.

	$290	$265	$235	$200	$180	$165	$150

Last Mfg.'s Sug. Retail was $348.

Model 1300 Win-Cam Turkey Gun — similar to Model 1300 Turkey Gun, except has greenish laminated hardwood stock and forearm. New 1987.

Mfg.'s Sug. Retail	$391	$325	$285	$245	$200	$180	$165	$150

Model 1300 Win-Cam National Wild Turkey Federation — 12 or 20 ga., Series I was released 1989 (12 ga. only) and included special receiver engraving, Series II was released 1990 with a choice of either 12 (disc.) or 20 ga. Ladies/Youth model.

Mfg.'s Sug. Retail	$411	$340	$295	$250	$200	$180	$165	$150

MODEL 1300 COMBO PACK WIN-CAM — 12 ga., supplied with 22 and 30 in. VR non-glare finished barrels, greenish laminated hardwood stock and forearm, camo sling, matte finished metal. Mfg. 1987-1988 only.

	$360	$320	$290	$260	$230	$200	$185

Last Mfg.'s Sug. Retail was $425.

MODEL 1300 SLUG HUNTER — 12 ga. only, 3 in. chamber, 22 in. rifled or smooth bore barrel with iron sights, checkered stock and forearm, satin walnut finish or brown laminate stock (Win-Tuff). Supplied with camo fabric sling. New 1988.

Mfg.'s Sug. Retail	$403	$335	$295	$250	$200	$180	$165	$150

Add $10 for smooth bore barrel with Sabot rifled tubes.

Add $20 for "Whitetails Unlimited" Model (new 1991).

MODEL 1300 RANGER SLIDE ACTION — 12 or 20 ga., 3 in. chamber, 24⅛ (disc. deer barrel), 26 (new 1991), 28 or 30 in. barrel, alloy receiver. New 1983.

Mfg.'s Sug. Retail	$277	$225	$180	$150	$135	$120	$110	$ 95

Subtract $20 without VR or Winchokes.

Add $4 for 22 in. cyl. bore deer barrel.

Add $28 for 22 in. rifled bore deer barrel.

Add $17 for 20 ga. for Ladies/Youth Model w/rearward forearm.

This model is also available in a deer combination package which includes a deer and regular Winchoke barrel in either 12 or 20 ga. — add approx. 20% to values listed above.

Grading	100%	98%	95%	90%	80%	70%	60%

Ranger Youth Model — 20 ga. only, 3 in. chamber, 22 in. barrel, youth stock dimensions - 13 in. length of pull.

Mfg.'s Sug. Retail	$294	$240	$200	$170	$150	$125	$110	$100

Subtract $35 if without Winchoke and vent rib.

MODEL 1300 DEFENDER — 12 or 20 ga., 3 in. chamber, available in Police (disc. 1989), Marine, and Defender variations, 18 in. cyl. bore barrel, 5, 7 (disc), or 8 shot mag., wood (high gloss), synthetic (matte finish), or pistol grip (matte finish) stock, 5½- 7 lbs.

Mfg.'s Sug. Retail	$243	$210	$180	$150			

Add $90 for Combo Package (includes extra 28 in. VR barrel).

Stainless Marine Defender — a new Sandstrom 9A phosphate coating was released late 1989 to give long lasting corrosion protection to all receiver and internal working parts, 7 shot mag., synthetic pistol grip or stock configuration, 6 - 7 lbs.

Mfg.'s Sug. Retail	$423	$375	$325	$250			

MODEL 1400 SEMI-AUTO — 12, 16, or 20 ga., 26, 28, or 30 in. barrels, alloy receiver, various chokes, gas operated, checkered pistol grip stock. Mfg. 1964-1981.

	$275	$250	$220	$200	$175	$155	$140
Vent rib	$315	$265	$240	$220	$195	$165	$150

Add 33% for Hydro-coil recoil system.

NEW MODEL 1400 WALNUT SEMI-AUTO — 12 or 20 ga., 2¾ in. chamber, 22 (disc.), 26 (new 1991), or 28 (12 ga. only) in. VR barrel, checkered walnut stock and forearm, Winchokes standard, 3 shot mag., rotary bolt system, 7-7½ lbs. New 1989.

Mfg.'s Sug. Retail	$398	$340	$300	$275	$250	$225	$195	$165

MODEL 1400 CUSTOM HIGH GRADE — 12 ga. only, 28 in. VR Winchoke barrel, special order only through the Custom Gun Shop, features deluxe hand checkered walnut and special engraving. New 1991.

Mfg.'s Sug. Retail	$1,695	$1,695	$1,100	$750			

MODEL 1400 SKEET GRADE — same as 1400, 12 or 20 ga., with 26 in. vent rib barrel, skeet bore, select skeet style stock. Mfg. 1965-1973.

	$360	$330	$305	$275	$220	$195	$165

MODEL 1400 TRAP GRADE — same as 1400, with 30 in. full choke vent rib barrel, select trap style stock. Mfg. 1965-1973.

	$360	$330	$305	$275	$220	$195	$165

MODEL 1400 DEER GUN — same as 1400, with 22 in. barrel, rifle sights, 12 ga. only. Mfg. 1965-1974.

	$265	$240	$220	$200	$175	$165	$140

Note: In 1968 the model 1400 series was modified. The action release was improved and the checkering redesigned. From 1968-1972, they were designated MKII, which was then dropped. The values for the later guns mfg. from 1968-1973 may run approx. 10% higher; values shown are for guns mfg. from 1965-1968.

MODEL 1400 SLUG HUNTER — 12 ga. only, 22 in. smooth bore cyl. or rifled Sabot choke-tubed barrel, drilled and tapped for scope, includes bases or iron sights, 7¼ lbs. New 1990.

Mfg.'s Sug. Retail	$442	$370	$325	$275	$250	$225	$195	$165

MODEL 1500 XTR SEMI-AUTO — 12 or 20 ga., 2¾ inch only, 28 inch barrel, plain or vent rib, Winchoke tubes, gas operation. Mfg. 1978-1982.

	$300	$260	$240	$220	$200	$180	$160

Grading	100%	98%	95%	90%	80%	70%	60%

MODEL 1400 RANGER SEMI-AUTO — 12 or 20 ga., gas operation, alloy receiver, 22 cyl. deer, 26 (new 1991), or 28 in. Winchoke barrel, new 1983, vent rib became standard 1985, 7¼ lbs.

Mfg.'s Sug. Retail	$358	$275	$230	$200	$180	$160	$140	$120

Add $46 for deer comb. (includes extra 22 in. cyl. bore barrel).
Subtract $30 without VR.

SUPER X MODEL 1 SEMI-AUTO — 12 ga., 26, 28, or 30 in. vent rib barrel, various chokes, steel receiver, gas operated - self compensating, checkered pistol grip stock and forearm. Mfg. 1974-1981.

	$425	$365	$345	$315	$295	$275	$240

SUPER X MODEL 1 SKEET — same as Standard, with 26 in. skeet bore barrel, select skeet style stock. Mfg. 1974-1981.

	$475	$425	$400	$385	$330	$305	$275

SUPER X MODEL 1 TRAP — same as Standard, with 30 in. barrel, imp. mod. or full choke, select trap style stock.

	$475	$425	$400	$385	$330	$305	$275

SUPER X MODEL 1 CUSTOM TRAP OR SKEET — 12 ga. only, limited production from the Custom Shop, deluxe checkered walnut stock and forearm, extensive scroll engraving on receiver, built to custom order. Limited mfg. starting 1987.

Mfg.'s Sug. Retail	$1,295	$1,295	$850	$650

Add $700 for factory gold inlays (8 flying ducks).

SHOTGUNS: RECENT MFG. OVER AND UNDER

Model 101 dates of manufacture and serialization data can be found in the SERIALIZATION section in the back of this text.

In November of 1987 Olin/Winchester disc. the Model 101. Classic Doubles (listed separately in this text) is now importing this model under their own trademark. With the discontinuance of the Model 101 and its many variations, both dealers and collectors have created a lot more demand for this model recently. As a result, prices have escalated and the scramble is on to try and pick off those rare and desirable variations. Since there have been a lot of limited editions and production changes in the 101 O/U series, it could very well be that this model might become very collectible in upcoming years (as in look what happened to the Model 12).

MODEL 101 FIELD GRADE O/U — 12, 20, or .410 ga., 26, 28, or 30 in. barrels, various chokes, boxlock, auto ejectors, SST, engraved receiver, checkered American walnut pistol grip stock. Mfg. 1963-present. Values below assume Winchokes (standard since 1983) - subtract $60 if without.

Older production — checkered walnut stock and forearm, ejectors, SST, blued metal with light engraving on receiver.

	$750	$695	$650	$620	$585	$550	$500

Add 40% for 28 ga. or .410 ga.

Field Special — 12 or 20 ga., 3 in. chambers, vent rib, 27 in. barrels with Winchokes, blued receiver with scroll engraving ejectors, 7 lbs. Disc. 1987.

	$995	$840	$775	$695	$600	$500	$450

Last Mfg.'s Sug. Retail was $1,185.

Lightweight Field — 12 or 20 ga., similar to regular Field Grade, except has coin finished receiver, vent barrels, and solid rubber recoil pad, 6½ - 7 lbs. Disc. 1987.

	$1,285	$1,030	$965	$895	$800	$700	$600

Last Mfg.'s Sug. Retail was $1,425.

Grading	100%	98%	95%	90%	80%	70%	60%

Waterfowl Model — 12 ga. only, 3 in. chambers, 30 or 32(disc.) in. Winchoked barrels, vent rib, matte blued receiver with moderate engraving, low gloss walnut stock with vent recoil pad, 7 ¾ lbs. Disc. 1987.

	$1,410	$1,175	$995	$895	$800	$700	$600

Last Mfg.'s Sug. Retail was $1,570.

Model 101 Field Grade 2 Barrel Hunting Set — 12 or 20 ga. barrels, both with Winchokes, 26 in. barrels - 20 ga., 28 in. barrels - 12 ga., scroll engraved, blued receiver with game scene engraving and borders, cased. Mfg. 1984-1987.

	$2,020	$1,825	$1,550	$1,375	$1,220	$1,050	$975

Last Mfg.'s Sug. Retail was $2,345.

Quail Special — 12, 20 (disc.1984), 28 (new 1987) or .410 (new 1987) ga., 25½ in. Winchoke barrels, 6¾ lbs. - 12 ga., straight grip stock, vent barrels and rib, coin finished receiver with game scene engraving. Imported 1984-1987.

	$1,475	$1,245	$1,100	$1,000	$900	$825	$750

Add $120 for 28 or .410 ga.
Last Mfg.'s Sug. Retail was $1,950.

National Wild Turkey Federation Commemorative — only 300 mfg.

	$1,350	$1,100	$950				

American Flyer Live Bird — 12 ga. only, 28 or 29½ (new 1988) in. separated barrels with special competition VR, blued frame with gold wire borders and pigeon inlay, 8 - 8½ lbs. Imported 1987 only.

	$2,595	$2,275	$1,950	$1,775	$1,600	$1,425	$1,300

Add $925 for Combo Model (extra set of 29½ in. barrels).

Add $265 for 29½ in. barrel with WT4 choke tubes.
Last Mfg.'s Sug. Retail was $2,910.

MODEL 101 MAGNUM O/U — same as 101 Field, 12 or 20 ga., 3 in. Mag. chambering, recoil pad, 30 in. barrels, full and mod., or full and full choke. Mfg. 1966-1981.

	$775	$715	$660	$605	$550	$500	$460

MODEL 101 SKEET GRADE — same as 101 Field, with 26 in. skeet bored barrels, skeet style stock. Mfg. 1966-1984.

	$1,000	$825	$770	$700	$650	$595	$540

MODEL 101 THREE GAUGE SKEET SET — same as Skeet 101, with 20, 28, and .410 ga. barrels, cased. Mfg. 1974-1984.

	$2,950	$2,500	$2,250	$2,000	$1,850	$1,700	$1,550

MODEL 101 TRAP GRADE — 12 ga. only, 30 or 32 in. barrels, imp. mod. and full or full and full choke, trap style stock. Mfg. 1966-1984.

	$1,320	$1,100	$935	$825	$715	$660	$605

MODEL 101 SINGLE BARREL TRAP — similar to O/U Trap, with 32 or 34 in. full choke barrel, Monte Carlo trap style stock. Mfg. 1967-1971.

	$880	$660	$550	$495	$385	$360	$330

Grading	100%	98%	95%	90%	80%	70%	60%

MODEL 101 XTR PIGEON GRADE — 12, 20, 28 or .410 (disc. 1986) ga.,barrels are vented, deluxe engraved silver receiver version of 101, select checkered wood. Mfg. 1974-1987.
Lightweight Field Model — lightweight variation, Winchokes standard, 6½ - 7 lbs. Disc. 1987.

	$1,500	$1,375	$1,120	$940	$785	$675	$600

Last Mfg.'s Sug. Retail was $1,950.

This model was previously available without Winchokes in 28 ga. only - deduct 5%.

Lightweight two barrel set — includes 28 and .410 ga. 27 in. barrels, 28 ga. has Winchokes; .410 ga. has fixed M/F chokes. Disc. 1986.

	$2,275	$1,950	$1,775	$1,600	$1,425	$1,300	$1,100

Last Mfg.'s Sug. Retail was $2,500.

Featherweight — 12 or 20 ga., English straight stock, 25½ in. barrels bored IC/IM, 6½ - 6¾ lbs. Disc. 1987.

	$1,325	$1,175	$975	$850	$750	$675	$600

Last Mfg.'s Sug. Retail was $1,580.

Skeet Grade — 12 or 20 ga.

	$1,100	$1,045	$990	$880	$770	$715	$660

Trap Grade — 12 ga. only, vent barrels and rib, coin finish receiver with fine scroll engraving, engraved pigeon on floorplate, Winchoke standard, 8¼ lbs. Disc. 1985.

	$1,300	$1,180	$990	$880	$770	$715	$660

Last Mfg.'s Sug. Retail was $1,475.

Super Pigeon Grade — 12 ga. only, blued receiver with elaborate engraving including multiple gold inlays, extra select walnut with fleur-de-lis checkering on stock and forearm, Winchoke standard, 7½ lbs. Imported 1985-1987 only.

	$4,025	$3,625	$3,225	$2,835	$2,500	$2,150	$1,920

Last Mfg.'s Sug. Retail was $4,590.

101 DIAMOND GRADE — Trap or Skeet O/U, 12 (Trap only), 20, 28, or .410 ga., vent barrels and rib, Winchoke standard on Trap — add $75 on Skeet model (disc.1986), select hand checkered walnut, engraved satin-finish receiver. Trap model has extra high vent rib. Skeet model has raised rib and muzzle vents.

Standard Trap — 12 ga. only, 30 or 32 in. vent barrels, 8¾ - 9 lbs. Disc. 1987.

	$1,620	$1,440	$1,230	$1,075	$900	$780	$640

Last Mfg.'s Sug. Retail was $1,860.

Unsingle Trap — 12 ga. only, lower single barrel, 32 or 34 in. barrel, extended rib. Add $60 for Winchoke. Disc. 1986.

	$1,575	$1,430	$1,200	$995	$895	$830	$740

Last Mfg.'s Sug. Retail was $1,760.

Oversingle Trap — 12 ga. only, Winchokes, 34 in. upper barrel only, 8½ lbs. Imported 1986-1987 only.

	$1,985	$1,695	$1,545	$1,395	$1,200	$995	$895

Last Mfg.'s Sug. Retail was $2,145.

Oversingle Combo — includes one set of O/U barrels and an oversingle barrel, cased. Imported 1987 only.

	$3,075	$2,750	$2,525	$2,300	$2,000	$1,750	$1,625

Last Mfg.'s Sug. Retail was $3,550.

Grading	100%	98%	95%	90%	80%	70%	60%

Trap Combo — 12 ga. only, includes a set of 30 or 32 in. vent O/U barrels and a 32 or 34 in. high ribbed unsingle (lower) barrel, standard or Monte Carlo stock, approx. 9 lbs. Disc. 1987.

	$2,570	$2,320	$1,975	$1,800	$1,600	$1,400	$1,200

Add $275 for ATA Trap set.
Last Mfg.'s Sug. Retail was $2,940.

Standard Skeet — 12, 20, 28, or .410 ga., 27½ in. vent barrels and competition rib, 6½ - 7¼ lbs. Disc. 1987.

	$1,650	$1,465	$1,240	$1,075	$900	$780	$640

Last Mfg.'s Sug. Retail was $1,950.

Four gauge Skeet set — includes 12, 20, 28, and .410 ga. 27½ in. separated barrel assemblies, cased. Imported 1985-1987 only.

	$4,600	$3,975	$3,600	$3,200	$2,800	$2,500	$2,150

Last Mfg.'s Sug. Retail was $5,025.

Sporting Clays Grade — 12 ga. only, 28 or 30 in. barrels with Winchokes, designed for Sporting Clay competition. Disc. 1987.

	$1,675	$1,475	$1,230	$1,075	$900	$780	$640

Last Mfg.'s Sug. Retail was $1,965.

501 GRAND EUROPEAN — Trap or Skeet, 12 or 20 (Skeet only) ga., 27, 30, or 32 in. barrels, extra select hand checkered walnut with oil finish, Schnabel forearm, entensive scroll engraving on satin-finished receiver, vent barrels and rib. Mfg. 1981-86.

	$1,520	$1,385	$1,200	$1,050	$900	$780	$640

Last Mfg.'s Sug. Retail was $1,720.

Grand European Featherweight — 20 ga. only, straight grip stock, 25½ in. vent rib barrels, 5¾ lbs. Disc. 1986.

	$1,520	$1,385	$1,200	$1,050	$900	$780	$640

Last Mfg.'s Sug. Retail was $1,720.

PRESENTATION GRADE — 12 ga. only, available in both Trap and Skeet models, blued action-extensively engraved with gold inlays, special crotch walnut, 27 (Skeet) or 30 in. vent barrels, hand checkered, gold lining on perimeter of receiver. Imported 1984-1987 only.

	$3,475	$2,850	$2,510	$2,280	$1,950	$1,800	$1,600

Last Mfg.'s Sug. Retail was $3,840.

SHOTGUN/RIFLE COMBINATION — combination 12 ga./.30-06 O/U, 25 in. barrels, top barrel is Winchoked, Grand European engraving and finish, 8½ lbs. Mfg. 1983-1985.

	$2,245	$2,040	$1,800	$1,650	$1,450	$1,300	$1,200

Also available in limited quantities in .222 Rem., .223 Rem., or 9.3 x 74R cal. Last Mfg.'s Sug. Retail was $2,550.

DOUBLE EXPRESS RIFLE — .30-06, .270 Win., .257 Roberts, 9.3 x 74R, or 7.7 x 65R cal., O/U configuration, ejectors, 23½ in. barrels, game scene engraved, satin finish receiver, 8½ lbs. Mfg. 1984 - 1985 only.

	$1,750	$1,495	$1,250	$1,125	$1,000	$875	$750

Last Mfg.'s Sug. Retail was $2,995.

MODEL 91 O & U — 12 ga. only, mfg. by Laurona in Spain for international sales including Europe, SST, ejectors optional, vent rib, distinguishable by black chrome finish on metal parts. Disc.

Prices hard to evaluate because of limited importation domestically. In some regions they are bought as medium priced field guns, while in others they are sold as a rare Winchester O&U.

Grading	100%	98%	95%	90%	80%	70%	60%

MODEL 96 XPERT O&U FIELD GRADE — similar action to Model 101, 12 or 20 ga., auto ejectors, SST, various barrel lengths and chokes, action similar to 101, no engraving, checkered pistol grip stock and forearm. Mfg. 1976-1982.

	$650	$575	$500	$450	$410	$370	$330

MODEL 96 XPERT SKEET GRADE — same as Field Grade, with 27 in. skeet barrels, skeet style stock. Mfg. 1976-1982.

	$700	$625	$550	$500	$450	$410	$370

MODEL 96 XPERT TRAP GRADE — same as Field, 12 ga. only, 30 in. imp. mod. and full or full and full choke, trap style stock. Mfg. 1976-1982.

	$650	$575	$525	$470	$430	$395	$360

Note: Model 101 and Model 96 Xpert guns were made by Olin Kodensha located in Tochigi, Japan.

SHOTGUNS: RECENT MFG. SIDE-BY-SIDE

MODEL 21: RECENT MFG. — since 1960 Model 21 production has been limited to high grade, built from special order, U. S. Repeating Arms currently offers the Model 21 in 12, 16 or 20 ga. U.S.R.A. has disc. the mfg. of the Model 21 temporarily beginning in 1990 as their Custom Gun Shop is backordered on many other projects. Very few new Model 21's have been produced during the past three years. Values below reflect 1989 information. Standard Custom guns (12 ga.) are currently trading in the $5,750 range if NIB.

Custom Built — standard model with no engraving.

Mfg.'s Sug. Retail	$8,100	$8,100	$5,000	$3,750

Custom Grade — includes No. 6 engraved receiver and vent rib.

Mfg.'s Sug. Retail	$11,080	$11,080	$7,250	$5,500

Grand American Grade — includes 2 sets of barrels with forearms, No. 6 engraved with gold inlays, cased.

Mfg.'s Sug. Retail	$22,745	$22,745	$15,000	$11,500

Grand American Small Gauge — 28 or .410 ga.

Mfg.'s Sug. Retail	$34,460	$34,460	$25,000	$17,500

Add 10% for 28/.410 ga. combo.

Grand American "1 of 8" set — includes 20, 28, and .410 ga. VR barrels. Only 8 sets mfg.

Mfg.'s Sug. Retail	$55,000	$55,000	$39,500	$27,500

Note: See Model 21 listing also under Pre-64 shotguns.

MODEL 22 DOUBLE BARREL — 12 ga. only, subcontracted by Winchester and manufactured in Spain by Laurona circa 1975 for international sales including Europe, field configuration only with 28 in. barrels, DT, oil finished checkered walnut stock and semi-beavertail forearm, matted rib, black-chrome finish on metal parts, hand engraved receiver, limited mfg.

	$1,200	$995	$825	$700	$600	$525	$475

MODEL 23 XTR — 12 or 20 ga., 3 in. chambers, 25½, 26, 28, or 30 in. barrels, various chokes, single trigger, vent rib, auto ejectors, scroll engraved, silver grey satin finish, blued barrel, checkered select walnut stock and forearm, first commercial gun to employ interchangeable chokes. Mfg. 1978-present.

Grade 1 (disc.)	$915	$820	$750	$650	$575	$500	$440

Grading	100%	98%	95%	90%	80%	70%	60%

Pigeon Grade — standard weight model, 6½ - 7 lbs, coin finished receiver with scroll engraving. Winchoke option became standard in 1986. Subtract $150 without Winchokes. Disc. 1986.

	$995	$875	$750	$675	$600	$550	$495

Last Mfg.'s Sug. Retail was $1,460.

Pigeon Grade Lightweight — 25½ in. barrels only, 6¼ - 6¾ lbs., coin finished receiver with scroll engraving. English stock, Winchoke not available. Disc. 1986.

	$1,265	$1,150	$995	$880	$760	$730	$680

Last Mfg.'s Sug. Retail was $1,420.

Pigeon Grade Ducks Unlimited — only 500 mfg. 1981, "SPO" serial no. suffix, cased.

	$1,450	$1,200	$995	$880	$760	$730	$680

Golden Quail Model Series — 12 ga. (1986), 20 ga. (1984), 28 ga. (1985), or .410 ga. (1987), 25½ in. barrels bored IC/M, beavertail forearm, straight grip English stock with recoil pad. Only 500 mfg. each year per gauge. Disc. 1987.

	$1,450	$1,150	$995	$875	$780	$700	$640

Add $165 for .410 and earlier ga.'s.
This limited production series is now complete with the release of the .410 ga. 1987.

Last Mfg.'s Sug. Retail was $1,950.

Model 23 Light Duck — limited edition, 500 mfg., introduced 1985, blued receiver and barrels, select walnut, 20 ga., 28 in.- F&F, 8½ lbs.

	$1,475	$1,225	$995	$900	$825	$775	$725

Last Mfg.'s Sug. Retail was $1,660.

Model 23 Heavy Duck — limited edition, 500 mfg. 1984 only, blued receiver and barrels, select walnut, 12 ga., 30 in.- F&F, 8½ lbs.

	$1,500	$1,265	$1,025	$920	$840	$785	$730

Custom 2 Barrel Set — interchangeable 20 and 28 ga. 26 in. barrels, blue engraved receiver with gold inlays, "B" checkering on stock and forearm, leather cased with accessories, only 500 sets mfg. 1986. Disc. 1987.

	$3,700	$3,300	$2,995	$2,750	$2,500	$2,150	$1,920

Last Mfg.'s Sug. Retail was $4,625.

MODEL 23 CUSTOM — 12 ga. only, 27 in. Winchoke barrels, high lustre bluing, no engraving, SST, ejectors, solid red rubber recoil pad, 7 lbs. Imported 1987 only.

	$1,675	$1,350	$1,100	$925	$875	$775	$650

Last Mfg.'s Sug. Retail was $1,975.

MODEL 23 CLASSIC — 12, 20, 28, or .410 ga., 26 in. VR barrels, single trigger, deluxe hand checkered walnut stock and beavertail forearm, solid recoil pad, brass name plate, gold inlay on bottom of receiver, ebony inlay in forearm, 5¾ - 7 lbs. Imported 1986-1987 only.

	$1,300	$1,175	$995	$925	$875	$780	$640

Add $150 for 28 or .410 ga.
The 28 and .410 ga.'s in this model feature a smaller frame.

Last Mfg.'s Sug. Retail was $1,975.

COMMEMORATIVES: U.S. PRODUCTION

Until recently, commemoratives in general have experienced poor liquidity because of oversupply versus consumer demand. Commemorative production in some trademarks has totalled well over 250,000 units, and some collectors are weighing the "limited production" factor on each model before paying a premium over the standard production model of that particular commemorative. The values below reflect actual prices paid recently in various

Grading		100%	98%	95%	90%	80%	70%	60%

areas of the U.S. In some regions it is possible to purchase a Winchester 94 commemorative made in substantial quantity for almost no premium over a standard production Winchester 94. Because of this, prices could fluctuate over 25% depending on the geographic location of purchase or sale. It is also important to remember that N.I.B. becomes especially important with commemoratives. Values below assume boxes, informational material, and warranty cards - subtract $75-$100 if without box and literature. Commemoratives having been shot as little as 3 times can only be classified as fancy hunting guns with little premium if any over the standard hunting model from which they were derived.

During the course of a year, I receive many phone calls and letters on special editions and limited editions that do not appear in this section. It should be noted that a commemorative issue is a gun that has been manufactured, marketed, and sold through the auspices of the specific trademark (in this case Winchester). Many "special interest" limited editions have been ordered through outside private contracts with Winchester (including General Motors, Dodge, Coca-Cola, etc.). These variations do not have the special suffix serialization (and may not have had a retail price when issued) and many times, the embellishments were subcontracted outside of the factory. While these guns do have special interest, they do not have the collectability or desirability of the below listed factory models. Typically, these limited editions sell in the $195-$350 range.

Many commemorative dealers have told me that recent changes in overseas currency rates have made domestic guns less expensive to own for Europeans especially. For this reason, many commemoratives are being sold overseas resulting in less supply for the domestic market. This secondary demand factor has strengthened commemorative prices. Desirability is the key to determining values on these firearms. More information on these special and limited editions not listed in the following pages can be obtained by contacting the factory.

A final note on commemoratives: As a rule, what determines the bottom of the market in commemoratives is the top of the market for their standard model production relatives. A problem with limited editions is that over the years of ownership, most of the original amount manufactured stays in the same N.I.B. condition. Thus, if supply always is constand and in one condition (NIB), demand has to increase before price appreciation can occur. Taking into consideration thte inflation factor during the past 2 decades, many older, high manufacture commemoratives/Limited editions have not performed very well as investments. Yet, others have. After 24 years of special edition production, many models' performance record can be accurately analyzed and any appreciation (or depreciation) can be compared against other purchases of equal vintage. You be the judge.

U.S. Repeating Arms has announced in 1990 that they will once again resume the production of factory commemorative firearms.

Grading	100%	issue price	qty made
1964 WYOMING DIAMOND JUBILEE 94 CARBINE			
	$1,295	$100	1,501
1966 CENTENNIAL '66 RIFLE			
	$375	$125	
1966 CENTENNIAL '66 CARBINE — total mfg. of both the rifle and carbine was 102,309.			
	$375	$125	102,309

Add $50-$75 over individual prices for consecutively serial numbered rifle and carbine set.

1966 NEBRASKA CENTENNIAL 94 RIFLE			
	$1,295	$100	2,500
1967 CANADIAN '67 CENTENNIAL RIFLE			
	$325	$125	

Grading	100%	issue price	qty made

1967 CANADIAN '67 CENTENNIAL CARBINE — total mfg. of both the rifle and carbine was 90,301.

	$325	$125	90,301

Add $50-$75 over individual prices for consecutively serial numbered rifle and carbine set.

1967 ALASKAN PURCHASE CENTENNIAL CARBINE

	$1,500	$125	1,501

1968 ILLINOIS SESQUICENTENNIAL 94 CARBINE

	$325	$110	37,468

1968 BUFFALO BILL RIFLE "1 OF 300" PRES.

	$2,000	$1,000	300

1968 BUFFALO BILL RIFLE

	$350	$130	

1968 BUFFALO BILL CARBINE — total mfg. of both the rifle and carbine was 112,923.

	$350	$130	112,923

Add $50-$75 over individual prices for consecutively serial numbered rifle and carbine set.

1969 GOLDEN SPIKE CARBINE

	$350	$120	69,996

1969 THEO. ROOSEVELT RIFLE

	$350	$135	

1969 THEO. ROOSEVELT CARBINE — total mfg. of both the rifle and carbine was 52,386.

	$350	$135	52,386

1970 COWBOY COMMEMORATIVE CARBINE

	$450	$125	27,549

1970 COWBOY CARBINE "1 OF 300"

	$1,995	$1,000	300

1970 LONE STAR RIFLE

	$395	$140	

1970 LONE STAR CARBINE — total mfg. of both the rifle and carbine was 38,385.

	$395	$140	38,385

1971 NRA CENTENNIAL MUSKET

	$325	$150	23,400

1971 NRA CENTENNIAL RIFLE

	$325	$150	21,000

1974 TEXAS RANGER CARBINE

	$695	$135	4,850

1974 TEXAS RANGER PRESENTATION

	$2,000	$1,000	150

1976 U.S. BICENTENNIAL CARBINE

	$600	$325	19,999

1977 WELLS FARGO

	$450	$350	19,999

1977 "LIMITED EDITION I"

	$1,295	$1,500	1,500

Grading	100%	issue price	qty made
1977 LEGENDARY LAWMEN			
	$450	$375	19,999
1978 ANTLERED GAME CARBINE			
	$450	$375	19,999
1979 LEGENDARY FRONTIERSMAN RIFLE			
	$450	$425	19,999
1979 "LIMITED EDITION II"			
	$1,295	$1,750	1,500
1979 MATCHED SET OF 1000			
	$2,250	$3,000	1,000
1980 BAT MASTERSON CARBINE			
	$650	$650	8,000
1980 "OLIVER WINCHESTER"			
	$550	$375	19,999
1981 U.S. BORDER PATROL			
	$895	$1,195	1,000
1981 U.S. BORDER PATROL — MEMBERS MODEL			
	$600	$695	800
1981 JOHN WAYNE			
	$795	$600	49,000

Optional accessories were also available for this model: the gun rack with leather insert is currently selling for approx. $40 and the leather scabbord is trading for $60.

1981 "DUKE"			
	$2,950	$2,250	1,000
1981 JOHN WAYNE "1 OF 300" SET			
	$6,500	$10,000	300
1982 GREAT WESTERN ARTIST I			
	$995	$2,200	999
1982 GREAT WESTERN ARTIST II			
	$995	$2,200	999
1982 ANNIE OAKLEY			
	$595	$699	6,000
1982 OKLAHOMA DIAMOND JUBILEE			
	$1,500	$2,250	1,001
1982 AMERICAN BALD EAGLE - SILVER			
	$600	$895	2,800
1982 AMERICAN BALD EAGLE - GOLD			
	$2,000	$2,950	200
1983 CHIEF CRAZY HORSE			
	$450	$600	19,999

Grading	100%	issue price	qty made

1984 WINCHESTER-COLT COMMEMORATIVE SET — 1 each of the Model 1894 Carbine and Colt Peacemaker, serial numbered 1 WC-4440 WC. .44-40 cal., elaborate gold etching, cased.

| | $2,000 | $3,995 | 2,300 |

Approx. 2,300 sets were actually put together in this combination. These sets have been split up with individual prices being discounted (Colt SAA's have been trading in the $700-$800 range).

1985 BOY SCOUTS 75TH ANNIVERSARY — Model 9422 action, .22 cal., rifle configuration, 6¼ lbs.

Eagle Scout — 1,000 mfg., serial numbered Eagle 1 - Eagle 1,000, receiver has triple level gold etching, select American walnut stock and forearm, gold plated lever, hammer, and forearm cap.

| | $1,695 | $1,710 | 1,000 |

Boy Scout — 15,000 mfg., serial numbered BSA 1 - BSA 15,000, roll engraved, antique pewter receiver, hooded front sight.

| | $425 | $495 | 15,000 |

1985 MODEL 94 TEXAS SESQUICENTENNIAL — .38-55 cal., available in carbine or rifle.

Model 94 Rifle — 24 in. round barrel, elaborate gold etching, includes Bowie knife, oak cased, 586 mfg.

| | $2,400 | $2,995 | 1,500 |

Model 94 Carbine — 18½ in. round barrel, gold finished receiver and barrel bands, roll engraved receiver, 2,600 mfg., serial numbered TEX 1 and up.

| | $550 | $695 | 15,000 |

Rifle/Carbine Set — includes one each of the Model 94 rifle and carbine, Bowie knife, 150 mfg.

| | $6,250 | $7,995 | 150 |

1986 120TH ANNIVERSARY MODEL 94 CARBINE — .44-40 cal. only, 20 in. barrel, hoop-type finger lever, crescent butt plate, deluxe checkered walnut stock and forearm, extensive gold etching on barrel and framesides, 1,000 mfg. ser. no. WRA001-WRA1000.

| | $850 | $995 | 1,000 |

1986 STATUE OF LIBERTY MODEL 94 — Model 94 rifle in .30-30 cal. with octagon barrel, extensive C. Giovanelli scroll engraving with multiple 22Kt. gold inlays, deluxe walnut with fine checkering, also includes 29 in. hand carved wooden statue of the Statue of Liberty, serial numbered SL1-SL100.

| | $6,500 | $6,500 | 100 |

1986 MODEL 94 DU — .30-30 cal., approx. 2,800 rifles were mfg. in the U.S. Since each Model 94 DU was bid on for ownership, prices will vary from points of origin. An average bid price seems to be in the $700-$995 range with lower and completing set ser. no.'s selling at premiums. Serial numbered DU-86 0001 on up.

This model is not a factory commemorative, but rather a trade gun commissioned by Ducks Unlimited.

1987 U.S. CONSTITUTION 200TH ANNIVERSARY

| | $13,000 | $12,000 | 8 |

WINCHESTER COMMEMORATIVES: NON-DOMESTIC — 1970 TO DATE

1970 NORTH WEST TERRITORIES (CANADIAN)

| | $650 | $150 | 2,500 |

Grading	100%	issue price	qty made
1970 NORTHWEST TERRITORIES DELUXE (CANADIAN)			
	$1,100	$250	500
1973 YELLOW BOY (SOLD IN EUROPE ONLY)			
	$795	$150	4,903
1973 M.P.X. (MADE ESPECIALLY FOR A MOVIE)			
	$8,500	$ 78	32
1973 R.C.M.P. (CANADIAN)			
	$650	$190	9,500
1973 R.C.M.P. MEMBERS ISSUE (CANADIAN)			
	$695	$190	4,850
1973 M.P. (MOUNTED POLICE) - (CANADIAN)			
	$1,275	$190	5,100
1974 APACHE (CANADIAN)			
	$650	$150	8,600
1975 KLONDIKE GOLD RUSH (CANADIAN)			
	$650	$230	10,500
1975 K.G.R. (DAWSON CITY ISSUE) - (CANADIAN)			
	$8,500	N/A	25
1975 COMMANCHE (CANADIAN)			
	$650	$230	11,500
1976 SIOUX (CANADIAN)			
	$650	$280	10,000
1976 LITTLE BIG HORN (CANADIAN)			
	$650	$230	11,000
1977 CHEYENNE (CANADIAN) — .44-40 Cal.			
	$650	$300	11,225
1977 CHEYENNE (CANADIAN) — .22 Cal.			
	$500	$320	5,000
1978 CHEROKEE (CANADIAN) — .30-30 Cal.			
	$650	$385	9,000
1978 CHEROKEE (CANADIAN) — .22 Cal.			
	$500	$385	3,950
1978 ONE OF ONE THOUSAND (SOLD IN EUROPE ONLY)			
	$7,995	$5,000	250
This model was not advertised in the U.S.			
1980 ALBERTA DIAMOND JUBILEE (CANADIAN)			
	$650	$650	2,700
1980 A.D.J. DELUXE PRESENTATION (CANADIAN)			
	$1,500	$1,900	300
1980 SASKATCHEWAN DIAMOND JUBILEE (CANADIAN)			
	$650	$695	2,700
1980 S.D.J. DELUXE PRESENTATION (CANADIAN)			
	$1,495	$1,995	300

Grading	100%	issue price	qty made
1981 CALGARY STAMPEDE (CANADIAN)			
	$1,100	$2,200	1,000
1981 CANADIAN PACIFIC CENTENNIAL (CANADIAN)			
	$550	$800	2,700
1981 CANADIAN PACIFIC CENTENNIAL PRESENTATION (CANADIAN)			
	$1,100	$2,200	300
1981 CANADIAN PACIFIC (EMPL.) - (CANADIAN)			
	$550	$800	2,000
1981 JOHN WAYNE (CANADIAN)			
	$995	$995	1,000
1986 SECOND SERIES EUROPEAN 1 OF 1,000 — mfg. for European sales only 1986.			
	$6,500	$6,000	150

WINSLOW ARMS COMPANY
Camden, SC.

WINSLOW BOLT ACTION SPORTING RIFLE — offered with various actions, FN Supreme, Mark X Mauser, Rem. 700 and 788, Sako and Win. 70, offered in all popular calibers from .17 Rem. to .458 Mag., standard calibers have 24 in. barrels and 3 shot magazines, magnum calibers have 26 in. barrels and 2 shot magazines, two style stocks, "Bushmaster Conventional", slender pistol grip and beavertail forearm, "Plainsmaster", full curl, hooked pistol grip and flat wide forearm, both are Monte Carlo with cheek pieces, recoil pads and swivels, walnut, maple, and myrtle are used with rosewood forend tip and pistol grip cap, rifle comes in 8 basic grades, custom embellishments can increase values greatly, discretion must be used, values are for basic models.

Grading	100%	98%	95%	90%	80%	70%	60%
COMMANDER GRADE							
	$495	$475	$440	$385	$360	$330	$305
REGAL GRADE							
	$605	$590	$560	$525	$470	$440	$415
REGENT GRADE							
	$725	$700	$670	$640	$605	$550	$495
REGIMENTAL GRADE							
	$935	$890	$855	$800	$745	$660	$605
CROWN GRADE							
	$1,375	$1,265	$1,155	$990	$910	$825	$715
ROYAL GRADE							
	$1,540	$1,375	$1,210	$1,100	$1,020	$965	$825
IMPERIAL GRADE							
	$3,520	$3,080	$2,860	$2,475	$2,200	$1,925	$1,320
EMPEROR GRADE							
	$6,215	$5,500	$4,950	$4,400	$3,300	$2,750	$2,200

Grading	100%	98%	95%	90%	80%	70%	60%

WISEMAN, BILL AND CO.

Custom rifle manufacturer/retailer located in College Station, TX.

Wiseman/McMillan also manufactures rifle barrels and custom stocks.

RIFLES

HUNTER MODEL — available in various cal.'s, sako action, stainless steel barrel by Wiseman/McMillan, laminate stock, teflon finished metal parts, Pachmayr decelerator pad, sling swivels, glass bedded action.

Mfg.'s Sug. Retail	$1,745	$1,745	$1,475	$1,200	$1,050	$875	$775	$675

HUNTER DELUXE — similar to Hunter Model except has custom checkering.

Mfg.'s Sug. Retail	$1,945	$1,945	$1,675	$1,400	$1,200	$995	$875	$775

MAVERICK — similar to Hunter but with black fiberglass stock.

Mfg.'s Sug. Retail	$1,545	$1,545	$1,200	$995	$875	$795	$695	$600

VARMENTER — similar to Hunter but with thumbhole stock.

Mfg.'s Sug. Retail	$1,845	$1,845	$1,575	$1,275	$1,125	$925	$825	$725

SILHOUETTE PISTOL

SILHOUETTE PISTOL — various cal.'s, Sako action, 14 in. Wiseman/McMillan fluted stainless barrel, 5 or 7 shot magazine, laminate pistol grip stock, no sights, 4½-5½ lbs. New 1989.

Mfg.'s Sug. Retail	$1,295	$1,295	$1,000	$900	$800	$750	$700	$650

WOODWARD, JAMES AND SONS

Previously mfg. in London, England. Acquired by James Purdey & Son spprox. 1935.

SHOTGUNS: DOUBLE AND SINGLE BARREL

Woodward made one of the world's finest shotguns. Prior to WWII, they were acquired by Purdey and Sons. Many of the weapons they made were custom built and grading and pricing should be done individually. We will list some of the general models with approximate values as a guideline, but strongly urge competent professional appraisal when contemplating purchase or sale.

BEST QUALITY DOUBLE BARREL SHOTGUN — custom built in all gauges, barrel lengths and chokes, sidelock, auto ejectors, stocked to specifications, pre-WWII.

$26,000	$23,000	$19,950	$17,000	$14,250	$12,000	$10,000

20 gauge — add 20%.

28 gauge — add 40%.

.410 gauge — add 60%.

SST — add $1,000.

BEST QUALITY O/U SHOTGUN — custom built in all gauges, barrel lengths, and chokes, vent rib, sidelock, auto ejectors, stocked to customer specifications, pre-WWII.

$29,500	$25,500	$21,500	$18,500	$15,750	$13,800	$12,000

20 gauge — add 35%.

28 gauge — add 75%.

.410 gauge — too rare to accurately predict.

Single trigger — add $1,000.

BEST QUALITY SINGLE BARREL TRAP GUN — 12 ga. only, limited mfg. - pre-WWII only.

$12,750	$10,000	$8,950	$7,725	$6,500	$5,750	$4,900

Grading	100%	98%	95%	90%	80%	70%	60%

WYOMING ARMS MFG. CORP.
Manufacturer located in Thermopolis, WY.

PARKER PISTOLS: STAINLESS STEEL

STANDARD PISTOL — 9mm Para., 10mm, .40 S&W, or .45 ACP cal., 3⅜, 5, or 7 in. barrel, 7 (.45 ACP), 8 (10mm & .40 S&W), or 9 (9mm Para.) shot mag., Millet adj. sights, grooved synthetic grips, 29-39 oz.

Mfg.'s Sug. Retail	$399	$350	$300	$250

Add $50 for 7 in. barrel.

.357 MAG. — .357 Mag. cal., single action semi-auto, 7 in. barrel, adj. sights, 8 shot mag., lifetime warranty, 44 oz.

Mfg.'s Sug. Retail	$479	$425	$350	$300

NOTES

Grading	100%	98%	95%	90%	80%	70%	60%

Z-B RIFLE
Brno, Czechoslovakia.

Grading	100%	98%	95%	90%	80%	70%	60%

Z-B MAUSER VARMINT RIFLE — small Mauser bolt action, .22 Hornet, 23 in. barrel, double set triggers, 3 leaf sight, checkered pistol grip stock, (also known as Brno Hornet).

	$825	$745	$690	$605	$550	$470	$415

ZABALA HERMANOS, S.A.
Manufacturer located in Eibar, Spain. Z. Hermanos has had limited importation to date (American Arms located in Kansas City is private labeling a few models).

Zabala Hermanos manufactures quality boxlock SxS or O/U shotguns and sidelock side-by-sides. For more information regarding this trademark, (including current models and prices) please contact the manufacturer directly (see Trademark Index).

ZANARDINI
Manufacturer located in Brescia, Italy since 1946. Shotguns and rifles are imported into the U.S. by Navy Arms Co. Located in Ridgefield, NJ and Morton's Ltd. Located in Lexington, KY.

For further information regarding Zanardini rifles and shotguns, either distributor should be contacted directly regarding availability and prices. Oxford rifles are imported by Navy Arms Co. Inc. - please contact directly for further information.

Prices could change rapidly on this trademark because of the fluctuating U.S. dollar.

COMBINATION GUNS O/U

PRINCESS — super light variation.

Mfg.'s Sug. Retail	$2,542	$2,542	$2,200	$1,925	$1,675	$1,400	$1,200	$1,000

BOXER MODEL — H&H styled sidelocks, top quality engraving.

Mfg.'s Sug. Retail	$6,246	$6,246	$5,750	$5,150	$4,600	$4,000	$3,550	$3,000

BOXER 4-LOCKS MODEL

Mfg.'s Sug. Retail	$4,562	$4,562	$3,900	$3,400	$2,975	$2,625	$2,300	$2,050

402 STRAUSS — top-of-the-line combination gun with best quality engraving and wood.

Mfg.'s Sug. Retail	$10,548	$10,548	$9,000	$8,000	$7,000	$6,000	$5,000	$4,000

RIFLES

403 OXFORD SxS — 9.3 x 74R and smaller cal.'s.

Mfg.'s Sug. Retail	$3,835	$3,835	$3,400	$3,000	$2,700	$2,425	$2,150	$1,875

Larger cal.'s .375 H&H, .458 Win. Mag., or .470 Nitro cal.

Mfg.'s Sug. Retail	$7,555	$7,555	$6,700	$6,000	$5,500	$5,000	$4,500	$3,950

Add approx. 135% for .470 Nitro cal.

Grading	100%	98%	95%	90%	80%	70%	60%

EXPRESS RIFLE SxS — .470 NE cal., boxlock action, ST, checkered walnut stock (with cheek piece), express sights. Other cal.'s available upon special order.

Mfg.'s Sug. Retail	$8,500	$8,150	$7,625	$6,800	$6,000	$5,500	$5,000	$4,500

This model is imported exclusively by Mandall's Shooting Supplies, Inc. located in Scottsdale, AZ.

409 BRISTOL SxS — priced by individual request.

407 OXFORD SL SxS — sidelock action.

Mfg.'s Sug. Retail	$17,095	$17,095	$15,000	$13,250	$11,950	$10,000	$9,250	$8,500

MODEL 403 KOENIG O/U — 7.65R or 9.3 x 74R cal.

Mfg.'s Sug. Retail	$7,368	$7,368	$6,500	$5,850	$5,350	$4,850	$4,350	$3,800

MODEL 403 DELUXE O/U

Mfg.'s Sug. Retail	$4,188	$4,188	$3,650	$3,200	$2,875	$2,525	$2,250	$1,925

SHOTGUNS

HAMMER LONDON MODEL SxS — features external hammers.

Mfg.'s Sug. Retail	$10,735	$10,735	$9,150	$8,125	$7,100	$6,100	$5,050	$4,000

HAMMERLESS LONDON MODEL SxS

Mfg.'s Sug. Retail	$4,936	$4,936	$4,200	$3,700	$3,175	$2,825	$2,500	$2,100

DONAU STANDARD MODEL SxS — boxlock action.

Mfg.'s Sug. Retail	$10,548	$10,548	$9,000	$8,000	$7,000	$6,000	$5,000	$4,000

DONAU SIDELOCK SxS — H&H style sidelock action.

Mfg.'s Sug. Retail	$18,966	$18,966	$16,500	$14,750	$12,950	$11,000	$9,950	$9,000

PRESTIGE TRAP AND SKEET SxS

Mfg.'s Sug. Retail	$2,598	$2,598	$2,250	$1,950	$1,675	$1,400	$1,200	$1,000

HASE CACCIA MONTECATINI SxS — boxlock action, double set triggers, extractors.

Mfg.'s Sug. Retail	$1,027	$1,027	$900	$800	$700	$600	$550	$495

Add 30% for ejectors.

HORN MODEL SxS — boxlock action, double set triggers, extractors.

Mfg.'s Sug. Retail	$1,102	$1,102	$950	$850	$750	$625	$550	$495

Add 40% for ejectors.

ZANOTTI, FABIO

Manufacturer located in Brescia, Italy since 1625. Currently imported and distributed by New England Arms, Co. located in Kittery Point, ME. Fabio Zanotti became part of the Renato Gamba Group in 1985.

Fabio Zanotti is one of the world's oldest quality shotgun manufacturers. Current domestic importation is often times done on a custom order only basis. For more information on Zanotti models and their values, contact New England Arms Co.

Grading	100%	98%	95%	90%	80%	70%	60%

SHOTGUNS: OVER/UNDER

MODEL 725 — 28 or .410 ga. only, scalloped case hardened shallow frame, DT or ST, ejectors, game scene and scroll engraving, custom built to individual specifications.
Mfg.'s Sug. Retail $4,500 $4,200 $3,800 $3,400 $2,950 $2,450 $2,000 $1,875

CASSIANO — 12, 20, 28, or .410 ga., Boss style shallow action, best quality gun built to individual specifications. Prices start at $15,000 and go up accordingly.

SHOTGUNS: SIDE BY SIDE
Add $300 for ST.
Add $250 for beavertail forearm.
Add $450 for leather case.

MODEL 625 BOXLOCK
Mfg.'s Sug. Retail $4,250 $3,750 $3,250 $2,850 $2,500 $2,200 $1,900 $1,800

MODEL 626 BOXLOCK — scroll, game scene, or combination engraving.
Mfg.'s Sug. Retail $5,000 $4,700 $3,950 $3,650 $3,375 $3,100 $2,950 $2,600

MODEL GIACINTO — hammer gun.
Mfg.'s Sug. Retail $4,950 $4,600 $3,850 $3,175 $2,450 $2,000 $1,825 $1,430

MODEL MAXIM SIDELOCK
Mfg.'s Sug. Retail $7,500 $7,000 $6,000 $5,250 $4,600 $3,850 $3,175 $2,450

MODEL EDWARD SIDELOCK
Mfg.'s Sug. Retail $9,500 $9,100 $7,750 $6,875 $6,275 $5,250 $4,000 $3,575

MODEL CASSIANO I SIDELOCK
Mfg.'s Sug. Retail $10,750 $8,950 $7,950 $6,500 $5,900 $5,250 $4,600 $3,850

MODEL CASSIANO II
Mfg.'s Sug. Retail $12,000 $11,000 $9,750 $8,950 $7,950 $6,500 $5,900 $5,250

CASSIANO EXECUTIVE — prices vary per individual order, top-of-the-line model. Prices start at $15,000 and go up.

ZASTAVA ARMS
Manufacturer located in Yugoslavia. Currently imported by T.D. Arms located in New Baltimore, MI. Distributed by Guns USA located in Southampton, PA.

HANDGUNS

MODEL CZ 99/CZ 40 SEMI-AUTO — 9mm Para. or .40 S&W (new 1991-Model CZ 40) cal., double action, semi-auto, 15 shot (9mm Para.) or 11 shot (.40 S&W) mag., 4¼ in. barrel, short recoil, Browning locking system, ambidextrous controls, 3-dot Tritium sighting system, alloy frame, firing pin block, chamber indicator, squared-off trigger guard, checkered walnut grips, 32 oz. New mid-1990.
No Mfg.'s Retail $650 $550 $440 $400 $365 $330 $300
Choice of finishes include matte top with polished slide bluing and black anodized frame or Nigrosines Military finish.

MODEL CZ 99R REVOLVER — .357 Mag., 6 shot, double action, 2½ or 4 in. VR barrel with full shroud, choice of finishes, checkered walnut grips, 2.2 lbs. New late 1991.
No Mfg.'s Retail $335 $265 $230 $200 $175 $150 $135

Grading	100%	98%	95%	90%	80%	70%	60%

RIFLES

MODEL CZ 99 PRECISION — .22 LR, bolt action, 5 shot mag., 20 in. barrel, adj. rear sight, checkered walnut stock and forearm with sling swivels, 6.2 lbs. New 1990.

No Mfg.'s Retail	$259	$205	$180	$160	$145	$135	$125

MODEL CZ 99 FOX HORNET — .22 Hornet cal., bolt action, 5 shot mag., 20 in. barrel, adj. rear sight, checkered walnut stock and forearm with sling swivels, 6.2 lbs. New 1990.

No Mfg.'s Retail	$350	$275	$225	$190	$170	$155	$140

ZEPHYR

Manufacturer located in Spain, and imported by Stoegers 1930's-1972.

RIFLES

Stoeger's has imported a wide variety of bolt action rifles during the past 60 years. Rather than list the many models individually, each Zephyr rifle should be compared to a gun of equal caliber, quality, and features to ascertain an approximate value range.

SHOTGUNS: SxS OR SINGLE SHOT

WOODLANDER II DOUBLE BARREL SHOTGUN — 12 or 20 ga., various chokes, boxlock, double triggers, extractors, engraved, checkered pistol grip stock.

	$495	$440	$385	$360	$305	$275	$250

UPLANDER (4E) SXS — 12, 16, 20, 28, or .410 ga., sidelock action, double triggers, ejectors, engraved.

	$775	$695	$640	$585	$570	$480	$440

STERLINGWORTH II DOUBLE BARREL SHOTGUN — similar to Woodlander, with sidelock action.

	$825	$725	$660	$605	$580	$525	$495

UPLAND KING SXS — 12 or 16 ga., sidelock, single trigger, vent rib, ejectors, fully engraved.

	$1,000	$900	$800	$725	$650	$600	$550

THUNDERBIRD SXS — 10 ga. Mag, 32 in. barrels, double triggers, French walnut, engraved. Add $175 for ejectors.

	$850	$750	$625	$550	$510	$490	$475

HONKER — 10 ga. Mag, single shot, 36 in. vent rib barrel, lightly engraved.

	$500	$460	$420	$350	$310	$290	$270

VANDALIA — 12 ga. Trap Model, 32 in. barrel, engraved.

	$700	$620	$575	$525	$475	$425	$390

VICTOR SPECIAL DOUBLE BARREL SHOTGUN — 12 ga., 25, 28, or 30 in. barrels, various chokes, double triggers, extractors, checkered pistol grip stock.

	$440	$385	$330	$305	$250	$220	$195

ZOLI, ANGELO

Previous manufacturer located in Brescia, Italy. Previously imported and distributed exclusively by Angelo Zoli USA located in Addison, IL. Mfg. 1985-87.

Angelo Zoli went out of business in December, 1987 and was taken over by the Italian Bank of Brescia in 1989. Many people tend to confuse the shotguns of Angelo and Antonio Zoli. There is no correlation between these trademarks and Antonio Zoli DOES NOT have parts for these earlier Angelo Zoli long arms. Even t hough both trademarks may indicate

Grading	100%	98%	95%	90%	80%	70%	60%

"A. ZOLI" for a barrel address, they are discernable by the model listings under both headings in this section.

Cape Outfitters (see Trademark Index under Angelo Zoli for address) has parts for most Angelo Zoli guns and should be contacted directly for availability and prices. All repairs are strickly non-warranty.

SHOTGUNS: OVER AND UNDER

SNIPE — .410 ga., 3 in. chambers, 26 or 28 in. barrels, single trigger. Disc. 1987.

	100%	98%	95%	90%	80%	70%	60%
	$230	$200	$185	$170	$155	$145	$135

Last Mfg.'s Sug. Retail was $265.

TEXAS — all ga.'s, 26 or 28 in. barrels, double triggers, folding design, lever action. Disc. 1987.

	100%	98%	95%	90%	80%	70%	60%
	$250	$220	$200	$185	$170	$155	$145

Last Mfg.'s Sug. Retail was $291.

DOVE — .410 ga. only, 3 in. chambers, 26 or 28 in. barrels, single trigger. Disc. 1987.

	100%	98%	95%	90%	80%	70%	60%
	$260	$230	$200	$185	$170	$155	$145

Last Mfg.'s Sug. Retail was $306.

FIELD SPECIAL — 12, 20, or 28 ga., 3 in. chambers, various barrel lengths and chokings, single trigger. Disc. 1989.

	100%	98%	95%	90%	80%	70%	60%
	$450	$400	$360	$330	$300	$270	$240

Last Mfg.'s Sug. Retail was $699.

PIGEON MODEL — 12 or 20 ga., 3 in. chambers, various barrel lengths, single trigger. Disc. 1987.

	100%	98%	95%	90%	80%	70%	60%
	$350	$295	$270	$250	$220	$195	$175

Add $60 for 20 ga.
Last Mfg.'s Sug. Retail was $394.

STANDARD MODEL — 12 or 20 ga., 3 in. chambers, various barrel lengths and chokings, single trigger. Disc. 1987.

	100%	98%	95%	90%	80%	70%	60%
	$395	$345	$320	$300	$280	$260	$245

Last Mfg.'s Sug. Retail was $459.

SILVER SNIPE — 12 or 20 ga., 3 in. chambers on the 20 ga., single trigger, ejectors, light engraving. Disc. 1987.

	100%	98%	95%	90%	80%	70%	60%
	$675	$585	$530	$485	$440	$400	$375

Add $50 for multi-chokes (12 ga. only).
This model was distributed by Euroarms of America, Inc.
Last Mfg.'s Sug. Retail was $739.

CONDOR MODEL — 12 ga. skeet model, 28 in. barrels, SST, ejectors, wide vent rib, engraved silver finished receiver, recoil pad. Disc. 1987.

	100%	98%	95%	90%	80%	70%	60%
	$795	$700	$640	$585	$530	$485	$440

This model was distributed by Mandall Shooting Supplies, Inc.
Last Mfg.'s Sug. Retail was $895.

TARGET MODEL 208 — 12 ga. only, available in either Trap, Skeet, or Monotrap configuration. Disc. 1987.

	100%	98%	95%	90%	80%	70%	60%
	$895	$775	$695	$620	$575	$500	$450

Add $494 for Monotrap II 208 Model.
Last Mfg.'s Sug. Retail was $996.

Grading	100%	98%	95%	90%	80%	70%	60%

TARGET MODEL 308 — 12 ga. only, available in either Trap, Skeet, or Monotrap configuration. Disc. 1987.

	$1,375	$1,125	$950	$875	$795	$725	$650

Add $76 for multi-chokes.
Add $824 for Monotrap II 308 Model.
Last Mfg.'s Sug. Retail was $1,581.

SPECIAL MODEL — 12 ga. only, 3 in. chambers, various barrel lengths and chokings, SST. Disc. 1987.

	$465	$395	$355	$325	$290	$270	$250

Add $120 for multi-chokes.
Last Mfg.'s Sug. Retail was $528.

DELUXE MODEL — similar to Special Model, except better wood and engraving. Disc. 1987.

	$645	$550	$495	$450	$400	$360	$320

Add $80 for multi-chokes.
Last Mfg.'s Sug. Retail was $730.

PRESENTATION MODEL — 12 ga. only, includes sideplates. Disc. 1987.

	$740	$630	$575	$495	$450	$395	$350

Add $42 for multi-chokes.
Last Mfg.'s Sug. Retail was $842.

ST. GEORGE'S TARGET — 12 ga. only, trap or skeet gun, SST, fixed choke. Disc. 1987.

	$900	$730	$645	$550	$495	$450	$400

Last Mfg.'s Sug. Retail was $1,024.

St. George's Competition — 12 ga. only, includes 30 in. O/U barrels and single barrel multi-choke. Disc. 1989.

	$1,995	$1,750	$1,550	$1,250	$995	$875	$775

Last Mfg.'s Sug. Retail was $1,627.

PATRICIA MODEL — .410 ga. only, 3 in. chambers, 28 in. barrels, SST. Disc. 1987.

	$1,175	$1,010	$900	$895	$820	$740	$650

Add $121 for case.
Last Mfg.'s Sug. Retail was $1,345.

SHOTGUNS: SIDE-BY-SIDE

QUAIL SPECIAL — .410 ga., 3 in. chambers, single trigger, 28 in. barrels. Disc. 1987.

	$205	$185	$170	$150	$125	$110	$100

Last Mfg.'s Sug. Retail was $243.

FALCON II — .410 ga., 3 in. chambers, 26 or 28 in. barrels, double triggers. Disc. 1987.

	$205	$185	$170	$150	$125	$110	$100

Last Mfg.'s Sug. Retail was $246.

SILVER SNIPE — 12 or 20 ga., various barrel lengths, vent rib, single trigger, engraved.

	$485	$440	$400	$360	$330	$300	$280

PHEASANT — 12 ga. only, 3 in. chambers, 28 in. barrels only, single trigger. Disc. 1987.

	$370	$320	$300	$280	$260	$240	$220

Last Mfg.'s Sug. Retail was $428.

ALLEY CLEANER — 12 or 20 ga., 3 in. chambers, 20 in. barrels, riot configuration, SST. Disc. 1987.

	$575	$495	$460	$420	$390	$350	$310

Add $65 for multi-chokes.
Last Mfg.'s Sug. Retail was $649.

Grading	100%	98%	95%	90%	80%	70%	60%

CLASSIC — 12 or 20 ga., 3 in. chambers, 26-30 in. barrels, ST. Disc. 1989.

	$995	$875	$750	$650	$550	$475	$400

Add $80 for multi-chokes.
Last Mfg.'s Sug. Retail was $706.

SHOTGUNS: SINGLE BARREL AND LEVER ACTION

DIANO I — 12, 20, or .410 ga., 3 in. chambers, top lever single barrel action, folding configuration, vent rib. Disc. 1987.

	$115	$95	$85	$80	$75	$70	$65

Last Mfg.'s Sug. Retail was $129.

DIANO II — similar to Diano I, except has bottom lever opening. Disc. 1987.

	$115	$95	$85	$80	$75	$70	$65

Last Mfg.'s Sug. Retail was $129.

LONER I — similar to Diano I. Disc. 1987.

	$95	$80	$75	$65	$55	$45	$35

Last Mfg.'s Sug. Retail was $109.

LONER II — similar to Diano II. Disc. 1987.

	$95	$80	$75	$65	$55	$45	$35

Last Mfg.'s Sug. Retail was $109.

APACHE — 12 ga. only, lever action, 3 in. chambers, 20 in. barrel, SST. Disc. 1987.

	$410	$355	$325	$300	$280	$260	$245

Add $80 for multi-chokes.
Last Mfg.'s Sug. Retail was $473.

SHOTGUNS: SLIDE ACTION

PUMP ACTION — 12 ga. only, available in riot, field, or deer (slug) barrel configurations, 3 in. chamber, hunter model has multi-chokes standard. Disc. 1987.

	$290	$245	$205	$185	$170	$150	$125

Last Mfg.'s Sug. Retail was $329.

COMBINATION GUNS

AIRONE — 12 ga./.30-06 or .308 Win. cal., boxlock with false sideplates, double triggers, checkered walnut stock and forearm, swivels. Disc. 1987.

	$1,450	$1,275	$1,050	$900	$800	$700	$600

CONDOR — similar to Airone, except does not have false sideplates. Disc. 1987.

	$1,295	$1,050	$900	$800	$700	$600	$500

DOUBLE RIFLES

LEOPARD EXPRESS — .30-06, .308 Win., .375 H&H, or 7 x 65R cal., boxlock action, double triggers, checkered walnut stock and forearm. Disc. 1987.

	$1,325	$1,150	$975	$900	$840	$775	$725

Last Mfg.'s Sug. Retail was $1,529.

Grading	100%	98%	95%	90%	80%	70%	60%

ZOLI, ANTONIO

Manufacturer located in Brescia, Italy. Imported and distributed exclusively by Antonio Zoli U.S.A. Inc. located in Fort Wayne, IN. Previously imported and distributed by Fiocchi of America, Inc. located in Ozark, MO. and by Mandall Shooting Supplies, Inc. located in Scottsdale, AZ.

All models within this heading are currently distributed exclusively by Antonio Zoli U.S.A. Located In Fort Wayne, IN.

Antonio Zoli firearms are totally unrelated to those guns of Angelo Zoli. Parts are not interchangeable and warranties from Antonio Zoli firearms DO NOT apply to Angelo Zoli guns.

RIFLES: O/U

The rifles listed below (including O/U, side by side, and bolt action) are imported exclusively by Euroarms of America.

EXPRESS — 7 x 65R, 7 x 57, .30-06, .308 Win. or 9.3 x 74R cal., 25.6 in. barrels, hand checkered walnut stock with cheekpiece, set trigger for bottom barrel, extractors.

Mfg.'s Sug. Retail	$4,190	$3,750	$3,250	$2,900	$2,600	$2,200	$1,950	$1,650

Add $700 for E Model (with ejectors).

EXPRESS EM — 7 x 65R, .30-06, .308 Win., or 9.3 x 74R cal., mechanical single trigger, ejectors. Importation disc. 1990.

	$4,450	$3,850	$3,300	$2,900	$2,600	$2,200	$1,900

Add $2,395 for De Luxe Model.

Add $7,200 for E3 De Luxe Model.

The Express E3 De Luxe Model includes 2 extra sets of barrels - 1 set is shotgun (20 ga. - 2¾ or 3 in. chambers).

Last Mfg.'s Sug. Retail was $4,600.

RIFLES: S X S

SAVANA E — 7 x 65R, .30-06, .308 Win. or 9.3 x 74R cal., boxlock action, ejectors. Importation disc. 1990.

	$5,175	$4,675	$3,950	$3,200	$2,700	$2,250	$1,950

Add $135 for Savana EM Model (single trigger - disc.).

Last Mfg.'s Sug. Retail was $5,695.

Savana Deluxe — similar to Savana E, except has elaborate game scene engraving. Importation disc. 1990.

	$7,750	$7,100	$6,500	$6,000	$5,500	$5,000	$4,600

Last Mfg.'s Sug. Retail was $8,295.

TROPHY MODEL — similar to Savana E, except is also available in .375 H&H cal., 25½ in. barrels, 8 lbs. Importation began 1991.

Mfg.'s Sug. Retail	$5,895	$5,275	$4,200	$3,600	$3,150	$2,750	$2,400	$2,050

RIFLES: BOLT ACTION

AZ 1900C — .243 Win., .270 Win., 6.5 x 55, .30-06, .308 Win., 7mm Rem. Mag., or .300 Win. Mag. cal., 21 or 24 (Mag. cal.'s) in. barrel, checkered walnut stock with weatherproof stock finish, sling swivels, iron sights, 7.4 lbs.

Mfg.'s Sug. Retail	$1,125	$1,000	$840	$740	$660	$585	$500	$450

Add approx. 10% for AZ 1900 Deluxe (better walnut).

Add 60% for AZ 1900 Super Deluxe (select walnut and moderate engraving).

Add approx. 10% for Model AZ 1900 DL (photo engraved receiver and floorplate).

Grading	100%	98%	95%	90%	80%	70%	60%

MODEL AZ 1900M — .243 Win., 6.5 x 55mm, .270 Win., .30-06, or .308 Win. cal., 21 in. barrel, composite stock is composed of fiberglass, Kevlar, and graphite and features baked on walnut wood grain finish with checkering, drilled and tapped receiver. Importation began 1991.

Mfg.'s Sug. Retail	$840	$725	$625	$550	$495	$450	$415	$375

Add approx. 10% for Model AZ 1900M DL (photo engraved receiver and floorplate).

SHOTGUNS: CURRENT MFG. O/U

SILVER FALCON — 12 or 20 ga., 3 in. chambers, boxlock action, SST, ejectors, 26 or 28 in. barrels with multi-chokes, coin finished receiver with engraving, checkered Turkish walnut stock and forearm with weatherproof finish. Importation disc. 1991.

	$795	$650	$575	$500	$450	$400	$365

Last Mfg.'s Sug. Retail was $1,395.

WOODSMAN — 12 ga. only, 3 in. chambers, 23 in. vent barrels are designed to shoot rifle slugs at 55 yards and to accept 5 interchangeable choke tubes, SST, ejectors, quarter rib on barrels with pop-up rifle sights, checkered Circassian walnut stock and forearm with swivels (waterproof finish).

Mfg.'s Sug. Retail	$1,545	$1,325	$1,100	$950	$800	$700	$600	$500

Woodsman Combo — includes 2 sets of barrels (3 in. chambers) with Zoli interchangeable choke system.

Mfg.'s Sug. Retail	$2,320	$2,050	$1,700	$1,475	$1,200	$1,050	$925	$800

MODEL Z-90 TARGET MODEL — 12 ga. only, boxlock action, adj. SST, black competition receiver, deluxe checkered Turkish walnut stock with recoil pad and forearm, vent barrels and rib, SST, ejectors.

Trap Gun — 29½ or 32 in. barrels with screw-in chokes and raised VR, Monte Carlo stock, blue finish.

Mfg.'s Sug. Retail	$1,795	$1,625	$1,400	$1,200	$995	$850	$700	$600

Mono Trap Gun — 32 or 34 in. barrel with screw-in chokes and raised VR, Monte Carlo stock.

Mfg.'s Sug. Retail	$1,795	$1,625	$1,400	$1,200	$995	$850	$700	$600

Z-90 Combo Trap Set — includes O/U trap barrels as well as Mono trap barrel on same receiver, available as 30/32 in. sets or 32/34 in. sets. New 1991.

Mfg.'s Sug. Retail	$2,700	$2,350	$1,900	$1,650	$1,400	$1,150	$950	$825

Skeet Gun — 28 in. barrels only with screw-in chokes.

Mfg.'s Sug. Retail	$1,795	$1,625	$1,400	$1,200	$995	$850	$700	$600

Sporting Clays Gun — 28 in. barrels with screw-in chokes, coin finished receiver with engraved sideplates, separated barrels, Schnabel forend, solid recoil pad. Importation disc. 1990.

	$875	$750	$675	$600	$550	$500	$465

Last Mfg.'s Sug. Retail was $1,595.

SHOTGUNS: DISC. MFG. O/U

GOLDEN SNIPE — 12 or 20 ga, various barrel lengths, vent rib, single trigger, ejectors, engraved.

	$560	$520	$475	$430	$395	$360	$330

DELFINO — 12 or 20 ga., 3 in. chambers, 26 or 28 in. barrels, ejectors, vent rib, single non-selective trigger, blued frame with delicate engraving, walnut pistol grip stock and forearm. Disc.

	$500	$425	$375	$325	$295	$280	$265

Grading	100%	98%	95%	90%	80%	70%	60%

RITMO HUNTING — 12 ga. only, 3 in. chambers, 26 or 28 in. vent barrels and rib, SST, ejectors, select checkered walnut, blued frame and barrels with moderate engraving, recoil pad, 7¼ lbs. Disc.

		$575	$510	$465	$410	$370	$350	$335

ANGEL MODEL — 12 ga. only, field grade, SST, ejectors, wide vent rib, engraved receiver, recoil pad. Disc.

		$850	$775	$700	$640	$585	$530	$485

This model was distributed by Mandall Shooting Supplies, Inc.

RITMO PIGEON GRADE IV — 12 ga. only, live pigeon gun, 28 in. barrels, SST, ejectors, superbly engraved silver finished receiver, extra fine checkering on deluxe walnut, vent barrels and rib, cased, 7½ lbs. Disc.

	$1,600	$1,450	$1,200	$1,000	$875	$795	$725

M85 RITMO TRAP OR SKEET — 12 ga. only, 28 in. (Skeet only), 30, or 32 in. barrels, ejectors, SST, special stock dimensions, engraved blue receiver, select checkered walnut stock and forearm, cased, 7¾ lbs. Disc.

		$595	$500	$465	$440	$415	$395	$370

This model was also available in a single barrel trap model at no extra charge.

> **M85 Ritmo Trap Combination** — 12 ga. only, supplied with O/U and single barrel sets, various barrel lengths, cased. Disc.

		$995	$895	$800	$700	$620	$575	$500

SHOTGUNS: CURRENT MFG. SIDE-BY-SIDE

UPLANDER — 12 or 20 ga., 3 in. chambers, 25 in. barrels with fixed chokes (IC/M), ST, ejectors, color casehardened receiver, English style checkered Circassian walnut stock and forearm with oil or polyurethane finish. Importation disc. 1990.

		$750	$625	$560	$520	$485	$450	$425

Last Mfg.'s Sug. Retail was $1,295.

SILVER FOX — 12 or 20 ga., 3 in. chambers, 26 or 28 (12 ga. only) in. barrels with fixed chokes, ST, ejectors, hand engraved silver finished receiver with "AZ" in gold, straight grip checkered Circassian walnut stock and forearm. Importation disc. 1990.

	$1,650	$1,425	$1,200	$995	$875	$750	$625

Last Mfg.'s Sug. Retail was $2,995.

SHOTGUNS: DISC. MFG. SIDE-BY-SIDE

SILVER HAWK — 12 or 20 ga., double trigger, engraved.

		$420	$395	$360	$330	$300	$280	$260

ARIETE M3 — 12 ga. only, 26 or 28 in. barrels, matted rib, single non-selective trigger, ejectors, blued receiver with fine scroll engraving, cased. Disc.

		$550	$475	$400	$360	$330	$310	$285

EMPIRE — 12 or 20 ga. Mag., 27 or 28 in. barrels, moderate engraving, coin finished receiver. Disc.

	$1,425	$1,175	$975	$875	$795	$725	$650

Add $100 for 3 in. Mag. chambers.
This model was distributed by Euroarms of America, Inc.

Grading	100%	98%	95%	90%	80%	70%	60%

VOLCANO RECORD — 12 ga. only, 28 in. barrels, H&H type sidelocks, ejectors, SST, treble Purdey locks, silver finished receiver with elaborate engraving, best quality fine checkered walnut, special order only. Disc.

	$5,300	$4,475	$3,950	$3,400	$2,950	$2,650	$2,300

Volcano Record ELM — 12 ga. only, built to individual customer specifications, best quality H&H style sidelock. Discs.

	$13,250	$11,000	$9,750	$8,600	$7,400	$6,300	$5,450

This model was distributed by Euroarms of America, Inc.

CUSTOM SERIES — s x s, individual custom order only, every refinement is used in the construction of these extremely rare and expensive shotguns. These guns have to be appraised individually since their numbers are so few.

COMBINATION GUNS

COMBINATO — 12 or 20 ga. over .243 or .222 cal., boxlock action, game scene engraved receiver with silver finish, double triggers, folding rear sight, skipline checkering, with sling swivels.

Mfg.'s Sug. Retail	$1,995	$1,750	$1,500	$1,300	$1,100	$950	$775	$600

Combinato Set — includes one set of either 20 or 12 ga. barrels and an additional rifle/shotgun barrel set, same cal.'s as Combinato, cased.

Mfg.'s Sug. Retail	$2,700	$2,400	$2,150	$1,850	$1,600	$1,400	$1,200	$995

SAFARI DELUXE — similar to Combinato, except has sideplates with elaborate game scene engraving.

Mfg.'s Sug. Retail	$5,200	$4,850	$4,400	$3,950	$3,550	$3,175	$2,800	$2,400

Add approx. 50% for Safari Deluxe 2 (includes 2 sets of shotgun barrels).

EXPRESS E3 SET — includes one set of .30-06 O/U barrels, one set of 20 ga./.243 cal. barrels, one set of 20 ga./20 ga. barrels, special order, elaborate game scene engraving, includes German claw mount 4X scope and case. Disc.

	$2,750	$2,400	$2,100	$1,850	$1,650	$1,500	$1,375

NOTES

MODERN AIRGUNS

Last summer Minneapolis and St. Paul hosted the regional Olympic Festival. A broad range of activities including karate, archery, skeet, trap, air rifle and pistol competitions. I thought, "what better birthday gift to give Steve (the author) than a set of tickets to the shooting events."

The morning of the competition, we got off to a typical late start, missing most of the early events (competitions were limited to 10 shooters so they ended sooner than we had anticipated). At lunch we discussed our misfortune but concluded we could pick off the highlights on the evening news.

That evening we watched with anticipation as the local news showed highlights of karate, sailing, kayaking, and archery. They covered every aspect of the Olympic Festival <u>except</u>, the shooting events. What happened, I know the reporters were there, most of the events were held at the same location?

The next day I attacked the morning paper to see what events were covered. The only mention of a shooting competition was a "what's a pretty girl like you doing in a place like this" article about a female target shooter who had to choose between the competition and a modeling career.

Given every opportunity to cover a story on the safe use of <u>firearms</u> for <u>recreation</u>, the media choose to ignore it (remember this is a hunters paradise).

That evening the news glamorized a shooting in North Minneapolis. No less than sixteen shows on various stations showed the reckless, irresponsible use of guns, but still nothing about the Olympic shooting competitions.

Perhaps the media needs to look at itself, its programming and its conscience, before blaming gun enthusiasts for problems they choose to exploit as news and entertainment.

1991 is going to be another exceptional year for Airgun enthusiasts. Due to a low dollar, prices are up substantially on all but domestic models. There is, however, good news on the product front.

Beeman/Feinwerkbau has introduced a new rapid fire CO2 Pistol (the C5), along with the A replacement for the C10 (the C20). Beeman, under its own label has introduced the P2 (a target version of the P1) and has guarenteed introduction of the RX.

Daisy is importing a new CO2 target pistol from Hungary (the Model 91). Gamo is now being distributed by RWS. Air rifle specialists are importing both air arms and a few BSA rifles, along with a new retro market Theoben Gas Ram to convert B.S.A. sporting guns to this new technology.

A note about Pricing: You can see this section, like Black Powder, only contains pricing down to 95% grading. Due to the mechanical complexity of Airguns, and the fact that most sophisticated Airguns are used solely for target practice (many have had several thousand rounds through them), guns under 95% condition retain very little of their original value. Most collector guns (i.e. old Benjamins, Crossmans and Daisy's) trade for under $100 with only a few 100% guns trading for more.

Medium priced airguns from large distributors, such as Marksman, RWS, Norica and Gamo are so heavily discounted to the Distributor/Dealer that many "new-in-the-box" guns can be purchased for the price of a 98% gun. Also, the lack of available parts for older collectibles and non-functioning airguns contribute to a reduced value. It should also be noted that prices in this section have to cover a broad range of vendors. Used guns purchased from factory importers with test facilities or from dealers with factory authorized repair centers will command a higher sales price.

AS WITH THE SECTION OF BLACK POWDER GUNS, AIRGUNS UNDER $100 ARE NOT SHOWN. ENGRAVED GUNS OR GUNS WITH FANCY WOOD SHOULD BE DISCOUNTED A MINIMUM OF 50% IF UNDER 95% CONDITION.

Sincerely,

Robert M. Lucking

Patrick M. Lucking
Modern Airguns Editor
Blue Book of Gun Values

ARS/FARCO

Manufactured in the Philippines. Imported by Air Rifle Specialists located in Elmira, NY.

Grading	100%	98%	95%

AIR RIFLES

AR6 (6 SHOT REPEATING AIR RIFLE)—.22 CO_2 or compressed air powered, 23¼ in. barrel, capable of delivering 18 shots at 50 ft/lbs. power (1,000 FPS) using compressed air or up to 80 shots at 19-22 ft/lbs. power using CO_2 (single fill), checkered walnut stock, 6 lbs. 12 oz.

Mfg.'s Sug. Retail	$550	$455	$395	$320

AIR SHOTGUNS

FARCO AIR SHOTGUN — 28 ga., CO_2 powered, 30 in. barrel, 100 FT/LBS. of energy (standard airgun has 12-14 lbs.), charged by refillable (and removeable) 10 oz. cylinder, hardwood stock, 7 lbs. Importation began in 1988.

Mfg.'s Sug. Retail	$395	$360	$295	$235

AIR MATCH

Previously imported by Kendall International located in Paris, KY.

AIR MATCH MODEL 600 PISTOL — .177 cal., side lever action, adj. trigger, professional target model, 2 lbs.

	$395	$250	$185

AIR ARMS

Imported by Air Rifle Specialists located in Elmira, NY.

Editors note: These guns are filled from high pressure scuba tanks allowing many shots to be fired from one charge. This also allows one to adjust the power level of each shot. All guns are made with Walther barrels that float so that expansion of contraction of the air chamber will not affect its accuracy. Add $160 for Olympic trigger, $240 for regulator, and $60 for lever bolt.

Grading	100%	98%	95%	

SM100 — .177 or .22 cal. precharged pneumatic, 22 in. barrel, power can range from 12 to 19 ft/lbs. in .177 or 12 to 22 ft/lbs. in .22 cal, two stage trigger (adjustable), beech stock, 8 lbs. 8 oz.

Mfg.'s Sug. Retail	$870	$750	$630	$505

Add $60 for left hand.

XM100 — same as above but with quick release tank connector, and walnut stock, 8 lbs.

Mfg.'s Sug. Retail	$1,060	$940	$700	$630

Add $60 for left hand.

TM100 — same as above but with adj. cheek piece and shoulder pad, (target style stock), 8 lbs. 12 oz.

Mfg.'s Sug. Retail	$1,300	$1,170	$1,010	$800

Add $60 for left hand.

NJR100 — same as above but with hand picked barrel for accuracy, adj. cheek piece, forearm and shoulder pad, designed by and named after Nick Jenkinson (one of England's top field target shooters), 10 lbs. 12 oz.

Mfg.'s Sug. Retail	$1,800	$1,670	$1,430	$1,045

Add $60 for left hand.

AIR LOGIC
Manufacturer/distributor located in Forest Row, Sussex, England.

Air Logic has limited importation into the U.S. More information can be obtained by contacting Air Logic directly at: Air Logic Limited, 3 Medway Bldg.'s, Lower Road Forest Row, East Sussex ENGLAND RH18 5HE.

GENESIS — .22 cal., single stroke pneumatic, 630 FPS, unique bolt action sliding barrel (by L. Walther), recoilless, adj. trigger, side lever action, 9½ lbs. New for 1988.

Mfg.'s Sug. Retail	$750	$675	$400	$350

AMERICAN ARMS, INC.
Manufacturer/importer located in North Kansas City, MO.

Even though American Arms, Inc. imports Norica airguns, they are listed in this section because of their private label status. Importation began in late 1988 and was discontinued in 1989.

RIFLES

JET RIFLE — .177 cal., barrel break action, 855 FPS, adj. double set triggers, hardwood stock, 7 lbs.

	$120	$100	$85	

Last Mfg.'s Sug. Retail was $160.
Deduct $65 for Junior Model.

COMMANDO — .177 cal., barrel break action, 540 FPS, adj. sights, 5 lbs.

	$90	$80	$65	

Last Mfg.'s Sug. Retail was $115.

PISTOLS

IDEAL — .177 cal., barrel break action, 400 FPS, adj. sights, 3 lbs.

	$85	$65	$45	

Last Mfg.'s Sug. Retail was $105.

Grading	100%	98%	95%

ANSCHUTZ

Manufactured in Ulm, W. Germany.

Models 333, 335, and 380 were previously imported by Crossman from 1986-1988. While discontinued, some dealers may still have remaining inventories of these models. Model 380 now imported by Marksman.

MODEL 333 — .177 cal., barrel cocking action, 700 FPS, adj. trigger, 18 in. barrel, 6 lbs. 13 oz.

	$155	**$110**	**$85**

Last Mfg.'s Sug. Retail was $175.

MODEL 335 — .177 cal., barrel cocking, 700 FPS, adj. trigger, 18½ in. barrel, 7 lbs. 10 oz. Add $10 for 335 Mag. (20% higher velocity).

	$160	**$125**	**$95**

Last Mfg.'s Sug. Retail was $200.

MODEL 380 — .177 cal., under lever cocking, 600-640 FPS, professional match model, removable cheekpiece, adj. trigger, stippled walnut grips. Add $30 for left hand, $60 for moving target.

Mfg.'s Sug. Retail	**$1,000**	**$750**	**$650**	**$495**

MODEL 2001 — .177 cal., single stroke pneumatic, side lever action, exceptional target model, 10 lbs. 8 oz. Add $80 for left hand.

Mfg.'s Sug. Retail	**$1,800**	**$1,370**	**$895**	**$795**

Add $80 for Running Target Model.

Model 2001 imported by Precision Sales, Westfield, Mass.

B S A GUNS (U.K.), LTD.

Manufactured in Birmingham, England. Some guns imported by Air Rifle Specialists in Elmira, NY.

AIRSPORTER/AIRSPORTER SUPER: — .177 or .22 cal., under lever action, 700-550 FPS/825-600 FPS. (Super), 8 lbs. Add $50 for Super, $25 for Monte Carlo stock Stutzen Model.

	$125	**$100**	**$85**

CENTENNIAL COMMEMORATIVE — .177 or .22 cal., designed to commemorate BSA's 100th year.

	$225	**$190**	**$125**

Last Mfg.'s Sug. Retail was $650.

MERCURY/MERCURY SUPER — .177 or .22 cal., barrel cocking action, 700-550 FPS/825-600 FPS (super), 7¼ lbs. Add $35 for Super.

	$100	**$80**	**$70**

MERCURY CHALLENGER — .177 or .22 cal., barrel cocking action, 850-625 FPS, 7 lbs. 4 oz. Disc. 1988.

	$100	**$80**	**$70**

Last Mfg.'s Sug. Retail was $205.

METEOR/METEOR SUPER — .177 or .22 cal., barrel cocking action, 650-500 FPS, 6 lbs. Add $15 for Super.

	$70	**$45**	**$35**

SUPER SPORT/SUPER SPORT CUSTOM — .177 or .22 cal., barrel cocking action, 950-700 FPS, approx. 7 lbs. Add $90 for custom model, $120 for guns equipped with Theoben Gas Ram (spring).

Mfg.'s Sug. Retail	**$275**	**$240**	**$210**	**$160**

Importation began in 1990.

Grading	100%	98%	95%

SUPERSTAR — .177 or .22 cal., underlever action, unique rotating breech for loading pellets directly into bore, checkered beech stock, maxi grip scope rail, two stage trigger, approx. 8 lbs.

Mfg.'s Sug. Retail	$395	$365	$320	N/A

Add $120 for guns equipped with Theoben gas ram (spring).

VS 2000 — .177 or .22 cal., 9 shot repeater, side lever action, 850-625 FPS, 9 lbs. Add $65 for custom model. Disc. 1988.

	$295	$200	$140

Last Mfg.'s Sug. Retail was $330.

Only 20 or so of this model ever made.

PISTOLS

SCORPION PISTOL — .177 or .22 cal., barrel-cocking action 510-380 FPS, 3.6 lbs. Add $50 for carbine stock, Shadow Model.

	$75	$50	$45

B.S.F. (BAYERISCHE SPORTWAFFENFABRIK)

Manufactured in W. Germany. Previously imported by Kendell International located in Paris, KY. and Beeman Precision Arms under the Wischo label.

B.S.F. tooling and machinery have been purchased by Weihrauch and is being utilized to manufacture older versions of B.S.F. Models for Marksman (Marksman Models 55, 59 and 75).

RIFLES

BAVARIA MODEL 35 — .177 cal., barrel-cocking action, 500 FPS, 4½ lbs.

	$120	$100	$85

Last Mfg.'s Sug. Retail was $125.

BAVARIA MODEL 45 — .177 cal., barrel-cocking action, 700 FPS, 6 lbs.

	$125	$105	$80

Last Mfg.'s Sug. Retail was $125.

BAVARIA MODEL 50 — .177 cal., barrel-cocking action, 700 FPS, 6 lbs.

	$130	$105	$80

BAVARIA MODEL S54 — .177 or .22 cal., under barrel-cocking action, 685/500 FPS, 8 lbs. Add $15 for Sport Model (discontinued 1986), $30 for M Model.

	$190	$160	$100

BAVARIA MODEL 55 — .177 or .22 cal., barrel-cocking action, 800/570 FPS, 6½ lbs. Add $15 for Deluxe Model, $30 for Special Model (both discontinued 1986).

	$150	$130	$100

BAVARIA MODEL S60 — .177 or .22 cal., barrel-cocking action, 800/570 FPS, 6½ lbs.

	$155	$135	$80

BAVARIA MODEL S70 — .177 or .22 cal., barrel-cocking action, 800/570 FPS, 7 lbs.

	$160	$140	$100

BAVARIA MODEL S80 — .177 or .22 cal., barrel-cocking action, 800/570 FPS, 8¼ lbs.

	$175	$150	$125

Last Mfg.'s Sug. Retail was $185.

Grading	100%	98%	95%

BEEMAN PRECISION ARMS, INC.

Importers and distributors located in Santa Rosa, CA. Beeman has exclusive rights to any items marketed in the U.S. under the names Beeman, Feinwerkbau, Weihrauch and Webley.

Beeman imported Feinwerkbau and Weihrauch Airguns will appear under their respective headings in this section.

RIFLES

BEEMAN R1—.177, .20, .22 or .25 cal., barrel-cocking action, 1000-610 FPS, 8.8 lbs. Add $300 for custom grade, $335 for custom fancy, $400 for X fancy, $30 for left-hand, $60 for adj. cheek piece.

Mfg.'s Sug. Retail	$440	$345	$275	$220

Add $450 for Laser Model.
Add $110 for Field Target.
Add $10 for .20 or .25 cal.

BEEMAN R7 — .177, .20 cal., barrel-cocking action, 700 - 620 FPS, 6.1 lbs. Add $10 for .20 cal.

Mfg.'s Sug. Retail	$270	$195	$170	$140

BEEMAN R8 — .177 cal., barrel-cocking action, 720 FPS, 7.2 lbs.

Mfg.'s Sug. Retail	$350	$255	$220	$170

BEEMAN R10 — .177, .20, or .22 cal., barrel-cocking action, 1,000- 750 FPS, 7.9 lbs. Add $300 for custom grade, $335 for custom fancy, $400 for X fancy, $50 for left-hand, and $50 for deluxe, $10 for .20 cal.

Mfg.'s Sug. Retail	$350	$260	$230	$210

Add $400 for Laser Model.

BEEMAN RX — .177, .20, .22, and .25 cal., Theoben "Gasram" airspring system (See Theoben), up to 1200 FPS/.177 cal., adj. velocity, (release delayed until summer 1991). Add $10 for .20 and .25 cal., $140 for Field Target, and $60 for left hand.

Mfg.'s Sug. Retail	$470	$400	$330	$280

BEEMAN CARBINE C1 — .177 or .22 cal., barrel-cocking action, 830-670 FPS, 6.2-6.3 lbs.

Mfg.'s Sug. Retail	$250	$200	$175	$130

BEEMAN FALCON 1 & 2 — .177 cal., barrel-cocking action, 620-680 FPS/560-600 FPS, 6.7/5.9 lbs. Add $30 for Falcon 2. Discontinued in 1984.

	$100	$80	$60

Last Mfg.'s Sug. Retail was $110.

BEEMAN FX 1 & 2 — same as Beeman Falcon 1 & 2. Add $30 for FX 1.

Mfg.'s Sug. Retail	$140	$110	$90	$75

BEEMAN/HARPER AIR CANE — .22 or .25 cal., pneumatic (reuseable gas cartridge), 650 FPS, reproduction of 19th century Walking Cane Gun, 1 lbs. Add $50 for decorative head piece.

Mfg.'s Sug. Retail	$595	$500	$425	$340

BEEMAN/WEBLEY OMEGA — .177 or .22 cal., barrel break action, 830-675 FPS, 7.8 lbs.

Mfg.'s Sug. Retail	$430	$340	$265	$175

BEEMAN/WEBLEY ECLIPSE—.177, .22 or .25 cal., underlever action, 990 FPS (in .177 cal.). New 1990.

Mfg.'s Sug. Retail	$460	$370	$320	$255

Grading	100%	98%	95%

BEEMAN/WEBLEY VULCAN III AND VULCAN III DELUXE — .177 or .22 cal., barrel-cocking action, 830-675 FPS, 7.6-7.7 lbs. Add $60 for Deluxe.

Mfg.'s Sug. Retail	$250	$195	$170	$130

PISTOLS

BEEMAN/FAS 604 — .177 cal., top lever spring pneumatic action, 380 FPS, 2.3 lbs. Add $30 for left-hand. Disc. 1988.

	$295	$225	$175

Last Mfg.'s Sug. Retail was $495.

BEEMAN/HARPER CLASSIC PISTOL — .22 or .25 cal., similar Harper Air Cane rifle action, 300 FPS, 4 oz. Add $10 for .25 cal., $35 for deluxe.

Mfg.'s Sug. Retail	$285	$245	$200	$150

Add $210 if cased. Retail for a cased pair is $700.

BEEMAN/HARPER PEPPERBOX PISTOL — .22 cal., pneumatic (like above), 9.8 oz.

Mfg.'s Sug. Retail	$575	$500	$400	$250

BEEMAN P1 — .177, .20 or .22 cal. Mag., top cocking action, 350-600 FPS, walnut grips, Colt .45 look alike.

Mfg.'s Sug. Retail	$330	$260	$210	$175

Add $10 for .20 cal.

Add $35 for stainless steel style finish.

Add $295 for gold plating.

BEEMAN P2 — .177 and .20 cal., single stroke pneumatic, similar to above but professional mid-priced match gun. New 1991.

Mfg.'s Sug. Retail	$375	$275	N/A	N/A

Add $10 for .20 cal.

Add $15 for match grips.

BEEMAN/WEBLEY HURRICANE — .177 or .22 cal., barrel-cocking action, 470-400 FPS, 2.4 lbs. Add $40 for M20 scope combo.

Mfg.'s Sug. Retail	$190	$150	$130	$100

BEEMAN/WEBLEY TEMPEST — .177 or .22 cal., barrel-cocking action, 470-400 FPS, 2 lbs.

Mfg.'s Sug. Retail	$160	$130	$115	$90

BENJAMIN AIR RIFLE COMPANY
Manufacturer located in Racine, WI.

CENTENNIAL MODEL 87 — .177 or .22 cal., multi-stroke pneumatic, 750/650 FPS, polished brass barrel, all nickel trim, Williams aperature, built to commemorate the 100th anniversary, bronze medallion in stock, 6 lbs, 6,086 mfg.

Mfg.'s Sug. Retail	$250	$225	$170	$125

BENJAMIN MODEL 340, 342, AND 347 — BB, .177 or .22 cal., pneumatic pump action, 750-650 FPS, 4½ lbs., (340-BB), (342-.22), (347-.177). Add $15 for Williams sight, $30 for 4 x 15 scope.

Mfg.'s Sug. Retail	$110	$85	$65	$50

Grading	100%	98%	95%	

BENJAMIN MODEL 392/397 — .177 and .22 cal. (392), CO2 or pneumatic pump action, 750-700 FPS, 19⅜ in. barrel, available in chrome or black matte finish, walnut stock, 5 lbs. 8 oz. New 1991.

Mfg.'s Sug. Retail	$110	$100	$85	N/A

Add $5 for chrome.
Add $20 for Williams peepsight.
Subtract $10 for CO2 (600-500 FPS).

PISTOLS

BENJAMIN AIR PISTOL MODEL 130, 132, AND 137 — .177 cal., pneumatic pump action, 380 FPS, 2 lbs.

Mfg.'s Sug. Retail	$85	$70	$50	$35

BENJAMIN AIR PISTOL MODEL 242, 247 — .177 and .22 cal., pneumatic pump action, 418/315 FPS, 2 lbs. 8 oz.

Mfg.'s Sug. Retail	$90	$75	$65	$50

BENJAMIN/SHERIDAN AIR PISTOL MODEL H/HB—.177, .20 and .22 cal., pneumatic pump action, 400 FPS, 9⅜ in. barrel, available in chrome (H) or black matte finish (HB), walnut grips, 2 lbs. 8 oz. New in 1991.

Mfg.'s Sug. Retail	$110	$95	$80	N/A

CROSMAN AIR GUNS
East Bloomfield, NY.

Other than the continued sale of the Model 84 and Skanaker, Crosman has dropped adult precision Airguns. The Crosman/Anschutz models listed below should be watched for collectors value due to their limited U.S. distribution using Crosman model numbers.

MODEL 84 AIR RIFLE — .177 cal., CO2 powered, match rifle, 0-720 FPS (fully adj.), adj. sights, walnut stock with adj. cheekplate and butt plate, 11 lbs.

Mfg.'s Sug. Retail	$1,295	$995	$600	$500

Crosman Model 84 is the first U.S. made air rifle designed to compete with established European models. Unlike its competitors, it is CO2 powered with a digital gauge mounted on the forearm to show remaining pressure.

6500 (ANSCHUTZ MODEL 335) — .177 cal., barrel break action, 700 FPS, 18½ in. barrel, 7 lbs. 10.5 oz. Disc. in 1989.

	$160	$125	$95	

Last Mfg.'s Sug. Retail was $200.

6300 (ANSCHUTZ MODEL 333) — .177 cal., barrel break action, 700 FPS, 18½ in. barrel, 6 lbs. 13 oz. Disc. in 1989.

	$155	$110	$85	

Last Mfg.'s Sug. Retail was $175.

MODEL 6100 (MADE BY DIANAWERK) — .177 cal., barrel break action, 780/830 FPS, 20½ in. barrel, 8 lbs. 6 oz. Disc. in 1989.

	$145	$115	$85	

Last Mfg.'s Sug. Retail was $235.

PISTOLS

SKANAKER PISTOL (AVAILABLE 1987) MODEL 88 — .177 cal., CO2 powered, 550 FPS, professional target model. Add $65 for carrying case.

No Mfg.'s Retail	$795	$600	$425	$300

DAISY MANUFACTURING CO., INC.

Manufactured and distributed in Rogers, AR.

Even though Daisy is one of the largest airgun manufacturers in the world, only 6 weapons would fall into the category of adult precision airguns - these are the Daisy 126 El Gamo, Model 128 Gamo Olympic, Model 953, Model 753, and their 2 target pistols (Models 747 and 777). The Daisy 126 El Gamo rifle and Model 128 Gamo Olympic are manufactured in Spain and assembled in the U.S. All 6 airguns have barrels made by Lothar Walther.

RIFLES

EL GAMO 126 SUPER MATCH TARGET RIFLE — .177 cal., single stroke pneumatic, 590 FPS, adj. sights, hardwood stock, 10 lbs. 9 oz.

Mfg.'s Sug. Retail	$525	$435	$300	$200

MODEL 128 GAMO OLYMPIC — same as above except with adj. cheek and butt piece, high quality European diopter sight.

Mfg.'s Sug. Retail	$735	$650	$425	$350

MODEL 753 COMPETITION — .177 cal., single stroke pneumatic, 480 FPS, competition sights, 6lbs. 8 oz.

Mfg.'s Sug. Retail	$280	$225	$180	$145

953 TARGET — .177 cal., single stroke pneumatic, 480 FPS, Lothar Walther barrel, adj. sights, 5 lbs. 8 oz.

Mfg.'s Sug. Retail	$135	$135	$120	$90

853 TARGET — .177 cal., same as Model 953 which is being phased out in 1991.

Mfg.'s Sug. Retail	$160	$140	N/A	N/A

PISTOLS

MODEL 747 TARGET PISTOL — .177 cal., side lever action, single stroke pneumatic, 360 FPS, 3 lbs. 3 oz.

Mfg.'s Sug. Retail	$110	$90	$70	$50

MODEL 777 TARGET PISTOL — .177 cal., side lever action, single stroke pneumatic, 360 FPS, wood target style grips, 3 lbs. 3 oz.

Mfg.'s Sug. Retail	$235	$180	$150	$110

MODEL 91 — .177 cal., CO2 powered, 425 FPS, 10¼ in. barrel, imported from Hungary, 2 lbs. 7 oz. New spring 1991.

Mfg.'s Sug. Retail	$425	$360	N/A	N/A

This is being imported by Daisy as an entry level professional target pistol, similar in design to Feinwerkbau or Crosman's Skanaker pistol.

DIANAWERK, MAYER AND GRAMMELSPACHER

Manufacturer located in West Germany.

Dynamit Nobel RWS Inc. is the exclusive Dianawerk importer located in Northvale, NJ.

Grading	100%	98%	95%

RIFLES

MODEL 24 — .177 or .22 cal., barrel-cocking action, 700/400 FPS, 17¼ in. barrel, 6 lbs. Deduct $25 for Model 24J. New in 1987.

Mfg.'s Sug. Retail	$145	$115	$95	$75

MODEL 25D — .177 or .22 cal., barrel-cocking action, 525/380 FPS, 15¾ in. barrel, 5¾ lbs. (sport). Disc. in 1987.

	$95	$75	$55

Last Mfg.'s Sug. Retail was $120.

MODEL 26 — .177 or .22 cal., barrel-cocking action, 750/500 FPS, 17¼ in. barrel, 6 lbs. 1 oz.

Mfg.'s Sug. Retail	$175	$150	$115	$75

MODEL 27 — .177 or .22 cal., barrel-cocking action, 550/415 FPS, 17¼ in. barrel, 6 lbs. (sport). Disc. in 1987.

	$150	$110	$90

Last Mfg.'s Sug. Retail was $150.

MODEL 28 — .177 or .22 cal., barrel-cocking action, 750/500 FPS, 15¾ in. barrel, 6 lbs. 12 oz.

Mfg.'s Sug. Retail	$190	$145	$120	$90

MODEL 34 — .177 or .22 cal., barrel-cocking action, 950/700 FPS, 19½ in. barrel, 7 lbs. 6 oz. Add $10 for 100 year Diana Commemorative Model (new in 1990).

Mfg.'s Sug. Retail	$205	$155	$110	$90

MODEL 35 — .177 or .22 cal., barrel-cocking action, 665/540 FPS, 19 in. barrel, 8 lbs. (sport/target). Disc. in 1987.

	$100	$75	$60

Last Mfg.'s Sug. Retail was $160.

MODEL 36 AND 36 CARBINE — .177 or .22 cal., barrel break action, 1000/700 FPS, 19½ in. barrel, 8 lbs. Add $40 for new S Model, deduct $10 for muzzle break model without factory sights.

Mfg.'s Sug. Retail	$295	$185	$140	$105

MODEL 38 — .177 or .22 cal., barrel break action, 1000/700 FPS, 19½ in. barrel, 8 lbs., walnut stock.

Mfg.'s Sug. Retail	$345	$250	$200	$140

Model 38 is the deluxe version of the Model 36 listed above.

MODEL 45 S / 45 DELUXE — .177 or .22 cal., barrel-cocking action, 900/650 FPS, 20½ in. barrel, 7 lbs. 9 oz., S Model equipped w/factory sling and scope. Add $40 for deluxe, $70 for S model with scope.

Mfg.'s Sug. Retail	$225	$145	$120	$85

MODEL 48 — .177 or .22 cal., side lever action, 1,100/780 FPS, 17 in. barrel, 8½ lbs.

Mfg.'s Sug. Retail	$345	$230	$160	$120

MODEL 50T/T01 — .177 or .22 cal., under lever action, 745/600 FPS, 18½ in. barrel, 8 lbs., (sport/target), parkerized finish. Add $20 for blue finish, $100 for T01 Model. Disc. 1988.

	$200	$160	$125

Last Mfg.'s Sug. Retail was $210.

MODEL 52 — .177 or .22 cal., side lever action, 1,100/780 FPS, 17 in. barrel, 8½ lbs.

Mfg.'s Sug. Retail	$385	$260	$180	$140

MODEL 70 — .77 cal., barrel cocking action, 450 FPS, 13½ in. barrel. This is a junior sized adult air rifle.

Mfg.'s Sug. Retail	$190	$130	$105	$85

Grading	100%	98%	95%	

MODEL 72 — .177 cal., same as above but with recoilless action.

Mfg.'s Sug. Retail	$340	$250	$200	$160

MODEL 75, 75 HV, 75U, 75K, 75S — .177 cal., side lever action, 580 FPS, 19 in. barrel (professional target), 11 lbs. Add $30 for left-hand, $165 for U, $100 for K, $80 for 75S with adj. cheek piece and micrometer sight. Model 75 HV and Model 75 U were disc. in 1989. Model K disc. 1990.

Mfg.'s Sug. Retail	$850	$650	$550	$380

MODEL 100 — .177 cal., single stroke pneumatic, 580 FPS, 19 in. barrel, adj. cheekpiece, professional target model, 11 lbs. New in 1989.

Mfg.'s Sug. Retail	$850	$650	$550	$380

MODEL 1000 — .177 cal., barrel-break action, unique colored plastic stocks (black, red, blue, white, and yellow). Disc. 1991.

	$140	$100	$80

Last Mfg.'s Sug. Retail was $215.

Model 1000 is the sport model of the standard Model 34.

PISTOLS

MODEL 5G/GS — .177 or .22 cal., barrel-cocking action, 450/300 FPS, 7 in. barrel, (sport) 2 lbs. 12 oz. GS Model equipped w/factory scope. Add $70 for GS.

Mfg.'s Sug. Retail	$175	$120	$90	$70

MODEL 6G/6M/6GS — .177 cal., barrel-cocking action, 450 FPS , 7 in. barrel, (professional target), 3 lbs. GS Model equipped with factory scope. Add $70 for GS model, $20 for left hand.

6G

Mfg.'s Sug. Retail	$285	$200	$150	$115

6M

Mfg.'s Sug. Retail	$390	$265	$185	$140

MODEL 10 — .177 cal., barrel-cocking action, 450 FPS, 7 in. barrel, (professional target) 3 lbs. 4 oz. Add $50 for cased model, $40 for left-hand.

Mfg.'s Sug. Retail	$670	$525	$375	$280

ENSIGN ARMS CO., LTD.

Previous international distributors for Saxby Palmer Airguns located in Newbury, England.

Ensign Arms previously distributed the Saxby Palmer line of airguns into the U.S. Please refer to the Saxby Palmer section for these guns. "Ensign" designated models were trademarked by Ensign Arms Co., Ltd. Marksman Products was the most recent importer located in Huntington Beach, CA.

F.A.S.

Previously imported by Beeman until 1988. Line now distributed by Nimbus Ltd., Winthrop, MA. Nygord Products La Crescenta, CA. and Mandall Shooting Supplies, Scottsdale, AZ. Manufactured in Italy.

FAS 604—.177 cal., top lever spring, pneuamtic action, 7½ in. barrel, 380 FPS, 2 lbs. 6 oz.

Mfg.'s Sug. Retail	$720	$410	$360	$280

Grading		100%	98%	95%

FAS 606 — .177 top lever spring, pneumatic action, 7½ in. barrel, professional target model, walnut grips, 2 lbs. 3 oz.

Mfg.'s Sug. Retail	$1,340	$800	$680	$590

F.E.G.

Imported by K.B.I. INC. (formerly Kassnar Imports). (Model GPM also imported as Daisy Model 91). Manufactured in Hungary.

RIFLES

CLG-462 — .177 or .22 cal., CO2 cartridge or cylinder charge, 490-410 FPS, 16½ in. barrel, (24 in. .22 cal.), 5 lbs. 8 oz.

Mfg.'s Sug. Retail	$550	$420	N/A	N/A

CLG-468 — .177 or .22 cal., CO2 cartridge or cylinder charge, 705-525 FPS, 26¾ in. barrel, 5 lbs. 12 oz.

Mfg.'s Sug. Retail	$600	$480	N/A	N/A

PISTOLS

MODEL GPM-01.177 cal., CO2 cartridge or cylinder charge, 425 FPS, 10¼ in. barrel, 2 lbs. 7 oz.

Mfg.'s Sug. Retail	$500	$360	N/A	N/A

FEINWERKBAU

Manufactured in Oberndorf, West Germany. Imported and distributed by Beeman Precision Arms Inc. located in Santa Rosa, CA.

The Feinwerkbau trademark is now owned in the U.S. by Beeman Precision Arms, Inc. Feinwerkbau has been responsible for developing many of the current technical innovations used in fabricating target Air Pistols and Rifles. In 1988, Feinwerkbau Airguns swept the Olympic competition in this newly formed Olympic sport. Feinwerkbau has always been a leader in Airgun technology.

RIFLES

MODEL 124 — .177 cal., barrel-cocking action, 780-830 FPS, 7.2 lbs. Add $35 for deluxe, $20 for left-hand deluxe, $400 for custom select, $425 for custom fancy, $475 for custom extra fancy. Disc. 1989.

		$385	$330	$275

Last Mfg.'s Sug. Retail was $490.

MODEL 127 — .22 cal., barrel-cocking action, 620-680 FPS, 6-7.1 lbs. Additions same as above. Disc. 1989.

		$385	$330	$275

Last Mfg.'s Sug. Retail was $490.

MODEL 300S — .177 cal., side lever action, 640 FPS, 8.8-10.8 lbs. Add $100 for Running Boar, $75 for left-hand (all styles), $100 for Universal, $75 for barrel sleeve.

Mfg.'s Sug. Retail	$1,095	$990	$800	$650

Add $200 for Tyrolean stock.

Add $75 for Running Boar stock configuration on Universal Model.

MODEL 600 — .177 cal., sidelever action, single stroke pneumatic operation, top of the line match rifle with aperture sights, unique hardwood laminate stock, 585 FPS, 10½ lbs. Add $30 for left-hand. Disc. 1988.

	$950	$855	$750

Last Mfg.'s Sug. Retail was $900.

Grading	100%	98%	95%

This model was also available in a Running Boar variation with extra-long barrel that unscrews for transporting.

MODEL 601 — .177 cal., side lever action, single stroke, pneumatic operation, replaces Model 600 (see above). 10 lbs. 8 oz. Add $110 for left hand, $150 for Running Boar.

Mfg.'s Sug. Retail	$1,495	$1,300	$1,100	$800

MODEL C60 — .177 cal., CO2 powered, 570 FPS, similar in style to Model 600/601 above, 9.2 to 10.6 lbs. Add $110 for left hand, deduct $30 for running target.

Mfg.'s Sug. Retail	$1,390	$1,150	$995	$700

PISTOLS

MODEL 65 MK I AND II — .177 cal., side lever action, 525 FPS, 2.6-2.9 lbs., short barrel Mark II only. Add $60 for left adj., $20 for adj. right.

Mfg.'s Sug. Retail	$965	$795	$600	$430

MODEL 80 — .177 cal., side lever action, 475-525 FPS, 2.8-3.2 lbs. Discontinued in 1983. (Like Model 65 with stacking barrel weightss and fine mechanical trigger).

	$695	$550	$450

Last Mfg.'s Sug. Retail was $625.

MODEL 90 — specifications same as above but with electric trigger. Add $45 for short barrel, $50 for left-hand. Disc. 1990.

	$750	$600	$495

Last Mfg.'s Sug. Retail was $1,155.

MODEL 100 — .177 cal., pneumatic action, 460 FPS, 2½ lbs.

Mfg.'s Sug. Retail	$1,100	$960	$760	$625

Add $40 for left hand variation.

MODEL 2 — .177 cal., CO2 cylinder, 425-525 FPS, 2½ lbs. Add $40 for left, deduct $20 for mini. Disc. 1989.

	$650	$550	$350

Last Mfg.'s Sug. Retail was $780.

MODEL C5 — .177 cal., CO2 powered 5 shot rapid fire, 7⅓ in. barrel, 510 FPS, 2 lbs. 6 oz. New in 1991. Add $75 for left hand.

Mfg.'s Sug. Retail	$1,350	$1,230	$1,080	N/A

MODEL C 10 — .177 cal., CO2 cartridge, 510 FPS, 2½ lbs. Disc. 1990.

	$750	$600	$450

Last Mfg.'s Sug. Retail was $965.
Add $60 for left hand model.

MODEL C20 — .177 cal., CO2 powered, 510 FPS. Add $60 for left hand, 2 lbs. 8 oz. (replacement for the C2 and C10 new in 1991).

Mfg.'s Sug. Retail	$965	$845	$735	N/A

FIOCCHI OF AMERICA, INC.

Manufacturer/importer/distributor located In Ozark, MO.

MODEL K58 — .177 cal., underlever pneumatic, 9 in. barrel, 2 lbs. 6 oz., professional target model.

Mfg.'s Sug. Retail	N/A	$660	$500	N/A

MODEL K60 — .177 cal., CO2 cylinder charge, 9½ in. barrel, 2 lbs. 4 oz.

Mfg.'s Sug. Retail	N/A	$660	$500	N/A

Grading	100%	98%	95%

MODEL P10 — .177 cal., underlever pneumatic, 7¾ in. barrel, 2 lbs. 3 oz., being phased out in 1990.

Mfg.'s Sug. Retail	$560	$425	$355	$295

GAMO

Previously imported by Stoeger Industries - importation discontinued in 1986. A few models are currently being imported by Daisy. Line now imported and distributed by Dynamit Nobel, RWS INC., Northvale, NJ.

PISTOLS

CENTER — .177 cal., under barrel lever cocking, 400-435 FPS, 14 in. barrel, 2.8 lbs.

	$90	$75	$55

PR-45 — .177 cal., pneumatic, 9¼ in. barrel, 1 lb 9 oz., looks similar to a Beeman P1.

Mfg.'s Sug. Retail	$125	$95	$80	$65

COMPACT — .177 cal., pneumatic, 9¼ in. barrel, two stage trigger, walnut grips, adj. sights, target model, 2 lbs.

Mfg.'s Sug. Retail	$190	$145	$120	$95

RIFLES

CF 20—.177 and .22 cal., underlever action, 790-625, 17¾ in. barrel, checkered stock, 6 lbs. 6 oz.

Mfg.'s Sug. Retail	$190	$155	$125	$100

CADET—.177 cal., barrel break action, 570 FPS, beechwood stock, 5 lbs.

	$70	$60	$50

CONTEST — .177 cal., side lever action, 543 FPS, beechwood stock, 10.1 lbs.

	NA	NA

CUSTOM 600—.177 or .22 cal., barrel break action, 690 FPS, 17¾ in. barrel, two stage adj. trigger, checkered stock, 6 lbs. 3 oz.

Mfg.'s Sug. Retail	$170	$130	$105	$80

DELTA — .177 cal., barrel break action, 525 FPS, 15¾ in. barrel, two stage trigger, automatic safety, adj. sights, plastic stock, 5 lbs. 5 oz.

Mfg.'s Sug. Retail	$105	$80	$70	$55

EXPO — .177 or .22 cal., barrel break action, 625 FPS, adj. trigger, special-sights, 5 lbs. 8 oz.

	$75	$60	$50

EXPOMATIC—.177 cal., repeating barrel break action, 575 FPS, adj. trigger, 5 lbs. 5 oz.

	$115	$95	$75

GAMO 68 — .177 or .22 cal., barrel locking action, 600 FPS, 6 lbs. 8 oz.

	$80	$65	$50

GAMATIC 85 — .177 cal., barrel break action, 560 FPS, 17¾ in. barrel, two stage trigger, unique loading system for up to 25 pellets, pistol grip stock, 6 lbs. 3 oz.

Mfg.'s Sug. Retail	$160	$120	$100	$80

Grading	100%	98%	95%

G-1200 — .177 cal., CO2 cylinder, 560 FPS, 17¾ in. barrel, unique pump action loading system for up to 12 pellets (styled like a pump centerfire rifle), 6 lbs. 6 oz.

Mfg.'s Sug. Retail	$185	$150	$120	$95

MAGNUM 2000 — .177 and .22 cal., barrel break action, 820-660 FPS, 17¾ in. barrel, adj. two stage trigger, checkered stock, 7 lbs. 2 oz.

Mfg.'s Sug. Retail	$200	$170	$140	$110

SUPER — .177 cal., side lever action, 593 FPS, 10 lbs. 8 oz.

	$140	$120	$100

MARKSMAN
Division of S/R Industries, Huntington Beach, CA.

JUNIOR MODEL 28 — .177 cal., barrel cocking action, 600 FPS, 16¾ in. barrel, 6 lbs. Mfg. for Marksman by Weihrauch.

Mfg.'s Sug. Retail	$185	$140	$120	$90

MODEL 29/30 — .177 or .22 cal., barrel cocking action, 800/625 FPS, 18½ in. barrel, 6 lbs. Mfg. for Marksman by BSA. Disc. 1991.

	$180	$140	$90

Last Mfg.'s Sug. Retail was $200.

MODEL 40 — .177 cal., barrel cocking action, 720 FPS, 18⅜ in. barrel, 7 lbs. 5 oz.

Mfg.'s Sug. Retail	$240	$160	$140	$100

MODEL 55 (RIFLE) & 59 CARBINE — .177 cal., barrel cocking action, 925 FPS, 19¾ (rifle) or 14 (carbine) in. barrel, 7 lbs. 8 oz. Mfg. for Marksman by Weihrauch.

Mfg.'s Sug. Retail	$260	$190	$165	$110

MODEL 56/56K — .177 cal., barrel cocking action, 925 FPS, 19⅝ in. barrel, adj. cheekpiece and trigger, 8 lbs. 11 oz.

Mfg.'s Sug. Retail	$415	$325	$280	$230

Add $180 for 56K Model with Marksman Model 6941 scope.
The Model 56/56K is manufactured for Marksman by Weihrauch.

MODEL 58/58K—.177 cal., barrel cocking action, 925 FPS, 16 in. heavy bull barrel, adj. trigger, designed for silhouette shooting, 8 lbs. 8 oz.

Mfg.'s Sug. Retail	$360	$275	$230	$195

Add $180 for 58K Model with Marksman Model 6941 scope.
The Model 58/58K is manufactured for Marksman by Weihrauch.

MODEL 60/61 CARBINE — .177 cal., under lever cocking action, 810-840 FPS, 8 lbs. 12 oz.

Mfg.'s Sug. Retail	$400	$280	$240	$210

Improved version of HW77 by Weihrauch.

MODEL 70, 71, 72 — .177, .20, or .22 cal., barrel cocking action, 925/760 FPS, 19¾ in. barrel, 8 lbs. Add $10 for .20 cal. Mfg. for Marksman by Weihrauch.

Mfg.'s Sug. Retail	$300	$220	$190	$110

The Model 72 is a .20 cal.

Grading	100%	98%	95%

MAUSER

Mauser Airguns are subcontracted under license to use the Mauser trademark and are not manufactured by Mauser-Werke. Previously imported and distributed by Marksman located in Huntington Beach, CA.

RIFLES

MATCH 300SL/SLC — .177 cal., under-lever action, 550/450 FPS, adj. sights and hardwood stock, 8.8 lbs. Add $75 for SLC Model with diopter sights.

Mfg.'s Sug. Retail	$330	$240	$200	$140

This model is mfg. in Hungary.

PISTOLS

U90/U91 JUMBO AIR PISTOLS — .177 cal., barrel break action, 260 FPS, 2 lbs.

	$80	$65	$45

Add $15 for deluxe model U91 with adj. sights and checkered grips.
Last Mfg.'s Sug. Retail was $100.

This model was mfg. by Record.

NORICA

Imported by KBI (Kassnar) Imports located in Harrisburg, PA and American Arms, Inc. located in North Kansas City, M0. Previously imported by S.A.E. located in Miami, FL.

Norica airguns imported by American Arms, Inc. will appear under the American Arms, Inc. heading in this text.

MODEL 47 — .177 cal., side lever action, 600 FPS, unique black pistol grip handle, 5½ lbs.

Mfg.'s Sug. Retail	$175	$120	$85	$65

MODEL 61C — .177 cal., barrel break action, 600 FPS, 5.8 lbs.

Mfg.'s Sug. Retail	$130	$90	$65	$45

MODEL 73 — .177 or .22 cal., barrel break action, 580/525 FPS, 6.4 lbs.

Mfg.'s Sug. Retail	$155	$105	$75	$50

MODEL 80G — .177 or .22 cal., barrel break action, 635/570 FPS, 7.2 lbs.

Mfg.'s Sug. Retail	$200	$135	$100	$70

MODEL 90 — .177 cal., barrel break action, 650 FPS, factory equipped with scope,

Mfg.'s Sug. Retail	$185	$125	$90	$65

MODEL 92 — .177 cal., side lever action, 650 FPS, 5.75 lbs.

Mfg.'s Sug. Retail	$175	$120	$85	$65

NORICA YOUNG — .177 cal., barrel break action, 600 FPS, unique colored stock.

Mfg.'s Sug. Retail	$120	$80	$60	$40

BLACK WIDOW — .177 or .22 cal., barrel break action, 500/450 FPS, unique black plastic stock, 5 lbs.

Mfg.'s Sug. Retail	$150	$115	$75	$50

Grading	100%	98%	95%

R W S
Importers located in Northvale, NJ.

See Dianawerk.

S G S (SPORTING GUNS SELECTION)
Previously Imported By Kendell International.

DUO 300AP — .177 or .22 cal., top cocking action, 455/430 FPS.

$125 $65 $50

DUO 300AR — .177 or .22 cal., top cocking action, 455/430 FPS, with extra stock and barrel assembly to create a 3-in-1 gun.

$250 $125 $80

SAXBY PALMER
Manufactured by Saxby Palmer located in Stratford-Upon-Avon, England. Previously imported/distributed by Marksman Products located in Huntington Beach, CA.

Saxby Palmer has developed the world's first cartridge loading air rifle. This is not a CO2 or other type of compressed gas gun. The cartridges are pressurized (2250 PSI) and reusable facilitating speed of loading and much greater velocities. New rifles are supplied with the table pump (for reloading brass or plastic cartridges) and 10 cartridges. You must have these accessories in order to operate air rifles or pistols. Deduct 50% for used guns without these accessories.

RIFLES: DISCONTINUED

ENSIGN ELITE — .177 or .22 cal., bolt action cartridge, 1000-800 FPS auto safety.

$120 $100 $80

      Last Mfg.'s Sug. Retail was $175.

ENSIGN ROYAL — .177 or .22 cal., bolt action cartridge, 1000-800 FPS auto safety, walnut stock.

$130 $110 $85

      Last Mfg.'s Sug. Retail was $275.

RIFLES

GALAXY — .177 or .22 cal., bolt action cartridge, 1,000/800 FPS, auto safety, walnut stain, hardwood stock. 6½ lbs. Current mfg.

$130 $110 $85

SATURN — .177 or .22 cal., bolt action cartridge, 1,000/800 FPS, auto safety, hi-strength black polymer stock. 6½ lbs. Disc. in 1987.

$130 $110 $85

      Last Mfg.'s Sug. Retail was $175.

REVOLVERS: DISCONTINUED

ORION AIR REVOLVER — .177 cal., 6 shot, compressed gas cartridges (reusable), 550 FPS, 6 in. barrel, 2 lbs. 3 oz. Disc. 1988.

$200 $160 $135

Grading	100%	98%	95%

This model is manufactured by Weihrauch of W. Germany and includes a Slim Jim pump and 12 reuseable cartridges.

This model also came with a 30 grain 38 cal. zinc pellet to allow cartridges to be used in a .38 Special pistol for practice.

MODEL 54 — .177 cal., 5 shot, compressed gas cartridges (reusable), 4 in. barrel, 1 lb. 5 oz. Disc. 1988.

$135 $100 $70

This model is manufactured by Weihrauch of W. Germany and includes a Slim Jim pump and 12 reuseable cartridges.

SHARP
Japan (Imported By Beeman).

SHARP INNOVA — .177 or .22 cal., pneumatic pump action, 920/720 FPS, 4 lbs. 6 oz. Disc. 1988.

$150 $130 $95

Last Mfg.'s Sug. Retail was $175.

SHARP ACE — .177 or .22 cal., pneumatic pump action, 920/750 FPS, 6 lbs. 4 oz. Disc. 1988.

$255 $220 $150

Last Mfg.'s Sug. Retail was $295.

SHERIDAN
Manufactured by Benjamin Air Rifle Co. located in Racine, WI.

SHERIDAN BLUE STREAK/SILVER STREAK — 20 cal., pneumatic pump or CO_2 action, 700 FPS, 6 lbs. Add $5 for Silver Streak, $25 for William S. sight, $30 for 4 x 15 scope, $25 for paint pellet rifle. Deduct $15 for CO_2.

Mfg.'s Sug. Retail	$125	$110	$95	$60

SHERIDAN AIR PISTOL
Model E — 20 cal., CO_2 cartridge, 400 FPS, 6⅜ in. barrel, 2 lbs. 4 oz. Add $40 for paint pellet pistol.

Mfg.'s Sug. Retail	$100	$80	$65	$45

SIG HAMMERLI
Imported by Mandall Shooting Supplies, Inc. located in Scottsdale, AZ.
Sig Hammerli Airguns are not mfg. by Sig in Switzerland, but rather subcontracted to other airgun manufacturers (including El Gamo), these models are German made. Prices may increase or decrease based on the value of dollar on international markets.

RIFLES

MODEL 403 — .177 cal., side lever action, 700 FPS, adj. sight target model, 9¼ lbs.

Mfg.'s Sug. Retail	$400	$275	$200	$150

MODEL 420 — .177 cal., side lever action, 700 FPS, military style plastic stock, 7½ lbs.

Mfg.'s Sug. Retail	$300	$200	$150	$100

STERLING
Manufactured by Benjamin Air Rifle Company located in Racine, WI.

Grading	100%	98%	95%

RIFLES

HR 81—.177 or .20, .22 cal., under lever cocking action, 700/660 FPS, adj. V type rear sight, 8½ lbs. Add $10 for .22 cal.

Mfg.'s Sug. Retail	$300	$260	$200	$145

HR 83—.177, .20 or .22 cal., under lever cocking action, 700/660 FPS, adj. Williams "FP" peep sight, walnut stock, 8½ lbs. Add $5 for .22 cal.

Mfg.'s Sug. Retail	$425	$330	$270	$200

STEYR

Manufactured by Steyr located in Austria. Imported and distributed by Guns South Inc. located in Trussville, AL. and Nygold Precision Products, La Crescents, CA.

CO2 RIFLE — .177 cal., CO2 powered match rifle with precision receiver sight and adj. butt plate. New in 1988.

Mfg.'s Sug. Retail	$1,250	$1,145	$995	$650

Add $150 for left hand.

CO2 PISTOL — .177 cal., CO2 powered match pistol, 15 ⅓ in. overall, 2 lbs. 8 oz.

Mfg.'s Sug. Retail	$965	$895	$760	N/A

THEOBEN ENGINEERING

Manufacturer located in England. Imported by Air Rifle Specialists located in Elmira, NY.

Add $75 for Theoben pump.

SIROCCO COUNTRYMAN — .177 or .22 cal., Anschutz barrel break action, 1,100/800 FPS, unique precharged sealed gas system replaces the springs used in most modern air rifles, not to be confused with a modern gas powered (CO2) air rifle, includes scope rings, barrel weight, walnut stained beech stock, 7½ lbs. Importation disc. in 1987.

	$465	$350	$275

Last Mfg.'s Sug. Retail was $585.

SIROCCO DELUXE — similar to Countryman, except has hand checkered walnut stock. Importation disc. in 1987.

	$750	$500	$300

Last Mfg.'s Sug. Retail was $650.

SIROCCO CLASSIC — similar to Sirocco Deluxe, except has updated floating inertia system in piston chamber and auto safety, variable power, 900/1100 FPS. New in 1987. Add $60 for left hand.

Mfg.'s Sug. Retail	$960	$930	$700	$550

This model is available with either a choked or unchoked Anschutz barrel as standard equipment.

SIROCCO GRAND PRIX — similar specifications to the Sirocco Classic, except has checkered walnut thumbhole stock.

Mfg.'s Sug. Retail	$1,070	$1,040	$940	$600

In 1987, this model was updated with a floating inertia system in piston chamber and auto safety, variable power.

Add $60 for left hand.

Subtract 50% for older models without safety and new piston design.

This model is available with either a choked or unchoked Anschutz barrel as standard equipment.

Grading	100%	98%	95%

ELIMINATOR — .177 or .22 cal., barrel break action, 1100/1400 FPS, variable power, deluxe checkered thumb hole stock with cheekpiece and pad. 9½ lbs. New in 1987.

Mfg.'s Sug. Retail	$1,650	$1,600	$1,300	$750

Add $60 for left hand.

This model incorporates an improved barrel design featuring pronounced rifling for the higher velocity pellets.

IMPERATOR — .22 cal., underlever action, 750 FPS, variable power, walnut hand checkered stock, auto safety. New in 1989.

Mfg.'s Sug. Retail	$1,500	$1,500	$1,350	$850

IMPERATOR SLR 88 — similar to above but with a 7 shot mag.

Mfg.'s Sug. Retail	$1,680	$1,550	$1,400	$950

VENOM ARMS CUSTOM GUNS
United Kingdom.

Venom Arms specializes in customizing Weihrauch firearms manufactured in Germany. A quick review of their latest pricing scedule for custom guns indicate prices may run nearly 100% over the initial cost of the uncustomized gun (see Weihrauch). Many of their airguns are available through MAC-1 Airgun Distributor, Inglewood, CA.

WALTHER
Manufactured in West Germany. Imported by Interarms located in Alexandria, VA.

RIFLES

CG 90 — .177 cal., CO2 powered, tilting block action, 18.9 in. barrel, 10 lbs. 2 oz. New in 1989.

Mfg.'s Sug. Retail	$1,300	$1,125	$975	$650

LG 90 — side lever action, single stroke pneumatic mechanism, professional target, 11 lbs. Prices were not available as this edition went to press.

LGR RIFLE — .177 cal., side lever action, single stroke pneumatic mechanism, 580 FPS (professional target) 10.8 lbs. Add $100 for universal, 10% for left-hand.

Mfg.'s Sug. Retail	$1,250	$1,090	$940	$560

Add $150 for Running Boar Model.

PISTOLS

CP 2 — .177 cal., CO2 powered, 9 in. barrel, 2½ lbs, professional target model.

Mfg.'s Sug. Retail	$850	$735	$500	$400

CP-3 — .177 cal., CO2 powered, professional target model.

Mfg.'s Sug. Retail	$960	$820	$650	$400

CP-5 — .117 cal., CO2 powered, professional target model.

Mfg.'s Sug. Retail	$1,650	$1,425	$1,000	$600

LP 3 AIR PISTOL — .177 cal., single stroke pneumatic action, 405 FPS, 2.8-3.0 lbs. Add $60 for match grade.

	$495	$425	$325

Add $50 for shaped barrel rather than round.

LP 53 — .177 cal.

	$395	$300	$200

Grading	100%	98%	95%

WEBLEY
Manufactured in England. See Beeman.

WEBLEY TRACKER — .177 and .22 cal., barrel cocking action. Add $50 for deluxe.

Mfg.'s Sug. Retail	$250	$240	$210	$170

WEIHRAUCH
Manufactured in W. Germany. Imported by Beeman Precision Arms Inc. located in Santa Rosa, CA.

RIFLES

MODEL 30 — .177 or .20 cal., barrel cocking action, 660 FPS/600 FPS, 40 in. overall, 5.5 lbs. Add $5 for .20 cal.

Mfg.'s Sug. Retail	$180	$145	$125	$100

MODEL 35EB — .177 or .22 cal., barrel-cocking action, 755/660 FPS, 8 lbs. Add $50 for chrome, $10 for .22 cal. Deduct $20 for 35L.

Mfg.'s Sug. Retail	$450	$275	$235	$170

MODEL 50 — .177 cal., barrel cocking action, 705 FPS, 43.1 in. overall, 6.9 lbs.

Mfg.'s Sug. Retail	$200	$160	$140	$110

MODEL 55 — .177 cal., barrel-cocking action, 660-700 FPS, 7.8 lbs. Add $40 for left-hand, $100 for Match, $140 for Tyrolean.

Mfg.'s Sug. Retail	$480	$375	$300	$250

MODEL 77/77CARBINE — .177, .20, or .22 cal., under lever cocking action, 830-710 FPS, 8.9 lbs. Add $30 for left-hand, $15 for .20 cal. (5mm) or .22 cal., $40 for Deluxe, $100 for tyrolean stock.

Mfg.'s Sug. Retail	$450	$360	$285	$225

PISTOLS

HW MODEL 70 — .177 cal., barrel-cocking action, 410 FPS, 2.4 lbs. Add $45 for chrome.

Mfg.'s Sug. Retail	$170	$135	$115	$90

WISCHO
Previously imported by Beeman Precison Arms, Inc. located in Santa Rosa, CA.

WISCHO AIR PISTOL MODEL S-20 STANDARD — .177 cal., barrel-cocking action, 450 FPS, 2.8 lbs. Disc. 1988.

	$95	$80	$45

Last Mfg.'s Sug. Retail was $130

MODEL CM — same as above but target style. Disc. in 1988.

	$110	$100	$70

Last Mfg.'s Sug. Retail was $160.

NOTES

BLACK POWDER

MODERN BLACK POWDER GUNS

Editors Note: With the forecast of war in the gulf following the holidays, I found myself renting a barrage of war movies, perhaps to prepare myself psychologically for what may lie ahead.

On January 15, (the day before Desert Storm), I rented the film "Glory", an outstanding movie depicting events of a Black regiment during the Civil War. This movie made clear what incredible loss of life could be needed to achieve a small military goal.

My mind wondered what uncertainty lie ahead for our troops in the desert. Imagine if we were to fight this war using the technology of more than a century ago. Over a million men on either side of a line in the sand, armed with percussion rifles. Eyes and bayonets fixed, waiting for the call to charge...Even though both sides were confident of their technological edge, Saddam still hoped and prepared for a bloody Civil War style battle.

As "Desert Storm" unfolded I watched our cruise missiles, rockets and laser guided bombs destroy targets with surgical accuracy. Saddam did not get his wish and our ground campaign was conducted with the same expertise as our air strategy, with little loss of coalition forces.

Unlike Saddam, our military was capable of not only developing new technology, but also the strategy to join it into a winning combination.

Congratulations to all who participated in Desert Storm!!

Once again the United States is leading the technological revolution in Black Powder hunting arms. The Kahnke .54 cal., the Thompson Center Scout and the new modern Muzzleloaders Hawk are setting new standards for modern Big Bore Black Powder pistol hunting (the Kahnke .54, actually introduced in 1989, set this trend). Big Bore pistols can provide a true hunting challenge or that sometimes necessary second shot.

1991 is a good year to sell, a cautious year to buy. Due to a lower than normal dollar, many prices on non-domestic goods have increased up to 30%. The good news, many large importers saw this trend and increased inventories to cover this hopefully short lived increase.

A note about pricing: The following section differs from the rest of the book in the number of pricing lines contained. You will notice guns under 95% are not listed and should be heavily scrutinized by the Buyer if one is presented to him (or her) at the trading table. Although many fine shooters exist under 95% condition, their value as collector pieces are negligable. This is due to limited demand for used guns and the relatively low price of many fine guns that are still in "new-in- the-box" condition.

Collectors and shooters wanting to enter the world of black powder guns would be far better off to buy a new gun that is being liquidated because of a blemish or overstock conditions, than to invest in the unknown mechanical condition of a less than 95% gun. Of course, if you find a gun in excellent mechanical shape under 95% condition feel free to buy it for pleasure but not as an investment.

The guns listed in this section are factory assembled, kit guns are also available from many of the below listed manufacturers at substantial savings. They are not included in this section, however. Also, most Black Powder guns under $100 in value are not listed, all prices are rounded to the nearest $5.

ALL ADD-ON'S FOR PRICING LISTED IN THIS SECTION ARE RETAIL WITHOUT DEALER DISCOUNTING. ENGRAVING PRICES ON LESS THAN 100% GUNS SHOULD BE DISCOUNTED BY A MINIMUM OF 50%.

Sincerely,

Patrick M. Lucking

Patrick M. Lucking
Black Powder Editor
Blue Book of Gun Values

ALLEN FIREARMS

Previous importer located in Santa Fe, NM Importing A. Uberti firearms until early in 1987. After Allen Firearms closed, Old-West Gun Co. (now called Cimarron Arms) located in Houston, TX purchased the remaining inventory and is currently selling the balance of Allen Firearms (in addition to ordering new products under their name). Values below have intentionally not been discontinued as they will approximate values for Old- West Gun Co. Uberti Firearms.

Add the following amounts for engraving on handguns:
Add $325 for "A" style engraving (30% coverage).
Add $425 for "B" style engraving (50% coverage).
Add $750 for "C" style engraving (100% coverage).
Add $800 for "Texas Cattlebrands" engraving pattern.

REVOLVERS: PERCUSSION

Grading	100%	98%	95%

1847 WALKER — .44 cal., percussion, charcoal finish, color case hardened frame, hammer, and load lever, brass trim, engraved cylinder, 4.4 lbs.

	100%	98%	95%
	$295	$255	$205

1848 BABY DRAGOON — .31 cal., percussion, 3, 4, or 5 in. barrel, 5 shot, color case hardened frame, hammer, no load lever, engraved cylinder, 1.4 lbs. Add $15 for silver straps and trigger guard.

	$230	$200	$160

DRAGOON (1ST, 2ND, OR 3RD) — .44 cal., percussion, 6 shot, brass grip straps, color case hardened frame, hammer, and load lever, brass trim, 3.9 lbs. Add $15 for silver-plated straps, or cut for stock on 3rd Dragoon Model.

	$245	$215	$170

1849 WELLS FARGO — .31 cal., percussion, 3, 4, or 5 in. octagonal barrel, 5 shot, color case hardened frame, hammer, no load lever, brass trim, 1½ lbs. Add $15 for silver straps.

	$230	$200	$160

1849 POCKET — .31 cal., percussion, with loading lever, 3, 4, or 5 in. barrel, 5 shot, color case hardened frame, hammer, and load lever, brass trim, 1½ lbs. Add $15 for silver straps and trigger guard.

	$235	$205	$165

1851 NAVY — .36 cal., percussion, many styles, loading lever, 6 shot engraved cylinder, 2.8 lbs. Add $95 for stock, $30 for stainless steel, $15 for silver plated strap and trigger guard, or steel strap and trigger guard.

	$235	$205	$165

Grading	100%	98%	95%

1860 ARMY — .44 cal., percussion, 8 in. barrel, 6 shot, loading lever, color case hardened frame, hammer, and load lever, all brass back strap and trigger guard, or steel backstrap and brass trigger guard on fluted cylinder model, 2.6 lbs. Add $95 for stock, $10 for silver plated strap and trigger guard, $25 for stainless steel.

$240 $210 $170

1861 NAVY — .36 cal., percussion, 5 in. barrel, many styles, brass back strap or trigger guard, color case hardened frame, hammer, and load lever, 2½ lbs. Add $15 for silver plated strap and trigger guard, $15 for fluted military cylinder, $25 for stainless steel.

$255 $220 $175

1862 POLICE — .36 cal., percussion, 4½, 5½, or 6½ in. barrel, color case hardened frame, hammer, and load lever, cylinder, semi-fluted or engraved, 1.6 lbs. Add $15 for silver plated straps and trigger guard, $25 for stainless steel.

$230 $200 $160

AUGUSTA CONFEDERATE — .36 cal., percussion, 7½ in. octagonal barrel, color case hardened hammer and trigger, all brass frame, engraved cylinder, 2½-2¾ lbs.

$200 $160 $100

GRISWOLD CONFEDERATE — .36 and .44 cal., percussion, same as above except round barrel, forward of lug, does not have engraved cylinder.

$200 $160 $100

LEECH AND RIGDON CONFEDERATE — .36 cal., percussion, same as above except all steel frame.

$230 $200 $160

TEXAS CONFEDERATE DRAGOON — .44 cal., percussion, 7½ in. round barrel, color case hardened frame, hammer, and load lever, brass trim, "Tucker, Sherrard, & Co.", 4 lbs. Add $35 for stainless steel.

$210 $175 $140

1858 REMINGTON — .44 cal., percussion, 7½ in. barrel, 6 shot, blued steel, brass trigger guard, 2.6 lbs. Add $15 for adj. sights.

$200 $175 $140

1858 REMINGTON STAINLESS — same as above, has brass strap and trigger guard. Add $15 for adj. sights.

$280 $245 $195

1858 REMINGTON NEW NAVY — .36 cal., percussion, 6½ in. octagonal barrel, 6 shot, blue frame, 2½ lbs. Add $15 for adj. sights.

$185 $160 $120

1866 REVOLVING CARBINE — 44 cal., percussion, 18 in. barrel, 6 shot, blued steel, brass trigger guard, walnut stock, 4.6 lbs.

$335 $280 $150

RIFLES

HAWKEN SANTA FE — .53 cal., percussion, single shot, 32 in. oct. barrel, damascened finish, double set triggers, 9½ lbs., walnut stock.

$395 $345 $250

Grading	100%	98%	95%

ST. LOUIS RIFLE — .45, .50, .54, or .58 cal., flintlock and percussion, color case hardened hammer lock and trigger guard, octagonal barrel. Add $15 for .54 or .58 cal., percussion, $15 for flint lock, $30 for 50 cal. flint lock.

$300 $265 $190

SQUIRREL RIFLE — .32 cal., percussion or flintlock, color case hardened hammer and lock, brass trigger guard, 28 in. octagonal barrel. Add $15 for flint lock.

$250 $205 $150

BLACKPOWDER CARTRIDGE

See "Uberti".

ARMI SAN MARCO

Mfg. in Italy, currently imported by Denver Arms (formerly House Of Muskets) Located in Pagosa Springs, CO. and Muzzle Loaders Inc located in Burke, VA, And E.M.F., Located In Santa Ana, CA.

REVOLVERS: PERCUSSION

WALKER MODEL 1847 — .44 cal., percussion, 9 in. barrel, color case hardened frame, loading lever and hammer, brass trigger guard and steel backstrap, 4½ lbs.

$190 $165 $120

BABY DRAGOON — .31 cal., percussion, 5 in. octagonal barrel, 5 shot cylinder, color case hardened frame, hammer and load lever, silver plated brass backstrap and trigger guard.

$180 $150 $90

1ST MODEL DRAGOON — .44 cal., percussion, 8 in. barrel, color case hardened frame, loading lever and hammer, silver plated brass backstrap and trigger guard.

$200 $175 $130

2ND MODEL DRAGOON — same as 1st Model Dragoon, except 7½ in. barrel.

$200 $175 $130

3RD MODEL DRAGOON — .44 cal., percussion, 7½ in. barrel, Western Model has silver plated brass backstrap, Military Model has steel backstrap - cut for stock, Texas Model has brass backstrap. Add $15 for Western Model.

$200 $175 $130

1851 NAVY — .36 or .44 cal., percussion, 7½ in. octagonal barrel, engraved (roll) cylinder, color case hardened frame and load lever, silver plated brass backstrap and square back trigger guard. Sheriff's Model has 5 in. barrel, brass trigger guard and backstrap. Deduct $20 for brass back strap and trigger guard, $25 for brass frame.

$105 $90 $70

1860 ARMY — .44 cal., percussion 8 in. round barrel, color case hardened frame, hammer and load lever, Sheriff's Model has 5 in. barrel, 2¾ lbs. Add $5 for Sheriff's Model. Deduct $25 for brass frame or fluted cylinder model.

$105 $90 $70

Grading	100%	98%	95%

1861 NAVY — .36 cal., percussion, 7½ in. round barrel, color case hardened frame, hammer and load lever, silver plated brass backstrap and trigger guard (very similar to 1860 Army, except cal. and shorter Navy grips).

$175 $150 $110

RIFLES

HAWKENS — .50 cal., percussion, 30 in. octagonal chrome lined barrel, brass patchbox, target sights, double set triggers, 8 lbs.

$245 $215 $160

ST. LOUIS HAWKEN — .50, .54, or .58 cal., percussion, color case hardened hammer and lock, 28 in. octagonal barrel, brass trim, 7 lbs. 15 oz. Add $65 for curly maple stock.

$225 $200 $140

ROCKY MOUNTAIN SHORT RIFLE — .50 cal., percussion, 24 in. octagonal barrel, brass furniture.

$225 $200 $140

ARMI SAN PAOLO

Mfg. in Italy. Armi San Paolo is a wholly owned subsidiary of Euroarms of Europe which also owns Euroarms of America. See Euroarms section for pricing. Previously imported by Kendall International located in Paris, KY and Muzzle Loaders, Inc. located in Burke, VA).

ARMSPORT

Importers located in Miami, FL.

PISTOLS

CORSAIR PISTOL — .44 cal., percussion, double barrel, blued finish, color case hardened hammer and lock, brass trim.

$250 $200 $130

DUELING PISTOL — .45 cal., percussion, blued finish, color case hardened hammer and lock, brass trim.

$150 $130 $100

KENTUCKY PISTOL — .45 or .50 cal., percussion or flintlock, blued finish, color case hardened hammer and lock, brass trim. Add $10 for flint lock.

$130 $105 $80

MODEL 1847 COLT WALKER REVOLVER — .44 cal., percussion, color case hardened frame, hammer, and load lever, brass trigger guard, steel backstrap, 6 shot, 4½ lbs.
Mfg.'s Sug. Retail $295 $255 $220 $145

MODEL 1851 COLT NAVY — .36 or .44 cal., percussion, brass or color case hardened frame, brass trigger guard and backstrap, 6 shot. Add $30 for color case hardened steel with engraved cylinders. Add $130 for engraved gold and silver.
Mfg.'s Sug. Retail $150 $125 $110 $80

Grading	100%	98%	95%	

MODEL 1860 COLT ARMY — .44 cal., percussion, brass frame, trigger guard, and backstrap, color case hardened hammer and load lever, 6 shot. Add $50 for color case hardened steel, $25 for Steel Sheriff Model, $180 for stainless steel, $130 for engraved gold and silver.

Mfg.'s Sug. Retail	$150	$125	$110	$80

MODEL 1858 REMINGTON ARMY— .44 cal., percussion, blued frame, brass trigger guard, steel backstrap, 6 shot. Add $130 for stainless steel, $80 for engraved gold and silver, $170 for stainless Target Model. Deduct $50 for brass frame, $25 for nickel plated brass.

Mfg.'s Sug. Retail	$210	$185	$160	$115

REMINGTON BUFFALO TARGET — .44 cal., percussion, 12 in. octagonal barrel, brass frame and trigger guard, adj. sights, based on 1858 Navy frame, 38 oz. Add $20 for nickel plated brass.

Mfg.'s Sug. Retail	$200	$175	$150	$110

RIFLES

BRISTOL KID RIFLE— .32 or .36 cal., percussion. Add $15 for standard version, $25 for deluxe. Discontinued in 1984.

	$175	$150	$100

HAWKEN RIFLE — .45, .50, .54 or .58 cal., percussion or flintlock, color case hardened hammer and lock, percussion cap holder in stock, chrome lined barrels. Add $25 for flintlock.

	$200	$175	$130

HAWKENTUCKY RIFLE — .36, or .50 cal., percussion or flintlock, color case hardened hammer and lock, percussion cap holder in stock, chrome lined barrels. Add $10 for flintlock.

	$195	$160	$125

KENTUCKY RIFLE — .36, .45, or .50, cal., percussion or flintlock, color case hardened hammer and lock, percussion cap holder in stock, chrome lined barrels, brass trim. Add $10 for flintlock, $55 for deluxe with engraved white steel hammer and lock.

	$225	$195	$155

TRYON TRAILBLAZER — .50, .53, or .54 cal., percussion, color case hardened hammer and lock, cap holder in stock. Add $45 for deluxe engraved.

	$310	$265	$205

SHOTGUNS

KENTUCKY RIFLE/SHOTGUN COMBO — .45 or .50 cal., 20 ga., percussion only, same as above.

	$310	$250	$165

DOUBLE BARREL SHOTGUN— 12 or 10 ga., percussion only, blued finish, color case hardened hammer and lock. Add $50 for 10 ga.

	$410	$350	$250

CANNONS

BORDA CANNON — .50 cal. wick, nickle plated.

Mfg.'s Sug. Retail	$195	$165	$145	$110

Add $100 for gold plating.

NAPOLEON CANNON — .45 or .75 wick, nickel plated. Deduct $250 for .45 cal. Add for gold plating .75 cal. $175, .45 $110.

Mfg.'s Sug. Retail	$575	$495	$430	$315

YORKTOWN CANNON— .50 cal. wick, nickle plated. Add $100 for gold plating.

Mfg.'s Sug. Retail	$195	$165	$145	$110

Grading	100%	98%	95%

ASSOCIATION FOR THE PRESERVATION OF WESTERN ANTIQUITY

Distributed by William Benjamin Ltd. in Ashville, NC.

1862 COLT NAVY— .36 cal., percussion, standard construction, roll engraved cylinder with 24Kt. gold inlay, only 100 revolvers made, sold in custom cameo art presentation case depicting a miner panning for gold, some sets may come with the addition of a seated Liberty silver dollar and a Double Eagle gold piece, coins value should be based on current numismatic value, present retail for entire set including gold pieces is $2,395.

Mfg.'s Sug. Retail　　　$995　$895　$795　$695

BENSON FIREARMS, LTD.

Previous importer/distributor of A. Uberti Firearms mfg. in Italy. Benson Firearms was located in Seattle, WA.

Benson Firearms was a recent importer (1987-1988) and imported A. Uberti firearms that were marked "Benson Firearms Seattle, WA". In 1989 Benson Firearms, Ltd. combined with Uberti USA, Inc. located in New Milford, CT.

All guns were manufactured to the same exact specifications as the originals. Crafted with an unmistakable fire blue finish. A. Uberti is one of the largest manufacturers of black powder firearms.

Add the following amounts for engraving on handguns:
Add $325 for "A" style engraving (30% coverage).
Add $425 for "B" style engraving (50% coverage).
Add $750 for "C" style engraving (100% coverage).
Add $800 for "Texas Cattlebrands" engraving pattern.

REVOLVERS

1847 WALKER—.44 cal., percussion, charcoal finish, color case hardened frame, hammer, and load lever, brass trim, engraved cylinder, 4.4 lbs.

　　　　$295　$255　$205

1848 BABY DRAGOON — .31 cal., percussion, 3, 4, or 5 in. barrel, 5 shot, color case hardened frame, hammer, no load lever, engraved cylinder, 1.4 lbs. Add $15 for silver straps and trigger guard.

　　　　$230　$200　$160

DRAGOON (1ST, 2ND, OR 3RD) — .44 cal., percussion, 6 shot, brass grip straps, color case hardened frame, hammer, and load lever, brass trim, 3.9 lbs. Add $15 for silver-plated straps, or cut for stock on 3rd Dragoon Model.

　　　　$245　$215　$170

1849 WELLS FARGO — .31 cal., percussion, 3, 4, or 5 in. octagonal barrel, 5 shot, color case hardened frame, hammer, no load lever, brass trim, 1½ lbs. Add $15 for silver straps.

　　　　$230　$200　$160

1849 POCKET — .31 cal., percussion, with loading lever, 3, 4, or 5 in. barrel, 5 shot, color case hardened frame, hammer, and load lever, brass trim, 1½ lbs. Add $15 for silver straps and trigger guard.

　　　　$235　$205　$165

Grading	100%	98%	95%

1851 NAVY — .36 cal., percussion, many styles, loading lever, 6 shot engraved cylinder, 2.8 lbs. Add $95 for stock, $30 for stainless steel, $15 for silver plated strap and trigger guard, or steel strap and trigger guard.

$235 $205 $165

1860 ARMY — .44 cal., percussion, 8 in. barrel, 6 shot, loading lever, color case hardened frame, hammer, and load lever, all brass back strap and trigger guard, or steel backstrap and brass trigger guard on fluted cylinder model, 2.6 lbs. Add $95 for stock, $10 for silver plated strap and trigger guard, $25 for stainless steel.

$240 $210 $170

1861 NAVY — .36 cal., percussion, 5 in. barrel, many styles, brass back strap or trigger guard, color case hardened frame, hammer, and load lever, 2½ lbs. Add $15 for silver plated strap and trigger guard, $15 for fluted military cylinder, $25 for stainless steel.

$255 $220 $175

1862 POLICE — .36 cal., percussion, 4½, 5½, or 6½ in. barrel, color case hardened frame, hammer, and load lever, cylinder, semi-fluted or engraved, 1.6 lbs. Add $15 for silver plated straps and trigger guard, $25 for stainless steel.

$230 $200 $160

AUGUSTA CONFEDERATE — .36 cal., percussion, 7½ in. octagonal barrel, color case hardened hammer and trigger, all brass frame, engraved cylinder, 2½-2¾ lbs.

$200 $160 $100

GRISWOLD CONFEDERATE—.36 and .44 cal., percussion, same as above except round barrel, forward of lug, does not have engraved cylinder.

$200 $160 $100

LEECH AND RIGDON CONFEDERATE — .36 cal., percussion, same as above except all steel frame.

$230 $200 $160

TEXAS CONFEDERATE DRAGOON — .44 cal., percussion, 7½ in. round barrel, color case hardened frame, hammer, and load lever, brass trim, "Tucker, Sherrard, & Co.", 4 lbs. Add $35 for stainless steel.

$210 $175 $110

1858 REMINGTON— .44 cal., percussion, 7½ in. barrel, 6 shot, blued steel, brass trigger guard, 2.6 lbs. Add $15 for adj. sights.

$200 $175 $140

1858 REMINGTON STAINLESS — same as above, has brass strap and trigger guard. Add $15 for adj. sights.

$280 $245 $195

1858 REMINGTON NEW NAVY — .36 cal., percussion, 6½ in. octagonal barrel, 6 shot, blue frame, 2½ lbs. Add $15 for adj. sights.

$185 $160 $120

1866 REVOLVING CARBINE— 44 cal., percussion, 18 in. barrel, 6 shot, blued steel, brass trigger guard, walnut stock, 4.6 lbs.

$335 $280 $150

RIFLES

HAWKEN SANTA FE — .53 cal., percussion, single shot, 32 in. oct. barrel, damascened finish, double set triggers, 9½ lbs., walnut stock.

$395 $245 $250

Grading	100%	98%	95%

BLACKPOWDER CARTRIDGE
See "Uberti".

BERETTA
Manufacturer located in Brescia, Italy. 1680-present.
SHOTGUNS

COMMEMORATIVE O/U MODEL M1000 — 12 ga., percussion, 30 in. barrel, limited production.

$365 $285 $225

Last Mfg.'s Sug. Retail was $840.

BONDINI
Manufacturer located in Italy. Imported by Helmut Hofman, Inc. located in Placitas, NH. Previously imported by House Of Muskets located in Pagosa Lakes, CO, some models now imported by Austin-Sheridan, USA Middlefield, CT.
PISTOLS

ASHABELLA COOK UNDERHAMMER — .45 cal., unique underhammer design uses trigger guard as mainspring. Very accurate.

$150 $110 $80

WM. PARKER PISTOL — .45 cal., flintlock or percussion, 11 in. octagonal browned barrel, silver plated furniture, double set triggers. Add $10 for flintlock.

$220 $185 $150

F. ROCHATTE — .45 cal., percussion, round barrel, single set triggers, hand checkered stock.

$220 $185 $150

RIFLES

SANFTL SCHUETZEN RIFLE — .45 cal., percussion, 31 in. octagonal barrel, unique backward lock, both peep and open iron sights, Schuetzen style butt plate and trigger guard, brass furniture.

$595 $495 $385

SHOTGUNS

GALLYON SHOTGUN — 12 ga., percussion, blued barrel, single shot. Add $150 for extra 12 ga. barrel.

$250 $210 $180

BROWNING
Headquarters located in Morgan, UT.

RIFLES

JONATHAN BROWNING MOUNTAIN RIFLE — 50 cal., percussion, 30 in. octagon barrel, single set trigger, engraved lock plate, select walnut stock, cased with medallion, 1,000 produced in 1978. Issue price — $650.

$500 $420 $375

Grading	100%	98%	95%

MOUNTAIN RIFLE— same as Jonathan Browning Mountain Rifle, without Centennial embellishments, not cased. Also in .45 or .54 cal.

	$225	$200	$170

CHARLES DALY
See Daly, Charles.

CHENEY RIFLE WORKS
Williamstown, WV. Distributed by Mountain State Muzzle Loading Supplies. Manufactured by Mowrey Gun Works, Waldron, IN.

PLAINS RIFLE — .50 & .54 percussion, 32 in. octagonal barrel, fancy maple stock, furniture is brass or browned steel, single set double action trigger, 9 lbs.

Mfg.'s Sug. Retail	$495	$415	$365	$290

PRAIRIE RIFLE— .36, .40, .45 and .50 cal., percussion, 32 in. barrel, furniture is brass or browned steel, double set triggers, fancy figure maple stock, wt. 8 lbs.

Mfg.'s Sug. Retail	$495	$455	$395	$310

SUMMIT RIFLE — .50 and .54 cal. percussion, 30 in. octagonal barrel, furniture is brass or browned steel, single set double action trigger, fancy figure maple stock, wt. 9 lbs.

Mfg.'s Sug. Retail	$485	$450	$390	$300

CIMARRON ARMS COMPANY
Importer/distributor of custom crafted A. Uberti Modern and Blackpowder Firearms. Cimarron Arms is located in Houston, TX.

Cimarron Arms was previously named Old-West Gun Company.

> After years of research, Cimarron Arms Co. has contracted A. Uberti to manufacture the most authentic western firearms reproductions to date, including such exact modifications as changing the taper of the cylinder face to exactly match the original Colt's. Also, serial number location, cylinder scenes, stock configuration, etc. have all been carefully manufactured to duplicate the original.

Add the following amounts for engraving on handguns:

Add $325 for "A" style engraving (30% coverage).

Add $425 for "B" style engraving (50% coverage).

Add $750 for "C" style engraving (100% coverage).

Add $800 for "Texas Cattlebrands" engraving pattern.

REVOLVERS

1847 WALKER— .44 cal., percussion, charcoal finish, color case hardened frame, hammer, and load lever, brass trim, engraved cylinder, 4.4 lbs.

Mfg.'s Sug. Retail	$270	$260	$225	$180

1848 BABY DRAGOON — .31 cal., percussion, 3, 4, or 5 in. barrel, 5 shot, color case hardened frame, hammer, no load lever, engraved cylinder, 1.4 lbs. Add $15 for silver straps and trigger guard.

Mfg.'s Sug. Retail	$215	$205	$180	$145

DRAGOON (1ST, 2ND, OR 3RD) — .44 cal., percussion, 6 shot, brass grip straps, color case hardened frame, hammer, and load lever, brass trim, 3.9 lbs. Add $20 for silver-plated straps, or cut for stock on 3rd Dragoon Model. Add $145 for stock.

Mfg.'s Sug. Retail	$230	$220	$190	$150

Grading	100%	98%	95%

1849 WELLS FARGO — .31 cal., percussion, 3, 4, or 5 in. octagonal barrel, 5 shot, color case hardened frame, hammer, no load lever, brass trim, 1½ lbs. Add $15 for silver straps.

Mfg.'s Sug. Retail	$215	$205	$180	$145

1849 POCKET — .31 cal., percussion, with loading lever, 3, 4, or 5 in. barrel, 5 shot, color case hardened frame, hammer, and load lever, brass trim, 1½ lbs. Add $15 for silver straps and trigger guard.

Mfg.'s Sug. Retail	$215	$205	$180	$145

1851 NAVY — .36 cal., percussion, many styles, loading lever, 6 shot engraved cylinder, 2.8 lbs. Add $130 for stock, $45 for stainless steel, $15 for silver plated strap and trigger guard, or steel strap and trigger guard, for London model or cut for stock 3rd model.

Mfg.'s Sug. Retail	$215	$205	$180	$145

1860 ARMY — .44 cal., percussion, 8 in. barrel, 6 shot, loading lever, color case hardened frame, hammer, and load lever, all brass back strap and trigger guard, or steel backstrap and brass trigger guard on fluted cylinder model, 2.6 lbs. Add $145 for stock, $15 for silver plated strap and trigger guard, $10 for cut for stock or fluted cylinder model (except on civilian model), $50 for stainless steel.

Mfg.'s Sug. Retail	$230	$220	$190	$150

1861 NAVY — .36 cal., percussion, 5 in. barrel, many styles, brass back strap or trigger guard, color case hardened frame, hammer, and load lever, 2½ lbs. Add $15 for silver plated strap and trigger guard, $10 for cut- for-stock or fluted military cylinder (except on civilian model), $50 for stainless steel, $145 for shoulder stock.

Mfg.'s Sug. Retail	$230	$220	$195	$155

1862 POLICE — .36 cal., percussion, 4½, 5½, or 6½ in. barrel, color case hardened frame, hammer, and load lever, cylinder, semi-fluted or engraved, 1.6 lbs. Add $15 for silver plated straps and trigger guard, $50 for stainless steel.

Mfg.'s Sug. Retail	$215	$205	$180	$145

1862 POCKET NAVY — .36 cal., percussion, 4½, 5½, or 6½ in. barrel, color case hardened frame, hammer, and load lever, cylinder, semi-fluted or engraved, 1.6 lbs. Add $15 for silver plated straps and trigger guard, $50 for stainless steel.

Mfg.'s Sug. Retail	$215	$205	$180	$145

AUGUSTA CONFEDERATE — .36 cal., percussion, 7½ in. octagonal barrel, color case hardened hammer and trigger, all brass frame, engraved cylinder, 2½-2¾ lbs.

	$175	$150	$120

Last Mfg.'s Sug. Retail was $150.

GRISWOLD AND GUNNISON CONFEDERATE— .36 or .44 cal., percussion, same as above except round barrel, forward of lug, does not have engraved cylinder.

	$175	$150	$120

Last Mfg.'s Sug. Retail was $150.

LEECH AND RIGDON CONFEDERATE — .36 cal., percussion, same as above except all steel frame.

	$185	$160	$125

Last Mfg.'s Sug. Retail was $200.

TEXAS CONFEDERATE DRAGOON — .44 cal., percussion, 7½ in. round barrel, color case hardened frame, hammer, and load lever, brass trim, "Tucker, Sherrard, & Co.", 4 lbs.

	$195	$170	$125

Last Mfg.'s Sug. Retail was $210.

Grading	100%	98%	95%

1858 REMINGTON— .44 cal., percussion, 7½ in. barrel, 6 shot, blued steel, brass trigger guard, 2.6 lbs. Add $25 for adj. sights.

Mfg.'s Sug. Retail $200 $190 $165 $130

1858 REMINGTON STAINLESS — same as above, has brass strap and trigger guard. Add $20 for adj. sights.

$240 $215 $180

Last Mfg.'s Sug. Retail was $260.

1858 REMINGTON NEW NAVY — .36 cal., percussion, 6½ in. octagonal barrel, 6 shot, blue frame, 2½ lbs. Add $25 for adj. sights.

$190 $165 $130

Last Mfg.'s Sug. Retail was $185.

1866 REVOLVING CARBINE— .44 cal., percussion, 18 in. barrel, 6 shot, blued steel, brass trigger guard, walnut stock, 4.6 lbs.

$300 $260 $200

Last Mfg.'s Sug. Retail was $320.

RIFLES: PERCUSSION

HAWKEN SANTA FE — .53 cal., single shot, 32 in. oct. barrel, damascened finish, double set triggers, 9½ lbs., walnut stock.

$360 $315 $250

Last Mfg.'s Sug. Retail was $350.

JEREDIAH SMITH SANTA FE HAWKENS — .50 and .54 cal. percussion, similar to above. Add $35 for Flintlock.

Mfg.'s Sug. Retail $380 $360 $315 $250

LEMAN TRADE RIFLE— .45, .50, .54, and .58 cal. percussion. Add $15 for .54 and .58 cal.

Mfg.'s Sug. Retail $250 $230 $200 $160

ST. LOUIS RIFLE — .45, .50, .54, or .58 cal., flintlock and percussion, color case hardened hammer lock and trigger guard, octagonal barrel. Add $15 for .54 and .58 cal. percussion, $15 for flintlock, $30 for 50 cal. flintlock.

$300 $250 $210

Last Mfg.'s Sug. Retail was $280.

BLACKPOWDER CARTRIDGE

ROLLING BLOCK SPORTING RIFLE — .45/.70 blackpowder catridge, 30 in. barrel. Add $100 for deluxe sporting rifle.

Mfg.'s Sug. Retail $620 $560 $495 $395

COLT'S FIREARMS

Hartford, CT. Colt subcontracted mfr. of these Black Powder pistols to Aldo Uberti in Italy. Parts were shipped into the U.S. and assembled stateside. **SEE PAGE 922 FOR THIS 2ND GENERATION SERIALIZATION AND PRODUCTION TOTALS.**

WALKER MODEL— .44 cal., 9 in. barrel, color case hardened frame, hammer, and loading lever, 73 oz., mfg. 1979-1981. Add $100 for cased Heritage Walker Commemorative Model.

$750 $575 $465

Last Mfg.'s Sug. Retail was $500.

Grading	100%	98%	95%

BABY DRAGOON — .31 cal., 4 in. barrel, unfluted straight cylinder, color case hardened frame, short frame. Discontinued.

	$300	$240	$200

Last Mfg.'s Sug. Retail was $500.

"1 of 500" cased set

	$600	$450	$350

Last Mfg.'s Sug. Retail was $900.

1ST MODEL DRAGOON—.44 cal., 7½ in. barrel, oval bolt cuts in cylinder, color case hardened frame, loading lever, plunger, and hammer, one piece stocks, 66 oz. Discontinued in 1981.

	$395	$250	$195

Last Mfg.'s Sug. Retail was $300.

2ND MODEL DRAGOON — .44 cal., 7½ in. barrel, rectangular bolt cuts in cylinder, color case hardened frame, loading lever, plunger, and hammer, one piece stocks, 66 oz. Discontinued in 1981.

	$395	$250	$195

Last Mfg.'s Sug. Retail was $300.

3RD MODEL DRAGOON — .44 cal., 7½ in. barrel, rectangular bolt cuts in cylinder, color case hardened frame, loading lever, plunger, and hammer, round trigger guard, one piece stocks, 66 oz. Discontinued in 1981. Add $400 for cased Giuseppe Garibaldi Commemorative Model.

	$395	$250	$195

Last Mfg.'s Sug. Retail was $300.

1851 NAVY — .36 cal., 7½ in. octagonal barrel, color case hardened frame, loading lever, plunger, and hammer, square trigger guard, one piece stocks, 42 oz. Discontinued in 1981.

	$375	$225	$180

Last Mfg.'s Sug. Retail was $350.

1851 Stainless Navy — stainless steel, only 498 mfg.

	$695	$500	$395

1860 ARMY—.44 cal., 8 in. round barrel, color case hardened frame, loading lever, plunger, and hammer, round trigger guard, one piece stocks, 42 oz. Discontinued in 1981. Two versions made, one has an engraved rebated cylinder and the other has a blued fluted cylinder. Add $125 (over Fluted Cylinder Model) for 1982 Stainless Steel version.

Fluted Cylinder	$495	$375	$250
Rebated Cylinder	$525	$400	$300

Last Mfg.'s Sug. Retail was $350.

1861 NAVY — .36 cal., 7½ in. round barrel, color case hardened frame, loading lever, plunger, and hammer, round trigger guard, one piece stocks, 42 oz. Discontinued in 1981. Add $125 for 1982 Stainless Steel version.

	$395	$250	$200

Last Mfg.'s Sug. Retail was $300.

1862 POCKET NAVY — .36 cal., 5½ in. octagonal barrel, color case hardened frame, loading lever, plunger, and hammer, round trigger guard, one piece stocks, 27 oz. Discontinued in 1981. Add $200 for 1982 Stainless Steel version.

	$375	$275	$225

Last Mfg.'s Sug. Retail was $300.

"1 of 500" cased set

	$525	$440	$320

Last Mfg.'s Sug. Retail was $500.

Grading	100%	98%	95%	

1862 POCKET POLICE — .36 cal., 5½ in. round barrel, color case hardened frame, loading lever, plunger, and hammer, round trigger guard, fluted cylinder, one piece stocks, 25 oz. Discontinued in 1981. Add $175 for 1982 Stainless Steel version.

	$375	$225	$200

Last Mfg.'s Sug. Retail was $300.

"1 of 500" cased

	$500	$400	$320

Last Mfg.'s Sug. Retail was $500.

CONNECTICUT VALLEY ARMS

Distributed in Norcross, GA.

All pistols have color case hardened finishes with solid brass trim.

PISTOLS

COLONIAL PISTOL — .45 cal., percussion, 6¾ in. octagonal barrel, 31 oz. New in 1989.

Mfg.'s Sug. Retail	$150	$115	$100	$80

CVA "HAWKINS" PISTOL — .50 cal., percussion or flintlock, 9¾ in. octagonal barrel, 50 oz. Add $10 for flintlock.

Mfg.'s Sug. Retail	$220	$165	$145	$115

STANDARD KENTUCKY PISTOL — .45 or .50 cal., percussion, 10¼ in. octagonal barrel, brass blade front sight, 40 oz.

Mfg.'s Sug. Retail	$200	$155	$135	$110

MOUNTAIN PISTOL — .45 or .50 cal., percussion, 9 in. octagonal barrel, German silver wedge plate with pewter cap, 40 oz.

	$150	$115	$80

PHILADELPHIA DERRINGER — .45 cal., percussion, 3¼ in. octagonal barrel, 16 oz.

Mfg.'s Sug. Retail	$120	$90	$80	$65

SIBER PISTOL — .45 cal., percussion, 10½ in. octagonal, white steel engraved barrel, lock also engraved white steel, checkered walnut grip, 38 oz.

Mfg.'s Sug. Retail	$580	$445	$385	$260

TOWER PISTOL — .45 cal., percussion, 9 in. octagonal barrel at breach tapers to round, antique brass trigger, 36 oz.

	$125	$100	$80

REVOLVERS

All revolvers have solid brass trim and walnut grips.

COLT WALKER MODEL — .44 cal., percussion, 9 in. barrel, color case hardened frame, hammer, and loading lever, 72 oz.

Mfg.'s Sug. Retail	$360	$275	$240	$180

3RD MODEL DRAGOON — .44 cal., percussion, 7½ in. barrel, rectangular bolt cuts in cylinder, color case hardened frame, loading lever, plunger, and hammer, round trigger guard, one piece stocks, 66 oz.

Mfg.'s Sug. Retail	$305	$240	$205	$140

WELLS FARGO — .31 cal., percussion, 3, 4, or 5 in. octagonal barrel, 5 shot, color case hardened frame, hammer, no load lever, brass trim, 1½ lbs. Add $65 for steel frame.

Mfg.'s Sug. Retail	$165	$130	$110	$85

Grading	100%	98%	95%

1851 NAVY — .36 cal., percussion, 7½ in. octagonal barrel, brass frame, 38 oz. Add $50 for steel frame.

Mfg.'s Sug. Retail	$180	$140	$120	$90

CVA COLT POCKET POLICE — .36 cal., 5½ in. round barrel, color case hardened frame, loading lever, plunger, and hammer, round trigger guard, fluted cylinder, one piece stocks, 25 oz. Add $55 for steel frame.

Mfg.'s Sug. Retail	$180	$140	$120	$90

1860 ARMY—.44 cal., percussion, 8 in. round barrel, 6 shot engraved cylinder, color case hardened frame, trigger, and load lever, 44 oz.

Mfg.'s Sug. Retail	$300	$230	$200	$140

1861 NAVY — .36 or .44 cal., percussion, 7½ in. round barrel, 6 shot engraved cylinder, color case hardened frame, trigger, and load lever, or brass frame (.44 cal. only), 44 oz. Add $60 for color case hardened steel frame, $60 for presentation grade Sheriff's Model (new in 1986).

Mfg.'s Sug. Retail	$185	$145	$125	$90

Add $10 for brass frame on Standard Sheriff Model.

Add $25 for steel frame on Standard Sheriff Model.

WAR AND PEACE — .36 cal., 1851 Navy and 1851 Sheriff's Model, heavily engraved in rosewood presentation case.

	$500	$420	$335

Last Mfg.'s Sug. Retail was $630.

1873 COLT SINGLE ACTION — .44 cal. percussion, 7 in. round barrel, brass back strap and trigger guard, color case hardened frame and cylinder, new in 1991 (this is a ball and cap version of the 1873 Colt Cartridge gun).

Mfg.'s Sug. Retail	$420	$325	N/A	N/A

1858 REMINGTON ARMY — .44 cal., percussion, 8 in. octagonal barrel, color case hardened hammer, steel or brass frame, 38 oz. Add $60 for steel.

Mfg.'s Sug. Retail	$215	$160	$140	$95

REMINGTON BISON — .44 cal., percussion, 1858 Remington Army frame brass, 10¼ in. octagonal barrel, adj. sights, 3 lbs.

Mfg.'s Sug. Retail	$315	$245	$210	$155

REMINGTON POCKET — .31 cal., percussion, 5 shot, 4 in. octagonal barrel, brass frame, 15 oz. New in 1989.

Mfg.'s Sug. Retail	$165	$125	$110	$80

REMINGTON TARGET — .44 cal., percussion, 12 in. octagonal barrel, brass frame and trigger guard, adj. sights, based on 1858 Navy frame, 38 oz.

Mfg.'s Sug. Retail	$310	$235	$205	$140

OFFICER AND THE GENTLEMAN—matched set .44 cal., 1858 Rem. Army and .31 cal. Pocket Rem., heavily engraved in rosewood presentation case.

	$500	$420	$335

Last Mfg.'s Sug. Retail was $650.

Grading	100%	98%	95%

RIFLES

APOLLO 90 RIFLE/CARBINE — .50 cal. percussion, straight-thru ignition, 27 in. round tapered barrel with chrome bore, slide bolt design, similar to Gonic Arms, Monte Carlo stock, adj. sights, 7 lbs., 8 oz. Add $75 for premier grade.

Mfg.'s Sug. Retail $450 $345 $300 $225

Subtract $125 for laminated stock (new 1991).

BLAZER RIFLE — .50 cal., percussion, straight ignition (like Percussion Revolver), 28 in. octagonal barrel, stainless steel nipple, brass tipped ramrod, 6 lbs, 12 oz. Deduct $10 for Blazer II.

Mfg.'s Sug. Retail $210 $160 $140 $100

BLUNDERBUSS — .69 cal., flintlock, 16 in. tapered to flared muzzle barrel, brass trim, available right or left-hand, 5 lbs. 5 oz.

                              $220 $185 $150

Last Mfg.'s Sug. Retail was $255.

EXPRESS RIFLE — .50 or .54 cal., percussion, double barrel, 28 in. tapered round barrel, color case hardened plate, hammers and trim, adj. sights. Add $375 for presentation grade (new in 1986).

Mfg.'s Sug. Retail $650 $490 $430 $330

Add $160 for extra set of 12 ga. barrels.

FRONTIER RIFLE — .45 or .50 cal., percussion or flintlock, 28 in. octagonal barrel, brass trim, right or left hand, 7 lbs. 15 oz. Add $10 for flintlock, $10 for left-hand, deduct $40 for carbine model.

Mfg.'s Sug. Retail $260 $200 $175 $125

HAWKEN RIFLE/CARBINE — .50 or .54 cal., percussion or flintlock, 28 in. octagonal chrome bore barrel, brass trim, beaver tail select walnut stock, 7 lbs. 15 oz. Add $10 for flintlock.

Mfg.'s Sug. Retail $390 $300 $260 $165

Deduct $120 for Hunter Hawken rifle or Carbine.

HUNTER HAWKEN RIFLE/CARBINE — .50 and .54 cal., percussion, 28 in. (24 in. carbine) octagonal barrel, color casehardened lock and nipple, sling swivels, adj. hunting sights. 8 lbs.

Mfg.'s Sug. Retail $360 $255 $220 $160

Add $70 for premier grade (.50 cal. only).

KENTUCKY RIFLE/HUNTER — .45 or .50 cal., percussion or flintlock, 33½ in. octagonal barrel, color case hardened hammer and plate, antique brass trigger, 7 lbs. 4 oz. Add $10 for flintlock, or adj. hunting sights.

Mfg.'s Sug. Retail $330 $255 $220 $150

MISSOURI HUNTER RIFLE — .50 cal. percussion, 28 in. octagonal barrel, adjustable hunting sights, color case hardened hammer and lock recoil pad, 9 lbs. 6 oz. New 1991.

Mfg.'s Sug. Retail $300 $240   N/A   N/A

MISSOURI RANGER — .50 cal., percussion, 28 in. octagonal barrel, color case hardened trim, right or left hand, 7 lb. 8 oz.

                              $170 $150 $110

MOUNTAIN RIFLE — .50 and .54 cal., percussion or flintlock, 32 in. octagonal barrel, German silver wedge plate and patch box, pewter or German silver nose cap, 7 lbs. 14 oz.

Mfg.'s Sug. Retail $360 $275 $240 $175

Add $80 for premier grade (chrome bore and German silver trim).

Grading	100%	98%	95%

OVER/UNDER DOUBLE BARREL CARBINE — .50 cal., percussion, O/U 26 in. octagonal tapering to round barrels, color case hardened lock, hammers, and triggers, checkered walnut stock, 8½ lbs.

Mfg.'s Sug. Retail	$800	$520	$430	$340

PENNSYLVANIA LONG RIFLE — .50 cal., percussion or flintlock, 40 in. octagonal barrel, color case hardened hammers and plate, brass trim, 8 lbs. 3 oz. Add $15 for flintlock.

Mfg.'s Sug. Retail	$700	$535	$465	$300

PLAINSMAN RIFLE — .50 cal., percussion, 26 in. octagonal barrel, color casehardened lock and nippel, 6 lbs. 9 oz.

Mfg.'s Sug. Retail	$230	$170	$150	$110

SQUIRREL RIFLE — .32 cal., percussion or flintlock, 25 in. octagonal barrel, color case hardened hammer and plate, brass trim, stainless steel nipple, 5 lbs. 12 oz. Add $10 for flintlock, $10 for left-hand.

Mfg.'s Sug. Retail	$330	$255	$220	$140

ST. LOUIS HAWKEN — .50, .54, or .58 cal., percussion or flintlock, 28 in. octagonal barrel, brass trim, 7 lbs. 13 oz. Add $15 for flintlock, $75 for 12 ga. combo. barrel, $70 for 1-48 twist extra .50 cal. barrel, $15 for left hand.

Mfg.'s Sug. Retail	$340	$260	$225	$150

STALKER RIFLE — .50 cal. percussion, 28 in. octagonal barrel, hunting style sight (click adjustable) color case hardened hammer and lock recoil pad, 7 lbs. 4 oz. New 1991.

Mfg.'s Sug. Retail	$280	$215	N/A	N/A

Add $100 for premier grade.

ZOUAVE RIFLE — .58 cal., percussion, 32½ in. tapered barrel with bayonet mount, brass trim and lands, adj. sight, 9¾ lbs. New in 1989.

Mfg.'s Sug. Retail	$445	$340	$295	$235

SHOTGUNS

BRITTANY SHOTGUN — 12 ga., 28 in. double barrel, 7 lbs. 7 oz. Disc. after 1989.

	$320	$250	$200

Last Mfg.'s Sug. Retail was $295.

BRITTANY SHOTGUN II — .410 ga., 24 in. double barrel, 6 lbs. 4 oz. Disc. after 1989.

	$180	$150	$125

Last Mfg.'s Sug. Retail was $210.

SHOTGUN — 12 or .410 ga., percussion, 28 in. (24 in. on .410) double barrel, 6 lbs. 10 oz (6 lbs. 4 oz. on .410). Deduct $85 for .410 ga. New in 1987. Presentation grade side by side add $350. Disc. 1989.

	$300	$225	$170

Last Mfg.'s Sug. Retail was $275.

TRAPPER SHOTGUN — 12 ga., 28 in. single barrrel, color case hardened hammer and lock, blued barrel, 3 chokes, recoil pad ,5 lbs. 10 oz. New in 1988.

Mfg.'s Sug. Retail	$430	$325	$285	$200

Add $60 for extra 1-66 twist .50 cal. barrel combo.

CLASSIC TURKEY SXS — 12 ga., percussion, 28 in. round barrel, color casehardened lock, stainless steel nipple, recoil pad, 9 lbs.

Mfg.'s Sug. Retail	$520	$395	$345	$250

Grading	100%	98%	95%

D.P. (DAVIDE PEDERSOLI & CO.)
Imported by Navy, E.M.F., House of Muskets, and Sile Distributors.

PISTOLS

ENGLISH DUELING PISTOL — .45 cal., percussion, 11 in. octagonal barrel, silver thimble and nosecap.

$230 $200 $160

HARPERS FERRY 1806 — .58 cal., flintlock, 10 in. barrel, color case hardened lock, brass furniture.

$235 $205 $150

KENTUCKY PISTOL — .44 cal., flintlock or percussion, available engraved or with brass barrel. Add $25 for flintlock, $35 for brass barrel, or $25 for engraved percussion.

$215 $180 $130

LEPAGE PISTOL—.45 cal., flintlock or percussion, 10½ in. browned octagonal barrel, white steel hammer, and lock, adj. triggers, 2 lbs. (cased set, gold trim, consecutive serial number). Deduct $70 for percussion.

$330 $285 $220

   Cased set — custom order only.

$820 $680 $500

MANG TARGET PISTOL — .38 cal., percussion, 10$7/16$ in. octagonal browned barrel, color case-hardened hammer and lock, 2 lbs. 8 oz.

$535 $465 $370

PENNSYLVANIA PISTOL — .44 cal, percussion, 10 in. octagonal barrel, brass fruniture, locks left in white.

$115 $100 $80

RIFLES

ALAMO — .38, .45. or .50 cal., percussion or flintlock, with double set triggers. Add $30 for flintlock.

$275 $240 $190

BROWN BESS MUSKET — .75 cal., flintlock, 31½ or 42 in. smooth bore barrel. Deduct $20 for carbine.

$495 $435 $340

   Add $65 for bayonet.

CHARLEVILLE MUSKET — .69 cal., flintlock, 44⅝ in. white steel barrel, hammer, and lock, brass trim, 8¾ lbs. New in 1989.

$390 $340 $260

FREDERICKSBURG MUSKET — .75 cal., flintlock.

$575 $500 $400

KENTUCKY— .38, .45. or .50 cal., percussion or flintlock, 35½ in. barrel. Add $5 for flintlock, $20 for luxury version, $110 for Silver Star.

$230 $200 $140

MORTIMER RIFLE — .54 cal. Flintlock, 36¼ in. octagonal to round barrel, color case hardened hammer, lock and trigger guard, waterproof pan.

$545 $475 $380

Grading	100%	98%	95%

PENNSYLVANIA RIFLE — .32 and .50 cal., percussion, brass trim, color case hardened lock, hammer, and trigger. New in 1989.

	$275	$240	$190

PLAINSMAN RIFLE — .38, .45. or .50 cal., percussion. Add $20 for luxury version.

	$350	$250	$200

TRYON RIFLE— .45, .50, or .54 cal., percussion, 34½ in. octagonal barrel. Add $10 for luxury version.

	$355	$300	$250

WAADTLANDR RIFLE — .44 cal., percussion, 31 in. octagonal browned barrel, target sights, 15 lbs.

	$1,315	$1,145	$920

KODIAK DOUBLE RIFLE — see Epress Combo below.

	$545	$500	$370

SHOTGUNS

CLASSIC TURKEY SXS — 12 ga., percussion, 28 in. round double barrel, color casehardened lock, stainless steel nipple, recoil pad, 9 lbs.

	$340	$295	$225

SXS SHOTGUN — 12 ga., percussion, 28 in. barrel, chrome bore, double triggers. Add $175 for hand checkered walnut stock, $20 for cavalry model.

	$370	$320	$210

KODIAK SXS SHOTGUN/EXPRESS/COMBO.— 10 or 12 ga. x .50, .12 x .58, or .50 x .58 cal., percussion. Add $10 for .10 ga., $300 for rifle or comb. barrels.

	$545	$500	$370

DALY, CHARLES

Previously distributed by Outdoor Sports, Hdqtrs., in Dayton, OH.

All rifles feature adj. sights, investment cast brass trim, patch boxes, color case hardened hammer and locks, octagonal, rifle barrels, adj. double set triggers, and European hard wood stocks.

HAWKEN RIFLE — .45 cal., percussion, 28 in. barrel, right-hand only.

	$260	$180	$130

Last Mfg.'s Sug. Retail was $240.

HAWKEN RIFLE — .50 cal., percussion, 28 in. barrel, right and left- hand. Add $20 for left-hand.

	$260	$180	$130

Last Mfg.'s Sug. Retail was $240.

HAWKEN RIFLE — .50 cal., flintlock, 28 in. barrel, right and left- hand. Add $20 for left-hand.

	$280	$205	$145

Last Mfg.'s Sug. Retail was $280.

HAWKEN CARBINE — .50 cal., flintlock, 22 in. barrel.

	$260	$180	$130

Last Mfg.'s Sug. Retail was $240.

Grading	100%	98%	95%

DIXIE GUN WORKS

Union City, TN — manufacturer and distributor.

Short descriptions are for models of standard construction. Also, new for 1986, many models are imported from Uberti (to eliminate duplications see Uberti, Aldo & Co.).

REVOLVERS: PERCUSSION

WALKER — .44 cal., percussion, 9 in. barrel, 6 shot, color case hardened frame, hammer, and load lever, brass trim, 4½ lbs. Add $75 for Deluxe version.

Mfg.'s Sug. Retail	$195	$175	$155	$120

1ST MODEL DRAGOON — .44 cal., percussion, 6 shot, brass grip straps, color case hardened frame, hammer, and load lever, brass trim, 3.9 lbs. Add $15 for silver-plated straps.

Mfg.'s Sug. Retail	$230	$210	$185	$140

2ND MODEL DRAGOON — .44 cal., percussion, 6 shot, brass grip straps, color case hardened frame, hammer, and load lever, brass trim, 3.9 lbs. Add $15 for silver-plated straps.

Mfg.'s Sug. Retail	$230	$210	$185	$140

3RD MODEL DRAGOON — .45 cal., percussion, 7⅜ in. barrel, color case hardened frame, hammer, and load lever, brass trigger guard and back strap. Add $60 for Deluxe version.

Mfg.'s Sug. Retail	$195	$175	$155	$120

BABY DRAGOON— .31 cal., 6 in. barrel, color case hardened frame. Add $45 for Deluxe version.

Mfg.'s Sug. Retail	$175	$160	$140	$110

MODEL 1849 POCKET — .31 cal., percussion, with loading lever, 3, 4, or 5 in. barrel, 5 shot, color case hardened frame, hammer, and load lever, brass trim, 1½ lbs. Add $15 for silver straps and trigger guard.

Mfg.'s Sug. Retail	$235	$200	$190	$150

1851 NAVY — .36 cal., brass frame. Add $30 for engraved model, $40 for steel, $130 for Deluxe or London marked version, or $35 for steel frame.

Mfg.'s Sug. Retail	$95	$85	$75	$60

TEXAS PATERSON HOLSTER PISTOL— .36 cal., percussion, 7½ or 9 in. barrel, has hidden trigger and no loading lever. Add $20 for 9 in. barrel.

Mfg.'s Sug. Retail	$310	$280	$250	$200

1860 ARMY— .44 cal., percussion, half-fluted cylinder, 8 in. barrel, color case hardened hammer, frame, and load lever, and brass trigger guard. Add $65 for Deluxe version, $20 for silver plated backstrap and trigger guard.

Mfg.'s Sug. Retail	$150	$140	$120	$90

MODEL 1861 NAVY REVOLVER — .36 cal., percussion, 5 in. barrel, many styles, brass back strap or trigger guard, color case hardened frame, hammer, and load lever, 2½ lbs. Add $15 for silver plated strap and trigger guard, $15 for fluted military cylinder, $50 for stainless steel. Add $100 for shoulder stock.

Mfg.'s Sug. Retail	$245	$225	$195	$140

MODEL 1862 POLICE — .36 cal., percussion, 4½, 5½, or 6½ in. barrel, color case hardened frame, hammer, and load lever, cylinder, semi-fluted or engraved, 1.6 lbs. Add $15 for silver plated straps and trigger guard, $50 for stainless steel.

Mfg.'s Sug. Retail	$220	$200	$175	$140

Grading	100%	98%	95%	

1858 REMINGTON— .44 cal., percussion, 8 in. octagonal barrel, blue finish. Add $50 for Deluxe version. Add $80 for stainless steel or new "Shooters" Revolver.

Mfg.'s Sug. Retail	$200	$185	$160	$130

REMINGTON NAVY— .36 cal., percussion, 6¼ in. octagonal barrel, .36 cal. variation of the 1858 Remington, 2½ lbs. New in 1989.

Mfg.'s Sug. Retail	$210	$195	$170	$135

LEECH & RIGDON — .36 cal., percussion, 7 in. round barrel, Confederate copy of the Colt Navy, 2¾ lbs. New in 1989.

Mfg.'s Sug. Retail	$220	$200	$175	$140

SPILLER & BURR— .36 cal., percussion, octagonal barrel, color case hardened hammer and load lever, brass frame and trigger guard.

Mfg.'s Sug. Retail	$125	$115	$100	$65

WYATT EARP— .44 cal., percussion, 6 shot, 12 in. oct. barrel, brass frame.

Mfg.'s Sug. Retail	$130	$115	$100	$70

PISTOLS BLACK POWDER CARTRIDGE

CATTLEMAN S.A. REVOLVER — .44-40 cal., 4¾, 5½, 7½ in. barrel, color case hardened frame, brass trigger guard.

Mfg.'s Sug. Retail	$370	$340	$295	$230

1875 ARMY S.A.— .44-40 cal. cartridge, 7½ in. barrel, fluted cylinder, color case hardened frame, brass trigger guard. Add $50 for nickle.

Mfg.'s Sug. Retail	$315	$290	$250	$200

1890 ARMY — .44-40 cal., 6 shot, 5½ in. barrel, color case hardened frame. Add $40 for nickle.

Mfg.'s Sug. Retail	$345	$315	$275	$220

PISTOLS

This is an alphabetized listing.

ABILENE DERRINGER — .41 cal., percussion with case.

Mfg.'s Sug. Retail	$80	$75	$65	$40

BLACK WATCH SCOTTISH PISTOL — .577 cal., flintlock, 7 in. smooth bore barrel.

Mfg.'s Sug. Retail	$150	$135	$120	$85

BRASS FRAME DERRINGER — percussion. Add $35 for engraving.

Mfg.'s Sug. Retail	$50	$45	$40	$35

CHARLEVILLE PISTOL — .69 cal., flintlock, 7½ in. white steel barrel.

Mfg.'s Sug. Retail	$165	$150	$130	$95

ENGLISH DUELING PISTOL — .45 cal. percussion, 11 in. octagonal barrel, silver thimble and nose cap.

Mfg.'s Sug. Retail	$250	$230	$200	$160

HARPERS FERRY — .58 cal., flintlock, 10 in. barrel, color case hardened hammer and lock.

Mfg.'s Sug. Retail	$210	$195	$170	$135

KENTUCKY PISTOL — percussion. Discontinued in 1983.

	$95	$80	$65	

Last Mfg.'s Sug. Retail was $100.

LEPAGE DELUXE TARGET PISTOL — .45 cal., percussion, 9¼ in. white steel barrel, adj. sights.

Mfg.'s Sug. Retail	$355	$330	$285	$220

Grading	100%	98%	95%	

LEPAGE DUELING PISTOL — .45 cal., percussion, 10 in. barrel.

| Mfg.'s Sug. Retail | $260 | $240 | $210 | $165 |

LINCOLN DERRINGER — .41 cal., percussion, 2 in. barrel, with case.

| Mfg.'s Sug. Retail | $285 | $260 | $225 | $150 |

MANG TARGET PISTOL — .38 cal. percussion, 10⁷⁄16 in. octagonal browned barrel, white steel hammer and lock.

| Mfg.'s Sug. Retail | $580 | $535 | $465 | $370 |

MOUSE KILLER

| Mfg.'s Sug. Retail | $20 | $20 | $15 | $12 |

MOORE AND PATRICK PISTOL — .45 cal., flintlock, 10 in. browned octagonal barrel.

| Mfg.'s Sug. Retail | $340 | $310 | $270 | $215 |

MURDOCK SCOTTISH HIGHLANDERS PISTOL — .52 cal., flintlock, 7¾ in. white steel barrel, hammer, lock, and furniture, 4 lbs. New in 1989.

| Mfg.'s Sug. Retail | $300 | $260 | $225 | $190 |

OVERCOAT DERRINGER

| Mfg.'s Sug. Retail | $35 | $35 | $30 | $25 |

PENNSYLVANIA PISTOL — .44 cal., flintlock or percussion, 10 in. barrel. Add $10 for flintlock.

| Mfg.'s Sug. Retail | $120 | $115 | $100 | $80 |

PHILADELPHIA DERRINGER

| Mfg.'s Sug. Retail | $45 | $40 | $35 | $30 |

QUEEN ANNE PISTOL — .50 cal., flintlock, 7½ in. bronzed steel barrel.

| Mfg.'s Sug. Retail | $170 | $155 | $135 | $110 |

TORNADO TARGET — .44 cal., percussion, 10 in. octagonal barrel. Built on Remington 1860 army frame.

| Mfg.'s Sug. Retail | $200 | $185 | $160 | $130 |

WILLIAM PARKER PISTOL— .45 cal., flintlock, 11 in. barrel, hand checkered half stock, 2 lbs. 8 oz.

| Mfg.'s Sug. Retail | $310 | $285 | $250 | $200 |

RIFLES

BROWN BESS MUSKET — .74 cal., flintlock, 41½ in. barrel, 9 lbs. 8 oz. add $75 for 2nd Model (1762).

| Mfg.'s Sug. Retail | $475 | $440 | $380 | $305 |

BUFFALO HUNTER — .58 cal., percussion, 26 in. barrel.

| | $225 | $190 | $140 | |

CHARLEVILLE MUSKET — .69 cal., flintlock, 44⁵⁄8 in. white steel barrel, hammer, lock, and furniture, 8¾ lbs. New in 1989. Add $200 for 1777 French Model.

| Mfg.'s Sug. Retail | $450 | $390 | $340 | $260 |

DELUXE CUB RIFLE — .40 cal., flintlock or percussion, 28 in. octagonal barrel, color case hardened hammer, plate and triggers, brass trim and patch box, double set triggers.

| Mfg.'s Sug. Retail | $250 | $220 | $190 | $145 |

HAWKEN RIFLE— .45, .50, .54 or .58 cal., percussion, color case hardened hammer and lock, brass patch box.

| Mfg.'s Sug. Retail | $225 | $200 | $175 | $130 |

Grading	100%	98%	95%	

HARPERS FERRY RIFLE — .54 and .58 cal. Flintlock, 35½ in. octagonal to round barrel, color case hardened hammer and lock, brass trigger guard and patchbox.

Mfg.'s Sug. Retail	$505	$465	$405	$320

Subtract $50 for .54 caliber.

INDIAN GUN — same as Brown Bess Musket except 31 in. barrel.

Mfg.'s Sug. Retail	$455	$420	$365	$290

J.P. MURRAY CARBINE — .58 cal. percussion, 23½ in. round barrel, color case hardened hammer and lock, brass buttplate trigger guard and barrel bands (2), factory sling swivels.

Mfg.'s Sug. Retail	$375	$345	$300	$240

KENTUCKIAN CARBINE — .45 cal., flintlock or percussion, 27½ in. barrel. Add $15 for flintlock.

Mfg.'s Sug. Retail	$210	$195	$160	$120

KENTUCKY RIFLE — .45 cal., flintlock or percussion, 33½ in. barrel, 27½ in. carbine barrel also available. Add $10 for flintlock.

Mfg.'s Sug. Retail	$245	$225	$195	$155

KODIAK DOUBLE RIFLE — .50, .54 and .58 cal. percussion, S x S, 28 in. barrels, hand checkered walnut stock, adjustable sights.

Mfg.'s Sug. Retail	$660	$610	$530	$425

KODIAK MKIII RIFLE SHOTGUN COMBO — same as above but with one 12 ga. barrel, .50 and .58 cal. percussion.

Mfg.'s Sug. Retail	$660	$610	$530	$425

LANCASTER COUNTY RIFLE — .45 cal., flintlock or percussion (same as Pennsylvania Rifle above, except less ornate trigger guard and patch box). Add $5 for flintlock.

	$190	$175	$160	

MISSISSIPPI RIFLE — U.S. rifle model 1841, .58 cal., percussion, 33½ in. barrel, color casehardened hammer and lock, solid brass furniture.

Mfg.'s Sug. Retail	$430	$400	$345	$250

MORTIMER RIFLE — .54 cal. Flintlock, 36¼ in. octagonal to round barrel, color case hardened hammer, lock and trigger guard, waterproof pan.

Mfg.'s Sug. Retail	$595	$545	$475	$380

PENNSYLVANIA RIFLE — .45 cal., flintlock or percussion, 41½ in. octagonal barrel, browned hammer, lock and barrel, 8 lbs.

Mfg.'s Sug. Retail	$395	$360	$315	$230

SANFTL SCHUETZEN TARGET RIFLE — .45 cal., percussion, 29 in. barrel, adj. sights.

Mfg.'s Sug. Retail	$595	$570	$475	$385

SHARPS RIFLE/CARBINE — .54 cal., percussion. 28 in. barrel. Deduct $30 for carbine. Disc. in 1987.

	$310	$280	$235	

TENNESSEE MOUNTAIN/SQUIRREL RIFLE — .32 or .50 cal., percussion or flintlock (.32 cal. is a small cal. squirrel rifle), right or left hand.

Mfg.'s Sug. Retail	$335	$315	$300	$200

TRYON CREEDMORE RIFLE — .50 cal., percussion, 32 in. octagonal all black barrel, matte finish, patchbox adjustable sights.

Mfg.'s Sug. Retail	$625	$575	$500	$400

TYRON RIFLE — .50 cal. percussion, 32 in. octagonal barrel, color case hardened furniture and patchbox, chrome bore.

Mfg.'s Sug. Retail	$390	$355	$310	$250

Grading	100%	98%	95%	

WAADTLANDER RIFLE — .44 cal. percussion, 31 in. octagonal browned barrel, color case hardened hammer, lock and trigger guard and heavy butt plate, adj. sights, professional target model

Mfg.'s Sug. Retail	$1,430	$1,315	$1,145	$920

WESSON RIFLE — .50 cal., percussion, 28 in. barrel, adj. sights.

Mfg.'s Sug. Retail	$395	$375	$325	$255

YORK COUNTY RIFLE — .45 cal., flintlock or percussion, 36 in. barrel. Add $15 for flintlock. Disc. in 1987.

	$205	$170	$135

Last Mfg.'s Sug. Retail was $210.

ZOUAVE RIFLE — .58 cal., percussion, 33½ in. blued barrel, color casehardened hammer and lock. Deduct $35 for carbine barrel.

Mfg.'s Sug. Retail	$370	$340	$295	$195

1858 2-BAND ENFIELD — .58 cal., percussion, 2 barrel bands, 9 lbs. 4 oz.

Mfg.'s Sug. Retail	$400	$370	$320	$255

1862 3-BAND ENFIELD — .58 cal., percussion, 3 barrel bands, 10 lbs. 8 oz.

Mfg.'s Sug. Retail	$395	$375	$315	$255

LONDON ARMORY ENFIELD MUSKETOON — .58 cal. percussion, 24 in. round barrel, color case hardened hammer and lock, brass buttplate, trigger guard and nose cap.

Mfg.'s Sug. Retail	$345	$315	$275	$220

1861 SPRINGFIELD MUSKET — .58 cal., percussion, 40 in. round tapered barrel, white steel furniture, 9 lbs. 8 oz.

Mfg.'s Sug. Retail	$450	$425	$385	$275

1863 SPRINGFIELD MUSKET — .58 cal., percussion, 41½ in. barrel.

Mfg.'s Sug. Retail	$450	$420	$375	$275

SHOTGUNS

MORTIMER SHOTGUN — 12 ga. Flintlock, similar to Mortimer Rifle listed in rifle section.

Mfg.'s Sug. Retail	$550	$505	$440	$350

BLACKPOWDER CARTRIDGE

HENRY RIFLE — .44-40 cal., brass frame, 24½ in. barrel. Add $235 for engraving.

Mfg.'s Sug. Retail	$800	$735	$640	$540

1866 CARBINE — .44-40 cal., brass receiver, 19 in. round barrel.

Mfg.'s Sug. Retail	$525	$490	$420	$330

1873 SPORTING RIFLE — .44-40 cal., color casehardened steel receiver, 24¼ in. octagonal barrel. Also available with slight engraving. Add $200 for deluxe, $275 for engraving.

Mfg.'s Sug. Retail	$725	$670	$580	$465

1873 CARBINE — .44-40 cal., steel receiver, 19 in. round barrel.

Mfg.'s Sug. Retail	$625	$605	$530	$420

CATTLEMAN REVOLVING CARBINE — .44-40 cal., 18 in. barrel, brass backstrap, with shoulder stock.

Mfg.'s Sug. Retail	$400	$380	$340	$270

Grading	100%	98%	95%

SHOTGUNS

DOUBLE BARREL: PERCUSSION — 10 or 12 ga., 30 in. barrels, brown finish, checkered European walnut. Add $20 for 10 ga.

Mfg.'s Sug. Retail	$400	$370	$320	$210

NORTHWEST TRADE — 20 ga., flintlock, 36 in. octagonal tapering to round barrel, browned barrel and lock assembly, 11 lbs. New in 1989.

Mfg.'s Sug. Retail	$495	$425	$370	$295

E.M.F. COMPANY

Manufactured & distributed in Santa Ana, CA.

Most percussion revolvers are available in a cased presentation set. Add $100 for cased set.

PISTOLS

1775 BLACK WATCH SCOTTISH PISTOL— .58 cal., flintlock, 7 in. smooth bore white steel barrel, brass frame, ram's horn grips with round ball trigger.

Mfg.'s Sug. Retail	$310	$195	$170	$120

CHARLES MOORE — .45 cal. flintlock, 10 in. octagonal barrel, 2 lbs.

Mfg.'s Sug. Retail	$400	$310	$270	$215

1777 CHARLEVILLE PISTOL — .69 cal., flintlock, 7½ in. white steel barrel, brass frame.

Mfg.'s Sug. Retail	$325	$240	$210	$130

CORSAIR PISTOL— .36 or .44 cal., percussion, double barrel, color case hardened hammer and lock, brass trim. Disc. in 1987.

	$300	$200	$130

Last Mfg.'s Sug. Retail was $160.

HARPERS FERRY — .58 cal., flintlock, brass mounted brown barrel.

Mfg.'s Sug. Retail	$325	$240	$210	$130

HAWKEN PISTOL— .54 cal. percussion, 9 in. octagonal barrel, adj. trigger, 2 lbs. 9oz.

Mfg.'s Sug. Retail	$370	$270	$235	$180

KENTUCKY PISTOL — .44 cal., flintlock or percussion, available engraved or with brass barrel. Add $30 for percussion, $20 for brass barrel, $25 for engraved percussion.

Mfg.'s Sug. Retail	$225	$145	$125	$100

LE PAGE PISTOL— .45 cal. percussion, 9 in. octagonal white steel barrel and trim, adj. sights, 2 lbs. 2 oz.

Mfg.'s Sug. Retail	$400	$310	$270	$200

REMINGTON STYLE TARGET PISTOL — .44 cal., percussion, 9 in. octagonal barrel, factory engraved, adj. sights (windage only), based on Rem. frame, 43 oz. Add $120 for stainless steel.

Mfg.'s Sug. Retail	$310	$225	$195	$135

WM. PARKER PISTOL — .45 cal. percussion, 10 in. octagonal barrel, German silver lock and trim, adj. double set of triggers, 2 lbs. 8 oz.

Mfg.'s Sug. Retail	$400	$310	$270	$200

REVOLVERS

All percussion revolvers are available in cased sets. Add $80 for cased set.

Grading	100%	98%	95%

1847 WALKER — .44 cal., percussion, 9 in. barrel, color case hardened frame and load lever, brass trim, 4 lbs. 8 oz. Add $75 for nickel plate, $135 for engraving.

Mfg.'s Sug. Retail	$265	$190	$165	$120

1ST MODEL DRAGOON — .44 cal., percussion, 7½ in. barrel, color case hardened frame, brass trim, engraved cylinder, 4 lbs. 2 oz.

Mfg.'s Sug. Retail	$285	$200	$175	$130

2ND MODEL DRAGOON — .44 cal., percussion, 7½ in. barrel, color case hardened frame, brass trim, engraved cylinder, 4 lbs.

Mfg.'s Sug. Retail	$285	$200	$175	$130

3RD MODEL DRAGOON — .44 cal., percussion, 7½ in. barrel, color case hardened frame and loading lever, brass trim, engraved cylinder, 4 lbs. 2 oz., adj. target sights. Add $25 for buntline model. Add $20 for Texas Dragoon Model (Tucker & Sherrard & Co., Confederate States, Texas Star engraved on cylinder, square brass trigger guard).

Mfg.'s Sug. Retail	$285	$200	$175	$130

BABY DRAGOON — .31 cal., percussion, 5 shot, 4 and 6 in. barrel, color case hardened frame and loading lever, brass trim, Add $20 for engraving, $30 for steel frame.

	$180	$150	$90

WELLS FARGO MODEL 1849 — .31 cal., percussion, 5 shot, 5 in. barrel, no loading lever.

	$180	$150	$90

1851 NAVY — .36 or .44 cal., percussion, 7½ in. barrel, brass frame, color case hardened hammer, and load lever, brass trim, engraved cylinder. Add $30 for engraving, brass, $140 for steel, $30 for steel frame, $25 for nickel plated brass (Mason Dixon Model), $45 for square trigger guard (on steel model), $55 for silver trimmed steel, $100 for 3 barrel set (.44 cal. only). Add $140 for commemorative issued with special grip.

Mfg.'s Sug. Retail	$140	$105	$90	$70

1851 NAVY BALLISTER — .44 cal., percussion, same as above, except with 12 in. barrel.

	$105	$90	$70

1851 NAVY SHERIFF'S MODEL — .36 or .44 cal., percussion, 5 in. round or octagonal barrel, (shorter barrel version of 1851 Navy), brass frame - add $25 for steel, $65 for square trigger guard.

Mfg.'s Sug. Retail	$140	$105	$90	$70

The same add on's apply to this model as the 1851 Navy.

1851 GRISWOLD CONFEDERATE — .36 and .44 cal. percussion, 7½ in. round barrel, brass frame, 2 lbs. 12 oz.

Mfg.'s Sug. Retail	$140	$105	$90	$70

1860 ARMY — .44 cal., percussion, 8 in. barrel, brass frame, 2 lbs. 9 oz. Add $40 for steel frame, $150 for stainless steel, engraving, add $25 for brass, $150 for steel. Add $80 for steel Sheriff's Model, $90 for fluted cylinder (steel), $60 for shoulder stock, $145 for deluxe engraving.

Mfg.'s Sug. Retail	$140	$105	$90	$70

1861 NAVY — .36 cal., percussion, steel frame. Disc. in 1987.

Mfg.'s Sug. Retail	$240	$175	$150	$110

Last Mfg.'s Sug. Retail was $115.

1862 POLICE — .36 cal., percussion, 5 shot, color case hardened frame. Add $100 for engraved steel.

Mfg.'s Sug. Retail	$215	$155	$135	$105

1862 POCKET NAVY — .36 cal., percussion, 5 shot, color case hardened frame.

Mfg.'s Sug. Retail	$200	$145	$125	$100

Grading	100%	98%	95%

NAVY SQUAREBACK — .36 or .44 cal., percussion, 7½ in. barrel, color case hardened frame and load lever, Dragoon style square back trigger guard.

Mfg.'s Sug. Retail	$130	$80	$70	$55

The same add on's apply to this model as the 1851 Navy.

1858 REMINGTON ARMY— .36 and .44 cal., percussion, 8 in. barrel, brass frame, blue finish, 2 lbs. 8 oz. For engraving, add $30 brass, $140 steel. Add $35 for steel frame, $140 for stainless steel, $100 for 12 in. Buffalo Model.

Mfg.'s Sug. Retail	$140	$105	$90	$70

RIFLES

BOSTONIAN — .45 cal., percussion. New in 1989.

Mfg.'s Sug. Retail	$305	$220	$190	$150

ALAMO COMMEMORATIVE — .45 cal., percussion, embellished to commemorate the anniversary of the Alamo. New in 1989.

	$305	$265	$210

Last Mfg.'s Sug. Retail was $435.

DELUXE BROWN BESS MUSKET — .75 cal., flintlock. Add $60 for bayonet.

Mfg.'s Sug. Retail	$850	$575	$500	$400

HAWKEN RIFLE — .50 cal., percussion, brass trim, color case hardened lock and hammer, adj. sights, and stainless steel nipple.

Mfg.'s Sug. Retail	$345	$245	$215	$160

KENTUCKY RIFLE—.36, .44, or .45 cal., percussion and flintlock, factory engraved, brass trim, color case hardened lock and hammer. Add $20 for flintlock, $30 for deluxe model, $50 for deluxe engraved.

	$210	$180	$140

"LONDON ARMORY" ENFIELD— .58 cal., percussion. Add $30 for 3 Band Model. Deduct $20 for Musketoon Model. Disc. in 1987.

	$290	$250	$200

Last Mfg.'s Sug. Retail was $285.

MINUTEMAN KENTUCKY RIFLE — .45 cal., flintlock or percussion, 36 in. octagonal barrel, brass blade front sight, brass trim, color case hardened lock, hammer, and trigger. Add $15 for engraving, $15 for flintlock.

	$210	$190	$140

PENNSYLVANIA KENTUCKY RIFLE — .50 cal., percussion, brass trim, color case hardened lock, hammer, and trigger.

	$295	$250	$200

Last Mfg.'s Sug. Retail was $440.

PLAINSMAN KENTUCKY RIFLE — .44 cal., percussion, shorter forearm than Pennsylvania with more ornate finish.

	$350	$250	$200

Last Mfg.'s Sug. Retail was $450.

PURDEY DELUXE — .50 cal., percussion, half stock English style, select checkered walnut, color case hardened nose cap, lock, tang, butt plate and patch box, adj. sights, double set triggers. Carbine or rifles.

	$310	$260	$210

SAN FRANCISCO TO ST. LOUIS COMMEMORATIVE — .45 cal., Kentucky rifle, highly embellished, made to commemorate the 130th anniversary of the stage coach crossing "2,400 miles in 24 days". New in 1989.

Mfg.'s Sug. Retail	$395	$280	$230	$190

Grading	100%	98%	95%

WESSON BERDAN RIFLE — .45 cal., percussion, engraved brass frame.

$210 $190 $140

ZOUAVE RIFLE — .58 cal., percussion, brass trim, color case hardened lock and hammer, blue finish, adj. "Sniper Sight". Add $220 for deluxe.

Mfg.'s Sug. Retail $200 $170 $140 $110

SHOTGUNS

SHOTGUN—.12 ga., S X S, percussion, based on early English design, brown barrel, color case hardened lock and hammer, im ported from Italy.

$420 $350 $250

Last Mfg.'s Sug. Retail was $535.

SHOTGUN O/U — 12 ga., percussion, O/U design. New in 1989.

Mfg.'s Sug. Retail $640 $460 $400 $300

EUROARMS OF AMERICA
Manufacturer/importer, Winchester, VA.

REVOLVERS

1851 NAVY "SCHNEIDER & GLASSICK"— .36 or .44 cal., percussion, 5 or 7 in. octagonal barrel, brass frame, 38-40 oz.

Mfg.'s Sug. Retail $125 $115 $100 $80

1851 NAVY "GRISWOLD & GUNNINSON" — .36 or .44 cal., percussion, 7½ in. octagonal round barrel, brass frame, 39-41 oz. Disc. in 1987.

$115 $100 $80

Last Mfg.'s Sug. Retail was $100.

1851 NAVY— .36 or .44 cal., percussion, 7½ in. barrel, steel frame, 39-43 oz. Add $10 for square back trigger, $25 for silver strap.

Mfg.'s Sug. Retail $165 $150 $130 $100

1851 NAVY POLICE MODEL— .36 cal., percussion, 5 or 7½ in. octagonal barrel, steel frame, 5 shot fluted cyliinder, 38-41 oz.

$150 $130 $100

Last Mfg.'s Sug. Retail was $135.

1851 NAVY SHERIFF'S MODEL—.36 or .44 cal., percussion, 5 in. barrel, steel frame, 39 oz.

$140 $125 $95

Last Mfg.'s Sug. Retail was $105.

1860 ARMY — .44 cal., percussion, 5 or 8 in. barrel, steel frame, 41 oz. Add $50 for steel, $75 for stainless steel, $50 for engraving. Deduct $40 for brass frame.

Mfg.'s Sug. Retail $130 $120 $105 $85

1861 NAVY—.36 cal., percussion, 7½ in. barrel, steel frame, 42 oz.

Mfg.'s Sug. Retail $205 $190 $165 $120

1862 POLICE— .36 cal., percussion, 7½ in. barrel, steel frame, 40 oz. Disc. in 1987.

$130 $115 $95

Last Mfg.'s Sug. Retail was $135.

Grading	100%	98%	95%	

REMINGTON REPLICAS

1858 ARMY — .36 or .44 cal., percussion, 6½ and 8 in. octagonal barrel, 40 oz. Add $90 for engraving, $60 for stainless steel, $40 for target adj. sights, deduct $50 for brass frame.

Mfg.'s Sug. Retail	$190	$175	$150	$110

1858 NAVY — .36 cal., percussion, 6½ in. octagonal barrel, 40 oz.

Mfg.'s Sug. Retail	$190	$175	$150	$110

ROGERS & SPENCER — .44 cal., percussion, 7½ in. octagonal barrel, 47 oz. Add $30 for target sights, $30 for London grey finish, $80 for engraving.

Mfg.'s Sug. Retail	$205	$190	$165	$120

RIFLES

BROWN BESS MUSKET "TOWER FLINTLOCK" — .75 cal. flintlock, 41¾ in. barrel, smooth bore.

Mfg.'s Sug. Retail	$755	$695	$605	$480

BUFFALO CARBINE — .58 cal., percussion, 26 in round barrel, color case hardened hammer and lock, brass patch box and furniture, 7¾ lbs. New in 1989.

Mfg.'s Sug. Retail	$455	$390	$340	$250

CAPE GUN RIFLE — .50 cal., percussion, 32 in. barrel, engraved with walnut stock. New in 1989.

Mfg.'s Sug. Retail	$460	$390	$350	$250

COOK & BROTHER RIFLE/CARBINE — .58 cal., percussion, 24 in. barrel, adj. front sight (windage only), 2 barrel bands, walnut stock, 7½ lbs. Add $25 for rifle.

Mfg.'s Sug. Retail	$435	$370	$325	$250

ENFIELD RIFLE MUSKET (LONDON ARMORY CO.), 1853 — .58 cal., percussion, 39 in. barrel, adj. rear sight (windage only), 3 barrel bands, walnut stock, 9½ lbs. Add $35 for white steel barrel.

Mfg.'s Sug. Retail	$475	$400	$350	$280

ENFIELD RIFLE MUSKET (LONDON ARMORY CO.), 1858 — .58 cal., percussion, 33 in. barrel, adj. rear sight (windage only), 2 barrel bands, walnut stock, 8 lbs.

Mfg.'s Sug. Retail	$450	$390	$340	$250

ENFIELD MUSKETOON (LONDON ARMORY CO.), 1861 — .58 cal., percussion, 24 in. barrel, adj. rear sight (windage only), 2 barrel bands, walnut stock, 8 lbs.

Mfg.'s Sug. Retail	$420	$360	$315	$240

FRENCH MODEL 1777 MUSKET — .69 cal. flintlock, 44¾ in. white steel barrel, smooth bore.

Mfg.'s Sug. Retail	$835	$770	$670	$530

HARPER'S FERRY MODEL 1803 — .54 and .58 cal., flintlock, 35/33 in. browned barrel, walnut stock, 9 lbs.

Mfg.'s Sug. Retail	$600	$520	$450	$320

HAWKEN RIFLE — .58 cal., percussion, 28 in. octagonal barrel, double set triggers, target model, 9 lbs. 6 oz. Disc. in 1989.

	$215	$185	$145

Last Mfg.'s Sug. Retail was $295.

J.P. MURRAY MODEL 1863 — .58 cal., percussion, 23 in barrel, 7 lbs. 9 oz.

Mfg.'s Sug. Retail	$445	$385	$335	$250

MISSISSIPPI RIFLE MODEL 1841 — .58 cal., percussion, 33 in. barrel, 9 lbs. 8 oz.

Mfg.'s Sug. Retail	$520	$450	$390	$300

Grading	100%	98%	95%	

PENNSYLVANIA RIFLE— .45 or .50 cal., flintlock or percussion, 36 in. barrel, adj. rear sight (windage only), walnut stock, 7 lbs. Add $30 for flintlock. Disc. in 1987.

$255 $225 $180

Last Mfg.'s Sug. Retail was $285.

REMINGTON 1862 RIFLE — .58 cal., percussion, 33 in. barrel, 3 leaf folding rear sight, 3 barrel bands, beelia stock, 9½ lbs. Disc. in 1987.

$310 $270 $200

Last Mfg.'s Sug. Retail was $285.

SPRINGFIELD RIFLE MUSKET — .58 cal. percussion, 40 in. barrel with 3 bands.

Mfg.'s Sug. Retail $495 $455 $395 $315

ZOUAVE RIFLE — .58 cal., percussion, brass trim, color casehardened lock and hammer, blue finish, adj. sniper sight.

Mfg.'s Sug. Retail $395 $340 $295 $230

Add $60 for "Range" grade Target Model.

SHOTGUNS

MAGNUM CAPE SHOTGUN— 12 ga., percussion, 32 in. barrel, engraved with walnut stock, 5½ lbs.

Mfg.'s Sug. Retail $460 $390 $350 $250

DUCK SHOTGUN— 8, 10, or 12 ga., percussion, 33 in. round barrel, color case hardened hammer and lock, brass patchbox and furniture, 8½ lbs. New in 1989.

Mfg.'s Sug. Retail $455 $390 $340 $240

DOUBLE BARREL SHOTGUN—12 ga., percussion, 28 in. barrel, engraved with walnut stock, 6 lbs.

$400 $350 $250

Last Mfg.'s Sug. Retail was $405.

F.I.E.

Firearms import & export - Miami, FL.

In 1986, F.I.E. ceased importation of black powder weapons.

PISTOLS

BABY DRAGOON — .31 cal., engraved. Discontinued in 1982.

$115 $100 $75

1851 NAVY — .44 cal., steel frame. Discontinued in 1982.

$140 $120 $90

1858 REMINGTON — .36 or .44 cal., Discontinued in 1982.

$140 $125 $95

1776 KENTUCKY — .44 cal., flintlock, color case hardened hammer and lock.

$140 $120 $90

RIFLES

KENTUCKY RIFLE — .45 cal., percussion or flintlock.

$200 $170 $130

Grading	100%	98%	95%

FABER BROTHERS
Distributor located in Chicago, IL.

Faber Brothers is currently marketing customized C.V.A. Hawkens Rifles. These rifles come drilled and tapped for scope with offset hammers and chrome bores. Even though these rifles trade for prices equal to the C.V.A. Hawken, Faber Brothers could command a slight premium (see Connecticut Valley Arms).

FEDERAL ORDNANCE CORPORATION
Manufacturer/importer located in South El Monte, CA. discontinued importation of Blackpowder Arms in 1990.

PISTOLS

DURS EGG SAW HANDLED PISTOL — .45 cal., flintlock or percussion, 9½ in. blued octagonal barrel, unique stock, hand checkered, German silver trim, white steel hammer and lock.

$210 $175 $140

Last Mfg.'s Sug. Retail was $225.

F. ROCHATTE — .45 cal., percussion, single set triggers, hand checkered stock.

$220 $185 $150

Last Mfg.'s Sug. Retail was $250.

KENTUCKY PISTOL — .45 cal., percussion, 10¼ in. octagonal barrel, brass blade front sight, 40 oz.

$130 $115 $90

Last Mfg.'s Sug. Retail was $110.

WILLIAM MOORE PISTOL — .45 cal., flintlock or percussion, 10 in. octagonal barrel, white steel hammer and lock, silver plated trim, 2 lbs. Add $10 for flintlock.

$160 $140 $105

Last Mfg.'s Sug. Retail was $230.

NAPOLEON LEPAGE PISTOL — .45 cal., percussion, 10 in. octagonal white steel barrel and lock, brass trim, adj. double set triggers, fluted grip, 2 lbs. 7 oz.

$160 $140 $105

Last Mfg.'s Sug. Retail was $185.

WILLIAM PARKER PISTOL — .45 cal., flintlock or percussion, 11 in. octagonal browned barrel, silver plated furniture, double set triggers. Add $10 for flintlock.

$220 $185 $150

Last Mfg.'s Sug. Retail was $200.

REVOLVERS

1858 REMINGTON — .44 cal., percussion, 7½ in. octagonal barrel, 6 shot, brass frame and trigger guard, 2 lbs. 10 oz. Add $30 for steel, $85 for stainless steel frame.

$135 $105 $80

Last Mfg.'s Sug. Retail was $110.
Add $75 for target model.

1860 ARMY — .44 cal., percussion, 8 in. barrel, 6 shot, color case hardened hammer, lock, and load lever, brass backstrap and trigger guard. Add $15 for Sheriff's Model, $75 for shoulder stock.

$125 $105 $85

Last Mfg.'s Sug. Retail was $125.

Grading	100%	98%	95%

1862 POCKET NAVY— .36 cal., percussion, 6½ in. barrel, color casehardened frame, hammer and load lever, cylinder semi-fluted, or engraved. 1 lb. 9 oz.

	$185	$160	$125

Last Mfg.'s Sug. Retail was $205.

ROGERS & SPENCER — .44 cal., percussion, 7½ in. octagonal barrel, blued steel, 3 lbs.

	$195	$170	$120

Last Mfg.'s Sug. Retail was $200.

RIFLES

P-1853 3-BAND ENFIELD — .58 cal., percussion, 39 in. round barrel, color case hardened hammer and lock, brass trim, blued bands, adj. rear sight, 9½ lbs.

	$370	$325	$230

Last Mfg.'s Sug. Retail was $400.

MODEL 1858 2-BAND ENFIELD— similar to P-1853 3-Band Enfield except has 33 in. round barrel, 10 lbs.

	$325	$285	$220

Last Mfg.'s Sug. Retail was $340.

ENFIELD MUSKETOON — .58 cal., percussion, 24 in. barrel, adj. rear sight (windage only), 2 barrel bands, walnut stock, 8 lbs.

	$235	$200	$160

Last Mfg.'s Sug. Retail was $480

HARPERS FERRY — .58 cal., flintlock, 35 in. round barrel, color case hardened hammer and lock, brass trim, 8½ lbs.

	$380	$330	$260

Last Mfg.'s Sug. Retail was $440.

HAWKENS RIFLE — .45 or .50 cal., flintlock or percussion, 28½ in. octagonal barrel, color case hardened hammer and lock, double set triggers, 7¾ lbs.

	$215	$185	$140

Last Mfg.'s Sug. Retail was $220.

KENTUCKY RIFLE — .45 cal., percussion, color casehardened hammer and lock, percussion cap holder in stock, brass trim.

	$220	$190	$150

Last Mfg.'s Sug. Retail was $210.

THE J.P. MURRAY CARBINE— .58 cal., percussion, 23½ in. browned round barrel, color case hardened hammer and lock, brass trim and bands, 7½ lbs.

	$275	$240	$155

Last Mfg.'s Sug. Retail was $370.

MISSISSIPPI RIFLE— .58 cal., percussion, 33 in. browned round barrel, color case hardened hammer and lock, brass trim and bands, 9½ lbs.

	$390	$340	$235

Last Mfg.'s Sug. Retail was $410.

SANFTEL SCHUETZEN RIFLE — .45 cal., percussion, 31 in. octagonal barrel, both peep and iron sights, Schuetzen style butt plate and trigger guard, brass furniture.

	$595	$495	$385

Last Mfg.'s Sug. Retail was $590.

ZOUAVE RIFLE— .58 cal., percussion, 32½ in. round barrel, color case hardened hammer, lock and trigger, brass trim, adj. rear sight, 9 lbs.

	$345	$300	$220

Last Mfg.'s Sug. Retail was $360.

Grading	100%	98%	95%

FREEDOM ARMS
Manufactured and distributed in Freedom, WY.

REVOLVERS

STAINLESS MINI-REVOLVER — .22 cal., percussion, 5 shot, 1, 1¾, or 3 in. barrel, stainless steel.
Add $15 for 3 in. barrel, $40 for brass buckle.

$200 **$165** **$130**

Last Mfg.'s Sug. Retail was $205.

Due to an increase in demand for Freedom Arms .454 Casull, the .22 cal. percussion pistol is temporarily out of production. It is unknown if production of this gun will ever begin again.

GONIC ARMS INC.
Manufacturer located in Gonic, NH.

Gonic Arms has designed a true hunters Black Powder rifle. Equipped with an ambidextrous safety, it eliminates the noisy "click" often associated with bringing a hammer back from half cock or setting the first of double set triggers. A specially designed firing pin and housing allow spent caps to blow out the bottom of the rifle, thus eliminating the need to "dig out" the spent cap from the breech. This combined with it's modern appearance and newly designed loading system make it a true hunters rifle without the problems associated with most Black Powder arms.

MODEL GA-87 RIFLE/CARBINE — .308 Spitfire and .458 Express, and .50 cal. (rifle only), 26 in. round barrel, single stage trigger with left or right safety, cap is placed in breech, hand checkered walnut stock (deluxe model), 6 lbs. New in 1987.

Mfg.'s Sug. Retail   **$480**   **$380**   **$320**   **$260**

Add $40 for sights, $40 for laminated stock, $250 for 1- 1000 limited addition.

HATFIELD RIFLE WORKS
Manufactured in St. Joseph, MO. Sold by Mountain State Muzzleloading Supplies.

MOUNTAIN RIFLE — .50 and .54 cal. percussion, 32 in. octagonal barrel, browned furniture, ½ stock, 9 lbs.

Mfg.'s Sug. Retail   **$665**   **$575**   **$500**   **N/A**

Over the last two years extensive work has been done to all internal working parts to insure greater longevity for target or field use. All internal parts now U.S. made.

SQUIRREL RIFLE — .32, .36, .45, or .50 cal., flintlock or percussion, 39 in. barrel, adj. sights, double set triggers, brass trim, 7½ lbs. Add $20 for flintlock.

Mfg.'s Sug. Retail   **$600**   **$520**   **$450**   **$360**

Add $65 for extra fancy maple Grade II.

Add $175 for hand selected fancy Grade III.

Custom guns could easily run 200% over standard.

This gun is a one-of-a-kind model with exceptional craftsmanship in both wood and metal.

HEGE
Uberlingen, West Germany (imported by Beeman).

This item is no longer stocked by Beeman, but can be special ordered. Price is set at time of order.

HEGE-MANTON — .44 cal., flintlock, 6 lbs. Add $100 for engraving.

$1,470 $1,270   **$900**

Last Mfg.'s Sug. Retail was $1,695.

Grading	100%	98%	95%

HEGE-SIBER PISTOL— .33 or .44 cal., percussion, 10 in. blue octagonal barrel, exceptional finish, world class target model, color case hardened hammer and lock.

$900 $800 $500

Last Mfg.'s Sug. Retail was $1,000.

FRENCH STYLE HEGE-SIBER PISTOL— .33 or .44 cal. percussion, 10 in. blue octagonal barrel, exceptional finish, world class target model, London gray finish, 24 Kt. gold inlays, blue trigger guard.

$1,570 $1,365 $1,000

Last Mfg.'s Sug. Retail was $1,795.

Matched set — same serial number.

$2,750 $2,410 $1,675

Last Mfg.'s Sug. Retail was $2,995.

IVER JOHNSON
Manufactured in Jackson, AR.

OVER/UNDER DOUBLE RIFLE MODEL BP50HB — .50 cal., percussion, double barrel, separate hammers and triggers, color case hardened hammer and furniture.

$380 $330 $275

KBI
Harrisburg, PA.

PISTOLS

1851 NAVY— .44 cal., percussion, 7½ in. barrel, steel frame, 39-43 oz. Add $50 for engraving.

Mfg.'s Sug. Retail $170 $140 $120 $95

1860 ARMY — .44 cal., percussion, 5 or 8 in. barrel, steel frame, 41 oz.

$200 $170 $130

Last Mfg.'s Sug. Retail was $240.

1858 REMINGTON ARMY — .36 or .44 cal., percussion, 6½ and 8 in. octagonal barrel, 40 oz. Add $40 for steel frame, $140 for stainless steel. Add $30 for 12 in. Buffalo Model.

Mfg.'s Sug. Retail $200 $145 $125 $90

RIFLES

HAWKEN RIFLE — .45, .50, .54, or .58 cal., flintlock or percussion, 28 in. octagonal barrel, color case hardened hammer and lock, 9 lbs. Add $40 for flintlock and $30 for left hand.

Mfg.'s Sug. Retail $315 $290 $250 $180

KAHNKE GUNWORKS
Manufacturer/retailer located in Redwood Falls, MN.

KAHNKE .54 CAL. MODEL — .54 cal., percussion, single-shot hunting pistol, adj. sights, unusual combination of utilizing both old and new technologies, staight through ignition system, 3½ lbs. New in 1988.

Mfg.'s Sug. Retail $285 $285 $190 $140

This model is available direct from the factory only.

Grading	100%	98%	95%

LOVEN-PIERSON INC.
Apalachin Arsenal - Apalachin, NY.

RIFLES: PERCUSSION

All rifles have a unique rotating over and under set of barrels to speed a 2nd shot.

LOVEN MODEL 10 — .45 cal., percussion swivel breech, 22 in. carbine or 28 in. rifle, octagonal or ½ in. round barrel, blued furniture, maple stock, 7¾ - 8½ lbs.

$265 $220 $175

Last Mfg.'s Sug. Retail was $330.

LOVEN MODEL 13 — .45, .50 or .54 cal., percussion, same as Loven Model 10, except brass furniture and walnut stock.

$320 $270 $210

Last Mfg.'s Sug. Retail was $440.

LOVEN MODEL 16 — .45, .50 or .54 cal., percussion, same as above except color case hardened lock and furniture, browned barrels and curly or bird's-eye maple or figured walnut stock.

$650 $550 $440

Last Mfg.'s Sug. Retail was $880.

LYMAN GUNS
Middlefield, CT.

Discontinued models still sold by Dixie Gun Works.

PISTOLS

REMINGTON .44 ARMY — .44 cal., 6 shot, percussion. Discontinued.

$175 $150 $110

Last Mfg.'s Sug. Retail was $170.

1851 NAVY — .36 cal., percussion. Discontinued.

$150 $130 $100

Last Mfg.'s Sug. Retail was $165.

1860 ARMY — .44 cal., percussion. Discontinued.

$120 $105 $85

Last Mfg.'s Sug. Retail was $170.

PLAINS PISTOL— .50 or .54 cal., percussion, color case hardened hammer and lock.

Mfg.'s Sug. Retail $200 $165 $140 $105

RIFLES

GREAT PLAINS RIFLE — .50 or .54 cal., flintlock or percussion, color case hardened hammer and lock, blackened steel furniture, 32 in. octagonal barrel, 11 lbs. 6 oz. Add $15 for flintlock.

Mfg.'s Sug. Retail $335 $290 $250 $200

TRADE RIFLE — .50 or .54 cal., percussion or flintlock, color case hardened hammer and lock, 11 lbs. Add $10 for flintlock.

Mfg.'s Sug. Retail $240 $215 $180 $140

Grading	100%	98%	95%	

DEERSTALKER— .50 and .54 cal., flintlock or percussion, 24 in. octagonal barrel, color casehardened hammer and lock, sling swivels, adj. sights, 10 lbs. 6 oz. Add $15 for flintlock.

Mfg.'s Sug. Retail	$300	$250	$210	$165

MANDALL SHOOTING SUPPLIES, INC.
Importer and distributor located in Scottsdale, AZ.

FRENCH DUELING PISTOL — .44 cal., percussion, single trigger, classic fluted handle, sold with velvet lined display case and accessories.

	$240	$200	$160	

Last Mfg.'s Sug. Retail was $295.

"NAPOLEON" CANNON — .69 ball, detailed scaled down model of the original used by both the Union and Confederacy during the Cival War, brass furniture, with carriage, 18 lbs.

Mfg.'s Sug. Retail	$290	$275	$225	$185

MICHIGAN ARMS CORPORATION
Manufactured in Troy, MI.

Michigan Arms has made a long needed change for Black Powder enthusiasts. It is now possible with their 3 models — the Wolverine, the Friendship Special Match, and the Silver Wolf — to enjoy Black Powder shooting without the drawbacks commonly associated with it. Rather than using a percussion cap or flint, Michigan Arms has designed an extremely accurate and reliable ignition system using a Model 209 Win. shotgun primer. It is unsure whether any of these guns were produced. Shortly after beginning production an ATF ruling stated that the use of a primer rather than a percussion cap changed the classification of this from a Blackpowder gun to a firearm, requiring a dealers liscence for purchase. Because of this, any gun that could be aquired would have a unique collectors value.

WOLVERINE RIFLE — .45, .50 or .54 cal., positive ignition Win. Model 209 centerfire primer, 25¼ in. octagonal barrel, adj. sights, Dayton Traister rifle trigger with adj. pull, 8 lbs.

Mfg.'s Sug. Retail	$400	$320	$265	$210

FRIENDSHIP SPECIAL MATCH — .45, .50 or .54 cal., positive ignition Win. Model 209 centerfire primer, 25¼ in. octagonal barrel, fully adj. target sights with custom Maple stock, Dayton Traister rifle trigger with adj. pull, 8 lbs.

Mfg.'s Sug. Retail	$600	$470	$390	$310

SILVERWOLF — same as Wolverine, only available in stainless steel.

Mfg.'s Sug. Retail	$600	$470	$390	$310

MITCHELL ARMS
Manufacturer/importer, located in Santa Ana, CA.

REVOLVERS

1851 NAVY— .36 and .44 cal., percussion, 7½ in. round barrel, many styles, 6 shot engraved cylinder, 2 lbs. 12 oz.

Mfg.'s Sug. Retail	$200	$180	$155	$115

Prices are equal on Sheriff's Model.

SPILLER & BURR— .36 cal., percussion, 7½ in. barrel, brass frame, color casehardened hammer and loading lever, 2 lbs. 8 oz.

Mfg.'s Sug. Retail	$200	$180	$155	$115

Grading	100%	98%	95%	

1860 ARMY— .44 cal., percussion, 7½ in. barrel, 6 shot rebated cylinder, color casehardened frame, hammer and load lever, all brass backstrap and trigger guard, 2 lbs. 9 oz.

Mfg.'s Sug. Retail $200 $180 $155 $115

1861 NAVY— .36 and .44 cal., percussion, 7½ in. barrel, brass backstrap and trigger guard, color casehardened frame, hammer, and load lever, 2 lbs. 8 oz.

Mfg.'s Sug. Retail $200 $180 $155 $115

1858 REMINGTON — .36 and .44 cal., percussion, 8 in. octagonal barrel, 6 shot, brass frame and trigger guard.

Mfg.'s Sug. Retail $200 $180 $155 $115

1858 REMINGTON — same as above, has steel frame with brass backstrap and trigger guard.

Mfg.'s Sug. Retail $200 $180 $155 $115

BLACKPOWDER CARTRIDGE

1858 HENRY RIFLE — .44-40 cal., 24½ in. barrel, brass frame.

Mfg.'s Sug. Retail $875 $805 $700 $560

1866 WINCHESTER RIFLE/CARBINE — .44-40 cal., brass receiver, 24¼ in. octagonal barrel (19 in. round on carbine).

Mfg.'s Sug. Retail $700 $640 $560 $450

1873 WINCHESTER RIFLE— .44-40 cal., color casehardened steel receiver, 24 ¼ octagonal barrel.

Mfg.'s Sug. Retail $795 $750 $650 $520

MODERN MUZZLE LOADING, INC.

Distributor located in Lancaster, MO.

The Knight MK Series is the forerunner of the modern Black Powder rifle designed as a true hunting/sporting rifle. These Black Powder rifles feature a unique straight through sure-fire ignition system, double safety, inline bolt assembly, and Timney deluxe trigger system. The Knight rifle is extremely accurate (especially with MMP Sabot bullets) and weighs under 7 lbs. New in 1988.

PISTOLS

R-K 88 HAWK — .45, .50 and .54 cal. percussion, same action as MK rifles, modern (swept back)black composite stock. New in 1991.

Mfg.'s Sug. Retail $430 $365 N/A N/A

RIFLES

MK-85 BACK COUNTRY CARBINE— .45, .50, and .54 cal., percussion, 20 in. round barrel, Monte Carlo stock, double safety, 6 lbs. 10 oz. Add $60 for stainless steel.

Mfg.'s Sug. Retail $520 $445 $385 $310

KNIGHT MK-85 HUNTER— .45, .50 or .54 cal., percussion rifle, straight through ignition system, 24 in. round barrel drilled and tapped for scope, walnut stock, double safety system, under 7 lbs.

Mfg.'s Sug. Retail $520 $445 $385 $310

KNIGHT MK-85 STALKER — .45, .50 or .54 cal., percussion, 22 in. round barrel, monte carlo stock, double safety system, under 7 lbs.

Mfg.'s Sug. Retail $580 $495 $435 $350

Grading	100%	98%	95%	

KNIGHT MK-85 PREDATOR— .50 or .54 cal., percussion, 20 in. round barrel, black synthetic stock, double safety system, under 7 lbs.

Mfg.'s Sug. Retail	$650	$555	$485	$395

BK-89 SQUIRREL— .36 cal., percussion, 24 in. barrel, Monte Carlo stock, double safety, 5 lbs. 8 oz.

Mfg.'s Sug. Retail	$500	$420	$370	$295

T-5 WOODSMAN— .50 and .54 cal. percussion, 20 in. round barrel, hardwood stock, double safety, adj. sights, approx. 7 lbs. New in 1991.

Mfg.'s Sug. Retail	$230	$215	N/A	N/A

MK-85 GRIZZLY "PLB"— .54 cal. percussion, brown laminate stock, double safety. New in 1991.

Mfg.'s Sug. Retail	$650	$560	N/A	N/A

MOWREY GUN WORKS, INC.
Currently manufactured in Waldren, IN, previously manufactured in Saginaw, TX.

Mowrey Gun Works has recreated the guns designed by Ethan Allen and marketed under the name Allen & Thurber in the early and mid 1800's. The guns themselves are beautifully hand crafted with "cut rifled" browned barrels (each groove cut individually using as many as 20 passes) and actions using only 5 moving parts creating exceptional accuracy and reliability. The 1 in 30 inch rifling was designed specifically to stabilize conical bullets. Each gun is available with a number of features and options (listed below).

Standard: curly maple stocks and forearms, front blade- buckhorn rear and hand rubbed finish, brass or browned steel receivers.

Options: premium curly maple, cherry or walnut stock and forearm, barrel length from 22-40 in., primative fixed sight, target sights, Scheutzen style butt plate. Add $38 for fancy Grade Curly Maple, $25 for other than standard barrel length or modern sights, $25 for brass forearm on Plains Rifle, $30 for fancy brass or steel Scheutzen butt plate.

RIFLES: PERCUSSION

1-N-30 CONICAL RIFLE — .45, .50 and .54 cal., percussion, 28 in. octagonal barrel, brass furniture, special 1-N-30 twist rifling for conical bullets, 8 lbs.

Mfg.'s Sug. Retail	$350	$315	$275	$200

PLAINS RIFLE — .50 or .54 cal., percussion, 28 or 32 in. full octagonal barrel, brass furniture, 10 lbs. Add $25 for brass forearm.

Mfg.'s Sug. Retail	$350	$315	$275	$200

ROCKY MOUNTAIN HUNTER— .50 or .54 cal., percussion, 28 in. full octagonal barrel, all browned steel furniture, 8 lbs.

Mfg.'s Sug. Retail	$350	$315	$275	$200

SILHOUETTE RIFLE — .40 cal., percussion, 28 or 32 in. octagonal barrel, brass furniture.

Mfg.'s Sug. Retail	$350	$315	$275	$200

SQUIRREL RIFLE — .32, .36 or .45 cal., percussion, 28 in. full octagonal barrel, brass furniture, 7 lbs., deduct $10 for all steel furniture.

Mfg.'s Sug. Retail	$350	$315	$275	$200

SHOTGUNS: PERCUSSION

12 GAUGE SHOTGUN— 12 ga., percussion, 32 in. full octagonal barrel, brass or steel furniture, 7½ lbs.

Mfg.'s Sug. Retail	$350	$315	$275	$200

Grading	100%	98%	95%	

28 GAUGE SHOTGUN— 28 ga., percussion, 28 in. full octagonal barrel, brass or steel furniture, built on squirrel frame, 7½ lbs.

Mfg.'s Sug. Retail	$350	$315	$275	$200

MUZZLE LOADERS, INC.
Previous importer/distributor located in Burke, VA.

REVOLVERS

1847 WALKER— .44 cal., percussion, charcoal finish, color case hardened frame, hammer, and load lever, brass trim, engraved cylinder. 4.4 lbs.

	$180	$155	$115

1848 1ST MODEL DRAGOON — .44 cal., percussion, 6 shot, brass grip straps, color case hardened frame, hammer, and load lever, brass trim, 3.9 lbs.

	$180	$155	$115

1850 2ND MODEL DRAGOON — .44 cal., percussion, 6 shot, brass grip straps, color case hardened frame, hammer, and load lever, brass trim, 3.9 lbs.

	$180	$155	$115

1851 3RD MODEL DRAGOON — .44 cal., percussion, 6 shot, brass grip straps, color case hardened frame, hammer, and load lever, brass trim, 3.9 lbs. Add $15 for silver-plated straps, or cut for stock, add $35 for Military Model.

	$180	$155	$115

1851 NAVY — .36 or .44 cal., percussion, 7½ in. octagonal barrel, engraved (roll) cylinder, color case hardened frame and load lever, silver plated brass backstrap and square back trigger guard. Sheriff's Model has 5 in. barrel, brass trigger guard and backstrap. Deduct $10 for Sheriff's Model, $20 for brass backstrap and trigger guard, $50 for brass frame.

	$175	$150	$110

1860 ARMY — .44 cal., percussion, 8 in round barrel, color case hardened frame, hammer and load lever, 2 lbs. 9 oz. Deduct $25 for brass frame.

	$180	$150	$100

1862 POLICE — .36 cal., 5½ in. round barrel, color case hardened frame, loading lever, plunger, and hammer, round trigger guard, fluted cylinder, one piece stocks, 25 oz.

	$180	$150	$100

1858 REMINGTON — .36 or .44 cal., percussion, blued frame, brass trigger guard, steel backstrap, 6 shot, 2 lbs. 7 oz. Add $80 for stainless, deduct $20 for brass frame.

	$180	$150	$100

ROGERS & SPENCER— .44 cal., percussion, 7½ octagonal barrel, 2 lbs. 15 oz. Add $15 for target sights, $25 for engraved London grey finish.

	$170	$145	$100

PISTOLS

DELUXE KENTUCKY PISTOL— .44 cal., percussion or flintlock, 10¼ in. octagonal barrel, brass blade front sight, 40 oz. Add $15 for flintlock.

	$140	$110	$75

RIFLES

1853 2-BAND ENFIELD — .58 cal., percussion, 33 in. barrel, 2 barrel bands.

	$400	$350	$280

Grading	100%	98%	95%	

DELUXE HAWKEN RIFLE — .45 or .50 cal., percussion or flintlock, color case hardened hammer and lock, percussion cap holder in stock, chrome lined barrels.

	$215	$185	$145

DELUXE KENTUCKY RIFLE — .45 or .50 cal., percussion or flintlock, color case hardened hammer and lock, percussion cap holder in stock, chrome lined barrels, brass trim. Add $15 for flintlock.

	$255	$220	$150

ST. LOUIS HAWKENS — .50 cal., percussion, color case hardened hammer and lock, 28 in. octagonal barrel, brass trim, 7 lbs. 15 oz.

	$225	$175	$130

ZOUAVE RIFLE — .58 cal., percussion, brass trim, color case hardened hammer and lock, blue finish.

	$300	$295	$230

NAVY ARMS CO.
Manufacturer/importer/distributor located in Ridgefield, NJ.

PISTOLS: SINGLE SHOT

1775 BLACK WATCH SCOTTISH PISTOL — .58 cal., flintlock, 7 in. smooth bore white steel barrel, brass frame, ram's horn grip with round ball trigger.

Mfg.'s Sug. Retail	$145	$130	$115	$90

BRITISH DRAGOON PISTOL — .614 cal., flintlock, white steel with brass trim, first 240 production models will be used in Governor's palace restoration, Colonial Williamsburg. Add $100 for official Williamsburg crest.

	$360	$300	$240

Last Mfg.'s Sug. Retail was $395.

CHARLEVILLE 1777 PISTOL — .69 cal. flintlock, 7½ in. white steel smooth bore barrel, brass furniture, belt hook, walnut stock, 12 lbs. 12 oz.

Mfg.'s Sug. Retail	$160	$145	$125	$100

DURS EGG SAW HANDLED PISTOL — .45 cal., flintlock, 9½ in. blued octagonal barrel, unique stock, hand checkered, German silver trim, white steel hammer and lock.

	$210	$175	$140

Last Mfg.'s Sug. Retail was $235.

HARPERS FERRY MODEL 1855 — .58 cal., flintlock or percussion, 11¾ in. barrel, color case hardened lock and hammer, brass trim, 3 lbs. 14 oz. Add $35 for cased gun. Deduct $25 for percussion.

Mfg.'s Sug. Retail	$195	$175	$155	$120

J.S. HAWKINS PISTOL — .50 or .54 cal., percussion, 9 in. octagonal barrel, German silver trim, blued barrel, adj. trigger, 2 lbs. 9 oz.

	$195	$170	$120

Last Mfg.'s Sug. Retail was $200.

KENTUCKY PISTOL — .44 cal., flintlock or percussion, 10⅛ in. barrel, color case hardened lock and hammer, brass trim, 2 lbs. Add $16 for brass barrel. Deduct $20 for percussion (each gun).

Mfg.'s Sug. Retail	$145	$130	$115	$90

Cased

Mfg.'s Sug. Retail	$230	$210	$185	$150

Double cased set

Mfg.'s Sug. Retail	$350	$320	$280	$230

Grading	100%	98%	95%	

LEPAGE PISTOL— .45 cal., flintlock or percussion, 9 in. octagonal white steel barrel and trim, adj. sights, engraved spur type trigger guard, 2 lbs. 2 oz. Deduct $70 for percussion, $80 for percussion cased set, $160 for percussion cased pair. Values also apply to smooth bore model (flintlock only).

Mfg.'s Sug. Retail	$435	$395	$345	$240
Cased				
Mfg.'s Sug. Retail	$625	$575	$500	$360
Cased pair				
Mfg.'s Sug. Retail	$1,100	$1,000	$875	$650

1985 cased set— custom order only, gold trim, consecutive serial number.

	$1,800	$1,200	$1,000

Last Mfg.'s Sug. Retail was $1,975.

JOHN MANTON MATCH PISTOL — .45 cal., percussion, 10 in. white steel barrel and lock, brass trim, 2 lbs. 4 oz.

$215	$185	$135

Last Mfg.'s Sug. Retail was $225.

MOORE AND PATRICK PISTOL — .45 cal., flintlock or percussion, 10 in. octagonal barrel, white steel hammer and lock, German silver trim, 2 lbs. Disc. in 1987.

$235	$195	$165

Last Mfg.'s Sug. Retail was $295.

MOUNTAIN PISTOL — .50 cal., flintlock or percussion, 10 in. octagonal barrel, color casehardened hammer and lock, brass furniture, 2 lbs. 4 oz. Add $10 for flintlock.

Mfg.'s Sug. Retail	$145	$130	$115	$90

NAPOLEON LEPAGE PISTOL—.45 cal., percussion, 10 in. octagonal white steel barrel and lock, brass trim, adj. double set triggers, fluted grip, 2 lbs. 7 oz.

$160	$140	$105

Last Mfg.'s Sug. Retail was $175.

W. PARKER PISTOL — .45 cal., percussion, 10 in. blued octagonal barrel, German silver lock and trim, adj. double set triggers, 2 lbs. 8 oz.

$220	$185	$150

Last Mfg.'s Sug. Retail was $250.

QUEEN ANNE PISTOL — .50 cal., flintlock, 7½ in. smooth bore, unique cannon style bronzed steel barrel, 2 lbs. 4 oz.

Mfg.'s Sug. Retail	$145	$130	$115	$90

F. ROCHETTE PISTOL — .45 cal., percussion, 10 in. round barrel with flat top, white steel lock and trim, adj. double set triggers, 2 lbs. 8 oz.

$220	$185	$150

Last Mfg.'s Sug. Retail was $250.

PISTOLS: DERRINGER STYLE

ELGIN CUTLAS — .44 cal., percussion, combination knife pistol, white steel hammer and barrel, brass trim, 2 lbs.

$80	$65	$50

Last Mfg.'s Sug. Retail was $80.

PHILADELPHIA DERRINGER — .45 cal., percussion, 3 in. barrel, color case hardened lock and hammer, German silver trim, checkered stock, ¾ lb.

$120	$100	$80

Last Mfg.'s Sug. Retail was $130.

Grading	100%	98%	95%

ENGRAVED "SNAKE EYES" PISTOL — .36 cal., percussion, 2⅝ in. brass double barrel, double hammers, 1½ lbs. Deduct $75 if not engraved.

	$145	$120	$95

REVOLVERS

1847 WALKER — .44 cal., percussion, 9 in. round barrel, color case hardened hammer, frame, and load lever, brass trim, engraved barrel and cylinder, 4 lbs. 11 oz. Add $85 for cased set, $200 for deluxe Uberti cased set.

Mfg.'s Sug. Retail	$225	$210	$185	$145

COLT 1851 NAVY - YANK — .36 or .44 cal., percussion, 7½ in. octagonal barrel, color case hardened hammer, frame, and load lever, brass trim. Add $5 for silver plated back strap and trigger guard, $60 for shoulder stock.

Mfg.'s Sug. Retail	$125	$115	$100	$80
Cased set				
Mfg.'s Sug. Retail	$225	$200	$175	$130
Double cased set				
Mfg.'s Sug. Retail	$325	$315	$275	$210

AUGUSTA CONFEDERATE — .36 cal. percussion, 5 or 7 in. barrel, brass frame (confederate copy of 1851 Navy), walnut grips.

Mfg.'s Sug. Retail	$200	$175	$150	$120

1861 NAVY—.36 cal., percussion, 7½ in. round barrel, cylinder engraved with navy scene, color case hardened hammer, frame, and load lever, brass trim, 2¾ lbs. Add $60 for shoulder stock. Also available in 5½ in. barrel Sheriff's model.

	$115	$100	$80

Last Mfg.'s Sug. Retail was $140.

Cased set

	$200	$175	$130

Last Mfg.'s Sug. Retail was $230.

Double cased set

	$315	$275	$210

Last Mfg.'s Sug. Retail was $385.

1860 ARMY — .44 cal., percussion, 8 in. round barrel, color case hardened hammer, frame, and load lever, roll engraved or fluted cylinder, 2 lbs. 12 oz. Add $60 for shoulder stock. Deduct $40 for 5½ in. barrel Sheriff's model for each gun in cased set (Sheriff's Model available in .36 or .44 cal.).

Mfg.'s Sug. Retail	$145	$135	$115	$95
Cased set				
Mfg.'s Sug. Retail	$220	$200	$175	$140
Double cased set				
Mfg.'s Sug. Retail	$365	$335	$290	$230

REB MODEL 1860 "GRISWOLD AND GUNNINSON" — .36 or .44 cal., percussion, 7½ in. round barrel, brass frame, color case hardened hammer and load lever, 5½ in. barrel Sheriff's Model, 2 lbs. 12 oz.

Mfg.'s Sug. Retail	$100	$95	$80	$65

Due to overstock, several 1860 Reb revolvers were factory de-activated and cannot be re-activated. These guns can be used only as props — values currently are in the $55 range.

Cased set				
Mfg.'s Sug. Retail	$190	$175	$150	$120
Double cased set				
Mfg.'s Sug. Retail	$300	$270	$235	$180

Grading	100%	98%	95%

1862 POLICE — .36 cal., percussion, 5½ in. round to octagonal barrel, color case hardened hammer, frame, and load lever, brass trim, 1 lb. 10 oz. Add $50 for cased Law & Order set (book style presentation case).

Mfg.'s Sug. Retail $210 $185 $160 $125

COLT PATERSON — .36 cal., percussion, 7½ in. octagonal barrel, standard "hidden trigger" design, blued steel hardware, no loading lever, 2 lbs. 9 oz. Add $120 for engraved version.

Mfg.'s Sug. Retail $310 $275 $240 $185

LEECH & RIGDON — .36 cal., percussion, 7½ in. barrel, color case hardened hammer, frame, and load lever, brass trim, 2 lbs. 10 oz.

     $120 $100 $80

LEMATE REVOLVER—.44 cal., percussion, 9 shot cylinder, plus 1 shot center barrel (maximum fire power for its day), 7⅝ in. octagonal barrel, white steel frame, 3 lbs. 7 oz. Add $350 for engraved Beauregard model, $160 for 18th Georgia engraved model.

Mfg.'s Sug. Retail $595 $550 $480 $375

Add $85 for single case, $110 for double case (not including guns).

REMINGTON 1858 NEW ARMY— .36. or .44 cal., percussion, 6½ in. barrel, brass trim. Add $20 for nickel or target model, $80 for stainless steel, $160 for Deluxe Uberti Model. Deduct $20 for brass frame (each gun in a cased set).

Mfg.'s Sug. Retail $145 $135 $115 $90
Cased set
Mfg.'s Sug. Retail $220 $200 $175 $140
Double cased set
Mfg.'s Sug. Retail $365 $320 $290 $220

ROGERS & SPENCER — .44 cal., percussion, 7½ in. octagonal barrel, blued trim, 3 lbs. Add $15 for satin finish, $35 for Target Model.

Mfg.'s Sug. Retail $215 $195 $170 $120

SPILLER & BURR— .36. cal., percussion, 7 in. barrel, brass frame, color case hardened hammer and load lever, 2 lbs. 8 oz.

Mfg.'s Sug. Retail $125 $115 $100 $75
Cased set
Mfg.'s Sug. Retail $215 $195 $170 $130
Double cased set
Mfg.'s Sug. Retail $325 $290 $250 $200

RIFLES

BROWN BESS MUSKET — .75 cal., flintlock, 42 in. white steel barrel, hammer, and lock, brass trim, 9½ lbs. Add $100 for Colonial Williamsburg seal. Deduct $30 for carbine model.

Mfg.'s Sug. Retail $550 $505 $440 $350

BROWN BESS MUSKET (ECONOMY MODEL) — same as above, all brass hardware. Disc. in 1987.

     $430 $375 $300

Last Mfg.'s Sug. Retail was $470.

BUFFALO HUNTER — .58 cal., percussion, 26 in. round barrel, color case hardened hammer and lock, brass trim, 8 lbs.

     $240 $200 $160

1763 CHARLEVILLE MUSKET — .69 cal., flintlock, 44⅝ in. white steel barrel, hammer, and lock, brass trim, 8¾ lbs. Add $45 for 1777 model, or 1816 Mt. Wickman model with steel ramrod and brass flash pan.

Mfg.'s Sug. Retail $550 $490 $425 $320

Grading	100%	98%	95%	

COUNTRY BOY — .32, .36, .45 or .50 cal., percussion, 26 in. octagonal barrel, matte black metal "no glare" finish on all parts, based on mule ear percussion lock, adj. sights, 6 lbs. Add $60 each for extra barrels.

| Mfg.'s Sug. Retail | $165 | $145 | $125 | $100 |

CUB RIFLE — .36 cal., percussion, 26 in. octagonal barrel, adj. sights, color case hardened lock, walnut stock, 5 lbs. 12 oz. Add $60 for extra barrel.

| Mfg.'s Sug. Retail | $175 | $160 | $140 | $110 |

MODEL 1853 3 BAND ENFIELD — .58 cal., percussion, 39 in. round barrel, color case hardened hammer and lock, brass trim, blued bands, adj. rear sight, 9½ lbs. Add $160 for Parker Hale version.

| Mfg.'s Sug. Retail | $400 | $370 | $325 | $230 |

MODEL 1858 2 BAND ENFIELD — .58 cal., percussion, 33 in. round barrel, color case hardened hammer and lock, brass trim, blued bands, adj. rear sight, 10 lbs. Add $165 for Parker Hale version.

| Mfg.'s Sug. Retail | $350 | $325 | $285 | $220 |

MODEL 1861 ENFIELD MUSKETOON — .58 cal., percussion, 24 in. round barrel, color case hardened hammer and lock, brass trim, blued bands, adj. rear sight, 7 lbs. Add $135 for Parker Hale version.

| Mfg.'s Sug. Retail | $300 | $280 | $245 | $190 |

HAWKEN RIFLE — .50, .54, or .58 cal., flintlock and percussion, 28 in. octagonal barrel, double set triggers, brass trim, 8 lbs. 8 oz. Deduct $15 for percussion.

| Mfg.'s Sug. Retail | $230 | $215 | $185 | $140 |

HAWKEN MARK 1 RIFLE—.50 or .54 cal., flintlock or percussion. 26 in. octagonal barrel, adj. double set triggers and sights, brass trim, 9 lbs. Add $15 for flintlock, $140 for commemorative model.

| | $215 | $185 | $140 |

Last Mfg.'s Sug. Retail was $260.

HUNTER RIFLE/CARBINE— .50, .54, or .58 cal., percussion, 28½ in. octagonal barrel, (.22½ carbine), color case hardened hammer and lock, double set triggers, 7 lbs. 12 oz. (6 lbs. 12 oz. carbine).

| Mfg.'s Sug. Retail | $230 | $215 | $185 | $140 |

ITHACA-NAVY HAWKENS— .50 or .54 cal., flintlock or percussion. 26 in. octagonal barrel, adj. double set triggers and sights, brass trim, 9 lbs. Add $65 for flintlock. (Left hand version disc. in 1987, .54 cal. disc. in 1991).

| Mfg.'s Sug. Retail | $365 | $340 | $295 | $225 |

HARPERS FERRY 1803 RIFLE — .58 cal., flintlock, 35 in. round barrel, color case hardened hammer and lock, brass trim, 8 lbs. 8 oz.

| Mfg.'s Sug. Retail | $475 | $430 | $380 | $290 |

J.P. MURRY ARTILLARY CARBINE— .58 cal., percussion, 23½ in. browned, round barrel, color case hardened hammer and lock, brass trim and bands, 7½ lbs.

| Mfg.'s Sug. Retail | $300 | $275 | $240 | $155 |

KENTUCKY RIFLE— .45 or .50 cal., percussion or flintlock, 35 in. barrel, color case hardened hammer and lock, brass trim, adj. brass rear sight (windage only), 6 lbs. 14 oz. Add $15 for flintlock or .45 cal. standard, $125 for .45 cal. deluxe.

| Mfg.'s Sug. Retail | $240 | $220 | $190 | $150 |

KODIAK DOUBLE RIFLE— .50, .54, or .58 cal., percussion, 28 in. double barrel, white steel furniture. New in 1989.

| Mfg.'s Sug. Retail | $550 | $520 | $450 | $360 |

Grading	100%	98%	95%

MISSISSIPPI RIFLE 1841— .58 cal., percussion, 33 in. browned round barrel, color case hardened hammer and lock, brass trim and bands, 9½ lbs.

Mfg.'s Sug. Retail $425 $390 $340 $235

MORSE RIFLE — .50 cal., percussion, 26 in. octagonal barrel, brass trim and action, blued barrel and hammer, adj. rear sight, windage only, 6 lbs.

     $210 $175 $140

MORTIMER RIFLE — .54 cal., flintlock, 36 in. browned barrel, color case hardened furniture, waterproof flash pan, chrome lined bore, 9 lbs. New in 1989. Add $250 for extra 12 ga. barrel.

Mfg.'s Sug. Retail $535 $490 $425 $340

MULE EAR MOUNTAIN MAN'S SQUIRREL RIFLE — .32, .36, or .45 cal., percussion, 26 in. octagonal barrel, brass trim, blued barrel, hammer, lock, and trigger, 5½ lbs.

     $205 $180 $140

Last Mfg.'s Sug. Retail was $185.

PARKER HALE VOLUNTEER RIFLE (IMPORTED)—.451 cal., percussion, 32 in. barrel, brass trim, blued band, color case hardened hammer and lock, adj. sights, 9½ lbs. Add $55 for 3-Band model.

Mfg.'s Sug. Retail $750 $690 $600 $480

PARKER HALE WHITWORTH VOLUNTEER RIFLE (IMPORTED) — .45 cal., percussion, 36 in. barrel, brass trim, blued barrel and bands, color case hardened hammer and lock, adj. sights, detented lock hammer, long range accuracy app. 1000 yds., comes with accessories, 9¼ lbs.

Mfg.'s Sug. Retail $815 $750 $650 $520

PENNSYLVANIA HALF STOCK HUNTER — .50 cal., percussion, 30 in. octagonal barrel, white steel hammer and lock, brass patchbox and trim, walnut stock, 6 lbs. 4 oz.

Mfg.'s Sug. Retail $220 $190 $165 $130

PENNSYLVANIA LONG RIFLE — .32 or .45 cal., flintlock or percussion, 40½ in. octagonal barrel, color case hardened hammer and lock, brass patchbox and trim, walnut stock, 7 lbs. 8 oz. Deduct $15 for percussion.

Mfg.'s Sug. Retail $300 $275 $240 $190

PIONEER RIFLE — .45 or .50 cal., flintlock, 30 in. octagonal barrel, color case hardened hammer and lock, walnut stock, 6 lbs. 4 oz.

Mfg.'s Sug. Retail $190 $175 $150 $120

RIGBY STYLE TARGET—.451 cal., 32 in. round blued barrel, color case hardened hammer and lock, hand checkered walnut stock, very similar to a modern day firearm, adj. vernier sights, 7 lbs. 12 oz.

Mfg.'s Sug. Retail $645 $595 $515 $370

1808/1835 SPRINGFIELD — .69 cal., flintlock, 44 in. round barrel, all white steel, walnut stock, 8 lbs. 12 oz.

Mfg.'s Sug. Retail $575 $500 $435 $350

The Model 1835 Springfield is a more refined version of the Model 1808. This was the last flintlock issued by the U.S. Army.

1863 SPRINGFIELD — .58 cal., percussion, 40 in. barrel, all white steel, 3 barrel bands, 9½ lbs.

Mfg.'s Sug. Retail $550 $505 $440 $325

Grading	100%	98%	95%	

SMITH ARTILLERY/CAVALRY CARBINE — .54 cal., percussion, 20½ in. octagonal tapering to round barrel, white steel hammer and receiver. New in 1989.

| Mfg.'s Sug. Retail | $595 | $535 | $465 | $370 |

SWISS FEDERAL TARGET RIFLE — .45 cal., percussion, 32 in. octagonal barrel, color case hardened hammer, lock, and trim, double set triggers, classic Bristlen and Morges design, adj., sights, 13¼ lbs. Add $35 for palm rest. Imported from West Germany by Neumann Co.

| | $1,050 | $900 | $725 | |

Last Mfg.'s Sug. Retail was $1,200.

TRYON RIFLE — .45 cal., percussion, 34 in octagonal barrel, white steel hammer and engraved lock and patchbox, double set triggers, walnut stock, 9 lbs. 12 oz. Add $35 for target sights, $150 for Creedmore Target Model.

| Mfg.'s Sug. Retail | $335 | $305 | $265 | $200 |

ZOUAVE RIFLE — .58 cal., percussion, 32½ in. round barrel, color case hardened hammer, lock, and trigger, brass trim, adj. rear sight, 9 lbs. Add $140 for deluxe.

| Mfg.'s Sug. Retail | $375 | $345 | $300 | $220 |

RIFLES: BLACK POWDER CARTRIDGE

CREEDMOOR TARGET — 45/70 rimfire, 30 in. tapered barrel, color case hardened action, beautiful reproduction, adj. sights, 9 lbs.

| Mfg.'s Sug. Retail | $640 | $565 | $490 | $400 |

IRON FRAME HENRY — .44-40, or .44 rimfire, 24 in. barrel, cast iron action, color case hardened receiver, lever and hammer, beautiful reproduction, adj. sights, 9¼ lbs. Add $10 for blued receiver.

| Mfg.'s Sug. Retail | $885 | $785 | $685 | $500 |

HENRY MILITARY/CARBINE RIFLE — .44-40, or .44 rimfire, 24 in. barrel, brass frame and trim, color case hardened lever and hammer, beautiful reproduction, military version has sling swivels, mounted on left side, adj. sights, 9¼ lbs.

| Mfg.'s Sug. Retail | $875 | $775 | $675 | $495 |

For engraving add $330 for 25%, $540 for 35%, $900 for 50%.

HENRY TRAPPER — .44-40, or .44 rimfire, 16½ in. barrel, brass frame and trim, color case hardened lever and hammer, beautiful reproduction, adj. sights, 7¼ lbs.

| Mfg.'s Sug. Retail | $875 | $775 | $675 | $495 |

For engraving add $330 for 25%, $540 for 35%, $900 for 50%.

ROLLING BLOCK BUFFALO RIFLE (REMINGTON STYLE) — 45/70 rimfire, varying barrel length, ½ round or octagonal, color case hardened action, brass trigger guard, beautiful reproduction, adj. sights, approx. 9 lbs. Add $25 for Creedmoor Model.

| Mfg.'s Sug. Retail | $485 | $425 | $375 | $290 |

SHARPS PLAINS RIFLE/CAVALRY CARBINE — 45/70 rimfire, 28½ in. barrel, (22 in. barrel carbine), color case hardened hammer and reciever, walnut stock, 7 lbs. 12 oz.

| Mfg.'s Sug. Retail | $650 | $570 | $495 | $390 |

Cavalry Model also available in .54 cal. percussion.

WINCHESTER 1873 RIFLE/CARBINE — .44-40 cal. rimfire, 20 in. round barrel, 11 shot walnut stock, trapdoor buttplate for cleaning rod, 7 lbs. Add $20 for rifle.

| Mfg.'s Sug. Retail | $800 | $700 | $610 | $460 |

1866 YELLOW BOY RIFLE/CARBINE — .44-40 cal. rimfire, 19 in. round barrel, walnut stock, 7½ lbs. Add $15 for rifle.

| Mfg.'s Sug. Retail | $660 | $580 | $505 | $395 |

Grading	100%	98%	95%

SHOTGUNS

CLASSIC SXS — 12 or 10 ga., percussion, 28 in. barrel, color case hardened hammer, lock, and trim, 7¾ lbs. Add $20 for .10 ga. (10 ga. disc. in 1987).

Mfg.'s Sug. Retail	$395	$355	$295	$240

FOWLER SHOTGUN— 10 or 12 ga., 28 in. barrel, color case hardened hammer and lock, 7 lbs. 6 oz.

Mfg.'s Sug. Retail	$295	$270	$235	$170

Add $100 for steel shot 10 ga. model.

Add $100 for extra 10 ga. barrel.

HUNTER SHOTGUN — 20 ga., 28½ in. barrel, round chrome lined color case hardened hammer and lock, double set triggers, 7 lbs. 12 oz. Disc. in 1989.

	$230	$200	$165

Last Mfg.'s Sug. Retail was $190.

MORSE SHOTGUN — .12 ga., percussion, 26 in. barrel, brass receiver and trim, blued hammer and butt plate, 5¾ lbs. Disc. in 1987.

	$240	$210	$175

Last Mfg.'s Sug. Retail was $165.

MORTIMER SHOTGUN — 12 ga., flintlock, 36 in. browned barrel, color case hardened furniture, walnut stock, waterproof pan and chrome bore. New in 1989.

Mfg.'s Sug. Retail	$535	$490	$425	$340

TURKEY AND TRAP — 12 ga., percussion s x s, 28 in. blued barrels, color case hardened locks and furniture, walnut stock.

Mfg.'s Sug. Retail	$375	$340	$295	$225

OLD-WEST GUN CO.

Importer and distributor that took over the inventory of Allen Fireams after they went out of business in early 1987. Old-West Gun Co. became Cimarron Arms Co. in 1987. Older guns marked Old West have the same values as those of Cimarron Arms Co. (Please refer to the Cimarron heading in this text).

RICHLAND ARMS

Previously distributed in Blissfield, MI.

PISTOLS

ANDREW TARGET — .32, .36. or .45 cal., percussion, 10 in. octagonal barrel, white steel hammer, barrel, frame, and sights, brass trigger guard, adj. trigger and sights, blued and engraved, 2 lbs. 10 oz. Add $55 for deluxe grade.

	$150	$120	$90

Last Mfg.'s Sug. Retail was $150.

REVOLVERS

1860 ARMY — .44 cal., percussion, 8 in. barrel, color case hardened hammer, frame, trigger and load lever, brass trigger guard, engraved cylinder. Deduct $25 for brass frame.

	$135	$115	$95

Last Mfg.'s Sug. Retail was $160.

Grading	100%	98%	95%

3rd MODEL DRAGOON — .44 cal., percussion, 7½ in. barrel, color case hardened hammer, frame, trigger and load lever, engraved cylinder, 66 oz.

| | $165 | $135 | $100 |

Last Mfg.'s Sug. Retail was $165.

1851 NAVY — .36 cal., percussion, 7½ in. octagonal barrel, color case hardened load lever and hammer, brass frame and trigger guard, 44 oz. Add $25 for steel frame.

| | $115 | $100 | $80 |

Last Mfg.'s Sug. Retail was $100.

WALKER — .44 cal., percussion, 9 in. round barrel, color case hardened hammer, frame, trigger and load lever, engraved cylinder, brass trigger guard, 73 oz.

| | $200 | $175 | $130 |

Last Mfg.'s Sug. Retail was $185.

REMINGTON REPLICAS

1858 ARMY — .44 cal., percussion, 8 in. octagonal barrel, brass frame and trigger guard, 44 oz. Add $25 for steel frame.

| | $145 | $125 | $100 |

Last Mfg.'s Sug. Retail was $125.

BUFFALO TARGET — .44 cal., percussion, 12 in. octagonal barrel, brass frame and trigger guard, adj. sights, based on 1858 Navy frame, 38 oz.

| | $235 | $205 | $160 |

Last Mfg.'s Sug. Retail was $150.

RIFLES

BRISTOL HUNTER — .50 or .54 cal., percussion, 28 in. octagonal barrel, color case hardened hammer and lock, rubber recoil pad, adj. rear sights, chrome plated bore, double set triggers.

| | $205 | $180 | $155 |

Last Mfg.'s Sug. Retail was $240.

HAWKEN RIFLE — .50 cal., percussion, 28 in. octagonal barrel, color case hardened hammer and lock, brass trim, adj. sights, double set triggers.

| | $200 | $175 | $130 |

Last Mfg.'s Sug. Retail was $225.

KODIAK DOUBLE BARREL RIFLE — .50 or .58 cal., percussion, 28 in. octagonal barrel. Add $280 for extra .12 ga. shotgun barrels.

| | $545 | $500 | $370 |

Last Mfg.'s Sug. Retail was $560.

SHOTGUNS

MUZZLE LOADING SHOTGUNS — .10 or .12 ga., percussion. Add $55 for .10 ga.

| | $270 | $235 | $170 |

Last Mfg.'s Sug. Retail was $320.

RUGER
Manufactured in Southport, CT.

OLD ARMY — .44 cal., 6 shot, percussion, 7½ in. barrel, adj. rear sight, blue or stainless.

| Mfg.'s Sug. Retail | $320 | $275 | $240 | $180 |

Grading	100%	98%	95%	

Stainless Old Army — stainless steel variation of the Old Army.

Mfg.'s Sug. Retail $405 $355 $310 $235

SILE DISTRIBUTORS

Importer and distributor of Invest Arms Brand and D. Pederson Brand., located in New York, NY.

REVOLVERS

1860 COLT ARMY — .44 cal., percussion, 8 in. blued round barrel, brass or color case hardened steel frame, brass trigger guard and back strap, color case hardened hammer, trigger, and load lever, 2 lbs. 11 oz. Deduct $15 for brass frame.

     $125 $110 $90

1858 REMINGTON ARMY — .44 cal., percussion, 8 in. white octagonal barrel, white steel frame, brass trigger guard, 2 lbs. 9 oz. Add $50 for stainless steel, $75 for stainless steel target.

     $140 $120 $95

RIFLES

BROWN BESS MUSKET — .75 cal., flintlock, 41¾ in. smooth bore barrel, brass furniture, white steel barrel, hammer, and lock, engraved lock, 9 lbs.

     $375 $325 $275

HAWKEN RIFLE— .45, .50 or .54 cal., flintlock or percussion (.50 cal. only in flintlock), 29 in. octagonal barrel, solid brass furniture, color case hardened engraved lock, coil spring mechanism with adj. set triggers, stainless steel nickel, chrome bore, brass patch box, adj. sights, 8 lbs. 10 oz. Add $10 for flintlock.

Mfg.'s Sug. Retail $245 $200 $175 $130

HAWKEN RIFLE CARBINE— .45, .50 or .54 cal., flintlock or percussion (.50 cal. only in flintlock), 22 in. octagonal barrel, solid brass furniture, color case hardened engraved lock, coil spring mechanism with adj. set triggers, stainless steel nickel, chrome bore, brass patch box, adj. sights, 7 lbs. Add $10 for flintlock.

Mfg.'s Sug. Retail $245 $200 $175 $130

HAWKEN HUNTER CARBINE—.45, .50 or .54 cal., flintlock or percussion (.50 cal. only in flintlock), 22 in. octagonal barrel, solid brass furniture, color case hardened engraved lock, coil spring mechanism with adj. set triggers, stainless steel nickel, chrome bore, brass patch box, adj. sights, 7 lbs. Add $10 for flintlock.

Mfg.'s Sug. Retail $265 $210 $185 $140

KENTUCKY RIFLE — .45 or .50 cal., flintlock or percussion, 32 in. blued octagonal barrel, solid brass furniture, color case hardened hammer and engraved lock, brass patch box, adj. rear sight, 7 lbs. 2 oz. Add $10 for flintlock.

     $230 $200 $150

PENNSYLVANIAN SQUIRREL RIFLE — .32 cal., flintlock, 40½ in. browned octagonal barrel, adj. double set triggers, polished white steel hammer and lock, 9 lbs.

     $275 $240 $180

SHOTGUNS

SXS DOUBLE BARREL — 10 or 12 ga., percussion, 28 in. double blued barrels, engraved furniture, color case hardened hammer and engraved lock, chrome lined bores, 7 lbs. 12 oz. (8 lbs. 12 oz. for 10 ga.). Add $45 for 10 ga.

     $340 $295 $210

Grading	100%	98%	95%

SOUTHWEST MUZZLE LOADERS SUPPLY
Located in Angleton, TX.

Importer of Uberti, Italian replicas. See Uberti.

DANCE REVOLVER — .36 or .44 cal., exact reproduction of the original J.H. Dance & Brothers revolver manufactured in Dance, Texas, 500 total production, manufactured by Alto Uberti & Co. from Brescia, Italy, cased. New in 1985.

| | $400 | $310 | $270 |

Last Mfg.'s Sug. Retail was $1,500.

TAYLOR'S & CO., INC.
Importer/distributor located in Winchester, VA.

PISTOLS: SINGLE SHOT

KENTUCKY PISTOL — .45 cal., percussion, 10¼ in. octagonal barrel, brass blade front sight, 2½ lbs.

| Mfg.'s Sug. Retail | $170 | $150 | $130 | $100 |

NAPOLEON LEPAGE PISTOL — .45 cal., percussion, 10 in. barrel, white steel barrel and lock, fixed sights with single barrel wedge, silver plated butt cap and trigger guard, double set triggers, 2 lbs. 7 oz.

| | $240 | $210 | $170 |

Last Mfg.'s Sug. Retail was $310.

F. ROCHATTE DUELLING PISTOL — .45 cal., percussion, 10 in. round barrel with flat top, white steel lock and trim, adj. double set triggers, 2½ lbs.

| | $275 | $225 | $190 |

Last Mfg.'s Sug. Retail was $395.

REVOLVERS

1847 WALKER — .44 cal., percussion, 9 in. blued barrel, color case hardened frame, hammer, and loading lever, brass trigger guard and steel backstrap, 4 lbs. 6 oz.

| Mfg.'s Sug. Retail | $215 | $185 | $160 | $125 |

DRAGOON (1ST, 2ND, OR 3RD) — .44 cal., percussion, 7½ in. barrel, roll engraving cylinder, brass backstrap.

| Mfg.'s Sug. Retail | $215 | $185 | $160 | $125 |

1851 NAVY — .36 or .44 cal., percussion, 7½ in. octagonal barrel, rolled cylinder scene, color case hardened frame, hammer, and loading lever, brass backstrap and trigger guard. Sheriff's Model has 5 in. barrel.

| Mfg.'s Sug. Retail | $140 | $120 | $105 | $85 |

Deduct $30 for brass frame.

1860 ARMY — .44 cal., percussion, 8 in. round barrel, color case hardened frame, hammer, and loading lever, 2¾ lbs.

| Mfg.'s Sug. Retail | $160 | $135 | $120 | $90 |

Deduct $30 for brass frame.

Grading	100%	98%	95%	

1858 REMINGTON ARMY — .36 or .44 cal., percussion, 6½ and 8 in. octagonal barrel, color case hardened hammer, steel or brass frame, 2 lbs. 6 oz.

Mfg.'s Sug. Retail	$170	$150	$130	$100

Deduct $40 for brass frame.

RIFLES

C.S. RICHMOND MUSKET — .58 cal., percussion, white steel hammer and furniture, brass nosecap, similar to Charleville Musket.

Mfg.'s Sug. Retail	$525	$425	$370	$295

CHARLEVILLE 1777 MUSKET — .69 cal., flintlock, 44¾ in. smooth bore barrel, white steel lockplate, hammer, and ramrod, brass barrel bands, trigger guard, and buttplate, walnut stock.

Mfg.'s Sug. Retail	$550	$540	$470	$340

DELUXE HAWKEN RIFLE — .50 cal., percussion, 30 in. octagonal chrome lined barrel, brass patchbox, target sights, double set triggers, 8 lbs.

Mfg.'s Sug. Retail	$235	$200	$175	$130

HAWKEN HUNTER CARBINE — .50 cal., percussion, 24 in. octagonal chrome lined barrel, rubber recoil pad, sling swivels, double set triggers.

Mfg.'s Sug. Retail	$255	$220	$190	$140

KENTUCKY RIFLE — .45 and .50 cal., percussion, 35 in. octagonal barrel, color casehardened lock, brass buttplate, trigger guard, patchbox, sideplates, thimbles and nosecap, walnut stock with large or small patchbox, rifle weighs 7½ lbs., carbine is 6 lbs.

Mfg.'s Sug. Retail	$300	$275	$240	$135

Add $10 for large patchbox.

Carbine Model — .50 cal., percussion, chrome lined barrel.

Mfg.'s Sug. Retail	$325	$300	$260	$200

Add $20 for large patchbox.

PENNSYLVANIA RIFLE—.45 cal., percussion, octagonal barrel, color case hardened hammer and lock, small brass patchbox, approx. 7 lbs.

Mfg.'s Sug. Retail	$215	$190	$165	$130

1861 SPRINGFIELD — .58 cal., percussion, 40 in. round barrel, white steel barrel, hammer, lock, trigger, and trim, 10¼ lbs.

Mfg.'s Sug. Retail	$525	$410	$355	$285

ST. LOUIS HAWKEN RIFLE—.50 cal., percussion, 30 in. octagonal barrel, all black steel furniture, adj. rear sight, double set triggers, approx. 8 lbs.

Mfg.'s Sug. Retail	$235	$200	$175	$130

1863 ZOUAVE RIFLE—.58 cal., percussion, 32½ in. round barrel, color case hardened hammer, lock, and trigger, brass patchbox, trigger guard, and barrel bands, 9 lbs.

Mfg.'s Sug. Retail	$365	$340	$295	$190

THOMPSON/CENTER ARMS
U.S. manufacturer located in Rochester, NH.

Grading	100%	98%	95%	

PISTOLS

PATRIOT — .36 or .45 cal., percussion, 9 in. barrel, double set triggers, target stock, walnut, color case hardened hammer and lock. Disc. 1987.

	$240	$200	$145	

Last Mfg.'s Sug. Retail was $235.

SCOUT PISTOL — .50 and .54 cal., percussion, 12 in. barrel, in-line ignition, walnut grips, 4 lbs. 6 oz.

Mfg.'s Sug. Retail	$275	$255	$220	$175

Similar in design to old style single shot Remington Target. Add $125 for extra barrel.

RIFLES

BIG BOAR — .58 cal. percussion, 26 in. octagonal barrel, color case hardened hammer and lock, single hunting style trigger, American walnut stock, recoil pad and swivels, 7 lbs. 12 oz.

Mfg.'s Sug. Retail	$330	$305	$265	N/A

NEW ENGLANDER RIFLE — .50 and .54 cal., percussion, 24 and 28 in. barrel, brass furniture, walnut or rynite (new 1991) stock, 5 lbs. 2 oz. Add $95 for extra .50 cal. barrel, $15 for left hand.

Mfg.'s Sug. Retail	$260	$240	$210	$160

HAWKEN COUGAR — .45 or .50 cal., stainless steel version of Hawken, percussion only, select hardwood stock.

	$350	$290	$230	

PENNSYLVANIA HUNTER — .50 cal., flintlock or percussion, 31 in. octagonal barrel, color case hardened hammer and lock, 7 lbs. 9 oz. Add $15 for left hand, $15 for flintlock.

Mfg.'s Sug. Retail	$310	$290	$250	$200

RENEGADE—.50 or .54 cal., percussion or flintlock, 26 in. octagonal barrel, color case hardened hammer and lock, double set triggers, 8 lbs. Also in .56 cal. — smooth bore. Add $10 for flintlock, add $105 for 12 ga. barrel. Deduct $20 for single trigger Hunter Model (new in 1987).

Mfg.'s Sug. Retail	$325	$300	$260	$200

SCOUT RIFLE — .50 and .54 cal., percussion, 21 in. round barrel, in- line ignition, 7 lbs. 4 oz.

Mfg.'s Sug. Retail	$370	$340	$295	$235

Similar in design to old style single shot Remington Target. Add $135 for extra barrels.

SENECA — .36 or .45 cal., percussion, 27 in. octagonal barrel, color case hardened hammer and lock, double set triggers, American walnut, 6 lbs. Disc. in 1987.

	$270	$235	$200	

Last Mfg.'s Sug. Retail was $300.

HAWKEN — .45, .50, or .54 cal., percussion or flintlock, 28 in. octagonal barrel, color case hardened hammer and lock, double set triggers, 8½ lbs. Add $15 for flintlock, add $105 for 12 ga. barrel.

Mfg.'s Sug. Retail	$365	$340	$295	$220

CHEROKEE— .32, .36 or .45 cal., percussion, 24 in. octagonal barrel, double set triggers, color case hardened hammer and lock, brass trim, American walnut. Add $115 for extra barrel.

Mfg.'s Sug. Retail	$320	$295	$255	$200

WHITE MOUNTAIN CARBINE — .50 cal., flintlock or percussion, 21 in. octagonal tapering to a round barrel, color case hardened furniture, single hunting trigger, walnut stock, 6½ lbs. New in 1989.Add $20 for flintlock.

Mfg.'s Sug. Retail	$325	$300	$260	$200

Grading	100%	98%	95%

SHOTGUNS

NEW ENGLANDER SHOTGUN — 12 ga., percussion, 26 and 28 in. barrel, brass furniture, 5 lbs. 2 oz. Add $95 for extra .50 cal. barrel, $15 for left hand.

Mfg.'s Sug. Retail	$260	$240	$210	$170

TRADITIONS, INC.
Deep River, CT.

PISTOLS

PIONEER PISTOL — .45 cal. percussion, 9⅝ octagonal barrel, German silver furniture, blackened hardware, 2 lbs. 4 oz. New in 1991.

Mfg.'s Sug. Retail	$160	$140	$120	N/A

TRAPPER PISTOL — .45 or .50 cal., percussion or 10 in. octagonal barrel, double set triggers, adj. sights, brass trim, 3 lbs. 4 oz.

Mfg.'s Sug. Retail	$160	$140	$120	$90

WILLIAM PARKER PISTOL — .45 cal., percussion, 10⅜ in. barrel, all white steel, double set triggers, 2 lbs. 8 oz.

Mfg.'s Sug. Retail	$240	$205	$180	$145

RIFLES

BUCKSKINNER CARBINE — .50 cal. flintlock or percussion, 21 in. octagonal to round barrel, German silver furniture, blackened hardware, 6 lbs. (New 1991).

Mfg.'s Sug. Retail	$260	$245	$215	N/A

Add $20 for flintlock.

FRONTIER RIFLE/FRONTIER CARBINE— .45 or .50 cal., percussion or flintlock, 28 in. octagonal barrel (24 in. carbine), double set triggers, adj. sights, brass trim, 6 lbs. 14 oz (6 lbs. 8 oz. carbine). Add $15 for flintlock (.50 cal. only).

Mfg.'s Sug. Retail	$230	$195	$170	$120

FRONTIER SCOUT RIFLE— .45 or .50 cal., flintlock or percussion, 26 in. octagonal barrel, double set triggers, adj. sights, brass trim, 5 lbs. 8 oz., lock has adj. sear. Add $10 for flintlock, $20 for carbine.

Mfg.'s Sug. Retail	$215	$185	$160	$115

HAWKEN RIFLE— .50, .54, or .58 cal., percussion or flintlock, 32¼ in. octagonal barrel, double set triggers, adj. sights, brass trim, 8 lbs. 2 oz. Add $10 for flintlock (.50 and .54 cal. only).

Mfg.'s Sug. Retail	$395	$340	$295	$190

A fiberglass ramrod and deluxe rear sight were introduced in 1989.

HAWKEN WOODSMAN RIFLE — .50 cal., percussion, 29 in. octagonal barrel, color case hardened hammer and lock, brass trim and patchbox, 7½ lbs.

Mfg.'s Sug. Retail	$260	$225	$195	$140

HUNTER RIFLE— .50 or .54 cal., percussion, 28 in. long octagonal barrel, double set triggers, adj. sights, black chrome brass trim with German silver wedge plates, lock has adj. sear, walnut stock, 8 lbs., 10 oz.

Mfg.'s Sug. Retail	$405	$345	$300	$220

A fiberglass ramrod and deluxe rear sight were introduced in 1989.

Grading	100%	98%	95%

KENTUCKY 2-PIECE RIFLE — .45 or .50 cal., percussion, 33½ in. octagonal barrel, color case hardened hammer and lock, unique full length two piece stock is joined with brass plate, 7 lbs. 4 oz. Disc. in 1989.

	$150	$125	$90

Last Mfg.'s Sug. Retail was $145.

KENTUCKY SCOUT RIFLE — .45 or .50 cal., percussion or 26 in. octagonal barrel, double set triggers, adj. sights, brass trim, full length stock, lock has adj. sear, 5 lbs. 8 oz. Add $10 for flintlock.Disc. 1989.

	$150	$125	$90

Last Mfg.'s Sug. Retail was $135.

PENNSYLVANIA RIFLE — .45 or .50 cal., flintlock or percussion, 40½ in. octagonal barrel, double set triggers, adj. sights, brass trim, 9 lbs. 13 oz. Add $20 for flintlock.

Mfg.'s Sug. Retail	$445	$385	$335	$240

PIONEER RIFLE — .50 or .54 cal., percussion, 27¼ in. octagonal barrel, color case hardened hammer, lock and furniture, German silver blade front sight, recoil pad, carbine style stock.

Mfg.'s Sug. Retail	$200	$170	$150	$110

SHENANDOAH RIFLE — .45 or .50 cal., flintlock or percussion, color case hardened hammer and lock, 33½ in. long octagonal barrel, brass furniture, 7 lbs. 4 oz. Add $10 for flintlock.

	$170	$150	$110

Last Mfg.'s Sug. Retail was $185.

TRAPPER RIFLE — .36, .45 and .50 cal., percussion, 25 in. octagonal barrel, color case hardened hammer and lock, brass trim, 5 lbs. Disc. 1989.

	$170	$150	$110

Last Mfg.'s Sug. Retail was $200.

TROPHY RIFLE — .50 or .54 cal., percussion, 27½ in. octagonal tapering to round barrel, adj. trigger, fiberglass ramrod, carbine style walnut stock, 7 lbs.

Mfg.'s Sug. Retail	$405	$345	$300	$230

SHOTGUNS

SINGLE BARREL — 12 ga., percussion, 32 in. octagonal tapering to round barrel, German silver wedge plate, blued furniture, scroll engraving, and polished steel furniture on Deluxe version, 4 lbs. Add $85 for Deluxe.

	$240	$210	$180

Last Mfg.'s Sug. Retail was $315.

TRAIL GUNS ARMORY
League City, TX. (guns manufactured by D. Pedersoli Co. Italy).

ALAMO LONG RIFLE — .45 or .50 cal., percussion or flintlock. Add $10 for flintlock.

Mfg.'s Sug. Retail	$350	$275	$240	$190

KODIAK MK-I, MK-II & MK-III DOUBLE RIFLE — .50 and .58 cal., or 12 ga. percussion, 28 in. barrel, adj. sights. Add $300 for spare combo. barrels (.50 cal. x 12 ga.). $215 for 12 ga. barrels.

Mfg.'s Sug. Retail	$595	$545	$500	$370

Grading	100%	98%	95%	

TRYON PLAINS RIFLE — .50 or .54 cal., percussion, 31 in. browned octagonal barrel, browned furniture, white steel hammer and lock, 9 lbs. 6 oz.

Mfg.'s Sug. Retail	$385	$325	$285	$175

As of 1990 only the deluxe engraved version is currently sold.

Mfg.'s Sug. Retail	$450	$390	$340	$240

RIFLES: BLACK POWDER CARTRIDGE

CREEDMOOR ROLLING BLOCK — 45/70 cal., rimfire, 30 in. tapered barrel, color case hardened action, adj. sights, 9 lbs.

Mfg.'s Sug. Retail	$695	$605	$530	$360

Add $115 for deluxe version.

REMINGTON SPORTING RIFLE — .45/70 cal. rimfire, same as above but without Creedmore sight, straight stock.

Mfg.'s Sug. Retail	$530	$450	$390	$300

KODIAK DOUBLE RIFLE—.45-70 cal. rimfire, 24 in. tapered round barrel, color case hardened hammer and lock, 2 piece high gloss walnut hand checkered stock, adj. twin sights, patterned after the very rare Colt Side X Side Double Rifle of the 1870's.

Mfg.'s Sug. Retail	$1,705	$1,595	$1,495	$1,195

SHOTGUNS

KODIAK 10 DOUBLE BARREL — 10 ga., percussion, goose gun barrels. Add $200 for spare barrel.

Mfg.'s Sug. Retail	$485	$460	$400	$300

UBERTI, ALDO & CO

Manufactured in Italy by Aldo Uberti & Co. Uberti guns are imported and distributed by Various U.S. companies under both the Uberti trademark as well as a multitude of others (Uberti Usa, Inc., Cimarron Arms Co., (formerly Old-West Gun Co.), Navy Arms, Dixie Gun Works, Etc.). Also previously imported by Allen Firearms and Benson Firearms Ltd.

All guns are to the exact specifications of the original manufacture. Crafted with an unmistakable fire blue finish. A. Uberti is one of the largest manufacturers of black powder firearms.

Add the following amounts for engraving on handguns:

> Add $325 for "A" style engraving (30% coverage).
> Add $425 for "B" style engraving (50% coverage).
> Add $750 for "C" style engraving (100% coverage).
> Add $800 for "Texas Cattlebrands" engraving pattern.
> Prices may fluctuation due to the recent devaluation of the U.S. dollar in international markets.

REVOLVERS

PATERSON MODEL— .36 cal., 7½ octagon barrel, hidden trigger design, without loading lever, 2 lbs. 9 oz. New in 1988.

Mfg.'s Sug. Retail	$385	$315	$275	$220

Add $20 for load lever.

1847 WALKER — .44 cal., percussion, 9 in. barrel, charcoal finish, color case hardened frame, hammer, and load lever, brass trim, engraved cylinder, 4.4 lbs.

Mfg.'s Sug. Retail	$360	$295	$255	$205

Grading	100%	98%	95%

1848 BABY DRAGOON — .31 cal., percussion, 3, 4, or 5 in. barrel, 5 shot, color case hardened frame, hammer, no load lever, engraved cylinder, 1.4 lbs. Add $15 for silver straps and trigger guard.

Mfg.'s Sug. Retail	$280	$230	$200	$160

DRAGOON (1ST, 2ND, OR 3RD) — .44 cal., percussion, 6 shot, brass grip straps, color case hardened frame, hammer, and load lever, brass trim, 3.9 lbs. Add $20 for silver-plated straps, or cut for stock on 3rd Model Dragoon, $100 for shoulder stock for 3rd Model Dragoon.

Mfg.'s Sug. Retail	$300	$245	$215	$170

1849 WELLS FARGO — .31 cal., percussion, 3, 4, or 5 in. octagonal barrel, 5 shot, color case hardened frame, hammer, no load lever, brass trim, 1½ lbs. Add $20 for silver straps.

Mfg.'s Sug. Retail	$280	$230	$200	$160

1849 POCKET — .31 cal., percussion, with loading lever, 3, 4, or 5 in. barrel, 5 shot, color case hardened frame, hammer, and load lever, brass trim, 1½ lbs. Add $15 for silver straps and trigger guard.

Mfg.'s Sug. Retail	$285	$235	$205	$165

1851 NAVY/NAVY SHERIFF — .36 cal., percussion, 5 (Sheriff's Model) or 7½ in. barrel, many styles, loading lever, 6 shot engraved cylinder, 2.8 lbs. Add $100 for stock, $50 for stainless steel, $15 for silver plated strap and trigger guard, or steel strap and trigger guard, $15 for "London" Model w/steel backstrap and trigger guard or if cut for stock (3rd Model Navy).

Mfg.'s Sug. Retail	$285	$235	$205	$165

1860 ARMY — .44 cal., percussion, 8 in. barrel, 6 shot, loading lever, color case hardened frame, hammer, and load lever, all brass back strap and trigger guard, or steel backstrap and brass trigger guard on fluted cylinder model, 2.6 lbs. Add $100 for stock, $15 for silver plated strap and trigger guard, $50 for stainless steel.

Mfg.'s Sug. Retail	$295	$240	$210	$170

1861 NAVY — .36 cal., percussion, 5 in. barrel, many styles, brass back strap or trigger guard, color case hardened frame, hammer, and load lever, 2½ lbs. Add $15 for silver plated strap and trigger guard, $15 for fluted military cylinder or cut for stock, $50 for stainless steel, $100 for shoulder stock.

Mfg.'s Sug. Retail	$305	$255	$220	$175

1862 POCKET NAVY — .36 cal., percussion, 4½, 5½, or 6½ in. barrel, color case hardened frame, hammer, and load lever, cylinder, semi-fluted or engraved, 1.6 lbs. Add $15 for silver plated straps and trigger guard, $50 for stainless steel.

Mfg.'s Sug. Retail	$280	$230	$200	$160

1862 POLICE — .36 cal., percussion, 4½, 5½, or 6½ in. barrel, color case hardened frame, hammer, and load lever, cylinder, semi-fluted or engraved, 1.6 lbs. Add $15 for silver plated straps and trigger guard or fluted cylinder model, $50 for stainless steel.

Mfg.'s Sug. Retail	$280	$230	$200	$160

AUGUSTA CONFEDERATE — .36 cal., percussion, 7½ in. octagonal barrel, color case hardened hammer and trigger, all brass frame, engraved cylinder, 2½-2¾ lbs.

	$200	$160	$100

Last Mfg.'s Sug. Retail was $170.

Grading	100%	98%	95%

GRISWOLD CONFEDERATE—.36 or .44 cal., 5½ or 7½ in. barrel, percussion, same as above except round barrel, forward of lug, does not have engraved cylinder.

	$200	$160	$100

Last Mfg.'s Sug. Retail was $170.

LEECH AND RIGDON CONFEDERATE — .36 cal., percussion, same as above except all steel frame.

	$230	$200	$160

Last Mfg.'s Sug. Retail was $220.

TEXAS CONFEDERATE DRAGOON — .44 cal., percussion, 7½ in. round barrel, color case hardened frame, hammer, and load lever, brass trim, "Tucker, Sherrard, & Co.", 4 lbs. Add $35 for stainless steel.

	$210	$175	$110

Last Mfg.'s Sug. Retail was $235.

1858 REMINGTON— .44 cal., percussion, 7½ in. barrel, 6 shot, blued steel, brass trigger guard, 2.6 lbs. Add $30 for adj. sights.

Mfg.'s Sug. Retail	$245	$200	$175	$140

1858 REMINGTON STAINLESS — same as above, has brass strap and trigger guard. Add $30 for adj. sights.

Mfg.'s Sug. Retail	$330	$280	$245	$195

1858 REMINGTON NEW NAVY — .36 cal., percussion, 6½ in. octagonal barrel, 6 shot, blue frame, 2½ lbs. Add $30 for adj. sights.

	$185	$160	$120

Last Mfg.'s Sug. Retail was $210.

1866 REVOLVING CARBINE— .44 cal., percussion, 18 in. barrel, 6 shot, blued steel, brass trigger guard, walnut stock, 4.6 lbs.

Mfg.'s Sug. Retail	$370	$335	$280	$150

RIFLES: PERCUSSION

HAWKEN RIFLE — .50 and .54 cal., 32 in. octagonal barrel, double set triggers, approx. 9 lbs.

Mfg.'s Sug. Retail	$535	$440	$385	$310

SANTA FE HAWKEN — .50 and .54 cal., percussion, single shot, 32 in. oct. barrel, damascened finish, double set triggers, 9½ lbs., walnut stock.

Mfg.'s Sug. Retail	$480	$395	$345	$250

ST. LOUIS RIFLE — .45, .50, .54, or .58 cal., flintlock and percussion, color case hardened hammer lock and trigger guard, octagonal barrel. Add $25 for .54 and .58 cal. percussion, $15 for flintlock, $30 for 54 cal. flintlock.

	$300	$265	$190

Last Mfg.'s Sug. Retail was $265.

SQUIRREL RIFLE — .32 cal., percussion or flintlock, color case hardened hammer and lock, brass trigger guard, 28 in. octagonal barrel. Add $15 for flintlock.

	$250	$205	$150

BLACKPOWDER CARTRIDGE

Grading	100%	98%	95%

RIFLES REPRODUCTIONS

HENRY RIFLE/CARBINE— .44-40 cal., brass frame, 24½ in. barrel on rifle, 22½ in. barrel on carbine.

Mfg.'s Sug. Retail	$900	$785	$685	$540

Can also be special ordered withGrade A engraving ($234 extra), Grade B engraving ($412 extra), and Grade 3 (C) engraving ($635 extra).

Henry 1 of 1,000 — discontinued several years ago, premiums are slightly higher than a C engraved gun.

1866 CARBINE— .44-40 cal., brass receiver, 19 in. round barrel. "Indian" model - add $40.

Mfg.'s Sug. Retail	$685	$600	$525	$400

1866 Trapper Carbine — .44-40 cal., 16 or 18½ in. barrel.

Mfg.'s Sug. Retail	$795	$720	$610	$490

1866 Yellowboy Indian Carbine — .44-40 cal., 19 in. barrel.

Mfg.'s Sug. Retail	$685	$600	$525	$400

Subtract $20 without brass tacks.

Red Cloud Commemorative Carbine— .44-40 cal., special engraving and brass tacks in forearm and stock.

Mfg.'s Sug. Retail	$685	$600	$525	$400

1866 RIFLE — .44-40 cal., brass receiver, 24¼ in. octagonal barrel.

Mfg.'s Sug. Retail	$750	$670	$570	$440

Yellowboy Indian Rifle — .44-40 cal., 19 in. rifle.

Mfg.'s Sug. Retail	$750	$620	$570	$440

This model comes without brass tacks.

1873 CARBINE — .44-40 cal., steel receiver, 19 in. round barrel.

Mfg.'s Sug. Retail	$850	$740	$640	$510

Add $95 for nickel plating.

1873 Trapper Carbine — .44-40 cal., 16 in. barrel.

Mfg.'s Sug. Retail	$850	$740	$640	$510

1873 RIFLE— .44-40 cal., case hardened receiver, 24¼ in. octagonal barrel. Add $40 for 30 in. barrel, also available in 20 in. barrel.

Mfg.'s Sug. Retail	$900	$785	$685	$540

ULTRA LIGHT ARMS

Manufacturer located in Granville, WV.

MODEL 90 — .45 or .50 cal., 28 in. button rifle barrel, adj. Timney trigger, in-line action, Kevlar/graphite stock with colors optional, Williams rear sight, 6 lbs., includes hard case.

Mfg.'s Sug. Retail	$950	$895	$775	$675

U.S. HISTORICAL SOCIETY

Marketing organization which subcontracts special editions/commemoratives. Located in Richmond, VA.

Please refer to listing in the Modern Firearms section of this text also.

WESTERN ARMS GUNS

More information available from manufacturer.

Grading	100%	98%	95%

COLT 1ST MOD. DRAGOON—.44 cal., 7½ in. barrel, oval bolt cuts in cylinder, color case hardened frame, hammer, and loading lever, one piece stock, 4 lbs. 2 oz.

	$170	$145	$110

COLT 2ND MOD. DRAGOON—.44 cal., 7½ in. barrel, oval bolt cuts in cylinder, color case hardened frame, hammer, and loading lever, one piece stock, 4 lbs. 2 oz.

	$170	$145	$110

COLT 3RD MOD. DRAGOON—.44 cal., 7½ in. barrel, oval bolt cuts in cylinder, color case hardened frame, hammer, and loading lever, one piece stock, 4 lbs. 2 oz.

	$180	$150	$120

1860 ARMY—.44 cal., 8 in. round barrel, color case hardened frame, hammer, and load lever, round trigger guard, one piece stock, 2 lbs. 10 oz.

	$165	$140	$110

1851 NAVY — .36 cal., 7½ in. octagonal barrel, color case hardened frame, hammer, and load lever, square trigger guard, one piece stock, 2 lbs. 10 oz.

	$150	$130	$100

1861 NAVY — .36 cal., 7½ in. octagonal barrel, color case hardened frame, hammer, and load lever, square trigger guard, one piece stock, 2 lbs. 10 oz.

	$180	$150	$120

COLT BLACKPOWDER
2ND GENERATION SERIALIZATION

MODEL NO.	SERIAL # RANGE	TOTAL PROD.	PROD. BEGAN	PROD. ENDED

MODEL 1851 NAVY

C-1121	4201 25100	20900	1971	1978
C-1122	As above but at higher range of numbers			
	Unk'n	—	1978	

MODEL 1851 NAVY, R. E. LEE

C-9001	251REL 5000 REL	4750	—	1971

MODEL 1851 NAVY, U. S. GRANT

C-9002	251USG 5000 USG	4750	—	1971

MODEL 1851 GRANT-LEE PAIR

C-9003	01 GLP 250 GLP	250	—	1971

3rd MODEL DRAGOON

C-1770	20801 208	25	1974	1978
	Prototype			
	20901 24501	3601		
C-1770MN	S/N's As Above	20	1984	1984

MODEL 1851 NAVY

F-1100	24900 29150	4250	5/80	10/81
F-1101	S/N's As Above	300	10/81	11/81
W/Blank Cylinders				
F-1110	29151s 29640s	489	6/82	10/82
Stainless Steel				

MODEL 1860 ARMY

F-1200	201000 212835	7593	11/78	11/82
Rebated Cylinder				
F-1200 EBO	S/N's As Above	500	1979	1979
Butterfield				
F-1200 LNK	S/N's As Above	Unk'n	Unk'n	Unk'n
Electroless Nickel				
F-1200MN	S/N's As Above	12	1984	1984
Nickel/Ivory				
F-1202	S/N's As Above	500	1979	1979
Limited Edition				
F-1203	207330 211250	2670	7/80	10/81
Fluted Cylinder				
F-1210	211263s 212540s	1278	1/82	4/82
Stainless Steel				

1861 NAVY

F-1300	40000 43165	3166	9/80	10/81

1862 POCKET NAVY

F-1400	48000 58850	5765	12/79	11/81
	and skip odd no's.			
F-1400MN	S/N's As Above	25	1984	1984
Nickel/Ivory				
F-1401	S/N's As Above	500	1979	1980
Limited Edition				

1862 POCKET POLICE

F-1500	49000 57300	4801	1/80	9/81
	and skip even no's.			
F-1500MN	S/N's As Above	25	1984	1984
Nickel/Ivory				
F-1501	S/N's As Above	500	1979	1980
Limited Edition				

1847 WALKER

F-1600	1200 4120	2573	6/80	4/82
	32256 32500	245	5/81	9/81

1st MODEL DRAGOON

F-1700	25100 34500	3878	1/80	2/82

2nd MODEL DRAGOON

F-172	S/N's As Above and Mix at Random for			
	1st, 2nd & 3rd	2676	1/80	2/82

3rd MODEL DRAGOON

F-140	S/N's As Above and Mix at Random for			
	1st, 2nd & 3rd	2856	1/80	2/82
	31401 31450	50	10/81	11/81
F-1740 EGA	Unk'n Unk'n	200	1982	1982
(Garabaldi Model– "GCA" prefix)				

BABY DRAGOON

F-1760	16000 17851	1852	2/81	4/81
F-1761	S/N's As Above	500	1979	1980
Limited Edition				

1860 ARMY

F-9005	US 001/001 US to			
	US 3025/3025 US	3025	9/77	1/80
Cavalry Commemorative (Two Gun Set)				

HERITAGE WALKER

F-9006	01 1853	1853	6/80	6/81

PROOF MARKINGS

The proof marks shown below will assist in determining nationality of manufacturers
when no other markings are evident. Since the U.S. has no federalized proofing
houses (as in England, France, Germany and other European countries), most U.S.
built guns voluntarily proof their firearms with a specified style of proofmark (i.e.—
the interlocked "WP" synonymous with nitro-proofed Winchesters is one example).
Remember, only guns with the definitive nitro-proof mark can be fired using modern
(smokeless powder) shells. Pre-1850 European firearms oftentimes do not exhibit any
commercial proof marks and with the exception of an occasional barrel address, they
represent the single hardest bracket of firearms I can research properly. Captured
weapons from major wars occasionally show 2 different nationalities of proofmarks.
This is acceptable since the gun was proofed in a national proof house after original
manufacture and again when the gun was "exported" to a different country as a
military acquisition.

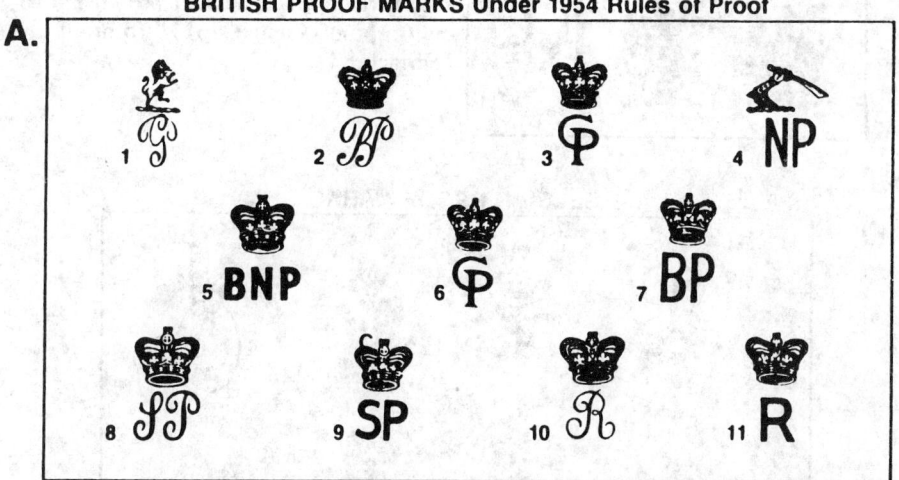

BRITISH PROOF MARKS Under 1954 Rules of Proof

A.

A. British rules of proof-1954: (1) London provisional proof, (2) Birmingham provisional proof, (3) Definitive proof for nitro powder (or modern ammo), (4) Definitive
London proof for nitro powder (or modern ammo), (5) Definitive Birmingham nitro
proof for barrel and action, (6) London proof for black powder only, (7) Birmingham
proof for black powder only, (8) Special definitive proof-London, (9) Special definitive
proof-Birmingham, (10) Reproof marking for London, (11) Reproofing marking for
Birmingham.

B. England: 1925 Rules of Proof –
(1) London proof, (2) London view,
(3) London nitro proof, (4) Birmingham
proof, (5) Birmingham view, (6)
Birmingham nitro proof.

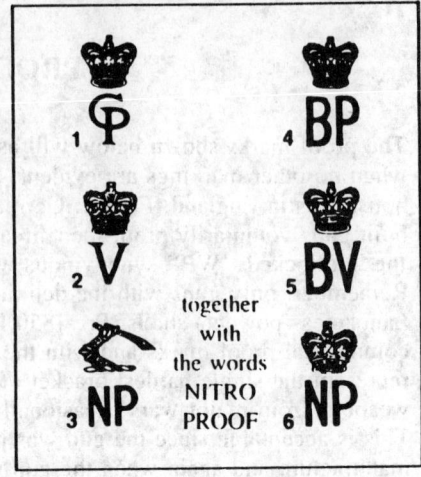

BRITISH PROOF MARKS
Under 1925 Rules of Proof

AUSTRIAN PROOF MARKS

C. Austrian proof marks – (1) Vienna
provisional proof, (2) Ferlach provisional
proof, (3) Vienna black powder proofing,
(4) Ferlach black powder proofing, (5)
Nitro proof-Vienna, (6) Nitro proof-
Ferlach.

BELGIAN PROOF MARKS

D. Belgium liege proof marks – (1) Provisional proof, (2) Double proofed provisional
marking, (3) Triple proofed provisional marking, (4) Definitive proofing, (5) View
proof, (6) Rifled arms definitive proof, (7) Nitro proof, (8) Superior nitro proof.

FRENCH PROOF MARKS The Paris Proof House

E.

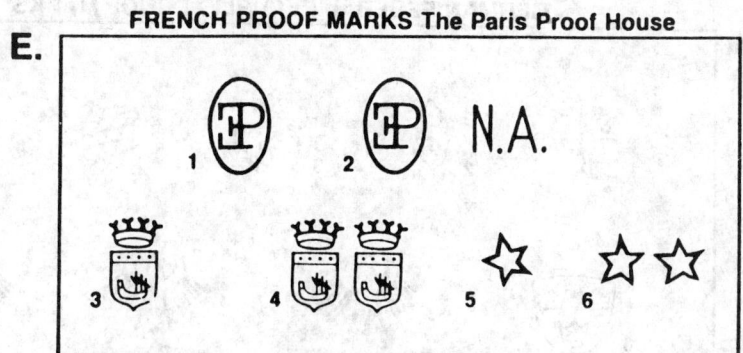

E. French proofings from Paris Proof House – (1) Assembly of tubes, seen in single, double, or tiple configuration, (2) Barrels proofed separately, not assembled, (3) Definitive proof for black powder, (4) Superior proof for black powder, (5) Smokeless powder ordinary proof, (6) Superior proof for smokeless powder.

F.

FRENCH PROOF MARKS The St. Etienne Proof House

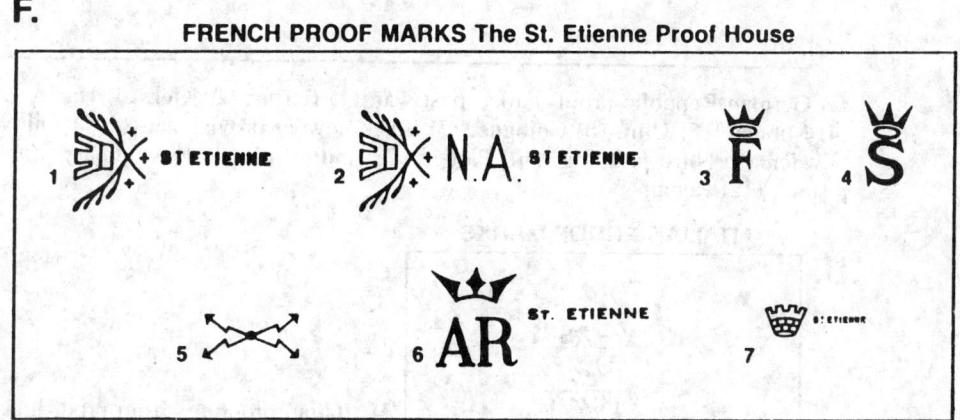

F. French proofs from the St. Etienne Proof House – (1) Ordinary assembled tubes proof—can be single, double, or triple. (2) Separate tube proofing—not assembled. (3) Black powder, (4) Superior black powder, (5) Ordinary smokeless proof. (6) Superior smokeless powder, (7) Short-barreled firearms.

G.

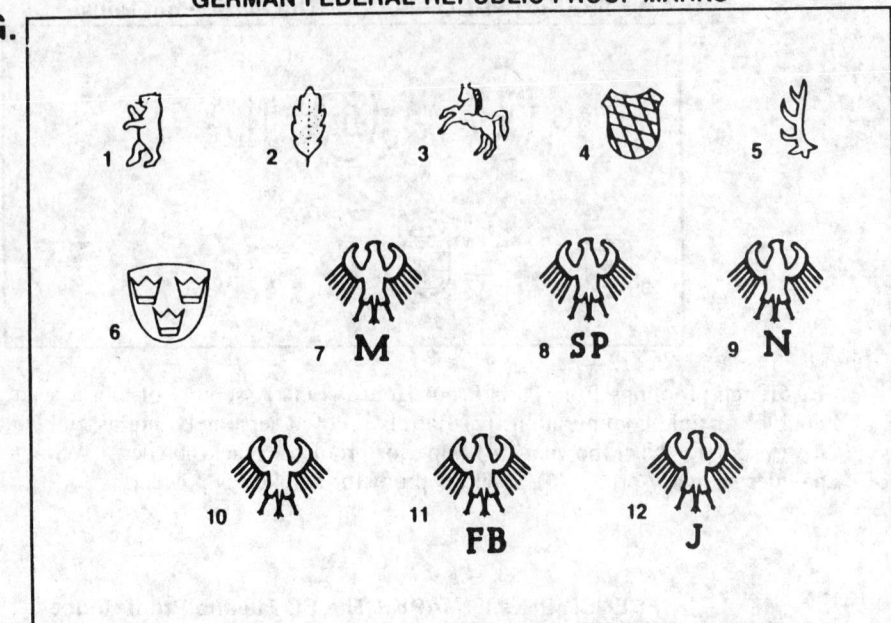

G. German Republic proof marks, post-war: (1) Berlin, (2) Kiel, (3) Hanover, (4) Munich, (5) Ulm, (6) Cologne, (7) Black powder provisional, (8) Definitive black powder, (9) Nitro proofing, (10) Flobert .22 rimfire rifles, (11) Voluntary proofing for pistols, (12) Repair.

ITALIAN PROOF MARKS

H.

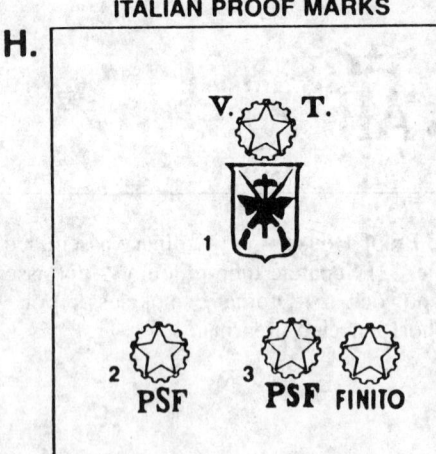

H. Italian proofings from proof house near Brescia – (1) Provisional proof, (2) Definitive proof, (3) Finish proof—firearm is now saleable.

SERIALIZATION

BROWNING BELGIUM PRODUCTION

A-5 (AUTOMATIC 5) SHOTGUN —
approximate recapitulation — 12 ga.

Year	Serial Number Beginning of Year	Serial Number at End of Year
1924	1	3000
1925	3001	18000
1926	18001	33000
1927	33001	48000
1928	48001	63000
1929	63001	78000
1930	78001	93000
1931	93001	108000
1932	108001	123000
1933	123001	138000
1934	138001	153000
1935	153001	168000
1936	168001	183000
1937	183001	198000
1938	198001	213000
1939	213001	229000
1940-1945	No production	
1946	229001	237000
1947	237001	249000
1948	249001	270000
1949	270001	285000
1950	285001	315000
1951	315001	346000
1952	346001	387000
1953	387001	438000
1954	Standard model	
	H1	H39000
	Lightweight model	
	L1	L42000
1955	Standard model	
	H39001	H83000
	Lightweight model	
	L42001	L83000
1956	Standard model	
	H83001	H99000
	M1	M22000
	Lightweight model	
	L83001	L99000
	G1	G23000

Year	Serial Number Beginning of Year	Serial Number at End of Year
1957	Standard model	
	M22001	M85000
	Lightweight model	
	G23001	G85000
1958	Standard model	
	M85001	M99000
	Lightweight model	
	G85001	G99000
1958-1976		

Ser. No. sequence changed in include a one or two digit numeral followed by an alpha character. "M" prefix designates standard models, "G" includes lightweight models, and "V" shows magnum models. To illustrate, an A-5 with a Ser. No. of 8G19264 would indicate a lightweight model manufactured in 1958. Ser. No. 71V24690 would specify a 3 inch magnum gun built in 1971.

SUPERPOSED MODEL — O & U — 12 GA.

Year	Serial Number Beginning of Year	Serial Number at End of Year
1931	1	2000
1932	2001	4000
1933	400l	6000
1934	6001	8000
1935	8001	10000
1936	10001	12000
1937	12001	14000
1938	14001	17000
1939-1947	No production	
1948	17001	17200
1949	17201	20000
1950	20001	21000
1951	21001	27000
1952	27001	33000
1953	33001	37000
1954	37001	43000

Year	Serial Number Beginning of Year	Serial Number at End of Year
1955	43001	48000
1956	48001	54000
1957	54001	59000
1958	59001	68500
1959	68501	76500
1960	76501	86500
1961	86501	96500
1962	96501	99999
1963	S3 suffix after Ser. No.	
1964	S4 suffix after Ser. No.	
1965	S5 suffix after Ser. No.	
1966	S6 suffix after Ser. No.	
1967	S7 suffix after Ser. No.	
1968	S8 suffix after Ser. No.	
1969	S69 suffix after Ser. No.	
1970	S70 suffix after Ser. No.	
1971	S71 suffix after Ser. No.	
1972	S72 suffix after Ser. No.	
1973	S73 suffix after Ser. No.	
1974	S74 suffix after Ser. No.	
1975	S75 suffix after Ser. No.	
1976	S76 suffix after Ser. No.	
1976 to date	"P" or Presentation Models only	

LIEGE O & U — Approximately 10,000 produced

Year		
1973	73J prefix before Ser. No.	
1974	74J prefix before Ser. No.	
1975	75J prefix before Ser. No.	

DOUBLE AUTOMATIC SHOTGUN

1952-1959	N/A	
1960-1971	1st or both digits indicate last 2 digits in year of manufacture (i.e. — 0A1947 — 1960 mfg., 70A245671 — 1970 mfg.)	

Year	Serial Number Beginning of Year	Serial Number at End of Year
HI-POWER (9 mm) PISTOL		
1955-1956	No records available	
1957	70000	80000
1958	80001	85267
1959	85268	89687
1960	89688	93027
1961	93028	109145
1962	109146	113548
1963	113549	115822
1964	115823	T136538
1965	T136569	T146372
1966	T146373	T173285
1967	T173286	T213999
1968	T214000	T258000
1969	69C prefix before Ser. No.	
1970	70C prefix before Ser. No.	
1971	71C prefix before Ser. No.	
1972	72C prefix before Ser. No.	
1973	73C prefix before Ser. No.	
1974	74C prefix before Ser. No.	
1975	75C prefix before Ser. No.	
1976	76C prefix before Ser. No.	
1977 to date	New style serialization	

BROWNING .380

1955-1964	No records exist	
1965	500000	598804
1966	598805	603890
1967	603891	619474
1968	619475	N/A
1969-1970	Discontinued due to GCA of 1968. New model has longer barrel, adj. rear sight, modified grip.	
1971	71N prefix before Ser. No.	
1972	72N prefix before Ser. No.	
1973	73N prefix before Ser. No.	
1974	74N prefix before Ser. No.	
1975	75N prefix before Ser. No.	

Year	Serial Number Beginning of Year	Serial Number at End of Year

.25 CAL. BABY BROWNING PISTOL

Year	Serial Number Beginning of Year	Serial Number at End of Year
1955-1958	Records not available	
1959	181000	206349
1960	206350	230999
1961	231000	250999
1962	251000	278999
1963	279000	286099
1964	286100	308499
1965	308500	329999
1966	333000	367443
1967	367444	412999
1968	413000	479000
1969	Discontinued because of GCA of 1968	

.22 CAL. PISTOLS (NOMAD-CHALLENGER-MEDALIST)

One or two digit suffix after single capital letter. "P" designates Nomad, "U" designates Challenger model, "T" designates Medalist model. "P5" suffix would indicate a Nomad built in 1965. "U71" suffix would indicate a Challenger built in 1971. Nomad models were manufactured from 1962 to 1973. Challenger and Medalist models were produced from 1962 to 1974.

BOLT ACTION RIFLES (SAFARI, MEDALLION, & OLYMPIAN MODELS)

Year	
1959-1962	No prefix (numeral-letter) before Ser. No. (i.e., only digits)
1963	3-single letter prefix or suffix by Ser. No.
1964	4-single letter prefix or suffix by Ser. No.
1965	5-single letter prefix or suffix by Ser. No.
1966	6-single letter prefix or suffix by Ser. No.
1967	7-single letter prefix or suffix by Ser. No.
1968	8-single letter prefix or suffix by Ser. No.
1969	Single letter (Y, Z, or L) followed by last 2 digits of year of mfg. Prefix only.
1970	"Y70" prefix
1971	"L71" prefix
1972	"Z72" prefix
1973	"Y73" prefix
1974	"Z74" prefix
1975	"L75" prefix

B.A.R

Year	
1967	"M7" suffix after Ser. No.
1968	"M8" suffix after Ser. No.
1969	"M69" suffix after Ser. No.
1970	"M70" suffix after Ser. No.
1971	"M71" suffix after Ser. No.
1972	"M72" suffix after Ser. No.
1973	"M73" suffix after Ser. No.
1974	"M74" suffix after Ser. No.
1975	"M75" suffix after Ser. No.
1976	"M76" suffix after Ser. No.
1977 to date	New sequence with "RT" appearing in middle of Ser. No.

.22 AUTO RIFLE (Grades I, II, and III)

Year	
1956-1964	Numeric only — 5 digits or less.
1965	"5T" or "5E" prefix before Ser. No.
1966	"6T" or "6E" prefix before Ser. No.
1967	"7T" or "7E" prefix before Ser. No.
1968	"8T" or "8E" prefix before Ser. No.
1969	"69T" or "69E" prefix before Ser. No.

Year	Serial Number Beginning of Year	Serial Number at End of Year
1970	"70T" or "70E" prefix before Ser. No.	
1971	"71T" or "71E" prefix before Ser. No.	
1972	"72T" or "72E" prefix before Ser. No.	
1973	Japan production	

T-BOLT RIFLE (T1 and T2)

Year	
1965	"X5" suffix after Ser. No.
1966	"X6" suffix after Ser. No.
1967	"X7" suffix after Ser. No.
1968	"X8" suffix after Ser. No.
1969	"X69" suffix after Ser. No.
1970	"X70" suffix after Ser. No.
1971	"X71" suffix after Ser. No.
1972	"X72" suffix after Ser. No.
1973	"X73" suffix after Ser. No.
1974	"X74" suffix after Ser. No.
1975	"X75" suffix after Ser. No.

MODEL SERIALIZATION
COLTS FIREARMS

This section is included to identify year of manufacture dates on Brownings, Colt pistols, Mauser broomhandles, Parker shotguns, and Winchester rifles. To use these tables, simply locate the Ser. No. of the above-mentioned trademarks, locate the proper bracket it falls into by model, and refer to the adjacent year to determine the year of manufacture. In several cases, caliber rarity can also be determined.

Year	Serial Number Beginning of Year	Serial Number at End of Year	Total Guns Produced in Year
MODEL 1849 POCKET REVOLVER			
1849	1	11999	11999
1850	12000	15999	3999
1851	16000	24999	8999
1852	25000	54999	29999
1853	55000	84999	29999
1854	85000	99999	14999
1855	100000	109999	9999
1856	110000	129999	19999
1857	130000	139999	9999
1858	140000	149999	9999
1859	150000	159999	9999
1860	160000	183999	23999
1861	184000	196999	12999
1862	197000	222999	25999
1863	223000	249999	26999
1864	250000	269999	16999
1865	270000	279999	9999
1866	280000	289999	9999
1867	290000	299999	9999
1868	300000	309999	9999
1869	310000	319999	9999
1870	320000	324999	4999
1871	325000	329999	4999
1872	330000	330999	999
1873	331000	340000	9000
MODEL 1849 POCKET REVOLVER — LONDON BARREL ADDRESS			
1853	1	999	999
1854	1000	4999	3999

Year	Serial Number Beginning of Year	Serial Number at End of Year	Total Guns Produced in Year
1855	5000	8999	3999
1856	9000	11000	2000
MODEL 1851 NAVY			
1850	1	2499	2499
1851	2500	9999	7499
1852	10000	19999	9999
1853	20000	34999	14999
1854	35000	39999	4999
1855	40000	44999	4999
1856	45000	64999	19999
1857	65000	84999	19999
1858	85000	89999	4999
1859	90000	92999	2999
1860	93000	97999	4999
1861	98000	117999	19999
1862	118000	131999	13999
1863	132000	174999	42999
1864	175000	179999	4999
1865	180000	184999	4999
1866	185000	200000	14999
1867	200000	203999	3999
1868	204000	206999	2999
1869	207000	209999	2999
1870	210000	211999	1999
1871	212000	213999	1999
1872	214000	214999	999
1873	215000	215348	348
MODEL 1851 NAVY — LONDON BARREL ADDRESS			
1853	1	3999	3999
1854	4000	14999	10999
1855	15000	40999	25999
1856	41000	42000	1000
MODEL 1860 ARMY			
1860	1	1999	1999
1861	2000	24999	22999
1862	25000	84999	59999
1863	85000	149999	64999
1864	150000	152999	2999
1865	153000	155999	2999
1866	156000	161999	5999

Year	Serial Number Beginning of Year	Serial Number at End of Year	Total Guns Produced in Year
1867	162000	169999	7999
1868	170000	176999	6999
1869	177000	184999	7999
1870	185000	189999	4999
1871	190000	197999	7999
1872	198000	198999	999
1873	199000	200500	1500

MODEL 1861 NAVY

Year	Serial Number Beginning of Year	Serial Number at End of Year	Total Guns Produced in Year
1861	1	4599	4999
1862	4600	9999	5399
1863	10000	16999	6999
1864	17000	24999	7999
1865	25000	27999	2999
1866	28000	29999	1999
1867	30000	30999	999
1868	31000	32999	1999
1869	33000	33999	999
1870	34000	34999	999
1871	35000	35999	999
1872	36000	36999	999
1873	37000	38843	1843

MODEL 1862 POLICE

Year	Serial Number Beginning of Year	Serial Number at End of Year	Total Guns Produced in Year
1861	1	8499	8499
1862	8500	14999	6499
1863	15000	25999	10999
1864	26000	28999	2999
1865	29000	31999	2999
1866	32000	34999	2999
1867	35000	36999	1999
1868	37000	39999	2999
1869	40000	41999	1999
1870	42000	43999	1999
1871	44000	44999	999
1872	45000	45999	999
1873	46000	47000	1000

MODEL 1873 — SINGLE ACTION ARMY (SAA) — PRE-WAR

Year	Caliber	Serial Number Beginning of Year
1873	.45 Colt Caliber, Standard	1
1874		200
1875	.44 Rimfire series (own serials, 1-1863; made through 1880	15000
1876	.476 Eley introduced	22000
1877		33000
1878	.44-40 introduced in quantity	41000
1879		49000
1880		53000
1881		62000
1882	Sheriff's model introduced	73000
1883	.22 rimfire introduced	85000
1884	.32-20 and .38-40 introduced	102000
1885	.41 Colt introduced	114000
1886	.38 Colt introduced	117000
1887	.32 Colt and .32 S&W introduced	119000
1888	Flattop Target S.A.A. began; no. 126530	125000
1889	.32 rimfire; .32-44 S&W, .38 S&W; and .44 Russian introduced	128000
1890	.44 Smoothbore; .380 and .450 Eley; and .44 S&W introduced	130000
1891	.38-44 introduced	136000
1892	Transverse cylinder latch introduced; screw lock at front of frame dropped	144000
1893		149000

Year	Caliber	Serial Number Beginning of Year
1894	Beginning of Bisley models	154000
1895		159000
1896		163000
1897		168000
1898		175000
1899		182000
1900	Revolvers built to handle smokeless powder	192000
1901		203000
1902		220000
1903		238000
1904		250000
1905		261000
1906		273000
1907		288000
1908		304000
1909		308000
1910		312000
1911		316000
1912	Discontinue Bisley model	321000
1913	.44 Russian and S&W Special introduced	325000
1914		328000
1915	Long flute cylinders; range no. 330001 to 331480	329500
1916		332000
1917		335000
1918		337000
1919		337200
1920		338000
1921		341000
1922		343000
1923		344500
1924	.45 ACP introduced, requiring special cylinders	346400
1925		347300
1926		348200
1927		349800

Year	Caliber	Serial Number Beginning of Year
1928		351300
1929		352400
1930	.38 Special introduced	353800
1931		354100
1932		354500
1933		354800
1934		355000
1935	.357 Magnum introduced	355200
1936		355300
1937		355400
1938		356100
1939		356600
1940	A few S.A.A. made during and just after the war	357000 thru 357859

COLT SINGLE ACTION ARMY — POST-WAR PRODUCTION
"SA" suffix from 1956 to 1978. "SA" prefix 1978 to 1981

Year	Serial Number Beginning of Year	Serial Number at End of Year
1956	0001SA	8799SA
1957	8800SA	18499SA
1958	18500SA	23399SA
1959	23400SA	28499SA
1960	28500SA	33599SA
1961	33600SA	35649SA
1962	35650SA	37299SA
1963	37300SA	38499SA
1964	38500SA	39999SA
1965	40000SA	41499SA
1966	41500SA	43799SA
1967	43800SA	46299SA
1968	46300SA	48999SA
1969	49000SA	52599SA
1970	52600SA	59399SA
1971	59400SA	61699SA
1972	61700SA	64399SA
1973	64400SA	69399SA

Year	Serial Number Beginning of Year	Serial Number at End of Year
1974	69400SA	73319SA
1975	None produced	
1976	80000SA	82000SA
	(start of 3rd generation of production)	
1977	82001SA	95999SA
1978	96000SA	99999SA
1978	Start of "SA" prefix on front of Ser. No.	
Mid-1978	SA01000	SA12999
1979	SA13000	discontinuance in 1981

NEW FRONTIER SINGLE ACTION ARMY

1961	3000NF	3005NF
1962	3006NF	3849NF
1963	4325NF	4699NF
1964	4700NF	4974NF
1965	4975NF	5399NF
1966	5400NF	5674NF
1967	5675NF	5699NF
1968	5700NF	
1969	5701NF	5924NF
1970	5925NF	6874NF
1971	6875NF	7049NF
1972	7050NF	7074NF
1973	7075NF	7174NF
1974	7175NF	7264NF
1975	7265NF	7288NF
1978	7501NF	discontinuance in 1981

COLT SINGLE ACTION ARMY — CALIBER BREAKDOWN

Caliber	S.A.A.	Flattop Target	Bisley	Bisley Target
.22 Rimfire	107	93	0	0
.32 Rimfire	1	0	0	0
.32 Colt	192	24	160	44
.32 S&W	32	30	18	17
.32-44	2	9	14	17
.32-20	29,812	30	13,291	131

Caliber	S.A.A.	Flattop Target	Bisley	Bisley Target
.38 Colt (through 1914)	1,011	122	412	96
.38 Colt (post-1922)	1,365	0	0	0
.38 S&W	9	39	10	5
.38 Colt Special	82	7	0	0
.38 S&W Special	25	0	2	0
.38-44	2	11	6	47
.357 Magnum	525	0	0	0
.380 Eley	1	3	0	0
.38-40	38,240	19	12,163	98
.41	16,402	91	3,159	24
.44 Smoothbore	15	0	1	0
.44 Rimfire	1,863	0	0	0
.44 German	59	0	0	0
.44 Russian	154	51	90	62
.44 S&W	24	51	29	64
.44 S&W Special	506	1	0	0
.44-40	64,489	21	6,803	78
.45	150,683	100	8,005	97
.45 Smoothbore	4	0	2	0
.45 ACP	44	0	0	0
.450 Boxer	729	89	0	0
.450 Eley	2,697	84	5	0
.455 Eley	1,150	37	180	196
.476 Eley	161	2	0	0
Total quantities	310,386	914	44,350	976

Year	Serial Number Beginning of Year	Serial Number at End of Year

MODEL 1911 AND 1911A1 — Commercial production — Capital "C" prefix — .45 cal.

1912	C1	C1899

Year	Serial Number Beginning of Year	Serial Number at End of Year		Year	Serial Number Beginning of Year	Serial Number at End of Year
1913	C1900	C5399		1956	272550C	276699C
1914	C5400	C16599		1957	276700C	281999C
1915	C16600	C27599		1958	282000C	283799C
1916	C27600	C74999		1959	283800C	285799C
1917	C75000	C98999		1960	285800C	287999C
1918	C99000	C105999		1961	288000C	289849C
1919	C106000	C120999		1962	289850C	291299C
1920	C120000	C126999		1963	291300C	293799C
1921	C127000	C128999		1964	293800C	295999C
1922	C129000	C133999		1965	296000C	300299C
1923	C134000	C134999		1966	300300C	308499C
1924	C135000	C139999		1967	308500C	315599C
1925	C140000	C144999		1968	315600C	324499C
1926	C145000	C150999		1969	324500C	332649C
1927	C151000	C151999		1970	332650C	336169C
1928	C152000	C154999		new		
1929	C155000	C155999		range	70G01001	70G05550
1930	C156000	C158999		1971	70G05551	70G18000
1931	C159000	C160999		1972	70G18001	70G34400
1932	C161000	C164799		1973	70G34401	70G43000
1933	C164800	C174599		1974	70G43001	70G73000
1934	C174600	C177999		1975	70G73001	70G88900
1935	C178000	C179799		1976	70G88901	70G99999
1936	C179800	C183199		new		
1937	C183200	C188699		range	01001G70	13900G70
1938	C188700	C189599		1977	13901G70	45199G70
1939	C189600	C198899		1978		
1940	C198900	C199299		to		
1941	C199300	C208799		date	45200G70	
1942	C208800	C215018				

Year	Serial Number Beginning of Year	Serial Number at End of Year	Manufacturer

1943-1945: Commercial production interrupted by WWII

MODEL 1911 AND 1911A1 MILITARY PRODUCTION

Year	Serial Number Beginning of Year	Serial Number at End of Year	Manufacturer
1946	C221001	C222000	
1947	C222001	C231999	
1948	C232000	C238500	
1949	C238501	C240000	
1950	C240000	247701C	
1912	1	500	Colt
	501	1000	Colt USN
	1001	1500	Colt
	1501	2000	Colt USN
	2001	2500	Colt
1951	247701C	253179C	
1952	253180C	259549C	
1953	259550C	266349C	
1954	266350C	270549C	
1955	270550C	272549C	
	2501	3500	Colt USN
	3501	3800	Colt USMC
	3801	4500	Colt

"C" suffix started with Ser. No. 240228

Year	Serial Number Beginning of Year	Serial Number at End of Year	Manufacturer
	4501	5500	Colt USN
	5501	6500	Colt
	6501	7500	Colt USN
	7501	8500	Colt
	8501	9500	Colt USN
	9501	10500	Colt
	10501	11500	Colt USN
	11501	12500	Colt
	12501	13500	Colt USN
	13501	17250	Colt
1913	17251	36400	Colt
	36401	37650	Colt USMC
	37651	38000	Colt
	38001	44000	Colt USN
	44001	60400	Colt
1914	60401	72570	Colt
	72571	83855	Springfield — (These numbers reserved Springfield
	83856	83900	Colt
	83901	84400	Colt USMC
	84401	96000	Colt
	96001	97537	Colt
	97538	102596	Colt
	102597	107596	Springfield —(Reserved for Springfield
1915	107597	109500	Colt
	109501	11000	Colt USN
	110001	113496	Colt
	113497	120566	Springfield —(Reserved for Springfield
	120567	125566	Colt
	125567	133186	Springfield —(Reserved for Springfield
1916	133187	137400	Colt
1917	137401	151186	Colt
	151187	151986	Colt USMC
	151987	185800	Colt
	185801	186200	Colt USMC
	186201	209586	Colt
	209587	210386	Colt USMC
	210387	215386	Colt frames (Reserved for receivers
	215387	216186	Colt USMC
	216187	216586	Colt
	216587	216986	Colt USMC
1918	216987	217386	Colt USMC
	217387	232000	Colt
	232001	233600	Colt USN
	233601	594000	Colt
	1	13152	Rem UMC
1919	13153	21676	Rem UMC
	594001	629500	Colt
	629501	700000	Unknown
1924	700001	710000	Colt
1937	710001	712349	Colt
1938	712350	713645	Colt
1939	713646	717281	Colt USN
1940	717282	721977	Colt
1941	721978	756733	Colt
1942	756734	800000	Colt
	S800001	S800500	Singer
	800501	801000	These numbers assigned to H&R
1943	801001	958100	Colt
	958101	1088725	US&S
	1088726	1208673	Colt
	1208674	1279673	Ithaca
	1279674	1279698	re no AA
	1279699	1441430	Remington-Rand
	1441431	1471430	Ithaca
	1471431	1609528	Remington-Rand
1944	1609529	1743846	Colt
	1743847	1890503	Ithaca
	1890504	2075103	Remington-Rand

Year	Serial Number Beginning of Year	Serial Number at End of Year	Manufacturer
1945	2075104	2134403	Ithaca
	2134404	2244803	Remington-Rand
	2244804	2380013	Colt
	2380014	2619013	Remington-Rand
	2619014	2693613	Ithaca

Date	Serial Number
PARKER SHOTGUNS	
1866-1868	0-6,800
1868-1877	9,700
1877-1879	15,700
1880	17,600
1881	22,700
1882	27,300
1883	34,900
1884	36,000
1885	46,450
1886	48,125
1887	56,650
1889	59,500
1890	61,350
1891	66,800
1892	71,600
1893	77,000
1894	80,300
1895	82,400
1896	85,200
1897	86,450
1898	89,350
1899	92,450
1900	97,300
1901	105,750
1902	113,100
1903	121,900
1904	129,200
1905	132,000
1906	138,300
1907	144,250
1908	148,250
1910	153,000

Date	Serial Number
1911	157,050
1912	157,800
1913	165,000
1914	168,200
1915	171,500
first year of Trojan grade	
1916	173,450
1917	175,650
first single barrel trap gun	
1918	180,250
1919	184,900
1920	190,100
1921	195,000
1922	200,500
first Parker single trigger	
1923	205,150
1924	207,600
first beavertail forend	
1925	214,400
1926	218,050
first ventilated rib, first .410	
1927	222,650
1928	228,200
PH grade dropped	
1929	230,700
1930	234,200
1931	235,950
1932	236,100
1933	236,300
1934	236,650
first skeet guns, takeover of factory by Remington	
1935	237,000
1936	239,900
last regular catalog	
1937	240,300
1938-1942	242,385

Serial # Range	Date	Nature of Changes

MAUSER BROOMHANDLES
produced from 1896 to late '30's

before #25	1896	— The cone hammer used in place of spur hammer.
#50	1896	— *"SYSTEM MAUSER"* marked on top of the chamber.
before #200	1897	— The locking system changed from one to two lugs. — The barrel contour at the chamber is tapered instead of stepped.
#390	1897	— *"WAFFENFABRIK MAUSER OBERNDORF A/N"* marked on top of the chamber.
#975	1897	— The center section of the rear panel on the left side of the frame is not milled out (this feature appears earlier on a few 20-shot pistols). This area is sometimes used for special markings on contract pieces such as the Turkish and Persian.
#12,200- #14,999	1898	— The large ring hammer replaces the cone hammer.
#21,000	1899	— There is no panel milling on either side of the frame. — A single lug bayonet type mount adopted for retaining the firing pin instead of the dovetail plate. — The trigger is mounted directly to the frame by two integral lugs rather than attached to a removable block. — The position of the serial number moved from the rear of the frame above the stock slot to the left side of the chamber.
#22,000	1900	— Two integral lugs used to mount the rear sight instead of a pin.
#29,000	1902	— Very shallow panels milled into the frame on both sides.*
#31,200	1903	— *"WAFFENFABRIK MAUSER OBERNDORF A NECKAR"* added to the right rear frame panel.*
#34,000	1904	— The depth of the frame panel milling increased.*
#35,000	1904	— The barrel extension side rails lengthened about a half inch.* — An additional lug for mounting added to the firing pin.* — The hammer changed to the small ring pattern.* — The safety mechanism altered to require that the lever be pushed up to engage it instead of down.* — The center of the safety lever knob is no longer milled out.*
#38,000	1905	— The short extractor with two ribs replaces the long thin extractor.*
#100,000- #130,000	1910 to 1911	— The rifling changed from four groove to six groove.
#270,000	1915	— "NS" *(Neues Sicherung* or New Safety) appears on the back of the hammer. The hammer must be moved back beyond the cocked position to engage the safety.
#440,000	1921	— The lanyard ring stud is rotated 90 degrees.
#501,000	1923	— The Mauser "banner" appears on the left rear frame panel.
#800,000	1930	— The Mauser banner is enlarged. — A step is added to the barrel contour just ahead of the chamber. — The safety is changed to allow the hammer to be dropped from a cocked position, without danger, by pulling the trigger (called Universal Safety).

Serial # Range	Date	Nature of Changes
		— The front of the grip frame widened to equal the rear part where the stock slot is.
#850,000	1932	— "D.R.P.u.A.P." (Deutsches Reich Patenten und Anderes Patenten) added below the inscription on the right rear frame panel.
#860,000	1932	— The lettering in the frame inscription is slanted forward.
#900,000	1934	— The serial number is moved to the rear of the barrel extension behind the sight.
		— The two grooves in each side of the barrel extension side rails are eliminated.

*These nine changes appear out of sequence (either early or late) on three small batches of guns (29,000 to 29,900, 40,000 to 41,000, and 42,600 to 43,900). Most of these pistols are of the "bolo" style, that is they have 3.9-inch barrels, small grips, six or 10-shot magazines and fixed or adjustable rear sights. A few of these pistols show non-standard barrel contours, barrel extension milling and hammer safety devices. Apparently the factory withheld these numbers from the regular production series and reissued them at later dates.

REMINGTON FIREARMS SERIAL NUMBER IDENTIFICATION
(CODE LOCATED ON BARREL, LEFT SIDE AT FRAME).

MONTH OF MANUFACTURE
(CODE LETTER CORRESPONDS TO NUMERAL UNDERNEATH)

B	L	A	C	K	P	O	W	D	E	R	X
1	2	3	4	5	6	7	8	9	10	11	12

YEAR OF MANUFACTURE

Year	Code	Year	Code	Year	Code	Year	Code	Year	Code	Year	Code
1921	M	1931	Z	1941	K	1951	XX	1961	H	1971	U
1922	N	1932	A	1942	L	1952	YY	1962	J	1972	W
1923	P	1933	B	1943	MM	1953	ZZ	1963	K		
1924	R	1934	C	1944	NN	1954	A	1964	L		
1925	S	1935	D	1945	PP	1955	B	1965	M		
1926	T	1936	E	1946	RR	1956	C	1966	N		
1927	U	1937	F	1947	SS	1957	D	1967	P		
1928	W	1938	G	1948	TT	1958	E	1968	R		
1929	X	1939	H	1949	UU	1959	F	1969	S		
1930	Y	1940	J	1950	WW	1960	G	1970	T		

The following Winchester serial numbers appear courtesy of U.S. Repeating Arms, New Haven, CT. I would like to thank U.S. Repeating Arms and Mr. Pardee for making these production figures available (many for the first time).

WINCHESTER RIFLES

Records at the factory indicate the following serial numbers were assigned to guns at the end of the calendar year.

MODEL 1866

1866 -	12476 to 14813
67 -	15578
68 -	19768
69 -	29516
70 -	52527
71 -	88184
72 -	109784
73 -	118401
74 -	125038
75 -	125965
76 -	131907
77 -	148207
78 -	150493
79 -	152201
80 -	154379
81 -	156107
82 -	159513
83 -	162376
84 -	163649
85 -	163664
86 -	165071
87 -	165912
88 -	167155
89 -	167401
90 -	167702
91 -	169003
92 -	None
93 -	169007
94 -	169011
95 -	None
96 -	None
97 -	169015
98 -	170100
99 -	Discontinued

MODEL 1873

1873 -	1 to 126
74 -	2726
75 -	11325
76 -	23151
77 -	23628
78 -	27501
79 -	41525
80 -	63537

81 -	81620
82 -	109507
83 -	145503
84 -	175126
85 -	196221
86 -	222937
87 -	225922
88 -	284529
89 -	323956
90 -	363220
91 -	405026
92 -	441625
93 -	466641
94 -	481826
95 -	499308
96 -	507545
97 -	513421
98 -	525922
99 -	541328
1900 -	554128
01 -	557236
02 -	564557
03 -	573957
04 -	588953
05 -	602557
06 -	613780
07 -	None
08 -	None
09 -	630385
10 -	656101
11 -	669324
12 -	678527
13 -	684419
14 -	686510
15 -	688431
16 -	694020
17 -	698617
18 -	700734
19 -	702042

No last # available —
20, 21, 22, 23, 720609

MODEL 1876

1876 -	1 to 1429
77 -	3579

78 -	7967
79 -	8971
80 -	14700
81 -	21759
82 -	32407
83 -	42410
84 -	54666
85 -	58714
86 -	60397
87 -	62420
88 -	63539
89 -	None
90 -	None
91 -	None
92 -	63561
93 -	63670
94 -	63678
95 -	None
96 -	63702
97 -	63869
98 -	63871

MODEL 1885 — SINGLE SHOT

1885 -	1 to 375
86 -	6841
87 -	18328
88 -	30571
89 -	45019
90 -	None
91 -	53700
92 -	60371
93 -	69534
94 -	None
95 -	73771
96 -	78253
97 -	78815
98 -	84700
99 -	85086
1900 -	88501
01 -	90424
02 -	92031
03 -	92359
04 -	92785
05 -	93611

06 -	94208
07 -	95743
08 -	96819
09 -	98097
10 -	98506
11 -	99012
12 -	None
13 -	100352

No further serial numbers were recorded until the end of 1923. The last number recorded was: 139700

MODEL 1886

1886 -	1 to 3211
87 -	14728
88 -	28577
89 -	38401
90 -	49723
91 -	63601
92 -	73816
93 -	83261
94 -	94543
95 -	103708
96 -	109670
97 -	113997
98 -	119192
99 -	120571
1900 -	122834
01 -	125630
02 -	128942
03 -	132213
04 -	135524
05 -	138838
06 -	142249
07 -	145119
08 -	147322
09 -	148237
10 -	150129
11 -	151622
12 -	152943
13 -	152947
14 -	153859
15 -	154452
16 -	154979
17 -	155387
18 -	156219
19 -	156930
20 -	158716
21 -	159108
22 -	159337

No further serial numbers were recorded until the discontinuance of the model which was in 1935 - at - 159994

MODEL 1887

1887 -	1 to 7431
88 -	22408
89 -	25673
90 -	29105
91 -	38541
92 -	49763
93 -	54367
94 -	56849
95 -	58289
96 -	60175
97 -	63952
98 -	64855

According to these records no guns were produced during the last few years of this model and it was therefore discontinued in 1901.

Records on the Model 1890 are somewhat incomplete. Our records indicate the following serial numbers were assigned to guns at the end of the calendar year beginning with 1908. Actual records on the firearms which were manufactured between 1890 and 1907 will be available from the "Winchester Museum", located at The "Buffalo Bill Historical Center" P.O. Box 1020, Cody, Wy. 82414

MODEL 1890

1908 -	330000 to 363850
09 -	393427
10 -	423567
11 -	451264
12 -	478595
13 -	506936
14 -	531019
15 -	551290
16 -	570497
17 -	589204
18 -	603438
19 -	630801
20 -	None

21 -	634783
22 -	643304
23 -	654837
24 -	664613
25 -	675774
26 -	687049
27 -	698987
28 -	711354
29 -	722125
30 -	729015
31 -	733178
32 -	734454

The Model 1890 was discontinued in 1932, however, a clean up of the production run lasted another 8+ years and included another 14 to 15000 guns. Our figures indicate approximately 749,000 guns were made.

MODEL 1892

1892 -	1 to 23701
93 -	35987
94 -	73508
95 -	106721
96 -	144935
97 -	159312
98 -	165431
99 -	171820
1900 -	183411
01 -	191787
02 -	208871
03 -	253935
04 -	278546
05 -	315425
06 -	376496
07 -	437919
08 -	476540
09 -	522162
10 -	586996
11 -	643483
12 -	694752
13 -	742675
14 -	771444
15 -	804622
16 -	830031
17 -	853819
18 -	870942
19 -	903649
20 -	906754
21 -	910476
22 -	917300

23 -	926329	27 -	990883	30 -	999730
24 -	938641	28 -	996517	31 -	1000727
25 -	954997	29 -	999238	32 -	1001324
26 -	973896				

Records at the factory, and in some years, estimates, indicate the following serial numbers were assigned to guns at the end of the calendar year.

MODEL 94

1894 -	1 to 14579	1924 -	953198	1954 -	2071100
95 -	44359	25 -	978523	55 -	2145296
96 -	76464	26 -	997603	56 -	2225000
97 -	111453	27 -	1027571	57 -	2290296
98 -	147684	28 -	1054465	58 -	2365887
99 -	183371	29 -	1077097	59 -	2410555
1900 -	204427	30 -	1081755	60 -	2469821
01 -	233975	31 -	1084156	61 -	2500000
02 -	273854	32 -	1087836	62 -	2551921
03 -	291506	33 -	1089270	63 -	2586000
04 -	311363	34 -	1091190	*1964 -	2700000 - 2797428
05 -	337557	35 -	1099605	65 -	2894428
06 -	378878	36 -	1100065	66 -	2991927
07 -	430985	37 -	1100679	67 -	3088458
08 -	474241	38 -	1100915	68 -	3185691
09 -	505831	39 -	1101051	69 -	3284570
10 -	553062	40 -	1142423	70 -	3381299
11 -	599263	41 -	1191307	71 -	3557385
12 -	646114	42 -	1221289	72 -	3806499
13 -	703701	43 -	No Record Avail.	73 -	3929364
14 -	756066	44 -	No Record Avail.	74 -	4111426
15 -	784052	45 -	No Record Avail.	75 -	4277926
16 -	807741	46 -	No Record Avail.	76 -	4463553
17 -	821972	47 -	No Record Avail.	77 -	4565925
18 -	838175	48 -	1500000	78 -	4662210
19 -	870762	49 -	1626100	79 -	4826596
20 -	880627	50 -	1724295	80 -	4892951
21 -	908318	51 -	1819800	81 -	5024957
22 -	919583	52 -	1910000	82 -	5103248
23 -	938539	53 -	2000000		

*The post-64 Model 94 began with serial number 2,700,000.

Serial number 1,000,000 was presented to President Calvin Coolidge in 1927.

Serial number 1,500,000 was presented to President Harry S. Truman in 1948.

Serial numbers 2,500,000 and 3,000,000 were presented to the Winchester Gun Museum, now located in Cody, Wyoming.

Serial number 3,500,000 was not constructed until 1979 and was sold at auction in Las Vegas, Nevada.

Serial number 4,000,000 — whereabouts unknown at this time.

Serial number 4,500,000 — shipped to Italy by Olin in 1978. Whereabouts unknown.

Serial number 5,000,000 — in New Haven, not constructed as of March 1983.

Records at the factory indicate the following serial numbers were assigned to guns at the end of the calendar year.

MODEL 1895

1895 -	1 to 287
96 -	5715
97 -	7814
98 -	19871
99 -	26434
1900 -	29817
01 -	31584
02 -	35601
03 -	42514
04 -	47805
05 -	54783
06 -	55011
07 -	57351
08 -	60002
09 -	60951
10 -	63771
11 -	65017
12 -	67331
13 -	70823
14 -	72082
15 -	174233
16 -	377411
17 -	389106
18 -	392731
19 -	397250
20 -	400463
21 -	404075
22 -	407200
23 -	410289
24 -	413276
25 -	417402
26 -	419533
27 -	421584
28 -	422676
29 -	423680
30 -	424181
31 -	425132
32 -	425825

MODEL 1903

1903 -	# Not Available ..
04 -	6944
05 -	14865
06 -	23097
07 -	31852
08 -	39105
09 -	46496
10 -	54298
11 -	61679

12 -	69586
13 -	76732
14 -	81776
15 -	84563
16 -	87148
17 -	89501
18 -	92617
19 -	96565
20 -	# Not Available ..
21 -	97650
22 -	99011
23 -	100452
24 -	101688
25 -	103075
26 -	104230
27 -	105537
28 -	107157
29 -	109414
30 -	111276
31 -	112533
32 -	112992

This model was discontinued in 1932, however, a clean up of parts was used for further production of approximately 2000 guns. Total production was stopped at serial number ...... 114962 ... in 1936.

MODEL 1905

1905 -	1 to 5659
06 -	15288
07 -	19194
08 -	20385
09 -	21280
10 -	22423
11 -	23503
12 -	24602
13 -	25559
14 -	26110
15 -	26561
16 -	26910
17 -	27297
18 -	27585
19 -	28287
20 -	29113

MODEL 1906

1906 -	1 to 52278
07 -	89147
08 -	114138
09 -	165068
10 -	221189
11 -	273355
12 -	327955
13 -	381922
14 -	422734
15 -	453880
16 -	483805
17 -	517743
18 -	535540
19 -	593917
20 -	None
21 -	598691
22 -	608011
23 -	622601
24 -	636163
25 -	649952
26 -	665484
27 -	679892
28 -	695915
29 -	711202
30 -	720116
31 -	725978
32 -	727353

A clean up of production took place for the next few years with a record of production reaching approximately 729305.

MODEL 1907

1907 -	1 to 8657
08 -	14486
09 -	19707
10 -	23230
11 -	25523
12 -	27724
13 -	29607
14 -	30872
15 -	32272
16 -	36215
17 -	38235
18 -	39172
19 -	40448
20 -	No # Available
21 -	40784
22 -	41289

23 -	41658		14 -	12311		

23 -	41658
24 -	42029
25 -	42360
26 -	42688
27 -	43226
28 -	43685
29 -	44046
30 -	44357
31 -	44572
32 -	44683
33 -	44806
34 -	44990
35 -	45203
36 -	45482
37 -	45920
38 -	46419
39 -	46758
40 -	47296
1941 -	47957
42 -	48275
43 -	None
44 -	None
45 -	48281
46 -	48395
47 -	48996
48 -	49684
**49 -	50662
**50 -	51640
**51 -	52618
**52 -	53596
**53 -	54574
**54 -	55552
**55 -	56530
**56 -	57508
**57 -	58486

**Actual records on serial numbers stops in 1948. The serial numbers ending each year from 1948 to 1957 were derived at by taking the last serial number recorded (58486) and the last number from 1948, (49684) and dividing the years of production (9), which relates to 978 guns each year for the nine year period.

MODEL 1910

1910 -	1 to 4766
11 -	7695
12 -	9712
13 -	11487
14 -	12311
15 -	13233
16 -	13788
17 -	14255
18 -	14625
19 -	15665
20 -	No # Available.
21 -	15845
22 -	16347
23 -	16637
24 -	17030
25 -	17281
26 -	17696
27 -	18182
28 -	18469
29 -	18893
30 -	19065
31 -	19172
32 -	19232
33 -	19281
34 -	19338
35 -	19388
36 -	19445

A cleanup of production continued into 1937 when the total of the guns was completed at approximately 20786 ...

MODEL 1911 S.L.

1911 -	1 to 3819
12 -	27659
13 -	36677
14 -	40105
15 -	43284
16 -	45391
17 -	49893
18 -	52895
19 -	57337
20 -	60719
21 -	64109
22 -	69132
23 -	73186
24 -	76199
25 -	78611

The Model 1911 was discontinued in 1925. However, guns were produced for three years after that date to clean up production and excess parts. When this practice ceased there were approximately 82774 guns produced.

MODEL 52

1920 -	None indicated
21 -	397
22 -	745
23 -	1394
24 -	2361
25 -	3513
26 -	6383
27 -	9436
28 -	12082
29 -	14594
30 -	17253
31 -	21954
32 -	24951
33 -	26725
34 -	29030
35 -	32448
36 -	36632
37 -	40419
38 -	43632
39 -	45460
40 -	47519
41 -	50317
42 -	52129
43 -	52553
44 -	52560
45 -	52718
46 -	56080
47 -	60158
48 -	64265
1949 -	68149
50 -	70766
51 -	73385
52 -	76000
53 -	79500
54 -	80693
55 -	81831
56 -	96869
57 -	97869
58 -	98599
59 -	98899
60 -	102200
61 -	106986
62 -	108718
63 -	113583
64 -	118447
65 -	120992
66 -	123537
67 -	123727
68 -	123917
69 -	E 124107
70 -	E 124297
71 -	E 124489

72 -	E 124574		
73 -	E 124659		
74 -	E 124744		
75 -	E 124828		
76 -	E 125019		
77 -	E 125211		
78 -	E 125315		

This Model was discontinued in 1978. A small clean up of production was completed in 1979 with a total of -   125419.

MODEL 53

In the case of the Model 53 the following list pertains to the amount of guns produced each year rather than a serial number list.

The Model 53 was serially numbered concurrently with the MODEL 92.

MODEL 53s PRODUCED

1924 -	1488
25 -	2861

26 -	2531
27 -	2297
28 -	1958
29 -	1733
30 -	920
31 -	621
32 -	206

This Model was discontinued in 1932, however, a clean up of production continued for 9 more years with an additional 486 guns.

TOTAL PRODUCTION APPROXIMATELY — 15100

Records at the factory indicate the following serial numbers were assigned to guns at the end of the calendar year.

MODEL 54

1925 -	1 to 3140
26 -	8051
27 -	14176
28 -	19587
29 -	29104
30 -	32499
31 -	36731
32 -	38543
33 -	40722
34 -	43466
35 -	47125
36 -	50145

MODEL 55 CENTERFIRE

1924 -	1 to 836
25 -	2783
26 -	4957
27 -	8021
28 -	10467
29 -	12258
30 -	17393
31 -	18198
32 -	19204
33 -	Clean - up 20580

MODEL 61

1932 -	1 to 3532
33 -	6008
34 -	8554
35 -	12379
36 -	20615
37 -	30334
38 -	36326

39 -	42610
40 -	49270
41 -	57493
42 -	59871
43 -	59872
44 -	59879
45 -	60512
46 -	71629
47 -	92297
48 -	115281
49 -	125461
50 -	135641
51 -	145821
52 -	156000
53 -	171000
54 -	186000
55 -	200962
56 -	215923
57 -	229457
58 -	242992
59 -	262793
60 -	282594
61 -	302395
62 -	322196
63 -	342001

This Model was discontinued in 1963. For some unknown reason there are no actual records available from 1949 through 1963. The serial number figures for these years are arrived at by taking the total production figure of

342001, subtracting the last known # of 115281, and dividing the difference equally by the amount of remaining years available, (15).

MODEL 62

1932 -	1 to 7643
33 -	10695
34 -	14090
35 -	23924
36 -	42759
37 -	66059
38 -	80205
39 -	96534
40 -	116393
41 -	137379
42 -	155152
43 -	155422
44 -	155425
45 -	156073
46 -	183756
47 -	219085
48 -	252298
49 -	262473
50 -	272648
51 -	282823
52 -	293000
53 -	310500
54 -	328000
55 -	342776
56 -	357551
57 -	383513
58 -	409475

MODEL 63			59 -	465040		40 -	67085
1933 -	1 to 2667		60 -	504257		41 -	114355
34 -	5361		61 -	545446		42 -	128293
35 -	9830		62 -	565592		43 -	None
36 -	16781		63 -	581471		44 -	128295
37 -	25435		All post - 64 Model 70s			45 -	128878
38 -	30934		began with the serial			46 -	145168
39 -	36055		number 700,000			47 -	173524
40 -	41456		64 -	740599		48 -	223788
41 -	47708		65 -	809177		49 -	249900
42 -	51258		66 -	833795		50 -	276012
43 -	51631		67 -	869000		51 -	302124
44 -	51656		68 -	925908		52 -	328236
45 -	53853		69 -	G941900		53 -	354348
46 -	61607		70 -	G957995		54 -	380460
47 -	71714		71 -	G1018991		55 -	406574
48 -	80519		72 -	G1099257			
49 -	88889		73 -	G1128731			
50 -	97259		74 -	G1175000		MODEL 88	
51 -	105629		75 -	G1218700		1955 -	1 to 18378
52 -	114000		76 -	G1266000		56 -	36756
53 -	120500		77 -	G1350000		57 -	55134
54 -	127000		78 -	G1410000		58 -	73512
55 -	138000		79 -	G1447000		59 -	91890
56 -	150000		80 -	G1490709		60 -	110268
57 -	162345		81 -	G1537134		61 -	128651
58 -	174692					62 -	139838
			MODEL 71			63 -	148858
MODEL 70			1935 -	1 to 4		64 -	160307
1935 -	1 to 19		36 -	7821		65 -	162699
36 -	2238		37 -	12988		66 -	192595
37 -	11573		38 -	14690		67 -	212416
38 -	17844		39 -	16155		68 -	230199
39 -	23991		40 -	18267		69 -	H239899
40 -	31675		41 -	20810		70 -	H258229
41 -	41753		42 -	21959		71 -	H266784
42 -	49206		43 -	22048		72 -	H279014
43 -	49983		44 -	22051		73 -	H283718
44 -	49997		45 -	22224			
45 -	50921		46 -	23534			
46 -	58382		47 -	25728		MODEL 100	
47 -	75675		48 -	27900		1961 -	1 to 32189
48 -	101680		49 -	29675		62 -	60760
49 -	131580		50 -	31450		63 -	78863
50 -	173150		51 -	33225		64 -	92016
51 -	206625		52 -	35000		65 -	135388
52 -	238820		53 -	37500		66 -	145239
53 -	282735		54 -	40770		67 -	209498
54 -	323530		55 -	43306		68 -	210053
55 -	361025		56 -	45843		69 -	A210999
56 -	393595		57 -	47254		70 -	A229995
57 -	425283					71 -	A242999
58 -	440792		MODEL 74			72 -	A258001
			1939 -	1 to 30890		73 -	A262833

WINCHESTER SHOTGUNS

Records at the factory indicate the following serial numbers were assigned to guns at the end of the calendar year.

MODEL 1897

Year	Serial
1897 -	1 to 32335
98 -	64668
99 -	96999
1900 -	129332
01 -	161665
02 -	193998
03 -	226331
04 -	258664
05 -	296037
06 -	334059
07 -	377999
08 -	413618
09 -	446888
10 -	481062
11 -	512632
12 -	544313
13 -	575213
14 -	592732
15 -	607673
16 -	624537
17 -	646124
18 -	668383
19 -	691943
20 -	696183
21 -	700428
22 -	715902
23 -	732060
24 -	744942
25 -	757629
26 -	770527
27 -	783574
1928 -	796806
29 -	807321
30 -	812729
31 -	830721
32 -	833926
33 -	835637
34 -	837364
35 -	839728
36 -	848684
37 -	856729
38 -	860725
39 -	866938
40 -	875945
41 -	891190
42 -	910072
43 -	912265
44 -	912327
45 -	916472
46 -	926409
47 -	936682
48 -	944085
49 -	953042
50 -	961999
51 -	970956
52 -	979913
53 -	988860
54 -	997827
55 -	1006784
56 -	1015741
57 -	1024700

Records on this Model are incomplete. The above serial numbers are estimated from 1897 thru 1903 and again from 1949 thru 1957. The actual records are in existence from 1904 through 1949.

MODEL 1901 SHOTGUN

Year	Serial
1904 -	64,856 to 64,860
05 -	66453
06 -	67486
07 -	68424
08 -	69197
09 -	70009
10 -	70753
11 -	71441
12 -	72167
13 -	72764
14 -	73202
15 -	73509
16 -	73770
17 -	74027
18 -	74311
19 -	74872
20 -	77000

MODEL 12

Year	Serial
1912 -	5308
13 -	32418
14 -	79765
15 -	109515
16 -	136412
17 -	159391
18 -	183461
19 -	219457
20 -	247458
21 -	267253
22 -	304314
23 -	346319
24 -	385196
25 -	423056
26 -	464564
27 -	510693
28 -	557850
29 -	600834
30 -	626996
31 -	651255
32 -	660110
33 -	664544
34 -	673994
35 -	686978
36 -	720316
37 -	754250
38 -	779455
39 -	814121
40 -	856499
41 -	907431
42 -	958303
43 -	975640
44 -	975727
45 -	990004
1946 -	1029152
47 -	1102371
48 -	1176055
49 -	1214041
50 -	1252028
51 -	1290015
52 -	1328002
53 -	1399996
54 -	1471990
55 -	1541929
56 -	1611868
57 -	1651435
58 -	1690999
59 -	1795500
60 -	1800000
61 -	1930029
62 -	1956990
63 -	1962001

A clean up of production took place from 64 through 66 with the ending serial # 1970875

New Style M/12

1972 -	Y200 0100 -
	Y2006396
73 -	Y2015662
74 -	Y2022061
75 -	Y2024478
76 -	Y2025482
77 -	Y2025874
78 -	Y2026156
79 -	Y2026399

MODEL 24

1939 -	1 to 8118
40 -	21382
41 -	27045
42 -	33670
43 -	None recorded
44 -	33683
45 -	34965
46 -	45250
47 -	58940
48 -	64417

There were no records kept on this model from 1949 until its discontinuance in 1958. The total production was approximately 116280.

MODEL 42

1933 -	1 to 9398
34 -	13963
35 -	17728
36 -	24849
37 -	30900
38 -	34659
39 -	38967
40 -	43348
41 -	48203
42 -	50818
43 -	50822
44 -	50828
45 -	51168
46 -	54256
47 -	64853
48 -	75142
49 -	81107
50 -	87071
51 -	93038
52 -	99000
53 -	108201
54 -	117200
55 -	121883
56 -	126566
57 -	131249
58 -	135932
59 -	140615
60 -	145298
61 -	149981
62 -	154664
63 -	159353

MODEL 50

1954 -	1 to 24550
55 -	49100
56 -	73650
57 -	98200
58 -	122750
59 -	147300
60 -	171850
61 -	196400

BEGINNING SERIAL NUMBER AND CORRESPONDING DATE OF MANUFACTURE-

HIGH STANDARD AUTOMATIC PISTOL

1958-1984

1958	8192XX	1976	ML19XXX
1959	9854XX	1977	ML23XXX
1962	12606XX	Feb.1981	ML71000
1963	12954XX	Apr.1981	ML84000
1965	14204XX	May 1981	ML85000
1965	15709XX	June 1981	ML86000
1966	16078XX	June 1981	SH10000
1967	17509XX	Sept.1982	SH14000
1967	18141XX	Oct. 1982	SH15000
1968	18891XX	Nov. 1982	SH16000
1968	19909XX	Dec. 1982	SH17000
1969	20485XX	Jan. 1983	SH18000
1969	21609XX	Feb. 1983	SH19000
1970	21971XX	Apr. 1983	SH21000
1971	22662XX	May 1983	SH23000
1972	22874XX	Oct. 1983	SH24000
1972	23337XX	Feb. 1984	SH25000
1973	23639XX	Apr. 1984	SH26000
1973	24140XX	May 1984	SH27000
1974	24337XX	June 1984	SH29000
1975	ML15XXX	Sept 1984	SH34000

WINCHESTER MODEL 101 SERIALIZATION

Serial No	Mon of Mfg	Year	Serial No	Mon of Mfg	Year	Serial No	Mon of Mfg	Year
50,000	10	1959	67,000	5	1964	83,500	8	1965
50,500	3	1960	67,500	5	1964	84,000	9	1965
51,000	5	1960	68,000	5	1964	84,500	9	1965
51,500	6	1960	68,500	5	1964	85,000	10	1965
52,000	9	1961	69,000	6	1964	85,500	10	1965
52,500	3	1962	69,500	6	1964	86,000	10	1965
53,000	4	1962	70,000	7	1964	86,500	10	1965
53,500	5	1962	70,500	7	1964	87,000	10	1965
54,000	8	1962	71,000	8	1964	87,500	10	1965
54,500	9	1962	71,500	9	1964	88,000	11	1965
55,000	10	1962	72,000	9	1964	88,500	11	1965
55,500	12	1962	72,500	10	1964	89,000	11	1965
56,000	1	1963	73,000	10	1964	90,000	12	1965
56,500	2	1963	73,500	11	1964	90,500	12	1965
57,000	3	1963	74,000	11	1964	91,000	12	1965
57,500	3	1963	74,500	12	1964	91,500	1	1966
58,000	4	1963	75,000	12	1964	92,000	1	1966
58,500	5	1963	75,500	1	1965	92,500	2	1966
59,000	6	1963	76,000	2	1965	93,000	2	1966
59,500	6	1963	76,500	2	1965	93,500	2	1966
60,000	7	1963	77,000	3	1965	94,000	3	1966
60,500	8	1963	77,500	4	1965	94,500	3	1966
61,000	8	1963	78,000	4	1965	95,000	5	1966
61,500	11	1963	78,500	4	1965	95,500	5	1966
62,000	11	1963	79,000	4	1965	96,000	6	1966
62,500	11	1963	79,500	4	1965	96,500	7	1966
63,000	12	1963	80,000	5	1965	97,000	7	1966
63,500	1	1964	80,500	6	1965	97,500	7	1966
64,000	1	1964	81,000	6	1965	98,000	8	1966
64,500	2	1964	81,500	6	1965	98,500	8	1966
65,000	3	1964	82,000	6	1965	99,000	9	1966
65,500	3	1964	82,500	8	1965	99,500	9	1966
66,000	3	1964	83,000	8	1965	100,000	10	1966
66,500	3	1964				100,500	10	1966

Serial No	Mon of Mfg	Year	Serial No	Mon of Mfg	Year	Serial No	Mon of Mfg	Year
101,000	10	1966	127,000	9	1969	207,000	9	1966
101,500	11	1966	127,500	10	1969	207,500	9	1966
102,000	11	1966	128,000	11	1969	208,000	9	1966
102,500	12	1966	128,500	11	1969	208,500	12	1966
103,000	1	1967	129,000	11	1969	209,000	2	1967
103,500	1	1967	129,500	2	1970	209,500	7	1967
104,000	2	1967	130,000	2	1970	210,000	10	1967
104,500	3	1967	130,500	3	1970	210,500	12	1967
105,000	4	1967	131,000	3	1970	211,000	1	1968
105,500	5	1967	131,500	4	1970	211,500	1	1968
106,000	5	1967	132,000	4	1970	212,000	10	1968
106,500	5	1967	132,500	4	1970	212,500	10	1968
107,000	9	1967	133,000	4	1970	213,000	10	1968
107,500	10	1967	133,500	5	1970	213,500	11	1968
108,000	10	1967	134,000	5	1970	214,000	12	1968
108,500	11	1967	134,500	5	1970	214,500	12	1968
109,000	11	1967	135,000	6	1970	215,000	1	1969
109,500	11	1967	135,500	6	1970	215,500	2	1969
110,000	12	1967	136,000	6	1970	216,000	5	1969
110,500	1	1968	136,500	8	1970	216,500	6	1969
111,000	2	1968	137,000	8	1970	217,000	9	1969
111,500	3	1968	137,500	8	1970	217,500	10	1969
112,000	3	1968	138,000	8	1970	218,000	11	1969
112,500	3	1968	138,500	11	1970	218,500	12	1969
113,000	3	1968	139,000	12	1970	219,000	12	1969
113,500	4	1968	139,500	12	1970	219,500	12	1969
114,000	5	1968	140,000	12	1970	220,000	12	1969
114,500	5	1968	140,500	1	1971	220,500	1	1970
115,000	6	1968	141,000	2	1971	221,000	1	1970
115,500	6	1968	141,500	2	1971	221,500	2	1970
116,000	7	1968	142,000	2	1971	222,000	3	1970
116,500	7	1968	142,500	3	1971	222,500	7	1970
117,000	9	1968	143,000	3	1971	223,000	9	1970
117,500	10	1968	143,500	4	1971	223,500	9	1970
118,000	1	1969	144,000	4	1971	224,000	9	1970
118,500	1	1969	144,500	4	1971	224,500	9	1970
119,000	2	1969	145,000	4	1971	225,000	10	1970
119,500	3	1969	145,500	5	1971	225,500	10	1970
120,000	4	1969	200,000	3	1966	226,000	11	1970
120,500	4	1969	200,500	3	1966	226,500	11	1970
121,000	4	1969	201,000	3	1966	227,000	11	1970
121,500	4	1969	201,500	3	1966	227,500	12	1970
122,000	5	1969	202,000	4	1966	228,000	12	1970
122,500	6	1969	202,500	4	1966	228,500	4	1971
123,000	6	1969	203,000	4	1966	229,000	4	1971
123,500	6	1969	203,500	5	1966	229,500	4	1971
124,000	7	1969	204,000	6	1966			
124,500	7	1969	204,500	6	1966			
125,000	7	1969	205,000	7	1966			
125,500	8	1969	205,500	8	1966			
126,000	8	1969	206,000	8	1966			
126,500	9	1969	206,500	8	1966			

Cartridge Interchangeability

This section is for the shooter whose motto is "If it fits, I'll shoot it". Many apparent "fits" are not adapted for a shorter round, and either immediate or future damage can occur to the firearm by firing ammunition not specifically adapted to the chambering of a particular gun. As an example, many people think that shooting .22 Shorts in a barrel marked for .22 Long Rifle is acceptable. In fact, repeated firing can cause erosion of the chamber to the point that shell extraction can become difficult in addition to experiencing velocity loss in extreme cases. Below is a listing of recommended caliber interchangeability. No other cartridge switching is recommended nor does this chart work vise-versa. For shotguns, there is no interchangeability for gauges. Only shells that are shorter than the specified chamber length in the same gauge may be used (ie. 2#3/4 in. 12 ga. ammunition may be used in a 12. ga. gun with a 3 in. chamber).

RIMFIRE INTERCHANGEABILITY

Firearm marked for:	Can also be used with:
.22 Short	.22 BB Cap, .22 CB Cap, .22 Short Blank, 22 CB Short
.22 Long	.22 BB Cap, .22 CB Cap, .22 Short Blank, .22 Short, .22 CB Short, .22 CB Long
.22 Long Rifle	.22 BB Cap, .22 CB Cap, .22 Short Blank, .22 CB Short, .22 CB Long, .22 Long, .22 L.R. Shot
.22 Win. Mag. R.F	..22 Win. R.F., .22 Rem. Spl.
.22 Rem. Spl	.22 Win. R.F.
.22 Win. R.F.	.22 Rem. Spl.
.25 Stevens	.25 Stevens Short
.32 Long	.32 Short

CENTERFIRE HANDGUN INTERCHANGEABILITY

Firearm marked for:	Can also be used with:
.32 Smith & Wesson Long	.32 Smith & Wesson, .32 Smith & Wesson Blank, .32 Colt New Police
.32 Colt New Police	.32 Smith & Wesson, .32 Smith & Wesson Blank, .32 Smith & Wesson Long
.32 Long Colt	.32 Short Colt
.38 Long Colt	.38 Short Colt
.38 Smith & Wesson	.38 Colt New Police, .38 Smith & Wesson Blank
.38 Colt New Police	.38 Smith & Wesson, .38 Smith & Wesson Blank
.38 Special	.38 Short Colt, .38 Long Colt, .38 Special Blank
.357 Magnum	.38 Short Colt, .38 Long Colt, .38 Special Blank, .38 Special, .38 Special +P
.38-40 Winchester	5 in 1 Blank
.38 Super Auto	.38 Auto Colt
.44 S&W Special	.44 S&W Russian
.44 Remington Magnum	.44 S&W Special
.44-40 Winchester	5 in 1 Blank
.45 Colt	5 in 1 Blank

GUNS ALSO CALLED CENTERFIRE PISTOLS

Full name:	Also called:
.25 Automatic	.25 Auto, .25 ACP, .25 C.A.P., 6.35mm Auto, 635mm Browning (Auto)
.30 Luger	7.65 Luger, 7.65 Parabellum
.32 Automatic	.32 Auto, .32 ACP, .32 C.A.P., 7.65 Auto, 7.65mm Browning (Auto)
9mm Luger	9mm Parabellum
380 Automatic	9mm Corto, 9mm Kurtz
.38-40 Winchester	.38-40, .38 W.C.F., .38 Winchester, .38-40 Remington, .38-40 Marlin
.44-40 Winchester	.44-40, .44 W.C.F., .44 Winchester, .44-40 Remington, .44-40 Marlin

CENTERFIRE RIFLES

Full name:	Also called:
6mm Remington	(formerly) .244 Remington
.25-20 Winchester	.25-20, .25 W.C.F., .25-20 Marlin
.30-30 Winchester	.30-30, .30 Winchester, .30 Marlin, .30 Savage, .30 W.C.F.
.32-20 Winchester	.32-20, .32 Winchester, .32 Marlin, .32 Remington, .32 W.C.F., .32 Colt L.M.R.
.38-40 Winchester	.38-40, .38 W.C.F., .38 Winchester, .38-40 Remington, .38-40 Marlin
.44-40 Winchester	.44-40, .44 W.C.F., .44 Winchester, .44-40 Remington, .44-40 Marlin
.45-70 Government	.45-70, .45-70 Marlin, .45-70-405, .45-70-500

TRADEMARK INDEX

The following directory has been provided to assist you when trying to learn more about each individual trademark and its respective current manufacturer/importer/distributor. Each trademark or brandname listed in bold typeface on the following pages has its respective contact organization/company/individual (several in some cases) listed below in italics with address and FAX or telephone number. This information will save you a lot of time when trying to access these companies/individuals (it took me over 3 days to compile these listings using a variety of source materials and other data cross-referencing).

If you need a firearm that needs service work or parts of some kind, DO NOT automatically write or FAX to that company regarding this request as this is what their dealer network has been established for (if they have one). Check with the local dealers/gunsmiths in your area to learn more about where the firearm should be sent for any service work. If you are not able to find out any information using this approach, then write/FAX/phone the company/individual listed in this section. Remember, most of the companies listed on the following pages do not have extra personnel to service these types of requests on an immediate basis, so use your patience and give them some courtesy.

If you are requesting more information than what is shown is this publication on a specific model or need other data involving an older discontinued model you may or may not obtain this knowledge from those contacts listed in this directory. Remember, firms like Winchester, Colt's and others have a customer charge for conducting this oftentimes tedious research - please locate their respective headings in this text to find out the amount. Smaller companies may not have any people with enough longevity to remember past models and production variances/ rarities. It is also no secret that doing the research necessary to assist with customer service will not add to the daily bank deposit of many of the smaller companies (as in sales are always a priorty when time is an issue).

Value related questions should be directed to me - most of these companies do not take an active part in hanging price tags from out of production trigger guards (except on current mfg). If you should have any further questions requesting additional information on these (or other) trademarks, please contact me for further assistance. I will help you as much as much as I can. Send requests or FAX to me at:

Blue Book of Gun Values
Attn: Mr. Steven P. Fjestad
One Appletree Square
Minneapolis, MN 55425
FAX Number: 612-853-1486
Telephone Number: 612-854-5229

As I receive thousands of phone calls and hundreds of letters yearly, I will try to respond as fast as time permits.

Steven P. Fjestad   Author - Blue Book of Gun Values

P.S. If you are looking for older gun parts only, I would contact The Gun Parts Corp. located in W. Hurley, NY 12491, Phone No. 914-679-2417, FAX No. 914-679-5849 and be specific about what you need.

TRADEMARK INDEX

Please direct all correspondence to "Attn: Customer Service"

Editor's note - As the 12th edition goes to press, we feel confident that the information listed below is both up-to-date and accurate. However, there are always last minute changes, deletions, and insertions. Because of this , if you should require additional assistance in "tracking" any of the firearms manufacturers, distributors, or importers listed in this publication who are currently engaged in the business of selling newly manufactured goods, please call or FAX us and we will try to help you regarding these specific requests.

AMAC, INC.
2202 Redmond Road
Jacksonville, AR 72076
FAX No.: 501-982-8075

AMT/IAI
Arcadia Machine & Tool
6226 Santos Diaz Street
Irwindale, CA 91702
FAX No.: 818-969-5247

A-SQUARE
Rt. 4 Simmons Road
Madison, IN 47250
FAX No.: 812-273-3649

ACCU-TEK
4525 Carter Court
Chino, CA 91710
FAX No.: 714-627-7817

ACTION ARMS
P.O. Box 9573
Philadelphia, PA 19124-0573
FAX No.: 215-533-2188

AMERICAN ARMS INC.
715 E. Armour Road
N. Kansas City, MO 64116
FAX No.: 816-474-1225

AMERICAN DERRINGER CORPORATION
127 N. Lacy Dr.
Waco, TX 76705
FAX No.: 817-799-9334

AMERICAN HISTORICAL FOUNDATION
Attn: Mary Hill or Pam Ellett
1142 W. Grace St., #C175
Richmond, VA 23220
Phone No.: 804-353-1812
FAX No.: 804-354-4895

ANSCHUTZ
Precision Sales Int'l,Inc
P.O. Box 1776
Westfield, MA 01086
FAX No.: 413-562-5056

ARMES DE CHASSE
P.O. Box No. 827
Chadds Ford, PA 19317
Phone No.: 215-388-1146

ARMITAGE INTERNATIONAL LTD.
Attn: Skorpion Customer Service
P.O. Box 1099
Seneca, SC 29679
Phone No.: 803-882-5900
FAX No.: 803-885-0948

ARMS CORPORATION OF THE PHILIPPINES
Armscor Precision Inc.
1175 Chess Dr., Suite 204
Foster City, CA 94404
FAX No.: 415-349-0259

ARMS RESEARCH ASSOCIATES
1800 Mannheim Rd.
Stone Park, IL 60165

ARMSCORP OF AMERICA, INC.
4424 John Avenue
Baltimore, MD 21227
FAX No.: 301-247-6205

ARMSPORT
3590 NW 49th St.
Miami, FL 33142
FAX No.: 305-633-2877

ARRIETA, S.L.
Arrieta Manufacturas S.L.
Barrio Urasandi
E-20870 Elgoibar (Guipuzcoa)
Phone No.: 43/74-3150-54

FAX No.: 43/74-3154

ARRIZABLAGA
Arrizabalaga, Pedro, S.A.
Errekatxu, 5
E-20600 Eibar (Guipuzcoa)
Phone No.: 43/11-1743

FAX No.: 43/11-1743

ASTRA
Interarms
10 Prince Street
Alexandria, VA 22314
FAX No.: 703-549-7826

AUSTRALIAN AUTOMATIC ARMS PTY. LTD.
California Armory, Inc.
119 El Camino Real
San Bruno, CA 94066
FAX No.: 415-871-0713

AUTO-MAG
Gibbons Sporting Arms
P.O. Box 751
Torrance, CA 90508

AUTO-ORDNANCE CORP.
Williams Lane
West Hurley, NY 12491
FAX No.: 914-679-2698

BSA GUNS LTD.
Armory Rd., Small Heath
Birmingham, ENGLAND B11 2PX
FAX No.: 021-773-0845

BAILONS GUNMAKERS LTD.
Woodcock Hill
RD #1 Box 147
Vinton, PA 17814
US FAX No. 717-864-3232
Factory FAX No.:44-21-236-3396

BARRETT FIREARMS MANUFACTURING,
8211 Manchester Highway
Murfreesboro, TN 37133
FAX No.: 615-896-7313

BAVARIAN RIFLES
H & S, Inc.
P.O. Box 325
Middlefield, CT 06455
FAX No.: 203-349-1771

BENELLI
Sile Distributors
Attn: Handgun Customer Service
7 Centre Market Place
New York, NY 10013
FAX No.: 212-925-3149
Heckler & Koch, Inc.
Attn: Shotgun Customer Service
21480 Pacific Blvd.
Sterling, VA 22170-8903
FAX No.: 703-450-8160

BERETTA, DR. FRANCO
Via Donizetti, 4/a
1-25062 Concesio, ITALY
FAX. No.: 030/ 2180414

BERETTA, PIETRO
Beretta U.S.A. Corp
17601 Beretta Drive
Accokeek, MD 20607
FAX No.: 301-283-0435

BERNARDELLI
Magnum Research
7110 University Ave. NE
Mpls, MN 55432
FAX No.: 612-574-0109

BERSA
Eagle Imports Inc.
1907 Hwy #35
Ocean, NJ 07712
FAX No.: 201-531-1520

BERTUZZI
New England Arms Co.
Attn: Import Customer Service
Lawrence Lane - Box 278
Kittery Point, ME 03905
Phone No.: 207-439-0593
FAX No.: 207-439-6726

BLASER
Autumn Sales Inc.
1320 Lake Street
Fort Worth, TX 76102
FAX No.: 817-246-0301

BOSWELL, CHARLES
Charles Boswell Gunmakers
212 E. Morehead Street
Charlotte, NC 28202
FAX No.: 704-372-9656

BRETTON
Mandall Shooting Supplies
3616 N. Scottsdale Rd.
Scottsdale, AZ 85252
Phone No.: 602-945-2553
FAX No.: 602-949-0734

BRITARMS
Mandall Shooting Supplies
3616 N. Scottsdale Rd.
Scottsdale, AZ 85252
Phone No.: 602-945-2553
FAX No.: 602-949-0734

BRNO ARMS
T.D. Arms
30464 No.2 - 23 Mile Road
New Baltimore, MI 48047
FAX No.: 313-949-1989

BROWN PRECISION CO.
Brown Precision Inc.
7786 Molinos Avenue
Los Molinos, CA 96055
Phone No.: 916-384-2506
FAX No.: 916-384-1638

BROWNING
Route 1
Morgan, UT 84050
FAX No.: 801-876-3331

BRUCHET
8139 San Benito Way
Dallas, TX 75218
Phone No.: 214-328-4000

BRYCO ARMS
Jennings Firearms, Inc.
3656 Research Way
Carson City, NV 89706
Phone/FAX No.: 702-882-4007

CABANAS
Mandall Shooting Supplies
3616 N. Scottsdale Rd.
Scottsdale, AZ 85252
Phone No.: 602-945-2553
FAX No.: 602-949-0734

CABELA'S INC.
812 13th Ave.
Sidney, NE 69160
Phone No.: 308-254-5505

CALICO
405 East 19th Street
Bakersfield, CA 93305
FAX No.: 805-323-7844

CASARTELLI, CARLO
New England Arms Co.
Attn: Import Customer Service
Lawrence Lane - Box 278
Kittery Point, ME 03905
Phone No.: 207-439-0593
FAX No.: 207-439-6726

CASPIAN ARMS
14 North Main Street
Hardwick, VT 05843
FAX No.: 802-472-6709

CENTURY GUN DIST., INC.
1467 Jason Road
Greenfield, IN 46140

CENTURY INTERNATIONAL ARMS, INC.
5 Federal St./PO Box 714
St. Albans, VT 05478
FAX No.: 802-524-5631

CHAMPLIN FIREARMS, INC.
Woodring Municipal Airport
Enid, OK 73702
Phone No.: 405-237-7388
FAX No.: 405-233-1724

CHAPIUS ARMES
Armes De Chasse
P.O. Box No. 827
Chadds Ford, PA 19317
Phone No.: 215-388-1146

CHARTER ARMS
430 Sniffens Lane
Stratford, CT 06497
FAX No.: 203-378-2846

CHURCHILL
Ellett Brothers
P.O. Box 128
Chapin, SC 29036
FAX No.: 803-345-1820

CHURCHILL, E.J., (GUNMAKERS) LTD.
Ockley Road, Dorking
Surrey, ENGLAND RH5 4PU

CIMARRON, F.A. MFG. CO.
9439 Katy Freeway
Houston, TX 77024
FAX No.: 713-461-8320

CLARIDGE HI-TECH
8946 Winnetka Ave.
Northridge, CA 91324
FAX No.: 818-700-0026

CLASSIC DOUBLES
Guns Unlimited
4325 S. 12oth St
Omaha, NE 68137
FAX No.: 402- 330- 8029

CLIFTON ARMS
P.O. Box 531258
Grand Prairie, TX 75053
Phone No.: 214-647-2500

COLT'S FIREARMS
P.O. Box 1868, Talcott Rd.
Hartford, CT 06101
FAX No.: 203-244-1442

CONNECTICUT VALLEY ARMS, INC.
5988 Peachtree Corners E.
Norcross, GA 30071
FAX No.: 404-242-8546

COONAN ARMS, INC.
830 Hampden Ave.
St. Paul, MN 55114
FAX No.: 612-646-8257

COSMI, AMERICO & FIGLIO
New England Arms Co.
Attn: Import Customer Service
Lawrence Lane - Box 278
Kittery Point, ME 03905
Phone No.: 207-439-0593
FAX No.: 207-439-6726

DAISY MANUFACTURING CO., INC.
P.O. Box 220
Rodgers, AR 72757
FAX No.: 501-636-1601

DAKOTA ARMS, INC.
Whitewood Rd.
HC55 Box 326
Sturgis, SD 57785
FAX No.: 605-347-4459

DAKOTA SINGLE ACTION REVOLVERS
EMF Company
1900 E. Warner Ave. 1-D
Santa Ana, CA 92705
FAX No.:714-756-0133

DALY, CHARLES: MODERN MFG.
Outdoor Sports Hdqtrs.
Attn: C. Daly Customer Service
967 Watertower Lane
Dayton, OH 45449
FAX No.: 513-865-5962

DAN ARMS OF AMERICA
P.O. Box 3126
Allentown, PA 18106-3126

DARNE S.A.
Please refer to Bruchet.

DAVIS INDUSTRIES
15150 Sierra Bonita Lane
Chino, CA 91710
FAX No.: 714-393-9771

DETONICS MANUFACTURING CORP.
Please refer to New Detonics

DOMINO
Mandall Shooting Supplies
3616 N. Scottsdale Rd.
Scottsdale, AZ 85252
Phone No.: 602-945-2553

FAX No.: 602-949-0734

DUBIEL ARMS COMPANY
1724 Baker Rd.
Sherman, TX 75090

**DUMOULIN-DELEYE, MANUFACTURE D'AR-
MES**
Rue Florent Boclinville, 8-10
B-4041 Votten, Belgium
Phone No.: 41/27 78 92

DUMOULIN, ERNEST
Rue Florent Boclinville, 8-10
B-4041 Votten, Belgium
Phone No. 41/ 27 7892

DUMOULIN, HENRI & FILS
New England Arms Co.
Attn: Import Customer Service
Lawrence Lane - Box 278
Kittery Point, ME 03905
Phone No.: 207-439-0593

FAX No.: 207-439-6726

EMF COMPANY
1900 E. Warner Ave. 1-D
Santa Ana, CA 92705
FAX No.: 714-756-0133

EAGLE ARMS INC.
131 E. 22nd Ave.
Coal Valley, IL 61240
Phone No.: 309-799-5619

FAX No.: 309-799-5150

ERMA-WERKE
Precision Sales Int'l, Inc.
P.O. Box 1776

Westfield, MA 01086
FAX No.: 413-562-5056
Mandall Shooting Supplies
3616 N. Scottsdale Rd.

Scottsdale, AZ 85252
Phone No.: 602-945-2553

FAX No.: 602-949-0734

EXCAM
4480 E. 11th Ave.

Hialeah, FL 33013
FAX No.: 305-681-3774

F.I.E. FIREARMS CORP.
Please refer to Quality Firearms,
Inc.

FAS
BEEMAN PRECISION ARMS, INC.
3440 Airway Drive

Santa Rosa, CA 95403-2040
FAX No.: 707-578-4751

FABARM
St. Lawrence Sales, Inc.
12 W. Flint Street

Lake Orion, MI 48035
Phone No.: 313-693-7760

FAX No.: 313-693-7718

FABBRI, ARMI
New England Arms Co.
Attn: Import Customer Service

Lawrence Lane - Box 278

Kittery Point, ME 03905
Phone No.: 207-439-0593

FAX No.: 207-439-6726

FABRIQUE NATIONALE
Gun South, Inc.
Attn: FN Customer Service

108 Morrow Ave.

Trussville, AL 35173
FAX No.: 205-655-7078

FALCON FIREARMS
P.O. Box 3748
Granada Hills, CA 91344
FAX No.: 213-349-5717

FAMARS, A & S
Via Cinelli, 29
I-25063 Gardone V.T. ITALY
FAX No.: 030/837122

The Sporting Fieldf, Inc.
Rt 116 & Keeler Rd.
North Salem, NY
Phone No.: 914-669-8962

FEATHER INDUSTRIES, INC.
2300 Central Ave. Unit K
Boulder, CO 80301
FAX No.: 303-447-0944

FEDERAL ORDNANCE, INC.
1443 Potrero Ave.
South El Monte, CA 91733
FAX No.: 818-350-1538

FEINWERKBAU
Beeman Precision Arms
3440 Airway Drive
Santa Rosa, CA 95403-2040
FAX No.: 707-578-4751

FERLACH GUNS
Attn: Customer Service
Waagplatz, 6
A-9170 Ferlach, AUSTRIA
Telex.: 422893

FERLIB
New England Arms Co.
Attn: Import Customer Service
Lawrence Lane - Box 278
Kittery Point, ME 03905
Phone No.: 207-439-0593
FAX No.: 207-439-6726

FIOCCHI OF AMERICA, INC.
Rt. 2, Box 90-8
Ozark, MO 65721
FAX No.: 417-725-1039

FRANCHI, LUIGI
American Arms, Inc.
715 E. Armour Road
N. Kansas City, MO 64116
FAX No.: 816-474-1225

FRANCOTTE, AUGUSTE & CIE. S.A.
Armes De Chasse
P.O. Box 827
Chadds Ford, PA 19317
Phone No.: 215-388-1146

FRASER FIREARMS CORP.
34575 Commerce
Fraser, MI 48026

FREEDOM ARMS
P.O. Box 1776
Freedom, WY 83120
FAX No.: 307-883-2005

FRIGON GUNS
627 West Crawford
Clay Center, KS 67432
Phone No.: 913-632-5607

GAMBA, RENATO
Heckler & Koch, Inc.
Attn: Shotgun Customer Service
21480 Pacific Blvd.
Sterling, VA 22170-8903
FAX No.: 703-450-8160
Armscorp of America, Inc.
Attn: Handgun Customer Service
4424 John Ave.
Baltimore, MD 21227
FAX No.: 301-247-6205

GARBI
Wlm. Larkin Moore & Co.
31360 Via Colinas, SE 109
Westlake Village, CA 91361
Phone No.: 818-889-4160

GASTINE RENETTE
39 Avenue Franklin D. Roosevelt
Paris, FRANCE

GATLING GUN COMPANY
J & G SALES, INC.
440 Miller Valley
Prescott, AZ 86301
Phone No.: 602-445-9650

GLOCK, INC.
6000 Highlands Pkwy.
Smyrna, GA 30082
FAX No.: 404-433-8719

GRANGER, G.
66, Cours Fauriel
F-42100 Saint-Etienne, FRANCE
Phone No.: 77/25-1473

GREENER, W. W.
Cardigan St.
GB-Birmingham,ENGLAND
B4 7SA
FAX No.: 021/359-4300

GRENDEL, INC.
P.O. Box 908
Rockledge, FL 32955
FAX No.: 407-633-6710

H-S PRECISION, INC.
1301 Turbine Dr.
Rapid City, SD 57701
FAX No.: 605-342-8964

HAMMERLI
Mandall Shooting Supplies
3616 N. Scottsdale Rd.
Scottsdale, AZ 85252
Phone No.: 602-945-2553

FAX No.: 602-949-0734
Beeman Precision Arms
Attn: Customer Service
3440 Airway Drive
Santa Rosa, CA 95403-2040
FAX No.: 707-578-4751

HATFIELD INTERNATIONAL INC.
224 N 4th
St. Joseph, MO 64501
FAX No.: 816-279-2716

HECKLER & KOCH
21480 Pacific Blvd.
Sterling, VA 22170-8903
FAX No.: 703-450-8160

HEYM, FRIEDRICH WILH.
Heckler & Koch
21480 Pacific Blvd.
Sterling, VA 22170-8903
FAX No.: 703-450-8160

HOFER-JAGDWAFFEN, PETER
Franz-Lang-StraBe 13
A-9170 Ferlach, AUSTRIA
Phone No.: 04227-3683

FAX No.: 04227/3683

HOLLAND & HOLLAND LTD.
Attn: Customer Service-BB
31 & 33 Bruton Street
London, ENGLAND WIX 8JS
Phone No.: 01-499 4411

FAX NO.: 01-499 4544

Telex No.: 269021

IGA SHOTGUNS
Stoeger Industries
55 Ruta Court
S. Hackensack, NJ 07606
FAX No.: 201-440-2707

INTERARMS
10 Prince Street
Alexandria, VA 22314
FAX No.: 703-549-7826

INTRATEC
12405 SW 130th St.
Miami, FL 33186
FAX No.: 305-253-7207

IRWINDALE ARMS, INC.
6226 Santos Diaz St.
Irwindale, CA 91702
FAX No.: 818-969-5247

ITHACA GUN
891 Route 34-B
King Ferry, NY 13081
FAX No.: 315-364-5134

JENNINGS FIREARMS, INC.
3680 Research Way, Ste.#1
Carson City, NV 89706
Phone/FAX No.: 702-882-4007

JERICHO
K.B.I., Inc.
P.O. Box 11933
Harrisburg, PA 17108
FAX No.: 717-540-8567

IVER JOHNSON
 AMAC
   2202 Redmond Road
   Jacksonville, AR 72076
   FAX No.: 501-982-4954

K.B.I., INC.
   P.O. Box 6346
   Harrisburg, PA 17112
   FAX No.: 717-540-8567

KDF, INC.
   2485 Highway 46 North
   Seguin, TX 78155
   FAX No.: 512-379-5420

KIMBER OF OREGON, INC.
   2036 S. Green Mountain Rd
   Cotton, OR. 97017
   Phone No. 800-842-0852
   FAX No.: 503-654-4997

KIMEL INDUSTRIES
 AAArms
   3800 Old Monroe Road
   Matthews, NC 28105
   FAX No.: 704-821-6339

KLEINGUENTHER FIREARMS
   1604 N. Heideke St.
   Seguin, TX 78155
   Phone No. 512-372-5050

KORRIPHILA
   No Current Importer

KORTH
 Mandall Shooting Supplies
   3616 N. Scottsdale Rd.
   Scottsdale, AZ 85252
   Phone No.: 602-945-2553
   FAX No.: 602-949-0734
 Beeman Precision Arms
   Attn: Customer Service
   3440 Airway Drive
   Santa Rosa, CA 95403-2040
   FAX No.: 707-578-4751

KRICO
 Mandall Shooting Supplies
   3616 N. Scottsdale Rd.
   Scottsdale, AZ 85252
   FAX No.: 602-949-0734

KRIEGHOFF, H., GUN CO.
 Krieghoff Intl., Inc.
   P.O. Box 549
   Ottsville, PA 18942
   FAX No.: 215-847-8691

L.A.R. MANUFACTURING, INC.
   4133 West Farm Road
   West Jordan, UT 84084
   FAX No.: 801-569-1972

LAKE FIELD ARMS LTD.
   Ellett Brothers
   P.O. Box 128
   Chapin, SC 29036
   FAX No.: 803-345-1820

LANBER
 Lanber Armas, S.A.
   Attn: Customer Service-BB
   Zubiaurre, 5
   Zaldibar, 48250 Vizcaya, SPAIN
   FAX No.: 34-4-6827999

LAURONA
 Galaxy Imports Inc.
   P.O. Box 3361
   Victoria, TX 77903
   Phone No.: 512-573-4867
   FAX No. 512- 576-9622

LAW ENFORCEMENT ORDNANCE CORP.
   P.O. Box 336
   Ridgway, PA 15853

LEBEAU-COURALLY
 New England Arms Co.
   Attn: Import Customer Service
   Lawrence Lane - Box 278
   Kittery Point, ME 03905
   Phone No.: 207-439-0593
   FAX No.: 207-439-6726

LEFORGERON
 No Current Importer

LJUTIC INDUSTRIES, INC.
   P.O. Box 2117
   Yakima, WA 98907
   Phone No.: 509-248-0476

LLAMA PISTOLS
Stoeger Industries
55 Ruta Court

S. Hackensack, NJ 07606
FAX No.: 201-440-2707

LORCIN ENGINEERING CO., INC.
6471 Mission Blvd.

Riverside, CA 92509
FAX No.: 714-683-8029

LUGER (New Mfg. Only)
Precision Imports, Inc.
5040 Space Center Drive

San Antonio, TX 78218
FAX No.: 512-666-2723

MK ARMS INC.
P.O. Box 16411

Irvine, CA 92713
Phone No.: 714-261-2767

M.O.A. CORPORATION
7996 Brookville-Salem Rd

Brookville, OH 45309
Phone No.: 513-833-5559

MAGNUM RESEARCH INC.
7110 University Ave. NE

Minneapolis, MN 55432
FAX No.: 612-574-0109

MALIN, F.E.
Cape Horn Outfitters
212 E. Morehead Street

Charlotte, NC 28202
FAX No.: 704-372-9656

MANURHIN HANDGUNS
Atlantic Bus. Org., Inc.
845 Third Ave. Suite 1400

New York, NY 10022
FAX No.: 212-593-1318

MARLIN FIREARMS
100 Kenna Drive

North Haven, CT 06473
FAX No.: 203-234-7991

MAROCCHI
Precision Sales Int.'l Inc.
Attn: Avanza Customer Service

P.O. Box 1776

Westfield, MA 01086

Sile Distributors, Inc.
7 Centre Market Place

New York, NY 10013
FAX No.: 212-925-3149

MAUSER-WERKE
Precision Imports, Inc.
5040 Space Center Drive

San Antonio, TX 78218
FAX No.: 512-666-2723

MAVERICK ARMS, INC.
P.O. Box 586

Eagle Pass, TX 78852
FAX No.: 512-773-8862

MCMILLAN, G. & CO. INC.
21438 N. 7th Ave. Suite E

Phoenix, AZ 85027
FAX No.: 602-582-5178

MERKEL & GEBRUDER
Armes De Chasse
P.O. Box No. 827

Chadds Ford, PA 19317
Phone No.: 215-388-1146

MITCHELL ARMS, INC.
3400 I-West MacArthur Blvd.

Santa Ana, CA 92704
FAX No.: 714-957-5732

MODERN MUZZLE LOAIDNG, INC.
Rural Route 1, Box 234A

P.O. Box 130

Centerville, IA 52544
FAX No.: 515-856-2628

MOSSBERG
O.F. Mossberg & Sons, Inc
7 Grasso Ave.

North Haven, CT 06473
FAX No.: 203-288-2404

MUSGRAVE
Musgrave Mfr.'s and Dist. Ltd.
P.O. Box 183

Bloemfontein 9300, Jagersfontein

REPUBLIC of S. AFRICA

NAVY ARMS CO.
689 Bergen Blvd.

Ridgefield, NJ 07657
FAX No.: 201-945-6859

NEW DETONICS MANUFACTURING CORP.
21438 N. 7th Ave., Suite F
Phoenix, AZ 85027
FAX No.: 602-582-0059

NEW ENGLAND ARMS CO.
Lawrence Lane - Box 278
Kittery Point, ME 03905
Phone No.: 207-439-0593
FAX No.: 207-439-6726

NEW ENGLAND FIREARMS CO., INC.
Industrial Rowe
Gardner, MA 01440
FAX No.: 508-632-2300

NORINCO
China Sports, Inc.
P.O. Box 3250
Ontario, CA 91761
FAX No.: 714-923-0775

NORTH AMERICAN ARMS
P.O. Box 707
Spanish Fork, UT 84660
FAX No.: 801-798-9418

OLYMPIC ARMS, INC.
624 Old Pacific Hwy. S.E.
Olympia, WA 98503
FAX No.: 206-491-3447

OMEGA PISTOL
Springfield Armory, Inc.
420 W. Main St.
Geneseo, IL 61254
FAX No.: 309-944-3676

OMEGA SHOTGUNS
K.B.I., Inc.
P.O. Box 11933
Harrisburg, PA 17108
FAX No.: 717-540-8567

ORVIS
5848 Westheimer
Houston, TX 77057
Phone No.: 713-783-2111

P.A.W.S., INC.
Sile Distributors
7 Centre Market Place
New York, NY 10013
FAX No.: 212-925-3149

P.S.M.G. GUN CO.
10 Park Avenue
Arlington, MA 02174
FAX No.: 617-648-7482

PARA-ORDNANCE MFG. INC.
3411 McNicoll Avenue #14
Scarborough, Ontario
CANADA M1V 2V6
FAX No.: 416-297-1289

PARDINI
Fiocchi of America, Inc.
Rt. 2, Box 90-8
Ozark, MO 65721
FAX No.: 417-725-1039

PARKER REPRODUCTIONS
Parker Reproduction Div.
124 River Road
Middlesex, NJ 08846
FAX No.: 201-469-9692

PARKER-HALE LTD.
Precision Sports
3736 Kellogg Road
Cortland, NY 13045-5588
FAX No.: 607-753-8835

PERAZZI
Perazzi USA, Inc.
1207 South Shamrock
Monrovia, CA 91016
FAX No.: 818-303-2081

PIOTTI
Wlm. Larkin Moore & Co.
31360 Via Colinas, Se 109
Westlake Village, CA 91361
Phone No.: 818-889-4160

POLY TECHNOLOGIES, INC.
PTK International, Inc.
2814 New Spring Rd., 340
Atlanta, GA 30339
FAX No.: 404-438-7839

PURDEY, JAMES, & SONS, LTD.
57-58 S Audley Street
London, ENGLAND W1Y 6ED

QUALITY FIREARMS, INC.
4541 Northwest 133 St.
Opa-Locka, Fl 33054
FAX No 305-687-6721

QUALITY PARTS
999 Roosevelt Trail Bldg. 3
Windham, ME 04062
FAX No.: 207-892-8068

RWS
Dynamit Nobel of America
105 Stonehurst Ct.
Northvale, NJ 07647
FAX No.: 201-767-1589

RANDALL FIREARMS CO.
KK Manufacturing
Attn: Older Randall Research
P.O. Box 1586
Lomita, CA 90717-5586
FAX No.: 213-539-3483

RAVELL LTD.
289 Diputacion Street
08009 Barcelona, SPAIN
Telex. No.: 51114 RAVE-E

RAVEN ARMS
1300 Bixby Drive
Industry, CA 91745
Phone No.: 818-961-2511

REMINGTON
Remington Arms Co., Inc.
1007 Market Street
Wilmington, DE 19898
FAX No.: 302-774-5776

RIGBY, JOHN & CO. (GUNMAKERS), LTD.
Suffolk Street
London, ENGLAND

RIPAMONTI RIFLES
Morton's, Ltd.
156 Trade Street
Lexington, KY 40510
FAX No.: 606-252-1399

RIPAMONTI SHOTGUNS
8139 San Benito Way
Dallas, TX 75218
Phone No.: 214-328-4000

RIZZINI
Wlm. Larkin Moore & Co.
31360 Via Colinas, SE 109
Westlake Village, CA 91361
Phone No.: 818-889-4160

New England Arms Co.
Attn: Import Customer Service
Lawrence Lane - Box 278
Kittery Point, ME 03905
Phone No.: 207-439-0593
FAX No.: 207-439-6726

ROSSI
Interarms
10 Prince Street
Alexandria, VA 22313
FAX No.: 703-549-7826

SKB ARMS CO.
G. U., Inc.
4325 S 120th Street
Omaha, NE 68137
FAX No.: 402- 330 - 8029

SSK INDUSTRIES
Rt. 1 Della Drive
Bloomingdale, OH 43910

S.W.D., INC.
1872 Marietta Blvd.
Atlanta, GA 30318
FAX No.: 404-432-6536

SAKO
Stoeger Industries
55 Ruta Court
S. Hackensack, NJ 07606
FAX No.: 201-440-2707

SARDIUS
Armscorp of America
4424 John Avenue
Baltimore, MD 21227
FAX No.: 301-247-6205

SAUER, J.P. & SOHN
G. U., Inc.
4325 S 120th Street
Omaha, NE 68137
FAX No.: 402- 330 - 8029

SAVAGE
  Savage Industries, Inc.
  Springdale Road
  Westfield, MA 01085
  FAX No.: 413-562-1145

SCOTT, W.C.
  Holland & Holland Ltd.
  31 & 33 Bruton Street
  London, ENGLAND W1X 8JS
  FAX No.: 01-499 4544

SEDCO INDUSTRIES, INC.
  506 N. Spring St., Unit E
  Lake Elsinore, CA 92330
  FAX No.: 714-245-2748

SEECAMP, LW.C.
  301 Brewster Road
  Milford, CT 06460
  Phone No.: 203-877-3429

SEMMERLING
  American Derringer Corp.
  127 N. Lacy Drive
  Waco, TX 76705
  FAX No.: 817-799-9334

SHILOH RIFLE MFG. CO., INC.
  P.O. Box 279, Ind. Park
  Big Timber, MT 59011
  Phone No.: 406-932-4454

SIG SAUER
  Sigarms, Inc.
  Corporate Park
  Exeter, NH 03833
  FAX No.: 603-772-9082

SILMA
  Via 1- Maggio, 76
  I-25060 Zanano di Sarezzo, ITALY
  FAX No. 030/ 80 1493

SMITH & WESSON
  2100 Roosevelt Avenue
  Springfield, MA 01102-2208
  Phone No.: 413-781-8300
  Roy Jinks is S&W Historian
  FAX No.: 413-731-8980

SNAKE CHARMER
  Sporting Arms Mfg. Inc.
  P.O. Box 191
  Littlefield, TX 79339
  FAX No.: 806-385-3394

SOKOLOVSKY CORP.
  P.O. Box 70113
  Sunnyvale, CA 94086

SPECIAL SERVICE ARMS MFG. INC.
  P.O. Box 500
  Aiken, South Carolina 29802
  FAX No.: 803-642-9188

SPRINGFIELD ARMORY, INC.
  420 W. Main Street
  Geneseo, IL 61254
  FAX No.: 309-944-3676

STAR
  Interarms
  10 Prince Street
  Alexandria, VA 22313
  FAX No.: 703-549-7826

STEEL CITY ARMS, INC.
  1883 Main Street
  Pittsburgh, PA 15215
  Phone No.: 412-461-3100

STERLING ARMAMENT, LTD.
  No Current Importer

STEVENS, J., ARMS COMPANY
  Savage Arms, Inc.
  Springdale Road
  Westfield, MA 01085
  FAX No.: 413-562-1145

STEYR MANNLICHER
  Gun South, Inc.
  108 Morrow Avenue
  Trussville, AL 35173
  FAX No.: 205-655-7078

STREET SWEEPER
  Sales of Georgia
  P.O. Box 94168
  Atlanta, GA 30318
  FAX No.: 404-350-9714

STURM, RUGER & CO.
35 Lacey Place
Southport, CT 06490
FAX No.: 203-259-6688

SUNDANCE INDUSTRIES
8216 Lankershim Blvd. #11
North Hollywood, CA 91605
Phone No.: 818-768-1083

TALON
Ports of Call
1091 Airport Road
Minden, NV 89423
FAX No.: 702-782-2613

TANNER, ANDRE
Mandall Shooting Supplies
3616 N. Scottsdale Rd.
Scottsdale, AZ 85252
Phone No.: 602-945-2553
FAX No.: 602-949-0734

TAURUS FIREARMS
4563 S.W. 71st Avenue
Miami, FL 33155
FAX No.: 305-661-8187

TECNI-MEC
Via Gitti S.N.
25060 Marcheno ITALY
FAX No.: (030) 8610179

TEXAS LONGHORN ARMS, INC.
P.O. Box 703
Richmond, TX 77469
Phone No.: 713-341-0775

THOMPSON/CENTER ARMS
P.O. Box 5002
Rochester, NH 03867
FAX No.: 603-332-5133

TIKKA
Stoeger Industries
55 Ruta Court
S. Hackensack, NJ 07606
FAX No.: 201-440-2707

U.S.A.S.
Gilbert Equipment Co., Inc.
P.O. Box 11047
Mobile, AL 36609
Phone No.: 205-344-3322

UBERTI
362 Limerock Road
Lakeville, CT 06039
FAX No.: 203-435-2846

UGARTECHEA, IGNACIO
P.O. Box 21
Eibar, SPAIN
FAX No.: 34-43-121669

ULTRA LIGHT ARMS
214 Price Street
Granville, WV 26534
Phone No.: 304-599-5687

UNIQUE (from Beeman)
3440 Airway Drive
Santa Rosa, CA 95403-2040
FAX No. 707- 578- 4751

U.S. HISTORICAL SOCIETY
First & Main Streets
Richmond, VA 23219
FAX No.: 804-648-0002

UZI
Action Arms Ltd.
P.O. Box 9573
Philadelphia, PA 19124-0573
FAX No.: 215-533-2188

VALMET (Disc.)
Stoeger Industries
55 Ruta Court
S. Hackensack, NJ 07606
FAX No.: 201-440-2707

VARNER SPORTING ARMS, CO.
1004F Cobb Parkway N.E.
Marietta, GA 30062
Phone No.: 404-422-5468

VICTORY ARMS CO. LTD.
Magnum Research Inc.
7110 University Avenue N.E.
Minneapolis, MN 55432
FAX No.: 612-574-0109

WALTHER
Interarms
10 Prince Street
Alexandria, VA 22313
FAX No.: 703-549-7826

WEATHERBY INC.
2781 Firestone Blvd.
South Gate, CA 90280
FAX No.: 213-569-5025

WEAVER ARMS CORP.
Monarch Court Suite 201
6265 Greenwich Drive
San Diego, CA 92122
FAX No.: 619-452-2064

WEBLEY & SCOTT LTD.
Frankley Industrial Park
Tay Road, Rubery, Rednal
GB-Birmingham B45 OPA
Phone No.: 021/453-1864
FAX No.: 021/457-7846

WEIHRAUCH, HANS-HERMANN
Beeman Precision Arms
Attn: Customer Service
3440-SS90 Airway Drive
Santa Rosa, CA 95403-2040
FAX No.: 707-578-4751

WESSON, DAN, ARMS
293 Main Street
Monson, MA 01057
FAX No.: 413-267-3601

WESTLEY RICHARDS & CO. LTD.
40 Grange Road
Birmingham, ENGLAND B29 6AR
FAX No.: 021-4141138
Telex. No.: 334049 DETACH

WICHITA ARMS, INC.
P.O. Box 11371
Wichita, KS 67211
Phone No.: 316-265-0760

WILDEY INC.
P.O. Box 475
Brookfield, CT 06804
FAX No.: 203-354-7759

WINCHESTER (U.S.Repeating Arms)
U.S. Repeating Arms Co.
275 Winchester Avenue
New Haven, CT 06511
FAX No.: 203-789-5071

WINCHESTER/OLIN
Models 101 & 23 only (Disc.)
Attn: Shotgun Customer Service
427 N. Shamrock Street
East Alton, IL 62024
FAX No.: 618-258-3393

WISEMAN, BILL & CO.
P.O. Box 3427
Bryan, TX 77805
Phone No.: 409-690-3456
FAX No.: 409-690-0156

WYOMING ARMS MFG. CORP.
HCR 77 Box 209 B
Thermopolis, WY 82443
FAX No.: 307-864-5738

ZANARDINI
Morton's, Ltd.
156 Trade Street
Lexington, KY 40510
FAX No.: 606-252-1399
Navy Arms Company
689 Bergen Blvd.
Ridgefield, NJ 07657
FAX No.: 201-945-6859

ZANOTTI, FABIO
New England Arms Co.
Attn: Import Customer Service
Lawrence Lane - Box 278
Kittery Point, ME 03905
FAX No.: 207-439-6726

ZASTAVA ARMS
T.D. Arms
30464 No. 2 - 23 Mile Road
New Baltimore, MI 48047
FAX No.: 313-949-1989

ZOLI, ANTONIO
Antonio Zoli, U.S.A., Inc.
P.O. Box 6190
Fort Wayne, IN 46896
FAX No.: 219-447-5772

Firearms Inventory Record

1. Type of firearm: Pistol _____ Rifle _____ Shotgun _____ Antique _____

   Manufacturer _____ Model _____

   Ser. No. _____ Cal./ga. _____ Barrel length _____ in./cm.

   Overall condition _____ Remarks _____

   _____

   Date purchased _____ Purchase price $ _____ Purchased from _____

   Sell date _____ Sell price $ _____ Sold to _____

2. Type of firearm: Pistol _____ Rifle _____ Shotgun _____ Antique _____

   Manufacturer _____ Model _____

   Ser. No. _____ Cal./ga. _____ Barrel length _____ in./cm.

   Overall condition _____ Remarks _____

   _____

   Date purchased _____ Purchase price $ _____ Purchased from _____

   Sell date _____ Sell price $ _____ Sold to _____

3. Type of firearm: Pistol _____ Rifle _____ Shotgun _____ Antique _____

   Manufacturer _____ Model _____

   Ser. No. _____ Cal./ga. _____ Barrel length _____ in./cm.

   Overall condition _____ Remarks _____

   _____

   Date purchased _____ Purchase price $ _____ Purchased from _____

   Sell date _____ Sell price $ _____ Sold to _____

4. Type of firearm: Pistol _____ Rifle _____ Shotgun _____ Antique _____

   Manufacturer _____ Model _____

   Ser. No. _____ Cal./ga. _____ Barrel length _____ in./cm.

   Overall condition _____ Remarks _____

   _____

   Date purchased _____ Purchase price $ _____ Purchased from _____

   Sell date _____ Sell price $ _____ Sold to _____

5. Type of firearm: Pistol _____ Rifle _____ Shotgun _____ Antique _____

   Manufacturer _____ Model _____

   Ser. No. _____ Cal./ga. _____ Barrel length _____ in./cm.

   Overall condition _____ Remarks _____

   _____

   Date purchased _____ Purchase price $ _____ Purchased from _____

   Sell date _____ Sell price $ _____ Sold to _____

6. Type of firearm: Pistol _____ Rifle _____ Shotgun _____ Antique _____

   Manufacturer _____ Model _____

   Ser. No. _____ Cal./ga. _____ Barrel length _____ in./cm.

   Overall condition _____ Remarks _____

   _____

   Date purchased _____ Purchase price $ _____ Purchased from _____

   Sell date _____ Sell price $ _____ Sold to _____

7. Type of firearm: Pistol _____ Rifle _____ Shotgun _____ Antique _____

   Manufacturer _____ Model _____

   Ser. No. _____ Cal./ga. _____ Barrel length _____ in./cm.

   Overall condition _____ Remarks _____

   _____

   Date purchased _____ Purchase price $ _____ Purchased from _____

   Sell date _____ Sell price $ _____ Sold to _____

8. Type of firearm: Pistol _____ Rifle _____ Shotgun _____ Antique _____

   Manufacturer _____ Model _____

   Ser. No. _____ Cal./ga. _____ Barrel length _____ in./cm.

   Overall condition _____ Remarks _____

   _____

   Date purchased _____ Purchase price $ _____ Purchased from _____

   Sell date _____ Sell price $ _____ Sold to _____

9. Type of firearm: Pistol _____ Rifle _____ Shotgun _____ Antique _____

   Manufacturer _____ Model _____

   Ser. No. _____ Cal./ga. _____ Barrel length _____ in./cm.

   Overall condition _____ Remarks _____

   _____

   Date purchased _____ Purchase price $ _____ Purchased from _____

   Sell date _____ Sell price $ _____ Sold to _____

10. Type of firearm: Pistol _____ Rifle _____ Shotgun _____ Antique _____

    Manufacturer _____ Model _____

    Ser. No. _____ Cal./ga. _____ Barrel length _____ in./cm.

    Overall condition _____ Remarks _____

    _____

    Date purchased _____ Purchase price $ _____ Purchased from _____

    Sell date _____ Sell price $ _____ Sold to _____

11. Type of firearm: Pistol _____ Rifle _____ Shotgun _____ Antique _____

    Manufacturer _____ Model _____

    Ser. No. _____ Cal./ga. _____ Barrel length _____ in./cm.

    Overall condition _____ Remarks _____

    _____

    Date purchased _____ Purchase price $ _____ Purchased from _____

    Sell date _____ Sell price $ _____ Sold to _____

12. Type of firearm: Pistol _____ Rifle _____ Shotgun _____ Antique _____

    Manufacturer _____ Model _____

    Ser. No. _____ Cal./ga. _____ Barrel length _____ in./cm.

    Overall condition _____ Remarks _____

    _____

    Date purchased _____ Purchase price $ _____ Purchased from _____

    Sell date _____ Sell price $ _____ Sold to _____

13. Type of firearm: Pistol _____ Rifle _____ Shotgun _____ Antique _____

    Manufacturer _____ Model _____

    Ser. No. _____ Cal./ga. _____ Barrel length _____ in./cm.

    Overall condition _____ Remarks _____

    _____

    Date purchased _____ Purchase price $ _____ Purchased from _____

    Sell date _____ Sell price $ _____ Sold to _____

14. Type of firearm: Pistol _____ Rifle _____ Shotgun _____ Antique _____

    Manufacturer _____ Model _____

    Ser. No. _____ Cal./ga. _____ Barrel length _____ in./cm.

    Overall condition _____ Remarks _____

    _____

    Date purchased _____ Purchase price $ _____ Purchased from _____

    Sell date _____ Sell price $ _____ Sold to _____

15. Type of firearm: Pistol _____ Rifle _____ Shotgun _____ Antique _____

    Manufacturer _____ Model _____

    Ser. No. _____ Cal./ga. _____ Barrel length _____ in./cm.

    Overall condition _____ Remarks _____

    _____

    Date purchased _____ Purchase price $ _____ Purchased from _____

    Sell date _____ Sell price $ _____ Sold to _____

16. Type of firearm: Pistol _____ Rifle _____ Shotgun _____ Antique _____

    Manufacturer _____ Model _____

    Ser. No. _____ Cal./ga. _____ Barrel length _____ in./cm.

    Overall condition _____ Remarks _____

    _____

    Date purchased _____ Purchase price $ _____ Purchased from _____

    Sell date _____ Sell price $ _____ Sold to _____

17. Type of firearm: Pistol _____ Rifle _____ Shotgun _____ Antique _____

Manufacturer _____ Model _____

Ser. No. _____ Cal./ga. _____ Barrel length _____ in./cm.

Overall condition _____ Remarks _____

_____

Date purchased _____ Purchase price $ _____ Purchased from _____

Sell date _____ Sell price $ _____ Sold to _____

18. Type of firearm: Pistol _____ Rifle _____ Shotgun _____ Antique _____

Manufacturer _____ Model _____

Ser. No. _____ Cal./ga. _____ Barrel length _____ in./cm.

Overall condition _____ Remarks _____

_____

Date purchased _____ Purchase price $ _____ Purchased from _____

Sell date _____ Sell price $ _____ Sold to _____

19. Type of firearm: Pistol _____ Rifle _____ Shotgun _____ Antique _____

Manufacturer _____ Model _____

Ser. No. _____ Cal./ga. _____ Barrel length _____ in./cm.

Overall condition _____ Remarks _____

_____

Date purchased _____ Purchase price $ _____ Purchased from _____

Sell date _____ Sell price $ _____ Sold to _____

20. Type of firearm: Pistol _____ Rifle _____ Shotgun _____ Antique _____

Manufacturer _____ Model _____

Ser. No. _____ Cal./ga. _____ Barrel length _____ in./cm.

Overall condition _____ Remarks _____

_____

Date purchased _____ Purchase price $ _____ Purchased from _____

Sell date _____ Sell price $ _____ Sold to _____

21. Type of firearm: Pistol _____ Rifle _____ Shotgun _____ Antique _____

    Manufacturer _____ Model _____

    Ser. No. _____ Cal./ga. _____ Barrel length _____ in./cm.

    Overall condition _____ Remarks _____

    _____

    Date purchased _____ Purchase price $ _____ Purchased from _____

    Sell date _____ Sell price $ _____ Sold to _____

22. Type of firearm: Pistol _____ Rifle _____ Shotgun _____ Antique _____

    Manufacturer _____ Model _____

    Ser. No. _____ Cal./ga. _____ Barrel length _____ in./cm.

    Overall condition _____ Remarks _____

    _____

    Date purchased _____ Purchase price $ _____ Purchased from _____

    Sell date _____ Sell price $ _____ Sold to _____

23. Type of firearm: Pistol _____ Rifle _____ Shotgun _____ Antique _____

    Manufacturer _____ Model _____

    Ser. No. _____ Cal./ga. _____ Barrel length _____ in./cm.

    Overall condition _____ Remarks _____

    _____

    Date purchased _____ Purchase price $ _____ Purchased from _____

    Sell date _____ Sell price $ _____ Sold to _____

24. Type of firearm: Pistol _____ Rifle _____ Shotgun _____ Antique _____

    Manufacturer _____ Model _____

    Ser. No. _____ Cal./ga. _____ Barrel length _____ in./cm.

    Overall condition _____ Remarks _____

    _____

    Date purchased _____ Purchase price $ _____ Purchased from _____

    Sell date _____ Sell price $ _____ Sold to _____

25. Type of firearm: Pistol _____ Rifle _____ Shotgun _____ Antique _____

Manufacturer _____ Model _____

Ser. No. _____ Cal./ga. _____ Barrel length _____ in./cm.

Overall condition _____ Remarks _____

_____

Date purchased _____ Purchase price $ _____ Purchased from _____

Sell date _____ Sell price $ _____ Sold to _____

26. Type of firearm: Pistol _____ Rifle _____ Shotgun _____ Antique _____

Manufacturer _____ Model _____

Ser. No. _____ Cal./ga. _____ Barrel length _____ in./cm.

Overall condition _____ Remarks _____

_____

Date purchased _____ Purchase price $ _____ Purchased from _____

Sell date _____ Sell price $ _____ Sold to _____

27. Type of firearm: Pistol _____ Rifle _____ Shotgun _____ Antique _____

Manufacturer _____ Model _____

Ser. No. _____ Cal./ga. _____ Barrel length _____ in./cm.

Overall condition _____ Remarks _____

_____

Date purchased _____ Purchase price $ _____ Purchased from _____

Sell date _____ Sell price $ _____ Sold to _____

28. Type of firearm: Pistol _____ Rifle _____ Shotgun _____ Antique _____

Manufacturer _____ Model _____

Ser. No. _____ Cal./ga. _____ Barrel length _____ in./cm.

Overall condition _____ Remarks _____

_____

Date purchased _____ Purchase price $ _____ Purchased from _____

Sell date _____ Sell price $ _____ Sold to _____

29. Type of firearm: Pistol _____ Rifle _____ Shotgun _____ Antique _____

Manufacturer _____ Model _____

Ser. No. _____ Cal./ga. _____ Barrel length _____ in./cm.

Overall condition _____ Remarks _____

_____

Date purchased _____ Purchase price $ _____ Purchased from _____

Sell date _____ Sell price $ _____ Sold to _____

30. Type of firearm: Pistol _____ Rifle _____ Shotgun _____ Antique _____

Manufacturer _____ Model _____

Ser. No. _____ Cal./ga. _____ Barrel length _____ in./cm.

Overall condition _____ Remarks _____

_____

Date purchased _____ Purchase price $ _____ Purchased from _____

Sell date _____ Sell price $ _____ Sold to _____

31. Type of firearm: Pistol _____ Rifle _____ Shotgun _____ Antique _____

Manufacturer _____ Model _____

Ser. No. _____ Cal./ga. _____ Barrel length _____ in./cm.

Overall condition _____ Remarks _____

_____

Date purchased _____ Purchase price $ _____ Purchased from _____

Sell date _____ Sell price $ _____ Sold to _____

32. Type of firearm: Pistol _____ Rifle _____ Shotgun _____ Antique _____

Manufacturer _____ Model _____

Ser. No. _____ Cal./ga. _____ Barrel length _____ in./cm.

Overall condition _____ Remarks _____

_____

Date purchased _____ Purchase price $ _____ Purchased from _____

Sell date _____ Sell price $ _____ Sold to _____

33. Type of firearm: Pistol _____ Rifle _____ Shotgun _____ Antique _____

Manufacturer _____ Model _____

Ser. No. _____ Cal./ga. _____ Barrel length _____ in./cm.

Overall condition _____ Remarks _____

_____

Date purchased _____ Purchase price $ _____ Purchased from _____

Sell date _____ Sell price $ _____ Sold to _____

34. Type of firearm: Pistol _____ Rifle _____ Shotgun _____ Antique _____

Manufacturer _____ Model _____

Ser. No. _____ Cal./ga. _____ Barrel length _____ in./cm.

Overall condition _____ Remarks _____

_____

Date purchased _____ Purchase price $ _____ Purchased from _____

Sell date _____ Sell price $ _____ Sold to _____

35. Type of firearm: Pistol _____ Rifle _____ Shotgun _____ Antique _____

Manufacturer _____ Model _____

Ser. No. _____ Cal./ga. _____ Barrel length _____ in./cm.

Overall condition _____ Remarks _____

_____

Date purchased _____ Purchase price $ _____ Purchased from _____

Sell date _____ Sell price $ _____ Sold to _____

36. Type of firearm: Pistol _____ Rifle _____ Shotgun _____ Antique _____

Manufacturer _____ Model _____

Ser. No. _____ Cal./ga. _____ Barrel length _____ in./cm.

Overall condition _____ Remarks _____

_____

Date purchased _____ Purchase price $ _____ Purchased from _____

Sell date _____ Sell price $ _____ Sold to _____

37. Type of firearm: Pistol _____ Rifle _____ Shotgun _____ Antique _____

Manufacturer _____ Model _____

Ser. No. _____ Cal./ga. _____ Barrel length _____ in./cm.

Overall condition _____ Remarks _____

_____

Date purchased _____ Purchase price $ _____ Purchased from _____

Sell date _____ Sell price $ _____ Sold to _____

38. Type of firearm: Pistol _____ Rifle _____ Shotgun _____ Antique _____

Manufacturer _____ Model _____

Ser. No. _____ Cal./ga. _____ Barrel length _____ in./cm.

Overall condition _____ Remarks _____

_____

Date purchased _____ Purchase price $ _____ Purchased from _____

Sell date _____ Sell price $ _____ Sold to _____

39. Type of firearm: Pistol _____ Rifle _____ Shotgun _____ Antique _____

Manufacturer _____ Model _____

Ser. No. _____ Cal./ga. _____ Barrel length _____ in./cm.

Overall condition _____ Remarks _____

_____

Date purchased _____ Purchase price $ _____ Purchased from _____

Sell date _____ Sell price $ _____ Sold to _____

40. Type of firearm: Pistol _____ Rifle _____ Shotgun _____ Antique _____

Manufacturer _____ Model _____

Ser. No. _____ Cal./ga. _____ Barrel length _____ in./cm.

Overall condition _____ Remarks _____

_____

Date purchased _____ Purchase price $ _____ Purchased from _____

Sell date _____ Sell price $ _____ Sold to _____

977

41. Type of firearm: Pistol _____ Rifle _____ Shotgun _____ Antique _____

Manufacturer _____ Model _____

Ser. No. _____ Cal./ga. _____ Barrel length _____ in./cm.

Overall condition _____ Remarks _____

_____

Date purchased _____ Purchase price $ _____ Purchased from _____

Sell date _____ Sell price $ _____ Sold to _____

42. Type of firearm: Pistol _____ Rifle _____ Shotgun _____ Antique _____

Manufacturer _____ Model _____

Ser. No. _____ Cal./ga. _____ Barrel length _____ in./cm.

Overall condition _____ Remarks _____

_____

Date purchased _____ Purchase price $ _____ Purchased from _____

Sell date _____ Sell price $ _____ Sold to _____

43. Type of firearm: Pistol _____ Rifle _____ Shotgun _____ Antique _____

Manufacturer _____ Model _____

Ser. No. _____ Cal./ga. _____ Barrel length _____ in./cm.

Overall condition _____ Remarks _____

_____

Date purchased _____ Purchase price $ _____ Purchased from _____

Sell date _____ Sell price $ _____ Sold to _____

44. Type of firearm: Pistol _____ Rifle _____ Shotgun _____ Antique _____

Manufacturer _____ Model _____

Ser. No. _____ Cal./ga. _____ Barrel length _____ in./cm.

Overall condition _____ Remarks _____

_____

Date purchased _____ Purchase price $ _____ Purchased from _____

Sell date _____ Sell price $ _____ Sold to _____

Index of Manufacturers

Index of Manfacturers, cont'd